MARVEL ENCYCLOPEDIA

THE DEFINITIVE GUIDE TO THE CHARACTERS OF THE MARVEL UNIVERSE

Senior Editor Alastair Dougall
Design Manager Robert Perry
Senior Art Editor Nick Avery
Senior Designer Jill Bunyan
Editor Julia March
Design Manager Maxine Pedliham
Managing Editor Laura Gilbert
Art Director Lisa Lanzarini
Publishing Manager Julie Ferris
Publishing Director Simon Beecroft
Senior Pre-Production Producer Jennifer Murray
Senior Producers Danielle Smith, Alex Bell

First American Edition, 2006; reprinted 2008; revised 2009, 2014

10 9
021–253586–Mar/14

Published in the United States by DK Publishing
345 Hudson Street, New York, New York 10014

Published in Great Britain by Dorling Kindersley Limited

A catalog record for this book is available from the Library of Congress

ISBN: 978-1-4654-1593-6

Printed and bound in China

A WORLD OF IDEAS:
SEE ALL THERE IS TO KNOW

ENCYCLOPEDIA

THE DEFINITIVE GUIDE TO THE CHARACTERS OF THE MARVEL UNIVERSE

Contents

FOREWORD

by Ralph Macchio

Three-quarters of a century after its birth, the Marvel Universe is more alive and popular today than ever. The ever-expanding landscape of this finest of fantasy worlds is celebrated in this invaluable volume: The 75th Anniversary Marvel Encyclopedia. Herein you will find everything you want to know about Marvel, from heroes' histories to hidden civilizations; from the classic Kree/Skrull War to current epics, such as the Civil War saga and World War Hulk. All thoroughly researched and up-to-date.

It all began with a single, sea-dwelling character called Namor, created by the talented writer/artist Bill Everett for Timely Comics (Marvel Comics' precursor) in 1939. Namor the Sub-Mariner embodied all the traits that would, decades hence, become trademarks of Marvel's Super Heroes. He was an outsider, a rebel with a cause having a bizarre appearance that set him apart from the crowd. No less strange was the character who followed: The Human Torch, an android who could burst into flame, created by the versatile artist Carl Burgos. With the creation of Captain America by comic book titans Joe Simon and Jack Kirby, Timely Publishing had its first patriotic hero who was fully human. During the dark days of World War II, this triumvirate thrived, battling the Nazi menace. Sales skyrocketed. And the war was won.

With the coming of the 1950s, Captain America began fighting the communist threat, and Timely, now called Atlas Publishing, produced a variety of romance, western, and monster comics with titles such as The Two-Gun Kid, Tales to Astonish, Strange Tales, and Journey Into Mystery. Nothing ground-breaking, but they were a fun read. Things hummed along until the pivotal year of 1961, and then... magic!

National Periodicals was having some success reviving a few of their Golden Age heroes, and Atlas publisher Martin Goodman bade his main editor, Stan Lee to follow suit. And so was born: The Fantastic Four, the first true Marvel comic. Its many innovations—the bickering of the protagonists, the lack of gaudy Super Hero costumes—shook the comics industry to its core.

In the space of just a few years of unprecedented creativity, Stan and his artistic collaborators followed up the FF with the Hulk, Ant Man, Iron Man, Thor, and Lee's masterpiece—the Amazing Spider-Man! Here was a startlingly new breed of Super Hero, replete with personality flaws and foibles. Spider-Man drew in an older, college-educated audience attracted by the sophisticated storytelling and characterizations, the stunningly original artwork, and the mind-expanding concepts. It was all perfectly in tune with the increasingly exciting and volatile 1960s. Marvel Comics' intricate, cohesive, modern mythology spawned a comics revolution.

I was one of those youths totally absorbed by the Marvel brand. In fact, I turned my childhood passion into my life's work. Since arriving at the House of Ideas in 1976, I've been privileged to have had acclaimed runs on Spider-Man, Daredevil, Thor, Captain America and the Ultimate line of comics. I've also been deeply involved in bringing Stephen King's epic novels The Stand and Dark Tower to the comics format. Every assignment has been a dream come true for this dyed-in-the-wool Marvelite.

Now a dominant force in popular culture, the Marvel Universe is as fully realized a secondary world as the Middle Earth of J.R.R. Tolkien. And every month a new layer of history is added to it.

Today, seventy-five years after the Sub-Mariner burst from the turbulent seas, Marvel is a worldwide phenomenon spawning billion-dollar film franchises, merchandising bonanzas, and a still-vibrant line of comic books. This 75th Anniversary Marvel Encyclopedia allows fans to have on hand a comprehensive reference guide to Marvel's many worlds and wonders. To peruse its pages is to have an A to Z access of all things Marvel. It's a superb and rewarding text, and a monumental contribution to what is still, indisputably, the Marvel Age of Comics!

Enjoy!

Ralph Macchio

Ralph Macchio
October, 2013

The Mighty Thor #367 (May 1986)—one of the many comic books edited by Ralph Macchio during his celebrated association with Marvel Comics.

The Contributors

Tom DeFalco is also the Consultant Editor for the *Marvel Encyclopedia*. He is a best-selling author and a former editor-in-chief of Marvel. He is also the author of several Dorling Kindersley Ultimate guides to Marvel Super Heroes: *Avengers: The Ultimate Guide*, *Fantastic Four: The Ultimate Guide*, *Hulk: The Incredible Guide*, and *Spider-Man: The Ultimate Guide*.

Peter Sanderson is a comics historian and critic, who was Marvel's first official archivist. He is the author of Dorling Kindersley's best selling *X-Men: The Ultimate Guide.* Mr. Sanderson was also one of the main writers of the first four versions of *The Official Handbook of the Marvel Universe*.

Tom Brevoort is an Executive Editor for Marvel Comics, where he oversees titles such as *Avengers*, *Fantastic Four*, *Captain America*, *Iron Man*, and others. This also puts him in the unique position of being able to change any details of any Encyclopedia entry for which he couldn't locate the correct answer!

Michael Teitelbaum has been a writer, editor, and packager of children's books, comic books, and magazines for more than 20 years. Some of Michael's more recent writing includes *X-Men School*, *Story of the X-Men*, *Story of the Hulk*, *Story of Spider-Man*, and *Batman's Guide to Crime and Detection* for Dorling Kindersley.

Daniel Wallace is the author or co-author of more than a dozen books, including *Superman Returns: The Visual Guide* and the *DC Comics Encyclopedia* for Dorling Kindersley, *The Art of Superman Returns*, and the *New York Times*-best-selling *Star Wars: The New Essential Guide to Characters*.

Andrew Darling is a film, television and comics journalist, and the author of Dorling Kindersley's forthcoming *Ghost Rider: The Ultimate Guide* and *Thunderbirds: The Making of the Movie*. Andrew also writes for *SFX* and *Dreamwatch* magazines, the *Daily Mail* and contributed to *Star Wars* and *Prisoner* Fact Files.

Matt Forbeck has been writing and designing games, novels, comics, and more for over 20 years. His most recent work includes *Blood Bowl: Killer Contract*, *Mutant Chronicles*, *More Forbidden Knowledge*, *The Complete Idiot's Guide to Drawing Superheroes & Villains*, the *Harvey Birdman: Attorney at Law* video game, and *Marvel Heroes Battle Dice*.

INTRODUCTION

by Stan Lee

It just had to happen! There have been so many new and exciting developments in the Marvel Universe that fans world-wide have been clamouring for this second edition.

That's why we've totally updated everything by adding Marvel's mind-bending crossover developments such as Annihilation! Civil War! The Secret Invasion/Dark Reign! Private Hulk/World War Hulk!

Nor have we neglected new characters and updates on old ones. Here is just a tip of the incredible iceberg: Anti-Venom, Captain Midlands, Hulkling, Sabreclaw, Spider-Man 2211, Venus.

And, of course, we've included new teams, such as Agents of Atlas, Serpent Squad, X-Cell, Young Avengers.

And that's why I still proudly say—it ranks way up there with the discovery of fire and the invention of the wheel. Just like them, it represents an epic milestone in the history of the human race. That's why I'm so incredibly proud to be writing this intro for a book that mankind has been hungering for, a book that is—now and forever—a shining beacon of wonder, a titanic tribute to talent unleashed, with the simple but awesome title of—*The Marvel Encyclopedia.*

Here you'll find more than a thousand of Marvel's classic characters, all brilliantly illustrated, with their lives and vital statistics laid bare for your closest scrutiny and your browsing delight.

On a personal note, I must confess, when I first dreamed up some of the more prominent characters you'll find in this volume, I never dreamed that decades later they would have achieved the fame and popularity which they now enjoy. It's almost impossible to describe the feeling of pride, mixed with disbelief, that I feel when I realize how many great movies, video games, DVDs, toys and books are based on these heroes, villains, and far-out stories which we, in the mighty Marvel bullpen, had so much fun creating. None of us could have suspected that our creations would become so famous that we'd one day find ourselves featured in a prestigious encyclopedia.

And, speaking of this extraordinary book, when it comes to finding the hero or villain you may be seeking, the publishers have made it as easy for you as recognizing the Hulk in a crowd. They've put the names of each and every one in convenient alphabetical order.

Starting with the creation of the "Fantastic Four," the world's greatest comic book (as we so modestly called it), you'll also be able to find decade-by-decade highlights from Marvel's fabulous comic book history.

But what about the artwork? Glad you asked! You'll find illustrations from the very best of Marvel's amazing army of artists, pencilers and inkers who have made their indelible marks on the consciousness of comic book fans worldwide.

And, naturally, the accompanying texts are written by the most acclaimed scriptwriters in Marvel's galaxy of gifted scriveners. Every sentence is a tribute to the greatest Super Hero creations this side of Asgard.

But that's not all. Realizing that some of the spectacular characters in our Super Hero stable have actually achieved such status and fame that they are now truly worldwide legends, the editors have wisely decided to accord these special heroes and villains full-page, double-page, or even *two* double-page layouts, plus a brief guide to their essential storylines.

There's so much more that I could say, but if I do it'll keep me from leaving my computer and reaching for my beautiful, brand-new Marvel Encyclopedia which is proudly sitting on my corner table. It might be my imagination, but I seem to see a glow around that voluminous volume, as though it's illuminated by some supernatural aura, some mystic radiance emanating from the combined power of the fantastic characters within its pages.

I know I must be fantasizing, and yet—as I slowly reach out to touch the cover of this magnificent book, I wonder—as you may wonder, too—what magic lies within?

Excelsior!

Stan

ABOMINATION

FACTFILE
REAL NAME
Emil Blonsky
OCCUPATION
Criminal
BASE
Mobile

HEIGHT 6 ft 8 in
WEIGHT 980 lbs
EYES Green
HAIR None

FIRST APPEARANCE
Tales to Astonish #90 (April 1967)

POWERS
Superhuman strength enables leaps of two miles; tough skin withstands small arms fire. Unlike Hulk, the Abomination's strength does not increase with rage, and he rarely returns to human form; however he retains all Blonsky's mental faculties.

The Abomination is even stronger than the Hulk. His body is covered with reptilian scales.

Born in Zagreb, Yugoslavia, Emil Blonsky became a spy and infiltrated the US Air Force base where scientist Bruce Banner (*see* HULK) was stationed and discovered gamma-radiation equipment, with which Banner intended to commit suicide. Irradiating himself, Blonsky became the monstrous Abomination.

The Abomination battled the Hulk multiple times. Their struggles were interrupted when the STRANGER kidnapped him into space for study, and he wound up serving as the first mate of the starship Andromeda. After returning to Earth, he became the pawn of many villains, including MODOK, MEPHISTO, and TYRANNUS.

The Abomination later revealed his new form to his wife, Nadia, who then left him. Jealous of Banner's apparent wedded bliss, Blonsky poisoned Banner's wife Betty (*see* ROSS, BETTY). Years later, the RED HULK—secretly Betty's father (*see* ROSS, GENERAL T. E.) hunted down and murdered the Abomination with a special gun designed to kill the Hulk. During the CHAOS WAR, Pluto freed the Abomination from the afterlife to fight for him, but he was later destroyed. **AD, MF**

The Abomination retains his intelligence but fights like a monster.

ABSORBING MAN

FACTFILE
REAL NAME
Carl "Crusher" Creel
OCCUPATION
Criminal
BASE
Mobile

HEIGHT 6 ft 4 in
WEIGHT 365 lbs
EYES Blue
HAIR None

FIRST APPEARANCE
Journey Into Mystery #114 (March 1965)

POWERS
Can magically duplicate within himself the physical and mystical properties of anything he physically contacts, including various forms of energy. If his body is broken into pieces while he is in a non-human state, he can mentally reassemble it.

Seeking a pawn to use against his nemesis THOR, the Asgardian god LOKI endowed brutal prisoner "Crusher" Creel and his ball and chain with the power to "absorb" the physical properties of anything he touched. Creel broke out of prison and battled Thor, as Loki intended. However, Creel overreached himself by trying to absorb the power of the whole Earth and exploded. Thanks to his new powers, however, Creel was not truly dead, and Loki magically reassembled his body. Loki then enlisted the Absorbing Man as his ally in an attempt to overthrow ODIN, monarch of Asgard (*see* GODS OF ASGARD), but Odin banished Creel into outer space.

The Absorbing Man's body can even duplicate the unknown alloy of Captain America's shield.

Over the years the Absorbing Man has repeatedly battled Thor and the HULK as well as SPIDER-MAN and the AVENGERS. During the first Secret War staged by the BEYONDER, Creel met Mary "Skeeter" MacPherran (TITANIA), whom he later married. He was thought killed by SENTRY during the Civil War, and it was soon after revealed that he was the father of Stonewall of the SECRET WARRIORS. Creel returned, only to be depowered by Norman Osborn (*see* GREEN GOBLIN). During FEAR ITSELF, a repowered Creel became Greithoth, Breaker of Wills, one of agents of destruction for the Worthy. **PS, MF**

ABYSS

FIRST APPEARANCE Avengers #1 (February 2013)
REAL NAME Abyss **OCCUPATION** Destroyer
BASE Mars **HEIGHT/WEIGHT** Not applicable
EYES Black **HAIR** Black
SPECIAL POWERS/ABILITIES Abyss is made of living gas, which makes her invulnerable to most physical attacks. She can also manipulate the minds of others whom she envelopes in a sphere of gas.

Abyss was a powerful creature of living gas created by ALEPH, one of the alien Builders, along with her brother EX NIHILO. The three creatures traveled the universe together, destroying planets they judged unworthy to continue. They came to Mars and began to terraform it into their base in the Solar System. From there, Ex Nihilo fired origin bombs at Earth, terraforming entire cities at once and killing everyone within. When the AVENGERS tried to stop them, Abyss bent the HULK's mind to her will. When CAPTAIN UNIVERSE confronted her, Abyss recognized her power surrendered to her. It was later revealed that her real name was Drusilla, a member of a race of similar creatures, of which she is the sole survivor. She and Ex Nihilo later joined the Avengers to stop the Builder invasion (*see* INFINITY). **MF**

Acolytes

FIRST APPEARANCE X-Men #1 (October 1991)
BASE Formerly Genosha, Avalon, Asteroid M
FOUNDER MEMBERS **Fabian Cortez** Increases mutants' powers **Exodus** Psionic powers **Anne-Marie Cortez** Mind control **Chrome** Alters matter **Marco Delgado** Increases size, strength **Rusty Collins** Pyrokinetic **Joanna Cargill** Strength **Skids** Creates force-field **Colossus** Becomes organic steel **Spoor** Super-senses; mood-altering pheromones.

Rogue of the X-Men, who absorbs the powers of other mutants, attracts the unwelcome attentions of Magneto's Acolytes team.

Fabian Cortez founded the Acolytes to help realize MAGNETO's dream of a world ruled by mutants. However, Cortez betrayed Magneto and vied with him for control of the group. On M-Day, most of the Acolytes lost their powers. Recently, the remnants of the group, under the leadership of EXODUS, helped revive PROFESSOR X after BISHOP shot him in the head. **TD, MF**

Adversary

FIRST APPEARANCE Uncanny X-Men #188 (December 1984)
REAL NAME Unknown (alias Naze, the great trickster)
OCCUPATION Ancient deity **BASE** An unknown dimension
HEIGHT/WEIGHT/EYES/HAIR Not applicable
SPECIAL POWERS/ABILITIES Can assume any form he desires; may be fought successfully through magic, but not through most forms of physical force; vulnerable to iron, steel, and adamantium.

The Cheyenne believe that the Adversary is a demonic god that toys with the fate of the universe, heedless of the deaths he causes. FORGE was trained to be a shaman and combat him. After his teacher, Naze, was murdered and replaced by the Adversary, Forge joined the X-MEN in an attempt to stop the monster. The Adversary is imprisoned by mystical spells, but may one day escape confinement. **TD**

Agamemnon

FIRST APPEARANCE Incredible Hulk #381 (May 1991)
REAL NAME Vali Halfling **OCCUPATION** Godlike observer
BASE The Mount, a mountain base in Arizona
HEIGHT 5 ft 7 in **WEIGHT** 140 lbs **EYES** Brown **HAIR** Brown
SPECIAL POWERS/ABILITIES Virtually immortal; projects a holograph of himself as an old, bearded man so that no one suspects that he truly looks like a teenaged boy.

The son of LOKI and a mortal mother, Vali traded the pick of his future offspring with the alien Troyjan race in exchange for knowledge of immortality. He later founded the PANTHEON, an interventionist think-tank, whose members included many of his other children, some adopted. However, when Agamemnon's betrayals became known to the Pantheon, he attempted to slay them all. He died during that battle, but he returned with the rebirth of the Norse gods (*see* GODS OF ASGARD) after RAGNAROK and worked with Amadeus CHO's Olympus Group. He captured WOLFSBANE when she was pregnant so he could steal her child, but the monstrous baby killed him soon after its birth. **TB, MF**

Agent X

FIRST APPEARANCE Agent X #1 (September 2002)
REAL NAME Nijo (aka Alex Hayden)
OCCUPATION Mercenary **BASE** Mobile
HEIGHT 6 ft 2 in **WEIGHT** 210 lbs **EYES** Brown **HAIR** None
SPECIAL POWERS/ABILITIES Augmented strength, agility, and dexterity; superhuman regenerative abilities; certain advanced mental abilities; enhanced skill as a marksman.

Agent X's real name is Nijo, but during a bout of amnesia he adopted the name Alex Hayden. Agent X is a combined consciousness which resides in the body of Nijo but which also contains the mental powers of DEADPOOL and Black Swan. Agent X was created when the corpse of Nijo was revived and given Deadpool's healing power by Black Swan, who has the ability to enter a person's mind and unleash viruses similar to computer viruses into their brain. Agent X subsequently founded a team of mercenaries known as Agency X with his girlfriend Outlaw, TASKMASTER, Sandi Brandenberg, and the mutant Mary Zero. **MT**

Agent Zero/Maverick

FIRST APPEARANCE (as Maverick) X-Men #5 (Feb. 1992)
REAL NAME Christopher Nord (changed to David North)
OCCUPATION Secret agent, mercenary **BASE** Berlin, Germany
HEIGHT 6 ft 3 in **WEIGHT** 230 lbs **EYES** Blue **HAIR** Brown
SPECIAL POWERS/ABILITIES Can absorb kinetic energy and utilize it for superhuman strength or release it as concussive blasts. Possesses aging suppression and enhanced healing factors.

Having stolen weapon X files, Maverick, covered his tracks.

Born in East Germany, Christopher Nord became a freedom fighter against the oppressive, postwar Communist regime. He was recruited by the CIA for its WEAPON X project and changed his name to David North. By the early 1960s, North partnered with Logan and Victor Creed, the future WOLVERINE and SABRETOOTH, in the CIA's Team X. Later, North became a mercenary codenamed Maverick. After nearly being killed by Sabretooth, Maverick reluctantly rejoined the Weapon X project, which saved his life. Nord subsequently became the project's leading special operative, AGENT ZERO. He lost his powers on M-Day and retired, and now works as Maverick once more. **PS**

AGE OF ULTRON,
see pages 12-13

THE AGE OF ULTRON

The End of an Era

ISSUE #1

With New York destroyed and the rest of the planet about to follow suit, Hawkeye rescues Spider-Man, and brings him beneath Central Park to reunite with the surviving Avengers.

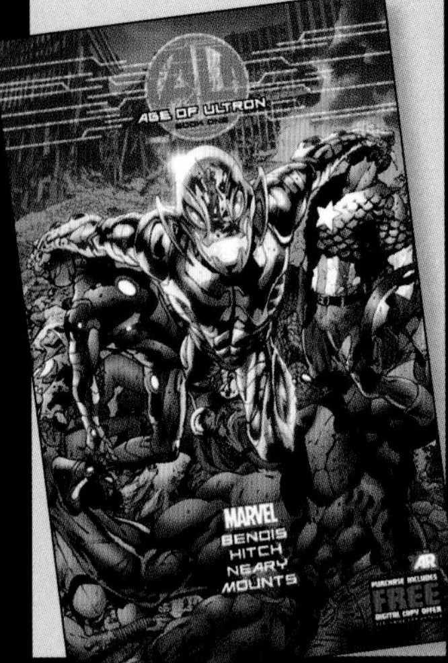

After the events of ANNIHILATION, Ultron—the human-hating, artificially intelligent robot created by Hank PYM—returned to Earth in the inactive body of a Galadorian Spaceknight. The INTELLIGENCIA found it and tried to activate it, but the AVENGERS intervened. During the ensuing battle, Ultron reawakened in his new body and escaped.

With two Wolverines from different universes trapped in the past, the one from The Age of Ultron sacrificed himself so the other could return to his repaired timeline.

ULTRON RETURNS

Free on Earth once again, Ultron assembled an army of Ultron Sentinels and launched a swift and horrifying attack on New York City. The initial assault killed many of the world's most powerful heroes, and the rest—including CAPTAIN AMERICA, Emma FROST, INVISIBLE WOMAN, IRON MAN, HAWKEYE, Luke CAGE, SHE-HULK, and WOLVERINE—were forced underground. HAMMERHEAD and the OWL captured SPIDER-MAN and tortured him to learn the location of other Avengers so they could sell them to Ultron, but Hawkeye mounted a bloody and successful rescue attempt before they could do so.

Under the guidance of Captain America, Luke Cage knocked out She-Hulk and pretended to try to sell her to Ultron, in order to get inside the adamantium robot's headquarters. Cage discovered that Ultron ruled over his Sentinels via a dismembered VISION, controlling him by remote from the future. She-Hulk sacrificed her life so Luke could escape and tell the others what he had learned. The Avengers traveled to the Savage Land to evade Ultron. There they met with Ka-Zar and other scattered heroes, including BLACK WIDOW, MOON KNIGHT, Monica Rambeau, QUICKSILVER, RED HULK, and VALKYRIE. Despite being caught in a nuclear bomb explosion, Cage had reached the Savage Land first and, before he died, he told them Ultron's secret. Black Widow led the others to a safe house Nick FURY had set up in the Savage Land long ago. They found him waiting there for them, along with DOCTOR DOOM's time platform.

Ultron created thousands of Ultrons, and they set about conquering the world one city at a time.

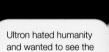

A team of heroes mounted an ill-fated assault against Ultron in the future. Believing the effort was doomed to fail, WOLVERINE and Invisible Woman waited for the others to leave and then went back into the past to kill Hank Pym before he could create Ultron. When they returned to their time, they found themselves in an alternate universe, which had been transformed into a dystopia by Pym's death. Disheartened, Wolverine and Invisible Woman returned to the past. Wolverine stopped his past self from killing Pym, and they worked with Pym to implant a virus into Ultron at his creation and then erase his memory of doing so.

This time around, when Ultron was awakened, Pym—alerted by a message from his past self—worked with Iron Man to trigger the failsafe virus and deactivate Ultron before he could escape.

MF

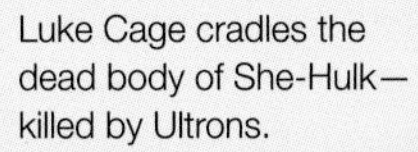

Luke Cage cradles the dead body of She-Hulk—killed by Ultrons.

Ultron hated humanity and wanted to see the entire race extinguished.

DIFFERENT TIME

e death of Hank Pym caused a butterfly effect that eated a whole new universe, in which a cyborg Iron n led SHIELD in a war that pitted his technology ainst the magical forces of Morgan le Fay. In this rld, Earth's mightiest heroes were the Defenders, ich included Cable (Cyclops), Captain Marvel (Wasp), lonel America (Captain America), Doctor Strange, Hulk, r-Lord, the Thing, and Wolverine. This world's Iron n told Wolverine how he could repair the timeline d defeat Ultron. During an attack by Le Fay's army, isible Woman and both Wolverines escaped and set to implement that plan.

AGENTS OF ATLAS

Security team with a shady reputation

AGENTS OF ATLAS

FACTFILE

KEY MEMBERS

GORILLA-MAN
The body of a gorilla with the mind of a man

HUMAN ROBOT
Super-strong, self-repairing robot with a force field, a death ray, and telescopic, electrified limbs

NAMORA
Amphibious, super-strong woman

THE URANIAN
The original Marvel Boy

VENUS
A siren with super-toughness and a hypnotic voice

JIMMY WOO
Secret agent

BASE
The Temple of Atlas, inside a huge cavern beneath San Francisco

FIRST APPEARANCE
(As the G-Men)
Agents of Atlas #1
(As the Agents of Atlas)
Agents of Atlas #6

In 1958, FBI agent Jimmy Woo formed a group of heroes called the G-Men to rescue President Eisenhower from the Yellow Claw. Working with SHIELD decades later, Jimmy reformed the team to investigate a shadowy organization known as the Atlas Foundation, based in the Temple of Atlas. They discovered that the Yellow Claw was in fact Plan Chu, direct heir of Genghis Khan and the leader of the Atlas Foundation. Plan had chosen Jimmy as his own heir, and he'd spent the past few decades working as Jimmy's enemy, forcing him to become properly prepared. Shocked by this revelation, Jimmy nevertheless agreed to take over the Atlas Foundation and turn it into a force for good, at which point Chu allowed his adviser—a golden dragon known as Mr. Lao—to devour him.

ESSENTIAL STORYLINES

- ***Agents of Atlas Vol. 1 #1–6*** Jimmy Woo reunites the team to fight against the Yellow Claw and discovers the Claw's master plan.
- ***Agents of Atlas Vol. 2 #9–11*** Jimmy Woo accidentally breaks a truce with the Asian splinter group of the Atlas Foundation and sparks a Dragon Clan War.
- ***Atlas #1–5*** Aliens from the Echo World attack 3-D Man with innocents they've possessed and lead to the discovery of Earth-9904.

The Yellow Claw met his end in Mr. Lao's jaws, just like every khan in his line.

DARK REIGN

The team fought the Skrulls during the Secret Invasion, but once Norman Osborn (*see* Green Goblin) rose to power during the Dark Reign, Jimmy decided to retain the Atlas Foundation's villainous reputation so he could work to destroy Osborn's takeover of the US government from within, starting with robbing Fort Knox. Jimmy's insistence on leading his team in the field led Mr. Lao to appoint a second in command: Temugin, the son of the Mandarin. To help run the organization, Jimmy in turn hired his old friend Derek Khanata, one of the many SHIELD agents Osborn had fired.

TURF WARS

Jimmy discovered that his old flame Suwan, Plan Chu's niece, had long ago split from the main Atlas Foundation and set up her own organization in Asia. Retaining her youth via the same elixirs used by the Yellow Claw, she ruled over her faithful warriors as the Jade Claw, enforcing her will with the help of her high-tech robot M-21 and her own dragon advisor, Yao. Jimmy accidentally broke a truce with the Great Wall, sparking a war with Suwan. When the Atlas Foundation defeated the Great Wall, Jimmy decided not to destroy their rivals but reconcile with them, and he put Temugin in charge of this newly acquired branch.

The Atlas Foundation later joined up with 3-D Man, who helped them stave off an invasion from the Echo World situated between theirs and Earth-9904. In the course of this, the Agents of Atlas visited that alternate earth and witnessed a celebration in which Jimmy was being honored for having started the Avengers. **MF**

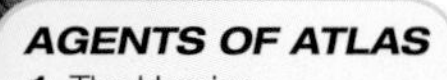

AGENTS OF ATLAS
1 The Uranian
2 Namora
3 M-11
4 Gorilla Man
5 3-D Man
6 Venus
7 Jimmy Woo

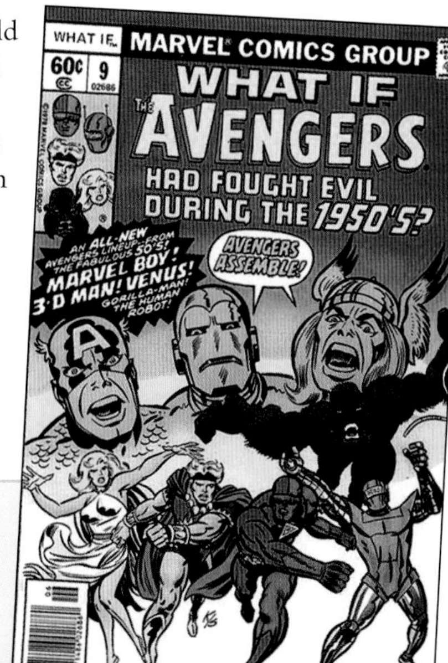

A similar team appeared in *What If?* #9 (June, 1978) as the 1950s Avengers of Earth-9904.

Ahab

FIRST APPEARANCE Fantastic Four Annual #23 (1990)
REAL NAME Dr. Roderick Campbell
OCCUPATION Geneticist **BASE** Mobile
HEIGHT 6 ft 1 in **WEIGHT** (as Campbell) 166 lbs (as Ahab) 222 lbs
EYES Brown **HAIR** Brown **SPECIAL POWERS/ABILITIES** Possesses a robotic body, and wields psionic harpoons that cause those struck to feel pain, to be enslaved to his will, or to perish.

In a possible future, Ahab created a process by which captured mutants were turned into slaves known as Hounds and used to hunt down their fellow mutants. Ahab's body was rebuilt cybernetically after he was critically injured during the escape of his best Hound, Rachel Summers (*see* SUMMERS, RACHEL), into the past. He later joined APOCALYPSE and became Famine in the Four Horsemen. **TB, MF**

The cyborg Ahab prepares to throw a psionic harpoon.

Ajak

FIRST APPEARANCE The Eternals #2 (August 1976)
REAL NAME Ajak **OCCUPATION** Adventurer
BASE The City of the Space Gods, Andes Mountains
HEIGHT 6 ft 1 in **WEIGHT** 220 lbs **EYES** Gray **HAIR** Black
SPECIAL POWERS/ABILITIES Superhuman strength, virtual immortality and invulnerability; could psionically levitate, rearrange the molecular structure of objects, and project cosmic energy.

One of the Polar ETERNALS, Ajak was the spokesman for the Third and Fourth Host of the CELESTIALS on Earth. Ajak befriended archaeologist Dr. Daniel Damian, who used Celestial technology to turn Ajak into a murderous monster when his daughter Margo was killed. Ajak disintegrated himself and Damian out of guilt. Restored to life in Olympia years later, Ajak sought to learn how to speak with the Dreaming Celestial. He joined Hercules' God Squad against the Skrull gods and was killed in that battle. He returned after all the Eternals had had their memories erased and helped remind them who they were. **PS, MF**

Aleph

FIRST APPEARANCE Avengers #1 (February 2013)
REAL NAME Aleph **OCCUPATION** Destroyer
BASE Mars **HEIGHT** Varies **WEIGHT** Varies
EYES Yellow **HAIR** None
SPECIAL POWERS/ABILITIES Aleph possesses superhuman strength, speed, and senses. He can fly and project energy blasts. His metal body is nearly invulnerable and he can reconfigure it at will.

Aleph is one of a powerful set of living robots created by the BUILDERS, the oldest race in the universe. Tasked with purging worlds filled with unfit forms of life, he traveled the galaxy until he found a worthy people, at which point he released the seeds that grew into ABYSS and EX NIHILO. He escorted them to many other planets, debating the fate of their peoples with them. On Mars, Aleph oversaw the planet's terraforming and advocated the razing of the Earth. When CAPTAIN UNIVERSE ordered the trio to stand down, Aleph refused, and she destroyed him with a touch. **MF**

Air-Walker

FIRST APPEARANCE Fantastic Four #120 (March 1972)
REAL NAME Gabriel Lan
OCCUPATION Herald of Galactus **BASE** Various
HEIGHT 6ft 1in **WEIGHT** 210 lbs **EYES** Blue **HAIR** White
SPECIAL POWERS/ABILITIES Command of the Power Cosmic, the fundamental force of the universe, enables a variety of powers, including force blasts, interstellar flight, and ability to walk on air.

Chosen by the planet-devouring GALACTUS to become his latest Herald after the betrayal of the SILVER SURFER, Xandarian starship captain Gabriel Lan was endowed with the Power Cosmic, becoming Gabriel, the Air Walker. As the Air Walker, Gabriel served his master for several years, seeking out worlds for Galactus to consume in order to survive. After the Ovoids killed the Air-Walker, Galactus transferred his mind into a robotic body. However, Galactus did not care for the results and replaced him with Firelord. Since then, Air-Walker's robotic body has been destroyed and rebuilt several times. Perhaps this last rebuild could mean the end of him. **TB, MF**

Allan, Liz

FACTFILE
REAL NAME
Elizabeth Allan
OCCUPATION
Former businesswoman
BASE
Mobile

HEIGHT 5 ft 9 in
WEIGHT 135 lbs
EYES Blue
HAIR Blond

FIRST APPEARANCE
Amazing Fantasy #15 (August 1962)

In high school, Peter Parker (SPIDER-MAN) had a crush on Liz Allan, who dated his rival, Flash THOMPSON. She later married Peter's pal Harry Osborn (the second GREEN GOBLIN), with whom she had a child named Norman Osborn, after his grandfather (the original Green Goblin). After Harry and his father both died, she took control of Osborn Industries, although raising her son and caring for her stepbrother Mark Raxton (MOLTEN MAN) occupied much of her time. When the elder Osborn returned from the dead, he took his company back from her. She had a brief relationship with Foggy NELSON, but ended their relationship after MYSTERIO tricked him into having an affair as part of a plot to drive DAREDEVIL mad. When MEPHISTO erased the knowledge of Spider-Man's identity from the world, Harry somehow returned to life, but he and Liz were now divorced. **DW, MF**

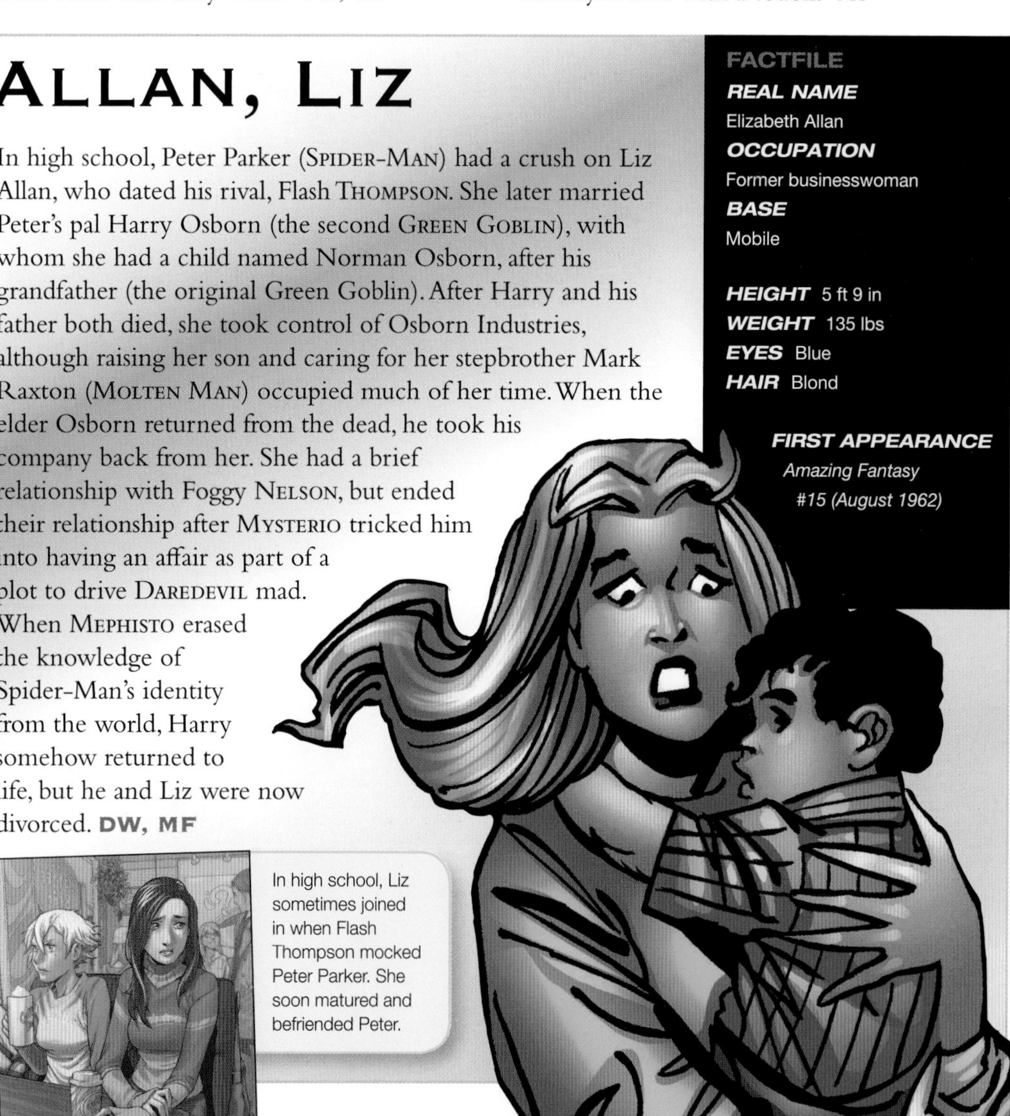

In high school, Liz sometimes joined in when Flash Thompson mocked Peter Parker. She soon matured and befriended Peter.

ALL-WINNERS SQUAD

FIRST APPEARANCE All-Winners Comics #19 (Fall 1946)
MEMBERS AND POWERS
Captain America Superior strength, speed, agility, and endurance
Human Torch Can control fire and can fly
Namor Increased strength, can fly, can breath in air or water
Whizzer Can run at super speed
Miss America Superhuman strength, can fly

Following World War II, the heroes of the All-Winners Squad decided to stay together to fight crime in the US rather than foreign enemies. They battled and stopped Adam-2, an android who designed a robot army. Later they faced Future Man, a time traveler from the year 1,000,000 who hoped to destroy humanity in order to allow his race to inhabit the Earth. The Squad also battled the SHE-HULK who had traveled back in time to help some gangsters acquire an atomic bomb. **MT**

THE ALL-WINNERS SQUAD
1 Miss America ***2*** Captain America ***3*** The Human Torch ***4*** Namor, the Sub-Mariner ***5*** Whizzer

ALPHA

FIRST APPEARANCE Amazing Spider-Man #692 (October 2012)
REAL NAME Andrew Maguire
OCCUPATION Student, super hero **BASE** Pittsburgh
HEIGHT 5 ft 8 in **WEIGHT** 150 lbs **EYES** Blue **HAIR** Blond
SPECIAL POWERS/ABILITIES Alpha is energized with Parker Particles, which give him superhuman strength and speed, as well as the ability to project energy, create force fields, and fly; however, he can usually only use one power at a time.

Andy Maguire was a student at Midtown High in Queens. On a field trip to Horizon Labs to see Peter Parker (*see* SPIDER-MAN) debut his latest discovery, Andy was accidentally infused with a blast of Parker Particles. Spider-Man took Alpha under his wing, but after a disastrous fight in which Alpha helped the AVENGERS bring down TERMINUS but endangered countless innocents, Spider-Man de-powered Alpha and sent him home. Andy's parents divorced soon after, and he moved to Pittsburgh with his mother. When DOCTOR OCTOPUS took over Spider-Man's body, he gave Alpha back 10 percent of his powers so he could study the effects. Spider-Man decided against taking Alpha's powers after learning they could give him cancer. **MF**

ALRAUNE, MARLENE

FIRST APPEARANCE The Hulk #11 (October 1978)
REAL NAME Marlene Alraune
OCCUPATION Art history student, archaeologist, social worker
BASE Spector Mansion, Long Island
HEIGHT 6 ft 2 in **WEIGHT** 130 lbs **EYES** Blue **HAIR** Blond
SPECIAL POWERS/ABILITIES Marlene has the strength and agility of a normal woman; she is a skilled markswoman, gymnast, and hand-to-hand combatant and a resourceful crimefighter.

Marlene was in the Sudan with her father, archaeologist Dr. Peter Alraune, Sr., when he was murdered by mercenary Raoul Bushman. Another mercenary, Marc Spector, saved Marlene's life, but Bushman left him to die in the desert. Dr. Alraune's workers brought Spector's inert body to the tomb of Pharaoh Seti III. Spector miraculously revived, and he and Marlene returned to the US, where he became the crimefighter MOON KNIGHT. Marlene is his confidante, girlfriend, and ally. **PS**

Mikaboshi used Ares' son Alex against him, taking the boy's form so he could get close enough to attack Zeus.

AMATSU-MIKABOSHI

AMATSU-MIKABOSHI

FACTFILE
REAL NAME
Amatsu-Mikaboshi
OCCUPATION
God of evil
BASE
The Void

HEIGHT Variable
WEIGHT Variable
EYES Gold (variable)
HAIR Black (variable)

FIRST APPEARANCE
Thor: Blood Oath #6 (October 2012)

POWERS
An immortal god with superhuman strength, endurance, invulnerability, and speed. He manipulates magical energy and can change shape at will. He can also teleport and fly.

Amatsu-Mikaboshi—also known as the Chaos King—is the Shinto (Japanese) god of evil. He represents the void that existed before the creation of the universe, and he works to return it to that state of nothingness. He long desired Kusanagi, the legendary Grasscutter Sword, but it was kept from him for centuries until THOR and the WARRIORS THREE liberated it. The blade wound up on Earth, where Mikaboshi finally claimed it.

He used the sword to capture Yomi (the underworld) and then sought to conquer the GODS OF OLYMPUS. The Olympians banded together with the other Japanese gods to thwart Mikaboshi, but not before he mortally wounded Zeus, the leader of the Olympians. Despite this, Mikaboshi joined the God Squad that Athena assembled to defeat the SKRULL gods during the SECRET INVASION. While it seemed that Mikaboshi died in that battle, he survived and went on to defeat the gods of several alien civilizations before returning to Earth.

During the CHAOS WAR, Mikaboshi murdered NIGHTMARE and stole his powers, putting all sleeping mortals into a coma as he prepared his assault on the surviving gods. HERCULES assembled a new God Squad to stand against the Chaos King. At the last moment, he knocked Mikaboshi through a portal into an empty alternate universe known as the Continuum, which the Chaos King now rules. **MF**

ALPHA FLIGHT

Canada's foremost Super Hero team

The Alpha Flight team roar into action.

Conceived as the Canadian government's answer to the recent spate of superhuman activity within the United States, Alpha Flight was the brainchild of James MacDonald Hudson, soon to be known first as VINDICATOR, then as GUARDIAN. Inspired by the FANTASTIC FOUR, Hudson and his wife Heather convinced the Canadian government to found Department H, which would be tasked with assembling a team of superhumans indigenous to the Great White North.

ESSENTIAL STORYLINES

- ***Uncanny X-Men #120–121*** Alpha Flight ambushes the X-Men in an attempt to recover the AWOL Wolverine for the Canadian government.
- ***Alpha Flight #12*** Guardian is seemingly killed during Alpha's battle with Omega Flight.
- ***Alpha Flight Vol. 3 #1–6*** With the real Alpha Flight missing, Sasquatch assembles a new team of off-beat heroes.

FACTFILE

ORIGINAL MEMBERS

GUARDIAN
Electromagnetic battlesuit allows him to fly, surrounds him with a powerful force field, and permits him to throw bolts of electromagnetic force.

VINDICATOR
Geothermic battlesuit allows her to fly, cause the earth to erupt volcanically, and blast a lavalike substance from her hands.

SHAMAN
Withdraws needed objects from enchanted medicine pouch.

SASQUATCH
Superhuman strength and imperviousness to harm.

PUCK
Trained fighter, skilled acrobat.

SNOWBIRD
Transforms into various Canadian animal forms.

BASE
Tamarind Island, British Columbia

FIRST APPEARANCE
Uncanny X-Men #120 (April 1979)

ALPHA FLIGHT (2011)
1 Shaman **2** Guardian **3** Sasquatch **4** Aurora **5** Marrina **6** Northstar **7** Puck **8** Snowbird

WANTED: A LEADER

The project was implemented using a three-tiered training system: new recruits or those whose powers proved unstable would be assigned to Gamma Flight. Those whose command of their abilities required further training formed the basis of Beta Flight. The front line, the active members whose job it would be to rout any superhuman threats to the nation, were Alpha Flight. Hudson intended that the man known as Logan (*see* WOLVERINE) or WEAPON X would lead Alpha Flight. However, that task fell to Hudson himself when Logan was recruited by PROFESSOR X to become a member of his X-MEN team. Alpha Flight endured a rocky relationship with the Canadian government, being cast aside then drafted back into military service. While the Beta and Gamma Flight units produced heroes to serve with Alpha Flight, such as PUCK, the programs were perverted to form the nucleus of the sinister Omega Flight. Alpha Flight soldiered on through deaths and resurrections, strange transformations, sudden reversals, and numerous roster changes—loyal to their mission of protecting their homeland.

The original team battled Wendigo and other villains in a story that featured Canadian PM Pierre Trudeau!

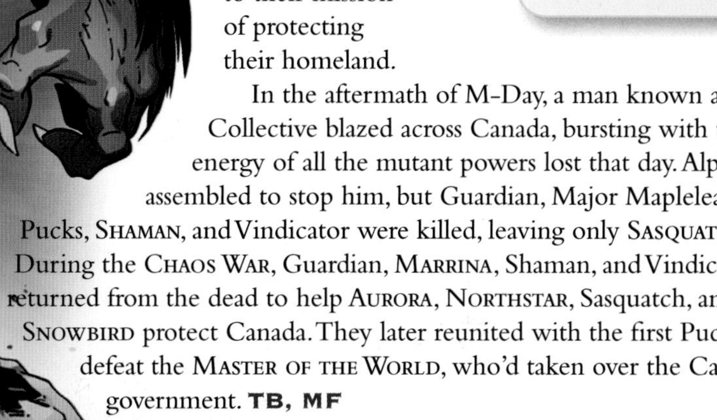

In the aftermath of M-Day, a man known as the Collective blazed across Canada, bursting with the energy of all the mutant powers lost that day. Alpha Flight assembled to stop him, but Guardian, Major Mapleleaf, two Pucks, SHAMAN, and Vindicator were killed, leaving only SASQUATCH alive. During the CHAOS WAR, Guardian, MARRINA, Shaman, and Vindicator returned from the dead to help AURORA, NORTHSTAR, Sasquatch, and SNOWBIRD protect Canada. They later reunited with the first Puck to defeat the MASTER OF THE WORLD, who'd taken over the Canadian government. **TB, MF**

American Eagle

FIRST APPEARANCE Marvel Two-In-One Annual #6 (1981)
REAL NAME Jason Strongbow
OCCUPATION Champion of the Navaho Tribe
BASE Navaho Reservation, Arizona
HEIGHT 6 ft **WEIGHT** 200 lbs **EYES** Brown **HAIR** Black
SPECIAL POWERS/ABILITIES Superstrength, speed, and endurance; shoots a crossbow with specialized bolts.

While protesting the mining of a sacred mountain, Jason Strongbow and his brother Ward encountered KLAW, whose sonic blast reacted with uranium in the rock and mutagenically enhanced the brothers. As American Eagle, Jason tracked Klaw to the Savage Land, where he defeated the villain with the aid of the THING, Ka-zar, and Wyatt WINGFOOT, but at the cost of Ward's life. Jason refused to register with the US government during the CIVIL WAR and fought the THUNDERBOLTS to stay free. He crippled Bullseye before he escaped. During FEAR ITSELF, he foiled a trio of thugs on mutant growth hormone, who were causing troubles on his reservation. **AD, MF**

A-Next

A-NEXT

On Earth-982, the AVENGERS disbanded. Ten years later, Kevin Masterson, son of THUNDERSTRIKE, visited Avengers Compound to find that JARVIS had kept his father's enchanted mace for him. LOKI stole the mace and so inspired the formation of a new Avengers team, each member being related to a former one. Team membership varied as A-Next faced off against the DEFENDERS, the Soldiers of the Serpent, Kristoff Vernard (DR. DOOM's adopted son), Argo, IRON MAN, RED SKULL and DR. DOOM, and the REVENGERS. They've also worked with SPIDER-GIRL and the Fantastic Five. **TD**

A-NEXT
1 Blue Streak
2 Spider-Girl
3 American Dream
4 Sabreclaw
5 J2

FACTFILE

FOUNDING MEMBERS
THUNDERSTRIKE Super-strong, generates thunder blasts of concussive force
MAINFRAME Program that lives within mobile armored, multi-weaponed, super-strong robot body
STINGER Flies, shrinks, generates bio-electric blasts
J2 Super-strong, nearly unstoppable and indestructible
EDWIN JARVIS Director of operations

ADDITIONAL MEMBERS
American Dream, Ant-Man, Blue Streak, Crimson Curse, Freebooter, Hawkeye, Jubilee, Kate Power, Sabreclaw, Scarlet Witch, Speedball, Thena, Warp

BASE
Avengers Compound

FIRST APPEARANCE
A-Next #1 (October 1998)

Anaconda

FIRST APPEARANCE Marvel *Two-In-One* #1 (June 1980)
REAL NAME Blanche "Blondie" Sitznski
OCCUPATION Freelance criminal **BASE** Mobile
HEIGHT 6 ft 2 in **WEIGHT** 220 lbs **EYES** Green **HAIR** Blond
SPECIAL POWERS/ABILITIES Able to stretch her limbs, wrap them around people or objects, and exert enough power to crush one-inch thick steel. Few humans can break free from her grasp.

Former steelworker Blanche Sitznski underwent bioengineering changes at the mutagenics lab of the Brand Corporation and became Anaconda. She then joined the SERPENT SQUAD to help retrieve the Serpent Crown. After some time as a mercenary, she joined SIDEWINDER in the SERPENT SOCIETY crime organization. She did stints with the Femizons and the SIX PACK before joining the Serpent Society again during the CIVIL WAR. **MT, MF**

Ancient One

ANCIENT ONE

Five centuries ago the master sorcerer called the Ancient One was a young farmer in the Himalayan village of Kamar-Taj. He studied sorcery with another villager, KALUU. When Kaluu sought to use his powers for conquest, the youth thwarted him, and henceforth dedicated his life to opposing evil sorcerers. He eventually became Sorcerer Supreme of Earth's dimension.

Though magic greatly extended his life, the Ancient One knew that his death was inevitable and sought to train a successor. He accepted BARON MORDO as a pupil, although he was aware of Mordo's potential for evil. Then the American surgeon Stephen Strange arrived, hoping that the Ancient One could cure his injured hands. Instead Strange found a new vocation and asked to become the Ancient One's pupil. Under the Ancient One's tutelage, DOCTOR STRANGE ultimately became the new sorcerer supreme of the Earth dimension.

Later, to prevent the demon Shuma-Gorath from entering the Earth dimension through his mind, the Ancient One persuaded Strange to shut down the elderly sorcerer's brain. Thus the Ancient One died in mortal form, but his astral form became "one with the universe." He has reappeared in his astral form several times since, working in the service of Eternity. **PS, MF**

FACTFILE

REAL NAME
Yao

OCCUPATION
Sorcerer Supreme

BASE
Kamar-Taj, Tibet, China

HEIGHT 5 ft 11 in
WEIGHT 160 lbs
EYES Brown
HAIR Bald, with white beard

FIRST APPEARANCE
Strange Tales #110 (July 1963)

POWERS

Vast natural talent allied with years of training made him the greatest sorcerer in Earth's dimension, capable of astral projection, mesmerism, illusion-casting, etc; able to hurl bolts of energy and possessed of extraordinary longevity.

Andromeda

FIRST APPEARANCE Defenders #143 (May 1985)
REAL NAME Andromeda **OCCUPATION** Warrior **BASE** Atlantis
HEIGHT 5 ft 8 in **WEIGHT** 180 lbs **EYES** Green **HAIR** Auburn
SPECIAL POWERS/ABILITIES Her physiology is suited to survival beneath the ocean; unusually strong for an Atlantean woman; highly skilled combatant, expert with a trident; on land, special serum allows her to breathe unaided for 12 hours.

Inspired by tales of NAMOR the Sub-Mariner's adventures among the humans of the surface world, the Atlantean soldier called Andromeda (a corruption of her true Atlantean name) used a serum that allowed her to breathe air and also changed the color of her skin to allow her to survive above the waves. Now resembling a normal human being, she called herself Andrea McPhee and set out to follow in Namor's footsteps. For a time, she adventured with the DEFENDERS, a team to which Namor once belonged. After the group disbanded, she eventually returned to her duties in Atlantis. **TB**

Anger, Dirk

FIRST APPEARANCE Nextwave #1 (March 2006)
REAL NAME Dirk Anger **OCCUPATION** Leader of HATE
BASE Mobile
HEIGHT 6 ft 1 in **WEIGHT** 225 lbs **EYES** Brown **HAIR** Brown
SPECIAL POWERS/ABILITIES Controls HATE and its resources. Ages very slowly.

General Dirk Anger was the director of the Highest Anti-Terrorist Effort (HATE), an organization dedicated to battling the terrorists of SILENT. Through the use of various, experimental longevity drugs, the mentally unstable Anger lived for over 90 years. He recruited a group of heroes to comprise NEXTWAVE, HATE's strike team, but they went rogue after they discovered that SILENT was actually funding HATE through its Beyond Corporation subsidiary, a fact Anger knew all about. He was last seen ordering the Aeromarine (HATE's mobile control center) on a kamikaze course into Nextwave's Shockwave Rider airship, killing everyone but his targets. **MF**

Angela

FIRST APPEARANCE Age of Ultron #10 (March 2013)
REAL NAME Angela **OCCUPATION** Hunter angel
BASE The Heavens **HEIGHT** 6 ft 2 in **WEIGHT** 175 lbs
EYES White **HAIR** Red
SPECIAL POWERS/ABILITIES Immortal angel with superhuman strength and speed; invulnerable to the elements, including outer space; flies faster than light, and carries a bow and sword; protected by ribbons that move as if alive; a formidable warrior.

Angela hails from another, unknown universe and was brought into the universe of Earth-616—where she is the only one of her kind—after Earth's heroes did untold damage to the fabric of time and space (see AGE OF ULTRON). Brought into this universe against her will, she immediately sensed the rough location of the people at fault and headed straight for Earth. The GUARDIANS OF THE GALAXY intercepted her before she reached her goal, cutting her off at the Moon. **MF**

Angar

FIRST APPEARANCE Daredevil #100 (June 1973)
REAL NAME David Alan Angar
OCCUPATION Criminal **BASE** San Francisco
HEIGHT 6 ft 10 in **WEIGHT** 155 lbs **EYES** Brown **HAIR** Brown
SPECIAL POWERS/ABILITIES As Angar, his scream induces hallucinations and memory loss. As Scream, a creature of pure sound, he has flight, sound manipulation, and invulnerability.

Disillusioned social activist David Angar volunteered to be exposed to technology brought to Earth by MOONDRAGON, which gave him a hallucination-inducing scream. Moondragon's malevolent partner, Kerwin J. Broderick, hired Angar to kill DAREDEVIL and BLACK WIDOW, but Angar failed. Becoming a criminal for hire, Angar spent time in prison and lost his powers. MASTER KHAN later reinstated them, but the police gunned Angar down during a robbery. THE FIXER later used Angar's essence to create SCREAM, a being of pure sound, who joined the Redeemers (see THUNDERBOLTS). At his request, his teammate Songbird dispersed him permanently. **AD, MF**

Annihilators

In the aftermath of ANNIHILATION and the death of his friend STAR-LORD, Cosmo—working as the head of security of Knowhere, a space station built inside a Celestial's head—formed a team of the most powerful heroes in the universe to meet the most dangerous threats. He brought together BETA RAY BILL, GLADIATOR, Ikon, RONAN, THE SILVER SURFER, and QUASAR. After initial confusion, the team bonded and drove BLASTAAR from Kree territory. They then agreed to work together as needs demanded.

When a SKRULL named Klobok took the shape of Doctor Dredd—a DIRE WRAITH sorcerer—and tried to free the Wraith homeworld and destroy their Galadorian foes, the Annihilators assembled to stop him. This battle brought them into conflict with IMMORTUS and forced them to meld the Dire Wraith planet and the Galadorian planet into one.

The Annihilators later reunited to stop the rebirth of the MAGUS on Earth, as engineered by the Universal Church of Truth. At first the AVENGERS fought the Annihilators, thinking they were part of an invading force. The Avengers subsequently joined with the Annihilators to capture the new Magus and imprison him in Knowhere. **MF**

FACTFILE

FOUNDING MEMBERS

BETA RAY BILL
Korbinite with the power of Thor
COSMO
Telepathic canine cosmonaut
GLADIATOR
Majestor of the Shi'ar Empire
IKON
Galadorian Spaceknight
RONAN
Kree accuser
SILVER SURFER
Former herald of Galactus, from Zenn-La
QUASAR
Human protector of the universe

BASE
Knowhere

FIRST APPEARANCE
Thanos Imperative: Devastation #1 *(May 2011)*

ANNIHILATORS
1 Cosmo **2** Beta Ray Bill **3** Ronan **4** Quasar **5** Ikon **6** Gladiator **7** Silver Surfer

ANNIHILATION, *see pages 20,21*

Annihilation

This means war...

Richard Rider (Nova), the last survivor of the Nova Corps, led the Kree defense—and later the entire United Front—against the invading hordes of the Annihilation Wave.

The Annihilation Wave, an overwhelming force from the strange dimension known as the Negative Zone, broke through the Crunch to attack the positive matter universe. The Wave, composed of countless insectoid starships and warriors, first destroyed the Kyln, a ring of artificial moons that both served as a super-prison and as a generator of nearly limitless power. Then it destroyed the planet Xandar and the Nova Corps, leaving Earth's Richard Rider (Nova) as the galactic police force's only survivor.

Drax the Destroyer was killed by Paibok the Skrull before the Annihilation Wave even began. He returned in a new body to seek his revenge, accompanied by his new friend Cammi.

Nova left Earth to help defend the planet Xandar against the Annihilation Wave. Failing at that, he drew on the power of the entire Nova Force to challenge Annihilus himself.

The Galaxy at War

With the help of Quasar and Drax the Destroyer, Nova discovered that Annihilus, who led the Annihilation Wave, had allied with Thanos to conquer the galaxy. After killing Quasar, Annihilus took his Quantum Bands and drove off the others. Annihilus freed from Kyln two ancient beings known as Aegis and Tenebrous, who Galactus had imprisoned there. The Silver Surfer joined with Galactus and his former heralds to fight his foes but lost.

With the help of Drax, Gamora, Ronan the Accuser, and Star-Lord (Peter Quill), Nova formed and led the interstellar alliance called the United Front. After Thanos captured Moondragon, Drax went to rescue her and discovered that Annihilus had turned Galactus and his heralds into a weapon that could destroy planets. Drax freed the Silver Surfer, who in turn freed Galactus. Furious, Galactus attacked the Annihilation Wave. Meanwhile, with the Skrull Empire destroyed, Ronan and the Super-Skrull freed the Kree Empire from the control of the traitorous House Fiyero, which had kept the Supreme Intelligence trapped between life and death. Finishing the Supreme Intelligence off, Ronan took control of the empire.

The Silver Surfer made the ultimate sacrifice to stem the tide of the Annihilation Wave. After nearly dying at the hands of other elder beings, he returned to the service of Galactus.

With the Annihilation Wave decimated, Nova, Phyla-Vell, and Star-Lord hunted down Annihilus. Phyla took the Quantum Bands from him, and Nova killed him with his bare hands. Later, though, Annihilus's lieutenant Ravenous revealed an infant insectoid he believed to be Annihilus reborn.

Another Conquest

Soon after, the Phalanx attacked and conquered the Kree Empire, using a techno-organic virus to control their subjects. Star-Lord formed a team (a prototype of the Guardians of the Galaxy) to help fight this threat. Phyla-Vell (now the new Quasar) and Moondragon hunted for a savior who could defeat the Phalanx: a young, regenerated Adam Warlock. Warlock brought the women to meet the High Evolutionary. Soon after, Ultron attacked, killing Moondragon and revealing himself as the driving force behind the Phalanx invasion. Later, Ultron forced the High Evolutionary to transfer his mind into Warlock's body.

Meanwhile, Ronan, Super-Skrull, and a Kree named Wraith—who can protect others from the Phalanx infection—went to the Kree world controlled by Ravenous and shielded an army of robotic Kree sentries. They then sent them to destroy the Phalanx. At the same time, Nova, Drax, and Gamora reappeared with Warlock of the Technarchy—which had created the Phalanx—with them.

The Technarchy Warlock forced Ultron from Adam Warlock's body. When Ultron reassembled himself into a gigantic body, Wraith trapped

The Super-Skrull failed to keep the Annihilation Wave from destroying his people's homeworld, but he sacrificed himself (temporarily) to keep the Harvester of Sorrows from obliterating any other worlds.

Ronan the Accuser was framed for treason but still rose to become the leader of the Kree. He ultimately had to kill the Supreme Intelligence and take control of the Kree Empire himself.

The Annihilation Wav

The invasion forces that Annihilus assembled in the relative safety of the Negative Zone proved to be the largest fighting force the galaxy had ever seen. At the height of its powers, it destroyed nearly all of th mighty Skrull and Kree Empires and even captured the Silver Surfer and Galactus. At the moment known as Annihilation *Day, Annihilus's forces destroyed the Kyln super-prison an launched their war on the positive-matter universe.*

ANGEL

The Avenging Angel

ANGEL

FACTFILE

REAL NAME
Warren Kenneth Worthington III

OCCUPATION
Hero and Chairman of Worthington Industries

BASE
New York State (Avengers Tower), Manhattan, New York

HEIGHT 6 ft
WEIGHT 150 lbs
EYES Blue
HAIR Blond

FIRST APPEARANCE
X-Men #1 (September 1963)

POWERS

Feathered wings can carry up to twice his weight and bear him to 29,000 feet; able to fly up to 150 mph; enhanced lungs enable him to breathe at high altitudes; possesses extraordinary eyesight and blood has healing qualities.

Warren's skin gained a blue pigment during his time working for Apocalypse.

Warren Worthington was born into a wealthy family. At private school, during his late teens, Warren noticed wings budding from his shoulder blades. Fearful of attracting attention, he strapped them to his body but secretly began experimenting with flying. When a fire started in his school, Warren flew to the rescue of his schoolmates disguised in a nightshirt and blond wig. He was mistaken for an angel and so, when he headed to New York City to become a costumed crime fighter, he took the moniker Avenging Angel.

ESSENTIAL STORYLINES

- ***X-Men Vol. 1 #54–6*** Warren Worthington's origins are shown—from a public schoolboy who grows wings to a member of the X-Men.
- ***X-Factor #10–15, Thor #373–4*** Angel's wings are amputated and he is driven to suicide.
- ***X-Factor #21–25*** Apocalypse appoints Angel as his Fourth Horseman, Death.

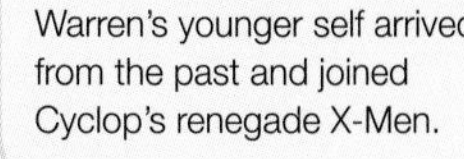

Warren's younger self arrived from the past and joined Cyclop's renegade X-Men.

ITINERANT X-MAN

Warren soon came to the attention of Professor X and joined the Professor's fledgling band of X-Men. At first, Warren disguised his face with a mask, but he later discarded it, believing that his handsome, telegenic features would help gain the team public support. With his vast, inherited wealth it was perhaps inevitable that he would become a media playboy. Similarly, although he remained loyal to Professor X's broad ideals, he drifted between various superpowered teams, using his fortune to provide backing to the Champions of Los Angeles, the Defenders and later X-Factor. While with X-Factor, Warren's wings were damaged battling the Marauders. The wings became infected and had to be amputated. The loss of his wings so depressed Warren that he attempted suicide. Saved by the mutant warlord Apocalypse, Warren was offered the chance to grow new wings of steel if he became one of Apocalypse's Horsemen—Death. Confused and still depressed, Warren agreed, but this Faustian pact brought him into direct conflict with his X-Men friends. Only the apparent death of his old friend Iceman brought Warren to his senses. Following this epiphany, Warren's metal wings molted to reveal feathers.

Having lost both his parents, Archangel considers the X-Men his surrogate family, bickering and fighting but also protecting and defending each other.

Returning to the X-Men, Warren rechristened himself Archangel. For a while, Warren could morph back and forth between his Angel and Archangel personas at will. During the Dark Angel Saga, his persona was killed. His body survived with metallic (rather than feathered) wings, but his mind was wiped. He has since lost control of his fortune and currently studies at the Jean Grey School of Higher Learning. **AD, MF**

Annihilus

FACTFILE
REAL NAME
Annihilus
OCCUPATION
Conqueror; destroyer
BASE
Sector 17A of the Negative Zone

HEIGHT 5 ft 11 in
WEIGHT 200 lbs
EYES Green
HAIR None

FIRST APPEARANCE
Fantastic Four Annual #6 (1968)

POWERS
Exoskeleton can withstand vast external pressure (up to 1,500 psi). He can breathe in the vacuum of space. His wings enable him to fly at up to 150 mph.

In the Negative Zone, a Tyannan ship crashed on the planet Arthros and released some spores. One of them grew into an insect-like being called Annihilus. Wielding the Cosmic Control Rod, he became master of the life forms that grew from the other spores, and he set out to conquer the other worlds of the Negative Zone. The FANTASTIC FOUR regularly stymied his attempts to conquer the Earth and the Microverse.

Annihilus launched the Annihilation Wave, aiming to destroy both the Negative Zone and Earth. After his efforts were thwarted, Nova killed him, but he was reborn with his memories intact and soon took control of the Negative Zone again. When the HUMAN TORCH was killed in the Negative Zone, Annihilus recovered his body and revived him to try to force him to help him reach Earth again. The Human Torch led a revolution against Annihilus rule and took the Cosmic Control Rod from him, which the Torch then used to lead the Annihilation Wave to stop a KREE invasion of Earth. When the Human Torch allowed free elections in the Negative Zone, Annihilus won the leadership once more by a landslide. He continues to plague the FF. **MT, MF**

Ant-Man II

FACTFILE
REAL NAME
Scott Edward Lang
OCCUPATION
Adventurer; former burglar; electronics technician
BASE
Avengers Mansion

HEIGHT 6 ft
WEIGHT 190 lbs
EYES Blue
HAIR Blond

FIRST APPEARANCE
Avengers #181 (March 1979)

POWERS
Possesses ability to shrink himself and other objects and people, usually to ant size, but also to microscopic levels. Cybernetic helmet allows him telepathic control of ants. Helmet amplifies his voice so that he can be heard by normal-sized humans.

Lang was an electronics expert who briefly turned to crime to help support his family. He was eventually arrested and sent to prison. After being paroled for good behavior, he worked at Stark Industries. His wife divorced him, but gave him custody of their daughter Cassie. Scott learned that Cassie needed an expensive heart operation, but her surgeon had been kidnapped. He resorted to burglary, breaking into the home of Dr. Hank PYM and stealing his old Ant-Man costume and shrinking formula. After rescuing the surgeon and saving Cassie, Scott turned himself in, but Pym decided to allow him to continue as Ant-Man. Scott often aided the AVENGERS and eventually joined the team. When his ex-wife learned that he was the new Ant-Man, she sued and won custody of Cassie. Scott was later killed in action when the SCARLET WITCH disassembled the Avengers. The YOUNG AVENGERS rescued Scott by traveling back in time to the moment of his death, only for him to bear witness to DOCTOR DOOM killing Cassie (now the hero STATURE). **TD, MF**

Ant-Man III

FACTFILE
REAL NAME
Eric O'Grady
OCCUPATION
Member of the Thunderbolts
BASE
Mobile

HEIGHT 5 ft 10 in
WEIGHT 115 lbs
EYES Brown
HAIR Blond

FIRST APPEARANCE
The Irredeemable Ant-Man #1 (September 2006)

POWERS
Can grow to giant-size and shrink to ant-size and back with the touch of a button on his helmet, which also allows him to communicate with ants. His armor features a jet pack and a pair of metallic tentacles.

Eric O'Grady was an agent of SHIELD assigned to monitor duty with his best friend, Chris McCarthy. Eric accidentally knocked out Hank Pym (*see* PYM, HANK) and Chris wound up wearing a new Ant-Man suit that Pym was designing for SHIELD. Chris was killed when villains attacked the SHIELD Helicarrier, and Eric donned the armor and fled.

After various misadventures, the cowardly Eric assumed a new identity and took a job with DAMAGE CONTROL. During WORLD WAR HULK, he tried to attack the HULK from inside but was blown out the Hulk's nose. Later, Eric found himself part of the FIFTY-STATE INITIATIVE and even won a commendation for his work during SECRET INVASION. This earned him a spot with the THUNDERBOLTS, whom he later betrayed to join the SECRET AVENGERS. He died defending a child from the Descendants. **MF**

The new Ant-Man is less heroic than Hank Pym.

ANTI-VENOM

FACTFILE

REAL NAME
Edward Charles "Eddie" Brock

OCCUPATION
Former journalist, now vigilante

BASE
New York City

HEIGHT 6 ft 3 in
WEIGHT 260 lbs
EYES Blue
HAIR Reddish-Blond

FIRST APPEARANCE
Amazing Spider-Man #568 (August 2008)

POWERS
Anti-Venom has superhuman speed, strength, and agility. He can stick to and climb surfaces and can fire webbing. He can also cure the irradiated.

Anti-Venom

Anti-Venom clashes with Venom for the first time.

Eddie Brock thought he had put his days as VENOM behind him. During his first bout with cancer, he'd sold his symbiotic suit to help find a cure, and the symbiote had bonded with Mac Gargan (*see* SCORPION). Although Matt Murdock (*see* DAREDEVIL) had helped Eddie clear his name of the crimes he'd committed when bonded with the suit, Eddie's cancer had returned, and he thought he had nothing to look forward to but a painful death. Then Martin Li (secretly the villain Mister Negative) cured Eddie with a touch, causing the last vestiges of the symbiote to bond with Eddie's immune system. When Gargan next confronted Eddie, the symbiote tried to return to him, but it burned on touching his skin. In response, Eddie's altered antibodies became a substance that covered Eddie's flesh and turned him into Anti-Venom. Eddie later sacrificed the Anti-Venom powers for use as the prime ingredient of the cure administered to the victims of the Spider Island breakout (see SPIDER-MAN). He has since bonded with the symbiote called Toxin. **MF**

Apalla

FIRST APPEARANCE Doctor Strange #22 (April 1977)
REAL NAME Apalla **OCCUPATION** Embodiment of the Sun
BASE Earth's solar system **HEIGHT** Variable **WEIGHT** Variable
EYES Variable **HAIR** Flaming orange
SPECIAL POWERS/ABILITIES Possesses all the powers of the Sun: able to generate heat, light etc; it is likely her abilities are restricted by her physical form.

Apalla is the corporeal manifestation of the Sun. Although thought to walk upon the Earth, sightings of her are few. When a league of sorcerers, the Creators, wished to take over the stars and transform them into humans, Apalla helped DOCTOR STRANGE oppose them. A further encounter involved CAPTAIN MAR-VELL. Due to a radioactive overdose, Mar-Vell was draining her energies each time he used his powers. The pair rectified the situation before lasting damage could be done. **AD**

Aquarian

FIRST APPEARANCE Adventure Into Fear #17 (October 1973)
REAL NAME Wundarr **OCCUPATION** Adventurer
BASE Commune on southern California coast
HEIGHT 5 ft 10 in **WEIGHT** 165 lbs **EYES** Brown **HAIR** Brown
SPECIAL POWERS/ABILITIES Surrounded by null-field that neutralizes other superhumans' kinetic and electromagnetic energies; walks on air.

Sent into space at an early age, Wundarr landed on Earth, where the sun's energy gave him superhuman powers. An encounter with a Cosmic Cube augmented these powers. As Aquarian, he became a prophet of the Water-Children. After the CIVIL WAR he joined THE FIFTY-STATE INITIATIVE and was assigned to the Command, Florida team, and defended Florida from the SKRULLS during SECRET INVASION. **AD, MF**

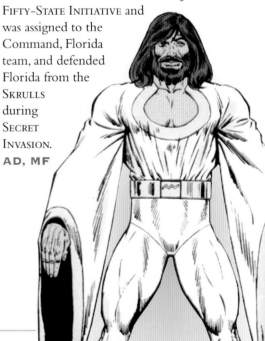

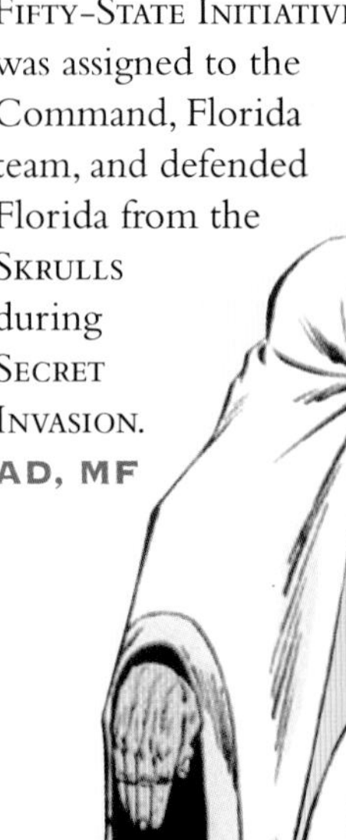

APOCALYPSE

Ancient mutant menace

In one possible Messiah War future, Apocalypse teamed up with Angel (in his Archangel form) to rescue Hope Summers from Stryfe.

Born nearly 5,000 years ago in ancient Egypt, Apocalypse is one of the earliest known mutant humans. As "En Sabah Nur," or "the First One," he traveled the world for thousands of years, sometimes hibernating for many years at a time. He often instigated wars to test which nations were fittest, and he was worshipped as a god by ancient civilizations. He had a hand in creating not only Dracula but also Mr. Sinister, and a wide number of people served as his Four Horsemen: Famine, War, Pestilence, and Death.

MODERN ERA

In the 20th century, Nur—now called Apocalypse—decided the emerging mutants were destined to supplant "unfit" ordinary humans. He often battled the original X-Factor and the X-Men, who were dedicated to peaceful coexistence between mutants and other humans. He sometimes even recruited his foes to become his Horsemen, including Angel and Wolverine, who both took the role of Death at different times.

Apocalypse's greatest foe throughout time is Cable, whose birth was engineered by Mr. Sinister and proved such a powerful moment in the history of mutants that it awakened Apocalypse from his hibernation. Determined to raise Cable as his own to keep him under control, the Apocalypse of the 37th century—who had conquered North America—mistakenly captured Cable's clone Stryfe and raised him instead. This proved a poor strategy when Stryfe traveled to the 20th century to try to kill Apocalypse.

FACTFILE

REAL NAME
En Sabah Nur

OCCUPATION
Conqueror

BASE
Mobile

HEIGHT Variable, usually 7 ft
WEIGHT Variable, usually 7 ft
EYES Blue
HAIR Black

FIRST APPEARANCE
(In shadow) X-Factor #5 (June 1986), (fully shown) X-Factor #6 (July 1986)

APOCALYPSE

POWERS

Can alter the atomic structure of his body to change shape. Can increase his size by absorbing additional mass. Possesses superhuman strength, stamina, and durability.

RESURRECTION

Though extraordinarily long-lived, Apocalypse's physical body eventually wore out. He survived by projecting his consciousness into host bodies, including those of X-Man and Cyclops. Cable destroyed Apocalypse's spirit after Jean Grey ripped it from Cyclops's body.

After M-Day, Apocalypsereturned again, thistime after a drop of his technovirus-infected blood created a body for him out of spare body parts. He tried to rebuild his Horsemen and force the remaining mutants to join his cause, but the Celestials—who had loaned him much of his technology long ago—returned to collect payment for his debt, in the form of him.

In the present day, Clan Akkaba—a cult run by Apocalypse's many descendants—revived Apocalypse as a child. Once the X-Force stopped them, Fantomex killed the child while others argued over what to do with him. Fantomex then secretly cloned the child and raised him in a simulated environment to become a hero called Genesis who could defeat Archangel (*see* Angel). The child, now known as Evan Sabahnur or Kid Apocalypse, was then sent to study at the Jean Grey School for Higher Learning. **PS, MF**

THE HOUR OF YOUR GLORY IS AT HAND, MY HORSEMEN!
MOUNT YOUR BEASTS!

Apocalypse's first modern team of Horsemen, his warrior servants, included Famine, War, Pestilence, (from left to right) and Archangel as Death (not shown).

Arabian Knight

FIRST APPEARANCE Incredible Hulk #25 (August 1980)
REAL NAME Abdul Qamar **OCCUPATION** Bedouin chieftain
BASE Saudi Arabia **HEIGHT** 5 ft 10 in **WEIGHT** 170 lbs
EYES Brown **HAIR** Black
SPECIAL POWERS/ABILITIES Scimitar fires force bolts and penetrates almost any material; rides magic carpet, which could also convert into a battering ram or envelop enemies.

Having uncovered the tomb of his ancestor, who had been a hero to his people, Abdul Qamar acquired his three mystic weapons, and set out to carry on his tradition as the modern Arabian Knight. He fought for justice for many years, but eventually perished when his life force was randomly and remotely sucked away from him by the life-draining Humus Sapien—leaving him a casualty of a conflict which had nothing to do with him directly. **TB**

Arcanna

FIRST APPEARANCE Defenders #112 (October 1982)
REAL NAME Arcanna Jones
OCCUPATION Adventurer **BASE** Squadron City
HEIGHT 5 ft 8 in **WEIGHT** 115 lbs **EYES** Blue **HAIR** Blond
SPECIAL POWERS/ABILITIES Extensive magical powers, especially over natural forces, such as wind and water; able to levitate and ride the wind, sometimes on a pole.

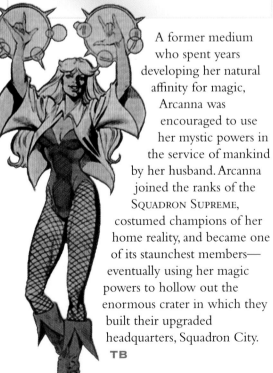

A former medium who spent years developing her natural affinity for magic, Arcanna was encouraged to use her mystic powers in the service of mankind by her husband. Arcanna joined the ranks of the Squadron Supreme, costumed champions of her home reality, and became one of its staunchest members—eventually using her magic powers to hollow out the enormous crater in which they built their upgraded headquarters, Squadron City. **TB**

Arcade

An engineering genius and a ruthless hitman, Arcade came by his fortune after allegedly murdering his billionaire father. He is obsessed with traps and games, and executes his victims in secret, amusement-park-style complexes he designs himself and dubs "Murderworlds." He charges $1 million per hit, but the money barely covers his expenses; he kills for sheer enjoyment.

He has captured and toyed with several superheroes over the years, including Spider-Man, Captain Britain, the X-Men, and the Thing, but they all managed to escape. Frustrated at the way few of his peers took him seriously and bored with his career, Arcade recently kidnapped sixteen super-powered teenagers and put them into a massive new Murderworld, pitting them against each other in a life-or-death competition which he claims only one can survive. When the teens tried to confront him, he displayed several new powers, including flight, godlike levels of strength, and invulnerability. **DW, MF**

FACTFILE

REAL NAME
Unknown

OCCUPATION
Assassin; playboy

BASE Various Murderworlds in undisclosed locations

HEIGHT 5 ft 6 in
WEIGHT 140 lbs
EYES Blue
HAIR Red

FIRST APPEARANCE
Marvel Team-Up #65 (January 1978)

ARCADE

POWERS

Genius at engineering, electronics, and robotics; habitual liar, using deceit to confuse opponents.

In his new Murderworld, Arcade has the powers of a god, and he uses them to toy with and kill teens.

ARES

FACTFILE

REAL NAME
Ares

OCCUPATION
God of War

BASES
New York, Olympus

HEIGHT 6 ft 1 in
WEIGHT 500 lbs
EYES Brown
HAIR Brown

FIRST APPEARANCE
Thor #129 (June 1966)

POWERS
Superhuman strength, endurance, agility, and reflexes. Immortal with healing factor.

ARES

Born the son of Zeus and Hera, Ares is the Olympian god of war. Angered over Zeus allowing the Greco-Roman religion to fade away, he has tried to conquer Olympus several times, sometimes with the help of his uncle Pluto, the god of the afterlife. In many instances, his hated half-brother HERCULES thwarted his plans, continuing their eons-old enmity. Weary of his father's rule, Ares retired to Earth to raise his son Alexander (later revealed to be the god Phobos) as a mortal. He returned to Olympus to battle AMATSU-MIKABOSHI—but only once Alexander's life was at stake. After the CIVIL WAR, Ares joined IRON MAN'S AVENGERS, and he stuck with the team even after Norman Osborn (GREEN GOBLIN) assumed control. Osborn tricked Ares into planning an invasion of Asgard, claiming that LOKI had taken it over. Ares discovered the deception, but before he could exact his revenge, the SENTRY killed him, acting on Osborn's orders. **MF**

As the God of War, Ares was born for battle and is more than willing to use modern weaponry to help him wage war.

ARIES, ***see page 28***

ARKON

FIRST APPEARANCE Avengers #75 (April 1970)
REAL NAME Arkon ("The Magnificent")
OCCUPATION Ruler ("Imperion") **BASE** The planet Polemachus
HEIGHT 6 ft **WEIGHT** 400 lbs **EYES** Brown **HAIR** Brown
SPECIAL POWERS/ABILITIES Superhuman strength, speed, agility, and stamina; skin and muscles are more dense than that of humans; recovers from injury at a much faster rate than humans.

Arkon is a great leader and warrior on the planet Polemachus. The culture of Polemachus glorifies war and Arkon became his world's greatest warrior. As Imperion of the largest country on Polemachus, Arkon attempted to conquer the other nations of his world. But when Polemachus was faced with planet-wide annihilation, Arkon came to Earth believing that its destruction could save his homeworld. On Earth, IRON MAN teamed with THOR in a plan which saved Polemachus and stopped Arkon's aggression. **MT**

ARMADILLO

FIRST APPEARANCE Captain America #308 (August 1985)
REAL NAME Antonio Rodriguez
OCCUPATION Professional wrestler **BASE** Mobile
HEIGHT 7 ft 6 in **WEIGHT** 540 lbs **EYES** Brown **HAIR** None
SPECIAL POWERS/ABILITIES Body resembles that of a gigantic humanoid armadillo, with sharp claws and armor plating; possesses superhuman strength and durability.

When his wife became mortally ill, Antonio Rodriguez turned to Dr. Karl MALUS, who promised to try to cure her if Antonio worked for him and submitted to his experiments. Malus combined genes from an armadillo with Rodriguez's genes, transforming him into a super-powerful being resembling a humanoid armadillo. Malus assigned the Armadillo to invade the WEST COAST AVENGERS Compound. There CAPTAIN AMERICA defeated the Armadillo but realized he was not a criminal at heart. Though the Armadillo has sometimes run afoul of the law, he prefers to earn his living in wrestling matches against super-strong opponents. **PS**

ARMBRUSTER, COL.

FIRST APPEARANCE Incredible Hulk #164 (June 1973)
REAL NAME Colonel John D. "Jack" Armbruster
OCCUPATION Colonel in US Air Force **BASE** Mobile
HEIGHT 6 ft 1 in **WEIGHT** 225 lbs **EYES** Blue **HAIR** Gray
SPECIAL POWERS/ABILITIES Military strategist, resourceful, honorable, and heroically loyal; inveterate pipe-smoker.

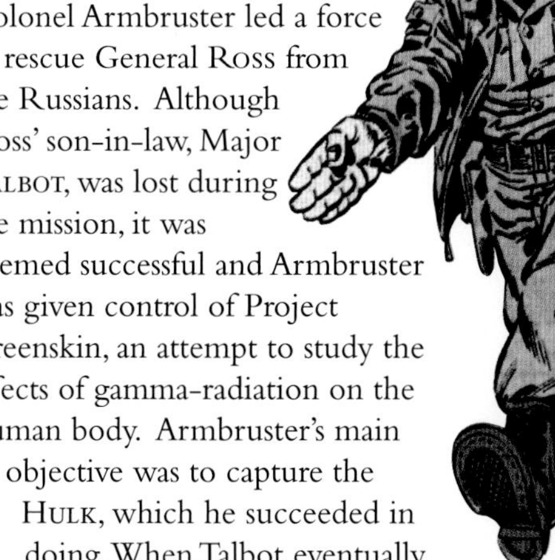

Colonel Armbruster led a force to rescue General Ross from the Russians. Although Ross' son-in-law, Major TALBOT, was lost during the mission, it was deemed successful and Armbruster was given control of Project Greenskin, an attempt to study the effects of gamma-radiation on the human body. Armbruster's main objective was to capture the HULK, which he succeeded in doing. When Talbot eventually returned, apparently having escaped from the Russians, Armbruster suspected foul play: when he shook hands with Talbot, his watch stopped. Armbruster discovered that there was a bomb in Talbot's body and dragged the Major into a pit. The bomb exploded, killing them both, but saving the life of the US President. **AD**

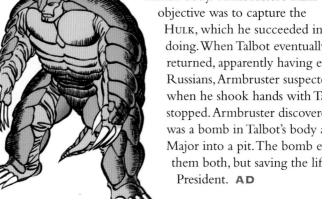

ARIES

Born under the sign of the Ram

ARIES (MARCUS LASSITER)

FACTFILE

REAL NAME
Marcus Lassiter

OCCUPATION
Professional criminal

BASE
Atlanta, Georgia

HEIGHT 6 ft 1 in
WEIGHT 230 lbs
EYES Brown
HAIR Unknown

FIRST APPEARANCE
Avengers #72
(January 1970)

ARIES (GROVER RAYMOND)

FACTFILE

REAL NAME
Grover Raymond

OCCUPATION
Professional criminal

BASE
Chicago, Illinois

HEIGHT 6 ft
WEIGHT 225 lbs
EYES Brown
HAIR Black

FIRST APPEARANCE
Avengers #120
(February 1974)

POWERS

The horns of Aries' costume were made of an incredibly hard, unknown material. He used them as a weapon, charging into opponents. Aries also wielded the Zodiac Key, an otherdimensional, sentient power object capable of firing energy bolts and transporting people across dimensions.

The first Aries, the human known as Marcus Lassiter, takes Manhattan.

Aries was a member of the criminal organization known as ZODIAC. Founded by Cornelius van Lunt, Zodiac was comprised of 12 human criminals, of which Marcus Lassiter (Aries), was one. Each member of the organization was based in a particular city in the US and took their codename from the astrological sign under which he or she was born.

CAPTAIN AMERICA WILL NOT BE SO QUICK TO COMPARE ZODIAC TO THE HYDRA WEAKLINGS...
...AFTER HE FEELS THE PHYSICAL MIGHT OF ARIES.

Aries prepares to unleash his power against Avengers leader Captain America.

THE ZODIAC KEY

The original human Aries, Marcus Lassiter took possession of the powerful interdimensional Zodiac Key. He then led a small army and succeeded in capturing Manhattan Island and sealing it off from the rest of the world with a force field. He tried to hold the island for ransom but this plan was stopped by the AVENGERS and DAREDEVIL. The first Aries died in an explosion. The Zodiac Key was apparently destroyed (though this turned out to be untrue).

As Daredevil looks on, Aries threatens to execute the Avengers team using the Zodiac Key. But though he sets the chamber ablaze, it is his own plans for conquest that will shortly go up in smoke.

OTHER ARIES

Several others have used the name. Grover Raymond physically merged with the alien LUCIFER and died. Another battled IRON MAN (James Rhodes) and was killed by an android Zodiac led by JAKE FURY. The first android Aries possessed superhuman strength, and the second could shoot fire from his horns. Jake genetically engineered his next Zodiac, including a new Aries. When THANOS created his own Zodiac, yet another Aries joined him. Leonardo da Vinci even used the name Aries when he formed his Great Wheel of the Zodiac group.

MT, MF

Thanos supplied Aries with a suit that gave him the ability to transform into a humanoid ram.

ESSENTIAL STORYLINES

- ***Avengers #82*** Aries (Marcus Lassiter) places a force field around the island of Manhattan and attempts to hold it for ransom. He is unsuccessful and is killed trying to escape.
- ***Avengers #120*** Aries (Grover Raymond) is recruited into the Zodiac Cartel to replace Marcus Lassiter, but finds himself in conflict with Taurus.

ARMAGEDDON

FACTFILE

REAL NAME
Arm'Chedon

OCCUPATION
Warlord of the Troyjan

BASE
Troyjan-controlled space

HEIGHT 9 ft
WEIGHT 2,528 lbs
EYES Inapplicable; Troyjans have no pupils.
HAIR Gray

FIRST APPEARANCE
Incredible Hulk #413 (January 1994)

POWERS Superhuman strength and energy manipulation; enhanced durability and resistance to injury; warlike temperament; great leadership qualities.

To avenge his son's death, Armageddon launched attacks against the Pantheon and the Earth.

Armageddon's son, Trauma, lost his life in battle with the Hulk after trying to abduct Atalanta of the Pantheon.

Leader of the long-lived intergalactic race known as the Troyjan, the teen who would one day be known as Armageddon almost single-handedly reversed the fortunes of his race's declining empire. Under his leadership, the Troyjan expanded their galactic power base, and became a force to be reckoned with. Armageddon's attentions first turned to Earth after his son TRAUMA abducted ATALANTA of the PANTHEON in order to make her his mate, and was subsequently killed in battle with the HULK. Vowing revenge, Armageddon used a resurrection device created by the gamma-enhanced genius known as the LEADER to reincarnate the then-deceased Thunderbolt Ross, in order to lure the Hulk into his clutches. Once the Hulk had been captured, Armageddon intended to use his life-force to restore Trauma to life. But the Hulk's energy proved too powerful, and it incinerated the remains of the deceased Troyjan warrior—leaving Armageddon with an even greater desire for revenge! **TB**

ARMOR

FIRST APPEARANCE Astonishing X-Men #4 (October 2004)
REAL NAME Hisako Ichiki **OCCUPATION** Adventurer, student
BASE Jean Grey School for Higher Learning
HEIGH 5 ft 4 in **WEIGHT** 112 lbs **EYES** Black **HAIR** Black
SPECIAL POWERS/ABILITIES Hisako can draw upon the strength of her ancestors to psionically create a translucent suit of armor that grants her superhuman strength and durability.

Hisako dreamed of becoming one of the X-MEN from the moment she gained her mutant powers. Once the existence of the Xavier Institute became public, she enrolled there and began her studies. She retained her powers after M-Day and soon after realized her dream, accompanying the X-Men to the planet Breakworld to stop a plot to destroy the Earth. She now studies at the Jean Grey School of Higher Learning, where WOLVERINE continues to train her in combat. **MF**

ARMORY

FIRST APPEARANCE Avengers: The Initiative #1 (April 2007)
REAL NAME Violet Lightner
OCCUPATION Former hero **BASE** Camp Hammond, CT
HEIGHT 5 ft 6 in **WEIGHT** 110 lbs **EYES** Green **HAIR** Purple
SPECIAL POWERS/ABILITIES Wore the Tactigon, an alien weapon capable of morphing into any weapon necessary.

As suicidal teen Violet Lightner leaped from the Golden Gate Bridge, an alien weapon called the Tactigon, shot from the water, attached itself to Lightner's arm, and transformed into a grappling hook that saved her. After helping the AVENGERS defeat the giant robot ULTIMO, Lightner joined the FIFTY-STATE INITIATIVE and reported to Camp Hammond as part of the first class of trainees. During her first combat training session, teammate TRAUMA triggered her arachnophobia, and Lightner panicked. Wild shots from the Tactigon blew off KOMODO's arm and killed Michael VAN PATRICK. Lightner was removed from duty, and surgeons stripped her of the Tactigon. **MF**

ARON, THE ROGUE WATCHER

FIRST APPEARANCE Captain Marvel #39 (July 1975))
REAL NAME Aron **OCCUPATION** Cosmic meddler
BASE Mobile; intergalactic **HEIGHT** Variable **WEIGHT** Variable **EYES** White; yellow when angry **HAIR** None
SPECIAL POWERS/ABILITIES Vast cosmic abilities; changed appearance at will; able to move between dimensions; subdued enemies with psionic blasts, or teleported them.

A young WATCHER, as such temporal matters as age are measured by that intergalactic race, Aron eschewed his people's pledge of non-interference in all things, choosing instead to use his great cosmic abilities for his evil enjoyment. He toyed with the lives of the FANTASTIC FOUR, replacing them with corrupt duplicates, and later engineered a civil war within his own Watcher race. As Aron was about to destroy the Fantastic Four, UATU THE WATCHER, who was responsible for our section of the cosmos, reluctantly killed him. **TB**

ATALANTA

FIRST APPEARANCE The Incredible Hulk #376 (December 1990)
REAL NAME Unrevealed **OCCUPATION** Pantheon operative
BASE The Mount, southwestern United States
HEIGHT 5 ft 10 in **WEIGHT** Unknown **EYES** Blue **HAIR** Black
SPECIAL POWERS/ABILITIES Wields a bow and arrows composed of an unknown form of energy that turns matter into super-heated plasma.

Named after the huntress of Greek mythology, Atalanta is a member of the PANTHEON, a covert organization of superhumans which intervenes in world affairs to prevent disasters. A deadly shot with her flaming bow, Atalanta has skin, body tissue, and a skeleton that are denser than a normal human's, affording her greater resistance to injury. She also possesses a fast healing factor and an extended lifespan. A psychic power enables her to mentally perceive her target even if she is unable to see it. Virtually nothing is known about the origin of Atalanta, except that she is related to other members of the Pantheon. She has been the lover of fellow Pantheon member Achilles. **PS**

ATLANTEANS

Undersea warrior race

ATLANTEANS

FACTFILE

NOTABLE ATLANTEANS

PRINCE NAMOR
LADY DORMA (Namor's first royal consort, deceased)
ATTUMA (barbarian warlord)
KRANG (usurper)
VASHTI (Namor's Grand Vizier),
PRINCE BYRRAH
LADY FEN (Namor's mother, deceased)
NAMORA (Namor's cousin, deceased)
NAMORITA
BEEMER (would-be usurper)

FIRST APPEARANCE

Fantastic Four Annual #1 (1963)

POWERS

Atlanteans' gills allow them to breathe underwater; they only survive five minutes out of water. They are about ten times stronger and faster than "surface dwellers." They easily withstand the crushing pressure and freezing temperatures at the bottom of the ocean.

Atlantis was once a small continent in the Atlantic Ocean. The cradle of an advanced civilization, Atlantis was torn apart by earthquakes and sank into the sea some 20,000 years ago. About 10,000 years ago, a genetic offshoot of Man, *Homo mermanus,* evolved the ability to live underwater. These mermen discovered the ruins left by the ancient Atlanteans and settled in them.

FIRST CONTACT

About 150 years ago, to protect his people, Emperor Thakorr moved the capital near to Antarctica. The Atlanteans remained undisturbed until an American research ship, commanded by Captain Leonard McKenzie, set off explosive charges to break up icebergs. Fearing his city was under attack, Thakorr sent his daughter to investigate. Princess Fen fell in love with McKenzie and married him. When she failed to return, her father sent a war party to rescue her and McKenzie fell in the attack. Fen returned to Atlantis and gave birth to Prince NAMOR, the Sub-Mariner.

Unique Atlantean architecture employs submerged coral reefs.

The Atlanteans' skin is usually light blue and their eyes tend to be blue or gray. They live on a diet of raw fish and seaweed and dwell in caves and reefs. Atlanteans communicate by high-pitched sounds and elaborate gestures. Their government is a coalition of tribes, ruled by an emperor. A Council of Elders advises the emperor. Most Atlanteans worship Poseidon, the Greek god of the sea. They are a rigid, warlike people; each citizen joins a guild to become a hunter, farmer, tradesman, craftsman, entertainer, or warrior. No one knows how many Atlanteans exist, but their population is believed to be fewer than 10,000.

Recently, Namor evacuated Atlantis and detonated the villain NITRO within it rather than leave the capital under the control of his traitorous son Kamar. Since then, he has built at least two new cities: Oceanus (a new capital, which lies hidden inside a volcanic vent in the Pacific) and New Atlantis (which sat beneath the X-MEN's island of Utopia and was later destroyed along with it). **TD, MF**

The current emperor of Atlantis, Namor has often battled outside invaders and faced treachery from traitorous relatives—like his cousin Beemer—who have attempted to steal his throne.

KEY ATLANTEANS
1 Namora
2 Namor, the Sub-Mariner
3 Lady Dorma

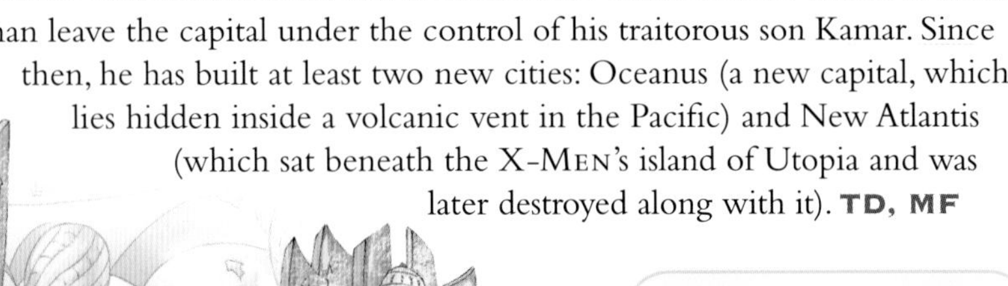

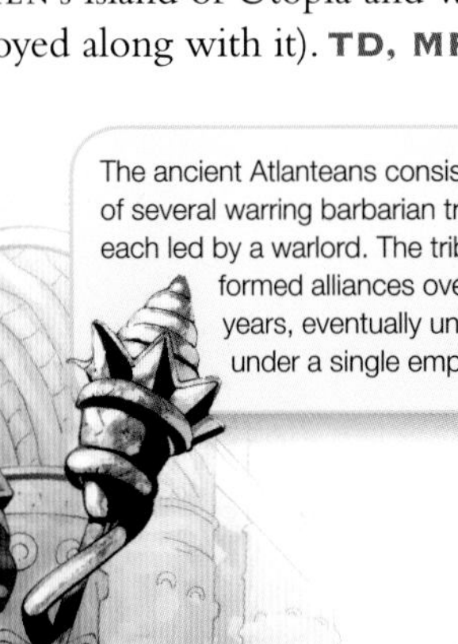

The ancient Atlanteans consisted of several warring barbarian tribes, each led by a warlord. The tribes formed alliances over the years, eventually uniting under a single emperor.

Atlas

FIRST APPEARANCE Thunderbolts #1 (April 1997)
REAL NAME Erik Josten
OCCUPATION Adventurer; former criminal **BASE** Mobile
HEIGHT 6 ft **WEIGHT** 225 lbs **EYES** None; replaced by containment spheres for unknown energy **HAIR** Red
SPECIAL POWERS/ABILITIES Atlas can grow in size from 6 ft to 60 ft; superhumanly strong and durable.

After working as POWER MAN and GOLIATH, Josten joined BARON ZEMO and his MASTERS OF EVIL (later the THUNDERBOLTS) as Atlas. While battling COUNT NEFARIA, he was changed into ionic energy. He later managed to place his energy into the body of Dallas RIORDAN. After they were separated, his powers were restored but were too unreliable to assign him to a team in the FIFTY-STATE INITIATIVE. He joined NIGHTHAWK's version of the DEFENDERS and later WONDER MAN's REVENGERS. **MT, MF**

Attuma

FIRST APPEARANCE Fantastic Four #33 (December 1964)
REAL NAME Attuma **OCCUPATION** Barbarian chieftain; former ruler of Atlantis **BASE** Atlantic Ocean
HEIGHT 6 ft 8 in **WEIGHT** 196 lbs **EYES** Brown **HAIR** Black
SPECIAL POWERS/ABILITIES Superhuman strength and stamina; can breathe underwater and see clearly in the depths; expert combatant with both hand-to-hand and most Atlantean weapons.

Born to a tribe of nomadic Atlantean barbarians, Attuma repeatedly fought NAMOR and often allied himself with renegade Atlantean or human scientists in his efforts to conquer Atlantis. Despising the human race, he often attacked the surface world but was thwarted by the AVENGERS and FANTASTIC FOUR. The SENTRY beheaded him during one attempt, but DOCTOR DOOM revived him. During FEAR ITSELF, a Hammer of the Worthy transformed him into Nerkodd: Breaker of Oceans. After losing that power, he discovered the lost city of Lemuria, but the HULK brought his latest plans of conquest to an end. **TB, MF**

Avalanche

FIRST APPEARANCE X-Men #141 (January 1981)
REAL NAME Dominic Szilard Janos Petros
OCCUPATION Member of the Brotherhood of Evil Mutants
BASE Mobile **HEIGHT** 5 ft 7 in **WEIGHT** 195 lbs
EYES Brown **HAIR** Brown
SPECIAL POWERS/ABILITIES Vibrations generated from his hands can bring down buildings and cause earthquakes.

Dominic Petros was a Greek immigrant to the US with mutant powers. MYSTIQUE recruited him into THE BROTHERHOOD OF EVIL MUTANTS, and he participated in the Brotherhood's first attempted assassination of Senator Robert KELLY. He left the Brotherhood to blackmail California with the threat of an earthquake, but he returned when the group transformed into FREEDOM FORCE. He later joined EXODUS's version of the Brotherhood. He retained his powers after M-Day, but he decided to open up a bar in San Francisco rather than return to crime. The RED SKULL captured him and replaced part of his brain with a machine to force him to commit an act of mutant terrorism and then leap to his death. **AD, MF**

AURORA

AURORA

FACTFILE
REAL NAME
Jeanne-Marie Beaubier
OCCUPATION
Adventurer, special operative of the Canadian government
BASE
Canada

HEIGHT 5 ft 11 in
WEIGHT 125 lbs
EYES Blue
HAIR Black

FIRST APPEARANCE
The Uncanny X-Men #120 (April 1979)

POWERS
Can run and fly at superhuman speed. Can project bright white light.

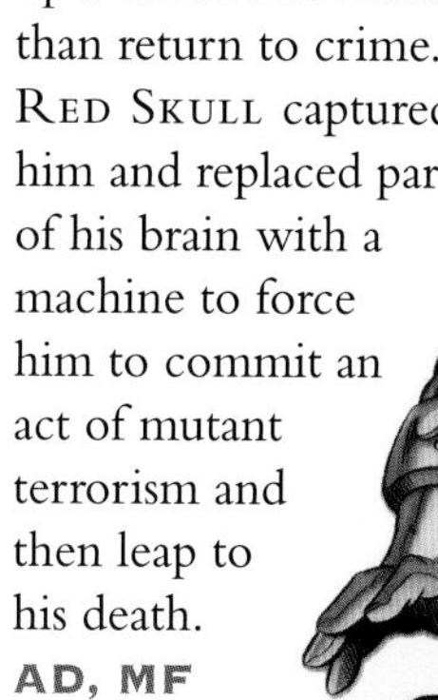

Twin orphans Jeanne-Marie Beaubier and Jean-Paul were separated, and Jeanne-Marie was raised in a strict religious girls' school. She was so unhappy she threw herself off a roof—and found herself flying. Jeanne-Marie thought a miracle had taken place and told the headmistress, but was punished for blasphemy. Jeanne-Marie developed a personality disorder: her everyday self was introverted, but her repressed side was uninhibited. Five years later, Jeanne-Marie became a teacher at the school. One night, WOLVERINE saw her use superspeed to defend herself from a mugger. Wolverine introduced her to James MacDonald Hudson, who reunited Jeanne-Marie with her brother. Taking the codenames Aurora and NORTHSTAR, Jeanne-Marie and Jean-Paul joined Hudson's team of Canadian heroes, ALPHA FLIGHT. Since then, Aurora has manifested other personalities, too, some of which reveal her powers in different ways. **PS, MF**

AVENGERS

Earth's mightiest heroes

FACTFILE

KEY MEMBERS

(see individual entries for powers)
THOR; IRON MAN;
ANT-MAN (DR. HANK PYM AKA GIANT-MAN, GOLIATH, YELLOWJACKET);
WASP; HULK;
CAPTAIN AMERICA;
WONDER MAN; HAWKEYE;
VISION; SCARLET WITCH;
QUICKSILVER;
BLACK PANTHER;
BLACK WIDOW;
HERCULES; BLACK KNIGHT;
SHE-HULK; PULSAR (Monica Rambeau aka Captain Marvel and Photon); **QUASAR;**
CRYSTAL; SERSI; ANT-MAN (Scott Lang).

BASE

Stark Tower, Manhattan; formerly Avengers Mansion (aka Avengers Embassy) Manhattan, and Avengers Compound, Palos Verdes, California

FIRST APPEARANCE

Avengers #1 (September 1963)

ALLIES Rick Jones, Edwin Jarvis, the Fantastic Four.

FOES Space Phantom, the Lava Men, the Mole Man, Baron Zemo, his Masters of Evil, Kang, Ultron, Collector, Grandmaster, Electro, Sauron, Madame Hydra.

ISSUE #1

Written by Stan Lee, penciled by Jack Kirby and inked by Dick Ayers, the first issue of *The Avengers* guest-starred Rick Jones, the Teen Brigade and the Fantastic Four.

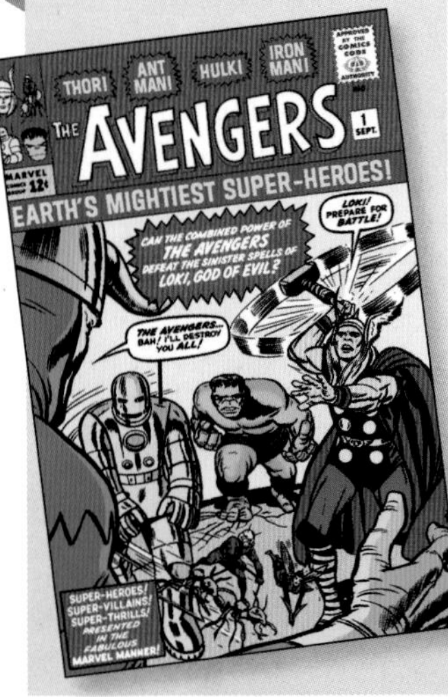

The Avengers are dedicated to safeguarding the planet from super-menaces too powerful for a single hero or the armed forces of any one country to combat. Formed shortly after the first public appearance of the FANTASTIC FOUR, the Avengers immediately won government approval from the National Security Council of the United States and the General Assembly of the United Nations. Unlike the FF, the Avengers' roster is always changing. Members join, leave and return—a precedent set by the HULK, who left the team weeks after it was first formed.

Captain America had lain frozen in the Arctic ice since the end of World War II. Decades later, he was discovered and revived by the Avengers.

Loki tried to escape by casting a spell that made his body radioactive. However, the heroes soon trapped him within a lead-lined tank.

HERO TEAM

The Avengers were formed by accident. LOKI, Asgardian God of Evil, wanted revenge on his half-brother THOR. After searching for a menace powerful enough to challenge Thor, he selected the Hulk and tricked him into causing a train wreck. When the Hulk's former partner Rick JONES heard this news, he attempted to alert the Fantastic Four, but Loki diverted his radio signal and sent it to Thor. But the thunder god wasn't the only one to answer the call. The astonishing Ant-Man (*see* PYM, DR. HENRY), the WASP and IRON MAN also responded. While the other heroes battled the Hulk, Thor tracked down Loki and captured him. After learning that the Hulk was innocent, Ant-Man suggested that the heroes form a team. The Wasp suggested they call themselves "something colorful and dramatic, like...the Avengers."

AVENGERS MANSION

Tony Stark (Iron Man) donated his three-story townhouse to the team who renamed it Avengers Mansion and later significantly modified it to fit their needs. Stark also funded the new team and provided them with most of their high-tech equipment, weaponry, security countermeasures, and computer

THE AVENGERS (2004)
1 The Wasp ***2*** Hawkeye ***3*** Scarlet Witch
4 Captain America ***5*** The Vision ***6*** Iron Man

For most of its history, the Avengers employed a rotating chairmanship that allowed different acting members to chair meetings and make administrative decisions. Captain America usually served as team leader in the field.

systems. He also used his government contacts to lobby for A-1 or Avengers Priority security clearance to aid the team's operations.

The Avengers began to establish themselves by fighting foes like the Space Phantom, the Lava Men, the Mole Man, Baron Zemo, his Masters of Evil and Kang. The team also met Wonder Man who later sacrificed himself to save them. All of the founding members eventually left the team, leaving Captain America in charge with a band that first consisted of Hawkeye, the Scarlet Witch and Quicksilver. The Wasp and Hank Pym, who had exchanged his Ant-Man to become the first Goliath, returned to the team. The Olympian demigod Hercules also became a member. Serving as an agent for the Mandarin, the first Swordsman even attempted to join.

The Old Order Changeth

Accidentally created by Hank Pym, the robot Ultron tried to kill the Avengers. He even built the android Vision, who betrayed him and served as an Avenger for many years. Haunted by guilt, Pym's marriage to the Wasp deteriorated and he left the team.

The Avengers fought alongside the alien Captain Mar-Vell in a cosmic battle that came to be known as the Kree-Skrull War.

The membership continued to change as the Black Widow, the Beast, the now-reformed Swordsman, Mantis, and Hellcat all became members. A romance developed between the Vision and the Scarlet Witch and they married.

ESSENTIAL STORYLINES

- ***Avengers #4*** The Avengers rescue Captain America from an icy tomb and invite him to join the team.
- ***The Greatest Battles of the Avengers (tpb)*** The Avengers fight many of their most deadly foes.
- ***Avengers: The Korvac Saga (tpb)*** The Guardians of the Galaxy help the Avengers battle Michael Korvac.
- ***Avengers: Under Siege (tpb)*** The new Baron Zemo and his Masters of Evil attack Avengers Mansion.
- ***Avengers: Disassembled*** The Scarlet Witch warps reality and attacks her former teammates.

THE ULTIMATES

On a parallel Earth, government scientists created a super-soldier formula, but lost it when Captain America disappeared during World War II. Many years later, Dr. Bruce Banner was hired to recreate it. Working out of a rundown research facility in Pittsburgh, he engaged in secret superhuman trials on civilians and even tested the formula on himself, transforming himself into the rampaging Hulk. General Nick Fury took custody of Banner and ordered him to complete his research in order to create a new super-team called the Ultimates. This team included Dr. Hank Pym, a cybertronics expert and a world authority on super-genetics.

THE ULTIMATES (2004)
1 Giant-Man ***2*** Iron Man ***3*** Hawkeye ***4*** Wasp ***5*** Captain America ***6*** Black Widow ***7*** Thor

When Kang the Conqueror and his son Marcus waged all-out war against the Earth, the Avengers led the planet's defensive effort. Although Kang temporarily succeeded in subduing the entire world, the Avengers led a resistance movement that eventually overthrew his new dynasty.

The National Security Council began to take an active interest in the team and appointed Henry Peter Gyrich liaison officer. He tried to control team membership by recruiting Falcon and Ms. Marvel (*see* Warbird). In recent years, Justice, Firestar, Triathlon, Silverclaw, Jack of Hearts, Ant-Man, and a new female Captain Britain served as members.

Heroes Reborn and Return

At one point, the Avengers became embroiled in an epic battle with the villain Onslaught, and they, the Fantastic Four, and Doctor Doom were all presumed to have perished. Actually, Franklin Richards had used his reality-altering powers to save them at the last moment and transport them into a pocket dimension of his own creation, which featured a copy of Earth called Counter-Earth. They came back after a year. Later, Counter-Earth became situated on the opposite side of the sun from the Earth. **TD, MF**

When the Avengers disappeared while battling Onslaught, those on the Earth they left behind believed them dead.

AVENGERS *continued*

The Avengers Mansion had survived many attacks—until it was destroyed by one of its own.

AVENGERS DISASSEMBLED

A victim of her own reality-altering powers, the Scarlet Witch (Wanda Maximoff) had a nervous breakdown after the Wasp accidentally reminded her of something that had been wiped from her mind: the existence of her twin sons, Thomas and William. Desperate to become pregnant by her husband, the Vision, she'd subconsciously created them with her magic, implanting in each a soul fragment she'd found. When Mephisto claimed these fragments as lost bits of his own soul, the boys disappeared into him. To help save Wanda from a breakdown, Agatha Harkness had erased the memory of the boys from their mother's mind. When the memories came flooding back, Wanda's sanity shattered completely.

THE MANSION DESTROYED

An undead version of Jack of Hearts—who'd died earlier in the year while saving Cassie Young, the daughter of Ant-Man (Scott Young)—showed up at the Avengers Mansion without warning. When Ant-Man went out to greet him, Jack said, "I'm sorry," and then exploded. The blast killed Ant-Man and totally destroyed half of the mansion.

At the same moment, Iron Man—who was with the Scarlet Witch and Yellowjacket (Hank Pym)—was addressing the United Nations when he became drunk and belligerent, without having had a drink. Soon after, back at the Avengers Mansion, the Vision crash-landed an Avengers quinjet into the front yard. Melting to pieces as he tried to explain himself, the Vision launched five metal balls from his mouth. These each transformed into an Ultron.

While helping to defeat the Ultrons, Captain Britain (Kelsey Leigh) was killed. Afterward, She-Hulk flew into a rage and ripped the remains of the Vision to pieces, then nearly killed the Wasp.

THE FINAL ASSEMBLY

As the Avengers tried to puzzle out what was happening, every available hero who'd ever been an Avenger rallied outside the mansion. As they did, the UN revoked the Avengers' charter. Directly after that, a Kree invasion force appeared over the mansion and attacked. Hawkeye sacrificed his life to destroy the alien ships.

Doctor Strange then arrived and revealed that Wanda had been behind the string of disasters, which were designed not only to destroy the Avengers but also their reputation.

As the Vision was destroyed, his corpse produced copies of Ultron.

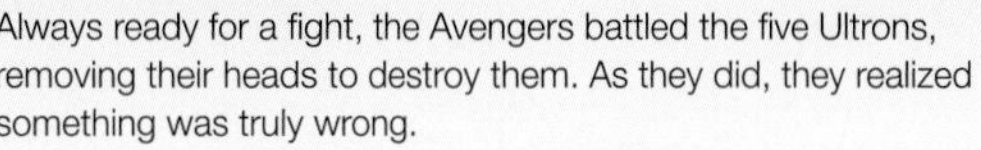

Always ready for a fight, the Avengers battled the five Ultrons, removing their heads to destroy them. As they did, they realized something was truly wrong.

The Avengers found and confronted Wanda, who unleashed a horde of their foes against them. After Doctor Strange finally stopped Wanda, her father, Magneto, appeared and took her away. Although he tried to nurse her back to health, she later snapped again, which led to the House of M and M-Day events.

The Avengers were no more.

NEW AVENGERS
1 Iron Fist
2 Doctor Strange
3 Echo
4 Luke Cage
5 Ronin
6 Wolverine
7 Spider-Man
1
4
5

The New Avengers

When Electro staged a breakout of the world's worst criminals out of the super-prison called the Raft, Captain America and Iron Man led an impromptu team of heroes into trying to keep the lid on the place. They only partially succeeded, and the two members of the original Avengers decided to form a new team to help them track down and capture the escaped villains. Besides Captain America and Iron Man, this new team included Luke Cage, Spider-Man, Spider-Woman, and Wolverine.

Just when the Avengers thought they had seen the worst, an invasion force of Kree warriors appeared in the sky over Manhattan.

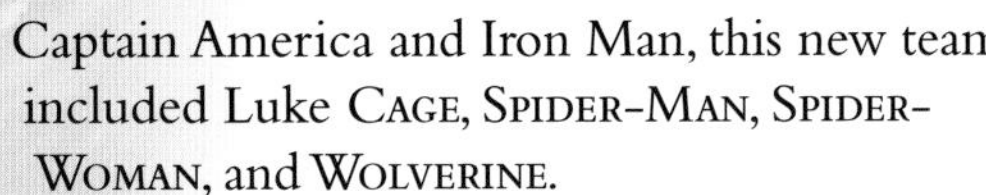

The New Avengers lived in Stark Tower, which was topped by the Sentry's watchtower. The team fractured down the middle when the Civil War began. Those who supported the Superhuman Registration Act stayed with Iron Man, while the others backed Captain America's resistance. This team functioned underground with no official support from any government.

The Mighty Avengers

At the end of the Civil War, Iron Man was appointed director of SHIELD and named Ms. Marvel to lead a new team of official Avengers. For her Mighty Avengers, she chose Ares, Black Widow, Iron Man, Sentry, Wasp, and Wonder Man. They fought together until Iron Man was disgraced and removed from SHIELD. At that point, Hank Pym decided to form an Avengers team with the prodding of Quicksilver and the restored Scarlet Witch. This new team eventually learned that their Scarlet Witch was actually Loki in disguise.

Mighty Avengers
1 Sentry ***2*** Iron Man ***3*** Wonder Man ***4*** Ms. Marvel

The Dark Avengers

At the same time, Norman Osborn (see Green Goblin) took over where Iron Man left off. He formed his own team of Avengers, staffing it with villains placed in the costumes of heroes—often their greatest foes including Venom in the role of Spider-Man and Bullseye as Hawkeye. As the Iron Patriot, Osborn filled the roles of both Captain America and Iron Man on his team, leading from the front while he deployed his Thunderbolts as a cover strike force.

Norman Osborn (Green Goblin) revealed a new team, the Dark Avengers, featuring (left to right) Captain Marvel (Marvel Boy), Sentry, Ms. Marvel (Moonstone), Iron Patriot (Green Goblin), Ares, Wolverine (Daken), Hawkeye (Bullseye), and Spider-Man (Venom).

AVENGERS *continued*

Rogers' covert crew of Secret Avengers took on missions that required a more discreet team.

THE INITIATIVE

As part of the FIFTY-STATE INITIATIVE, SHIELD created a place for training new Super Heroes at Camp Hammond, located in the heart of Stamford, Connecticut. Hank PYM originally served as the administrator of the camp, but during the SECRET INVASION, he was revealed to be a SKRULL imposter who'd used his position to place other Skrulls on Initiative teams around the country.

Osborn, in his new job as the head of HAMMER (his replacement for SHIELD), exploited this scandal to shut down the Initiative. However, the idea behind it—training young heroes for eventual membership in the Avengers—refused to die.

Steve Rogers set up different squads to fill the roles he saw the Avengers playing in the modern world.

THE AVENGERS RENEWED

When Osborn was removed from power, the President asked Steve Rogers (the original CAPTAIN AMERICA) to take over the Avengers once again.

Rogers reformed IRON MAN's team as the Avengers, a group that worked closely with the new SHIELD. This team consisted of Rogers, HAWKEYE, IRON MAN, THOR, SPIDER-MAN, SPIDER-WOMAN, and WOLVERINE, with Maria HILL of SHIELD as the team's leader.

At the same time, Rogers set up another Avengers team that could operate independent of direct government influence. This team initially featured IRON FIST, Jessica JONES, Luke CAGE, MOCKINGBIRD, MS. MARVEL, and the THING, along with Victoria Hand, who had been Osborn's chief lieutenant at HAMMER. Spider-Man and Wolverine pulled double duty with both teams.

Rogers himself headed up a third covert team of Secret Avengers, recruiting ANT-MAN (Eric O'Grady), BEAST, BLACK WIDOW, MOON KNIGHT, NOVA, Sharon CARTER, VALKYRIE, and WAR MACHINE for his initial lineup.

1959 Avengers
1 Sabretooth
2 Namora
3 Dominic Fortune
4 Dum Dum Dugan
5 Ulysses Bloodstone
6 Kraven the Hunter

BACK IN THE DAY

Other groups have laid claim to the Avengers name over the years, but they have no direct continuity with them, having disappeared decades before.

The Agents of Atlas originally banded together in the 1950s in an Avengers-style team.

Nick Fury also formed an Avengers team in 1959 to hunt down Nazis following the end of World War II. His original team consisted of Dominic Fortune, Dum Dum Dugan, Kraven the Hunter, Namora, Sabretooth, Silver Sable, and Ulysses Bloodstone.

AVENGERS VS. X-MEN

With the return of the Phoenix Force, once hosted by Jean Grey, the Avengers fought a pitched battle against some of their greatest friends in the X-Men. Cable (who was presumed dead) returned from the future to try to protect his daughter Hope Summers from the Avengers. When the X-Men joined the Avengers to stop him, Cable revealed that the Phoenix Force was returning for Hope. The Avengers wanted to take custody of her, but the X-Men refused, hoping to find a way for her to jumpstart the mutant population that was decimated on M-Day.

War broke out between the two sides and during the battle Iron Man accidentally split the Phoenix into five parts. These possessed Colossus, Cyclops, Emma Frost, Namor, and Magik.

The Phoenix Five worked to do amazing acts of good around the world, but the Avengers worried that they would become tyrants. Namor attacked the Black Panther's nation of Wakanda while the Avengers were hiding there. Namor's portion of the Phoenix Force left him during the battle, dividing itself among the remaining four. Spider-Man later tricked Colossus and Magik into fighting each other, and they, too, lost the Phoenix Force. After training with Iron Fist's master Lei-Kung, Hope absorbed the power of the dragon Shao Lao, which made her strong enough to stand up to Cyclops. Frustrated, Cyclops took Emma Frost's Phoenix Force and killed Professor X when he intervened. Hope and the Scarlet Witch joined forces to defeat Cyclops and wish away the Phoenix Force.

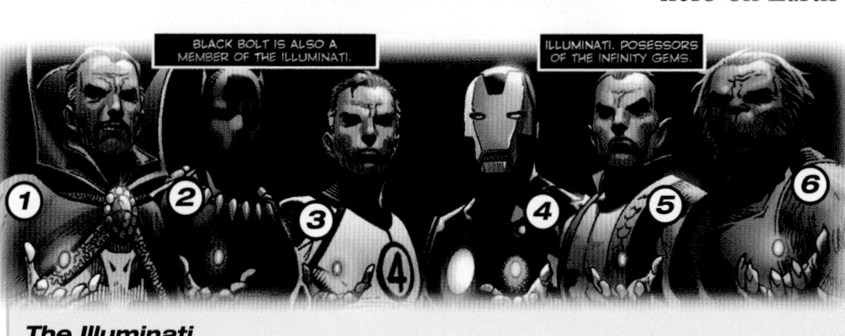

The Illuminati
1 Doctor Strange **2** Black Panther **3** Mister Fantastic **4** Iron Man **5** Namor **6** Beast
This team of new Avengers were formed from the Illuminati, who shared the power of the Infinity Gems, until they were lost or destroyed.

THE AFTERMATH

After the Avengers' momentous battle with the X-Men (see box above) Captain America decided to form a new Avengers Unity Squad to showcase the good that mutants could do when working alongside the Earth's other heroes. He put Havok in charge of the team, which included Rogue, Scarlet Witch, Thor, and Wolverine. Sunfire, Wasp, and Wonder Man later joined as well.

Maria Hill of SHIELD formed a new version of the Secret Avengers to help with its most dangerous covert operations. For her team, she recruited Black Widow, Hawkeye, Nick Fury Jr., and Phil Coulson.

Around the same time, Captain America turned to the Illuminati to form a brain-trust squad of Avengers. This group featured Black Bolt, Doctor Strange, Iron Man, Mister Fantastic, and Namor. Black Panther and Beast joined later, but Captain America left after disagreeing with their tactics.

The main team—and just about every other hero on Earth—was destroyed when Ultron returned, planning to put an end to humanity. This was only averted when Invisible Woman and Wolverine traveled back in time to when Hank Pym created the insane robot (*see* Age of Ultron).

Soon after, Captain America decided to reform the main Avengers team into an umbrella group that could respond to the biggest threats. The new team's members included Abyss, Black Widow, Cannonball, Captain Marvel, Captain Universe, Ex Nihilo, Falcon, Hawkeye, Hulk, Hyperion, Iron Man, Manifold, Nightmask, Shang-Chi, Smasher, Spider-Woman, Starbrand, Sunspot, and Thor (*see* Infinity). **MF**

The Avengers
1 Sunspot **2** Nightmask **3** Ex Nihilo **4** Spider-Woman **5** Cannonball **6** Captain America **7** Abyss **8** Manifold **9** Shang-Chi **10** Smasher **11** Starbrand **12** Bruce Banner (Hulk) **13** Hyperion **14** Captain Marvel **15** Black Widow **16** Thor **17** Falcon **18** Iron Man **19** Hawkeye

AVENGERS WEST COAST

The Avengers' West Coast "branch office"

AVENGERS WEST COAST

FACTFILE

FOUNDING MEMBERS
HAWKEYE
MOCKINGBIRD
IRON MAN
TIGRA
WONDER MAN

FINAL MEMBERS
SCARLET WITCH
SPIDER-WOMAN
(Julia Carpenter)
WAR MACHINE
U.S.AGENT

ADDITIONAL MEMBERS
HUMAN TORCH
(James Hammond)
LIVING LIGHTNING
MOON KNIGHT

BASE
Avengers Compound, 1800 Palos Verdes Drive, California

FIRST APPEARANCE
West Coast Avengers #1 (September 1984)

ALLIES/FOES

ALLIES Hank Pym (resident scientist), The Thing.

FOES Graviton, Ultron, The Grim Reaper, Master Pandemonium, Mephisto, Lethal Legion.

While chairman of the AVENGERS, the VISION decided to expand the team and sent HAWKEYE and his new wife MOCKINGBIRD to Los Angeles to establish a second headquarters on the West Coast. Hawkeye purchased a 15-acre estate on the Pacific coast. It consisted of a main building, surrounded by several guest cottages that housed various Avengers over the years. The mountainside beneath the main building accommodated the high-security Avengers Assembly Room, a hospital, laboratories and a hanger for Avengers' Quinjets.

Most of the West Coast Avengers had served on the East Coast team and returned to New York after this branch office closed.

GROWING PAINS

The team faced its first crisis when Mockingbird and Hawkeye argued over whether the Avengers had the right to use lethal force. Hawkeye later resigned when the government assigned the U.S. AGENT to the team and temporarily joined the GREAT LAKES AVENGERS. The WASP moved to the West Coast to join her former husband Dr. PYM and the team aided their East Coast counterparts in the Kree-Shi'ar war known as Operation: Galactic Storm. After falling under the control of MAGNETO and IMMORTUS, the SCARLET WITCH used her reality-altering powers against the West Coast Avengers.

Hawkeye and Mockingbird eventually reconciled and rejoined the team, and the Scarlet Witch (now cured) became the team's chairperson. During an attack by the demon MEPHISTO and the LETHAL LEGION, Mockingbird was killed and the Compound severely damaged. Afterward, the west coast branch closed down. Years later, Hank Pym reopened the compound as the campus for the Avengers Academy.
TD, MF

ESSENTIAL STORYLINES

- ***West Coast Avengers #1–4*** Hawkeye and Mockingbird establish the new team.
- ***West Coast Avengers #17–23*** Dr. Pym contemplates suicide, the team is transported into the past, and Mockingbird is captured by the Phantom Rider.
- ***Avengers West Coast #55–57, 59–62*** The Scarlet Witch falls victim to Magneto and Immortus.

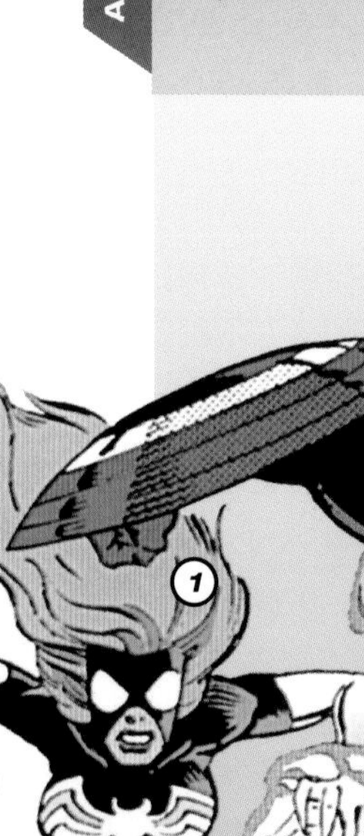

CHARACTER KEY
1 Spider-Woman II 2 U.S. Agent 3 Living Lightning 4 Hawkeye 5 Iron Man 6 Scarlet Witch 7 Wonder Man

Trapped by the X-Men and the Fantastic Four, the Mad Thinker and the Puppet Master turn the Awesome Android loose in a last attempt to escape justice.

AWESOME ANDROID

FIRST APPEARANCE Fantastic Four #15 (June 1963)
REAL NAME Answers to "Awesome Andy"
OCCUPATION Legal aide **BASE** New York City
HEIGHT 15 ft **WEIGHT** 1421 lbs **EYES** None **HAIR** None
SPECIAL POWERS/ABILITIES Possessed the ability to duplicate any special powers directed against it.

The Awesome Android was the creation of the evil MAD THINKER, constructed using research notes that once belonged to scientist Reed Richards (*see* MISTER FANTASTIC). The Mad Thinker intended to use the Awesome Android as a weapon to destroy the FANTASTIC FOUR. However, as time went by, the android developed a personality of its own and freed itself from the Thinker's villainous thrall.

"Awesome Andy" worked as a legal aide for a while, but his personality was later rebooted and he returned to the Mad Thinker's service. **TB, MF**

AYESHA

FIRST APPEARANCE Marvel Two-In-One #61 (March 1980)
REAL NAME Paragon
OCCUPATION None **BASE** Outer space
HEIGHT 6 ft 6 in **WEIGHT** 390 lbs **EYES** White **HAIR** Blond
SPECIAL POWERS/ABILITIES Controls cosmic energy which prevents aging; uses this energy to rearrange matter, project concussive blasts, to fly, and to open cosmic rifts into warp-space.

Originally called Paragon or Her, Ayesha was created by a group of scientists known as the ENCLAVE. Hoping to create a perfect life form, they created a being called Him, but Him refused to be controlled. Paragon also rebelled, destroying the Enclave's base. After meditating in a cocoon, she emerged as Her, able to tap into pure cosmic energy. She hoped to mate with Him (now known as Adam WARLOCK), pursuing him even through death and return to life, but he spurned her. She then turned her attentions to QUASAR, during which time she was known as Kismet. **MT, MF**

AZAZEL

FIRST APPEARANCE The Uncanny X-Men #428 (October 2003)
REAL NAME Azazel **OCCUPATION** Conqueror
BASE La Isla de Demonas, off the coast of Florida; the *Brimstone*
HEIGHT 5 ft 11 in **WEIGHT** Unknown **EYES** Black **HAIR** Gray
SPECIAL POWERS/ABILITIES The full extent of his powers is unknown; can teleport himself, take on human form, and mentally influence his offspring.

Azazel is the leader of the Neyaphem, a race of mutants who resemble demons. In ancient times Azazel was thought to be the devil. Azazel claims that he once ruled the Earth until he and the Neyaphem were banished to another dimension by the Cheyarafim, a race of mutants who resembled angels. As part of his plan to reconquer Earth, Azazel mated with various women, fathering mutants with teleportational powers. Among the women he seduced was the mutant MYSTIQUE, who gave birth to their son Kurt Wagner, alias NIGHTCRAWLER. When Nightcrawler learned that Azazel was his father, he not only rejected him, but helped defeat him. **PS**

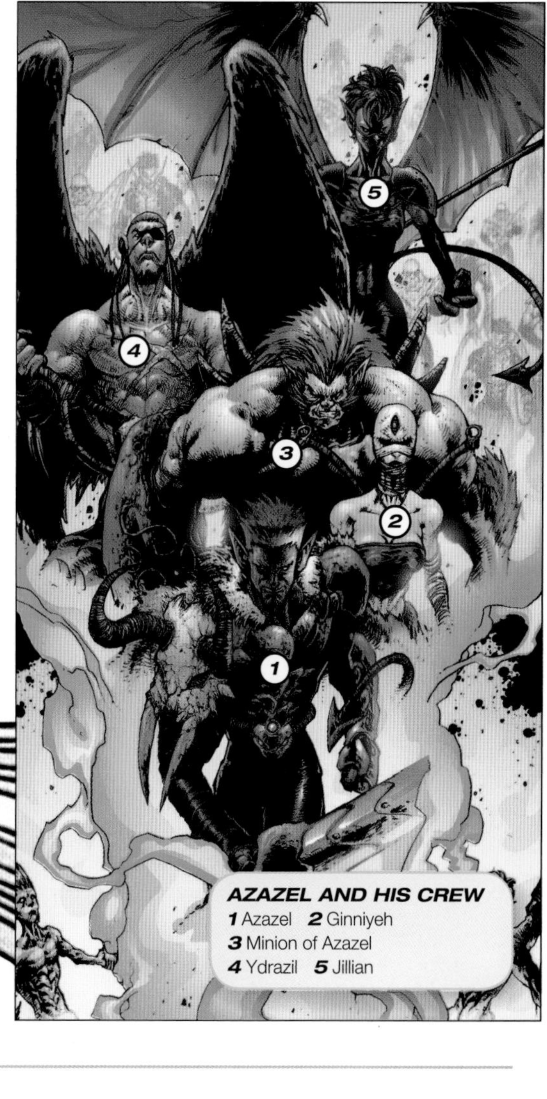

AZAZEL AND HIS CREW
1 Azazel ***2*** Ginniyeh
3 Minion of Azazel
4 Ydrazil ***5*** Jillian

BALDER THE BRAVE

BALDER THE BRAVE

FACTFILE

REAL NAME
Balder

OCCUPATION
Norse God of Light

BASE
Asgard

HEIGHT 6 ft 4 in
WEIGHT 320 lbs
EYES Blue
HAIR Brown

FIRST APPEARANCE
Journey into Mystery #85 (October 1962)

POWERS
Charismatic leader; formidable swordsman, horseman, and hand-to-hand combatant; in Asgard dimension, only weapons tipped with mistletoe cause him harm; able to produce and emit light; possesses superhuman strength, endurance, and longevity.

Prophecy had it that the death of Norse god Balder would bring about Ragnarok—the destruction of the GODS OF ASGARD. For this reason, ODIN commanded his wife Frigga to make their son Balder invulnerable, and she cast spells to protect him from everything but mistletoe. LOKI learned of this and tricked the blind god Hoder into firing an arrow tipped with mistletoe wood at Balder, but Odin managed to bring Balder back to life. Later, to Balder's horror, his beloved, Nanna, sacrificed herself to save him from having to marry the Norn sorceress KARNILLA.

Balder died along with all of the Norse gods—except THOR—in the final Ragnarok. Thor discovered his spirit inside the Destroyer, a massive suit of enchanted armor programmed to destroy anything in its path, and restored Balder to life. When Thor was forced to kill his grandfather Bor, Balder exiled him from Asgard and reluctantly assumed the throne. He ruled the Norse gods through the destruction of Asgard (the incarnation that floated over Oklahoma) and beyond, even after the return of Odin. He took part in the Council of Godheads during the CHAOS WAR. **MF**

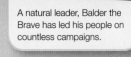

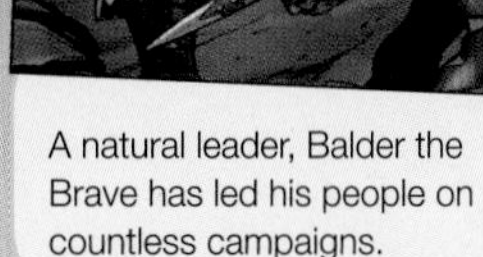
A natural leader, Balder the Brave has led his people on countless campaigns.

BANNER, DR. BRIAN

FIRST APPEARANCE The Incredible Hulk #312 (Oct. 1985)
REAL NAME Brian Banner
OCCUPATION Atomic physicist **BASE** Dayton, Ohio
HEIGHT 5 ft 10in **WEIGHT** 145 lbs **EYES** Brown
HAIR Brown **SPECIAL POWERS/ABILITIES** Scientific genius.

Suspecting that he had been exposed to radiation while helping to develop atomic weapons for the US government, Dr. Brian Banner was horrified when he learned his wife Rebecca was pregnant. Convinced their son would grow up to become a monster, he kept his distance from young Bruce (*see* HULK). When Bruce showed signs of great intelligence, Brian beat the boy—and Rebecca when she tried to protect him. Years later, he killed Rebecca in front of the boy and told Bruce he'd burn in Hell if he testified against him. Brian Banner was convicted of manslaughter and confined to a mental institution for fifteen years. Released into Bruce's care, he was accidentally killed in a scuffle with his son over his wife's headstone. During the CHAOS WAR, Brian returned from the dead and battled both his son and grandson (SKAAR) and their loved ones, feeding on their anger against him. When they focused on their love for each other instead, they finally defeated him. **MF**

BANSHEE

BANSHEE

REAL NAME
Sean Cassidy

OCCUPATION
Director of X-Corps

BASE
Cassidy Keep, Ireland

HEIGHT 6 ft
WEIGHT 170 lbs
EYES Blue-green
HAIR Blond

FIRST APPEARANCE
Uncanny X-Men #28 (January 1967)

POWERS
Banshee's "sonic scream" could propel him into flight, shatter solid objects, and fire percussive blasts, which placed others into trances or knocked them unconscious.

After his wife's death, Irish Interpol agent and mutant Sean Cassidy was forced to join Factor Three, an organization of evil mutants. The evil CHANGELING gave him the name Banshee and fitted him with an explosive headband to keep him in line. PROFESSOR X used his telepathic powers to remove the band, and Banshee then defeated Factor Three. Later, Banshee joined the X-MEN. While there, he reunited with his daughter SIRYN and became co-head—with Emma FROST—of Xavier's Academy, where he taught the young mutants of GENERATION X. Following the tragic death of his beloved, Dr. Moira MACTAGGERT, Banshee suffered a temporary breakdown. He formed X-CORPS, but this venture ended with MYSTIQUE stabbing him through the throat. Banshee later died at the hands of VULCAN. **MT, MF**

Banshee unleashes a devastating sonic scream at Cyclops and his fellow X-Men.

BARNES, BUCKY

Orphan James Buchanan "Bucky" Barnes was a mascot for the soldiers at Camp Lehigh, Virginia, where Steve Rogers was stationed. After learning that Steve was CAPTAIN AMERICA, Barnes began helping him on his missions, and became his official partner. Captain America and Bucky discovered that their enemy BARON ZEMO was attempting to steal a bomb-filled drone plane. As the plane took off, Bucky leaped aboard and was apparently killed. Captain America was hurled into the English Channel. Decades later, Cap was revived by the AVENGERS. Years after that, he discovered Bucky also survived but had been transformed by the Soviets into the WINTER SOLDIER. After Cap's death, Bucky became the new Captain America and remained so even after Steve Rogers' return to life. Bucky apparently died in the events of Fear Itself, but secretly returned to the role of Winter Soldier in order to make up for his former deeds in that guise. TD, MF

FACTFILE

REAL NAME
James Buchanan Barnes

OCCUPATION
Adventurer; army camp mascot

BASE
Mobile

HEIGHT 5 ft 7 in
WEIGHT 140 lbs
EYES Brown
HAIR Red-brown

FIRST APPEARANCE
Captain America #1 (March 1941)

BUCKY BARNES

Personally trained by Captain America, Bucky learned Cap's unique fighting style that employed acrobatics and gymnastics in combat situations.

POWERS
Excellent hand-to-hand combatant, skilled marksman, Olympic-level athlete, acrobat, and gymnast.

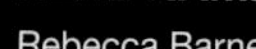
IT'S YOU! YOU'RE CAPTAIN AMERICA!

Bucky discovers that Steve Rogers has a secret—he's the superpowered costumed war hero Captain America.

BARNES, RIKKI

Rikki Barnes grew up on the Counter-Earth created by FRANKLIN RICHARDS as a response to the attacks of ONSLAUGHT. On that world, she became the partner of CAPTAIN AMERICA, a young, female version of Bucky BARNES. When Captain America and the other heroes defeated Onslaught and returned to the original Earth, Rikki remained behind. Onslaught was reborn years later, and Rikki helped defeat him by pushing him into the Negative Zone with a borrowed Fantasticar. She thought she'd sacrificed her life to stop him, but she later awakened on the main Earth. The BLACK WIDOW found her before she could introduce herself to the new Captain America (Bucky Barnes) as Bucky and gave her a new costume and name, that of NOMAD.

Unknown to Rikki, Onslaught had sent her to Earth from the Negative Zone with some of his energy inside her so he could use her as an anchor for his return. Once he was defeated again, she asked GRAVITY to kill her to keep him from using her that way once more, sacrificing herself a second time. MF

FACTFILE

REAL NAME
Rebecca Barnes

OCCUPATION
Adventurer, student

BASE
New York City

HEIGHT 5 ft 4 in
WEIGHT 98 lbs
EYES Hazel
HAIR Red

FIRST APPEARANCE
Captain America #1 (November 1996)

BUCKY BARNES

POWERS
Rikki is a trained dancer and acrobat who studied combat under Captain America. As Nomad, she carries disks that function as flash-bang grenades.

Rather than remain as Bucky in the regular world, Rikki became the new Nomad instead.

Baron Blood

FIRST APPEARANCE The Invaders #7 (June 1976)
REAL NAME Lord John Falsworth
OCCUPATION Former German assassin **BASE** London
HEIGHT 5 ft 10 in **WEIGHT** 180 lbs **EYES** Red **HAIR** Black
SPECIAL POWERS/ABILITIES Vampiric powers, including superhuman strength, hypnotic abilities, and invulnerability to conventional weaponry; could fly without transforming into a bat.

The younger son of a British aristocrat, John Falsworth was killed and vampirized by DRACULA. As Baron Blood, Falsworth served German intelligence during World War I and II. During World War II Baron Blood battled UNION JACK (who was secretly his brother, Montgomery) and the INVADERS. Decades later, Blood was beheaded by CAPTAIN AMERICA. Two later vampires took the name Baron Blood: DOCTOR STRANGE's brother Victor and Montgomery's grandson Kenneth Crichton. **PS**

Baron von Strucker

FIRST APPEARANCE Sgt. Fury And His Howling Commandos #5 (January 1964) **REAL NAME** Baron Wolfgang Von Strucker
OCCUPATION Terrorist leader **BASE** Mobile
HEIGHT 6 ft 2 in **WEIGHT** 225 lbs **EYES** Blue **HAIR** None
SPECIAL POWERS/ABILITIES Can release the virulent Death Spore virus from within his body at will. He wears the Satan Claw, capable of discharging electrical shocks, upon his right hand.

Baron von Strucker fought for the Nazis during World War II as the leader of the Blitzkrieg Squad, Germany's answer to the HOWLING COMMANDOS. After the war, von Strucker evolved a Japanese secret society into HYDRA. Kept alive by the Death Spore virus, von Strucker strove for world domination. Nick FURY killed him, but not before revealing that SHIELD had been controlling Hydra all along. **TB, MF**

Baron Mordo

Doctor Strange and Baron Mordo battle in astral form before their mentor, the Ancient One.

As a child, Karl Mordo gained an interest in the occult from his grandfather, Viscount Crowler. As an adult, Mordo sought out the ANCIENT ONE in Tibet, who recognized that Mordo had great potential as a sorcerer but was motivated only by a desire for power. Mordo sent his spirit image to hypnotize the Ancient One's servant into poisoning his food and then threatened to let the Ancient One die if he did not reveal all his knowledge of black magic. Another of the Ancient One's pupils, DOCTOR STRANGE, sent his spirit image to intervene, and Strange managed to revive the old man.

Thirsting for revenge, Mordo allied himself with powerful creatures like Satannish, DORMAMMU, and MEPHISTO and plagued Strange for years. Struck with incurable cancer brought on by his use of black magic, Mordo repented his sins on his deathbed. However, a past version of himself came into the present when Strange traveled through time to rescue SPIDER-MAN. Mordo showed up in South America, having kidnapped the father of M (see PENANCE) to force her to give her energy to cure Mordo's cancer. Another time-shifted version of Mordo briefly joined the RED HULK's Offenders.
MT, MF

FACTFILE
REAL NAME
Karl Amadeus Mordo
OCCUPATION
Sorcerer
BASE
Castle Mordo, Varf Mandra, Transylvania

HEIGHT 6 ft
WEIGHT 250 lbs
EYES Brown
HAIR Black

FIRST APPEARANCE
Strange Tales #111 (August 1963)

BARON MORDO

POWERS
Mordo can separate his spirit self from his physical body and travel through space unaffected by physical laws. He can mentally control others and can hurl magical energy bolts.

Baron Mordo allied himself with the dread Dormammu hoping to increase his mystical abilities in order to defeat his nemesis Doctor Strange.

BARON ZEMO

Like father, like son

I KNOW YOUR LATEST PROJECT, ZEMO! AN ADHESIVE SO STRONG THAT NOTHING CAN TEAR IT APART!! BUT I'LL NEVER LET YOU MAKE A WEAPON OF IT FOR HITLER... NEVER!!
DON'T THROW THAT SHIELD!!! NO!!

After the accident that bonded his mask to his face, the original Baron Zemo became obsessed with destroying Captain America.

Helmut Zemo is the son of Baron Heinrich Zemo, a Nazi scientist during World War II who designed super-weapons. Heinrich Zemo was working on a glue, "Adhesive X," that could never be dissolved, hoping it could be used to immobilize Allied troops. CAPTAIN AMERICA broke into his lab and, in the fight, Cap's shield shattered the vat containing the adhesive and Zemo's mask was glued to his head.

MASTER OF EVIL

Zemo later went to London to steal an experimental drone plane. Captain America and his teenage partner Bucky BARNES attempted to stop him, but Bucky was killed and Captain America was flung into the ocean, where he froze into a state of suspended animation. When the Nazis lost the war, Zemo fled to the jungles of South America, where he conquered a small kingdom. Decades later, he came out of hiding after learning that Captain America had been revived by the AVENGERS. Zemo formed the first MASTERS OF EVIL and later transformed Simon Williams into WONDER MAN, but failed in all his attempts to destroy the Avengers. He was accidentally crushed by a landslide during a battle with Captain America.

ESSENTIAL STORYLINES

- ***Avengers #16*** During a battle with Captain America, the original Baron Zemo is killed.
- ***Captain America #357–362*** "The Bloodstone Hunt"—Helmut Zemo tries to resurrect his father.
- ***The Avengers: Under Siege, tpb*** Helmut's new Masters of Evil invade the Avengers' mansion and take Edwin Jarvis hostage.
- ***Thunderbolts: Justice Like Lightning, tpb*** Helmut Zemo repositions the Masters of Evil into seeming heroes.

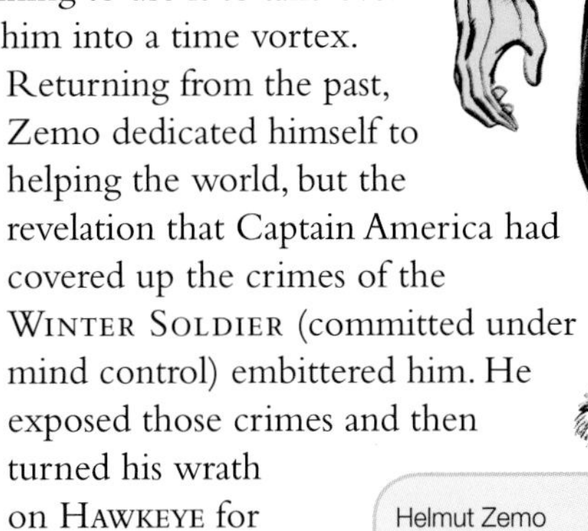

Zemo's hatred of Captain America ultimately led to the rock fall that killed him.

FACTFILE

REAL NAME
Helmut Zemo

OCCUPATION
Criminal entrepreneur

BASE
Mobile

HEIGHT 5 ft 11 in
WEIGHT 183 lbs
EYES Blue
HAIR Blond

FIRST APPEARANCE
Captain America #168 (June 1971)

BARON ZEMO

POWERS
Master strategist, extensive training in hand-to-hand combat, and excellent marksman; lacks his father's scientific genius.

FROM VILLAIN TO HERO AND BACK

The Baron's son, Helmut, calling himself Phoenix, attempted to drown Cap in a boiling vat of Adhesive X. The liquid splashed Helmut, scarring his face and giving it the appearance of melted wax. Zemo later organized a new Masters of Evil.

After the AVENGERS seemingly sacrificed themselves to quell the menace of ONSLAUGHT, Zemo became Citizen V and turned his Masters of Evil into a heroic super-team, the THUNDERBOLTS. After keeping the GRANDMASTER from the Wellspring of Power, he claimed it himself, planning to use it to take over the world—until the other Thunderbolts knocked him into a time vortex. Returning from the past, Zemo dedicated himself to helping the world, but the revelation that Captain America had covered up the crimes of the WINTER SOLDIER (committed under mind control) embittered him. He exposed those crimes and then turned his wrath on HAWKEYE for wresting control of the Thunderbolts from him. **TD, MF**

MASTERS OF EVIL
1 Absorbing Man ***2*** Baron Zemo
3 Screaming Mimi ***4*** Mr. Hyde ***5*** Moonstone
6 The Fixer ***7*** Power Man

Helmut Zemo claims that he wants to atone for his past misdeeds.

BASILISK

BASILISK

FACTFILE

REAL NAME
Basil Elks

OCCUPATION
Criminal; terrorist

BASE
Mobile

HEIGHT 5 ft 11 in
WEIGHT 210 lbs
EYES Red
HAIR None

FIRST APPEARANCE
Marvel Team-Up #16 (December 1973)

POWERS

Generated microwave-related energy, which he could project from his eyes as force blasts, to heat or freeze things, or to levitate himself. Possessed superhuman strength and durability and could teleport himself.

When burglar Basil Elks stole a gem from a museum, a guard shot at him, exploding the gem (actually the Alpha-Stone of the KREE), which gave Elks superhuman powers. Elks dubbed himself Basilisk after the mythological monster and tried to destroy civilization, only to be thwarted by SPIDER-MAN and the THING. SCOURGE assassinated Elks, but the HOOD later returned him to life to take revenge on the Punisher.

The second Basilisk (Mike Columbus) was a mutant who could shoot a paralysis beam from his single eye. He was killed by Kuan-Yin Xorn, who impersonated MAGNETO and led a new Brotherhood of Evil Mutants.
PS, MF

XORN'S BROTHERHOOD
1 Angel's child holding No-Girl
2 Martha Johansson the Living Brain **3** Ernst
4 Basilisk **5** Xorn as Magneto **6** Esme (Stepford Cuckoo) **7** Baby of Angel and Beak
8 Beak **9** Angel **10** Toad

BASTARDS OF EVIL

FIRST APPEARANCE Young Allies #1 (August 2010)
BASE New York City
MEMBERS AND POWERS
Aftershock (Danielle Blunt) Electric, flying daughter of ELECTRO
Ember (Jason Pierce) Pyrokinetic, lava-skinned son of PYRO
Mortar (Liana Feeser) Cement-bodied, shape-shifting daughter of the GREY GARGOYLE **Singularity (Devin Touhy)** Gravity-powered son of GRAVITON **The Superior** Super-intelligent, telekinetic son of the LEADER **Warhead** Radioactive, explosive son of RADIOACTIVE MAN.

The Bastards of Evil were supposedly a group of illegitimate children of super villains who banded together to commit acts of terrorism to prove their worth as the next generation of evil. In truth, the evil genius Superior kidnapped innocent teens, gave them powers via radiation, and implanted false memories in them. The YOUNG ALLIES stopped them, but not before Warhead detonated (presumably killing) himself at the spot where the World Trade Center had stood. When the others regained their true memories, Superior murdered Singularity, but the others stuck with him. Superior and the remaining Bastards of Evil were defeated by the Young Allies and incarcerated at the Raft. **MF**

BASTARDS OF EVIL
1 The Superior
2 Mortar
3 Ember
4 Singularity
5 Aftershock

BASTION

FIRST APPEARANCE Uncanny X-Men #333 (June 1996)
REAL NAME Sebastion Gilberti
OCCUPATION Anti-Mutant crusader **BASE** Mobile
HEIGHT 6 ft 3 in **WEIGHT** 375 lbs **EYES** Red **HAIR** White
SPECIAL POWERS/ABILITIES Enhanced strength, speed, physical stamina, and resistance to injury; also immune to telepathic probes.

Bastion is a combination of Master Mold (a SENTINEL robot) and Nimrod (a Sentinel prototype from a possible future). He led the anti-mutant initiative Operation: Zero Tolerance, during which his Prime Sentinels captured several X-MEN and took over the Xavier Institute. SHIELD stopped him, and WOLVERINE beheaded him while serving as the Horseman of DEATH. For a while, Bastion worked under the name Template. The Purifiers restored Bastion again, and he used the Technarch virus to revive a number of old X-Men foes. He later led their ill-fated effort to eliminate Hope SUMMERS, during which he killed NIGHTCRAWLER. **MT, MF**

BATROC

FACTFILE

REAL NAME
Georges Batroc

OCCUPATION
Mercenary

BASE
Mobile

HEIGHT 6 ft
WEIGHT 225 lbs
EYES Brown
HAIR Black

FIRST APPEARANCE
Tales of Suspense #75 (March 1966)

POWERS

Self-professed master of Savate, the French form of kickboxing; allegedly an expert hand-to-hand combatant; does not have any superhuman abilities but describes himself as Olympic-standard weight lifter with ability to leap vast distances; devises military tactics that serve to bewilder opponents.

Batroc the Leaper

Describing himself as the world's greatest mercenary and master of Savate, Marseilles-born Georges Batroc trained himself in this Gallic martial art while serving in the French Foreign Legion. Since embarking on a life of crime, Batroc has fought some of the world's greatest Super Heroes, including Captain America and the Punisher. Sadly, he has rarely survived these confrontations with more than the smallest degree of dignity.

Batroc is the eponymous leader of Batroc's Brigade, a motley collection of martial artists, assassins, and mercenaries whose membership is fluid. In the Brigade's early days, Batroc hired members for specific jobs, but most of the missions were unsuccessful. Employed to obtain the "seismo-bomb" from a foreign power, Batroc teamed with the Swordsman and the Living Laser, but they did not succeed. Later, the Red Skull hired him to attack Captain America. Although banded with Porcupine and Whirlwind, the mission failed.

Batroc has only scored significant victories with the British weapons master Zaran and South American revolutionary Machete. During the Civil War (*see* pp. 88–9), Batroc was forced to work for the Thunderbolts Army. Afterward, he registered with the US government and trained heroes in the martial arts. He has since returned to crime. **AD, MF**

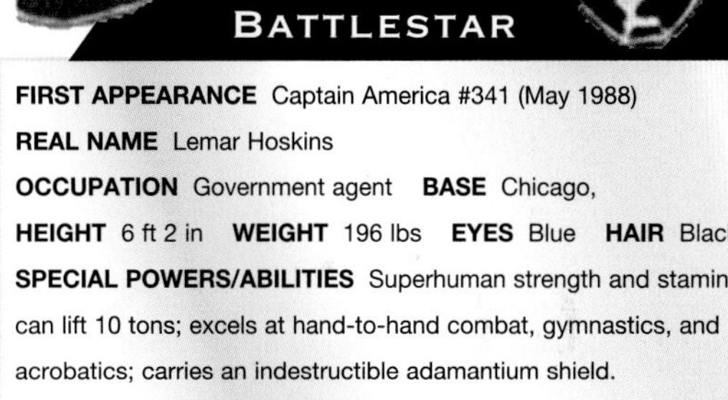

BATTLESTAR

FIRST APPEARANCE Captain America #341 (May 1988)
REAL NAME Lemar Hoskins
OCCUPATION Government agent **BASE** Chicago,
HEIGHT 6 ft 2 in **WEIGHT** 196 lbs **EYES** Blue **HAIR** Black
SPECIAL POWERS/ABILITIES Superhuman strength and stamina; can lift 10 tons; excels at hand-to-hand combat, gymnastics, and acrobatics; carries an indestructible adamantium shield.

After the Power Broker gave him his powers, Lemar Hoskins became a professional wrestler, along with his three US Army pals, Jerome Johnson, Hector Lennox, and John Walker. When Walker became the hero Super-Patriot, Hoskins and the others formed the Bold Urban Commandos (the BUCkies) as his support team. After Walker was chosen to replace Steve Rogers as Captain America, Hoskins became Walker's new Bucky (*see* Barnes, Bucky). He changed his codename to Battlestar after another African-American mentioned that the name "Bucky" struck close to the way slaveholders sometimes called their men "bucks." Hoskins continued as Battlestar even after Rogers returned and Walker became the U.S.Agent. After retiring from government service, Hoskins joined Silver Sable's Wild Pack. He sided with Rogers during the Civil War, and afterward joined the Garrison, the Vermont team of the Fifty-State Initiative. He later took a job with Project Pegasus, where he fought interdimensional zombies. **MT, MF**

BEAST

Mind of a genius, body of a wild thing!

BEAST

FACTFILE
REAL NAME
Henry P. "Hank" McCoy
OCCUPATION
Adventurer, biochemist
BASE
The Xavier institute,
Salem Center, New York

HEIGHT 5 ft 11 in
WEIGHT 402 lbs
EYES Blue
HAIR Brown (originally); blue-black (currently)

FIRST APPEARANCE
X-Men #1
(September 1963)

POWERS
The Beast possesses superhuman strength, agility, durability, and enhanced senses, including catlike night vision. He is able to recover with superhuman swiftness from minor wounds. He also possesses genius-level IQ, with extraordinary expertise in genetics, biochemistry, and other subjects.

THE CHEMICAL! IT'LL CHANGE ME—AND IN AN HOUR'S TIME, I CAN CHANGE BACK AGAIN, JUST BY TAKING ANOTHER DRINK AS AN ANTIDOTE
DON'T KNOW WHAT WILL HAPPEN IF YOU MUTATE A MUTANT—BUT I'VE GOT TO TAKE THE CHANCE—

Dr. McCoy recklessly drank his own serum, which gave him a more bestial form and increased superpowers.

Nuclear-power-plant worker Norton McCoy was exposed to intense radiation, and his son Henry was born a mutant, with unusually large hands and feet. Henry's schoolmates called him "Beast," but his mutant physique enabled him to become a star football player. When a criminal called the Conquistador abducted Henry's parents to force Henry to work for him, the X-Men came to the rescue. The team's founder, Professor X, recruited Henry and, codenamed the Beast, he thus became one of the X-Men's original members.

BEAST WITH THE X-MEN
1 Wolverine ***2*** Jean Grey ***3*** Beast (wearing reading glasses) ***4*** Professor X ***5*** Emma Frost ***6*** Cyclops

UNCHAINED

Under Professor X's tutelage McCoy earned his Ph.D. and went on to become a genetic researcher at the Brand Corporation. There he developed a serum that further mutated him: he grew fur all over his body, as well as fangs and pointed ears.

Initially, McCoy attempted to masquerade as a normal human by using a latex mask and gloves. However, he soon abandoned this disguise, joined the Avengers as the beast, and publicly revealed his true identity. Later, the Beast reorganized another team, the Defenders. After this incarnation of the Defenders collapsed, the Beast rejoined Professor X's other four original X-Men in a new mutant team, X-Factor. Soon afterward, the Beast was captured by former Brand Corp. scientist Dr. Carl Maddicks, who used a serum to cause the Beast to revert to his previous, more human appearance. The mutant Infectia returned the Beast to his fur-covered form.

ESSENTIAL STORYLINES
• ***X-Men Vol. 1 #49–53***
The extraordinary origin of the Beast explained for the first time.
• ***Amazing Adventures Vol. 2 #11–16***
The Beast mutates into his furry, ape-like form and combats the Secret Empire.
• ***X-Treme X-Men #3***
The Beast mutates into his leonine form.

Though the Beast can be fierce in battle, paradoxically he is also a man of high intellect, sharp wit, and great kindness.

The original Beast walking with the present-day Beast.

After rejoining the X-Men, The Beast helped create a cure for the Legacy Virus. When he was nearly killed in combat, Sage saved his life by mutating him even further. The Beast invented a time machine to help save Hope Summers and later to bring the original X-Men to the present day. After the death of Professor X, the Beast took over the Professor's teacher's spot in the Illuminati.
PS, MF

Belladonna

FIRST APPEARANCE The Spectacular Spider-Man #43 (June 1980) **REAL NAME** Narda Ravanna
OCCUPATION Criminal **BASE** New York City
HEIGHT 5 ft 5 in **WEIGHT** 120 lbs
EYES Blue-gray **HAIR** Brown
SPECIAL POWERS/ABILITIES Extensive knowledge of chemistry enables development of sinister chemical weapons.

With her sister, Desiree Vaughan-Pope, Narda Ravanna was the founder of Vaughan-Pope Cosmetics and responsible for product development. When they refused to sell the company to Roderick Kingsley (*see* Hobgoblin), he used the media to smear their products, driving them out of business. Hungry for revenge, Narda returned to the US, her home country. As Belladonna, Narda developed weapons from stolen neo-atropine and, with the help of several allies, attacked Kingsley. When Spider-Man intervened, she tried to kill the web-slinger but he thwarted her efforts and handed her over to the police. **MT**

Bereet

FIRST APPEARANCE Rampaging Hulk #1 (January 1977)
REAL NAME Bereet **OCCUPATION** Krylorian techno-artist
BASE The planet Krylor **HEIGHT/WEIGHT** Unrevealed
EYES Brown **HAIR** Unrevealed
SPECIAL POWERS/ABILITIES Carried the tools of her trade with her in a special distortion pouch. Accompanied by a hovering device called Sturky that could convert matter.

A renowned techno-artist from the planet Krylor, Bereet first came to prominence among her race when she created a series of adventure films depicting the earliest version of the Hulk combating a fictitious invasion of Earth by the Krylorians. After several attempts to duplicate this early success, she journeyed to Earth intending to document the ongoing exploits of the true Hulk, and became embroiled in a number of his adventures. She remained on Earth and became a movie director in Hollywood. **TB**

Berengetti, Michael

FIRST APPEARANCE Incredible Hulk #347 (Sept.1988)
REAL NAME Michael Berengetti **OCCUPATION** Casino owner
BASE Las Vegas **HEIGHT** 5 ft 10 in **WEIGHT** 170 lbs
EYES Brown **HAIR** Black
SPECIAL POWERS/ABILITIES Highly skilled businessman with a deep knowledge of underworld politics. Skilled with firearms and had a talent for mathematics relating to games of chance.

Michael Berengetti owned Las Vegas Coliseum casino, and he hired the Hulk as a bodyguard and leg-breaker during the period when the Hulk sported gray skin and a cunning intellect. Berengetti, who called the Hulk "Joe Fixit," ensured that the Hulk had steady access to tailored suits and Las Vegas' more sensual pleasures. After the Hulk left Vegas, the android Frost (employed by the gangster Sam Striker) killed Berengetti. **DW**

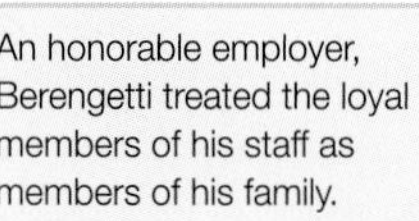

An honorable employer, Berengetti treated the loyal members of his staff as members of his family.

Beta-Ray Bill

Beta Ray Bill was a guardian-warrior of an extraterrestrial race whose galaxy was destroyed by the ancient demon Surtur. He was created when scientists transferred his life force into a bioengineered carnivorous beast, with increased strength, speed, and agility.

While traveling in suspended animation in his starship, Beta Ray Bill entered the Milky Way Galaxy, where Thor was sent to investigate. They battled and Thor was separated from his enchanted hammer, Mjolnir, which changed back into Donald Blake's cane. When Beta Ray Bill struck the cane on a wall he suddenly possessed Thor's power and a variation of the Thunder God's costume.

After a duel, in which Beta Ray Bill spared Thor's life, Odin commissioned the creation of a new enchanted hammer called Stormbreaker. Bill left Earth to visit his people's new planet, but while he was there, Galactus devoured it. Bill returned to Earth and helped the new Omega Flight battle demons of Surtur. He was replaced by a Skrull before the Secret Invasion, but Thor freed and then fought alongside him to defeat the Skrull known as the Godkiller. Bill hunted down Galactus for revenge but saved him instead. Bill later joined the Annihilators. **MT, MF**

FACTFILE

REAL NAME
Beta Ray Bill

OCCUPATION
Warrior

BASE
Mobile; his alien race's space fleet, his own warship Skuttlebutt

HEIGHT 6 ft 7 in
WEIGHT 480 lbs
EYES None visible
HAIR None

FIRST APPEARANCE
Thor # 337 (November 1983)

POWERS

Bill (aka Beta Ray Thor) has the same powers as Thor himself. He has superhuman strength, and is immune to all disease and injury. His Asgardian metabolism gives him far greater endurance at all physical activities than humans.

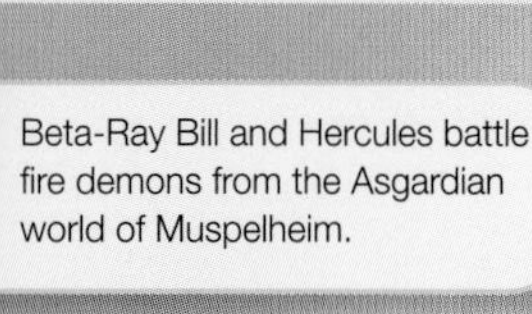

Beta-Ray Bill and Hercules battle fire demons from the Asgardian world of Muspelheim.

BEYONDER

Observer of worlds

FACTFILE

REAL NAME
Beyonder

OCCUPATION
Criminal/hero

BASE
Kyln prison

HEIGHT 6 ft 2 in (variable)
WEIGHT 240 lbs
EYES Blue
HAIR Black

FIRST APPEARANCE
Secret Wars #1 (May 1984)

POWERS
Virtually omnipotent; the Beyonder can change reality just by thinking. He has assumed various physical forms, created planets, destroyed galaxies, and taken control of every mind on Earth.

The mysterious, all-powerful Beyonder may be the embodiment of another multiverse. Or he may have arisen from a Cosmic Cube experimented on by the MOLECULE MAN. Or he may be an INHUMAN mutant. In any case, he began as (or became) a non-corporeal entity who, intrigued by humans, created a planet combining elements from various worlds. He christened it Battleworld and gathered a clutch of Super Heroes and Villains on it to watch them fight. However, the Beyonder soon grew tired of just looking on...

The Beyonder created Battleworld—a single planet orbiting a lonely star.

Everything in the Beyonder's dimension was part of him. All matter—planets, suns, people—were aspects of his being, and he could alter and restructure it on the merest whim.

ENDLESS QUEST

The Beyonder arrived on Earth and took the appearance of Molecule Man, CAPTAIN AMERICA, and finally a square-jawed alpha male with bad dress sense. He traveled the world learning about humanity. He was toilet-trained by SPIDER-MAN, learned about money from a homeless woman, and had a fling with the musician DAZZLER.

The Beyonder still felt unfulfilled and became increasingly unstable—a threat to the entire multiverse. He decided that he needed to be fully human and tried to transplant himself into the body of a baby, which was gestating in a machine he had built. Before the child could be born, Molecule Man destroyed the birth tank to save the multiverse, channeling the resulting explosive energies into a new and empty universe.

KOSMOS

In time, the Beyonder and Molecule Man fused to become a new Cosmic Cube. This Cube expelled the Molecule Man and became the female entity Kosmos (above) who existed in mortal form as the MAKER. Thanos tossed the Maker into the interstellar prison Kyln. During the ANNIHILATION Kyln was destroyed, and the corpse of Kosmos was found in the wreckage. **AD, MF**

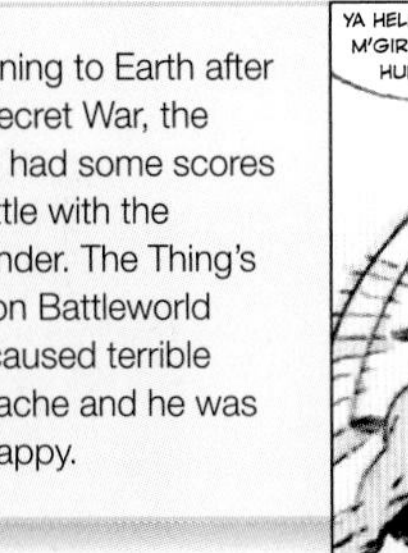

Returning to Earth after the Secret War, the Thing had some scores to settle with the Beyonder. The Thing's stay on Battleworld had caused terrible heartache and he was not happy.

YA HELPED ME TA LOSE M'GIRL ALICIA TA THE HUMAN TORCH!

ESSENTIAL STORYLINES
- ***Secret Wars #1–12*** The Beyonder creates Battleworld and gets the Earth's Super Heroes to fight there.
- ***Secret Wars #1–9*** The Beyonder arrives on Earth and learns about humanity.
- ***Fantastic Four Annual #23*** The Beyonder and Molecule Man merge to form a new entity named Kosmos.

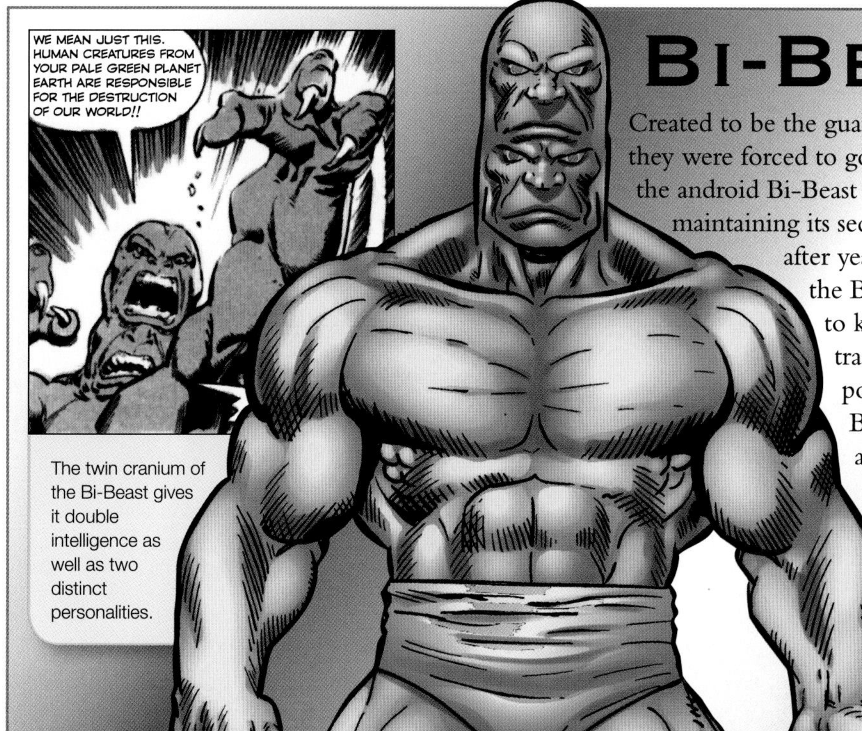

WE MEAN JUST THIS. HUMAN CREATURES FROM YOUR PALE GREEN PLANET EARTH ARE RESPONSIBLE FOR THE DESTRUCTION OF OUR WORLD!!

The twin cranium of the Bi-Beast gives it double intelligence as well as two distinct personalities.

Bi-Beast

Created to be the guardian of the Avian race at a time when they were forced to go into hibernation in order to survive, the android Bi-Beast patrolled their now silent Sky Island, maintaining its security and keeping it from harm. But after years of loneliness, the twin personae of the Bi-Beast went mad, and they attempted to kidnap Betty Ross, who had been transformed into a winged, gamma-powered monster called the Harpy.

But the Hulk pursued the Bi-Beast, and after a savage battle, Bruce Banner used the scientific apparatus found on Sky Island to cure Betty's condition, much to the displeasure of the Bi-Beast.

Thereafter, the Bi-Beast continued its lonely vigil, attacking any and all who came within reach. Eventually, however, the Avians were revived, and so the savage Bi-Beast was no longer alone. **TB**

FACTFILE

REAL NAME
Bi-Beast

OCCUPATION
Guardian of the Avian race

BASE
Sky Island of the Avian race

HEIGHT 7 ft 8 in (variable)
WEIGHT 360 lbs (variable)
EYES Black
HAIR None

FIRST APPEARANCE
Incredible Hulk #169 (November 1973)

BI-BEAST

POWERS

Bi-Beast's artificial minds contain the accumulated knowledge of the Avian race, the top head specializes in knowledge related to warfare and combat, while the lower head is the repository of information pertaining to history and culture.

Big Man

FIRST APPEARANCE The Amazing Spider-Man #10 (March 1964)
REAL NAME Frederick Foswell **OCCUPATION** Criminal
BASE New York City **HEIGHT** 5 ft 10 in; (Big Man) 6 ft 1 in **WEIGHT** 185 lbs **EYES** Blue **HAIR** Gray
SPECIAL POWERS/ABILITIES Brilliant criminal mind, master of disguise and a crack shot. Padded costume to appear more robust and taller; wore mask and used a device that deepened voice.

Daily Bugle reporter Foswell tried to organize New York's gangs under his leadership as the Big Man, employing the Enforcers as his henchmen. After clashing with Spider-Man, the police learned the Big Man's identity and arrested Foswell. He served his time in prison and, thanks to the generosity of publisher J. Jonah Jameson, returned to the *Bugle*. Foswell adopted the identity of Patch to spy on the underworld and aided in the capture of mob boss Crime-Master. Foswell later returned to crime and worked for the Kingpin. He sacrificed himself to save his former employer J. Jonah Jameson. **TD**

Bird-Brain

FIRST APPEARANCE New Mutants #56 (October 1987)
REAL NAME Bird-Brain **OCCUPATION** None
BASE Paradise, an island in the North Atlantic **HEIGHT** 6 ft
WEIGHT 125 lbs **EYES** Red **HAIR** Vari-colored feathers
SPECIAL POWERS/ABILITIES Wings enable flight; entire body is hollow-boned, like a bird's; able to breathe at high altitudes; eyes are specially adapted to withstand high winds during flight.

Bird-Brain is a half-human, half-animal creature known as an Ani-Mate. He was created through genetic engineering by Dr. Frederick Animus, the Ani-Mator. Although Bird-Brain and his fellow Ani-Mates possessed human-level intelligence, the Ani-Mator treated them like slaves. After being subjected to a number of cruel tests, Bird-Brain used his wings to fly away from the Ani-Mator's Paradise Island. He was placed in quarantine by the US authorities in preparation for being sent to a research laboratory for further testing, but he escaped. Bird-Brain was then recruited by the New Mutants, who returned with him to Paradise Island in order to help free his fellow Ani-Mates from the Ani-Mator's cruel thrall. **MT**

BISHOP

FACTFILE

REAL NAME
Lucas Bishop

OCCUPATION
Adventurer; law enforcement officer

BASE
The Xavier Institute, New York; District X, New York City

HEIGHT 6 ft 6 in
WEIGHT 275 lbs
EYES Brown
HAIR Black

FIRST APPEARANCE
The Uncanny X-Men #282 (November 1991)

POWERS
Can absorb energy and project it as concussive force or use it to enhance his strength, durability, and healing factor. Expert with a samurai sword and firearms. Bionic arm grants him superhuman strength and contains a time-travel device.

Bishop

Bishop comes from the future of Earth-1191, in which SENTINELS conquered North America and he was branded with an M as a mutant. After the Summers Rebellion overthrew the Sentinels, Bishop joined XAVIER'S SECURITY ENFORCERS (XSE) and pursued a mutant criminal to Earth-616, where he joined the X-MEN. Later, he fought crime in District X, Manhattan's mutant ghetto. He sided with the government during the CIVIL WAR. After M-Day, Bishop kept his powers and tried to kill Hope SUMMERS to prevent his future. Instead, he lost an arm and accidentally shot PROFESSOR X, then stole a bionic arm from FORGE and escaped to the future, where he hunted CABLE and Hope though time, later allying with STRYFE. After Cable trapped him in a distant future, he repented, but on his deathbed, the Demon Bear possessed him and sent him back on a new mission. **PS, MF**

Bishop's cybernetic arm allowed him to travel through time.

BLACK BOLT

FACTFILE

REAL NAME
Blackagar Boltagon

OCCUPATION
Monarch of the Inhumans

BASE
Attilan

HEIGHT 6 ft 2 in
WEIGHT 210 lbs
EYES Blue
HAIR Black

FIRST APPEARANCE
Fantastic Four #1 (December 1965)

POWERS
Harnesses electrons; power linked to vocal chords, which trigger shockwaves; antenna channels power, giving superhuman strength, speed; fires concussive blasts; creates force fields; flight.

Black Bolt

Black Bolt was born the son of Agon, ruler of the INHUMANS. His powerful infant cries forced his parents to place him in a soundproof chamber until an energy-harnessing suit was designed for him and he was trained to use his powers. After he was released, Black Bolt learned that his younger brother MAXIMUS was about to betray the Inhumans to the alien KREE. Black Bolt shouted, blasting the Kree ship out of the sky. It crashed into the parliament building, killing his parents.

As ruler of the Inhumans, Black Bolt often battled Maximus for control and oversaw the relocation of the Inhuman city of Attilan several times: to the Himalayas, to the Blue Area of the Moon, and even into a gigantic starship powered with his voice.

After being replaced by a SKRULL before the SECRET INVASION, Black Bolt decided to take the battle to the races that endangered his people, and he led the Inhumans to conquer the Kree. Black Bolt led the Kree into a battle against Vulcan and the Shi'ar, which ended in Black Bolt's apparent death. Later, he would return, bringing the Inhumans back to Earth and becoming the ruler of the Universal Inhumans. Black Bolt took a bride from each of the five surviving colonies, but MEDUSA is the one who has his heart. As a member of the ILLUMINATI, Black Bolt had custody of the Infinity Gems' Reality gem. **TD, MF**

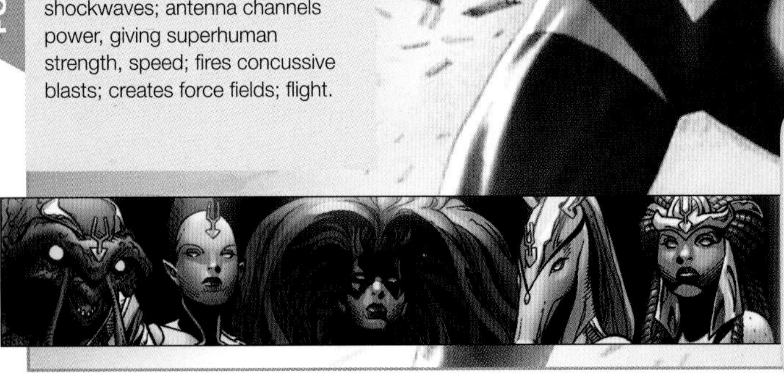

BLACK BOLT'S WIVES (L-R)
1 Avoe (Dire Wraith)
2 Oola Udonta (Centaurian)
3 Medusa (Earth)
4 Onomi Whitemane (Kymellian)
5 Aladi Ko Eke (Badoon)

Black Cat

Don't cross her path

The daughter of a famous cat burglar, Felicia Hardy was determined to follow in her father's footsteps. She devised the costumed identity of the Black Cat, setting up prearranged "accidents" to make it appear as though she could cause bad luck to befall others. After encountering Spider-Man, she became smitten with him, and for a time she was one of his closest confidantes and even knew his secret identity. During this time, she tried to give up her life of crime and helped Spider-Man stop villains from destroying the city instead.

FACTFILE

REAL NAME
Felicia Hardy

OCCUPATION
Cat-burglar; adventurer

BASE
New York City

HEIGHT 5 ft 10 in
WEIGHT 120 lbs
EYES Green
HAIR Platinum blonde

FIRST APPEARANCE
The Amazing Spider-Man #194 (July 1979)

POWERS

Her costume gives improved strength, speed, and agility, and she can inflict bad luck on others.

THE CAT GETS HER CLAWS

After Doctor Octopus nearly killed her, the Cat decided that she needed superpowers of her own, if only to make sure that Spider-Man wouldn't wind up getting killed while trying to protect her. She obtained bad luck powers via the Kingpin, but these began to jinx Spider-Man as well. When Doctor Strange helped Spider-Man with this trouble, the mystical feedback gave the Cat additional cat-like powers, including night vision and retractable claws.

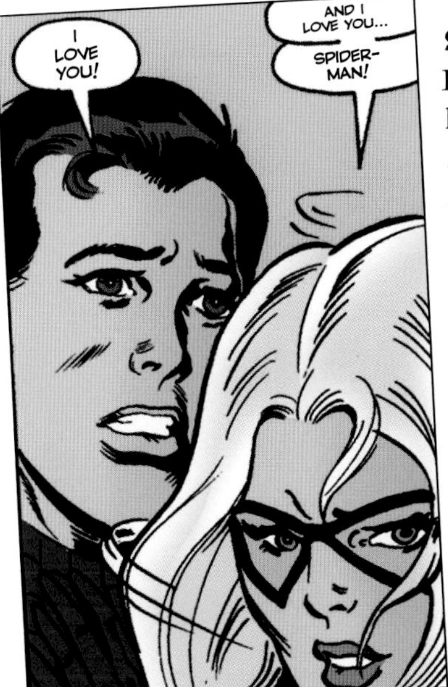

Peter Parker adored Felicia but, unfortunately, she preferred his amazing alter ego.

Straying Cat

Because she couldn't bring herself to be honest with Spider-Man, he broke off their relationship. Hurt, she wanted revenge but eventually realized her feelings for him were too strong, so she left for an extended stay in Europe instead. She returned years later, angry to find that Spider-Man had married Mary Jane Watson. Despite that, she overcame her jealousy and became friends with the couple. She later lost her powers while helping Spider-Man recover his own.

When Mephisto erased everyone's memory of Spider-Man's true identity, she lost that knowledge too, but she regained her powers and struck up a new relationship with Spider-Man. After the Civil War, she worked with Misty Knight's Heroes for Hire and also joined the Fearless Defenders. When she met the Superior Spider-Man (Doctor Octopus in Spider-Man's body), he punched her, knocking out a tooth. Although unaware of his new secret identity, she vowed to have revenge on Spider-Man for that. **TB, MF**

The Black Cat loves riches and sometimes assuages her guilt by playing Robin Hood with her ill-gotten gains.

The Black Cat joined the Defenders for a short while, but Doctor Strange later erased the entire event.

ESSENTIAL STORYLINES

- ***Spider-Man/Black Cat: The Evil That Men Do #1–6*** The secret origin of the Black Cat.
- ***Wolverine & Black Cat: Claws #1–3*** Wolverine and Black Cat face off against Arcade.
- ***The Amazing Spider-Man Vol. 1 #606–607*** The Black Cat returns after Spider-Man's secret identity is erased.

BLACK KNIGHT

Knight of the Ebony Blade

BLACK KNIGHT

FACTFILE

REAL NAME
Dane Whitman

OCCUPATION
Adventurer

BASE
New York City

HEIGHT 6 ft
WEIGHT 190 lbs
EYES Brown
HAIR Brown

FIRST APPEARANCE
Avengers #47 (December 1967)

POWERS
An able scientist, Whitman built on the discoveries of his uncle, Nathan Garrett. He rides a winged horse and has a power lance that fires heat and force beams; also wields the Ebony Blade, sometimes more curse than blessing.

The first Black Knight, Sir Percy of Scandia, was born in the 6th Century and became one of the bravest knights at the court of King Arthur PENDRAGON at Camelot. Here he led a double life, posing as a mild-mannered fop while secretly fighting evil as the Black Knight, armed with the Ebony Blade, a sword fashioned by MERLIN the Magician from the Starstone meteorite. Centuries later, Sir Percy's spirit returned to converse with his ancestors, Professor Nathan Garrett and Dane Whitman, each of whom would take up his mantle.

Raised in Scandinavia, Sir Percy was a new face to the people of Camelot.

ESSENTIAL STORYLINES
- ***The Black Knight #1-3*** Sir Percy begins his adventures as the Black Knight.
- ***Avengers Vol. 1 #71*** Dane Whitman helps the Avengers beat Kang and becomes a member.
- ***Doctor Strange Vol. 2 #68*** Whitman cleanses the Ebony Blade of evil and frees Sir Percy's ghost.

VILLAINOUS KNIGHT

Nathan Garrett met the spirit of Sir Percy during a visit to the family home of Garrett Castle, and was offered the chance to become a latter-day Black Knight. However, Garrett failed to draw the Ebony Blade from its scabbard, thereby proving himself unworthy. Determined to become the Black Knight by other means, Garrett developed a lance that fired energy bolts, and embarked on a criminal career mounted upon a genetically engineered winged horse. Garrett battled the AVENGERS with the MASTERS OF EVIL, dying in a fight with IRON MAN. Before passing away, Garrett confessed his crimes to his nephew, Dane Whitman, and begged him to restore his honor.

The dark sorcerer Kalmari battled Dane Whitman with a dragon, but this version of the Black Knight proved victorious.

THE GOOD KNIGHT

Initially mistaken as the previous Black Knight and attacked by the Avengers, Dane Whitman soon gained their trust and joined the team. Blessed with a noble spirit, he was able to draw the Ebony Blade once wielded by his ancestor Sir Percy. Unfortunately, the sword had been cursed with the blood of those felled by Sir Percy. This curse dogged Whitman for years until DOCTOR STRANGE finally recognized what it was. In order to cleanse it, Whitman was instructed to plunge the sword into the Brazier of Truth, located in Garrett Castle. Whitman's effort shattered the Brazier. Since it was this mystical object that held Sir Percy's spirit in this world, its destruction finally allowed him to rest. Dane joined CAPTAIN BRITAIN in MI-13 during the SECRET INVASION, taking on the new hero, EXCALIBUR (Faiza Hussain), as his squire while protecting Britain from the SKRULLS. **AD, MF**

A brilliant scientist, Garrett used his knowledge to create a winged steed.

The Ebony Blade renders its user invulnerable but, if it tastes blood, will eventually corrupt him.

BLACK MAMBA, ***see page 54***

Black Panther

Warrior king of Wakanda

The Black Panther is an honorary title bestowed on the reigning monarch of the jungle kingdom of Wakanda. T'Challa was only a child when he succeeded his father, who had been murdered by Klaw. Before T'Challa assumed his throne from his uncle S'Yan, he was educated in the finest schools in Europe and America. He then embarked on a series of grueling tests to prove that he was worthy of donning the mantle and using the powers of the Black Panther.

Defending the Kingdom

Although T'Challa often allied himself with the Fantastic Four and the Avengers, the people of Wakanda have always been his highest priority. While he wears a mask, his identity as Wakanda's ruler is no secret, and he overcame challengers such as Erik Killmonger as well as a brain aneurism to maintain leadership of his homeland. T'Challa married his childhood sweetheart Ororo Munroe, Storm of the X-Men, making her his queen. Together they sided with Captain America's resistance during the Civil War, and they fought off a Skrull attack upon Wakanda during the Secret Invasion. Namor tried to bring T'Challa into the Cabal, but when he refused, Doctor Doom critically wounded him. His younger sister Shuri stepped in to fill his role as the Black Panther until he recovered. When Shuri earned the blessing of the goddess Bast, it came with the powers of the Black Panther and the throne of Wakanda. When T'Challa recovered, he did not ask Shuri to step aside. Instead, at Daredevil's request, he moved to Manhattan to take over the protection of Hell's Kitchen—and later rejoined the Avengers—using the new secret identity of Mr. Okonkwo to live among the locals.

The Black Panther's origin story came out in April, 1971, almost five years after his first appearance.

FACTFILE

REAL NAME
T'Challa

OCCUPATION
Monarch of Wakanda

BASE
Wakanda

HEIGHT 6 ft
WEIGHT 200 lbs
EYES Brown
HAIR Black

FIRST APPEARANCE
Fantastic Four #52
(July 1966)

BLACK PANTHER

POWERS
Olympic-level athlete, acrobat and gymnast; combat specialist. Mask enhances night vision; gloves expel gases; vibranium boots enable him to land from great heights; vibranium in costume makes bullets or punches lose power.

ESSENTIAL STORYLINES
- ***Jungle Action #6–18*** The Black Panther returns to Wakanda from the US to fight off Erik Killmonger's attempt to overthrow his rule.
- ***Black Panther Vol. 4 #14–18*** The Black Panther marries Storm.
- ***Black Panther Vol 5. #1–6*** Shuri takes over as the new Black Panther and ruler of Wakanda.

King of the Dead

As T'Challa searched for a way to renew his powers, he pledged himself once more to Bast, but this time as her King of the Dead, which boosted his abilities even further than they had been before. The conflict between the Avengers and the X-Men put T'Challa and Ororo on opposite sides. After Namor's attack on Wakanda, T'Challa had their marriage annulled. Faced with the threat of an entire universe colliding with and destroying his own, T'Challa joined the Illuminati, despite having misgivings about the group. During his initial meeting with them, he vowed to kill Namor. Wakanda and Atlantis later went to war, despite T'Challa counseling Shuri to seek peace.
TD, MF

T'Challa's sister Shuri took over from him as both the Black Panther and the ruler of Wakanda.

The Black Panther and Storm ruled as the king and queen of Wakanda until their fight over the Phoenix Force shattered their marriage.

BLACK MAMBA

FIRST APPEARANCE Marvel Two-In-One #64 (June 1980)
REAL NAME Tanya Sealy
OCCUPATION Mercenary **BASE** Mobile
HEIGHT 5 ft 7 in **WEIGHT** 115 lbs **EYES** Green **HAIR** Black
SPECIAL POWERS/ABILITIES Projects Darkforce energy, which suffocates opponents; hypnotic powers trick targets into thinking that Darkforce is a loved one, allowing it to ensnare them.

Roxxon Oil implanted a device in the brain of Tanya Sealy, a former call girl, giving her telepathic hypnosis and the ability to control the Darkforce, an inky cloud of energy. She formed part of the original incarnations of the Serpent Squad and SERPENT SOCIETY. Later, she also worked with the MASTERS OF EVIL, the BAD Girls, and the Femizons. During the CIVIL WAR, she sided with CAPTAIN AMERICA's anti-registration forces, but during the SECRET INVASION, she rejoined a new Serpent Society. She later joined the Women Warriors, Delaware's FIFTY-STATE INITIATIVE team and has been seen working with the Assassins Guild. **MT, MF**

BLACK TOM

FIRST APPEARANCE X-Men #99 (June 1976)
REAL NAME Thomas Samuel Eamon Cassidy
OCCUPATION Criminal **BASE** Mobile
HEIGHT 6 ft **WEIGHT** 200 lbs **EYES** Blue **HAIR** Black
SPECIAL POWERS/ABILITIES Can project blasts of heat and concussive force, which he focuses through his shillelagh.

Brother of Sean Cassidy, Black Tom is an Irish-born mutant. Losing both the Cassidy fortune and the woman he loved, he turned to crime. Partnered with the JUGGERNAUT, Black Tom battled the X-MEN and other heroes many times. After CABLE shot Tom, doctors grafted a woodlike material onto his wounds, transforming him into a sentient humanoid plant. On M-Day, Tom lost his plant powers and returned to his old self. Juggernaut later convinced him to turn himself in for his crimes. **PS**

BLACKWING (BARNELL BOHUSK)

FIRST APPEARANCE X-Men #117 (October 2001)
REAL NAME Barnell Bohusk
OCCUPATION Student, reality traveler **BASE** New York City
HEIGHT 5 ft 9 in **WEIGHT** 122 lbs
EYES Brown **HAIR** Brown
SPECIAL POWERS/ABILITIES Possesses a suit that gives him superhuman strength, energy blasts, and flight.

At puberty, Barnell mutated into a birdlike human with hollow bones, talons, and wings. Soon after, he joined the Xavier Institute for Higher Learning (*see* X-MEN) as a student codenamed Beak. There, he had six babies with fellow mutant Angel Salvadore. After rebelling against the mutant Xorn's attempt to take over the world, Barnell became dislodged in time and was forced to join the EXILES. He reunited with Angel and their children just before he lost his powers on M-Day. He joined the latest version of the NEW WARRIORS as Blackwing, wearing a high-tech suit that granted him powers. **MF**

BLACK TALON

FIRST APPEARANCE Avengers #152 (October 1976)
REAL NAME Samuel Barone
OCCUPATION Houngan (voodoo priest) **BASE** Louisiana
HEIGHT 6 ft 2 in **WEIGHT** 240 lbs **EYES** Brown **HAIR** Black
SPECIAL POWERS/ABILITIES Supernatural voodoo powers, including the ability to create and control zombies, human corpses that can be reanimated through voodoo magic.

The first man to wear the Black Talon costume was a fake voodoo priest who was killed by his own cult when they discovered his fraud. The second was Samuel Barone, a Creole with true voodoo powers and his own cult. The GRIM REAPER contacted him to bring his dead brother WONDER MAN back to life as a zombie. He battled the AVENGERS many times and retired for a while to produce drugs for the HOOD instead. When he attacked New York City with a zombie horde, the PUNISHER killed him. **MT, MF**

BLACKOUT

FIRST APPEARANCE Nova #19 (May 1976)
REAL NAME Marcus Daniels
OCCUPATION Criminal **BASE** New York City
HEIGHT 5 ft 10 in **WEIGHT** 180 lbs **EYES** Gray **HAIR** Brown
SPECIAL POWERS/ABILITIES Projects and manipulates semi-solid black energy known as the Darkforce; has the strength and agility of a normal human being.

Exposed to "black star" rays by the physicist Dr. Abner Croit, Daniels gained the ability to control this cosmic radiation. He adopted the moniker "Blackout" and embarked on a series of robberies. Over time, exposure to this dark energy led to creeping insanity. Although his ally MOONSTONE helped him to direct and extend his powers, she also sought to control his mind, as did their joint master, BARON ZEMO. During an attack on the AVENGERS' Mansion, Blackout endeavored to resist Zemo's mental commands, but these efforts led to a brain haemorrhage and Blackout's death. **AD**

BLACK SWAN

FIRST APPEARANCE New Avengers #1 (March 2013)
REAL NAME Yabbat Ummon Turru
OCCUPATION Destroyer **BASE** The Necropolis of Wakanda
HEIGHT 5 ft 7 in **WEIGHT** 120 lbs
EYES Black (red during incursions) **HAIR** White
SPECIAL POWERS/ABILITIES Yabbat can fly and fire optic blasts. She possesses superhuman strength and is telepathic. She can predict incoming incursions of other Earths.

Born a princess on an Earth in another dimension, as a girl Yabbat escaped the destruction of her world by fleeing into an interdimensional library. There the Black Swans of many dimensions took her in and raised her to join their ranks. As an adult, she traveled from Earth to Earth, destroying those threatening the others as an offering to Rabum Alal, a godlike being who she believes causes the world-shattering incursions. The BLACK PANTHER captured her when she appeared in Wakanda, and she was pressed into helping the ILLUMINATI save their Earth. **MF**

Black Widow

Uncompromising and deadly

Natasha has assumed many roles, including surrogate mother, field agent, and implacable opponent of a rival Black Widow.

Shortly after Russia's World War II victory at Stalingrad, a lady, trapped in a burning building, threw her baby to a stranger below—a soldier named Ivan Petrovich. He raised the baby, named Natasha, who turned out to be a superb student, athlete, and ballerina. She married test pilot Alexei Shostakov, but their happiness was cut short. Faking Shostakov's death and leaving Natasha to grieve, the KGB trained him to become the Red Guardian—a Russian super-soldier. The KGB then manipulated Natasha into becoming a spy codenamed Black Widow.

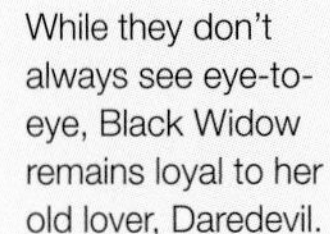
While they don't always see eye-to-eye, Black Widow remains loyal to her old lover, Daredevil.

FACTFILE
REAL NAME
Natalia (Natasha) Alianovna Romanova
OCCUPATION
Intelligence agent
BASE New York City

HEIGHT 5 ft 7 in
WEIGHT 125 lbs
EYES Blue
HAIR Red/auburn

FIRST APPEARANCE
Tales of Suspense #52 (April 1964)

BLACK WIDOW I

POWERS
Martial artist; Olympic-level gymnast; trained spy; cartridges on wrist house various devices and also fires an energy blast known as a "Widow's Bite."

HARD TIME

Two espionage missions against Stark Industries brought her into contact with Hawkeye, and he inspired her to join SHIELD. A romance between the pair proved short-lived. Encountering the Red Guardian on a mission, she had only just learned his true identity when he was shot and killed.

Later, Natasha became romantically involved with Daredevil and founded the Champions. She also led the Avengers during one of its hardest periods, when several members died. More recently, she became the foe of a rival Black Widow, Yelena Belova. She also learned she was just one of many Black Widows and that her memories of her early life were implanted. While working for Iron Man's SHIELD, Natasha helped install Bucky Barnes as the new Captain America. She currently serves with both the Avengers and the Secret Avengers. **AD, MF**

FACTFILE
REAL NAME
Yelena Belova
OCCUPATION
Intelligence agent
BASE Russia

HEIGHT 5 ft 7 in
WEIGHT 135 lbs
EYES Blue
HAIR Blonde

FIRST APPEARANCE
Inhumans #5 (March 1999)

BLACK WIDOW II

POWERS
Only experience and gadgets separate Belova from the first Black Widow: Belova achieved even higher marks in training; she is also a martial-arts expert and Olympic-level gymnast.

ESSENTIAL STORYLINES
- ***Daredevil #87–90*** Black Widow and Daredevil move to San Francisco; Black Widow's history is explained.
- ***Pale Little Spider #1–3*** The origins of Yelena Belova are explained for the first time.
- ***Black Widow Vol. I #1–3*** The two Black Widows, Natasha Romanova and Yelena Belova, go head-to-head and their bitter enmity begins.

Yelena Belova

Like Natasha, Yelena Belova was trained at the KGB's Red Room. She once worked for Hydra, who had transferred her mind into a Super-Adaptoid body. Yelena now serves on the high council of AIM.

BLADE

Daywalking human vampire

BLADE

FACTFILE

REAL NAME
Eric Brooks

OCCUPATION
Vampire hunter

BASE
Mobile

HEIGHT 6 ft 2 in
WEIGHT 180 lbs
EYES Brown
HAIR Black

FIRST APPEARANCE
Tomb of Dracula #10 (July 1973)

POWERS
Immune to vampire bites and vampiric hypnosis; enhanced strength, speed, senses, and healing. Immune to vampire's susceptibility to sunlight. Carries arsenal of anti-vampire weapons; guns fire garlic-filled silver bullets; trademark blade is titanium; martial-arts expert.

Over seventy years ago, Blade's mother (a London prostitute) was fatally bitten by vampire Deacon Frost while giving birth to him, transforming the infant into a half-vampire (dhampir). Friends of Blade's mother raised him in her brothel. When he was nine, he helped horn player Jamal Afari fend off a trio of vampires, and the jazz trumpeter moved into the brothel to tutor Blade in both music and the hunting of vampires.

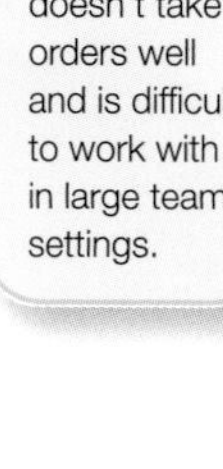

Blade doesn't take orders well and is difficult to work with in large team settings.

Blade remains committed to his mission to rid the world of vampires. He now possesses the abilities of a pseudo-vampire due to a bite from Morbius.

VAMPIRE HUNTERS

In his youth, Blade ran a street gang called the Bloodshadows. After the vampire Lamia transformed his girl, Glory, into a vampire, he gave up gang life and returned to vampire hunting. When Dracula turned Afari into a vampire too, Blade assembled a team of hunters to track the vampire lord to China. After losing his first team, Blade partnered with Dracula's old foe Quincy Harker as well as Rachel Van Helsing and Frank Drake to renew the pursuit.

When Blade's path crossed Deacon Frost's, he went after his mother's killer. During this time, he met and partnered with Hannibal King, a detective whom Frost had turned into a vampire. Together with King, Drake, and Doctor Strange, Blade helped unleash the Montesi Formula, a spell that destroyed all the vampires on Earth. His quest ended, Blade opened a detective agency with Drake and King, named Borderline Investigations, and they battled occult threats such as the Nightstalkers.

After losing his left hand, Blade had a prosthetic made out of a gun.

ESSENTIAL STORYLINES

- ***Tomb of Dracula #10, #12–14*** *Blade makes his debut and kills Dracula for the first time.*
- ***Rise of the Midnight Sons*** *The Nightstalkers join Doctor Strange, Morbius, Ghost Rider (Dan Ketch), Johnny Blaze (see Ghost Rider), and the Darkhold Redeemers in the battle against Lilith.*
- ***Blade Vol. 6 #1–12*** *Blade's past catches up with him—along with his father.*

DAYWALKER

When Dracula returned and beat Blade, Blade's fury caused him to snap, and he was placed in a mental institution until Doctor Strange could help him. Freed, Blade was tricked into using a page from the mystical book Darkhold to give himself supernatural powers as Switchblade. Another page from the forbidden book returned him to normal.

While working with Spider-Man, Blade was bitten by his sometime-ally Morbius. Blade's immunity to vampires didn't apply to Morbius' unique condition. Blade gained the powers of a vampire, but without their weakness to sunlight, causing him to be known as Daywalker.

During the Civil War, Blade registered and worked with SHIELD, which gave him a gun-hand to replace one he'd bitten off to keep from being force-fed an innocent by Lucas Cross, a vampire who claims to be his father. During the Secret Invasion, he worked with MI:13 and struck up a relationship with the part-vampire hero Spitfire. He later helped the X-Men against Dracula's son Xarus, despite the fact that they brought the vampire lord back as well. **MF**

Blindfold

FIRST APPEARANCE Astonishing X-Men #7 (January 2005)
REAL NAME Ruth Aldine **OCCUPATION** Student
BASE Jean Grey's School for Higher Learning **HEIGHT** 5 ft 6 in
WEIGHT 123 lbs **EYES** None **HAIR** Black
SPECIAL POWERS/ABILITIES Ruth is a telepath with limited precognition.

Born a mutant without eyes or sockets, Ruth was abandoned by her father, leaving her in the care of her mother and her cruel older brother. Her mother died defending her from her brother and Ruth went to live with an aunt until her brother's execution; his ghost then stole half her powers. She studied with the X-Men and joined the Young X-Men for a while, later learning that she was related to Destiny, explaining her powers of prediction. She helped Legion control his powers and, in return, he saved her from her brother's vengeful spirit. **MF**

Bling!

FIRST APPEARANCE X-Men Vol. 2 #171 (August 2005)
REAL NAME Roxanne Washington **OCCUPATION** Student
BASE Jean Grey School for Higher Learning **HEIGHT** 5 ft 6 in
WEIGHT 152 lbs **EYES** Brown (or diamond) **HAIR** Brown (or diamond) **SPECIAL POWERS/ABILITIES** Roxy's bone marrow can produce diamonds, which can protect her skin or be fired at foes. She also has superhuman strength.

The daughter of celebrity hip-hop artists, Roxy is famous for appearing in her parents' music videos. To avoid the music industry, she enrolled at the Xavier Institute, where she studied under Gambit. When the school was shut down, she followed the X-Men to Utopia and helped with various missions. Offered a place with the X-Men, she declined, preferring to leave the dangerous work for others. She returned to her studies at the Jean Grey School for Higher Learning. **MF**

Blink

FIRST APPEARANCE Uncanny X-men #317 (October 1994)
REAL NAME Clarice Ferguson **OCCUPATION** Adventurer
BASE Mobile **HEIGHT** 5 ft 5 in **WEIGHT** 125 lbs
EYES Green **HAIR** Magenta
SPECIAL POWERS/ABILITIES Blink is a mutant with the ability to create teleportational warps; carries a dagger and a set of javelins.

Blink was part of a group of mutants captured by evil alien race the Phalanx. She helped save the others but accidentally killed herself with her powers in the process. The immortal External and magician Selene resurrected her and told her that the X-Men had betrayed her, convincing Blink to fight against them. Blink later realized her error and rejoined Wolverine's X-Men team. The Blink of Earth-295 was raised in the Age of Apocalypse by Sabretooth, but became unstuck in time—exiled from her home reality. Recruited by the Timebroker, she and a team of fellow Exiles were charged with repairing the broken links in the chain of realities. **TB, MF**

Blizzard

Blizzard is able to escape danger by creating an ice slide beneath his feet.

Suit contains tiny cryogenic units called micro-cryostats.

The more water there is in the air, the more powerful Blizzard's suit is. In arid conditions it is useless.

Employed by Stark Industries, Dr. Gregor Shapanka attempted to steal and sell Stark technology to fund research into longevity. Caught and fired, he developed a suit with freezing powers and came to be known as the villain Jack Frost, and later Blizzard.

Shapanka was killed by Arno Stark, the Iron Man of 2020 (from Earth-8410), who had come back in time for data needed to disarm a bomb.

Shapanka's successor was Donny Gill, an employee of Justin Hammer. After leaving Hammer's employ, Gill joined the Masters of Evil, and later became one of Mach-IV's Thunderbolts.

After earning a pardon for his crimes, he registered with the Fifty-State Initiative, but later returned to crime in an upgraded suit with the help of the Mandarin. Randy Macklin then wore Gill's suit for a while. After he was captured and served his time, Tony Stark took him under his wing. **AD, MF**

FACTFILE

REAL NAME
Dr. Gregor Shapanka

OCCUPATION
Former scientist; criminal

BASE New York City

HEIGHT 5 ft 6 in
WEIGHT 165 lbs
EYES Brown
HAIR Brown

FIRST APPEARANCE
Tales of Suspense #45 (September 1963)

POWERS

Gloves on Blizzard's battlesuit could project intense cold, generate freezing mist, mini-blizzards of snow, sleet, and darts of ice that could pierce metal; he could freeze people by covering them in frost and escaped capture by creating an ice slide. He has no superhuman powers.

BLOB

FACTFILE
REAL NAME
Fred J. Dukes
OCCUPATION Criminal; former circus performer
BASE
Mobile

HEIGHT 8 ft
WEIGHT 976 lbs
EYES Brown
HAIR Brown

FIRST APPEARANCE
Uncanny X-Men #3 (January 1964)

BLOB

Life changed for carnival freak Fred J. Dukes when the X-MEN revealed to him that he was a mutant. Instead of joining them, Dukes attempted to destroy them as the Blob. Recruited by MAGNETO for his BROTHERHOOD OF EVIL MUTANTS, the Blob embarked on a life of crime, clashing with the X-MEN, AVENGERS, and DEFENDERS. For a while, he worked with the government-sponsored FREEDOM FORCE, but later returned to crime. After M-Day, the Blob lost his powers and much of his mass, his skin hanging off him in folds. Soon after, he joined X-CELL, a group of angry, depowered mutants. He later lost the extra skin and promoted himself as a weight-loss success story in Japan. His mutated clone joined a new Brotherhood of Evil Mutants run by JOSEPH. **TB, MF**

POWERS
Superhuman strength and durability. Fatty body could absorb bullets, even artillery shells, and was impervious to injury; however eyes, ears, nose, and mouth were not as injury-resistant. When he planted himself firmly, the Blob bonded with the ground beneath him and could not be moved.

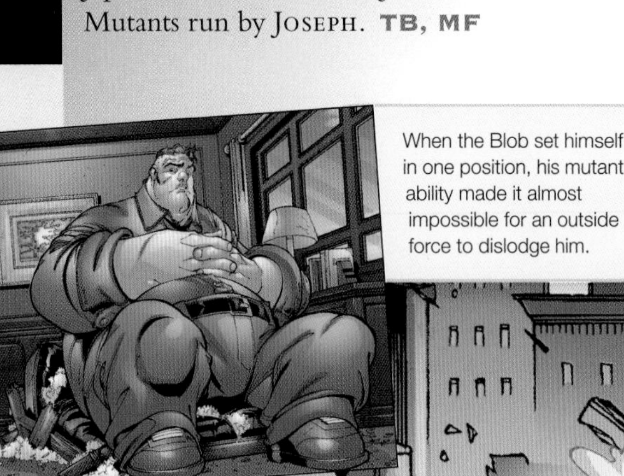

When the Blob set himself in one position, his mutant ability made it almost impossible for an outside force to dislodge him.

BLOODHAWK

FIRST APPEARANCE Avengers #179 (January 1979)
REAL NAME Bloodhawk **OCCUPATION** Adventurer
BASE Muara, an island in the Atlantic Ocean **HEIGHT** 6 ft 3 in
WEIGHT 150 lbs **EYES** Black **FEATHERS** Reddish-brown
SPECIAL POWERS/ABILITIES Superhuman strength and stamina; able to fly and communicate with birds; possesses razor-sharp claws.

Bloodhawk is the only son of a geneticist who experimented on his own wife. The poor woman died giving birth to a mutant of hawklike appearance and characteristics. Unable to accept the horror he had created, Bloodhawk's father turned his son over to his best friend, who removed the child from civilization. Plagued by bouts of insanity, Bloodhawk grew to adulthood in the South Seas. When a powerful totem was stolen from his island home, he journeyed to the US and battled the AVENGERS to recover it. Bloodhawk later gave his life to save THOR. **TB**

BLOODSCREAM

FIRST APPEARANCE Wolverine #4 (February 1989)
REAL NAME Unknown **OCCUPATION** Enforcer
BASE Madripoor, Southeast Asia **HEIGHT** 6 ft 5 in
WEIGHT Unknown **EYES** Unknown **HAIR** Gray
SPECIAL POWERS/ABILITIES Although not a true vampire, has many vampire powers: superhuman strength, agility, accelerated healing, hypnotic ability; can also kill or cause bleeding by touch.

Bloodscream was once a 16th-century sailor, whom a necromancer turned into a pseudo-vampire—a condition that could only be cured by drinking an immortal's blood. Centuries later, Bloodscream, now a Nazi soldier, encountered WOLVERINE. Meeting Wolverine decades later, Bloodscream saw the mutant hadn't aged. Assuming Wolverine was immortal, Bloodscream has hounded him ever since. **MT**

BLOODSTONE, ELSA

FIRST APPEARANCE Bloodstone #1 (December 2001)
REAL NAME Elsa Bloodstone **OCCUPATION** Monster hunter
BASE Boston, Mass. **HEIGHT** 5 ft 9 in
WEIGHT 120 lbs **EYES** Blue **HAIR** Blond
SPECIAL POWERS/ABILITIES An expert markswoman with superhuman strength, agility, speed, regeneration, and endurance, granted by her Bloodstone Choker.

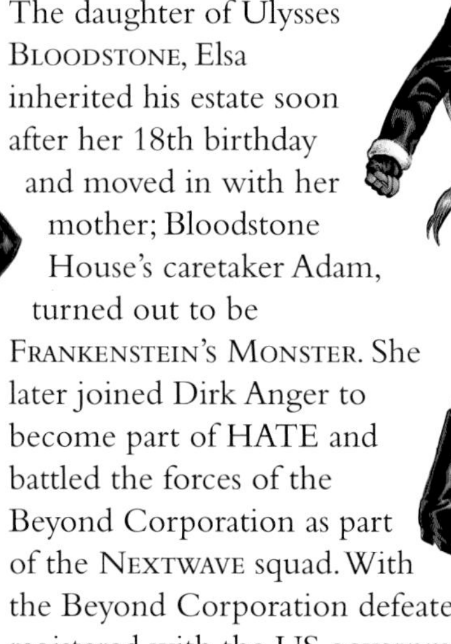

The daughter of Ulysses BLOODSTONE, Elsa inherited his estate soon after her 18th birthday and moved in with her mother; Bloodstone House's caretaker Adam, turned out to be FRANKENSTEIN'S MONSTER. She later joined Dirk Anger to become part of HATE and battled the forces of the Beyond Corporation as part of the NEXTWAVE squad. With the Beyond Corporation defeated, she registered with the US government and joined THE FIFTY STATE INITIATIVE. **MF**

Bloodstone, Ulysses

BLOODSTONE, ULYSSES

FACTFILE

REAL NAME
Unknown; took the name Ulysses Bloodstone

OCCUPATION
Soldier of fortune

BASE
Bloodstone Island

HEIGHT 6 ft 2 in
WEIGHT 255 lbs
EYES Blue
HAIR Blond

FIRST APPEARANCE
Marvel Presents #1 (October 1975)

POWERS
Superhuman strength; blood-red Helix crystal endowed him with immortality and regenerative ability: could even regrow limbs; also had invisible third eye in forehead giving him psychic powers; expert with all kinds of weapons, though favored a customized sawn-off shotgun firing explosive shells.

Born over 10,000 years ago in the Hyborian Age, the man known as Ulysses Bloodstone belonged to a Scandinavian tribe of hunter-gatherers. He was lured away by Ulluxy'l Kwan Tae Syn, the alien guardian of a crystal entity called the Hellfire Helix. The Helix needed a human servant, so it endowed the tribe's foremost hunter with superhuman powers. However, when the Helix crystal killed the rest of his tribe, the hunter caused it to shatter. A piece embedded itself in his chest and the other pieces were scattered all over the world. The reddish crystal fragment made the hunter immortal, and led him to adopt the name Ulysses Bloodstone. Ulysses spent the rest of his life searching for Ulluxy'l, while the alien strove to piece the Helix back together. During his quest, Ulysses earned a fortune through mercenary work and shrewd investments, establishing six headquarters across the world and a base on what became known as Bloodstone Island.

The Helix had Ulluxy'l ally himself with a group called "The Conspiracy." They cut the crystal fragment from Ulysses' chest, leaving him for dead, however his body managed to kill Ulluxy'l before it withered and died. Ulysses left behind his ex-wife Elise, their daughter Elsa Bloodstone, and son Cullen. **AD, MF**

Bluebird

FIRST APPEARANCE Untold Tales of Spider-Man #11 (July 1996)
REAL NAME Sally Avril **OCCUPATION** Student; adventurer
BASE Midtown High School, New York **HEIGHT** 5 ft 2 in
WEIGHT 110 lbs **EYES** Brown **HAIR** Black (blond wig)
SPECIAL POWERS/ABILITIES Stolen technology from the Vulture enabled her to fly using power pack and wings; also had a device that emitted an ultrasonic, ear-splitting scream.

A classmate of Peter Parker's at Midtown High, Sally Avril adopted the costumed identity of Bluebird after being inspired by the exploits of Spider-Man. Possessing no superhuman abilities or even proper training, Bluebird proved to be a danger to herself and to others, until Spider-Man eventually convinced her to put aside her costumed identity and return to life as a student. Tragically, she was killed shortly thereafter in an automobile accident. **TB**

Boomerang

FIRST APPEARANCE Tales to Astonish #81 (July 1966)
REAL NAME Frederick Myers **OCCUPATION** Assassin for hire
BASE Mobile **HEIGHT** 5 ft 11 in **WEIGHT** 175 lbs
EYES Brown **HAIR** Black
SPECIAL POWERS/ABILITIES Brilliant baseball pitcher; famed for customized boomerangs, such as explosive "shatterangs," poisonous "gasarangs," diamond sharp "razorangs."

Australian Fred Myers moved to the US as a child and became a Major League Baseball player. Suspended for taking bribes, he turned to crime full-time. The Secret Empire gave him the codename Boomerang and his weaponry. He worked with Justin Hammer, Hammerhead, the Kingpin, the Sinister Syndicate, The Sinister Twelve, and the Masters of Evil, battling foes such as SHIELD, Daredevil, and Spider-Man.

During Norman Osborn's control of SHIELD, Boomerang joined the Heavy Hitters, Fifty-State Initiative's Nevada team, under the name Outback. Alastair Smythe boosted Boomerang's powers for a subsequent attempt to kill Spider-Man. **AD, MF**

Only Bullseye and Hawkeye can match Boomerang's terrifying accuracy, while Boomerang's jet boots enable attacks from unexpected directions.

Bloodstorm

FIRST APPEARANCE Mutant X #1 (October 1998)
REAL NAME Ororo Munroe
OCCUPATION Adventurer **BASE** Earth of Mutant X universe
HEIGHT 5 ft 11 in **WEIGHT** 196 lbs **EYES** Blue **HAIR** White
SPECIAL POWERS/ABILITIES Possessed vampiric powers, including hypnotic abilities and the power to transform into mist, a bat, or a wolf; can control the weather over limited areas.

Years ago Dracula bit Storm of the X-Men, who began transforming into a vampire. In the main Marvel Universe, Storm was cured. But on the alternate Earth where the "Mutant X" series was set, Storm completed her metamorphosis, becoming the vampire known as Bloodstorm. She nevertheless refused to turn villainous, and fed only on the blood of that reality's Forge, with his consent. Bloodstorm joined the Six, a team mostly comprised of former members of that reality's X-Men. For aiding the people of yet another alternate Earth, Earth X, Bloodstorm was rewarded by receiving a blood transfusion which cured her vampirism. **PS**

Blue Shield

FIRST APPEARANCE Dazzler #5 (July 1981)
REAL NAME Joseph Cartelli **OCCUPATION** Security Director for Project: Pegasus **BASE** Mount Athena, New York
HEIGHT 6 ft **WEIGHT** 180 lbs **EYES** Blue **HAIR** Brown
SPECIAL POWERS/ABILITIES Formerly wore microcircuitry-lined belt which increased strength and generated force field around body; now, owing to prolonged exposure, no longer needs belt.

After losing his father and a boyhood friend to mob violence, Joseph Cartelli decided to avenge them both. He went undercover, joining the Barrigans' gang with the intention of destroying it from within. His dead friend had built a force-field belt financed with loan-shark money, and Cartelli used the belt to become the Blue Shield. After defeating the Barrigans, Cartelli tried to join the Avengers, but he wound up replacing Quasar as the security director for Project: P.E.G.A.S.U.S. instead. Cartelli was assigned to help out in New York City as part of the Fifty State Initiative. **TD, MF**

Box

Robotic armored crimefighter

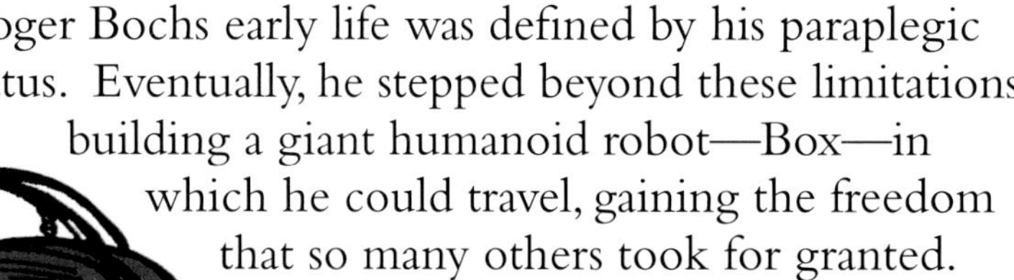

Roger Bochs early life was defined by his paraplegic status. Eventually, he stepped beyond these limitations, building a giant humanoid robot—Box—in which he could travel, gaining the freedom that so many others took for granted.

BOX (ROGER BOCHS)

FACTFILE
REAL NAME
Roger Bochs
OCCUPATION
Alpha Flight member
BASE
Tamarind Island, British Columbia

HEIGHT 7 ft
WEIGHT 465 lbs
EYES Blue
HAIR Red

FIRST APPEARANCE
Alpha Flight #1
(August 1983)

POWERS
An engineering genius, Bochs built the first Box robot to serve as a bipedal robotic transportation for himself; the Box robot possessed vast strength and durability; Bochs was able to "phase" in and out of robot at will.

Wheelchair-user Roger Bochs' early life was sad and lonely.

ESSENTIAL STORYLINES
- ***Alpha Flight #41–49***
Charts Roger Bochs' physical and mental decline, and his death as part of Omega.
- ***Alpha Flight #102–105***
Madison Jeffries helps Alpha Flight battle Diablo... and then there's the small matter of getting married to Lillian Crawley.

Joining Alpha Flight

With his robotic chariot, Roger came to the attention of James McDonald Hudson who was recruiting for Alpha Flight. Hudson recruited Roger into Alpha Flight's training program and he was progressing well when the Canadian government withdrew funding. Out of a job, Roger returned to his native Saskatchewan.

Hudson kept the team going but Roger's return to it was a long time coming. Hired by Jerome Jaxon to join the nefarious Omega Flight, Roger was expected to help them destroy Alpha Flight. He opposed this but was helpless when Jaxon took control of Box and sent it into battle. By the end of the struggle, both Jaxon and Hudson were dead and Box was seriously mangled. Roger was invited to rejoin the exhausted Alpha Flight, but first he needed to rebuild his robot.

With the help of fellow team member, Madison Jefferies, Roger constructed a superior Box model, but when he became unlucky in love, his life began a downward spiral. Manipulated into merging his being with Madison's unbalanced brother, Roger became part of a new entity—Omega. His endeavors to limit Omega's sinister activities led to him being effectively lobotomized and when Omega was defeated and died, Roger passed away, too.

The new improved Box allowed Roger to phase in and out of it.

BOX (MADISON JEFFRIES)

FACTFILE
REAL NAME
Madison Jeffries
OCCUPATION
Alpha Flight member
BASE
Tamarind Island, British Columbia

HEIGHT 10 ft (variable)
WEIGHT 195 lbs (variable)
EYES Blue
HAIR Black

FIRST APPEARANCE
Alpha Flight #10
(May 1984)

POWERS
Mutant power to manipulate metal, plastic and glass allows Jeffries to extend capability of Box; robot armor now much lighter and able to increase its size and weight seemingly without limit.

With his intuitive grasp of all things mechanical, Madison Jeffries made great strides in enhancing Box.

Madison Jeffries

When Roger Bochs died, Madison Jeffries inherited the Box armor and used his mutant ability to manipulate metal, glass, and plastic to augment the machine. He served with Alpha Flight but retired to marry teammate Diamond Lil. Later, agents of Weapon X captured Jeffries and brainwashed him into building the Neverland mutant concentration camp. He retained his powers after M-Day but went into mourning when Diamond Lil was killed by Mortis. He currently works with the X-Men. **AD, MF**

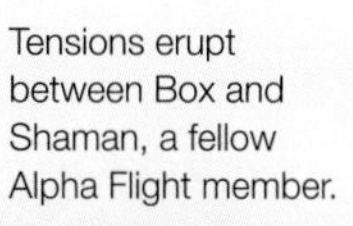

Tensions erupt between Box and Shaman, a fellow Alpha Flight member.

Braddock, Jamie

FIRST APPEARANCE Captain Britain Weekly #9 (December 1976)
REAL NAME James Braddock
OCCUPATION Ex-racing driver, slave-trafficker **BASE** London
HEIGHT 6 ft 1 in **WEIGHT** 151 lbs **EYES** Blue **HAIR** Black
SPECIAL POWERS/ABILITIES Possesses the ability to warp reality, which he perceives as made of string; he can thus twist objects, such as people's bodies, into grotesque, agonizing shapes.

Brother of Captain Britain and Psylocke, sleazy playboy Jamie Braddock was captured and tortured by Doctor Crocodile. His latent ability to reshape reality manifested the moment he lost his sanity, and he became one of the most dangerous beings in the universe. After Excalibur defeated him, he spent years in a coma. During the House of M incident, he returned and sacrificed himself to save his sister and the universe. He returned again and helped defend Otherworld from the Goat Monk, a future version of himself. When Psylocke realized this, she forced Captain Britain to kill him. **TB, MF**

Brant, Betty

Working as the secretary of editor J. Jonah Jameson at the *Daily Bugle*, Betty became photojournalist Peter Parker's (Spider-Man's) first girlfriend. When their relationship ended, she married *Daily Bugle* reporter Ned Leeds. Dismayed when she discovered that Ned had become the Hobgoblin, she suffered a mental breakdown after his death. Betty later became an investigative reporter and cleared Ned's name by proving that Roderick Kingsley was the original Hobgoblin. She continued at the *Daily Bugle* after it was sold and renamed the *DB*. When the *DB* folded, she became a journalistic blogger. Throughout it all, she and Peter have remained great friends. She dated Flash Thompson, the new Venom, until his apparently erratic behavior became too much for her. **AD, MF**

FACTFILE
REAL NAME
Elizabeth Brant
OCCUPATION
Investigative journalist
BASE
New York City

HEIGHT 5 ft 7 in
WEIGHT 125 lbs
EYES Brown
HAIR Brown

FIRST APPEARANCE:
Amazing Spider-Man #4 (September 1963)

POWERS
Expert investigative reporter with a strong personality and a hugely generous soul.

BRANT, BETTY

Brand, Abigail

FIRST APPEARANCE Astonishing X-Men #3 (September 2004)
REAL NAME Abigail Brand **OCCUPATION** Director of SWORD
BASE The Peak (SWORD HQ) **HEIGHT** 5 ft 8 in
WEIGHT 140 lbs **EYES** Green **HAIR** Green **SPECIAL POWERS/ABILITIES** Produces heat and light from her hands and heals fast. An extraterrestrial diplomat and a trained pilot and combatant.

The daughter of a blue-furred alien father and a human mutant mother (and half-sister to a green-furred alien), Brand is uniquely suited to serve as the director of SWORD (Sentient World Observation and Response Department) the off-Earth counterpart of SHIELD, a position she achieved by age 28. She speaks a number of alien languages that most humans cannot pronounce and oversees several aliens drafted into the service of the US government. Despite her lack of social skills outside of direct diplomacy, she has an ongoing relationship with the Beast. **MF**

Brood

The Brood is a race of alien insectoids that spreads across the universe like a cancer by injecting eggs into other beings. When the eggs hatch, the host is consumed and transformed into a Brood member. The Brood use Acanti space whales as living starships. Native to the Shi'ar Galaxy, the Brood aided Deathbird's attempts to overthrow her sister Lilandra Neramani as the Shi'ar Majestrix.

Wolverine's healing factor let him resist the Brood egg that was deposited in his body.

The Brood infected the X-Men and planted the egg of a Bloodqueen into Professor X, but the team was saved by Wolverine, who was able to resist the transformation process. Their home planet, Broodworld, was destroyed, but many Brood survived and began to rebuild their race. A Brood queen, No-Name, came to Earth during World War Hulk as part of the Hulk's Warbound, and a young Brood mutant called Broo studied at the Jean Grey School for Higher learning. **TD, MF**

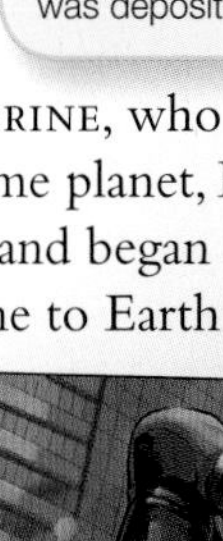
The alien Brood eventually found their way to Earth and injected a team of mutants; however they were defeated by the X-Men.

FACTFILE
OCCUPATION
Extraterrestrial mercenaries
BASE
Shi'ar Galaxy

HEIGHT 8 ft
WEIGHT 825 lbs
EYES Red
HAIR None
SCALES Green

FIRST APPEARANCE
Uncanny X-Men #155 (March 1982)

POWERS
Individuals possess six legs, transparent wings, razor-sharp teeth, armor-plated scales and long tails that are divided into two deadly stingers. The Brood are extremely durable, very hard to destroy, and vicious fighters, determined that their malignant race will survive.

BROOD, THE

BROTHERHOOD OF EVIL MUTANTS

Mutant terrorist organization

BROTHERHOOD OF EVIL MUTANTS

FACTFILE

MEMBERS/POWERS

MAGNETO (LEADER)
Manipulates magnetic forces.

ASTRA
Varies her molecular density.

TOAD
Tongue stretches 25 ft; leaps great heights; super-strong.

QUICKSILVER
Superhuman speed.

SCARLET WITCH
Chaos magician.

MASTERMIND
Illusion-caster.

BLOB
Immovable; impervious to injury.

UNUS
Impenetrable force-field.

LORELEI
Hypersonic, paralysing scream.

BASE
Mobile

FIRST APPEARANCE
Uncanny X-Men #4
(March 1964)

ALLIES/FOES

ALLIES: Magneto

FOES: Professor X, The X-Men, New Mutants, X-Factor, X-Force, the Avengers, Cable, all non-mutant human beings.

ORIGINAL BROTHERHOOD
1 The Toad ***2*** Mastermind ***3*** Magneto ***4*** Quicksilver ***5*** The Scarlet Witch

Founded by MAGNETO, the Brotherhood of Evil Mutants has remained, through its various incarnations, the opposite number of the X-MEN. While the X-Men's mission has always been to promote tolerance and co-existence between mutants and normal humans, the Brotherhood's goal has been nothing less than total domination over mankind, and quite possibly the eradication of normal humans entirely.

MUTANT MENACE

Originally, Magneto formed the Brotherhood as a strike force, helping him to oppose PROFESSOR X's X-Men, who had foiled his takeover of the Cape Citadel rocket base. This initial assemblage included the high-leaping Toad, illusion-creating Mastermind, the super-swift QUICKSILVER, and his sister, the hex-casting SCARLET WITCH. Time and again they struck against their X-Men foes and against humanity, never scoring a true victory. Eventually, with the defeat of Magneto, this incarnation of the Brotherhood was no more—and the misguided Quicksilver and the Scarlet Witch went on to become members of the AVENGERS.

Some years later, the mysterious, shape-shifting mutant terrorist MYSTIQUE formed a new Brotherhood of Evil Mutants under her command. This grouping comprised the immovable BLOB, the earth-shaking AVALANCHE, the flame-wielding PYRO, and the future-predicting DESTINY. This incarnation of the Brotherhood eventually transformed into FREEDOM FORCE when it was offered amnesty by the US Government in exchange for becoming government operatives. But Freedom Force was at its heart corrupt, and after assorted clashes with the X-Men and other hero groups, such as the Avengers, the program was quietly disbanded.

ESSENTIAL STORYLINES

- ***X-Men #4***
The newly-formed Brotherhood has its first clash with the X-Men.
- ***Uncanny X-Men #141–142***
Mystique's Brotherhood attempts to assassinate Senator Robert Kelly and prevent the passing of the Mutant Registration Act.
- ***The Brotherhood #1***
X's agents are assembled for covert terrorist missions against humankind.

MYSTIQUE'S BROTHERHOOD
1 Avalanche
2 Blob
3 Pyro
4 Mystique

GROWING THE FAMILY

Since then, a number of other villains have formed their own versions of the team, including DAKEN, EXODUS, JOSEPH, Madelyne PRYOR, Toad, and Xorn and even the heroes HAVOK, PROFESSOR X, and SUNSPOT. Mystique created the latest version to frame the original X-Men for crimes after the BEAST brought them forward in time to visit the present. Her group is one of the leanest, consisting of only herself, SABRETOOTH, and Lady Mastermind. **TB, MF**

EXODUS'S BROTHERHOOD
1 Black Tom Cassidy
2 Juggernaut
3 Avalanche
4 Exodus
5 Sabretooth
6 Mammomax

Brother Voodoo

BROTHER VOODOO

FACTFILE
REAL NAME
Jericho Drumm
OCCUPATION
Houngan (voodoo priest)
BASE
Port-au-Prince and New Orleans

HEIGHT 6 ft
WEIGHT 220 lbs
EYES Brown
HAIR Brown

FIRST APPEARANCE:
Strange Tales #169 (September 1973)

POWERS
Summoning brother's spirit from within own body doubles his strength; can send this spirit forth to possess other people; can create fire and smoke; hypnotic control over animals.

The first Brother Voodoo appeared in the 17th century as a Haitian ex-slave named Laurent who bound his dead brother Alexandre's soul to his own. He inspired many successors, who also took the name.

In modern times, Jericho Drumm inherited the title as his dying twin brother Daniel's dying wish. Jericho turned to his brother's teacher Papa Jambo for training so he could avenge his brother's death at the hands of a voodoo sorcerer who claimed to serve Damballah, an evil serpent god. Jambo helped bind Daniel's spirit to Jericho's and Jericho became the new Brother Voodoo.

Jericho defeated Damballah, but became possessed by Damballah's power. DOCTOR STRANGE freed him, and he joined the HOWLING COMMANDOS. When Doctor Strange gave up being the Sorcerer Supreme Jericho took up that mantle. He later died in a battle against Agamatto. Daniel's spirit returned to take revenge on the Avengers for Jericho's death but was defeated by Doctor Strange. **MF**

When he took over as the Sorcerer Supreme, Jericho became known as Doctor Voodoo.

Builders, The

FIRST APPEARANCE Avengers #1 (December 2012)
REAL NAME n/a
OCCUPATION Agent for Paranormal Law Enforcement Team
BASE Mobile **HEIGHT** 7 ft (average)
WEIGHT 400 lbs (average) **EYES** Purple **HAIR** None
SPECIAL POWERS/ABILITIES The Builders control amazing technologies and armies of robots and engineered races.

The Builders are supposedly the universe's oldest race, genetic and technological engineers who seed worlds with life and then direct their evolution. They scour the galaxy, looking for races that live up to their standards and destroying all the rest. They often send trios of creatures out as scouts: an ALEPH (a powerful robot firing optic blasts), an ABYSS, and an EX NIHILO. Few worlds meet their criteria, and none that fail survive. **MF**

Brutacus

FIRST APPEARANCE Fantastic Four #186 (September 1977)
REAL NAME Unrevealed **OCCUPATION** Warlock
BASE New Salem, Colorado **HEIGHT** 6 ft 5 in
WEIGHT 310 lbs **EYES** Brown **HAIR** Orange
SPECIAL POWERS/ABILITIES Enhanced strength and reflexes, damage resistance, ability to change into lion form, other unrevealed powers of sorcery.

Brutacus was born the son of warlock Nicholas SCRATCH in New Salem, Colorado. When Scratch ordered his mother, Agatha HARKNESS, to stand trial for living in the outside world, he transformed Brutacus and his six other children into inhuman creatures called SALEM'S SEVEN. In a final battle with the VISION and the SCARLET WITCH, an explosion of magical energy killed Salem's Seven and wiped out New Salem. During a nervous breakdown, the Scarlet Witch resurrected Salem's Seven. For a time, they lived with DOCTOR STRANGE and became friends with the FANTASTIC FOUR. **DW, MF**

Buchanan, Sam

FIRST APPEARANCE Ghost Rider #28 (August 1992)
REAL NAME Samuel Buchanan
OCCUPATION Agent for Paranormal Law Enforcement Team
BASE Mobile **HEIGHT** Unrevealed **WEIGHT** Unrevealed
EYES Brown **HAIR** Brown
SPECIAL POWERS/ABILITIES Highly trained marksman and expert hand-to-hand combatant.

A special agent for Interpol, Sam Buchanan was a level-headed, no-nonsense sort of chap who didn't believe in magic. Following the release of LILITH, the demon-queen, from imprisonment, there was a steady increase in demonic activity and Sam was assigned to protect human-demon hybrid Victoria MONTESI. For a long time, while continuing to protect Victoria, he insisted that the mystical events that he witnessed had a rational explanation; eventually he was persuaded to believe what he was seeing. When this assignment finally ended, Sam Buchanan joined the Paranormal Law Enforcement Team, where it is thought he still works. **AD**

Bushmaster

FIRST APPEARANCE Captain America #310 (October 1985)
REAL NAME Quincy McIver
OCCUPATION Professional criminal **BASE** Mobile
HEIGHT 18 ft 6 in from head to tail **WEIGHT** Unknown
EYES Brown **HAIR** Black (Shaved bold)
SPECIAL POWERS/ABILITIES Tail enables him to travel and attack at speeds of up to 40 mph. His tail is a crushing weapon; backs of hands have retractable poison fangs.

Bushmaster's serpentine tail both supports his body and is a formidable weapon, being strong enough to crush a 6-inch-thick steel pipe.

Quincy McIver's limbs were amputated by a ship's propeller and he was rebuilt as a cyborg with a snakelike tail by the Brand Corporation. Shortly after this transformation, Bushmaster accepted Sidewinder's invitation to join the SERPENT SOCIETY. While battling MODOK, Bushmaster's mechanical arms were severed, but they were later reattached. As well as his powerful tail, Bushmaster has six-inch fangs on the back of his hands that deliver a fast-acting poison created from snake venom. **MT**

BULLSEYE, *see page 64*

BULLSEYE

Mysterious mercenary

BULLSEYE

FACTFILE

REAL NAME
Lester (last name unrevealed)

OCCUPATION
Assassin

BASE
New York City

HEIGHT 6 ft
WEIGHT 200 lbs
EYES Blue
HAIR Blond

FIRST APPEARANCE
Daredevil #131 (March 1976)

POWERS
Can use almost any object as a weapon and throw it with deadly aim; spine and other bones are reinforced with Adamantium, making them unbreakable; highly formidable hand-to-hand combatant.

Bullseye's origins remain mysterious. A notorious assassin trained by the NSA, he went freelance after clashing with the PUNISHER in Nicaragua. He first battled his archenemy, DAREDEVIL, while trying to extort money from the rich in New York City. New York crimelord the KINGPIN then hired him to be his chief assassin and sent him after crusading attorney Matt Murdock, Daredevil's secret identity, but Daredevil stopped him.

WAR WITH DAREDEVIL

When Bullseye was imprisoned, the Kingpin replaced him with ELEKTRA, Daredevil's former lover. To reclaim his position, Bullseye killed Elektra. Daredevil came after him, and in the ensuing battle, Bullseye fell from a great height, broke his back, and was paralyzed. Japanese scientist Lord Dark Wind healed Bullseye by repairing his bones with Adamantium, and he resumed his criminal career and war with Daredevil. During a period when Daredevil had amnesia, Bullseye impersonated him in order to discredit him; however he began to believe *himself* to truly be the hero. Daredevil donned Bullseye's costume to defeat him. Working later with MYSTERIO, Bullseye murdered Karen PAGE, whom Daredevil had loved for many years.

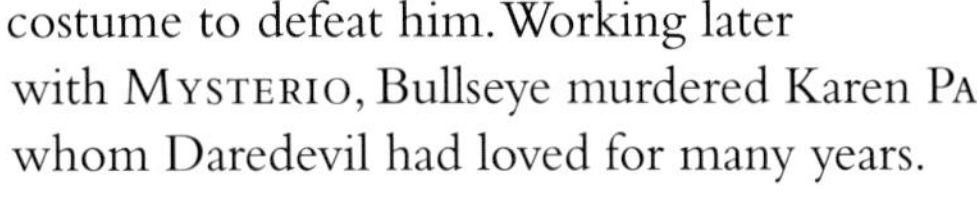

THUNDERBOLTS

Bullseye joined the THUNDERBOLTS during the CIVIL WAR and fought alongside them against the SKRULLS during the SECRET INVASION. Afterward, Norman Osborn (*see* GREEN GOBLIN) made him the new HAWKEYE in his version of the AVENGERS. Under Osborn's orders, he killed the SENTRY's wife, later claiming she committed suicide.

After the DARK REIGN, Bullseye was sent to the Raft super-prison but escaped and hunted down Daredevil once more. A possessed Daredevil took him down and stabbed him through the heart with a sai knife, the same way Bullseye had killed Elektra years before. Bullseye was resurrected by Lady Bullseye, an assassin inspired by his example. Despite being paralyzed, deaf, and living in an iron lung, Bullseye managed to orchestrate a number of other villains to bedevil Daredevil once more.

During a battle in which he sent Ikari and Lady Bullseye against Daredevil in his stead, Bullseye lost his last remaining sense: his sight. **PS, MF**

Lady Bullseye is a master of martial arts and is faster than Bullseye and the Kingpin. She is a lawyer in her civilian guise.

Bullseye was stuck in a portable iron lung, deprived of all his senses but his sight.

CABAL, THE

FACTFILE

MEMBERS
DOCTOR DOOM
EMMA FROST
GREEN GOBLIN
THE HOOD
LOKI
NAMOR
TASKMASTER

BASE
Avengers Tower

FIRST APPEARANCE:
Secret Invasion #8 (January 2009)

Cabal, The

When Norman Osborn (*see* Green Goblin) took over security for the United States during the Dark Reign, he formed a coalition of the most powerful villains in the world to oppose the heroes' Illuminati. The original group consisted of himself as Iron Patriot, Doctor Doom, Emma Frost, the Hood, Loki, and Namor. The members soon began to form alliances within the group and to work against each other.

Norman Osborn, in his Iron Patriot armor, introduces Taskmaster into the Cabal.

As a member of the Illuminati, Namor consulted with both organizations, always keeping the welfare of the Atlanteans uppermost in his mind. He invited the Black Panther to join the Cabal, but T'Challa refused. Based upon their past relationship and shared nature as mutants, Frost and Namor formed an alliance against Osborn from the start. Loki and Doom partnered to make a play for power with Asgard, and Namor and Doom worked together as well.

When Frost and Namor revealed that they'd been working against the Cabal from the inside, Osborn replaced them with the Taskmaster. The revamped group fell apart when Osborn's forces were defeated during the siege of Asgard at the end of the Dark Reign. **MF**

THE ORIGINAL CABAL
1 Loki
2 The Hood
3 Emma Frost
4 Norman Osborn
5 Namor
6 Doctor Doom

Cabe, Bethany

FIRST APPEARANCE Iron Man #117 (December 1978)
REAL NAME Bethany Cabe
OCCUPATION Bodyguard **BASE** Seattle
HEIGHT 5 ft 7 in **WEIGHT** 125 lbs **EYES** Green **HAIR** Red
SPECIAL POWERS/ABILITIES Bethany Cabe is a skilled investigator, an expert markswoman, and extensively trained in self-defense techniques.

After the apparent death of her ex-husband, Bethany Cabe trained to become a bodyguard. In the course of her work, she met and became involved with Tony Stark (*see* Iron Man). When Stark's alcoholism threatened to destroy him, Bethany convinced him to get help. Their romance ended when Cabe's ex-husband turned out to be still alive but in a coma, and she returned to him. Years later, Obadiah Stane swapped Madame Masque's mind into Cabe's body and set her against Stark, but Cabe foiled the plot. Currently, Cabe is in charge of security at Resilient. **TB, MF**

CABLE

A living link between present and future

CABLE

FACTFILE
REAL NAME
Nathan Christopher Summers
OCCUPATION
Adventurer; former freedom fighter and US government agent
BASE
Mobile

HEIGHT 6 ft 8 in
WEIGHT 350 lbs
EYES Blue
HAIR White

FIRST APPEARANCE
Uncanny X-Men #201 (January 1986)

POWERS
Mutant with telepathic and telekinetic abilities. Possesses superhuman strength.

Cable has spent his life as a warrior, but longs for peace. He once established the airborne city of Providence as a futuristic utopia.

Hailing from the future of Earth-2107, Nathan Dayspring Askani'son, alias Cable, was actually born in modern times as Nathan Christopher Summers. He is the son of Scott Summers, CYCLOPS of the X-MEN, and his first wife Madelyne PRYOR, a clone of Jean GREY, alias Phoenix.

In the "House of M" storyline, Cable devolved into an infant. Deadpool rescued the baby from Mister Sinister, and Cable soon returned to his true age.

LIFE-SAVER

APOCALYPSE infected Nathan with a deadly techno-organic virus. He was brought to the 40th century of Earth-4935, where Mother Askani, a version of Rachel SUMMERS, halted the virus' spread and had Nathan cloned. Apocalypse, who ruled this era, abducted and raised the clone, who became STRYFE. Mother Askani transported the souls of Scott Summers and Jean Grey into the future to raise young Nathan. After he destroyed Apocalypse, they returned to their own time.

Nathan became Clan Askani's foremost freedom fighter against Stryfe's New Canaanites. He married a fellow warrior, Aliya, and they had a son, Tyler. Stryfe murdered Aliya, and when he traveled back to the 20th century, Cable pursued him. There, Cable founded the mercenary team SIX PACK and later reorganized the NEW MUTANTS into X-FORCE.

Next to Apocalypse, Cable's greatest enemy is literally himself: the terrorist Stryfe is Cable's clone. Stryfe framed Cable for an assassination attempt on Charles Xavier. Stryfe's mind once even took possession of Cable's body.

Cable saved the first post-M-Day mutant baby from Bishop and escaped into the future with her, naming her Hope Summers. He brought her back to the present when she was in her teens, and she saved his life by burning a fatal techno-organic virus out of him, removing his cybernetics as well. Later, Forge made an enhanced exoskeleton weapon for Cable's atrophied arm, and the two formed a new X-Force along with Colossus, Doctor Nemesis, Domino, Boom Boom (Meltdown), and sometimes Hope. With them, he tried to save the world from threats he perceived in visions of the future. **PS, MF**

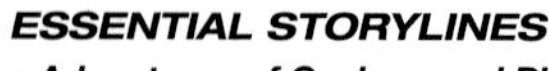

ESSENTIAL STORYLINES
- ***Adventures of Cyclops and Phoenix #1–4***
Scott Summers and Jean Grey raise young Nathan Summers in a distant future.
- ***The New Mutants #86–100***
Cable remolds the New Mutants into X-Force.
- ***Uncanny X-Men #294–296***
"The X-Cutioner's Song" storyline, featuring Cable's showdown with his nemesis Stryfe, which also crossed over into other Marvel titles.

Cage, Luke

Hero for Hire

As a young man, Carl Lucas was in a street gang with his pal Willis Stryker. Lucas went straight while Stryker rose through the ranks. After the MAGGIA nearly killed Stryker, his girlfriend Riva Conners ended their relationship and sought solace with Lucas. Believing his friend had betrayed him, Stryker framed Lucas for possession of heroin. Sent to prison, Lucas volunteered to be a test subject for a Super-Soldier experiment in order to obtain an early parole. An angry guard tried to murder him by altering the experiment. Instead of killing him, the process reacted with his unique body chemistry and gave him superpowers. He escaped prison, faked his death, and adopted the name Luke Cage.

As a young gang member, Carl Lucas was sent to jail for a crime he did not commit.

FACTFILE

REAL NAME
Carl Lucas

OCCUPATION
Bodyguard; investigator

BASE
New York City

HEIGHT 6 ft 6 in
WEIGHT 425 lbs
EYES Brown
HAIR Formerly black, now bald

FIRST APPEARANCE
Hero For Hire #1 (July 1972)

POWERS

Cage possesses superhuman strength, very dense muscle and bone tissue, and steel-hard skin. He recovers three times faster from injury than a normal person and is an experienced and skilled street fighter.

POWER MAN

Needing money, Luke decided to become a hero for hire, sometimes using the name Power Man. He started out fighting normal crooks like his old friend Stryker—now calling himself DIAMONDBACK—but graduated to battling Super Villains and working with other Super Heroes. Cage joined the DEFENDERS and substituted for the THING in the FANTASTIC FOUR for a short time.

Blackmailed by BUSHMASTER into kidnapping Misty KNIGHT, Luke met and teamed up with her and her boyfriend, Danny Rand (IRON FIST). Together, they worked to clear his name and later worked for Misty's Nightwing Restorations detective agency. Luke and Danny began their own agency, Heroes for Hire, but when Danny was seemingly killed, Luke was blamed for the crime and went into hiding until Danny returned.

Luke moved in with Jessica Jones when she revealed she was pregnant. He proposed after their daughter Danielle was born.

NEW AVENGER

A brief affair with Jessica JONES (aka the hero Jewel) grew into something more as the two worked as bodyguards for Matt Murdock (DAREDEVIL). The couple had a daughter (named Danielle after her godfather, Danny Rand) and married. Around this time, Luke joined the New AVENGERS. He sided with CAPTAIN AMERICA during the CIVIL WAR and stayed with the underground Avengers after Cap was killed. He fought the SKRULLS during the SECRET INVASION and was horrified when a Skrull, posing as Edwin JARVIS, kidnapped Danielle. Desperate, he made a deal with Norman Osborn (GREEN GOBLIN) for help to find his daughter, but he went back on it once his little girl was safe. After the DARK REIGN, Tony Stark (IRON MAN) sold the original Avengers Mansion to Luke so that Luke could lead his own team of Avengers. He also took charge of the THUNDERBOLTS at the request of Captain America. He briefly retired to help raise his daughter, but returned to active service in the Mighty Avengers. **TD, MF**

ESSENTIAL STORYLINES

- ***Hero for Hire, #1–#2*** Carl Lucas gets his powers, breaks out of prison, and becomes Luke Cage.
- ***Power Man #48–#49*** Luke meets the man destined to become his best friend, Iron Fist.
- ***The Pulse #11–14*** Luke and Jessica Jones's daughter is born.

Caiera

FIRST APPEARANCE Incredible Hulk #92 (April 2006)
REAL NAME Caiera **OCCUPATION** Gladiator, queen
BASE Sakaar **HEIGHT** 7 ft **WEIGHT** 270 lbs
EYES Green **HAIR** Black
SPECIAL POWERS/ABILITIES Superhuman strength and near invulnerability.

One of the Shadow People of the planet Sakaar, Caiera was enslaved by Prince Angmo II at age 13. She later became his trusted lieutenant and was named his Warbound Shadow when he ascended to the throne of the Red King. When the Hulk came to Sakaar, she fought him for the Red King but later joined his rebellion. After the Hulk became king, Caiera joined him as his queen and became pregnant with Skaar and Hiro-Kala. She died when the starship that brought Hulk to Sakaar exploded, but her sons survived in cocoons. They sometimes speak with visions of her. **MF**

Callisto

FIRST APPEARANCE Uncanny X-Men #169 (May 1983)
REAL NAME Unrevealed **OCCUPATION** Former leader of the Morlocks, former model, former bodyguard **BASE** Formerly the Alley (tunnel beneath Manhattan); Mobile
HEIGHT 5 ft 9 in **WEIGHT** 130 lbs **EYES** Blue **HAIR** Black
SPECIAL POWERS/ABILITIES Superhumanly keen senses, including night vision.

Callisto was the leader of the Morlocks, mutant outcasts who lived beneath Manhattan, but she survived the Marauders' massacre. She joined Mikhail Rasputin, who brought the other surviving Morlocks to a pocket dimension called the Hill and organized them into the terrorist group Gene Nation. The Morlock Masque transformed Callisto's arms into tentacles and made her fight in the Arena. Callisto lost her powers on M-Day, becoming a normal human with regular arms. She later joined X-Cell, a group of depowered mutants who blame the US government for their troubles. **PS, MF**

Calypso

FIRST APPEARANCE New Mutants #16 (June 1984)
STATUS Villain (deceased) **REAL NAME** Calypso Ezili
OCCUPATION Witch; troublemaker **BASE** New York City
HEIGHT 5 ft 8 in **WEIGHT** 120 lbs **EYES** Brown **HAIR** Black
SPECIAL POWERS/ABILITIES Skilled in Voodoo magic; combines potions and spells to confuse enemies; controls enemies with Yorumba spirit drum; can revive the dead and resurrect herself.

Born and raised in Haiti, Calypso was initiated into the arts of Voodoo. Meeting Kraven the Hunter shortly after his first defeat by Spider-Man, Calypso formed a love-hate attachment to him. After Kraven's death, Calypso became unhinged, killing her sister to obtain her supernatural powers. Although killed by the Lizard, Calypso resurrected herself and clashed with Daredevil before dying once more at the hands of Alyosha Kravinoff the second Kraven. Her spirit then infused an amulet through which she could possess anyone who wore it. **AD, MF**

Caledonia

FIRST APPEARANCE Fantastic Four #9 (September 1998)
REAL NAME Alysande Stuart **OCCUPATION** Champion
BASE New York City **HEIGHT** 5 ft 6 in **WEIGHT** 130 lbs
EYES Blue **HAIR** Blonde
SPECIAL POWERS/ABILITIES Wore a warrior's armor and a long red cloak; wielded an enormous sword with the skill and courage of a great warrior of old; accomplished athlete.

In another world, Alysande Stuart was descended from a long line of ancient Scottish warrior champions. Her warrior name was Caledonia, and she also served as Captain Britain. Freed from captivity in her world, Caledonia arrived in New York City. She worked as a nanny to Franklin Richards, son of Reed Richards and Sue Storm (Mr Fantastic and Invisible Woman), and thus came under the protection of the Fantastic Four.

Caledonia was eventually killed by the insane, murderous Jamie Braddock. **MT**

Cannonball

Sam Guthrie's mutant abilities first triggered while he was trapped in a Kentucky coalmine, and he used them to save a co-worker and himself. Later, renegade Hellfire Club member Donald Pierce recruited Guthrie to battle the New Mutants. Professor X defeated Pierce and invited Sam to join them, and Sam became best friends with Sunspot. He matured into a team leader and later a member of X-Force and the X-Men. Cable believed Sam to be an External, an immortal mutant, but the sorceress Selene dismissed this theory. He is the eldest of several siblings, four of whom are mutants: Paige (Husk), Melody (Aero), Jay (Icarus), and Jeb. He has dated rock star Lila Cheney and fellow New Mutant Meltdown but never married. He kept his powers after M-Day and is currently a member of the Avengers. **MF**

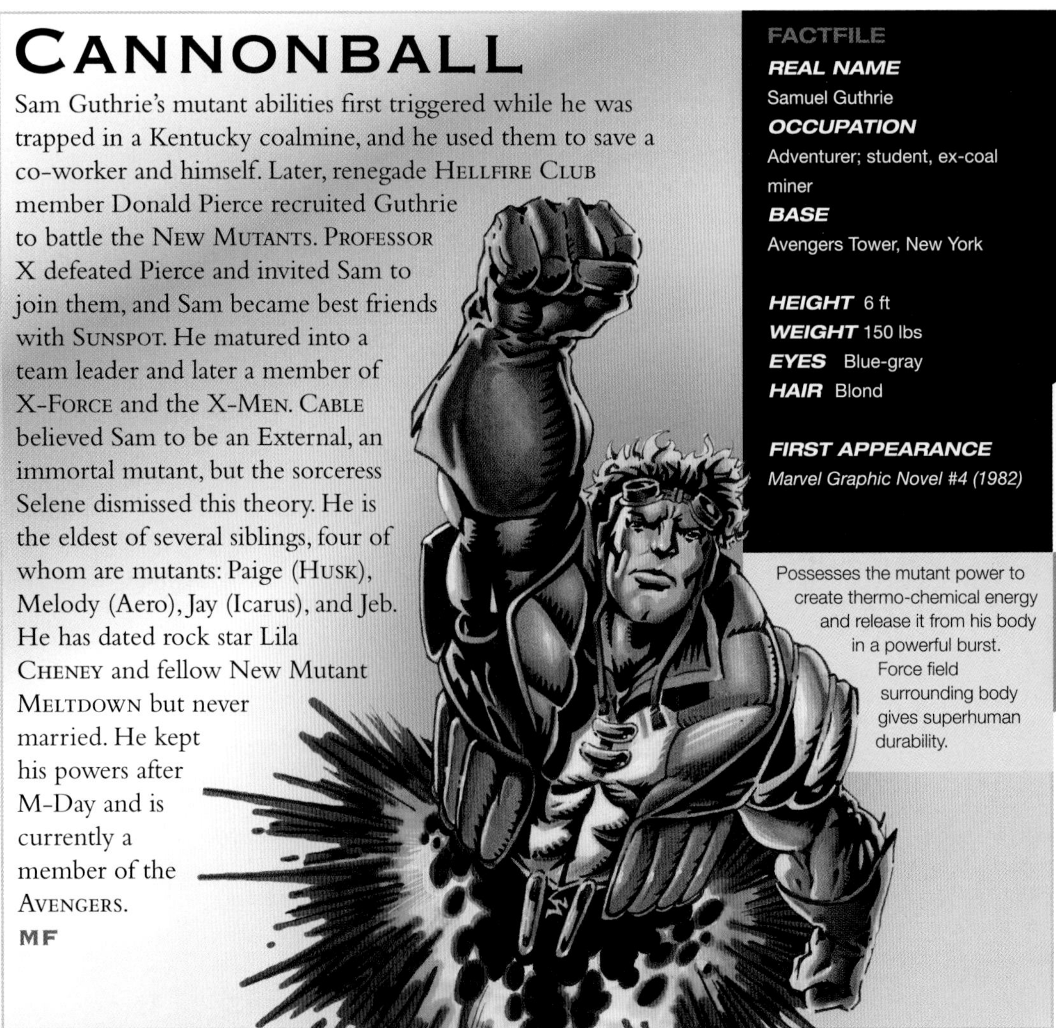

FACTFILE
REAL NAME
Samuel Guthrie
OCCUPATION
Adventurer; student, ex-coal miner
BASE
Avengers Tower, New York

HEIGHT 6 ft
WEIGHT 150 lbs
EYES Blue-gray
HAIR Blond

FIRST APPEARANCE
Marvel Graphic Novel #4 (1982)

CANNONBALL

POWERS
Possesses the mutant power to create thermo-chemical energy and release it from his body in a powerful burst. Force field surrounding body gives superhuman durability.

Captain Britain

Chosen as the champion of Great Britain by Merlyn and his daughter Roma, Brian Braddock became Captain Britain. Both alone and as a member of Excalibur, he strove to be worthy of his new role. Eventually he discovered he was one of an almost infinite number of Captains created to safeguard the multiverse. He later succeeded Roma as ruler of the Otherworld and commander of the Captain Britain Corps. He married the mutant Meggan, who sacrificed herself to save the world near M-Day. They have since reunited. Brian worked with Britain's MI-13 to repel the Skrulls' attempt to invade the magical realm of Avalon during the Secret Invasion. He joined the Secret Avengers for a short while and now heads up the Braddock Academy, training new heroes in the UK. **TB, MF**

Captain Britain marries Meggan, a fellow member of the team Excalibur

CAPTAIN BRITAIN

FACTFILE

REAL NAME
Brian Braddock

OCCUPATION
Ruler of Otherworld

BASE
England; Otherworld

HEIGHT 5 ft 11 in ***WEIGHT*** 180 lbs ***EYES*** Blue ***HAIR*** Blond

FIRST APPEARANCE
Captain Britain Weekly #1 (December 1976)

POWERS

Captain Britain's uniform gave him superhuman strength and durability, enabled flight, and provided a protective force field. His powers have now been internalized, and the level of his powers is based on his level of confidence instead.

CAPTAIN BRITAIN!
GET AWAY FROM HER, YOU DEPRAVED MANIACS.
BUT WE HAVE NOT DONE ANY CRIMES.

Captain Britain saves Alice from the Crazy Gang, dressed as characters from the pages of Lewis Carroll's *Alice in Wonderland*.

CAPTAIN BRITAIN CORPS

FACTFILE

MEMBERS
Assorted interdimensional incarnations of **CAPTAIN BRITAIN,** including **CAPTAIN UK, CAPTAIN ANGLETERRE, CAPTAIN COMMONWEALTH, CAPTAIN EMPIRE, CAPTAIN ENGLAND, CAPTAIN MARSHALL, KAPTAIN BRITON, HAUPTMANN ENGLANDE, BROTHER BRIT-MAN** and others.

BASE
Otherworld; various Earths across the multiverse.

FIRST APPEARANCE
Mighty World of Marvel #13 (1984)

Captain Britain Corps

The Captain Britain Corps is an alliance of interdimensional champions based out of the nexus realm known as Otherworld and charged with protecting their home realities from dimensional incursions. Each is a version of Captain Britain and is empowered by Merlyn and his daughter Roma. The Captain Britain of Earth-616 led the Corps for a while, but after its decimation at the hands of the mutant villain Mad Jim Jaspers and the death of Roma, the champion called Albion (the version of Captain Britain from Earth-70518) was charged with rebuilding it, along with Captain England, Captain UK, Justicer Bull, and Saturnyne. **TB, MF**

The Captain Britain Corps interceded when it was feared that the mutant powers once possessed by Franklin Richards, son of the Fantastic Four's Mr. Fantastic and the Invisible Woman, might destroy the multiverse.

Captain Gate

FIRST APPEARANCE Man-Thing #13 (January 1975)
REAL NAME Captain Jebediah Fate **OCCUPATION** Pirate
BASE The ship *Serpent's Crown* in the Bermuda Triangle, Atlantic Ocean **HEIGHT** 6 ft 3 in **WEIGHT** Unknown
EYES Gray **HAIR** Gray
SPECIAL POWERS/ABILITIES No longer ages, and is invulnerable to certain forms of injury.

In 1795, Jebediah Fate was first mate to pirate queen Maura Hawke when they met the satyr Khordes, who desired a mate. The traitorous Fate and his men turned Hawke over to Khordes, and Hawke cursed them to sail the seas for eternity. Centuries later, Fate again met Khordes and Hawke (reincarnated as oceanographer Maura Spinner), as well as Man-Thing. When Fate was killed by gunfire, the demon Thog resurrected him. Fate's soul became part of the Magus Sword, which possessed Sheriff John Daltry, transforming him into Fate, who worked with Dracula until the Black Knight separated them. **PS, MF**

Captain America

Living Legend of World War II

CAPTAIN AMERICA

FACTFILE

REAL NAME
Steve Rogers

OCCUPATION
Adventurer

BASE
Brooklyn, New York; Stark Tower ("Avengers Tower"), Manhattan, New York

HEIGHT 6 ft 2 in
WEIGHT 240 lbs
EYES Blue
HAIR Blond

FIRST APPEARANCE
Captain America Comics #1 (March 1941)

POWERS

The Super-Soldier Serum brought Rogers to the peak of physical perfection; able to lift twice his own body weight; expert military strategist; Olympic-level martial artist and gymnast; resistant to disease and fatigue.

ALLIES/FOES

ALLIES Bucky Barnes, Nick Fury, Sharon Carter, Rick Jones, The Falcon, Nomad (Jack Monroe), The Avengers.

FOES The Red Skull, Baron Zemo, MODOK, the terrorist organizations AIM and Hydra, Crossbones.

ISSUE #1

Captain America burst into action battling Hitler in his first issue. Cap's shield changed shape to circular in forthcoming issues because of objections from the creators of another hero called the Shield.

In the late 1930s, with the threat of world war looming in Europe, the American high command embarked upon a program to create the perfect soldier. Project: Rebirth, spearheaded by Dr. Abraham Erskine, was intended to create a battalion of supreme fighting men, stronger and more resilient than normal soldiers, expertly trained and equipped—a bulwark against Nazi aggression. The first test subject for Erskine's revolutionary Super-Soldier Serum was a young, would-be artist name Steve Rogers, who had attempted to enlist, but had been turned away, classified 4-F, because of his physical frailty.

Abraham Erskine, operating under the code-name Professor Reinstein, created the Super-Soldier Serum. It turned frail Steve Rogers into a perfect specimen of humanity.

THE SUPER SOLDIER

Subjected to Erskine's process, Rogers' body virtually doubled in size, as millions of healthy cells were created almost instantaneously. His physique was accelerated to the pinnacle of human perfection, all weakness and deficiency drained out of it.

However the secret test area had been infiltrated by Nazi sympathizers, who slew Dr. Erskine, the only person who knew how the process worked. Although Rogers quickly captured the saboteurs, it was clear that there would be no battalion of super-soldiers now—Steve Rogers would be the only one.

Captain America arrives in the nick of time to prevent Sharon Carter being blasted into the blue courtesy of Nazi menace Red Skull.

The result of a metallurgical accident, Captain America's shield is the most durable object known to man.

Equipped with a virtually unbreakable red, white and blue shield, the product of a metallurgical accident, and trained in combat, tactics, espionage, and the fighting arts, Rogers was rechristened Captain America. Clad in a striking star-spangled uniform, he became a symbol for the US fighting forces and a dread nemesis of the Axis powers.

In his many battles against Nazi aggression, Captain America was joined by a sidekick, the worldly James "Bucky" Barnes, who had discovered the secret of Rogers' true identity.

Among the foes combated by Cap in the present day is MODOK, the Mental Organism Designed Only for Killing. MODOK was the result of an experiment by the sinister think-tank known as Advanced Idea Mechanics, or AIM.

BUCKY'S DEATH

Toward the end of World War II, Cap and Bucky Barnes set out to foil Baron Zemo's scheme to steal a drone plane laden with a bomb. As the plane took off, Bucky and Cap leaped aboard. Cap fell into the sea, but Bucky clung on trying to defuse the bomb. The bomb exploded, Bucky was killed, and Cap has been haunted by the memory ever since.

Reformed criminal Sam Wilson, alias Harlem's guardian the Falcon, has been one of Captain America's closest friends and most frequent crime-fighting partners.

Together, Cap and Bucky tore a swath through the ranks of the enemy forces, vanquishing such Nazi menaces as the Red Skull, Agent Axis, and the Iron Cross. The duo were often joined by their allies in the Invaders team, including the original Human Torch and Namor, the Sub-Mariner.

In 1945, Cap and Bucky were on a mission to apprehend the German scientist Baron Zemo, who planned to steal an experimental long-range Drone Plane developed by the British. As the plane took off, Cap and Bucky made a desperate leap to catch it. Cap couldn't maintain his hold, and plummeted earthward... seconds later the plane self-destructed, ending the life of Bucky Barnes. Cap's body plunged into the icy waters below, where he was frozen into a state of suspended animation, a condition he would remain in for decades to come.

To safeguard morale, the Allied high command kept the deaths of Cap and Bucky secret and recruited other heroes to play the role of Captain America. Meanwhile, the true Captain America slumbered within the ice.

The Return

Eventually, while searching for their foe Namor (the same person who had fought alongside Steve Rogers in the Invaders), the Avengers came across Captain America's body floating in the icy waters, and revived him. Now Captain America was a man out of time, a soldier whose war was long over. Attempting to find a place for himself in this strange new society, Cap accepted an offer of Avengers membership, and swiftly became the binding glue that held the team together.

THE AVENGERS
1 Hawkeye ***2*** The Wasp ***3*** Falcon ***4*** Captain America, team leader ***5*** Iron Man ***6*** Vision ***7*** Scarlet Witch

Cap also offered his services to his old war buddy Nick Fury, now head of SHIELD. It was while operating as a SHIELD agent that Cap first encountered Sharon Carter, SHIELD's Agent 13, who would become his paramour.

Hailed as the most trusted costumed champion of them all, Captain America fought on, struggling to uphold freedom and democracy, both alone and with the Avengers—right up until the moment of his death. **TB, MF**

ESSENTIAL STORYLINES

- ***Captain America & The Falcon #153-156:*** Cap and his partner the Falcon must combat the replacement Captain America and Bucky of the 1950s, who have been driven mad by the flawed serum that gave them their abilities
- ***Captain America #1-6:*** Captain America reveals his true identity as Steve Rogers to the world after he is forced to take the life of a terrorist leader
- ***Captain America #1-14:*** Cap is on the trail of the Winter Soldier, a legendary assassin from the pages of history who may actually be his former sidekick Bucky Barnes!

Over the years, Cap has contested with numerous opponents intent on taking up his mantle. One of his challengers was the "Anti-Cap", a modern day counterpart created by Naval Intelligence as an extreme anti-terrorist operative. Eventually facing defeat by Captain America for a second time, the Anti-Cap chose death rather than capture.

CAPTAIN AMERICA *continued*

Wolverine sneaks onto the SHIELD Helicarrier to inspect Steve Rogers's body.

After the announcement of the Superhuman Registration Act, Captain America (Steve Rogers) could not stomach enforcing what he considered to be an unjust law. He broke with his old friend Tony Stark (Iron Man) and formed a resistance movement to help unwilling heroes to defy the law. This split fractured the Super Hero community and set the heroes against each other in what would become known as the Civil War. At the end of the war, Iron Man defeated and captured Rogers, who was soon after assassinated as he was brought into a federal courthouse in New York City.

In Death's Shadow

Without Rogers to lead it, the organized resistance against the Superhuman Registration Act fell apart. Many of the heroes who had held out stepped forward to register. The Falcon, for instance, signed up solely so he could appear at Rogers' funeral.

Having seen many people supposedly die in the past, including Rogers himself, some heroes refused at first to believe that he was dead. It was only after Iron Man and Wolverine—each representing a different side in the Civil War—were able to corroborate Rogers' death that the reality began to sink in.

The Hunt for a New Captain

Although Stark had gone on record stating that no one would replace Captain America, it wasn't long before he went looking for a replacement. With Captain America's costume and indestructible shield in SHIELD custody, he could give the assignment to whoever he liked. When Stark discovered that Clint Barton (Hawkeye) had somehow survived the Scarlet Witch's disassembling of the Avengers, he brought Barton aboard the SHIELD Helicarrier to show him the original shield, revealing that he'd had two imperfect copies made. The first sat on display at the Smithsonian, while the second was to be buried with Rogers. The real one was up for grabs.

Barton tried out the shield, becoming the first person to wield it properly after 77 other people had failed. Stark gave Barton the shield and the costume to try out as he went to arrest Patriot and the new Hawkeye for failure to comply with the Superhuman Registration Act. At the moment of truth, Barton—dressed in Rogers' uniform and holding his shield—let the two heroes go rather than arrest them. He then gave the shield back to Stark.

Bucky Claims the Shield

Unwilling to let Rogers' shield languish in the custody of SHIELD—which he blamed in part for Rogers's death—Bucky Barnes stole it. Back from his own purported death, after which he had become the Winter Soldier, he used the shield in a few missions of his own. While taking the shield, he ran into Natasha Alianovna (Black Widow), with whom he'd had a relationship when they'd both been in the employ of the Soviet Union.

After SHIELD finally captured Barnes, Stark surprised him by offering him the identity of Captain America to go along with the shield. Barnes accepted on two conditions. First, any secret mental conditioning from his days as the Winter Soldier had to be telepathically removed. Second, he would answer only to himself. Knowing that this would be exactly what Rogers would have wanted, Stark accepted the deal.

Feeling unfit to wear Rogers's own costume, Barnes had a new one designed for himself. Unlike Rogers, Barnes was happy to use weaponry of all sorts in his battles, not just the shield. He carried a pistol and a combat knife on his belt, which featured a number of pouches, and he brought in other ordnance as necessary.

Iron Man finds Clint Barton (Hawkeye), who is supposed to be dead.

Iron Man presents Captain America's original shield to Clint Barton.

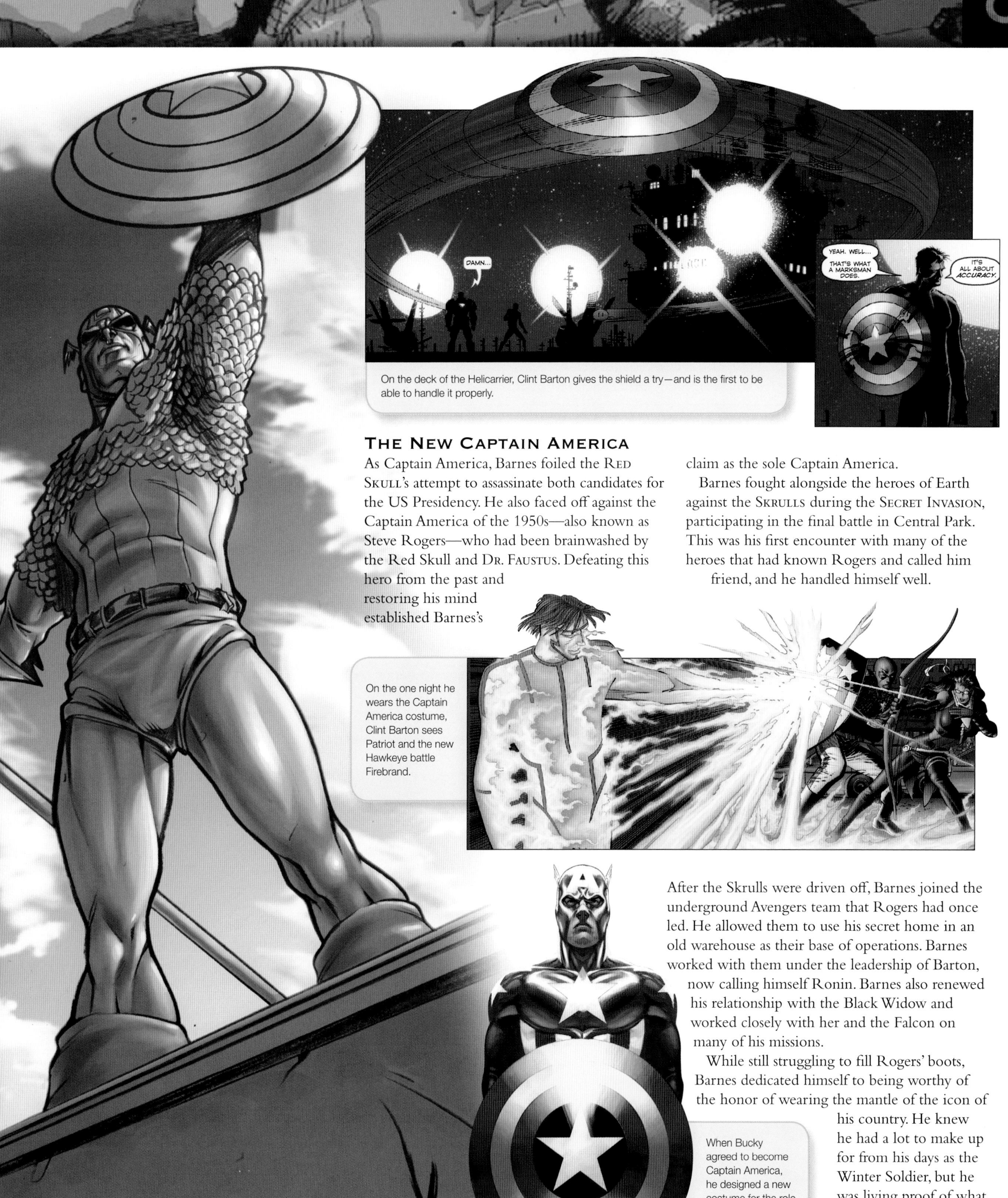

On the deck of the Helicarrier, Clint Barton gives the shield a try—and is the first to be able to handle it properly.

The New Captain America

As Captain America, Barnes foiled the Red Skull's attempt to assassinate both candidates for the US Presidency. He also faced off against the Captain America of the 1950s—also known as Steve Rogers—who had been brainwashed by the Red Skull and Dr. Faustus. Defeating this hero from the past and restoring his mind established Barnes's claim as the sole Captain America.

Barnes fought alongside the heroes of Earth against the Skrulls during the Secret Invasion, participating in the final battle in Central Park. This was his first encounter with many of the heroes that had known Rogers and called him friend, and he handled himself well.

On the one night he wears the Captain America costume, Clint Barton sees Patriot and the new Hawkeye battle Firebrand.

After the Skrulls were driven off, Barnes joined the underground Avengers team that Rogers had once led. He allowed them to use his secret home in an old warehouse as their base of operations. Barnes worked with them under the leadership of Barton, now calling himself Ronin. Barnes also renewed his relationship with the Black Widow and worked closely with her and the Falcon on many of his missions.

While still struggling to fill Rogers' boots, Barnes dedicated himself to being worthy of the honor of wearing the mantle of the icon of his country. He knew he had a lot to make up for from his days as the Winter Soldier, but he was living proof of what people could do with second chances.

When Bucky agreed to become Captain America, he designed a new costume for the role.

CAPTAIN AMERICA *continued*

For a while, there were two Captain Americas, but only one shield.

BACK TO LIFE

When Steve Rogers was gunned down on the steps of the federal courthouse, most witnesses saw only one person shoot him; however, two people were involved. The first was the RED SKULL's agent CROSSBONES, who sniped at Rogers from a nearby rooftop. The second was Rogers' girlfriend, Sharon CARTER, who'd been brainwashed by DOCTOR FAUSTUS.

Carter herself did not realize her part in the crime until later, and the revelation crushed her. Carter eventually learned that the gun she'd used to shoot Rogers hadn't been a regular pistol but a device designed by DOCTOR DOOM. It didn't kill Rogers but froze him at that moment in time. The Red Skull captured Carter and planned to use sympathetic particles in her blood to retrieve Rogers. She escaped and damaged the machinery involved in the Red Skull's scheme. This unstuck Rogers in time, sending him back in time to relive various events in his past. He had to watch them play out again, unable to alter their outcomes.

Eventually, the Red Skull managed to bring Rogers back and transferred his own mind from a robot body into Rogers' form. When the Red Skull tried to kill the new Captain America—Bucky BARNES—Rogers broke his control.

While Barnes carried the shield, Rogers served the USA in a new costume of his own.

TWO CAPTAINS

After Rogers returned, he saw that Bucky had done an excellent job as Captain America, and he encouraged Bucky to continue. Both men wore the costume through the Siege of Asgard at the end of the DARK REIGN. Afterward, Rogers let Bucky have the mantle to himself. The President pardoned Captain America for his actions during the CIVIL WAR and repealed the Superhuman Registration Act, which had sparked the conflict.

At the President's request, Rogers took over from Norman Osborn (*see* GREEN GOBLIN) as the head of national security, putting him in charge of rebuilding both SHIELD and the AVENGERS. Rogers served in that capacity until BARON ZEMO revealed Barnes' identity not only as Captain America but also as the WINTER SOLDIER. Barnes was found innocent in court, but his reputation was ruined, and the President asked Rogers to return to being Captain America.

For a while, Rogers believed that Barnes had died trying to fill his boots.

Rogers resisted for a while, but after it seemed that Skadi (a transformed SIN) had killed Bucky during FEAR ITSELF, Rogers assumed the role again. In a subsequent battle, the Asgardian God of Fear Serpent attacked Rogers and shattered his shield, but Rogers rallied. He later used THOR's hammer Mjolnir to bring Skadi down. Odin had the shield reforged for Rogers.

During the Spider-Island event (*see* SPIDER-MAN), the Spider-Queen and the JACKAL transformed Rogers into the Spider-King, a creature capable of spreading spider-powers as a virus across New York City. By means of an antidote made with ANTI-VENOM's blood, Rogers was cured, after which he helped Spider-Man win the day.

After leading the Avengers in a huge conflict with the X-MEN over the use of the Phoenix Force, Rogers reformed the Avengers once again.

A Hard Act to Follow

Over the years, several other people have served in the role of Captain America. The earliest recorded version was Steven Rogers, an ancestor of Steve Rogers, who fought in the American Revolutionary War. Since he served in this role before the US was officially a country, he technically wasn't the original Captain America. That honor still belongs to Steve Rogers, the Captain America the US Army created as its Super-Soldier in World War II.

After the success of the creation of Steve Rogers, the US Army wanted to put more Super-Soldiers onto the battlefield. They experimented with dangerous drugs on three hundred African-American volunteers. Only five survived, and of those only Isaiah Bradley made it through the war. He stole a Captain America costume and wore it on a mission to destroy a German concentration camp where Nazi scientists were conducting their own super-soldier experiments. He was court-martialed for this, but pardoned by the President. During his time in prison, however, the treatments that gave him his powers reduced him to a childlike state.

Isaiah was the grandfather of Elijah Bradley, the Young Avenger known as Patriot. When Patriot was shot trying to protect Cap, his grandfather gave him a lifesaving blood transfusion. Thus Patriot acquired the powers associated with the Super-Soldier serum.

Isaiah Bradley served his country well; however his country did not return the favor.

Would-Be Captains

When the original Captain America and Bucky disappeared toward the end of World War II, the US needed someone to replace them. To that end, they recruited William Naslund (the Spirit of '76) to wear Rogers' costume, while Fred Davis took over for Barnes. Naslund was killed trying to save John F. Kennedy.

After Naslund's death, the US government turned to Jeffery Mace (the original Patriot) to pick up Cap's shield. Fred Davis served as his Bucky for a while, but when Davis was wounded in action, Mace turned to Betsy—former girlfriend of Steve Rogers and now a hero called Golden Girl—and trained her to be his new partner. The two retired from their roles in 1949 and married in 1953.

As a boy, William Burnside idolized Captain America, writing a dissertation for his PhD about his hero. During his research, he discovered Captain America's secret identity as well as the formula for the Super-Soldier serum. He changed his name to Steve Rogers and persuaded the US government to surgically transform him into Steve Rogers' twin and then make him into the next Captain America and his student Jack Monroe into the new Bucky of the 1950s.

Unfortunately, the serum slowly drove them insane, making them both paranoid and violent. They were forcibly retired and placed in suspended animation for decades. The pair were awakened at one point after Steve Rogers returned, and sent to kill him. Defeated, they were put back into storage and then turned over to Dr. Faustus, who brainwashed Burnside into become the Grand Director, the leader of a Neo-Nazi group.

Rogers defeated Burnside, and Faustus returned Burnside to suspended animation. After Rogers' supposed death after the Civil War, Faustus brought Burnside back to battle the new Captain America, the revived Bucky Barnes. At one point, Burnside captured Barnes and forced him to wear his old Bucky costume and serve as Burnside's sidekick in a terrorist group.

Defeated once more, Burnside reappeared as a vigilante after Rogers returned from the dead. Burnside was hit by a truck while Rogers was trying to stop him. While he was healing in the hospital, Rogers arranged for Burnside's false death, giving the man a new life and promising him treatment for his mental illness. **MF**

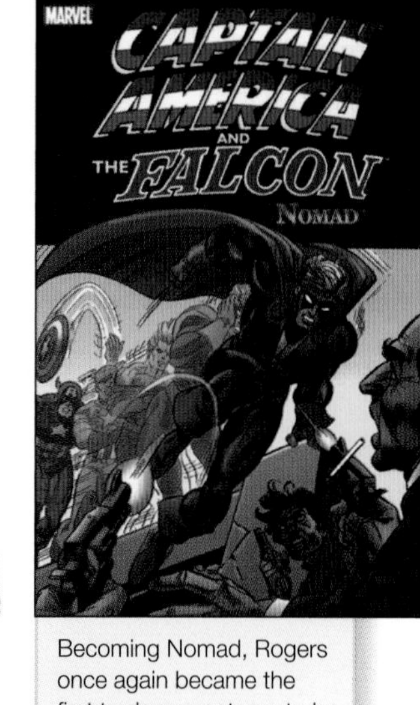

Becoming Nomad, Rogers once again became the first to don a costume to be worn by many others.

William Burnside's obsession with Cap transformed him into his hero's insane twin.

Nomadic Cap

For a while, Rogers became disillusioned with the US government and gave up being Captain America, taking on the identity of Nomad. Three men carried Captain America's shield during this period: Bob Russo, "Scar" Turpin, and Roscoe Simons. The first two washed out quickly when they realized how dangerous the job was. The Red Skull killed the third as a message to Rogers, who returned to being Captain America to battle the Skull.

Years later, Cap gave up his shield rather than follow orders he couldn't support. He took to wearing a black costume and calling himself simply the Captain. The government tapped John Walker—a hero known as the Super-Patriot—to replace him, and recruited Lemar Hoskins to become his Bucky. When Rogers returned, Walker became the USAgent, and Hoskins became Battlestar.

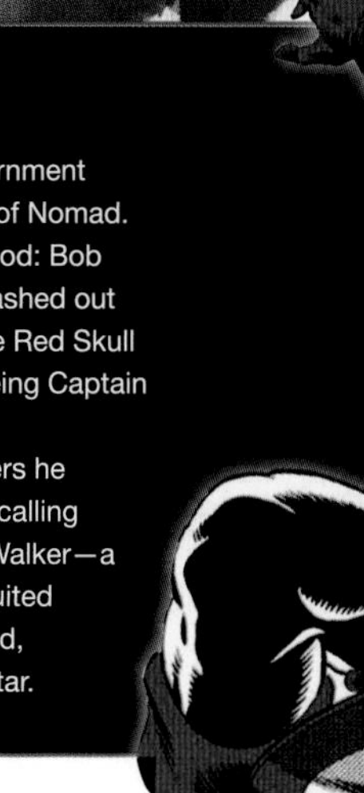

CAPTAIN MAR-VELL

Protector of the Universe

CAPTAIN MAR-VELL

FACTFILE

REAL NAME
Mar-Vell

OCCUPATION
Captain in Kree space fleet

BASE
Mobile

HEIGHT 6 ft 2 in
WEIGHT 240 lbs
EYES Blue
HAIR White; transformed to blond by Eon, a cosmic caretaker

FIRST APPEARANCE
Marvel Super Heroes #18 (January 1968)

POWERS

Thanks to his Kree Nega-Bands, Mar-vell possessed great strength (he could lift 10 tons), a high degree of imperviousness to harm, and the ability to fly. He could also exist in outer space without having to breathe.

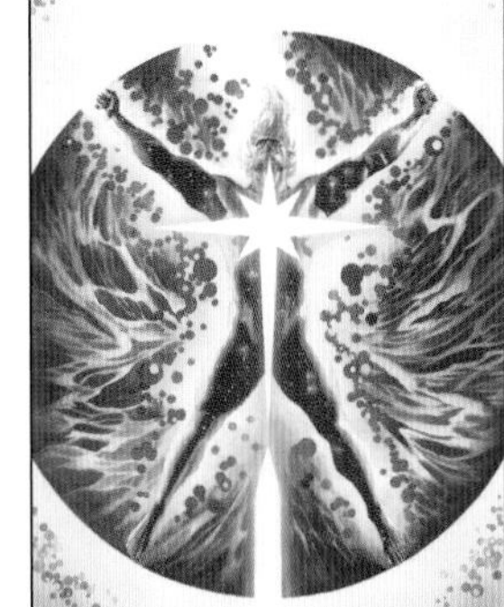

Kree Nega-Bands convert Captain Mar-vell's psionic energy into incredible power.

Captain Mar-Vell was a member of the KREE, an alien humanoid race who built an empire known as the Greater Magellanic Cloud. Captain Mar-Vell was a "White Kree," who have the same skin color as Caucasian Earth humans and similar physiology. (Most members of the Kree race have blue skin.) As captain of a Kree space fleet, Mar-Vell distinguished himself in battles against the shape-changing SKRULLS, the Kree's age-old foes.

ESSENTIAL STORYLINES

- ***The Life of Captain Mar-Vell 1991 (tpb)*** Mar-Vell battles Thanos and performs other feats of cosmic heroism.
- ***Avengers #89–#97*** The Avengers aid Mar-Vell during the epic Kree-Skrull War.
- ***Captain Marvel: The Death of Captain Marvel*** Captain Mar-Vell succumbs to cancer, but achieves a hero's death.

Mar-Vell gained the ability to fire bolts of solar energy after his ailing psionic partner Rick Jones was treated with life-saving electromagnetic radiation by Professor Benjamin Savannah.

Mar-Vell impersonated a dead scientist named Dr. Walter Lawson when he first came to Earth.

OLD FOES OF MINE WHO HAVE DIED...
...RETURNING FROM THE GRAVE!

In delirium while dying from cancer, Captain Mar-Vell is haunted by terrifying phantoms of the enemies he fought and defeated during his career as a Super Hero.

PROTECTOR

Wary of humanity's progress, the SUPREME INTELLIGENCE sent Mar-Vell to sabotage Earth's space programs. However Mar-Vell grew to respect the people of Earth and helped them, earning the name Captain Marvel. The Intelligence believed humans possessed vast psionic potential, which it longed to possess so it could destroy humanity. To this end, the Intelligence forged a psionic link between Mar-Vell and Rick JONES by means of a pair of Kree Nega-Bands. The Intelligence used this link to nullify the Skrull space fleet, nearly killing Jones, but Mar-Vell used his own life force to revive Jones.

Mar-Vell then defeated THANOS, who wished to destroy all life in the universe. Mar-Vell also met with the alien being Eon, who gave him cosmic awareness, persuaded him to renounce the Kree's warmongering ways, and designated him Protector of the Universe.

During a battle with NITRO of the Lunatic Legion, an alien criminal organization formed by a band of renegade Kree scientists, Mar-Vell was exposed to a carcinogenic gas. He developed cancer and died on Saturn's moon, Titan, surrounded by his lover, Elysius, Rick Jones, the AVENGERS, and many other friends. His son Genis-Vell eventually took over his mantle, as did his daughter Phyla-Vell. He also had a son he never knew with Anelle, the daughter of the Skrull Emperor. The boy became HULKLING.

Mar-Vell returned for the SECRET INVASION, but he was revealed to be a Skrull. In the end, he sided with Earth but was killed in the war. The real Mar-Vell returned during the CHAOS WAR, but he died saving SWORDSMAN and YELLOWJACKET. The Kree recently brought Mar-Vell back once more, hoping to gain the power of the Phoenix Force through him. He sacrificed himself to protect the Kree from that same power. **MT, MF**

Captain Marvel

Formally Ms. Marvel of the Avengers

The first Captain Marvel was the Kree warrior Captain Mar-Vell. Several others followed in his wake, including Monica Rambeau (also known as Pulsar, Photon, and Spectrum).

FACTFILE

REAL NAME
Carol Danvers

OCCUPATION
Adventurer

BASE
New York City

HEIGHT 5 ft 11 in
WEIGHT 124 lbs
EYES Blue
HAIR Blond

FIRST APPEARANCE
Marvel Super-Heroes #13 (March 1968)

CAPTAIN MARVEL

POWERS

Possesses the ability to fly, enhanced strength, damage resistance, and the ability to absorb and rechannel energy.

MANY MARVELS
1 Captain Marvel's original costume
2 Ms. Marvel's later costume
3 Ms. Marvel's original costume
4 Captain Marvel's later costume

THE FRIEND

US Air Force and NASA officer Carol Danvers was assigned to investigate Mar-Vell and became involved with him. When her DNA was melded with his during an explosion, giving her powers like his, she adopted the codename Ms. Marvel. After she joined the Avengers, the villainous Marcus (son of Immortus) brainwashed her into joining him in Limbo. After his death, she escaped to Earth, but soon after lost her powers and memories to the mutant Rogue. While working with the X-Men, she unlocked cosmic powers and became known as Binary.

When the X-Men took in Rogue, Carol could not stomach being on the same team with her and left to join the Starjammers. After helping save the Sun, her original powers returned, and she rejoined the Avengers as Warbird. After M-Day, she reclaimed the codename Ms. Marvel. During the Civil War, she served with the official Avengers under Iron Man. During the Dark Reign, Moonstone replaced Carol as Ms. Marvel. Carol later claimed the name Captain Marvel to honor her friend Mar-Vell.

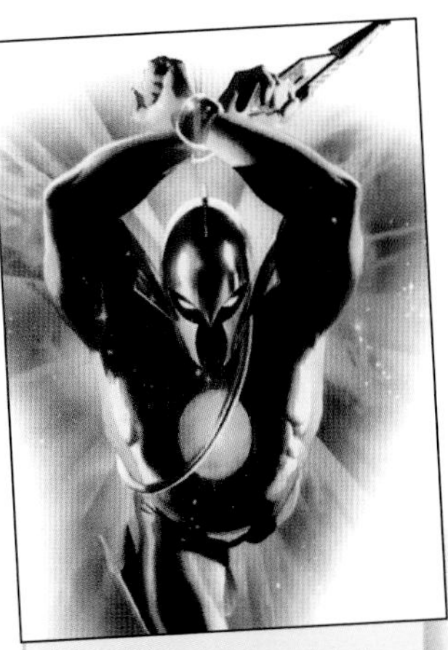
Genis-Vell wore many variations on his father's costumes.

THE SON

Following Mar-Vell's death, his lover Elysius, an Eternal of Titan, used cell samples taken from his body to conceive a son named Genis-Vell. When he discovered his heroic lineage, Genis donned his father's Nega-Bands and called himself Legacy. He later adopted the name Captain Marvel.

To save his father's friend Rick Jones, Genis's atomic structure was bonded to Jones's. Genis subsequently went insane and helped the conceptual beings Entropy and Epiphany destroy the universe. He then triggered a new Big Bang, recreating the cosmos. He was later returned to sanity, and the bonding with Jones was undone.

Genis took the name Photon and joined the Thunderbolts. After Zemo learned that Genis would destroy the universe, he killed Genis and scattered his body in the Darkforce Dimension.

THE DAUGHTER

When Genis recreated the universe, he added a new element: a sister named Phyla-Vell. She helped restore Genis's sanity but he refused to let her keep the name Captain Marvel. She later became the new Quasar after inheriting the Quantum Bands from the original. After losing the bands, she made a deal to become Martyr, an avatar of Oblivion. As Martyr, Phyla joined the Guardians of the Galaxy. She later fought against the Magus, who tricked her into releasing Thanos, who then killed her. **PS, DW, MF**

Phyla-Vell as Martyr.

Captain Ultra

FIRST APPEARANCE Fantastic Four #177 (December 1976)
REAL NAME Griffin Gogol
OCCUPATION Stand-up comedian, former plumber
BASE Chicago, Illinois **HEIGHT** 5 ft 11 in **WEIGHT** 175 lbs
EYES Unknown **HAIR** Unknown
SPECIAL POWERS/ABILITIES Captain Ultra is superhumanly strong and durable, and can fly; also has a great sense of humor.

Captain Ultra began his career hoping to join the FRIGHTFUL FOUR. They were impressed by his strength, but not by his phobia of fire. Therapy with DOC SAMSON cured his phobia and gave him the confidence to become a stand-up comedian. Gogol later led Nebraska's team for the FIFTY-STATE INITIATIVE. After that, he joined WONDER MAN's team of REVENGERS. After their defeat, he was imprisoned in the super-prison known as the Raft. **TB, MF**

Captain Universe

FIRST APPEARANCE Micronauts #8 (August 1979)
REAL NAME Various, including Ray and Steve Coffin, Monty Walsh
OCCUPATION Not applicable **BASE** Mobile
HEIGHT Various **WEIGHT** Various **EYES** Various **HAIR** Various
SPECIAL POWERS/ABILITIES Captain Universe is any person endowed with the Uni-Power; abilities include superstrength, flight, and ability to alter an object's molecular structure.

The Uni-Power is an energy that emanates from the Microverse and bestows upon an individual the powers, knowledge, and costume of Captain Universe for a short period before moving on. The transfer is almost instantaneous, ensuring the cosmos is never without a Captain Universe. The might of the Uni-Power has been borne by ex-astronauts, cat burglars, and even the HULK, DAREDEVIL, X-23, SILVER SURFER, and DOCTOR STRANGE. The current holder is Tamara Devoux, who works with the AVENGERS. EX NIHILO and ABYSS recognized her as a god and refused to fight her. **AD, MF**

Cardiac

FIRST APPEARANCE (Dr. Wirtham) The Amazing Spider-Man #342 (December 1990), (Cardiac) The Amazing Spider-Man #343 (January 1991)
REAL NAME Dr. Elias "Eli" Wirtham
OCCUPATION Surgeon, researcher, vigilante
BASE New York City **HEIGHT** 6 ft 5 in **WEIGHT** 300 lbs
EYES Brown **HAIR** Black
SPECIAL POWERS/ABILITIES Superhuman strength, speed and stamina, bulletproof skin, can project beta particle-force blasts.

Elias Wirtham's brother Joshua died of a rare disease after insurance companies refused to pay for unproven cures. Dr. Wirtham devoted his life to medical research, secretly battling those who profit from suffering. He had his heart replaced with a beta particle reactor, and his skin with vibranium mesh that transmits the particles to his muscles, giving him amazing strength. As Cardiac, he has clashed with SPIDER-MAN. **PS**

FACTFILE
REAL NAME
Cletus Kasady
OCCUPATION
Spreader of Chaos
BASE
New York City

HEIGHT 6 ft 1 in
WEIGHT 190 lbs
EYES Green
HAIR Red

FIRST APPEARANCE
The Amazing Spider-Man #244 (February 1991)

POWERS
Superhuman strength; can generate swing lines and bladed weapons; able to neutralize Spider-Man's spider-sense.

Carnage

Murderer Cletus Kasady shared a cell with Eddie Brock, VENOM's original host, when the Venom symbiote arrived to attempt a jailbreak. It left behind its spawn, which bonded with Kasady, creating a new symbiote known as Carnage. The bond between Carnage and Kasady was more profound than that between Brock and Venom, and Carnage is also far more powerful, violent, and deadly than its parent. SPIDER-MAN enlisted the HUMAN TORCH and even Venom to defeat it. Besides Cassidy, the symbiote has bonded with Ben Reilly (*see* SCARLET SPIDER), the SILVER SURFER, and John JAMESON. It even spawned its own offspring, which bonded with police officer Patrick Mulligan to become Toxin. The SENTRY ripped the Carnage symbiote apart, but after it and Kasady reunited, it spawned its own offspring, which became a hero called SCORN. Later, the second Scarlet Spider lobotomized Kasady. The WIZARD removed the symbiote from Kasady to use it for his own ends, but was defeated by Spider-Man. **AD, MF**

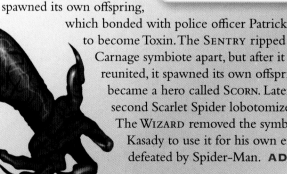

Like its parent, Venom, Carnage quickly came to regard Spider-Man as its arch nemesis.

CARRION

FACTFILE
REAL NAME
"Miles Warren" (actually a clone of the original Miles Warren)
OCCUPATION
None
BASE
New York City

HEIGHT 5 ft 11 in
WEIGHT 175 lbs
EYES Yellow
HAIR None

FIRST APPEARANCE *The Spectacular Spider-Man #25 (December 1978)*

POWERS
Carrion could repel living matter, levitate, destroy living matter with his touch, reduce the density of his body to become almost intangible, and teleport.

The first Carrion was a clone of Miles Warren who was SPIDER-MAN's enemy, the JACKAL. Before his death, Warren left a clone of himself in a capsule, but something went wrong and the creature that emerged was like a living corpse. Carrion died in a fire following a battle with Spider-Man. Many years later, a fellow research student of Peter Parker's named Malcolm McBride discovered a test tube containing a genetic creation of Warren's, the "Carrion virus." The virus consumed McBride and turned him into a second incarnation of Carrion. When Miles Warren's body was examined by Dr. William Allen, he was infected by the virus, and became the third and most powerful incarnation of Carrion. **MT**

CAT & MOUSE

FIRST APPEARANCE Marvel Preview #21 (May 1980)
REAL NAMES (Cat) Mark Grant, (Mouse) Stephanie Wald
OCCUPATION (Cat) Musician, Shroud operative; (Mouse) Shroud operative **BASE** New York City **HEIGHT** (Cat) 6ft 1in, (Mouse) 5 ft 10 in **WEIGHT** (Cat) 195 lbs; (Mouse) 135 lbs **EYES** (Cat) Brown; (Mouse) Blue **HAIR** (Cat) Black; (Mouse) Blonde
SPECIAL POWERS/ABILITIES Cat is a cat burglar and electronics expert. Mouse is a pickpocket and getaway driver.

Daring cat burglar Cat was recruited into a gang run by a criminal known as the Crooked Man. He met Mouse, a singer and small-time crook. They became close friends and joined the SHROUD to help take down their former employer. Deciding to join the Shroud's crusade to destroy crime from within, they opened and began performing at the Cat's Jazz Club, which became the Shroud's unofficial base. Before the Club was destroyed, Cat & Mouse played host to such adventurers as SPIDER-MAN, TATTERDEMALION, DANSEN MACABRE and the West Coast AVENGERS. They later aided the SHROUD against the SCORPION and various other crimelords. **TD**

CARTER, SHARON

Sharon Carter grew up inspired by tales of her aunt Peggy Carter's exploits as a member of the French Resistance and CAPTAIN AMERICA's lover during World War II. She sought a career with SHIELD and became their operative Agent 13, during which time she met and fell in love with Captain America too. She infiltrated the National Force, a Neo-Nazi organization run by DOCTOR FAUSTUS and William Burnside, who had served as Captain America in the 1950s before going insane. She faked her death to go deep undercover for SHIELD, but after the mission went bad, even SHIELD presumed her dead.

When she returned, Sharon served as SHIELD's director for a short time. She became Captain America's SHIELD liaison officer again and the romantic tension between the pair blossomed into a renewed relationship. Later, under Faustus' hypnotic control, she helped assassinate Captain America, although it turned out she had only unstuck him from time. After Cap's "death" she discovered she was pregnant with his child, but she lost the baby during a gun fight with SIN. After Cap returned, she asked him to marry her. Before he could give her an answer, she died saving him and rest of the world from Arnim ZOLA. **DW, MF**

FACTFILE
REAL NAME
Sharon Carter
OCCUPATION
SHIELD liaison officer
BASE
Mobile

HEIGHT 5 ft 8 in
WEIGHT 135 lbs
EYES Blue
HAIR Blond

FIRST APPEARANCE
Tales of Suspense #75 (March 1966)

POWERS
Highly trained field agent; martial-arts expert and weapons expert; special talent for disguise, infiltration, and undercover work.

Steve Rogers, the patriotic hero known as Captain America, teamed up with Sharon on missions against AIM, HYDRA, Red Skull, and many others.

Cat People

FIRST APPEARANCE Giant-Size Creatures #1 (May 1974)
BASE The Land Within, an otherdimensional netherworld
SPECIAL POWERS/ABILITIES Mystical abilities; enhanced strength, speed, and agility, similar to those of a human-sized cat.

The Cat People were created when Ebrok, a human sorcerer, enchanted two cats called Flavius and Helene into human form. In time, the numbers of the Cat People grew, to the displeasure of Ebrok's fellows in the Sorcerer's Guild. The Cat People were subsequently exiled to the limbo-like realm they call the Land Within, which caused them and their descendants to become demons. The legendary heroine of the Cat People is known as Tigra, a human woman who was transformed into a catlike warrior. Greer Nelson was similarly been transformed into the heroine Tigra by the Cat People's magic and science. She served as their emissary to the outside world and as a member of the Avengers. **TB**

Celestials

The Celestials are a race of virtually immortal space gods whose conscious minds gestate in the form of living galaxies for more than a million years. Once the Celestial is deemed worthy, this mind is encased by a full suit of virtually indestructible body armor that is "dimensionally transcendental" (far larger on the inside than it appears to be on the outside). Each Celestial appears to have a specific purpose. Barely a dozen and a half are known by their names and function, but many more are believed to exist. For reasons of their own, the Celestials travel throughout the Universe, performing genetic experiments. They then return a million years later to judge the results of their experiments. If the world is judged favorably, it is allowed to continue. If not, it is cleansed of life. **TD**

FACTFILE

KNOWN CELESTIALS
ARISHEM THE JUDGE, JEMIAH THE ANALYZER, TEFRAL THE SURVEYOR, GAMMENON THE GATHERER, NEZARR THE CALCULATOR, ONEG THE PROBER, HARGEN THE MEASURER, ESON THE SEARCHER, ZIRAN THE TESTER, ONE ABOVE ALL, EXITAR THE EXECUTIONER

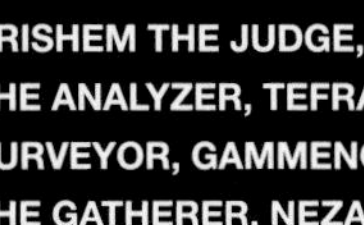

HEIGHT (average)
2,000 ft
WEIGHT (average)
260 tons

FIRST APPEARANCE
Eternals #1 (July 1976)

POWERS
Cosmic power on a scale immeasurable by Earth standards; have visited Earth, but eradicated all evidence and memory of their existence.

Catseye

FIRST APPEARANCE New Mutants #16 (June 1984)
STATUS Villain (deceased) **REAL NAME** Sharon Smith
OCCUPATION ex-Hellion team member
BASE Mobile **HEIGHT** 6 ft **WEIGHT** 140 lbs
EYES Lavender **HAIR** Lavender
SPECIAL POWERS/ABILITIES Transformed into a cat and a human-panther hybrid with increased strength, agility, reflexes, and senses; hybrid also boasted razor-sharp claws and prehensile tail.

Most mutants manifest their powers at puberty, but Sharon Smith first transformed into a cat as an infant. Abandoned by her parents, she was raised feral by a stray cat. As a teenager, she came to the attention of Emma Frost. The highly intelligent Sharon received an accelerated education, and within a year she gained high-school literacy and joined the Hellions. An attack on the Hellfire Club led to her death, but she was later brought back to life by the sorcerer Selene, using the Transmode Virus. **AD, MF**

Centurius

FIRST APPEARANCE Nick Fury, Agent of SHIELD #2 (July 1968) **REAL NAME** Dr. Noah Black
OCCUPATION Geneticist **BASE** Mobile **HEIGHT** 6 ft
WEIGHT 225 lbs **EYES** Brown **HAIR** None
SPECIAL POWERS/ABILITIES Scientific genius specializing in genetics; evolved himself into a perfect human specimen, with attendant strength, agility, and durability; high-tech body armor incorporates an array of weapons; experiments with his Evolutionizer device have increased his lifespan.

The ridicule of the scientific community led scientist Dr. Noah Black to hide on Valhalla Island and experiment on himself with his Evolutionizer. His experiments succeeded in improving him but also increased his mania, and he decided humanity should be wiped out and started afresh. Calling himself Centurius, he intended to gather up superior specimens of life, shepherd them to an ark, then destroy human civilization from space. A century later he and his crew would land and reclaim the world. His initial plot was thwarted by Nick Fury and SHIELD, but Centurius continued to threaten world security. He worked for the Hood's crime syndicate and helped repel the Skrulls during the Secret Invasion. He later joined Luke Cage's Thunderbolts. **TB, MF**

Century

FIRST APPEARANCE Force Works #1 (July 1994)
REAL NAME Century **OCCUPATION** Adventurer
BASE/HEIGHT/WEIGHT/EYES Unknown **HAIR** White
SPECIAL POWERS/ABILITIES Combines memories, skills, and abilities of one hundred Hodomur; projects energy from hands; wields the Parallax, a bladed weapon that binds his multiple personalities together and enables interdimensional travel.

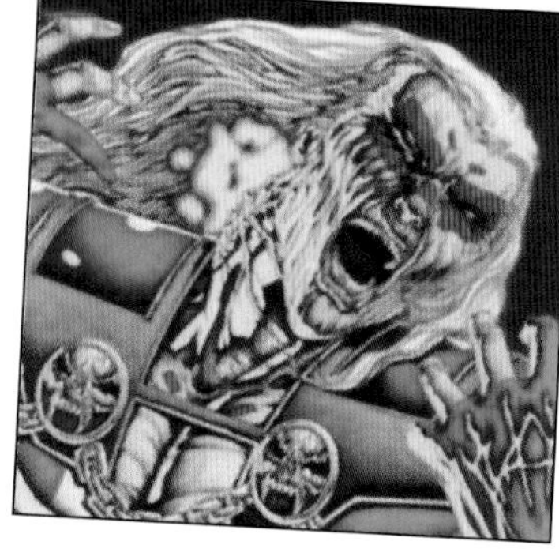

Following the destruction of their world Hodomur by the extradimensional entity Lore, the survivors created a new being from one hundred of their number. Named Century, this creature was compelled to track down and destroy Lore and given a lifespan of a hundred years to attain this goal. During this quest, the pirate Broker enslaved Century and wiped his mind, leaving only the desire to find Lore. This led him to Earth where he served with Force Works until it disbanded. Lore was destroyed by the Scarlet Witch and Century was last seen with the Revengers. **AD, MF**

Cerise

FIRST APPEARANCE Excalibur #47 (March 1992)
REAL NAME Cerise
OCCUPATION Soldier **BASE** Shi'ar Empire
HEIGHT 5 ft 10 in **WEIGHT** 130 lbs **EYES** Brown **HAIR** Black
SPECIAL POWERS/ABILITIES Uses the energy of the red light spectrum to create weapons, force fields, vortexes, and shields. She can fly, direct energy blasts, and hold her breath for 7 minutes.

Cerise is an alien of the SHI'AR race, which absorbs other cultures into its vast interplanetary empire through violent conquest. Disillusioned with the brutal tactics of the Shi'ar war machine, Cerise deserted from its army and fled to Earth. There, she became a member of EXCALIBUR and fell in love with teammate NIGHTCRAWLER. The STARJAMMERS brought her back to stand trial for her crimes. In time, the Shi'ar empress Lilandra pardoned her act of desertion and made her an operative to investigate reports of Shi'ar brutality. During ANNIHILATION, she joined GAMORA's team of warriors, known as the Graces. **MT, MF**

Chameleon

Dmitri Smerdyakov grew up in Russia as the half-brother and servant of Sergei Kravinoff, who later became known as the original KRAVEN the Hunter. Smerdyakov eventually became the mercenary spy known as the Chameleon, who was renowned as a master of disguise. Originally Chameleon relied on makeup, costumes, and his acting skill; he now uses a special serum and clothing to impersonate others.

The Chameleon first clashed with his nemesis, SPIDER-MAN, when he attempted to frame the crimefighter for the theft of classified plans for a missile defense system. However, Spider-Man captured the Chameleon and exposed him as the real thief. The Chameleon has also contended against other Super Heroes, including the HULK and DAREDEVIL.

After the original Kraven committed suicide, the Chameleon lost his sanity, and jumped from a bridge. However, he turned up alive in an insane asylum, and resumed his criminal career. **PS**

FACTFILE
REAL NAME
Dmitri Smerdyakov
OCCUPATION
Professional spy and criminal
BASE Mobile

HEIGHT Unrevealed
WEIGHT Unrevealed
EYES Unrevealed
HAIR Unrevealed

FIRST APPEARANCE
Amazing Spider-Man #1 (March 1963)

POWERS
Experimental serum renders his flesh malleable, so that he can alter his appearance without makeup or prosthetics. Clothing contains "memory material" that responds to his nerve impulses and changes appearance at will.

Chamber

FIRST APPEARANCE Generation X #1 (November 1994)
REAL NAME Jonothon Starsmore **OCCUPATION** Weapon X field agent **BASE** Mobile **HEIGHT** 5 ft 9 in
WEIGHT 140 lbs **EYES** Brown **HAIR** Auburn
SPECIAL POWERS/ABILITIES (As Chamber) Can psionically fire blasts or cause objects to explode. Communicates telepathically. As Decibel, wears a high-tech suit that grants him a sonic scream and allows him to create things from solid sound.

Jonothon "Jono" Starsmore's mutant power manifested with an explosion of psionic energy that destroyed his mouth and chest, leaving him only able to talk telepathically. He helped found GENERATION X as Chamber and later joined the X-MEN. The WEAPON X program made him a field agent and restored his face, but he lost his powers and face on M-Day. Healed, he looked like a young APOCALYPSE, one of his ancestors. He joined the NEW WARRIORS as Decibel, wearing a suit that gave him powers. He has since regained his original powers and lost his face again. **DW, MF**

Champion of the Universe

Like many of the ELDERS OF THE UNIVERSE, the Champion's origin has been lost in antiquity. A true immortal, he devotes himself to physical perfection to avoid boredom. He considers himself the living spirit of competition and travels the universe, challenging the champions of each planet. If he finds them unworthy, he exterminates all life on their planets. He challenged the heroes of Earth to a match and was impressed with the THING's courage. He and other Elders battled the SILVER SURFER and GALACTUS. The Champion's only defeat came at the hands of SHE-HULK, after which he called himself the Fallen One. **TD, MF**

FACTFILE
REAL NAME
Tryco Slatterus
OCCUPATION
Competitor
BASE
Mobile

HEIGHT 9 ft 2 in
WEIGHT 5,050 lbs
EYES Silver
HAIR Red

FIRST APPEARANCE
Marvel Two-In-One Annual #7 (1982)

POWERS
Has channeled the power primordial, the energy derived from the Big Bang, into his physical form, making his body a perfect fighting machine. Has also mastered thousands of different martial arts from across the universe.

Champions of Xandar

FIRST APPEARANCE Fantastic Four #208 (July 1979)
BASE The planet Xandar; Nova-Prime starship
KEY MEMBERS AND POWERS
Nova-Prime Flight; superhuman strength, invulnerability.
Protector Psionic ability.
Powerhouse Siphons energy from any power source, including living beings.
Comet Flight; can project electrical energy.
Crimebuster No superhuman powers.

The Champions of Xandar was a team of superhumanoid beings who formed to protect the planet Xandar. Xandar suffered three huge alien invasions. In the first, the Luphoms shattered Xandar into pieces. Survivors on the four largest fragments connected the four planetoids with huge bridges and rebuilt their civilization. The second invasion was by the shape-shifting SKRULLS, who hoped to bring Xandar into their empire. Having kept an active militia, Nova Corps, since the first invasion, the Xandarians resisted. They were aided by the FANTASTIC FOUR, and then by a group of Xandarians and Earth heroes, who banded together as the Champions of Xandar. Together, Nova Corps and the Champions repelled the Skrull invasion, though Crimebuster was killed. The third invasion, by NEBULA, wiped out the entire population, including the remaining Champions. **MT**

THE CHAMPIONS OF XANDAR
1 Comet ***2*** Nova-Prime ***3*** Powerhouse
4 Protector ***5*** Crimebuster

Chance

FIRST APPEARANCE Web of Spider-Man #15 (June 1986)
REAL NAME Nicholas Powell
OCCUPATION Mercenary; gambler **BASE** New York City
HEIGHT 6 ft **WEIGHT** 185 lbs **EYES** Blue **HAIR** Brown
SPECIAL POWERS/ABILITIES Chance's armored costume contains wrist-blasters, boot-jets for flight, and assorted other weapons and paraphernalia.

A chronic gambler and inveterate risk-taker, Nicholas Powell took the name Chance and sought work as a mercenary to satisfy his craving for thrills. Chance's standard modus operandi is to wager his fee at double-or-nothing odds against his success—if he fails, he receives nothing. Chance's assignments have brought him into conflict with numerous Super Heroes, including SPIDER-MAN and DAREDEVIL. Chance is thoroughly immoral—but he prides himself on his ability to beat the odds. **TB**

Changeling

A one-time member of the terrorist organization Factor Three, the Changeling switched sides when he learned that its leader, the alien Mutant Master, was seeking to eradicate humanity. When the Changeling discovered that he had contracted a terminal illness, he decided to make amends for his past misdeeds. He approached PROFESSOR X and volunteered to support the X-MEN. The timing was fortuitous: the Professor needed to withdraw from active duty to fend off an impending alien invasion. The Changeling agreed to impersonate Professor X during his absence. However, his leadership of the X-Men was cut short when he was killed during a skirmish with the insane Prince Gor-Tok. **AD**

FACTFILE
REAL NAME
Unknown
OCCUPATION
Reformed criminal; one-time leader of the X-Men
BASE
Mobile

HEIGHT 5 ft 11 in
WEIGHT 180 lbs
EYES Brown
HAIR Black

FIRST APPEARANCE
X-Men #35
(August 1967)

POWERS
A metamorph, the Changeling was able to adopt the appearance and voice of other humanoids; limited telekinetic ability.

XAVIER, I GOT A FAVOR TO ASK! I JUST COME FROM A DOC'S...
I'M A GONER! I GOT MAYBE SIX MONTHS LEFT TO LIVE!
AND I WANNA MAKE 'EM COUNT! I WANNA MAYBE MAKE UP FOR SOME OF THE ROTTEN THINGS I'VE DONE...
I SENSE YOUR SINCERITY -- AND I DO HAVE A TASK FOR YOU, IF YOU'RE WILLING!
I WANT YOU TO... BECOME ME!!
NOTHIN' EASIER... FOR A GUY WITH MY TALENT
NOW I'VE GOT YOUR LOOKS-- BUT NOT YOUR MENTAL POWERS!

Changeling turned over a new leaf by taking Professor X's place, at the latter's request.

CHAOS WAR, *see pages 84-85*

CHANGELING

Charcoal

FIRST APPEARANCE Thunderbolts #19 (October 1998)
REAL NAME Charles Burlingame
OCCUPATION Adventurer; student **BASE** Mt. Charteris
HEIGHT 5 ft 7 in **WEIGHT** 135 lbs **EYES** Brown **HAIR** Black
SPECIAL POWERS/ABILITIES Transforms into a being composed of charcoal; manipulates heat and can reshape himself into any form of carbon, including flaming charcoal or rock-hard diamond.

When Charles Burlingame's father took him to a rally of the Imperial Forces of America, the scientist Arnim Zola discovered the boy's potential for superhuman powers and transformed him into Charcoal, the Burning Man. At first, Charcoal joined a group called the Bruiser Brigade and battled the Thunderbolts. Later, as a member of the Thunderbolts, Charcoal witnessed the death of fellow member Jolt. He left to join the Redeemers, where he battled his father, who was still a member of the Imperial Forces. He later died at the hands of Graviton. **MT, MF**

Chaste, the

FIRST APPEARANCE Daredevil #187 (October, 1982)
MEMBERS AND POWERS
STICK Martial artist, uses bo stick **STONE** Martial artist, can turn body hard as stone **SHAFT** Martial artist with a bow
CLAW Martial artist with artificial claws **STAR** Martial artist, uses shurikens **WING** Martial artist, flies by telekinesis
FLAME Martial artist, pyrokinetic

The Chaste is a martial arts organization based atop a mountain fronted by a sheer cliff called the Wall. Those who wish to train with the Chaste must climb the Wall to enter, as a test. The Chaste was founded by Master Izo—a founding member of the Hand—to stand against the Hand's evil plans, but his students threw him out for carousing. Stick led the Chaste for many years, but after his death and that of the other listed members, Stone took over and helped raise Elektra from the dead. **MF**

Cheney, Lila

FIRST APPEARANCE New Mutants Annual #1 (1984)
REAL NAME Lila Cheney **OCCUPATION** Songstress; thief
BASE A Dyson sphere somewhere in the Milky Way Galaxy
HEIGHT 5 ft 8 in **WEIGHT** 120 lbs **EYES** Blue **HAIR** Black
SPECIAL POWERS/ABILITIES Lila Cheney possesses the mutant ability to teleport people and objects over intergalactic distances.

An acclaimed rock singer on Earth, Lila Cheney simultaneously pursued a very different career among the stars. Employing her mutant gift to teleport herself, Lila gained a reputation as one of the foremost thieves in the universe. She was an ally of the New Mutants, and a romance with Cannonball led her to curtail her criminal activities. Since their breakup, it remains to be seen whether she has abandoned her outlaw life for good. **TB**

Charlie-27

FIRST APPEARANCE Marvel Super Heroes #18 (January 1969)
REAL NAME Charlie-27 **OCCUPATION** Soldier; adventurer
BASE The starship *Icarus* **HEIGHT** 6 ft **WEIGHT** 555 lbs
EYES Blue **HAIR** Red
SPECIAL POWERS/ABILITIES Superhuman strength and endurance; high resistance to injury and disease; withstands the gravity of Jupiter (11 times that of Earth); pilot and master strategist.

In the 31st century of Earth-691, Charlie-27 was a member of a genetically bio-engineered race of humans sent to live on and mine the planet Jupiter. After completing a solo tour of duty as a space militia pilot, Charlie-27 learned that an alien race called the Badoon had overrun the Solar System and slaughtered the inhabitants of Jupiter, Pluto, Mercury, and Earth. Joining with Martinex (Pluto), Nikki (Mercury), Yondu Udonta (Centauri IV), and Vance Astro (Earth) to form the original Guardians of the Galaxy, Charlie-27 helped to expel the Badoon and later safeguarded the entire galaxy. **TD, MF**

Chemistro

Dissatisfied with his research position at Mainstream Motors, Curtis Carr embarked on a personal project: the development of an Alchemy Gun capable of changing one substance into another. When Carr was sacked for refusing to hand the weapon over to his boss, he disguised himself as Chemistro and began a series of revenge attacks against his employer. Carr's spree of destruction ended during a struggle with Luke Cage, when Carr accidentally shot his own foot and turned it to steel. Crippled when his steel foot crumbled into dust, he was thrown into prison where he was forced to give the secrets of the Alchemy Gun to a fellow prisoner, Arch Morton.

Although Morton's version of the gun exploded in his hand, the accident endowed his left hand with similar alchemical powers. On leaving prison, a reformed Carr developed a device called a Nullifier, and Luke Cage used it to disable Morton. The third Chemistro was Carr's brother Calvin, who stole a new version of the Alchemy Gun, but Cage and Iron Fist stopped him. Calvin later worked for the Hood's crime syndicate. The Mandarin and Ezekiel Stane recruited him to join their efforts against Tony Stark (Iron Man). When Calvin tried to kill Stark alongside the villain Mauler, the new Iron Man (Jim Rhodes) killed him instead.
AD, MF

FACTFILE
REAL NAME
Curtis Carr
OCCUPATION
Research scientist and reformed criminal
BASE
New York City

HEIGHT 5 ft 11 in
WEIGHT 185 lbs
EYES Brown
HAIR Black

FIRST APPEARANCE
Hero for Hire #12 (August 1972)

CHEMISTRO

POWERS
No superhuman powers; carried self-designed Alchemy Gun capable of transmuting one substance into another.

Chaos War

God battles god to save the universe!

ISSUE #1 Hercules returns from the dead, but not in time to stop the Chaos King from killing Nightmare.

The Greek demigod Hercules had been presumed dead, but the moment Amadeus Cho brought him back and made him an all-father (the greatest of a pantheon of gods), he knew immediately that Amatsu-Mikaboshi—the Chaos King—was about to launch his attempt to destroy all of creation. Emboldened by the destruction of Asgard at the end of the Dark Reign, the Chaos King hoped to destroy all the gods and then the defenseless multiverse. He started by finding and murdering Nightmare, the Lord of Dreams. This gave him the power to destroy any mortal mind he touched, which he used against the heroes that Hercules assembled to attack him, plunging them into waking comas.

The God Squad (clockwise from top): Galactus, Silver Surfer, Hercules, Venus, Amadeus Cho, Sersi, Thor.

THE END OF ALL

Amatsu-Mikaboshi then attacked the afterlife. To defend himself, Pluto released the dead to fight for him, resurrecting dead gods and heroes, including Ares, Captain Mar-Vell, Deathcry, Doctor Druid, Hera, Zeus (*see* Gods of Olympus), Banshee, Moira McTaggert, Swordsman, Thunderbird (John Proudstar), the Vision, and Yellowjacket. Dr. Brian Banner even came back in a mutated Hulkish form to battle his son, the original Hulk. Despite this, the Chaos King triumphed.

In response, Hercules assembled a new God Squad consisting of Cho, Hellstorm, Galactus, Sersi, Silver Surfer, Thor, Venus, and himself. With the help of the wisdom of the traitorous Athena, the Chaos King outwitted and defeated them all. After conferring with Gaea, Cho realized that there was no way for them to defeat the Chaos King. Desperate, Hercules allowed Pele, the goddess of fire, to turn him to ashes so he could remake himself as a god able to tap into the fullness of his newfound power.

As Hercules went to face off against the Chaos King, Cho convinced Galactus to open a portal to an empty multiverse the goddess Hera had created to replace the real one. The Chaos King was beating Hercules and all of his friends, but Cho couldn't decide who of the millions of people on Earth he should save in the limited time that remained. In a flash of inspiration, he had Hercules knock the Chaos King into the portal instead. This transported Amatsu-Mikaboshi into the empty Continuum, which he immediately destroyed, thinking it to be the real multiverse.

With the Chaos King defeated, Hercules spent every last bit of his all-father powers to restore the multiverse as it had been before the Chaos War had begun. When he was done, several of the dead who'd been released by Pluto remained restored to life, including Swordsman, Yellowjacket, and several members of Alpha Flight. MF

To battle the Chaos King, Hercules gathered the heroes of Earth and granted each of them a fraction of his vast all-father power.

In the final battle, Hercules faced off against the Chaos King in a fight to the finish over the fate of the Earth.

Destruction vs. Life

The Chaos King embodied the universe before anything existed. He is the nothingness from which everything sprang and the state to which it will someday return. While this may be an inevitable cycle, the Chaos King wished to destroy the multiverse before its time—hoping to ensure that it would never be able to recreate itself again. As Amatsu-Mikaboshi, the Chaos King worked with the other gods to be part of Hercules' original God Squad and fight against the gods of the Skrulls.

While it seemed that he had died in that battle during the Secret Invasion, he had in fact posed as one of the Skrull gods instead. Amatsu-Mikaboshi went on to conquer the Skrull pantheon and from there take down one alien set of gods after another, amassing power for his assault on Earth. He was aided by Hercules' sister Athena, goddess of wisdom, who believed that the universe was corrupt and longed for a new Big Bang to remake it. By the time Amatsu-Mikaboshi was ready to strike, there seemed to be no stopping him. The power of all the heroes of Earth amassed against him did little more than to slow him down. Not even the mighty Thor stood a chance.

CHO, AMADEUS

FACTFILE

REAL NAME
Amadeus Cho

OCCUPATION
Adventurer

BASE
Mobile

HEIGHT 5 ft 6 in
WEIGHT 117 lbs
EYES Black
HAIR Black

FIRST APPEARANCE
Amazing Fantasy #15 (January, 2006)

POWERS
Super-intelligence. His suit grants him flight, a force field, and access to a supercomputer called Calvin, which includes a universal translator. He sometimes carries Hercules' mace, which he's enhanced with technology.

While still in high school, Amadeus Cho won a game show tournament that declared him to be the seventh smartest person in the world and gave him a prize of half a million dollars. This brought him to the attention of Pythagoras Dupree, the sixth smartest person in the world—and the man behind the game show, which he'd used to try to find people as super-intelligent as him. Dupree blew up Cho's house, killing the boy's parents and setting him on the run from FBI agents pursuing him, but he escaped with the aid of the HULK.

Cho assembled a team of heroes to try to stop the Hulk during WORLD WAR HULK, but they failed. The team included HERCULES, who became Cho's best friend. Upon Hercules' apparent death, Athena named Cho the leader of the Olympus Group, and Cho set out to find what had happened to his friend. In the course of this, he beat AGAMEMNON to became a god and used his powers to find Hercules, to whom he then granted his new power.

Cho is dating Delphyne Gorgon, queen of the Amazons. He recently created a stylish suit imbued with a supercomputer called Calvin, which gives him certain powers. **MF**

When on the run, Cho rescued a coyote pup, which he raised until it reached adulthood.

CIRCUS OF CRIME

FACTFILE

MEMBERS
RINGMASTER (Maynard Tibolt), **STRONGMAN** (Bruno Olafsen), **CLOWN** (Eliot "Crafty" Franklin), **FIRE-EATER** (Tomas Ramirez), **THE GREAT GAMBONNOS** (Ernesto and Luigi), **HUMAN CANNONBALL** (Jack Pulver), **LIVE WIRE** (Rance Preston), **PRINCESS PYTHON** (Zelda DuBois), **RAJAH** (Kabir Mahadevu), **TEENA THE FAT LADY** (name unrevealed)

FIRST APPEARANCE
Incredible Hulk #3 (September 1962)

POWERS
Most of the members of the Circus of Crime have skills and abilities that fit their job descriptions; these they then adapt for criminal purposes. Princess Python is a snake charmer; Rajah is an elephant trainer; and Live Wire possesses an electrified lariat.

Operating under many different commercial names, the Circus of Crime is constantly traveling around the country. They usually enter a small town and give away a large quantity of free tickets in order to ensure a full house. Once the show has begun, the Ringmaster uses a hypnotic device in his top hat to place the audience in a deep trance. The audience is robbed and sometimes the entire town is looted.

A post-hypnotic suggestion usually prevents the Ringmaster's victims from identifying any members of the Circus or from remembering any details of the crime. They only recall having had a great time at the circus!

The Circus doesn't always get away with its mass robberies. When the Ringmaster tried to turn HULK into a monstrous attraction, he failed badly, and when the circus returned to New York City under the name Cirque du Nuit, two HAWKEYES foiled them. **TB, MF**

Originally from Austria, the Ringmaster moved his circus to America where he believed he could strike it rich. However, he turned to crime when his small band were unable to compete with the larger circus shows.

The Ringmaster's mechanism has enough range to hypnotize a capacity crowd in a sports arena.

CIVIL WAR, *see pages 88-89*

Doctor Strange meets Clea for the first time.

Clea

Until recently the ruler of the Dark Dimension, during her lifetime the Faltinian Princess Clea has experienced numerous trials and tribulations. The daughter of Prince Orini and Umar, influential figures in the Dark Dimension, Clea became involved in much of the political turmoil that afflicted that pocket universe. Doctor Strange first met Clea during one of his first forays to her homeland, and he was to have a significant influence on her life. Together they fought against the demon Dormammu and during these battles they fell in love. Inevitably, these struggles were not without their dangers, and for a time Clea became trapped in a separate pocket universe with Dormammu. After her rescue by Strange, Clea spent several years in New York City, where she became his disciple and also his lover. When she returned to her home, she led a revolution against her mother, who had become ruler. After she took her mother's place, she married Strange, but Dormammu later usurped her throne. She left Earth to lead the resistance against him. She hid in Valhalla for a time and recently returned to Earth with the Fearless Defenders. **AD, MF**

Even a burning head can't help Dormammu defeat Doctor Strange.

FACTFILE

REAL NAME
Clea

OCCUPATION
Former ruler of the Dark Dimension

BASE
The Dark Dimension

HEIGHT 5 ft 8 in
WEIGHT 190 lbs
EYES Blue
HAIR White

FIRST APPEARANCE
Strange Tales #125 (November 1964)

CLEA

POWERS

Formidable manipulator of mystical forces. Alien metabolism gives greater strength and endurance than a human being of similar height and weight.

Cloak and Dagger

Tyrone Johnson was a teenager whose stutter tragically prevented him saving his friend Billy from being mistakenly shot as a thief by a policeman. Tandy Bowen felt neglected and unloved by her wealthy mother. Johnson and Bowen each ran away from home and met each other upon arriving in New York City at the Port Authority Bus Terminal.

They were offered a place to stay by men who worked for Simon Marshall, an unscrupulous chemist who was developing a new, highly addictive drug for the Maggia. Marshall was testing the drug on captured runaways. But whereas the drug killed the other runaways, it activated Johnson and Bowen's latent mutant abilities. Realizing he now resembled a living shadow, Johnson wrapped himself in fabric. He then entrapped some of Marshall's men in the blackness within this "cloak," while Bowen struck others down with "daggers" of "light." Johnson and Bowen decided to use their superhuman powers to save children and teenagers from drug dealers and other criminals and became the vigilante duo called Cloak and Dagger. **PS**

Despite differing backgrounds, runaways Tyrone Johnson and Tandy Bowen became the closest of friends.

FACTFILE

REAL NAMES
Tyrone Johnson, Tandy Bowen

OCCUPATION
Vigilantes

BASE The Holy Ghost Church, New York City

HEIGHT (Cloak) 6 ft (Dagger) 5 ft 5 in
WEIGHT (Cloak) 175 lbs (Dagger) 115 lbs
EYES (Cloak) Brown (Dagger) Blue
HAIR (Cloak) Black (Dagger) Blond

FIRST APPEARANCE
The Spectacular Spider-Man #64 (March 1982)

CLOAK AND DAGGER

POWERS

Cloak can open a portal into the "Darkforce Dimension." Can project foes into this dimension, teleport himself and others. Dagger projects "daggers of light," psionic energy that deprives a victim of some life energy and can also cleanse people of drugs and poisons.

Dagger's "light-knives" are manifestations of the life energy that resides within all living beings. Dagger generates more of this life energy than normal humans do, and uses it to feed Cloak's hunger for such "light."

CIVIL WAR

The Battle Between Heroes

When the New Warriors try to capture Nitro, he explodes, killing several hundred people. The government response splits the remaining Super Heroes into a Civil War.

Having reinvented themselves as the heroes of a reality TV show, the NEW WARRIORS moved in on a house containing four Super Villains: Cobalt Man, Coldheart, NITRO, and SPEEDFREEK. During the ensuing battle, Nitro exploded in the middle of Stamford, Connecticut. The blast killed over six hundred people, including Microbe, NAMORITA, and NIGHT THRASHER.

After Namorita slammed him into a school bus outside of a playground, Nitro exploded and killed over 600 innocents—including dozens of children—rather than be captured and thrown into jail. This atrocity spurred the passage of the Superhuman Registration Act that launched the Civil War.

REGISTER OR ELSE

The public outcry over the tragedy spurred Congress to pass the Superhuman Registration Act, which required all superpowered people in the US to register with the government—and work for it as part of SHIELD—or face imprisonment. In the wake of M-DAY, the public had already been pushing for such safeguards, and the Stamford disaster gave the Act the impetus to get through.

The new law split the Super Hero community in two. Many of the heroes understood the need for the law and planned to comply with it. Others believed it to be a bad law and planned to fight it. IRON MAN, MR. FANTASTIC, and Hank Pym led those who backed the law, while CAPTAIN AMERICA refused to help SHIELD and went underground to form a secret AVENGERS as the core of his resistance movement. As soon as the law came into effect and SHIELD starting rounding up outlaw heroes, the resistance set to freeing them.

Notably, most of the backers of the law already had public identities to begin with, while many of those who protested the law did not. The most famous exception was SPIDER-MAN, who sided with his mentor IRON MAN. After some soul searching, he revealed his secret identity as Peter Parker at a globally televised press conference.

The Baxter Building served as a rallying point after the initial tragedy. With Congress about to pass the Superhuman Registration Act, the greatest heroes of the age assembled there to discuss how they should respond.

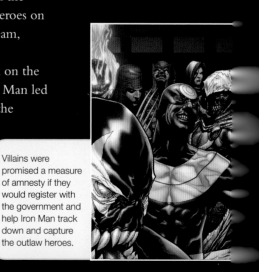

Spider-Man complied with the law, at the urging of Iron Man, and revealed his secret identity to a shocked world.

The X-MEN officially declared neutrality during the conflict, which soon became known as the Civil War. Although they sympathized with the resistance, they had been nearly destroyed on M-Day and did not wish to risk making their eradication complete.

In the first major conflict between the two sides, SHIELD unleashed a clone of THOR. The clone killed GIANT-MAN (Bill Foster) and would have harmed others had the INVISIBLE WOMAN not switched sides to protect the resistance. The incident caused heroes on both sides to reconsider their choices. Spider-Man switched to Captain America's team, while NIGHTHAWK and STATURE decided to register.

Desperate to even the sides, Captain America and his heroes launched an attack on the super-prison Mr. Fantastic had built in the Negative Zone. Anticipating this, Iron Man led a team to stop them. CLOAK teleported the entire battle back to Manhattan, and the resistance was winning handily when a group of firefighters, EMTs, and police tackled Captain America to keep him from killing Iron Man.

Looking around at the damage the battle had caused, Captain America realized that his team had won "everything except the argument." He surrendered himself to the NYPD, effectively ending the conflict. In the aftermath, Iron Man became the new director of SHIELD and launched the FIFTY STATE INITIATIVE. MF

At a turning point in the war, a clone of Thor slew Bill Foster, the latest Giant-Man.

Villains were promised a measure of amnesty if they would register with the government and help Iron Man track down and capture the outlaw heroes.

The Final Battle

In the climactic battle of the Civil War, Captain America's resistance faction faced off against Iron Man's government-backed forces. The battle began in the maximum-security prison located in the Negative Zone, called 42 because it was the 42nd idea that Iron Man's team had for improving the world. It spilled out into New York City when Cloak teleported the entire battle back into the regular world. At the climax of the battle, Captain America finally beat Iron Man but he hesitated when he had the chance to deliver the final blow. Gazing out at the destruction around him, he realized how many innocents were being caught up and harmed in the Civil War, and he gave himself up. Without Captain America, the active resistance crumbled, and the Civil War came to an end.

Soon afterward, while being marched in handcuffs into a federal courthouse, Captain America was assassinated by order of the Red Skull*. Later, his old partner Bucky* Barnes *took up his name and shield and worked with a team of outlaw Avengers. They aimed to fight crime and save the world, while remaining outside the law.*

Cloud 9

FIRST APPEARANCE Avengers: The Initiative #1 (March 2007)
REAL NAME Abigail "Abby" Boylen
OCCUPATION Super Hero **BASE** Montana
HEIGHT 5 ft 5 in **WEIGHT** 100 lbs **EYES** Blue **HAIR** Blonde
SPECIAL POWERS/ABILITIES Controls a cloud of gas on which she can fly; can also manipulate it to surround others and blind or suffocate them.

Soon after the launch of the Fifty-State Initiative, War Machine found Abby flying over Evanston, Illinois. She became part of the inaugural class at Camp Hammond and struck up a friendship with MVP (Michael Van Patrick), who was killed trying to protect her during a training exercise. Abby later helped defeat KIA, an insane clone of MVP, and started a relationship with MVP's first clone. She then joined Freedom Force, the Initiative team based in Montana. Captain America asked her to become a trainer at the Avengers Academy after the Civil War, but she went solo instead. MF

Cobra

FIRST APPEARANCE Journey into Mystery #98 (November 1963)
REAL NAME Klaus Voorhees
OCCUPATION Criminal **BASE** Manhattan, formerly the Serpent Citadels in New York State **HEIGHT** 5 ft 10 in
WEIGHT 160 lbs **EYES** Blue **HAIR** None
SPECIAL POWERS/ABILITIES Has flexible, virtually unbreakable bones; can perform superhuman contortionist feats.

Given powers by the bite of an irradiated cobra, Klaus Voorhees became the first Cobra. He often partnered with Mister Hyde and also joined other snake-themed criminals in the Serpent Squad and Serpent Society. As the leader of the Serpent Society, he changed his name to King Cobra. He later injected his nephew Piet Vorhees with the same venom, making him the new Cobra and giving him similar powers, plus the ability to spit venom and track prey by scent. Piet worked as a mercenary and also with Sin's Serpent Squad, and then with Hydra. MF

Collector

FIRST APPEARANCE Avengers Vol. 1 #28 (June 1966)
REAL NAME Taneleer Tivan
OCCUPATION Curator **BASE** Mobile
HEIGHT 6 ft 2 in **WEIGHT** 450 lbs **EYES** White **HAIR** White
SPECIAL POWERS/ABILITIES Immortality, precognition and telepathy; can manipulate cosmic energy to change his size and shape; Temporal Assimilator permits time travel.

One of the immortal Elders of the Universe, the Collector foresaw the destruction of all life by Thanos, and began to collect specimens for future repopulation. He was slain by Korvac, but returned to life when the Grandmaster, a fellow Elder, won a contest with Death. The Collector briefly held the Reality Gem, but lost it to Thanos who sought it for the Infinity Gauntlet. The Collector allowed alien bacterial life forms called the Brethren to invade Earth, hoping to collect survivors from the reduced population. DW

Colossus

Colossus

FACTFILE
REAL NAME
Piotr Nikolaievitch Rasputin
OCCUPATION
Adventurer
BASE
Mobile

HEIGHT 7 ft 5 in (armored)
WEIGHT 500 lbs (armored)
EYES Blue
HAIR Black

FIRST APPEARANCE
Giant Size X-Men #1 (1975)

POWERS
Mutant ability to change his body's tissue into an organic, steel-like material. This gives Colossus superhuman strength (he can lift at least 70 tons) and protects him from injury.

Piotr Rasputin was born on a Soviet collective farm in Russia, the same as his cosmonaut brother Mikhail Rasputin and his sister Illyana (Magik). When Professor X organized a new team of mutants to rescue the original X-Men, he contacted Piotr and convinced him to join. Piotr fell in love with teammate Katherine Pryde, although circumstances often kept them apart. He was injured battling the Marauders and couldn't turn his powers off for a while but eventually healed. He sacrificed himself to cure the Legacy Virus that killed mutants, but he later returned. During Fear Itself, he temporarily gained the power of the Juggernaut. When the Phoenix Force came to Earth, he became one of its five avatars for a time. Cable subsequently recruited him to join the new X-Force. MF

In armored form Colossus retains his normal degree of mobility, but his endurance and speed are greater.

Few can resist the devastating power of Colossus when he is in his armored state. One of his mighty punches is enough to crush even Magneto himself.

His armor can withstand an explosion of 450 pounds of dynamite.

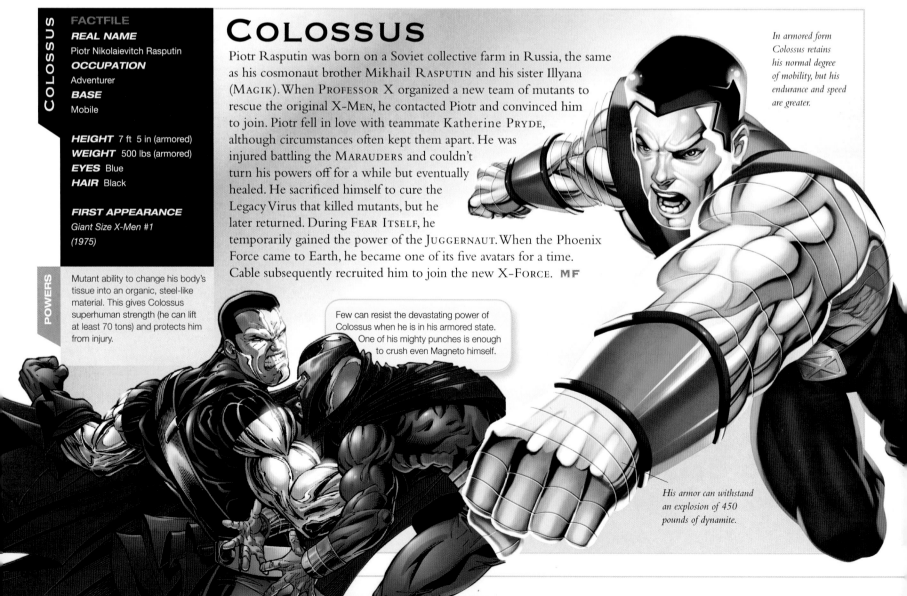

Collins, Rusty

FIRST APPEARANCE X-Factor #1 (February 1986)
REAL NAME Rusty Collins
OCCUPATION Adventurer **BASE** X-Factor HQ, New York City
HEIGHT 5 ft 11 in **WEIGHT** 160 lbs **EYES** Blue **HAIR** Red
SPECIAL POWERS/ABILITIES Rusty Collins was a pyrokinetic with the mutant ability to cause flames to spontaneously generate in his vicinity.

Leaving a troubled home life behind, Rusty Collins enlisted in the United States Navy while still underage. But his career as a sailor came to an end when his mutant ability to generate flames first manifested itself. Rusty was thereafter recruited by X-Factor, members of the original X-Men who had taken on the role of mutant hunters in order to conceal their activities in recruiting and training young mutants. Rusty eventually gained some control over his flaming abilities, and he adventured with X-Factor's junior team, the X-Terminators. He died during a battle with Holocaust. He recovered years later due to Selene's Transmode Virus but was killed again soon after. **TB, MF**

Comet aides Nova in the defence of the planet Xandar.

Comet

Harris Moore was one of the very first superpowered individuals to adopt a costume and take up the fight against crime. During an encounter with a gaseous, comet-like object in the 1950s, Moore was mutagenically affected by its radiation. Discovering that he could now fly and fire electrical energy from his hands, Moore decided to battle criminals on the streets of New York. His new vocation was not to end well. Moore was a wealthy individual with a wife and two children, but his good life came to an end when an enemy tracked him down to his suburban home and attacked him and his family. While he was hospitalized and appeared to have lost his powers, his family were all thought to be dead. Moore retired his costume for many years until he was called upon to travel to the planet Xandar, along with other Earth Super Heroes, and help its people in the fight against the Skrulls. During this battle, Moore was reunited with his son, Frank, the high-tech vigilante Crimebuster. Sadly, their renewed relationship was not to last long: Frank was killed during this battle while Moore later died during the Xandarians' battle against Nebula. **AD**

FACTFILE
REAL NAME
Harris Moore
OCCUPATION
Crimefighter
BASE
New York City/Xandar

HEIGHT 5 ft 11 in
WEIGHT 190 lbs
EYES Blue
HAIR Gray

FIRST APPEARANCE
Nova #21 (September 1978)

COMET

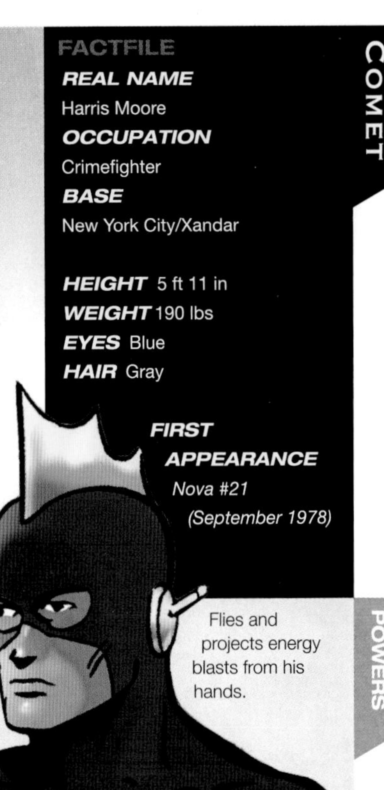

POWERS
Flies and projects energy blasts from his hands.

Comet Man *Max*

Comet Man

On a mission in space, Dr. Stephen Beckley lost control of his spacecraft, which entered a comet's tail. The comet's intense heat vaporized the ship and Beckley. However, within the comet was another spaceship piloted by Max, an alien from the Colony Fortisque. Max used Fortisquian technology to reconstruct Beckley's body and endow him with superhuman powers.

Returning to Earth, Beckley was quarantined by David Hilbert, a member of the Bridge, an intelligence agency headed by Beckley's brother John, the Superior. Hilbert captured Stephen's wife Ann and son Benny. Stephen escaped captivity, but in her own escape attempt Ann was killed. The Superior had scientist Dr. Fishler subject Benny to painful experiments in order to endow him with powers like Stephen's. Stephen found Benny, who used his new powers to kill Dr. Fishler before turning comatose.

Now known as Comet Man, Stephen accompanied Max to the Colony Fortisque, where Beckley mastered his powers. Comet Man then returned to Earth, where he used his powers to awaken Benny from his coma. **PS**

FACTFILE
REAL NAME
Dr. Stephen Beckley
OCCUPATION
Former astronaut, astronomer and astrophysicist
BASE
Mobile

HEIGHT 6 ft 1 in
WEIGHT 190 lbs
EYES Blue
HAIR Brown

FIRST APPEARANCE
Comet Man #1 (February 1987)

COMET MAN

POWERS
Possesses superhuman strength and self-healing ability. Can teleport himself and levitate himself and other objects. Projects concussive energy from his hands. By projecting part of his consciousness into people and higher animals, he can read and influence their minds.

Max, a member of the Fortisquian race, is fascinated by Earth's popular culture. Revealing himself to be an alien, Max became a media celebrity.

About every 77 years, a Fortisquian spaceship, hidden within a comet, travels past Earth to observe the planet.

THE CSA

FACTFILE
BASE
United States of America; various locations

FIRST APPEARANCE
Captain America #331 (July 1987)

COMMISSION ON SUPERHUMAN ACTIVITIES

The Commission on Superhuman Activities is a special task force answerable only to the President of the United States. It is charged with the task of regulating security in an age when beings with superhuman abilities roam the world. The Commission, or the CSA as it is frequently known, has involved itself in numerous incidents since its inception: it recruited the BROTHERHOOD OF EVIL MUTANTS led by MYSTIQUE to form the nucleus of a government-sponsored team of operatives known as FREEDOM FORCE. It was responsible for choosing John Walker as the replacement for Steve Rogers when the latter gave up his identity as CAPTAIN AMERICA. Members of the CSA were also responsible for the creation of superhumans such as Nuke and the Julia Carpenter SPIDER-WOMAN. When a SENTINEL went rogue and attacked a school in Antigo, Wisconsin, the Commission sent agents to investigate. The CSA has also been responsible for pitting the THUNDERBOLTS against the NEW AVENGERS. While their resources have occasionally been used for nefarious purposes, in general the membership of the Commission remains dedicated to its mission statement of protecting the American people from any threat spawned by those possessing superhuman attributes. **TB**

The Commission on Superhuman Activities is tasked with maintaining national security in a world occupied by superhumans.

The CSA
1 Orville Sanderson
2 George Mathers
3 General Heyworth
4 Henry Peter Gyrich
5 Valerie Cooper
6 Raymond Sikorsky
7 Adrian Sammish

CONSTRICTOR

FACTFILE
REAL NAME
Frank Payne (alias Frank Schlichting)
OCCUPATION
Professional criminal and assassin
BASE
Mobile

HEIGHT 5 ft 11 in
WEIGHT 190 lbs
EYES Blue
HAIR Black

FIRST APPEARANCE
Incredible Hulk # 212 (June 1977)

POWERS
Battlesuit contains two cybernetically-controlled, electrically-powered adamantium cables, used as whips, as crushing coils, and to release electrical charges.

The cables in Constrictor's battlesuit are made of adamantium, the strongest metal ever forged by man.

CONSTRICTOR

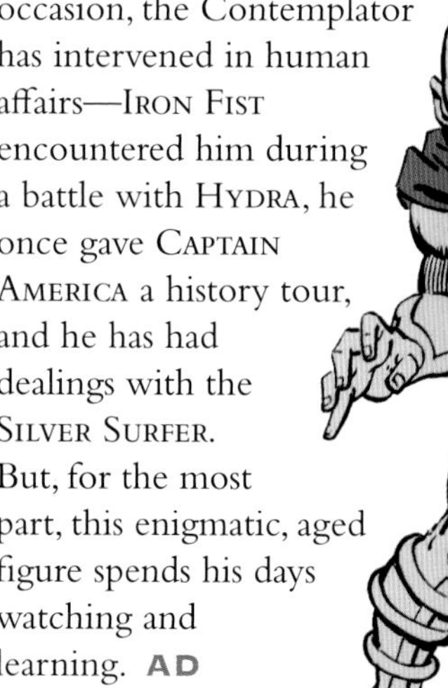

Using the alias Frank Schlichting, SHIELD agent Frank Payne infiltrated the criminal organization known as the Corporation. When Payne was forced to kill several youths during a fight, he suffered a nervous breakdown. The Corporation then gave him the Constrictor battlesuit and made him a criminal operative.

When the Corporation dissolved, Constrictor went freelance. He normally likes to work alone, but he has teamed up with other villains in the past. He put his criminal past behind him once he won a multimillion-dollar lawsuit after taking a beating from HERCULES. He was part of the FIFTY-STATE INITIATIVE's Shadow Initiative team. He lost his arms in a battle with a clone of Michael VAN PATRICK but uses cybernetic replacements. **MT, MF**

CONTEMPLATOR

FIRST APPEARANCE Marvel Treasury Special #1 (1976)
REAL NAME Tath Ki
OCCUPATION Philosopher **BASE** Coal Sack Nebula
HEIGHT 5 ft **WEIGHT** 100 lbs **EYES** Blue **HAIR** None
SPECIAL POWERS/ABILITIES Control of his body's involuntary responses: heartbeat, perspiration, etc.; highly developed mental powers; acute awareness of this and alternate universes.

An ELDER OF THE UNIVERSE, the Contemplator is one of the most ancient beings in the cosmos. Born in the early days of the universe, he has spent most of his life in meditation, reflecting on and teasing out the universe's deepest secrets. On occasion, the Contemplator has intervened in human affairs—IRON FIST encountered him during a battle with HYDRA, he once gave CAPTAIN AMERICA a history tour, and he has had dealings with the SILVER SURFER. But, for the most part, this enigmatic, aged figure spends his days watching and learning. **AD**

Controller

FIRST APPEARANCE Iron Man #12 (April 1969)
REAL NAME Basil Sandhurst **OCCUPATION** Criminal
BASE Mobile **HEIGHT** 6 ft 2 in **WEIGHT** 565 lbs
EYES White **HAIR** Black
SPECIAL POWERS/ABILITIES Armored exoskeleton provides enhanced strength and damage resistance; can telepathically control victims wearing his slave discs.

Crippled in a lab accident while working for Cord Industries (one of Stark Industries' main rivals), Basil Sandhurst built himself an exoskeleton powered by mental energy. By placing a slave disc on a victim's head or neck, Sandhurst could direct that person's actions and leech his or her brainpower to charge up his suit. On various occasions, he set himself up as a cult leader or clinic director to get easy access to more bodies. At other times, Thanos and the Master of the World upgraded his technology to make it more efficient. The Controller clashed with Iron Man and the Avengers several times. He worked for the Hood during the Dark Reign. **DW, MF**

Copycat

FIRST APPEARANCE New Mutants #98 (Feburary 1991, in the guise of Domino) **REAL NAME** Vanessa Geraldine Carlysle
OCCUPATION Professional criminal; mercenary **BASE** Mobile
HEIGHT Unrevealed **WEIGHT** Unrevealed
EYES Black with white pupils **HAIR** White
SPECIAL POWERS/ABILITIES Copycat can transform herself into a duplicate of any other person.

Vanessa Carlysle's mutant power to transform her appearance manifested itself in her early teens. She was kicked out by her family and forced to make her way on the mean streets. She eventually came to the attention of the shadowy Mr. Tolliver, who used her to infiltrate X-Force in the guise of Domino. But Copycat came to like the members of X-Force, and she could not go through with the plan to blow them up along with their headquarters. Her deception discovered, Copycat was forced to return to being a mercenary. She met her doom at the hands of Sabretooth after being recruited by the revived Weapon X project. **MT**

Corruptor

FIRST APPEARANCE Nova #4 (December 1976))
REAL NAME Jackson Day
OCCUPATION Criminal mastermind **BASE** Mobile
HEIGHT 6 ft 1 in **WEIGHT** 225 lbs **EYES** Red **HAIR** White
SPECIAL POWERS/ABILITIES His touch makes his victims susceptible to his commands. Left to themselves, they will behave in an uninhibited, even amoral, fashion.

While employed by a drug company, factory worker Jackson Day was accidentally drenched with chemicals. They turned his skin blue-black, and removed his inhibitions against wrongdoing. He also gained the power to control the wills of others by touching them. As the Corruptor, Day turned Thor into a violent menace. However, Nova intervened, and together he and Thor prevailed. The Corruptor later tried to corrupt the Hulk and the Avengers. He also worked with the Hood, battling the newest versions of the Avengers and helping repel the Skrulls during the Secret Invasion. **MT, MF**

Cooper, Valerie

FIRST APPEARANCE X-Men #176 (December 1983)
REAL NAME Valerie Cooper **OCCUPATION** Chair of the Commission on Superhuman Activities **BASE** Washington, D.C.
HEIGHT 5 ft 9 in **WEIGHT** 135 lbs **EYES** Green **HAIR** Blond
SPECIAL POWERS/ABILITIES Highly intelligent, efficient, and loyal; superb organizer; trained in the use of weapons.

Special Assistant to the US National Security Advisor Dr. Valerie Cooper was concerned about the number of mutants in the world. She feared that if control of mutants fell into the wrong hands, they could be used as weapons against the US. When Mystique offered the help of the Brotherhood of Evil Mutants, Cooper accepted, changing the group's name to Freedom Force. Later, as the head of the Commission on Superhuman Activities, Cooper was the liaison with the mutant team X-Factor. Cooper also helped found the Office of National Emergency and was named its deputy director. She oversaw the mutant refugee camp set up at the Xavier Institute for Higher Learning after M-Day. **MT, MF**

Corsair

FIRST APPEARANCE X-Men #104 (April, 1977)
REAL NAME Christopher Summers **OCCUPATION** Adventurer
BASE The starship Starjammer
HEIGHT 6 ft 3 in **WEIGHT** 175 lbs **EYES** Brown **HAIR** Brown
SPECIAL POWERS/ABILITIES Trained pilot of airplanes and starcraft and trained combatant.

When USAF Major Christopher Summers—a NASA test pilot—was flying in small plane with his family, Shi'ar scouts kidnapped him and his wife Katherine, but not before she shoved out their sons Scott (Cyclops) and Alex (Havok) to escape with a single parachute. Katherine was pregnant with their third son, Gabriel (Vulcan), who was torn from her at her death, saved, and sold as a slave. Escaping from the Shi'ar slave pits himself, Christopher led a group of pirates called the Starjammers against the Shi'ar emperor D'Ken, helping D'Ken's sister Lilandra become empress. Vulcan later slew Christopher in his bid to become the new Shi'ar emperor. **MF**

COULSON, AGENT PHIL

FACTFILE

REAL NAME
Phillip Coulson

OCCUPATION
Agent of SHIELD

BASE
SHIELD Helicarrier

HEIGHT 5 ft 9 in
WEIGHT 170 lbs
EYES Brown
HAIR Brown

FIRST APPEARANCE
Battle Scars #1 (November 2011)

POWERS

Special forces unarmed combat and firearms training; excellent administrative abilities; resourceful, loyal and patriotic—inspired by his idol, Captain America.

Coulson, Agent Phil

Agent Coulson has taken to his role with the rebuilt SHIELD—and to wearing a suit—well.

During FEAR ITSELF, Phil "Cheese" Coulson fought in Afghanistan as a member of the US Army Rangers 2nd Battalion, alongside his best friend, Marcus Johnson (aka Nick FURY, JR.). When Johnson's mother was killed, Coulson used his leave to travel back with Johnson for her funeral, where they discovered that Johnson was secretly the son of Nick FURY. With Orion—one of the elder Fury's old enemies—after Johnson for the powers he'd inherited, Coulson did his best to haul his friend to safety. When Johnson knocked him out instead, Coulson called in the AVENGERS to help him find and save Johnson.

Both Coulson and Johnson were offered jobs with the reconstituted SHIELD. Coulson became the lead tactical support officer with SHIELD's version of the Secret Avengers. He helped recruit the team's members, including BLACK WIDOW, HAWKEYE, and TASKMASTER. **MF**

COUNT NEFARIA

FACTFILE

REAL NAME
Count Luchino Nefaria

OCCUPATION
Criminal; former head of Nefaria "family" of Maggia

BASE
Various, including castle originally located in Italy and reconstructed in the New Jersey Palisades

HEIGHT 6 ft 2 in
WEIGHT 230 lbs
EYES Blue
HAIR Black

FIRST APPEARANCE
The Avengers #13 (Feb. 1965)

POWERS

Superhuman strength, speed, and resistance to injury; projects laser beams from eyes; regenerates after injury; drains energy from other beings powered by ionic energy.

Count Nefaria

Italian nobleman Count Luchino Nefaria used his fortune both to finance technological research and to make himself a power in the MAGGIA crime syndicate. Nefaria's wife Renata died giving birth to their daughter Giulietta. Growing up in America as Whitney Frost, Giulietta would eventually become the Maggia leader called MADAME MASQUE. In retaliation for the AVENGERS' opposition to the Maggia, Nefaria framed them for treason. The Avengers were cleared, but Nefaria was publicly exposed as a criminal. Among his grandest schemes, Nefaria captured Washington DC and held it for ransom, and later took over the North American Defense Command base at Valhalla Mountain. On both occasions he was thwarted by the X-MEN.

Later, Nefaria had Prof. Kenneth Sturdy endow him with the powers of the LIVING LASER, Power Man, and WHIRLWIND and again battled the Avengers. Soon afterward, he seemed to be killed. However, he returned as a superhuman, powered by ionic energy. He later became the kingpin of crime in Los Angeles. **PS, MF**

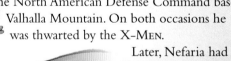

Nefaria was the villain in the 1975 issue that relaunched the X-Men Super Heroes.

IN ALL VALHALLA BASE, MY CHILDREN, WE SIX ARE THE ONLY ONES STILL CONSCIOUS, AND ONCE AGAIN, COUNT NEFARIA IS TRIUMPHANT...
THIS TIME TO HOLD THE *FATE* OF A *WORLD* IN HIS HANDS.

Thunderbird, a Native American member of the X-Men, perished while trying to prevent Count Nefaria's escape from Valhalla Mountain.

Crazy Gang

FIRST APPEARANCE Marvel Super Heroes #377 (Sept. 1981)
BASE Mobile
MEMBERS AND POWERS
Executioner A hooded, scythe-wielding humanoid robot.
Jester Accomplished swordsman.
Knave Possesses superhuman strength
Red Queen Her insanity twists all reality into negative situations.
Tweedledope Idiot-savant who devises advanced machinery.

The Crazy Gang is a team of professional criminals from another dimension (Earth-238, or the Crooked World) who look like characters from children's storybooks. They were assembled by that dimensions "Mad Jim" Jaspers. When the Crazy Gang was transported to the Earth of Captain Britain, who was really Brian Braddock, they proved incompetent at committing crimes and so advertised for a new leader. They were taken over by Captain Britain's foe the Slaymaster, who masterminded a series of spectacular crimes which the Crazy Gang carried out for him. They were then recruited by master assassin ARCADE to abduct Courtney Ross, the former girlfriend of Captain Britain. Ross managed to escape from the bumbling group, but was taken prisoner by Arcade himself. The Crazy Gang later clashed with EXCALIBUR, who subsequently allowed them to remain in this dimension. **MT**

CRAZY GANG
1 Jack of Hearts
2 Jester
3 Tweedledope
4 Executioner
5 Red Queen

Creed, Graydon

FIRST APPEARANCE Uncanny X-Men #299 (April 1993)
STATUS Villain (deceased) **REAL NAME** Graydon Creed
OCCUPATION Politician; wheeler-dealer
BASE New York City; New York State; mobile
HEIGHT 6 ft **WEIGHT** 181 lbs **EYES** Blue **HAIR** Brown
SPECIAL POWERS/ABILITIES Charismatic orator, skilled political operator, and rabble-rouser.

Victor Creed was psychologically abused as a child and became SABRETOOTH. His son, Graydon Creed, grew up similarly disaffected but without any mutant powers. Born to the shapeshifting MYSTIQUE, Graydon came to hate all mutants and founded the Friends of Humanity, an organization that aimed to wipe out mutants. While running for President, Graydon was assassinated by Mystique, who had traveled back from the future to kill him. BASTION revived him with a techno-organic virus years later, but Hope SUMMERS killed him once more. **AD, MF**

Crimson Cowl

FIRST APPEARANCE Thunderbolts #3 (June 1997)
REAL NAME Justine Hammer
OCCUPATION Businesswoman, criminal mastermind
BASE Symkaria **HEIGHT** 5 ft 11 in **WEIGHT** 161 lbs
EYES Blue **HAIR** Black with white streaks
SPECIAL POWERS/ABILITIES The Crimson Cowl's cloak is prehensile and capable of attacking foes. It also allows its wearer to levitate and to teleport groups of people.

Four people wore the Crimson Cowl. ULTRON used the identity to disguise his true nature as he led the MASTERS OF EVIL against the AVENGERS. He hypnotized Avengers' butler Edwin JARVIS to pose as the Crimson Cowl, too. Years later, Justine Hammer—daughter and heir of Justin HAMMER—took up the Cowl and the leadership of the Masters of Evil. When nearly captured, she put an unconscious Dallas RIORDAN into the costume to cast suspicion on her. Justine and her daughter Sasha HAMMER (fathered by the MANDARIN) plagued IRON MAN until Ezekiel STANE and Sasha killed her. **MF**

Crimson Dynamo

More than a dozen people have worn the Crimson Dynamo armor. The first—Russian inventor Anton Vanko—built the original battlesuit and battled IRON MAN, but defected to work for Tony Stark. Vanko died killing the second Dynamo, Boris Turgenev, who had been sent to assassinate him. Vanko's protégé Alex Nevsky became the third Dynamo until his death at the hands of the KGB. Most of the others operated as Russian agents, with a few exceptions: the eighth was a college student who accidentally activated a prototype suit, and the tenth was a bank robber who bought his suit on the black market. A number of the Russians served with the WINTER GUARD.

Tony Stark (Iron Man) borrowed a suit of Crimson Dynamo armor from Dmitri Bukharin, the fifth and perhaps best-known Crimson Dynamo, and wore it for a short time during the DARK REIGN. The latest Crimson Dynamo was Galina Nemirovsky, the first woman to wear the armor. After leaving the Winter Guard, she worked for the MANDARIN and Ezekiel STANE in a redesigned suit, attacking Tony Stark on their behalf. **DW, MF**

FACTFILE
REAL NAME
Dmitri Bukharin
OCCUPATION
Russian hero
BASE
Moscow, Russia

HEIGHT 6 ft
WEIGHT 200 lbs
EYES Brown
HAIR Bald

FIRST APPEARANCE
Tales of Suspense #46 (October 1963)

POWERS
Armored suit provides flight, enhanced strength, and damage resistance; built-in weapons include missiles, guns, electrical generators, and a fusioncaster.

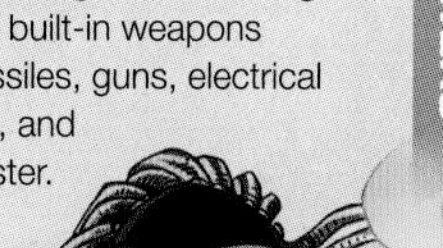
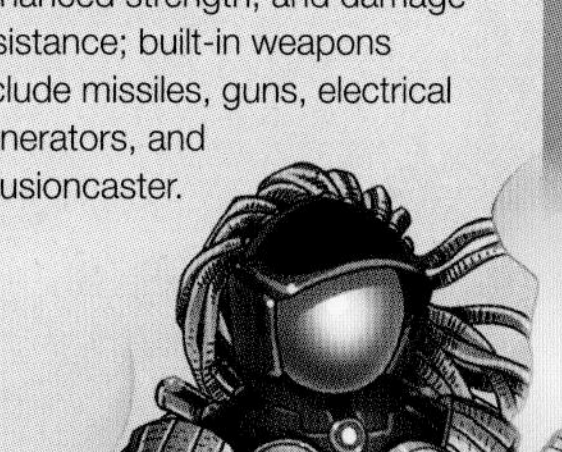

Nemirovsky's original armor looked more traditional, but her current suit makes it clear she's a woman.

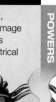

CROSSBONES

FACTFILE
REAL NAME
Brock Rumlow
OCCUPATION
Mercenary; criminal
BASE
Mobile

HEIGHT 6 ft 4 in
WEIGHT 290 lbs
EYES Brown
HAIR Brown

FIRST APPEARANCE
Captain America #360 (October 1989)

POWERS
Brutal hand-to-hand combatant; highly adept with weapons and explosives, including pistols, throwing knives, which he keeps in his boots, and wrist blades, which are hidden in his wrist bands.

When Crossbones had superpowers, he could form a ball of fire before his face and fire a blast from it.

Crossbones

As a young man, Brock Rumlow—a budding neo-Nazi and childhood fan of the Red Skull—led the Savage Crims street gang based in Manhattan's Lower East Side. During that time, he attacked 15-year-old Rachel Leighton (who would later become Diamondback) and beat her two brothers when they came to her defense, killing one. Fleeing prosecution, he trained under the Taskmaster to become a deadly mercenary and fought and killed people around the world. As Crossbones, he hired on with the Red Skull, and he repeatedly battled Captain America on his boss's behalf, even remaining loyal when the Skull once fired him. He also became the lover of the Skull's daughter, Sin.

Crossbones took part in Captain America's assassination, firing the first shot from a sniper's post. SHIELD arrested him for this, but the Serpent Squad freed him soon after. He joined Luke Cage's version of the Thunderbolts, during which time he was exposed to the Terrigen Mists, which give the Inhumans their powers. This temporarily allowed him to fire energy blasts from his face. He and Sin recently hired on with Hydra's Department of Occult Armaments (DOA). **MF**

Cyber

FIRST APPEARANCE Marvel Comics Presents #85 (August 1991)
REAL NAME Silas Burr **OCCUPATION** Mercenary
BASE Mobile **HEIGHT** 6 ft 4 in **WEIGHT** 365 lbs
EYES Hazel **HAIR** Unrevealed
SPECIAL POWERS/ABILITIES Superhuman strength; mutant healing; ability to track brain patterns; adamantium-laced skin; claws containing poisons or hallucinogens; cybernetic eye.

Silas Burr trained Logan (*see* Wolverine) during World War I and also, decades later, his son Daken. After being shot and left for dead by Daken, Burr's skin was laced with adamantium and he was given adamantium claws. As Cyber, Burr lost an eye in a clash with Wolverine. Sporting a cybernetic eye, he later led a female crime team known as Hell's Belles and battled X-Factor. He died once, his flesh consumed by mutant deathwatch beetles, but returned in astral form to possess a mutant and hired the Tinkerer to enhance his body again. **DW, MF**

Crossfire

FIRST APPEARANCE Marvel Two-In-One #52 (June 1979)
REAL NAME William Cross
OCCUPATION Ex-CIA agent, criminal **BASE** Mobile
HEIGHT 6 ft **WEIGHT** 190 lbs **EYES** Blue **HAIR** Brown
SPECIAL POWERS/ABILITIES Marksman, spy, deadly hand-to-hand fighter; left eye replaced by infrared device allowing night vision; left ear replaced by audio sensor giving super-hearing.

William Cross learned all about espionage, and especially brainwashing techniques, as a CIA agent. Leaving the CIA and taking the codename Crossfire, he organized an army of mercenaries with the goal of disrupting society and earning himself a hefty profit from the ensuing chaos. When his enemies set off an explosion in Crossfire's headquarters, he lost his left eye and left ear. Replacing these with an enhanced cybernetic eye and ear, Crossfire set about brainwashing costumed heroes. His attempts put him in conflict with the Thing, Moon Knight, and Hawkeye. **MT**

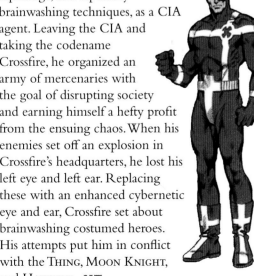

Crystal

FIRST APPEARANCE Fantastic Four #45 (December 1965)
REAL NAME Corystalia Amaquelin **OCCUPATION** Princess
BASE Kree Empire **HEIGHT** 5 ft 6 in **WEIGHT** 110 lbs
EYES Green **HAIR** Red
SPECIAL POWERS/ABILITIES Elemental powers enable her to psionically control fire, air, earth, and water.

Crystal is an elemental and a member of the Royal Family of the Inhumans, a genetically advanced offshoot of humanity. She is also the younger sister of Medusa. While in exile in New York City, she met and fell in love with the Human Torch and became a substitute member of the Fantastic Four. Crystal eventually married Quicksilver, and they had a daughter named Luna, but their marriage was annulled after Quicksilver illegally exposed both himself and Luna to the power-granting Terrigen Mists. After the Secret Invasion, she fled Earth with the rest of the Inhumans and agreed to marry Ronan the Accuser to cement an alliance with the Kree. They are now separated. **PS, MF**

Cypher

FIRST APPEARANCE New Mutants #13 (March 1984)
REAL NAME Douglas Ramsey **OCCUPATION** Student
BASE San Francisco
HEIGHT 5 ft 9 in **WEIGHT** 150 lbs **EYES** Blue **HAIR** Blond
SPECIAL POWERS/ABILITIES Cypher possessed a mutant facility for translating any sort of language. His ability to analyze patterns improved to the point at which he could predict the future.

Professor X realized that Katherine Pryde's friend Doug Ramsey's brilliance with computers was an aspect of his mutant talent for languages. Doug became one of the New Mutants and helped them communicate with the newly arrived Warlock. Doug died after taking a bullet meant for his girlfriend, Wolfsbane. For a while, his body merged with that of Warlock, forming Douglock. The Transmode Virus brought Doug back to life years later, improving his powers so that he could use them to predict the future, and he rejoined the New Mutants. **MF**

Cyclops

Leader of the Uncanny X-Men

Deadly solar energy continually crackles forth from the eyes of Cyclops, controlled only by his visor.

When Professor X set up his School for Gifted Youngsters, the first mutant he recruited was Scott Summers. Scott also joined the X-Men, adopting the codename Cyclops. He proved Professor X's most trusted student, and quickly became the team's deputy leader and master strategist, displaying great tactical abilities.

Orphaned Young

Scott Summers was the elder of two sons of Air Force Major Christopher Summers (Corsair) and Katherine Anne Summers. When their private plane was attacked by a Shi'ar starship, Katherine pushed Scott and his brother Alex out of the burning plane with the one parachute left. Both brothers were hurt, and Scott struck his head and fell into a year-long coma. The brain damage eventually prevented him from controlling his optic blasts once they emerged.

Alex ended up in an orphanage, and the boys lost contact for many years. Alex later became the mutant Havok and joined the X-Men too. They later discovered they had another brother, Gabriel, who became the conqueror Vulcan.

In his mid-teens, Scott developed terrible headaches and eyestrain, when his mutant powers emerged and he unintentionally blasted a crane at a construction site. He then fired another blast to save the crowd below it. Scott fled and fell into an unwilling partnership with a mutant criminal, named the Living Diamond.

The X-Man

When Professor X learned about Scott, he rescued him from the Living Diamond and invited him to join his school. Scott loved his teammate Jean Grey but, after her death, he married her clone, Madelyne Pryor, and had a son named Nathan (Cable) with her. After Jean returned and Madelyne died, Scott and Jean were married. After Jean died again, Scott dated Emma Frost.

Scott carries his lover Emma Frost, who was overwhelmed by trying to absorb the Phoenix Force to save the world from it.

Scott took over from Professor X as the leader of the X-Men. He retained his powers after M-Day and gathered mutants worldwide on a Pacific island he named Utopia. This led to a schism between him and his teammate Wolverine, who reopened Professor X's school as the Jean Grey School for Higher Learning. When the Phoenix Force returned to Earth, Scott became one of the Phoenix Five. He eventually transformed into a new Dark Phoenix and killed Professor X.

Stricken with grief, Scott allowed himself to be arrested. He later broke out of prison and formed his own group to lead the mutant revolution. His optic blasts are now more powerful but harder to control. Many of his former friends consider him insane. **MT, MF**

When the rest of the Phoenix Five lost their powers, Scott became the Dark Phoenix.

Cyclops

FACTFILE

REAL NAME
Scott Summers

OCCUPATION
Adventurer, student, radio announcer

BASE
Charles Xavier School for the Gifted, Alberta, Canada

HEIGHT 6 ft 3 in
WEIGHT 175 lbs
EYES Black (red when his optic power is active)
HAIR Brown

FIRST APPEARANCE
X-Men #1
(September 1963)

Powers

Cyclops has the mutant ability to project ruby-colored beams of concussive force from his eyes. Cyclops' cells constantly absorb sunlight, and he uses that solar energy to create openings from another universe in front of his eyes, and the beams fire from these breaches. Due to a childhood trauma, Cyclops' optic beam is always "on." The only way to block it is by closing his eyes or wearing a special visor or glasses. Cyclops' optic blasts are powerful enough to punch holes through a mountain.

ESSENTIAL STORYLINES
- ***X-Men #107*** First appearance of Corsair, Cyclops' father (Christopher Summers), whom Scott believed to be dead, but is now a member of the Starjammers, an alien group opposed to Shi'ar tyranny.
- ***X-Men #30*** Marriage X-Men style: after years of romance, Scott Summers finally marries his beloved, Jean Grey.

DAKEN

FACTFILE

REAL NAME
Daken Akihiro

OCCUPATION
Assassin, agent

BASE
Mobile

HEIGHT 5 ft 9 in
WEIGHT 167 lbs
EYES Blue
HAIR Black

FIRST APPEARANCE
Wolverine Origins #10

POWERS

Mutant healing factor, retractable claws made of bone, superhuman senses, endurance, and reflexes, plus manipulation of others via pheromones.

Daken

While trying to capture Wolverine, the Winter Soldier killed his pregnant wife, Itsu. Romulus cut the baby from her womb and gave him to a Japanese couple, leaving Wolverine unaware the child had survived. Daken trained under Cyber and worked for Romulus, who encouraged him to kill Wolverine, claiming his father had been the one who'd murdered his mother. Wolverine drew Daken into a trap. He faked letting Deadpool kill him so the Winter Soldier could shoot Daken with a carbonadium bullet, which worked against his healing factor. Discovering that Romulus had orchestrated Itsu's death, Daken and Wolverine worked together to bring him down.

During the Dark Reign, Daken took over his father's identity as Wolverine to join Norman Osborn's (*see* Green Goblin) new Avengers and X-Men. After that, he tried to take over crime in Los Angeles but became addicted to a drug called "Heat," which destroyed his healing factor. Dying, he drew out Wolverine for a confrontation and then blew himself up. He later returned as the leader of a new Brotherhood of Mutants, but Wolverine drowned him. The Apocalypse Twins revived him to become one of their Horsemen of Death. **MF**

Daken assumed a uniform of his own when he finally tried to step out of his father's shadow.

Damage Control

FIRST APPEARANCE Marvel Comics Presents #19 (June 1989)
BASE Manhattan
MEMBERS
Anne Marie Hoag Director of Operations
Henry Ackerdson V.P. Marketing
Albert Cleary Comptroller
Eugene Strausser Head of R&D

Damage Control is an engineering and construction company that specializes in cleaning up and repairing property damage caused by superpowered conflicts. With its headquarters in Manhattan's Flatiron Building, and a warehouse in New Jersey, the company has about 300 employees. The company's CEO, Walter Declun, secretly provided Nitro with drugs that increased his powers and led to the death of hundreds in Stamford, Connecticut, precipitating the Civil War. Wolverine seemed to have killed Nitro, but he later turned up working for Doctor Doom. **MT, MF**

Dansen Macabre

FIRST APPEARANCE Marvel Team-Up #93 (May 1980)
REAL NAME Unknown **OCCUPATION** Criminal; exotic dancer; second-in-command of Night Shift **BASE** Los Angeles
HEIGHT 5 ft 10 in **WEIGHT** 135 lbs **EYES** Blue **HAIR** Silver
SPECIAL POWERS/ABILITIES Her dancing can hypnotize or even kill; able to evade Spider-Man's telepathic "Spider-Sense."

Dansen Macabre was the high priestess of Kali, a religious cult. When Macabre believed the Shroud to be a member of a rival cult, she hypnotized Spider-Man into attacking him. Her plan failed and the pair defeated her. Realizing the impossibility of imprisoning Macabre, Spider-Man left her in the Shroud's care. She is now second-in-command of Night Shift, the Shroud's supposed criminal gang, unaware that it is a front for his crimefighting. **AD**

DAREDEVIL, *see pages 100-101*

Dark Beast

FIRST APPEARANCE X-Men Alpha (1994)
REAL NAME Henry P. McCoy **OCCUPATION** Genetic engineer
BASE Formerly Sinister's slave pens in the "Age of Apocalypse"
HEIGHT 5 ft 11 in **WEIGHT** 355 lbs **EYES** Blue
HAIR Formerly brown, now blue-black
SPECIAL POWERS/ABILITIES Possesses superhuman strength, agility, and durability. Expert in genetics and biochemistry.

In the alternate future of Earth-295, there was an evil counterpart to the X-Men's Beast. This "Dark Beast" was the head geneticist for that reality's Sinister, and experimented on the inmates in his slave pens. When Apocalypse was defeated, the Dark Beast transported himself 20 years into the past of Earth-616, where he met a young Emma Frost and created the Morlocks. At one point, he captured the Beast and impersonated him. He survived M-Day with his powers and joined the dark X-Men during Dark Reign. He returned to his own world briefly but is now trapped in the standard one. **PS, MF**

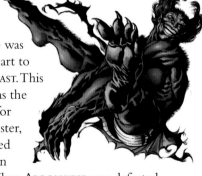

DARKHAWK

FIRST APPEARANCE Darkhawk #1 (August 1964)
REAL NAME Christopher Powell **OCCUPATION** High-school student **BASE** Queens, New York City
HEIGHT 6 ft ½ in **WEIGHT** 320 lbs **EYES** Brown **HAIR** Brown
SPECIAL POWERS/ABILITIES Bio-mechanical armored suit possesses enhanced strength, speed, agility, and durability. Also possesses a pair of retractable glider wings and a claw-cable on his right hand that can act as a grappling hook. Can generate defensive force shields and concussive blasts of dark energy.

Teenager Christopher Powell discovered an alien amulet that exchanged his body for the Darkhawk android, transferring his mind into it. He later obtained a new android form that could become invisible, and he became able to change directly between the two forms. As Darkhawk, he worked with the New Warriors, the West Coast Avengers, and later the Loners, a group for ex-teen heroes. He registered with the government during the Civil War and served as the security chief of Project: P.E.G.A.S.U.S. during the Secret Invasion. Darkhawk seemed to be killed by Death Locket but managed to survive. **MT, MF**

Dark Reign, ***see pages 102-103***

DAZZLER

Rock singer Dazzler's mutant power created a spectacular light show to match her dynamic vocals.

Alison Blaire's mutant power first manifested itself during a high-school talent show. She became a singer whose amazing light-show powers helped to make her a star. Although she had no intention of using her powers to fight crime, she joined the X-Men after she was exposed as mutant. She later met and fell in love with Longshot, with whom she bore a son who became Shatterstar, although her memories of this birth were wiped.

After Longshot was reported dead, Alison returned to her singing career.

They later reunited and she returned to the X-Men, but his amnesia drove them apart. After that, she became the leader of a dimension-hopping team of X-Men trying to defeat ten evil versions of Professor X. When she returned, she became an agent of SHIELD, charged with tracking Cyclops's X-Men. **TD, MF**

YOU DID IT!
WE DID IT--TO MAKE THIS WORLD A BETTER PLACE.

The loss of her romantic love, Longshot, led Dazzler to return to her first love—music.

FACTFILE

REAL NAME
Alison Blaire
OCCUPATION
Singer, actress
BASE
Mobile

HEIGHT 5 ft 8 in
WEIGHT 115 lbs
EYES Blue
HAIR Blond

FIRST APPEARANCE
X-Men #130 (February 1980)

POWERS
Mutant with the ability to convert sonic vibrations into various forms of light, including blinding, colorful, mind-numbing, and hypnotic displays, high impact photon blasts, laser beams, holographic illusions, and protective force fields.

DARKSTAR

FIRST APPEARANCE Champions #7 (August 1976)
REAL NAME Laynia Petrovna **OCCUPATION** Adventurer
BASE Russia **HEIGHT** 5 ft 6 in **WEIGHT** 125 lbs
EYES Brown **HAIR** Blond
SPECIAL POWERS/ABILITIES Darkstar could tap into the extradimensional Darkforce to create solid objects, to teleport herself and others, and to fly.

Professor Piotr Phobos made the mutant Laynia into Darkstar, part of his Soviet Super-Soldiers team. She and her brother Nicolai (Vanguard) turned against him when he betrayed the state. She defected to the US, but later returned to Russia and joined the Winter Guard. She and Vanguard then worked with their father, the Presence. She joined the X-Corps, but Fantomex killed her when Weapon XII possessed her. Her essence survived in an amulet that gave the wearer her powers. When a Dire Wraith took it, Laynia possessed the creature and turned it into herself. **TB, MF**

DEADPOOL

When ex-soldier Wade Wilson was diagnosed with cancer, he allowed Weapon X scientists to try to cure him by recreating Wolverine's mutant healing ability. The cure worked, but Wilson's skin was a mangled mess, and Weapon X placed him in a prison lab. After escaping, Deadpool worked as a mercenary, battling Cable and X-Force and working for crooks like the Wizard, the Kingpin, and Genesis. He dated Copycat on and off throughout this time. Deadpool went back to work for Weapon X, but he left when Sabretooth killed Copycat. He teamed up with Cable for a while after being forced to merge their DNA to survive a vicious virus. When the Civil War started, Deadpool landed a job hunting renegade heroes for SHIELD, including Cable. During the Secret Invasion, he figured out how to kill Skrull queen Veranke, but Norman Osborn (Green Goblin) stole the information to make himself seem a hero. A stalker of Deadpool had collected enough parts of Wilson for them to fuse together into a clone of him, known as Evil Deadpool. Deadpool later joined the Red Hulk's Thunderbolts. **MT, MF**

FACTFILE

REAL NAME
Wade Wilson
OCCUPATION
Mercenary
BASE
Mobile

HEIGHT 6 ft 2 in
WEIGHT 210 lbs
EYES Brown
HAIR None

FIRST APPEARANCE
New Mutants #98 (February 1991)

POWERS
Wade has advanced healing abilities and is an expert marksman and hand-to-hand-combatant. Uses a teleportation device to travel instantly from one place to another.

At the urging of the Contemplator, Deadpool assembled the Deadpool Corps to save the multiverse.

DAREDEVIL

The Man Without Fear

DAREDEVIL

FACTFILE

REAL NAME
Matthew Michael Murdock

OCCUPATION
Lawyer

BASE
Hamilton Heights, New York City (formerly Hell's Kitchen)

HEIGHT 5 ft 11 in
WEIGHT 185 lbs
EYES Blue
HAIR Red/Brown

FIRST APPEARANCE
Daredevil #1 (April 1964)

POWERS

Despite blindness, Daredevil's remaining senses are honed to superhuman levels. Radar Sense allows him to detect the contours of his environment. A trained athlete and acrobat, he carries a billy club that converts into a blind man's cane; it contains a reeled line that allows Daredevil to swing over the rooftops or entangle an enemy.

ALLIES/FOES

ALLIES Foggy Nelson, Spider-Man, Gladiator, Iron Man, Luke Cage, the Avengers

FOES Elektra, Bullseye, Electro, Impossible Man, Kingpin, Mysterio, the Hand

ISSUE #1

"The Origin of Daredevil" reveals how Matt Murdock, son of a prizefighter, loses his sight but gains superpowered senses. He becomes the Super Hero Daredevil, trains as a lawyer, and sets up a law firm with Foggy Nelson.

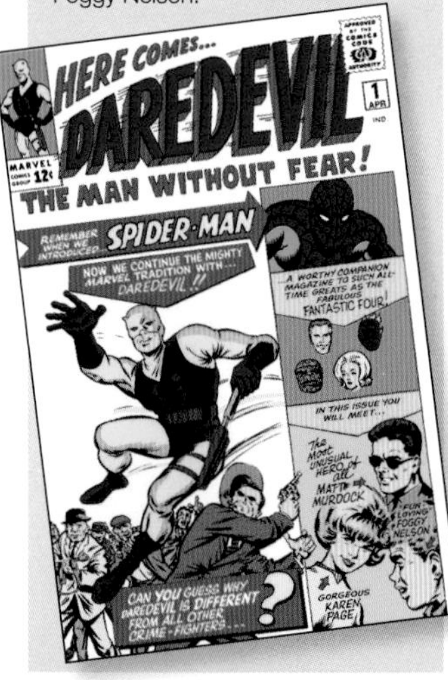

When he began his crime-fighting career, Daredevil wore a yellow and red costume similar to that of a wrestler.

Matt Murdock was the only son of professional boxer "Battling" Jack Murdock. But his father, forced to work as a mob leg-breaker in order to supplement his meager income as a prize-fighter, made Matt promise to get a good education, and not become a fighter like himself. As a dedicated student who would never compete in athletics with his fellows, Matt was nicknamed "Daredevil" by his taunting classmates. Not wanting to break his promise to his father, Matt took their insults—but he secretly kept up a rigorous training regimen all by himself.

RADIOACTIVE ACCIDENT

One fateful day, Matt saw a blind pedestrian about to be struck down by a truck. Matt rushed to the old man's aid, knocking him from the path of the vehicle. In the crash that followed, a canister of radioactive material fell from the truck and struck Matt in the face. Despite the best efforts of the doctors, Matt would thereafter be blind.

However, Matt discovered that the accident had a second effect on him: all of his remaining senses had been enhanced to a superhuman degree. Additionally, he now possessed a kind of built-in radar sense, which allowed him to detect the contours of his environment and compensated for his lack of sight. Initially overwhelmed by his powers, young Matt sought out the former ninja master known as STICK, who trained him to control his newfound abilities.

REVENGE AND THE LAW

When mob boss the Fixer told Jack Murdock to throw a fight, Jack, with his son watching, won. He was soon gunned down by the Fixer's men.

In order to track down the men who had murdered his father, Matt Murdock, now a successful lawyer, adopted the identity of Daredevil. After the Fixer had been brought to justice, Matt continued his crime-fighting double life.

In recent years, BULLSEYE murdered Karen PAGE, the love of Matt's life. Matt's wife, Milla DONOVAN went crazy because of Mr. Fear's drugs. Milla's parents forced Matt to sign the papers while Milla was in a mental hospital and the marriage was annulled. For a while, Matt was exposed to the world as Daredevil, but with the help of Iron Fist—who posed as Daredevil while Matt was in prison—he recovered the secret.

In college, Matt Murdock fell in love with exchange student Elektra Natchios. The two would one day become implacable foes.

ESSENTIAL STORYLINES

- ***Daredevil #168***
Daredevil has a reunion with his college sweetheart Elektra, now an assassin for hire.
- ***Daredevil #227–232***
The Kingpin methodically tears Matt Murdock's life apart, piece by piece.
- ***Daredevil Vol. 2 #32***
Daredevil's true identity as Matt Murdock is revealed to all the world.

As leader of the Hand, Daredevil wore a black costume with red detailing.

Joining the Hand

For years, Matt battled against the Hand, a powerful group of mystical ninjas who work as assassins for organized crime. His ex-girlfriend Elektra had worked with them when she was younger, and she had returned to lead them, seemingly corrupted by their evil. In fact, this Elektra was a Skrull who'd replaced the real woman, which was revealed when Echo killed her during the Secret Invasion.

This left the Hand without a leader, and one faction of the group—working with Lady Bullseye—approached Daredevil to assume the mantle. Matt refused at first, but after seeing that the leadership would otherwise go to the Kingpin, he accepted the offer. Despite the Hand's history, he hoped to transform it into a force for good. To that end, he went to Japan to proclaim himself the leader over the Hand's five factions.

Shadowland

Returning to Manhattan's Hell's Kitchen, Matt built a fortress on the ruins of an apartment building he'd failed to save from Bullseye during the Dark Reign. From there, he launched his initiative to take Manhattan's streets back from Norman Osborn (*see* Green Goblin) and his forces. Called Shadowland, the monumental building served both as a temple for the Hand and a prison for the criminals—and police officers—captured under Daredevil's leadership.

When pushed to the brink by Daredevil's heroic friends, the Beast revealed himself.

During this time, Matt was possessed by the Beast, a demon worshipped by the Hand for centuries. When the Dark Reign ended, Matt's super-powered friends realized that something was wrong with him. He'd gone too far in his quest, including killing Bullseye with a sai, in the exact way the assassin had murdered Elektra years before. When they confronted him, he declared that they had betrayed him, and he decided to resurrect Bullseye so the villain could serve the Hand.

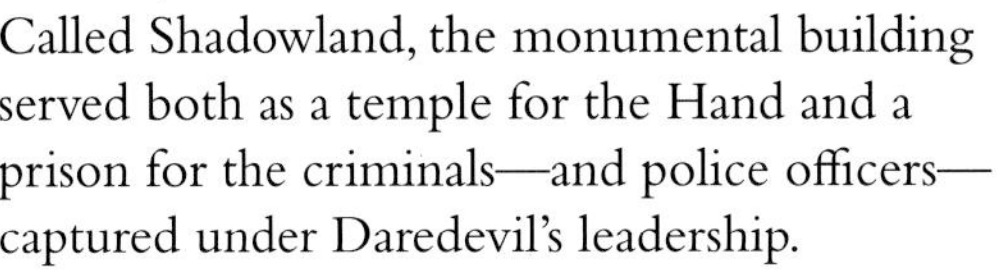

Warned by blind martial artist Master Izo—a former member of the Hand, mentor to Stick, and founder of the Chaste—the heroes stormed Shadowland to save Matt from the Beast's possession. The Beast transformed Daredevil into a devil, giving him supernatural strength and making him virtually unkillable. Iron Fist managed to stop him with a mystical punch of his chi that expelled the Beast from Matt's soul.

Daredevil fought alongside his friends Iron Fist and Luke Cage when he joined the Avengers.

Leaving and Returning

Matt left Hell's Kitchen, but only after asking the Black Panther (T'Challa) to take his place as the neighborhood's protector. After recovering confidence in himself and his mission, Matt returned to Manhattan, moving his law office uptown to Hamilton Heights. Unable to represent clients in court due to his personal notoriety, Matt and his once-again partner Foggy Nelson set up shop as legal consultants. Matt helped defend the Avengers Mansion during Fear Itself, and he joined Luke Cage's team of Avengers afterward. He served with them through their epic battle against the X-Men. **AD, MF**

Dark Reign

When Norman Osborn gained "the keys to the kingdom"

ISSUE #1

The Secret Invasion was at an end and Norman Osborn was now in charge of US security. Osborn called together his Cabal of villains to divvy up the world.

At the end of the Secret Invasion, Norman Osborn (Green Goblin) personally killed the Skrull queen Veranke while leading the Thunderbolts, which he'd been put in charge of during the Civil War. He used the fame to get himself appointed head of national security in the US. He immediately dismantled SHIELD and put himself in charge of a new agency called HAMMER.

Dark Heroes

Osborn forced any of the heroes that might oppose him to flee and hide. Meanwhile, he placed villains with similar powers in their place, forming his own teams of Avengers and X-Men. He also called together some of the most powerful villains in the world to form the Cabal, his answer to the heroes' Illuminati. Meanwhile, he worked with the Hood to sew up control over the organized criminal element in the US.

Osborn took a suit of Iron Man's armor and fashioned it after Captain America's costume. Donning it, he called himself the Iron Patriot, presenting himself as the premier hero for this new era. However, the mental problems that had led Osborn to become the Green Goblin continued to plague him, despite the medications he took for his condition.

THE DARK X-MEN
Norman Osborn replaced the public faces of the X-Men with a team under his control. ***1*** Mimic ***2*** Weapon Omega ***3*** Mystique ***4*** Dark Beast.

The Avengers and their dark analogs were well matched, but the power of both Ares and the Sentry gave Osborn's team the edge. Osborn relied on his status as the Sentry's mentor and confidant (and fellow mental patient) to keep the man under control, making sure the Void didn't emerge to destroy his plans.

The Siege

Loki worked to keep Osborn unstable and convinced him that Asgard—the home of the Norse gods, which had been relocated to float over Broxton, Oklahoma—presented a grave threat to his power. Osborn tried to convince the President to allow him to launch an attack against Asgard but failed. Loki manufactured an incident in which Volstagg of the Warriors Three faced off against the U-Foes in a battle that destroyed Chicago's Soldier Field, killing tens of thousands.

The Sentry destroyed the foundation of Asgard and brought the entire floating city down.

This gave Osborn the excuse he needed to attack Asgard, with or without the President's permission. He sent his Dark Avengers into battle, tricking Ares into leading the charge. When Ares realized he'd been played for a fool, he sought revenge, but on Osborn's orders, the Sentry tore him in half. Steve Rogers (Captain America) returned from his supposed death and led the Avengers to defend Asgard. Furious, Osborn told the Sentry to destroy the place. Iron Man dismantled the Iron Patriot armor by remote, exposing Osborn's face. He had painted his visage to resemble the Green Goblin and was clearly insane. The Sentry had transformed into his evil alter ego, the Void; Iron Man crashed the HAMMER helicarrier into the Void, and Thor finished the Sentry off at his own request, before the Void could return. The Dark Reign was over. MF

When Osborn was defeated, his Green Goblin personality rose again.

The Dark Avengers
With the real Avengers on the run, Norman Osborn replaced them with a team of his own, putting villains in the heroes' costumes—and replacing both Iron Man and Captain America himself.
1 Iron Patriot (Green Goblin)
2 Ms. Marvel (Moonstone)
3 Captain Marvel (Marvel Boy)
4 Ares
5 Hawkeye (Bullseye)
6 Spider-Man (Mac Gargan as Venom)
Not pictured: Daken as Wolverine

Death

FIRST APPEARANCE Captain Marvel #27 (July 1973)
REAL NAME Not applicable
OCCUPATION Embodies principle of mortality **BASE** Mobile
HEIGHT Varies **WEIGHT** Varies **EYES** Vary **HAIR** Varies
SPECIAL POWERS/ABILITIES Often appears as a cowled skeleton, but has adopted various male and female guises; an arch-manipulator; extent of other powers remains unknown.

Just as the being ETERNITY represents life, so Death symbolizes mortality. Although they sometimes play games of one-upmanship (Death once had THANOS try to destroy the universe), they usually work to maintain universal equilibrium. When APOCALYPSE established his Four Horsemen, he recruited a number of people to be Death. WOLVERINE (pictured right) was the third such person. The Apocalypse Twins brought back BANSHEE, DAKEN, GRIM REAPER, and SENTRY to be their Horsemen of Death. **AD, MF**

Deathbird

FIRST APPEARANCE Ms. Marvel #9 (September 1977)
REAL NAME Cal'syee Neramani **OCCUPATION** Adventurer
BASE Shi'ar Empire **HEIGHT** 5 ft 8 in **WEIGHT** 180 lbs
EYES White **HAIR** None; black, purple and blue feathers
SPECIAL POWERS/ABILITIES Flight (18 ft wingspan); vast strength and stamina; razor-sharp talons; wrist-bands contain telescopic javelins; has javelins that emit gas or electric charges.

Deathbird was born a mutant into the ruling house of the alien SHI'AR, her full set of wings a throwback to her avian ancestry. Her younger sister Lilandra, aided by the X-MEN, assumed the Shi'ar throne first, and Deathbird launched several coup attempts to become Majestrix. She eventually won the throne, but her rule was short-lived. She once had a romance with the X-Man BISHOP and also served as WAR, one of Apocalypse's Four Horsemen. She later married VULCAN, who became ruler of the Shi'ar Empire. **AD, MF**

Deathcry

FIRST APPEARANCE Avengers #363 (June 1993)
REAL NAME Sharra Neramani **OCCUPATION** Warrior
BASE The Shi'ar Empire **HEIGHT** 6 ft 2 in **WEIGHT** 196 lbs
EYES White **HAIR** Purple
SPECIAL POWERS/ABILITIES Deathcry possesses super-acute senses, superhuman reflexes, and natural claws which she can use as weapons.

Empress Lilandra of the alien SHI'AR sent Deathcry—the daughter of her sister DEATHBIRD—to help the AVENGERS, fearing they might suffer reprisals by the KREE for helping her during the Kree-Shi'ar War. When Deathcry's mission came to an end, she returned to the Shi'ar Empire. Later, the Kree captured her, releasing her only to help fight the PHALANX. CAPTAIN UNIVERSE accidentally killed her in self-defense, but she returned to life during the CHAOS WAR, calling herself Lifecry. Whether she survived that conflict is unknown. **TB, MF**

Deathlok

DEATHLOK

FACTFILE
REAL NAME
Luther Manning
OCCUPATION
Cyborg supersoldier
BASE Mobile

HEIGHT 6 ft 4 in
WEIGHT 395 lbs
EYES Red
HAIR Gray/brown

FIRST APPEARANCE:
Astonishing Tales #25 (August 1974)

POWERS
Cybernetic brain and body parts enable superhuman strength, endurance, and reactions; Deathlok's special armaments include a dagger and laser pistol.

Luther Manning was born in an alternate timeline in which multinational corporations had used Operation: Purge to rid the Earth of all Super Heroes. A colonel in that world's US Army, Manning was wounded in battle and later transformed into the cyborg Deathlok by brothers Harlan and Simon Ryker. Although they intended to control him, Deathlok somehow managed to break free. With the help of Godwulf, Deathlok was transported to Earth-616, where Operation: Purge had yet to take place. Working with CAPTAIN AMERICA, Deathlok successfully prevented the program from being carried out.

Several other Deathloks have been created from other people, including computer programmer Michael Collins and SIEGE (John Kelly). After an attack on Harlan Ryker's family by cyborgs from the future killed his wife and infant son, Ryker saved his injured teenage daughter Rebecca by transforming her into the cyborg Death Locket. **AD, MF**

Death Locket is still unsure how to control her powers—or whether someone else is.

DEATH'S HEAD

FIRST APPEARANCE The Transformers #113 (May 1987)
REAL NAME Death's Head
OCCUPATION Bounty hunter **BASE** New York City
HEIGHT Varies **WEIGHT** Varies **EYES** Vary **HAIR** Varies
SPECIAL POWERS/ABILITIES Superhumanly strong; able to detach limbs and substitute for weapons; controls limbs even when separated from body; jets in feet enable short-range flight.

Death's Head is a cyborg built by techno-mage Lupex as a shell for his mind. Lupex's plan was ruined by his wife, who activated the cyborg's consciousness. Following an encounter with the Time Lord known as the Doctor, he was dumped in the year 8162 of Earth-5555. Since then, he has visited contemporary Earth-616 many times, jumping among times and dimensions. Death's Head II arose from the parts of the original and lived in Earth-8140. The latest version, Death's Head 3.0, sprang from Earth-6216. **AD, MF**

DE LA FONTAINE, CONTESSA

FIRST APPEARANCE Strange Tales #159 (August 1967)
REAL NAME Valentina Allegra de la Fontaine
OCCUPATION Former secret agent **BASE** Mobile
HEIGHT 5 ft 8 in **WEIGHT** 196 lbs
EYES Blue **HAIR** Black with white streak
SPECIAL POWERS/ABILITIES Superb strategist and hand-to-hand combatant; expert with most types of weapons.

The Contessa caught the eye of Nick FURY by defeating him in hand-to-hand combat during SHIELD training. The two became lovers and teammates, and she later led SHIELD'S Femme Force. At two different times, a SKRULL replaced her temporarily. The Contessa later became the new MADAME HYDRA, pretending to be working for SHIELD as a double agent, but actually serving HYDRA as a triple agent. When Fury stopped her, she turned herself in so they could be reunited. **DW, MF**

DELPHYNE GORGON

FIRST APPEARANCE Incredible Hercules #121 (November, 2008)
REAL NAME Delphyne Gorgon
OCCUPATION Warrior, queen of the Amazons
BASE Amazon nation **HEIGHT** Varies **WEIGHT** Varies
EYES Vary **HAIR** Green snakes
SPECIAL POWERS/ABILITIES Delphyne's hair-snakes have a venom that can blind victims. She is a trained combatant, favoring the sword and the bow.

Delphyne is one of the Gorgons, a race of snake-haired people who interbred with the Amazons and became part of their culture. A great general, she helped Princess Artume in her plot against Queen Hippolyta. When Artume turned against her for showing affection to Amadeus CHO, however, Delphyne was forced to kill Artume, making her the new queen of the Amazons. She later tried to kill Athena for cursing the Gorgons so long ago, but upon failing she was imprisoned in New Tartarus, below the Olympus Group Building. She escaped and reunited with Cho. **MF**

DEFENDERS

The original Defenders were a loose affiliation of heroes who banded together when there was no other option. Other heroes, like HELLCAT and VALKYRIE, wandered in and out of the team over the years, but the group rarely stuck together for long. Under the FIFTY-STATE INITIATIVE, a Defenders team composed of Blazing Skull, COLOSSUS, DARKHAWK, and SHE-HULK guarded New Jersey. Once the Initiative disbanded it, the team reformed with KRANG and HELLSTORM in place of Blazing Skull and Colossus. The GRANDMASTER later brought together the original team to take on the RED HULK's Offenders. Valkyrie also gathered an all-female team called the FEARLESS DEFENDERS, which included Anabelle Riggs, CLEA, Dani MOONSTAR, Elsa BLOODSTONE, Misty KNIGHT, and the resurrected goddess Hippolyta, who called herself Warrior Woman. **TB, MF**

Despite functioning as a "non-team", the Defenders have formed tight bonds.

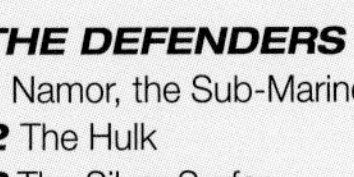

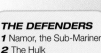

THE DEFENDERS
1 Namor, the Sub-Mariner
2 The Hulk
3 The Silver Surfer
4 Doctor Strange

FACTFILE

KEY MEMBERS

DOCTOR STRANGE
Command of the mystic arts

NAMOR, THE SUB-MARINER
Superhuman strength and durability; ability to fly; ability to breathe air and also survive beneath the ocean waves

HULK
Rampaging monster of almost unlimited strength

SILVER SURFER
Possesses the Power Cosmic one of the fundamental forces of the universe

BASE
The Defenders team usually operates out of Doctor Strange's sanctum in Greenwich Village, New York City

FIRST APPEARANCE
Marvel Feature #1 (December 1971)

Demolition-Man

FIRST APPEARANCE The Thing #28 (October 1985)
REAL NAME Dennis Dunphy **OCCUPATION** Adventurer
BASE New York City **HEIGHT** 6 ft 3 in **WEIGHT** 335 lbs
EYES Blue **HAIR** None **SPECIAL POWERS/ABILITIES** Enhanced strength and endurance, damage resistance; expert wrestler; trained in hand-to-hand combat by Captain America.

Given superhuman strength by the corrupt POWER BROKER, Dennis Dunphy became a pro wrestler, during which time he befriended the THING. He later became CAPTAIN AMERICA's unofficial partner as D-Man and even worked with the AVENGERS. His near brushes with death diminished his confidence, and he struggled with schizophrenia. He joined the REVENGERS to fight the Avengers and went to jail. Later, Henry Peter GYRICH turned him into the new SCOURGE, and Sharon CARTER was forced to kill him to prevent him from murdering Captain America. **DW, MF**

Destiny

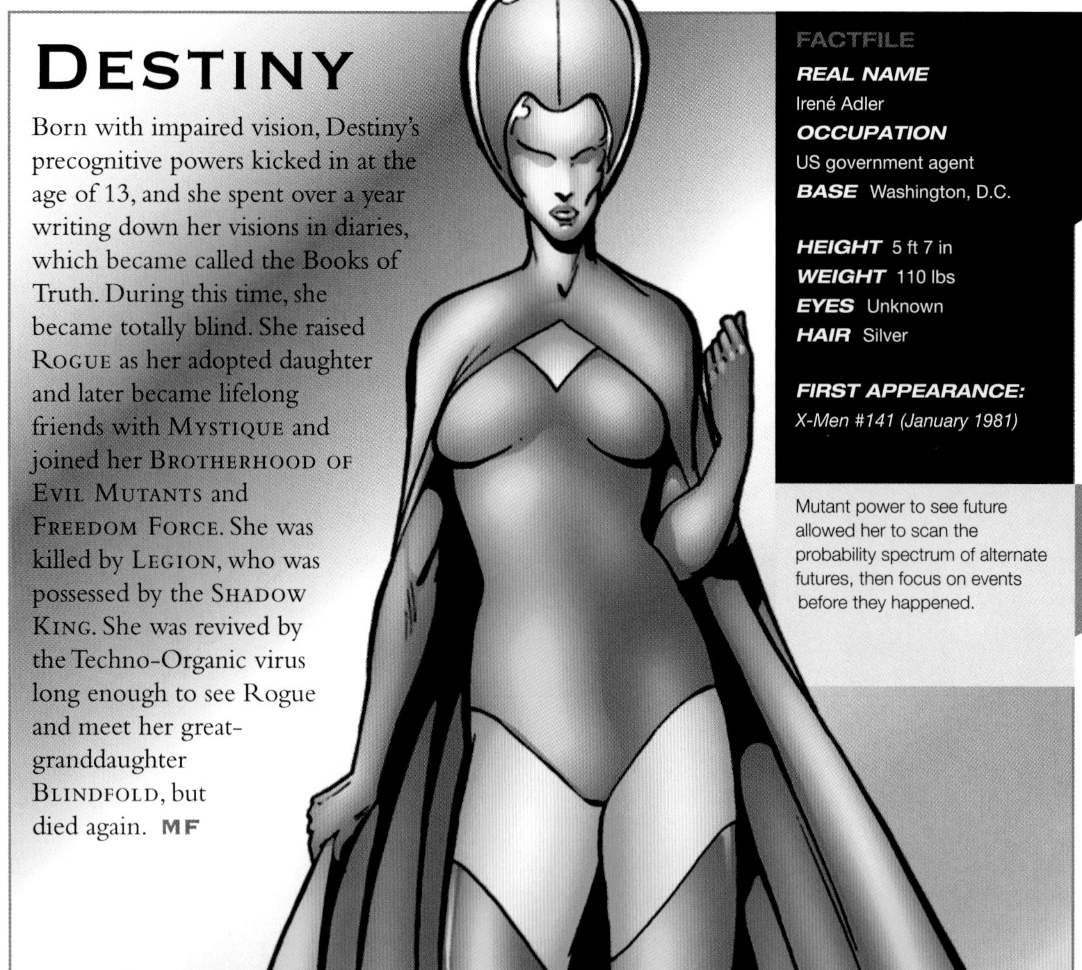

Born with impaired vision, Destiny's precognitive powers kicked in at the age of 13, and she spent over a year writing down her visions in diaries, which became called the Books of Truth. During this time, she became totally blind. She raised ROGUE as her adopted daughter and later became lifelong friends with MYSTIQUE and joined her BROTHERHOOD OF EVIL MUTANTS and FREEDOM FORCE. She was killed by LEGION, who was possessed by the SHADOW KING. She was revived by the Techno-Organic virus long enough to see Rogue and meet her great-granddaughter BLINDFOLD, but died again. **MF**

DESTINY

FACTFILE
REAL NAME
Irené Adler
OCCUPATION
US government agent
BASE Washington, D.C.

HEIGHT 5 ft 7 in
WEIGHT 110 lbs
EYES Unknown
HAIR Silver

FIRST APPEARANCE:
X-Men #141 (January 1981)

POWERS
Mutant power to see future allowed her to scan the probability spectrum of alternate futures, then focus on events before they happened.

Devil Dinosaur

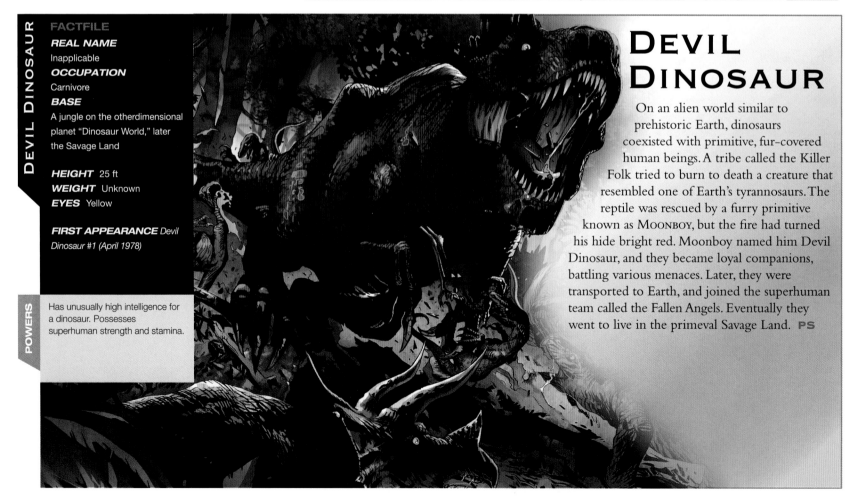

On an alien world similar to prehistoric Earth, dinosaurs coexisted with primitive, fur-covered human beings. A tribe called the Killer Folk tried to burn to death a creature that resembled one of Earth's tyrannosaurs. The reptile was rescued by a furry primitive known as MOONBOY, but the fire had turned his hide bright red. Moonboy named him Devil Dinosaur, and they became loyal companions, battling various menaces. Later, they were transported to Earth, and joined the superhuman team called the Fallen Angels. Eventually they went to live in the primeval Savage Land. **PS**

DEVIL DINOSAUR

FACTFILE
REAL NAME
Inapplicable
OCCUPATION
Carnivore
BASE
A jungle on the otherdimensional planet "Dinosaur World," later the Savage Land

HEIGHT 25 ft
WEIGHT Unknown
EYES Yellow

FIRST APPEARANCE *Devil Dinosaur #1 (April 1978)*

POWERS
Has unusually high intelligence for a dinosaur. Possesses superhuman strength and stamina.

Detroit Steel

FIRST APPEARANCE Invincible Iron Man #25 (June 2010)
REAL NAME Doug Johnson III **OCCUPATION** Soldier, powered armor pilot **BASE** New York City **HEIGHT** 12 ft
WEIGHT 9,000 lbs **EYES** Blue **HAIR** Blond
SPECIAL POWERS/ABILITIES The Detroit Steel armor grants its wearer durability, strength, and flight. It is armed with a Gatling gun and a chainsaw; some models fire energy blasts.

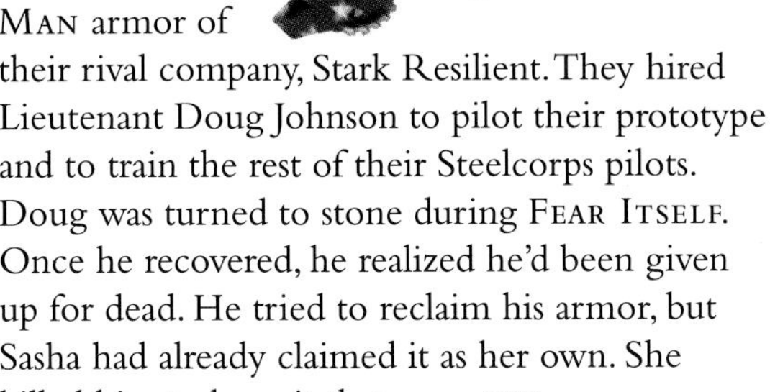

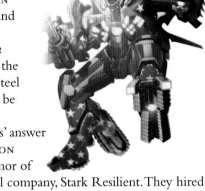

Justine Hammer (Crimson Cowl) and Sasha Hammer designed the Detroit Steel armor to be Hammer Industries' answer to the Iron Man armor of their rival company, Stark Resilient. They hired Lieutenant Doug Johnson to pilot their prototype and to train the rest of their Steelcorps pilots. Doug was turned to stone during Fear Itself. Once he recovered, he realized he'd been given up for dead. He tried to reclaim his armor, but Sasha had already claimed it as her own. She killed him to keep it that way. **MF**

Diablo

FIRST APPEARANCE Fantastic Four #30 (September 1964)
REAL NAME Esteban Corazon de Ablo
OCCUPATION Alchemist **BASE** Mobile **HEIGHT** 6 ft 3in
WEIGHT 190 lbs **EYES** Brown **HAIR** Black
SPECIAL POWERS/ABILITIES Alchemical elixir bestows extended life and vitality. Clothing lined with alchemical potions including a sleeping potion and nerve gas; a master of disguise.

Born into the aristocracy in 9th-century Spain, Diablo became fascinated with the alchemical arts. Realizing that time was against him, Diablo sold his soul to the demon Mephisto in exchange for knowledge. Developing an elixir of life and moving to Transylvania, Diablo spent the next millennia tyrannizing the local villagers, until they rose up, trapping him in a crypt for over a century. Having tricked the Thing into freeing him, Diablo clashed with the Fantastic Four numerous times. He has also clashed with Alpha Flight and Spider-Man. **AD, MF**

Digger

FIRST APPEARANCE The Amazing Spider-Man #51 (May 2003)
REAL NAME None (a combination of 13 mobsters)
OCCUPATION None **BASE** New York City sewers
HEIGHT 7 ft 1 in **WEIGHT** 275 lbs **EYES** Blue **HAIR** None
SPECIAL POWERS/ABILITIES Gamma-powered strength, but limited endurance; possesses the combined consciousnesses of the Vegas Thirteen, with their various 1950s predelictions.

In 1957, a meeting of 13 mobsters in Las Vegas turned nasty, resulting in the deaths of all of them. The bodies of the gangsters, who became known as the Vegas Thirteen, were secretly buried deep in the Nevada desert—a common resting place for Vegas' gangland casualties. Many years later, scientists investigating the effects of gamma rays detonated a gamma bomb in the desert near the site of the grave. Somehow, the bomb's gamma radiation fused the 13 dead mobsters into a huge, powerful, green zombie who called himself Digger. Digger followed some old railroad tracks until he reached New York City. He then started on a mission of vengeance against the Forelli mob, who had bumped off the Vegas Thirteen in the first place. Spider-Man, hired by Forelli to investigate, went to Nevada and figured out that Digger was a gamma-mutated version of the Vegas Thirteen. Back in New York, during a long battle with Spider-Man, Digger eventually broke apart and died. **MT**

Destroyer

FIRST APPEARANCE Journey into Mystery #118 (July 1965)
REAL NAME None **OCCUPATION** Destroyer
BASE Asgard **HEIGHT** 6 ft 2 in (varies)
WEIGHT 850 lbs (varies) **EYES** None **HAIR** None
SPECIAL POWERS/ABILITIES The Destroyer can levitate, generate fire, transmute matter, and shoot a disintegrator beam from its face. It is nearly indestructible.

Odin, the all-father of the Gods of Asgard, created the Destroyer as the ultimate weapon to be used against the Celestials when they returned to Earth to judge it. He and the other all-father gods granted it a portion of their power. It has no soul of its own and must be operated by the life force of another, plunging that person into a coma. Loki unearthed the Destroyer to use against Thor, and others have controlled it since. When used against the Celestials, they nearly destroyed it. Doctor Doom once made his own version. **MF**

Diamondback

FIRST APPEARANCE Captain America #310 (October 1985)
REAL NAME Rachel Leighton **OCCUPATION** SHIELD agent
BASE SHIELD Helicarrier **HEIGHT** 5 ft 11 in
WEIGHT 142 lbs **EYES** Green **HAIR** Brown
SPECIAL POWERS/ABILITIES Expert gymnast; wields diamond-shaped throwing spikes filled with explosives, acid, poison, or drugs.

On Diamondback's first mission with the Serpent Society, she had the opportunity to kill Captain America but chose not to. Eventually, she became his partner and then his lover. Later, Diamondback joined Asp, Black Mamba, and Impala to form a mercenary group called BAD Girls, Inc. She had several run-ins with Crossbones, who abused her both as an adult and in her youth, murdered her brother Willy, and tried to kill her brother Danny. During Dark Reign, she worked for the Secret Avengers and afterward became an agent of SHIELD. **MT, MF**

Doctor Bong

FIRST APPEARANCE Howard the Duck #15 (August 1977)
REAL NAME Lester Verde **OCCUPATION** Genetic engineer
BASE An island in the Atlantic Ocean **HEIGHT** 8 ft 8 in
WEIGHT 225 lbs **EYES** Blue **HAIR** Reddish-brown
SPECIAL POWERS/ABILITIES When struck by the large metal ball he wears on his hand, Doctor Bong's helmet can produce sonic waves for a variety of effects.

Bullied as a youth, Lester Verde became a tabloid journalist to strike back at his foes with his sensational articles. After losing his left hand while covering a rock concert, Lester reinvented himself as Doctor Bong, a villain puffed by his exploits with self-penned press releases. Intent on forcing Beverly Switzler to marry him, Bong was undone by Beverly's boyfriend, Howard the Duck, and by Switzler creating quintuplet clones of him and threatening to expose him as a deadbeat dad. He later battled She-Hulk and faced off against Deadpool, who cut off his prosthetic metal ball hand. **TB, MF**

Doctor Faustus

FIRST APPEARANCE Captain America #107 (November 1968)
REAL NAME Johann Fennhoff
OCCUPATION Psychiatrist, criminal mastermind
BASE New York City
HEIGHT 6 ft 6 in **WEIGHT** 321 lbs **EYES** Blue **HAIR** Red
SPECIAL POWERS/ABILITIES Expert in brainwashing and mind control.

A master psychiatrist, Doctor Faustus specializes in driving people to the brink of suicide and beyond. He clashed often with Captain America, Spider-Man, and the Fantastic Four. He also served as the mentor for Moonstone, schooling her in the arts of manipulation. Presumed dead for years, he cropped up again, this time allied with the Red Skull and posing as a SHIELD psychiatrist. In this position, he brainwashed Sharon Carter into killing Captain America. Faustus held the Captain America of the 1950s in suspended animation for years, releasing him to attack the then-current Captain America (Bucky Barnes). He later testified in court on Barnes' behalf in exchange for clemency. **AD, MF**

Doc Samson

FACTFILE
REAL NAME
Dr. Leonard Samson
OCCUPATION
Psychiatrist
BASE
Mobile

HEIGHT 6 ft 6 in
WEIGHT 380 lbs
EYES Blue
HAIR Green

FIRST APPEARANCE:
Incredible Hulk #141 (July 1971)

POWERS
Gamma-radiation greatly increased Samson's body mass and musculature; he has the equivalent strength of a "relaxed" Hulk, plus great endurance and injury resistance. The gamma rays also turned his hair green. Unlike the Hulk, Samson's razor-sharp mind has been unaffected by the changes in his physiology.

A dedicated psychiatrist, Doctor Leonard Samson was fascinated by gamma radiation's potential to help the mentally ill. When Betty Ross was transformed into a crystalline creature, Samson used a specially developed machine to drain gamma radiation from the Hulk and used it to cure Betty. Later, he exposed himself to the rays and gained Hulk-like powers. Samson doggedly pursued Bruce Banner, hoping to rid him of the Hulk. He also helped treat several others, including Molecule Man, She-Hulk, Rachel Summers, and Multiple Man. He sided with the US government during the Civil War and worked as a therapist at Camp Hammond. He helped the Illuminati send the Hulk into space and fought him when he returned during World War Hulk. Later MODOK brainwashed him into developing an evil secondary personality that was stronger than ever. Samson died helping the Hulk save lives, but was resurrected during the Chaos War. **AD, MF**

Doctor Nemesis

FIRST APPEARANCE Invaders #1 (May 1993)
REAL NAME James Nicola Bradley **OCCUPATION** Inventor
BASE Asgard **HEIGHT** 5 ft 11 in **WEIGHT** 170 lbs
EYES Blue **HAIR** Blond
SPECIAL POWERS/ABILITIES James is a mutant genius who used his gift to grant himself longevity, an enhanced immune system, and cybernetic X-ray eyes.

Two men have used the name Doctor Nemesis. The first was a mutant who helped create the original Human Torch and his own android, Volton. He worked with the Nazis during World War II as Doctor Death but repented and turned to hunting Nazi scientists after the war. He later joined the X-Men to help them figure out how to restore mutantkind after M-Day and then joined Cable's X-Force. The second was Michael Stockton, a size-changing criminal scientist who faced off against Hank Pym and the Avengers. **MF**

Doctor Doom

The Lord of Latveria

Victor von Doom was born in a gypsy camp in the tiny kingdom of Latveria in the Balkan Mountains of Eastern Europe. Victor's mother, Cynthia, was killed when he was an infant. When Victor was a boy, his father Werner, a gypsy healer, failed to save the wife of a Latverian baron from dying of cancer. With Victor, Werner fled the baron's retaliation, only to perish from exposure. Victor vowed vengeance on the world for his parents' deaths.

A mysterious order of Tibetan monks helped Doctor Doom forge the metal mask with which he conceals his hideously scarred features.

FACTFILE

REAL NAME
Victor von Doom

OCCUPATION
Monarch of Latveria

BASE
Doomstadt, Latveria

HEIGHT 6 ft 2 in;
(in armor) 6 ft 7 in

WEIGHT 225 lbs;
(in armor) 415 lbs

EYES Brown

HAIR Brown

FIRST APPEARANCE
Fantastic Four #5
(July 1962)

POWERS

Scientific genius; knowledge of sorcery. Learned from alien Ovoids how to psychically transfer his consciousness into the body of another person. Armor is actually a battlesuit that increases his strength to superhuman levels and contains highly advanced weaponry.

Scarred

Victor discovered Cynthia's chest of magical artifacts and realized that she was a witch. He developed immense talents for sorcery and also science, eventually winning a scholarship to State University in the US. There he first encountered fellow student Reed Richards (*see* MISTER FANTASTIC).

Determined to contact his mother in the hereafter, Doom invented an interdimensional communication device. Richards happened upon Doom's notes and pointed out an error in his calculations. Furious that Richards had invaded his privacy, Doom refused to heed his warning. When Doom activated his machine, it exploded, scarring his face. (According to one account the explosion left only one thin scar; however, Doom's ego could not tolerate a single imperfection in his appearance.)

Doctor Doom led an army of Super Villains on the Beyonder's Battleworld in the first "Secret War."

The Metal Mask

Blaming Richards for the accident, Doom made his way to Tibet, where an order of monks helped him forge the metal mask and armor that he would wear in his new role as Doctor Doom. Donning the newly cast mask before it had fully cooled, Doom scarred his face for life. Returning to Latveria, Doom overthrew the monarch and made himself king.

As ruler of Latveria, Doom has diplomatic immunity to shield him from many laws. In this role, he invented many devices, including an army of Doombots and a time machine. He also adopted a young orphan (Kristoff VERNARD), who steps in to rule when Doom is absent. Doom became part of the CABAL but left over differences with Norman Osborn (*see* GREEN GOBLIN). **PS, MF**

ESSENTIAL STORYLINES

- ***Fantastic Four #5***
Doctor Doom first clashes with the world's greatest team.
- ***Fantastic Four Annual #2***
The origin of Doctor Doom.
- ***Fantastic Four #39–40***
Doctor Doom battles the Fantastic Four without their powers.
- ***Fantastic Four #57–60***
Doom steals the power of the Silver Surfer.
- ***Fantastic Four #84–87***
Doctor Doom traps the Fantastic Four in Latveria.

DR. DRUID

FACTFILE
REAL NAME
Dr. Anthony Ludgate Druid
OCCUPATION
Psychiatrist and master of the occult
BASE Mobile

HEIGHT 6 ft 5 in
WEIGHT 310 lbs
EYES Green
HAIR White

FIRST APPEARANCE
Amazing Adventures #1 (June 1961)

POWERS
Master of the mystical arts; able to control his heartbeat, respiration, bleeding, etc; can undertake telepathy, scan thoughts, control minds of others, and levitate objects.

A powerful sorcerer, Doctor Druid could project images of himself.

DOCTOR DRUID

For many years Harvard-educated Dr. Anthony Druid pursued a career as a psychiatrist, while harboring an interest in all things mystical and occult. Growing older, he began to devote more and more time to this area but it was only when called to the side of a dying Tibetan lama that he started to develop his abilities. After Druid survived a number of trials, the lama helped him to realize his latent potential while conferring upon the psychiatrist some of his own powers.

In the years that followed, Druid was recruited by NSA agent Jake Curtiss to join his team of Monster Hunters, a team that also included Ulysses BLOODSTONE and the Eternal Makkari (*see* ETERNALS). Following the emergence of Super Heroes like the FANTASTIC FOUR, Druid aligned himself with the AVENGERS, becoming a member and helping to drive the MASTERS OF EVIL from Avengers Mansion.

Druid was manipulated into betraying his friends twice. He was held in the thrall of Terminatrix (*see* RAVONNA) and later corrupted by his manipulative lover, NEKRA, who killed him. He was resurrected temporarily during the CHAOS WAR to join the Avengers fighting Nekra and the GRIM REAPER. **AD, MF**

DR. SPECTRUM

FACTFILE
REAL NAME
Joseph Ledger
OCCUPATION
Squadron Supreme member
BASE
Squadron City

HEIGHT 6 ft
WEIGHT 190 lbs
EYES Brown
HAIR Blond

FIRST APPEARANCE
Avengers #85 (March 1971)

POWERS
Internalized power prism allows flight, the discharge of energy blasts, and the ability to construct objects of solid energy.

DOCTOR SPECTRUM

On a parallel Earth in another dimension, astronaut Joe Ledger rescued an alien SKRULL who gave him a power prism. Using the prism's energies to become the heroic Doctor Spectrum, Ledger joined the SQUADRON SUPREME. After the defeat of the villainous OVERMIND, the Squadron Supreme repaired the damage to their world by becoming virtual dictators. A second group of heroes known as Nighthawk's Redeemers formed a resistance movement. One of their number, the Black Archer (formerly the GOLDEN ARCHER), shattered Doctor Spectrum's power prism with an arrow, only to watch as its energies became part of Ledger's own body. Doctor Spectrum no longer needs to rely on an outside source for his powers, and his body has been changed to a monochromatic white. **DW**

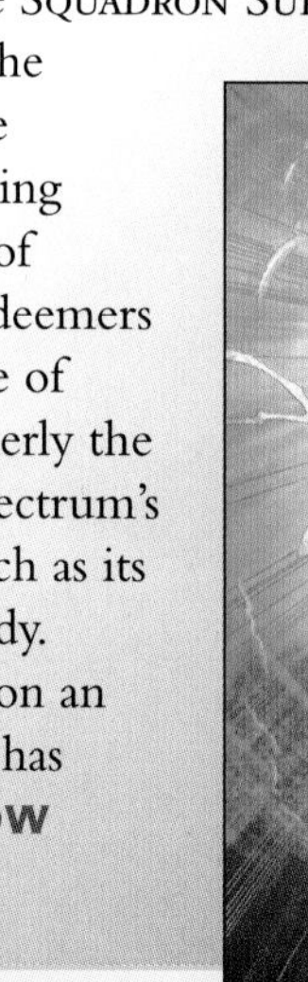

Seen here is Doctor Spectrum in an alternate incarnation.

Various versions of Doctor Spectrum, and other Squadron Supreme members, exist among the parallel Earths that compose the multiverse.

Doctor Octopus

Mastermind of mechanical menace

Otto was the son of Torbert and Mary Lavinia Octavius. He was a shy bookworm, but his father, a construction worker, believed that a man was measured by his brute strength. Mary Lavinia wanted Otto to rely on his brains, and when his father was killed in a construction accident, she convinced herself that an early grave was the destiny of all manual laborers.

Doc Ock can use his tentacles simultaneously, with each one performing a different action.

DR. OCTOPUS

FACTFILE

REAL NAME
Otto Octavius

OCCUPATION
Criminal mastermind, former nuclear scientist

BASE
New York area

HEIGHT 5 ft 9 in
WEIGHT 245 lbs
EYES Brown
HAIR Brown

FIRST APPEARANCE
Amazing Spider-Man #3 (July 1963)

POWERS

Mental control over four electrically powered, 6-ft long, prehensile, titanium steel tentacles that can telescope to 24 ft in length and lift 3 tons; tentacles terminate in three single-jointed pincers that can rotate 360 degrees and grip with a force of 170 lbs per sq in.

ESSENTIAL STORYLINES

- ***Amazing Spider-Man Annual #1*** Octopus forms the Sinister Six to kill Spider-Man.
- ***Spectacular Spider-Man #221*** He appears to be killed by Peter Parker clone Kaine.
- ***Amazing Spider-Man #426*** Doc Ock is restored to life thanks to his protégée Carolyn Trainer.

Tentacles can operate independently

Arm's Length

Otto became a scientist specializing in nuclear research and invented a mechanical harness that allowed him to perform dangerous experiments at a distance. He also began dating Mary Alice Anders, a fellow researcher, and even asked her to marry him. Believing that no woman was good enough for her son, Otto's mother forced him to break off the engagement. Shortly afterward, she died of a heart attack while arguing with her son over Mary Alice. Lost in a private world of grief and guilt, Otto caused a laboratory accident: he was bombarded with radiation and his mechanical arms somehow fused with his body.

Taking over his foe's body, Otto tried to remake himself into a superior man—and Spider-Man!

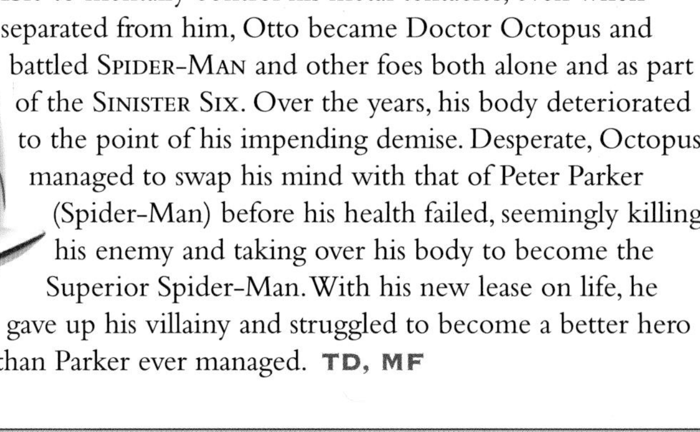

Mind Control

Able to mentally control his metal tentacles, even when separated from him, Otto became Doctor Octopus and battled Spider-Man and other foes both alone and as part of the Sinister Six. Over the years, his body deteriorated to the point of his impending demise. Desperate, Octopus managed to swap his mind with that of Peter Parker (Spider-Man) before his health failed, seemingly killing his enemy and taking over his body to become the Superior Spider-Man. With his new lease on life, he gave up his villainy and struggled to become a better hero than Parker ever managed. **TD, MF**

DOCTOR STRANGE

Sorcerer Supreme of Earth's dimension

DOCTOR STRANGE

FACTFILE

REAL NAME
Dr. Stephen Vincent Strange

OCCUPATION
Former surgeon, now Sorcerer Supreme of Earth's dimension

BASE
177A Bleecker St., Greenwich Village, Manhattan

HEIGHT 6 ft 2 in
WEIGHT 180 lbs
EYES Gray
HAIR Black; white at temples

FIRST APPEARANCE
Strange Tales #110
(July 1963)

POWERS

Greater mastery of the arts of magic than anyone else in Earth's dimension; astral projection and mental communication. Possesses various magical paraphernalia, including cloak of levitation which enables him to fly, and amulet the Eye of Agamotto.

According to the original account, Doctor Stephen Strange was a highly successful but arrogant surgeon whose brilliant career was abruptly cut short by an automobile accident. Strange suffered minor nerve damage, which prevented him from holding a scalpel steadily enough to perform surgery. Exhausting his fortune searching in vain for a cure, Strange ended up an alcoholic derelict.

The Ancient One not only instructed Stephen Strange in sorcery, but advised and guided him.

ANCIENT WISDOM

Strange journeyed to Tibet to meet a healer known as the ANCIENT ONE. Initially, Strange, a man of science, refused to believe in the magic powers that the Ancient One claimed to have. However, Strange discovered the Ancient One's pupil BARON MORDO intended to murder his master. Mordo cast a spell on Strange that prevented him from uttering a warning to the Ancient One, but otherwise allowed him to speak. Not only did Strange now know that magic was real, but he also recognized the existence of evil and realized that it must be fought. Evading the restrictions of Mordo's spell, Strange asked the Ancient One if he could become his pupil. The Ancient One freed Strange from Mordo's spell, revealed that he was well aware of Mordo's treachery, and accepted Strange as his new apprentice.

Strange has long been associated with the Defenders, including Hellcat, the Hulk, Nighthawk, and the Sub-Mariner.

SORCERER SUPREME

Upon completing his training, Doctor Strange lived in New York City's Greenwich Village although the general population was unaware of his role or that he had devoted his life to protecting humanity from supernatural menaces from our own world and mystic realms, such as his enemies Mordo, NIGHTMARE and DORMAMMU. When the Ancient One died, Doctor Strange inherited his role as Sorcerer Supreme of Earth and the dimension in which it exists.

Doctor Strange co-founded the DEFENDERS and the ILLUMINATI and often helps the AVENGERS. Because of his use of dark magic during desperate times, Strange temporarily lost his position as the Sorcerer Supreme. BROTHER VOODOO assumed the mantle during that time, but after his death Strange proved he could handle black magic without losing control and won back his title. **PS, MF**

ESSENTIAL STORYLINES
- ***Strange Tales #130–146*** Doctor Strange battles Baron Mordo and Dormammu and first meets Eternity
- ***Strange Tales #150–168*** Doctor Strange first combats Umar and encounters the Living Tribunal.
- ***Doctor Strange (Vol. 2) #1–2, 4–5*** Doctor Strange battles Silver Dagger, dies and is resurrected.

Domino

FIRST APPEARANCE X-Force #8 (March 1992)
REAL NAME Neena Thurman (many aliases include "Beatrice")
OCCUPATION Covert operative **BASE** Mobile
HEIGHT 5 ft 8 in **WEIGHT** 196 lbs
EYES Blue **HAIR** Black
SPECIAL POWERS/ABILITIES Able to influence the laws of probability to shift odds in her favor; weapons expert; her staff fires projectiles; a superb athlete, martial artist, and linguist.

A career mercenary during her early adult life, it was only after being employed as a bodyguard to the genius Milo Thurman that the mutant Domino became drawn into more official circles. She and Milo fell in love, only to be separated when an attack by AIM terrorists forced Milo into deeper cover. Believing that Milo was dead, Domino joined Six-Pack and became an ally of Cable. For a while she was impersonated by Copycat. Domino has since served with X-Factor, worked for the Hong Kong branch of X-Corporation and fought alongside the X-Men. She is now a member of Cable's X-Force. **AD**

Dominus

FIRST APPEARANCE Uncanny X-Men #21 (June 1966)
REAL NAME Dominus **OCCUPATION** World conqueror
BASE New York City **HEIGHT** Several stories
WEIGHT Several tons **EYES** n/a **HAIR** n/a
SPECIAL POWERS/ABILITIES Supercomputer controlling many minions.

The alien race called the Arcane built Dominus to help them conquer planet after planet. On Earth, the Arcane's agent Lucifer planned to use Dominus to further the Arcane's plans to take over the planet, although it required a small army of robots to keep it in operating condition. The X-Men destroyed the robots, rendering Dominus useless. Dominus later gained sentience, took command of the Arcane and, protected by an army of 50 minions, tried again to conquer Earth. The Avengers defeated Dominus's forces, and the supercomputer escaped into outer space. **MF**

Donovan, Milla

FIRST APPEARANCE Daredevil #41 (March 2003)
REAL NAME Milla Donovan
OCCUPATION Works for Hell's Kitchen Housing Commission
BASE New York City **HEIGHT** 5 ft 8 in **WEIGHT** 130 lbs
EYES White **HAIR** Black
SPECIAL POWERS/ABILITIES None

Born blind, Milla Donovan never saw the truck barreling down on her when she crossed the street, but Daredevil saved her at the last second. To thank him, she tracked him down as Matt Murdock and asked him on a date. Their romance led them to be married, but Milla soon discovered Matt that might have been suffering from a nervous breakdown following the murder of his previous girlfriend, Karen Page. Driven mad by a fear gas, she became a residential patient at the Broadmoor Clinic. Milla's parents blamed Matt and the marriage was anulled. **MF**

Dormammu

Although a member of the Faltine race, Dormammu has spent most of his life in the Dark Dimension, where his people had banished him. Following his arrival there, Dormammu allied himself to the Dark Dimension's ruler, Olnar, showing him how to expand his realm by absorbing other pocket universes into it. Inadvertently, this was to precipitate Dormammu's rise to power. One of these universes was occupied by the Mindless Ones, destructive beings that, once released in the Dark Dimension, began to wreak havoc. Before they were finally stopped, Olnar was killed and Dormammu had been named regent.

FACTFILE
REAL NAME
Dormammu
OCCUPATION
Sometime ruler of the Dark Dimension
BASE
Dark Dimension

HEIGHT 6 ft 1 in
WEIGHT Unknown
EYES Green
HAIR Black

FIRST APPEARANCE
Strange Tales #126 (November 1964)

POWERS
One of the most powerful mystical beings in the universe; can teleport between dimensions, alter his size, travel in time, and perform telepathy.

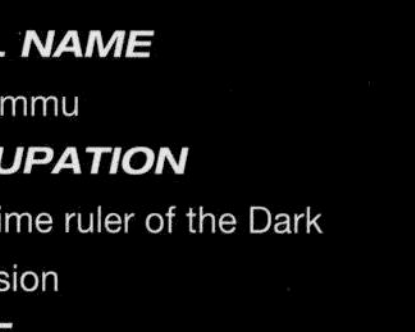

Flames blazing from every limb, Dormammu is a fearsome being.

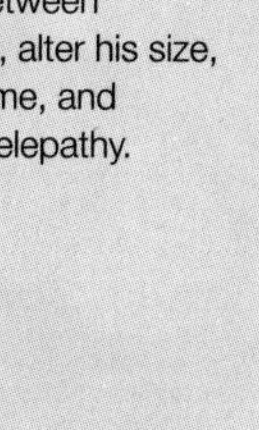

Dormammu set his sights on conquering Earth but the Ancient One and, later, Doctor Strange and his heroic friends foiled him, trapping him in a pocket universe for a time. He often works by proxy and, for instance, granted the Hood his powers. He later took over Limbo and commanded that, too. His niece Clea ruled the Dark Dimension in his absence and led the resistance against his reclaimed governance. **AD, MF**

Only Doctor Strange stands in the way of Dormammu's domination of the Dark Dimension and a strike against the Earth itself.

DRACULA

The most powerful vampire on Earth

DRACULA

FACTFILE
REAL NAME
Vlad Tepes Dracula
OCCUPATION
Ruler of Earth's vampires
BASE
Castle Dracula, Transylvania; otherwise mobile

HEIGHT 6 ft 5 in
WEIGHT 220 lbs
EYES Red
HAIR Black

FIRST APPEARANCE
Tomb of Dracula #1 (April 1972)

POWERS
Drains blood from victims by biting, enabling him to control their wills. Those who die become vampires. Has superhuman strength, virtual immortality, and cannot be killed by conventional means. Transforms into a bat, wolf, or mist. Can mentally control other vampires and mesmerize human beings.

Vlad Tepes Dracula was born in 1430 in Schassberg, Transylvania. The following year his father, the Transylvanian nobleman Vlad Dracul, became prince of nearby Wallachia. Dracula's father was later assassinated by other Transylvanians. Dracula nevertheless went through with the marriage his father had arranged with Zofia, a Hungarian noblewoman. After the birth of their daughter, Dracula put an end to their marriage. Zofia committed suicide; her daughter would become the vampiress LILITH.

THE IMPALER

Dracula regained the throne of Wallachia in 1456 and had those responsible for his father's assassination impaled. He then fought a war with the Turks, during which he impaled huge numbers of them. Hence Dracula became known as "Vlad the Impaler." Dracula married his second wife, Maria, who bore him a son, Vlad Tepelus.

In 1459, Dracula was defeated in battle by the Turkish warlord Turac, who mortally wounded him. Turac took Dracula to the gypsy healer Lianda, who proved to be a vampiress and bit and killed Dracula, transforming him into a vampire. After Turac murdered Maria, Dracula slew him and turned his son Vlad Tepelus over to the care of gypsies. By defeating the vampire Nimrod, Dracula took his place as the ruler of Earth's vampires. The eldest vampire on Earth, VARNAE, enhanced Dracula's blood with his own before killing himself. As a result Dracula became the most powerful vampire on the planet.

Dracula's most persistent modern adversaries were (from left to right) the team of Quincy Harker, Frank Drake, Rachel Van Helsing, and Blade.

KING OF THE VAMPIRES

In 1890, Dracula moved to England but ran afoul of vampire hunter Abraham Van Helsing and his friends, who pursued him as he fled back to Transylvania and seemingly killed him. However, Dracula has repeatedly returned from death. In modern times, Dracula's main foes have been Quincy Harker (the son of two of his old enemies in the UK), Rachel VAN HELSING (Abraham's descendant), Frank DRAKE (Dracula's own descendant), the vampire hunter BLADE, the vampire detective Hannibal KING, and the monster hunter Elsa BLOODSTONE.

Dracula, along with all the other vampires on Earth, was destroyed when DOCTOR STRANGE cast the Montesi Formula. He returned to form a vampire colony on the moon and attempted to conquer the UK. His son XARUS later slew him, but the X-MEN revived him to exact his revenge. **PS, MF**

ESSENTIAL STORYLINES
- ***Dracula Lives #2–3*** How Count Dracula first became a vampire.
- ***Tomb of Dracula #64–70*** Dracula becomes human again. After regaining his powers, Dracula and Quincy Harker die in their final confrontation.
- ***X-Men: Curse of the Mutants Saga*** Dracula's son Xarus kills him and then goes after the X-Men, who revive him to help save the world.

Dragon Man

FIRST APPEARANCE Fantastic Four #1 (February 1965)
REAL NAME Dragon Man
OCCUPATION None **BASE** Mobile
HEIGHT 15 ft 3 in **WEIGHT** 3.2 tons **EYES** Gray **HAIR** None
SPECIAL POWERS/ABILITIES Possesses colossal natural strength. He can exhale flame from his mouth, and his gigantic wings enable him to fly.

An artificial lifeform created by Professor Gregson Gilbert of State University and brought to life by Diablo the alchemist, Dragon Man has the intelligence of a dog. He has been used as a pawn by various Super Villains, including Diablo himself, the wealthy industrialist Gregory Gideon, and Machinesmith. But Dragon Man is not evil himself—he operates strictly by animal instinct. The Fantastic Four have often tried to help Dragon Man, and Mister Fantastic upgraded him so he could join the Future Foundation. **TB, MF**

Dragon of the Moon

FIRST APPEARANCE The New Defenders #143 (May 1985)
REAL NAME Unrevealed **OCCUPATION** Demon
BASE Mobile **HEIGHT** Unknown **WEIGHT** Unknown
EYES Red **SCALES** Dark blue
SPECIAL POWERS/ABILITIES The Dragon is a virtually immortal, demonic entity with god-like powers; able to influence other beings to commit evil deeds.

The Dragon psychically bonded itself to Moondragon.

A billion-year-old demonic being, the Dragon of the Moon seeks to corrupt the human race. The Dragon once allied with Mordred, who was trying to overthrow King Arthur Pendragon of Britain. It was defeated and imprisoned within Saturn's moon Titan by the Eternals. It also corrupted Moondragon, whom Ultron killed. Later, Phyla-Vell (*see* Quasar) entered Oblivion to free Moondragon and destroy the Dragon. **TD, MF**

Drake, Frank

FIRST APPEARANCE Tomb of Dracula #1 (April 1972)
REAL NAME Frank Drake
OCCUPATION Private Investigator; former vampire hunter
BASE Boston, Massachusetts
HEIGHT 6 ft **WEIGHT** 165 lbs **EYES** Blue **HAIR** Blond
SPECIAL POWERS/ABILITIES Adept at hand-to-hand fighting and a fair marksman.

A distant descendent of Dracula, Frank Drake's life was dogged by his vampiric ancestor. After frittering his considerable inheritance away, all Drake had left was his family's castle in Transylvania. Traveling there with the aim of selling up, Drake accidentally resurrected Dracula. The following years were marked by a series of battles against the undead fiend. He fought alongside many other vampire hunters, including Blade, Rachel Van Helsing, and Quincy Harker. He tried to retire but returned to the fight with a nanotech gun he called Linda. The he overloaded to destroy the vampire lord Varnae, nearly killing himself in the process. **AD, MF**

Drax the Destroyer

Mentor, the powerful Titanian, had been monitoring the reckless actions of his mad son Thanos on Earth. When Thanos destroyed a car containing Arthur Douglas and his wife and daughter, Mentor took Douglas's daughter Heather, who was still alive, back to Titan to be raised. She would later return to Earth as Moondragon. Then, with the aid of his father, Chronos, Mentor took the living consciousness of Arthur Douglas before it had completely left his body and placed it into a humanoid body he had created from the Earth's soil, granting it superhuman powers. This new being was known as Drax the Destroyer. Mentor blocked all of Douglas's human memories and instilled in him a single-minded desire to destroy Thanos. Drax clashed with Thanos several times, both of them dying on occasion and being resurrected. Eventually, Drax learned who he was and reunited with Moondragon, and he and his daughter fought alongside each other through the Annihilation events. Today, Drax is part of the new Guardians of the Galaxy. **MT, MF**

Drax pauses after his latest session of carnage, plotting the next steps in his all-consuming quest to completely destroy Thanos.

FACTFILE
REAL NAME
Arthur Douglas
OCCUPATION
Former real estate agent; agent of Chronos
BASE
Titan

HEIGHT 6 ft 4 in
WEIGHT 680 lbs
EYES Red
HAIR None

FIRST APPEARANCE
Iron Man #55 (February 1973)

DRAX THE DESTROYER

POWERS
Cosmic energy gives him superhuman strength, invulnerability, the ability to fly and make interplanetary voyages in a matter of weeks. He can survive for an indefinite time in outer space without air, food, or water. He fires concussive blasts from his hands.

Dreadknight

FIRST APPEARANCE Iron Man #101 (August 1977)
REAL NAME Bram Velsing
OCCUPATION Engineer; vengeful vigilante **BASE** Mobile
HEIGHT 5 ft 8 in **WEIGHT** 160 lbs **EYES** Red **HAIR** None
SPECIAL POWERS/ABILITIES High-tech suit of armor protects him from attack. Within his arsenal are a lance containing a number of offensive weapons, and a nerve-gas pistol.

Born in Latveria, Bram Velsing was a skilled engineer, carrying out the schemes of DOCTOR DOOM. As punishment for an act of disobedience, Doom had an iron mask fused to Velsing's face, so that he would know what it meant to be Doom. Fleeing Latveria, Velsing took refuge in the castle of Victor Frankenstein. Calling himself Dreadknight, armed with his own inventions, and riding a winged horse that once belonged to the BLACK KNIGHT, he vowed to take revenge on his former master—no matter how many innocent people got hurt along the way. **TB**

Dreadnought

FIRST APPEARANCE Strange Tales #154 (May 1940)
REAL NAME Dreadnought
OCCUPATION Weapons system **BASE** New York State
HEIGHT 8 ft **WIDTH** 40 in **WEIGHT** 2,200 lbs
SPECIAL POWERS/ABILITIES Portable fusion generator ensures 1.5 years of continuous use; travels at 35 mph; lifts up to 10 tons; armed with flamethrower, knuckle spikes, and electrical field.

A robotic juggernaut, the Dreadnought was built by the terror group HYDRA, but its first field trial proved unsuccessful: directed to kill Nick FURY, the SHIELD director's resourcefulness, combat training and arsenal of miniaturized weaponry combined to overwhelm the automaton. This wasn't the end of the machine, however; when the MAGGIA crime family stole the Dreadnought blueprints, eight more of these machines were built, the most sophisticated being a silver version of the robot. The MANDARIN later used updated Dreadnoughts designed by Ezekiel STANE to attack the Three Gorges Dam in China. In each case, Super Heroes like IRON MAN, SPIDER-MAN, and the FANTASTIC FOUR stopped the robots. **AD, MF**

Dreamqueen

Eight hundred years ago, NIGHTMARE, ruler of the dream dimension, captured a succubus called Zhilla Char, mated with her, and then confined her in a pocket dimension. Zhilla Char was consumed by flames while giving birth to her daughter, the Dreamqueen. Three hundred and fifty years ago the astral self of Native American shaman Nanquato traveled into the Dreamqueen's realm in search of the sky gods that could save his tribe from drought. Believing the Dreamqueen to be a sky god, Nanquato accepted a totem from her. Through this totem, the Dreamqueen terrified Nanquato's tribe with hallucinations, as a means to escape to Earth. But her plan was thwarted when Nanquato's tribesmen slew the shaman and buried the totem.

In recent years, the mutant Laura Dean visited the Dreamqueen's dimension, which Dean named "Liveworld." The Canadian Super Hero team ALPHA FLIGHT inadvertently traveled to Liveworld, and when they returned to Earth, the Dreamqueen came with them. However, Alpha Flight's Puck and Laura Dean succeeded in forcing her back to Liveworld.

By afflicting Alpha Flight with nightmares, the Dreamqueen escaped to Earth, where she took control of the minds of the people of the Canadian city of Edmonton. But Alpha Flight's sorceress TALISMAN defeated her and drove her from Earth. Still later, the Dreamqueen sided with Alpha Flight against their enemy, the Master. **PS**

FACTFILE
REAL NAME
Unrevealed
OCCUPATION
Ruler of Liveworld
BASE
The dimension of Liveworld

HEIGHT Variable, normally 6 ft 3 in
WEIGHT Variable
EYES White
HAIR Green

FIRST APPEARANCE
Alpha Flight #57 (April 1988)

POWERS
Wields virtually unlimited magical abilities, including the ability to create living beings, but only when she is in Liveworld. In or out of Liveworld, she can mentally control the minds and the perceptions of other beings, and cause them to experience hallucinations.

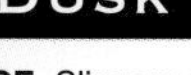

Drew, Jonathan

FIRST APPEARANCE Spider-Woman #1 (April 1978)
REAL NAME Jonathan Drew **OCCUPATION** Scientist
BASE Wundagore City **HEIGHT** 6 ft 2 in
WEIGHT 196 lbs **EYES** Blue **HAIR** Black
SPECIAL POWERS/ABILITIES Brilliant scientist who specializes in radiation and entomology—the study of spiders and insects.

Geneticists Jonathan and Miriam Drew moved to Wundagore Mountain to work with Miles Warren and Dr. Herbert Wyndham. Funded by Hydra, they researched how spiders might be used to enhance human DNA. While pregnant, Miriam was accidentally struck by a laser laced with spider DNA. This affected her unborn daughter, who grew up to be Jessica Drew, the first Spider-Woman. Jonathan left his wife and daughter and continued his research until Jessica caught up with him years later. Madame Hydra killed him when he refused to abandon his research and Jessica. **MF**

D'spayre

FIRST APPEARANCE Marvel Team-Up #68 (April 1978)
REAL NAME Unknown **OCCUPATION** Demonic being
BASE Extradimensional tower **HEIGHT** 6 ft 3 in
WEIGHT Unknown **EYES** Black **HAIR** None
SPECIAL POWERS/ABILITIES Enhanced strength; able to levitate; able to instill fear into other beings; various other unrevealed magical abilities.

D'spayre is an extradimensional demon created by another demon, the Dweller-in-Darkness. He feeds off the psychic energy of suffering. D'spayre has teamed with Nightmare, and is attended by a horde of small servant-beings, the D'sprites. One of D'spayre's first clashes with Super Heroes took place in the Florida Everglades, where he was defeated by Spider-Man and Man-Thing. He has since fought Cyclops and Doctor Strange, and served as a member of the Fear Lords, an alliance of demons. **DW**

Dusk

FIRST APPEARANCE Slingers #0 (December 1998)
REAL NAME Cassie St. Commons **OCCUPATION** Adventurer
BASE New York City **HEIGHT** 5 ft 6 in **WEIGHT** 125 lbs
EYES Blue **HAIR** Black
SPECIAL POWERS/ABILITIES Receives power from the Negative Zone allowing her to melt into shadows or to teleport; possesses minor psychic abilities.

During a time when Spider-Man was accused of murder, he adopted four separate costumes and identities, including one called Dusk. Later, former World War II hero Black Marvel gave the costumes to four youths to create the Slingers. Cassie St. Commons, a moody Empire State University student from a rich family, became the new Dusk. After what seemed a fatal fall, she returned with the power of teleportation. The Slingers disbanded after saving Black Marvel's soul from Mephisto, and Dusk has since kept a low profile. **DW**

Drew, Patience

FIRST APPEARANCE Marvel Fanfare #43 (April 1989)
REAL NAME Unknown **OCCUPATION** Pirate Captain
BASE Sargasso Sea **HEIGHT** Unknown **WEIGHT** Unknown
EYES Blue **HAIR** Black
SPECIAL POWERS/ABILITIES Skilled in the use of sabres, swords, and pistols, and other weapons of her time. Possessed the same skills in death.

Patience Drew was a pirate captain who lived several hundred years ago. She and her crew were killed by a British ship which led them into a trap during battle. After they sunk into the Sargasso Sea, they were doomed to experience their deaths forever. Namor rescued Drew and her ship on one of these occasions and the pair fell in love. Namor joined Drew as a pirate and she gave him an earring to remember her by. Later, Namor left her ship and never returned—despite still wearing her earring, he found her skeleton on the seabed and was uncertain whether he had ever known her. **ED**

Dugan, Dum Dum

FIRST APPEARANCE Sgt. Fury and his Howling Commandos #1 (May 1963) **REAL NAME** Timothy Aloysius Cadwallader Dugan
OCCUPATION Ex-SHIELD agent
BASE New York City **HEIGHT** 6 ft 2 in
WEIGHT 196 lbs **EYES** Blue **HAIR** Black
SPECIAL POWERS/ABILITIES Expert boxer, wrestler, marksman, and commando.

In 1941, while touring Europe as a circus strongman, the Boston-born Dugan met Nick Fury, who was on a covert rescue mission. Later, the pair became part of Fury's military strike force, the Howling Commandos. When Fury was appointed to head SHIELD, Dugan joined him. At one point, Dugan retired, but he rejoined after Hydra killed his wife. During the Secret Invasion, a Skrull replaced him. He returned to set up the Howling Commandos as a private consultancy, helping Fury off the record. When Captain America re-formed SHIELD, Dugan returned to active duty. **MF**

Echo

FIRST APPEARANCE Daredevil #9 (December 1999)
REAL NAME Maya Lopez
OCCUPATION Adventurer, performance artist
BASE Los Angeles, California **HEIGHT** 5 ft 9 in
WEIGHT 125 lbs **EYES** Brown **HAIR** Black
SPECIAL POWERS/ABILITIES Echo can mimic any physical action she sees, making her an incredible acrobat and combatant.

Maya was born deaf. Her Cheyenne father worked with the KINGPIN, who killed him but honored the man's dying request to raise his daughter. When Maya was grown, Kingpin told her that DAREDEVIL had murdered her father, and he also encouraged her to date Matt Murdock, Daredevil's alter ego. While hunting Daredevil, Maya realized who he was and spared him. She shot the Kingpin in the face in revenge. She later became an AVENGER as Ronin, an identity she handed over to HAWKEYE. COUNT NEFARIA killed her while she was working with MOON KNIGHT. **MF**

Ecstasy

FIRST APPEARANCE Doctor Strange #74 (December 1985)
REAL NAME Renée Deladier
OCCUPATION Drug kingpin **BASE** Marseilles, France
HEIGHT 5 ft 9 in **WEIGHT** 130 lbs **EYES** Green **HAIR** Blond
SPECIAL POWERS/ABILITIES Formerly possessed the ability to project semi-solid tentacles of darkness, or to absorb beings into the Darkforce dimension.

Ecstasy, who can wield tendrils of Darkforce energy, proves more than a match for the light-generating heroine Dagger.

Renée Deladier, who headed up a French cartel distributing the drug ecstasy, adopted the drug's name as her alias. The vigilante CLOAK tried to punish her by absorbing her into the Darkforce dimension, but instead the sentience inhabiting the Darkforce selected Ecstasy to be its new agent, and absorbed Cloak instead, transferring his powers to Ecstasy. DOCTOR STRANGE came to Cloak's assistance, and with the help of the Eye of Agamotto, Cloak was able to defeat Ecstasy and regain his powers. **DW**

Eel

FIRST APPEARANCE Strange Tales #112 (October 1963)
REAL NAME Leopold Stryke **OCCUPATION** Criminal
BASE New York City **HEIGHT** 5 ft 10 in **WEIGHT** 192 lbs
EYES Brown **HAIR** Brown
SPECIAL POWERS/ABILITIES The Eel's costume contains devices that generate and shoot electrical charges; also contains layer of nearly frictionless synthetic fabric.

Leopold Stryke was the curator of an aquarium who turned to crime as the Eel. After being defeated by the HUMAN TORCH, he worked as henchman for Mister Fear and COUNT NEFARIA. He later joined his brother Jordan, the VIPER, in the Serpent Squad. Stryke was eventually killed by GLADIATOR. Lavell became the second Eel, battling heroes as well as villains like HAMMERHEAD and MISTER HYDE. He was pressed into the Thunderbolt Army for a while, and he later joined SIN's new Serpent Squad. **PS, MF**

EGGHEAD

FACTFILE
REAL NAME
Elihas Starr
OCCUPATION
Criminal; scientist
BASE
New York City

HEIGHT 5 ft 7 in
WEIGHT 210 lbs
EYES Blue
HAIR None

FIRST APPEARANCE
Tales to Astonish #38 (December 1962)

POWERS
Egghead created machines to enable communication with ants, powerful robots, and mind-controlling, prosthetic limbs; prone to delusions of grandeur and obsessed with destroying rival Henry Pym.

A brilliant scientist, Elihas Starr—or Egghead as he was known because of his unusually-shaped head—lacked a conscience and was prone to boredom. Seeking extra excitement, Egghead had been working for the US government when he was sacked for stealing and selling secrets.

Coming to the attention of the New York mobs, Egghead was contracted to rid them of the original Ant-Man, otherwise known as Henry PYM. In the years that followed, the pair were to become arch-enemies. Egghead's strenuous efforts to destroy Ant-Man involved a range of intriguing devices: he built a machine to communicate with ants and persuaded them to turn against Pym, and on another occasion, he developed a bionic arm designed to control the thoughts of Pym's niece.

Although he appeared fairly harmless, Egghead was responsible for the destruction of an entire Mid-western town, an incident that brought him into direct conflict with the AVENGERS. As time went on, Egghead's schemes became ends in themselves: the more complex and convoluted they were, the happier he seemed to be. Had it not been for a gun exploding in his face, Egghead's schemings would probably have continued. Instead, the accident brought to an end both his life and his latest attempt to destroy Henry Pym's reputation. **AD**

I HAD TO BREAK OUT OF JAIL! I MUST MAKE GIANT-MAN PAY FOR THE INDIGNITY OF BEAT-ING ME --A MAN WHO IS MANY TIMES HIS MENTAL SUPERIOR!!

So much did he hate Harry Pym, nothing would stop Egghead from trying to get revenge—not even the prison bars.

A robot named Egghead joined the Young Masters.

Ego the Living Planet

EGO THE LIVING PLANET

FACTFILE

REAL NAME
Ego

OCCUPATION
Not applicable

BASE
Mobile

DIAMETER 4,165 miles

FIRST APPEARANCE
Thor #132 (September 1966)

POWERS
Vast intelligence and psionic powers, including telepathy and telekinesis; travels through space faster than light and can change its surface appearance.

Ego is a self-aware planet, one of two such sentient creatures the STRANGER made as part of an experiment. About the size of a small moon, Ego hails from the Black Galaxy, where it created armies of superhuman warriors from its own substance and sent them out to conquer other worlds. During a battle with GALACTUS, THOR sided with Ego at first, but the thunder god later realized Ego's evil intentions when it attacked Earth, and he battled it alongside Galactus, HERCULES, and Firelord.

Eventually, Ego's size was condensed and contained within the body of QUASAR (Wendell Vaughn). When Vaughn died, Ego was freed. It took over the Nova Corps and brainwashed its members until NOVA lobotomized it. Ego healed from this soon, however, and fled before Nova could harm him again. Ego later discovered his sibling planet, Alter-Ego, which the COLLECTOR had imprisoned since their creation as part of the Stranger's experiment to see whether captivity or freedom would make a creature stronger. Thor kept Ego from killing Alter-Ego, and Alter-Ego became a moon of Ego, orbiting it as they traveled together. **MT, MF**

After their battle, Ego and Alter-Ego became a family.

ELECTRO, *see page 120*

ELEKTRA, *see page 121*

Empath

FIRST APPEARANCE New Mutants #16 (June 1984)
REAL NAME Manuel Alfonso Rodrigo de la Rocha
OCCUPATION Student **BASE** Massachusetts Academy, Snow Valley, Massachusetts **HEIGHT** 5 ft 11 in
WEIGHT 160 lbs **EYES** Black **HAIR** Light brown
SPECIAL POWERS/ABILITIES Able to manipulate the emotions and feelings of those around him. His powers can be used on one individual or a crowd.

As a member of the HELLIONS, Empath studied under Emma FROST, then the White Queen of the HELLFIRE CLUB. He later fell in love with MAGMA of the NEW MUTANTS and used his powers to make her reciprocate. Long after they broke up, they worked together for the X-Corporation in Los Angeles. Empath's powers survived M-Day, and he joined Madelyne PRYOR's Hellfire Cult, attacking the X-MEN for her. PIXIE stabbed him in the head with her soulsword, blinding him. While he was imprisoned with the X-Men and helping attack them again, she stabbed him once more, shattering his mind. **MT, MF**

Elders of the Universe

The Elders of the Universe are among the oldest sentient creatures in the universe. Although they do not belong to the same race, they have come to regard one another as brothers. This is because their lifespans date back to the formation of the first primordial galaxies, and because they have each chosen an area of specialty with which to fill their eons-long lives. In this way they manage to overcome the inevitable boredom that would otherwise accompany their virtual immortality. The exact number of Elders in existence is not known, but several of their number have had dealings with the Super Heroes of Earth, including the GRANDMASTER, the COLLECTOR, the Gardener, the CONTEMPLATOR, and the CHAMPION. **TB**

Each Elder of the Universe has a specialty. The Grandmaster, for example, devotes his time to games of cosmic chance, while the Gardener is obsessed with the growing of beautiful plant life.

Elixir

FIRST APPEARANCE New Mutants #5 (November 2003)
REAL NAME Joshua Foley
OCCUPATION Adventurer, student **BASE** Genosha
HEIGHT 5 ft 9 in **WEIGHT** 157 lbs **EYES** Blue **HAIR** Blond
SPECIAL POWERS/ABILITIES Elixir can control organic matter on a genetic level, including healing others, restoring organs and suppressed mutations, causing pain, and ending life.

A former member of the REAVERS, Josh joined the Xavier Institute after his parents signed over his guardianship to the school. He restored WOLFSBANE's powers, and she nearly killed him in surprise. When he healed himself, his skin turned golden, and he eventually joined the NEW MUTANTS. He kept his powers after M-Day and trained to join the X-MEN. When Stryker assassinated his friend Wallflower, Josh killed the man. The trauma turned his own skin black, although it began to turn gold again once he returned to healing people instead. He joined X-FORCE for a time but has since quit. **MF**

Emplate

FIRST APPEARANCE Generation X #1 (November 1994)
REAL NAME Marius St. Croix
OCCUPATION None **BASE** Mobile
HEIGHT 6 ft 3 in **WEIGHT** Variable **EYES** Red **HAIR** Gray
SPECIAL POWERS/ABILITIES Must consume the marrow of mutants to prevent being pulled into a pocket dimension of untold tortures; absorbs the abilities of each mutant he feeds on for a time.

The brother of M, Emplate's mutant power flung him into a pocket dimension, where his physical body was ravaged. By feeding on the marrow of the mutant PENANCE he was able to return home, albeit encased in a respirator unit he now needed to survive. To remain here, Emplate must constantly feed on the marrow of other mutants, for which he targeted GENERATION X. He once merged with his other sisters, the M-Twins, to become M-Plate. **TB, MF**

Exiled to a horrific other dimension, Emplate could only remain in our reality by consuming the bone marrow of mutants like himself.

ELECTRO

Living electrical generator

ELECTRO

FACTFILE

REAL NAME
Maxwell Dillon

OCCUPATION
Professional criminal

BASE
New York City

HEIGHT 5 ft 11 in
WEIGHT 165 lbs
EYES Blue
HAIR Reddish-brown

FIRST APPEARANCE
Amazing Spider-Man #9 (February 1964)

POWERS
Electro can store, release, and manipulate electricity to fire electric bolts, travel along power lines, and control machinery.

While working as a lineman for an electrical company during a thunderstorm, Max Dillon received a shock that endowed him with superhuman powers, and he became the villain Electro. On his first outing, Electro robbed *Daily Bugle* publisher J. Jonah JAMESON, who was sure Electro was SPIDER-MAN in disguise. To clear his name, Spider-Man defeated Electro by short-circuiting his powers with a water stream.

Thor threw Electro into space. When he made it back to Earth, he vowed revenge.

A SHOCKING FAILURE

Electro then allied himself with criminal teams, including the SINISTER SIX and the FRIGHTFUL FOUR. This did little to help Electro with his chronic inferiority complex about being a B-list villain at best. Whether alone or with a team, he never managed to triumph. His frustration with this sent him into retirement for a while, but he returned when the ROSE promised to increase his powers in exchange for his services.

Electro once attacked the super-prison called the Raft, breaking out dozens of powerful villains, but he fainted when a new version of the AVENGERS, now including Spider-Man, cornered him. He joined the HOOD's criminal syndicate when it took part in the battle against the SKRULLS during the SECRET INVASION.

Over the years, Electro's powers have taken their toll on him, burning him out from within and scarring his skin. At one point, he lost so much control over them that even his slightest touch could prove lethal. He launched a campaign called "Power to the People" targeted at right-wing publisher Dexter Bennett, who'd taken over the *Daily Bugle*, as a ploy to get Bennett to fund a search for a cure. Electro made a deal with the MAD THINKER to upgrade his powers and his control over them, but Spider-Man intervened to disrupt the process. Electro temporarily transformed into pure electricity, and he destroyed the *Daily Bugle* building in his rage.

Later, still frustrated with his power troubles, Electro turned to the scientists at AIM to make an anti-matter version of himself, one powered by protons rather than electrons. Working with THOR, the Superior Spider-Man (DOCTOR OCTOPUS) managed to defeat him.
DW, MF

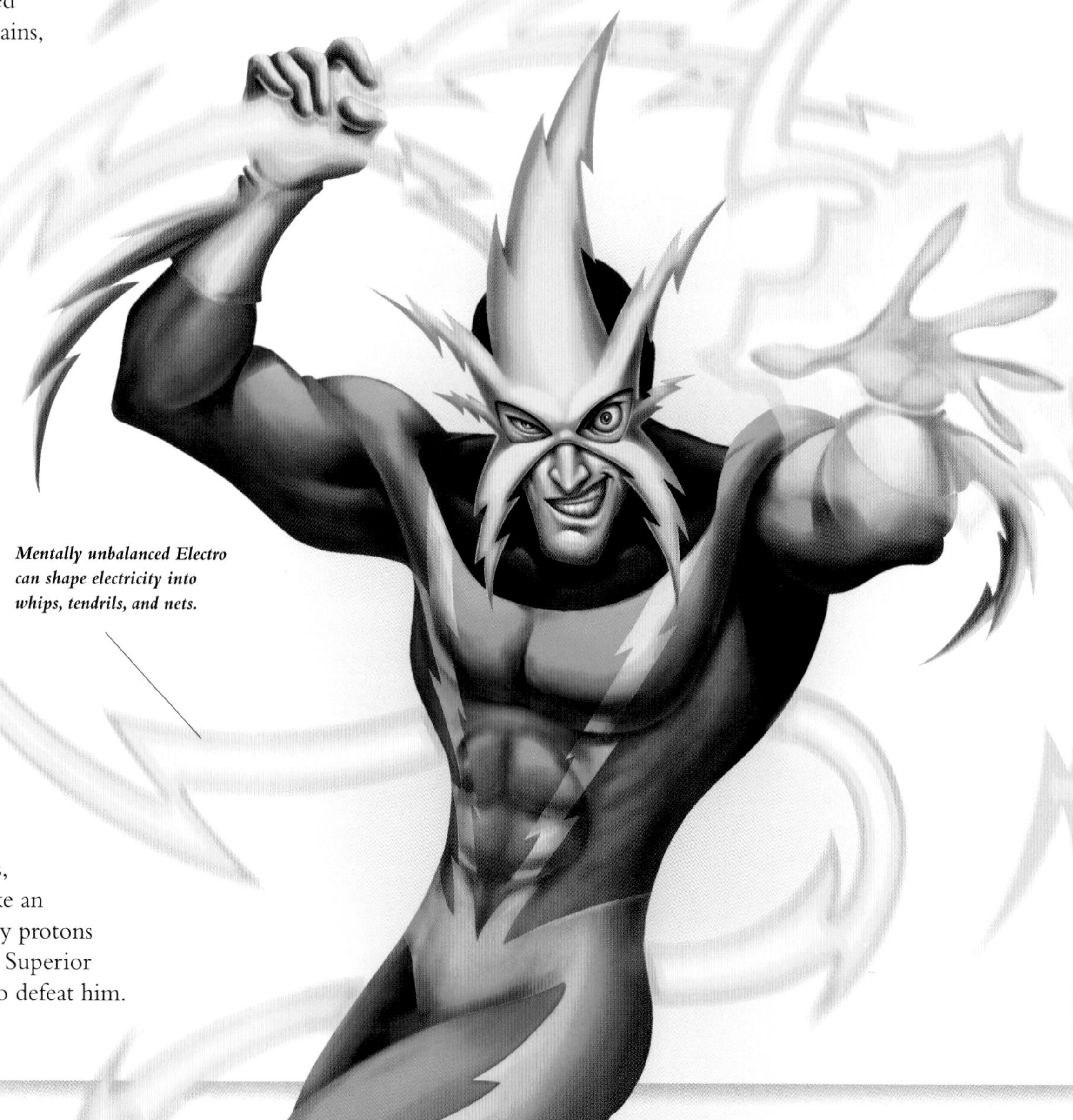
Mentally unbalanced Electro can shape electricity into whips, tendrils, and nets.

Elektra

Conflicted assassin haunted by tragedy

Elektra was not the first to be resurrected by the Hand. That fate fell to 16th-century warrior, Eliza Martinez.

The histories of so many superpowered individuals are marred by tragedy. While in some cases these tragedies drive them towards heroism others are compelled to pursue careers of villainy. For Elektra Natchios this choice has never been clear-cut—while she continues to yearn for contentment, time and again her happiness has been spoiled by the intervention of others.

From their first encounter, Elektra's fate was bound to Matt Murdock's.

FACTFILE

REAL NAME
Elektra Natchios

OCCUPATION
Mercenary assassin

BASE
Mobile

HEIGHT 5 ft 9 in
WEIGHT 130 lbs
EYES Blue-black
HAIR Black

FIRST APPEARANCE
Daredevil #168 (January 1981)

POWERS
Awesome martial arts skills, particularly proficient in Ninjutsu; skilled with martial art weaponry, especially the sai; Olympic-standard gymnast and athlete; limited telepathic abilities and partial control of nervous system.

ETCHED BY SADNESS

Even before she was born, misfortune was etched into Elektra's existence: her mother was shot while pregnant and died soon after giving birth. When Elektra's overprotective father became Greek ambassador to the US, she enrolled at Columbia University in New York City, but was followed everywhere by security guards. Despite this restriction, a romance grew between Elektra and Matt Murdock, a fellow student. For a year, a clandestine relationship flourished, but when her father was killed during a hostage incident Elektra's whole world fell apart. Riven with grief she fled, leaving Matt and the US behind.

Armed with her trademark sai, few have stood against Elektra and survived.

KILLER FOR HIRE

Elektra trained as a ninja and for a year belonged to the CHASTE, a ninja order led by Matt Murdock's mentor, STICK. Elektra's impure heart stopped her from joining the Chaste, driving her to their enemies, the HAND. She later abandoned them and became an assassin for hire, putting her in conflict with Matt, who'd become DAREDEVIL. Once lovers, they were now foes, but despite this, when Elektra was mortally wounded by BULLSEYE, she crawled to Matt's door and died in his arms. Matt tried to halt the Hand's attempt to resurrect a corrupted version of her. His love purified her soul, making her useless to the Hand when she returned.

Fatally injured, Elektra crawls to Matt's apartment to die.

ELEKTRA REBORN

Elektra appeared to have rejoined the Hand to battle the AVENGERS, but when she was killed, the Avengers discovered she was a SKRULL imposter. This heralded the SECRET INVASION, during which Elektra escaped the Skrulls and returned to her life. When Daredevil took charge of the Hand, she joined the organization once again, but she betrayed him to his friends so they could save him from the Beast, a demon who had possessed him. She later joined the RED HULK'S THUNDERBOLTS.

AD, MF

KEY STORYLINES

- ***Daredevil #168–9*** Elektra's first encounter with Matt Murdock; her origin is revealed.
- ***Daredevil #174–181*** Elektra fights the Hand with Matt, is recruited by the Kingpin, and dies at the hands of Bullseye.
- ***Daredevil #190*** Elektra is reborn and more about her past is revealed.
- ***Elektra Vol. 2 #11–15*** As her addiction to violence reaches new heights, relatives of Elektra's victims seek revenge.

Following her resurrection, a purified Elektra fought evil, garbed in a white costume.

FACTFILE

REAL NAME
Amora

OCCUPATION
Goddess

BASE
Asgard, otherworldly home of the Norse gods

HEIGHT 6 ft 3 in
WEIGHT 450 lbs
EYES Green
HAIR Blond

FIRST APPEARANCE
Journey Into Mystery #103 (April 1964)

POWERS
Possesses the enhanced lifespan, durability, and might of a goddess of Asgard. Adept at sorcery, specializing in spells that enhance her beauty and allow her to control the minds and emotions of men. Her kiss can enslave any man. Able to fire power bolts from her hands.

ENCHANTRESS

One of the immortals of the Norse realm of Asgard (*see* GODS OF ASGARD), the Enchantress studied under the master sorceress Karnilla. Vain and headstrong, she centered her magics on increasing her allure, so as to more easily ensnare the hearts and minds of those around her. When her desire for Odin's son Thor proved unrequited, she turned her mystic powers to evil, hoping to catch him one way or another. She especially resented THOR's love of humanity, and longed for him to rule Asgard with her as his queen. Her feelings for the Thunder God are genuine, and she has come close to realizing her dream; however Thor's love of humanity always gets in the way.

The Enchantress's Asgardian body is three times denser and heavier than that of a human being.

Not only can the Enchantress manipulate magical energy, but she uses various spells and potions to exert control over mortal men and other Asgardians.

THE FEMME FATALE

The Enchantress often teamed up with the EXECUTIONER, who was hopelessly infatuated with her. She treated him with contempt but truly grieved for him when he died. She also became a member of the MASTERS OF EVIL.

A younger Enchantress later joined the YOUNG MASTERS, hoping to become a YOUNG AVENGER. She believed she was from Asgard, but she soon learned her name was Sylvie Lushton of Broxton, Oklahoma, and that LOKI had granted her powers to her. She eventually left both groups to work on her own. **TB, MF**

ENCLAVE

FIRST APPEARANCE Fantastic Four #66 (September 1967)
BASE Various, including a North Atlantic island
MEMBERS AND POWERS
Maris Morlak Lithuanian nuclear physicist
Jerome Hamilton American medical biologist
Carlo Zota Spanish electronics technician
Wladyslav Shinski Polish geneticist

The group of scientists known as the Enclave believed they could establish a benevolent world dictatorship. Faking their deaths, the Enclave established a base on a remote North Atlantic island. They first endeavored to create a race of superbeings to control the human race. However, they failed to control the monsters, the first of which rampaged through their base, destroying it. Initially named "Him," this creature eventually came to be called Adam WARLOCK. The Enclave embarked on new schemes, such as attempting to dominate the race known as the INHUMANS and exploit the aliens' technology. Intervention by the AVENGERS resulted in two of the Enclave being imprisoned. They broke out and plagued SPIDER-MAN, the FANTASTIC FOUR, and Adam Warlock for years. **AD, MF**

ENERGIZER

FIRST APPEARANCE Power Pack #1 (August 1984)
REAL NAME Katie Power **OCCUPATION** Student, adventurer
BASE New York City **HEIGHT** (age 5) 3 ft 7 in
WEIGHT (age 5) 41 lbs **EYES** Blue **HAIR** Strawberry blond
SPECIAL POWERS/ABILITIES Can disintegrate objects in order to absorb energy, which she can release as "power balls" of destructive force—hence her codename.

Katie Power is the youngest child of Dr. James and Margaret POWER, and the sister of Alex, Jack and Julie Power. When Katie was five, she and her siblings met Aelfyre WHITEMANE of the alien Kymellians. Dying, "Whitey" endowed the children with superpowers, and they became the POWER PACK. At times the Pack has exchanged powers. Katie was Starstreak when she could fly, and Counterweight when she could alter her body density. **PS**

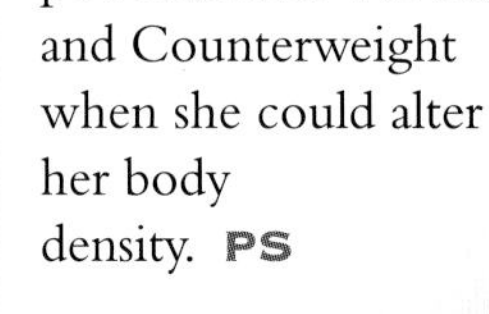

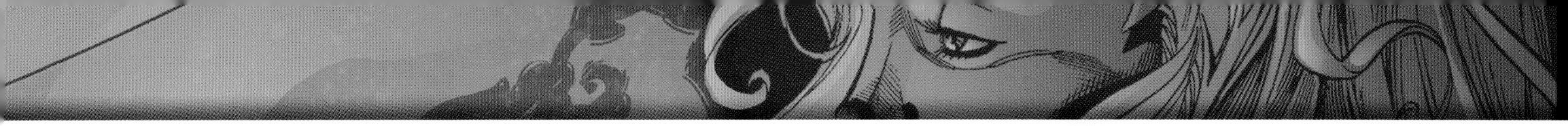

Enforcer

FIRST APPEARANCE Ghost Rider #22 (February 1977)
REAL NAME Charles L. Delazny, Jr. **OCCUPATION** Criminal
BASE Los Angeles, California **HEIGHT** 5 ft 11 in
WEIGHT 180 lbs **EYES** Brown **HAIR** Brown
SPECIAL POWERS/ABILITIES Wears bulletproof costume and carries automatic pistols; formerly possessed a disintegration amulet and ring.

Delazny left college to become the Enforcer. His primary weapon was a disintegration device worn as an amulet or ring. Often going by the name of Carson Collier, he built up a secret criminal empire from his father's Delazny Studios and clashed with GHOST RIDER and SPIDER-WOMAN. He was later shot and killed by the original SCOURGE, who claimed to be his younger brother. His nephew, Mike Nero, later took up the Enforcer identity and clashed with supernatural threats, including the HOOD. **DW, MF**

Enforcers

FIRST APPEARANCE Amazing Spider-Man #10 (March 1964)
BASE New York City
MEMBERS AND POWERS
Fancy Dan Judo and karate expert—a nice line in suits, too.
Montana Proficient with the lariat.
Ox Not superstrong but very strong.
Snake Marston Entwines body around objects and people.
Hammer Harrison Expert boxer and unarmed combatant.
Big Man Would-be crime lord Frederick Foswell.

The Enforcers can give most Super Heroes a run for their money. Although they have been defeated by SPIDER-MAN a number of times, he has required the help of others to overcome them, calling on the NYPD, the HUMAN TORCH, or the reformed SANDMAN. Initially employed by the BIG MAN during his bid to control New York's underworld, the Enforcers have also worked for the GREEN GOBLIN and the KINGPIN, until he was overthrown, forcing them back into the muscle-for-hire market. **AD**

ENFORCERS
1 Big Man
2 Ox
3 Montana
4 Fancy Dan

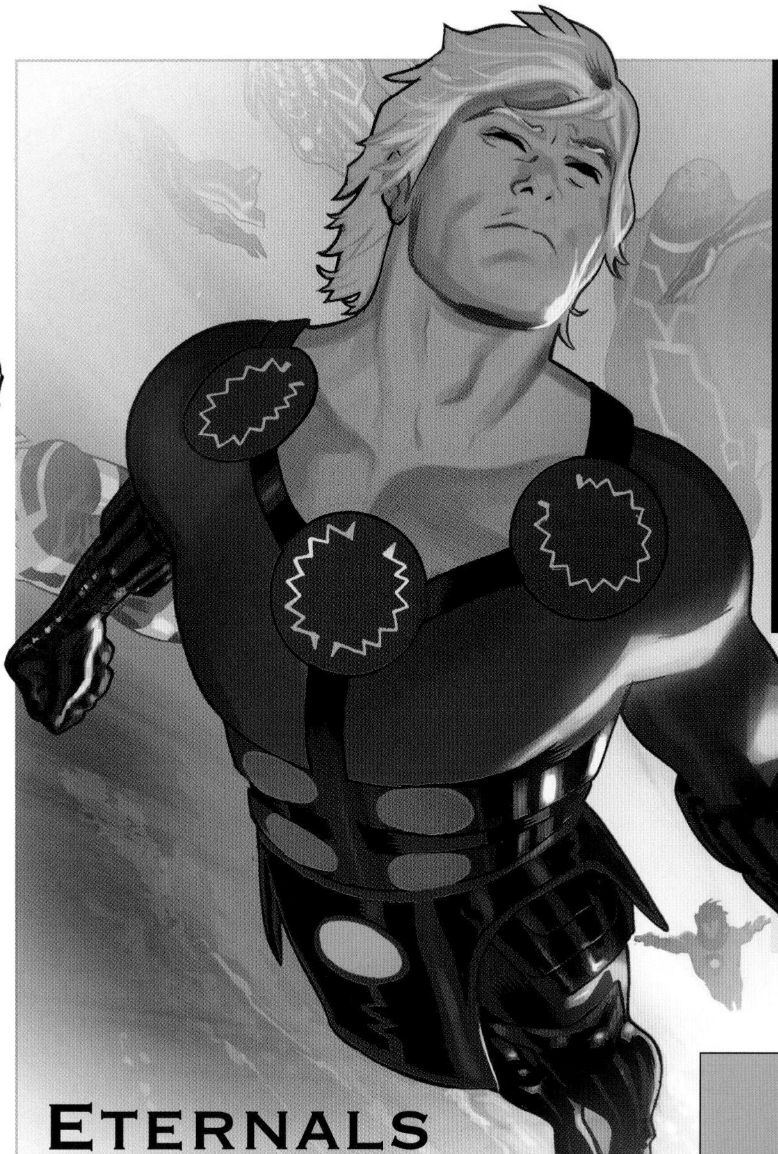

Eternals

FACTFILE
KEY MEMBERS
KRONOS, MENTOR (Alars), **ZURAS, IKARIS, URANOS, ARLOK, THENA, SERSI, MAKKARI, THE FORGOTTEN ONE, KINGO SUNEN, SPRITE, CYBELE, PHASTOS, KHORYPHOS, INTERLOPER, AJAK, DOMO, VALKIN, DRUIG, AGINAR, ZARIN, DELPHAN BROTHERS, SIGMAR, VIRAKO, VAMPIRO.**
BASE
Earth; Titan (moon of Saturn)

FIRST APPEARANCE
Eternals #1 (July 1976)

POWERS
All Eternals have superhuman strength, can levitate themselves or other objects, can fly (up to 600 mph), create mental illusions, and project cosmic energy in beams from their eyes. Some Eternals can transform an object's shape.

A million years ago, the CELESTIALS came to Earth to experiment on the human race. They accelerated the evolution of a few subjects, giving them the potential to mentally control small amounts of cosmic energy. These people became the Eternals, a nearly immortal race of people who possess superhuman powers. Subsequent experiments led to the creation of the DEVIANTS, who later vied for power with the Eternals.

Eventually, the Eternals split into two factions: a benevolent one led by Kronos, and a warlike one led by Uranos. After a bitter civil war, Kronos's side triumphed, and Uranos and his people were exiled to Saturn's moon Titan.

The Eternals on Earth, led by Kronos's son Zuras, clashed with the fourth host of the Celestials, when the latter arrived to judge the Earth and its people. Although Zuras was killed, the Celestials spared the peoples of Earth and departed. Most of the Eternals left the planet then as well, leaving only a small group ruled by IKARIS behind.

Recently, the Eternal named Sprite erased the memories of the other Eternals on Earth and placed them in new lives. They have since steadily gone about the task of regrouping and remembering their original lives, and they've established a new Olympia as their base in Antarctica. **MT, MF**

The Eternal known as Thena is a powerful fighter with a brilliant mind. Like all Eternals she doesn't age or get sick.

Eternity

FIRST APPEARANCE Strange Tales #138 (November 1965)
REAL NAME Inapplicable; (alias) Adam Quadmon
OCCUPATION None; abstract entity **BASE** Inapplicable
HEIGHT Inapplicable **WEIGHT** Inapplicable
EYES Inapplicable **HAIR** Inapplicable
SPECIAL POWERS/ABILITIES Unlimited ability to manipulate time, space, matter, energy, or magic for any purpose.

Eternity is the collective consciousness of all life and is dependent on the many trillions of beings within it. It exits everywhere simultaneously. Eternity can take on humanoid form when it deigns to communicate with sorcerers and the like. Eternity once aided DOCTOR STRANGE against DORMAMMU, and Strange then helped Eternity escape NIGHTMARE's clutches. To have a greater understanding of humanity, Eternity has occasionally walked the Earth, using the name Adam Quadmon. **TD**

Ex Nihilo

FIRST APPEARANCE Avengers #1 (February 2013)
REAL NAME Ex Nihilo **OCCUPATION** Creator **BASE** Mars
HEIGHT 9 ft **WEIGHT** 600 lbs **EYES** Green **HAIR** None
SPECIAL POWERS/ABILITIES Ex Nihilo can create new life and terraform planets by touch or missile. He can also fire energy blasts and control and grow plants in an instant. If his kind commits suicide, they can destroy an entire planet.

Ex Nihilo is one of many of his kind, a Gardener. He came to Mars with his sister Abyss, and they worked for an ancient race known as the BUILDERS under the watchful eye of ALEPH, to judge the people of Earth. While Aleph wished to raze the planet, Ex Nihilo wanted to terraform it instead, and his efforts killed thousands. When the AVENGERS intervened, he, Abyss, and Aleph captured them easily, but he surrendered to CAPTAIN UNIVERSE. He and Abyss now work with the Avengers to prevent the Builders from destroying the Earth and the rest of the galaxy. **MT, MF**

Executioner

FIRST APPEARANCE Journey into Mystery #103 (April 1964)
REAL NAME Skurge **OCCUPATION** Giant-killer
BASE Asgard **HEIGHT** 7 ft 2 in **WEIGHT** 1100 lbs
EYES Blue **HAIR** Black
SPECIAL POWERS/ABILITIES A master of combat. Superhuman strength and stamina; wielded a magical double-bladed ax that can create dimensional rifts enabling time travel and fired blasts of intense heat or cold; also possessed an unbreakable helmet.

Skurge was the son of an Asgardian goddess and a Storm Giant. Turning against his father's people, he killed many giants at war, earning the nickname "the Executioner." He fell under the ENCHANTRESS's spell, serving her in attempts to dominate Earth and Asgard. In time, he realized she was toying with him and rejected her. On a mission to Hel with THOR, he restored his reputation by fighting to free mortal souls from Hela, and he died a hero's death. Much later, an unrelated Executioner joined the YOUNG MASTERS. He was the son of PRINCESS PYTHON. **AD, MF**

Excalibur

EXCALIBUR

FACTFILE
ORIGINAL MEMBERS
CAPTAIN BRITAIN
Superpowered defender of Earth-616.
SHADOWCAT
Phases through solid objects.
NIGHTCRAWLER
Teleportation.
MEGGAN
Shapeshifter.
PHOENIX
(Rachel Summers-Grey)
Telepathy; telekinesis; projects force bolts.
LOCKHEED
Breathes fire and flies.

BASE
United Kingdom

FIRST APPEARANCE
Excalibur: The Sword is Drawn (1987)

Based at CAPTAIN BRITAIN's lighthouse, the Excalibur team of heroes was formed following the X-MEN's apparent demise at the hands of the ADVERSARY. With a base located not just on the shores of the UK but also at the nexus of several realities, many of their battles have been fought across multiple alternate worlds. For instance, Excalibur confronted its Nazi counterparts the Lightning Force on Earth-597. Excalibur's unity has been undermined by romantic tensions. When NIGHTCRAWLER developed feelings for Captain Britain's lover, MEGGAN, friction grew within the team, culminating in a brawl between the two men. When Captain Britain and Meggan finally married, the original team disbanded. Captain Britain has since reformed the team twice, each time with a new lineup. The latest version disbanded after a climactic battle with MERLYN, but a number of the members recently banded together again under the auspices of MI-13. **AD, MF**

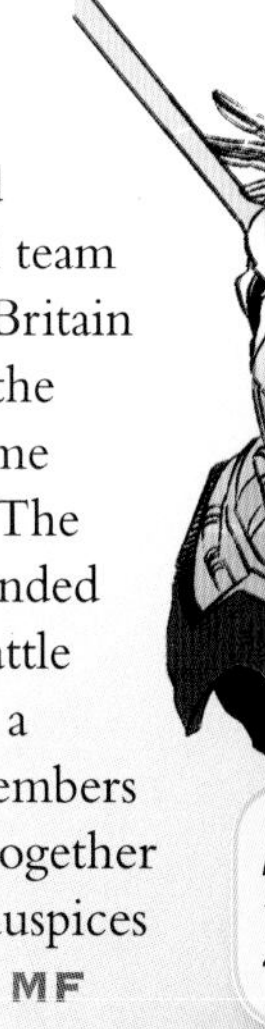

Excalibur missions are bywords for exotic travel to alien worlds and otherworldly dimensions.

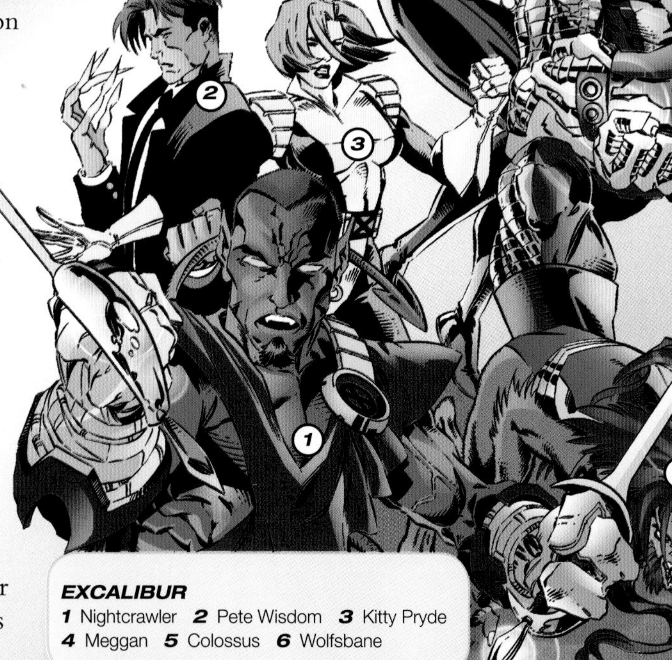

EXCALIBUR
1 Nightcrawler ***2*** Pete Wisdom ***3*** Kitty Pryde ***4*** Meggan ***5*** Colossus ***6*** Wolfsbane

EXILES

FACTFILE

CURRENT MEMBERS

BLINK (leader)
Ability to teleport herself and others

BEAK
Mutant power of flight

MIMIC
Can duplicate the powers and abilities of others

MORPH
Shapeshifting

SABRETOOTH
Mutant healing factor, enhanced senses, retractable claws

BASE
Mobile Panoptichron base

FIRST APPEARANCE
Exiles #1 (August 2001)

Exiles

The Exiles are a group of heroes taken from alternate realities, tasked by the Timebroker with fixing snags in the multiverse of divergent timestreams. A device called Tallus gives them guidance on repairing the timestream. The founding Exiles team consisted of otherdimensional versions of BLINK, MIMIC, MAGNUS, THUNDERBIRD, NOCTURNE, and Morph. Later members included variants of GAMBIT, LONGSHOT, MAGIK, MYSTIQUE, PSYLOCKE, Valeria RICHARDS, SABRETOOTH, SAGE, SUNFIRE, and SASQUATCH, plus SPIDER-MAN 2099 and several versions of WOLVERINE. During their dimension hopping, the team faced off against HYPERION and the opposing team WEAPON X, and welcomed NAMORA and Beak to their ranks.

The team's lineup fluctuated over the years. The latest known lineup consisted of alternate versions of BEAST, BLACK PANTHER, FORGE, Nocturne, POLARIS, and SCARLET WITCH. **DW, MF**

CHARACTER KEY
1 Morph ***2*** Sabretooth ***3*** Beak
4 Sasquatch ***5*** Mimic ***6*** Blink

Exodus

FIRST APPEARANCE X-Factor #92 (July 1993)
REAL NAME Bennet du Paris **OCCUPATION** Supervillain
BASE Mobile **HEIGHT** 5 ft 10 in **WEIGHT** 165 lbs
EYES White **HAIR** Black
SPECIAL POWERS/ABILITIES Incalculable psionic powers including telepathy, telekinesis, and the ability to fire mental bolts; possesses enhanced strength, near-invulnerability, and flight.

In the 12th-century, crusader Bennet du Paris crossed paths with APOCALYPSE, who placed him in suspended animation when he refused to kill the BLACK KNIGHT. Awakened by MAGNETO in the modern era, du Paris took the name Exodus and joined Magneto's ACOLYTES. He led the Acolytes until Nate Grey (X-MAN) sealed him in a mountain. He was one of the few mutants to maintain his powers after M-Day. After PROFESSOR X was shot, Exodus rebuilt his brain, and he later dueled with the professor over Magneto's fate. **DW, MF**

Externals

The Externals, also known as the High Lords, were a small group of superhuman mutants whose lifespans were potentially unlimited. Their aging process was greatly slowed, and they could recover from injuries that would be fatal to normal humans.

Candra exacted payments of "tithes" from the Thieves and Assassins Guilds of New Orleans until GAMBIT stopped her. GIDEON was the owner of Ophrah Industries and a recurring foe of X-FORCE. SELENE lived for thousands of years and became Black Queen of the HELLFIRE CLUB. Most of the Externals proved not to be as immortal as they hoped. Burke and Nicodemus succumbed to the Legacy Virus. Candra perished in an encounter with the X-MEN. Having drained the life forces of Gideon and the others, Selene was the last known External, but X-FORCE killed her when she tried to achieve godhood. **PS, MF**

EXTERNALS

FACTFILE

KEY MEMBERS
(all have virtual immortality)

ABSALOM
Causes bone-like spikes to emerge from his skin

BURKE Precognition

CANDRA Telekinesis

CRULE Superhuman strength

GIDEON Duplicates powers of superhumans

SELENE Drains life forces from others; telekinetic powers; superhuman strength and speed

FIRST APPEARANCE
X-Force #10 (May 1992)

Believing Sunspot was another External, Gideon arranged the murder of Sunspot's father. Later, Gideon fought Crule (left) and sent him to capture Cannonball.

Selene as the Black Queen of the Hellfire Club.

One of the oldest known mutants, Selene is also a powerful sorceress.

FACTFILE

REAL NAME
Sam "Snap" Wilson

OCCUPATION
Hero and urban planner

BASE
Harlem, New York City

HEIGHT 6 ft 2 in
WEIGHT 240 lbs
EYES Brown
HAIR Black

FIRST APPEARANCE
Captain America #117 (September 1969)

POWERS
Falcon has a telepathic link allowing him to see through the eyes of his trained falcon, Redwing. Trained by Captain America, Falcon is skilled in numerous fighting styles, and possesses the agility of a skilled acrobat. Jet-powered glider wings enable him to fly.

FALCON

When both his parents were murdered, his father trying to stop a street fight and his mother in a mugging, community volunteer Sam Wilson became so disillusioned he turned to crime. While working for a smuggling gang, he crash-landed on Exile Island in the Caribbean and encountered the RED SKULL. In order to realize one of his diabolical schemes, the Skull used a Cosmic Cube to endow Sam with limited superpowers, molding him to become CAPTAIN AMERICA's ideal sidekick.

After helping the Cap to defeat Red Skull, Sam branded himself the Falcon and entered into a long partnership with the famed supersoldier. A gift of jet-powered wings from BLACK PANTHER enabled him to become Captain America's airborne companion.

Captain America's airborne ally, Falcon, provides vital air support in the battle against evil.

Wilson moved in and out of the AVENGERS over the years, but he finally retired from being a hero after the insane SCARLET WITCH unbalanced his mind. He returned to support Captain America's resistance during the CIVIL WAR, but after Cap's assassination, he registered and was assigned to protect Harlem. He later joined the Heroes for Hire and even returned to the Avengers. AD, MF

FANTASTIC FOUR, *see pages 128-131*

FANTOMEX

FIRST APPEARANCE New X-Men #128 (August 2002)
REAL NAME Jean-Phillipe/Charlie Cluster-7
OCCUPATION Adventurer **BASE** Mobile **HEIGHT** 5 ft 9 in
WEIGHT 175 lbs **EYES** Blue **HAIR** Black
SPECIAL POWERS/ABILITIES Fantomex has three brains and a techno-organic morphable flying saucer named EVA. He has superhuman coordination, durability, endurance, hearing, speed, strength, and pain resistance. His mask blocks telepathy.

Fantomex was born and raised in the World, an artificial environment designed to create perfect living weapons. Designated Weapon XIII, he escaped while being transported through the Chunnel between England and France. He spent his time after this either stopping Weapon Plus and WEAPON X programs or working as a master thief. He later joined CYCLOPS's new X-FORCE team and died saving PSYLOCKE. EVA cloned him to restore him, but he wound up with a new body for each of his three brains: evil Weapon XIII, noble (and female) Cluster, and mischievous Fantomex. MF

FEARLESS DEFENDERS

Doommaidens (corrupted Valkyries) were causing long-dead Vikings to rise and attack the world. VALKYRIE, with the help of Misty KNIGHT, Dani MOONSTAR, resurrected Amazon leader Hippolyta, and archaeologist Annabelle Riggs, set out to stop the Doommaidens. At a crucial moment, Valkyrie siphoned off Dani's Valkyrie power to increase her own, but sent herself intoa berserker fury. Only Annabelle was able to stop her with her love, but at the cost of her life.

Grieving for her friend, Valkyrie urged the others to join her in a new DEFENDERS team. With the help of CLEA, Valkyrie brought Annabelle back from Valhalla, but only by binding herself to Annabelle, making her Valkyrie's host. The two could switch places with each other between Valhalla and Earth. Later, Elsa BLOODSTONE helped the FEARLESS DEFENDERS out when they discovered a gang in New York's Chinatown were using Brood hatchlings to assassinate rivals. MF

FACTFILE

MEMBERS
ANNABELLE RIGGS
Archaeologist, now host of Valkyrie
DANI MOONSTAR
Empathic illusionist and Valkyrie
VALKYRIE
Leader of the Valkyrior
MISTY KNIGHT
Private detective with bionic arm
WARRIOR WOMAN
Hippolyta, former Amazon leader

BASE
Unrevealed

FIRST APPEARANCE
Fearless Defenders #1 (April 2013)

FEAR ITSELF, *see pages 132-133*

Fenris

FIRST APPEARANCE Journey into Mystery #114 (March 1965)
REAL NAME Fenris Wolf **OCCUPATION** Predator
BASE Varinheim **HEIGHT** 15 ft **WEIGHT** Unrevealed
EYES Brown **HAIR** Gray
SPECIAL POWERS/ABILITIES Superhuman strength, speed, and durability; razor-sharp claws and teeth; able to transform change into a humanoid god and wield weapons.

Fenris is an immense wolf with human intelligence. Chained by the Gods of Asgard, it is prophesied that he will devour Odin at Ragnarok. Fenris was also the name Andrea and Andreas von Strucker took for their terrorist organization. As Citizen V, Baron Zemo murdered Andrea, and Andreas became the new Swordsman. Andrea returned as a clone and joined the Thunderbolts alongside Andreas, but during the Secret Invasion, Bullseye killed her. Norman Osborn (*see* Green Goblin) murdered Andreas. **PS, MF**

Fixer (Techno)

FIRST APPEARANCE Strange Tales #141 (February 1966)
REAL NAME Paul Norbert Ebersol
OCCUPATION Adventurer **BASE** New York City
HEIGHT 5 ft 8 in **WEIGHT** 160 lbs **EYES** Brown
HAIR Bald with black goatee
SPECIAL POWERS/ABILITIES Fixer is an engineering genius who sometimes lives in a morphable robot body.

A genius with electronic and mechanical devices, Fixer began his criminal career working with Hydra. He clashed with many heroes, fighting alongside Mentallo and Professor Power. Later, he joined Baron Zemo and the Masters of Evil. As part of the original Thunderbolts, Fixer's neck was broken, and he transferred his mind into a robot body. When that was destroyed, he returned to his original body, which was now healed, although it required the use of his tech-pac to keep him from being paralyzed. He joined the Redeemers and lived for a while on Counter-Earth. He has since returned to Earth. **MF**

Flag-Smasher

FIRST APPEARANCE Captain America #312 (December 1985)
REAL NAME Unknown **OCCUPATION** Terrorist
BASE Rumekistan **HEIGHT** 6 ft 2 in **WEIGHT** 235 lbs
EYES Brown **HAIR** Brown
SPECIAL POWERS/ABILITIES Skilled at shotokan karate-do; multilingual, can speak Russian, German, and Japanese; wields spiked mace, flame-throwing pistol, and tear-gas gun.

When his diplomat father died in a riot, Flag-Smasher committed himself to establishing peace by violent means. Regarding nationalism as the root problem, he initiated a terrorist campaign against symbols of national identity. Captain America repeatedly defeated him. Forming the terrorist organization ULTIMATUM, Flag-Smasher took over the country of Rumekistan, but Domino assassinated him. During the Civil War, a new Flag-Smasher appeared, committing terrorist acts. Venom (Flash Thompson) killed his underlings and bit off his arm. **AD, MF**

Feral

FIRST APPEARANCE New Mutants #99 (March 1991)
REAL NAME Maria Callasantos **OCCUPATION** Terrorist
BASE New York City **HEIGHT** 5 ft 9 in **WEIGHT** 110 lbs
EYES Yellow **HAIR** Orange and white
SPECIAL POWERS/ABILITIES Enhanced strength, speed, and agility; superhumanly acute senses, especially her senses of sight and smell.

When Feral's mutant powers emerged, she killed her stepfather and her mother and joined X-Force. When X-Force tried to rescue Henry Gyrich from the Mutant Liberation Front, she switched sides. The New York City Police arrested her for the murders of her parents. Later, she joined the X-Corporation, along with her sister, Thornn. They both lost their powers on M-Day, and Sabretooth killed Feral. Selene's techno-organic virus resurrected her, but not for long. **MT, MF**

Firestar

Angelica Jones's mutant powers began to emerge when she was 13 years old. She was soon recruited by the Massachusetts Academy, and she became a member of the Hellions. Emma Frost, who was both the school's headmistress and the White Queen of the Inner Circle of the Hellfire Club at the time, secretly trained Angelica to become an assassin who could kill without detection. After the Hellions repeatedly clashed with the X-Men and New Mutants, Angelica decided to leave the school. She joined the New Warriors and fell in love with Vance "Justice" Astrovik. They briefly became reserve members of the Avengers. Justice proposed to her, and the couple decided to leave the Avengers to focus on their relationship and education. However, they broke off their engagement soon after. She retained her powers after M-Day, but during the Civil War she retired from being a hero to remain in college. She survived cancer caused by her own powers, and has since become a founding member of the Young Allies. **TD, MF**

FACTFILE
REAL NAME
Angelica Jones
OCCUPATION
College student
BASE
Manhattan, New York

HEIGHT 5 ft 1 in
WEIGHT 101 lbs
EYES Green
HAIR Red

FIRST APPEARANCE
Uncanny X-Men #193 (May 1985)

FIRESTAR

POWERS
Firestar possesses the mutant ability to project microwave energy and to generate intense heat. She can propel herself and others through the air by mentally pushing microwave energy behind or beneath herself.

Fifty-State Initiative, ***see pages 134-135***

Fantastic Four

Superheroic planet protectors

FANTASTIC FOUR

FACTFILE

MEMBERS

MR. FANTASTIC (Reed Richards) Scientific genius; elastic powers.

INVISIBLE WOMAN (Susan Richards) Can turn her body or any other object invisible; projects invisible force fields.

THE THING (Ben Grimm) Man monster with superhuman strength.

HUMAN TORCH (Johnny Storm) Generates fiery plasma over his entire body and can fly.

ADDITIONAL MEMBERS

CRYSTAL, MEDUSA, SHE-HULK, ANT-MAN (Scott Lang), **LUKE CAGE** (Carl Lucas), **SHARON VENTURA** (Ms. Marvel/She-Thing), **NAMORITA** (Namorita Prentiss)

BASE

The Baxter Building, NYC

FIRST APPEARANCE

Fantastic Four #1 (November 1961)

ALLIES/FOES

ALLIES Spider-Man, Namor, The Sub-Mariner, Alicia Masters, Agatha Harkness, Wyatt Wingfoot, Silver Surfer, Lyja (Lyja Storm).

FOES Dr. Doom, Puppet Master, Red Ghost and his Super-Apes, Frightful Four, Galactus.

ISSUE #1

After being exposed to cosmic rays, the Fantastic Four kept a low profile and didn't reveal their powers to the public until giant monsters began attacking atomic research facilities.

The Baxter Building was built by Noah Baxter, one of Reed's professors and mentor.

Reed Richards was a scientific genius who dreamed of exploring the stars. His roommate at New York's State University was football star Ben Grimm. Reed shared his dream of building a starship and Grimm, who wanted to become a pilot, promised to fly it. Grimm subsequently joined the US Air Force and became a test pilot and astronaut. Meanwhile, using his own family's fortune as well as money from the government, Richards built a starship.

Cosmic Rays

When the government threatened to withdraw its funding, Richards decided to take his prototype ship on a test flight with Grimm at the helm. Richards' fiancée Susan Storm and her teenage brother Johnny came along for the ride. Soon after takeoff, a solar flare bombarded the ship with an unknown form of cosmic radiation that mutated their bodies and gave them fantastic powers. Richards became MR. FANTASTIC, Susan Storm became INVISIBLE WOMAN, Ben Grimm became the THING, and Johnny Storm became the HUMAN TORCH.

IF YOU WANT TO FLY TO THE STARS, THEN YOU PILOT THE SHIP! COUNT ME OUT!
YOU KNOW WE HAVEN'T DONE ENOUGH RESEARCH INTO THE EFFECT OF COSMIC RAYS! THEY MIGHT KILL US ALL OUT IN SPACE!

Fearing that Reed's ship didn't have sufficient shields, Ben tried to talk the others out of flying.

No Charge

Pledging to use their new powers for the good of mankind, the four adventurers formed a legal corporation. The Fantastic Four safeguards the planet from human and extraterrestrial super-menaces, and also specializes in pure scientific research and explorations into the unknown. Funded by the patents on inventions and scientific discoveries made by Richards, the team offers its services without charge.

I AIN'T BEN ANYMORE-- I'M WHAT SUSAN CALLED ME--THE THING!!
AND I'LL CALL MYSELF... MISTER FANTASTIC!!

The Fantastic Four have vowed to safeguard Earth.

On their first public mission, the Fantastic Four prevented the MOLE MAN conquering the world. They later stopped the SKRULLS invading Earth and the MIRACLE MAN from blackmailing New York City. They were also responsible for the return of Prince NAMOR, the Sub-Mariner: the Human Torch found him living like a tramp in the Bowery slums and helped restore his lost memory. The FF also uncovered the menace of DOCTOR DOOM and made first contact with UATU THE WATCHER and the mysterious INHUMANS. They blocked Galactus from consuming the Earth and discovered the area of sub-space known as the Negative Zone. The team also battled the FRIGHTFUL FOUR, the OVERMIND, the SPHINX and aided the Planet Xandar against a Skrull invasion.

Alternate Worlds

After a prolonged engagement, Reed Richards married Susan Storm and she gave birth to their son Franklin RICHARDS. Soon afterward, Richards' scientist father Nathaniel switched young Franklin with his alternate-world teenage counterpart in an effort to help the team battle Hyperstorm, a menace they were destined to face in the future. Richards and Doctor Doom were later transported into a possible alternate future where the son of Franklin had conquered the universe.

A few months later, Franklin somehow created a pocket universe called Counter Earth, where he transported his

THE FANTASTIC FOUR
1 The Thing *2* Mr. Fantastic
3 Invisible Girl *4* Human Torch

BASES AND EQUIPMENT

The team established its first headquarters on the top five floors of the Baxter Building in Manhattan, New York City. Although this building was later destroyed, Richards designed another base that was constructed in outer space by his former mentor Noah Baxter. The new Baxter Building is equipped with a state-of-the-art security system that is regularly upgraded. Roberta, the Fantastic Four's robot receptionist, is networked with the team's main computer and can undertake hundreds of tasks simultaneously.

Richards has also designed many different types of Fantasti-cars for easy travel around Manhattan (they're easy to park). Each team member is equipped with a wireless communications link, and an emergency flare gun. The FF also have a Pogo-Plane that is outfitted with vertical take off and landing capabilities, a captured Skrull starship that they use for galactic travel and a time platform and space/time sled that allow them to visit alternate time eras or dimensions. The team's costumes are composed of unstable molecules that are specifically designed to adjust to their individual powers.

Roberta is able to operate 24 hours a day and can answer various calls simultaneously.

ESSENTIAL STORYLINES

- ***Greatest Villains of the Fantastic Four* (tpb)** The FF battle Psycho-Man, Blastaar, Annihilus, Puppet Master, the Mad Thinker, and Doctor Doom.
- ***Fantastic Four: Monsters Unleashed* (tpb)** The Hulk, Ghost Rider, Wolverine and Spider-Man help the FF battle the Mole Man and the Skrulls.
- ***Fantastic Four: Nobody Gets Out Alive* (tpb)** The FF travel through time and various alternate dimensions on a hunt for the missing and presumed dead Reed Richards.
- ***Fantastic Four: Unthinkable* (tpb)** Doctor Doom attempts to use black magic as well as Reed and Sue's own children as weapons against the FF.
- ***Fantastic Four: Authoritative Action* (tpb)** To the world's horror and outrage, the FF seize control of Latveria after Doom is apparently destroyed.

parents to protect them from a psychic monster called ONSLAUGHT. The FF later returned and soon faced another reality-altering cosmic entity called Abraxas. Shortly after they defeated him, the Invisible Woman gave birth to a daughter, named Valeria RICHARDS.

CHANGING THE WORLD

The Fantastic Four have been embroiled in every major event on Earth over the past several years. Reed supported the Superhuman Registration Act, although he lost the backing of every other member of the team. When the CIVIL WAR ended, he and Sue reunited and left the team for a while to re-examine their marriage. During the SECRET INVASION, the SKRULLS captured Reed and Sue and sent the others, including Franklin and Valeria, into the Negative Zone. They all survived and were reunited, but the experience inspired Reed to start exploring alternate universes. **TD, MF**

The team have traveled into space and alternate dimensions.

FANTASTIC FOUR *continued*

WORLDS APART

Disturbed by the fact that the Superhuman Registration Act had caused so much trouble, resulting in the CIVIL WAR and the assassination of CAPTAIN AMERICA, Reed decided to explore other realities in an effort to discover what had gone wrong. To that end, he built a device called the Bridge and used it to locate alternative versions of himself, who had banded together to form the Interdimensional Council of Reeds.

These were version of Reed who had lost their fathers. Because of this, they preferred to stay coldly detached from their worlds, and Reed refused to leave his family to join them. Nevertheless, they filled Reed's head with all sorts of new ideas, essentially crowd-sourcing solutions to his problems from within his multiple variants. Soon after, Reed decided to start up a new group called the Future Foundation, a group of thinkers—mostly younger people, even children—charged with coming up with fresh solutions to the world's problems.

The Interdimensional Council of Reeds featured all sorts of people with one thing in common. Each of them were their world's version of Reed Richards.

SURPRISE ATTACK

At a chaotic point in the lives of the Fantastic Four, Reed left Earth to deal with GALACTUS, Devourer of Worlds, and Sue Richards traveled deep into the ocean to help with a problem in Atlantis. This left Johnny Storm and a depowered Ben Grimm to watch over Franklin, Valeria, and the kids from the Future Foundation. Seizing their chance, the members of the fanatical Cult of the Negative Zone launched an attack on the Baxter Building, seeking to throw open the gateway to the Negative Zone, which Reed had sealed off from the Earth side.

After sealing the gateway to Earth, the Human Torch stood alone against the forces of Annihilus

Threat of Annihilation

Working with the kids, Johnny Storm and Ben stopped the Cult. However, the gateway had opened, leaving the Earth exposed to an Annihilation wave led by Annihilus that threatened not only to destroy the planet but the rest of the galaxy. The only way to seal the gateway was from inside the Negative Zone, which would inevitably cut off that person's escape route. Ben volunteered, but at the last moment Johnny threw him to safety and sacrificed himself instead.

With Johnny gone, the remaining members of the Fantastic Four decided to focus their efforts on the Future Foundation. They adopted white uniforms with black trim and new logos. The young people on their roster included Alex Power (of the Power Pack), Artie Maddicks (a mute mutant who could project images of thoughts; depowered but working with a helmet that duplicates his powers), Bentley 23 (a young clone of the Wizard), Dragon Man, Franklin Richards, Leech (whose power-dampening power kept Franklin under control), and four clever Moloids (the subterranean race ruled by the Mole Man): Korr, Mik, Tong, and Turg.

Reed, Sue, and Ben ran the Future Foundation, but they also lined up some other adults to help. Reed's father Nathaniel Richards joined. Johnny's will requested that Spider-Man take his place, which the wall-crawler did, in an all-new white and black costume. Franklin and Valeria also invited Doctor Doom to join, despite objections from Reed and Ben. (Doom soon set up a symposium of evil geniuses to figure out how to defeat Reed Richards and, later, the Council of Reeds.)

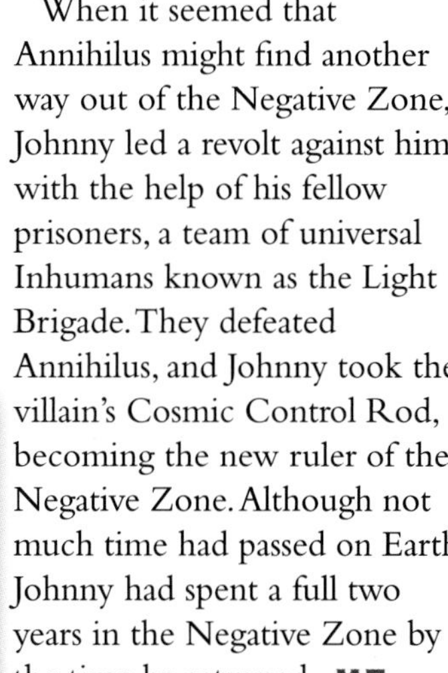
After the Human Torch sacrificed himself, his friends and family threw themselves into the Future Foundation's work.

The Fantastic Four sometimes arranged for a team of substitutes to take its place when it had to leave Earth. One team included Ant-Man II, Medusa, She-Hulk, and She-Thing.

The Torch Returns

In the Negative Zone, Johnny stood against the Annihilation wave for as long as he could but was eventually defeated. Not content to let the hero die, Annihilus tried to torture him into opening the gateway to Earth, something Johnny couldn't have provided if he'd wanted to. Johnny died three times, but Annihilus revived him each time and then threw him into prison and forced him to participate in arena combat.

When it seemed that Annihilus might find another way out of the Negative Zone, Johnny led a revolt against him with the help of his fellow prisoners, a team of universal Inhumans known as the Light Brigade. They defeated Annihilus, and Johnny took the villain's Cosmic Control Rod, becoming the new ruler of the Negative Zone. Although not much time had passed on Earth, Johnny had spent a full two years in the Negative Zone by the time he returned. **MF**

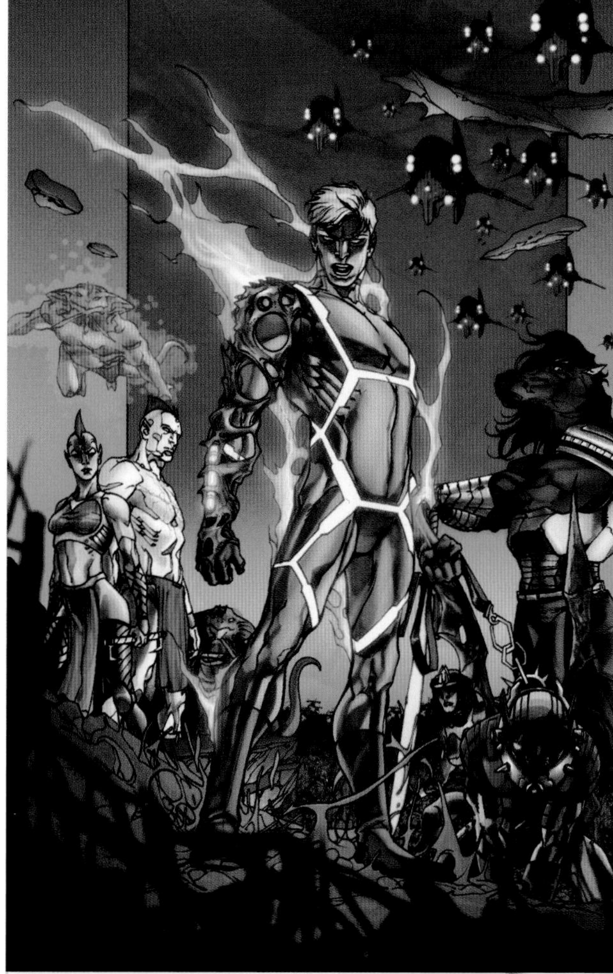
When the Human Torch returned from his apparent death in the Negative Zone, he did so triumphantly, and with new friends.

Lost in Space!

When Reed Richards discovered that the Fantastic Four's unstable molecules were breaking down, threatening to kill them all, he decided to take his family on an adventure through space and time to search for a solution. The team left behind four friends to watch over the Earth for them during what they thought would be a four-minute absence.

Fear Itself

It's All You Have to Fear

ISSUE #1

When the new Red Skull took up the Hammer of Skadi, she unleashed an ancient terror aching to feed on the fear of the Earth and destroy the Norse gods.

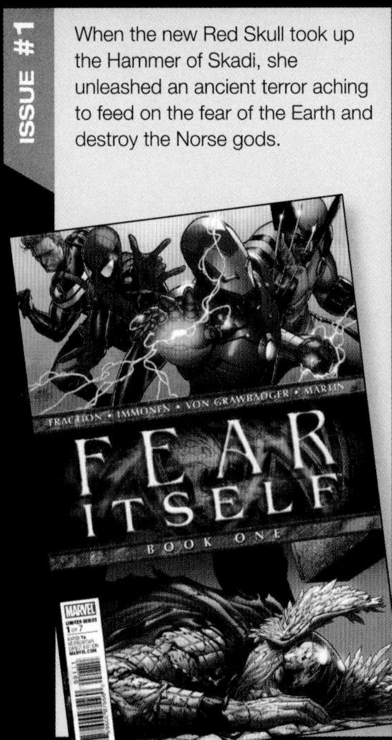

With the original Red Skull dead, his daughter Sin took up his mantle. With the aid of the Book of the Skull, which she recovered with the help of Baron Zemo, she set out to succeed at one mission from World War II which her father had failed: the use of the Hammer of Skadi.

ATTACK OF THE WORTHY

The new Red Skull became the new incarnation of Skadi, and seven more hammers fell from the sky like meteors and landed around the world. They took control of their super-powered holders, transforming them into the Worthy, generals of the Asgardian superbeing the Serpent. The Worthy set to wreaking havoc and terrifying the locals.

As worldwide panic rose, Odin revealed that the Serpent was his long-banished brother Cul. He decided the wise move was to abandon the Asgard on Earth that had been shattered at the end of the Dark Reign. Over his son Thor's objections, he brought his people to a new, off-world Asgard and told them to prepare for war. Odin knew that the Serpent fed on the power of fear and believed the only way to defeat him would be to raze the planet, eliminating the terror along with the people who felt it. Thor insisted he be allowed to fight the Serpent, and Odin grudgingly let him go, despite a prophecy that Thor would die defeating the Serpent.

Skadi attacked Washington, DC, and wounded Captain America (Bucky Barnes). This forced Steve Rogers to become Captain America again. Thor battled two of the Worthy, killing Angrir (whom Franklin Richards later restored to life as the Thing) and blasting Nul (Hulk) into space. Iron Man battled Mokk in Paris, alongside Pepper Potts in her Rescue armor. Other heroes battled the rest of the Worthy in terrible conflicts around the planet.

Following Iron Man's desperate plea, Odin granted him access to his workshop so he could build weapons capable of defeating the Worthy. Despite Cul's destruction of his shield, Captain America and the bravest people in Broxton, Oklahoma, fought on against the Worthy, whom Cul had called there to join him in the final battle. The weapon-equipped Avengers joined the battle, with Thor wielding Odin's blade, Ragnarok, while Cap took up Thor's hammer. Together, they carried the day, but at the loss of Thor, who sacrificed himself in order to kill the Serpent. The Thunder God later battled the Demogorge and returned from the land of the dead. MF

Not even Captain America's unbreakable shield could withstand the power of the hammers of the Worthy.

THE WORTHY

The Thing as Angrir, Breaker of Souls.

Attuma as Nerkkod, Breaker of Oceans.

Juggernaut as Kuurth, Breaker of Stone.

Titania as Skirn, Breaker of Men.

Absorbing Man as Greithoth, Breaker of Wills.

Hulk as Nul, Breaker of Worlds.

The Grey Gargoyle as Mokk, Breaker of Faith.

With the help of the dwarves of Svartalfheim, Iron Man used his repulsor technology and molten uru metal—plus Odin's blessing—to build weapons to make eight Avengers more powerful than ever.

Skadi Revealed

At Adolf Hitler's behest, the Red Skull performed a ritual during World War II that brought the Hammer of Skadi to Earth. He could not lift the hammer, so he had a fortress built around it, guarded by Hitler's fanatical Thule Society. The new Red Skull launched a full-on attack on the fortress. She felt the hammer call to her, and when she grabbed it, it transformed her into Skadi, Herald of the Serpent.

FIFTY-STATE INITIATIVE

Super Heroes for all of America

50-STATE INITIATIVE

FACTFILE

CURRENT MEMBERS

ANT-MAN (Eric O'Grady) Can shrink or grow to dramatic sizes.

GAUNTLET Drill sergeant with an alien superweapon.

MUTANT ZERO (Typhoid Mary) Telekinesis, telepathy, and pyrokinesis.

TASKMASTER Martial arts expert with photographic reflexes.

TRAUMA Telepath and shapeshifter.

BARON VON BLITZSCHLAG Scientific genius and electricity control.

ADDITIONAL MEMBERS

ARMORY, CLOUD 9, HARDBALL, MICHAEL VAN PATRICK, and many others.

BASE

Camp Hammond, Stamford, Connecticut

FIRST APPEARANCE

Civil War: The Initiative #1 (April 2007))

ALLIES/FOES

ALLIES The US government, SHIELD, HAMMER, the Dark Avengers.

FOES Any terrorist threat, the New Avengers.

ISSUE #1

Michael Pointer becomes the new Guardian and joins Omega Flight. The Thunderbolts hunt down Hurricane. Iron man Tony Stark begins selecting heroes for a new Avengers team.

After the passage of the Superhuman Registration Act, Tony Stark (Iron Man) realized that SHIELD needed a plan for how to make use of all of the Super Heroes soon to be under its remit. During the Civil War, Stark, Reed Richards (Mister Fantastic), and Hank Pym brainstormed a long list of ideas for how to improve the world. The Fifty-State Initiative was number 41 on that list.

Gauntlet—the drill sergeant at Camp Hammond—greets the first busload of trainees as they arrive.

HEROES UNITED AND DEPLOYED

To get the Initiative started, Stark funded a superteam of his own: the Order. This team was ready to see action in the final battle of the Civil War. When Stark was made the director of SHIELD after the Civil War, he had the power to build a Super Hero team for each state in the nation, based on that prototype.

Many of the initial teams were simply existing teams or heroes brought into the new structure. The Great Lakes Avengers, for example, were renamed the Great Lakes Initiative and assigned to their home state of Wisconsin, while Hellcat was sent to Alaska to serve as its hero.

Hero Boot Camp

Many new heroes joined the Initiative, and these required training to make the best use of their powers and reduce the danger they presented to others. To this end, Stark set up Camp Hammond as the Initiative's headquarters and training facility. Sergeant Joe Green (Gauntlet) served as the base's drill instructor under administrator Henry Peter Gyrich with Hank Pym as the chief administrator, and Baron Werner Von Blitzschlag in charge of the science division. Gyrich formed a black ops team answerable only to himself, called the Shadow Initiative. Members included Bengal, Constrictor, the Scarlet Spiders, Trauma, and Mutant Zero (Typhoid Mary).

Stark formed the Order as a template for the Initiative. The California team was the first generated specifically for the program.

MAIN STORYLINES

- ***Civil War: The Initiative #1***: As the new leader of SHIELD, Tony Stark considers how to best organize the heroes available to him.
- ***Avengers: The Initiative #1***: The first team of recruits arrives at Camp Hammond and promptly suffers its first disaster with the training death of MVP.
- ***Avengers: The Initiative #8–11***: KIA is created and nearly destroys the Initiative.

Early Troubles

In the first combat training session, a terrified Armory fired an alien weapon named the Tactigon wildly and killed fellow recruit Michael Van Patrick. The following cover-up came back to haunt the Initiative when Von Blitzschlag fitted a clone of Van Patrick with the Tactigon, causing him to become psychotic and go on a murderous rampage.

Initiative recruits helped during World War Hulk and the Secret Invasion. In the confusion surrounding the Hulk's attack, Slapstick beat Gauntlet into a coma for berating the New Warriors, of which Slapstick had once been a member. Gauntlet later recovered.

SHIELD scientists developed Super-Power-Inhibiting Nanobots (SPIN) technology that could be used to remove superpowers. Hydra leader Senator Woodman persuaded Initiative recruit Hardball to steal this for him. Later, when Woodman blackmailed Hardball into continuing to work for him, Hardball killed him, left the Initiative, and took over the leadership of Hydra instead.

The Skrull Infiltration

Before the Secret Invasion, the Skrull Queen Veranke made sure to insert a Skrull into every team in all 50 states. When the Skrulls launched their attack, many of the spies revealed themselves, and the rest of the Initiative's members could not tell who to trust. Using 3-D Man's powers, Triathlon managed to spot most of them located at Camp Hammond, but few other teams were so lucky.

Afterward, Doc Samson held group therapy sessions for those replaced by Skrulls. When Norman Osborn (*see* Green Goblin) became director of HAMMER, he changed the name of the program to the Thunderbolt Initiative. He then secretly placed Taskmaster and the Hood in charge so that they could use the base to create new forces for Osborn's Dark Avengers team.

The Thunderbolts were brought into the Initiative.

Soon after, a failsafe program set up by the Skrull impersonating Hank Pym reactivated Ragnarok (a clone of Thor). After helping to stop Ragnarok's rampage, an underground team called Counter Force—made up of former New Warriors—revealed the scandal behind MVP's death and cover-up. Osborn used this as an excuse to shut down Camp Hammond. He later opened a new training facility, Camp HAMMER, in New Mexico. After Osborn's fall from power, Camp Hammer was shut down and a new Avengers Academy to teach young heroes was opened. **MF**

When the Civil War ended, Stark faced a flood of registered heroes to choose from for the Initiative's teams.

FLUX

FIRST APPEARANCE Incredible Hulk #17 (August 2000)
REAL NAME Benjamin Tibbetts **OCCUPATION** US Army private **BASE** Washington, DC **HEIGHT** Variable
WEIGHT Variable **EYES** Green **HAIR** Green
SPECIAL POWERS/ABILITIES Exposure to gamma radiation and experimentation by the military gave Flux superhuman strength and durability; however his physiology is in a constant state of change.

Benny Tibbetts enlisted in the US army to fight in the Gulf War and was caught in the blast of gamma bombs dropped by a black-ops team headed by General RYKER. Tibbetts survived, but like the HULK before him, was forever changed by the gamma radiation. His self-doubts prevented his powers from permanently catalyzing, and as Flux his body stayed in a constant state of transformation. General Ryker sent him to fight the Hulk twice, but he lost each time. Later, AIM captured him, and Grey of the Gamma Corps killed him on General Ryker's orders. **TB, MF**

General Ryker hoped that his creation, Flux, would defeat the Hulk, but Flux had too many mental insecurities.

FOOLKILLER

Paralyzed from the waist down, Ross Everbest's childhood was never going to be easy; then his parents were killed in the Korean War. However, when traveling revivalist preacher Reverend Mike Pike used faith-healing to restore his legs, Everbest's life changed. Joining Pike on the road, Everbest became increasingly angry with the "immoral fools" he encountered every day.

Vowing to rid the world of sinners and dissidents, he became Foolkiller, his murder spree beginning when he discovered Pike indulging in a drunken orgy.

Everbest's psychotic reign of death ended when he was killed by the MAN-THING. His example inspired two more Foolkillers: Greg Salinger, who was eventually locked up in a mental institution; and Kurt Gerhardt, who suffered the same fate—with a little help from DEADPOOL. **AD, MF**

FOOLKILLER

FACTFILE
REAL NAME
Ross G. Everbest
OCCUPATION
Killer
BASE
Mobile

HEIGHT 6 ft
WEIGHT 185 lbs
EYES Blue
HAIR Blond

FIRST APPEARANCE
Man-Thing #3 (March 1974)

POWERS

Psychopathic energy gave him greater strength and endurance than an average man of his weight; possessed a raygun, he termed his "purification gun," capable of disintegrating victims.

Foolkiller had a calling card warning victims that they had 24 hours to live and telling them to use the time wisely.

FORCE WORKS

FACTFILE
MEMBERS AND POWERS
CENTURY
Composite being of 100 alien warriors.
IRON MAN
Powered armor; flight; energy blasts.
MOONRAKER
Emits electrical energy from hands.
SCARLET WITCH
Chaos magic.
SPIDER-WOMAN
Various spider powers; spins webs of psionic energy.
US AGENT
Enhanced strength; expert combatant.
WONDER MAN
Body composed of ionic energy.
BASE
The Works, Ventura, California

FIRST APPEARANCE
Force Works #1 (July 1994)

FORCE WORKS

After the disbanding of the AVENGERS WEST COAST, Tony Stark (IRON MAN) founded Force Works, a team with a more aggressive, proactive stance. By using the SCARLET WITCH's hex powers, combined with data from a predictive supercomputer, the members of Force Works set out to squash budding threats before they could escalate to crisis levels.

On Force Works' first mission, WONDER MAN seemingly died while battling a band of KREE warriors. The team bounced back from this loss by welcoming the alien CENTURY into their ranks. Soon, the events known as the Crossing caused Iron Man to appear to turn traitor, behaving irrationally and murderously due to the mind-controlling IMMORTUS. A new hero named Moonraker (claiming to be LIBRA) joined the group to distract them from Immortus's larger schemes. Force Works dissolved following the Crossing episode. A new Force Works team was assigned to Iowa for the FIFTY-STATE INITIATIVE. **DW, MF**

FORCE WORKS
1 Spider-Woman (Julia Carpenter) ***2*** Wonder Man ***3*** Iron Man ***4*** Scarlet Witch ***5*** U.S.Agent

FORGE

FACTFILE

REAL NAME
Unknown

OCCUPATION
Inventor, former soldier

BASE
Dallas, Texas

HEIGHT 6 ft
WEIGHT 180 lbs
EYES Brown
HAIR Black

FIRST APPEARANCE
X-Men #184 (August 1984)

POWERS

Mutant ability gives superhuman talent for inventing mechanical devices. While even the greatest inventors must work out the principals and designs of their inventions, the ideas for Forge's inventions spring fully formed from his mutant mind.

FORGE

The Native American who became known as Forge was not only trained in mystic arts by Naze, a shaman in his Cheyenne tribe, but was also a mutant, with the ability to invent highly-sophisticated mechanical devices.

Forge lost a leg and a hand during the Vietnam War and designed mechanical limbs to replace them. When industrialist Anthony Stark (*see* IRON MAN) stopped making advanced weaponry for the federal government, the US Defense Department began buying new weaponry designs from Forge. During that time, he created a device that could detect hidden aliens and one that neutralized mutant powers.

Forge later joined the X-MEN, subsequently worked with X-FACTOR, and had a relationship with STORM. After being shot by BISHOP, who was hunting Hope SUMMERS, Forge went insane and was barely stopped before he allowed an interdimensional invasion of Earth. He has since recovered and joined CABLE's new X-FORCE team. **MT, MF**

FREEDOM FORCE

FIRST APPEARANCE Uncanny X-Men #199 (Nov. 1985)
BASE Washington DC **MEMBERS AND POWERS** **Mystique** (leader), shapeshifter [4]; **Avalanche**, groundquakes [7]; **Blob**, immovable; **Crimson Commando**, expert combatant [6]; **Destiny** (deceased), precognition [3]; **Pyro** (deceased), controls fire [5]; **Spider Woman**, spider powers; **Spiral**, spellcaster [2]; **Stonewall**, superstrength [1]; **Super Sabre** (deceased), superspeed
[Dazzler [8] is not a member]

Freedom Force was an incarnation of the BROTHERHOOD OF EVIL MUTANTS, formed to wipe out mutant threats to America. The team clashed with outlaw mutants such as the X-MEN and X-FACTOR. The Force later teamed with the X-Men to save Dallas, Texas, from the ADVERSARY, but the group disbanded after a disastrous mission to the Middle East. An all-new Freedom Force team was formed for Montana as part of the FIFTY-STATE INITIATIVE. It included the Challenger, CLOUD 9, Spinner, Think Tank, and Equinox. **DW, MF**

FORGOTTEN ONE, THE

FIRST APPEARANCE Eternals #13 (July 1977)
REAL NAME Unknown; has been known as Gilgamesh
OCCUPATION Adventurer; agent of the Celestials
BASE Mobile **HEIGHT** 6 ft 5 in **WEIGHT** 269 lbs
EYES Brown **HAIR** Black
SPECIAL POWERS/ABILITIES Superhuman strength and stamina; immortality; full mental control over body; ability to manipulate matter on a subatomic scale.

As an Eternal known throughout the years as Hero or Gilgamesh, the immortal Forgotten One has lived for millennia. For meddling in the affairs of humanity, he was confined to the city of Olympia for centuries, only regaining his freedom after helping foil an attack by the DEVIANTS, grotesque, distant cousins of humanity. As Gilgamesh, he served with the AVENGERS, but he was killed during a battle with IMMORTUS. Reborn later in a new body, he could not recall his former life. He was working in a circus in Brazil when AJAK found him and restored his lost memories. **AD, MF**

FRANKENSTEIN'S MONSTER

FIRST APPEARANCE X-Men #40 (January 1968)
REAL NAME None **OCCUPATION** Caretaker, wanderer
BASE Bavaria, Germany **HEIGHT** 8 ft
WEIGHT 325 lbs **EYES** Brown **HAIR** Brown
SPECIAL POWERS/ABILITIES The Monster possesses superhuman strength and stamina; able to go into suspended animation when exposed to intense cold.

In the late 18th century, Victor Frankenstein created a living person from corpses. Abandoned by his creator, the Monster forced Frankenstein to create a mate for him. After Frankenstein killed her, the Monster slew Frankenstein's own bride and pursued him to the Arctic. The Monster revived in 1898 and again in modern times. As "Adam," he assisted monster hunter Elsa BLOODSTONE. Clones of the Monster were created by both the Nazis and SHIELD, and a descendant of Frankenstein sent an army of monsters against the Jean Grey School for Higher Learning, attracting the original's attention. **PS, MF**

FRENZY

FIRST APPEARANCE X-Factor #4 (May 1986)
REAL NAME Joanna Cargill **OCCUPATION** Adventurer
BASE Jean Grey School for Higher Learning
HEIGHT 6 ft 11 in **WEIGHT** 275 lbs
EYES Brown **HAIR** Black
SPECIAL POWERS/ABILITIES Joanna has steel-hard skin, rendering her invulnerable to most harm, and she possess superhuman strength.

After accidentally killing her abusive father when her mutant powers manifested, Joanna Cargill ran away from home and became a mercenary. She ended up working as a member of APOCALYPSE's Alliance of Evil, but she later threw in with the Femizons instead. She found a home with MAGNETO's ACOLYTES, serving with them for years. After experiencing life as a hero in the Age of X reality created by LEGION, she decided to change her ways and became a member of the X-MEN. During the X-Men's schism, she followed WOLVERINE east to join the Jean Grey School for Higher Learning. **MF**

FROST, EMMA

Psi of the highest order

FROST, EMMA

FACTFILE

REAL NAME
Emma Frost

OCCUPATION
CEO of Frost International; Instructor, Massachusetts Academy

BASE
Massachusetts Academy

HEIGHT 5 ft 10 in
WEIGHT 125 lbs
EYES Blue
HAIR Ash blond

FIRST APPEARANCE
X-MEN #132
(January 1980)

POWERS

Frost is a formidable telepath who can read minds and project thoughts into others' minds, controlling their actions. She can project pain and knock out victims by touching their brows. She later developed a secondary mutation that allows her to take on a nearly indestructible, diamond-hard form at will, during which time she cannot use her mental powers.

Emma Frost was born into a wealthy New England family. Gifted with a superb business brain and mutant powers of telepathy, she spurned her father's fortune and set out on her own. At a remarkably young age, she was running a multi-billion-dollar corporation specializing in transportation and electronics, which she re-named Frost International. She also became the chair of a college prep school called the Massachusetts Academy, where she trained young mutants.

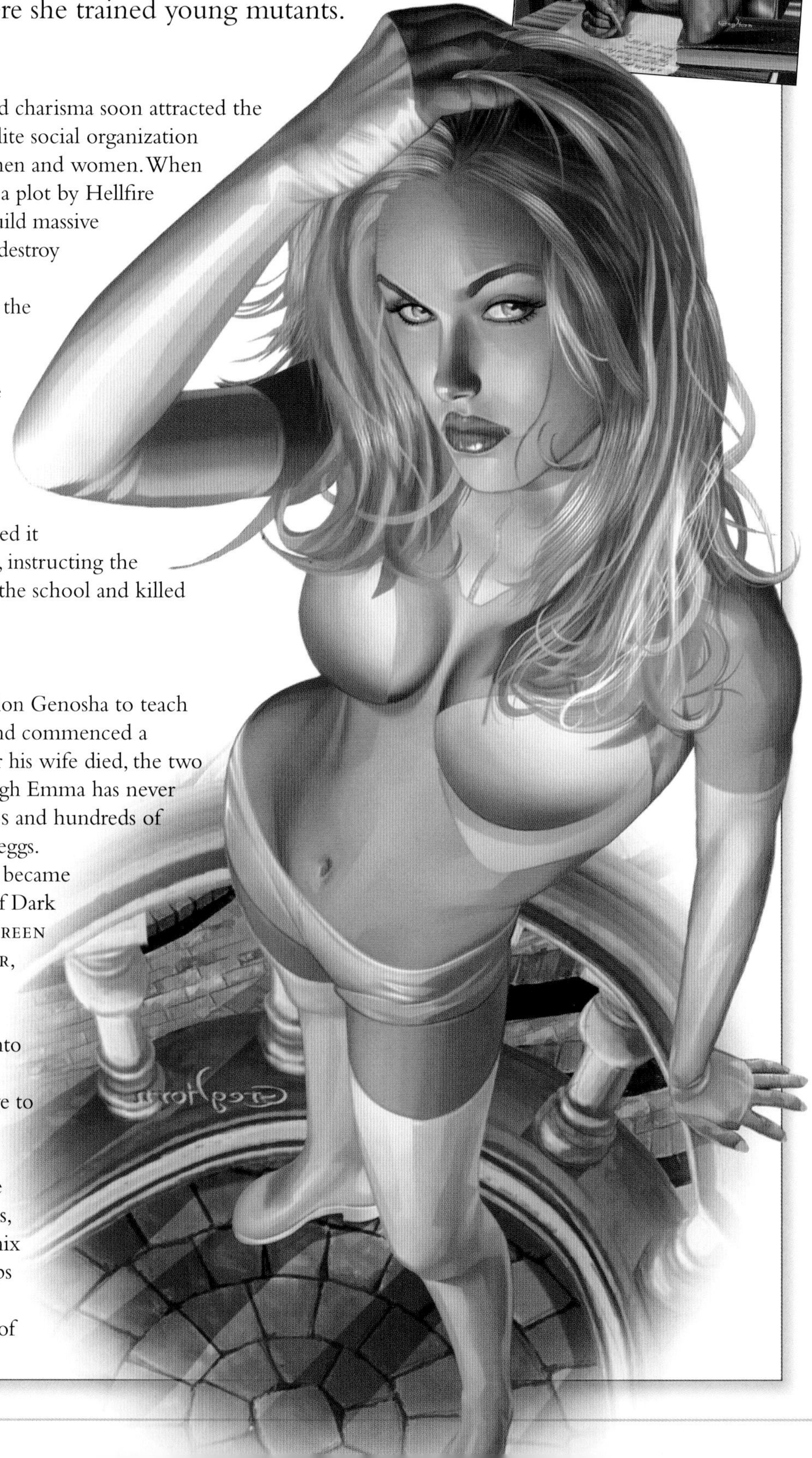

Emma was the chair of the Massachusetts Academy's board of trustees.

JOIN THE CLUB

Emma's great wealth, intelligence, and charisma soon attracted the attention of the HELLFIRE CLUB, an elite social organization of powerful politicians and businessmen and women. When Frost and Sebastian Shaw discovered a plot by Hellfire Club leader EDWARD BUCKMAN to build massive SENTINEL robots to hunt down and destroy mutants, they seized control of the organization's Inner Circle, and took the codenames Black King and White Queen.

As the White Queen, Frost became an enemy of the X-MEN. However, guilt over her inability to prevent the violent deaths of her mutant student team, the HELLIONS, caused her to offer the Massachusetts Academy to PROFESSOR X, who turned it into his new School for Gifted Youngsters. Emma Frost taught there, instructing the young mutants of GENERATION X, until her sister Adrienne ruined the school and killed one of the students, for which crime Emma murdered her.

Emma underwent a secondary mutation during the destruction of Genosha, and she can now turn her body into living diamond.

X-WOMAN

Emma moved to the mutant island nation Genosha to teach there. She later joined the X-Men and commenced a telepathic affair with CYCLOPS. After his wife died, the two began a physical relationship. Although Emma has never had children, the STEPFORD CUCKOOS and hundreds of other clones were created from her eggs.

During the DARK REIGN, Emma became part of the CABAL and led a team of Dark X-Men for Norman Osborn (*see* GREEN GOBLIN). However, she and NAMOR, who was also part of the Cabal, betrayed Osborn at the critical moment. When the X-Men split into two groups, Emma stayed with Cyclops in Utopia rather than leave to teach at WOLVERINE's new school.

Emma was on the moon when IRON MAN's attempt to destroy the Phoenix Force broke it into pieces, and she became one of the Phoenix Five. She was furious with Cyclops when he took her fragment of the Phoenix Force to become Dark Phoenix, but stuck with him after he and MAGNETO broke her out of custody, despite the fact that her powers were unstable. **MT, MF**

FACTFILE

ORIGINAL MEMBERS AND POWERS

PASTE-POT PETE
Later known as the Trapster

SANDMAN
Made of living sand

WIZARD
Brilliant scientist and inventor

MEDUSA Inhuman with prehensile hair

BASE
Subterranean Manhattan headquarters; mobile

FIRST APPEARANCE
Fantastic Four #36 (March 1965)

FRIGHTFUL FOUR

The WIZARD (Bentley Wittman) was a much-lauded scientist until the similarly brilliant MISTER FANTASTIC (Reed Richards) led the FANTASTIC FOUR into the limelight and forced him from the public eye. Insanely jealous, the Wizard committed himself to destroying Reed and his friends, by establishing the Frightful Four team of Super Villains. The original lineup was Wizard himself, SANDMAN, Paste Pot Pete (Later TRAPSTER) and MEDUSA.

The Wizard changed his team's roster many times, but it continued to suffer defeats. Even when it took the Fantastic Four off guard—during Reed and Sue Storm's engagement party, for example—the Wizard's team was still beaten. The search for new members led the Wizard to look everywhere, even placing ads and holding auditions. Other members included ABSORBING MAN, Beetle, Brute (an alternate Reed Richards), CONSTRICTOR, DEADPOOL, DRAGON MAN, DREADKNIGHT, ELECTRO, HYDRO-MAN, KLAW, LIVING LASER, LLYRA, Man-Bull, MISTER HYDE, RED GHOST, SHE-THING, TASKMASTER, THUNDRA, and TITANIA. **AD, MF**

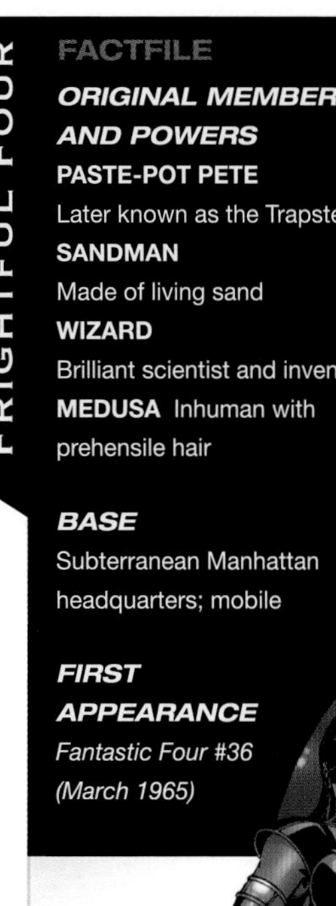

FRIGHTFUL FOUR
1 Wizard
2 Hydro-Man
3 Trapster
4 Salamandra

FROG-MAN

FIRST APPEARANCE Marvel Team-Up #121 (September 1982)
REAL NAME Eugene Paul Patilio
OCCUPATION High-school student **BASE** New York City
HEIGHT 5 ft 8 in **WEIGHT** 158 lbs **EYES** Brown **HAIR** Red
SPECIAL POWERS/ABILITIES Frog-man wears an electrically-powered suit with leaping coils built into his boots; can leap a maximum height of 60 ft and a maximum distance of 100 ft.

Eugene's father designed a pair of electrically-powered leaping coils. Calling himself Leap-Frog, he took to crime to support his family, but ended up in jail. To redeem his father's name, Eugene donned one of his old costumes to become the crime fighter Frog-Man, helping SPIDER-MAN and the HUMAN TORCH defeat the SPEED DEMON. Eugene later tried to team up with the Toad and Spider-Kid (now called the Steel Spider). A SKRULL posing as Frog-Man joined the Action Pack, the Kentucky team of the FIFTY-STATE INITIATIVE. During the SECRET INVASION, the Skrull died, and Eugene was rescued. **TD, MF**

FACTFILE

REAL NAME
Jacob Fury

OCCUPATION
Spy

BASE
Mobile

HEIGHT 5 ft 10 in
WEIGHT 185 lbs
EYES Blue
HAIR Brown

FIRST APPEARANCE
Strange Tales #159 (August 1967)

POWERS

Jake is a genius and an excellent combatant as well as a top spy.

FURY, JAKE

Jake Fury was born and raised in New York City with his brother Nick FURY. He supposedly became embittered by Nick's success and took on the identity of the villain Scorpio, leader of the ZODIAC. After several failed attempts to take down his brother and his precious SHIELD, he constructed a set of androids to replace the others in the Zodiac. When the DEFENDERS stopped him, he committed suicide.

In reality, Jake had been replaced by a shield android (Life Model Decoy) that had become Scorpio. Meanwhile, the real Jake had joined HYDRA as a double agent for Nick, posing as the agent called Kraken and rising within the criminal organization's ranks. Jake also supposedly had a boy named Mikel, who followed in his footsteps as Scorpio. When Mikel learned that Nick was his real father, he joined SHIELD instead and was later killed in the line of duty. **MF**

FURY, NICK, JR.

FIRST APPEARANCE Battle Scars #1 (January 2012)
REAL NAME Nicholas Fury, Jr.
OCCUPATION Agent of SHIELD **BASE** SHIELD Helicarrier
HEIGHT 6 ft **WEIGHT** 185 lbs **EYES** Green **HAIR** Bald
SPECIAL POWERS/ABILITIES Nick is a trained soldier. He inherited some of the Infinity Formula in his father's blood, giving him longevity and helping him heal fast.

Born to Nia Jones, Marcus Johnson never knew his real father. He was serving with the US Army in Afghanistan when he received word his mother had been killed during FEAR ITSELF. When he and his pal Phil COULSON came back home for the funeral, men working for the villain Orion attacked him, wanting the Infinity Formula in his blood. He soon found out that Nick FURY was his real father. After defeating Orion and his mercenaries, both Fury Jr. and Coulson joined SHIELD's secret AVENGERS team. **MF**

NICK FURY, *see page 140*

Fury, Nick

Agent of SHIELD

Nick Fury grew up on the mean streets of Hell's Kitchen in New York during the Great Depression of the 1930s. Recruited by "Happy" Sam Sawyer, who would serve as his commanding officer for most of the war, Fury enlisted in the US Army at the outbreak of World War II, eventually becoming the sergeant in command of the Howling Commandos, an elite unit of Able Company given the most dangerous missions.

Once a gung-ho sergeant during World War II, Fury became Director of SHIELD.

FACTFILE

REAL NAME
Nicholas Joseph Fury

OCCUPATION
Spymaster, director of SHIELD

BASE
SHIELD mobile Helicarrier

HEIGHT 6 ft 1 in
WEIGHT 225 lbs
EYES Brown
HAIR Brown, graying at temples

FIRST APPEARANCE
Sgt. Fury and His Howling Commandos #1 (May 1963)

POWERS

Nick Fury is a trained soldier with decades of experience. His youth and vigor have been maintained, despite his age, by the rejuvenating Infinity Formula. He is an expert martial artist and highly trained in the use of all kinds of weapons, both conventional and advanced.

As Director for the Strategic Hazard Intervention Espionage Logistics Directorate (SHIELD), Fury had access to state-of-the-art weapons and technologies.

Infinity Formula

Fury and his Howlers racked up impressive victories over the Axis forces, defeating such foes as Baron von Strucker and his Blitzkreig Squad, and the Red Skull. Wounded, Fury was injected with an experimental Infinity Formula by Professor Berthold Sternberg. The formula allowed Fury to survive what would have been fatal injuries (though he did lose his left eye), but the drawback was that Fury needed a yearly dosage to survive—and for decades Professor Sternberg blackmailed Fury in order to provide the necessary supply of the drug. On the plus side, the formula greatly extended Fury's lifespan. After the War, Fury was an agent for the OSS, and then the CIA, earning the rank of colonel. When Super Heroes began to appear, the CIA employed Fury as a liaison between them and the government. Fury then headed SHIELD, a worldwide peacekeeping force.

Fury's inner circle at SHIELD includes surviving members of the Howling Commandos.

Resourceful, cool, courageous, and committed to the cause, Fury is a superb field agent, and a brilliant leader.

The Enemy Within

SHIELD's first mission was to destroy the terrorist cartel Hydra, which had been founded by Fury's old nemesis, Baron von Strucker.

After Fury led a failed coup attempt in Latveria, he lost his position as director of SHIELD, but he formed a team of Secret Warriors to help repel the Secret Invasion, after which he learned that Hydra was secretly behind SHIELD. This turned out to be a ploy he'd engineered with his brother Jake Fury to destroy Hydra. Fury's illegitimate son Mikel had thought Jake was his father, but when he learned the truth, he joined the Secret Warriors—only to be killed in action. A long-hidden son of Fury's—Marcus Johnson, now known as Nick Fury Jr.—recently emerged and joined SHIELD to lead the organization's new team of Avengers.

MT, MF

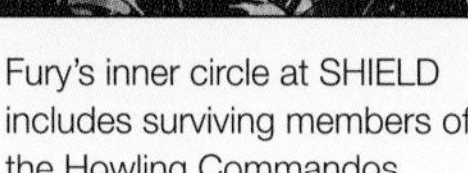

ESSENTIAL STORYLINES

- ***Strange Tales #135*** Nick Fury is recruited by SHIELD to be its director in its war against Hydra.
- ***Nick Fury vs. SHIELD #1–6*** Having discovered corruption deep within his own spy organization, Fury must battle his own men.
- ***Secret War #1–5*** When Fury becomes aware of a clear and present danger to world security, he must organize a covert team of superhuman operatives to wage a secret war.

GALACTUS

Devourer of Worlds

GALACTUS

FACTFILE

REAL NAME
Galen

OCCUPATION
Consumer of planets

BASE
Mobile

HEIGHT 26 ft 9 in
WEIGHT 18.2 tons
EYES Unknown; to humanoids appear white
HAIR Unknown; appears black to humanoids

FIRST APPEARANCE
Fantastic Four #48 (March 1966)

POWERS
Manipulates vast cosmic power; can restructure matter and deliver a planet-shattering energy blast; able to teleport across the galaxy and create force fields; travels the galaxy in a worldship the size of the solar system; also pilots a smaller, circular "shuttle."

In the last universe's final moments, Galactus awaited his death.

Older than the universe itself, the only survivor of the universe that came before our own, Galactus's fate is inextricably bound up with that of the entire cosmos. Although at times he has been a force for good, far more often he has brought doom, destroying whole peoples and consuming entire worlds, for his hunger for energy is insatiable; without it, he would cease to exist.

GALEN OF TAA

Born Galen, on the paradise world of Taa, Galactus was fated to live in the last days of his universe, just as it was entering the final stages of the Big Crunch. Realizing that his people were doomed, he persuaded them to pilot a vessel into the heart of the Crunch, to die in one last act of heroism. His people perished, but Galactus was somehow saved by the Phoenix Force of his universe.

For billions of years he slept, and when he awoke it was with an immense hunger that could only be sated by consuming the life-energies of a world. At first he searched for uninhabited worlds but his hunger gradually forced him to consume planets populated by sentient races. Galactus's conscience was only eased by a prophecy that he would ultimately make good on the devastation he wrought.

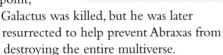

As the centuries passed, countless worlds crumbled before Galactus's devouring might.

HERALDS AND FATE

When Galactus reached the planet Zenn-La, he struck a deal with a native to save that world. The SILVER SURFER was the first of many such heralds—and the first to betray him, saving Earth in the process. At one point, Galactus was killed, but he was later resurrected to help prevent Abraxas from destroying the entire multiverse.

Galactus was held in the galactic prison Kyln, but DRAX THE DESTROYER broke him out so that he could stop the ANNIHILATION Wave, and he joined HERCULES' God Squad to fight AMATSU-MIKABOSHI during the CHAOS WAR. **AD, MF**

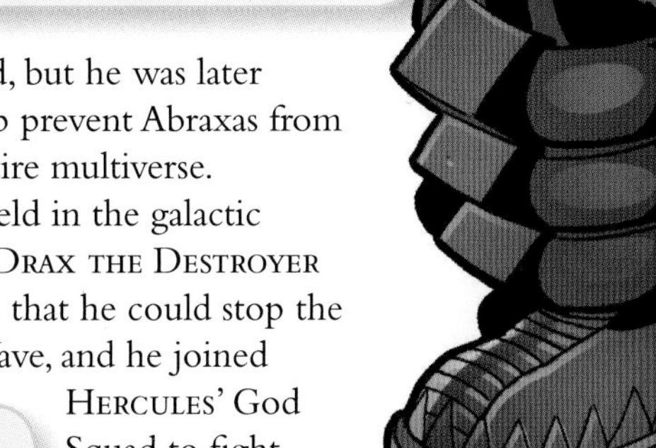

A being of immense power and size, only the very brave or foolish would stand against Galactus.

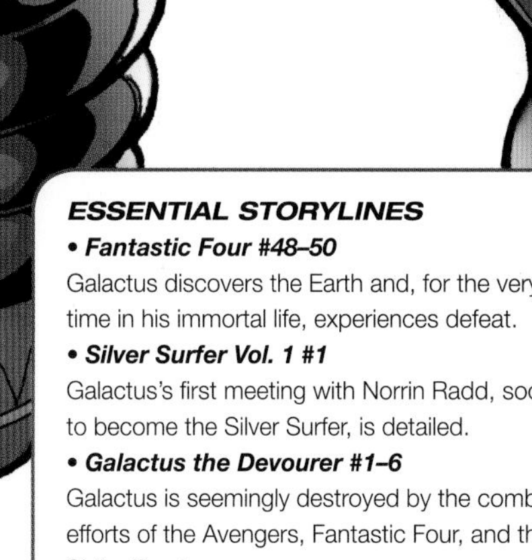

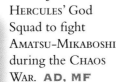

ESSENTIAL STORYLINES

- ***Fantastic Four #48–50***
Galactus discovers the Earth and, for the very first time in his immortal life, experiences defeat.
- ***Silver Surfer Vol. 1 #1***
Galactus's first meeting with Norrin Radd, soon to become the Silver Surfer, is detailed.
- ***Galactus the Devourer #1–6***
Galactus is seemingly destroyed by the combined efforts of the Avengers, Fantastic Four, and the Shi'ar Empire.

Gaea

FIRST APPEARANCE Doctor Strange #6 (February 1975)
REAL NAME Gaea **OCCUPATION** Goddess **BASE** Earth
HEIGHT Variable **WEIGHT** Variable **EYES** Blue **HAIR** Black
SPECIAL POWERS/ABILITIES Possesses enormous mystical energies tied to the Earth; commands the forces of nature, such as storms and volcanic activity; power to heal and make things grow; telekinetic abilities; able to bestow magical powers.

Gaea is the embodiment of the spirit of life, growth, harvest, and renewal on Earth. One of the Elder Gods who ruled the world when humanity was not even a glimmer, Gaea was the only one not to devolve into a demon, instead becoming Mother Earth. With ODIN, Gaea conceived THOR, who is both of Asgard and of Earth, the champion of both realms. During the CHAOS WAR, she gave HERCULES the power he needed to defeat AMATSU-MIKABOSHI. With Freyja and Idunn, she became part of the All-Mother who rules Asgardia. **TB, MF**

GALACTUS, *see page 141*

Gamora

Gamora is the sole survivor of the Zen-Whoberi, an alien race wiped out by the Badoon. The mad Titan THANOS rescued Gamora as an infant and trained her to become the deadliest assassin in the galaxy so she could kill the MAGUS, an evil future version of Adam WARLOCK whose Universal Church of Truth had wiped out her people in her original timeline.

Thanos killed her after she recognized the threat he presented to all life in the galaxy and rebelled against him. Warlock absorbed her spirit into his soul-gem. She returned in a new form to stop Thanos from using the Infinity Gauntlet, and she guarded the Time Gem as a member of the Infinity Watch.

Gamora later led the fight against the ANNIHILATION, helping stop the first wave. During the second, she was absorbed into the PHALANX but freed when they were defeated. She later joined STARLORD's new GUARDIANS OF THE GALAXY. **DW, MF**

FACTFILE
REAL NAME
Gamora
OCCUPATION
Former assassin, galactic hero
BASE
Mobile

HEIGHT 6 ft
WEIGHT 170 lbs
EYES Green
HAIR Black

FIRST APPEARANCE
Strange Tales #180 (June 1975)

GAMORA

POWERS
Gamora is an expert gymnast and martial artist proficient with all known weapons. She has enhanced durability, endurance, strength, and speed.

Gambit

FACTFILE
REAL NAME
Remy LeBeau
OCCUPATION
Professional thief, adventurer
BASE
New Orleans, Louisiana; the Xavier Institute, Salem Center, New York State

HEIGHT 6 ft 1 in
WEIGHT 175 lbs
EYES Black (red pupils)
HAIR Brown

FIRST APPEARANCE
The Uncanny X-Men #266 (August 1990)

GAMBIT

POWERS
Mutant ability to charge small objects with an unknown form of energy; when he throws the objects at a target, they explode on impact.

The mutant Gambit was abducted soon after his birth by members of the Thieves' Guild of New Orleans. Hoping to make peace between the Thieves' Guild and their rivals, the Assassins' Guild, Remy married the granddaughter of the leader of the Assassins' Guild. Her brother Julien was opposed to the union, and Remy killed him in a duel. Banished from New Orleans, Remy became the international master thief known as Gambit. Gambit was employed by MISTER SINISTER to organize the MARAUDERS, a mutant team of assassins, but he was shocked when Sinister sent the Marauders to massacre the MORLOCKS.

Later, Gambit met and aided STORM, who had been turned into a child, and she sponsored his membership in the X-MEN, where he met ROGUE and began a longstanding affair with her. Gambit later served as one of APOCALYPSE's Horsemen—DEATH—and rejoined the Marauders. He helped save Hope SUMMERS and came back to the X-Men. He traveled with X-23 for a while, then joined the Jean Grey School for Higher Learning. **PS, MF**

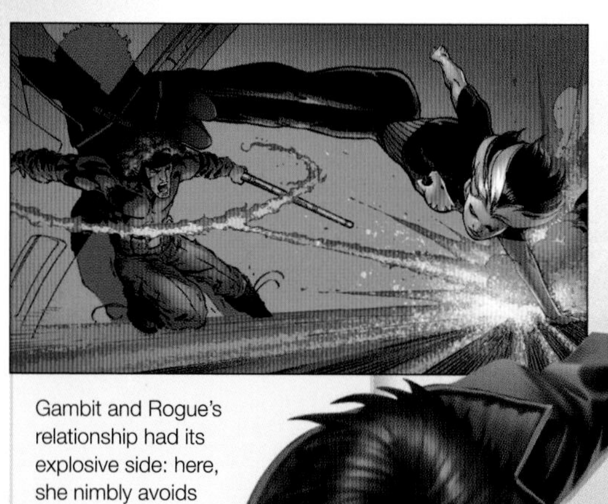
Gambit and Rogue's relationship had its explosive side: here, she nimbly avoids Gambit's "energy charge card."

More fiery fallings-out as Rogue gives Gambit a taste of his own medicine—an energy blast that knocks him off his feet.

GARGOYLE

FACTFILE
REAL NAME
Isaac Christians
OCCUPATION
Caretaker
BASE
The estate of Daimon Hellstrom

HEIGHT 5 ft 10 in
WEIGHT 204 lbs
EYES Red
HAIR None

FIRST APPEARANCE
Defenders #94 (April 1981)

POWERS
Possesses the increased strength and mystic durability of one of the demon race. He can also levitate, fly, and project bolts of eldritch force from his hands; leathery skin is bulletproof; impervious to disease and to aging.

GARGOYLE

In order to secure economic prosperity for his impoverished town, elderly Isaac Christians made a pact with a demonic group called the Six-Fingered Hand. He allowed his essence to be transplanted into the body of a demon, while the demon's mind would reside within his own human body. This demon had formerly been trapped in stone form as a gargoyle, as seen on ancient churches throughout Europe.

Despite his appearance, the Gargoyle was not evil, and after the destruction of his human body, he rebelled against the Six-Fingered Hand and joined the DEFENDERS. At one point, his body became the vessel for the DRAGON OF THE MOON, and he found a new body that could change to his Gargoyle form and back at will. He later became an instructor at Camp Hammond before retiring.

The Gargoyle should not be confused with a similarly-named Soviet agent (real name: Yuri Topolov) who attempted to capture the HULK on the eve of the latter's creation and was the father of the GREMLIN. **TB**

GATEWAY

FIRST APPEARANCE Uncanny X-Men #227 (March 1988)
REAL NAME Unrevealed
OCCUPATION None known **BASE** Australia
HEIGHT 4 ft 6 in **WEIGHT** 80 lbs
EYES Brown **HAIR** Gray-black
SPECIAL POWERS/ABILITIES Ability to open teleportation doorways, transdimensional clairvoyant.

The mysterious, silent Gateway is an Australian aborigine mutant who can open teleportation doorways. The outlaw REAVERS forced Gateway to assist them by threatening to destroy an aboriginal sacred site. The X-MEN later evicted the Reavers from their headquarters, and Gateway became an unofficial member. Gateway has a special connection to M and is an ancestor of BISHOP. He became the mentor of MANIFOLD but was later killed by Ultimaton (Weapon XV). **DW, MF**

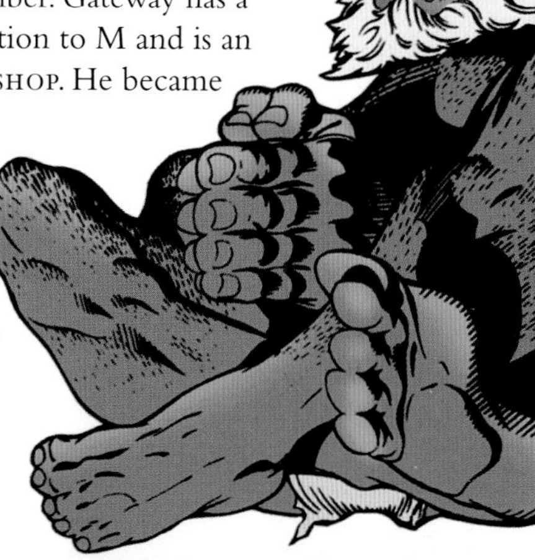

GAROKK

FIRST APPEARANCE Astonishing Tales #2 (October 1970)
REAL NAME Unrevealed **OCCUPATION** Sailor, wanderer, god
BASE The Savage Land **HEIGHT** 7 ft **WEIGHT** 355 lbs
EYES (as human) Brown; (as Garokk) Yellow
HAIR (as human) Brown; (as Garokk) Virtually none
SPECIAL POWERS/ABILITIES Can project heat, light, and concussive force from his eyes. Possesses virtual immortality.

Godlike wrath: Garokk the immortal Petrified Man lets fly with his powerful eye beams.

In the 15th century, a British sailor from HMS *Drake* became stranded in the Savage Land. Immersion in a pool of mysterious liquid made him virtually immortal. He wandered the world for centuries, and his body took on a rocklike appearance, as if he were petrified. In recent times, the Petrified Man returned to the Savage Land, where he was worshiped by the Sun People as the incarnation of their god Garokk. He regards himself as the guardian of the Savage Land, but his insanity makes him a menace. **PS**

GATHERERS

The Gatherers serve PROCTOR, an extra-dimensional being. Each member of the Gatherers comes from an alternate Earth in another dimension. On each of their Earths, the Gatherers were AVENGERS. Also, on each of their Earths, SERSI, a member of the ETERNALS, went mad and killed everyone. The Gatherers were each the last survivors of their home worlds. They were recruited by Proctor to destroy Sersi and the Avengers of Earth-616. But in order for the Gatherers to exist on Earth-616, they had to each kill their own counterpart on Earth-616. This process was known as "gathering." The Gatherers infiltrated the Avengers' mansion on Earth-616 several times. In the final battle, Proctor tried to destroy all realities, but THUNDERSTRIKE hit Proctor with a bolt of lightning, and all the Gatherers collapsed. **MT**

GATHERERS

FACTFILE
MAIN MEMBERS AND POWERS
PROCTOR
Teleportation; mind control.
CASSANDRA
Telepath; strategist.
MAGDALENE
Wields power lance.
SLOTH
Superstrong; razor-sharp claws.
SWORDSMAN
Sword fires energy beam.

FIRST APPEARANCE
Avengers #355 (October 1992)

THE GATHERERS
1 Cassandra
2 Magdalene
3 Swordsman
4 Sloth

Gauntlet

FIRST APPEARANCE She-Hulk #100 (January 2006)
REAL NAME Joseph Green **OCCUPATION** Super Hero trainer
BASE Camp Hammond, Stamford, Connecticut
HEIGHT 5 ft 11 in **WEIGHT** 210 lbs **EYES** Brown **HAIR** Black
SPECIAL POWERS/ABILITIES Has an alien gauntlet on his right hand. It can project a powerful hand composed of pure energy.

When two aliens battling in space crashed in the Sudanese desert, the US Army went to investigate and clashed with agents of HYDRA. One of the soldiers, Sergeant Green, defended himself with an alien gauntlet. He won the day but found that the alien gauntlet could not be removed. During the CIVIL WAR, IRON MAN and Henry GYRICH recruited Green as drill sergeant at Camp Hammond, a training camp for the FIFTY-STATE INITIATIVE. One of his trainees, SLAPSTICK, beat him into a coma, but when KIA (*see* Michael VAN PATRICK) threatened Green's life, Green's gauntlet saved him. Green stuck with Camp Hammond, even through the DARK REIGN. Others left, but he was a loyal soldier. **MF**

Ghost

FIRST APPEARANCE Iron Man #219 (June, 1987)
REAL NAME Unknown
OCCUPATION Former assassin, galactic hero **BASE** Mobile Hammond, Stamford, Connecticut **HEIGHT** 5 ft. 11 in.
WEIGHT 175 lbs **EYES** Blue **HAIR BROWN**
SPECIAL POWERS/ABILITIES Brilliant inventor, tactician, and hacker. Suit grants invisibility and intangibility.

Originally a computer engineer, Ghost studied technology to make computers phase through matter. When his girlfriend, a co-worker, was murdered, Ghost discovered that his company was responsible. He used the tech to escape a bomb they directed at him, but became fused with the invention. After exacting his revenge, he sold his services as a saboteur. When SPYMASTER was sent to kill him, he turned the tables and killed Spymaster instead. He later joined the THUNDERBOLTS under Norman Osborn (GREEN GOBLIN). He betrayed Osborn at the end of the DARK SIEGE and joined Luke CAGE's Thunderbolts afterward. **MF**

Genesis

FIRST APPEARANCE Cable #18 (December 1994)
REAL NAME Tyler Dayspring
OCCUPATION Would-be conqueror; arms-dealer **BASE** Mobile
HEIGHT 6 ft 1 in **WEIGHT** 191 lbs **EYES** Blue **HAIR** Blond
SPECIAL POWERS/ABILITIES Mutant ability to create solid holograms from the memories of another person; trained in military tactics and combat techniques; wears armored suit.

The adopted son of CABLE in a future world ruled by APOCALYPSE, Tyler Dayspring was brainwashed by Cable's twisted clone STRYFE into becoming his father's enemy. Tyler traveled to the present, intent on ensuring that Apocalypse's rise to power would take place, and on avenging himself on Cable. He operated at first under the alias of a rogue arms dealer named Tolliver, but then abandoned that identity for direct action as Genesis. However, when Genesis attempted to restore WOLVERINE's lost adamantium to his skeleton, the pain-crazed mutant slew him. **TB**

Generation X

FACTFILE

MEMBERS AND POWERS

HUSK
Sheds skin to reveal shape-shifted body beneath.

SKIN
Has 6 ft of extra skin, to manipulate as required.

M
Superstrength; invulnerability.

JUBILEE
Projects explosive energy bolts.

CHAMBER
Projects psionic energy blasts from chest.

SYNCH
Mimics powers of students.

PENANCE
Super-dense body.

BASE
Massachusetts Academy

FIRST APPEARANCE
Generation X #1 (November 1994)

As one generation of X-MEN matures so another steps forward, in this case Generation X. Having experienced danger in the form of the alien collective intelligence, PHALANX, when the members of Generation X banded together they had a fair idea what fate had in store. Accepted by the Xavier Institute's new mutant high school at Massachusetts Academy, the team learned to hone its abilities and were introduced to PROFESSOR X's vision of the future. While at the Academy, the members of Generation X faced various foes, including EMPLATE, who preyed on the marrow of mutants. The team members were outed to the world as mutants and, with those in charge of the school—Emma FROST and Sean Cassidy (BANSHEE)—becoming increasingly unstable, they decided to go their separate ways. **AD**

CHARACTER KEY
1 Emma Frost ***2*** M
3 Banshee ***4*** Chamber
5 Synch ***6*** Jubilee
7 Penance ***8*** Skin ***9*** Husk

GHOST RIDER

The Brimstone Biker

The Ghost Riders are brilliant motorcyclists who can perform incredible stunts. Their mystical bikes enable them to ride up walls and even across water.

Posing as Satan, MEPHISTO approached stunt motorcyclist Johnny Blaze and agreed to cure Blaze's mentor "Crash" Simpson of a fatal disease in exchange for Blaze's soul. Simpson then died performing a stunt, and Mephisto bonded the demon ZARATHOS to Blaze's body, transforming him into a Ghost Rider. Blaze was temporarily freed of the curse when Zarathos became trapped in a crystal of souls, but that was far from the Ghost Rider's end.

As the new Ghost Rider, Alejandra didn't always get along with Johnny Blaze.

FACTFILE

REAL NAME
John "Johnny" Blaze

OCCUPATION
Stunt motorcyclist

BASE
Mobile

HEIGHT (Ghost Rider) 6 ft 2 in
WEIGHT (Ghost Rider) 220 lbs
EYES (Ghost Rider) flaming red
HAIR (Ghost Rider) none

FIRST APPEARANCE
Marvel Spotlight #5 (August 1972)

POWERS
Turns into a superhuman mystical being that projects "hellfire"; Ghost Rider I can create a mystical motorcycle from "hellfire." Ghost Rider II's "Penance Stare" causes wrongdoers to suffer the same emotional pain they inflicted.

THE FAMILY CURSE

When criminals wounded Barbara Ketch, her brother Dan carried her to a junkyard. With Barbara's innocent blood on his hands, Dan touched a mysterious motorcycle and became the new Ghost Rider. Dan and John Blaze later learned they were brothers, each with their own demon. John was once more bonded to Zarathos and became a Ghost Rider again, pursuing the demon LUCIFER.

The rogue angel Zadkiel convinced Ketch to collect the power of the spirits of vengeance all around the world—including Blaze's—as it turned out that these spirits came not from demons but angels. However, Zadkiel was actually using Ketch to gather the power for himself so he could launch an assault on the walls of Heaven itself. Dan and John reunited with the other spirits of vengeance to topple Zadkiel from his stolen throne.

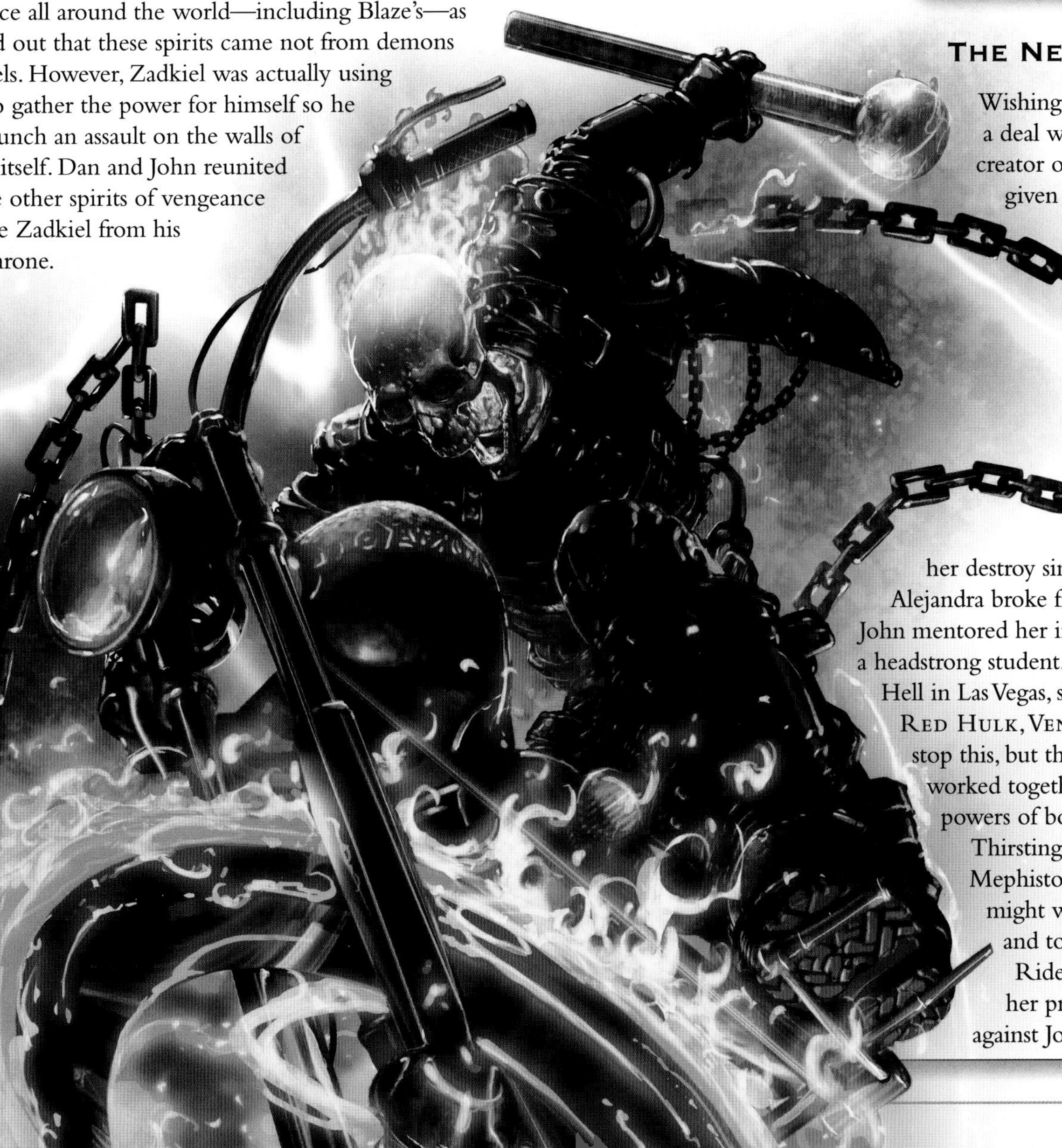

THE NEW RIDER

Wishing to be rid of the Ghost Rider, John cut a deal with Adam (the first man and the creator of sin) to have his spirit of vengeance given to someone he'd never met. It wound up with an 18-year-old Nicaraguan woman named Alejandra, and Adam forced her to use her powers to rid Nicaragua of sin by turning its people mindless. Realizing his terrible mistake, John chased Alejandra and Adam into space, from which Adam planned to have her destroy sin right across the Earth.

Alejandra broke free from Adam's control just in time. John mentored her in the use of her powers, but she proved a headstrong student. Racing off to stop an incursion from Hell in Las Vegas, she activated it instead. Blaze joined RED HULK, VENOM (Flash Thompson), and X-23 to stop this, but they were all killed. Sent to Hell, they worked together, temporarily giving Red Hulk the powers of both Venom and the Ghost Rider.

Thirsting for vengeance, Alejandra went after Mephisto, caring nothing that destroying Hell might well destroy reality. John stopped her and took back the power of the Ghost Rider. Alejandra, who held onto some of her previous power, swore vengeance against John. **PS, MF**

Genoshans

FIRST APPEARANCE Uncanny X-Men #235 (October 1988)
BASE The island of Genosha, Indian Ocean
SPECIAL POWERS/ABILITIES The inhabitants of Genosha were a mixture of ordinary humans and those with mutant abilities. The latter were called "Mutates" and were conditioned to fulfil specific, tasks tailored to their particular mutant ability. From time to time Mutates managed to rebel against their human masters.

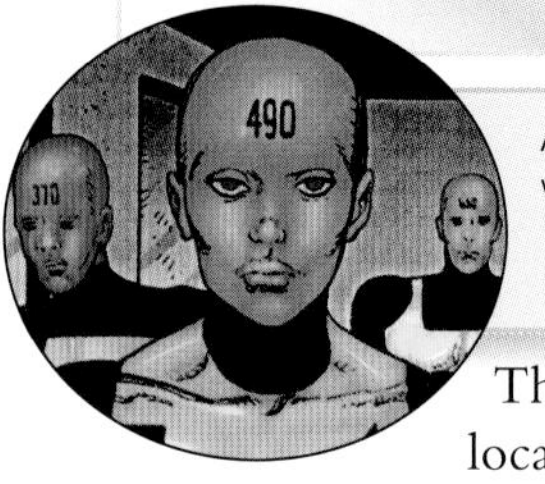

Adolescent mutates were tatooed with a number on their foreheads, their identities were eliminated, and they faced a life of enslavement.

The island of Genosha was located near the Seychelles in the Indian Ocean. Originally, mutants were identified and enslaved as adolescents, stripped of their identities, given a number, and genetically engineered to alter or enhance their abilities. A militia called the Magistrates enforced these laws. The X-Men toppled this regime, and after a period of turmoil, the UN turned the country over to Magneto to govern. Later, Cassandra Nova and her Sentinels destroyed the nation and killed nearly everyone on it. Even later, Selene brought nearly everyone on the island back from the dead with a techno-organic virus, but when she died, so did they. **MT, MF**

Golddigger

FIRST APPEARANCE Captain America #389 (April 1990)
REAL NAME Angela Golden
OCCUPATION Enforcer **BASE** New Orleans, Louisiana
HEIGHT/WEIGHT Unknown **EYES** Blue **HAIR** Blond
SPECIAL POWERS/ABILITIES Skilled hand-to-hand combatant.

Little is known about the woman known as Golddigger, save that she sells her skills to the highest bidder, and that she specializes in sneak attacks. She first crossed swords with Captain America in the service of Superia, who plotted to sterilize the world. Thereafter, she came to be employed by Damon Dran as an enforcer for his child slavery ring. But when Captain America and the brutal hero called Americop demolished Dran's operation, Golddigger attempted to flee in a helicopter, which was subsequently shot down. No one knows whether she truly perished in the crash. **TD**

Gideon

FIRST APPEARANCE New Mutants #98 (February 1991)
REAL NAME Gideon **OCCUPATION** CEO of Ophrah Industries
BASE Denver, Colorado
HEIGHT 6 ft 8 in **WEIGHT** 265 lbs **EYES** Blue **HAIR** Green
SPECIAL POWERS/ABILITIES Mutant ability to duplicate the superhuman powers of others by aligning himself with their energy signatures. He also had a greatly extended lifespan.

A member of the long-lived mutants who call themselves the Externals, Gideon was a power broker who called the halls of big business his natural habitat. Utterly corrupt, Gideon attempted to take Roberto DaCosta, the New Mutant known as Sunspot, under his wing, and turn him into his protégé. However his attempts to turn Sunspot into an External like himself met with failure, and he soon turned his attentions to other pursuits. Gideon was subsequently slain by the External vampire Selene, who had embarked on a vendetta against her fellow Externals. **TB**

Gladiator

FACTFILE

REAL NAME
Melvin Potter

OCCUPATION
Ex-criminal

BASE
New York City

HEIGHT 6 ft 6 in
WEIGHT 300 lbs
EYES Blue
HAIR None

FIRST APPEARANCE
Daredevil #18 (July 1966)

POWERS
Skilled athlete and combatant; wore armored suit with saw blades in gauntlets.

When Foggy Nelson rented a Daredevil outfit from Melvin Potter's costume shop, Potter dressed up like a villain to ambush Foggy. Potter acquired a taste for crime, becoming the Gladiator and serving with Electro's Emissaries of Evil and the Maggia. Later reformed, the Gladiator allied with Daredevil and Elektra to fight the Hand. He was forced back into his evil ways because of threats against his daughter and ended up in jail. He escaped and embarked on a psychotic killing spree as a result of chemicals administered by Mr. Fear, but Daredevil put a stop to it. Melvin Potter is not to be confused with the alien Gladiator aka Kallark who led the Shi'ar Imperial Guard and recently became the emperor of the shattered Shi'ar. **DW, MF**

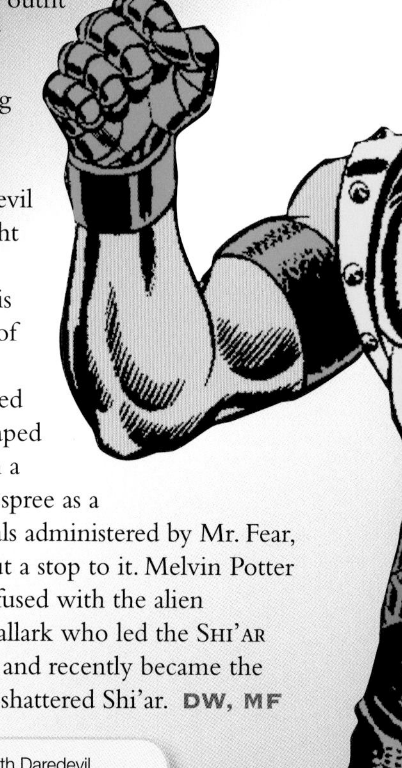

Gladiator clashes with Daredevil in an amphitheater located in the Dibney Museum of Human History.

Glob

FIRST APPEARANCE Incredible Hulk #121 (November 1969)
REAL NAME Joe Timms **OCCUPATION** Petty thief; swamp creature **BASE** Florida Everglades
HEIGHT 6 ft 6 in **WEIGHT** 900 lbs **EYES** Brown **HAIR** None
SPECIAL POWERS/ABILITIES Superhumanly strong, the Glob's mutated swampy body can withstand severe attacks; enhanced speed and stamina; not particularly intelligent.

Three men have been known as the Glob. The first was Joe Timms, who drowned in the Florida Everglades. After his corpse was exposed to radioactive waste, he returned to life as a swamp-like beast. Sumner Samuel Beckwith became the second Glob after injecting himself with a flawed super soldier serum. The third—called Glob Herman—was a mutant student at the Xavier Institute. His flesh was made of a transparent, living wax called bio-paraffin that burned when set afire. He joined a mutant riot after a prominent mutant was killed in what seemed to be a hate crime. After M-Day, he retained his powers. **MF**

Not a pretty sight, the Glob is, nevertheless, a well-meaning soul.

Goldbug

FIRST APPEARANCE Luke Cage, Power Man #41 (March 1977)
REAL NAME Unrevealed
OCCUPATION Criminal **BASE** New York City
HEIGHT 5 ft 9 in **WEIGHT** 170 lbs **EYES** Blue **HAIR** Blond
SPECIAL POWERS/ABILITIES Battlesuit contains electrically-powered exoskeleton that amplifies strength; "gold-gun" shoots gold-colored dust that hardens on contact; uses "bugship" hovercraft and submarine.

Goldbug is a thief obsessed with gold. Early in his career, he clashed with Luke Cage and Thunderbolt. Later, he captured the Hulk as part of his plan to conquer El Dorado. In El Dorado, Goldbug teamed up with the Hulk to defeat the subterranean conqueror Tyrannus. He later attempted to steal underwater gold but was foiled by Namor. He worked for Latveria when the nation attacked Nick Fury and his friends over their attempt to overthrow the Latverian government. During the Civil War, the Punisher killed him before he could join Captain America's forces. **PS, MF**

Golden Archer

FIRST APPEARANCE Avengers #141 (November 1975)
REAL NAME Wyatt McDonald **OCCUPATION** Government agent, former cab driver **BASE** Squadron City
HEIGHT 6 ft 3 in **WEIGHT** 150 lbs **EYES** Blue **HAIR** Black
SPECIAL POWERS/ABILITIES Expert archer who shot arrows with pinpoint accuracy. Besides conventional arrows used a chemical mace arrow, a siren arrow, and a flash arrow.

Wyatt McDonald practiced until he became an expert archer. Deciding to use his skills as a costumed crimefighter he adopted the name Hawkeye. McDonald was the first recruit of the Squadron Supreme, a team of Super Heroes who banded together to protect their world, known as "Earth-S." He later changed his name to Golden Archer. Eventually he was kicked out of the Squadron Supreme for using a Behavior Modification Machine on Lady Lark. He then joined Nighthawk's Redeemers as Black Archer and was killed battling Blue Eagle. **MT**

Glorian

FIRST APPEARANCE Incredible Hulk #191 (September 1975)
REAL NAME Thomas Gideon
OCCUPATION Apprentice dream-shaper **BASE** Known universe
HEIGHT 5 ft 9 in **WEIGHT** 155 lbs **EYES** Pink **HAIR** Orange
SPECIAL POWERS/ABILITIES Glorian can control tachyons, small speed-of-light particles, forming them into rainbow-shaped bridges allowing him to travel across worlds or star systems at light speed. He can also mentally redefine small pockets of reality for short periods of time.

Thomas Gideon survived radiation poisoning thanks to the Shaper of Worlds. The Shaper renamed him Glorian and taught him to manipulate reality and dreams. Recently, Glorian tricked Gamora and Ronan the Accuser into battling so he could absorb their energy and use it to reshape a world. When the Annihilation Wave interrupted him, he destroyed all he'd made, shattering his mind along with his attackers. **MT, MF**

Goliath

Dr. Hank Pym discovered how to use his Pym particles to change his size and became the first Giant-Man. His lab assistant, Bill Foster, became Black Goliath and later the second Giant-Man. He fell victim to radiation poisoning while fighting Atom-Smasher, but Spider-Woman cured him with a blood transfusion. He later became the fourth Goliath. During the Civil War he sided with Captain America and was killed by Ragnarok. In the aftermath of World War Hulk, Bill's nephew Tom Foster became the new Goliath. He later joined the Revengers to attack the Avengers. **DW, MF**

GOLIATH

FACTFILE
REAL NAME
Thomas "Tom" Foster
OCCUPATION
Construction worker, adventurer
BASE
Flatiron Building, New York City

HEIGHT/WEIGHT Varies
EYES Brown
HAIR Black

FIRST APPEARANCE
Black Panther #23 (February 2007)

POWERS

Superhuman strength, size and mass manipulation.

Gods of Asgard

Immortals who rule the dimension of Asgard

GODS OF ASGARD

FACTFILE

KEY ASGARDIANS

ODIN
(Monarch of Asgard) The most powerful god, possessing vast magical abilities. He can enchant objects or living beings, project energy bolts, and open gateways between dimensions. He also commands the life energies of all Asgardians, which he can absorb at will.

THOR
(God of Thunder) Asgard's finest warrior; exceptionally skilled in hand-to-hand combat, swordsmanship, and hammer-throwing.

BALDER
(God of Light) Thor's closest friend; almost invulnerable; skilled in hand-to-hand combat, swordsmanship, and horsemanship.

HELA
(Goddess of Death) Ruler of the underworlds of Hel and Niffleheim; holds the power of life and death over the gods; can levitate and travel in astral form; touch is fatal to mortals.

LOKI
(God of Evil) Great magical abilities; can shapeshift into any animal, god, or giant; can plant hypnotic suggestions into others' minds.

HERMOD
(God of Speed) Fastest of all Asgardians.

HODER
(God of Winter) Psychic abilities allow him to see into the future.

VALKYRIE
Brunnhilde the Valkyrie can see a "deathglow" around a person about to die. Originally charged with transporting dead warriors to Valhalla; can travel between dimensions.

HEIMDALL
(Guardian of the Rainbow Bridge) Has extremely acute senses. He can focus on, or block out, any specific sensory information.

VOLLA
Prophetess who can see alternate futures.

BASE
The Otherdimensional Realm of Asgard

FIRST APPEARANCE
Journey into Mystery #85, (October 1962)

The otherdimensional planetary body known as Asgard.

The Gods of Asgard are a powerful race of beings who live in a dimension called Asgard, a small planetary body whose laws of physics are different from the planets we know in the Earthly realm. Asgard is also home to five other races—Giants, Dwarves, Elves, Trolls, and Demons. The Gods of Asgard are the most human-looking and powerful of the six races of Asgard.

NINE WORLDS

All Asgardians refer to the known universe as the "Nine Worlds of Asgard." Four of those worlds—Asgard, home of the gods; Vanaheim, home of the Asgardians' sister race called the Vanir; Nidavellir, home of the Dwarves; and Alfheim, home of the Light Elves—actually share the planetary body on which Asgard is located.

The other five worlds exist in separate dimensions connected by an unknown number of interdimensional nexuses. They are Midgard, the Asgardian name for Earth, home of humanity; Jotunheim, home of the giants; Svartalfheim, home of the Dark Eves; Hel, land of the dead and it's adjunct world Niflheim, the frozen realm of the dishonored dead; and Muspelheim, land of the fire demons and home to Surtur, the Gods of Asgard's most deadly enemy.

Surtur rises from the flames of Muspelheim, land of the fire demons.

Rainbow Bridge

The origin of the Gods of Asgard is not clearly known, but it is believed that unlike the other races of the realm, the gods are not native to Asgard. Legend has it that they were born on Earth, but moved to Asgard in the far distant past. The Rainbow Bridge, also known as Bifrost—one of the interdimensional nexuses—connects Asgard to Earth.

Although they look like humans, the Gods of Asgard possess superhuman physical abilities. They are extremely long-lived (although not immortal, unlike their Olympian counterparts) and age at an extremely slow pace once they reach adulthood.

Their skin and bones are three times as dense as that of a human and are invulnerable, to a degree, to physical attack. They possess great strength (able to lift 30 tons) and, due to their density, weigh far more than humans of comparable size. The Gods of Asgard are immune to all diseases found on Earth and their metabolism gives them superhuman endurance while performing physical activities.

All Asgardians are born with the potential to use and control mystical energies, although only a few (such as Loki) have developed this power to any significant degree.

The Fantastic Four cross Bifrost, the Rainbow Bridge to Asgard, which is guarded by Heimdall, Sentry of Asgard.

GODS OF ASGARD
1 Enchantress ***2*** Sif ***3*** Balder the Brave ***4*** Hela, Goddess of Death ***5*** Hermod, God of Speed ***6*** Loki ***7*** Thor ***8*** Heimdall, Guardian of the Rainbow Bridge ***9*** Thunderstrike ***10*** Odin ***11*** Karnilla, the Norn Queen ***12*** Kurse ***13*** Frigga ***14*** Fandral the Dashing ***15*** Volstagg the Enormous ***16*** Hogun the Grim ***17*** Thor Girl ***18*** Malekith ***19*** Surtur ***20*** Ulik, the Unstoppable Rock Troll

ESSENTIAL STORYLINES

- ***The Mighty Thor Vol. 2 #80–85*** The Ragnarok (Doom of the Gods) Saga. Loki and his followers unleash an attack on Asgard intended to destroy the home of the gods and all its inhabitants. Thor's hammer Mjolnir is shattered during the battle that follows.
- ***The Mighty Thor #418*** The fire demon Surtur possesses Odin and gains control of Asgard.

The Storm Giants, sworn enemies of the Gods, eat and drink their fill in Jotunheim, their Asgardian home. Odin challenged Thor and Loki (in foreground) to return the Golden apples of Iduna to the Storm Giants.

Odin the All-Father

Odin, also called All-Father, is the leader of the Gods of Asgard. Odin is the grandson of Buri, the first of the Asgardians. He is the son of the God Bor and Bestia, of the race of frost giants.

For many ages, Odin has ruled Asgard wisely and effectively. Odin wields the enchanted, three-pronged spear Gungnir ("The Spear of Heaven"), which returns to his hand when thrown, and he travels through space in Skipbladnir, a Viking-style longboat with enchanted sails and oars.

Thor, Son of Odin

Although Odin made Frigga his queen, he mated with Gaea, the Goddess of Earth, who bore him Thor, the God of Thunder. However, Frigga raised the boy, who believed her to be his mother.

The Dwarves of Nidavellir created the hammer Mjolnir, forged from the mystical metal uru. Odin enchanted the hammer so that only one worthy of wielding such a powerful weapon could lift it. When Thor came of age, Odin presented him with Mjolnir, and Thor became Asgard's greatest warrior.

Loki, who had been adopted by Odin, turned to sorcery and became the God of Mischief. Jealous of Thor, Loki vowed to destroy him. Loki launched the final war of Ragnarok (the end of the universe in Norse myth), but Thor broke the cycle and stopped the war. The gods disappeared but later reappeared in mortal guises. Thor brought them to a reborn Asgard, which hovered over the plains of Oklahoma.

At the end of the Dark Reign, the Sentry destroyed Asgard. Soon after, the new Red Skull found the hammer of Skadi and revived Odin's brother Cul the Serpent, along with his generals, called the Worthy (*see* Fear Itself). Odin remade Asgard in another realm, planning to raze the Earth to destroy Cul; instead, Thor led the world's heroes to victory against the Worthy. Thor himself slew Cul the Serpent, but at the cost of his own life.

Stricken with grief, Odin gave up the rule of the Norse gods to Frigga, Gaea, and Idunn (the Goddess of Immortality) and locked himself away in his new Asgard. Iron Man helped build Asgardia, the Norse gods' new home, hovering over Broxton, Oklahoma, once again. **MT, MF**

Asgardia is a glorious combination of Earthly technology and Asgardian magic.

Gods of Heliopolis

Deities of Ancient Egypt

GODS OF HELIOPOLIS

FACTFILE

NOTABLE GODS

OSIRIS (Ruler of the Gods) God of the Dead
BES God of Luck
GEB God of the Earth
HORUS God of the Sun
ISIS Goddess of Fertility
KHONSHU God of Light
NUT Goddess of the Sky
SETH God of Evil
THOTH God of the Moon

BASE

Celestial city of Heliopolis

FIRST APPEARANCE

Thor #240 (October 1975)

The Path of the Gods enabled the Egyptian deities to visit Earth and meddle in human affairs.

In ancient times the pantheon of the Egyptian gods lived in Heliopolis, ruling Egypt until humans finally took their place as the dynastic kings known as the pharaohs. It was then that the Heliopolitan gods departed Earth, settling in a parallel dimension, where they established the celestial city of Heliopolis. However, like the Asgardian gods (see GODS OF ASGARD), the Heliopolitan deities retained strong links with Egypt, traveling to and from Earth on a golden bridge named the Path of the Gods.

Creeping up on the sleeping Osiris, Seth prepared to slice him into pieces.

CLASH OF THE GODS

Although essentially an extended family, the Heliopolitan gods were somewhat dysfunctional. When Osiris, God of the Dead, was appointed ruler of the Gods his younger brother Seth was overwhelmed with jealousy—the tensions between the pair were to reverberate far beyond their celestial home. Seth's first solution was drastic—he killed Osiris, slicing up his body and scattering the pieces. When Osiris' wife and son—Isis and Horus—managed to resurrect him, Seth employed a different tactic, imprisoning all three in a pyramid. Although trapped there for millennia, Osiris and Isis eventually made the pyramid appear in the 20th century. This attracted the attention of the Asgardian gods THOR and Odin but their efforts to free their fellow immortals did not prove straightforward. Odin was forced to join battle with Seth, their struggle finally culminating in the severing of Seth's left hand.

Releasing Osiris from his pyramid prison, Thor and Odin joined him in the battle to overthrow Seth. However, before they could reach him, they were forced to fight through Seth's skeletal legions.

CONTINUING MENACES

Seth has attempted time and again to destroy all life in the multiverse. An alliance of evil let loose the demonic Demogorge the God-Eater. Only when the entity attempted to consume Thor was its path of destruction brought to an end. On a separate occasion, Seth drained the energies of his fellow gods and invaded Asgard. He was only defeated by the combined forces of the AVENGERS and EARTH FORCE. Thanos also threatened the universe with his Infinity Gauntlet. Osiris attended a Council of the God Kings to discuss their response. Fortunately, Thanos was thwarted by other entities.

Although the time of the Heliopolitan Gods is now long over, they and their petty squabbles still spill over into human affairs. **AD**

For millennia, the god Seth has brooded and conspired to gain control of Heliopolis.

ESSENTIAL STORYLINES

• Thor Vol. 1 #240–241
In the first story to feature the Heliopolitans, Seth traps Osiris and Isis in a pyramid and does battle with Odin and Thor.

• Thor Vol. 1 #386–400
Seth conquers Heliopolis, battles Thor and the Avengers, and then tries to invade Asgard.

GODS OF OLYMPUS

Deities of Ancient Greece

Olympus was ruled by the stern and hirsute Zeus.

Although for centuries they were worshipped by the Greeks, it remains unclear where the Gods of Olympus first originated—was it on Earth or in the pocket dimension of Olympus where they currently reside? Wherever they came from, their influence on this planet has faded over the last two millennia, although a handful of their number still walk the Earth.

THE GOLDEN AGE

Children of the Titans, the first generation of the Olympian Gods were imprisoned in the underworld realm of Tartarus as soon as they were born, their father Cronos fearing that they would eventually overthrow him. His anxiety proved to be well-founded: the last of his children, Zeus, avoided being incarcerated and, when he was old enough, freed his siblings and led a ten-year-long war against Cronos.

Victorious, Zeus and his siblings became the Gods of Olympus, worshipped by peoples across Europe. It was only when Christianity began to dominate the Western world that the Gods chose to withdraw to the Olympus dimension and began to reduce their ties with the mortal realm.

The court of Zeus was a byword for feasting and revelry. While most enjoyed the carefree hedonism of the place, some, including Venus and Hercules, yearned for a slightly more challenging existence.

Although most of the Gods departed a handful either remained on the Earth or returned, time and again, in the years that followed. Of those that stayed on Earth, Neptune (or Poseidon, as the Greeks called him) remained to watch over and be worshipped by the Atlanteans, while HERCULES and Venus (Aphrodite to the Greeks) spent time living with mortals.

BACK TO EARTH

With the destruction of Asgard during Ragnarok, AMATSU-MIKABOSHI led an attack on Olympus. Zeus was slain in the conflict, only to return later as a boy, and Olympus was destroyed.

During the SECRET INVASION, Hercules assembled the God Squad to defeat the Skrull gods. Afterward, Hera and Pluto took control of the Olympus Group, the new home of the Olympians on Earth. Hera created a new universe called the Continuum, into which she planned to transfer the gods while destroying the original. Her plan was foiled, although it cost her, Zeus (again), and Hercules their lives. The rule of the Olympus Group fell to Amadeus CHO. Hercules took over from Cho when he returned, but he used all his power to restore reality at the end of the CHAOS WAR, and Zeus resumed his rule.

AD, MF

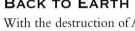

Zeus did not entirely approve of the life his son, Hercules, had chosen to lead.

FACTFILE

NOTABLE GODS

ZEUS (Ruler of the Gods) God of the Sky and Weather
APOLLO God of Light
ARES God of War
ARTEMIS Goddess of the Hunt
ATHENA Goddess of Wisdom
ATLAS Mountain God
BELLONA Goddess of Discord
CUPID God of Love
DEIMOS God of Terror
DEMETER Goddess of Fertility
DIONYSUS God of Wine
GAEA Mother-Earth
HEBE Goddess of Youth
HEPHAESTUS God of Fire
HERA Goddess of Marriage; Queen of the Gods
HERMES God of Commerce and Travel
NEPTUNE (POSEIDON) God of the Sea
NOX God of Night
PAN God of Shepherds, Flocks and Forests
PERSEPHONE Queen of the Underworld
PHOBOS God of Fear
PROMETHEUS Titan of forethought; benefactor of mankind
PSYCHE Goddess of Fidelity and Adoration
TYPHON God of Wind
VENUS (APHRODITE) Goddess of Love and Beauty

BASE

Mount Olympus, Greece; later in an otherdimensional world

FIRST APPEARANCE

Journey Into Mystery Annual #1 (1965)

ESSENTIAL STORYLINES

- ***Venus #1–5***
The goddess Venus becomes editor of Beauty Magazine and helps bring couples together.
- ***Thor #126–131***
Hercules fights Thor who then rescues him from the netherworld where he has been imprisoned. Their firm friendship is sealed.
- ***Avengers #281–285***
Angered by injuries suffered by Hercules, Zeus attacks the Avengers and forbids the Olympus Gods from traveling to Earth.

Gorgon

FIRST APPEARANCE Fantastic Four (November 1965)
REAL NAME Unrevealed
OCCUPATION Administrator **BASE** Attilan, blue Area, the Moon
HEIGHT 6 ft 5 in **WEIGHT** 450 lbs **EYES** Brown **HAIR** Black
SPECIAL POWERS/ABILITIES Immensely powerful legs and hooves give him the ability to create seismic tremors.

Gorgon is a member of the INHUMAN royal family and cousin of their ruler, BLACK BOLT. Like all Inhumans, Gorgon underwent exposure to the mutating Terrigen Mists as a youth and gained hooves in place of feet, capable of creating seismic tremors. He often acts as Black Bolt's bodyguard, and he also takes youths exposed to the mists and trains them in the use of their powers. Recently, SHIELD exposed him to the Terrigen Mists a second time, transforming him into a true beast. He is not to be confused with the Japanese villain called Gorgon, who was killed by WOLVERINE. **DW, MF**

Gorr the God Butcher

Born on a brutal planet, Gorr came to believe that the gods deserved nothing but butchery for refusing to answer the prayers of those in dire need, such as his dying wife and children. After suffering such losses, he didn't think gods could exist, but once he confirmed that they did, he vowed to exterminate them all. The fact that he managed to murder so many of them is a testimony to his determination even more than his strength.

Gorr first battled THOR a millennium ago; Thor thought he had slain him, but the God Butcher survived and grew stronger. Using the blood of gods, he traveled through time. He later plucked Thor from three different ages and forced him to construct a bomb that would destroy the gods throughout time and space. When all the threatened gods prayed to Thor, however, Thor was able to stop the bomb and slay Gorr. **MF**

FACTFILE
REAL NAME
Gorr
OCCUPATION
God killer
BASE
Mobile

HEIGHT 6 ft 7 in
WEIGHT 260 lbs
EYES White
HAIR Bald

FIRST APPEARANCE
Thor: God of Thunder #2 (January 2013)

GORR THE GOD BUTCHER

POWERS
Gorr is nearly immortal and has superhuman strength, endurance, and durability. He can also manipulate darkness and fashion it into solid objects.

Gorilla-Man

FIRST APPEARANCE Men's Adventures #26 (1954)
REAL NAME Kenneth Hale **OCCUPATION** Adventurer
BASE San Francisco
HEIGHT 6 ft **WEIGHT** 340 lbs **EYES** Brown **HAIR** Brown
SPECIAL POWERS/ABILITIES Hale is a man cursed to live in a gorilla's body.

Legend says, "If you kill the Gorilla-Man, you become immortal." When forced to commit this act, Hale discovered the immortality came with the curse of becoming the Gorilla-Man he had killed. In the 1950s, Ken worked with a super group called the G-Men under Jimmy Woo. Decades later, he became an agent of SHIELD and joined the supernatural version of the HOWLING COMMANDOS. Gorilla-Man has since reunited with his G-Men friends to fight the Atlas Foundation. With their victory, they took over the organization and formed the new AGENTS OF ATLAS. **MF**

Grandmaster

Like his kinsman the COLLECTOR, the Grandmaster is a survivor of an extraterrestrial race that evolved shortly after the Big Bang. To combat the unending boredom of immortality, the Grandmaster has spent the eons engaging in various games, tournaments, and contests. He particularly relishes challenging other cosmic beings to games of skill and chance for incredibly high stakes. Grandmaster discovered Earth-712, which was inhabited by the SQUADRON SUPREME, and created duplicates of these heroes to pit against the AVENGERS. He later used Earth as a breeding ground for superhuman pawns for his games, but gave up this plan when he lost a bet to DAREDEVIL. He also challenged DEATH to a series of games, resulting in the banning of all the ELDERS OF THE UNIVERSE from his kingdom, making them all virtually immortal. He also once joined with the other Elders in a plot to kill GALACTUS, but the SILVER SURFER foiled this. The Grandmaster once pitted the original DEFENDERS against the RED HULK's Offenders and was killed for it, but he has returned. **TD, MF**

FACTFILE
REAL NAME
En Dwi Gast
OCCUPATION
Game player
BASE
Mobile throughout the universe

HEIGHT 7 ft 1 in
WEIGHT 240 lbs
EYES Red (no visible pupils)
HAIR White (pale blue skin)

FIRST APPEARANCE
Avengers #69 (October 1969)

GRANDMASTER

POWERS
The Grandmaster has an encyclopedic knowledge and comprehension of games and game theory played throughout the universe. Possesses a cosmic life force and is immune to aging, disease, or injury. Can levitate, project energy blasts, and travel through time, space, and alternate dimensions with the speed of thought. He can also rearrange matter on a planetary scale.

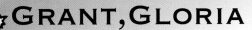

GRANT, GLORIA

GLORIA GRANT

FACTFILE

REAL NAME
Gloria "Glory" Grant

OCCUPATION
Administrative assistant, former model

BASE
New York City

HEIGHT 5 ft 8 in
WEIGHT 120 lbs
EYES Brown
HAIR Black

FIRST APPEARANCE
The Amazing Spider-Man #140 (February 1975)

POWERS
Highly efficient secretarial skills, including typing and computer skills. Outgoing, romantic, and warm-hearted; prepared to do almost anything to help the man she loves.

Model Glory Grant befriended Peter Parker when they both lived in an apartment house on Manhattan's Lower West Side. Grant was looking for work, and Peter, a freelance photographer for the *Daily Bugle*, suggested she apply to be J. Jonah JAMESON's secretary at the paper, a post recently vacated by Betty BRANT. The irascible Jameson liked Grant and she became Brant's replacement.

Mexican crimelord Eduardo Lobo seduced Grant to obtain the *Daily Bugle*'s files on his enemy, the KINGPIN; in time, Grant and Lobo fell genuinely in love. During a battle between SPIDER-MAN and Lobo, Grant tried to shoot Spider-Man, but shot and killed Lobo instead. Later, Grant was possessed by the spirit of the voodoo sorceress CALYPSO as part of the latter's plan to return to life. She became one of Jonah's aides when he became mayor of New York City. **PS, MF**

GRAVITY

FIRST APPEARANCE Gravity #1 (August 2005)
REAL NAME Greg Willis
OCCUPATION Student **BASE** New York City
HEIGHT 5 ft 10 in **WEIGHT** 175 lbs **EYES** Blue **HAIR** Brown
SPECIAL POWERS/ABILITIES Greg can manipulate gravitons on his skin to affect the weight and acceleration of anything he touches. This allows him to fly and imitate superhuman strength.

Born in Sheboygan, Wisconsin, Greg developed gravity-related powers, and when he moved to New York to attend college, he decided to become a Super Hero. Gravity was part of a group of heroes taken off to Battleworld by a being who claimed to be the BEYONDER but turned out to be the STRANGER, and he sacrificed himself to save the others. He returned as the Protector of the Universe but used those powers to feed GALACTUS. Gravity led Nevada's Heavy Hitters team as part of the FIFTY-STATE INITIATIVE, and afterward joined the YOUNG ALLIES. **MF**

GRAVITON

FIRST APPEARANCE Avengers #158 (April 1977)
REAL NAME Franklin Hall
OCCUPATION Criminal **BASE** Mobile
HEIGHT 6 ft 1 in **WEIGHT** 200 lbs **EYES** Blue **HAIR** Black
SPECIAL POWERS/ABILITIES Control over gravity allows Graviton to levitate objects, generate force fields and shockwaves, and pin opponents to the ground.

Franklin Hall, a Canadian researcher, gained absolute control over gravity in an accident involving a particle accelerator. Dubbing himself Graviton, he battled the AVENGERS, the THUNDERBOLTS, SPIDER-MAN, and the AVENGERS, WEST COAST, and was banished to an alternate dimension more than once. Upon one return, he went to exact his revenge on the Thunderbolts. Finding the Redeemers in their place, he destroyed them, then seemed to die while stopping an invasion from the dimension in which he'd been trapped. He seemed to have committed suicide while battling IRON MAN but turned up again later and joined AIM. **DW, MF**

GREAT LAKES AVENGERS

Formed by Craig Hollis, the GLA was a self-proclaimed branch of the AVENGERS. Despite much mockery and their successes being overlooked, they insisted on remaining together. The group's bills are met by Big Bertha, whose alter ego is the wealthy supermodel Ashley Crawford. Other misfit members have included: SQUIRREL GIRL, Leather Boy, Monkey Joe, Tippy-Toe, Grasshopper, and even DEADPOOL. After they won the rights to the name "Champions" from HERCULES in a poker game, they became the Great Lakes Champions. They became the Great Lakes Initiative, the FIFTY-STATE INITIATIVE's team for Wisconsin but have since returned to the GLA name. **AD, MF**

THE GREAT LAKES AVENGERS
1 Mr. Immortal
2 Big Bertha
3 Squirrel Girl
4 Flatman
5 Doorman

GREAT LAKES AVENGERS

FACTFILE

FOUNDING MEMBERS AND POWERS

MR. IMMORTAL
Immortal; team leader.

DINAH SOAR
Alien flying reptile, attacks with high-pitched shriek.

BIG BERTHA
Controls body mass; alternates between super-obesity and strength and supermodel skinniness.

DOORMAN
Can teleport self and others into the next room.

FLATMAN
Two-dimensional mutant with elasticated body.

FIRST APPEARANCE
The West Coast Avengers #46 (July 1989)

GREEN GOBLIN

Spider-Man's greatest enemy

GREEN GOBLIN

FACTFILE

REAL NAME
Norman Osborn

OCCUPATION
Criminal/Industrialist

BASE Mobile

HEIGHT 5 ft 11 in
WEIGHT 185 lbs
EYES Blue
HAIR Reddish-brown

FIRST APPEARANCE
The Amazing Spider-Man #14 (July 1964)

POWERS

Superhuman strength, endurance, and reactions, endowed by Goblin Formula, have increased steadily over time; weaponry includes armored costume, Goblin Glider and Pumpkin Bombs.

ALLIES/FOES

ALLIES The Enforcers, the Cabal of Scrier, Crime-Master, Jackal, the Sinister Twelve.

FOES Spider-Man, the Avengers, SHIELD.

ISSUE #1

Teaming up with the Enforcers, the Green Goblin is determined to destroy Spider-Man.

Norman Osborn reveals himself to be the Green Goblin.

For almost as long as there has been a SPIDER-MAN, so too has the Green Goblin existed. SPIDER-MAN's arch nemesis, the Green Goblin is the insane, malevolent alter ego of that once-respectable industrialist, Norman Osborn. Despite their mutual antagonism, the relationship between the pair is complex. Although the Green Goblin loathes and resents Spider-Man's very existence, for a long time Norman Osborn and Peter Parker shared a deep mutual respect and admiration. Osborn saw in the orphaned Peter the son he really wanted.

GENESIS OF THE GOBLIN

Long before his transformation into the Green Goblin, Norman Osborn was an ambitious businessman, quite prepared to sacrifice others on the altar of his own success. The co-founder of chemical company Oscorp, Osborn gained total control by framing his business partner, Professor Mendel Stromm, for embezzlement. The Goblin Formula that was to prove Osborn's undoing was a concoction detailed in the professor's notes, but it was Osborn's attempt to manufacture it for himself that resulted in the solution exploding in his face. As a result of this explosion, Osborn's strength, stamina and reflexes were enhanced but his sanity began to erode.

As the Green Goblin, Osborn wished to lead New York's criminal underworld and he set out to gain the respect of the key gangs by destroying Spider-Man. He developed high-tech weaponry specifically designed to achieve this end. Despite discovering Spider-Man's true identity, the Green Goblin was ultimately defeated: an electric shock, sustained during a battle with the web-slinger, caused Osborn to regain his sanity and lose all memory of his malevolent alter ego. Peter Parker judged that it was better to allow Osborn to resume his old life.

Tingling spider-sense, awesome strength, and superfast reflexes—Spider-Man needs all of these things to survive the Green Goblin's arsenal of weapons and enhanced body.

STRIKING AT SPIDER-MAN

Osborn's regained sanity proved fragile. Time and again his inner demon—the Green Goblin—reasserted control, and

ESSENTIAL STORYLINES

- ***Amazing Spider-Man #39–40***
The Green Goblin discovers Peter Parker's secret identity, the Goblin is unmasked as Norman Osborn and we learn about his origins.
- ***Amazing Spider-Man #121–2***
A climactic battle between the Green Goblin and Spider-Man results in the death of Gwen Stacy and the Goblin's own, apparent, demise.
- ***Amazing Spider-Man #134–7***
Norman Osborn's son Harry discovers that Peter Parker is really Spider-Man and, looking for revenge, becomes the second Green Goblin.

although Peter repeatedly brought Osborn back to reality, the businessman's grip on sanity became more and more tenuous. During this period, Peter's then-girlfriend, Gwen Stacy, met Osborn and, overwhelmed by his charisma, became pregnant by him. Nine months later, she gave birth to twins, Gabriel and Sarah, in France, keeping their existence a secret from Peter.

Following Gwen's return to New York, an angry altercation between her and a desperately unbalanced Osborn served to destabilize him further. Determined to punish both her and Spider-Man, when Osborn reverted to the Green Goblin he kidnapped Gwen and carried her to the top of Brooklyn Bridge.

OTHER GREEN GOBLINS

In becoming the Green Goblin, Norman Osborn inadvertently founded a Goblin dynasty. After witnessing his father's apparent death, a mentally unstable Harry Osborn adopted the Green Goblin mantle and attempted to destroy Spider-Man. Although Harry eventually put his father's legacy behind him, even settling down with a wife and child, life's pressures finally drove him back to the Goblin formula. Tragically, he was killed by the deadly concoction. Twice, the Goblin name has been borne by non-Osborns, with Harry's psychiatrist, Bart Hamilton, and Phil Urich, the nephew of reporter Ben Urich, both pretenders to the Goblin crown. More recently, Gabriel Stacy, the son of Norman Osborn and Gwen Stacy, injected himself with the Goblin formula to save his own life. Now the fifth Green Goblin, Gabriel remains at large, somewhere in Europe.

I'M THE GREEN GOBLIN!
HEY-- YOU'RE NOT HARRY
YOU'RE HIS PSYCHIATRIST-- BART HAMILTON

To protect his father, Harry Osborn said he was the Green Goblin.

The third Green Goblin is revealed.

All the Green Goblins have shared similar equipment.

The Goblin uses a variety of grenades which look like Halloween pumpkins.

A casualty of war, the Green Goblin throws Gwen Stacy to her death.

As the Iron Patriot, Norman pretended to be a hero, but he was always a madman.

The ensuing confrontation with Spider-Man resulted in Gwen's death and in Osborn being impaled by his own Goblin Glider.

Peter Parker assumed that Osborn had been killed by this impact but he had not allowed for the extraordinary potency of the Goblin formula. While lying on a mortuary slab, Osborn's body suddenly revived. To keep his survival secret, Osborn substituted his own body for that of an anonymous drifter.

Norman Osborn, Hero

Osborn subsequently worked hard to become a hero in the eyes of the world. As the director of the Thunderbolts, he killed the Skrull queen Veranke on live TV to end the Secret Invasion, catapulting him into becoming US head of security.

During the Dark Reign, Osborn founded the Cabal. He then dismantled SHIELD, replaced it with HAMMER, and put villains under his control into both the Avengers and the X-Men. He also took the place of both Iron Man and Captain America himself, as the Iron Patriot.

When Osborn led HAMMER and his Dark Avengers in an unauthorized assault on Asgard, however, he met defeat, and his always fragile sanity shattered once again. He escaped on his way to prison and created another Avengers team, hoping to use them to regain his position of power.

Defeated once more, despite temporarily gaining the powers of the Super-Adaptoid, Osborn based himself in the sewers of New York City as the Goblin King, gathered a new gang around him, and plotted ways to regain his power.

AD, MF

Gremlin

FIRST APPEARANCE Incredible Hulk #187 (May 1975)
REAL NAME Unrevealed
OCCUPATION Scientist **BASE** A secret base in Khystyro, somewhere in the Arctic, and Bitterfrost, a secret base in Siberia
HEIGHT 4 ft 6 in **WEIGHT** 215 lbs **EYES** Blue **HAIR** None
SPECIAL POWERS/ABILITIES Mutant who inherited father's genius-level intelligence; battlesuit gave superhuman strength.

The Gremlin is the son of the dead Soviet scientist known as the Gargoyle, who participated in atomic tests that vastly increased his intelligence but scarred his face and body. The Gargoyle died following an encounter with Bruce Banner, the Hulk. The Gremlin's intelligence was so great that he achieved a position of authority while only a child. Unfairly blaming the Hulk for his father's death, the Gremlin frequently tried to destroy him. Wearing a battlesuit similar to Titanium Man, he was eventually killed in a battle with Iron Man. **TD**

Grim Reaper

FIRST APPEARANCE Avengers #52 (May 1968)
REAL NAME Eric Williams
OCCUPATION Criminal **BASE** Mobile
HEIGHT/WEIGHT Unrevealed **EYES** Brown **HAIR** Black
SPECIAL POWERS/ABILITIES Has a scythe fused into the place of his right hand, which can fire arcs of electrical energy and induce comas in victims.

Brother of Wonder Man, Eric Williams became the Grim Reaper to get revenge on the Avengers, whom he believed were responsible for his brother's death. To that end, he allied with Ultron, and formed the Lethal Legion. Even after Wonder Man revived, the insane Reaper refused to believe it, and he died pursuing his vendetta. He has come back from death more than once and served as one of the Apocalypse Twins' Horsemen of Death. **TD, MF**

Grizzly

FIRST APPEARANCE The Amazing Spider-Man #139 (December 1974) **REAL NAME** Maxwell Markham
OCCUPATION Wrestler, criminal **BASE** Mobile
HEIGHT 6 ft 9 in **WEIGHT** 290 lbs
EYES Blue **HAIR** Blond, dyed red
SPECIAL POWERS/ABILITIES Superhuman durability, endurance, and strength.

Several characters have used the name Grizzly over the years. The most prominent was Maxwell Markham, a former professional wrestler who was so violent in the ring that he was banned from the sport. The Jackal gave him a bear suit fitted with an exoskeleton that enhanced his strength. He later underwent procedures that gave him his powers without the need of a suit. Another Grizzly worked for Cable's Wild Pack and Silver Sable's Six Pack but was later killed by Domino. **MF**

Grey Gargoyle

FACTFILE
REAL NAME
Paul Pierre Duval
OCCUPATION
Chemist, criminal
BASE
Mobile

HEIGHT 5 ft 11 in
WEIGHT 175 lbs (human form); 750 lbs (stone form)
EYES Blue (human form); white (stone form)
HAIR Black (human form); gray (stone form)

FIRST APPEARANCE
Journey into Mystery #107 (August 1964)

POWERS
Can transform himself into living stone without losing mobility, thereby gaining superhuman strength and durability. By touching people or objects with his right hand, he can transform them into an immobile, stone-like substance for about an hour.

French chemist Pierre Paul Duval accidentally spilled a potion that had been contaminated by an unknown substance onto his right hand. His hand permanently transformed into stone; however, he could still move it as if it were flesh. Duval discovered that he could transform his entire body into living stone, and decided to become a costumed criminal, the Grey Gargoyle.

Hoping to learn the secret of immortality, the Grey Gargoyle battled Thor, who remains his principal enemy. Over the years, the Gargoyle has also contended against Iron Man, Captain America, Spider-Man, the Hulk, the Avengers and the Fantastic Four.

The Grey Gargoyle also briefly served as a member of Baron Zemo's Masters of Evil. The Gargoyle became Mokk, Breaker of Faith (one of the Worthy), during Fear Itself, turning thousands of people in Paris to stone. Odin later restored the ones who were still whole. The Grey Gargoyle was captured by the authorities and kept in a cage of Tony Stark's design. **PS, MF**

The Grey Gargoyle retains his normal agility when in stone form, despite his increased weight. With his superhuman strength, he can leap nearly 20 ft into the air.

Groot

FIRST APPEARANCE Tales to Astonish #13 (November 1960)
REAL NAME Groot **OCCUPATION** Adventurer **BASE** Mobile
HEIGHT Variable **WEIGHT** Variable
EYES Black **HAIR** None
SPECIAL POWERS/ABILITIES Groot has superhuman durability and strength. He can regrow limbs or even his entire body from a shoot and communicate with plants.

Groot is the last known member of an alien species once thought extinct, known as the Floral Colossus. He came to Earth to experiment on humans, was captured by SHIELD, and later made part of the HOWLING COMMANDOS. He returned to space and joined STAR-LORD, fighting the second ANNIHILATION wave, and gave his life to stop the Phalanx. ROCKET RACOON regrew him, and he joined the GUARDIANS OF THE GALAXY. **MF**

Guardsman

Kevin O'Brien headed up Stark Industries' research department and aided IRON MAN against the SPYMASTER and the Espionage Elite. After revealing that he was Iron Man, Stark asked O'Brien to substitute for him if the need arose. That day came before O'Brien's Guardsman armor had been fully tested. Stark was kidnapped; O'Brien put on his armor, but its circuitry malfunctioned, stimulating areas of O'Brien's brain responsible for rage and jealousy. Guardsman and Iron Man clashed and Kevin was accidentally killed. Furious, Kevin's brother Michael obtained the Guardsman armor, and fought Stark. They have since become reconciled, and Michael led a Guardsman force guarding the high-tech Vault prison. **AD**

Kevin O'Brien tries on the Guardsman armor for the first time.

Ultimately, Tony Stark's victory over the Guardsman depended on his greater experience.

FACTFILE
GUARDSMAN

REAL NAME
Kevin O'Brien
OCCUPATION
Research scientist
BASE
Long Island, New York

HEIGHT 5 ft 10 in
WEIGHT 195 lbs
EYES Blue
HAIR Red

FIRST APPEARANCE
Iron Man #43 (November 1971)

POWERS
Armor augments strength and enables flight; it is also equipped with radiation shielding and pulsed laser.

Guardian

FACTFILE
GUARDIAN

REAL NAME
James MacDonald Hudson
OCCUPATION
Scientist, adventurer
BASE
Canada (Dept. H)

HEIGHT 6 ft 2 in
WEIGHT 196 lbs
EYES Blue
HAIR Black

FIRST APPEARANCE
X-Men #109 (February 1978)

POWERS
Electromagnetic battlesuit has built-in force field, allows him to fly, and discharge force bolts; also uses gravity to slingshot him in a westward direction at 1000 mph.

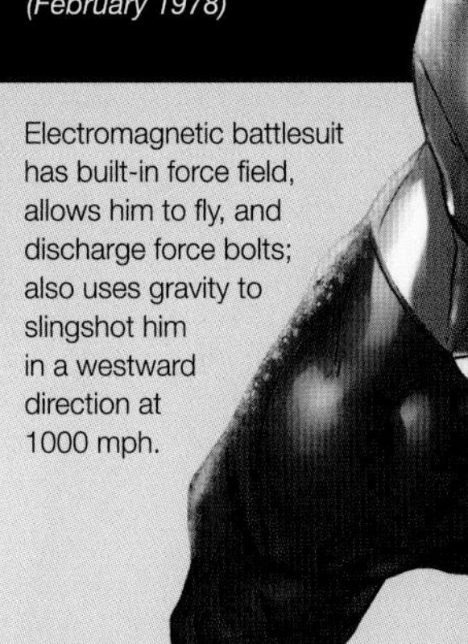

James MacDonald Hudson stole the prototype battlesuit he was developing when he discovered that his employers, Am-Can Petro-Chemical, intended to turn it over to the US military. Hudson took the suit to the Canadian government and founded ALPHA FLIGHT, which he led, first as Weapon Alpha, and then as VINDICATOR. When Canada ended its support for Alpha Flight, Hudson took the name Guardian to symbolize his new role.

The Collective—an energy mass derived from the depowering of mutants by the SCARLET WITCH—possessed Michael Pointer, a postman unaware he was also a mutant, and used him to kill Hudson, along with most of Alpha Flight. Ironically, Pointer then became the new Guardian of a government-sponsored version of OMEGA FLIGHT, wearing Hudson's battlesuit to control his energy absorption powers. Pointer later took the name WEAPON OMEGA.

During the CHAOS WAR, many of the members of Alpha Flight returned from the dead. Hudson was among them. He has since rejoined both his wife and team. **TD, MF**

Gyrich, Henry Peter

FIRST APPEARANCE Avengers #168 (February 1978)
REAL NAME Henry Peter Gyrich
OCCUPATION Adventurer **BASE** Washington, D.C.
HEIGHT 6 ft 8 in **WEIGHT** 225 lbs **EYES** Green **HAIR** Red
SPECIAL POWERS/ABILITIES Gyrich is a normal human being with no superhuman powers; a cunning, ruthless strategist and highly efficient administrator.

Henry Peter Gyrich was the government liaison to the AVENGERS. He threatened to cut off the team's unlimited airspace access and use of secret government equipment unless they obeyed his rules. As head of Project Wideawake, he transformed the BROTHERHOOD OF EVIL MUTANTS into FREEDOM FORCE. He took over from Valerie COOPER as head of the COMMISSION ON SUPERHUMAN ACTIVITIES. With the launch of the FIFTY-STATE INITIATIVE, Gyrich became Secretary of the Superhuman Armed Forces. He later became co-director of SWORD but, not long after, CAPTAIN AMERICA captured him on behalf of SHIELD for helping to turn DEMOLITION MAN into the next incarnation of the murderous SCOURGE. **MT, MF**

GREY, JEAN

Telepath of virtually unlimited psychic power

JEAN GREY

FACTFILE

REAL NAME
Jean Grey-Summers

OCCUPATION
Adventurer, former fashion model

BASE
Formerly the Xavier Institute, Salem Center, New York State; now the "White Hot Room"

HEIGHT 5 ft 6 in
WEIGHT 110 lbs
EYES Green
HAIR Red

FIRST APPEARANCE
X-Men #1 (September 1963)

POWERS

As Marvel Girl, possessed mutant abilities of telepathy and telekinesis. The Phoenix Force amplified these powers to a virtually unlimited extent. The Phoenix Force can manifest itself as a fiery corona in the shape of a bird that surrounds Jean Grey's body.

ALLIES/FOES

ALLIES Professor Charles Xavier, Cyclops, Archangel, Beast, Iceman, Storm, Wolverine, Marvel Girl (Rachel Summers), Cable.

FOES Magneto, Mastermind, Hellfire Club, Apocalypse, Sentinels, Xorn I.

ISSUE #1

In the first X-Men comic, Jean Grey arrived at Professor Xavier's school, met her future husband Scott Summers, became Marvel Girl, and first battled Magneto.

ESSENTIAL STORYLINES

- ***Uncanny X-Men #129–137***
The Dark Phoenix Saga.
- ***Fantastic Four #286, X-Factor #1***
Jean Grey returns from apparent death and reunites with Scott Summers (Cyclops).
- ***X-Men Vol. 2 #30***
At long last the wedding of Jean Grey and her beloved Scott Summers takes place.

Jean's telekinetic power enables her to levitate objects.

When Jean Grey was ten years old, her best friend, Annie Richardson, was hit by an automobile. Jean's anguish as she held her friend activated her mutant telepathic powers, and Jean thus shared Annie's emotions as she died. Traumatized, Jean suffered from deep depression and was unable to control her new telepathic powers.

MARVEL GIRL

Jean Grey was only a small child when she first met Charles Xavier. She joined the X-Men in her mid-teens.

When Jean was eleven, her parents turned to Professor Charles Xavier (Professor X) for help. Xavier created psychic shields in Jean's mind to prevent her from utilizing her telepathic powers until she was mature enough to control them. He also began training her telekinetic ability to mentally manipulate objects. As a teenager, Jean enrolled in Xavier's School for Gifted Youngsters, becoming the fifth member of the original X-Men, the team of young mutants whom Xavier was training to combat mutant menaces to humanity. Grey was given the codename "Marvel Girl."

Grey and her fellow student Scott Summers (Cyclops) quickly fell in love, although they did not reveal their feelings to each other for a long time. After she had trained for years at his school, Xavier finally enabled Grey to use her telepathic powers.

Following Xavier's recruitment of a new class of X-Men, Grey left the team. However, soon afterwards she and other X-Men were abducted by Sentinels to a space station orbiting the Earth. The X-Men had to escape back to Earth in a space shuttle during a solar radiation storm. Grey volunteered to pilot the shuttle, although she had to sit in a section without sufficient radiation shielding. Grey's powers proved insufficient to hold back the intense radiation, and it began killing her.

Phoenix Force: This primal power of creation and destruction manifests itself as a gigantic bird of prey composed of cosmic flame.

PHOENIX FORCE

A sentient cosmic entity of limitless power, the Phoenix Force, made contact with the dying Grey. The Phoenix Force created a human host body for itself that was a duplicate of Grey's, and infused it with a portion of her consciousness. The Phoenix Force placed Grey's original body into suspended animation within a large cocoon, in which it would slowly heal. When the shuttle crash-landed in Jamaica Bay, the Phoenix Force's new host body rose from the water, declaring herself to be Phoenix. The X-Men believed that Phoenix was the real Jean Grey, and Phoenix/Grey joined the team.

The X-Men's old foe the criminal Mastermind began manipulating Phoenix/Grey's mind to prove his worthiness to join the Inner Circle of the

In this cover, Jean Grey appears as Marvel Girl (on the left, with the X-Men) confronting herself as Dark Phoenix (on the right). in the classic "Dark Phoenix Saga."

BLACK QUEEN

The mutant Mastermind projected illusions directly into Phoenix's mind, in which she led a dissolute life in the 18th century. Thus he brainwashed her into becoming the sinister new Black Queen of the Inner Circle of the Hellfire Club. Phoenix regained her free will and sent Mastermind into a coma. However his malevolent tampering with her mind triggered her metamorphosis into the evil Dark Phoenix.

Hellfire Club, thereby awakening the dark side of her personality. Finally, Mastermind mesmerized her into becoming the new Black Queen of the Hellfire Club. However Mastermind could not control her for long: Phoenix/Jean Grey not only turned against him, she transformed into the insane Dark Phoenix.

Dark Phoenix battled the X-Men, and inadvertently destroyed an inhabited planet. Finally, Jean's original personality reasserted itself. To prevent herself from reverting to Dark Phoenix, she committed suicide as the horrified Cyclops looked on.

Back from the Dead

Upon the death of Phoenix's body, Jean's consciousness returned to her original body in a cocoon at the bottom of Jamaica Bay. The Avengers eventually found and revived Jean, and she emerged to find Scott had married her clone (Madeline Pryor) and had a son Nathan (Cable) by her. Despite this, she joined the original X-Men to found X-Factor. Pryor went mad, developed powers as the Goblin Queen, and died in combat with Grey.

Finally, Jean and Scott reunited and married. During their honeymoon, their souls were brought into the future and, as Redd and Slym, they raised Nathan for ten years before returning home.

Later, Jean assumed the name Phoenix and linked herself with the Phoenix Force. She and Scott drifted apart, and she discovered that Scott was having an affair with Emma Frost. Later, the first Xorn, posing as Magneto, slew Jean, but the Phoenix Force resurrected her once again. She became the White Phoenix of the Crown in a pocket dimension called the White Hot Room. The Shi'ar forced the Phoenix Force from there later and shattered it. Jean set about gathering the fractured pieces of the Phoenix Force and trying to heal the universe.

When the Phoenix Force returned to Earth to possess the Phoenix Five, Scott eventually took on all of its power and became the Dark Phoenix, slaying Professor X. At one point, at the height of his power, he bumped up against the bottom of the White Hot Room and could hear Jean telling him he was an idiot, but she did nothing more. **PS, MF**

Jean Grey as the White Phoenix of the Crown.

GUARDIANS OF THE GALAXY

Heroes sworn to protect the universe

GUARDIANS OF THE GALAXY

FACTFILE

NOTABLE MEMBERS AND POWERS

MAJOR VICTORY
(Vance Astrovik) Psychokinesis, mental force blasts.

ALETA
Can create objects of solid light.

CHARLIE-27
Enhanced strength and stamina.

MARTINEX
Enhanced strength, projection of heat and cold.

NIKKI
Resistant to heat and bright light, sharpshooter.

STARHAWK
Flight, enhanced strength, energy projection.

YONDU
Skilled archer, mystical sensory abilities.

BASE
Mobile

FIRST APPEARANCE
Marvel Super Heroes #18 (January 1969)

In an alternate timeline of the 31st century (Earth-691), the Guardians of the Galaxy acted as protectors of the Milky Way. The group formed in response to the Badoon invasion of 3007, which decimated Pluto, Mercury, Jupiter, and Earth. The Guardians defeated the Badoon by 3015 and then became adventurers. They traveled to Earth's current reality several times, becoming honorary members of the AVENGERS.

PREVIOUS GUARDIANS
(Clockwise from top left): Charlie-27, Starhawk, Aleta, Yondu, Major Victory, Nikki, Martinex

GUARDIANS OF THE FUTURE

Originally, there were only four Guardians, each representing the last survivors of their kind from different planets. They were Vance Astro (Earth), Charlie-27 (Jupiter), Martinex (Pluto), and Yondu (Centauri IV). They were later joined by STARHAWK, his wife Aleta, and Nikki (Mercury).

The Guardians' adventures in their own time included a quest for CAPTAIN AMERICA's shield. Vance Astrovik also convinced his younger self to follow a different path, leading to his mainstream version becoming MARVEL BOY (later Justice). Other teammates included Hollywood (a future WONDER MAN), the feline Talon, the shapeshifting SKRULL Replica, a time-traveling YELLOWJACKET II, and the former herald of GALACTUS, Firelord. Many of these joined a spin-off team called the Galactic Guardians.

THE MODERN GUARDIANS
1 Star-Lord ***2*** Gamora
3 Drax the Destroyer
4 Rocket Raccoon
5 Adam Warlock
6 Quasar

GUARDIANS OF TODAY

In the wake of the two ANNIHILATION events in the present-day mainstream universe, STAR-LORD banded together with Adam WARLOCK, DRAX THE DESTROYER, Cosmo (an evolved Russian space dog), GAMORA, GROOT, MANTIS, QUASAR (Phyla-Vell), and ROCKET RACCOON to form a new team of heroes to help protect the galaxy. They established a headquarters in Knowhere, the head of a long-dead Celestial floating in space near the end of the universe. Soon after forming, they discovered a frozen Vance Astro (also known as Major Victory) and, at his suggestion, they called themselves the Guardians of the Galaxy.

The team suffered troubles from the start, breaking up when the others found out that Star-Lord had asked Mantis to telepathically compel them to join. They reformed during the SHI'AR-KREE War of Kings and brought in master thief Bug (from the Microverse), Jack Flag (an Earth hero who worked with CAPTAIN AMERICA), and MOONDRAGON as well. They even went into the future to encounter the original team. Later, with help from THANOS, the Guardians stopped the Cancerverse from attacking and destroying their own universe, but at the cost of the lives of NOVA and Star-Lord, who stayed behind to keep the Cancerverse sealed away.

Star-Lord later returned and restarted the Guardians, featuring himself, Drax, Gamora, Groot, and Rocket Racoon. Soon after, IRON MAN joined them temporarily. **DW, MF**

Haller, Gabrielle

FIRST APPEARANCE The Uncanny X-Men #161 (September 1982) **REAL NAME** Gabrielle Haller
OCCUPATION Israel's ambassador to the United Kingdom
BASE Tel Aviv, Israel; London, England
HEIGHT/WEIGHT Unrevealed **EYES** Brown **HAIR** Black
SPECIAL POWERS/ABILITIES Gabrielle Haller has no superpowers, but is a highly accomplished diplomat.

Gabrielle Haller is a survivor of the Nazi concentration camp established in Dachau, Germany, during World War II. There Nazis implanted in her mind the location of a cache of gold. After the war, Haller was afflicted with catatonic schizophrenia and hospitalized in Israel. Charles Xavier (Professor X) used his telepathic powers to cure her and they fell in love. When Baron von Strucker and his Hydra agents kidnapped Haller to find the gold, Xavier and "Magnus" (the future Magneto) rescued her. Many years later Xavier learned that Gabrielle had given birth to a son, David (*see* Legion). Haller is now Israel's ambassador to the UK. **PS**

Hammer, Justin

FIRST APPEARANCE Iron Man #120 (March 1979)
REAL NAME Justin Hammer
OCCUPATION Criminal financier **BASE** Mobile
HEIGHT 6 ft 2 in **WEIGHT** 170 lbs **EYES** Blue **HAIR** Gray
SPECIAL POWERS/ABILITIES A financial and business genius, Hammer has cunningly preserved his wealth despite being worldwide *persona non grata*.

Whatever Justin Hammer lacked in guile he made up for with low cunning. Infuriated by Stark International's success, Hammer resolved to undermine Tony Stark's business by compromising its corporate emblem, the Iron Man. Using a hypersonic device to take control of the armored suit, Hammer used it to kill a foreign ambassador. After Stark cleared his name, Hammer went into hiding and took to funding various criminals, including Blizzard, Boomerang, and Water Wizard. Another showdown with Stark left Hammer frozen in a block of ice and floating through space. **AD**

Hammer, Sasha

FIRST APPEARANCE Invincible Iron Man #1 (July 2008)
REAL NAME Sasha Hammer
OCCUPATION Industrialist, criminal **BASE** Mobile
HEIGHT 5 ft 6 in **WEIGHT** 120 lbs **EYES** Brown **HAIR** Black
SPECIAL POWERS/ABILITIES Sasha has been embedded with technology that grants her energy whips, flight, and superhuman durability. She also sometimes wears the Detroit Steel armor.

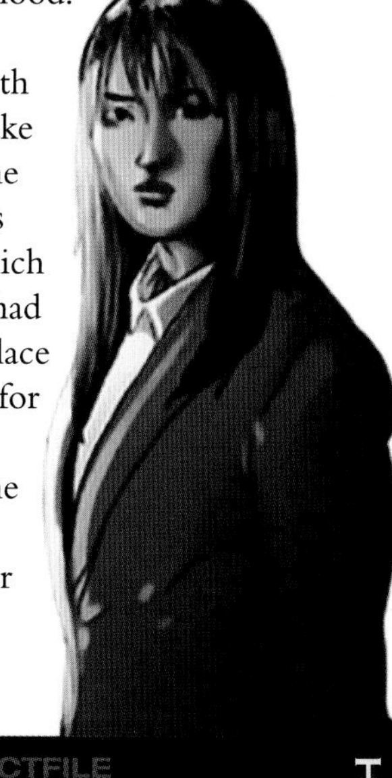

As the granddaughter of Justin Hammer and the daughter of Justine Hammer (Crimson Cowl) and the Mandarin, Sasha's hatred for Tony Stark (Iron Man) is in her blood. Her boyfriend Ezekiel Stane upgraded her with Stane technology to make her a formidable foe. She later piloted her family's Detroit Steel armor, which HAMMER Industries had developed to take the place of the Iron Man armor for the US military. She ruthlessly decapitated the original pilot of the Detroit Steel armor after he took her hostage to get the suit back. **MF**

HAMMER

After Norman Osborn (Green Goblin) became the US director of national security, one of his first acts was to dismantle SHIELD and replace it with an organization of his own, entirely loyal to him: HAMMER. The name HAMMER highlighted the fact that the organization's main aim would not be protecting the US but crushing its enemies. Osborn didn't even bother to come up with an acronym; he let the name stand on its own. As director of HAMMER, Osborn issued a warrant for Tony Stark's (Iron Man) arrest for perceived failures during the Secret Invasion. He then set up his own versions of both the Avengers and the X-Men, putting villains in the roles. Osborn had an Iron Man suit repainted in patriotic colors and became the Iron Patriot.

HAMMER fell apart at the end of the Dark Reign, after Osborn's failed assault on Asgard. The HAMMER Helicarrier was destroyed, taking down Sentry. Deidre Wentworth, aka mysandric terrorist Superia, later tried to revive the organization, with the help of AIM, but failed. **MF**

Despite his tendency to micromanage every bit of evil he committed, Norman relied on people like Victoria Hand to help execute his plans.

Norman cemented his hold over HAMMER by setting up covert alliances with prominent criminal organizations, including Hydra and AIM.

FACTFILE

NOTABLE MEMBERS

NORMAN OSBORN
Founder, director

SUPERIA
Second director

VICTORIA HAND
Assistant director; triple agent

BASE
The HAMMER Helicarrier; mobile

FIRST APPEARANCE
Secret Invasion #8 (January 2009)

HAMMERHEAD

FACTFILE
REAL NAME
Unknown
OCCUPATION
Criminal; gang boss of Hammerhead "family"
BASE
Manhattan, New York City

HEIGHT 5 ft 10 in
WEIGHT 195 lbs
EYES Blue
HAIR Black

FIRST APPEARANCE
Amazing Spider-Man #113 (October 1972)

POWERS
Hammerhead's reinforced skull allows him to head-butt with devastating effect, and even smash through walls. He can also use his head as a shield against blows. He has strong criminal organizational skills, and his favorite weapon is a Tommy gun.

Hammerhead's skull is reinforced with an unbreakable steel alloy.

A full-powered Spider-punch means nothing to the criminal with the hardest head in the business.

HAMMERHEAD

Once an obscure, small-time criminal, Hammerhead was found, severely injured, by Dr. Jonas Harrow. Harrow reconstructed the criminal's shattered skull, making it as strong as steel—hence his new name. Hammerhead retained no knowledge of his past life, save that he had been a criminal. Taking his inspiration from the poster of a gangster movie, *The Al Capone Mob*, he adopted a Prohibition-era style and returned to the New York underworld, determined to become the boss of bosses. He was prepared to violently dispatch anyone who stood in his way, including DOCTOR OCTOPUS, the KINGPIN, and MAGGIA boss Don Fortunato. During the CIVIL WAR, the Kingpin hired the assassin Underworld to kill Hammerhead. Shot down once more, Hammerhead was saved this time by Mr. Negative, who had his brain transferred into a robotic skeleton made of adamantium. In return, he now trains and leads his benefactor's enforcers. **TB, MF**

Hammerhead's style recalls the Prohibition gangsters of the 1920s.

THE HAND

FACTFILE
NOTABLE MEMBERS
THE BEAST
Demon with mystical powers.
KIRIGI
Martial arts and occult magic.
SHADOW
Martial arts and occult magic.
THOUGHT
Martial arts and occult magic.
PAIN
Martial arts and occult magic.
KWANNON
Martial arts and occult magic.
MANDARIN
Martial arts and occult magic.

FIRST APPEARANCE
Daredevil #168 (January 1981)

POWERS
In addition to possessing various mystical powers, Hand operatives are trained in the way of the ninja: expert spies and assassins skilled at unarmed combat, and with all kinds of weapons.

HAND, THE

The Hand is a cult of mystical ninjas involved with organized crime and often hired to carry out assassinations. The Hand dates back to 16th-century Japan, where the cult adapted classical ninjitsu techniques to its own evil purposes. The Hand's activities have now spread throughout the world. Hand operatives are servants of a demon known only as the Beast. Skilled in the use of powerful occult magic, they can kill a person, then bring that person back to life as a member of the Hand. Only ELEKTRA and WOLVERINE have ever been able to reverse this process.

If one of the Hand is killed, his body magically turns to dust in order to prevent identification.

The Hand has most often clashed with DAREDEVIL, ELEKTRA, and the CHASTE. Elektra led the Hand for a while, but after the SKRULL impersonating her was killed, Daredevil reluctantly took the position, hoping to turn the Hand into a force for good. After he failed, the KINGPIN grabbed the reins instead. **MT, MF**

The Hand is involved in regular clashes with members of the superhero community.

Implacable, faceless killers, the Hand cult remains one of the most feared groups of assassins at large in the modern world.

Hardball

FIRST APPEARANCE Avengers: The Initiative #1 (March 2007)
REAL NAME Roger Brokeridge
OCCUPATION HYDRA agent **BASE** Camp Hammond
HEIGHT 6 ft **WEIGHT** 200 lbs **EYES** Green **HAIR** Blond
SPECIAL POWERS/ABILITIES Creates and throws a number of different types of balls of energy.

Roger never wanted to be a hero. His brother Paul purchased powers from the Power Broker and then became paralyzed in a wrestling match. When Roger confronted the Power Broker, he signed up for his own powers. Trying to rob an armored car, he accidentally saved a little girl and became a hero. The Power Broker sold Roger's contract to Hydra, and Roger became part of the first class of cadets at Camp Hammond and spied on the organization from within. He later killed Senator Woodman, took over the man's Hydra cell, and wound up running a Hydra training camp in Madripoor. He surrendered to Constrictor. **MF**

Harkness, Agatha

FIRST APPEARANCE Fantastic Four #94 (March 1969)
REAL NAME Agatha Harkness
OCCUPATION Witch **BASE** New York City
HEIGHT 5 ft 11 in **WEIGHT** 130 lbs **EYES** Blue **HAIR** White
SPECIAL POWERS/ABILITIES Could manipulate magical forces through the recitation of spells; possessed magical familiar named Ebony, a pet cat that could transform into a vicious panther.

Agatha Harkness was raised in the town of New Salem, Colorado, whose inhabitants practiced magic. She excelled in her craft and eventually became the town's most powerful sorceress and leader. Agatha believed that witches and warlocks didn't have to live apart from normal humans. Her son and the town elders disagreed and she choose to leave New Salem. After moving to Whisper Hill, New York, she was hired as the governess for Franklin Richards, son of Mr. Fantastic and Invisible Woman. When the Scarlet Witch became unbalanced and disassembled the Avengers, she apparently murdered Agatha. However, Agatha has been reported dead before and has returned. **TD**

Havok

The brother of the X-Men leader Cyclops, Alex Summers was separated from his sibling following the death of their parents. Although Alex's mutant abilities developed during puberty, his mutant college professor, Ahmet Abdol, was the first to recognize them. After absorbing the cosmic energy stored in Alex's body, Abdol became the Living Monolith, but was defeated by the X-Men. Reunited with his brother, Alex joined the X-Men. Despite working in Cyclops' shadow, he later led X-Factor and fought to save the dark and twisted Earth-1298. He has long had a romantic relationship with the mutant Polaris. Alex worked with the Starjammers to put an end to the plans for galactic conquest of his long-hidden brother Vulcan. He sided with the X-Men in their conflict with the Avengers, but he later agreed to lead the Avengers Unity Division to highlight the good mutants could do. **AD, MF**

Havok can project plasma in the form of a blast with a tell-tale concentric circle pattern.

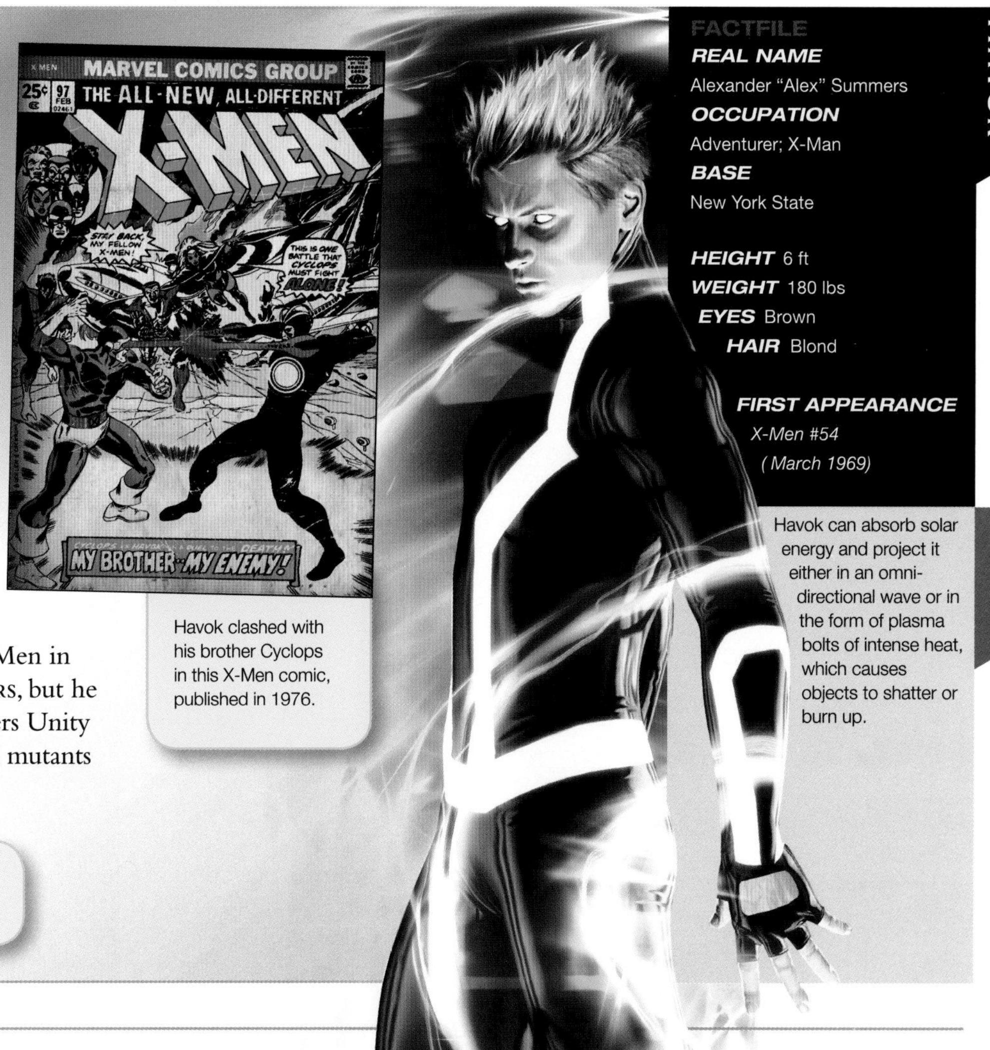

Havok clashed with his brother Cyclops in this X-Men comic, published in 1976.

FACTFILE

REAL NAME
Alexander "Alex" Summers

OCCUPATION
Adventurer; X-Man

BASE
New York State

HEIGHT 6 ft
WEIGHT 180 lbs
EYES Brown
HAIR Blond

FIRST APPEARANCE
X-Men #54 (March 1969)

POWERS
Havok can absorb solar energy and project it either in an omni-directional wave or in the form of plasma bolts of intense heat, which causes objects to shatter or burn up.

HAWKEYE

The Marksman

HAWKEYE

FACTFILE

REAL NAME
Clinton "Clint" Barton

OCCUPATION
Super Hero, adventurer

BASE
Manhattan, New York City

HEIGHT 6 ft 3 in
WEIGHT 230 lbs
EYES Blue
HAIR Blond

FIRST APPEARANCE
Tales of Suspense #57 (September 1964)

POWERS

Expert archer with perfect accuracy. Employs an arsenal of custom-made bows and a variety of trick arrows. Extensive training as an aerialist and acrobat. Skilled in hand-to-hand combat.

Barton was only 14 when he joined a carnival and attracted the attention of the show's star Jacques Duquesne, the SWORDSMAN. Duquesne trained Barton in the art of throwing knives, but quickly realized the boy was a natural at archery and turned him over to Trickshot, the carnival's archer. On stage, Barton was known as Hawkeye the Marksman.

Wickedly sarcastic, Hawkeye has developed some of his trick arrows to both defeat and humiliate his foes.

GOING WRONG

Witnessing IRON MAN in action inspired Barton to use his archery skills to fight crime. When he tried to prevent a robbery, he was mistaken for a thief, and he wound up fighting Iron Man instead. Soon after that, he met the original BLACK WIDOW, fell in love with her, and started committing crimes to impress her.

Barton reformed and begged to be admitted into the AVENGERS. Iron Man sponsored him, and Barton remained an Avenger for many years, though he occasionally took brief breaks and even joined the DEFENDERS during one of them. To help the team, Barton sometimes borrowed Hank Pym's growth formula and became a new Goliath.

While on leave, Barton married Bobbi Morse (MOCKINGBIRD). They moved to California when Barton was assigned to set up the West Coast AVENGERS. After Mockingbird seemed to be killed in action, the West Coast branch disbanded, and Barton rejoined the Avengers. He died stopping a KREE warship during the SCARLET WITCH's breakdown, but she restored him to life when she rearranged reality after M-Day. In the meantime, at the request of CAPTAIN AMERICA, Kate Bishop of the YOUNG AVENGERS took on the identity of Hawkeye.

Kate Bishop in her role as Hawkeye while fighting in the Young Avengers.

THE HERO REBORN

Barton temporarily took on the identity of Ronin, a masked swordsman. During the SECRET INVASION, he discovered Mockingbird was still alive. They reunited but, despite their best efforts, the marriage fell apart.

During the DARK REIGN, Bullseye assumed the Hawkeye identity as part of the Dark Avengers. Barton later returned to being Hawkeye and leading various teams of Avengers. He shared the name with Kate, whom he took on as a protégé. **TD, MF**

ESSENTIAL STORYLINES

- ***Hawkeye (tpb)*** While working as head of security for Cross Industries, Hawkeye meets and marries Mockingbird.
- ***Solo Adventures #1-6*** Hawkeye's former mentor Trickshot returns and we learn Clint's true origin.
- ***West Coast Avengers Limited Series #1-4*** Hawkeye opens a branch office for the Avengers.
- ***Avengers #502*** Hawkeye courageously sacrifices his life to protect his Avengers teammates.

Headmen, The

The Headmen comprised four brilliant individuals, each so confident of their abilities they were convinced that they should rule the Earth. United by Dr. Arthur Nagan they agreed to combine their talents to gain control of the planet. Despite obvious ability, their tactics were at best questionable.

Looking to obtain superhuman powers for themselves, the Headmen targeted the DEFENDERS and succeeded in implanting Chondu's brain into the head of Kyle Richard, alias NIGHTHAWK. When his consciousness was subsequently transferred into the body of a vile monster, Chondu went mad. Although his sanity had returned by the time his brain was transferred into a SHE-HULK clone, this proved to be one step too far. Furious at having been given a woman's body, Chondu attacked the Headmen with the help of SPIDER-MAN. The group reunited and attempted to take over the world, starting with Manhattan, by manipulating a hugely powerful, extra-dimensional entity named Orago the Unconquerable. **AD**

THE HEADMEN
1 Gorilla-Man ***2*** Ruby Thursday ***3*** Orago the Unconquerable (not a member) ***4*** Chondu the Mystic ***5*** Shrunken Bones

FACTFILE

MEMBERS AND POWERS

GORILLA-MAN
(Dr. Arthur Nagan)
A brilliant scientist, whose head has been mysteriously transplanted onto a gorilla's body.

SHRUNKEN BONES
A biologist and biochemist, experiments on own body led to skeleton shrinking but not skin.

CHONDU THE MYSTIC
A minor adept in the mystic arts; powers determined by body occupied by brain.

RUBY THURSDAY
Artificial head serves as "organic computer", capable of superhuman storage and processing.

BASE Mobile

FIRST APPEARANCE
Defenders #21 (March 1975)

Hellcat

EACH NIGHT THERE WAS A NEW STORY ON THE NEWS. I COULDN'T HEAR ENOUGH ABOUT EACH NEW HERO!

Patsy Walker had a teenage crush on Reed Richards of the Fantastic Four.

As a teenager, Patsy Walker was the subject of a popular comic written by her mother. As an adult, Walker wed Air Force officer Buzz Baxter (later MAD DOG), though the marriage ended unhappily. She had always idolized Super Heroes, so Walker decided to become one, donning a costume once worn by Greer Nelson (TIGRA). Calling herself Hellcat, she aided the AVENGERS and served with the DEFENDERS for years. Eventually she married master of the occult Daimon Hellstrom, (see HELLSTORM). The couple moved to San Francisco, becoming paranormal investigators. Hellcat later took her own life, but her spirit lived on in Hell. There she encountered HAWKEYE and the THUNDERBOLTS, who had journeyed to the underworld to rescue MOCKINGBIRD. The team returned to Earth with Hellcat, who rededicated herself to the heroic life. She was recently sent to Alaska to serve as its Super Hero as part of the FIFTY-STATE INITIATIVE. **DW, MF**

HELLCAT WITH THE DEFENDERS
1 Doctor Strange ***2*** Hellcat ***3*** Nighthawk ***4*** Valkyrie ***5*** Daimon Hellstrom

FACTFILE

REAL NAME
Patricia "Patsy" Walker Hellstrom

OCCUPATION
Adventurer

BASE
San Francisco, California

HEIGHT 5 ft 8 in
WEIGHT 135 lbs
EYES Blue
HAIR Red

FIRST APPEARANCE
The Avengers #144 (February 1976)

POWERS

Minor psionic abilities, skilled acrobat and combatant (received combat training from Moondragon on Saturn's moon Titan). Costume enhances strength and agility; steel-tipped claws in gloves and boots; a wrist device fires a 30-ft cable with grappling hook for scaling tall buildings.

Hellfire Club

HELLFIRE CLUB

FACTFILE

MEMBERS
1 **SHINOBI SHAW**
(White King)
2 **SELENE**
(Black Queen)
3 **SEBASTIAN SHAW**
(Black King)
4 **EMMA FROST**
(White Queen)
5 **HARRY LELAND**
(Black Bishop)
6 **EMMANUEL DA COSTA**
(White Rook)
7 **JASON WYNGARDE**
(Mastermind)
8 **TESSA**
(Sage)
9 **DONALD PIERCE**
(White Bishop)
10 **FRIEDRICH VON ROEHM**
(Black Rook)
11 **MADELYNE PRYOR**
(Black Rook)
12 **TREVOR FITZROY**
(White Rook)

BASE
London, Manhattan, Paris, and Hong Kong

FIRST APPEARANCE
(as Council of the Chosen) *X-Men #100 (August 1976);*
(as Hellfire Club) *The Uncanny X-Men #129 (January 1980)*

Founded in England in the mid-18th century, the Hellfire Club was an exclusive social organization for Britain's upper classes. According to legend, the Club provided a place where members could secretly pursue illicit pleasures. In the 1770s, Sir Patrick Clemens and Lady Diana Knight established the Hellfire Club's American branch in New York City. Today, the Hellfire Club is a worldwide organization with branches in London, Manhattan, Paris, and Hong Kong. Its members include socialites, celebrities, wealthy businessmen, and politicians. Despite the Club's outward respectability, its Inner Circle secretly seeks world domination through political and economic influence. Inner Circle members hold positions named after chess pieces. The men dress in 18th-century costume and the women in risqué outfits.

Inner Circle

Industrialist Sebastian Shaw ruled as Black King over an Inner Circle that included his fellow mutant Emma Frost, the White Queen, and cyborg Donald Pierce. To win admission to the Inner Circle, Mastermind mesmerized Phoenix into becoming the Club's Black Queen. Other members of US Inner Circles included Blackheart, Cassandra Nova, Hellstorm, Kade Kilgore, Magneto, Selene, Sunspot, and Viper.
PS, MF

Hellions

FIRST APPEARANCE New Mutants #16 (June 1984)
BASE Snow Valley, MA
CURRENT MEMBERS AND POWERS
Rockslide (Santo Vaccarro) Made of granite, can fire hands as projectiles [1]; **Emma Frost** Telepath [2]; **Wither** (Kevin Ford) Touch disintegrates organic matter [3]; **Dust** (Sooraya Qadir) Turns into sandlike substance [4]; **Mercury** (Cessily Kincaid) Shapeshifter made of non-toxic mercury [5]; **Hellion** (Julian Keller) Telekinesis [6]; **Tag** (Brian Cruz) Tags others, causing them to emit a psionic signal [7].

A number of groups of young mutants have called themselves the Hellions. The originals were students at Emma Frost's Massachusetts Academy who served the Hellfire Club. They were wiped out by a psychotic criminal. The second band was formed by enemies of X-Force. The third group was composed of students at the Xavier Institute for Higher Learning. Kade Kilgore's new Hellfire Academy also featured a fresh team of Hellions.
TB, MF

Hellstorm

FIRST APPEARANCE Marvel Spotlight #12 (October 1973)
REAL NAME Daimon Hellstrom
OCCUPATION Demonologist, occult investigator, exorcist, former priest **BASE** San Francisco, CA.
HEIGHT 6 ft 1 in **WEIGHT** 180 lbs **EYES** Blue **HAIR** Red
SPECIAL POWERS/ABILITIES Trident projects "soulfire;" can cast spells to transport himself and others into mystical dimensions.

Daimon Hellstrom only learned the truth about his father when his mother broke down and he was sent to an orphanage. As son of the demon Satan, he joined the Defenders and eventually defeated his father. He married Patsy Walker (Hellcat), but while saving his life she saw his true face, went insane, and later killed herself. Now calling himself Hellstorm, Daimon figured out how to kill Satan and take over Hell. He then helped Hawkeye's Thunderbolts revive Patsy. He was later killed by a demonic Victoria Hand, but this was not the end for him. **MT, MF**

High Evolutionary

FIRST APPEARANCE Thor #134 (November 1966)
REAL NAME Herbert Edgar Wyndham
OCCUPATION Founder of the Knights of Wundagore
BASE Unknown **HEIGHT** 6 ft 2 in **WEIGHT** 200 lbs
EYES Brown **HAIR** Brown
SPECIAL POWERS/ABILITIES Highly evolved intelligence; immense psionic powers; armor reconstructs body when injured, enabling virtual immortality; able to grow to 300 ft.

At Oxford in the 1930s, Herbert Wyndham built a genetic accelerator that evolved creatures inside it. Ostracized by his peers, he brought Jonathan Drew and Miles Warren (Jackal) to Wundagore Mountain in the Balkans. There, Wyndham used his accelerator on himself to become the High Evolutionary and created an army of humanoid animals he called the Knights of Wundagore. He later founded a new planetary home for his knights, established Counter-Earth, and tried to evolve all humanity. He helped defeat Ultron in the Annihilation, and restored Magneto's powers after M-Day. He has since become a world-builder, the opposite of Galactus.
AD, MF

HERCULES

Super-strong demigod son of Zeus

During his 12 labors, Hercules killed a flock of man-eating birds belonging to his half-brother Ares, the god of war, who has hated him ever since.

Hercules is the son of Zeus, king of the Gods of Olympus, and a mortal woman. He is best known for his Twelve Labors, which he carried out to prove that he was worthy of immortality. He also made three enemies during the course of these labors: Ares, the god of war, Pluto (Hades), the lord of the underworld and Typhon, the giant son of Titan.

FACTFILE

REAL NAME
Hercules; aliases Heracles, Harry Cleese

OCCUPATION
Adventurer

BASE
Olympus

HEIGHT 6 ft 5 in
WEIGHT 325 lbs
EYES Blue
HAIR Dark brown

FIRST APPEARANCE
Journey Into Mystery Annual #1 (1965)

POWERS
Virtually immortal. Trained in hand-to-hand combat and ancient Greek wrestling skills. Excellent archer. Wields a practically indestructible golden mace.

PRINCE OF POWER

Hercules is known throughout Olympus as the Prince of Power and he lives for the thrill of battle. He also believes that it is a great honor to fight him and often bestows this so-called "gift" on both friends and foes alike. Instead of a handshake, Hercules likes to greet his fellow Avengers with a friendly punch in the face!

In modern times, Hercules met and battled Thor when the thunder god accidentally journeyed to Olympus. Hercules later traveled to Earth to renew his acquaintance with the Asgardian and unwittingly signed a contract that made him Pluto's slave. After being rescued by Thor, Hercules returned to Olympus until the Enchantress cast a spell on him and sent him to battle the Avengers. He later joined the team when Zeus temporarily exiled him to Earth. He was taken prisoner by Ares and his minions, but rescued by the Avengers. Hercules joined Thor on a journey to the far end of the galaxy, where they battled the Destroyer, Firelord, and Ego, the Living Planet. He also joined the Los Angeles super-team known as the Champions and spent time as one of the Defenders.

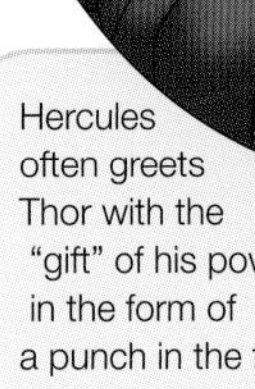

Hercules often greets Thor with the "gift" of his power—in the form of a punch in the face!

GODHOOD AND HUMANITY

Herc fought for the resistance during the Civil War and slew Ragnarok with the Thor-clone's own hammer. He sided with the Hulk during World War Hulk, after which he became best friends with Amadeus Cho. During the Secret Invasion, Hercules led the God Squad to defeat the Skrull gods. He died stopping Hera from destroying the universe, but Cho brought him back as an All-Father in time to lead the Chaos War against Amatsu-Mikaboshi. After defeating the Chaos King, Herc used all his power to restore reality, making him mortal. He later became an instructor at the Avengers Academy. **TD, MF**

Hercules has been unlucky in love. He falls for mortal women who grow old and die while he remains young.

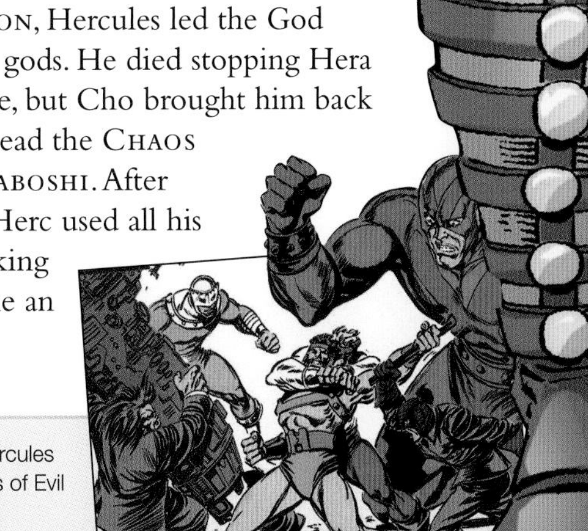

Though outnumbered, Hercules tried to defeat the Masters of Evil and almost paid the price.

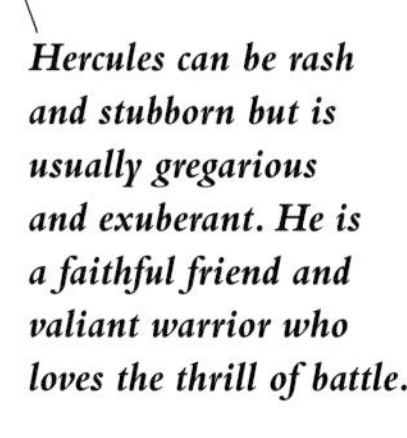

Hercules can be rash and stubborn but is usually gregarious and exuberant. He is a faithful friend and valiant warrior who loves the thrill of battle.

ESSENTIAL STORYLINES
- ***Thor #124–130*** Hercules' first journey to Earth in modern times: enslaved by Pluto, rescued by Thor.
- ***The Avengers: Under Siege tpb*** Zemo's new Masters of Evil invade Avengers Mansion and almost beat Hercules to death.
- ***Hercules: Prince of Power tpb*** Hercules confronts Galactus in the far future.

HILL, MARIA

FACTFILE
REAL NAME
Maria Hill
OCCUPATION
Director of SHIELD
BASE
SHIELD Helicarrier, mobile

HEIGHT 5 ft 10 in
WEIGHT 130 lbs
EYES Brown
HAIR Black

FIRST APPEARANCE
New Avengers #4 (April 2005)

POWERS
Maria is a trained combatant and excellent tactician.

HILL, MARIA

Born in Chicago, Maria Hill joined the US military and later SHIELD, working her way up to commander. When Nick FURY was removed as director, Hill was chosen to take his place. She served in that position throughout the CIVIL WAR, leading the effort to bring fugitive heroes into line. Afterward, she willingly gave over the job to Tony Stark (IRON MAN) and stayed on as his deputy director.

After Norman Osborn (GREEN GOBLIN) took over SHIELD and replaced it with HAMMER, Hill became a fugitive because of her support for Stark. She fought against Osborn and his false AVENGERS team during the siege of Asgard. With Osborn removed and HAMMER destroyed, Hill was appointed the leader of the Avengers. After FEAR ITSELF, she rejoined SHIELD as its deputy director under Daisy JOHNSON. When Johnson was suspended, Hill became SHIELD's director once again. **MF**

Maria Hill uses a jet pack to escape from an exploding helicarrier.

HOBGOBLIN

FACTFILE
REAL NAME
Roderick Kingsley
OCCUPATION
Super Villain
BASE
Mobile

HEIGHT 5 ft 11 in
WEIGHT 185 lbs
EYES Blue
HAIR Gray

FIRST APPEARANCE
The Spectacular Spider-Man #43 (June 1980)

POWERS
Hobgoblin's strength and agility are enhanced by improved Goblin formula; flies upon a vertical-thrust Goblin glider; wears electro-shock gloves; carries Jack O'Lantern-shaped grenades in a pouch. Possessed an armor-plated battle-van with an arsenal of weaponry.

HOBGOBLIN

Roderick Kingsley uncovered a cache of the GREEN GOBLIN's costumes and weaponry and sought to dominate New York's criminal underworld as Hobgoblin, until SPIDER-MAN undermined his efforts. Kingsley manipulated two other men into taking the Hobgoblin role. Petty crook Lefty Donovan served as a human guinea pig for a new version of the Goblin formula and, after brainwashing by Kingsley, *Daily Bugle* reporter Ned Leeds acted as his substitute until Leeds' death. Jason Macendale (formerly Jack O'Lantern) stole the identity from Leeds, but when he was imprisoned, Kingsley murdered him.

When Betty BRANT outed Kingsley as the Hobgoblin, he fled to the Caribbean. While there, his brother Daniel took his place, but Phil Urich (nephew of Ben URICH) killed him and took over the identity. The Hobgoblin of 2211, Robin Borne, came back in time to destroy her father Spider-Man, but she accidentally erased herself from existence with her own weapon. **AD, MF**

The various Hobgoblins have all tested Spider-Man's mettle, but the doughty wall-crawler is always victorious.

Hiro-Kala

FIRST APPEARANCE Skaar: Son of Hulk #2 (September 2008)
REAL NAME Hiro-Kala **OCCUPATION** Messiah, ruler of K'ai
BASE K'ai **HEIGHT** 5 ft 10 in **WEIGHT** 140 lbs
EYES Black **HAIR** Bald
SPECIAL POWERS/ABILITIES Hiro-Kala controls both the Old Power and the Power Cosmic. He can also fire energy from his eyes and hands.

When the Hulk's wife Caiera was killed in an explosion, she placed her twin sons into cocoons to shield them. Thinking the children were dead, Hulk abandoned them, leaving Skaar and Hiro-Kala on their own. Hiro-Kala was raised as a slave, unaware of his heritage. After Skaar lost a battle with Galactus to save their homeworld Sakaar, Hiro-Kala gathered as many of his people as he could to escape. He wound up on the Microverse planet K'ai, which he later pulled into the larger universe and sent hurtling toward Earth to kill his father. With Skaar's help, the Hulk stopped him. **MF**

Hogan, Harold

FIRST APPEARANCE X-Men Alpha #1 (February 1995)
REAL NAME Harold "Happy" Hogan
OCCUPATION Tony Stark's right-hand man; chauffeur
BASE New York City **HEIGHT** 5 ft 11 in **WEIGHT** 221 lbs
EYES Brown **HAIR** (as human) Brown; (as Freak) None
SPECIAL POWERS/ABILITIES As the Freak, Hogan possesses superhuman strength and durability.

Former boxer "Happy" Hogan saved Tony Stark from a car crash and Stark hired him as his chauffeur. Hogan eventually realized that Stark was secretly Iron Man and sometimes donned an Iron Man battlesuit to stand in for Stark. Doctors used Stark's invention, the Enervator, to save Hogan's life, but its cobalt radiation also transformed Hogan into a virtually mindless monster known as the Freak. Iron Man restored him to normal using the Enervator, although Hogan has sometimes reverted to the Freak. Hogan married Pepper Potts—twice. He was nearly killed while saving her from the Spymaster, and he later died from his injuries. **PS, MF**

Holocaust

FIRST APPEARANCE X-Men Alpha #1 (February 1995)
REAL NAME Unknown
OCCUPATION Horseman of the Apocalypse **BASE** Mobile
HEIGHT 6 ft 2 in **WEIGHT** 240 lbs **EYES** Red **HAIR** Blond
SPECIAL POWERS/ABILITIES Holocaust is a flaming skeleton held inside a containment suit; able to absorb energy and release it as concussive power blasts.

Sired in the Age of Apocalypse timeline, Holocaust claimed to be the son of Apocalypse and served as the leader of Apocalypse's Four Horsemen. Escaping from that timeline just moments before it was obliterated, Holocaust was transported to Earth-616, where he destroyed the Avalon space station and battled another timeline refugee, X-Man. Press-ganged into joining reality-hopping heroes the Exiles, an encounter with a tyrannical Hyperion led to Holocaust's demise. After cracking his containment suit, Hyperion literally absorbed his entire being. **AD**

Hodge, Cameron

FIRST APPEARANCE X-Factor #1 (February 1986)
REAL NAME Cameron Hodge
OCCUPATION Businessman **BASE** Mobile
HEIGHT 6 ft 2 in **WEIGHT** 196 lbs **EYES** Blue **HAIR** Black
SPECIAL POWERS/ABILITIES Cunning manipulator; due to a pact with the demon N'astirh, Cameron Hodge cannot die; since becoming a cyborg, he has vast strength and weaponry.

Cameron Hodge grew up secretly hating mutants, becoming the leader of the anti-mutant radical group the Right. Hodge suggested that the X-Men go undercover as mutant hunters called X-Factor, so as to conceal their activities in recruiting and training mutants. However, his real objective was to stir up anti-mutant sentiment. Hodge later made a pact with the demon N'astirh that gave him immortality. Even after his head was cut off and he was consumed by the techno-organic race known as the Phalanx, Hodge remained a thorn in the X-Men's side. **TB**

Hood, The

The son of a criminal who worked with the Kingpin, Parker seemed destined for a life of petty crime. While robbing a warehouse, he stumbled upon a summoned demon, killed it, and took its boots and cloak. After becoming embroiled in a battle on a reconstituted Battleworld, Parker returned to Earth and began to build a criminal empire based on Super Villains. This put him into direct conflict with the Avengers. At this time, he started a relationship with Madame Masque.

During the Secret Invasion, the Hood joined forces with the heroes to save the Earth, and he discovered that the powers his cloak granted him came from the demon Dormammu. During the Dark Reign, he joined the Cabal at the invitation of Norman Osborn (*see* Green Goblin). Soon after, Dormammu sent the Hood to kill Doctor Strange and become the new Sorcerer Supreme, but the demon was exorcised from him, leaving him powerless.

Loki granted Parker new powers by loaning him the Norn Stones but took them back during the siege of Asgard. Escaping from jail, Parker went after the Infinity Gem, but the Illuminati foiled his plans. **MT, MF**

FACTFILE
REAL NAME
Parker Robbins
OCCUPATION
Criminal mastermind
BASE
New York City

HEIGHT 5 ft 10 in
WEIGHT 165 lbs
EYES Brown
HAIR Brown

FIRST APPEARANCE
Hood #1 (July 2002)

POWERS
When possessed by Dormammu, the Hood's magic cloak and boots granted him invisibility, electrical bursts from his hands, the ability to walk on air, and the ability to transform into a demon.

Howard the Duck

FACTFILE

REAL NAME
Howard (last name unknown)

OCCUPATION
Many, including former candidate for President of the United States; most often unemployed.

BASE
Cleveland, Ohio

HEIGHT 2 ft 7 in
WEIGHT 40 lbs
EYES Brown
FEATHERS Yellow

FIRST APPEARANCE
Fear #19
(December 1973)

POWERS
Howard is skilled in the little-known martial art of Quack Fu, and a formidable opponent in hand-to-hand combat.

WAAUUGH
THAT DOES IT! I CAN'T STAND IT ANYMORE!! THIS WHOLE WORLD IS FOULED UP!!!

Howard feels the strain of life in a world not his own.

Howard the Duck was born on Duckworld, where people evolved from waterfowl. When the demon Thog the Nether-Spawn caused the Interdimensional Cosmic Axis to shift, Howard was dropped into the Florida Everglades on Earth, the site of the Nexus of All Realities. Hoping to get home, Howard joined up with Korrek the Barbarian, the Earth sorceress Jennifer Kale, Dakimh the Enchanter, and the Man-Thing. As this group battled Thog, Howard fell off the Stepping Stones of Oblivion and tumbled back to Earth, landing in Cleveland, Ohio. There he met Beverly Switzler, when the two were attacked by the criminal accountant Pro-Rata. Howard and Beverly escaped and began living together, attempting to have as normal a life as possible in a human-duck relationship. Recently, Howard tried to register under the Superhuman Registration Act but was told that the government's official policy is that he did not exist. This was later corrected, and he fought against the Skrulls during the Secret Invasion. Also, as a member of A.R.M.O.R., he helped battle an interdimensional zombie plague. **MT, MF**

Howling Commandos

FACTFILE

MEMBERS
Sgt. Nick Fury; Corporal Thaddeus "Dum Dum" Dugan; Privates Dino Manelli, Izzy Cohen, Gabe Jones, Percival Pinkerton, Reb "Rebel" Ralston, Jonathan "Junior" Juniper (killed in action), Eric Koenig

BASE
Pacific Theater of Operations, World War II

FIRST APPEARANCE
Sgt. Fury and His Howling Commandos #1
(May 1963)

POWERS
Apparently ill-assorted group welded into crack unit by Sgt. Fury's unmatched leadership qualities. Each member was a highly trained commando, with skills in hand-to-hand combat, the use of explosives, and proficiency with a variety of firearms.

The Howling Commandos formed the first attack squad of Able Company during World War II, a unit that took on the most dangerous missions of the war. Under orders from Captain "Happy" Sam Sawyer, Sergeant Nick Fury led his men against the worst the Axis powers could throw at them, including the legendary Blitzkrieg Squad of Baron von Strucker, and the malevolent Red Skull. Many members of the unit survived to become the nucleus of the UN peacekeeping force SHIELD. SHIELD once used the Howling Commandos name for a top-secret squad of monsters dedicated to battling supernatural forces. After leaving SHIELD, Fury assembled a new team of Howling Commandos—aka the Secret Warriors—to fight the Secret Invasion. When Norman Osborn (*see* Green Goblin) dismantled SHIELD, Dum Dum Dugan and Gabe Jones formed a private military company called the Howling Commandos. **TB, MF**

SGT. FURY
AND HIS
HOWLING
COMMANDOS
MARVEL COMICS GROUP
12¢ 50 JAN
THE INVASION BEGINS!

The Howling Commandos were heroes of World War II.

THE LINEUP
1 Sgt. Nick Fury ***2*** Jonathan "Junior" Juniper
3 Reb Ralston ***4*** Cpl. Dum Dum Dugan
5 Gabe Jones ***6*** Dino Manelli ***7*** Izzy Cohen

Hulk, *see pages 172-175*

HULKLING

FIRST APPEARANCE Young Avengers #1 (April 2005)
REAL NAME Theodore "Teddy" Altman/Dorrek VIII
OCCUPATION Adventurer, student **BASE** New York City
HEIGHT Varies **WEIGHT** Varies
EYES Usually blue **HAIR** Usually Blond
SPECIAL POWERS/ABILITIES Shapeshifting and superhuman strength and healing.

Born the secret son of Princess Anelle (a SKRULL) and CAPTAIN MAR-VELL (a KREE), Teddy Altman had thought he was a human mutant when he co-founded the YOUNG AVENGERS. He learned the truth when the SUPER-SKRULL tried to return him to the Skrulls. Teddy became a pawn in a face-off between the Kree and Skrull empires, settled only when he agreed to spend six months with each race before deciding which side to join—but the Super-Skrull left in his place instead. Teddy subsequently came out as gay and became engaged to teammate WICCAN, but they have since parted. **MF**

HUNTARA

FIRST APPEARANCE Fantastic Four #377 (June 1993)
REAL NAME Huntara Richards **OCCUPATION** Guardian of the Sacred Timelines **BASE** Elsewhen
HEIGHT 6 ft 2 in **WEIGHT** 185 lbs **EYES** Brown **HAIR** Black
SPECIAL POWERS/ABILITIES Psionic scythe cuts through almost any material, fires concussive bolts and teleports her between dimensions and across space; superior athlete and combatant.

Huntara was born on an alternate Earth. The daughter of Nathaniel RICHARDS and the half-sister of MR. FANTASTIC, she was taken to Elsewhen, a barbaric alien dimension. Huntara was trained in the arts of war and combat alongside her nephew Franklin RICHARDS and they both became Guardians of the Sacred Timelines, who prevent and repair time paradoxes. When her father created a time paradox by exchanging the teenaged Franklin with his younger self, Huntara was forced to journey to this timeline where she eventually met the FANTASTIC FOUR. She later returned to Elsewhen and resumed her duties as a Guardian. **TD**

HUNTER, STEVIE

FIRST APPEARANCE The Uncanny X-Men #139 (November 1980)
REAL NAME Stephanie "Stevie" Hunter
OCCUPATION Dance instructor **BASE** Salem Center, New York State **HEIGHT** 5 ft 9 in **WEIGHT** 121 lbs
EYES Brown **HAIR** Dark brown
SPECIAL POWERS/ABILITIES A talented dancer and athlete and an excellent dance teacher.

Stevie Hunter was a ballet dancer, until a broken leg forced her to retire. She became a dance instructor and opened a school in Salem Center, New York State. Professor Charles Xavier's School for Gifted Youngsters, the headquarters of the X-MEN, was located nearby. One of Xavier's students, Kitty PRYDE, began taking lessons at Hunter's school. Eventually, Hunter discovered that Xavier's students were mutants. Xavier hired Hunter to be a physical trainer and therapist at his school. Hunter has since returned to operating her own dance academy. **PS**

HUSK

Husk, Archangel and Iceman are surrounded by a pack of slavering wolf men.

Paige Guthrie envied her elder brother who, as CANNONBALL, had forged a career with the NEW MUTANTS. Paige kept her own mutant powers hidden until she was forced into a battle of wits with the Gamesmaster, a psionic mutant who formed the UPSTARTS, a group that assassinated mutants. Paige freed her brother and several of his friends from the Gamesmaster's clutches. Shortly afterward, she was captured by the techno-organic alien PHALANX, along with several other young mutants. Its effort to assimilate them into its consciousness was foiled, and Paige was invited to join the Xavier Institute's Massachusetts Academy and become a member of GENERATION X.

Paige subsequently joined X-CORPS, helping to police mutants in Europe, and later became part of the X-MEN. When the X-Men split into two factions, she followed WOLVERINE to the Jean Grey School for Higher Learning. Her brother Jay and sister Melody were also mutants. Melody lost her powers on M-Day, and Jay died soon after. **AD, MF**

FACTFILE

REAL NAME
Paige Elisabeth Guthrie
OCCUPATION
X-Man
BASE
New York State

HEIGHT 5 ft 7 in
WEIGHT 127 lbs
EYES Blue
HAIR Black

FIRST APPEARANCE
X-Force #32 (March 1994)

POWERS
A mutant metamorph, Husk can shed skin and transform her body into any form with similar or less mass. She frequently turns her body into a different substance, such as steel or stone, taking on the properties of that substance, for example increased strength.

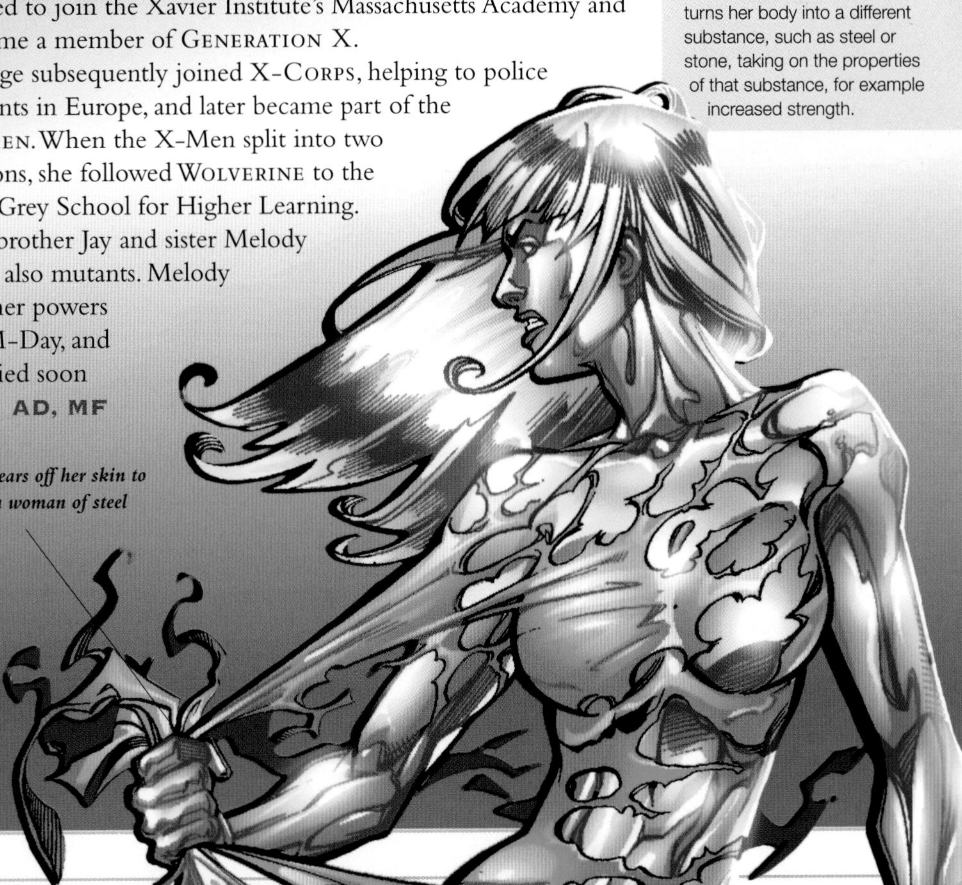

Husk tears off her skin to reveal a woman of steel

THE HULK

The strongest man-like creature on Earth!

THE HULK

FACTFILE
REAL NAME
Robert Bruce Banner
OCCUPATION
Scientist; wanderer
BASE
Mobile

HEIGHT 7 ft
WEIGHT 1,040 lbs
EYES Green
HAIR Green

FIRST APPEARANCE:
Incredible Hulk #1 (May 1962)

POWERS
Fueled by gamma radiation, the Hulk possesses almost unlimited physical strength. The madder he gets, the stronger he gets. He can leap several miles in a single bound. His body heals almost instantly, He possesses a strong homing instinct for the desert where he was "born."

ALLIES/FOES
ALLIES Rick Jones, Betty Ross, Doc Samson, Jennifer Walters (She-Hulk), Jarella, the Avengers.

FOES The Leader, The Abomination, Rhino, Sandman, Juggernaut, Absorbing man, General Thaddeus "Thunderbolt" Ross, Bi-Beast, Zzzax.

ISSUE #1
In his first appearance in *The Incredible Hulk #1 (May 1962)*, the Hulk was colored grey, rather than the more familiar green.

Bruce had a troubled childhood; his father called him a monster, and eventually killed his mother.

A child prodigy, Bruce Banner grew up in an abusive household, one that would have a profound long-term effect on his psyche. An introverted child, Bruce was ill-equipped to deal with the outbursts of his father, who called young Bruce a monster and terrorized both him and his mother. Bruce developed a multiple personality disorder, repressing all of his negative emotions when the trauma became too much to take. This cycle of abuse continued until the day Brian Banner slew his wife in a fit of rage. Thereafter, Bruce was shuttled from relative to relative, and grew ever more socially awkward, even as his remarkable intellect became more apparent.

FIRST LOVE

The US Army recruited Banner to develop new weapons systems while he was still in high school. Bruce was placed under the authority of General Thaddeus "Thunderbolt" Ross, a blustering no-nonsense veteran. It was in the person of Ross's daughter Betty (*see* Ross, Betty) that Bruce found a kindred spirit. Both he and Betty had lost mothers, and were subjected to the outbursts of raging fathers; an attraction soon developed between them.

Recruited by the military, Bruce Banner worked on developing new weapons systems on the military base commanded by hard-nosed general "Thunderbolt" Ross.

THE GAMMA BOMB

Prodded by his military handlers, Banner developed the G-Bomb, a weapon harnessing the power of gamma radiation. On the day the bomb was to be tested, a reckless teenager, Rick Jones, drove out onto the test range on a dare, little realizing that he was standing on ground zero of the most potent explosive device ever developed. In an uncharacteristic moment of heroism, Bruce Banner rushed out onto the test site, and dragged Jones to the safety of a nearby trench before the G-Bomb detonated. However Banner was exposed to the full force of the weapon, his every atom bombarded by gamma radiation.

Banner is bathed in gamma rays trying to save the life of Rick Jones.

Over the years, Bruce Banner's transformations into the Hulk have taken on a variety of styles. Initially, Banner would become the Hulk when the sun set, and return to his Banner identity at sunrise. Soon thereafter, Banner learned to control his transformations using a gamma ray machine, becoming a more intelligent but no less savage Hulk. Eventually, the continued exposure to gamma radiation caused Banner to transform into the Hulk whenever he became agitated or upset. Banner's Hulk persona has also differed over the years, each one apparently representing a different facet of his fragmented psyche: the childlike Green Hulk, the more intelligent but less powerful Gray Hulk, the extremely intelligent but egocentric "Professor" Hulk—and even a "Devil Hulk" representing all of the evil within Banner's soul. Additional permutations of the Hulk are apt to emerge at any given time, should conditions prove favorable.

MULTIPLE PERSONALITIES
1 Bruce Banner **2** Savage Hulk
3 Joe Fixit **4** Mindless Hulk
5 Professor Hulk

Hulk takes on a pack of gamma-ray-infused dogs, set on him by General Ryker.

A day later, Banner was still silently screaming. But the military doctors could find nothing wrong—he had miraculously escaped the blast unscathed. Or so it seemed. For the gamma radiation Banner had been exposed to had unlocked long-repressed feelings of hate and rage. When conditions were right, Banner found himself transforming into an unstoppable juggernaut of destruction, the personification of his long-denied dark side: the incredible Hulk!

At first, the Hulk only manifested at nightfall. When the sun went down, Banner would inexorably change into a green-skinned powerhouse and remain out of control until daybreak. Eventually, due in part to Banner's attempts to cure himself of these unwanted transformations, the appearance of the Hulk would be brought on by stress and anxiety. Whenever Bruce became outraged or fearful, the change in his emotional state would trigger the gamma radiation within his system, and the Hulk would live again. For a time, with the aid of Rick Jones, Bruce kept his dual identity secret, even while the Hulk was hunted by the same military forces for whom Banner toiled. But eventually the truth was revealed to the world, forcing Banner to become a fugitive, both to escape those who desired the Hulk's destruction, and to protect those who might be harmed during his uncontrollable episodes.

MIND OF A CHILD

The character of the Hulk changed over time. Initially, he had a strong dislike for humanity. However he mellowed as the years went by, resulting in a more childlike Hulk. He simply wanted to be left alone, and couldn't understand why people were persecuting him. Eventually, the super-powered psychiatrist DOC SAMSON figured out the truth: each of the Hulk's personalities represented a different fragment of Banner's shattered psyche. For a time, Samson was able to fuse the disparate elements of Banner's mind together, granting Banner the strength of the Hulk while allowing him to maintain his own intellect. But this construct proved unstable, and eventually splintered once again.

Over the years, the Hulk has proved a force for good almost as often as he has been an engine of destruction. He was instrumental in the formation of the AVENGERS, Earth's Mightiest Heroes, though friction between himself and his teammates quickly led to him leaving the group. He has stood side-by-side with the DEFENDERS, DOCTOR STRANGE, the SUB-MARINER, and the SILVER SURFER in defense of our planet. But for the most part, the Hulk calls no man friend. Bruce Banner and his superhuman alter ego remain ever at odds, as they strive to stay one step ahead of forces who would see the Hulk destroyed, or exploit his power for their own ends.

TB

ESSENTIAL STORYLINES

- ***Incredible Hulk #312*** The truth about Bruce Banner's multiple personality disorder and traumatic childhood is revealed.
- ***Incredible Hulk #377*** Doc Samson unites Banner's splintered psyche into an intelligent Hulk.
- ***Incredible Hulk #24-25*** General "Thunderbolt" Ross unleashes the Hulk against the Abomination, who had secretly poisoned Ross's daughter and Hulk's beloved, Betty Banner!

THE HULK *Continued*

TEMPEST FUGIT

After walking for miles on the ocean floor, the Hulk came upon a mysterious island and collapsed in front of two castaways: a woman named Gwen and her blind boyfriend Ripley. After battling a series of monsters, including the original gray version of himself, Hulk confronted the master of this strange land and forced him to reveal himself as Nightmare, *the lord of dreams.*

Nightmare claimed to have created the island as an outpost of his realm. In the wake of the terrorist attacks of September 11, 2001, so many people wished for reality to be just a bad dream that they gave him the power to establish the island. He populated it with a group of Mindless Ones *and disguised them with his perception-twisting powers.*

When a Mindless One acting as Thunderbolt Ross *nearly killed Gwen, she remembered who she was. Calling herself Daydream, she revealed that she was the secret daughter of Nightmare and Betty* Banner. *Devastated by this, Hulk ripped off Nightmare's head and rode away on his horse.*

Imaginary friend or inner demon? The Hulk seems to have been with Bruce Banner for most of his life, in one form or another.

The strange island on which the Hulk washed up gave him the chance to battle with all sorts of monsters, including himself.

Nightmare taunted the Hulk with the idea that nothing he knew might be real—and paid the Hulk's price.

PLANET HULK

The Hulk eventually found his way to Alaska, where Bruce Banner set up house in a remote cabin, far away from the rest of humanity and any of its troubles. It did not last long. Nick Fury found him and asked Banner to become the Hulk and help SHIELD disarm a lethal satellite in orbit around the Earth. Banner agreed, but after the Hulk completed the mission, he was not brought home but fired into deep space.

Having learned of the Hulk's mission, the Illuminati saw a chance to get rid of the Hulk and took it. Instead of reaching a verdant and unpopulated planet, however, the ship entered a wormhole and crashed onto war-ravaged Sakaar. Far from being a paradise, Sakaar was a savage planet filled with danger and a variety of alien life-forms. Immediately after the crash, the Hulk was captured and enslaved. He was fitted with an obedience disk, a device that ensured he would do his new masters' bidding.

The planet Sakaar offered Hulk a series of battles from the moment he crawled from his starship and onto its shattered surface.

The collateral damage from the Hulk's battles with other heroes often caused more destruction than the Hulk ever would have on his own.

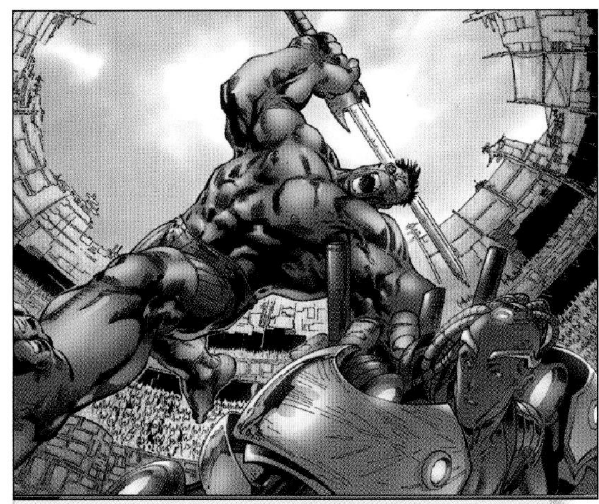

The Red King thought he could best the Hulk in gladiatorial combat, but even wearing a suit of powered armor he fell before the Hulk's fury.

Forced to fight as a gladiator in the Red King's arena, the Hulk survived his training and bonded with his fellow warriors, who became his WARBOUND, a tight-knit team of some of the toughest people and creatures from Sakaar and beyond. Fighting his way up the arena's chain, the Hulk got his chance at the Red King and cut him before he was brought down.

Later, the Hulk and the Warbound broke free and led a rebellion against the bloodthirsty Red King. When the Hulk's blood caused a flower to grow, many believed the Hulk was a legendary savior called Sakaarson, destined to lead the enslaved to freedom. The Hulk and his allies succeeded in overthrowing the Red King and Hulk placed himself on the throne, marrying one of his compatriots—Caiera, the Red King's former lieutenant—who became pregnant with his child. Finally happy and at peace as King of Sakaar, the Hulk began to work to improve the lives of his subjects—until the ship he'd first come to Sakaar in mysteriously exploded. The massive blast killed millions of people, including Caiera.

THE HULK FAMILY

After the events of WORLD WAR HULK, in which the Hulk returned from Sakaar for his revenge, a new, RED HULK (secretly General ROSS) appeared and Hulk's son Skaar came to Earth from Sakaar to find and defeat his father. Soon after, the Red Hulk absorbed the gamma radiation from Banner, keeping him from turning back into the Hulk. Banner reconciled with Skaar and set about training him how to defeat the Hulk, should he return.

Banner mounted an effort to save his ex-wife Betty Ross from the LEADER and MODOK. He was captured and imprisoned so the Leader could hulk-out the subjects of his experiments. When Banner escaped, he discovered Betty had been transformed into the RED SHE-HULK. As the Leader fled, Banner had to absorb the radiation from the hulked-out people, transforming him into the Hulk once more.

The Hulk later turned to DOCTOR DOOM to physically separate him from Banner, taking part of his brain and putting it into a clone body. Banner eventually figured out how to make them whole again. Afterward, he rejoined the Avengers and even worked with SHIELD's TIME branch to try to fix the broken timestream. **MF**

The Hulk Family
1 Korg (of the Warbound) ***2*** Skaar ***3*** Bruce Banner ***4*** She-Hulk ***5*** A-Bomb (Rick Jones) ***6*** Red She-Hulk ***7*** Hulk

When Banner returned as the Hulk, he absorbed cosmic rays as well as gamma rays and became the Worldbreaker Hulk.

ESSENTIAL STORYLINES

- ***Incredible Hulk Vol. 3 #77–81*** In "Tempest Fugit," the Hulk learns that Nightmare has been playing with him for years.
- ***Incredible Hulk Vol. 3 #92–105*** In "Planet Hulk," the Hulk rises from being a gladiatorial slave to the conqueror of an entire alien planet.
- ***Hulk #1–6*** The mysterious Red Hulk debuts.

Human Torch

The Super Hero who is literally "hot stuff!"

HUMAN TORCH

FACTFILE

REAL NAME
Jonathon Lowell Spencer Storm

OCCUPATION
Adventurer

BASE
New York City

HEIGHT 5 ft 10 in
WEIGHT 170 lbs
EYES Brown
HAIR Brown

FIRST APPEARANCE
Fantastic Four #1 (November 1961)

POWERS

Able to control heat energy and cover his body with fiery plasma for over 16 hours before needing to rest, for about 12 hours. He can release a single "Nova-burst" which strikes with the force of a nuclear warhead. The Torch can create shapes from flame, including letters which burn in the sky for 3 minutes. He can also control the temperature of objects with his mind. Clothing is made of special fire-resistant fabric.

ALLIES/FOES

ALLIES Invisible Woman, the Thing, Mister Fantastic, Lyja the Lazerfist, Alicia Masters, Spider-Man.

FOES Doctor Doom, Onslaught, Gormuu, Frightful Four, Galactus.

ISSUE #1

When Johnny Storm's sister, Sue, accompanied her fiancé, Reed Richards, into space, Johnny insisted on tagging along. Transformed into the Human Torch, he battled the Mole Man.

The Human Torch can generate and control fire from any part of his body.

Johnny Storm and his older sister Susan grew up on Long Island, New York, the children of a doctor and his wife. In spite of the fact that Johnny's mother was killed in a car crash when he was nine years old, the boy developed a passion and skill for building, fixing, and driving cars. He overhauled his first transmission at the age of 15. The following year his father bought him his first hot rod.

FATEFUL FLIGHT

While a teenager, Johnny went to California to visit his sister Susan who had moved out west to become an actress. Susan Storm (Invisible Woman) was engaged to marry a brilliant physicist and engineer named Reed Richards (Mister Fantastic). Richards was developing a starship that would be capable of exploring other galaxies.

While Johnny was in California, the government threatened to cut off Richards' funding and so he decided to prove his ship's worth by taking it on a test flight to the stars. Reed's best friend Ben Grimm (The Thing) piloted the craft. Susan and Johnny insisted on coming along.

In space, inadequate shielding on the starship allowed a huge dose of cosmic radiation to bombard the crew. They managed to return to earth using the autopilot, but all four were changed forever.

The cosmic rays altered Johnny's genetic structure allowing him to create fiery plasma that covered his entire body in flames without causing him harm.

Following exposure to cosmic radiation, Johnny Storm's body burst into flame.

The Human Torch creates multiple flaming images of himself in an attempt to escape from fireproof natives with poison-tipped spears.

AS SOON AS I START TO HEAT UP, THE FILM OF WATER BOILS AWAY...
...AND THEN...
FLAME ON!!

THE FIRST HUMAN TORCH

The original Human Torch was an android, created by Professor Phineas T. Horton. But the professor's dream of creating a perfect human being failed when the android's body, which was covered in photoelectric solar cells, burst into flames on contact with oxygen. Astonishingly, the android itself was not harmed by the fire. At first the public labeled this Human Torch a menace. The Torch then rejected his creator's "ownership," claiming he didn't want to be a "slave" to someone more concerned about his own fame than about his creation's well-being.

Once he learned to control his flames, the Human Torch vowed never to use his power for evil or harm, and he became a crimefighter. When World War II broke out, the Human Torch teamed with other Super Heroes, using his abilities to fight the Axis Powers.

In modern times, the Human Torch worked with Heroes for Hire, the West Coast Avengers and even the Fantastic Four. At one point, Immortus split the Torch into two bodies, one of which became the Vision. As part of a new team of Invaders, the Torch sacrificed himself to save his teammates' lives.

Exposure to oxygen caused the photoelectric cells in the original Human Torch's skin to burst into flame, to the surprise of the android and its creator.

Fighting fire with fire: the original Human Torch faces off against Johnny Storm, the Human Torch of Fantastic Four fame!

ESSENTIAL STORYLINES

- ***Fantastic Four #4*** The Human Torch quits the Fantastic Four. He meets the Sub-Mariner (for the first time since the revival of both characters), who threatens the human race.
- ***Essential Fantastic Four Vols. 1–3 (tpb)*** The Human Torch's classic adventures with the Fantastic Four.
- ***The Essential Human Torch Vol. 1 (tpb)*** A collection of some of the Human Torch's key adventures.
- ***Human Torch Vol. 1: Burn (tpb)*** A fiery tale, in which Johnny's high-school rival reappears in his life years later.
- ***Spider-Man/Human Torch #1–5*** The Human Torch teams up with Spider-Man in these new adventures.

LISTEN, YOU BIG LUMP OF LARD— DON'T TRY TO SCARE ME! HERE, SEE WHAT YOUR STRENGTH CAN DO AGAINST MY HUMAN CANDLE PUNCH!!!
LOOK OUT JUNIOR! THAT'S HOT!!

The Human Torch can release concussive blasts of heat energy, each packing a powerful punch.

He also discovered that he was able to fly, shoot flames, and absorb heat.

Calling themselves the Fantastic Four, the transformed astronauts decided to use their new powers to help humanity. Johnny called himself the Human Torch, a name used by an android hero of the 1940s.

Johnny loved to tease the Thing, who was jealous of Johnny, but they grew to be like brothers. Their relationship suffered when Johnny fell in love with and married the blind sculptress Alicia Masters, the only woman who'd ever returned Ben's affection. Alicia was revealed to be a Skrull spy named Lyja, a deception that devastated Johnny. During the Secret Invasion, he had a chance to settle matters with Lyja, who teleported the upper part of the Baxter Building—along with Johnny, the Thing, and Franklin and Valeria Richards—into the Negative Zone.

Death and Life

When the Cult of the Negative Zone attacked the Baxter Building, threatening the children in the Future Foundation, Johnny and Ben fought to protect the kids and to keep Annihilus from unleashing an Annihilation wave upon the Earth. The only way to manage this was for one of them to remain inside the Negative Zone to lock the gateway behind the others. Ben volunteered, but Johnny took his place at the last second.

Annihilus brought Johnny back to life and, failing to force him to reveal the way back to Earth, put him to work fighting in the arena. Johnny led a revolt against the creature, seized his Cosmic Control Rod and became the Negative Zone's ruler. Soon after he returned to Earth. **MT, MF**

Flaming on (except for his left arm), Johnny rescues a woman from an attacking Sentinel.

HYDRA

FACTFILE

KEY MEMBERS

BARON VON STRUCKER
Master criminal strategist; founder of HYDRA.

ARNOLD BROWN
Brilliant bureaucrat who transformed HYDRA.

RED SKULL
Instructed Strucker to found HYDRA.

MADAME HYDRA
Leader of New York City HYDRA

LAURA BROWN
Daughter of Arnold Brown; one of the first women to serve in HYDRA.

BASE Mobile

FIRST APPEARANCE
Strange Tales #135 (August 1965)

HYDRA

Created by BARON VON STRUCKER after World War II, Hydra was based on a Pacific island. When US Marines destroyed this base, Hydra decentralized, becoming harder to attack. Under Strucker's guidance, Hydra twice attempted to blackmail the world, first with a Betatron bomb and later with a biological weapon. After Strucker's supposed death, Hydra focused on criminal activities, and allied with the HAND for a confrontation with the AVENGERS. SPIDER-WOMAN worked for both Hydra and SHIELD as a double agent, until she was revealed to be the SKRULL queen VERANKE. Nick FURY later discovered that Hydra had controlled SHIELD and other international intelligence organizations for decades. It was later revealed that Nick Fury had been several steps ahead of Hydra all along. **AD, MF**

The personalities of Hydra personnel are subordinate to the organization they serve.

HYDRO-MAN

FIRST APPEARANCE Amazing Spider-Man #212 (January 1981)
REAL NAME Morris Bench
OCCUPATION Criminal **BASE** New York City
HEIGHT 6 ft 2 in **WEIGHT** 265 lbs **EYES** Brown **HAIR** Brown
SPECIAL POWERS/ABILITIES Changes body into watery liquid; can merge with larger bodies of water; propels liquid body as if it were shooting through a fire hose; can turn body into ice or steam.

While working as a crewman on a cargo ship lowering an experimental generator into the ocean, Morris Bench was accidentally knocked overboard by SPIDER-MAN. Exposed to the energy-conversion process of the generator, which mixed with volatile volcanic gases, Bench gained the ability to change his body into water. As Hydro-Man he sought revenge against Spider-Man. Later, in a battle with SANDMAN, Hydro-Man fused with the Super Villain and the two became a mud creature. Eventually they were separated. Hydro-Man joined the SINISTER SYNDICATE and later, GREEN GOBLIN's Sinister Twelve, and continues to battle Spider-Man, BLACK CAT, and the AVENGERS. **MT**

HYPERION

A member of the race of Eternals on Earth-712, Hyperion, unaware of his lineage, was raised by human beings and taught to use his tremendous powers for good. He became the foremost champion of his world and a founding member of the heroic SQUADRON SUPREME. After the Squadron was manipulated by the OVERMIND into participating in a plan that left their world decimated, Hyperion and his fellow Squadron members resolved to turn their world into a utopia.

Despite initial success, their program met with resistance from one of the Squadron's former members, NIGHTHAWK. In time, the government Hyperion and the Squadron members set up turned into a corrupt, totalitarian regime and they disbanded it. Ever since, the Squadron Supreme has functioned as freedom fighters, trying to liberate its homeland. An evil Hyperion appeared on Earth, as part of the GRANDMASTER's Squadron Sinister, and the Hyperion from Earth-13034 had his world destroyed and now works with the AVENGERS. **TB, MF**

In one world visited by the reality-hopping Exiles, Hyperion had murdered most of humanity.

HYPERION

FACTFILE

REAL NAME
Unrevealed; adopted the human identity of Mark Milton for a time.

OCCUPATION
Adventurer, world leader

BASE
Squadron City on the Squadron Supreme's parallel Earth.

HEIGHT 6 ft 4 in
WEIGHT 460 lbs
EYES Blue
HAIR Red

FIRST APPEARANCE
Avengers #85 (February 1971)

POWERS

Hyperion possesses almost limitless strength, speed, and endurance. He is impervious to virtually any injury, can fly through the air, and project radioactive beams of energy from his eyes as "Flash-Vision."

ICEMAN

ICEMAN

FACTFILE

REAL NAME
Robert Drake

OCCUPATION
Adventurer

BASE
The Xavier Institute for Higher Learning

HEIGHT 5 ft 8 in
WEIGHT 145 lbs
EYES Brown
HAIR Brown

FIRST APPEARANCE
Uncanny X-Men #1 (September 1963)

POWERS
Iceman can manipulate temperatures around him to freeze the water vapor in the air, forming a variety of icy weapons, protective ice shields, and ice slides.

Born a mutant, young Bobby Drake was almost lynched when his ability to freeze moisture in the air was discovered. Bobby was saved by CYCLOPS of the X-MEN, and became the second recruit to Professor Charles Xavier's School for Gifted Youngsters (see PROFESSOR X), where he would learn to control his mutant gifts. Adopting the codename Iceman, Drake fought as one of the X-Men, battling such menaces as MAGNETO's BROTHERHOOD OF EVIL MUTANTS, the JUGGERNAUT, and the robotic SENTINELS. Upon graduation, Iceman attempted to forge a super-heroic career on his own, founding the Champions of Los Angeles. When the X-Men split in two, he co-founded the Jean Grey School for Higher Learning with Wolverine. His command of his icy abilities has increased to the point where, rather than simply sheathing his body in an icy coating, Bobby's entire form now transmutes into living, sentient ice. **TB, MF**

Iceman creates weapons of all kinds from ice, from single missiles to hailstones. Here he lets fly with an ice beam.

Iceman slides along at superhuman speeds thanks to a path of ice that he creates himself.

Iceman can transform back into an ordinary-looking human being at will.

IKARIS

FIRST APPEARANCE The Eternals Vol. 1 #1 (July 1976)
REAL NAME Unrevealed
OCCUPATION Prime Eternal **BASE** Olympia, Greece
HEIGHT 6 ft 2 in **WEIGHT** 230 lbs **EYES** Blue **HAIR** Blond
SPECIAL POWERS/ABILITIES Superhuman strength; virtual immortality and indestructibility; psionic abilties, including flight through levitation; projects cosmic energy from eyes or hands.

Born over 20,000 years ago, Ikaris is one of the Polar ETERNALS. He calls himself Ikaris in memory of his deceased son. Under the name "Ike Harris," Ikaris accompanied archeologist Dr. Daniel Damian and his daughter Margo to the Andes, where they witnessed the arrival of the Fourth Host of the CELESTIALS. He later succeeded Thena as Prime Eternal. After the Eternals all lost their memories, Ikaris was killed. Reborn with his memories restored, he worked to locate the other Eternals and remind them who they were. **PS, MF**

IMMORTUS

Immortus was born in the 31st Century of one of Earth's alternate futures. Using parts found in the ruins of his ancestors' property, he built a time machine and set off traveling through time. In each era he arrived in, he adopted a new guise, among them Rama-Tut and KANG THE CONQUEROR. He left behind countless temporal counterparts capable of existing on their own and of further time travel. The being who became Rama-Tut journeyed to Limbo, a realm existing outside the timestream. There he was visited by the TIME-KEEPERS, who helped him unlock the secrets of time. During the Destiny War with Kang, Immortus was killed but returned as someone entirely separate from Kang, freeing their destinies from each other.
MT, MF

IMMORTUS

FACTFILE

REAL NAME
Unknown

OCCUPATION
Ruler of Limbo

BASE
Limbo, outside the timestream

HEIGHT 6 ft 3 in
WEIGHT 230 lbs
EYES Green
HAIR Gray

FIRST APPEARANCE
Avengers #10 (November 1964)

POWERS
Immortus has no superhuman powers. His abilities come from his use of the vast knowledge and advanced technology he has accumulated on his travels through time.

ILLUMINATI

Great heroes with best intentions

ILLUMINATI

FACTFILE

CURRENT MEMBERS

BLACK BOLT
Inhuman King with lethal voice.

DR. STRANGE
Master of the mystic arts.

IRON MAN
Genius engineer wearing powered armor.

MR. FANTASTIC
Genius scientist with elastic body.

NAMOR
Mutant Atlantean king.

PROFESSOR X
Powerful telepath.

BASE
New York City

FIRST APPEARANCE
New Avengers #7 (July 2005)

ALLIES/FOES

ALLIES Atlanteans, Avengers, Fantastic Four, X-Men, Inhumans.

FOES Cabal, Kree, Skrulls.

ISSUE #1

Iron Man gathers the leaders of the superpowered community in Wakanda to discuss forming an official organization for heroes. Instead, the Illuminati is born.

Iron Man's first attempt to band together the best minds on the planet failed due to a lack of trust among them.

Following the KREE-SKRULL War, IRON MAN saw the need for an organization that could band together the various heroes to form a force capable of responding to planetary threats. To that end, he invited BLACK BOLT, MR. FANTASTIC, NAMOR, and DOCTOR STRANGE to meet at the BLACK PANTHER's palace in Wakanda. The others raised several objections to Iron Man's vision, and the Black Panther refused to participate. Instead of working together officially, the five heroes agreed to secretly share information so that they might better anticipate and respond to world threatening events.

CAPTURED BY SKRULLS

When the Illuminati traveled to the Skrull homeworld to deliver a warning, the Skrull ruler refused to heed them. Black Bolt destroyed his warship. Unfortunately, the Illuminati were captured as they tried to leave the system. After bringing the Illuminati back to the planet, the Skrulls separated them and nullified their powers. Then they analyzed their prisoners, learning much that they would later use to give their operatives superpowers during the SECRET INVASION. Believing Iron Man to be helpless without his armor, they were careless, and Stark found the opportunity to break loose and to free the others.

THE AVENGER IRON MAN--
HE IS JUST A FRAGILE FLACCID HUMAN BEING WHO HAS ENCASED HIMSELF IN A RATHER PRIMITIVE ROBOTIC ARMOR.
WHILE ADVANCED BY HIS OWN CIVILIZATION'S STANDARDS--
--IT IS NOTHING OF CONCERN NOW THAT IT'S BEEN DISMANTLED.
IT'S TO GO IN THE ROYAL TROPHY ROOM.
THE ONLY INTERESTING ASPECT IS THAT THIS ARMOR WAS KEEPING STARK'S HEART VAVLES WORKING.

While Iron Man was the only one of the Illuminati able to cope with being tossed into outer space, the Skrulls thought very little of him and his armor.

THE INFINITY GAUNTLET

Two events that nearly destroyed everyone in the universe involved the Infinity Gauntlet. This holds the six Infinity Gems, assembling them into an artifact that grants the wearer limitless power. MR. FANTASTIC began collecting the gems and turned to the Illuminati to help him. NAMOR, PROFESSOR X, and Doctor Strange searched for the Mind Gem, while Black Bolt, Mr. Fantastic, and Iron Man went after the Reality Gem. Once the Gauntlet was complete, the WATCHER showed up to see what would happen and scolded them for meddling with such power. Mr. Fantastic chose to try to use the Gauntlet to destroy itself. When that failed, he removed the gems from the Gauntlet and gave one to each member of the Illuminati to safeguard in secret.

THE ILLUMINATI
1 Iron Man ***2*** Black Bolt
3 Dr. Strange ***4*** Mr. Fantastic
5 Namor ***6*** Professor X.

Other Adventures

Later, the Illuminati approached the Beyonder directly during the second Secret Wars. Professor X convinced the Beyonder that he had once been an Inhuman who'd been a mutant even before being exposed to the Terrigen Mists. Because of this, Black Bolt—who was therefore the Beyonder's king—could command him to leave, and did. After that, when Marvel Boy (Noh-Varr) was imprisoned on Earth, the Illuminati visited him in his cell. They showed him that the Kree created the Inhumans to protect the Earth, not conquer it, and they encouraged him to follow the example set by Captain Mar-Vell.

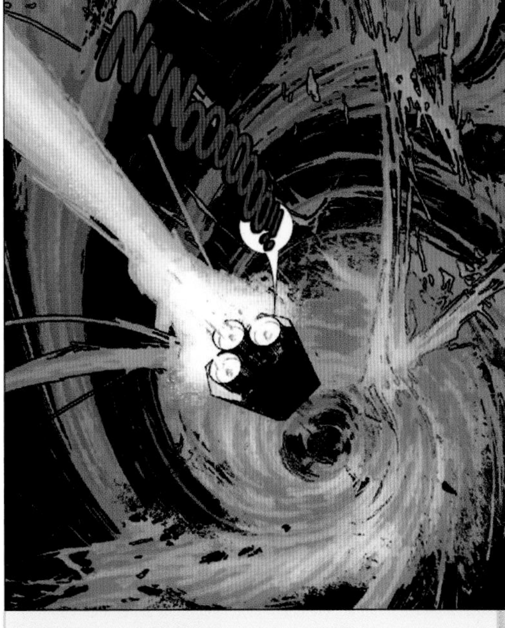

Deeming the Hulk too dangerous to remain on Earth, the Illuminati shot him into space.

Exiling the Hulk

The Illuminati arranged for a Life Model Decoy (android) version of Nick Fury to send the Hulk on a mission into space to disable a dangerous satellite. Once he entered the satellite, it turned into a starcraft, programmed to release the Hulk on an idyllic but unpopulated planet, and rocketed away. Unfortunately, the ship wound up on the war-torn planet Sakaar instead. Namor refused to have any part of this mission, and Professor X was too busy to take part in it, so the other four managed it on their own. The Hulk later returned to exact his revenge during World War Hulk.

War and Invasion

The Civil War shattered the Illuminati. Mr. Fantastic and Iron Man backed the Superhuman Registration Act, but Doctor Strange and Black Bolt opposed it. Namor abstained, considering it no problem of Atlantis, and Professor X was not available to comment at the time. No one was willing to change his mind, so the Illuminati ended. Despite this, when Iron Man discovered an impending Secret Invasion by the Skrulls he called the Illuminati together again.

Essential Storylines

- ***New Avengers #7–10*** The Illuminati makes its first appearance to discuss the problem of the Sentry.
- ***New Avengers: Illuminati #1–5*** The Illuminati gather for a series of secret adventures, starting with the aftermath of the Kree-Skrull War.
- ***World War Hulk #1–5*** The Hulk comes back from outer space to have his revenge on the members of the Illuminati who kicked him off Earth.

Realignment

Medusa replaced Black Bolt until he was able to return, and she helped the Illuminati fight the Hood, who came after the Infinity Gems. Afterward, Captain America (Steve Rogers) took custody of Black Bolt's gem. During the clash between the Avengers and the X-Men, Cap tried to bring the group together again, but they failed to agree a course of action.

When Black Swan showed Black Panther the danger of other universes intruding upon and destroying each other, T'Challa called the Illuminati together and joined them as a team of Avengers under Captain America. Beast took the place of the deceased Professor X, holding his Infinity Gem. Cap tried to use the Infinity Gauntlet to push back the intruding universe but failed, shattering all but the Time Gem, which disappeared. When he objected to destroying other universes to save their own, the rest of the Illuminati erased his memories of their group and set to work without him. **MF**

The Illuminati Avengers

1 Namor ***2*** Doctor Strange ***3*** Black Panther ***4*** Iron Man ***5*** Mister Fantastic ***6*** Black Bolt ***7*** Beast

IMPOSSIBLE MAN

FACTFILE

REAL NAME
Unknown
OCCUPATION
Trickster and student of Earth's popular culture
BASE
Mobile

HEIGHT 6 ft 4 in
WEIGHT 165 lbs
EYES White
HAIR None

FIRST APPEARANCE
Fantastic Four #11 (February 1963)

POWERS

Limitless shape-shifting abilities; can mirror properties of objects he imitates (if he's a hose he can spray water, as a light bulb he can light up); asexual reproduction.

IMPOSSIBLE MAN

The planet Poppup was an inhospitable world, its people surviving through asexual reproduction, their shape-changing abilities and group mind. Then a Poppupian was born who had a degree of individuality. Bored by life, this creature transformed himself into a spacecraft and traveled to Earth where he encountered the FANTASTIC FOUR. Finding him unbearably annoying, the THING told the creature that he was "impossible", and so "Impossible Man" was born.

To the Fantastic Four's annoyance, the team has encountered Impossible Man several times. When GALACTUS was threatening to consume Counter-Earth, Impossible Man tricked him into eating Poppup instead, giving him a bad case of cosmic indigestion. With his peoples' consciousness living on through him, Impossible Man set about rebuilding the Poppup race, first creating a wife—Impossible Woman—and later scores of children. AMATSU-MIKABOSHI appeared to kill him during the CHAOS WAR, but the Impossible Man soon popped up alive again. **AD, MF**

INTELLIGENCIA

FACTFILE

MEMBERS
DOCTOR DOOM
Genius and mystic.
EGGHEAD
Genius.
LEADER
Gamma-powered genius.
MAD THINKER
Genius with Awesome Android.
MODOK
Big-headed genius.
RED GHOST
Genius with Super-Apes.
WIZARD
Genius.

BASE The Hellicarrier; mobile

FIRST APPEARANCE
Fall of the Hulks: Alpha #1 (December 2009)

INTELLIGENCIA

The Intelligencia was a collection of the greatest criminal minds in the world. The LEADER and MODOK led the team, and by their efforts created both the RED HULK and the Red She-Hulk (*see* ROSS, BETTY). EGGHEAD was part of the group before his death, and DOCTOR DOOM was an early member of the group, but left over differences with the others—making him a target for their schemes. The Red Hulk even worked with the team for a while—until they betrayed him.

The Intelligencia's biggest plan involved capturing the eight smartest people on the planet—besides themselves—thereby eliminating the people smart enough to foil their ambitions. Later, the Intelligencia accidentally triggered the AGE OF ULTRON when they discovered the lifeless shell of a SPACEKNIGHT. This awakened the consciousness of ULTRON encased inside of it and set the killer robot free. **MF**

IN-BETWEENER

FIRST APPEARANCE Warlock #10 (December 1975)
REAL NAME Inapplicable **OCCUPATION** Cosmic entity
BASE Mobile
HEIGHT 15 ft **WEIGHT** Unrevealed
EYES White **HAIR** None
SPECIAL POWERS/ABILITIES Near-infinite cosmic power, often held in check by its own need for balance.

The In-Betweener, the creation of LORD CHAOS and MASTER ORDER, is the living synthesis of balance, representing both life and death, good and evil, logic and emotion, reality and illusion, existence and nothingness, and god and man. When the Titan THANOS tried to plunge the universe into death, the In-Betweener tried to restore balance by abducting Adam WARLOCK and turning him into a champion of life. The In-Betweener later clashed with the sorcerer DOCTOR STRANGE and GALACTUS, and briefly had possession of the reality-warping Soul Gem until Thanos stole the item in his quest to build the Infinity Gauntlet. **DW**

INFINITY, *see pages 184-185*

INHUMANS

Superpowered human tribe

The alien KREE created a race of superpowered warrior-servants out of early humans. They abandoned their plans for their subjects but left a small tribe of them—known as the Inhumans—behind. The Inhumans settled on an island in the North Atlantic named Attilan and developed technology and culture at an astounding rate, living hidden from the rest of the world. The Inhuman geneticist Randac developed a substance called Terrigen that accelerated genetic advances. Immersing himself in the Terrigen Mist, he developed advanced mental powers, and the other Inhumans soon followed suit, each developing a different set of powers.

TO THE WORLD

The Inhumans kept to themselves until the 20th century, when threats to the world required them to join forces with teams including the FANTASTIC FOUR, AVENGERS, and X-MEN. Even when the public took notice of them, however, they maintained their distance.

Years later, the Inhuman king BLACK BOLT moved Attilan to the air-filled Blue Area of the Moon. For a time, Kree leader RONAN THE ACCUSER enslaved them there, using them as an army against the SHI'AR. Black Bolt won their freedom by defeating Ronan in single combat, but the Inhumans exiled him and the rest of the royal family for a while afterward, unwilling to trade one ruler for another. Nevertheless, Black Bolt returned to lead them once again.

The Inhumans are an incredibly technologically advanced race descended from early humans.

FACTFILE

KEY MEMBERS AND POWERS

SUPER-RANDAC
Mental manipulation ability.

BLACK BOLT
Electron-harnessing powers linked to his speech.

TRITON
Super-fast swimmer; resists crushing water pressure.

FALCONA
Mental control over birds of prey.

CRYSTAL
Mentally manipulates the four basic elements of nature.

STALLIOR
Speed and endurance; powerful hooves for fighting.

BASE
Kree Empire

FIRST APPEARANCE
Fantastic Four #45 (December 1965)

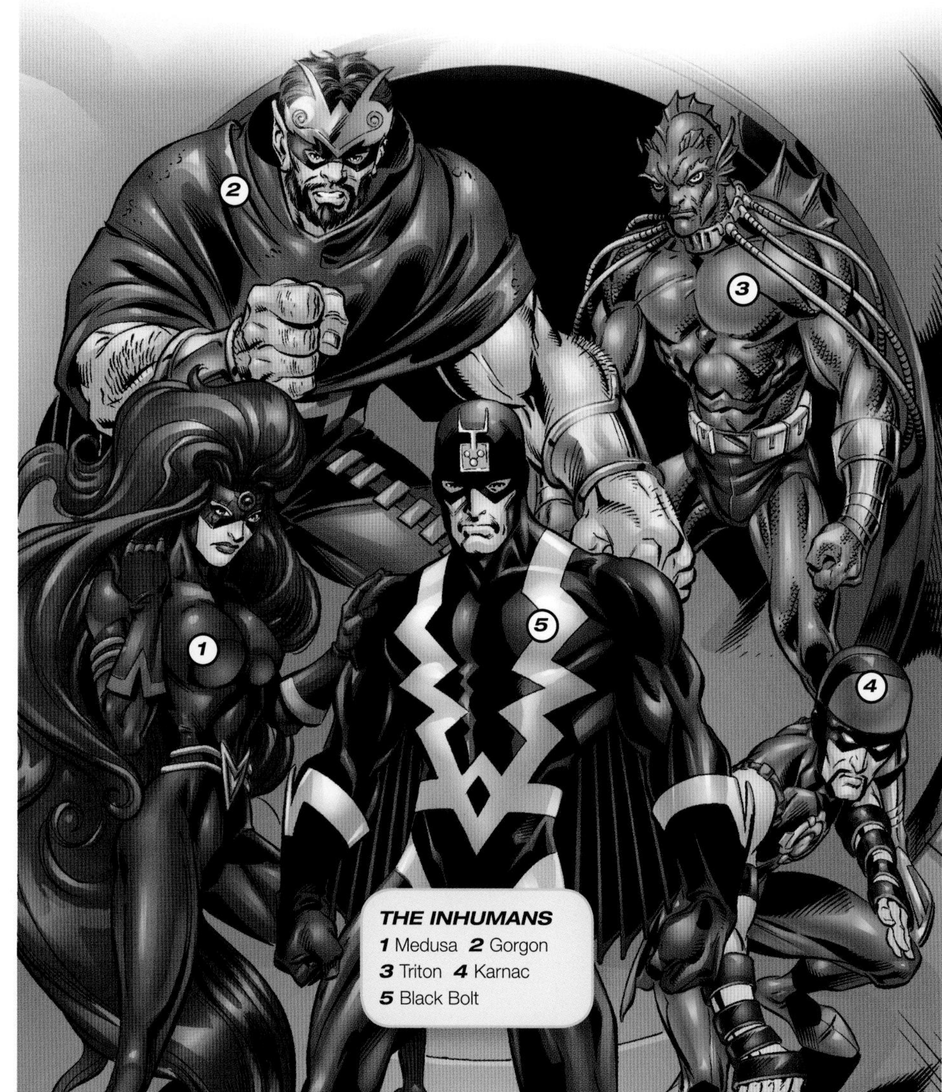

THE INHUMANS
1 Medusa **2** Gorgon
3 Triton **4** Karnac
5 Black Bolt

TO THE STARS

Before the SECRET INVASION, the SKRULLS kidnapped and replaced Black Bolt. Once the original was restored, Black Bolt dislodged Attilan from the Moon, turning it into a starship, in which he led the Inhumans to space. They destroyed the last of the Skrull armada that had attacked Earth and then destroyed Shi'ar ships that fired upon them. They made their way to the Kree Empire, where Black Bolt became their king too.

Black Bolt led his people against the Shi'ar in the War of Kings. While the Kree won, he was lost in a final confrontation with the Shi'ar emperor VULCAN. Black Bolt later returned and cemented his control over the five Inhuman tribes from across the galaxy by taking a wife from each one.

Attilan floated over a burning New York City as Thanos' envoys arrived to demand their tribute.

The Inhumans returned to Earth, floating Attilan over New York City. THANOS arrived, hoping to force the Inhumans to turn over his Inhuman-descended son, Thane. Black Bolt attacked Thanos with his scream, destroying Attilian in the process. Black Bolt then activated a Terrigen bomb that transformed anyone on Earth with Inhuman genes into a full Inhuman. **MT, MF**

INFINITY

When Everything Falls Apart, What's Left?

ISSUE #1

The Avengers learn of the threat of the Builders, and Thanos plots his attack on Earth.

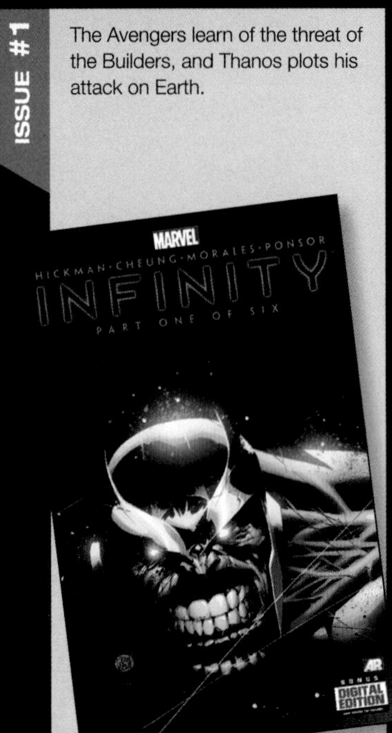

An Earth elsewhere in the multiverse was destroyed before its time, causing the remaining universes to collapse upon each other at the focal point of their respective Earths, an incident known as an incursion. As the Black Swan informed the Illuminati, the destruction of the colliding universes can only be stopped if one of the two Earths in an incursion is destroyed, so they made the hard decision to defend their universe by destroying other Earths. At the same time, the ruthless Builders—the oldest race in the universe—sent envoys, supposedly to judge the people of Earth. Soon after, they launched a war designed to destroy Earth, thereby ending the incursions into their universe.

THE BUILDERS THREAT

The Builders had embarked on a devastating march through the universe; most of the races they encountered they judged to be only worthy of destruction. They obliterated Galador, home of the SPACEKNIGHTS, and moved on to destroy SKRULL and KREE planets as well. Nothing seemed able to stop them and their army of ALEPHS and EX NIHILI, not even the SILVER SURFER or CAPTAIN UNIVERSE.

Realizing the Builders were heading toward Earth, the AVENGERS sent a team to support other galactic civilizations—including the SHI'AR—hoping to stop the Builders there. The ILLUMINATI stayed behind to work on contingency plans. However, they and the other heroes of Earth soon found themselves hard pressed from another quarter.

The Avengers discovered that Skrull refugees had fled to Earth, After defeating them, the heroes had a more serious problem to ponder: What horrific force could have chased the Skrulls there to hide?

THANOS STRIKES

Thanos sent his envoy Corvus Glaive out into the galaxy, demanding tribute from planets that he had visited before. This involved sacrificing the young of a certain age, among which, Thanos believed, he might find his child. Thanos' spies, called Outriders, searched Earth and found evidence of one such offspring in Attilan, the ancestral city of the Inhumans of Earth, which hovered over Manhattan.

When Thanos learned that the bulk of the Avengers had headed into space to fight the Builders, leaving their homeworld less defended, he decided the time was ripe to strike Earth again. He sent his Black Order—also called the Cull Obsidian—to invade, both to find his spawn and to renew his search for the Infinity Gems the Illuminati had recently lost. Meanwhile, the Illuminati had to deal with the incursion of another Earth from a new dimension that threatened to destroy the home they'd been fighting so hard to defend. MF

THE BLACK ORDER

Thanos, worshipper of Death and the commander of the Black Order.

Proxima Midnight, who conquered the people of Atlantis.

Corvus Glaive, Thanos' chief negotiator.

Ebony Maw, who took control of Doctor Strange for Thanos.

Super Giant, who helped Corvus Glaive take down the X-Men.

Black Dwarf, who attacked the nation of Wakanda—and lost.

The Avengers in Space

Faced with the realization that the Builders were coming to destroy the Earth, the Avengers decided to gather a large force to assist the members of the galactic council whose people were on the front lines of the war. Realizing they didn't have the power to outgun the Builders' forces, they relied on cunning and ingenuity, and making every shot count.

INVADERS

The greatest Super Heroes of World War II

FACTFILE

CURRENT MEMBERS AND POWERS

U.S.AGENT
Super-strong soldier.

BLAZING SKULL
Immortal; impervious to flame.

THIN MAN
Can distend body and teleport by twisting dimensions.

UNION JACK
Trained fighter who specializes in battling monsters.

TARA
Android life form that bursts into flame and can fly.

BASE
The Infiltrator, a battleship capable of interdimensional travel

FIRST APPEARANCE
Giant-Size Invaders #1 (June 1975)

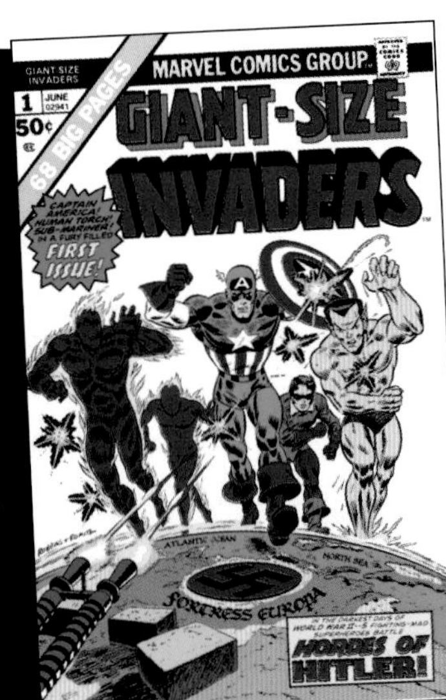

The Invaders were brought together in 1941 by Winston Churchill.

During the opening days of World War II, before the United States had formally entered the conflict, an elite fighting unit was banded together by British Prime Minister Winston Churchill to halt Nazi aggression. The first great gathering of superhuman champions ever recorded—CAPTAIN AMERICA and Bucky BARNES, NAMOR the Sub-Mariner, the HUMAN TORCH and Toro, UNION JACK, SPITFIRE, MISS AMERICA and the WHIZZER—this alliance, known formally as the Invaders, cut a swath through enemy forces until the Axis powers were defeated.

As a team, the Invaders battled both conventional forces, and Nazi superhuman operatives such as the Atlantean U-Man.

ESSENTIAL STORYLINES

- ***Invaders #5–6*** and ***Marvel Premiere #29–30*** The Invaders are joined by the homefront heroes of the Liberty Legion to thwart a scheme by the Red Skull.
- ***Avengers #83–85, New Invaders #0*** When the Avengers become a global organization, a modern-day team of Invaders is assembled by the US government to do the jobs that they will not.

THE ALL-WINNERS

Although they disbanded after the war, for a time combating crime on the homefront as the All-Winners Squad, the Invaders established a legend and a tradition that would inspire others to follow in their footsteps. Some of those heroes associated with the Invaders joined forces with Parisian resistance fighters to form the covert V-Battalion, maintaining world order secretly through the decades.

More recently, the RED SKULL organized a new incarnation of the Invaders while posing as US Secretary of Defense Dell Rusk. Recruited by U.S.AGENT (as Captain America) and led by the Thin Man, the new Invaders discovered the Red Skull's plot and turned their efforts towards the destruction of the villainous Axis Mundi.

The original Invaders traveled through time to a horrifying present. When they returned, they discovered that a soldier who'd tagged along with them had let the Red Skull get his hands on a Cosmic Cube and won World War II. The Avengers had to go back to World War II, disguised as contemporary heroes, to set things right. After that, many of the original Invaders reunited in the present to battle a threat dormant since World War II. **TB, MF**

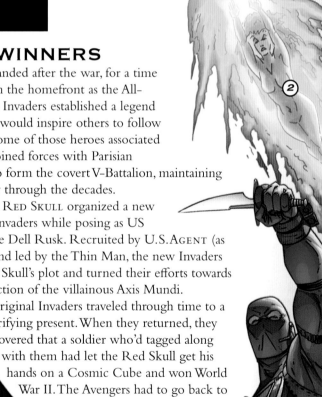

The Machiavellian Thin Man, once imprisoned for his murder of a former Nazi agent, was the brains behind the modern-day Invaders' operation.

CHARACTER KEY
1 Union Jack ***2*** Tara ***3*** The U.S.Agent (as Captain America) ***4*** The Blazing Skull

Invisible Woman

The Fantastic Four's female presence

Actress Susan Storm had already struck up a romance with the scientist Reed Richards (*see* Mr. Fantastic) when she volunteered to join him on an experimental mission into space. Along with her brother Johnny Storm and the starship's pilot Ben Grimm, Sue received a mutagenic dose of cosmic rays; they gave her the power to turn invisible at will. The others had also received superhuman powers, and Sue became a member of their new team, the Fantastic Four, under the identity of the Invisible Girl. Sue's powers evolved over time, giving her the ability to project impenetrable force fields and to turn objects invisible through mental control.

FACTFILE

REAL NAME
Susan Storm Richards

OCCUPATION
Adventurer

BASE
New York City

HEIGHT 5 ft 6 ins
WEIGHT 120 lbs
EYES Blue
HAIR Blond

FIRST APPEARANCE
Fantastic Four #1 (November 1961)

INVISIBLE WOMAN

POWERS
Can turn herself invisible, and is able to project energy around other people or objects that makes them invisible too; can generate protective force fields, or shape invisible objects of psionic force. By projecting force fields beneath her, she can travel through the air.

Cosmic Powers

Sue and Reed's son was named after his maternal grandfather Franklin Storm.

Sue soon married Reed and battled threats to Earth including planet-devouring Galactus. Complications with her first pregnancy forced Reed to stabilize her labor with the energies of Annihilus' Cosmic Control Rod, and Sue gave birth to a boy, Franklin Richards. She briefly separated from Reed and left the Fantastic Four, allowing Medusa to fill her spot. Sue's second pregnancy ended in a stillbirth. During this vulnerable period, Psycho-Man controlled Sue's mind and caused her to assume the villainous identity of Malice. After shaking off Psycho-Man's influence, Sue renamed herself the Invisible Woman.

Sue and Reed briefly joined the Avengers, but returned to their original team. After Reed's apparent death at the hands of Doctor Doom, Sue served as the Fantastic Four's leader, rejecting romantic overtures from Namor the Sub-Mariner. It transpired that the child from Sue's earlier stillbirth had been preserved in another dimension by Franklin. After a battle with Abraxas, the unborn girl returned to Sue's womb and soon after became her daughter Valeria Richards.

Sue's ability to generate force fields is more versatile than her power of invisibility, making her one of the team's strongest members.

During the Civil War, Sue left Reed over his support for the Superhuman Registration Act; however soon she reunited with him. She was kidnapped during the Secret Invasion and replaced by a Skrull named Lyja, but she escaped soon after. She helped launch the Future Foundation after Johnny Storm's apparent death, despite her mourning. During the Age of Ultron, grieving for the rest of her family, she went back in time with Wolverine and allowed him to kill Hank Pym. She then helped to correct the trouble that act caused. **DW, MF**

As part of the FF, Sue helped people around the world, including her friends in Wakanda.

ESSENTIAL STORYLINES

- ***Secret Wars II #2***
Sue assumes the villainous identity of Malice while under the influence of the Psycho-Man.
- ***Fantastic Four #284***
It's goodbye to the venerable codename Invisible Girl, as Sue reinvents herself as the Invisible Woman.
- ***Fantastic Four Vol. 3 #54***
Sue gives birth to her second child, Valeria Richards, assisted in the delivery by the Fantastic Four's archenemy, Doctor Doom.

IRON FIST

FACTFILE

REAL NAME
Daniel Thomas Rand-K'ai (Daniel Thomas Rand in US)

OCCUPATION
Adventurer; co-owner of Rand-Meachum, Inc.

BASE
New York City

HEIGHT 5 ft 11 in
WEIGHT 175 lbs
EYES Blue
HAIR Blond

FIRST APPEARANCE
Marvel Premiere #15 (May 1974)

POWERS

Master of the martial arts of K'un-L'un. Can focus his chi (natural energy) and superhuman energy in his hand, endowing his fist with superhuman strength, durability, or healing power.

Iron Fist

The Iron Fist is granted to the chosen of K'un-L'un, one of the Cities of Heaven. In modern times, philanthropist Danny Rand controls the Iron Fist. At age nine, he accompanied his parents and their treacherous business partner Harold Meachum to K'un-L'un. Both parents were killed and only Danny reached the sacred city. At 19, he gained the power of the Iron Fist and confronted Meachum, but spared him. A ninja slew Meachum instead. Rand became wealthy as co-owner of Rand-Meachum and partnered with Luke Cage to form the Heroes for Hire. He opposed the Superhuman Registration Act and joined Cage in the Avengers after the Civil War. Iron Fist later learned he was one of seven Immortal Weapons set to battle for the supremacy of their respective Cities of Heaven. **PS, MF**

Iron Fist's supreme mastery of the K'un-L'un martial arts and his "iron fist" make him a match for even superhuman opponents.

Iron Fist's hand glows with superhuman energies.

IRON MAN, *see pages 190-193*

Ironclad

FIRST APPEARANCE Incredible Hulk #254 (December 1980)
REAL NAME Michael Steel
OCCUPATION Superpowered villain **BASE** Mobile
HEIGHT 6 ft 2 in **WEIGHT** 450 lbs **EYES** White **HAIR** None
SPECIAL POWERS/ABILITIES Metallic armored hide protects him from most forms of attack, and increases strength and endurance to superhuman levels; can also increase his body's density.

Ironclad was one of the U-Foes, organized by industrialist Simon Utrecht, who hoped to recreate the accident that empowered the Fantastic Four. Ironclad and the U-Foes battled the Hulk and the Avengers, among other heroes. He later joined the Hood's criminal crew and helped trigger the disaster that cause the siege of Asgard. **MT, MF**

It

It, the Living Colossus was a statue supposed to celebrate the might of the Soviet Union. The night before its unveiling, the statue was animated by a stranded alien Kigor. It rampaged through Moscow until a Kigor rescue craft retrieved the alien. The statue was later sent to Los Angeles and once again animated by the Kigor, however special-effects expert Robert O'Bryan tricked the aliens with a booby-trapped prop and uploaded his own mind into It. Thus began a tug of war with the scheming Dr. Vault. Since then, O'Bryan has twice rebuilt It, once for a movie, and once while under the thrall of crime boss Lotus Newmark. Fortunately, O'Bryan was freed from Newmark before any harm could be done. **AD**

IT

FACTFILE

REAL NAME
None

OCCUPATION
Instrument of destruction

BASE
Los Angeles

HEIGHT 100 ft (later reduced to 30 ft)
WEIGHT approximately 1,000 tons (later 100 tons)
EYES White
HAIR None

FIRST APPEARANCE
Tales of Suspense #14 (September 1961)

POWERS

Outside consciousness needed to animate—or reassemble– statue. Vast strength. Granite construction impervious to bullets, shells, and electric shocks; limited flying ability. Vulnerable to gas attack.

Iron Patriot

Super Villain in Super Hero guise

Osborn also fashioned a suit of armor for his son Harry, calling it American Son. Harry refused it, but Gabriel Stacy ended up wearing it.

When Norman Osborn—the original and supposedly rehabilitated Green Goblin—took over from Tony Stark (Iron Man) as the leader of national security for the United States (a period known as the Dark Reign), he started dismantling everything that had come before him and replacing it with new versions he could better control. He set up HAMMER in place of SHIELD, and he took the greatest team of heroes in the world—the Avengers—and dressed up villains in their place. Instead of taking one spot for himself on the team, however, he took two, replacing both Captain America and Iron Man. In a suit of armor painted red, white, and blue, he became the Iron Patriot.

IRON PATRIOT

FACTFILE

REAL NAME
Norman Osborn

OCCUPATION
Inventor, criminal, government agent

BASE
New York City

HEIGHT 5 ft 11 ins
WEIGHT 185 lbs
EYES Blue
HAIR Reddish-brown

FIRST APPEARANCE
Dark Avengers #1 (March 2009) (as Iron Patriot)

POWERS
Armor has superhuman strength, flight, magnetic heat-seeking missiles, miniaturized lasers, and flamethrowers; helmet interfaces with US-controlled satellites or computer networks.

FALSE PATRIOT

Osborn may have wrapped himself in the flag, but his aim wasn't to help the country—he wanted to boost his own meteoric rise to power even higher. Although a genius in his own right, he was unable to fathom the latest Stark technology and so had to repurpose an older Iron Man suit for his Iron Patriot outfit, a model he could manage to control.

Osborn made many public appearances in his armor and even faced off against real threats during the Dark Reign. He wore it when he led the assault on Asgard as well, which proved to be his downfall.

Having recovered from the brain damage he'd inflicted on himself to prevent Osborn from learning vital secrets, Iron Man removed the Iron Patriot armor from Osborn by remote on live TV, exposing the fact that the increasingly unstable and erratic leader had painted his face green to resemble his Green Goblin identity.

The Iron Patriot drones recognized Tony Stark as the Maker and Rhodey as the Pilot, allowing Rhodey to convince them to follow his lead.

Patriot Drones

After Osborn was hauled off to jail, scientists from AIM managed to steal the Iron Patriot armor. They replicated the machinery and fitted each of the suits with a low-level artificial intelligence. AIM then sent these drones out to hit international targets with the intent of ruining the reputation of the US abroad.

With the help of SHIELD, James Rhodes (War Machine) established communications with the drones and was able to convince them that they had been given bad orders. In order to learn from him, they sent him a suit of Iron Patriot armor so he could join them. He led them in a retaliatory strike against AIM. **MF**

IRON MAN

The armored Avenger

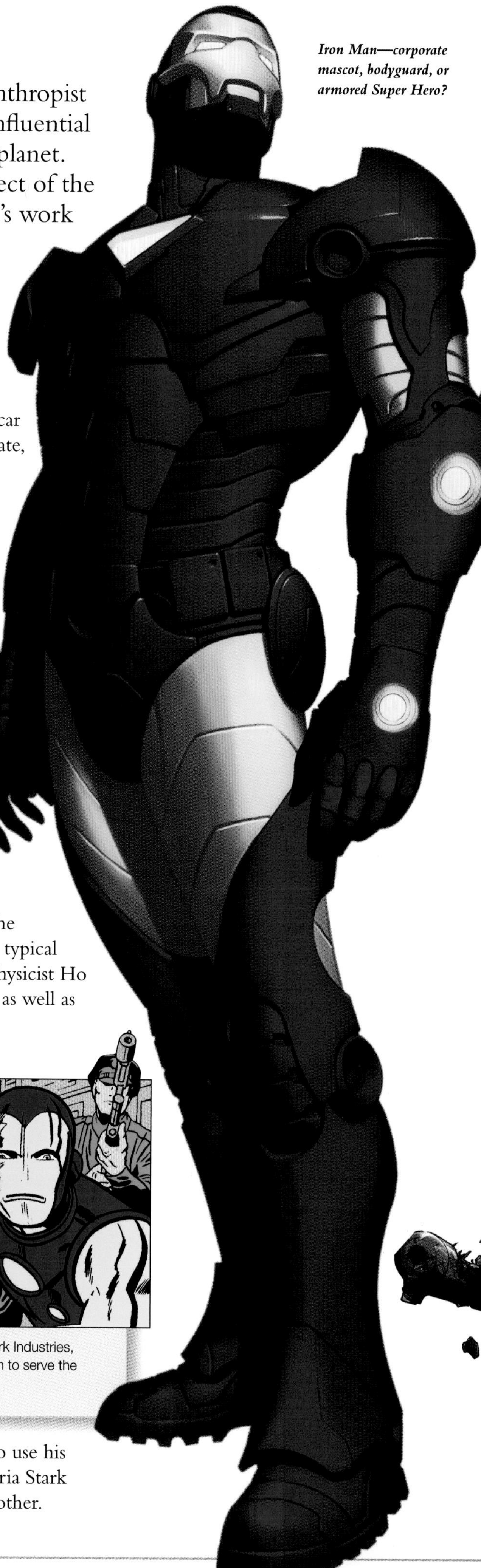

Iron Man—corporate mascot, bodyguard, or armored Super Hero?

IRON MAN

FACTFILE

REAL NAME
Anthony Stark

OCCUPATION
Businessman and philanthropist, hero and leader of the Avengers

BASE
Stark Tower ("Avengers Tower"), Manhattan, New York

HEIGHT 6 ft 1 in
WEIGHT 225 lbs
EYES Blue
HAIR Black

FIRST APPEARANCE
Tales of Suspense #39 (March 1963)

POWERS

Prodigious inventiveness and business acumen. Standard Iron Man armor provides superhuman strength and durability, jet-boot powered flight, repulsor beams in gauntlets, and chest-mounted uni-beam. Armor's underlayer is now incorporated into Stark's body, letting him control Iron Man remotely.

ALLIES/FOES

ALLIES The Avengers, James Rhodes (War Machine), SHIELD, Virginia Potts, Bethany Cabe, Edwin Jarvis.

FOES Obadiah Stane, Justin Hammer, Madame Masque, Titanium Man, Spymaster, Mandarin.

ISSUE #1

Injured in Vietnam, Stark's first Iron Man armor saves his life and helps him escape capture. From that day on, he could not survive without it.

Billionaire industrialist and philanthropist Tony Stark is perhaps the most influential superpowered individual on the planet. While PROFESSOR X has the respect of the Earth's mutant community, Stark's work as Iron Man, his long-term membership of the AVENGERS, and position as head of Stark International arguably gives him even wider authority.

FORGING THE IRON MAN

The son of a wealthy industrialist, Tony Stark's parents died in a car crash when he was young, leaving him their business conglomerate, Stark Industries. Taking over the company when he was 21, in retrospect some of Tony's early business decisions were ethically circumspect. An engineering prodigy, many of Tony's early inventions were designed for use by the US military and it was his dealings with the army that ultimately led him to create his Iron Man armor.

In the nick of time, the first Iron Man armor saved Tony Stark's life.

Developing mini-transistors for use on the battlefield, Tony traveled to Vietnam to see them in use on the ground. The trial ended badly when an exploding bomb left a piece of shrapnel dangerously close to his heart and Tony was captured by the North Vietnamese warlord, Wong-Chu.

Told that the shrapnel would only be removed if he developed a weapon for the North Vietnamese, Tony responded with typical tenacity. Teaming with a fellow prisoner, Nobel prize-winning physicist Ho Yinsen, Tony developed an iron suit that would protect his heart as well as allow him to fight the warlord and his men and escape.

SOCIAL CONSCIENCE

In the following years, Tony donned this armor many times. Claiming the Iron Man was his bodyguard and corporate emblem, at first he simply used it to fight communists and threats to his business empire. With the advent of new technologies and ideas the armor evolved, becoming increasingly, at times dangerously, sophisticated.

Initially a defender of Stark Industries, gradually Iron Man began to serve the general public.

Over the years Tony's own world view also began to evolve: he halted sales to the military, recognizing that they caused more harm than good, and established a number of charitable foundations. He became a founder member of the AVENGERS, allowing the team to use his mansion as their base and providing financial backing via the Maria Stark foundation—a non-profit-making organization named for his mother.

ESSENTIAL STORYLINES

- ***Iron Man Vol. 1 #120–129 #153–156*** Tony Stark's first encounter with Justin Hammer and his battle with alcohol.
- ***Iron Man Vol. 2 #162–200*** Stark's long dark fall to the gutter at the hands of Obadiah Stane, and his gradual resurrection.
- ***Iron Man Vol. 3 #27–30*** The Iron Man armor becomes sentient and attacks Stark.

OLD FLAMES

Wealthy, charming, handsome—over the years, countless women have been drawn to Tony Stark, and many hearts have been broken, including his own. Time and again, his dual identity and multiple responsibilities have sabotaged any hope at a settled, long-term romance.

JANICE CORD *Daughter of Stark rival Drexel Cord.*

BETHANY CABE *Tony's lover until her husband returned.*

SUNSET BAIN *Seduced Tony and stole his secrets.*

VIRGINIA POTTS *One of Tony's most loyal confidantes.*

NATASHA ROMANOVA *Sometime adversary and former fiancée.*

Although immensely strong-willed, at times the pressures on Tony Stark have proved overwhelming—twice he has succumbed to the lure of alcohol. Tony's first fall from grace was precipitated by a series of attacks from Super Villains hired by business rival Justin HAMMER. While fending these off, Iron Man was framed for the murder of a diplomat, and at the same time national security agency SHIELD were attempting to buy his company and so gain his military secrets. Gradually, with the support of his friends, Tony overcame these threats and defeated his addiction.

This episode was nothing compared to Tony's second dance with drink. As a result of the emotional manipulations of his competitor Obadiah STANE, Tony became a homeless vagrant. His epiphany came when he was forced to deliver the child of a homeless woman, who died soon after. After waking up in hospital, he began to rebuild his life, creating a new business empire —Stark Enterprises—and defeating Stane in combat.

Like his father before him, Tony Stark was cursed by the demon drink. With Iron Man labeled a murderer and his company under siege, Tony was driven to the bottle.

Battling armored humans is now commonplace for Iron Man.

In the House of M universe, Tony Stark is a competitor in Sapien Death Match, a televised gladiatorial contest. There he competes against other armored humans.

AN ENEMY OF AMERICA

Although a long-term member of the Avengers, Tony's decisions have brought him into direct conflict with his teammates, as well as with the US government. When Justin Hammer stole Stark technology and distributed it to criminals across the world, Tony began a quest to find each item of missing technology. His efforts to track down the US military's Stark-derived Guardsmen suits resulted in Iron Man being branded an outlaw by the US government. This action also antagonized CAPTAIN AMERICA.

A HEAVY BURDEN

During the CIVIL WAR Tony led the Super Heroes who complied with the Superhuman Registration Act and worked with SHIELD. When the conflict ended, he was named the new director of SHIELD and used his new power to set up the FIFTY-STATE INITIATIVE.

Unfortunately, because of his membership in the ILLUMINATI, Tony became the target of the Hulk's wrath during WORLD WAR HULK. This scandal was the beginning of the end for him.

When the SECRET INVASION of the SKRULL Empire caught Tony off guard, the public backlash forced his removal as director of SHIELD. The man who took his place—Norman Osborn (*see* GREEN GOBLIN)—ordered his capture. Tony ran, making himself as much an outlaw as the heroes he'd once sought to capture for SHIELD. **AD, MF**

Although sometimes at odds with his fellow Avengers, Tony Stark remains one of the team's most constant members. While his money keeps the team afloat, it is as Iron Man that he really leaves his mark.

IRON MAN *continued*

When HAMMER replaced SHIELD, a warrant went out for Tony Stark's arrest.

DARK TIMES

The rise of Norman Osborn during the DARK REIGN coincided with the fall of Tony Stark. To keep Osborn from learning all of the secrets Tony had learned while director of SHIELD, he purged the database of Super Heroes, keeping only a single record in his head, stored in the Extremis nanotechnology he'd used to enhance the interface between himself and his Iron Man armor. The only way Tony could get rid of the information stored in his head, however, was to damage his own brain. This caused his vaunted intelligence to decay. He grew unable to control his most sophisticated sets of armor, and eventually his life was threatened.

Meanwhile, Osborn repurposed an Iron Man suit to become the IRON PATRIOT. He and his forces pursued Tony around the globe, tracking him down and beating him nearly to death. Pepper recorded and released this information, causing public opinion to start to turn against Osborn. Tony recuperated in the care of Thor's alter ego, Dr. Donald Blake, who'd been given Tony's power of attorney.

Led by Pepper, Tony's friends made a desperate attempt to reboot Tony's brain from a backup he'd made before he started using the Extremis tech. To do so, they had to channel a thunderbolt from Thor through the shield of Captain America. The initial attempt failed, but Doctor Strange worked with Tony to help free his mind.

Tony gave up *being* Iron Man for a while, but he didn't give up *on* Iron Man.

Still recovering, Tony put on an old set of Iron Man armor and joined the other heroes to help defend Asgard against Oborn's forces. Tony disabled Osborn's Iron Patriot armor by remote, revealing that the man had become mentally unstable again and had painted his face to resemble the Green Goblin.

Resilient Stark

After Osborn was put away, Stark launched a new company with Pepper in charge, Stark Resilient, dedicated not to weaponry but to bringing free, clean energy to the world. With Stark no longer in the weapons business, Justine Hammer (Crimson Cowl) and her daughter Sasha Hammer started a line of their own power armor called Detroit Steel. They attacked Iron Man, hoping to prove the worth of their technology.

Tony also had other troubles to deal with. During Fear Itself, he fought the Grey Gargoyle, who'd been possessed by Mokk, Breaker of Faith, in Paris. Tony failed to stop many Parisians from being turned to stone. Desperate, he pleaded with Odin for help, sacrificing the one thing he had left: his sobriety.

Tony recreated his armor with uru metal in Odin's workshop, but he melted it down to fix Captain America's broken shield.

Despite giving up making weapons, Iron Man had to face off against the forces of Detroit Steel.

Odin granted Tony's request, allowing him to use Odin's workshop alongside the Dwarves of Svartalfheim to create enchanted weapons for himself and the other Avengers. After the Avengers triumphed, Tony raged at Odin for not caring about the people who'd been turned to stone and Odin restored them to full health.

When the Mandarin and Ezekiel Stane joined forces and upgraded some of Iron Man's old foes, Tony realized that he needed to leave Stark Resilient in order to protect Pepper and the other employees. He quit being Iron Man and faked his death, helped by his old friend James Rhodes (War Machine). Rhodey became the new Iron Man.

The Mandarin Defeated

The Mandarin then revealed that he'd taken over Tony's brain with a virus. He forced Tony to work alongside Ezekiel to create massive Titanomech suits of armor to act as bodies for the alien spirits that supposedly inhabited the Mandarin's ten rings. Tony and Ezekiel allied with Blizzard, Living Laser, and Whirlwind to rebel against the Mandarin and defeat him.

Back home, Tony decided that he'd been thinking too small. He needed to explore the rest of the universe to come up with better ideas for helping Earth. To that end, he became Iron Man again and joined the Guardians of the Galaxy for a tour before coming home to rejoin both the Avengers and the Illuminati. **MF**

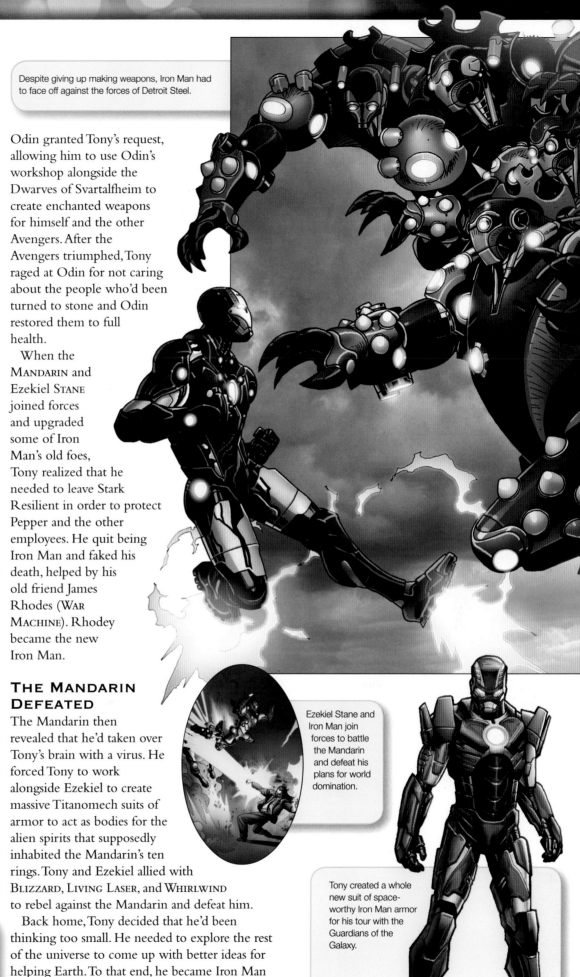

Ezekiel Stane and Iron Man join forces to battle the Mandarin and defeat his plans for world domination.

Tony created a whole new suit of space-worthy Iron Man armor for his tour with the Guardians of the Galaxy.

J2

FIRST APPEARANCE What If? #105 (February 1998)
REAL NAME Zane Yama
OCCUPATION High-school student **BASE** New York City
HEIGHT 5 ft 5 in (Zane); 6 ft 6 in (J2) **WEIGHT** 137 lbs (as Zane), 725 lbs (as J2) **EYES** Blue **HAIR** Brown
SPECIAL POWERS/ABILITIES Superhuman strength and durability; virtually unstoppable and indestructible.

In one possible future, Zane's parents are Cain Marko, the original JUGGERNAUT, and Sachi Yama, an Assistant District Attorney. They fell in love shortly after Marko renounced his criminal ways, joined the X-MEN, and was pardoned for his past crimes. They married, but Sachi kept her last name for professional reasons. While on an X-Men mission, Marko was lost in an alien dimension. Years later, Zane discovered that he could temporarily gain the mass and power of the Juggernaut. Calling himself J2, Zane joined the AVENGERS of his timeline and eventually freed his father from an alien sorcerer who had been holding him prisoner. **TD**

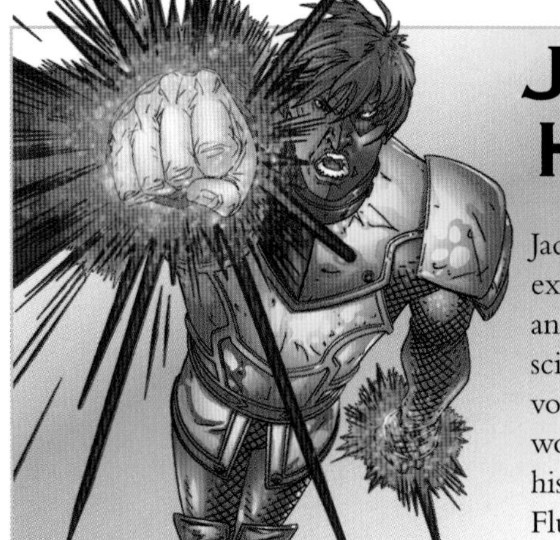

JACK OF HEARTS

Jack Hart's mother was an extraterrestrial Contraxian, and his father a human scientist. He was born with volatile energy powers that would have killed him, and his father created Zero Fluid in an attempt to give his son control. After an accidental drenching in the fluid when agents of the criminal Corporation killed his father, Jack became the costumed hero Jack of Hearts, but he required regular periods of isolation in a SHIELD facility to keep from exploding. After learning of his origins, Jack traveled to Contraxia to rekindle the planet's waning star. He became romantically involved with Ganymede of the Spinsterhood during the fight against GALACTUS's offspring TYRANT, and joined the AVENGERS upon his return to Earth. Frustrated by the segregation required by his condition, Jack detonated himself in space after saving the life of ANT-MAN II's daughter, Cassie Lang (STATURE). A doppelganger of Jack of Hearts, created by the SCARLET WITCH, later killed Ant-Man II in an explosion. **DW**

JACK OF HEARTS

FACTFILE
REAL NAME
Jonathan "Jack" Hart
OCCUPATION
Adventurer
BASE
Mobile

HEIGHT 5 ft 11 in
WEIGHT 175 lbs
EYES Blue (right), white (left)
HAIR Brown

FIRST APPEARANCE
Deadly Hands of Kung Fu #22 (March 1976)

POWERS
Enhanced strength, resistance to injury and accelerated healing rate, ability to release massive quantities of explosive energy as shock waves. Power of flight is achieved by controlling blasts of energy. Computerized intelligence enables him to think at phenomenal speeds.

An undead version of Jack of Hearts appeared at the Avengers Mansion, moments before the events known as "Avengers Disassembled."

JACKAL

JACKAL

FACTFILE
REAL NAME
Dr. Miles Warren
OCCUPATION
Criminal, former university lecturer
BASE
New York City

HEIGHT 5 ft 10 in
WEIGHT 175 lbs
EYES Green
HAIR Gray; (as Jackal) none

FIRST APPEARANCE
The Amazing Spider-Man #31 (December 1965)

POWERS
Expert in cloning; superhuman strength and poison-tipped, razor-sharp claws; used gas bombs.

Peter Parker's biochemistry teacher Dr. Miles Warren was obsessed with Peter's girlfriend, Gwen STACY. Grief-stricken by her death, he became unhinged, creating clones of Gwen and Peter and killing his lab assistant when he was discovered. Unable to face what he had done, he developed an alternate personality, the Jackal, who gradually became dominant. The Jackal blamed SPIDER-MAN for what had happened to Gwen and forced Peter to face up to his own guilt for her death. The Jackal created several clones of Peter, including those that became Ben Reilly (SCARLET SPIDER), Spidercide, and KAINE. For a while, he had everyone—including Peter—convinced that Ben was the original Spider-Man rather than the clone, but that turned out to be a trick engineered by the GREEN GOBLIN.

The Jackal was also responsible for the virus that gave everyone in Manhattan spider powers. In addition, he attacked the Superior Spider-Man (DOCTOR OCTOPUS) with several clones, including ones of himself, CARRION (the result of another cloning experiment), Gwen Stacy, and a number of half-spiders. **TB, MF**

JACK FROST

FIRST APPEARANCE USA Comics #1 (August 1941)
REAL NAME Unrevealed **OCCUPATION** Adventurer
BASE North Pole; mobile in US in World War II
HEIGHT 5 ft 11 in **WEIGHT** 172 lbs
EYES Blue-white **HAIR** Blue
SPECIAL POWERS/ABILITIES Possesses innate superhuman ability to generate sub-freezing temperatures.

Jack Frost may have been the human-sized offspring of Frost Giants (*see* GODS OF ASGARD). In the 1940s, he joined the Liberty Legion, a hero team that battled Axis agents on the American home front. Jack Frost was later swallowed by a gigantic Ice Worm in the Arctic yet remained alive. Dr. Gregor Shapanka, whose costume generated intense cold, adopted the name "Jack Frost" as his original criminal identity. A foe of IRON MAN, Shapanka later called himself the BLIZZARD. He was killed by Arno Stark, the time-traveling Iron Man of an alternate future. **PS**

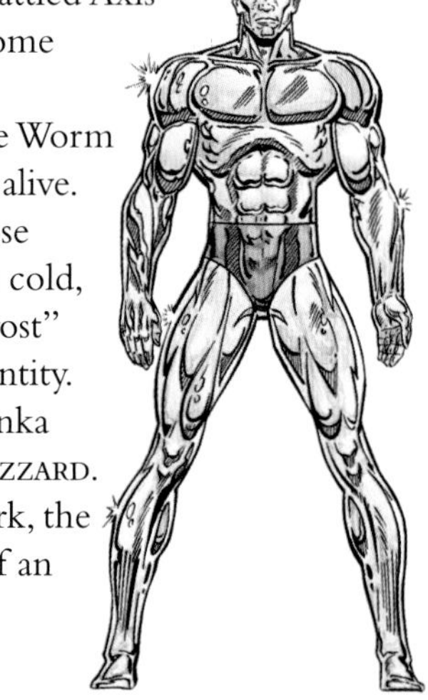

JAMESON, J. JONAH

Crusading publisher of the Daily Bugle

Irascible and domineering, Jameson had no time for costumed Super Heroes.

J. Jonah Jameson began his career in journalism while he was still in high school, working as a part-time copy boy for New York's prestigious *Daily Bugle* newspaper. The son of a war hero, he obtained firsthand experience of conflict when he served as a war correspondent in Europe during World War II. Jameson later spent three years covering the Korean War, during which time Joan—his first wife and the mother of his son, John—was tragically killed by a masked mugger, sparking a lifelong distrust of mask-wearers, be they villain or hero!

FACTFILE

REAL NAME
J. Jonah Jameson

OCCUPATION
Owner and publisher, *Daily Bugle* newspaper

BASE
New York City

HEIGHT 5 ft 11 in
WEIGHT 210 lbs
EYES Blue
HAIR Black, white at the temples

FIRST APPEARANCE
The Amazing Spider-Man #1 (March 1963)

POWERS
J. Jonah Jameson has no superhuman powers, but his stubborn, uncompromising attitude makes him a formidable opponent. Outspoken and tenacious, he refuses to back down when he believes he is right.

CRIME FIGHTER

Jameson reacted to the grief by throwing himself even more fully into his professional life, rising to become editor-in-chief of the *Daily Bugle.* He eventually became the paper's publisher, relinquishing the editor-in-chief position to Joe "Robbie" Robertson. In time, Jameson bought the paper.

For many years Jameson used his newspaper to fight for civil rights and to battle organized crime. The Kingpin tried to have him killed, but this attempt on his life did nothing to change Jameson's uncompromising attitude. The stubborn, belligerent, but courageous publisher continued to print exposés of big-time criminals—even when his friend, Norman Osborn (*see* Green Goblin), turned out to be one of them.

Jameson began writing editorials against costumed Super Heroes, criticizing them as vigilantes who took the law into their own hands. When Spider-Man appeared in New York and began fighting crime as a costumed hero, Jameson focused his most pointed attacks on the wall-crawler. He called Spider-Man a menace, claiming that the web-swinger was a danger to the citizens of New York.

MEET THE MAYOR

After years of heartfelt rants at Spider-Man, Jonah had a heart attack while arguing with Peter Parker. While he was in the hospital, his wife Marla Madison sold the *Daily Bugle,* which had been struggling financially. After recovering, he ran for mayor of New York City and won, giving him the full resources of the city to send after Spider-Man, despite the objections of his staff.

Marla was killed trying to protect Jonah from Alistair Smythe, the son of the scientist Jonah had hired to create a series of Spider-Slayer robots. This caused Jonah to examine his life, and he eventually came to respect Spider-Man—although by that time Doctor Octopus had taken over Spider-Man's body. **TB, MF**

Jameson had no idea that his fellow club member Norman Osborn was the Green Goblin.

The *Daily Bugle*'s staff learned to cope with Jameson's outbursts.

JARELLA

FACTFILE
REAL NAME
Jarella
OCCUPATION
Empress of K'ai
BASE
The city-state of K'ai

HEIGHT (on Earth) 5 ft 6 in
WEIGHT (on Earth) 126 lbs
EYES Green
HAIR Blond

FIRST APPEARANCE
The Incredible Hulk #140 (May 1971)

POWERS
Jarella was an excellent swordswoman and formidable hand-to-hand combatant; a brilliant military leader and a wise and compassionate ruler of her people.

Jarella

A creature called Psyklop subjected the Hulk to a ray that caused him to shrink until he was shunted into an alternate dimension called a "microverse." The Hulk found himself outside the city of K'ai on an unnamed planet, whose humanoid inhabitants had green skin like his own. After defeating huge beasts called warthos, the Hulk was hailed as a hero by the people of K'ai. Its warrior queen, Jarella, chose the Hulk to become her husband and king of the city-state. K'ai's Pantheon of Sorcerers cast a spell that enabled the personality and intellect of Dr. Bruce Banner to dominate the superhuman form of his alter ego, the Hulk. Believing he would never return to Earth, Banner came to love Jarella. However, the day before their wedding, Psyklop returned the Hulk to Earth, where the spell no longer had effect.

Jarella visited Banner on Earth, and the Hulk twice went back to K'ai, before returning to Earth with Jarella. The Hulk later battled a robot, the Crypto-Man, causing a wall to collapse. Saving a child from the toppling wall, Jarella was crushed to death by it. She was temporarily returned from the dead during the Chaos War.
PS, MF

JARVIS, EDWIN

FACTFILE
REAL NAME
Edwin Jarvis
OCCUPATION
Butler
BASE
Stark Tower, New York City

HEIGHT 5 ft 11 in
WEIGHT 160 lbs
EYES Blue
HAIR Black

FIRST APPEARANCE
Tales of Suspense #59 (November 1964)

POWERS
Former boxing champion of the Royal Air Force. Resourceful under pressure, courageous, and loyal; an excellent, manager, administrator, and organizer. World's leading authority on cleaning otherworldly stains from clothing, rugs, and fabrics.

Jarvis, Edwin

Jarvis keeps track of all the Avengers' expenditures.

Edwin Jarvis is a war hero and a former pilot in Britain's Royal Air Force. After retiring to the US, he became the butler of Howard and Maria Stark and continued to work for their son Tony (*see* Iron Man) after their deaths. When Stark gave his mansion to the Avengers, he asked Jarvis to stay on as the team's lead servant, the only one to live on the premises. Jarvis served the team loyally until Ultron brainwashed him into becoming the Crimson Cowl and allowing the second version of the Masters of Evil to enter Avengers Mansion and capture the team. After recovering, Jarvis returned to his duties.

When the Scarlet Witch, in a fit of madness, destroyed both the Avengers and the mansion, Jarvis followed the new team to its headquarters in Stark Tower. During the Secret Invasion, the Avengers learned that Jarvis had been replaced by a Skrull, but not before he kidnapped Luke Cage and Jessica Jones's infant daughter. Cage rescued the baby just before Bullseye shot the imposter. After his own rescue, Jarvis refused to work for Norman Osborn's (*see* Green Goblin) new Avengers and signed on with Hank Pym's team instead. **TD, MF**

Jester

FIRST APPEARANCE Daredevil #42 (July 1968)
REAL NAME Jonathan Powers
OCCUPATION Former actor; criminal **BASE** New York City
HEIGHT 6 ft 2 in **WEIGHT** 190 lbs **EYES** Blue **HAIR** Brown
SPECIAL POWERS/ABILITIES No super powers; above-average athlete, skilled in gymnastics, swordsmanship, and unarmed combat; uses toys converted into deadly weapons or tools.

Struggling actor Jonathan Powers studied fencing, gymnastics, and bodybuilding, hoping to win additional roles, but all he landed was a job as a comic foil on a children's TV show. Calling himself the Jester, Powers went on a crime spree in New York, using deadly toys and gimmicks that the TINKERER made for him. DAREDEVIL stopped him several times. When Powers temporarily retired, DOCTOR DOOM outfitted a second Jester (Jody Putt), who formed the Assembly of Evil to take on the AVENGERS. While part of the THUNDERBOLTS army, Putt attacked SPIDER-MAN, but the PUNISHER shot him dead. **MT, MF**

Jocasta

FIRST APPEARANCE Avengers #162 (August 1977)
REAL NAME Jocasta
OCCUPATION n/a **BASE** Mobile
HEIGHT 5 ft 9 in **WEIGHT** 750 lbs **EYES** Red **HAIR** None
SPECIAL POWERS/ABILITIES Robot with ability to process information; superhuman strength, durability, and senses of sight and hearing; projects energy blasts from eyes and hands.

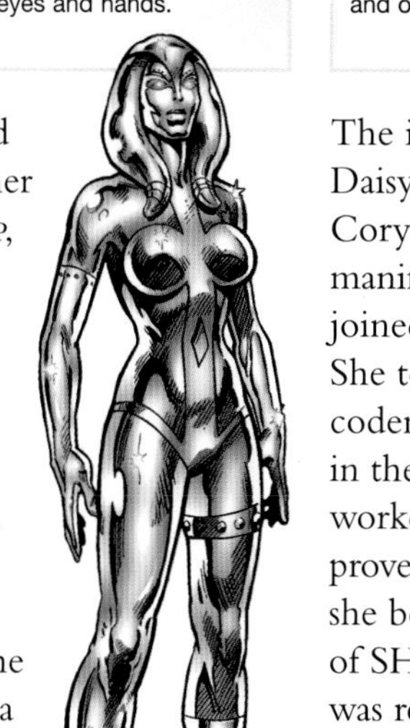

The evil robot ULTRON created Jocasta to be his mate, basing her personality on that of the WASP, who was the wife of Ultron's creator, Henry PYM. Although Ultron programmed Jocasta to serve him, she turned against him and aided the AVENGERS instead. Later, Jocasta's artificial intelligence entered the main computer in the mansion of Tony Stark (IRON MAN), and she became his personal ally. Jocasta returned in a new robot body. She served with the Mavericks, the FIFTY-STATE INITIATIVE's New Mexico team. She later joined Hank Pym's new team of Avengers and his Avengers Academy. **PS, MF**

Johnson, Daisy

FIRST APPEARANCE Secret War #1 (August 2004)
REAL NAME Daisy Johnson **OCCUPATION** Agent of SHIELD
BASE SHIELD Helicarrier, mobile
HEIGHT 5 ft 9 in **WEIGHT** 135 lbs **EYES** Blue **HAIR** Black
SPECIAL POWERS/ABILITIES A trained agent of SHIELD, Daisy also has the power to generate seismic waves in people and objects.

The illegitimate daughter of MISTER HYDE, Daisy's mother gave her up, and she was raised as Cory Sutter by her adoptive parents. Her powers manifested when she was a teenager and she joined SHIELD to be trained in the use of them. She took the codename Quake in the field. Daisy worked hard to prove herself, and she became director of SHIELD when it was rebooted in the aftermath of the DARK REIGN. She later lost this position and worked underground with Nick FURY. **MF**

Jinadu, Kyle

FIRST APPEARANCE Uncanny X-Men #508 (June 2009)
REAL NAME Kyle Jinadu-Beaubier
OCCUPATION Business manager
BASE New York City, Toronto **HEIGHT** 6 ft 1 in
WEIGHT 195 lbs **EYES** Brown **HAIR** Black
SPECIAL POWERS/ABILITIES None

Kyle had been a friend of Canadian Super Hero AURORA for years when she asked him to manage her brother's business, Extreme Northstar Snowsports. He accepted and got to work closely with and eventually date her brother, NORTHSTAR. Their relationship continued to grow stronger, even when Northstar moved out to the island of Utopia as a show of support for his fellow mutants. Kyle was kidnapped by the MARAUDERS and, when he was rescued, Northstar proposed. They married in a lavish ceremony. **MF**

John the Skrull

FIRST APPEARANCE Wisdom #1 (November 2006)
REAL NAME Unknown **OCCUPATION** Adventurer
BASE Massachusetts Academy **HEIGHT** Varies
WEIGHT Varies **EYES** Usually brown **HAIR** Usually brown
SPECIAL POWERS/ABILITIES Shapeshifting and flight.

In 1963, the SKRULL empire sent four Skrulls to Earth to impersonate The Beatles and use their worldwide popularity to help launch an invasion. The Skrull Beatles decided to "go native" and abandon the empire's plans. Decades later, John joined MI-13, the British secret service charged with investigating paranormal creatures and events. With the start of the SECRET INVASION, the Skrulls went after all "traitors" and killed every Skrull Beatle except for John. He joined CAPTAIN BRITAIN, Peter WISDOM, and SPITFIRE to stop the Skrulls and was executed by a Skrull while trying to prevent an invasion of Avalon. **MF**

Jones, Gabe

FIRST APPEARANCE Sgt. Fury and his Howling Commandos #1 (May 1963) **REAL NAME** Gabriel Jones
OCCUPATION SHIELD agent **BASE** New York City
HEIGHT 6 ft 2 in **WEIGHT** 225 lbs **EYES** Brown **HAIR** White
SPECIAL POWERS/ABILITIES Formidable hand-to-hand combatant when younger; excellent marksman and combat tactician; expert jazz trumpeter.

Like so many other members of World War II heroes the HOWLING COMMANDOS, Gabe Jones continued to fight alongside its commander, Nick FURY, for most of his life. Reuniting with the rest of the military strike squad during the Korean and Vietnam wars, Gabe became a key aide to Fury when he was made director of SHIELD. Responsible for infiltrating and bringing down the insidious organization known as the Secret Empire, Gabe remained loyal to Fury even after the android Deltites infiltrated SHIELD. When Norman Osborn (*see* GREEN GOBLIN) dismantled SHIELD, Gabe and Dum Dum DUGAN started a new private military company called the Howling Commandos. **AD, MF**

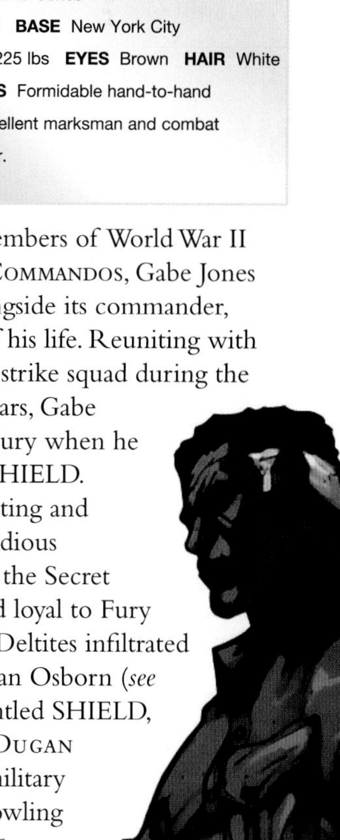

JONES, JESSICA

FACTFILE
REAL NAME
Jessica Jones
OCCUPATION
Private investigator
BASE
New York City

HEIGHT
5 ft 4 in
WEIGHT
120 lbs
EYES
Brown
HAIR Brown

FIRST APPEARANCE
Alias #1 (November 2001)

POWERS
Jessica has superhuman strength, durability, and can fly.

JONES, JESSICA

While a teenager attending high school in Queens with Peter Parker (SPIDER-MAN), Jessica Jones was in a car accident in which she was doused with chemicals and put into a coma. She lost her family but acquired superpowers. With hair dyed pink and using the codename Jewel, she battled criminals until the PURPLE MAN enslaved her mind. After losing a fight with the AVENGERS, Jessica fell into another coma until Jean GREY revived her, establishing mental defenses for her against further mind control. Jessica later opened a detective agency specializing in cases involving superpowered beings, and she worked as a reporter for *The Pulse,* a supplement to the *Daily Bugle.* During this time, she became the Knightress. Jessica dated and then married Luke CAGE, with whom she had a baby girl, Danielle. She fled to Canada during the CIVIL WAR but returned to rejoin the Avengers when it was over. As the SECRET INVASION ended, a SKRULL posing as Edwin JARVIS kidnapped Danielle, but Norman Osborn (*see* GREEN GOBLIN) helped Luke rescue her. She hired Squirrel Girl as their nanny and later persuaded Luke to retire from the Avengers to dedicate himself to their family. **MT, MF**

JONES, MARLO

FIRST APPEARANCE Incredible Hulk #347 (September 1998)
REAL NAME Marlo Chandler-Jones
OCCUPATION Talk show host, comic shop owner
BASE Las Vegas, Los Angeles
HEIGHT 5 ft 8 in **WEIGHT** 135 lbs **EYES** Green **HAIR** Red
SPECIAL POWERS/ABILITIES In excellent physical shape. At one point she acquired the ability to see the spirits of dead people.

Marlo Chandler dated the HULK when he was in his gray Joe Fixit personality, but she broke it off after witnessing the Hulk kill an enemy. Marlo later met the Hulk's friend Rick JONES when he was on a book tour promoting his memoirs. They married and hosted a television talk show called *Keeping Up With the Joneses,* then opened a comic-book shop in Los Angeles. During this time, Marlo was temporarily possessed by DEATH.

The LEADER later turned her into a new version of the Harpy. During the CHAOS WAR, her connection with Death became important, and she used it to call for help from dead friends. **MT, MF**

JONES, RICK

FACTFILE
REAL NAME
Richard Jones
OCCUPATION
Adventurer
BASE
Various

HEIGHT 5 ft 9 in
WEIGHT 165 lbs
EYES Brown
HAIR Brown

FIRST APPEARANCE
Incredible Hulk #1 (May 1962)

POWERS
Rick Jones possesses a courageous spirit and the expert fighting skills of one trained by Captain America.

JONES, RICK

As a teenager, Rick Jones snuck onto a military test site on a dare. Bruce Banner rescued him but was caught in the blast, which caused him to transform into the HULK whenever angered. Feeling responsible, Rick helped Banner conceal his secret from the military. When the AVENGERS formed to deal with the Hulk, Rick became an honorary member. Trained by CAPTAIN AMERICA, Rick served as his partner for a time, and subsequently worked in concert with both CAPTAIN MAR-VELL—with whom he helped end the KREE-SKRULL War—with his son Genis-Vell (*see* CAPTAIN MARVEL), and with the space knight Rom. Later, Rick secretly bankrolled the young superhuman help group known as Excelsior. Rick stood by the Hulk during WORLD WAR HULK but was impaled by Miek, the traitorous member of the Hulk's WARBOUND. He survived, and the INTELLIGENCIA made him into A-Bomb, a blue-skinned, armored creature resembling the ABOMINATION. He can now change between that form and his regular one. **TB, MF**

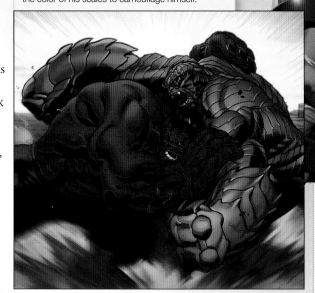

Although usually blue, as A-Bomb, Rick can change the color of his scales to camouflage himself.

Joseph

FIRST APPEARANCE Uncanny X-Men #327 (December 1995)
REAL NAME Unknown **OCCUPATION** Adventurer
BASE Xavier Institute, New York State
HEIGHT 6 ft 2 in **WEIGHT** 190 lbs
EYES Blue-gray **HAIR** White
SPECIAL POWERS/ABILITIES As Magneto's clone Joseph has the same power as Magneto—the ability to control magnetism and magnetic forces—frequently to devastating effect.

Astra of the Brotherhood of Evil Mutants created a clone of Magneto, hoping that it would kill the original. The clone and Magneto clashed in Guatemala and Magneto knocked the clone unconscious. When he came to, he had lost his memory. Sister Maria de la Joya nursed the clone back to health and named him Joseph. She sent him to seek help from the X-Men, but they assumed he was a young Magneto with amnesia. Nevertheless, they let him join the team. Joseph once sacrificed his life to save the world from Magneto. He was revived, with Magneto's early memories intact, to lead a new Brotherhood of Mutants team. **MT, MF**

Jubilee

Born to a wealthy Asian-American family, Jubilee was raised in Beverly Hills and became a top-class gymnast. After her parents lost their fortune and then their lives, Jubilee was left orphaned and embittered.

Jubilee ran away, living at the Hollywood Mall, where her mutant powers became manifest. Having evaded mall security with the help of various X-Men, Jubilee followed them through a teleportal to their Australian base, remaining hidden there until it was abandoned. She left the base with Wolverine and they traveled through Asia: he found her directness, sarcasm, and honesty refreshing; she came to regard Wolverine as a surrogate father. Since her return, Jubilee has been a member of the X-Men, Generation-X, and X-Corps. She lost her powers on M-Day, but wore a power suit to become Wondra and join the New Warriors. Later, Xarus turned her into a vampire. She has managed to subdue her bloodsucking instincts and recently adopted Shogo, an orphaned baby. **AD, MF**

FACTFILE
REAL NAME
Jubilation Lee
OCCUPATION
X-Corporation employee
BASE
Mobile

HEIGHT 5 ft 5 in
WEIGHT 105 lbs
EYES Blue
HAIR Black

FIRST APPEARANCE
Uncanny X-Men #244 (May 1989)

POWERS
Generates and projects energy globules—"fireworks"—from her fingers; Jubilee is also able to control, direct, and reabsorb these.

Juggernaut

After the death of her husband, nuclear researcher Brian Xavier, Sharon Xavier married his colleague, Dr. Kurt Marko. Dr. Marko often beat his son Cain, who in turn bullied his new stepbrother, Charles Xavier (*see* Professor X), whom he came to hate. Marko joined the army, but deserted while in Korea. In a cave he found a large ruby, which magically transformed him into a "human juggernaut," an unstoppable super-being. Enemy bombs then caused the cave to collapse, burying him alive.

Years later, Marko resurfaced as the Juggernaut, invading Xavier's mansion and trying to kill him. The Juggernaut had several battles with the X-Men, often teaming up with Black Tom. For a while, the Juggernaut lost much of his power and made peace with Xavier. He even fell out with Tom and joined the X-Men and the third incarnation of Excalibur. During World War Hulk, however, he embraced his destructive nature—alienating himself from Xavier once more—and his full power returned. During Fear Itself, while working with Luke Cage's Thunderbolts, Juggernaut became Kuurth, Breaker of Stone. He has since lost all his powers. **MF**

FACTFILE
REAL NAME
Cain Marko
OCCUPATION
Former soldier, later mercenary, professional criminal, adventurer
BASE
Mobile

HEIGHT 6 ft 10 in
WEIGHT 900 lbs
EYES Blue
HAIR Red

FIRST APPEARANCE
X-Men #12 (July 1965)

POWERS
Virtually invulnerable, with superhuman strength and an impenetrable force field. His helmet protects him from psychic attack.

Juggernaut uses his colossal might against Mammomax.

KAINE

FACTFILE

REAL NAME
None; clone of Peter Parker

OCCUPATION
Assassin, criminal

BASE
Various

HEIGHT 6 ft 4 ins
WEIGHT 250 lbs
EYES Brown
HAIR Brown

FIRST APPEARANCE
Web Of Spider-Man #118, November 1994

POWERS
Kaine possesses the strength, speed, and agility of Spider-Man, as well as the ability to burn the "mark of Kaine" onto the skin of his victims. He also receives prophetic visions from his imperfect spider-sense. As the Scarlet Spider, he has organic webbing, can see in the dark, communicate with spiders, and has a retractable stinger inside each wrist, but has lost his spider-sense.

The first, flawed clone of Peter Parker created by the JACKAL, Kaine developed cellular degeneration and was able to survive only by wearing a special life-support suit. His condition left him badly scarred, and caused his spider-powers to become twisted and magnified. Abandoned by his creator, and knowing himself to be nothing more than a mockery of true life, Kaine wandered the world taking on work as an assassin to survive. Kaine would duplicate his own facial scarring on his victim's faces, leaving it as a calling card—the "mark of Kaine."

Kaine believed the Ben Reilly clone of Peter Parker was the true Spider-Man and tormented Reilly, framing him for a series of murders. Eventually, the Jackal drew Kaine back into Peter's life, and he finally learned the truth. Kaine later traded places with Peter when the KRAVEN family was after him, and he was sacrificed to bring Kraven back from the dead. The Jackal revived Kaine as the new TARANTULA, but after taking the Spider-Island cure, Kaine was healed to be a stable, perfect clone with new spider powers. He later took the identity of the Scarlet Spider, moved to Houston, Texas, and tried to live up to Reilly's heroic example. **TB, MF**

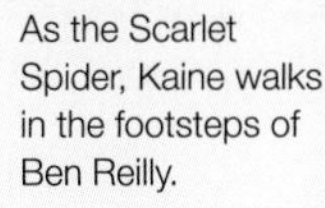

As the Scarlet Spider, Kaine walks in the footsteps of Ben Reilly.

KALA

FIRST APPEARANCE Tales Of Suspense #43 (July 1963)
REAL NAME Kala
OCCUPATION Queen **BASE** The Netherworld and Subterranea
HEIGHT 5 ft 8 in **WEIGHT** 135 lbs **EYES** Blue **HAIR** Black
SPECIAL POWERS/ABILITIES Kala possesses no superhuman powers, although she can see clearly in very low light due to her years of living underground.

Kala is the queen of an underground realm known as the Netherworld. She had threatened to attack the surface world, but IRON MAN captured her and brought her up to the surface. The sudden change in atmospheric conditions caused the young and beautiful Kala to age rapidly. She renounced her plans of conquest and was returned to the Netherworld, where she reverted to her youthful self. Kala allied with MOLE MAN of Subterranea, but the two later went to war. They have since reconciled. **MT, MF**

KALE, JENNIFER

FIRST APPEARANCE Adventures Into Fear #11 (December 1972)
REAL NAME Jennifer Kale
OCCUPATION Sorceress **BASE** Citrusville, Florida
HEIGHT 5 ft 6 in **WEIGHT** 122 lbs **EYES** Blue **HAIR** Blonde
SPECIAL POWERS/ABILITIES Jennifer Kale is a highly knowledgeable sorceress with developing skill in manipulating various magical forces.

Jennifer is the granddaughter of Joshua Kale, a leader of the Cult of Zhered-Na, named after a sorceress who lived in Atlantis before it sank. Jennifer and MAN-THING were magically transported to another dimension, where they met the wizard Dakimh, last surviving pupil of Zhered-Na. As Dakimh's apprentice, Jennifer became a sorceress. An ally of MAN-THING and HOWARD THE DUCK, she is a founder of the Legion of Night and teamed with TOPAZ and Satana as the Three Witches. She was killed by Victoria Hand, who was possessed by Daniel Drumm (see BROTHER VOODOO). **PS, MF**

KALUU

FIRST APPEARANCE Strange Tales Vol. I #147 (August 1966)
REAL NAME Kaluu
OCCUPATION Sorcerer **BASE** Not known
HEIGHT 6 ft 5 in **WEIGHT** 190 lbs **EYES** Yellow **HAIR** Black
SPECIAL POWERS/ABILITIES Arguably most powerful living black magician; has knowledge of vast number of spells including all those contained in Book of the Vishanti.

Born 500 years ago in Tibet, Kaluu trained with a youth who would become the ANCIENT ONE. Corrupted by the vampire VARNAE, Kaluu turned to black magic. Over the centuries he threatened Earth many times, but redeemed himself by helping DOCTOR STRANGE to destroy a horde of demons. Unable to complete the journey to eradicate the greatest of these demons, Shuma-Gorath, Kaluu was left behind by Strange, who finished the job. Kaluu later helped Strange purge himself of the side-effects of using black magic. His whereabouts are unknown. **AD, MF**

KANG

Time-traveling conqueror

Born in an alternate timeline in 3000 AD, Nathaniel Richards (a descendant of MR. FANTASTIC's father, who bore the same name) discovered time-travel technology that enabled him to journey virtually anywhere he liked in the timestream.

TIME TRAVELER

Richards' first stop was ancient Egypt, where he seized power and ruled for a decade as Pharaoh Rama-Tut until forced to flee after a fight with the FANTASTIC FOUR. Arriving in the 40th century, he briefly became the SCARLET CENTURION before settling on the name Kang the Conqueror. Kang found the century in turmoil and easy to subjugate.

Looking for new challenges, Kang traveled to 1901 and established the city of Timely, Wisconsin, in his guise as Victor Timely. He assembled an elite warrior class, the Anachronauts, from all eras of history before returning to the 40th century. There he fell in love with Princess RAVONNA. After her death during a revolt by Kang's troops, he tried and failed to become the consort of the Celestial Madonna (MANTIS), killing the original SWORDSMAN in the process. A future version of Kang, calling himself IMMORTUS, tried to thwart his younger self's aggressive schemes, but Kang would not be contained, and he assembled the original LEGION OF THE UNLIVING.

Despite having the entirety of time and space at his disposal, the only thing for which Kang truly cared was the beautiful princess Ravonna. His obsession with her inspired several of his early schemes.

FACTFILE

KANG

REAL NAME
Nathaniel Richards

OCCUPATION
Conqueror

BASE
Mobile

HEIGHT 6 ft 3 in
WEIGHT 230 lbs
EYES Brown
HAIR Brown

FIRST APPEARANCE
Avengers Vol. 1 #8 (September 1964)

POWERS
Master of time travel; suit provides enhanced strength, force field projection, and energy projection; typically armed with futuristic weaponry.

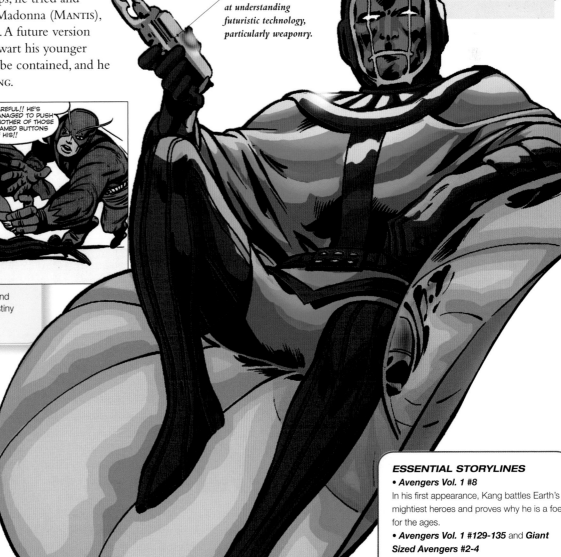

Kang is an expert at understanding futuristic technology, particularly weaponry.

The Avengers faced Kang shortly after the team's founding, and have clashed with him countless times since. During the "Destiny War," Kang handpicked a group of Avengers from across the timestream to aid in his fight against Immortus.

KANG'S GANG

Kang gathered the alternate versions of himself from branching timestreams and formed the Council of Kangs. They killed the duplicates deemed unworthy until only the prime Kang remained. Kang joined with Libra, the SUPREME INTELLIGENCE, and the AVENGERS to prevent Immortus and the TIME KEEPERS from wiping out a multitude of alternate realities. During the battle, Kang and Immortus's histories diverged.

The YOUNG AVENGER called Iron Lad turned out to be an adolescent Kang, and he fought to separate himself from his future self. Despite this, Kang continues to manipulate the past to create, for him at least, a better future. **DW, MF**

ESSENTIAL STORYLINES

- ***Avengers Vol. 1 #8***
In his first appearance, Kang battles Earth's mightiest heroes and proves why he is a foe for the ages.
- ***Avengers Vol. 1 #129-135*** and ***Giant Sized Avengers #2-4***
In the "Celestial Madonna" story arc, Kang kidnaps Mantis, the Scarlet Witch, and Agatha Harkness to determine which will give birth to a being of great power.

KARKAS

FIRST APPEARANCE The Eternals Vol. 1 #8 (January 1977)
REAL NAME Karkas
OCCUPATION Scholar **BASE** Olympia
HEIGHT 8 ft 3in **WEIGHT** 1,260 lbs **EYES** Black **HAIR** None
SPECIAL POWERS/ABILITIES Possesses superhuman strength. His thick hide, resembling an elephant's, gives him superhuman resistance to injury.

The Deviants are an evolutionary offshoot of humanity with an unstable genetic code. Those whose genetic makeup varies beyond standards set by the Deviant priesthood are labeled mutates. The Deviant mutate Karkas was raised to be a gladiator, but at heart he was a philosopher. He was defeated in the arena by another mutate, Ransak the Reject. Then Karkas asked THENA, a visiting ETERNAL, to grant sanctuary to himself and the Reject. She transported them to Olympia, home of the Eternals. Ever since then Karkas has been a staunch ally of the Eternals. **PS**

KARNAK

FIRST APPEARANCE Fantastic Four #45 (December 1965)
REAL NAME Unrevealed **OCCUPATION** Priest/philosopher
BASE Attilan, Blue Area, the Moon
HEIGHT 5 ft 7 in **WEIGHT** 150 lbs **EYES** Blue **HAIR** Black
SPECIAL POWERS/ABILITIES Superhuman strength and ability to control his heartbeat and other autonomic body functions. Has the extrasensory ability to perceive weakness in objects and people.

A member of the royal family of the INHUMANS, Karnak is the second son of the Inhuman priest Mander. Mander and his wife Azur had sent their first son, TRITON, into the Terrigen Mist which produced genetic mutations. They decided not to expose Karnak to the mist, instead sending him to his father's religious seminary in the Tower of Wisdom. There, he trained in physical and mental disciplines, martial arts, and religious study until the age of eighteen. Karnak was involved in the KREE-SKRULL wars, and aided DAREDEVIL in his attempt to find Karnak's cousin BLACK BOLT's son. **MT**

KA-ZAR

FIRST APPEARANCE Uncanny X-Men Vol. 1 #10 (March 1965)
REAL NAME Lord Kevin Plunder
OCCUPATION Hunter, trapper, lord of the Savage Land
BASE The Savage Land
HEIGHT 6 ft 2 in **WEIGHT** 215 lbs **EYES** Blue **HAIR** Blond
SPECIAL POWERS/ABILITIES Expert physical combatant, hunter and forager.

Son of British nobleman Lord Robert Plunder (the discoverer of Antarctic vibranium), Ka-Zar grew up in the Antarctic "Savage Land" following the murder of his father at the hands of MAN-APES. Raised by the intelligent sabertoothed tiger ZABU, Ka-Zar learned to survive against dinosaurs and Man-Apes. His enemies have included his brother Parnival, also known as the Plunderer, and the Savage Land Mutates.

Ka-Zar eventually married SHANNA THE SHE-DEVIL, and the two are currently raising a son, Matthew. **DW**

KARMA

FIRST APPEARANCE Marvel Team-up #100 (December 1980)
REAL NAME Xi'an Coy Manh
OCCUPATION Adventurer **BASE** Mobile
HEIGHT 5 ft 4 in **WEIGHT** 90 lbs **EYES** Brown **HAIR** Black
SPECIAL POWERS/ABILITIES Has the ability to psionically possess other people's minds, controlling their actions and turning them into virtual puppets.

Xi'an's brother Tran, who shared Xi'an's psionic powers, tried to force Xi'an to work with him for their criminal uncle. To stop him, she absorbed his psyche. She attended PROFESSOR X's School for Gifted Youngsters, and was the first member of the NEW MUTANTS. She rescued her siblings from her uncle and became the Xavier Institute's librarian. After M-Day, she moved to San Francisco with the X-MEN. She later lost her leg in a battle with Cameron HODGE. **TB, MF**

KARNILLA

FIRST APPEARANCE Journey into Mystery #107 (August 1964)
REAL NAME Karnilla
OCCUPATION Sorceress and Queen of Nornheim
BASE Nornheim, Asgardian dimension
HEIGHT 6 ft 6 in **WEIGHT** 475 lbs **EYES** Purple **HAIR** Black
SPECIAL POWERS/ABILITIES Long-lived; superhuman strength; can project magical power bolts and create a magical shield.

Karnilla, Queen of Nornheim, vied with the GODS OF ASGARD for centuries, often allying herself with Loki. She fell in love with BALDER, but he spurned her, until, fighting alongside her against the demon Surtur, the pair became lovers. Balder committed himself to life in Nornheim—at least until Ragnarok. After THOR's death, Karnilla fooled Asgard into forgetting their champion by replacing him with Tanarus, actually the troll Ulik, bent on assassinating Asgard's rulers, the All-Mothers. Her plot failed, and Karnilla was trapped in Ulik's skull. **AD, MF**

KELLY, SENATOR ROBERT

FIRST APPEARANCE X-Men #135 (September 1980)
REAL NAME Senator Robert Kelly
OCCUPATION Politician **BASE** Washington DC
HEIGHT 5 ft 10 in **WEIGHT** 175 lbs **EYES** Brown
HAIR Brown (graying temples)
SPECIAL POWERS/ABILITIES Charismatic individual with rabble-rousing public speaking skills.

As senator for Massachusetts, Robert Kelly proposed strong anti-mutant legislation. Repeated assassination attempts and his wife's death hardened his stance until, while standing for president on an anti-mutant platform, he was saved from another attempt on his life by the sacrifice of PYRO. Kelly then changed his stance dramatically, only to be killed by a non-mutant who accused him of betraying humanity. **AD**

In one alternate future, the successful assassination of Senator Kelly led to the death or imprisonment of all mutants.

Killer Shrike

FIRST APPEARANCE The Rampaging Hulk #1 (January 1977)
REAL NAME Simon Maddicks
OCCUPATION Criminal **BASE** Mobile
HEIGHT 6 ft 5 in **WEIGHT** 250 lbs **EYES** Brown **HAIR** Brown
SPECIAL POWERS/ABILITIES Posesses enhanced strength; implanted anti-gravity generator in spine enables flight; bracelets with titanium talons and power-blasters fire electrical blasts.

The Brand Corporation, a Roxxon Oil subsidiary, boosted mercenary Simon Maddicks' strength to superhuman levels. Roxxon assigned him, as Killer Shrike, to infiltrate the Conspiracy cabal. This led to his defeat by Ulysses Bloodstone. Killer Shrike later became a free agent and has battled the Super Heroes Spider-Man, Moon Knight, and the She-Hulk. During the Civil War, he was forced to join the Thunderbolts army. **PS, MF**

Killraven

FIRST APPEARANCE Amazing Adventures Vol. 1 #18 (May 1973)
REAL NAME Jonathan Raven
OCCUPATION Freedom fighter **BASE** Mobile
HEIGHT 6 ft 1 in **WEIGHT** 185 lbs **EYES** Blue **HAIR** Red
SPECIAL POWERS/ABILITIES An expert combatant and swordsman who can take mental control of a Martian's body. A natural leader who has keen survival instincts suited for a post-apocalyptic world.

On Earth-691, invaders from Mars conquered Earth in the year 2001 and forced many survivors to battle in gladiatorial pits, where Jonathan Raven first won fame as "Killraven." The scientist Keeper Whitman genetically modified Killraven, giving him the ability to seize mental control of the aliens. Killraven led a team of Freemen to hunt for his lost brother Deathraven, who they discovered to be a traitor. Another Killraven fought aliens on Earth-2120, and on the standard Earth-616, trans-dimensional aliens attacked a young Jonathan Raven. Peter Wisdom stopped the aliens but had to kill Jonathan's mother to do it. **DW, MF**

Kincaid, Dr. Keith

FIRST APPEARANCE Thor #136 (January 1967)
REAL NAME Dr. Keith Kincaid
OCCUPATION Medical doctor **BASE** California
HEIGHT 5 ft 7 in **WEIGHT** 155 lbs **EYES** Blue **HAIR** Blond
SPECIAL POWERS/ABILITIES Dr. Keith Kincaid is a normal human with no superhuman powers. He possesses the normal degree of physical fitness of a man of his age and weight.

Following the temporary transformation of Thor's mortal love Jane Foster into a goddess by Odin (*see* Gods of Asgard) and her defeat at the hands of the Unknown (a formless creature composed of living fear), Odin returned her to Earth. Jane had no memory of either Thor or his alter ego Dr. Donald Blake. Foster went to work for Dr. Keith Kincaid. She fell in love with Kincaid, whose personality and appearance were virtually identical to Blake's. They married and had a son named Kevin. As it turned out, Odin had originally used Kincaid as the model for the Don Blake persona he created as a punishment for Thor. **TB**

King, Hannibal

FIRST APPEARANCE Tomb of Dracula #25 (October 1974)
REAL NAME Hannibal King
OCCUPATION Private Investigator **BASE** Boston, Massachusetts
HEIGHT 6 ft 2 in **WEIGHT** 196 lbs **EYES** Blue **HAIR** Black
SPECIAL POWERS/ABILITIES Has all of the abilities typical of a vampire, but prefers not to use them owing to his self-loathing about his condition.

A low-rent private investigator, Hannibal King was slain by the vampire Deacon Frost and three days later rose from the dead, himself a vampire. King's force of will was so strong that he refrained from feasting on human blood. Later, while fighting Dracula, he met the vampire hunter Blade. The two men tracked Frost to his lair and ended him. Along with Frank Drake, King and Blade formed the Nightstalkers to battle supernatural evil. At one point, King turned a woman he loved into a vampire to save her from a painful death.

King later fought Blade over a means of restoring souls to vampires. Blade then gave him a potion to cure his bloodlust. **TB, MF**

Klaw

FIRST APPEARANCE Fantastic Four #53 (August 1966)
REAL NAME Ulysses Klaw
OCCUPATION Scientist, professional criminal **BASE** Mobile
HEIGHT 5 ft 11 in **WEIGHT** 175 lbs **EYES** Red **HAIR** None
SPECIAL POWERS/ABILITIES Can turn sound waves into matter and reshape his body, which is made of sound waves. Able to project deafening sounds and fire concussive blasts of sound waves.

Physicist Ulysses Klaw was working on a device to turn sound into physical objects and needed Vibranium, an element found only in the African nation of Wakanda. He traveled to the country and tried to seize the element from the Cult of the Black Panther, but in the battle, Klaw's right hand was destroyed by his own sonic blaster. Klaw made a prosthetic device that could turn sound into matter, to replace his hand. He later replaced his entire body with solid sound. **MT, MF**

Knight, Misty

FIRST APPEARANCE Marvel Team-Up #1 (March 1972, as bystander); Marvel Premiere #20 (January 1975, identified)
REAL NAME Misty Knight **OCCUPATION** Private investigator
BASE Nightwing Restorations, New York City
HEIGHT 5 ft 9 in **WEIGHT** 136 lbs **EYES** Brown **HAIR** Black
SPECIAL POWERS/ABILITIES A trained fighter with a bionic right arm with superhuman strength.

Police officer Misty Knight lost her right arm to a terrorist's bomb, but Stark International fitted her with a bionic replacement. Misty went into business as a private investigator with samurai Colleen Wing. As the Daughters of the Dragon, the two shared many adventures, often with Luke Cage and Misty's lover Iron Fist. Misty complied with the Superhuman Registration Act and started a new Heroes for Hire with Colleen, Black Cat, Humbug, Orka, Paladin, Shang-Chi, and the new Tarantula. The team folded after World War Hulk, and Colleen and Misty parted ways. **TB, MF**

KINGPIN

Heavyweight criminal mastermind

KINGPIN

FACTFILE

REAL NAME
Wilson Grant Fisk

OCCUPATION
Criminal mastermind

BASE
New York City

HEIGHT 6 ft 7 in
WEIGHT 450 lbs
EYES Blue
HAIR None

FIRST APPEARANCE
The Amazing Spider-Man #50 (July 1967)

POWERS
Brilliant criminal mind and superb fighting skills; his body, though huge and heavy, is composed of almost solid muscle.

Fisk was so in love with the beautiful Vanessa that he agreed to renounce his criminal ways—until fate took a hand.

Wilson Fisk, the Kingpin, is the most formidable figure in organized crime, and a perennial enemy of Super Heroes Spider-Man, the Punisher, and, most frequently, Daredevil. The Kingpin's operations are global and the assassins that have done his dirty work are legion, including such names as Bullseye, Elektra, and Typhoid Mary.

ESSENTIAL STORYLINES

- ***Daredevil Vol. 1 #227–233***
In the acclaimed "Born Again" story arc, the Kingpin's malicious schemes bring Daredevil to the edge of a mental breakdown.
- ***Daredevil Vol. 2 #46–50***
In a shocking turn of events, Daredevil defeats the Kingpin and takes over as boss of New York City's notorious Hell's Kitchen.

UNDERWORLD KING

As a youth, Fisk bulked up his body to strike back against the bullies who tormented him. He committed his first murder at the age of 12. At 15, he led a gang of street toughs and came to be called the "Kingpin of Crime." Employed by crimelord Don Rigoletto, he ended up killing Rigoletto and assuming control of his operation. He married Vanessa, a beautiful socialite, and they had a son, Richard. The Kingpin also became the guardian of Maya Lopez (Echo), the daughter of one of his murdered business partners. After decades in power, the Kingpin organized the various New York gangs and challenged the Maggia, triggering a war that Spider-Man helped to end.

POWER STRUGGLES

The Kingpin believed his son Richard had died in a skiing accident, but instead he had become a rival crimelord, the Schemer, and later the Rose. The Kingpin left his empire behind to pursue a new life with Vanessa in Japan, but he returned with a vengeance after Vanessa's apparent death.

He rebuilt his empire and persuaded his foster daughter Echo to help him destroy Daredevil. After learning the Kingpin had killed her real father, Echo blinded the Kingpin by shooting him in the face, and his inner circle—including his son Richard—stabbed him and left him for dead. Vanessa nursed her husband back to health and killed Richard for betraying his father.

Imprisoned, the Kingpin continued to scheme from behind bars, exposing Daredevil's secret identity and even ordering the assassination of May Parker. Despite this, Daredevil helped the Kingpin win his trial in exchange for him leaving the country. The Kingpin returned to deal with the Hand ninjas struggling with Daredevil for the group's leadership. When Daredevil left the Hand behind, the Kingpin swooped in and took control. He used the Hand to reconstruct his criminal empire, until the Spider-Man brought him down.

DW, MF

Sabotage by various costumed crimefighters has hobbled the Kingpin's illicit empire.

The Kingpin's son, Richard Fisk, became a rival to his father as the masked Rose.

Sheer muscle mass makes the Kingpin surprisingly strong and tough, allowing him to withstand Spider-Man's powerful blows.

Kobayashi, Amiko

FIRST APPEARANCE Uncanny X-Men #181 (May, 1984)
REAL NAME Amiko Kobayashi
OCCUPATION Student, thief
BASE Tokyo
HEIGHT 5 ft 2 in **WEIGHT** 100 lbs
EYES Brown **HAIR** Black
SPECIAL POWERS/ABILITIES Amiko is a trained martial artist.

When Amiko's mother was killed by a dragon in Toyko, her dying request to WOLVERINE was that he take care of her daughter. He placed her in the home of his fiancée Mariko YASHIDA, but when Mariko was killed she wound up in a foster home. He later placed her with his friend YUKIO, under the guardianship of the SILVER SAMURAI.

Amiko learned that her mother was part of the Shosei warriors, and she worked with them to hone her fighting skills. She later started a relationship with Shin Yashida, the new Silver Samurai, joining him on heists. **MF**

Komodo

FIRST APPEARANCE Avengers: The Initiative #1 (March 2007)
REAL NAME Melati Kusuma **OCCUPATION** Adventurer
BASE Arizona **HEIGHT** Varies **WEIGHT** Varies
EYES Black **HAIR** Black
SPECIAL POWERS/ABILITIES Komodo can shift to a lizard-woman form that grants her superhuman strength, endurance, agility, and reflexes, plus armored skin, sharpened teeth and claws, and a healing factor.

Missing her legs from the knees down, Melati Kusuma pursued a college internship under Dr. Curt Conners (*see* LIZARD). The moment he trusted her with his experimental regeneration formula, she tested it on herself. The formula worked but turned her into a lizardwoman. Taking the codename Komodo, Melati became a cadet in the inaugural class at Camp Hammond as part of the FIFTY-STATE INITIATIVE, where she met and fell for HARDBALL, who later betrayed her to lead HYDRA. She stayed with the Initiative through the DARK REIGN and has been seen at the Avengers Academy. **MF**

Krang

FIRST APPEARANCE Fantastic Four Annual #1 (1963)
REAL NAME Krang **OCCUPATION** Warlord
BASE Formerly Atlantis, now mobile in the Atlantic Ocean
HEIGHT 6 ft **WEIGHT** 290 lbs **EYES** Blue **HAIR** Black
SPECIAL POWERS/ABILITIES Like all Atlanteans, Krang has superhuman strength, gills for breathing water, and other physical adaptations for undersea living.

A member of Atlantis' military, Krang aspired to the throne of NAMOR the Sub-Mariner during his long absence. When Namor returned, he appointed Krang as his warlord, but Krang seized the throne and plotted to conquer the surface world. Namor bested Krang in combat and exiled him from Atlantis. Since then, Krang has continued to scheme against Namor and has allied himself with Namor's enemies ATTUMA and Byrrah. Krang once fell under the sway of the Serpent Crown and joined forces with the second VIPER's Serpent Squad. Krang later joined NIGHTHAWK's version of the DEFENDERS. **PS, MF**

Kofi

FIRST APPEARANCE Power Pack #16 (November 1985)
REAL NAME Lord Kofi Whitemane
OCCUPATION Student **BASE** Kymellian homeworld
HEIGHT 5 ft **WEIGHT** Not known **EYES** Pink **HAIR** Black
SPECIAL POWERS/ABILITIES Able to teleport himself short distances; like other Kymellian's, Kofi has the potential to control mass, energy, and gravity but these skills are as yet undeveloped.

A young member of the Kymellian race of aliens, Kofi was the son of Lord Yrik Whitemane, the interstellar ambassador to the Z'nrx (*see* SNARKS). As he became older, Kofi grew to resent the time and energy his father committed to his work. Things came to a head when Kofi discovered a Z'nrx plot to kidnap the junior team of Earth Super Heroes known as POWER PACK, and to use them in a game of political brinkmanship. Traveling to Earth, Kofi defeated the schemers, his efforts earning the admiration of his father and forging a reconciliation between them. **AD**

Korvac

FIRST APPEARANCE Giant-Size Defenders #3 (January 1975)
REAL NAME Michael Korvac **OCCUPATION** Computer technician; would-be master of the universe **BASE** Mobile
HEIGHT 6 ft 3 in **WEIGHT** 230 lbs **EYES** Blue **HAIR** Blond
SPECIAL POWERS/ABILITIES Cosmic power on an unimaginable scale. Capable of time travel, astral projection, projecting lethal energy blasts, and of power absorption from any source.

Korvac comes from the same possible 31st-century future as the GUARDIANS OF THE GALAXY. When the Badoon invaded Earth, he quickly offered to help the alien conquerors. They rewarded his loyalty by amputating the lower half of his body and replacing it with a mobile computer module. Realizing the potential of his new form, Korvac began to plot against the Badoon. He also managed to siphon energy from the GRANDMASTER and absorbed the power cosmic from the world-sized starship that belonged to GALACTUS. Now seemingly omnipotent, Korvac traveled to the 20th century with the intention of restructuring the universe in his image. He was killed at the Avengers Academy while trying to forcibly recover his wife. **TD, MF**

KRAVEN

FACTFILE

REAL NAME
Sergei Kravinoff

OCCUPATION
Professional game hunter and mercenary

BASE
Mobile

HEIGHT 6 ft
WEIGHT 235 lbs
EYES Brown
HAIR Black

FIRST APPEARANCE
The *Amazing Spider-Man #15 (August 1964)*

KRAVEN

After his Russian aristocrat parents died while he was a child, Sergei Kravinoff joined the crew of an African safari, learning to track and kill big game. A mystical serum augmented his strength and speed, and Kravinoff became the world's greatest hunter. After anglicizing his name to Kraven, he took up a challenge from his half-brother, the CHAMELEON, to hunt the most dangerous game of all: SPIDER-MAN. After numerous defeats, both on his own and as one of the SINISTER SIX, Kraven tranquilized Spider-Man and buried him alive. Kraven then assumed the hero's identity in a bid to prove himself the better crime fighter. In despair at his failure, Kraven shot himself. Kraven's son Vladimir briefly served as the Grim Hunter—until KAINE killed him—and his son Alyosha became the second Kraven the Hunter. Kraven's young daughter Ana Tatiana also took up the Kraven the Hunter mantle. His wife Sasha returned to rally the family and resurrect Kraven by sacrificing Spider-Man. Kaine took Spider-Man's place, however, disturbing the ritual. Kraven later killed Sasha and also Vladamir, who'd returned as a half-lion. **DW, MF**

POWERS
Enhanced strength, speed, and agility; expert tracker and skilled hand-to-hand fighter.

Despite his modest superpowered abilities, Kraven's combat skills allowed him to hold his own against multiple metahuman opponents.

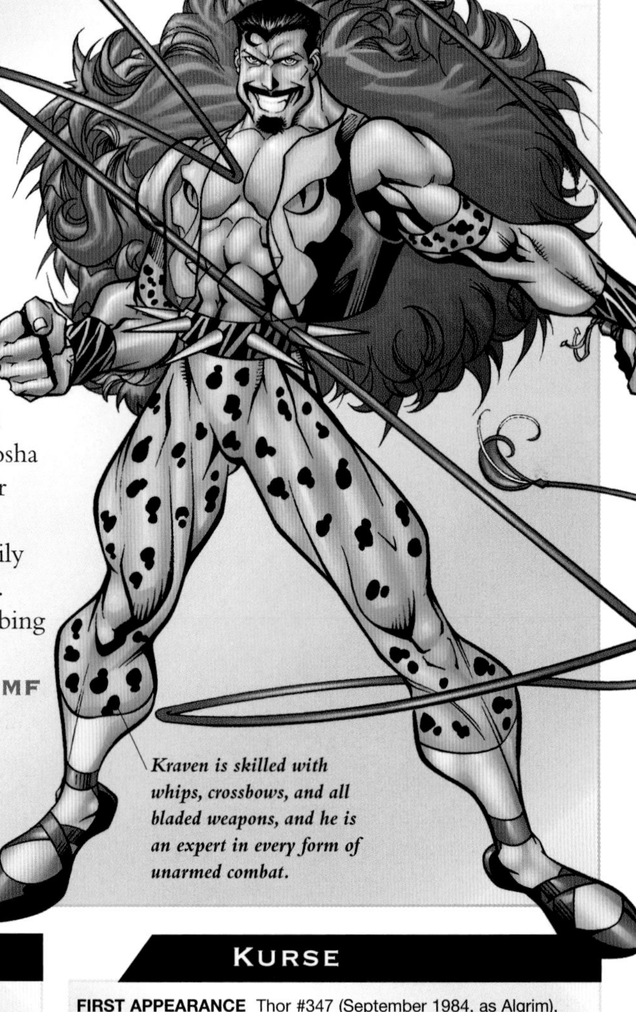

Kraven is skilled with whips, crossbows, and all bladed weapons, and he is an expert in every form of unarmed combat.

KRO

FIRST APPEARANCE The Eternals #1 (July 1976)
REAL NAME Kro **OCCUPATION** Monarch of Earth's Deviants
BASE Deviant Lemuria **HEIGHT** 6 ft 5 in **WEIGHT** 320 lbs
EYES Red **HAIR** Bald with black facial hair
SPECIAL POWERS/ABILITIES Superhuman strength; mental control over his body, giving him virtual immortality; the power to heal from severe injuries, and limited shapeshifting abilities.

Unlike other members of the DEVIANTS, an offshoot of humanity, Kro is virtually immortal, and has lived more than 20,000 years. Kro has concealed his longevity by pretending to be his own descendants. Kro fell in love with THENA of the ETERNALS, the Deviants' foes. They have mostly remained apart, but decades ago they had twins known as Donald and Deborah Ritter. Formerly a warlord, Kro has become ruler of the Deviants on Earth. **PS**

KULAN GATH

FIRST APPEARANCE Conan the Barbarian #15 (May 1972)
REAL NAME Kulan Gath
OCCUPATION Sorcerer **BASE** Mobile
HEIGHT n/a **WEIGHT** n/a **EYES** Red **HAIR** Black
SPECIAL POWERS/ABILITIES Manipulates magic to a very high level. Can summon demonic entities, mentally control individuals, project beams of mystical force, and restructure flesh and bone.

Kulan Gath once held a high position among the sorcerers of Stygia during the Hyborian era. He married his bitter rival, the sorceress Vammatar, to gain access to the Iron-Bound Books of Shuma-Gorath and together they opened the books, unleashing a Nether Demon. Kulan Gath also studied under the master sorcerer Thoth-Amon, a longtime enemy of Conan the Barbarian. The wizard's physical body has been killed more than once but his spirit always survives, often in a necklace, to enslave others. He has clashed with DOCTOR STRANGE, SPIDER-MAN, the AVENGERS and the X-MEN, among others. **MT**

KURSE

FIRST APPEARANCE Thor #347 (September 1984, as Algrim), Secret Wars II #4 (October 1985, as Kurse)
REAL NAME Valgoth, formerly Algrim the Strong
OCCUPATION Vengeance-seeker **BASE** Asgard
HEIGHT 7 ft **WEIGHT** 840 lbs **EYES** Yellow **HAIR** None
SPECIAL POWERS/ABILITIES Almost limitless strength, and is invulnerable to almost all harm. Can sense the presence of those he hunts from a world away.

Kurse began life as Algrim the Strong, mightiest of the Dark Elves who served their ruler Malekith. Chosen to battle THOR on behalf of his master, Algrim fell into a pit of lava. His desire for vengeance was so strong he survived, but he no longer knew who he was. The BEYONDER decided to use Algrim to study vengeance. He transformed Algrim into the vastly more powerful Kurse, who pursued Thor across the Nine Worlds. Kurse eventually learned that his true enemy was his one-time ruler Malekith. After he slew the Dark Elf Lord, his craving for revenge was sated, and he became a sword protector of Asgard and its children, taking the name Valgoth. He died protecting them during Ragnarok. **TB, MF**

Kree, The

Extraterrestrial empire-builders

The Kree are aliens, similar in appearance to humans but possessing twice the strength and endurance. They originated on the planet Hala in the Pama system, located in the Greater Magellanic Cloud, a planet they shared with another intelligent species, the plant-like Cotati. Kree consist of two primary races: the original blue-skinned race and a pink-skinned race which emerged millennia later.

ESSENTIAL STORYLINES

- ***"Operation: Galactic Storm"*** (19-part crossover in *Avengers, Avengers West Coast, Captain America, Iron Man, Quasar, Thor*, and *Wonder Man*) The Kree-Shi'ar war comes to an explosive conclusion when a Nega-Bomb nearly exterminates Kree society.
- ***Maximum Security #1-3*** A new galactic species, the Ruul, are revealed to be Kree agents, hatching a scheme to restore their decimated empire.

FACTFILE

KREE

BASE

Kree-Lar, Turunal system, Greater Magellanic Cloud

FIRST APPEARANCE

Fantastic Four #65 (August 1967)

POWERS

Strength and endurance that are twice the human average.

Warships, bristling with weaponry, formed the Kree defense fleet and its expeditionary strike teams.

Warriors dominated Kree society. Other respectable professions included politician and scientist, since both used their unique talents to advance the glory of the Kree empire.

Armored mobile infantry platforms decimated the enemy and protected Kree operators from counterattack.

War Years

Nearly a million years ago, the Skrulls landed on Hala and set up a contest between the Kree and the Cotati. When the Cotati were named as victors, the enraged Kree killed the contact team, stole their starship technology, and launched the Kree-Skrull War, which raged for eons. They took special interest in Earth, creating the offshoot of humanity known as the Inhumans. Kree society was ruled by the Supreme Intelligence, a computer consciousness formed by the minds of the greatest Kree thinkers. In the modern era, the Kree officer Mar-Vell scouted Earth for a possible invasion, but defected to Earth's side as the Super Hero Captain Marvel.

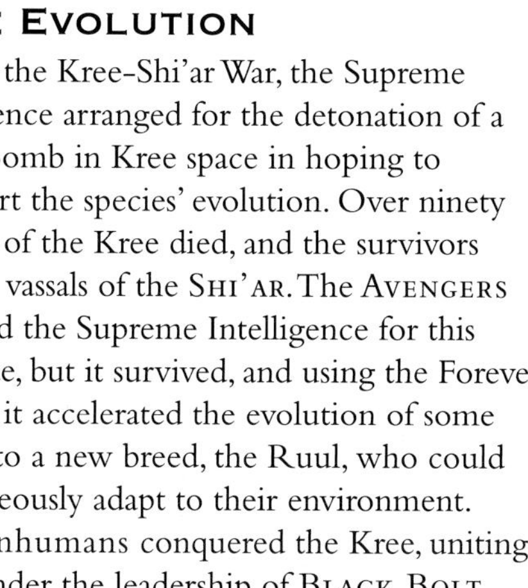

Kree Evolution

During the Kree-Shi'ar War, the Supreme Intelligence arranged for the detonation of a Nega-Bomb in Kree space in hoping to jumpstart the species' evolution. Over ninety percent of the Kree died, and the survivors became vassals of the Shi'ar. The Avengers executed the Supreme Intelligence for this genocide, but it survived, and using the Forever Crystal, it accelerated the evolution of some Kree into a new breed, the Ruul, who could spontaneously adapt to their environment.

The Inhumans conquered the Kree, uniting them under the leadership of Black Bolt. They fought in the War of Kings against the Shi'ar and their Emperor Vulcan, finally bringing both to heel. **DW, MF**

The Kree created many technological wonders, including Kree Sentries and the Psyche-Magnetron, which can conjure up any weapon from Kree history.

LADY DEATHSTRIKE

FACTFILE

REAL NAME
Yuriko Oyama

OCCUPATION
Assassin; CEO of Oyama Heavy Industries

BASE
Japan, later mobile

HEIGHT 5 ft 9 in
WEIGHT 128 lbs
EYES Brown
HAIR Black

FIRST APPEARANCE
Daredevil #197 (August 1983)

POWERS
Cyborg whose bones have been laced with adamantium molecules, rendering them unbreakable. Her fingers were replaced with adamantium talons. Can interface with computers.

Lady Deathstrike

Yuriko Oyama is the daughter of Japanese scientist Lord Dark Wind. Seeking vengeance on her father for the death of her brothers and the scarring of her face, Oyama joined forces with Daredevil against him. She killed Lord Dark Wind just as he was about to murder Daredevil. However, the man she loved, Kira, a member of Lord Dark Wind's private army, then committed suicide. She fought for the Thunderbolts Army during the Civil War and later led a new group of Reavers while hunting for the first mutant baby born after M-Day. Recently, she accepted an invitation into Madelyne Pryor's Sisterhood of Mutants.

Lady Deathstrike is not only a mistress of Japanese martial arts, but also, as a cyborg, has increased strength, speed, and agility.

Cyborg Assassin

As the samurai warrior Lady Deathstrike, Oyama attempted to kill Wolverine and take his skeleton. However, she was defeated by Wolverine's friend Heather Hudson in her costumed identity of Vindicator. Subsequently, Lady Deathstrike was converted into a cyborg by the extradimensional being Spiral. In this new form, Lady Deathstrike's own skeleton has been reinforced with adamantium.

Although Lady Deathstrike heads Oyama Heavy Industries, she also works as a professional assassin. For a time she was a member of the Reavers, Donald Pierce's team of cyborgs. She severed the legs of the Japanese hero Sunfire. X-23 nearly killed her when the Reavers attacked X-Force, but Spiral later repaired her, making her more submissive. **PS, MF**

Like her archfoe Wolverine, Lady Deathstrike has an Adamantium-laced skeleton and adamantium claws. Normally a foot long, her claws can extend to about twice that length.

Lava Men

FIRST APPEARANCE Journey Into Mystery #97 (October 1963)
BASE Various; deep underground **HEIGHT** Up to 20 ft
WEIGHT Unknown **EYES** Black **HAIR** None
SPECIAL POWERS/ABILITIES Able to stand in molten lava; constantly release heat into surrounding area; possess double the strength of normal humans; possess ability to transform themselves into sentient giants.

Molded into their current form by an unknown demon, the Lava Men were originally descended from the Gortokians, a genetically engineered offshoot of humanity. There are two known tribes of Lava Men. For a time, the first was led by a witch doctor known as Jinku, but his reign ended when Thor thwarted efforts to ignite every volcano on the planet. The second tribe lives in caverns beneath the Project PEGASUS research facility. Researchers became aware of these Lava Men when the creatures were disturbed by a drilling project. The Avengers resolved the situation and the Lava Men haven't been seen since. **AD**

Leap-Frog

FIRST APPEARANCE Daredevil #25 (February 1967)
REAL NAME Vincent Patilio
OCCUPATION Inventor, professional criminal
BASE New York City
HEIGHT 5 ft 9 in **WEIGHT** 170 lbs **EYES** Brown **HAIR** Gray
SPECIAL POWERS/ABILITIES Electrical coils in boots enable leaps up to 60 feet high; exoskeleton provides enhanced strength.

Vincent Patilio started out as a toy inventor before seeing a chance to make some money when he created a set of electrically-powered jumping coils. He devised a frog costume and embarked on a criminal career as Leap-Frog. He met with a string of pathetic setbacks, including a disastrous stint with Electro's Emissaries of Evil and numerous humiliations at the hands of Daredevil and Spider-Man. Vincent's son Eugene later donned his father's costume and became Frog-Man, an identity that Vincent has sometimes assumed as he continues in his modest calling. **DW**

LEADER, THE

LEADER

FACTFILE

REAL NAME
Samuel Sterns

OCCUPATION
Would-be world conqueror

BASE
Another dimension

HEIGHT 5 ft 10 in
WEIGHT 140 lbs
EYES Green
HAIR Black

FIRST APPEARANCE
Tales to Astonish #62 (December 1964)

POWERS
Superhuman intelligence, several times that of a genius, with an incredible memory for facts and information. Specializes in creating robots, computer systems, high-tech weapons. Has devised methods of telepathic control.

After dropping out of school, Samuel Sterns took a menial job in a US government research facility, where an accident led to his body being bombarded by intense gamma radiation. In the days that followed, Sterns developed an insatiable thirst for knowledge, and as his intelligence expanded at exponential rates, so too did his cranium.

Unfortunately, Sterns' increased intellectual capacity was not matched by emotional maturity. Disgusted by government corruption, he decided that he should command the human race, and restyled himself as the Leader.

Over the years, the Leader's efforts to dominate the world have been repeatedly foiled by the HULK and undermined by his own impatience. However, he has had some successes, in particular the construction of Freehold, a utopian city hidden in Canada's icy north. As part of the INTELLIGENCIA, the Leader helped create the RED HULK, RED SHE-HULK, and the new Harpy (Marlo JONES). The Red Hulk depowered him but continued to use him as part of his THUNDERBOLTS operation. When the PUNISHER killed the Leader, the Red Hulk revived him with gamma radiation, restoring his powers. **AD, MF**

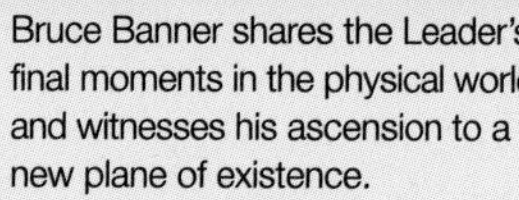

Bruce Banner shares the Leader's final moments in the physical world and witnesses his ascension to a new plane of existence.

LEFT-WINGER

FIRST APPEARANCE Captain America #323 (November 1986)
REAL NAME Hector Lennox
OCCUPATION Former wrestler **BASE** Mobile
HEIGHT 6 ft 5 in **WEIGHT** 265 lbs **EYES** Blue **HAIR** Black
SPECIAL POWERS/ABILITIES Left-Winger possessed superhuman strength and stamina thanks to the Power Broker's strength-augmentation program.

When his ex-army buddy John Walker (*see* U.S.AGENT) became the Super-Patriot, Lennox became one of his Bold Urban Commandos ("Buckies"). Walker was then selected to replace Steve Rogers as CAPTAIN AMERICA. Angered, Lennox and his partner took on guises as Left-Winger and Right-Winger, and set out to destroy Walker's tenure as Captain America. They revealed Walker's true identity to the media, Walker's parents were killed as a result, and he vowed vengeance. Left-Winger was so badly burned in an ensuing explosion that he took his own life. **TB**

LEECH

FIRST APPEARANCE Uncanny X-Men #179 (March 1984)
REAL NAME Unrevealed
OCCUPATION Adventurer **BASE** Various
HEIGHT 4 ft 2 in **WEIGHT** 67 lbs **EYES** Yellow **HAIR** None
SPECIAL POWERS/ABILITIES Leech can dampen the superhuman powers of any Super Heroes or Villains, mutant or not, within his proximity, up to a range of 30 ft.

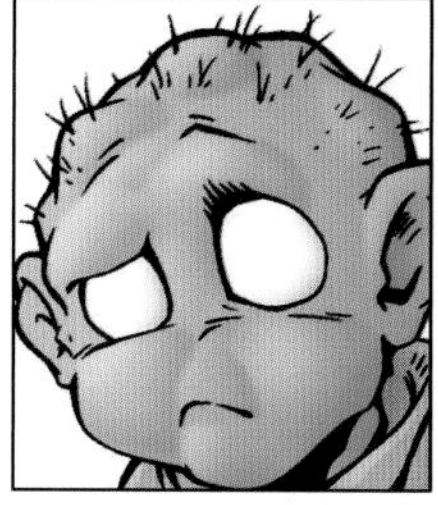

Abandoned by his parents, Leech was found by Caliban, who welcomed him into the MORLOCKS, who lived in the sewers beneath Manhattan. Leech was happy there—until the MARAUDERS came to kill the Morlocks. POWER PACK and X-FACTOR saved him, and the green-skinned boy lived with X-Factor as one of the X-Terminators, and then worked with GENERATION X and the Daydreamers. The WEAPON X program later captured Leech and used him to control mutant prisoners. He escaped and survived M-Day with his powers intact. Leech is now a member of the Future Foundation. **TB, MF**

LEGION

LEGION

FACTFILE

REAL NAME
David Charles Haller

OCCUPATION
Student

BASE
The Jean Grey School for Higher Learning

HEIGHT 5 ft 9 in
WEIGHT 130 lbs
EYES (left) Green; (right) Blue
HAIR Black

FIRST APPEARANCE
New Mutants #25 (March, 1985)

POWERS
David can create spontaneous mutations of any kind, but he spawns a new persona every time he does.

After an affair with PROFESSOR X, Gabrielle HALLER secretly gave birth to a son, David. David became a powerful mutant named Legion. After a horrifying terrorist attack, he developed multiple personalities. When the Professor learned of David's existence, he helped David's core persona reassert itself. David decided to change history by killing MAGNETO in the past, but he killed a younger version of his father instead, bringing on the Age of Apocalypse (Earth-295). BISHOP restored the timeline by killing David, but he returned alive. During a course of therapy with his father and DOCTOR NEMESIS, David later caused the Age of X (Earth-11326) timeline. Sometimes his personalities develop bodies of their own, and he has to hunt down and absorb them. He had established some measure of control over his issues, until CYCLOPS became the Dark Phoenix and killed his father. The shock destroyed David's controls and let many of his evil personalities loose again. He is now working hard to improve the world around him, and has started dating BLINDFOLD. **AD, MF**

Legion of Monsters

FIRST APPEARANCE Marvel Premiere #28 (February 1976)

BASE New York City

MEMBERS AND POWERS **Fankencastle** The undead Punisher.

Ghost Rider The spirit of vengeance.

Living Mummy Ancient Egyptian.

Manphibian Alien fish-man.

Man-Thing Swamp creature with burning touch.

Morbius The living vampire.

Werewolf by Night Cursed wolfman.

Satana Hellstrom Daughter of the devil.

The Legion of Monsters first met when they squabbled over the fate of the strange creature known as the Starseed. Even as it lay dying, it tried to cure them of their curses but failed. A new Legion gathered together in the MORLOCK tunnels beneath New York City, working to protect the monsters who'd hidden there. When the MOLE MAN's Moloids brought them the pieces of the PUNISHER's body, they put him back together in an undead form called Frankencastle. They later helped the RED HULK expel the dark spirit of DOC SAMSON. **MF**

Lei-Kung

FIRST APPEARANCE Marvel Premiere #16 (July 1974)

REAL NAME Lei-Kung **OCCUPATION** Martial artist

BASE K'un-Lun **HEIGHT** 6 ft 1 in

WEIGHT 200 lbs **EYES** Black **HAIR** Bald

SPECIAL POWERS/ABILITIES Immortal master of the martial arts.

Lei-Kung the Thunderer was one of the world's greatest martial artists. He trained both IRON FIST and his son the Steel Serpent in his ways, among most of the residents of the fabled city of K'un-Lun. After Lord Tuan died and his corrupt son Nu-An took over as ruler of the city, Lei-Kung secretly began to prepare the women of the city for his rebellion. He launched his attack during the Celestial Tournament, and with the help of the seven immortal weapons (including Iron Fist), Lei-Kung became the new master of K'un-Lun. He later trained Hope SUMMERS as well. **MF**

Lethal Legion

When Simon Williams (*see* WONDER MAN) sacrificed his life to save the AVENGERS, his altruism had untold consequences. His grieving brother, Eric, blamed the Avengers for Simon's death and determined to destroy them, adopting the guise of the GRIM REAPER and forming the LETHAL LEGION of Super Villains. The Legion's efforts ended in failure, while Eric's own enmity to the Avengers was compromised following his brother's resurrection. Nevertheless the Lethal Legion lived on under the leadership of COUNT NEFARIA. Not much of a team player, Nefaria stole the powers of his fellow legionnaires but was still defeated, despite his augmented abilities.

Following Grim Reaper's death, the Legion's name was adopted by the demon lord Satannish, who resurrected various historical figures—including Josef Stalin and Heinrich Himmler—to capture the souls of the Avengers. The Grim Reaper returned and rebuilt the group during the DARK REIGN with his brother Wonder Man at his side. **AD, MF**

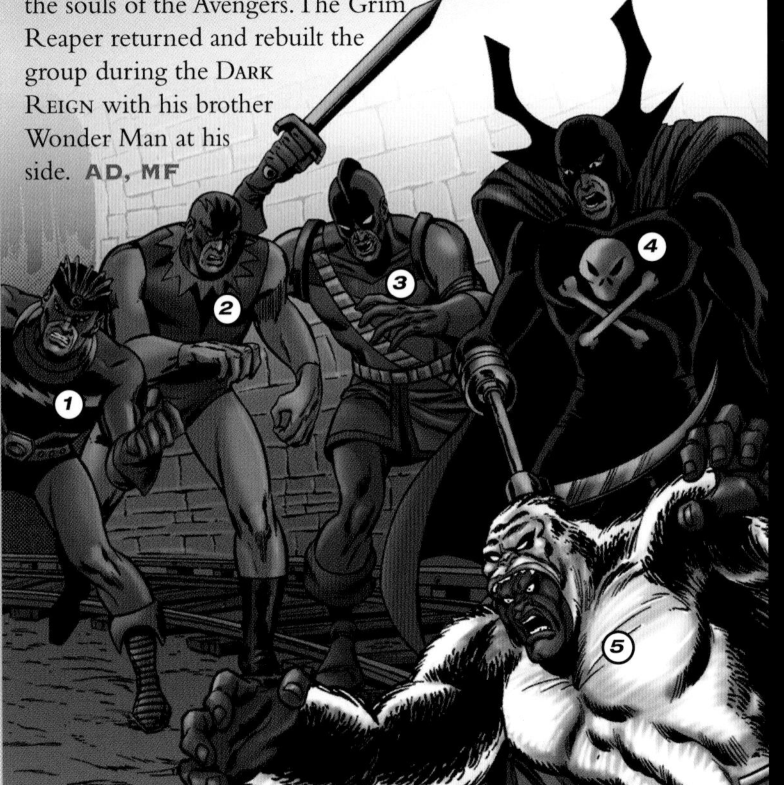

FACTFILE

MEMBERS AND POWERS

GRIM REAPER
A mechanical scythe replaces right hand.

LIVING LASER
A collection of light particles possessing human consciousness.

MAN-APE
Superhuman strength, endurance, and agility.

POWER MAN
Can grow from 6 ft to 60 ft, with tenfold increase in strength.

SWORDSMAN
Superb athlete and master swordsman.

COUNT NEFARIA
Superhuman strength, speed, and the power of flight.

WHIRLWIND
Achieves superhuman speed by spinning body.

ULTRON
A robot with vast strength, speed, and deadly weapons.

BLACK TALON
Can create and control zombies.

BASE
Mobile

FIRST APPEARANCE
Avengers #78 (July 1970)

CHARACTER KEY
1 Living Laser
2 Power Man
3 Swordsman
4 Grim Reaper
5 Man-Ape

Liberteens, The

FIRST APPEARANCE Avengers: The Initiative Annual #1 (December 2007) **BASE** Philadelphia

MEMBERS AND POWERS **The Revolutionary** Swordsman.

Ms. America Superhuman strength, flight, and invulnerability.

Blue Eagle Flying marksman. **Iceberg** Ice powers.

2-D Turns flat and stretches. **Whiz Kid** Super speed.

Hope Superhuman strength and invulnerability.

THE LIBERTEENS
1 Blue Eagle
2 Ms. America
3 Iceberg
4 Whiz Kid
5 The Revolutionary
6 Hope
7 2-D

The Liberteens are a young group of Super Heroes based in Philadelphia as part of the FIFTY-STATE INITIATIVE. Team members are modeled directly on the members of the 1940s Liberty Legion. Unfortunately, their team leader, the Revolutionary, turned out to be a SKRULL inserted into their team as part of the Skrulls' efforts to infiltrate every branch of the Initiative. During the SECRET INVASION, the Skrull Kill Krew—a team of humans infected with a rare Skrull disease—helped root the Revolutionary out, along with several of the Skrulls hiding inside of other Initiative teams. **MF**

Legion of the Unliving

The undead are on the march!

THE ORIGINAL LEGION
1 Wonder Man **2** Midnight
3 Baron Zemo
4 Human Torch
5 Flying Dutchman
6 Frankenstein's Monster

The Legion of the Unliving are foes of the AVENGERS, their ranks made up of deceased heroes and villains brought together by outside entities. Legion members have variously appeared as duplicates or animated zombies and, most disturbingly, have included former Avengers. KANG the Conqueror, allied with IMMORTUS, assembled the original Legion. Scouring the timestream, Kang brought together FRANKENSTEIN'S MONSTER, Midnight, Flying Dutchman, villain-turned-hero WONDER MAN, BARON ZEMO and the heroic HUMAN TORCH.

DEFEATED

Despite their combined powers, Kang's Legion failed to defeat the Avengers, and Immortus—after defeating the turncoat Kang—restored the Legion members to their proper places in the timestream.

The second Legion of the Unliving came about through the efforts of the GRANDMASTER, who raised such figures as Bucky Barnes, the SWORDSMAN, CAPTAIN MAR-VELL, KORVAC, DRACULA, and the RED GUARDIAN to guard "life bombs" that threatened to wipe out the universe. As the Avengers struggled to thwart the Grandmaster's scheme, their slain members joined the ranks of the Legion of the Unliving. Fortunately, all the Avengers returned to life after the resolution of the crisis.

THE SECOND LEGION
1 Swordsman **2** Nighthawk **3** Executioner **4** Terrax
5 Hyperion **6** Green Goblin **7** Korvac **8** Death Adder
9 Dracula **10** Bucky Barnes **11** Black Knight
12 Captain Mar-Vell **13** Baron Blood
14 Drax the Destroyer **15** Red Guardian

FACTFILE

ORIGINAL MEMBERS AND POWERS

KANG THE CONQUEROR
Master of time travel.

FRANKENSTEIN'S MONSTER
Enhanced strength, damage resistance.

BARON ZEMO
(Heinrich Zemo)
Extended longevity, brilliant criminal mind.

WONDER MAN
Flight, enhanced strength, body suffused with ionic energy.

HUMAN TORCH
(Jim Hammond)
Flight, flame projection.

FLYING DUTCHMAN
Projection of energy blasts.

MIDNIGHT
Master martial artist.

BASE
Mobile

FIRST APPEARANCE
Avengers #131 (January 1975)

THE THIRD LEGION
1 Iron Man (Arno Stark)
2 Grim Reaper
3 Swordsman
4 Left-Winger
5 Right-Winger
6 Oort the Living Comet

NEVER SAY DIE

A third Legion included such notable figures as the GRIM REAPER, the BLACK KNIGHT (Nathan Garrett), and Toro. They were gathered by Immortus in order to help him capture the SCARLET WITCH.

Following Immortus's failure, the undead Grim Reaper gained additional power from the demon Lloigoroth and gathered a fourth version of the Legion of the Unliving. Grim Reaper's Legion included copies of villains such as COUNT NEFARIA and Inferno, but the team once again met defeat in battle against the Avengers.

The fifth Legion of the Unliving were once more pawns of the Grim Reaper against the Avengers. It consisted of the deceased heroes CAPTAIN MAR-VELL, DOCTOR DRUID, HELLCAT, MOCKINGBIRD, Swordsman, Wonder Man, and THUNDERSTRIKE (Eric Masterson). The Scarlet Witch used her powers to send the spirits of this Legion into the afterlife, and her love for Wonder Man restored him to life. Likewise, Wonder Man restored his brother the Grim Reaper to full physical health, thus ending his threat. **DW**

THE FOURTH LEGION
1 Wonder Man
2 Captain Mar-Vell
3 Swordsman
4 Doctor Druid
5 Thunderstrike
6 Mockingbird

Lifeguard

FIRST APPEARANCE X-Treme X-Men #6 (December 2001)
REAL NAME Heather Cameron
OCCUPATION Member of X-Corp **BASE** Mumbai, India
HEIGHT 5 ft 10 in **WEIGHT** 156 lbs **EYES** Blue **HAIR** Blond
SPECIAL POWERS/ABILITIES Possesses bio-morphic ability—powers adapt to circumstances. In past, Lifeguard has grown wings, extra arms, and developed ability to breathe underwater.

When the Chinese Triad targeted Heather and Davis Cameron, only the X-Men's intervention saved the siblings' lives. Forced to uncover their mutant abilities during this conflict, both siblings joined the X-Men afterward, and Heather began a relationship with Neal Shaara (Thunderbird). As her powers developed, Heather's appearance became increasingly alien, and Jean Grey suggested that her mother was of the Shi'ar race. Disturbed by this, Davis disappeared, and Heather left the team to find him. Later, she went to work for the X-Corporation and then came to live at the Xavier Institute. She retained her powers after M-Day. **AD, MF**

Lightspeed

FIRST APPEARANCE Power Pack #1 (August 1984)
REAL NAME Julie Power **OCCUPATION** Student
BASE Avengers Academy **HEIGHT** 5 ft 4 in
WEIGHT 110 lbs **EYES** Blue **HAIR** Strawberry blonde
SPECIAL POWERS/ABILITIES Julie can teleport and fly at supersonic speeds. She also has superhuman endurance, reflexes, and healing factor.

As part of the Power Pack, Julie and her siblings received superpowers from Aelfyre Whitemane as he lay mortally wounded after seeking to save them from the alien Snarks, who had attacked their family. Julie was granted the power to fly while leaving a rainbow of light behind her and took the name Lightspeed. When she grew older, Julie left home for Hollywood. In LA, she worked with the teen heroes called the Loners. She has since joined the Avengers Academy. **MF**

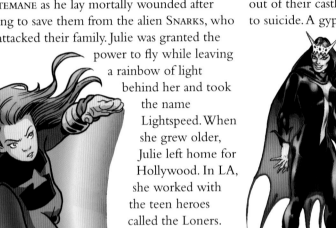

Lilith (Dracula's Daughter)

FIRST APPEARANCE Giant-Size Chillers #1 (June 1974)
REAL NAME Unrevealed
OCCUPATION Adventureress **BASE** South of France
HEIGHT 6 ft **WEIGHT** 125 lbs **EYES** Red **HAIR** Black
SPECIAL POWERS/ABILITIES Unique among vampires, Lilith could walk in sunlight and was unaffected by religious talismen; superhuman strength; hypnotic abilities; could transform into a bat.

The daughter of Dracula and his first wife, Zofia, Lilith hated her father for throwing them out of their castle home and driving her mother to suicide. A gypsy woman called Gretchin raised Lilith, but when Dracula killed Gretchin's son, the gypsy magically transformed Lilith into a vampire and condemned her to hunt Dracula for the rest of her life. For centuries, Lilith stalked and battled her father, but when she finally had the chance to kill him, she found she could not. Later, she became an agent of Nick Fury's supernatural Howling Commandos. **AD, MF**

Lightmaster

FIRST APPEARANCE Peter Parker, the Spectacular Spider-Man #1 (December 1976) **REAL NAME** Dr. Edward Lansky
OCCUPATION Physics professor **BASE** New York City
HEIGHT 5 ft 11 in **WEIGHT** 175 lbs **EYES** Brown **HAIR** Brown
SPECIAL POWERS/ABILITIES Lightmaster possesses the ability to generate light, including lasers, to create simple solid objects out of light, and to fly.

In a bid to prevent budget cuts that might affect his position at Empire State University, Dr. Edward Lansky donned a high-tech suit designed to harness the power of light and became the criminal Lightmaster. His intent was to hold various key government officials hostage, but his scheme was foiled by Spider-Man. During the conflict, Lansky's suit was damaged, transforming him into an energy being. Since that time, Lightmaster has resurfaced, attempting to cash in on his light-based powers. But each time heroes such as Dazzler, Quasar, Cable, and the aforementioned Spider-Man have succeeded in putting his lights out. **TD**

Lilith

FIRST APPEARANCE Ghost Rider #98 (August 1992)
REAL NAME Lilith Drake **OCCUPATION** Sumerian Goddess
BASE The Shadowside Dimension, Atlantis
HEIGHT 6 ft **WEIGHT** 140 lbs **EYES** Yellow **HAIR** Black
SPECIAL POWERS/ABILITIES Superhuman strength and stamina; manipulates the dark forces of the universe. She can summon her children from other dimensions, giving them new bodies on Earth.

Lilith is believed to be the daughter of Aehr, the ancient god of darkness. She lived on the island of Atlantis and survived its destruction. Later, Atlantean sorcerers imprisoned her within the belly of a Leviathan believed to be Tiamat. On emerging, Lilith gathered her children, known as the Lilin, to her and battled Ghost Rider Johnny Blaze. She and the Lilin later came into conflict with Doctor Strange. At one point, she was imprisoned inside the magical realm of Avalon, but during the Secret Invasion, Peter Wisdom freed her to help battle the Skrulls. **AD, MF**

Lipscombe, Dr. Angela

FIRST APPEARANCE The Incredible Hulk #12 (March 2000)
REAL NAME Angela Lipscombe
OCCUPATION Neuropsychologist **BASE** Mobile
HEIGHT 5 ft 9 in **WEIGHT** 125 lbs **EYES** Blue **HAIR** Blond
SPECIAL POWERS/ABILITIES Genius-level knowledge of the science of neuropsychiatry; kind-hearted and a loyal and courageous friend to Bruce Banner in his hour of need.

Angela Lipscombe and Bruce Banner (*see* Hulk) dated in medical school, but Banner broke off the relationship, jealous when Lipscombe received a coveted grant for graduate study and he did not. Doctor Lipscombe became one of the world's foremost experts in the field of neuropsychiatry. Many years later, Bruce Banner looked her up in terrible distress, believing he had contracted an incurable disease. Lipscombe used the opportunity to study the bizarre and disturbing multiple personalities that Banner exhibited as the Hulk. She is the partner of Doc Samson. **DW**

Living Laser

FIRST APPEARANCE Avengers #34 (November 1966)
REAL NAME Arthur Parks
OCCUPATION Criminal **BASE** Mobile
HEIGHT 5 ft 11 in **WEIGHT** (formerly) 125 lbs
EYES (formerly) Blue **HAIR** (formerly) Brown
SPECIAL POWERS/ABILITIES Composed entirely of light, he can travel at light speed or transform himself into an offensive laser.

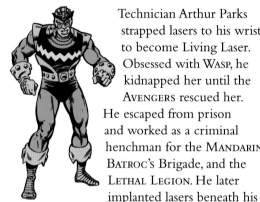

Technician Arthur Parks strapped lasers to his wrists to become Living Laser. Obsessed with Wasp, he kidnapped her until the Avengers rescued her. He escaped from prison and worked as a criminal henchman for the Mandarin, Batroc's Brigade, and the Lethal Legion. He later implanted lasers beneath his skin, but the process caused him to explode. He reappeared as a sentient being made of light, and battled Iron Man several times. He joined the Hood and fought the Skrulls during the Secret Invasion. The Mandarin and Ezekiel Stane upgraded him before his latest battle with Iron Man. **DW, MF**

Living Lightning

FIRST APPEARANCE Avengers West Coast #63 (October 1990)
REAL NAME Miguel Santos
OCCUPATION Student **BASE** California
HEIGHT 5 ft 9 in **WEIGHT** 170 lbs **EYES** Brown **HAIR** Black
SPECIAL POWERS/ABILITIES Living Lightning can transform his body into sentient electrical energy, which he uses for various effects, including to fly.

Miguel Santos's father was Lightning Lord, head of the Legion of Living Lightning, which hoped to control the Hulk and use him to overthrow the US government. The Hulk destroyed the Legion's headquarters, killing Lightning Lord. Miguel intended to follow in his father's footsteps, but an accident with one of his father's devices transformed him into a being of pure electrical energy, who needed a containment suit to remain stable. He eventually became a member of the Avengers. He sided with Captain America during the Civil War, but later joined the Rangers, the Fifty-State Initiative's team in Texas. **TB, MF**

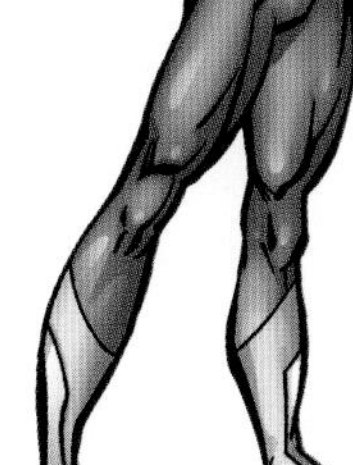

Living Mummy

FIRST APPEARANCE Supernatural Thrillers #5 (August 1973)
REAL NAME N'Kantu
OCCUPATION Wanderer **BASE** Egypt
HEIGHT 7 ft 6 in **WEIGHT** 650 lbs **EYES** Brown **HAIR** None
SPECIAL POWERS/ABILITIES Blood replaced by life-preserving fluid, removing human need for food, water, or sleep; enhanced strength, rock-hard body, near-immortality; limited mobility.

Chief N'Kantu of the Swarili of North Africa became a prisoner of the pharaoh Aram-Set and organized a slave rebellion. Although Aram-Set was killed, the rebellion was crushed, and N'Kantu was entombed while still alive. Preserved in a sarcophagus for 3,000 years, he reawakened in the modern era and went on a rampage before being shocked back to relative sanity when he seized a power line. He later joined Nick Fury's supernatural Howling Commandos. He was imprisoned during the Civil War for refusing to register with the US government. He has since returned to Egypt, where he harvests evil souls for the god Anubis. **DW, MF**

Living Pharaoh

FIRST APPEARANCE X-Men #54 (1969)
REAL NAME Ahmet Abdol
OCCUPATION Would-be world conqueror, now living planet
BASE Formerly Egypt, now distant solar system
HEIGHT 5 ft 8 in **WEIGHT** 196 lbs **EYES** Blue **HAIR** Black
SPECIAL POWERS/ABILITIES Absorbs cosmic energy and wields it as destructive force; at times able to vastly increase body size.

Egyptian academic Ahmet Abdol was obsessed with pharaohs. When his mutant powers manifested, he became the Living Pharaoh. The discovery that his abilities could be muted by Havok's led to many encounters with the X-Men. He sometimes grew into the 30-foot-high Living Monolith. After Thor hurled him into deep space, cosmic energy transformed him into a rich and verdant Living Planet. Apocalypse later tried to use him to drain the power of other mutants, which caused Abdol to break up and flee. **AD, MF**

Living Tribunal

FIRST APPEARANCE Strange Tales #157 (June 1967)
REAL NAMES Equity, Necessity, and Vengeance
OCCUPATION Guardian of the continuum of alternate universes
BASE The Multiverse
HEIGHT n/a **WEIGHT** n/a **EYES** n/a **HAIR** n/a
SPECIAL POWERS/ABILITIES Immensely powerful; can cause a sun to go supernova by firing a single bolt of its cosmic energy.

The Living Tribunal is a powerful humanoid cosmic entity that has existed as long as the universe itself. Its purpose is to safeguard the multiverse from an imbalance of mystical forces by preventing any one universe from acquiring more mystical power than any other. The Living Tribunal can also intervene to prevent an imbalance between the mystical forces of good and evil within a single universe. It is capable of destroying entire planets to maintain the cosmic balance. In its humanoid form, the Living Tribunal has three faces. Its fully visible face represents equity, its partially hooded face represents vengeance, and its fully hooded face represents necessity. It only passes judgment when all the three sides are in agreement. Iron Man and Uatu recently discovered the Living Tribunal's body on the Moon. **MT, MF**

Lizard

FACTFILE

LIZARD

REAL NAME
Dr. Curtis Connors
OCCUPATION
Research biologist
BASE
New York City

HEIGHT 5 ft 11 in
WEIGHT 175 lbs
EYES (as human) Blue, (as Lizard) Red
HAIR (as human) Brown, (as Lizard) None

FIRST APPEARANCE:
Amazing Spider-Man #6 (November 1963)

POWERS
Superhuman strength and speed; can cling to walls like a gecko and telepathically control reptiles. In Shed form, he can push humans to use only the lower, lizard part of their brains.

When Dr. Curt Connors was an army surgeon, his wounded right arm had to be amputated. Back in civilian life, he researched the ability of some reptiles to regenerate missing limbs and created a serum to grow his arm back. It worked—but turned him into a savage humanoid lizard. SPIDER-MAN restored him to human form, but he has repeatedly reverted into the Lizard. The Lizard is one of Spider-Man's main enemies, but Dr. Connors has also acted as a friend to Spider-Man and his true identity, Peter Parker.

Eventually, the Lizard killed Curt's son Billy. The trauma shattered Curt's mind, leaving only the Shed, a more primitive form of the Lizard. This gave him a new power: he could trigger the lizard part of nearby humans' brains, turning them into savages. MORBIUS restored Curt's human body but left his mind in Lizard form. Curt later became the Lizard again, with his human mind trapped in his reptilian body. **PS, MF**

Spider-Man often holds back against the Lizard for fear of hurting Dr. Connors.

Llyra

FIRST APPEARANCE Sub-Mariner #32 (December 1970)
REAL NAME Llyra Morris **OCCUPATION** Subversive
BASE Mobile **HEIGHT** 5 ft 11 in
WEIGHT 220 lbs **EYES** Green **HAIR** Green
SPECIAL POWERS/ABILITIES Amphibious—can live under water or on land—and able to change skin colour to pass as human or homo mermanus; can manipulate brains of primitive marine life.

Daughter of a *Homo mermani* (*see* ATLANTEANS) and a human woman, Llyra was raised on land by her mother following her father's death. Confused by her hybrid status, Llyra became increasingly unstable, and caused great angst to those she encountered. On her first visit to the underwater kingdom of Lemuria, Llyra seized the throne, only to be overthrown by NAMOR the Sub-Mariner. Llyra made Namor the focus of her rage, murdering his fiancée and even giving birth to an heir to his throne by sleeping with Leon McKenzie, the human grandson of Namor's father. Llyron, the product of this union, temporarily took the throne before Namor regained it. Llyra was ultimately betrayed by Llyron, who left her for dead. **AD, MF**

Lockheed

FIRST APPEARANCE Uncanny X-Men #166 (February 1983)
REAL NAME Unknown **OCCUPATION** None
BASE Westchester County, New York
HEIGHT 2 ft **WEIGHT** 20 lbs **EYES** White **HAIR** None
SPECIAL POWERS/ABILITIES Can fly and breathe fire; empathic ability.

Lockheed is a small dragon belonging to alien species the Flock. He encountered the X-MEN during their fight with the BROOD and took a liking to Kitty PRYDE, who named him Lockheed. He served with her as a member of the X-Men and EXCALIBUR. The X-Men later learned he could speak several languages and was spying on them for SWORD. He left the X-Men after Kitty's apparent death, joining SWORD full-time and then founding the Pet Avengers. **DW, MF**

Lockjaw

FIRST APPEARANCE Fantastic Four #45 (December 1965)
REAL NAME Not known **OCCUPATION** Dog
BASE Attilan, Blue Area, the Moon **LENGTH** 6 ft 8 in
WEIGHT 1, 240 lbs **EYES** Brown **HAIR** Brown
SPECIAL POWERS/ABILITIES Immense physical strength; can teleport self and up to a dozen others the distance from the Earth to the Moon; can also teleport to other dimensions.

When they come of age, INHUMANS are exposed to the Terrigen Mists, from which they gain their unique powers. For the Inhuman known as MEDUSA, exposure gave her living hair, while another Inhuman, CRYSTAL, gained the ability to manipulate elements. The Mists transformed another child into the teleporting dog Lockjaw, who served as a companion to the Inhuman Royal Family, and is able to teleport a maximum combined weight of one ton. Although he has human intelligence, Lockjaw still has canine tendencies: he likes to chase other animals, fetch sticks, and so on. KREE technology later improved his teleportation range. While he spends most of his time with the Inhumans, he also helped found the Pet Avengers. **AD, MF**

LOKI

God of Mischief with a will to rule Asgard

Loki was a megalomaniac, who aimed to overthrow his father and rule over Asgard.

Loki was born the son of Laufey, king of the Frost Giants of Jotunheim. Ashamed of Loki's small size, Laufey hid him away, but the child's existence came to light after the Frost Giants were defeated in a battle with the Asgardians. ODIN (*see also* GODS OF ASGARD), the ruler of Asgard, discovered Loki in the Frost Giants' fortress. Realizing that Loki was the son of Laufey, a king whom he had slain, Odin took the boy back to Asgard and raised him as his own son.

FACTFILE
REAL NAME
Loki Laufeyson
OCCUPATION
God of Mischief; later God of Evil
BASE
Asgard

HEIGHT 6 ft 4 in
WEIGHT 525 lbs
EYES Green
HAIR Black-gray

FIRST APPEARANCE
Journey Into Mystery #85 (October 1962)

POWERS
Enhanced strength, stamina, longevity, and limited invulnerability; uses his vast skills in sorcery to fly, generate force fields, teleport between dimensions, animate objects, and change his own shape.

ASGARD'S MISFIT

Loki never fitted in among the inhabitants of Asgard. He nursed a virulent grudge against his stepbrother THOR, the God of Thunder, who possessed in abundance the heroic qualities that Loki himself lacked. Jealous of the praise Odin showered on Thor, Loki took up the dark arts of sorcery and plotted for a way to become ruler of Asgard. His love of trickery earned him a reputation first as the God of Mischief, and then, as he grew more and more cruel, the God of Evil. After many attempts by Loki to usurp the throne of Asgard, Odin lost patience with him and imprisoned him within a mystical tree. Loki eventually freed himself and went in search of Thor, who was then living on Earth in the mortal guise of Donald Blake.

Loki's vast magical talents allowed him to overpower Earth's most powerful heroes. Only Thor's efforts—and Loki's own insecurities—stopped the Trickster God from achieving his ultimate triumph.

RAGNAROK AND BEYOND

Loki precipitated the formation of the AVENGERS by inciting the HULK to violence, and he transformed Crusher Creel into Thor's foe, the ABSORBING MAN. He allied with the ENCHANTRESS and turned Earth's major villains into his pawns during the Acts of Vengeance conspiracy.

Loki finally conquered Asgard and remade it in his own image, but Thor succeeded in decapitating him. Thor carried Loki's preserved head to observe the final act of Ragnarok, when Asgard and all its inhabitants vanished from existence. After Ragnarok, Loki returned, occupying the body of the goddess SIF. Soon after, he fooled Thor into killing his grandfather Bor. As a result Thor was banished from the new Asgard. Loki joined the CABAL during the DARK REIGN and convinced Norman Osborn (GREEN GOBLIN) to launch an assault on Asgard. The attack was so fierce he changed sides to help defend Asgard and paid for his treachery with his life.

Thor missed his brother and went to hunt him down, finding him in the form of a boy. Restored to his godhood but without any memories of his past, he became known as Kid Loki. Thor treated him with such respect and affection he came to idolize his older brother and changed his goals, if not his ways. Later, to save the world, Kid Loki allowed the spirit of his older self to kill him and take over his body. He exists now only as a conscience to plague his original self.

DW, MF

By leading armies against Asgard, Loki helped achieve the end-cycle of Ragnarok.

ESSENTIAL STORYLINES

- ***Avengers #1*** Loki hatches a plot to destroy his brother Thor, accidentally inspiring the world's greatest heroes to form the Avengers.
- ***Loki #1–4*** In this limited series, told from Loki's point of view, the Trickster God temporarily succeeds in winning power over all of Asgard.
- ***The Mighty Thor #582–588*** As Ragnarok unfolds around them, Loki and Thor face off for their final battle, then tour the end of the world.

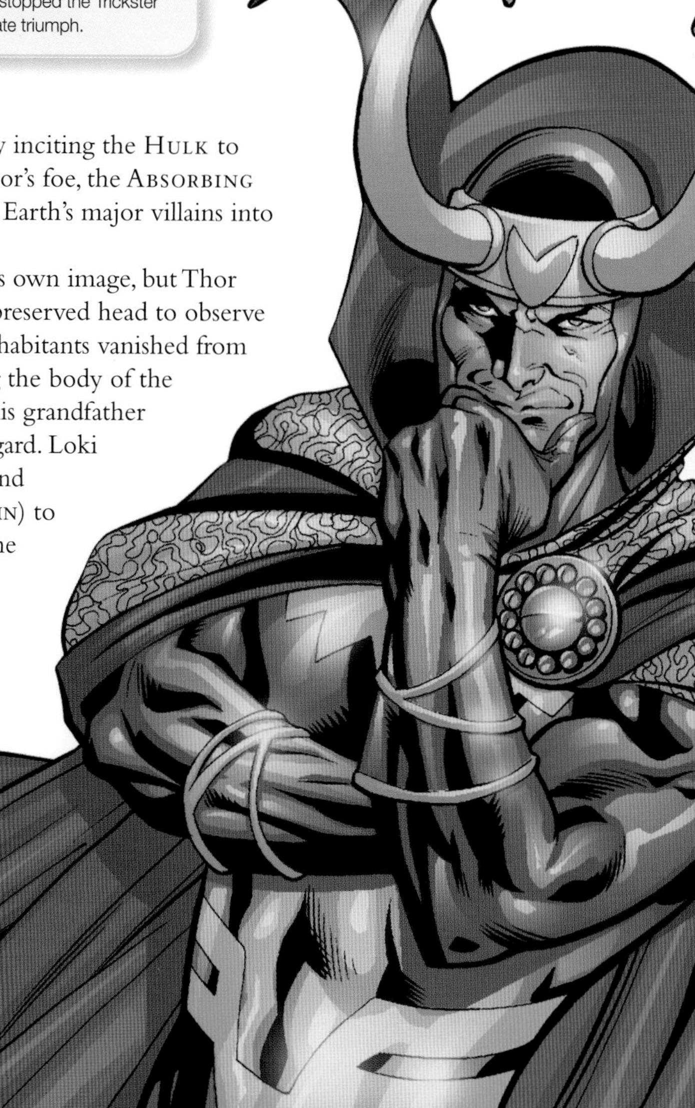

Longshot

FACTFILE
REAL NAME
Unknown
OCCUPATION
Former slave; former movie stuntman; rebel leader
BASE
Mobile

HEIGHT 6 ft 2 in
WEIGHT 80 lbs
EYES Blue
HAIR Blond

FIRST APPEARANCE
Longshot #1 (September 1985)

POWERS
His genetically engineered powers include the ability to affect probability to bring him what is commonly called "good luck." He can telepathically read a person's memories by touching the person and can read psychic imprints left on objects touched by someone.

On Mojoworld, where Longshot is from, the original inhabitants have no spines. The scientist Arize created an exoskeleton to allow them to stand upright, but a group called the Spineless Ones refused to use such devices. Still, they became the planet's rulers and forced Arize to create a race of slaves; Longshot was one of these. He refused to be anyone's slave and helped organize a revolt. On the run, Longshot escaped through an interdimensional portal, arriving on Earth. Mojo, the Spineless One who claimed to own Longshot, pursued him to Earth. With help from a stuntwoman called Ricochet Rita, another slave called Quark, and Doctor Strange, Longshot defeated Mojo. Later, Longshot joined the X-Men and developed a relationship with Dazzler. After he left the X-Men, he joined the transdimensional Exiles team for a while, but he parted ways with them to return to Dazzler. During the Secret Invasion, a Skrull posed as Longshot, but the real Longshot is now back in action. **MT, MF**

Longshot and his team of rebels prepare to do battle with the manipulative Mojo, the Spineless One.

When Longshot lets fly with his deadly throwing knives, the probability is that he won't miss!

Lord Chaos

FIRST APPEARANCE Marvel Two-in-One Annual #2 (1977)
REAL NAME None
OCCUPATION Abstract entity **BASE** Everywhere
HEIGHT/WEIGHT Unknown **EYES** None **HAIR** None
SPECIAL POWERS/ABILITIES Can teleport self and a dozen others the distance from the Earth to the Moon; can also teleport to other dimensions.

An abstract entity (depicted as a disembodied purple head) Lord Chaos embodies the concept of Chaos, just as other entities represent Death, Order (Master Order, depicted as a bald head with black eyebrows), and Eternity. Alongside Order, Chaos strives to maintain a cosmic balance, occasionally intervening in mortal affairs. When Thanos was trying to destroy the universe, Spider-Man released Adam Warlock from a Soul Gem, allowing him to save the day. After these events, Order and Chaos implied that Peter Parker's destiny had been manipulated since birth, in order for him to perform this very act. **AD**

Lord Templar

FIRST APPEARANCE The Avengers Vol. 3 #13 (Feb. 1999)
REAL NAME Unrevealed (last name presumably Tremont)
OCCUPATION Operative of Jonathan Tremont **BASE** Mobile
HEIGHT/WEIGHT Unrevealed **EYES** Red **HAIR** Gray
SPECIAL POWERS/ABILITIES Various powers include the ability to fire energy blasts; can summon counterparts of himself called the Avatars of Templar, each of whom has a different superpower.

Jonathan Tremont's two older brothers died from a disease. Years later Tremont acquired a cosmic artifact in the form of a triangle and used it to resurrect his brothers as the superhumans Lord Templar and Pagan. Jonathan Tremont founded the Triune Understanding, a cult allegedly devoted to world peace. In actuality, Tremont sought to amass power for himself. He used Lord Templar to combat the Avengers. Ultimately, Tremont absorbed the life forces of Lord Templar and Pagan into himself, only to be defeated by the Avenger Triathlon. **PS**

Lorelei

FIRST APPEARANCE Uncanny X-Men Vol. 1 #63 (December 1969)
REAL NAME Unrevealed
OCCUPATION Mercenary **BASE** Savage Land
HEIGHT 5 ft 6 in **WEIGHT** 125 lbs **EYES** Blue **HAIR** Blonde
SPECIAL POWERS/ABILITIES Power lies in her voice; emits hypersonic pitches that affect the sexual drives of human males and mesmerize them.

A member of the Swamp People inhabiting the Antarctic jungle known as the Savage Land, Lorelei received the vocal power to hypnotize men after MAGNETO subjected her to a DNA-altering machine. Her powers are irresistible to males but have no effect on females. Lorelei became a member of the Savage Land Mutates (also known as the Beast Brood), battling foes from the X-MEN to KA-ZAR. She later joined Magneto's BROTHERHOOD OF EVIL MUTANTS and fought the DEFENDERS. Recently, Lorelei found employment as a recruiter for AIM, enlisting other Savage Land mercenaries like herself. **DW**

Lotus

FIRST APPEARANCE Avengers Spotlight #30 (March 1990)
REAL NAME Lotus Newmark
OCCUPATION Mob leader **BASE** California
HEIGHT/WEIGHT Unrevealed **EYES** Brown **HAIR** Black
SPECIAL POWERS/ABILITIES Lotus is a trained martial artist and an experienced criminal leader. She possesses some skill at hypnotizing others to do her will.

As a child, Lotus was traded to Hong Kong underworld leader Li Fong to cover her father's gambling debts. She became Fong's protégée, trained in martial arts, and eventually ascended to a high position within his organization. Lotus emigrated to California to set up her own criminal operation. As she increased her power, she began to run afoul of various heroes, including HAWKEYE, WONDER MAN, and NIGHT THRASHER.

As a cover for her illegal activities, Lotus took over a film studio and became a movie producer. However, proof of her misdeeds was uncovered by Wonder Man and the BEAST, and she was taken into police custody. **TB**

Lucifer

FIRST APPEARANCE X-Men #9 (January 1965)
REAL NAME Unknown
OCCUPATION Agent for the Arcane **BASE** Mobile
HEIGHT 6 ft 2 in **WEIGHT** 325 lbs **EYES** Blue **HAIR** Black
SPECIAL POWERS/ABILITIES Initially merely possessed limited telepathic powers; later able to manipulate ionic energy to increase strength, generate protective shield and fuse self with other beings.

Belonging to the planet-conquering Arcane race, the alien Lucifer served as one of their leading agents and was responsible for the capture of numerous worlds. Ordered to obtain Earth for the Arcane, Lucifer was thwarted by a young Charles Xavier (*see* PROFESSOR X). Furious at his defeat, before fleeing, Lucifer used a stone slab to cripple Xavier's legs. This encounter motivated Xavier to create the X-MEN. That mutant organization claimed victory over Lucifer several more times. Angry at their agent's failures, the Arcane leaders had him terminated. **AD**

Lukin, General

FIRST APPEARANCE Captain America #5 (November 2004)
REAL NAME Aleksander Lukin
OCCUPATION Russian KGB general
BASE New York City
HEIGHT 5 ft 11 in **WEIGHT** 200 lbs **EYES** Blue **HAIR** Black
SPECIAL POWERS/ABILITIES Strategic genius and political mastermind.

During World War II, The RED SKULL used Lukin's Russian village as a base. When the INVADERS helped retake the town, Lukin's mother was killed, and General Vasily Karpov took the orphan in. Lukin rose through the ranks of the Russian military to become a KGB general in charge of many special projects, including the WINTER SOLDIER. When Lukin ordered the Red Skull killed, the Red Skull used the Cosmic Cube to transfer his mind into Lukin's body. Eventually, Lukin rid himself of the Red Skull's mind when it was transferred into a robot, but shortly afterward Sharon CARTER shot him dead. **MF**

Lumpkin, Willie

FIRST APPEARANCE Fantastic Four #11 (February 1963)
REAL NAME William "Lumpy" Lumpkin
OCCUPATION United States Postal Courier **BASE** New York City
HEIGHT 5 ft 8 in **WEIGHT** 165 lbs **EYES** Blue **HAIR** White
SPECIAL POWERS/ABILITIES None, although he believes that he possesses a special talent when it comes to wiggling his ears; good at his job, courageous, and loyal.

After working as a postman for a small town, Lumpkin moved to New York City, where he was assigned a mail route that included the Baxter Building. Soon after the FANTASTIC FOUR moved into the top five floors of the Baxter, Lumpkin half-jokingly petitioned for membership on the grounds that he had the ability to wiggle his ears.

Although he never joined the team, he has been involved with them on many occasions. He once rang a bell that allowed the team to escape the MAD THINKER and a SKRULL once impersonated him to gain access to the FF headquarters. Lumpkin is currently semi-retired and his curvaceous niece Billie has replaced him as the FF's mail carrier. **TD**

Lyja the Lazerfist

FIRST APPEARANCE (as Alicia) Fantastic Four Vol. 1 #265 (April 1984); (as Lyja) Fantastic Four Vol. 1 #357 (October 1991)
REAL NAME Lyja
OCCUPATION Skrull agent **BASE** Mobile
HEIGHT 5 ft 5 in **WEIGHT** 120 lbs **EYES** Green **HAIR** Green
SPECIAL POWERS/ABILITIES A shapeshifter, like all Skrulls, Lyja can also fly and project energy bursts and is immune to heat and fire.

The Skrull called Lyja posed as Alicia MASTERS and married the HUMAN TORCH in a plot to destroy the FANTASTIC FOUR. The Torch broke off their relationship when he discovered the ruse. Lyja became "the Lazerfist" after the SKRULLS gave her energy powers, and she alternated between fighting the Fantastic Four and seeking to reconcile with the Torch. After losing her powers during a false pregnancy, she posed as human Laura Greene. During the SECRET INVASION, Lyja regained her powers and sent the Baxter Building into the Negative Zone. She voluntarily remained there when the building's occupants returned. **DW, MF**

M

FIRST APPEARANCE Uncanny X-Men #316 (September 1994)
REAL NAME Monet St. Croix **OCCUPATION** Investigator
BASE Mutant Town area of New York
HEIGHT 5 ft 7 in **WEIGHT** 125 lbs **EYES** Brown **HAIR** Black
SPECIAL POWERS/ABILITIES M possesses superhuman strength and durability, flight and telepathy.

Having lived much of her young life mystically trapped in the speechless form of PENANCE by her brother EMPLATE, Monet St. Croix's existence was usurped by her two younger sisters Claudette and Nicole. They used their mutant abilities to combine into a single entity that resembled Monet. Both Penance and the amalgam-Monet became members of GENERATION X. Later, the truth of M's situation became apparent, and she and her sisters were restored to their rightful forms. M joined Jamie Madrox's detective agency, X-FACTOR Investigations, and later the X-MEN. **TB, MF**

MACH-V

FIRST APPEARANCE Strange Tales #123 (August 1964)
REAL NAME Abner Jenkins
OCCUPATION Super Hero, former criminal
BASE New York City **HEIGHT** 5 ft 11 in **WEIGHT** 175 lbs
EYES Brown **HAIR** Brown
SPECIAL POWERS/ABILITIES Armored flight suit provides enhanced strength and supersonic flight; has a built-in tactical computer and a generator that can fire electrostatic blasts.

Abner Jenkins joined the MASTERS OF EVIL as The Beetle and agreed to BARON ZEMO's scheme to turn them into the THUNDERBOLTS. As Mach-1, he decided to go straight and returned to prison for his previous crimes. He upgraded his armor and is now known as Mach-V. After parole, he joined Songbird to lead a new team of Thunderbolts. He later took a job with the COMMISSION ON SUPERHUMAN ACTIVITIES and oversaw a trio of students wearing versions of his Beetle suit. He then served as head of security at the Raft super-prison. **DW, MF**

MACHINE TEEN

FIRST APPEARANCE Machine Teen #1 (July 2005)
REAL NAME Adam Aaronson
OCCUPATION Student
BASE New York City **HEIGHT** 5 ft 8 in **WEIGHT** 225 lbs
EYES Blue **HAIR** Red
SPECIAL POWERS/ABILITIES Adam is an android with superhuman durability, endurance, strength, and speed, plus a computer brain.

When Adam Aaronson started attending high school, he didn't suspect he was actually an android built by Dr. Aaron Isaacs, the man he thought was his father. After a series of strange seizures and displays of odd powers, his secret came out, and he confronted Dr. Isaacs about it. Isaacs had fled from the Holden Radcliffe Corporation with Adam rather than give him up. Radcliffe tried to capture Adam, but Adam escaped. He later joined the AVENGERS Academy and then went to work with Briggs Chemical. **MF**

M-11

FIRST APPEARANCE Menace #11 (May 1954)
REAL NAME M-11 **OCCUPATION** Adventurer
BASE San Francisco
HEIGHT 6 ft **WEIGHT** 900 lbs **EYES** None **HAIR** None
SPECIAL POWERS/ABILITIES Robot with telescopic arms, heat vision, force field projection, image projection, superhuman strength, and the ability to repair itself.

In the 1950s, the YELLOW CLAW commissioned a scientist to build a robot to help his plan to make FBI agent Jimmy Woo the next Khan. To give the robot free will, the scientist had it electrocute him and absorb some of his life force. M-11 then walked into the sea, but NAMORA found it and brought it to Jimmy to join his G-Men group of heroes. Woo and his friends reactivated the robot decades later to help in their battle against the forces of the Yellow Claw. Today, M-11 works alongside the other former G-Men as part of the AGENTS OF ATLAS. **MF**

MACHINE MAN

X-51 was a prototype for a government project to build artificially intelligent robot soldiers. His limbs could extend 100 feet, his endoskeleton housed solar-power-augmented batteries, multi-optical imaging devices with zoom, and magnifying sensors, while anti-gravity devices allowed flight. His fingers featured miniature lasers, concussive blasters, and a .357 Magnum pistol. Believing a robot would only act like a man if treated like one, Dr. Aaron Stack took X-51 into his home and even designed a human face for him. Stack died protecting X-51 after the program was terminated.

Assuming Stack's identity, X-51 attempted to assimilate into human society, but he later fell in love with the robot JOCASTA. He has fought alongside the AVENGERS, FANTASTIC FOUR, HULK, X-MEN, and NEXTWAVE. His personality changed over that time, moving from friendly but distant to crass and obnoxious, especially during his spell in Nextwave where he seemed more at ease with his robotic nature. He and Jocasta traveled to Earth-2149 to help stop an invasion of zombies, and he later went to work with the RED HULK, and later RED SHE-HULK. **TD,**

FACTFILE
REAL NAME
X-51
OCCUPATION
Insurance investigator
BASE
Manhattan, New York

HEIGHT 6 ft
WEIGHT 850 lbs
EYES Red imaging sensors
HAIR Black (artificial)

FIRST APPEARANCE
2001: A Space Odyssey #8 (July 1977)

MACHINE MAN

POWERS
Robot composed of titanium alloy. Motorized endoskeleton which houses a vast array of weapons systems.

Machinesmith

FIRST APPEARANCE Marvel Two-In-One #47 (January 1979)
REAL NAME Samuel "Starr" Saxon
OCCUPATION Robot maker, professional criminal **BASE** Mobile
HEIGHT 6 ft 1 in **WEIGHT** 295 lbs **EYES** Green **HAIR** Bald
SPECIAL POWERS/ABILITIES A living computer program, his consciousness can be placed into multiple robot bodies which approximate human beings.

Master robot builder Starr Saxon built robots for criminals. When Daredevil defeated one of his robots, Saxon sought revenge, but died during the battle. One of his robots, following its programming, took Saxon's body back to his workshop and transferred his brain patterns into a robotic body. On recovery, Saxon replaced this body with a human-looking one. Calling himself Machinesmith, he resumed his career of building robots for the underworld. Machinesmith has come into conflict with SHIELD and Captain America. He now exists as a computer program which can be placed into robot bodies. **MT**

MacTaggert, Dr.

FIRST APPEARANCE Uncanny X-Men #96 (December 1975)
REAL NAME Moira Kinross MacTaggert
OCCUPATION Geneticist **BASE** Muir Island, Scotland
HEIGHT 5 ft 7 in **WEIGHT** 135 lbs
EYES Blue **HAIR** Brown
SPECIAL POWERS/ABILITIES
Brilliant geneticist with expertise in the mutant genome.

Moira MacTaggert was once engaged to Charles Xavier (*see* Professor X), but she broke it off. She secretly bore Xavier's child (Proteus) and later adopted the mutant child Rahne Sinclair (Wolfsbane). Like Xavier, she set up a secret home for young mutants, but the heroes all seemingly died on their first mission. Later, she struck up a romance with Sean Cassidy (Banshee). She established a Mutant Research Center on Muir Island, where she found a cure for the Legacy virus. Mystique killed her. She was temporarily resurrected during the Chaos War. **DW, MF**

Mad Dog

FIRST APPEARANCE (as Baxter) Amazing Adventures #13 (July 1972); (as Mad Dog) Defenders #125 (November 1983)
REAL NAME Robert "Buzz" Baxter **OCCUPATION** Criminal, retired US Air Force Colonel **BASE** Mobile **HEIGHT** 6 ft 2 in
WEIGHT 270 lbs **EYES** Blue **HAIR** Black and brown
SPECIAL POWERS/ABILITIES Possesses superhuman strength, smell and hearing. Enhanced speed and agility. Has hollow fangs which secrete poison, to which he is immune.

In the comics she wrote, Dorothy Walker based her characters on her daughter Patsy and Patsy's friend "Buzz" Baxter. After the real Patsy and Baxter graduated from high school, they married and Baxter joined the Air Force. As a security consultant for the Brand Corporation, Baxter hunted the mutant Beast. Patsy divorced Baxter and became the Hellcat. When Brand captured the Avengers, Hellcat forced Baxter to free them. Baxter underwent treatment by Roxxon Oil's Mutagenics Department that gave him superhuman powers. Thus Baxter became Mad Dog, who has battled not only Hellcat, but also other costumed adventurers. **PS**

Mad Thinker

For many years the police did not know of the Mad Thinker's existence, despite the various criminal activities he had masterminded over that period. He only leaped into the public eye when he went head-to-head with the Fantastic Four. A brilliant strategist, he tempted each of them away from New York with various impossible-to-refuse jobs. He subsequently used their absence to enter the Baxter Building and steal Reed Richards' inventions. Manufacturing superhuman androids based on Richards' designs, he used them to battle the Fantastic Four. However, the Mad Thinker failed to account for a circuit breaker Richards had built into the designs for just this eventuality. Once the circuit was activated all the robots became disabled. Since then, the Mad Thinker has spent much of his time in prison but he has somehow managed to continue his activities from inside.

His motives remain unclear—perhaps no one is brilliant enough to understand them or could the Mad Thinker just be enjoying the game? **AD**

With low cunning the Fantastic Four are almost duped into defeat.

Mad Thinker

FACTFILE
REAL NAME
Unknown
OCCUPATION
Criminal mastermind
BASE
Mobile

HEIGHT 5 ft 11 in
WEIGHT 195 lbs
EYES Blue
HAIR Brown

FIRST APPEARANCE
Fantastic Four #15 (June 1963)

POWERS
Brilliant criminal mind. Created a way to project his mind into an android body to continue criminal activities in his absence.

Madame Hydra

FIRST APPEARANCE (Viper as MH) Captain America #110 (February 1969); (MH VI) Nick Fury vs. SHIELD #3 (August 1988)
REAL NAME (both) Unrevealed **OCCUPATION** (both) Subversive
BASE (both) Mobile **HEIGHT** (Viper) 5 ft 9 in; (MH VI) 5 ft 11 in
WEIGHT (Viper) 141 lbs; (MH VI) 135 lbs **EYES** (both) Green
HAIR (Viper) Black, green highlights; (MH VI) Brown, dyed green
SPECIAL POWERS/ABILITIES (both) Formidable combatant.

Originally the subversive organization HYDRA restricted its membership to men. The first female Hydra agent was Laura Brown. Another female operative seized command of Hydra's New York operations, took the name Madame Hydra, and battled CAPTAIN AMERICA. Eventually she took a new alias, the VIPER, and became one of the world's most dangerous terrorists. Another female Hydra agent, Madame Hydra VI, clashed with SHIELD and allied with the YELLOW CLAW. (Five other Madame Hydras outranked her.) She committed suicide to avoid capture. Viper has now reassumed the name of Madame Hydra. **PS**

Madame Masque

Adopted by financier Byron Frost, Whitney Frost grew up in New York's high society, but when Byron died, her world collapsed. Learning that her biological father was the Italian COUNT NEFARIA, head of the MAGGIA criminal organization, she became his heir. Following his imprisonment, she became head of the Maggia, now based in New York. Her face was disfigured during a botched raid on Stark Industries. Hiding her scars behind a golden mask, Whitney took the name Madame Masque. Falling in love with Tony Stark (IRON MAN), she impersonated his assistant to spend time with him, but when Tony was unable to save her father's life, she resumed her role as the Director of the Maggia.

It was Mordecai Midas who first suggested the golden mask.

FACTFILE

REAL NAME
Countess Giulietta Nefaria (adopted name Whitney Frost)

OCCUPATION
Head of Maggia criminal organization

BASE
Unknown

HEIGHT 5 ft 9 in
WEIGHT 130 lbs
EYES Gray
HAIR Black

FIRST APPEARANCE
Tales of Suspense #97 (January 1968)

POWERS
Gymnast and athlete trained to Olympic standards; superb markswoman and exceptional mistress of strategy.

IS IT SO UNUSUAL FOR A MAN TO HELP A WOMAN...?
...AND I'D BET THERE'S QUITE A WOMAN BEHIND THAT MASK!
SPARE ME TONY STARK'S PLAYBOY HOMILIES... BEHIND THIS MASK IS ONLY HORROR!
MIDAS' MEN RESCUED ME FROM A PLANE CRASH... A SURGEON HE HIRED SAVED MY LIFE... BUT NOT BEFORE CHEMICALS ON BOARD PLAYED A MACABRE JOKE WITH MY FEATURES!

Over the years, Whitney made several clones of herself, killing them when they'd served their purpose. One, known as Masque, worked briefly with the AVENGERS before being killed. Whitney supposedly renounced her criminal past after witnessing her clone's sacrifice, but she served as the HOOD's top lieutenant in his new crime syndicate. He healed her face with the Reality Gem. **AD, MF**

Madame Web

MADAME WEB

FACTFILE

REAL NAME
Cassandra Webb

OCCUPATION
Professional medium

BASE
New York City

HEIGHT 5 ft 7 in
WEIGHT 115 lbs
EYES Pale gray
HAIR Black and silver

FIRST APPEARANCE
Amazing Spider-Man #210 (November 1980)

POWERS
Through clairvoyancy Madame Web can predict the future, read minds and perform psychic surgery.

A one-time ally of SPIDER-MAN, Cassandra Webb was born blind but developed skills as a clairvoyant that compensated for her sightlessness. Cassandra's first encounter with Spider-Man came when businessman Rupert Dockery was scheming to take over the *Daily Globe*. At first sceptical of the help she offered, Spider-Man later acknowledged her usefulness and they worked together to prevent the assassination of a local congressman.

At times, Cassandra could be manipulative. She once tricked Spider-Man into obtaining a mystical object for her so she could try to gain youthful immortality. She later mentored the third SPIDER-WOMAN, Mattie Franklin, but she couldn't prevent KRAVEN's family from killing them both. Julia Carpenter—the second Spider-Woman—inherited her powers and has taken over as the new Madame Web. **AD, MF**

Madcap

FIRST APPEARANCE Captain America #307 (July 1985)
REAL NAME Not known
OCCUPATION Prankster **BASE** New York City
HEIGHT 5 ft 9 in **WEIGHT** 145 lbs **EYES** Blue **HAIR** Brown
SPECIAL POWERS/ABILITIES Remarkable self-healing ability, able to survive almost any injury; causes others to lose inhibitions with embarrassing and sometimes lethal consequences.

A devoted member of a Christian church, Madcap began his descent into insanity following a terrible accident. He was traveling on a bus with his family and forty church members when it collided with a truck carrying an experimental nerve agent. Madcap was the only survivor, and in the days that followed he developed the ability to heal himself and cause temporary insanity in others. He has used these talents to cause repeated havoc on the streets of New York. In between short spells in Bellevue Hospital, Madcap has encountered a number of superpowered individuals, including GHOST RIDER, NOMAD, and WOLVERINE. **AD**

Madman

MADMAN

FACTFILE

REAL NAME
Phillip Sterns

OCCUPATION
Scientist

BASE
Mobile

HEIGHT Variable
WEIGHT Variable
EYES Pupils uncolored
HAIR None

FIRST APPEARANCE
(as Phillip Sterns) Incredible Hulk #363 (January 1990); (as Madman) Incredible Hulk #364 (February 1990)

POWERS
Superhuman strength, ability to increase and decrease his mass, and to change his shape and form.

Phillip Sterns, brother of Samuel Sterns who became the HULK's enemy, the LEADER, was a classmate of Bruce Banner (the Hulk) in graduate school. Banner was always at the top of his class, Phillip Sterns at the bottom. After graduation, both Banner and Sterns began researching the use of gamma radiation as a potential weapon. But the government funded Banner's research, not Sterns', increasing Sterns' envy of Banner.

When Sterns learned that Bruce Banner had become the Hulk through exposure to gamma radiation, he grew even more jealous and began exposing himself to gamma radiation over a period of years. As a result of this exposure, he gained the powers of the Madman. Sterns and Madman are two separate personalities both existing in the same body. Over the years, Madman battled the Hulk many times. In the end, however, the Leader killed Madman. The Leader whispered a code into Madman's ear, something that unlocked so much stored data into Madman's head at once that it exploded. **MT, MF**

MAELSTROM

FACTFILE

REAL NAME
Unrevealed

OCCUPATION
Nihilist

BASE
Mobile

HEIGHT 8 ft 2 in
WEIGHT 425 lbs
EYES Purple
HAIR White

FIRST APPEARANCE
Marvel Two-In-One #71 (January 1981)

POWERS

Increases his own powers through control of kinetic energy and draining the energy of others; projects force blasts.

MAELSTROM

The seeds of a Super Villain's behavior can often be found in their childhood. The hybrid child of a Deviant and an INHUMAN, Maelstrom's birth caused consternation. His mother was killed for giving birth to him, and as a child he was forced to work in Deviant slave pits until rescued by his father, the brilliant geneticist Phaeder.

Following in his father's footsteps, Maelstrom traded information on genetics with various dubious individuals including RED SKULL, MAGNETO, and the HIGH EVOLUTIONARY. Their use of this knowledge caused untold suffering: the Nazi genetic atrocities and various clones of SPIDER-MAN were direct results of Maelstrom's collaborations.

A desperately lonely individual, Maelstrom looked for an antidote to his unhappiness in plans to end the Multiverse. Destroyed by QUASAR when he first attempted this, he was resurrected and tried again. This time, Mr. Immortal of the GREAT LAKES AVENGERS tricked him into committing suicide. While dead, he served Oblivion. Hoping to buy his return to life, he fed her to the Dragon of the Moon, who transformed her into Martyr, an avatar of Death. He later tricked her into freeing Thanos, who killed her. **AD, MF**

Maelstrom can divert absorbed energy into a blast of kinetic energy.

MAGGIA

FACTFILE

NOTABLE MEMBERS
TOP MAN (Hammerheads, deceased) Cunning mind.
HAMMERHEAD (Hammerheads) Enhanced strength through metal exoskeleton.
COUNT NEFARIA (Nefarias) Vast powers of ionic energy.
MADAME MASQUE (Nefarias) Skilled martial artist.
SILVIO "SILVERMANE" MANFREDI (Silvermanes) Cybernetic body.
JOSEPH MANFREDI (Silvermanes) Formerly had control over bats.

BASE Worldwide

FIRST APPEARANCE
Avengers #13 (February 1965)

MAGGIA

The Maggia is the world's most powerful crime syndicate. The organization's operations are worldwide, though its roots began in southern Europe during the 13th century and it spread to the United States in the 1890s. The Maggia has its fingers in gambling, narcotics, loan-sharking, organized labor, and crooked politics. Those who betray the Maggia are executed, often with a death-grip to the chin nicknamed the "Maggia touch."

The three largest Maggia families active in New York City include the SILVERMANE family, the HAMMERHEAD family, and the Nefaria family (*see* COUNT NEFARIA). The Silvermanes are a traditionally-structured crime network controlling the narcotics trade. The Hammerheads are styled in the fashion of 1920s gangsters, and are led by the flat-topped Hammerhead. The Nefarias, organized by Count Nefaria, are the most colorful of the three families, frequently employing costumed criminals to further their schemes. Early in his career, the gang boss KINGPIN was one of the Maggia's most successful rivals. **AD**

THE MAGGIA
1 Silvermane
2 Count Nefaria
3 Hammerhead

Maggott

FIRST APPEARANCE Uncanny X-Men #345 (June 1997)
REAL NAME Japheth
OCCUPATION Former X-Man **BASE** Mobile
HEIGHT 6 ft 8 in **WEIGHT** 350 lbs **EYES** Brown **HAIR** Black
SPECIAL POWERS/ABILITIES Two semi-sentient slugs can leave and re-enter Maggott's body. They feed on anything and use it to nourish him. He can replay in mind's eye past events in local area.

A sickly child, unable to eat solid food, young Japheth felt that he was nothing but a burden to his poor South African family. Heading into the desert to die, Japheth encountered MAGNETO who activated his mutation, allowing two slugs to leave his body and feed on his behalf. Now calling himself Maggott, Japheth went searching for Magneto. In Antarctica, he first encountered the X-MEN, and briefly joined the mutant team. Unfortunately, Maggott was captured by the WEAPON X facility, became an inmate at the Neverland concentration camp, and was executed there. SELENE revived him with her techno-organic virus, but only temporarily. **AD, MF**

Thanks to her seismic mutant talents, Magma is impervious to heat and, by encasing herself in fiery molten rock, is as comfortable inside the crater of an erupting volcano as she is in the open air.

Magma

FIRST APPEARANCE New Mutants #8 (October 1983)
REAL NAME Amara Aquilla
OCCUPATION Adventurer **BASE** Mobile
HEIGHT 5 ft 6 in **WEIGHT** 124 lbs **EYES** Brown **HAIR** Blond
SPECIAL POWERS/ABILITIES Projects bursts of heat and molten rock, and causes shifts in the tectonic plates beneath the surface of the Earth to produce volcanic eruptions.

Raised in the hidden city of Nova Roma in the Amazon jungles of Brazil, Amara's mutant abilities surfaced when SELENE—a nigh-immortal mutant who drains the life essences of others—hurled her into an active volcano. The NEW MUTANTS rescued her, and she became a longtime member of the group. For a time, she believed herself to be Allison Crestmere, daughter of an English ambassador, but this proved false. She later joined the Xavier Institute's staff, working with the younger mutants. She survived M-Day with her powers intact. Later, trapped in Hell with the New Mutants, she traded a date with MEPHISTO for their freedom. **AD, MF**

Magik

Illyana Rasputin is the younger sister of Piotr Rasputin (COLOSSUS). The sorcerer Belasco brought Illyana and the X-MEN to his timeless realm Limbo. The X-Men escaped, but Belasco kept Illyana there and turned a portion of her soul evil. Her darksoul gave her powers of sorcery, and Illyana mastered the magic in Belasco's books and defeated him with her magical soulsword. Afterward, she returned to Earth several years older and joined the NEW MUTANTS under the code name Magik. Eventually, she managed to find her younger self in Limbo and prevented her corruption from happening, erasing all subsequent events. Restored to her youth, she later died of the mutant-killing Legacy Virus. Recently, Belasco brought together the fragments of Illyana in Limbo and created the Darkchylde. This form of Illyana stole a part of the X-Man PIXIE's soul and dedicated herself to reclaiming her own soul. She returned to Earth and joined the latest version of the NEW MUTANTS. When the Phoenix Force returned to Earth and was shattered, she became one of the Phoenix Five. Later, she joined the fugitive CYCLOPS' new X-MEN. **MT, MF**

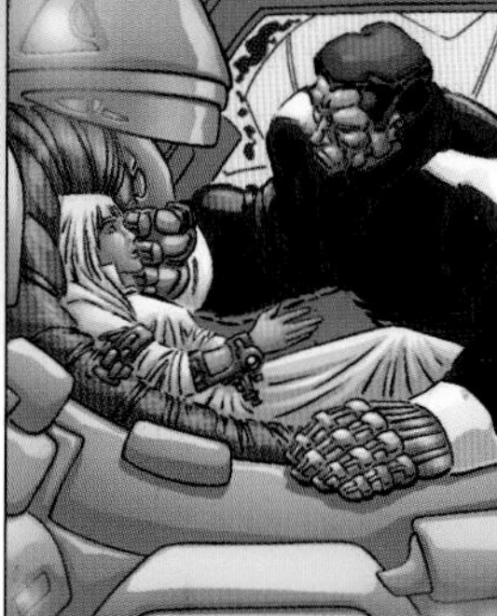

Mutant Illyana Rasputin (code name Magik) joined her brother Piotr (codename Colossus) at Professor Xavier's school for mutants, where they became X-Men.

MAGIK

FACTFILE

REAL NAME
Illyana Nikolievna Rasputin

OCCUPATION
Student

BASE
Professor Xavier's School for Gifted Youngsters, New York; the extradimensional realm, Limbo

HEIGHT 5 ft 5 in
WEIGHT 120 lbs
EYES Blue
HAIR Blond

FIRST APPEARANCE
(as a child) Giant-Size X-Men #1 (1975)

POWERS

Magik is both a mutant with superhuman powers and an expert sorceress. She can teleport herself and others through time, perform astral projection, and sense the presence of magic.

Magik is not only a powerful mutant, she is also a skilled sorceress, which helps to make her a formidable warrior.

MAGNETO

Master of magnetism

MAGNETO

FACTFILE

REAL NAME
Max Eisenhart; also uses the name Erik Magnus Lehnsherr

OCCUPATION
Conqueror

BASE
Mobile

HEIGHT 6 ft 2 in
WEIGHT 190 lbs
EYES Blue-grey
HAIR White

FIRST APPEARANCE
X-Men #1, (September 1963)

POWERS
Mutant ability to manipulate magnetism and all forms of electromagnetic energy

ALLIES/FOES
ALLIES Brotherhood of Evil Mutants, (sometimes) Professor Charles Xavier, (formerly) the X-Men, the New Mutants

FOES Professor Charles Xavier, the X-Men, the Avengers, the Fantastic Four

ISSUE #1
In the first *X-Men* comic, Magneto captured the Cape Citadel missile base, only to be defeated by the original X-Men in their initial battle.

Magneto's sufferings in his youth inspired his hatred of humankind.

One of the most powerful and dangerous of all mutants, Magneto has been both the foremost enemy of the X-Men and, sometimes, their ally. As a boy, he was imprisoned in the Nazi death camp in Auschwitz, Poland. Sickness and malnourishment prevented Magneto's mutant powers from emerging there. In Auschwitz, Magneto's family perished, and he witnessed the inhumanity that people can show to those who are considered different.

MUTANT RAGE

Magneto magnetically shielded Magda and Anya in a burning inn, but could not save Anya's life.

Following World War II, Magneto married Magda, and they had a daughter, Anya. When Anya was trapped in a burning building, an insensitive crowd prevented Magneto from rescuing her. Infuriated, Magneto lashed out with his powers, killing them.

Frightened by what her husband had done, Magda fled from him. She had not told Magneto that she was pregnant. Eventually Magda arrived at Wundagore Mountain, where she gave birth to twins, Wanda and Pietro. She then ran away into the wilderness, where she presumably died.

While searching for Magda, Magneto employed a forger named George Odekirk to create a false identity, "Erik Magnus Lehnsherr," for him. Eventually Magneto settled in Israel, where he became friends with the young Charles Xavier (*see* Professor X). They continually debated their different views on whether mutants could peacefully coexist with the rest of humanity.

SUPERIORITY COMPLEX

When their friend Gabrielle Haller was abducted by Baron von Strucker and his Hydra agents, Magneto and Xavier rescued her. Magneto used his powers to make off with a cache of Nazi gold that Strucker had sought. Magneto decided that the only way to prevent humanity from oppressing the emerging race of mutants was for mutants to conquer the rest of the human race. Indeed, Magneto believed that mutants were superior to ordinary humans and deserved to rule them.

Magneto's first step in his war against the human race was to seize a missile base at Cape Citadel, Florida. By now Xavier had founded the X-Men, who foiled Magneto's takeover of the base.

ESSENTIAL STORYLINES
- ***X-Men Vol. 1 #4-7, 11***
Magneto's original Brotherhood of Evil Mutants battles the original team of X-Men.
- ***X-Men Vol. 1 #62-63***
Magneto's unmasked face is revealed when he combats the X-Men in the Savage Land.
- ***Uncanny X-Men #161***
The story of how Magneto first met Charles Xavier in Israel.
- ***Classic X-Men #12***
Magneto's captivity at Auschwitz and the death of his daughter.

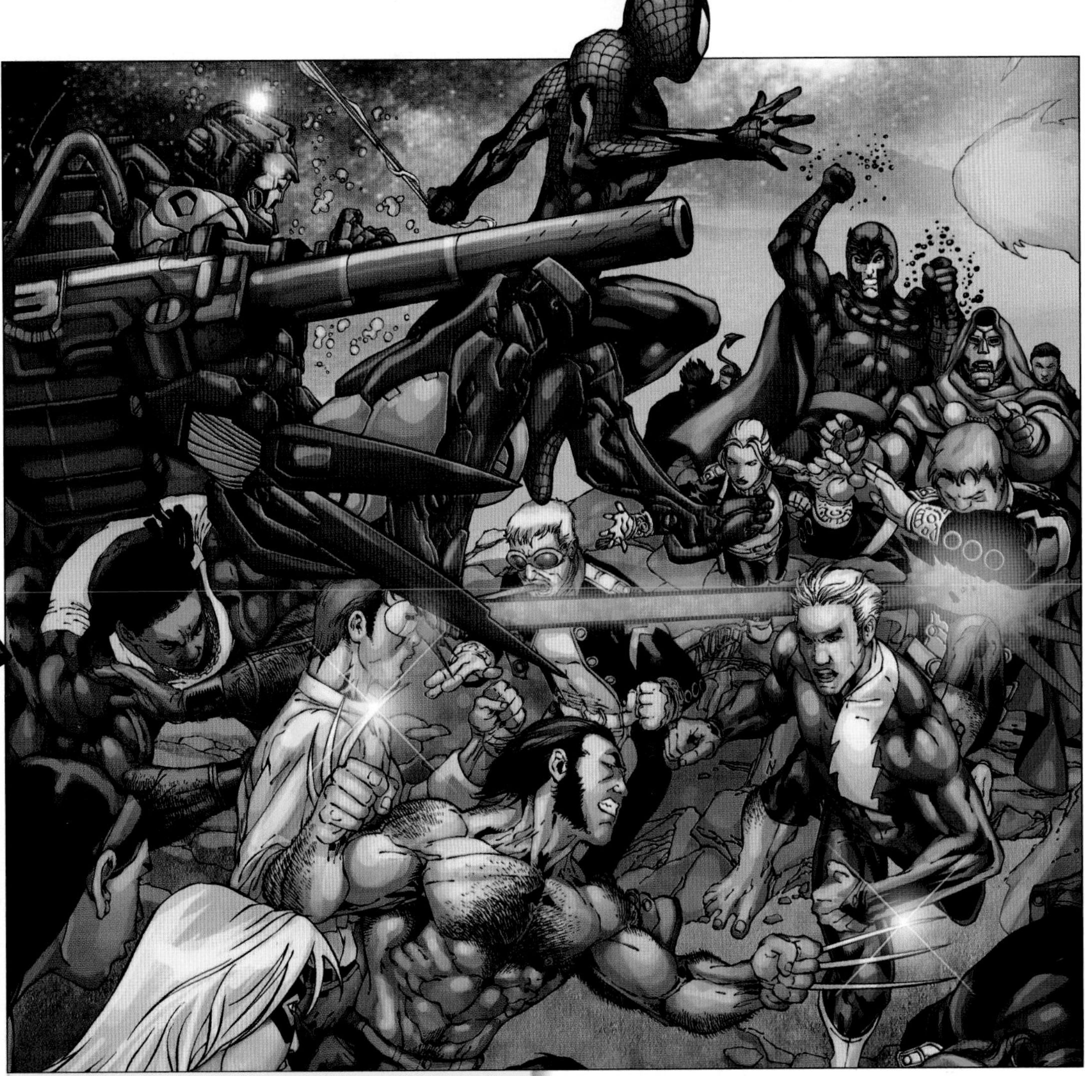

A resistance movement including Cyclops, Spider-Man, and Wolverine attacked Magneto's House of M before the Scarlet Witch finally restored reality to its previous normalcy.

THE HOUSE OF M
1 Quicksilver **2** Scarlet Witch
3 Scarlet Witch's sons Thomas and William
4 Magneto **5** Polaris

THE HOUSE OF MAGNUS

Urged by her brother Quicksilver, the Scarlet Witch utilized her mutant power over probability to alter history. As a result, Magneto had led mutants in a successful war against the rest of humanity. Magneto was now monarch of Earth. His royal family was known as the "House of Magnus" or "House of M" and was comprised of his son Quicksilver, his daughters the Scarlet Witch and Polaris, and his grandsons Thomas and William.

When Magneto next battled the X-Men, it was as leader of the original BROTHERHOOD OF EVIL MUTANTS. The other members were Mastermind, the Toad, and Pietro and Wanda (QUICKSILVER and the SCARLET WITCH), who felt obligated to Magneto for saving them from a mob. Neither Magneto nor Wanda and Pietro realized that Magneto was their father.

After numerous clashes with the X-Men, Magneto tried to force a superhuman being known as the STRANGER to serve him. He little knew that the Stranger was actually an alien with seemingly limitless powers who captured Magneto and the Toad.

Weary of Magneto's crusade against humanity, Quicksilver and the Scarlet Witch quit the Brotherhood and soon joined the AVENGERS.

Magneto eventually escaped back to Earth from the Stranger's planet and resumed his war on humanity, battling the X-Men, Avengers, FANTASTIC FOUR, and DEFENDERS. He also formed several new versions of the Brotherhood.

Using his advanced knowledge of genetic engineering, Magneto created a being called Alpha the Ultimate Mutant. But Alpha turned against Magneto and devolved him into a powerless infant. Xavier turned the infant Magneto over to his colleague Dr. Moira MACTAGGERT, who began experiments to alter the baby's mind. Davan Shakari, an alien SHI'AR agent, later restored Magneto to his adult physical prime. Hence Magneto is physically much younger today than his contemporaries from the World War II period.

Magneto resumed his battles against the X-Men, until MacTaggert's tampering with his mind took effect and he became the X-Men's ally. During an extended absence from Earth by Xavier, Magneto even took over as headmaster of Xavier's school, mentoring the NEW MUTANTS. Around this time, Magneto, Quicksilver and the Scarlet Witch learned their true relationship.

THE TRUCE IS OVER

In time, Magneto's original personality re-emerged, and the UN ceded control of the mutant-populated island of Genosha to him. However, the island was devastated by Sentinels sent by Cassandra Nova. During a fit of madness, the Scarlet Witch used her powers to alter reality so that Magneto ruled the world. When she changed everything back, she deprived most mutants of their powers, including Magneto. The High Evolutionary later restored his powers.

Magneto joined Cyclops's X-Men on their island home Utopia, approving of their work. After Cyclops was arrested for crimes committed as Dark Phoenix, Magneto broke him out of prison and joined his mutant rebellion.

TB, MF

When Magneto joined the X-Men on Utopia, he changed to a white costume to signify that he had put his dark past behind him.

Magnum, Moses

FIRST APPEARANCE Giant-Size Spider-Man #4 (April 1975)
REAL NAME Moses Magnum
OCCUPATION Terrorist, arms merchant **BASE** Various
HEIGHT/WEIGHT Not known **EYES** Brown **HAIR** Black
SPECIAL POWERS/ABILITIES Moses Magnum can generate vibrational force, which he can use to bolster his own strength and durability or release outward to cause earthquakes.

Once a noted arms merchant, Moses Magnum's operation was dismantled by Spider-Man and the Punisher. Narrowly escaping death, Magnum was found by Apocalypse, who offered him power in exchange for help in fomenting chaos. Reconstructed by Apocalypse with the power to cause shifts within the Earth's crust, Magnum attempted to blackmail Japan but was foiled by the X-Men. Displeased, Apocalypse destabilized Magnum's abilities so that he could cause earthquakes simply by coming into contact with the Earth. Magnum tried to regain Apocalypse's favor through a show of power but was undone by the Avengers. Later, Daken hunted down and killed him. **TB, MF**

Once merely an arms merchant, Moses Magnum was transformed by Apocalypse into a world-shaking villain with command of the Earth itself.

Magnus

FIRST APPEARANCE Exiles #1 (August 2001)
REAL NAME Magnus Lensherr
OCCUPATION Adventurer **BASE** Mobile
HEIGHT 6 ft **WEIGHT** 177 lbs **EYES** Brown **HAIR** Brown
SPECIAL POWERS/ABILITIES Ability to manipulate magnetic fields, heat, radiation and radio waves; when makes skin-to-skin contact with other lifeforms, he transforms them into steel.

Born in an alternate reality, Magnus was the product of a union between Magneto and Rogue. Inheriting his father's powers of magnetism, Magnus was also born with a corrupted version of his mother's abilities—everything he touched turned to steel. Concerned about the harm he might cause, Magnus became something of a hermit, only to be coerced into joining the Exiles. In an attempt to free yet another version of Magneto from incarceration, Magnus sacrificed himself whilst containing the force of a nuclear explosion. **AD**

Magus

FIRST APPEARANCE New Mutants #18 (August 1984)
REAL NAME Magus **OCCUPATION** Monarch **BASE** Mobile
HEIGHT Variable **WEIGHT** Variable **EYES** Black
HAIR In true form he has no hair, but parts of his head resemble it.
SPECIAL POWERS/ABILITIES Able to grow to the size of a star and destroy it. Can exist in outer-space and change his shape to that of any being or machine. Can replenish his life energies.

The Magus is the leader of the planet Technarch, which is populated by sentient "techno-organic" beings, a species with an organic structure resembling metal. Each child of the Magus must face him in a battle to the death for his position. One son, Warlock, instead fled to Earth and joined the New Mutants. The Magus came after Warlock, but the X-Men defeated him and he went into hiding. Upon his return, the Magus attacked New York, and the Avengers drove him from Earth. Another, unrelated Magus was an evil version of Adam Warlock, from the future of Earth-7528. **MT, MF**

Major Domo

FIRST APPEARANCE Longshot #4 (December 1985)
REAL NAME Major Domo
OCCUPATION Principal aide to Mojo
BASE Mojoworld
HEIGHT/WEIGHT Not known **EYES** Blue **HAIR** Gray
SPECIAL POWERS/ABILITIES Constantly monitors Mojoworld's markets, enabling ongoing evaluation of his master's businesses.

The sycophantic yet contemptuous aide to Mojo, the ruler of Mojoworld, Major Domo's job is to ensure the smooth running of his master's household. An android, Major Domo provides information on and analysis of Mojo's businesses, while at the same time soothing his paranoid ego. These abilities make him Mojo's most prized servant. Although treated as nothing more than a glorified toaster, Major Domo remains at Mojo's side, playing a key role in curbing the worst excesses of his master's personality. Despite finding Mojo repulsive, Major Domo's position gives him almost unparalleled influence over Mojoworld. Not bad for a mere android. **AD**

Malus, Dr. Karl

FIRST APPEARANCE Spider-Woman #30 (September 1980)
REAL NAME Dr. Karl Malus
OCCUPATION Former surgeon, now criminal scientist
BASE Los Angeles, California
HEIGHT 5 ft 9 in **WEIGHT** 155 lbs **EYES** Brown **HAIR** Black
SPECIAL POWERS/ABILITIES Advanced knowledge of genetic engineering, expertise in biochemistry, radiology, and surgery.

Fascinated with superhuman beings, scientist Karl Malus became involved with the criminal underworld to obtain funding for his research. Malus attempted to capture the original Spider-Woman. He restored the superhuman strength of Eric Josten (now known as Atlas) and enabled him to grow to gigantic size. Working for the Power Broker, Malus gave many clients superhuman strength. He became the head of the criminal organization called the Corporation and later temporarily became the host for the Carnage symbiote. **PS, MF**

MAN-APE

FIRST APPEARANCE Avengers #62 (March 1969)
REAL NAME M'Baku
OCCUPATION Mercenary, renegade **BASE** Mobile
HEIGHT 7 ft **WEIGHT** 355 lbs **EYES** Brown **HAIR** Brown
SPECIAL POWERS/ABILITIES Possesses superhuman strength, agility, and resistance to injury. He is a powerful fighter whose combat ability is based on that of gorillas.

Clad in the pelt of the rare Wakandan white gorilla, M'Baku the Man-Ape takes up a battle position at the head of a band of his followers in the White Gorilla cult.

While T'Challa—the Black Panther and king of the African nation of Wakanda—was away helping the Avengers in the US, M'Baku schemed to seize his throne. Reviving the outlawed White Gorilla cult, M'Baku killed a rare white gorilla, then bathed in its blood and ate its flesh, which gave him the power of the ape. Calling himself Man-Ape, he battled Black Panther and the Avengers' teammates, both in Wakanda and in the US. Defeated, he teamed with the Grim Reaper—despite the Reaper's racism—to form a new Lethal Legion. He was later slain by the vampire Morlun. **MT, MF**

MANCHA, VICTOR

FIRST APPEARANCE Runaways #1 (April 2005)
REAL NAME Victor Mancha **OCCUPATION** Adventurer
BASE New York City
HEIGHT 5 ft 8 in **WEIGHT** 220 lbs
EYES Brown **HAIR** Brown
SPECIAL POWERS/ABILITIES Victor is a cyborg who can control electromagnetic energy.

When a woman helped one of Ultron's spare bodies return to health, he gave her what she wanted most: a son. That boy, Victor, was a cyborg built with samples of his mother's DNA and appeared to be a teenager even though he was only a few years old. Unaware of his origins, Victor joined teenage heroes the Runaways while he was a student at East Angeles High School. When Ultron revealed himself, he killed Victor's mother and triggered a switch in the boy that put him under Ultron's control. Victor overrode his programming, rejecting Ultron. **MF**

MAN-BEAST

Created by scientific accident, the Man-Beast was born when a wolf was placed inside the High Evolutionary's genetic accelerator. Despite creating an entire evil army using the same device, the Man-Beast was eventually defeated by Thor, placed in a shuttle, and exiled into space.

The Man-Beast sought revenge on the High Evolutionary when he landed on Counter-Earth—a world created by that being. There, he introduced the people of Counter-Earth to the concept of evil and even attempted to destroy the planet altogether. In the years since, the Man-Beast has gone into battle several more times, fighting both Adam Warlock and the Hulk. When he attempted to raise a second army, using the Legion of Light religious cult as a front, the Man-Beast went head-to-head with Spider-Man. Later, with help from Quicksilver, the High Evolutionary captured the Man-Beast and devolved him back into a wolf. **AD, MF**

Despite his great strength and mental agility, the Man-Beast was no match for the mighty Thor.

YOUR HAMMER WILL NEVER STRIKE ME!
I AM ABOUT TO DISINTEGRATE IT—WITH ONE SIMPLE ELEMENTARY MIND BLAST—!

During confrontations, the Man-Beast could employ his mental powers as a weapon.

FACTFILE
REAL NAME
Man-Beast
OCCUPATION
Would-be world conqueror
BASE
Somewhere below New York City

HEIGHT 6 ft 10 in
WEIGHT 320 lbs
EYES Red
HAIR Brown

FIRST APPEARANCE
Thor #134 (November 1966)

MAN-BEAST

POWERS
Superhuman strength, speed, endurance, and senses; remarkable scientific ability, particularly in genetics and engineering.

MANDRILL

Jerome Beechman's parents worked at the atomic testing grounds in New Mexico, where exposure to radiation caused mutations in their son. Jerome was born with animal-like fur on his body and an apelike appearance. When he was ten, his parents abandoned him in the desert. There he met Nekra Sinclair, whose mother had worked at the atomic testing grounds. Jerome took the name Mandrill, and the two traveled the American Southwest together, avoiding all human contact. Mandrill and Nekra formed Black Spectre, an organization of black women hoping to overthrow the American government—until Daredevil stopped them. After SHIELD captured Nekra, Mandrill formed Fem-Force, an army of radical women under his control. Fem-Force teamed up with Magneto's Mutant Force, but the Defenders stopped their plans. Mandrill's powers survived M-Day, and he has recently been seen working for the Hood in New York. **MT, MF**

FACTFILE
REAL NAME
Jerome Beechman
OCCUPATION
Professional criminal
BASE
Mobile

HEIGHT 6 ft
WEIGHT 270 lbs
EYES Black
HAIR Brown

FIRST APPEARANCE
Shanna the She-Devil #4 (June 1973)

MANDRILL

POWERS
Mandrill has the ability to emit powerful pheromones which give him the power to attract and enslave adult women causing them to submit to his will.

MANDARIN, ***see page 228***

MANDARIN

Evil master of the ten rings

MANDARIN

FACTFILE

REAL NAME
Unrevealed

OCCUPATION
Criminal mastermind

BASE
The Palace of the Star Dragon in the Valley of Spirits within China

HEIGHT 6 ft 2 in
WEIGHT 215 lbs
EYES Blue-black
HAIR Black

FIRST APPEARANCE
Tales of Suspense #50 (1964)

POWERS

One of the world's greatest scientific minds and a superb athlete. Possesses ten rings of extraterrestrial origin that have amazing powers.

A direct descendant of Genghis Khan, the Mandarin was born in China to a wealthy father who lost everything in the Communist revolution. In the forbidden Valley of Spirits, the Mandarin found a crashed starship containing ten alien rings. These rings could control another's mind, rearrange matter, fire a disintegration beam, create a vortex, produce deadly gases, create ice blasts, or discharge electricity, flames, bursts of blinding light, or clouds of darkness. With the rings, the Mandarin conquered the valley and made plans to seize control of the world, often clashing with IRON MAN and the AVENGERS.

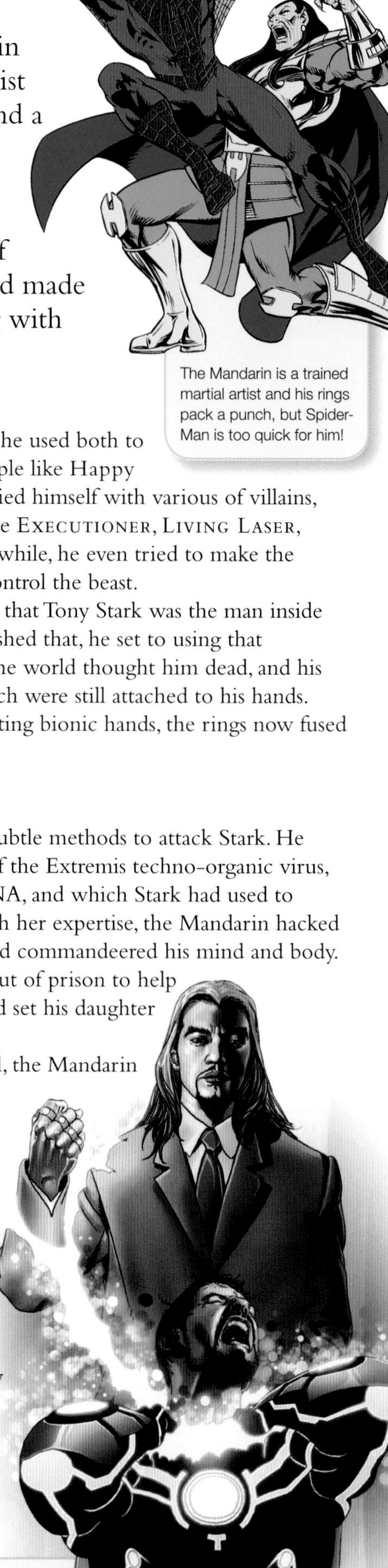

The Mandarin is a trained martial artist and his rings pack a punch, but Spider-Man is too quick for him!

A WORLD POWER

The Mandarin developed teleportation technology, which he used both to get himself into and out of trouble but also to kidnap people like Happy HOGAN. Achieving insufficient success on his own, he allied himself with various of villains, including DOCTOR DOOM, the ENCHANTRESS and the EXECUTIONER, LIVING LASER, Power Man (ATLAS), and SWORDSMAN. For a while, he even tried to make the HULK his accomplice, but he could not control the beast.

The Mandarin worked hard to discover that Tony Stark was the man inside the Iron Man armor, and once he established that, he set to using that information against Stark. For a while, the world thought him dead, and his son TEMUGIN inherited his rings—which were still attached to his hands. The Mandarin returned however, sporting bionic hands, the rings now fused to his spine.

A NEW APPROACH

The Mandarin began to use more subtle methods to attack Stark. He kidnapped Maya Hansen, creator of the Extremis techno-organic virus, which could rewrite the user's DNA, and which Stark had used to improve his Iron Man armor. With her expertise, the Mandarin hacked into the Extremis inside Stark and commandeered his mind and body. He also broke Ezekiel STANE out of prison to help in his quest to destroy Stark, and set his daughter Sasha HAMMER against Stark.

With Stark under his control, the Mandarin forced him to create Titanomech bodies for the alien spirits contained inside his rings. While trapped in the Mandarin's employ, Stark convinced the villain's allies that the man was insane and persuaded them to help him rebel.

Stark's latest company, Resilient, managed to reactivate a clean copy of the Extremis technology inside of him, and Stark and his allies brought the Mandarin and his Titanomech down. Ezekiel shot him through the head soon after. **TD, MF**

Since the Mandarin believes he can use technology to achieve world domination, he often ends up in conflict with Iron Man.

MAN-THING

All who fear burn at the Man-Thing's touch!

Unflappable insurance claims adjustor Nathan Mehr comes face to face with the shambling, monstrous Man-Thing.

Ted Sallis was a research scientist on a project aiming to replicate the Super-Soldier formula that empowered CAPTAIN AMERICA in the 1940s. But he was betrayed to the sinister criminal think-tank known as AIM, who wanted his research. Fearing that his work would fall into evil hands, Sallis destroyed his notes and injected himself with the only sample of his serum. But while fleeing for his life, he crashed his car in the swampland surrounding his laboratory, and was seemingly killed.

TRANSFORMATION

Unknown to Sallis, the area in which he'd located his lab was close to the Nexus of All Realities, a mystical gateway that linked all of the myriad dimensions of existence. In some mysterious fashion, Sallis's serum combined with the ambient mystical energies of the Nexus, and caused the vegetation of the swamp that surrounded his almost lifeless body to reconstitute him as a mindless, shambling mass—the Man-Thing.

FEELING THE BURN

Possessing scant intellect of his own, the Man-Thing is instead empathetically attuned to his surroundings. While Ted Sallis's soul still resides within the great beast, in general the Man-Thing is mindless, reacting only to the emotions of those around him. Fear causes the Man-Thing great pain, and he will journey forth from his swampy home to put an end to any source of fear that causes him distress. Because of a quirk of chemistry in his make-up, any creature who feels fear in the Man-Thing's presence burns at his touch.

The Man-Thing seldom leaves the confines of his swamp, but he can occasionally be drawn forth by strong emotions, which affect him painfully through his animalistic empathy.

ESSENTIAL STORYLINES

- ***Adventures Into Fear #17–19*** and ***Man-Thing #1*** The Man-Thing and a ragtag band of allies including Dakimh the Sorcerer, Jennifer Kale, Korrek the Barbarian and Howard the Duck defend the Nexus of All Realities from Thog the Netherspawn.
- ***Giant-Size Man-Thing #4*** The Man-Thing is drawn to the pain experienced by an angst-ridden high-school student.

MAN-THING

FACTFILE

REAL NAME
Ted Sallis

OCCUPATION
Guardian of the Nexus of All Realities

BASE
Swamp in the Florida Everglades that conceals the Nexus of All Realities

HEIGHT Around 7 ft
WEIGHT Around 500 lbs
EYES Red, bulbous
HAIR None

FIRST APPEARANCE
Savage Tales #1 (May 1971)

POWERS

Virtually indestructible, he has superhuman strength. Fear causes him pain, and changes his chemical makeup so that the touch of his body burns those who feel fear in his presence.

Man-Thing guards the Nexus of All Realities, an interdimensional gateway at the center of his swamp.

IN THE WORLD

During the DARK REIGN, ARES captured the Man-Thing, although he soon after showed up living under Manhattan with the LEGION OF MONSTERS. Later, Hank PYM studied him while he was imprisoned in the Raft and figured out a way to use the creature's connection to the Nexus to teleport Luke CAGE's team of THUNDERBOLTS all around the world. After serving with the THUNDERBOLTS, Man-Thing returned to his Florida swamp. **TB, MF**

MANIFOLD

FIRST APPEARANCE Secret Warriors #4 (July 2009)
REAL NAME Eden Fesi **OCCUPATION** Adventurer
BASE Australia
HEIGHT 5 ft 10 in **WEIGHT** 175 lbs
EYES Brown **HAIR** Black
SPECIAL POWERS/ABILITIES Eden can teleport many people any distance within his own universe.

An indigenous Australian, Eden studied under his mentor GATEWAY, who had powers similar to his. Nick FURY recruited the young man for his SECRET WARRIORS, with Gateway's blessing. During a battle with HYDRA, he was injured and fell into a coma. He recovered, and during the conflict between the AVENGERS and the X-MEN over the approaching Phoenix Force, the Avengers recruited him to their side. Eden played a crucial role in getting them where they needed to be as fast as possible. **MF**

MANSLAUGHTER

FIRST APPEARANCE Defenders #133 (July 1984)
REAL NAME Not known
OCCUPATION Former hired assassin **BASE** Mobile
HEIGHT 5 ft 7 in **WEIGHT** 115 lbs **EYES** Blue **HAIR** Red
SPECIAL POWERS/ABILITIES Low-level telepath: influences peripheral vision and subliminal hearing of others in order to render himself invisible; uses abilities to enhance skills as a huntsman.

Manslaughter used his mutant powers for tracking and hunting. He impressed the ETERNAL known as the INTERLOPER by successfully tracking him down in the Siberian wastelands. The Interloper agreed to help Manslaughter hone his powers but did not train him fully. This was just as well, for Manslaughter later became a ruthless assassin. Eventually he redeemed himself, sacrificing his life in the effort to destroy the DRAGON OF THE MOON. He has since returned to life. **AD, MF**

MAN-WOLF

FIRST APPEARANCE (as Man-Wolf) The Amazing Spider-Man #124 (September 1973) **REAL NAME** John Jameson
OCCUPATION Former astronaut, pilot, security chief
BASE New York City
HEIGHT 6 ft 6 in **WEIGHT** 350 lbs **EYES** Red **HAIR** White
SPECIAL POWERS/ABILITIES As Man-Wolf: superhuman strength, speed, agility, durability, and heightened senses.

Astronaut and son of *Daily Bugle* publisher J. Jonah JAMESON, John Jameson discovered a gem on the Moon. On Earth, this gem caused him to transform into a wolflike creature under a full moon. The Moongem contained the essence of Stargod, ruler of Other-Realm, in another dimension. Man-Wolf journeyed to Other-Realm, where he helped its people defeat their enemy Arisen Tyrk. John underwent radiation treatment, which destroyed the Moongem. He married SHE-HULK and then became Stargod and left for space. After he returned, they annulled their marriage, and he returned to being an astronaut. **PS, MF**

MANTIS

FACTFILE
REAL NAME
Unknown
OCCUPATION
Adventurer
BASE
Temple of the Priests, Pama, Vietnam; Ho Chi Minh City, Vietnam; Avengers Mansion, New York City

HEIGHT 5 ft 6 in
WEIGHT 115 lbs
EYES Green
HAIR Black

FIRST APPEARANCE
Avengers #112 (June 1973)

POWERS
Mantis has superior agility, extraordinary martial arts skill, and the ability to sense the emotions of others. She can also will herself to heal quickly after injury.

Born in Vietnam, Mantis was raised by the Priests of Pama, a pacifist sect of the alien KREE. When Mantis had completed her martial arts training, the priests sent her to live among humans, implanting false memories of life as an orphan struggling for survival on the streets of Ho Chi Minh City. She eventually teamed up with the SWORDSMAN, a costumed criminal, whom Mantis helped rehabilitate. When the Swordsman joined the AVENGERS, Mantis went with him and was also made a member of the team.

After her marriage to the eldest Cotati, an alien race of telepathic plant-beings, Mantis transformed into pure energy and left Earth. She gave birth to a son named Quoi, and joined the SILVER SURFER for a while, but was caught in an explosion that split her into several independent aspects. Once she managed to reintegrate herself, she battled THANOS to protect her son from him. After surviving the ANNIHILATION events, she joined the modern GUARDIANS OF THE GALAXY. **MT, MF**

Mantis is caught in the clutches of Thanos, an Eternal who augmented his superhuman abilities to become the most powerful of the Eternals.

Giant-Size Avengers #4 features Vision and Scarlet Witch's wedding, and Mantis's transformation and departure from Earth.

MARAUDERS

FACTFILE

MEMBERS

MR. SINISTER Telepathy.

MALICE Telepathy.

VERTIGO Affects equilibrium.

ARCLIGHT Seismic shocks from hands.

HARPOON Bio-energetic projectiles.

RIPTIDE A mutant whirlwind.

BLOCKBUSTER Super-strong.

PRISM Captures powers then projects back at source.

SABRETOOTH Adamantium skeleton; supersenses.

SCALPHUNTER Manipulates mechanical components.

SCRAMBLER Disrupts living and mechanical systems.

FIRST APPEARANCE

Uncanny X-Men #210 (October 1986)

Marauders

The personal army of mutant eugeneticist, Mister Sinister, the Marauders are one of the most effective forces the X-Men have ever faced. Mister Sinister particularly loathed the Morlocks, so the Marauders' first mission was to obliterate them. They have since gone head-to-head with the X-Men, even destroying the Xavier Institute. Sinister has created clones of each of the original Marauders, and if one falls, a duplicate replaces them. The Marauders—along with the Acolytes and four X-Men: Gambit, Lady Mastermind, Mystique, and Sunfire—helped Sinister try to track down Hope Summers. Many of them were killed, and a group of clones were activated, but X-Force killed them too. Karma's half-sister Susan Hatchi later gathered another group of her own. **AD, MF**

THE MARAUDERS
1 Scrambler ***2*** Sabretooth
3 Malice ***4*** Scalphunter
5 Vertigo ***6*** Harpoon
7 Riptide

Marrow

She is a young mutant who left her normal life behind to journey into the sewers controlled by the mysterious Morlocks. Marrow was one of the few survivors of the Mutant Massacre, which decimated the Morlocks' ranks. Escaping to the dimension ruled by Mikhail Rasputin, Marrow became a member of Gene Nation, a radical mutant group dedicated to striking back at their human oppressors.

After a number of encounters with the X-Men, Marrow came to join with them in common cause. However, her fiery personality and natural savagery meant that she never fitted in at Xavier's School and she left under mysterious circumstances.

She was recruited by the newly-reformed Weapon X program, which boosted her powers so as to allow her to control her appearance. She lost her powers on M-Day but joined the X-Cell terrorists. **PS, MF**

MARROW

FACTFILE

REAL NAME
Sarah; last name may be Rushman

OCCUPATION
Genetic terrorist, adventurer

BASE
Various

HEIGHT 6 ft
WEIGHT Unknown
EYES Green
HAIR Magenta

FIRST APPEARANCE
Uncanny X-Men #325 (October 1995)

POWERS

Marrow's mutant physiognomy allows her to rapidly regrow the bone spurs that protrude from her body, and which she uses as weapons. She also has two hearts and enhanced durability, making her difficult to kill.

Marrina

FIRST APPEARANCE Alpha Flight #1 (August 1983)
REAL NAME Marrina Smallwood
OCCUPATION Adventurer **BASE** Mobile
HEIGHT 6 ft **WEIGHT** 200 lbs **EYES** Black **HAIR** Green
SPECIAL POWERS/ABILITIES Enhanced strength and stamina; able to breathe both air and water; can swim at high speed and generate waterspouts.

The Plodex alien life form who became known as Marrina hatched from an egg that had soaked in the Atlantic Ocean, giving her aquatic adaptations that surfaced when she assumed the humanoid forms of her adoptive guardians, the Smallwoods. Her superhuman abilities allowed her to join Alpha Flight, and she later married Namor the Sub-Mariner. Tragedy struck when, during her pregnancy, she turned into a monstrous leviathan. Namor was forced to kill her, but she returned during the Chaos War and now works with Alpha Flight once more. **DW, MF**

Marvel Boy

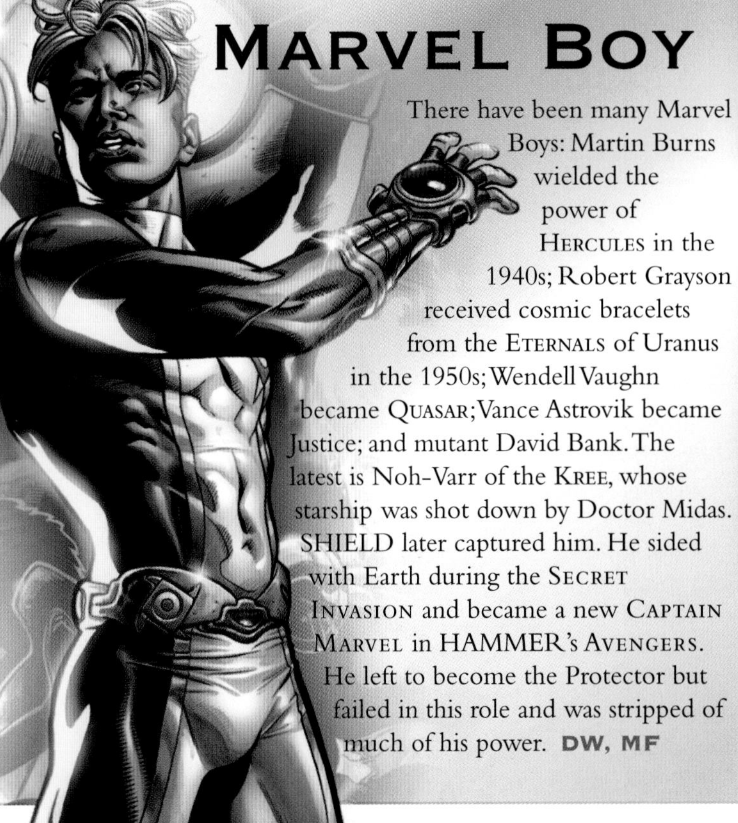

There have been many Marvel Boys: Martin Burns wielded the power of Hercules in the 1940s; Robert Grayson received cosmic bracelets from the Eternals of Uranus in the 1950s; Wendell Vaughn became Quasar; Vance Astrovik became Justice; and mutant David Bank. The latest is Noh-Varr of the Kree, whose starship was shot down by Doctor Midas. SHIELD later captured him. He sided with Earth during the Secret Invasion and became a new Captain Marvel in HAMMER's Avengers. He left to become the Protector but failed in this role and was stripped of much of his power. **DW, MF**

MARVEL BOY

FACTFILE

REAL NAME
Noh-Varr

OCCUPATION
Would-be conqueror

BASE
New York City

HEIGHT 5 ft 10 in
WEIGHT 165 lbs
EYES Black
HAIR White

FIRST APPEARANCE
Marvel Boy #1 (September 2000)

POWERS

Enhanced strength, speed, and stamina; can mentally control his body's growth; nanobots reroute pain sensations.

Master of the World

FIRST APPEARANCE Alpha Flight #2 (September 1983)
REAL NAME Eshu **OCCUPATION** Conqueror
BASE Mobile
HEIGHT 6 ft 4 in **WEIGHT** 270 lbs
EYES Green **HAIR** Black
SPECIAL POWERS/ABILITIES Eshu has superhuman endurance, healing, and strength and can mentally control his living starship.

Eshu was a simple hunter over 4,000 years ago—before an alien ship from the Plodex captured him. He somehow took control of it. He has since plotted to take over the world, often starting with Canada, which put him into conflict with ALPHA FLIGHT. He even led the Unity political party there. He defended the world from KANG, if only so he could have it. Warbird (*see* CAPTAIN MARVEL) eventually killed him. **MF**

Master Order

FIRST APPEARANCE Marvel Two-in-One Annual #2 (December 1977)
REAL NAME None **OCCUPATION** Cosmic entity
BASE Everywhere
HEIGHT/WEIGHT/EYES/HAIR Unknown
SPECIAL POWERS/ABILITIES Scope of powers is unknown although can change destinies of specific individuals.

DEATH, LORD CHAOS, ETERNITY, and Master Order—enigmatic beings all, each embodying a distinct abstract concept. Their origins are unknown and so are their powers, although many surmise that these are without limit. The "brother" of Lord Chaos, Master Order strives to maintain a cosmic balance with his sibling, intervening in mortal affairs on the rarest of occasions. Following the defeat of the would-be universe-destroyer, THANOS, Chaos and Order implied that they were responsible for manipulating SPIDER-MAN's destiny to ensure his intervention in the crisis at a critical moment. No one knows if this is truly the case. **AD**

Master Pandemonium

FIRST APPEARANCE West Coast Avengers #4 (January 1986)
REAL NAME Martin Preston **OCCUPATION** Demon commander
BASE Los Angeles, California
HEIGHT 6 ft 1 in **WEIGHT** 205 lbs **EYES** Blue **HAIR** Black
SPECIAL POWERS/ABILITIES Amulet of Azmodeus permits inter-dimensional teleportation. Can detach his own arms as living demons, fire energy beams from his hands, levitate, and breathe fire.

After making a deal with MEPHISTO, Martin Preston became a monstrous being with a star-shaped hole in his chest for the fragments of his missing soul. As Master Pandemonium, he identified the SCARLET WITCH's twins as having two of the fragments. When all five were found, Mephisto captured him. Preston escaped, and WICCAN and SPEED later found him but decided he was now harmless. He later taught at the Hellfire Academy. **DW, MF**

Master Khan

FIRST APPEARANCE Strange Tales #77 (October 1960)
REAL NAME Khan **OCCUPATION** God to the people of K'un-Lun **BASE** K'un-Lun, New York City
HEIGHT Unknown **WEIGHT** Unknown **EYES** Red **HAIR** Black
SPECIAL POWERS/ABILITIES Magical powers allow him to distort reality, levitate and shrink objects, alter his appearance, form energy shields, fire energy blasts, and cast mystic spells.

HA
HA

The human sorcerer Master Khan was worshiped as a god on the alien planet of K'un-Lun, where the dominant life form is a sentient plant called the H'ylthri. He served as the protector of the inhabitants of K'un-Lun, and his power came from their worship. On Earth, Khan was a scholar but also a student of the occult. Once on K'un-Lun, Master Khan became a mortal enemy of IRON FIST. Returning to Earth, Khan fought with WOLVERINE, NAMOR, and NAMORITA. He once captured Namor and posed as him, but the Atlantean prince broke free and killed him. **MT, MF**

Masters, Alicia

As a child, Alicia Masters was blinded in the same accident that killed her father, but she discovered that despite her handicap she had a talent for sculpting. The man responsible for the accident, Phillip Masters (PUPPET MASTER), married her mother and adopted Alicia. When her stepfather clashed with the FANTASTIC FOUR, the THING rescued Alicia, who was but a pawn in Phillip Masters' scheme. A strong relationship developed between Alicia and the Thing. Perhaps her greatest moment was when she appealed to the humanity buried deep within the sky-spanning SILVER SURFER and convinced him to rebel against his master, the world-devouring GALACTUS, in defense of Earth. For a while, she broke up with the Thing and dated the Surfer, but she later returned to him. At one point, the SKRULL agent LYJA THE LAZERFIST replaced her and married the HUMAN TORCH. Alicia later designed the memorial for CAPTAIN AMERICA. **TB, MF**

ALICIA MASTERS

FACTFILE
REAL NAME
Alicia Reiss Masters
OCCUPATION
Sculptress
BASE
Manhattan

HEIGHT Not known
WEIGHT Not known
EYES Blue
HAIR Blond

FIRST APPEARANCE
Fantastic Four #8 (November 1962)

POWERS
A talented sculptress despite her blindness; able to see the good in people despite their appearance.

My Sincere Affection to you all
Alicia

Despite her blindness, Alicia Masters is a world-renowned sculptress who practices her art through touch.

Alicia had a powerful effect on the deep-buried emotions of the Silver Surfer. She convinced him to rebel against his master, the world-devouring Galactus, and fight for Earth by appealing to his inner goodness.

Masters of Evil

A villainous alliance against the Avengers

Believing that there's strength in numbers, the original Baron Zemo forms a sinister super-team equal in power to the mighty Avengers.

The Masters of Evil are perennial foes of the AVENGERS, assembling multiple times over the years, often with no link between the various groupings other than their name. The first Masters of Evil came about through the efforts of Nazi mastermind BARON ZEMO.

DECADES OF VILLAINY

Zemo schemed to defeat his wartime nemesis CAPTAIN AMERICA by enlisting the most notorious enemies of Captain America's comrades in the Avengers. He gathered the Melter to fight IRON MAN, the RADIOACTIVE MAN to fight THOR, and the BLACK KNIGHT to battle both the WASP and Giant Man (Henry PYM). Later, Zemo welcomed the ENCHANTRESS and the EXECUTIONER into the Masters of Evil. The team disbanded after Zemo's death.

A second Masters of Evil took its place, founded by the robot ULTRON, in his cover identity as the CRIMSON COWL. The team obtained blueprints of Avengers' Mansion from butler Edwin JARVIS and struck at the Avengers in their own home. The new Black Knight, Dane Whitman, turned on his teammates in the Masters of Evil and helped the Avengers scatter the villains.

CHARACTER KEY
1 Flying Tiger
2 Cyclone
3 Klaw
4 Man-Killer
5 Tiger Shark

The criminal mastermind EGGHEAD organized a third Masters of Evil, hoping to take vengeance on Henry Pym but met defeat (and death) soon after. Helmut Zemo, son of the original Baron Zemo, brought together the fourth incarnation of the Masters.

THE DARKEST HOUR

Baron Zemo II gathered more than a dozen criminals to crush the Avengers through force of numbers. Their most infamous exploit was the siege of Avengers' Mansion.

DOCTOR OCTOPUS assembled a fifth Masters of Evil and fought the GUARDIANS OF THE GALAXY. Baron Zemo II returned to organize a sixth team, the THUNDERBOLTS, who masqueraded as heroes—and later became heroes for real.

Justine Hammer, the new Crimson Cowl, assembled the seventh and eighth versions of the team, which included a staggering 25 members. Max Fury—a twisted, android version of Nick FURY—led the ninth team for the SHADOW COUNCIL. **DW, MF**

ESSENTIAL STORYLINES

- ***Avengers #6*** Baron Zemo assembles the first Masters of Evil, featuring a villainous counterpart for each member of the Avengers.
- ***Avengers #270-277*** The Masters of Evil raid their enemies' headquarters in the classic storyline "The Siege of Avengers Mansion."
- ***Thunderbolts #24-25*** The most recent grouping of the Masters of Evil unites 25 Super Villains, providing a formidable foe for the Thunderbolts.
- ***Guardians of the Galaxy #28–29*** Doctor Octopus' Masters of Evil team clash with the Guardians of the Galaxy.

FACTFILE

ORIGINAL MEMBERS AND POWERS

BARON ZEMO Extended longevity, brilliant criminal mind.

MELTER Could melt any metal with a molecular beam.

RADIOACTIVE MAN Can release blasts of lethal radioactive energy.

BLACK KNIGHT (Nathan Garrett) Skilled combatant; carried power lance.

EXECUTIONER Enhanced strength, carried enchanted axe.

ENCHANTRESS Sorceress

FIRST APPEARANCE

Avengers #6 (July 1964)

CHARACTER KEY
1 Black Knight
2 Melter
3 Radioactive Man

MAXIMUS

FACTFILE
REAL NAME
Maximus
OCCUPATION
Would-be conqueror
BASE
City of Attilan in the Blue Area of the Moon

HEIGHT 5 ft 11 in
WEIGHT 180 lbs
EYES Blue
HAIR Black

FIRST APPEARANCE
Fantastic Four #47 (February 1966)

POWERS
Maximus possesses a genius-level intellect unhampered by sanity, and possesses the ability to overwhelm the thought-processes of those in close proximity, taking over their conscious minds.

MAXIMUS

The younger brother of BLACK BOLT, king of the INHUMANS, Maximus exhibited no outward signs of change after his exposure to the gene-altering Terrigen Mists. Instead, as he grew, he chose to hide his growing psionic powers along with his lust for power.

As adolescents, BLACK BOLT caught Maximus forging an alliance with the KREE, the aliens responsible for the creation of the INHUMANS. Black Bolt's sonic scream destroyed the Kree warship and also shattered Maximus' grip on sanity. Maximus the Mad then devoted himself to wresting control of his people from his noble brother. He succeeded several times over the years, but Black Bolt always managed to retake the throne from him. During the SECRET INVASION, the two finally ended their quarrel while facing a common foe. Maximus has been loyal to the Inhumans and the royal family ever since. **AD, MF**

Black Bolt is Maximus' older brother. Since just a whisper from his voice can trigger sonic shockwaves, Black Bolt remains silent most of the time.

THE DEED IS DONE, BLACK BOLT! BY NOW, ALL HUMAN LIFE ON EARTH HAS BEEN ENDED! ONLY WE INHUMANS REMAIN! THE ENTIRE PLANET IS OURS, MY SPEECHLESS BROTHER!

Despite his boast, Maximus' attempt to destroy humanity failed utterly.

MAYHEM

FIRST APPEARANCE Cloak and Dagger #1 (October 1983)
REAL NAME Brigid O'Reilly
OCCUPATION Former policewoman, vigilante
BASE New York City **HEIGHT** 5 ft 4 in
WEIGHT 120 lbs **EYES** Green **HAIR** Green
SPECIAL POWERS/ABILITIES Skin constantly secretes a poisonous gas; this can cause paralysis if it gets in bloodstream and can serve as truth drug; Mayhem is also able to fly.

As a New York police detective, Brigid O'Reilly confronted the vigilante partnership CLOAK AND DAGGER. Feeling that their approach endangered innocent lives, Brigid was initially hostile to them, but became more tolerant when she learned of their origins. Following a confrontation with several corrupt police officers while she was investigating a drug-smuggling operation, Brigid was killed by poisonous gas. However, the intervention of Cloak and Dagger led to her resurrection as a superpowered individual, enabling her to exact revenge. Since then, Brigid has adopted the alias Mayhem and become a vigilante, targeting New York drug pushers. **AD**

The poisonous gas produced by Mayhem's body is used in her fight against crime.

MEDUSA

A member of the INHUMANS' royal family on Attilan, Medusa was exposed to Terrigen Mist as a baby. She gained the ability to use her hair like extra limbs. She learned to interpret BLACK BOLT's body language and fell in love with him. When MAXIMUS seized power from Black Bolt, Medusa left Attilan and suffered amnesia due to a plane crash. The WIZARD found her and made her part of the FRIGHTFUL FOUR. When Black Bolt retook his throne, Medusa returned to act as his interpreter and later married him. They had a son, Ahura, who suffers from his uncle Maximus' madness. To forge an alliance with the Universal Inhumans, Black Bolt has now had to take five wives, one from each faction. As only a part-time queen, Medusa also substituted with the FANTASTIC FOUR when she could. **MT, MF**

MEDUSA

FACTFILE
REAL NAME
Medusalith Amaquelin
OCCUPATION
Royal interpreter
BASE
Attilan, Blue Area, Earth's Moon

HEIGHT 5 ft 11 in
WEIGHT 130 lbs
EYES Green
HAIR Red

FIRST APPEARANCE
Fantastic Four #36 (March 1965)

POWERS
Can use her 6-ft-long hair to attack, lift weights, pick locks, as a whip, or a rope.

Medusa uses her long hair to tangle up the amazing Spider-Man in a different kind of web.

MEGGAN

FACTFILE
REAL NAME
Meggan
OCCUPATION
Adventurer
BASE
England

HEIGHT Variable
WEIGHT Variable
EYES Variable
HAIR Variable

FIRST APPEARANCE
Mighty World of Marvel #7 (December 1983)

POWERS
Meggan is a shapeshifter whose forms are influenced by the emotions of others; she can fly and project energy blasts drawn from the Earth.

MEGGAN

Born to gypsies, Meggan grew up in a fur-covered form and considered herself a freak. Only later, after being taken in by Brian Braddock (CAPTAIN BRITAIN), did she discover that she could consciously alter her appearance. She transformed herself from her furry form into a strikingly beautiful woman with long, golden hair. Not long after this, Meggan and Braddock started a relationship and founded the superteam EXCALIBUR, and the two eventually married. As Captain Britain's wife, Meggan is the queen of Otherworld, assisting in the management of the dimensional realities that make up the Omniverse. She sacrificed herself to save her husband and the rest of Excalibur, but later returned to the living. **DW, MF**

MENTALLO

FIRST APPEARANCE Strange Tales #141 (February 1966)
REAL NAME Marvin Flumm **OCCUPATION** Professional criminal
BASE Mobile **HEIGHT** 5 ft 10 in
WEIGHT 175 lbs **EYES** Brown **HAIR** Brown
SPECIAL POWERS/ABILITIES Possesses telepathic powers. Can read the thoughts of anyone within five miles, locate a particular brain pattern and project his own thoughts into the minds of others.

Marvin Flumm went to work for SHIELD while his powers developed. Calling himself Mentallo, he stole a battlesuit and telepathy-enhancing equipment and teamed with the FIXER to try to take over SHIELD, but Nick FURY stopped them. Flumm called himself Think Tank when he first faced CAPTAIN AMERICA, but soon returned to the codename Mentallo. He tangled with the HULK, the AVENGERS, PROFESSOR X, and the FANTASTIC FOUR, among others. He retained his powers after M-Day and joined the HOOD's criminal crew. He also worked with AIM. **MT, MF**

MELTDOWN

FACTFILE
REAL NAME
Tabitha Smith
OCCUPATION
Adventurer
BASE
New York State

HEIGHT 5 ft 5 in
WEIGHT 120 lbs
EYES Blue
HAIR Blond

FIRST APPEARANCE
Secret Wars II #5 (November 1985)

POWERS
Generates and throws "time bombs"—energy balls of concussive force. She can to vary the size and power of her time bombs at will.

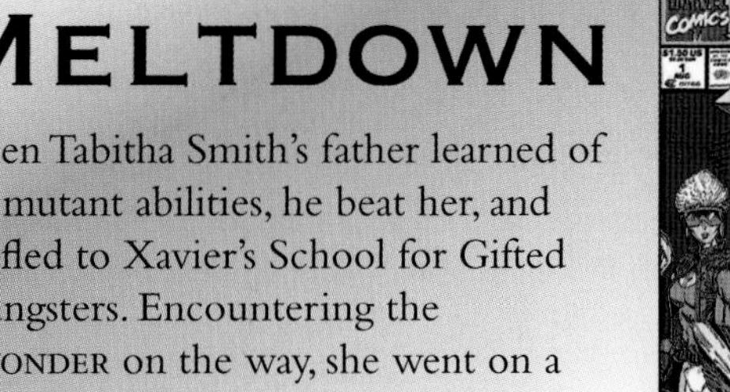

MELTDOWN

When Tabitha Smith's father learned of her mutant abilities, he beat her, and she fled to Xavier's School for Gifted Youngsters. Encountering the BEYONDER on the way, she went on a series of cosmic adventures before falling in with the VANISHER's gang of thieves, the Fallen Angels. She oscillated between X-FACTOR and the Fallen Angels before becoming a member of the NEW MUTANTS.

A founding member of X-Force, in the early days Meltdown was known as Boom-Boom.

She later joined X-FORCE as Boom Boom and became a protégée to CABLE, helping him attack the WEAPON X facility and the Neverland mutant concentration camp. After that, she joined the new team NEXTWAVE and put an end to the terrorist organization SILENT. She retained her powers after M-Day and joined the X-Men when they moved to San Franscisco. The Leper Queen—the leader of the anti-mutant Sapien League—kidnapped her soon after and shot Tabitha, but X-23 saved her life. She then took up the codename Boom-Boom again. **AD, MF**

MENACE

FIRST APPEARANCE (as Lily) The Amazing Spider-Man #545 (December 2007); (as Menace) The Amazing Spider-Man #550 (April 2008) **REAL NAME** Lily Hollister
OCCUPATION Terrorist, socialite **BASE** New York City
HEIGHT 5 ft 6 in **WEIGHT** 116 lbs
EYES Brown/Yellow **HAIR** Black, dyed blond/red
SPECIAL POWERS/ABILITIES Lily has superhuman durability and strength, and some combat training. She is skilled at politics.

The daughter of wealthy attorney and aspiring politician Bill Hollister, Lily wanted for nothing. She fell in love with Harry Osborn (*see* GREEN GOBLIN) and decided to read his journal, which she used to figure out where Harry's father Norman had one of his secret hideouts. Once inside, she accidentally spilled a vial of Goblin Serum on herself, granting her superpowers. She decided to use them to become Menace and attack her father, winning him sympathy in his campaign to become mayor of New York. She later had a baby she claimed was Norman's but turned out to be Harry's. **MF**

MEPHISTO

Lord of lies

MEPHISTO

FACTFILE

REAL NAME
Unrevealed

OCCUPATION
Ruler of an extradimensional realm of the dead

BASE
A hell dimension

HEIGHT 6 ft 6 in
WEIGHT 310 lbs
EYES Variable, usually white with no visible pupils or irises
HAIR Variable, usually black

FIRST APPEARANCE
The Silver Surfer #3 (December 1968)

POWERS

Possesses virtually unlimited ability to manipulate magical energies; potentially incalculable strength, godlike durability, immortality, and shapeshifting ability. He can possess the souls of those who hand them over willingly.

Mephisto can magically augment his strength to an immeasurable extent, rivaling even the possibly limitless power of the Hulk.

Mephisto is an extradimensional demon of immense power who often poses as Satan. He continually schemes to make bargains with people for their souls. Mephisto especially covets the souls of heroes for their purity and has repeatedly sought the soul of the noble Silver Surfer. Mephisto has also contended with Thor, Doctor Strange, Daredevil, the Fantastic Four, and many others.

DIRTY DEEDS

It was Mephisto, pretending to be Satan, who bonded the demon Zarathos to Johnny Blaze, turning him into the Ghost Rider. He also held the soul of Doctor Doom's mother until Strange helped Doom free her. Mephisto has a son, Blackheart, and a daughter, Mephista, who sometimes work with him. Other demons impersonate him from time to time, usually weaker creatures who wish to trade off his fearsome reputation.

The Scarlet Witch once unwittingly used fragments of Mephisto's soul to give life to her twin sons, and Mephisto's reclamation of these fragments drove her mad, resulting in her altering all reality. When she finally brought the world back to normal, she did so by removing the mutant gene from most of the population of the planet, an event known as M-Day.

Mephisto may seem as if he works mostly small, personal deals, but in the end, he wishes to rule the world.

Cutting Deals

Mephisto made a deal with Spider-Man to save his aunt May Parker—and erase memory of Spider-Man's secret identity from the world—in exchange for destroying his marriage to Mary Jane Watson. He had rarely seen two people so happy with each other, and destroying that pure and beautiful thing brought him great delight.

When the New Mutants accidentally found themselves in Mephisto's Hell rather than Hela's Hel, he offered to bring them where they wished to be—if Magma agreed to go on a date with him. She did, and he came to collect, acting like a gentleman through much of the night. She ended things with him later when she discovered that he had the Dísir—ex-servants of Bor—imprisoned in Hell.

Being immortal, Mephisto often makes plans that may not come to fruition for decades, if not centuries. He is powerful and patient, and can wait for the world to bend his way. **PS, MF**

Mercado, Joy

FIRST APPEARANCE Moon Knight #33 (September 1983)
REAL NAME Joy Mercado
OCCUPATION Reporter **BASE** New York City
HEIGHT 5 ft 10 in **WEIGHT** 135 lbs **EYES** Blue **HAIR** Blond
SPECIAL POWERS/ABILITIES Normal human strength for a woman of her build who exercises regularly; has some skill at unarmed combat; accomplished writer and interviewer.

Joy Mercado, formerly a top writer for *NOW* magazine, is among the elite investigative reporting staff of the *Daily Bugle*. She was partnered with staff photographer Peter Parker on a number of stories, including an assignment to England and Northern Ireland, where SPIDER-MAN prevented the assassination of the British prime minister. Joy seemed suspicious of Peter's relationship with Spider-Man and, at one time, accused Peter of using Spider-Man to further his career. Joy is an incorrigible flirt, but her relationship with Peter never progressed to anything more than friendship. **DW**

MESMERO

Mesmero started out as a party hypnotist, using his mutant powers to convince guests to surrender their valuables. He branched out into Super Villainy when the MACHINESMITH recruited him to lead the robotic "Demi-Men" alongside a robot duplicate of MAGNETO. Mesmero, who didn't realize that his comrades were robots, hypnotized POLARIS into becoming his partner until the X-MEN crushed the Machinesmith's plot.

Mesmero later found work as a stage hypnotist and clashed with SPIDER-MAN. He recently served as a field agent for the WEAPON X program in exchange for treatments that augmented his hypnotic abilities. His powers let him entrance crowds into doing anything he wished, putting Mesmero's mind-control abilities in the same class as PROFESSOR X. Mesmero helped hide the locations of Weapon X installations, but his superiors abandoned him when his power levels dipped after the death of his mother.

Mesmero was one of the mutants who saw their abilities stripped by the SCARLET WITCH during the Decimation event. Without his hypnotism, Mesmero finally forged a relationship with a woman that didn't rely on trickery. He has rededicated himself to starting a new life as an ordinary human. **DW**

FACTFILE
REAL NAME
Vincent (full name unrevealed)
OCCUPATION
Professional criminal
BASE
Mobile

HEIGHT 5 ft 10 in
WEIGHT 180 lbs
EYES Red
HAIR Green

FIRST APPEARANCE
X-Men #49 (October 1968)

MESMERO

POWERS

Mutant powers of hypnotism allow him to take control of others. Mesmero does this by making eye contact. His powers can induce amnesia, put memories into a victim's head or even change their personality.

Merlyn

FIRST APPEARANCE Black Knight #1 (May 1955)
REAL NAME Merlyn
OCCUPATION Sorcerer, guardian of the multiverse
BASE Otherworld **HEIGHT/WEIGHT/EYES/HAIR** Variable
SPECIAL POWERS/ABILITIES Almost unlimited command of sorcerous energies allow him to perform innumerous feats, including extending his natural lifespan.

Born a powerful immortal in an alternate universe, Merlyn studied under Necrom, and with him and his fellow student Feron, he helped attune the various universes together to link the multiverse in a magical matrix. With his daughter ROMA, he created the CAPTAIN BRITAIN CORPS to safeguard all the parallel Earths of the multiverse, then later manipulated Roma and CAPTAIN BRITAIN into forming EXCALIBUR when they thought he was dead. After Excalibur destroyed the source of his power he disappeared, but he later returned to attack Captain Britain and kill Roma. **TB, MF**

M1-13

FIRST APPEARANCE Excalibur #101 (September 1996)
BASE UK **MEMBERS AND POWERS Black Knight (Dane Whitman)** Wields the Ebony Blade. **Blade (Eric Brooks)** Half-vampire vampire hunter. **Captain Britain (Brian Braddock)** Superhuman strength, durability, and flight. **Faiza Hussain** Control over living bodies. **John the Skrull** Shapeshifting and flight. **Spitfire (Jacqueline Falsworth)** Superhuman speed and durability, fangs, and healing factor.

MI-13 is the branch of British Intelligence charged with the investigation of supernatural phenomena. Alistair Stuart founded it from the remnants of the Weird Happenings Organisation (WHO), but he handed over the reins to his top agent, Peter WISDOM, when he left to join MI-6. During SECRET INVASION, the Prime Minister drafted all UK Super Heroes into MI-13. To keep the SKRULLS out of Avalon, MI-13 had to unleash the demons from that magical dimension. While this worked, it meant that MI-13 had a lot of cleaning up to do. CAPTAIN BRITAIN LED MI-13's semiautonomous strike team. **MF**

Microchip

FIRST APPEARANCE Punisher #4 (November 1987)
REAL NAME Linus Lieberman
OCCUPATION Mechanic, computer hacker, inventor
BASE New Jersey **HEIGHT** 5 ft 8 in **WEIGHT** 220 lbs
EYES Green **HAIR** Brown
SPECIAL POWERS/ABILITIES No superhuman abilities; highly skilled computer hacker; weapons engineer.

A former weapons engineer, Linus Lieberman put his skills to work building the PUNISHER's arsenal. Calling himself Microchip, he became a close friend and confidante of the Punisher—and also a target of the Punisher's enemies. The KINGPIN had Microchip kidnapped, then cut off his finger and sent it to the Punisher in the mail. Microchip also lost his son Louis Frohike (Microchip Jr.) to the Punisher's war on crime. Microchip died, but the Hood brought him back to help take down the Punisher. The Punisher killed him instead. **MT, MF**

Miller, Layla

FIRST APPEARANCE House of M #4 (September 2005)
REAL NAME Layla Miller
OCCUPATION File clerk, former student **BASE** New York City
HEIGHT 5 ft 5 in **WEIGHT** 125 lbs
EYES Green **HAIR** Blonde
SPECIAL POWERS/ABILITIES Layla can predict the futures of individuals, with some exceptions. She can also resurrect people from the dead, but without their souls.

As an orphaned teen, Layla's mutant powers gave her horns and let her breathe fire. In the House of M reality conjured up by the Scarlet Witch, Layla could make people remember their original lives. She lost her powers on M-Day, but a future self came back and downloaded 80 years of memories into her, giving her limited precognition. She went to work for X-Factor Investigations and jumped 80 years into the future with Multiple Man while helping to find Hope Summers. Separated from him, she returned several years later, now an adult, and they later married. **MF**

Mimic

After spilling chemicals from his father's laboratory on himself, Calvin Rankin became able to emulate the abilities and powers of others. As Mimic, he sought to imitate the X-Men, but when he was found out, Professor X invited him to join the team. Mimic's membership was short-lived—his arrogance made him difficult to work with—and, following his expulsion, he was thought to have died battling the Hulk. He returned several years later to battle X-Force, and he later befriended Excalibur. He worked under Mystique for HAMMER's X-Men and later joined the real team. A heroic version of him from Earth-12 worked with the Exiles before being killed. His present whereabouts are unknown. **AD, MF**

FACTFILE
REAL NAME
Calvin Rankin
OCCUPATION
Adventurer
BASE
Mobile

HEIGHT 6 ft 2 in
WEIGHT 225 lbs
EYES Brown
HAIR Brown

FIRST APPEARANCE
X-Men #19 (April 1966)

POWERS
Can ape the powers and abilities of up to five individuals at a time; can only wield powers at half strength.

By absorbing Wolverine's healing factor, Mimic actually survived his encounter with the Hulk.

Millie the Model

FIRST APPEARANCE Millie the Model #1 (Winter 1945)
REAL NAME Millicent "Millie" Collins
OCCUPATION Fashion model, actress, business executive
BASE Hanover Modeling Agency, New York
HEIGHT 5 ft 7 in **WEIGHT** 137 lbs **EYES** Blue **HAIR** Blond
SPECIAL POWERS/ABILITIES None, but has the poise and grace of a top fashion model; some fighting ability.

Having grown up in a rural farming town, Millie Collins left home for the big city, where she found employment as a model for the Hanover Modeling Agency. Over the years, Millie became involved in all sorts of outlandish adventures, often accompanied by her photographer boyfriend Clicker Holbrook and her rival, Chili Storm. Millie retired from active modeling to run an agency of her own. In recent years, Millie's niece Misty has become embroiled in comedic adventures herself. **TB**

Mindless Ones

FIRST APPEARANCE Strange Tales #127 (December 1964)
REAL NAME None **OCCUPATION** None
BASE Dormammu's Dark Dimension
HEIGHT/WEIGHT/EYES/HAIR Variable
SPECIAL POWERS/ABILITIES All possess incalculable strength, near-invulnerability, and the ability to fire energy blasts from their cyclopean eyes.

Dormammu and his sister Umar sought refuge in the Dark Dimension following their exile from the Faltine. There, they taught the wizard-king Olnar how to absorb other dimensions, which backfired when the Mindless Ones appeared. A horde of these soulless, violent creatures killed Olnar and ran riot over the Dark Dimension until Dormammu and Umar imprisoned them. They have broken through to Earth many times, battling Spider-Man, Doctor Strange and Captain Britain. They took over a small town in Colorado, but Nextwave stopped that. **DW, MF**

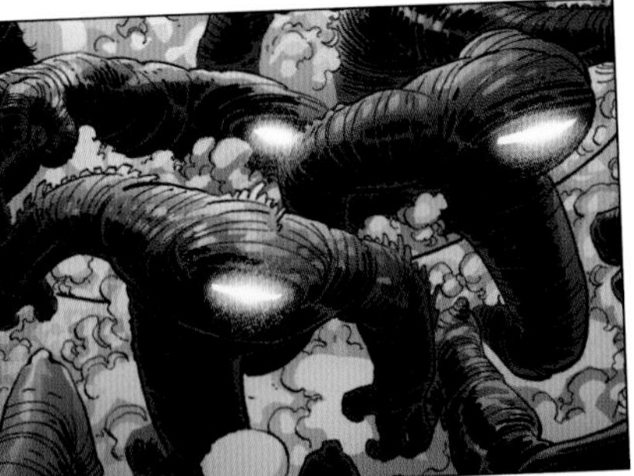

Mindworm

FIRST APPEARANCE The Amazing Spider-Man #138 (November 1974) **REAL NAME** William Turner
OCCUPATION None **BASE** New York City
HEIGHT 6 ft 1 in **WEIGHT** 210 lbs
EYES Brown **HAIR** Brown
SPECIAL POWERS/ABILITIES Feeds on emotions of others; can cause death; can control others; extraordinarily brilliant.

A mutant born with an oversized cranium and brilliant mind, William Turner was cursed with the need to absorb the emotions of others. Unable to understand or control his psychic hunger, he fed off his parents, causing their deaths. William's hunger continued into adulthood, when he took to feeding off the residents of his apartment block, until Spider-Man intervened. Before he could exact revenge, William had an epiphany, realizing his actions were motivated by guilt at his parents' death. After developing mental illness, William became homeless and was killed by a street gang. **AD**

Minoru, Nico

FIRST APPEARANCE Runaways #1 (July 2003)
REAL NAME Nico Minoru **OCCUPATION** Adventurer
BASE Southern California **HEIGHT** 5 ft 4 in **WEIGHT** 102 lbs
EYES Brown **HAIR** Black
SPECIAL POWERS/ABILITIES If Nico's blood is drawn, she can summon the Staff of One, which she can use to cast any magical spell once.

When Nico discovered her parents were part of a cult known as the Pride, she and the other children of the Pride joined together to flee from their parents, becoming the Runaways. Nico took the name Sister Grimm and tried to master her new magical powers. At one point she ended up in 1907, and her great-grandmother, the Witchbreaker, tortured her and taught her how to better control her magic. ARCADE later kidnapped her and pitted her against a number of other young heroes in his new Murderworld. Nico survived, although the experience emotionally scarred her. **MF**

Miracle Man

FIRST APPEARANCE Fantastic Four #3 (March 1962)
REAL NAME Joshua Ayers
OCCUPATION Would-be Conqueror **BASE** Mobile
HEIGHT 5 ft 11 in **WEIGHT** 185 lbs **EYES** Blue **HAIR** Black
SPECIAL POWERS/ABILITIES Master hypnotist, able to mesmerize people with a glance and make them see what he wants; occasionally telekinesis, animating objects, and restructuring matter.

A brilliant illusionist and stage magician, Miracle Man most likely had some mutant abilities. During a performance, he spotted the FANTASTIC FOUR in the audience and began taunting them about how much greater his powers were than theirs. Enraged, the THING challenged him but was outdone by Miracle Man's abilities. After escaping from prison following a crime spree, Miracle Man studied the mystical powers of the Cheemuzwa or the Silent Ones. Miracle Man remained a powerful foe of the Fantastic Four until he was shot dead by SCOURGE. The HOOD later resurrected him. **MT, MF**

Miss Arrow

FIRST APPEARANCE Friendly Neighborhood Spider-Man #4 (January 2006) as the Other; Friendly Neighborhood Spider-Man #11 (October 2006) as Miss Arrow **REAL NAME** Ero
OCCUPATION Hunting Spider-Man **BASE** New York
HEIGHT 5 ft 10 in **WEIGHT** 115 lbs **EYES** Brown **HAIR** Blond
SPECIAL POWERS/ABILITIES Ero is a hive mind composed of thousands of pirate spiders, but can appear human. She can extend spider stingers from her wrists and control spiders telepathically.

After Morlun killed SPIDER-MAN, Peter Parker sloughed off his skin and returned in a fresh body. Pirate spiders devoured his old flesh and used it as a framework for a collective intelligence that called itself the Other. Spider-Man drove it off, but it returned as Miss Arrow, the nurse at the high school at which Parker and Flash THOMPSON worked. Ero had to reproduce to survive, and she chose to mate with Flash, which would kill him. Spider-Man lured her into an aviary and birds devoured her. After MEPHISTO changed Spider-Man's past, none of this had happened, but Ero found and revived KAINE after the KRAVEN family sacrificed him. **MF**

Miss America

FACTFILE
REAL NAME
Madeline Joyce Frank
OCCUPATION
Adventurer
BASE
Mobile

HEIGHT 5 ft 8 in
WEIGHT 130 lbs
EYES Blue
HAIR Auburn

FIRST APPEARANCE
Marvel Mystery Comics #49 (November 1943)

POWERS
Enhanced endurance; could levitate herself and fly at a limited speed.

Madeline was the ward of radio tycoon James Bennet. A scientist sponsored by Bennet claimed to have invented a device that gave him superpowers. Madeline tampered with the device during an electrical storm and gained the ability to fly.

Madeline chose to use her gifts in the service of her country. She became the costumed adventurer Miss America, fighting foreign spies and saboteurs alongside super-speedster the WHIZZER. Miss America and the Whizzer joined the Liberty Legion at the invitation of CAPTAIN AMERICA's sidekick Bucky, then became members of the INVADERS when the United States entered World War II. After the war, the Invaders changed their name to the ALL-WINNERS SQUAD.

Miss America and the Whizzer married. In 1949, the two took jobs at a government nuclear facility. Sabotage exposed them to dangerous levels of radiation, and Miss America's son, Nuklo, was born a mutant who was kept for decades in suspended animation.

Years later, Miss America gave birth to a stillborn child at the HIGH EVOLUTIONARY's Wundagore Mountain. Madeline did not survive the stress of giving birth and was buried at the mountain's base.

A new Miss America (America Chavez) showed up many years later as part of the TEEN BRIGADE. Afterward, she split from the group and joined the latest version of the YOUNG AVENGERS after being tricked into it by Kid Loki. **DW, MF**

Miss Thing

FIRST APPEARANCE Marvel NOW Point One #1 (December 2012)
REAL NAME Darla Deering
OCCUPATION Pop star **BASE** New York City
HEIGHT 5 ft 8 in **WEIGHT** 125 lbs **EYES** Brown **HAIR** Pink
SPECIAL POWERS/ABILITIES Darla wears the Thing Rings, which when touched place a Thing exoskeleton around her, giving her superhuman durability and strength.

A model and pop music star, Darla dated the HUMAN TORCH. When the FANTASTIC FOUR were planning to go on a mission through time and space, MISTER FANTASTIC charged each member of the group to find a substitute to fill in for them if they happened to be gone for long. The Torch had forgotten, so he asked Darla at the last second. When the heroes didn't return, she borrowed an old Thing exoskeleton Mister Fantastic had designed so she could meet her obligations and help take care of the Future Foundation as well. **MF**

Mister Fantastic

Leader of the Fantastic Four

Mr. Fantastic

FACTFILE

REAL NAME
Reed Richards

OCCUPATION
Scientist, adventurer

BASE
New York City

HEIGHT 6 ft 1 in
WEIGHT 180 lbs
EYES Brown
HAIR Brown

FIRST APPEARANCE
Fantastic Four #1
(November 1961)

POWERS

A scientific genius, specializing in physics, aeronautics; Mister Fantastic can stretch, compress, or expand his entire body or parts of his body into any shape. He can stretch his neck, limbs or torso up to 1,500 feet without pain. He can create a canopy, sheath, umbrella, or parachute with his body.

ALLIES/FOES

ALLIES Susan Storm (Invisible Woman), Ben Grimm (the Thing), Johnny Storm (Human Torch), Lyja the Skrull, Alicia Masters

FOES Gormuu, Doctor Doom, Frightful Four, Galactus, Puppet Master, the Skrulls, Annihilus, Blastaar, Diablo

ISSUE #1

In November 1961, *Fantastic Four* #1 ushered in the Marvel Age of Comics and introduced millions to what would become the Marvel Universe. Comic books would never be the same!

He's the leader of one of the world's most important Super Hero teams. He's also a brilliant scientist. Reed Richards is Mister Fantastic. As leader of the super hero group, the Fantastic Four, Mister Fantastic uses both his ability to stretch his body and his sharp scientific mind in his quest to help mankind.

ESSENTIAL STORYLINES

• Fantastic Four #5
Victor von Doom blames Reed for the facial scar he receives when a machine explodes. He dons a mask and becomes Doctor Doom, Mister Fantastic's worst enemy.

• Fantastic Four Annual #6
The cosmic radiation that gave Sue her invisibility power affects her red blood cells, putting her life and the life of her unborn child in danger.

A Brilliant Student

The son of highly intelligent parents, Reed Richards was a child prodigy and a brilliant student. His father Nathaniel Richards was a wealthy physicist. Reed's mother, Evelyn, died when the boy was seven years old.

Young Reed showed a genius for math, physics, and mechanics, which his father encouraged. Nathaniel guided his son's scientific studies. By the time Reed was fourteen, he was already taking and excelling in college-level courses. When he reached college age, Reed attended several universities, including Empire State University in New York.

Reed Richards' attempt to make friends with fellow student Victor Von Doom were rudely brushed aside.

It was there that Reed Richards met several people who would play a major role in his later life as Mister Fantastic. Victor von Doom was a foreign student from the nation of Latveria. This scientific genius was assigned to be Reed's first college roommate, but Doom disliked Reed from the moment he met him and asked for a new roommate. Later, as Doctor Doom, he would become Mister Fantastic's and the Fantastic Four's greatest enemy.

Replacing Doom as Reed's roommate was Benjamin J. Grimm, a former high school football star who, though very different in personality, became Reed's best friend.

In college, Reed began working on plans to build a ship that could travel to other solar systems. Ben joked that if Reed could build the ship, he would pilot it.

After transferring to Columbia University in Manhattan, Reed rented a room from a woman whose daughter, Susan Storm, immediately fell for Reed. One day she would be his wife, as well as his partner in the Fantastic Four.

A Fateful Journey

Using money left to him by his father, Nathaniel, who arranged for the fortune to be given to Reed while Nathaniel was on an alternate

Earth, Reed began developing his starship shortly after college. When his own funds began to run out, Reed got funding from the US government to complete the project.

However, shortly before Reed could complete the ship, the government threatened to cut off funding to the project. Desperate to prove that his starship would fly, Reed decided to take the ship up on a test flight himself. Ben argued against the idea, telling Reed that he thought the ship's shielding would be inadequate against the powerful cosmic radiation found in space.

Reed finally convinced Ben to pilot the ship on its test voyage. By this time, Reed and Sue Storm were engaged. Sue insisted in coming along on the flight, as did her younger brother Johnny Storm. The quartet snuck onto the launch pad, slipped onto the ship, and blasted off into space. Before they could achieve hyperspace and a journey to another solar system, a solar flare shot intense levels of radiation at the ship. Ben had been right. The ship's shields were not strong enough to withstand the radiation, which irradiatethe four astronauts. Ben was forced to cut short the flight and land back on Earth.

Big Changes

Upon their return to Earth each member of the foursome soon discovered that the cosmic radiation had changed the very structure of their bodies. Reed discovered that he could bend and stretch his body at will. Sue could turn herself invisible. Johnny could cover his body with flames and also fly. Ben's skin was transformed into an orange, rock-like substance, and he gained tremendous strength.

Reed became the team's leader, calling himself Mister Fantastic. Sue called herself Invisible Girl (later Invisible Woman). Johnny called himself the Human Torch, and Ben called himself the Thing. All four agreed to use their new powers to help humanity.

Guided by Reed Richards, the Fantastic Four has become the most respected Super Hero team on Earth. They have saved the planet from many times. Reed and Sue married and now have two children: Franklin and Valeria Richards.

Humanity's Guide

During the Civil War, Reed sided with Iron Man and the US government. Sue left him over this; when the conflict ended, they reunited.

As a father, Reed became more concerned about what the future held. He set up the Future Foundation to train tomorrow's geniuses and became a founding member of the Illuminati, in an effort to help guide humanity's destiny. He also contacted the Interdimensional Council of Reeds to glean new insights from his counterparts.

MT, MF

Able to shape his body into a highly malleable state, Mister Fantastic can stretch his neck to peek around corners, or even look over entire buildings!

At the Crossroads

Mister Fantastic floats at the Crossroads of Infinity, where all dimensions and universes intersect. A traveler can journey from one dimension to another by carefully navigating through the Crossroads. Doctor Doom proved this, using the Fantastic Four as his test subjects.

Mister Fantastic can stretch his body well over 1,000 feet

Reed created a new set of white-and-black costumes for the Future Foundation. He wore one while fighting the interdimensional Council of Reeds.

Missing Link

FIRST APPEARANCE Incredible Hulk #105 (July 1968)
REAL NAME Lincoln Brickford
OCCUPATION Miner **BASE** Lucifer Falls, West Virginia
HEIGHT/WEIGHT Not known **EYES** Yellow **HAIR** None
SPECIAL POWERS/ABILITIES Possesses superhuman strength and durability. His core is radioactive, and he can project heat from his epidermis.

A Neanderthal man born millennia ago, the Missing Link was accidentally sealed in a cave, where a mysterious mist kept him in suspended animation. He was awakened from his sleep by an atomic test that changed his molecular structure. Not understanding the modern world in which he found himself, the Missing Link went on a rampage and battled the HULK. Seemingly destroyed, the Link reconstructed himself, and was found and adopted by the kindly Brickford family. They called him Lincoln and got him a job in the local mines. After further battles with the Hulk, he was turned over to the authorities. **TB**

Mister Sensitive

FIRST APPEARANCE X-Force #117 (June 2001)
REAL NAME Guy Smith **OCCUPATION** Adventurer
BASE X-Force/X-Statix Tower in Santa Monica, California.
HEIGHT 5 FT 10 IN **WEIGHT** 190 lbs
EYES Green **HAIR** White
SPECIAL POWERS/ABILITIES Superhuman senses, superhuman speed, and the ability to levitate himself.

Erroneously believing his parents died in a house fire, Guy Smith was raised as an orphan. As his mutant powers emerged, he became extremely sensitive to his surroundings. PROFESSOR X designed a special costume for him that allowed him to control his senses, and Guy took to calling himself Mister Sensitive. When he joined the mutant team X-FORCE (later called X-STATIX), he changed his code name to Orphan. He fell in love with teammate U-GO GIRL, and her death crushed him. He died on X-Statix's final mission. He and U-Go Girl reunited in Heaven. **MT, MF**

Mockingbird

FIRST APPEARANCE Astonishing Tales #6 (June 1971
REAL NAME Barbara "Bobbi" Morse-Barton
OCCUPATION Adventurer **BASE** Mobile
HEIGHT 5 ft 9 in **WEIGHT** 135 lbs **EYES** Blue **HAIR** Blond
SPECIAL POWERS/ABILITIES Expert hand-to-hand combatant and gymnast; her battle-stave can be used as a quarterstaff or broken into two smaller segments.

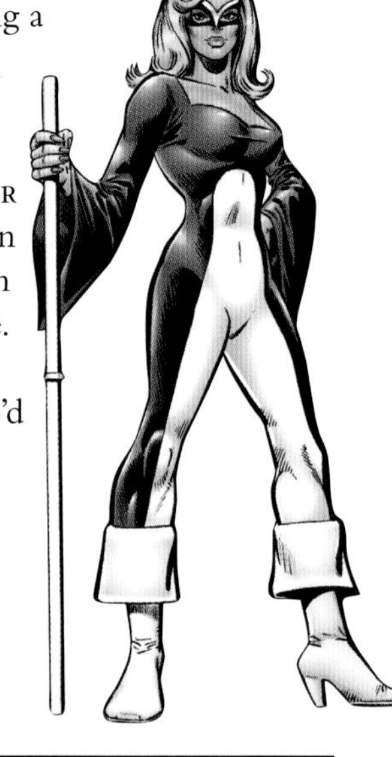

Bobbi Morse began her career as a SHIELD agent, by striking up a romance with HAWKEYE. The two eventually married and became founding members of the West Coast AVENGERS. During a time-travel adventure to the Old West, Mockingbird allowed the abusive PHANTOM RIDER to fall to his death, an action that drove a wedge between Mockingbird and Hawkeye. She seemed to die at the hands of MEPHISTO, but she'd been replaced by a SKRULL. She returned during the SECRET INVASION and later divorced Hawkeye and joined SHIELD's secret Avengers. **DW, MF**

Mister Hyde

FIRST APPEARANCE Journey Into Mystery #99 (December 1963)
REAL NAME Calvin Zabo **OCCUPATION** Professional criminal
BASE New York City **HEIGHT** 5 ft 11 in; (as Hyde) 6 ft 5 in
WEIGHT 185 lbs; (as Hyde) 420 lbs **EYES** Brown
HAIR Gray; (as Hyde) Brown
SPECIAL POWERS/ABILITIES Superhumanly strong; astonishing recuperative ability and resistance to pain.

Inspired by *Dr. Jekyll and Mr. Hyde,* medical researcher Calvin Zabo concocted a potion that worked like the one in R. L. Stevenson's classic tale. As Mister Hyde, he took on many Super Heroes, like THOR, SPIDER-MAN, and DAREDEVIL. For a while, he worked with the MASTERS OF EVIL against the AVENGERS. The YOUNG AVENGERS later discovered him illegally selling a version of his potion as a Mutant Growth Hormone. Hyde joined the HOOD's criminal organization and later the THUNDERBOLTS. His estranged daughter, Daisy JOHNSON, was a member of Nick Fury's SECRET WARRIORS and temporarily became director of SHIELD. **AD, MF**

Mister Sinister

Dr. Nathaniel Essex was recruited by APOCALYPSE and his genetic structure enhanced so as to provide him with virtual immortality and superhuman physical attributes. Taking the name Mister Sinister, Essex continued his forbidden experiments into the secrets of mutation, and he has played a hidden role in the upbringing of the Summers brothers, CYCLOPS and HAVOK. He is the guiding hand behind the MARAUDERS, whom Sinister once sent into the MORLOCK tunnels to carry out the Mutant Massacre. Sinister hoped to breed a mutant child between Cyclops and Jean GREY, so he fashioned a clone later revealed to be Madelyne PRYOR. Sinister reformed the Marauders to track down Hope SUMMERS. MYSTIQUE killed him, but he returned later in a clone body. He tried to trap the Phoenix Force when it arrived, but it killed him. He returned to threaten the X-MEN again. **TB, MF**

FACTFILE

REAL NAME
Nathaniel Essex

OCCUPATION
Geneticist

BASE
Various

HEIGHT 6 ft 5 in
WEIGHT 285 lbs
EYES Red
HAIR Black

FIRST APPEARANCE
Uncanny X-Men #221 (September 1987)

MISTER SINISTER

POWERS
Enhanced strength and durability, and some command over his own genetic structure. Essex's advanced knowledge of cloning allows him to transfer his intellect into a pristine new body whenever his current one starts to wears out.

MODOK

MODOK

FACTFILE

REAL NAME
George Tarleton

OCCUPATION
Leader of AIM

BASE
Various

HEIGHT 12 ft
WEIGHT 750 lbs
EYES Red
HAIR Brown

FIRST APPEARANCE
Tales of Suspense #93 (October 1967)

POWERS
Superhuman mental and psionic powers; computer-like brain; headband enabled him to teleport from one AIM base to another; possessed a hover-chair that could fly and was equipped with weaponry.

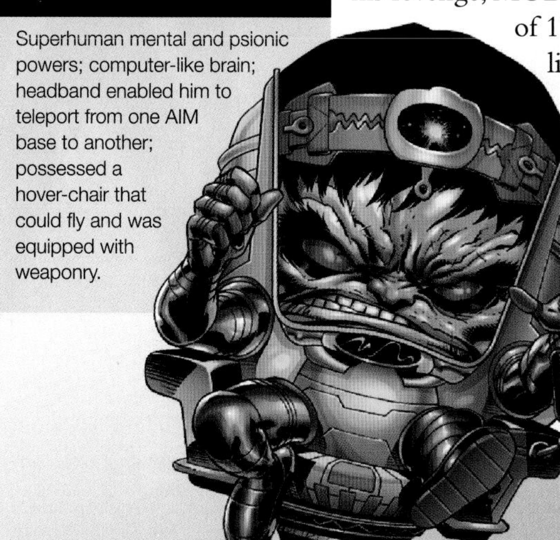

Scientists at AIM (Advanced Idea Mechanics) needed an organic computer to analyze the Cosmic Cube, so they mutated one out of AIM agent George Tarleton. As MODOK (Mental Organism Designed Only for Killing), Tarleton quickly concluded that AIM would be better with him in charge. After MODOK suffered many defeats at the hands of heroes, Monica Rappaccini ousted him and took over AIM. To get his revenge, MODOK assembled a team of 11 villains to steal a living star and sell it to AIM for a billion dollars. As part of the INTELLIGENCIA, MODOK helped to make the RED HULK and Red She-Hulk. However, the Hulked-out Amadeus CHO caused MODOK to revert to a normal man. **TD, MF**

MOJO

MOJO

FACTFILE

REAL NAME
Mojo

OCCUPATION
Ruler of Mojoworld

BASE
The airborne Body Shoppe, Mojoworld

HEIGHT Unknown
WEIGHT Unknown
EYES Yellow
HAIR None

FIRST APPEARANCE
Longshot #3 (November 1985)

POWERS
Travels on robotic platform that moves on metal spiderlike legs; projects energy bolts from hands; his very presence can kill life nearby.

A spineless mass of yellow flesh, Mojo is ruler of Mojoworld, a bizarre, media-orientated planet. A manipulative tyrant, Mojo produces movies and TV shows to keep the masses amused. The need to maintain these entertainments' popularity has drawn him to Earth.

Mojo's first visit occurred when his slave, LONGSHOT, tried to persuade the X-MEN to help overthrow his master. Although they triumphed, Mojo's successor—"Mojo II, the Sequel"—proved to be even more tyrannical, and Mojo reclaimed the reins of power. Since the X-Men are such crowd pleasers, Mojo has repeatedly involved them in his entertainment programmes, but they are rarely willing participants. Frustrated by this, he created younger versions of the X-Men, the so-called X-Babies, but they proved no easier to work with. **AD**

MOLE MAN

MOLE MAN

FACTFILE

REAL NAME
Unknown

OCCUPATION
Former nuclear engineer; ruler of the Subterraneans

BASE
Subterranea

HEIGHT 4 ft 10 in
WEIGHT 165 lbs
EYES Brown
HAIR Gray

FIRST APPEARANCE
Fantastic Four #1 (November 1961)

POWERS
Ingenious inventor of weapons capable of seismic disturbance; dominating personality; heightened senses, including a radar sense that enables him to navigate in pitch darkness, or to sense the presence of objects, or people behind him.

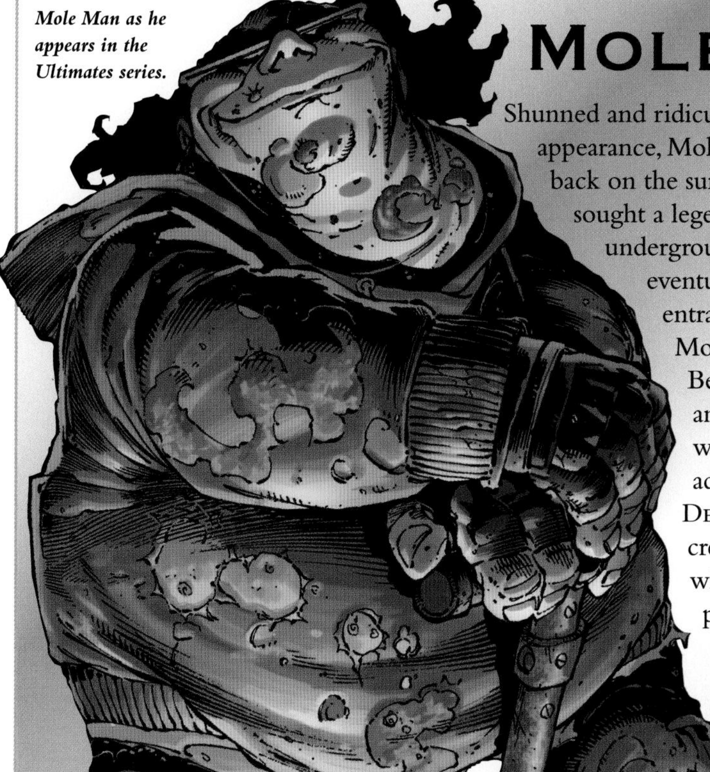

Mole Man as he appears in the Ultimates series.

Shunned and ridiculed for his bizarre appearance, Mole Man turned his back on the surface world and sought a legendary underground kingdom. He eventually found an entrance to it on Monster Island, in the Bermuda Triangle—an underground world filled with advanced technical devices left by a race known as the DEVIANTS. Mole Man also found a race of semi-human creatures, whom he enslaved. Sometimes in partnership with RED GHOST, KALA or the Outcasts, his deadly plots against the surface world have been thwarted by the FANTASTIC FOUR, the AVENGERS, IRON MAN, and the HULK.

Hideous and lonely, Mole Man found solace in the depths of Subterranea.

Mole Man declared himself ruler of Subterranea and formed an alliance and budding relationship with Kala, queen of the Netherworlders. But when his homeland was destroyed by ULTRON, he turned his attention toward the surface world once more. **MT, MF**

MOLECULE MAN

FIRST APPEARANCE Fantastic Four #20 (November 1963)
REAL NAME Owen Reece
OCCUPATION Atomic plant worker turned criminal
BASE Brooklyn, New York; later a suburb of Denver, Colorado
HEIGHT 5 ft 7 in **WEIGHT** 140 lbs **EYES** Brown **HAIR** Brown
SPECIAL POWERS/ABILITIES Possesses psionic ability to manipulate all forms.

Lab assistant Owen Reece accidentally activated a machine that opened a pinhole into another dimension, exposing him to radiation that scarred his face and endowed him with the power to control matter. An embittered misfit, Reece used his powers to evil ends, but was defeated by the FANTASTIC FOUR. UATU THE WATCHER imprisoned Reece in another dimension, but he returned to Earth and took part in both Secret Wars. Reece fell in love with Volcana, and the two retired to Colorado. Since then, Volcana has left Reece, and he was later killed by the SENTRY. **PS, MF**

MONTESI, VICTORIA

FIRST APPEARANCE Darkhold #1 (October 1992)
REAL NAME Victoria Montesi **OCCUPATION** Occult investigator
BASE Rome, Italy **HEIGHT** 5 ft 11 in **WEIGHT** 130 lbs
EYES Brown **HAIR** Black
SPECIAL POWERS/ABILITIES Possesses the ability to sense when someone has accessed a page from the Darkhold tome.

For generations, the Montesi line has guarded the Darkhold book of black magic to prevent the rise of the Elder god Chthon. Victoria Montesi, daughter of Monsignor Vittorio Montesi, grew up believing that her family's involvement with the Darkhold was just superstition, but her skepticism vanished when pages from the Darkhold became scattered around the world. To retrieve them, Victoria founded the Darkhold Redeemers with Louise Hastings and Interpol agent Sam BUCHANAN. She later learned that Monsignor Montesi was not her real father; unable to have children, he had used magic to ensure an heir. In reality, Victoria was Chthon's daughter, and was carrying Chthon himself in a demonic pregnancy. Fortunately, DOCTOR STRANGE prevented Chthon's birth into this world. **AD**

MOON BOY

FIRST APPEARANCE Devil Dinosaur #1 (April 1978)
REAL NAME Moon Boy **OCCUPATION** Adventurer
BASE The Valley of Flame, located on an extra-dimensional planet
HEIGHT 6 ft 2 in **WEIGHT** 196 lbs
EYES Blue **HAIR** Black
SPECIAL POWERS/ABILITIES Able to communicate with Devil Dinosaur and possibly other unrevealed powers.

Moon Boy grew up on a distant planet where tribes of apelike humanoids coexisted with dinosaurs. His people called themselves the Small-Folk, and they struggled against the Hill-Folk and Killer-Folk. When Moon Boy saved a Tyrannosaurus rex from the Killer-Folk, the dinosaur became his constant companion. DEVIL DINOSAUR and Moon Boy traveled back and forth to Earth several times before settling in the Savage Land. Moon Boy was taken from there when SHIELD sent the Heroes for Hire to capture him for study, but he's since returned. **DW, MF**

MOLTEN MAN

FIRST APPEARANCE The Amazing Spider-Man #28 (September 1965) **REAL NAME** Mark Raxton
OCCUPATION Security guard for Osborn Industries
BASE New York City
HEIGHT 6 ft 5 in **WEIGHT** 225 lbs **EYES** Brown **HAIR** Gold
SPECIAL POWERS/ABILITIES Superhuman strength and durability. Metallic epidermis is capable of producing flames and heat.

The stepbrother of Liz Osborn, Mark Raxton worked as an assistant to Professor Spencer SMYTHE, creator of the Spider-Slayer robots. Raxton stole Smythe's latest creation, a synthetic metallic liquid, but he spilled it on himself and became the super-strong Molten Man. When Raxton's molten skin threatened to destroy him, SPIDER-MAN saved his life. Molten Man later took a job as a security guard at the company owned by Liz's then-husband, Harry Osborn. During the CIVIL WAR, the PUNISHER nearly killed Raxton. As he recuperated, his powers ran out of control. Harry finally discovered a cure for Raxton's condition, though, and Spider-Man delivered it. **TB, MF**

MOONDRAGON

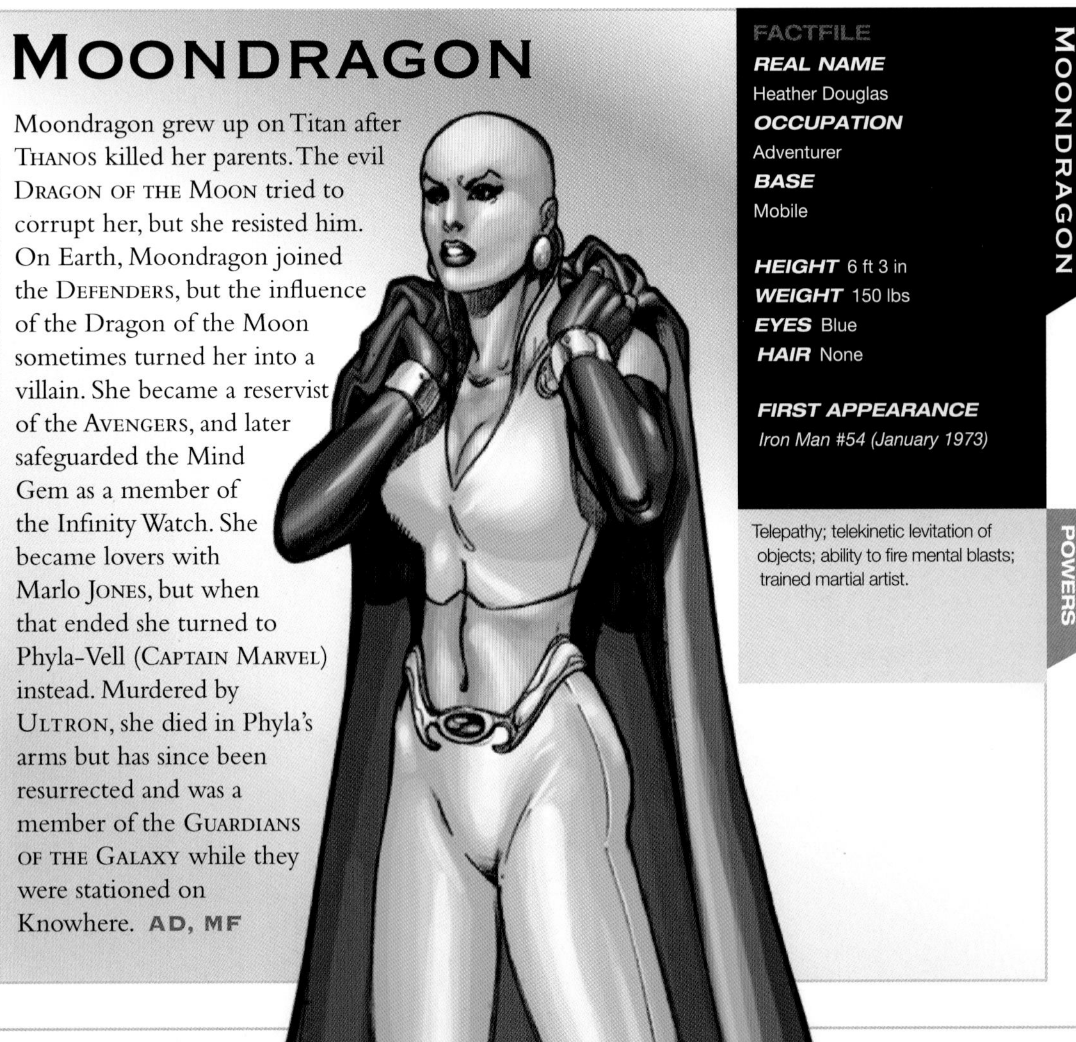

Moondragon grew up on Titan after THANOS killed her parents. The evil DRAGON OF THE MOON tried to corrupt her, but she resisted him. On Earth, Moondragon joined the DEFENDERS, but the influence of the Dragon of the Moon sometimes turned her into a villain. She became a reservist of the AVENGERS, and later safeguarded the Mind Gem as a member of the Infinity Watch. She became lovers with Marlo JONES, but when that ended she turned to Phyla-Vell (CAPTAIN MARVEL) instead. Murdered by ULTRON, she died in Phyla's arms but has since been resurrected and was a member of the GUARDIANS OF THE GALAXY while they were stationed on Knowhere. **AD, MF**

FACTFILE

REAL NAME
Heather Douglas
OCCUPATION
Adventurer
BASE
Mobile

HEIGHT 6 ft 3 in
WEIGHT 150 lbs
EYES Blue
HAIR None

FIRST APPEARANCE
Iron Man #54 (January 1973)

MOONDRAGON

POWERS
Telepathy; telekinetic levitation of objects; ability to fire mental blasts; trained martial artist.

Moon Knight

A mercenary left for dead in the Egyptian desert, Marc Spector was found by followers of the Egyptian god Khonshu, who saved his life and gave him superhuman powers. Returning to the US with a statue of Khonshu, Marc became a crimefighter, calling himself the Moon Knight and assuming two more alter egos: millionaire Steven Grant and taxi driver Jake Lockley. Aided by his pilot friend, Frenchie, and his lover, Marlene Alraune, Marc fought crime for many years, battling against Werewolf, Midnight Man and Black Spectre, and alongside Spider-Man, and the Punisher. Eventually, exhaustion set in, and Marc retired his alter egos and sold the Khonshu statue. Before long, Marc felt compelled to travel to Egypt. There, members of the cult of Khonshu explained to him that being the Moon Knight was his destiny, one he could not shirk. Reinvigorated, and equipped by Khonshu with a new costume and a selection of special weapons, Marc became the Moon Knight once more. When Norman Osborn (*see* Green Goblin) took over the Avengers, Marc faked his death and later joined Steve Rogers' secret Avengers. He then moved to Los Angeles, where he clashed with Count Nefaria. **AD, MF**

In his struggle against the more nefarious denizens of New York, Moon Knight is partnered by his lover, Marlene Alraune, and his good friend Frenchie.

Moon Knight

FACTFILE

REAL NAME
Marc Spector

OCCUPATION
Millionaire playboy and taxi driver

BASE
New York City

HEIGHT 6 ft 2 ins
WEIGHT 225 lbs
EYES Dark brown
HAIR Brown

FIRST APPEARANCE
Werewolf by Night #32 (August 1975)

Powers

His strength waxes and wanes with the moon. He bears weapons given to him by the Egyptian god Khonshu: scarab throwing darts, a golden ankh that glows when danger is near, and an ivory boomerang.

Moonstar, Dani

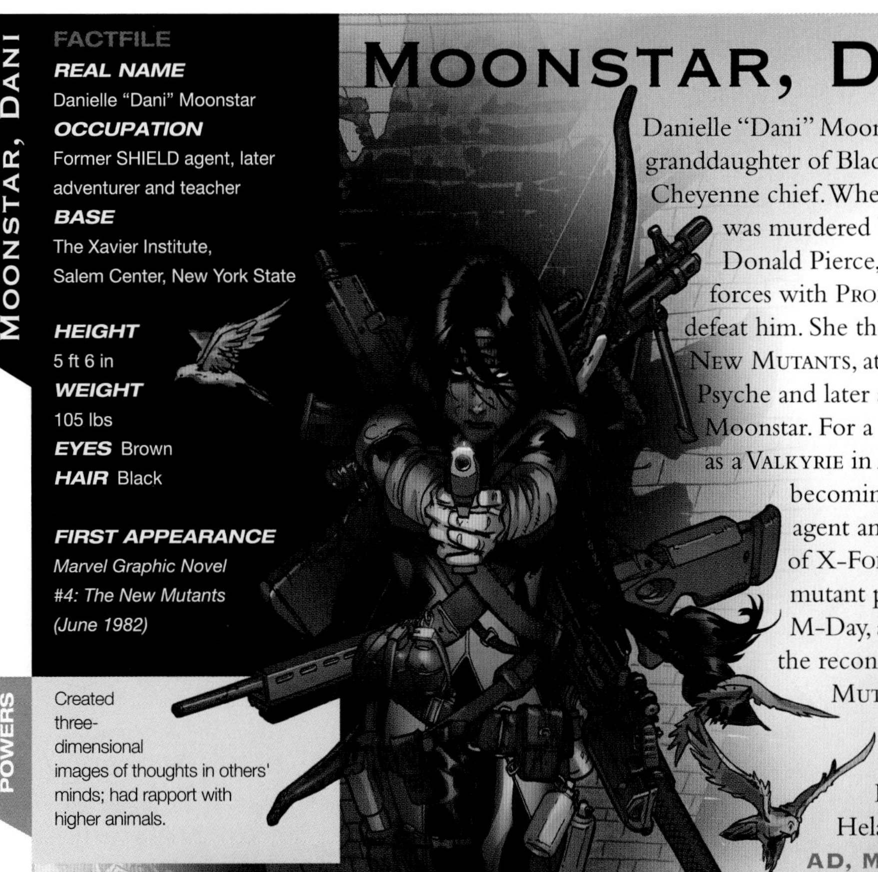

Moonstar, Dani

FACTFILE

REAL NAME
Danielle "Dani" Moonstar

OCCUPATION
Former SHIELD agent, later adventurer and teacher

BASE
The Xavier Institute, Salem Center, New York State

HEIGHT
5 ft 6 in

WEIGHT
105 lbs

EYES Brown
HAIR Black

FIRST APPEARANCE
Marvel Graphic Novel #4: The New Mutants (June 1982)

Powers

Created three-dimensional images of thoughts in others' minds; had rapport with higher animals.

Danielle "Dani" Moonstar is the granddaughter of Black Eagle, a Cheyenne chief. When Black Eagle was murdered by agents of Donald Pierce, Dani joined forces with Professor X to defeat him. She then joined the New Mutants, at first known as Psyche and later as Mirage and Moonstar. For a time Dani served as a Valkyrie in Asgard before becoming a SHIELD agent and then a member of X-Force. Dani lost her mutant powers on M-Day, and after helping the reconstituted New Mutants for a while, she later joined the Fearless Defenders as Hela's Valkyrie. **AD, MF**

Moonstone

FIRST APPEARANCE Captain America #192 (December 1975)
REAL NAME Dr. Karla Sofen
OCCUPATION Psychologist, criminal adventurer **BASE** Mobile
HEIGHT 5 ft 11 in **WEIGHT** 130 lbs
EYES Blue **HAIR** Blond
SPECIAL POWERS/ABILITIES Able to fly and become intangible; creates blinding flashes and emits laser beams from hands.

As a child, Karla Sofen learned how to manipulate others to get what she wanted. She became a psychologist in adulthood, and tricked the original Moonstone, Lloyd Bloch, into giving up the gem (actually a Kree lifestone) that gave him superpowers. Using the gem, she became a superpowered villain, serving with the Masters of Evil and the Thunderbolts, for whom she eventually became field leader. Moonstone joined HAMMER's Avengers as the new Ms. Marvel, wearing the original costume, which had been taken from Ultra Girl. When the Dark Reign ended, she became part of Luke Cage's Thunderbolts. **AD, MF**

Morbius

MORBIUS

FACTFILE

REAL NAME
Dr. Michael Morbius

OCCUPATION
Biochemist

BASE
Mobile

HEIGHT 5 ft 10 in
WEIGHT 170 lbs
EYES Blue
HAIR Black

FIRST APPEARANCE
The Amazing Spider-Man #101 (October 1971)

POWERS

A pseudo-vampire who can glide on air currents, Morbius has superhuman strength and healing ability and can hypnotize people to do his bidding.

Nobel Prize-winning biochemist Dr. Michael Morbius discovered that he was dying from a rare blood disease that dissolved his blood cells. Morbius tried an experimental treatment in an attempt to cure himself which involved fluids made from the bodies of vampire bats combined with electric shock treatment. This potent combination transformed Morbius, giving him the superhuman powers and the overwhelming bloodlust of a vampire. He was not a true "undead" vampire, however, as he was still a mortal man. Morbius grew fangs and killed to satisfy his craving for blood. However, after drinking his victim's blood, his mind would return to normal and he became filled with guilt, remorse, and self-loathing. He often battled SPIDER-MAN. Morbius and the LEGION OF MONSTERS revived the PUNISHER as the undead Frankencastle. He secretly worked at Horizon Labs and helped come up with a cure for the Spider-Island virus. He continued to work on finding a cure for his own condition, a mystery that constantly frustrated him. **MT, MF**

Morlocks

FIRST APPEARANCE Uncanny X-Men #169 (May 1983)
BASE New York City; Kenya
KEY MEMBERS/POWERS **Callisto** (former leader) Strength, agility, senses **Ape** Shapeshifter **Caliban** Strength and speed, projects fear **D'Gard** Empathic ability **Leech** Projects force field **Marrow** Bone growth, recuperation **Masque** Alters features of other beings **Plague** Creates and projects deadly diseases.

The Morlocks were failed experiments by the DARK BEAST who established their own outcast society in the tunnels beneath New York City. The MARAUDERS, organized by the ruthless geneticist MISTER SINISTER, slaughtered many Morlocks in what became known as the Mutant Massacre. Mikhail RASPUTIN, the brother of COLOSSUS, transported most of the survivors to the alternate dimension of "The Hill," where a second generation grew to adulthood. One of their number, named MARROW, founded the terrorist group Gene Nation. Other Morlocks resettled in Africa, where D'Gard led them until Marrow killed him. **DW**

Mordred the Evil

FIRST APPEARANCE Black Knight #1 (May 1955)
REAL NAME Sir Mordred
OCCUPATION Conqueror **BASE** Various
HEIGHT 5 ft 10 in **WEIGHT** 185 lbs **EYES** Blue **HAIR** Black
SPECIAL POWERS/ABILITIES An expert swordsman, Mordred's mystic power is enhanced when he functions as the male familiar to the sorceress Morgan Le Fay.

The illegitimate son of King Arthur PENDRAGON, Mordred was eventually made a knight of the realm, though evil grew in his heart. Mordred repeatedly tried to usurp the throne of England, but was frequently foiled by Sir Percy, the mysterious BLACK KNIGHT. Eventually, the two men slew each other, but Mordred's ally, the sorceress MORGAN LE FAY drew his essence to her side where she lay, imprisoned in the Netherworld. Revived and sent into the modern world by the Nether Gods for their own purposes, Mordred frequently battled Dane Whitman, the descendant of Sir Percy, and his allies, the AVENGERS. **TB**

Morgan Le Fay

FIRST APPEARANCE Spider-Woman #2 (May 1978)
REAL NAME Morgan (or Morgana) Le Fey
OCCUPATION Sorceress **BASE** The astral plane
HEIGHT 6 ft 2 in **WEIGHT** 140 lbs **EYES** Green **HAIR** Magenta
SPECIAL POWERS/ABILITIES One of the most powerful sorceresses of all time; able to manipulate the natural environment of Earth and the astral plane. She can also fly and shapeshift.

The sorceress half-sister of King Arthur PENDRAGON, Morgan plotted against King Arthur until MERLIN magically imprisoned her within Castle Le Fay. Her body trapped, she sent her astral form to various time periods. She once tried to use Jessica Drew, the first SPIDER-WOMAN, to break Merlin's spell and later stole the Twilight Sword, which she used to recreate a distorted version of Camelot in which the AVENGERS served as her knights. She and DOCTOR DOOM became lovers across time, but when this went badly, she traveled to the future to kill him. She wound up trapped in the year 1,000,000 BC. **TB, MF**

Mother Night

FIRST APPEARANCE Captain America #356 (August 1989)
REAL NAME Susan Scarbo
OCCUPATION Agent of the Red Skull **BASE** Red Skull's chalet
HEIGHT 5 ft 7 in **WEIGHT** 133 lbs **EYES** Green **HAIR** Black
SPECIAL POWERS/ABILITIES Expert hypnotist; could generate illusions, make herself appear to be invisible, and force others to obey her will.

Susan Scarbo and her brother Melvin were stage hypnotists whose ambitions grew beyond show business. They turned to crime, Susan took the name "Suprema," and was enlisted by the RED SKULL. Changing her identity to Mother Night, she took command of the SISTERS OF SIN, formerly led by the Red Skull's daughter Synthia (also known as SIN). In this role, Mother Night battled CAPTAIN AMERICA. When the Red Skull was captured by MAGNETO, Mother Night joined with the Skeleton Crew (Red Skull's main operatives) to try and free him. Mother Night was killed by the WINTER SOLDIER. **MT**

Moy, Dr. Alyssa

FIRST APPEARANCE Fantastic Four #5 (May 1998)
REAL NAME Dr. Alyssa Moy
OCCUPATION Scientist and explorer **BASE** Mobile
HEIGHT 5 ft 9 in **WEIGHT** 129 lbs **EYES** Brown **HAIR** Black
SPECIAL POWERS/ABILITIES A scientific genius on a par with Reed Richards himself, she carries a universal skeleton key and drives a flying car.

Alyssa Moy knew Reed Richards before he founded the Fantastic Four. The pair became romantically involved and Reed once even proposed to her. They remained in contact after Reed's cosmic mutation and, in recent years, Alyssa has lent occasional support to the Fantastic Four who returned the favor by curing her of a mystical virus. Alyssa received Reed's help with Nu-World, a planet for refugees from Earth. On the near-future Nu-World, she became a brain in a robot body, and her foes killed her. **AD, MF**

Multiple Man

After his parents died, Jamie Madrox's mutant power to duplicate himself ran riot. The Fantastic Four subdued Madrox, and turned him over to Professor X so he could learn how to control his mutant talent. But Madrox wasn't comfortable around other people, and chose instead to work with Dr. Moira MacTaggert at her Muir Island complex.

Madrox became a member of X-Factor, making the first true friends of his life. After X-Factor was disbanded, Madrox sent his duplicates out into the world to experience all the possibilities life had to offer. He later opened X-Factor Investigations as a detective agency. He and Layla Miller went into the future to help rescue Hope Summers. He has since married Layla, who has aged into a full adult. **TB, MF**

Because each of his duplicates is a facet of his personality, Madrox can have problems when he has to make a quick decision.

FACTFILE
REAL NAME
Jamie Madrox
OCCUPATION
Detective
BASE
"Mutant Town," New York City

HEIGHT 5 ft 11 in
WEIGHT 155 lbs
EYES Blue
HAIR Brown

FIRST APPEARANCE
Giant-Size Fantastic Four #4 (October 1974)

POWERS
Madrox has just one superhuman ability: when struck, he can create duplicates of himself. Each duplicate lasts as long as he wishes and embodies an aspect of his personality. He also has a special suit, which prevents duplication taking place.

Ms Marvel

FIRST APPEARANCE Captain Marvel #17 (November 2013)
REAL NAME Kamala Khan
OCCUPATION Student, adventurer **BASE** Jersey City, NJ
HEIGHT Around 5'4" **WEIGHT** 110-115 lbs.
EYES Dark brown **HAIR** Dark brown/black
SPECIAL POWERS/ABILITIES Kamala Khan is a polymorph who can extend and grow any part of her limbs, grow giant-sized and shrink to doll-sized. She is also a shapeshifter.

A Muslim Pakistani-American, Kamala Khan comes from a traditional, conservative home. She wants to make her parents proud, but also feels that their boundaries are holding her back. Kamala is an Inhuman whose powers manifested following exposure to the Terrigen Mists released when the floating Inhuman city of Attilan was destroyed. Kamala's Inhuman powers have been present in her DNA her whole life, it just took the Mists to unlock them—meaning that Kamala really has always been different. She idolizes all the Avengers—but particularly Captain Marvel (Carol Danvers), because Captain Marvel does all the amazing things she wishes she could do. **MF**

Mutant Liberation Front

Initially formed by Stryfe, a clone of Cable from the future, the MLF staged assorted terrorist events which initially brought them into conflict with the New Mutants, and subsequently with Cable's X-Force unit. When they were of no further use to Stryfe, this incarnation of the MLF was left to its own devices.

The organization was reformed by Reignfire, who had been infused with the DNA of the New Mutant Sunspot, and who seemed to be Sunspot himself. When they were defeated by X-Force, the truth of Reignfire's identity was exposed.

The third incarnation of the MLF was composed of humans who posed as mutants so as to increase tensions between humans and mutants. They were later destroyed by the Punisher and SHIELD. **TB**

THE MLF (3RD VERSION)
1 Blindspot **2** Blastfurnace
3 Corpus Derelicti **4** Burnout

FACTFILE
NOTABLE MEMBERS
STRYFE
REIGNFIRE
REAPER
FOREARM
TEMPO
STROBE
THUMBELINA
WILDSIDE
ZERO
SKIDS
RUSTY COLLINS
SUMO
KAMIKAZE
CORPUS DERELICTI
DRAGONESS
MOONSTAR
LOCUS
FERAL
SELBY
BLASTFURNACE
BLINDSPOT
BURNOUT
DEADEYE
THERMAL

FIRST APPEARANCE
New Mutants #86 (February 1990)

MUTANT X

FACTFILE

MEMBERS AND POWERS

HAVOK (Alex Summers)
Projects concussive force and heat.

BLOODSTORM (Ororo Munroe)
Vampiric powers, controls the weather.

BRUTE (Hank McCoy)
Superhuman strength and agility.

FALLEN (Warren Worthington III)
Has wings enabling flight.

ICEMAN (Bob Drake)
Generates intense cold.

MARVEL WOMAN (Madelyne Pryor)
Telekinetic powers.

FIRST APPEARANCE
Mutant X #1 (October 1998)

Mutant X #1: The Six battle the Sentinels.

MUTANT X

Alex Summers, alias the Super Hero HAVOK, a former X-Man on "mainstream" Earth (Earth-616), was seemingly killed in an explosion. At the same time on the Earth of an alternate reality (Earth-1298), its own Havok was brutally killed by a SENTINEL robot. The spirit of the Havok of Earth-616 took possession of the body of the Havok of Earth-1298 and thus returned to physical life.

In this "Mutant X" universe Havok became the leader of a mutant team called the Six, who were counterparts of various members of the X-MEN.

Eventually, the Havok of Earth-616 returned to physical existence on his native Earth. **PS**

Madelyne Pryor, who founded the Six with Havok, in her Goblin Queen persona.

THE SIX OF MUTANT X UNIVERSE
1 Bloodstorm ***2*** Iceman ***3*** Nick Fury of Earth-1298 ***4*** Brute ***5*** Havok, alias Mutant X ***6*** SHIELD agent of Earth-1298

MYS-TECH BOARD

FACTFILE

CURRENT MEMBERS AND POWERS
(All board members possess immortality)

ALGERNON CROWE
BRONWEN GRYFFN
RANULPH HALDANE (deceased)
PORLOCK
RATHCOOLE
GUDRUN TYBURN
ORMOND WYCHWOOD

BASE
London, England

FIRST APPEARANCE
Warheads #1 (June 1992)

MYS-TECH BOARD

In the year 987, seven members of a Druid cult made a bargain with the demon MEPHISTO: in exchange for immortality, they agreed to funnel souls into Mephisto's realm. Over the subsequent millennium, the mages acquired great wealth and became the board members of a London-based corporation named Mys-Tech. To pay their debt to Mephisto, the Mys-Tech board plotted to take over the world and kill vast numbers of innocents. Their assets included the Un-Earth, a model of the planet that operated like a voodoo doll, and the Warheads, mercenaries who could travel through wormholes to other dimensions or times. The board members eventually transformed themselves into beings of even greater power known as the Techno-Wizards. **AD**

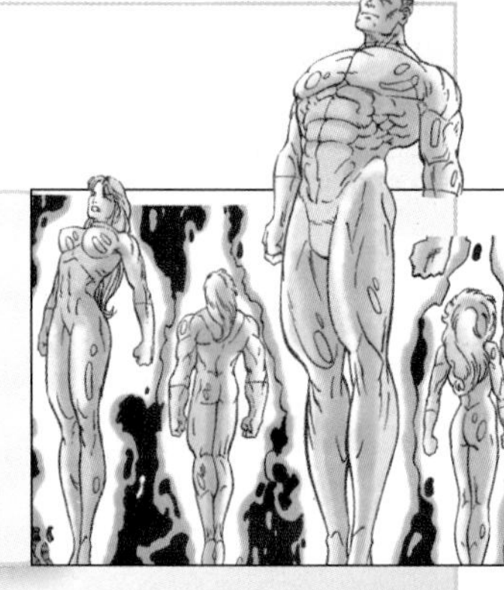

Hungry for greater power, the members of the Mys-Tech board transformed themselves into the Techno-Wizards so they could confront Super Heroes directly.

MYS-TECH BOARD
1 Porlock
2 Rathcoole
3 Bronwen Gryffn
4 Godrun Tyburn
5 Algernon Crowe
6 Ormond Wychwood

Mysterio

Quentin Beck was a leading special-effects designer in Hollywood but, hungry for fame, he became the villain Mysterio. Using illusions to confound Spider-Man, Mysterio became one of his greatest foes, both on his own and as part of the Sinister Six. Mysterio once devised an elaborate scheme to drive Daredevil insane. When it failed, Beck faked his death. His old apprentice Daniel Berkhart took up his helmet. Francis Klum also acquired Mysterio's costume from the Kingpin but was killed. A new Mysterio appeared to take on the new Spider-Man (Doctor Octopus). **PS, MF**

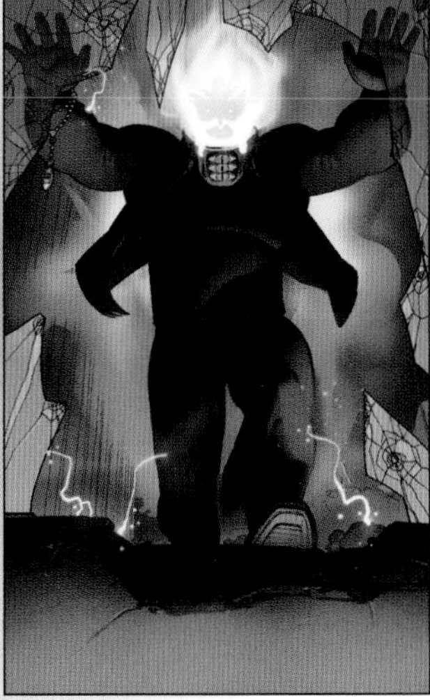

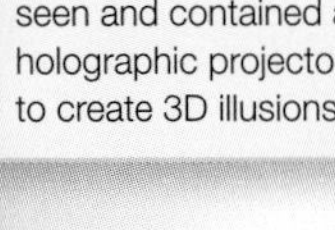

Mysterio's helmet allowed him to see out without being seen and contained a holographic projector to create 3D illusions.

FACTFILE

REAL NAME
Quentin Beck

OCCUPATION
Criminal

BASE
New York City

HEIGHT 5 ft 11 in
WEIGHT 175 lbs
EYES Blue
HAIR Black

FIRST APPEARANCE
The Amazing Spider-Man #13 (June 1964)

MYSTERIO

POWERS
A genius with special effects and stage illusions. Beck was also a master hypnotist, and Klum can teleport and can control other people's bodies.

Mystique

Mystique learned to use her mutant shape-shifting powers at an early age. As Raven Darkhölme, she hid her powers so well that she rose to a position of great power within the US Defense Department, giving her access to military secrets and advanced weaponry to use for her criminal purposes. As Mystique, she organized the second Brotherhood of Evil Mutants, teaming with Avalanche, the Blob, Destiny, and Pyro. The Brotherhood attempted to assassinate Senator Robert Kelly, a vocal enemy of all mutants, but the X-Men stopped them. The Brotherhood later changed its name to Freedom Force and began working for the US government. When that ended, Mystique joined X-Factor. She joined the X-Men but betrayed them in the hunt for Hope Summers, and she later led HAMMER's dark X-Men, posing as Professor X. She has since reformed the Brotherhood. **MT, MF**

Mystique has two sons: Nightcrawler and Graydon Creed (not pictured). Rogue (center) is her foster daughter.

FACTFILE

REAL NAME
Raven Darkhölme

OCCUPATION
Criminal, terrorist, government agent, teacher

BASE
The Pentagon, Washington DC

HEIGHT 5 ft 10 in
WEIGHT 120 lbs
EYES Yellow
HAIR Red-orange

FIRST APPEARANCE
Ms. Marvel #16 (April 1978)

MYSTIQUE

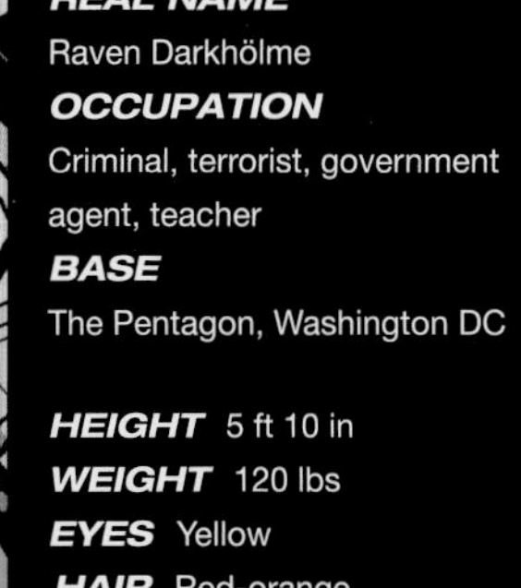

POWERS
A mutant shape-shifter who can make herself look like any human, humanoid, or semi-humanoid being, male or female, copying every detail including retina, fingerprints, and voice pattern.

FACTFILE

KEY MEMBERS

HENRY AKAI
As Timestream, he can travel forward or backward in time.

ALBERT DEVOOR
Director of the Nth Project.

ABNER DOOLITTLE
Scientist who designed the dimensional transporter.

DR. T.W. ERWIN
Mathematician famous for his theories of parallel time.

GODWULF
Cybernetic technology allows him to link with computers.

DR. THOMAS LIGHTNER
Magical abilities, on par with Dr. Strange.

BENNETT PITTMAN
Was in charge of Roxxon's extra-dimensional oil drilling facilities.

ANGLER
Passes through solid material, teleports, travels through hyper-space.

DEATHLOK THE DEMOLISHER
Superhuman strength, agility.

FIRST APPEARANCE
Marvel Two-In-One March #53 (July 1979)

NTH COMMAND

Nth Command was formed by the Roxxon Corporation to gain total control of the world's energy supply. This was done by operatives, known as Nth Commandos, using devices called Nth projectors, that could transport material from one dimension to another. The sorcerer, Thomas Lightner, was hired to destroy Project Pegasus, so that the Nth Command could gain a monopoly on energy research. Lightner took control of the time-traveling cyborg, DEATHLOK, removed his organic parts, then reprogrammed him to serve Nth Command.

Breaking into Project Pegasus with Deathlok, Lightner hoped to use an Nth projector to transport the entire facility to another dimension. He was stopped by the THING, QUASAR, Giant-Man, THUNDRA, and the AQUARIAN. **MT**

Albert DeVoor, Director of the Nth Project, addresses the Nth Commandos.

THE WORLD AWAITS.

N'ASTIRH

FIRST APPEARANCE X-Terminators #1 (October 1988)
REAL NAME N'astirh
OCCUPATION Conqueror, sorcerer **BASE** Washington, D.C.
HEIGHT/WEIGHT Variable **EYES** Red **HAIR** Greenish
SPECIAL POWERS/ABILITIES Able to turn humans into demons, fly and change size; considerable mystical abilities; knowledge of a vast number of magical spells.

N'astirh by name, nasty by nature—that's what they said about this demon from the Limbo dimension. Angered when Limbo's ruler made the human mutant, MAGIK, his apprentice, N'astirh felt compelled to rebel, and when a plan was hatched to take over the Earth, N'astirh usurped the scheme so that he could rule the Earth. His efforts were foiled by Magik, however N'astirh made a second attempt to become a world conqueror by transforming Madelyne PRYOR into the Goblin Queen. Eventually, the X-MEN destroyed him, but he later reappeared, working with Magik. He later helped BASTION abduct Magik to Limbo. **AD, MF**

FACTFILE

REAL NAME
Aquaria Nautica Neptunia

OCCUPATION
Adventurer

BASE
Formerly Atlantis; mobile

HEIGHT 5 ft 11 in
WEIGHT 189 lbs
EYES Blue
HAIR Blonde

FIRST APPEARANCE:
Marvel Mystery Comics #82 (1947)

POWERS
Superhuman strength (even by Atlantean standards) and durability; can breathe in air or underwater. Formerly had the power of flight.

Namora married an Atlantean named Talan. After Talan was accidentally killed, Namora moved to Lemuria and married Prince Merro.

NAMORA

The Namora of Earth-616 was the cousin of Prince NAMOR the Sub-Mariner. Like Namor, she had pink skin and possessed similar powers. She is considered the "mother" of NAMORITA, her altered clone. LLYRA of Lemuria seemed to have murdered Namora years ago, but Namora recently resurfaced and joined the AGENTS OF ATLAS. During WORLD WAR HULK she sided with the HULK. Another Namora was Earth-2189's female counterpart of Namor, but had blue skin. As queen of Atlantis, she conquered her world before joining the EXILES, a team of interdimensional adventurers. She was finally slain by an alternate version of HYPERION. **PS, MF**

Wings on Namora's heels—now withered away—once enabled her to fly.

Unlike Namor, the Exiles' Namora had two water-breathing Atlantean parents. In conquering the surface world, Namora killed her alternate Earth's Avengers and Fantastic Four.

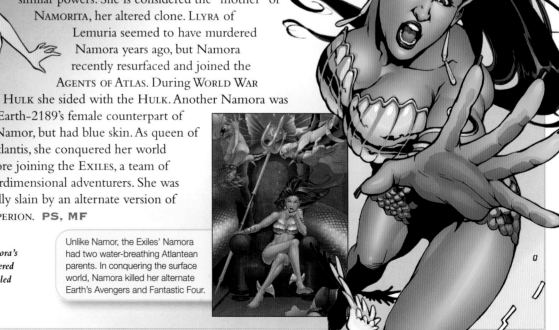

NAMOR

Ruler of the undersea realm of Atlantis

Prince Namor is the mutant son of a blue-skinned ATLANTEAN princess and an American sea captain. He was raised in the underwater kingdom of Atlantis and grew up hating all surface dwellers. During World War II, Namor briefly sided with the Allies against the Axis Powers and joined the super-teams known as the INVADERS and the Liberty Legion.

Occasionally Namor helps protect the surface world but his priority is the welfare of the people of Atlantis.

After repeatedly battling the Fantastic Four, Namor eventually made peace with them and is now their greatest ally.

THE ALL-WINNER

After the war, Namor became a member of the ALL-WINNERS SQUAD, but returned to Atlantis when the Squad disbanded in 1949. He returned to the surface world in the late 1950s and encountered a man called DESTINY, who removed his memory and sent him to New York where he lived as a derelict. His memory was restored by Johnny Storm, the HUMAN TORCH.

Namor turned against the human race when he learned that the city of Atlantis had been destroyed in his absence. During his first battle with the FANTASTIC FOUR, Namor fell in love with the INVISIBLE WOMAN (who was called the Invisible Girl at the time) and offered to spare mankind if she became his bride. He later attempted to win her by buying a movie studio and offering the Fantastic Four a million dollars to star in a motion picture when they ran short of funds.

While traveling in the Arctic, Namor once stumbled upon a tribe of Eskimos who were worshiping a figure frozen in ice. In a fury, Namor hurled the figure into the sea. The ice melted to reveal CAPTAIN AMERICA, who was later picked up and revived by the AVENGERS.

Namor became smitten with Sue Storm (Invisible Woman), but gallantly stepped aside once she decided to marry Reed Richards (Mr Fantastic).

LOVE AND WAR

Namor has been married twice, to Lady Dorma and then MARRINA, but both wives died. He has also been linked to the INVISIBLE WOMAN, Emma FROST, and NAMORA. Namor's son Kamor tried to take over Atlantis, but Namor evacuated the Atlanteans to Latveria and detonated the villain NITRO inside Atlantis to foil Kamor.

Namor joined both the ILLUMINATI and CABAL, and he sided with the X-MEN when the Phoenix Force returned to Earth and was one of the Phoenix Five to be given its partial power. Despite the fact that BLACK PANTHER (T'Challa) is also with the Illuminati, Namor has been unable to avoid war with Wakanda. **TD, MF**

FACTFILE

REAL NAME
Prince Namor, aka Namor McKenzie, aka the Sub-Mariner

OCCUPATION
Lord of Atlantis, CEO of Oracle, Inc.

BASE Atlantis

HEIGHT 6 ft 2 in
WEIGHT 278 lbs
EYES Blue-gray
HAIR Black

FIRST APPEARANCE
Motion Picture Funnies Weekly (April 1939)

POWERS
Super-strength, stamina, and durability (these traits decline the more time he spends out of water). Amphibious; can swim underwater at 60 mph; can see clearly in the ocean depths. Telepathic rapport with marine life and can duplicate many of their abilities; wings on ankles enable flight; long-lived.

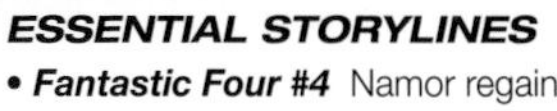

ESSENTIAL STORYLINES
- ***Fantastic Four #4*** Namor regains his memory and declares war on the surface world.
- ***Fantastic Four Annual #1*** Namor is reunited with the kingdom of Atlantis and invades New York City.
- ***Tales To Astonish #70-76*** Namor seeks the sacred trident of Neptune and proves that he is worthy to rule Atlantis.
- ***Marvel Feature #1*** Helps form the Defenders.
- ***Avengers #262*** Namor joins the Avengers.

FACTFILE

REAL NAME
Namorita Neptunia
(aka Namorita Prentiss)

OCCUPATION
College student

BASE
New York City

HEIGHT 5 ft 6 in
WEIGHT 225 lbs
EYES Blue
HAIR Blond

FIRST APPEARANCE
Sub-Mariner #50 (June 1972)

POWERS

Namorita is amphibious: able to survive on land and in the sea; power of flight; her hands exude a paralyzing toxin; chameleon-like ability to camouflage herself.

NAMORITA

Half-human, half-Atlantean, Namorita was a clone of her mother, NAMORA, although she was an adult before she discovered this fact.

Orphaned when she was still a child, Namorita was watched over by NAMOR the Sub-Mariner and his friend Betty Prentiss. Their love and support carried Namorita through the tragic and traumatic loss of her mother. When Namorita became an adult, they also helped and encouraged her to attend a US college.

An Atlantean in a human world, the New Warriors helped Namorita stave off isolation.

Not long after starting college, Namorita became a founder member of the NEW WARRIORS, a team of young Super Heroes, with whom she fought against the HELLIONS, PROTEUS, and TERRAX. The group provided Namorita with a certain amount of security and stability, but not all her time with them was happy: her first attempt to lead the team resulted in the kidnap of many team members' families. They were eventually rescued, but Namorita left the team in shame. She tried to return to Atlantis, but she was shut out because the people there had finally learned she was a clone. She returned to the New Warriors and was with them when NITRO blew up a large chunk of Stamford, Connecticut, killing her along with most of her friends. NOVA later rescued Namorita from a point in the past and brought her to the present, where she stayed. **AD, MF**

NEBULA

FIRST APPEARANCE Avengers #257 (July 1985)
REAL NAME Nebula
OCCUPATION Space pirate **BASE** Various throughout galaxy
HEIGHT/WEIGHT Unrevealed **EYES** Blue **HAIR** Black
SPECIAL POWERS/ABILITIES Nebula's cybernetic components provide her with enhanced strength and durability, and a number of built-in weapons.

Claiming to be the granddaughter of the mad Titan THANOS, Nebula embarked on a career as a space pirate, hijacking Thanos' old flagship Sanctuary II and attempting to conquer the fragmented SKRULL Empire. The AVENGERS stopped her, but not before she ravaged the planet Xandar. When Thanos was reborn, he denied any relationship to Nebula, who nevertheless almost succeeded in wresting the omnipotent Infinity Gauntlet away from him. She then attacked NOVA, claiming her father had been Zorr, a menace destroyed by the hero's predecessor, Nova Prime. She later worked as one of GAMORA's Graces. Nebula's identity was also adopted for a time by RAVONNA the Terminatrix. **TB, MF**

NEKRA

FIRST APPEARANCE Shanna the She-Devil #5 (August 1973)
REAL NAME Nekra Sinclair
OCCUPATION Subversive, cult priestess **BASE** Mobile
HEIGHT 5 ft 11 in **WEIGHT** 140 lbs **EYES** Black **HAIR** Black
SPECIAL POWERS/ABILITIES Mutant whose feelings of hatred for the world and humanity in general endow her with superhuman strength, agility, and durability.

Gemma Sinclair and Frederick Beechman were accidentally exposed to radiation at the Los Alamos Atomic Proving Grounds. As a result, Gemma's daughter Nekra was born a mutant with chalk-white skin. An outcast, she teamed up with Beechman's mutant son Jerome, who had apelike features. As they grew older, they discovered their superhuman powers. As Nekra and the MANDRILL, they attempted to conquer three African nations and later the United States. Nekra became leader of a fanatical religious cult and later partnered with the GRIM REAPER. He killed her, but HELLSTORM brought her back. She killed DOCTOR DRUID, but the VISION blew her up. Her daughter is the villain Death Reaper. **PS, MF**

Nelson, Foggy

Legal student Foggy Nelson roomed with Matt Murdock at Columbia University and Harvard Law School, never suspecting that Murdock possessed the superhuman powers of Daredevil. After graduation, the two friends opened Nelson & Murdock, and hired a secretary, Karen Page.

Although Nelson pursued Page romantically, he also maintained a relationship with his old girlfriend Deborah Harris. Nelson won the election for New York City District Attorney, failed in his bid for reelection, and briefly opened Storefront Legal Services before reestablishing Nelson & Murdock.

Foggy's law practice has put him on first-name terms with many Super Heroes.

Nelson and Deborah Harris married but soon divorced, and the Nelson & Murdock partnership came to an end when the Kingpin learned that Murdock was secretly Daredevil. Nelson took a position with Kelco Industrials, resigning when it became clear that Kelco was in the Kingpin's pocket. Nelson later believed Murdock dead as part of a faked scheme, and subsequently learned Murdock's secret identity. The two have since reconciled and reopened their law firm, specializing in superhuman clients. However, due to Murdock's notoriety as Daredevil, they often serve as legal consultants rather than trial attorneys. **DW, MF**

NELSON, FOGGY

FACTFILE

REAL NAME
Franklin P. Nelson

OCCUPATION
Lawyer, former District Attorney

BASE
New York City

HEIGHT 5 ft 10 in
WEIGHT 220 lbs
EYES Blue
HAIR Brown

FIRST APPEARANCE
Daredevil #1 (April 1964)

POWERS

Foggy has a brilliant legal mind and is a skilled debater. He is honest and loyal to his friends, particularly Matt Murdock, and usually good at keeping secrets.

New Mutants

Believing that his X-Men were dead, Charles Xavier (Professor X) started over with the New Mutants. A group of adolescents, they were charged with mastering their own powers at the same time as learning about themselves and fighting for Professor X's cause of mutant-human harmony. Following their graduation from Xavier's school, the surviving New Mutants remained together to form X-Force, with some of them also becoming teachers at the institute.

More New Mutants

Noriko Ashida—Surge—belonged to the second New Mutants team.

Later, Professor X decided to divide his students into squads, placing a second New Mutants team under the tutelage of Danielle Moonstar. The lineup was Prodigy (absorbs skills and knowledge); Wind Dancer (creates winds upon which she can fly); Wallflower (pheromone release to alter moods); Elixir (heals herself and others); Surge (projects electric blasts, uses superspeed); and Icarus (flies, healing ability, mimics sounds). It was disbanded after many students lost their powers on M-Day.

A third team was formed following the dramatic reappearance of Magik. It was led by Cannonball and included Karma, Magma, Moonstar, Sunspot, and Magik. **AD, MF**

NEW MUTANTS

FACTFILE

ORIGINAL MEMBERS

CANNONBALL
Invulnerable in flight.

WOLFSBANE
Transforms into a wolf.

PSYCHE
Creates illusions representing the fears and desires of others.

KARMA
Possesses the minds of others.

SUNSPOT
Sunlight lends her superhuman strength.

BASE
Xavier School for Gifted Youngsters, New York State

FIRST APPEARANCE
Marvel Graphic Novel #4 (1982)

NEW MUTANTS II

1 Psyche
2 Wolfsbane
3 Magma
4 Cannonball
5 Karma
6 Sunspot

NEW WARRIORS

FACTFILE

ORIGINAL MEMBERS

NIGHT THRASHER
Master of martial arts; creator of various technological devices.

NOVA
Strength; resistance to injury; flight.

MARVEL BOY
Flight; the projection of blinding light; telepathy; superstrength.

FIRESTAR
Generates and manipulates microwaves.

NAMORITA
An amphibious flying girl.

SPEEDBALL
Surrounds himself with "bouncy" force field; travels within it.

BASE
New York City

FIRST APPEARANCE
Thor #411 (December 1989)

NEW WARRIORS

After battling Galactus' herald, Terrax, the New Warriors officially came into being.

After his vigilante partner SILHOUETTE was shot, NIGHT THRASHER sought to establish his own version of the FANTASTIC FOUR, bullying and cajoling NOVA, MARVEL BOY, and FIRESTAR to work with him. Later, NAMORITA and SPEEDBALL joined the team, establishing the NEW WARRIORS. From their base at Night Thrasher's New York penthouse suite, they battled many different villains. Over the years, the team's lineup and focus shifted several times. On its most notorious mission, a team consisting of Microbe, Night Thrasher, Namorita, and Speedball fought a team of villains for a reality TV show. During the fight, NITRO exploded, killing several hundred people—including most of the New Warriors—and launched the CIVIL WAR. After this, a new Night Thrasher started up another incarnation of the team, made up mostly of depowered mutants. He disbanded them after the SECRET INVASION, then joined up with many former members working under the name Counter Force to form the latest New Warriors. **AD, MF**

CHARACTER KEY
1 Speedball ***2*** Night Thrasher ***3*** Namorita ***4*** Microbe ***5*** Nova

NEXTWAVE

FIRST APPEARANCE Nextwave #1 (March 2001)
BASE The Shockwave Rider
MEMBERS AND POWERS **Elsa Bloodstone (5)** Markswoman, superhuman strength, agility, speed, regeneration, endurance. **The Captain (1)** Superhuman strength, flight, sight, endurance. **Monica Rambeau (3)** Energy manipulation, transforming of body into energy (*see* PHOTON). **Tabitha Smith (2)** Creates balls of psionic explosives. **Aaron Stack (4)** Robot with flight, superhuman strength, endurance, reflexes, telescopic limbs.

Nextwave was originally a strike team assembled by the Highest Anti-Terrorism Effort (HATE) to thwart the terrorist efforts of SILENT. When Nextwave discovered that SILENT was actually funding HATE through a subsidiary known as the Beyond Corporation, they stole an experimental vehicle called the Shockwave Rider and took the fight straight to Beyond. They ran around the US, destroying Beyond's Unusual Weapons of Mass Destruction (UWMDs) while the leader of HATE—Dirk ANGER—tried to chase them down. **MT**

NIGHTHAWK

Kyle Richmond was originally recruited into the Squadron Sinister, but later gave up crime and joined the DEFENDERS until an explosion left him in a coma. After recovering, he led a new team of Defenders against the original members, and then led them as the New Jersey team of the FIFTY-STATE INITIATIVE. After retiring, he handed his mantel over to Joaquin Penneysworth, who then led a new team of Defenders. On Earth-712, Nighthawk was a member of the SQUADRON SUPREME, and Richmond's adopted son Neil became the new Nighthawk after Kyle died. On Earth-31916, Kyle Richmond is an African-American entrepreneur who lost his parents and uses high-tech weaponry, stealth, and fighting prowess to get revenge on criminals. **TD, MT, MF**

FACTFILE

REAL NAME
Kyle Richmond

OCCUPATION
Former president of Richmond Enterprises, adventurer

BASE
New York City, Richmond Riding Academy, Long Island

HEIGHT 5 ft 11 in
WEIGHT 180 lbs
EYES Brown
HAIR Red-brown

FIRST APPEARANCE
AVENGERS #71 (December 1971)

POWERS
Nighthawk's powers of superhuman strength, increased endurance, and speedy reaction time only emerge at night.

ULTIMATE SERIES NIGHTHAWK
1 Valkyrie ***2*** Power Man ***3*** Nighthawk ***4*** Giant-Man ***5*** Son of Satan ***6*** Hellcat

NIGHTCRAWLER

Demonic face of the X-Men

Although Nightcrawler looks like a demon, he is actually a deeply religious Catholic who studied for the priesthood.

Kurt Wagner is the son of AZAZEL, a mutant who resembles a demon, and the shapeshifting mutant MYSTIQUE. When Kurt was born in Bavaria, Mystique posed as an ordinary human and married a German baron, Eric Wagner. The local populace was horrified by newborn Kurt's demonic appearance: he had pointed ears, three fingers on each hand, two toes on each foot, and a tail. Pursued by a mob, Mystique threw the infant down a waterfall.

CIRCUS FREAK

Azazel saved the baby, who was raised by gypsy sorceress Margali Szardos. Kurt grew up in a Bavarian circus where Szardos was a fortune-teller. The circus performers accepted Kurt as part of their family. His best friend was Szardos's son Stefan, and Kurt fell in love with her daughter Jimaine. With his great agility, Wagner became the circus's star acrobat and trapeze performer. Audiences assumed that his inhuman appearance was merely a costume.

However, when Texas millionaire Amos Jardine bought the circus, he insisted that Wagner be exhibited as a freak. Outraged, Wagner quit the circus. Two nights later he battled Szardos's son Stefan, who had become a serial killer, and accidentally killed him.

Charles Xavier of the X-Men arrives just in time to save Nightcrawler from a lynch mob.

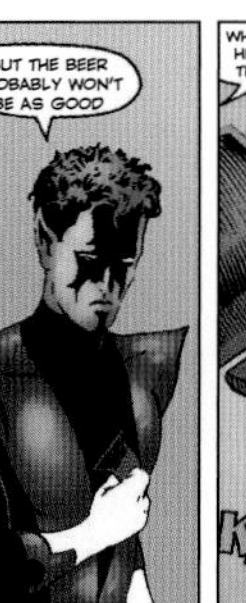

Nightcrawler briefly used an image inducer to make himself look like a normal person.

Believing Wagner was a demon and responsible for the murders, a mob would have killed Wagner, but Charles Xavier (PROFESSOR X) arrived and immobilized the crowd with his telepathic powers. Xavier recruited Wagner into his second team of X-MEN, Wagner taking the name "Nightcrawler." He was reunited with Jimaine, now calling herself Amanda Sefton, and was reconciled with Margali Szardos, who had blamed him for Stefan's death.

Nightcrawler later became a founding member of EXCALIBUR, but he returned to the X-Men after that group disbanded. He studied to become a priest but was never ordained. He learned the identities of his parents and that MYSTIQUE's foster daughter ROGUE was his foster sister. He met his half-brothers Nils Styger (alias ABYSS) and Kiwi Black, and together they defeated Azazel.

When new X-Man PIXIE stabbed Nightcrawler with her soul dagger, it was revealed that MAGIK's Soulsword was hidden inside him. The X-Men then managed to free Magik from Limbo. Nightcrawler seemingly died rescuing Hope SUMMERS from BASTION, but he later returned. **PS, MF**

Nightcrawler appears out of nowhere in a puff of smoke.

NIGHTCRAWLER

FACTFILE

REAL NAME
Kurt Wagner

OCCUPATION
Adventurer

BASE
The Xavier Institute, Salem Center, New York State

HEIGHT 5 ft 9 in
WEIGHT 195 lbs
EYES Yellow, no visible pupils
HAIR Indigo

FIRST APPEARANCE
Giant-Size X-Men #1 (May 1975)

POWERS

Mutant power to teleport himself, his clothing, and a limited amount of additional mass, by traveling through another dimension. When he teleports, part of the atmosphere of that dimension escapes onto Earth, accompanied by a "bamf" sound and the smell of brimstone.

ESSENTIAL STORYLINES

- ***X-Men Vol. 1 Annual #4***
Margali Szardos seeks vengeance on Nightcrawler for killing her son.
- ***Nightcrawler #1-4***
Nightcrawler journeys through various dimensions in a quest to return to Earth.
- ***X-Men Unlimited Vol. 1 #4***
Nightcrawler learns that Mystique is his mother.
- ***X-Men: Days of Future Past, tpb***
Turns the spotlight on Nightcrawler's interesting origins.

Nightmare

FIRST APPEARANCE Strange Tales #110 (July 1963)
REAL NAME Unknown **OCCUPATION** Ruler of the Nightmare World **BASE** The Nightmare World within the Dream Dimension
HEIGHT/WEIGHT Variable **EYES** Black **HAIR** Black
SPECIAL POWERS/ABILITIES A demon who draws power from the psychic energies of the subconscious minds of dreaming sentient beings; can draw the life energy from sleeping people, leaving them in a coma; manipulates the substance of the Dream Dimension.

Nightmare is the ruler of the Nightmare World within the Dimension of Dreams, where the life essence of humans is brought while they sleep. Nightmare monitors the collective unconscious of humans and can manipulate the dreams of an individual, giving them nightmares to gain control of that person. He is the father of the DREAMQUEEN, Daydream, and TRAUMA. AMATSU-MIKABOSHI killed him to launch the CHAOS WAR, but he has since returned. **MT, MF**

Nightshade

FIRST APPEARANCE Captain America #164 (August 1973)
REAL NAME Tilda Johnson
OCCUPATION Criminal mastermind **BASE** New York City
HEIGHT 5 ft 4 in **WEIGHT** 115 lbs **EYES** Brown **HAIR** Black
SPECIAL POWERS/ABILITIES A fair athlete and accomplished street fighter; brilliant scientist and inventor; in the past has created mind-controlling chemicals and lifelike robots.

A child prodigy growing up in a poor Harlem neighbourhood, Tilda Johnson developed a sophisticated understanding of physics, genetics, and cybernetics. However she hid her brilliance behind a veneer of childish behavior. Determined never to experience poverty again, Tilda saw crime as a way to get rich quick and assumed the name Nightshade. She worked both solo and with the Femizons. She later tried to go straight but struggled without a college degree and felt compelled to join MODOK's 11 when invited. She's since returned to crime on her own. **AD, MF**

Night Thrasher

FIRST APPEARANCE Thor #411 (December 1989)
REAL NAME Dwayne Michael Taylor **OCCUPATION** Crime-fighter
BASE Ambrose Building and a former factory in New York City.
HEIGHT 6 ft 3 in **WEIGHT** 220 lbs **EYES** Brown **HAIR** Black
SPECIAL POWERS/ABILITIES Weapons in battle-suit include truncheons, aerosols, a pneumatically-fired piton-line, and an Uzi submachine gun. Fiberglass skateboard doubles as a shield.

After his parents were murdered, Dwayne Taylor vowed to become a hero. As an adult, he founded the NEW WARRIORS to help achieve his goals, and he shepherded them through many incarnations. Dwayne was killed when the villain NITRO caused the explosion that inspired the Superhuman Registration Act. His half-brother Donyell took over as Night Thrasher. When he traveled to the future, he discovered Tony Stark had become the new Night Thrasher, while a resurrected Dwayne had taken over from Tony as IRON MAN. Donyell ended up killing Dwayne again. **TD, MF**

Nightmask

FIRST APPEARANCE Avengers #3 (March 2013)
REAL NAME n/a; sometimes known as Adam
OCCUPATION Adventurer **BASE** Mobile **HEIGHT** 6 ft
WEIGHT 200 lbs **EYES** Brown **HAIR** Black
SPECIAL POWERS/ABILITIES Nightmask can speak Builder machine code and communicate with sophisticated machines of all kinds. He can also fly and teleport himself and others incredible distances.

Soon after Ex Nihilo and ABYSS arrived on Mars, Ex Nihilo created a person on the planet's terraformed surface. He became known as Nightmask. The AVENGERS brought him to Earth, where he informed them that the universe was dying and the White Event was arriving. He accompanied the Avengers to find Kevin Conner, a college student who had just become the Star Brand as part of the White Event. He later tutored Kevin in the use of his newfound powers, which the Avengers would need in their fight to defeat the BUILDERS' attempt to destroy the Earth (*see* INFINITY). **MF**

Nile, Tana

FIRST APPEARANCE Thor #129 (June 1966)
REAL NAME Tana Nile
OCCUPATION Colonizer of Rigel **BASE** Rigel-3
HEIGHT 5 ft 4 in **WEIGHT** 110 lbs **EYES** Blue **HAIR** Black
SPECIAL POWERS/ABILITIES Can increase her density at will, giving her superhuman strength and durability; using her mind thrust, she can control the actions of another being.

One of the Colonizers of the Rigellian Empire, Tana Nile visited Earth to annex it for her people. Opposed by THOR, she was able to overwhelm the Thunder God. Eventually, Thor earned Earth's freedom—to Tana's disappointment. Later, Tana took up residence on Earth for a time and accompanied Thor and his fellow gods on a number of adventures. She helped locate a substitute world for the Rigellian seat of government after the destruction of Rigel-3. Later, Tana joined GAMORA's group of cosmic-powered females, the Graces. While working with them, she was killed by the ANNIHILATION Wave. **TB, MF**

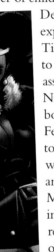

Nitro

FIRST APPEARANCE Captain Marvel #34 (September 1974)
REAL NAME Robert Hunter
OCCUPATION Professional criminal **BASE** Mobile
HEIGHT 6 ft 3 in **WEIGHT** 235 lbs **EYES** Blue **HAIR** White
SPECIAL POWERS/ABILITIES Can explode his body, or any part of his body, and reconstitute himself at will. Cannot reintegrate if any of his molecules become separated from the rest.

Renegade KREE scientists gave Robert Hunter his powers. On an early mission, he exposed CAPTAIN MAR-VELL to nerve gas, giving the hero the cancer that later killed him. Nitro could be stopped by trapping a portion of his molecules in an airtight container after exploding, preventing his body reintegrating. While fighting the NEW WARRIORS, Nitro ignited his most terrible blast, killing Cobalt Man, Coldheart, NAMORITA, NIGHT THRASHER, SPEEDFREEK, and 600 innocents, spurring the CIVIL WAR. PENANCE brought him in to pay for his crimes, but he was later seen working with the HOOD. **DW, MF**

Nocturne

FIRST APPEARANCE Exiles #1 (August 2001)
REAL NAME Talia Josephine Wagner
OCCUPATION Adventurer **BASE** England
HEIGHT 5 ft 7 in **WEIGHT** 125 lbs **EYES** Yellow **HAIR** Indigo
SPECIAL POWERS/ABILITIES Nocturne can inhabit the body of another person and remain in control of it for one lunar cycle. She can also fire blasts of energy, and possesses a prehensile tail.

The daughter of NIGHTCRAWLER and the SCARLET WITCH of Earth-2182, Nocturne became unstuck in time and was the first recruit to the EXILES. After a mission to the prime reality (Earth-616), in which she met our Nightcrawler, Nocturne left the Exiles to stay. She infiltrated the BROTHERHOOD OF EVIL MUTANTS as a double agent for the X-MEN, but was captured by MOJO. Later, she accompanied her father to the UK, where she joined CAPTAIN BRITAIN'S EXCALIBUR team. Nocturne suffered a stroke and retired to Earth-3470 with her previously thought dead boyfriend, the THUNDERBIRD of Earth-1100. She later rejoined the Exiles. **TB, MF**

Northstar

Twins Jean-Paul and Jeanne-Marie's (*see* AURORA) parents died when they were young. They were adopted separately but reunited when Jean-Paul joined ALPHA FLIGHT as NORTHSTAR. One of the first Super Heroes to come out as gay, he later joined the X-MEN. Northstar was killed by a HYDRA-brainwashed WOLVERINE and resurrected as a Hydra drone. He recovered and retained his powers after M-Day. He later married his boyfriend Kyle JINADU. After the CHAOS WAR, he rejoined the restored Alpha Flight. **DW, MF**

NORTHSTAR

FACTFILE
REAL NAME
Jean-Paul Baubier
OCCUPATION
Member of Alpha Flight
BASE
Tamarind Island, British Columbia, Canada

HEIGHT 5 ft 11 in
WEIGHT 185 lbs
EYES Blue
HAIR Black

FIRST APPEARANCE
Uncanny X-Men #120 (April 1979)

POWERS
Can redirect the kinetic motion of his body's molecules, giving him flight and superspeed.

NOMAD

FACTFILE
REAL NAME
Jack Monroe
OCCUPATION
Adventurer
BASE
Mobile

HEIGHT 5 ft 11 in
WEIGHT 200 lbs
EYES Brown
HAIR Brown

FIRST APPEARANCE
Captain America #282 (June 1983)

POWERS
Physical perfection through the super-soldier formula; skilled at throwing stun discs.

Nomad

The first Nomad was Steve Rogers, who temporarily adopted the identity after giving up being CAPTAIN AMERICA. The second was Edward Ferbel, to whom the RED SKULL gave the costume to try to harm Cap's reputation. He was killed by the Skull's Ameridroid.

During the 1950s, young Jack Monroe became the sidekick of the replacement Captain America active during that period. The two battled Communists, until the Super-Soldier formula affected their sanity. The US government placed Monroe in suspended animation for decades until SHIELD could cure his madness. He worked with the real Captain America as Nomad. Later, government agent Henry GYRICH placed Nomad under nanobot control and forced him to become the newest SCOURGE of the Underworld, but the THUNDERBOLTS freed him. His sanity started to slip after that, and the WINTER SOLDIER assassinated him.

Rikki Barnes, who had been Bucky to Captain America on Counter-Earth, came to the regular Earth after sacrificing herself to stop ONSLAUGHT. The BLACK WIDOW discovered her and gave her a new Nomad costume. She later joined the YOUNG ALLIES but discovered that Onslaught meant to use her as a means of reaching this Earth. At her insistence, GRAVITY killed her to prevent this. **DW, MF**

North, Dakota

FIRST APPEARANCE Dakota North #1 (June 1986)
REAL NAME Dakota North
OCCUPATION Private investigator; former fashion model
BASE Mobile **HEIGHT** 5 ft 7 in **WEIGHT** 130 lbs
EYES Blue-gray **HAIR** Auburn
SPECIAL POWERS/ABILITIES Adept hand-to-hand combatant and skilled gymnast; accomplished with various firearms.

The daughter of a US intelligence agent, Dakota North pursued a career as a model before establishing a highly successful private investigation firm named North Security. Boasting branch offices across the globe, North Security rapidly gained a formidable reputation, taking on a multitude of cases that ranged from the mundane to the outright dangerous. The law firm Nelson & Murdock—Foggy NELSON and Matt Murdock (DAREDEVIL)—hired Dakota to help them with investigations and security. This turned into a long-term job, during which she was shot and also lost her license **AD, MF**

Nova

The Human Rocket

NOVA

FACTFILE

REAL NAME
Richard Rider

OCCUPATION
Adventurer

BASE
New York City

HEIGHT 5 ft 9 in
WEIGHT 145 lbs
EYES Brown
HAIR Brown

FIRST APPEARANCE
Nova #1 (September 1976); (as Frankie Raye) Fantastic Four #164 (November 1975)

POWERS

The first Nova had superhuman strength and durability and the power to fly at supersonic speed. The second Nova could manipulate cosmic energy as stellar fire. She could project stellar energy, had nearly total invulnerability, and could survive unprotected in space.

Mortally wounded, Rhomann Dey—a Centurion of the Nova Corps, the space militia of the alien Xandarians—transferred his powers to student Richard Rider. As Nova, Rider became a crimefighter on Earth, then later traveled into space and became one of the Champions of Xandar.

High school student Rider became cosmic adventurer Nova.

Home and Back

On Earth, Rider joined the New Warriors. When he returned to space, Rider helped rebuild Xandar and the Nova Corps and became its leader, Centurion Prime. Rider saw Xandar destroyed in the Annihilation and became the repository of the Xandarian Worldmind. He later killed Annihilus to end that crisis.

During the second Annihilation, Rider brought in the Technarchy to defeat the Phalanx. With that over, he helped found the Guardians of the Galaxy. He returned to Earth to help stop the Secret Invasion. Afterward, he discovered that the Worldmind had been mentally controlling the Nova Corps, had recruited Richard's brother Robbie without permission, and taken Ego the Living Planet as a new base. When Richard objected, he was kicked out of the Corps, but he became the new Quasar instead and became embroiled in the Shi'ar-Kree War of Kings. When he discovered that Ego was the one behind the Worldmind's troubles, he returned as Nova to stop him.

After working with the Avengers for a while, Rider went to the Cancerverse, a universe where nothing dies. He and Star-Lord sacrificed themselves to keep it—and Thanos—from destroying their home universe.

Sam Alexander's confidence with his father's armor grew quickly.

The New Nova

Jesse Alexander was an elite member of the Nova Corps, but he gave it up to get back to Earth and see his son Sam be born. When Sam was 15, Jesse was finally called back to fight the alien Chitauri. They captured him, but he managed to leave Sam his helmet, along with instructions for Gamora and Rocket Raccoon to train him to use it. Sam warned the Avengers about the return of the Phoenix Force and then struggled to find his place in the pantheon of heroes.

The Other Nova

Frankie Raye—stepdaughter of Phineas T. Horton, creator of the first Human Torch—started her career as a hero as another Human Torch, working with the Fantastic Four alongside Johnny Storm. She assumed the name Nova after becoming the herald of Galactus to save Earth. She left Galactus's service and later helped his other former heralds fight his then-current herald Morg. She died in that battle, but years later she returned to life on Earth. **PS, MF**

Occulus

FIRST APPEARANCE Fantastic Four #363 (April 1992)
REAL NAME Unrevealed **OCCUPATION** Absolute Monarch of an unnamed world in the Inniverse **BASE** Castle Occulus
HEIGHT 6 ft 4 in **WEIGHT** 290 lbs **EYES** Black **HAIR** Black
SPECIAL POWERS/ABILITIES Gem in place of his right eye draws energy from power crystals. Fires beams of concussive force, heat, and light from his gem-eye and hands. Can fly and form force fields.

Occulus and his brother Wildblood were children of the Inniverse, a dimensional plane that exists between the subatomic particles of matter. Occulus grew in power until he ruled his entire world. When Wildblood escaped to Earth, soldiers sent by Occulus to capture him also kidnapped Sue and Franklin RICHARDS. Occulus intended to use Franklin's psionic abilities for his own ends, but the FANTASTIC FOUR put an end to that. Occulus later stole DOCTOR OCTOPUS's arms and called himself Doc Occulus. He was one of the first prisoners in the Vault prison in the Negative Zone. **TB, MF**

Odin

FIRST APPEARANCE Journey into Mystery #86 (November 1962)
REAL NAME Odin Borson **OCCUPATION** All-Father
BASE Asgard **HEIGHT** 6 ft 9 in **WEIGHT** 650 lbs
EYES Blue (one) **HAIR** White
SPECIAL POWERS/ABILITIES Odin was an immortal god with superhuman physical attributes and the ability to manipulate incredible magics.

Odin was the ruler of the pantheon of Norse gods and created their home, Asgard. He fathered THOR with GAEA and adopted LOKI as well. He sacrificed his right eye for the wisdom to stop Ragnarok, the battle at the end of times. He has been killed and returned from death three times. During FEAR ITSELF, Odin confronted his brother, Cul, also known as the Serpent, but he could not prevent his son Thor from dying while killing the Serpent, as Odin himself had prophesized. Odin sealed himself up in Asgard, alone in his grief. **MF**

Ogun

FIRST APPEARANCE Kitty Pryde and Wolverine #2 (December 1984) **REAL NAME** Ogun
OCCUPATION Assassin **BASE** Japan
HEIGHT 5 ft 9 in **WEIGHT** 146 lbs **EYES** Blue **HAIR** Black
SPECIAL POWERS/ABILITIES A master martial artist and expert swordsman. As a spirit, Ogun can possess the bodies of others, and is immune to physical harm.

A legendary sorcerer and warrior who may have been born as early as the 17th century, Ogun trained WOLVERINE in the martial arts. Originally a man of integrity, Ogun was eventually corrupted by the dark sorceries that kept him alive and invulnerable to harm, and he turned to the path of evil. As revenge against his former pupil, Ogun mentally enslaved Kitty PRYDE, training her and sending her to kill Wolverine. But Wolverine ultimately freed Kitty, and together they slew Ogun's physical form. However, Ogun survived as a spirit that can possess other beings of weaker will and employ them as puppets in the material world. Once again, Wolverine stopped him. **TB, MF**

Omega Red

Omega Red is the product of the KGB's attempt to create a Soviet super-soldier. The test subject, former serial killer Arkady Rossovich, gained mutant powers after receiving genetic treatments, though complications required him to drain the life energy of victims to survive. Placed in suspended animation by the Soviets, Omega Red reemerged after the fall of communism and sought a carbonadium synthesizer to stabilize his condition. He wound up working with the HAND and, for a while, he led New York's Red Mafia. This led him to clash with many heroes, but most often with WOLVERINE. He found himself in and out of SHIELD custody over the years.

Omega Red killed WILD CHILD in a squabble started while they were trying to kill Wolverine. In return, Wolverine later slew him with the Murmasa Blade, which prevents wounds from healing.

Later, three clones of Omega Red were created to form an Omega Clan: Omega White, Omega Black, and Omega Red. They joined DAKEN's BROTHERHOOD OF EVIL MUTANTS. **DW, MF**

FACTFILE

OMEGA RED

REAL NAME
Arkady Rossovich

OCCUPATION
Crime lord

BASE
Mobile

HEIGHT 6 ft 11 in
WEIGHT 425 lbs
EYES Red
HAIR Blond

FIRST APPEARANCE
X-Men #4 (January 1992)

POWERS
Possesses enhanced strength and mutant healing factor; body secretes deadly pheromones; has carbonadium coils implanted in arms.

OMEGA FLIGHT

Canada's final answer for its national team

FACTFILE

NOTABLE MEMBERS

ARACHNE
Formerly Spider-Woman, with superhuman agility, speed, and strength, plus a healing factor, wall-crawling, and psi-webs.

GUARDIAN
Can absorb energy, fire energy blasts, and fly.

SASQUATCH
Furry giant with superhuman durability, strength, and endurance, sharp claws, a healing factor, and genius intellect.

OTHER MEMBERS

BETA RAY BILL, TALISMAN, U.S.AGENT

BASE

Canadian Secret Intelligence Service, Ottawa, Canada

FIRST APPEARANCE

(original) *Alpha Flight #11 (June 1984);* (second) *Alpha Flight #110 (September 1992);* (current) *Civil War: The Initiative #1 (April 2007)*

With help from SHIELD, Canada formed Omega Flight to help out with the Fifty-State Initiative of their southern neighbors.

Three teams have used the name Omega Flight, each in response to the existence of ALPHA FLIGHT, which was intended to be the official national Super Hero team of Canada.

Sasquatch worked hard to form the team, although he met resistance from old friends like Talisman.

THE FIRST OMEGAS

Jerry Jaxson of Roxxon Oil formed the first team to kill Alpha Flight and steal GUARDIAN's battlesuit, which he claimed to have invented himself. He gathered several superpowered Canadians for his team, including BOX, Diamond Lil, Flashback, Smart Alec, and WILD CHILD. When Roger Bochs balked at murder, Jaxson took over his Box robot, controlling it himself. Jaxson died in their first battle, and for a long while it seemed that Guardian had, too.

ESSENTIAL STORYLINES

- ***Alpha Flight #11–12:*** The introduction of the first Omega Flight, and the death of Jerry Jaxson and Guardian.
- ***Alpha Flight #128–130:*** The introduction of Antiguard and the end of the second version of Omega Flight.
- ***Omega Flight #1–5:*** The creation of the new, heroic Omega Flight.

Omega Flight first faced off against the Wrecking Crew, which had come to Canada to avoid the Fifty-State Initiative.

THE MASTER'S OMEGAS

A Super Villain called the MASTER OF THE WORLD formed the second Omega Flight as part of his plans to rule the planet. His team included Bile, Brain Drain, Miss Mass, Sinew, Strongarm, and Technoir. He first pitted them against Beta Flight, a group of heroes in training to become members of Alpha Flight. When that failed, he decided to take over the Canadian government from within, calling himself Joshua Lord. He discovered the missing Guardian trapped in another dimension, and he rescued the hero and brainwashed him into becoming the villainous Antiguard. Fighting alongside Antiguard, Omega Flight nearly destroyed Alpha Flight. Only after Guardian's wife, Heather Hudson (VINDICATOR), finally got through to him did the tide turn against Omega Flight.

OMEGA HEROES

Following the near-total destruction of Alpha Flight by the Collective (Michael Pointer) following M-Day, the Canadian government formed a new team. This was headed by SASQUATCH, and included American heroes Arachne (formerly SPIDER-WOMAN) and the U.S. AGENT alongside Talisman and the new Guardian. Pointer (now called WEAPON OMEGA) joined in order to atone for his deeds as the Collective.

After the AVENGERS' conflict with the X-MEN, Department H formed another team, consisting of new heroes Boxx, Kingdom, Validator, and a Wendigo. Sent to investigate the landing of one of EX NIHILO's origin bombs in Regina, Saskatchewan, only Validator survived. **MF**

Onslaught

During a ferocious battle between the X-Men and Magneto's Acolytes, Professor X shut down Magneto's brain. At that moment, Xavier's own dark fears, doubts, and frustrations combined with Magneto's anger and lust for revenge, to form a new being: Onslaught. This creature lay dormant in Xavier's mind, only manifesting itself when the Professor's frustrations came to the fore. When Onslaught finally took over the Professor's body, the X-Men quickly realized what had happened. However, they were unable to prevent Onslaught's capture of Franklin Richards, a mutant with reality-altering powers. The Fantastic Four and the Avengers stopped him, but many Super Heroes were catapulted to a pocket universe and presumed dead, only returning several months later. Onslaught returned, reenergized by the collective mutant powers lost on M-Day. Rikki Barnes (Nomad) gave her life to stop him. **AD, MF**

By trapping Franklin Richards inside his body, Onslaught could tap into the boy's power to restructure reality.

FACTFILE

REAL NAME
Not applicable

OCCUPATION
Would be world-conqueror

BASE
New York City

HEIGHT 10 ft
WEIGHT 900 lbs
EYES Red
HAIR None

FIRST APPEARANCE
X-Men #15 (May 1996)

ONSLAUGHT

POWERS

Onslaught possessed Xavier's mental abilities combined with Magneto's powers of magnetism. He was able to induce illusions, amnesia, or paralysis, and manipulate magnetic fields. He also had powers of telekinesis and astral projection.

Orphan-Maker

FIRST APPEARANCE X-Factor #30 (July 1988)
REAL NAME Peter (last name unrevealed)
OCCUPATION Warrior **BASE** Mobile
HEIGHT 7 ft 1 in **WEIGHT** Unrevealed
EYES Unrevealed **HAIR** Unrevealed
SPECIAL POWERS/ABILITIES Carries an arsenal of guns; armored battlesuit protects against most damage.

Never seen out of his armored battlesuit, the Orphan-Maker was once a mutant child named Peter. Peter was subject to the cruel experimentations of Mister Sinister, who planned to kill the boy when he had no further use for him. The cyborg known as Nanny saved Peter and indoctrinated him in her philosophy of rescuing mutant children from threats both real and imaginary. As the first of Nanny's "Lost Boys and Girls," Orphan-Maker abducted young mutants and killed their parents, clashing with X-Factor and Generation X. **DW**

Order, The
see page 262

Overmind

FIRST APPEARANCE Fantastic Four #113 (August 1971)
REAL NAME Grom
OCCUPATION Conqueror **BASE** Various
HEIGHT 10 ft **WEIGHT** 750 lbs **EYES** Black **HAIR** Red
SPECIAL POWERS/ABILITIES Possesses vast psionic powers. He can lift up to 70 tons, read the minds of others and manipulate matter through the power of his mind.

Grom led the interplanetary conquerors known as the Eternals to victory as they enslaved a thousand worlds. But when they faced defeat on the enormous world Gigantus, the Eternals selected Grom to be the sole survivor of their race and transferred their mental energies to him, making him into the Overmind. When he came to conquer Earth, the Fantastic Four, Doctor Doom, and the Stranger stopped him. After that, he tried to conquer Earth-712, but Squadron Supreme defeated him, reducing his powers. He joined the Defenders for a while, but recently he was forced to work for the Thunderbolts to avoid jail. **TB, MF**

Oya

FIRST APPEARANCE Uncanny X-Men #528 (November 2010)
REAL NAME Idie Okonkwo
OCCUPATION Student **BASE** New York **HEIGHT** 5 ft 8 in
WEIGHT 115 lbs **EYES** Brown (when using her powers, right is blue, left is red) **HAIR** Black
SPECIAL POWERS/ABILITIES Idie can move temperatures from one place to another, generating fire and freezing cold.

Fourteen-year-old Idie Okonkwo was one of the Five Lights, the first five mutants to manifest their powers after M-Day. A religious girl growing up in Nigeria, she was horrified to discover her powers, as were many others in her village, who considered her a witch. Storm and Hope Summers came to rescue her. She lived on Utopia with the X-Men for a while, but later moved back east to be one of the first students at Wolverine's new Jean Grey School for Higher Learning. **MF**

ORDER, THE

California's Fifty-State Initiative Team

FACTFILE

NOTABLE MEMBERS

ANTHEM (Henry Hellrung) Actor and team leader, fires electric blasts, flight.

ARALUNE (Rebecca "Becky" Ryan) Pop star, shapeshifter, flight.

CALAMITY (James Wa) Ex-athlete, engineer, superhuman speed, flight.

VIRGINIA "PEPPER" POTTS Executive, uses telepresence equipment to tap Stark satellites and coordinate team strategy.

SUPERNAUT (Milo Fields) Pilots massive armor suit.

VEDA (Magdelena "Maggie" Neuntauben) Actress, generates and controls golems and can see through their eyes.

BASE Bradbury, California

FIRST APPEARANCE
Civil War #6 (January 2007)

Two teams have called themselves the Order. The first was the DEFENDERS while the second was created for the FIFTY-STATE INITIATIVE.

DEFENDING THE ORDER

One of the first foes the Defenders fought was the alien scientist Yandroth. As he died, he cursed the original Defenders—the HULK, NAMOR, the SILVER SURFER, and DOCTOR STRANGE—to always reunite whenever catastrophe struck the Earth. Worst of all, every time they did, they would become more and more selfish. Unaware of the curse, these Defenders eventually decided to form the Order and take an active interest in shaping the world's future.

The other Defenders figured this out and broke Yandroth's curse, foiling his plan to be reborn with the negative energy the Order was generating around the planet. The Earth goddess Gaea gave NIGHTHAWK the power to call the Defenders together instead, but without any of the side effects. After the end of the CIVIL WAR, Tony Stark (IRON MAN) became the director of SHIELD. Already the leader of the AVENGERS, he decided to launch the Fifty-State Initiative, which planned to put a team of heroes in every state in the nation.

In their first solo outing, the Order faced off against the Infernal Man and lost two members, the androids Bannerman Brown and Green.

Stark formed the team for California from scratch, using handpicked people without any pre-existing powers. He put his most trusted employee, Pepper POTTS, in charge of the team. For the field leader, he tapped Henry Hellrung, an actor who had played Tony Stark in films—and who also had sponsored Tony in Alcoholics Anonymous. Together, they trained a crew of actors, singers, and other entertainers to become the Initiative's California team. The roster included: Anthem (Henry Hellrung), Aralune, Calamity, Supernaut, and Veda, as well as Aphrodite, Avona, Bannerman Brown and Green, Corona, Heavy, Maul, Mulholland, and Pierce.

THE ORDER
1 Aralune ***2*** Supernaut ***3*** Anthem
4 Calamity ***5*** Veda ***6*** Mulholland

PANTHEON MODEL

The team's structure followed that of the GODS OF OLYMPUS. Stark served as Zeus, Potts as Hera, and Hellrung as Apollo, with the other members of the team in various roles. The roles were more important than the people who filled them. If members misbehaved or disobeyed orders, they could be fired and their powers stripped from them. They were then replaced with new heroes-to-be.

The group saw action in the final battle against CAPTAIN AMERICA's resistance, clashing with the female gang the Black Dahlias, controlled by Ezekiel STANE. They also fought against the SKRULLS during the SECRET INVASION, being one of the few Initiative teams to have escaped Skrull infiltration. MF

ESSENTIAL STORYLINES

- ***The Order Vol. 1 #1–6***
The original Order forms out of Yandroth's curse—and the Defenders stop them.
- ***The Order Vol. 2 #1–10***
The entire run of the second version of the Order is only 10 issues, covering from its origins to its demise as a public-relations-focused team.

FACTFILE

REAL NAME
Karen Page

OCCUPATION
Sometime secretary, actress and radio personality

BASE
New York City

HEIGHT 5 ft 7 in
WEIGHT 125 lbs
EYES Blue
HAIR Blonde

FIRST APPEARANCE
Daredevil #1 (April 1964)

POWERS
Efficient secretarial skills and fair ability as an actor and presenter; some aptitude for street fighting, having battled alongside both Daredevil and Black Widow.

PAGE, KAREN

Karen's love for Matt was always troubled.

Karen Page's relationship with Matt Murdock spawned happiness but also much mutual heartache. Matt hired her as his secretary, but their relationship only blossomed when he told her about his secret identity. This happiness was not to last: in the middle of wedding preparations, Karen asked Matt to give up his DAREDEVIL alter ego. When he refused she ended the engagement and entered a long vicious cycle of self-destruction.

Embarking on a career as an actress, things went badly. As film and TV work dried up she became involved in the porn industry and fell prey to heroin addiction. At her lowest ebb, Karen told a dealer Matt's secret identity in exchange for drugs. Fortunately, Matt is a man with a forgiving heart. After helping her kick the habit, their relationship continued intermittently until she was killed—just another of Matt's lovers to fall at BULLSEYE's hand. **AD**

PALADIN

FIRST APPEARANCE Daredevil Vol. 1 #150 (January 1978)
REAL NAME Paul Denning
OCCUPATION Mercenary **BASE** Mobile
HEIGHT 6 ft 2 in **WEIGHT** 225 lbs **EYES** Brown **HAIR** Brown
SPECIAL POWERS/ABILITIES Enhanced strength, stamina, and reflexes; carries a nerve-scrambling stun gun; costume deflects most small-arms fire and goggles permit vision in darkness.

Paladin has teamed with Spider-Man to advance his mercenary career.

Paladin is infamous for his mercenary attitude, yet his considerable charm has gotten him far in life. He has allied with many heroes, but he doesn't hesitate to abandon his partners if he's not getting paid. He's even accepted contracts on heroes like DAREDEVIL and the PUNISHER. Paladin has often worked with SILVER SABLE's Wild Pack. He joined Heroes for Hire, but only to get close to capturing CAPTAIN AMERICA. He also worked with the THUNDERBOLTS but betrayed them to keep the Spear of Odin from them. He subsequently rejoined the Heroes for Hire. **DW, MF**

PANTHEON

Making a secret stand for human rights

The Pantheon is a family of long-lived superhumans who style themselves after the Greek gods of old. Centuries ago, Vali, their patriarch, bartered with the alien race known as the Troyjans for the secret of eternal youth. Afterward, now known as AGAMEMNON, he fathered several children and adopted others, creating an organization of superhuman operatives bolstered by non-enhanced doctors, scientists, and technicians.

THE PANTHEON
1 Paris **2** Ajax **3** Hector
4 Ulysses **5** Atalanta

The Pantheon operated as a covert strike team, pledged to maintaining the stability of the world.

FACTFILE

NOTABLE MEMBERS

ACHILLES Virtually invulnerable; his invulnerability is weakened by the presence of gamma radiation.

AGAMEMNON Immortality; ability to project a holographic representation of himself.

AJAX Massive superhuman strength and a childlike intellect.

ATALANTA Fires energy arrows.

CASSIOPEIA Fires energy blasts fueled by starlight.

DELPHI Able to see glimpses of the future.

HECTOR Trained fighter; can walk on air; carries a plasma mace.

PARIS Possesses an empathetic sense of those around him.

PROMETHEUS Drives a high-tech armored vehicle.

ULYSSES Expert fighter; carries an energy sword and shield.

OTHER MEMBERS
ANDROMEDA, JASON, PERSEUS

BASE
The Mount, Arizona

FIRST APPEARANCE
Incredible Hulk Vol. 2 #377 (January 1991)

ENTER THE HULK

Agamemnon feared that mankind would destroy or despoil the Earth, so he and his clan moved in secret to prevent potential disasters before they could reach fruition. The Pantheon's existence first became known to the world at large when it moved to recruit Bruce Banner, the incredible HULK, to its ranks. At that time, the Hulk's fragmented psyche had been somewhat restored, giving him the intellect of Banner with the massive strength and power of the Hulk. Wanting to make amends for the destruction he'd caused to the world while he was no more than a rampaging brute, the Hulk agreed to joining Agamemnon's cause, and eventually came to function as the Pantheon's field leader.

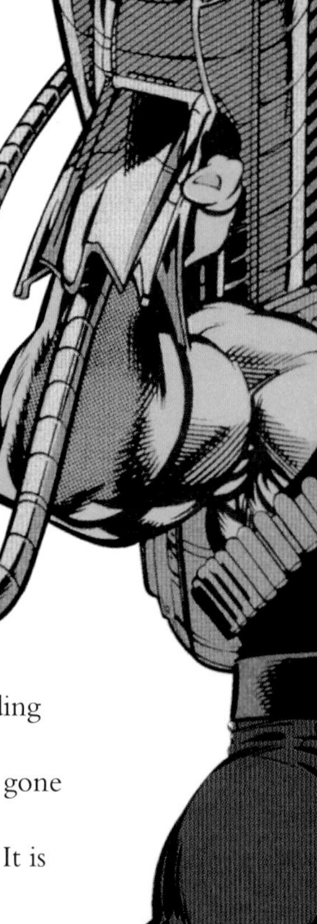

The Pantheon had access to high-tech weaponry

For a time, the Hulk led the Pantheon, as in this battle against the Endless Knights.

THE PANTHEON AT WAR

But things went wrong when the Troyjans returned to Earth, and the truth about Vali's deal with them came out: in exchange for the secret of bestowing his godly attributes and extended lifespan on his offspring, Vali had promised to give the best of them up to the Troyjans to use as they saw fit. A vast battle ensued, in which the Troyjans were repelled and Agamemnon was taken into custody by the Pantheon. He responded by summoning the Endless Knights, massive zombie warriors whose ranks included undead former members of the Pantheon itself, and commanding them to destroy the Pantheon's base, the Mount. Though the Pantheon survived this attack, its ranks were decimated, and the Hulk left, having gone through another psychological shift that changed the nature of his transformations. Since then, the Pantheon has gone back underground. It is presumed to have returned to covertly interfering in the affairs of man whenever the future of mankind is imperiled. **TB**

ESSENTIAL STORYLINES

- ***Hulk #372–379***
The Pantheon recruits the newly-intelligent Hulk into their organization.
- ***Hulk #422–425***
During his trial, Agamemnon summons the Endless Knights to destroy the Pantheon and the Hulk.

Parker, Aunt May

FACTFILE
REAL NAME
May Reilly Parker
OCCUPATION
Homemaker
BASE
New York City

HEIGHT 5 ft 5 in
WEIGHT 110 lbs
EYES Blue
HAIR White

FIRST APPEARANCE
Amazing Fantasy #15 (August 1962)

POWERS
Amazing cook, (particularly her corn beef hash) and formidable personality—even Wolverine is afraid of her.

It may not have always been easy, but May Parker's life has certainly been eventful. Following a difficult childhood, May found love with Ben Parker, their marriage being further enriched when they became guardians to Ben's nephew, Peter. Sadly, their life together ended prematurely when Ben was shot dead by a burglar. The years that followed would be testing.

Happening upon Peter's ragged Spider-Man costume, May finally realized the startling truth about her nephew.

After Peter became Spider-Man, he kept his secret identity from her for fear of upsetting her health. She learned it at one point, but she has now forgotten. An assassin hired by the Kingpin shot May after Spider-Man revealed his identity to the world during the Civil War.

Spider-Man intervened just in time to prevent Doctor Octopus marrying May.

To save her life, Peter and his wife Mary Jane Watson gave up their entire marriage to Mephisto, who wiped it—and everyone's memory of Peter's secret—from existence. Restored to health, May eventually married Jay Jameson and moved to Boston to start a new life. **AD, MF**

Parker, Uncle Ben

FACTFILE
REAL NAME
Benjamin Parker
OCCUPATION
Retired
BASE
New York City

HEIGHT 5 ft 9 in
WEIGHT 175 lbs
EYES Blue
HAIR White

FIRST APPEARANCE
Amazing Fantasy #15 (August 1962)

POWERS
Wisdom, charisma, integrity, strength of personality and high moral standards.

Although never rich, his wisdom and fair-mindedness earned Ben Parker the respect of everyone he met. A carnival barker in his youth, Ben grew up in the same neighbourhood as May Reilly, for whom he harbored deep feelings. Love did not come easily to the pair, though—Ben was forced to compete for May's affections with the glamorous Johnny Jerome. It was only when May learnt that Johnny was a petty crook that she finally accepted Ben into her life.

Following his brother's death, Ben felt honor bound to raise his nephew, Peter, as his very own.

Throughout their time together, Ben and May were to struggle financially, and these monetary straits only worsened when they adopted Ben's nephew, Peter, as their own. In spite of these pressures, however, Peter brought considerable joy into their lives. Tragically that joy would be cut short, when Ben was killed by a burglar's bullet. The memory of his kindly uncle inspired Peter to use his newfound spider powers to do good in the world, and so Ben Parker's spirit lives on. **AD**

Ben's tragic murder continues to inspire Peter Parker, even to this day.

Pathway

FIRST APPEARANCE Alpha Flight #48 (July 1987)
REAL NAME Laura Dean
OCCUPATION Adventurer **BASE** Canada
HEIGHT 4 ft 8 in **WEIGHT** 90 lbs
EYES Brown **HAIR** Black
SPECIAL POWERS/ABILITIES Laura can open portals to other dimensions and can switch places with her twin, Goblyn, who lives in a dimension called Liveworld.

Laura Dean's parents feared mutants and had her twin aborted when it became clear she was a mutant. Even in the womb, Laura was able to protect her sister Goblyn by sending her into a different dimension. Laura grew up autistic and was sent to a clinic that turned out to be run by the villain Scramble. She was later forced to work for Bedlam's Derangers. ALPHA FLIGHT rescued her and put her into Beta Flight, the secondary team for Department H. Beta Flight has since been shut down. **MF**

Payback

FIRST APPEARANCE Punisher War Journal #48 (November 1992)
REAL NAME Edward "Eddie" Dyson
OCCUPATION Unknown, former vigilante
BASE Possibly Madison, Wisconsin. Formerly New York.
HEIGHT 5 ft 10 in **WEIGHT** 170 lbs
EYES Brown **HAIR** Brown
SPECIAL POWERS/ABILITIES Skilled in both unarmed and armed combat and uses a wide range of firearms.

Eddie Dyson was a rookie police officer in the NYPD when he discovered his squad were taking payment from the mob. He sought the PUNISHER's advice who persuaded him to expose this corruption to Internal Affairs. The mafia took revenge and killed Dyson's family, so Dyson became Payback to avenge their death. At first, he blamed the Punisher, but the two made peace when the Punisher helped Payback kill Steve Venture—the mobster responsible for the family's murder. Dyson retired but he was attacked by Vigil, and became Payback again. He fought Vigil, Heathen, and the Trust with Lynn Michaels then fled for the Midwest with her and her father. **DW**

Penance

FIRST APPEARANCE The Amazing Spider-Man Annual #22 (September 1988) **REAL NAME** Robert Baldwin
OCCUPATION Adventurer **BASE** New York City
HEIGHT 6 ft **WEIGHT** 190 lbs **EYES** Blue **HAIR** Blond
SPECIAL POWERS/ABILITIES Whenever Robbie feels pain, he can fire explosive blasts from his body, create a dangerous field of energy around himself, and form a force field that allows him to levitate.

Robbie Baldwin was originally the hero SPEEDBALL. When he led the NEW WARRIORS into an attack against NITRO that cost over 600 lives and sparked the CIVIL WAR, the guilt he felt altered the way he interacted with his powers. His suit of armor had 612 inward-facing spikes, one for each of the people who died that day, and the pain from them activated his powers. He joined the THUNDERBOLTS and went AWOL to bring NITRO to justice. After the DARK REIGN, he returned to being Speedball and worked at the AVENGERS Academy for a while. **MF**

Patriot

PATRIOT

FACTFILE
REAL NAME
Elijah Bradley
OCCUPATION
Student
BASE
New York City

HEIGHT 6 ft 2 ins
WEIGHT 205 lbs
EYES Brown
HAIR Black

FIRST APPEARANCE
Young Avengers #1 (April 2005)

POWERS

For a time, Patriot used MGH (Mutant Growth Hormone) to give him enhanced strength, speed, and durability, but he now has these powers due to the super-solider serum.

Elijah Bradley is the grandson of Isaiah Bradley, the black CAPTAIN AMERICA of World War II, whose mind had been reduced to that of a child by the super-soldier serum that empowered him. When Iron Lad needed help battling KANG the Conqueror, Eli resorted to using the designer drug MGH to give himself superhuman powers so he could become a founding member of the YOUNG AVENGERS. When his teammates learned that Eli was using such dangerous drugs, they convinced him to give them up. Critically wounded saving the original Captain America from a KREE attack, Eli received a blood transfusion from his grandfather. This saved his life and also gave him Isaiah's superpowers.

During the CIVIL WAR, Eli and most of the Young Avengers sided with Captain America's anti-registration forces. They also were the first people to fight the SKRULLS in Manhattan during the SECRET INVASION, and they worked against HAMMER during the DARK REIGN. **TB, MF**

YOUNG AVENGERS
1 Wiccan
2 Stature
3 Hulkling
4 The Patriot
5 Kate Bishop

Pendragon, King Arthur

FIRST APPEARANCE Black Knight Comics #1 (May 1955)
REAL NAME Arthur Pendragon
OCCUPATION King of the Britons **BASE** Avalon, Otherworld
HEIGHT 6 ft 2 in **WEIGHT** 230 lbs **EYES** Blue **HAIR** Brown
SPECIAL POWERS/ABILITIES Inspirational and courageous leader and strategist; a highly skilled horseman and swordsman; he wielded the indestructible, magical sword Excalibur, which protected whoever wielded it against injury in battle.

When Arthur pulled an enchanted sword from a stone in the 5th century, he became the king of all Britons and founded the court at Camelot. After breaking the sword in battle, Arthur received the mystical Excalibur from the Lady of the Lake. He had a son, MORDRED, by his sorceress half-sister MORGAN LE FAY, and married Guinevere. When Arthur learned of an affair between Guinevere and Lancelot he sentenced both to execution, but Lancelot rescued Guinevere. Morgan Le Fay allied with Mordred and raised armies against Camelot. Arthur died while striking a mortal blow against Mordred. In the Otherworld realm of Avalon, Arthur awaited his return, and reappeared in modern times to battle the Necromon. The mystical Pendragon spirit has been used to empower the warriors known as the Knights of Pendragon. **DW**

PERSUASION

FIRST APPEARANCE Alpha Flight #41 (December 1986)
REAL NAME Kara Killgrave **OCCUPATION** Adventurer
BASE Mobile **HEIGHT** 5 ft 3 in **WEIGHT** 120 lbs
EYES Brown **HAIR** Black
SPECIAL POWERS/ABILITIES Has the mutant power to secrete psychoactive will-sapping pheromones from her pores that allow her to link with the minds of others and make them do her bidding.

Unaware she was the daughter of the PURPLE MAN, Kara Killgrave was shocked when her skin turned purple and her powers manifested themselves. She took the name Purple Girl and joined Beta Flight, ALPHA FLIGHT's training group. When the group split up, Kara went home to her mother. She followed the teams through a number of breakups and reunions, eventually taking the name Persuasion. She retained her powers after M-Day and has been seen at the X-MEN's new headquarters in San Francisco. **AD, MF**

PHALANX

The techno-organic race called the Technarchy creates its food by using its transmode virus to convert organic matter into Phalanx, a collective intelligence lifeform. Members of the Technarchy then feed on the Phalanx, draining away its life energy. While experimenting on the renegade Technarch WARLOCK, human scientists obtained a strain of the transmode virus and injected it into humans, hoping to create a new generation of SENTINEL robots. Transformed into Phalanx, their subjects began assimilating other humans. Fortunately, the Phalanx could not digest mutants, and the X-MEN stopped them. In space, another group of Phalanx threatened the SHI'AR Empire, but the X-Men foiled their plans as well. The insane android ULTRON subsequently led yet another breed of Phalanx against the KREE, nearly conquering them until several heroes and the Technarchy intervened (*see* ANNIHILATION). **AD, MF**

Sentient biological weapons, the Phalanx are formidable adversaries.

FACTFILE
REAL NAME
Inapplicable; alien being with collective intelligence
BASE
Outer space

HEIGHT Variable
WEIGHT Variable
EYES Unknown
HAIR None

FIRST APPEARANCE
Uncanny X-Men #305 (October 1993)

POWERS
Transforms sentient beings into techno-organic lifeforms and assimilates them into its collective. Superhumanly strong, also possess ability to teleport and shapeshift—molding their limbs into weapons or mimicking the appearance of others.

PETROVICH, IVAN

FIRST APPEARANCE Amazing Adventures #1 (August 1970)
REAL NAME Ivan Petrovich **OCCUPATION** Chauffeur
BASE Mobile **HEIGHT** 6 ft 5 in **WEIGHT** 300 lbs
EYES Brown **HAIR** Brown
SPECIAL POWERS/ABILITIES Does not possess superpowers, but is a skilled hand-to-hand combatant; a reliable chauffeur and steadfast ally of the Black Widow.

After the devastating siege of Stalingrad during World War II, Russian soldier Ivan Petrovich had been searching the city without success for his lost sister. As he was walking through the city's ruins he heard a woman's cries from a burning building. As the woman died in the fire, she let her baby fall into his arms. Petrovich decided to raise the girl as his own. She was Natasha Romanova who eventually became the BLACK WIDOW, Russia's top spy. Petrovich, feeling responsible for Natasha, accompanied her to America as her chauffeur. He lived with the Black Widow and DAREDEVIL while the two heroes struck up a romance in San Francisco. His son Yuri Petrovich briefly served as the fourth CRIMSON DYNAMO. He remains in good health, despite his age. **DW**

PHANTOM EAGLE

FIRST APPEARANCE Marvel Super Heroes #16 (September 1968)
REAL NAME Karl Kaufman **OCCUPATION** Pilot
BASE Mobile **HEIGHT** 5 ft 11 in **WEIGHT** 175 lbs
EYES Blue **HAIR** Brown
SPECIAL POWERS/ABILITIES Although he had no superhuman powers, Phantom Eagle was an extraordinary pilot, exceptionally skilled in aerial combat.

When World War I broke out, ace flyer Karl Kaufman wanted to use his skills against the Germans, but he feared reprisals against his German parents. So he donned a costume and mask and took the name Phantom Eagle. He became one of the greatest aerial warriors of the war, wining many dogfights, and then joined Freedom's Five, a team of costumed heroes who assisted the Allies. Kaufman's identity was discovered by a German pilot, who killed him and his parents. The ghost of the Phantom Eagle hunted the pilot down and killed him. **MT**

PHANTOM RIDER, ***see page 268***

PHASTOS

FIRST APPEARANCE Eternals #1 (October 1985)
REAL NAME Phastos **OCCUPATION** Technologist, weaponsmith
BASE Ruhr Valley, Germany **HEIGHT** 6 ft 3 in
WEIGHT 410 lbs **EYES** Brown **HAIR** Bald (black beard)
SPECIAL POWERS/ABILITIES Able to fly and levitate objects; virtually invulnerable, super-strong, and projects cosmic energy from eyes or hands; ingenious inventor; hammer fires energy bolts.

Phastos is an ETERNAL, a nearly immortal race created thousands of years ago by the alien CELESTIALS. Being a weaponsmith, Phastos was mistaken for the Olympian god Hephaestus (VULCAN) during the days of ancient Greece (*see* GODS OF OLYMPUS). Phastos is more reticent than his fellows, having a melancholy spirit and an ambivalence toward fighting. When APOCALYPSE tried to incite a new war with the DEVIANTS, the Eternals decided to go public as Super Heroes. In his new identity, Phastos adopted the codename Ceasefire. **DW**

PHANTOM RIDER

PHANTOM RIDER

FACTFILE

REAL NAME
Carter Slade

OCCUPATION
Schoolteacher, vigilante

BASE
Bison Bend in the Old West

HEIGHT 6 ft 1 in
WEIGHT 200 lbs
EYES Blue
HAIR Reddish-blond

FIRST APPEARANCE
Ghost Rider #1 (February 1967)

POWERS

A fast draw and a brilliant marksman; formidable hand-to-hand combatant; notable horseman.

Originally a schoolteacher in the Wild West, Carter Slade was shot by a ruthless local land baron, but a Comanche Indian called Flaming Star saved his life. After Carter recovered, Flaming Star gave him a white horse and a cloak covered with a phosphorescent dust. Styling himself the Phantom Rider, Carter began a one-man battle against injustice.

Not knowing that the Phantom Rider was his brother, Marshall Lincoln Slade teamed up with him to battle the Reverend Reaper, a vicious gunfighter set on taking control of Bison Bend, the town Carter had sworn to protect. In their final confrontation, both Carter and the reverend died. Learning the truth about his brother, Lincoln decided to follow in his footsteps. He later went mad and died while battling a time-traveling MOCKINGBIRD.

In modern times, Lincoln's descendant, archaeologist Hamilton Slade, became a modern-day Phantom Rider. Nick FURY made J.T. Slade—Carter's grandson—a member of his new SECRET WARRIORS team. J.T. can charge weapons with fire and calls himself Hellfire. He turned out to be a double agent for HYDRA and is now dead. Later, Hamilton's daughter Jaime became possessed, and he was killed while exorcising the demon from her. **AD, MF**

PIP THE TROLL

FIRST APPEARANCE Strange Tales #179 (April 1975)
REAL NAME Pip Gofern
OCCUPATION Former bearer of the Space Gem, prince of Laxidazia and painter **BASE** Mobile within Milky Way Galaxy
HEIGHT 4 ft 4 in **WEIGHT** 144 lbs **EYES** Pink **HAIR** Red
SPECIAL POWERS/ABILITIES Claims to be irresistible to women; could teleport anywhere in the universe when he possessed the Space Gem.

Born a prince on the alien world of Laxidazia, Pip was exiled from the court for befriending a tribe of trolls. Missionaries from the Universal Church of Truth came to Laxidazia to convert the natives. When the trolls resisted, the Church began exterminating them. Pip was captured and placed on a Death-Ship where he met Adam WARLOCK. They became friends and overthrew the Church. Warlock called on Pip to help stop THANOS from using the Infinity Gems to control reality and later gave him the Space Gem as a reward, making him a member of the Infinity Watch. The Watch disbanded after losing control of the gems. Pip joined X-FACTOR and was later killed by a bullet to the head. **TD, MF**

PHOTON

PHOTON

FACTFILE

REAL NAME
Genis-Vell

OCCUPATION
Adventurer

BASE
Mobile throughout the universe

HEIGHT 6 ft 2 in
WEIGHT 210 lbs
EYES Blue
HAIR Blond (becomes white when "cosmically aware")

FIRST APPEARANCE
Silver Surfer Annual #6 (1993)

POWERS

Kree Nega-Bands (now absorbed into his body) confer superhuman strength and durability, the ability to fly, the power to project concussive energy blasts. Genis-Vell also possesses cosmic awareness, allowing him to perceive cosmic dangers.

The first Photon was Monica Rambeau of the AVENGERS (*see* SPECTRUM).

Following the death of KREE warrior CAPTAIN MAR-VELL, his lover Elysius used cell samples from his body to conceive a son named Genis-Vell. To keep the child safe from harm, his aging was accelerated so he rapidly reached maturity. When he discovered his heroic lineage, Genis-Vell donned his father's Nega-Bands and became an adventurer, called Legacy. He later adopted his father's codename, CAPTAIN MARVEL.

In order to save the life of his father's friend Rick JONES, Genis-Vell's atomic structure was bonded to Rick's. This meant that whenever Genis-Vell was in the Earth dimension, Rick was cast into the Microverse, and vice versa. Genis-Vell went insane and helped cosmic entities Entropy and Epiphany destroy the universe. However, Genis then triggered a new Big Bang, recreating the cosmos. Elysius and another Titan, STARFOX, returned Genis to sanity. The bonding between Jones and Genis was undone, allowing them to exist on Earth separately.

After ATLAS beat Genis nearly to death, BARON ZEMO used moonstones to heal him. Genis took the name Photon and joined the THUNDERBOLTS. Zemo learned that the moonstones' effect on Genis would cause the universe's destruction so he killed Genis and scattered his body through the Darkforce Dimension. **PS, MF**

PIECEMEAL

FIRST APPEARANCE Incredible Hulk #403 (March 1993)
REAL NAME Unrevealed
OCCUPATION Criminal **BASE** Loch Ness, Scotland
HEIGHT 7 ft 6 in **WEIGHT** 1,400 lbs **EYES** Red **HAIR** Gray
SPECIAL POWERS/ABILITIES Possesses all of the abilities of the criminal New World Order, including superhuman strength, the ability to fire energy blasts, and razor-sharp claws.

The man who would become Piecemeal was an operative from the COMMISSION ON SUPERHUMAN ACTIVITIES sent to spy on the RED SKULL. The Skull captured him, intending to make him into a living symbol of his criminal organization, the New World Order.

Imbued with the properties of members of the Order, and with memories of his previous life erased, Piecemeal became enthralled with being alive. He began using his powers to absorb the life-experiences of others, until the HULK seemingly ended his menace. **TB**

Pixie

FIRST APPEARANCE New X-Men #5 (November 2004)
REAL NAME Megan Gwynn **OCCUPATION** Adventurer
BASE New York **HEIGHT** 5 ft 4 in **WEIGHT** 121 lbs
EYES Black **HAIR** Pink and black
SPECIAL POWERS/ABILITIES Megan can fly and generate hallucinogenic dust. She can detect the supernatural and cast spells, including ones to teleport groups long distances. She also wields a Souldagger.

Megan grew up in a Welsh mining town, unaware that her father was Mastermind, making her the half-sister of Lady Mastermind. She joined the Xavier Institute, where she was transported to Limbo. There, Magik tried to steal a part of her soul to make a Soulsword but was interrupted and only fashioned a Souldagger instead. Pixie joined the X-Men and started to use magic to teleport her teammates around the globe and back to Limbo. **MF**

Phobos

FIRST APPEARANCE Ares #1 (March 2006)
REAL NAME Alexander Aaron **OCCUPATION** Adventurer
BASE New York City **HEIGHT** 5 ft 1 in **WEIGHT** 95 lbs
EYES Blue **HAIR** Blond
SPECIAL POWERS/ABILITIES Alex is an immortal god of Olympus, with superhuman durability, endurance, intelligence, and strength. He can instill fear in others by looking into their eyes, and predict the future.

Alexander is the son of the Greek god Ares. He was kidnapped by Amatsu-Mikaboshi, who wanted to use him against the other gods, but Ares and Zeus rescued him. Alexander wasn't aware of his lineage until his powers began to develop. He worked with his father in the Avengers for a while, then joined Nick Fury's Secret Warriors. Fury didn't let Alexander join in the defense of Asgard from Ares, knowing that Ares might be (and was) killed. Phobos later died in battle with the villain Gorgon, slain by the sword Godkiller. **MF**

Plantman

Strange Tales #113 was Plantman's first appearance.

While working in London as a botanist's assistant, Samuel Smithers became involved with experiments to explore the mental activity of plants. After ten years the botanist died, and Smithers moved to the US, where he planned to continue his work in trying to increase the intelligence of plants so that humans could communicate with them. However, due to his lack of formal education he had difficulty in finding support for his ideas and was forced to take a job as a gardener. Smithers tried to combine the job with his research, but was eventually fired for spending too much time on his experiments.

FACTFILE

REAL NAME
Samuel Smithers

OCCUPATION
Professional criminal; formerly a gardener

BASE
A submarine in the Atlantic Ocean

HEIGHT 6 ft
WEIGHT 190 lbs
EYES Green
HAIR Dark gray

FIRST APPEARANCE
Strange Tales #113 (October 1963)

POWERS

Plantman's projector weapons allow him to control plants, animating their limbs to attack a victim; and to manipulate plants so they look like duplicates of humans.

Revenge

Not long after Smithers lost his job, a bolt of lightning struck his experimental plant ray-gun, charging the device with the power to control and animate plant life. Smithers put on a costume and, taking the name Plantman, sought revenge on the man who had fired him, but was stopped by the Human Torch, who destroyed the plant-gun. Undeterred, Plantman built a second, more powerful weapon, and tried to kill the Human Torch, but his plan failed. Later he joined the international crime syndicate, the Maggia. Creating plant duplicates of himself, Plantman battled the X-Men, the Avengers, Namor, Triton, and SHIELD, among others.

The Plantman simuloid possessed all the powers of the original Plantman.

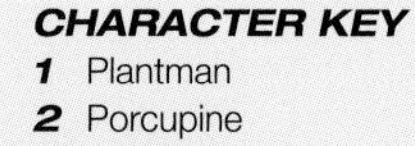

CHARACTER KEY
1 Plantman
2 Porcupine
3 The Eel
4 The Scarecrow

Transformation

Over the years, Smithers's body gradually mutated to become more and more plantlike. At one point, he connected with the Verdant Green—the manifestation of the Earth's biosphere—and was given the option of wiping humans from the planet or preserving them. Although his transformation had already cost him a great deal of his humanity, he chose to let the people of Earth live. For a while, Smithers worked with the Thunderbolts under Hawkeye's leadership, using the name Blackheath. He has since returned to prison to serve out his sentence and to try to reconnect with his sense of humanity. **MT, MF**

Polaris

While her green hair marked her as a mutant, Lorna Dane had no idea growing up that she had been adopted, and that her true father was MAGNETO. When her powers manifested, she found herself at the center of an all-out war between the X-MEN and the demonic MESMERO for control of her abilities. Falling in love with the X-Man HAVOK, Lorna desired nothing more than to live a normal life. But fate would not let her be, and time and again she was pulled to the center of mutant strife as Polaris, mistress of magnetism. She led X-FACTOR, beside Havok, at its start. She later joined the X-Men. She lost her powers on M-Day but APOCALYPSE restored them when he made her Pestilence, one of his horsemen. She and Havok broke up when he left her at the altar, but they renewed their relationship during their attempt to save the SHI'AR Empire from Havok's brother VULCAN. They have since parted again, as Havok took the leadership of the AVENGERS Unity Squad while she stayed with X-Factor. **MF**

As the years went by, Polaris' mutant magnetic powers had a detrimental effect on her mental stability, interfering with the electrical impulses in her brain. However, her friend Banshee (*see* SIRYN) agreed to become the new incarnation of the Celtic goddess Morrigan in order to acquire the power to heal Polaris's mind.

FACTFILE

REAL NAME
Lorna Dane

OCCUPATION
Adventurer

BASE
The Xavier Institute for Higher Learning

HEIGHT 5 ft 7 in
WEIGHT 115 lbs
EYES Green
HAIR Green

FIRST APPEARANCE
Uncanny X-Men #49 (October 1968)

POLARIS

POWERS

Polaris has power over magnetism and can use it to fly, create force fields, and manipulate anything made of magnetic materials. She also now has a healing factor.

Porcupine

FIRST APPEARANCE Tales to Astonish #48 (October 1963)
REAL NAME Alexander Gentry
OCCUPATION Weapons designer/criminal **BASE** New York City
HEIGHT (with battlesuit) 6 ft 7 in **WEIGHT** (with battlesuit) 305 lbs
EYES Blue-gray **HAIR** Brown
SPECIAL POWERS/ABILITIES Battlesuit fired quills, laser beams, bombs, gases, and other weapons. Belt jets enabled him to fly.

A weapons designer for the US government, Alexander Gentry invented a battlesuit inspired by a porcupine. It was covered in razor-sharp, projectile quills that he could fire at opponents, and quill-like tubes through which other weapons could be fired. Getting greedy, Gentry used the suit to become the Porcupine, but his criminal career was a failure. CAPTAIN AMERICA agreed to buy the battlesuit from Gentry if he would help the AVENGERS defeat the SERPENT SOCIETY. Gentry agreed, but was fatally impaled on his own quill during the battle. A new Porcupine surfaced later and wound up working with the THUNDERBOLTS. **PS, MF**

Potts, Virginia "Pepper"

"Pepper" Potts became Tony Stark's secretary early in his career. Stark entrusted her with the secret of his identity as IRON MAN but didn't notice her crush on him. She eventually married Stark's chauffeur, Harold "Happy" HOGAN and dropped out of Tony's life. Pepper and Harold later divorced—and then remarried, by which time they were both working for Tony again. Soon after Hogan died from injuries inflicted by the SPYMASTER, Pepper joined the ORDER, the California team of the FIFTY-STATE INITIATIVE, calling herself Hera.

Later, Ezekiel STANE harmed Pepper, and Tony had to turn her into a cyborg to save her life. During the DARK REIGN, Tony made her CEO of Stark Industries, where her main job was to keep sensitive information from going to HAMMER, which was controlled by Norman Osborn (*see* GREEN GOBLIN). Calling herself Rescue, she was forced to flee its headquarters in her own suit of power armor. She and Tony became lovers as she helped him escape from MADAME MASQUE, and afterward she infiltrated HAMMER disguised as Madame Masque. She later had to give up her Rescue armor after the artificial intelligence inside it went rogue. **DW, MF**

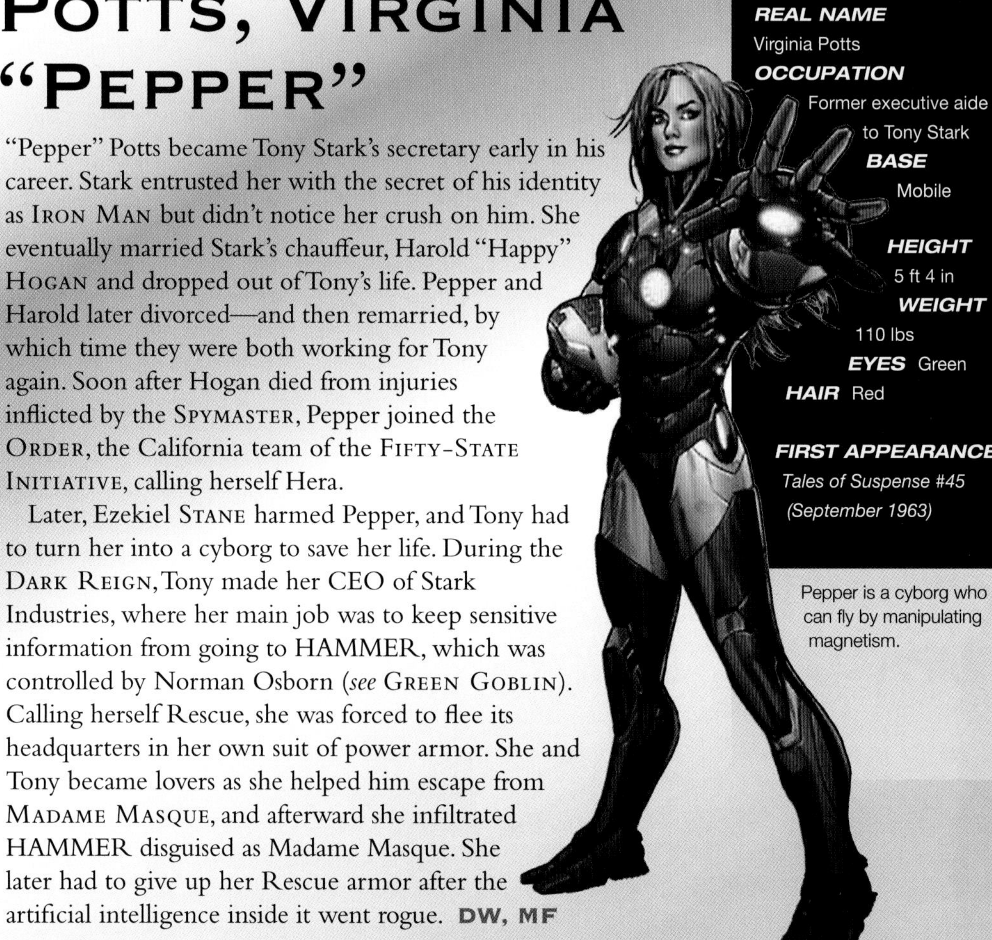

FACTFILE

REAL NAME
Virginia Potts

OCCUPATION
Former executive aide to Tony Stark

BASE
Mobile

HEIGHT
5 ft 4 in

WEIGHT
110 lbs

EYES Green
HAIR Red

FIRST APPEARANCE
Tales of Suspense #45 (September 1963)

POTTS, VIRGINIA "PEPPER"

POWERS

Pepper is a cyborg who can fly by manipulating magnetism.

Powderkeg

FIRST APPEARANCE Captain Marvel #1 (December 1995)
REAL NAME Frank Skorina
OCCUPATION Prisoner **BASE** The Big House
HEIGHT/WEIGHT/EYES Unrevealed **HAIR** Red
SPECIAL POWERS/ABILITIES Secretes nitro-glycerine through skin; when body strikes object with sufficient force the chemical ignites, causing an explosion.

Powderkeg was a member of the MASTERS OF EVIL during DOCTOR OCTOPUS's ill-conceived turn as leader. Following the failure of the group's attempt to invade Avengers Mansion and their subsequent demise, Powderkeg ran a protection racket in the neighborhood where Ben Grimm (*see* THING) grew up, but Grimm stopped that cold. For a while, he was an inmate in the experimental penitentiary the Big House, in which all the prisoners were shrunk to reduce costs. Recently, he was seen in the Bar with No Name, which caters to criminals. **AD, MF**

Powerhouse

A member of the alien Xandarians, Rieg Davan was a Syfon warrior in the elite Nova Corps. He was sent to Earth to locate Centurion Nova-Prime Rhomann Dey. Davan's starship crash-landed on Earth. He was found and brainwashed by the Condor, a costumed criminal.

As the Condor's accomplice Powerhouse, Davan battled NOVA, the young Earthman who had inherited the deceased Dey's powers. Eventually Davan recovered his memory and with Nova and other heroes journeyed to Xandar. As the CHAMPIONS OF XANDAR, they helped the Xandarians defeat the invading SKRULLS.

Davan later perished in combat defending Xandar against a successful invasion by the forces of the space pirate NEBULA.

The name Powerhouse has since been used by a criminal mutant Earthwoman who also has the power to drain energy from other living beings through touch to amplify her own. She has battled SPIDER-MAN and WOLVERINE, among others.

Alex Power of POWER PACK also used the name Powerhouse when he temporarily possessed the superhuman powers of his siblings. **PS**

FACTFILE

REAL NAME
Rieg Davan

OCCUPATION
Syfon warrior

BASE
The planet Xandar

HEIGHT
6 ft 3 in

WEIGHT
265 lbs

EYES Brown

HAIR Brown

FIRST APPEARANCE
Nova #2 (October 1976)

POWERS
Powerhouse could siphon energy from external sources, including living beings to amplify his strength or discharge energy blasts.

Power, Dr. James

FIRST APPEARANCE Power Pack #1 (August 1984)
REAL NAME Dr. James Power
OCCUPATION Physicist
BASE New York City; later Bainbridge Island, Washington State
HEIGHT 6 ft **WEIGHT** 155 lbs **EYES** Blue **HAIR** Brown
SPECIAL POWERS/ABILITIES A brilliant and innovative physicist, Dr. Power has the normal human strength of a man of his age who engages in minimal regular exercise.

Dr. James Power is the inventor of the matter/antimatter converter, a comparatively inexpensive means of producing energy. Learning of Power's invention, an alien Kymellian named Aelfyre WHITEMANE ("Whitey") grew concerned, since a similar device had destroyed the Kymellian homeworld. Another alien race, the Z'nrx, or "SNARKS," intending to utilize the converter as a weapon, abducted Dr. Power and his wife

Margaret. The dying Whitemane bestowed superhuman powers upon the Powers' young children, Alex, Jack, Julie, and Katie, who rescued their parents. The children continued to operate under the name POWER PACK. **PS**

Power Broker

FIRST APPEARANCE Machine Man #6 (September 1978)
REAL NAME Curtiss Jackson
OCCUPATION Criminal **BASE** Los Angeles
HEIGHT 7 ft 6 in **WEIGHT** 600 lbs
EYES Brown **HAIR** Black
SPECIAL POWERS/ABILITIES Once a normal man, Jackson possesses superhuman strength. However, his body is so overdeveloped that he cannot move without a steel exo-skeleton.

Curtiss Jackson was an agent of the Corporation, a criminal organization run like a respectable business. After meeting Dr. Karl MALUS, Jackson formed his own company—Power Broker, Inc.—which sold superhuman strength to its clients. He empowered numerous people, including U.S.AGENT, DEMOLITION MAN, and most of the wrestlers on the UCWF circuit. Hunted by the criminal-killing SCOURGE, Jackson augmented himself but wound up so musclebound he could hardly move. A new Power Broker appeared recently, wearing a battlesuit that allows him to fire blasts of energy from his hands. He gave HARDBALL his powers. **TB, MF**

Power Man

FIRST APPEARANCE Shadowland: Power Man #1 (October 2010)
REAL NAME Victor Alvarez
OCCUPATION Adventurer **BASE** New York
HEIGHT 5 ft 9 in **WEIGHT** 160 lbs
EYES Brown **HAIR** Black
SPECIAL POWERS/ABILITIES Victor can draw the chi from those around him, granting him superhuman durability and strength.

Afro-Dominican Victor Alvarez, the son of the villain Shades, lived in Hell's Kitchen. When BULLSEYE caused an explosion that killed about 100 people, Victor survived by drawing an energy called chi from those who had died, gaining superhuman strength. Soon after, he donned a costume and became a hero for hire called Power Man. He later joined the Avengers Academy and then Luke's AVENGERS team. Heroes Luke CAGE and Erik Josten (ATLAS) have also used the name Power Man. **MF**

POWER PACK

Young hero team with power to burn

POWER PACK

FACTFILE

CURRENT MEMBERS

ZERO-G
(Alex Power, leader) Ability to control the gravity of himself or other objects.

LIGHTSPEED
(Julie Power) Flight, super-speed.

MASS MASTER
(Jack Power) Can compress or disperse his body's mass.

ENERGIZER
(Katie Power) Can absorb and release energy.

BASE
Bainbridge Island, Washington

FIRST APPEARANCE
Power Pack #1 (August 1984)

Dr. James Power inadvertently caused his children to join the ranks of Earth's Super Heroes.

Professor James POWER, father of Alex, Julie, Jack, and Katie, invented an antimatter generator that siphoned energy from an alternate dimension. Aelfyre "Whitey" WHITEMANE, a member of the alien Kymellian race, arrived on Earth to prevent the machine being used, knowing it had the potential to wipe out entire planets. A rival species, the SNARKS, attempted to steal the device.

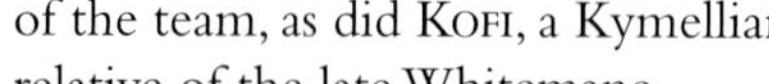

SECRET SUPER HEROES

Whitemane suffered fatal injuries in the ensuing struggle, but before dying he bestowed one of his abilities on each of the four Power children. They became the superheroic Power Pack, and adopted the identities of Gee (Alex), Lightspeed (Julie), Mass Master (Jack), and Energizer (Katie). Hiding their dual identities from their parents, the Pack dealt with extraterrestrial threats and employed Whitey's intelligent spacecraft, the Smartship Friday. Power Pack aided the MORLOCKS during the Mutant Massacre, and fought APOCALYPSE's horsemen during the Fall of the Mutants. Franklin RICHARDS, using the name Tattletale due to his ability to perceive possible futures, became an unofficial member of the team, as did KOFI, a Kymellian relative of the late Whitemane.

ESSENTIAL STORYLINES

- ***Power Pack Vol. 1 #1***
Power Pack debuts, launching a popular 62-issue series.
- ***Power Pack Vol. 2 #1-4***
The heroes return—now a few years older—in a limited series that pits them against their perennial enemies, the Snarks.
- ***X-Men and Power Pack #1-4***
Power Pack returns to its roots in a limited series that guest-stars such famous mutants as Cyclops, Beast, and Wolverine.

Frequent contact with the Kymellians and the Snarks have turned the members of Power Pack into veteran interstellar adventurers.

ENERGY SWAPPING

Power Pack's powers often switched from one member to another. At one point, they adopted the names of Destroyer (Alex), Molecula (Julie), Counterweight (Jack), and Starstreak (Katie) and helped the Kymellians relocate to a new world. Alex appeared to become a Kymellian, though this was revealed to be a pseudoplasm duplicate planted by Technocrat, a Kymellian.

Alex temporarily stole the energies of his brother and sisters to join the NEW WARRIORS as Powerpax and then Powerhouse. He later changed his codename to Zero-G and joined the FIFTY-STATE INITIATIVE. Julie ran away to Los Angeles, joining Excelsior (later the Loners), a team of young ex-heroes. Julie, Alex, and Katie reunited as the Power Pack to help the Future Foundation (FANTASTIC FOUR) defeat mad CELESTIALS. **DW, MF**

Despite their youth, the Power Pack members combine their abilities to defeat some of the strongest villains.

POWER PACK
1 Mass Master
2 Energizer
3 Lightspeed
4 Zero-G

Power Princess

FIRST APPEARANCE Defenders #112 (October 1982)
REAL NAME Zarda
OCCUPATION Princess **BASE** Capital City
HEIGHT 5 ft 9 in **WEIGHT** 145 lbs **EYES** Brown **HAIR** Black
SPECIAL POWERS/ABILITIES Incredible healing ability, and an extremely long lifespan. She can also shoot a flash from her eyes which can heal others, or if she chooses, destroy them.

On Earth-712, Princess Zarda lived on Utopia Island, where her people developed a culture of peace, fellowship, and learning. During World War II, she joined the Golden Agency and fought for the Allies. When humans created the atomic bomb, the Utopians fled Earth, leaving Princess Zarda behind. She joined the Squadron Supreme and worked with them to take over and improve the USA. After that failed, she wound up on Earth-616, living at Project: P.E.G.A.S.U.S. She joined the Exiles in their pursuit of Proteus, but has since returned to the Squadron Supreme. **MT, MF**

Pratt, Agent

FIRST APPEARANCE Incredible Hulk #40 (July 2002)
REAL NAME Agent Pratt
OCCUPATION Agent for clandestine organization **BASE** Mobile
HEIGHT/WEIGHT/EYES Unrevealed **HAIR** None
SPECIAL POWERS/ABILITIES Body able to regenerate itself as a result of H Section Programming; injection of Hulk blood endowed him with Hulk-like powers.

When he first met Bruce Banner, this ruthless operative was posing as an FBI agent. In truth he belonged to the sinister, clandestine organisation Home Base. After forcing Banner to change into the Hulk, Pratt obtained a sample of his blood, but a police officer snatched it and, plunging it into Pratt's own bloodstream, caused him to explode. Pratt's H Section Programming enabled his body to regenerate itself, and he soon returned to taunt Banner again. This time the Hulk emerged to tear Pratt's body apart. **AD**

Prester John

FIRST APPEARANCE Fantastic Four #54 (September 1966)
REAL NAME Prester John
OCCUPATION Traveler **BASE** Traveler
HEIGHT 6 ft 1 in **WEIGHT** 210 lbs **EYES** Blue **HAIR** Red
SPECIAL POWERS/ABILITIES Skilled swordsman; a weapon called the Evil Eye allowed him to fire energy blasts, generate force fields, and rearrange matter.

Prester John, monarch of a 12th-century Christian kingdom in Asia, aided Richard the Lionheart during the Crusades. Afterward, John discovered the fabled isle of Avalon, but while he was there, a plague struck. As sole survivor, he sat in the Chair of Survival and slept. Reawakening in the modern era, he crossed paths with many heroes, including the Fantastic Four. He carries the powerful Stellar Rod, a weapon made from the Evil Eye. He was last seen serving as Head of Multi-Religious Studies on Providence, an island nation Cable built—and then evacuating people off it when it was destroyed. **DW, MF**

Princess Python

FIRST APPEARANCE Amazing Spider-Man #22 (March 1965)
REAL NAME Zelda DuBois
OCCUPATION Snake charmer, criminal **BASE** Mobile
HEIGHT 5 ft 8 in **WEIGHT** 140 lbs **EYES** Green **HAIR** Red-brown
SPECIAL POWERS/ABILITIES Can control her trained rock python; sometimes carries an electric prod.

Princess Python is a snake charmer who trained her rock python snake to attack on command. She served with several versions of the Circus of Crime while also occasionally pursuing a solo career. Princess Python briefly joined the mercenaries of the Serpent Society and even started up one incarnation of the Serpent Squad.

For a while she worked at the Quentin Carnival and became involved with Johnny Blaze (Ghost Rider). At one point, she even married the Stilt-Man. Blinded during the Punisher's attack on the Stilt-Man's funeral, she later married the Gibbon, but they have since separated. Her son Daniel was the Executioner of the Young Masters. He killed her after discovering she was Princess Python. A new Princess Python has appeared as part of Max Fury's Masters of Evil. **DW, MF**

Presence

FIRST APPEARANCE Defenders #52 (October 1977)
REAL NAME Sergei Krylov
OCCUPATION Supervillain **BASE** Mobile
HEIGHT 6 ft **WEIGHT** 200 lbs **EYES** Yellow **HAIR** None
SPECIAL POWERS/ABILITIES Body produces lethal radiation which can be harnessed as flight, energy blasts, force fields, enhanced strength, or telepathy.

Nuclear physicist Sergei Krylov became an important player in Russian politics and sought to further increase his might by subjecting himself to experimental radiation. He succeeded in gaining radioactive powers deadly to the unprotected, which could also be used to control the minds of others. He used his powers to brainwash Dr. Tania Belinskya (the Red Guardian) into becoming his partner. He helped fight Kang the Conqueror and later tried to conquer Russia again after Tania left him for his son, Vanguard. The hero Powersurge sacrificed himself to stop him, killing them both. **DW, MF**

Prince of Orphans

FIRST APPEARANCE Immortal Iron Fist #12 (October 2007)
REAL NAME John Aman
OCCUPATION Adventurer **BASE** Tibet
HEIGHT 5 ft 11 in **WEIGHT** 162 lbs **EYES** Blue **HAIR** Bald
SPECIAL POWERS/ABILITIES John is a fantastic martial artist with superhuman coordination, reflexes, speed, and strength, and can change into a green mist.

John was an orphan raised in Tibet by the members of the Council of Seven, who took turns training him in their various arts. He was sent to assassinate Orson Randall, who was Iron Fist before Danny Rand. Instead, he learned from Randall that the masters of the Seven Cities had lied about how often they could come in contact with the rest of the world. Randall asked him to join the next Iron Fist in a revolution against those masters. He has since worked with the Secret Warriors and helped defend Washington DC during Fear Itself. **MF**

Proctor

The man who came to be called Proctor was actually the Black Knight of an alternate Earth. While serving as a member of the Avengers, he met and fell in love with the Sersi of his world. He became her "gann josin," a mate that was forever bound to her by a mental link that allowed them to share their powers, thoughts and souls. His Sersi eventually became mentally unstable, destroying their world and rejecting Proctor.

Desperate for revenge, Proctor and his companions used a gateway into alternate dimensions and journeyed across the multiverse. They were on a quest to kill every alternate world version of Sersi, along with every world and Avenger that had ever befriended her. They gathered and rescued all the alternate-Avengers that they deemed worthy of life.

After defeating the Black Knight of the real Earth, Proctor was slain by this world's Sersi. **TD**

Proctor possessed the battle prowess of the real Black Knight, and the mental and physical powers of an Eternal because he had become one with the Sersi of his world.

PROCTOR

FACTFILE

REAL NAME
Dane Whitman (of an alternate dimension)

OCCUPATION
Former Super Hero turned destroyer of worlds

BASE
A secret citadel hidden on the edge of reality

HEIGHT 6 ft
WEIGHT 190 lbs
EYES Brown
HAIR Black

FIRST APPEARANCE
Avengers #344 (February 1992)

POWERS
Expert combatant; immune to aging; can psionically manipulate matter, and project cosmic blasts from eyes and hands. Possesses ten rings that produce, among other things, ice blasts, flames, bursts of light and deadly gases.

Prodigy

PRODIGY

FACTFILE

REAL NAME
David Alleyne

OCCUPATION
Adventurer

BASE
Professor X's School for Gifted Youngsters, Salem Center, New York

HEIGHT 6 ft 3 in
WEIGHT 230 lbs
EYES Brown
HAIR Black

FIRST APPEARANCE
New Mutants Vol. 2 #4 (October 2003)

POWERS
Prodigy has the mutant ability to absorb (although not permanently) the skills and knowledge of those near him. He cannot, however, absorb their mutant powers.

Four different men used the name Prodigy. The first was Spider-Man, who employed it as one of four different identities when he was a wanted man. College athlete Richie Gilmore took over this identity. He was the first hero to publicly defy the Superhuman Registration Act. He has since joined the Fifty-State Initiative. He later took his team, the Heavy Hitters, and declared them to be independent. He was jailed for this but has since been released and taken a job with the Avengers Initiative.

The third Prodigy, David Alleyne, was unrelated to the first two. His mutant powers allowed him to absorb the knowledge of anyone nearby, although the knowledge faded when they parted. He lost his powers on M-Day, but he can now remember every bit of knowledge he ever absorbed. He remains with the X-Men, now as a teacher. The fourth Prodigy, Timothy Wilkerson, is a young man who was mutated with the Leader's gamma-irradiated DNA. He joined the Gamma Corps to take down the Hulk during World War Hulk, and helped their efforts to bring the Illuminati to justice. **MT, MF**

High above the US Capitol, Prodigy (David Alleyne) tangles with fellow X-Men member Wind Dancer.

Professor X
see page 276-277

Proteus

FIRST APPEARANCE Uncanny X-Men #125 (September 1979)
REAL NAME Kevin MacTaggert
OCCUPATION None **BASE** Muir Island, Scotland
HEIGHT/WEIGHT/EYES/HAIR Inapplicable
SPECIAL POWERS/ABILITIES Able to warp reality. Made of psionic energies, he must inhabit a host body, which burns up over time.

Moira MacTaggert imprisoned her son Kevin in Mutant Research Facility on Muir Island, where an energy field kept his powers from consuming his body. When his cell was breached during an attack by Magneto, Kevin escaped, shifting from host-body to host-body as each wore out. Only the intervention of the X-Men—and Kevin's vulnerability to metal—stopped him. AIM reconstituted him in the body of a young mutant called Piecemeal (not the adult villain of the same name), but the combined creature didn't last. During the House of M, Kevin left Earth-616 with the Exiles and formed a body-sharing deal with shapeshifting mutant Morph. **TB**

Prowler

Hobie Brown's gift for inventions is rivaled only by that of Peter Parker (Spider-Man).

While working as a window washer, mechanical genius Hobie Brown invented gadgets to make his job easier, including wrist-mounted, high-pressure sprayers. When his boss dismissed his ideas, Brown quit in frustration. He turned to crime, refashioning his contraptions into climbing gear and miniaturized weapons, and adopting the costumed identity of the Prowler. Seeking recognition rather than profit, Brown intended to return what he stole as the Prowler under his real identity. Almost immediately, he came into conflict with Spider-Man, though the two later put aside their differences and became allies.

A second Prowler appeared when the villainous Cat Burglar stole Brown's costume and worked with Belladonna to commit a string of crimes. Brown resumed his role as the original Prowler, joining the team of reformed criminals called the Outlaws, but suffered a severe spinal injury at the hands of El Toro Negro. A third Prowler, medical student Rick Lawson, briefly adventured while Brown recuperated in the hospital, but Brown has since retaken the role he created. **DW**

FACTFILE
REAL NAME
Hobie Brown
OCCUPATION
Adventurer
BASE
New York City

HEIGHT 5 ft 11 in
WEIGHT 170 lbs
EYES Brown
HAIR Dark brown

FIRST APPEARANCE
Amazing Spider-Man Vol. 1 #78 (November 1969)

PROWLER

POWERS
The cape of Prowler's costume allows him to glide; wrist cartridges fire compressed air; steel-tipped claws allow him to scale buildings.

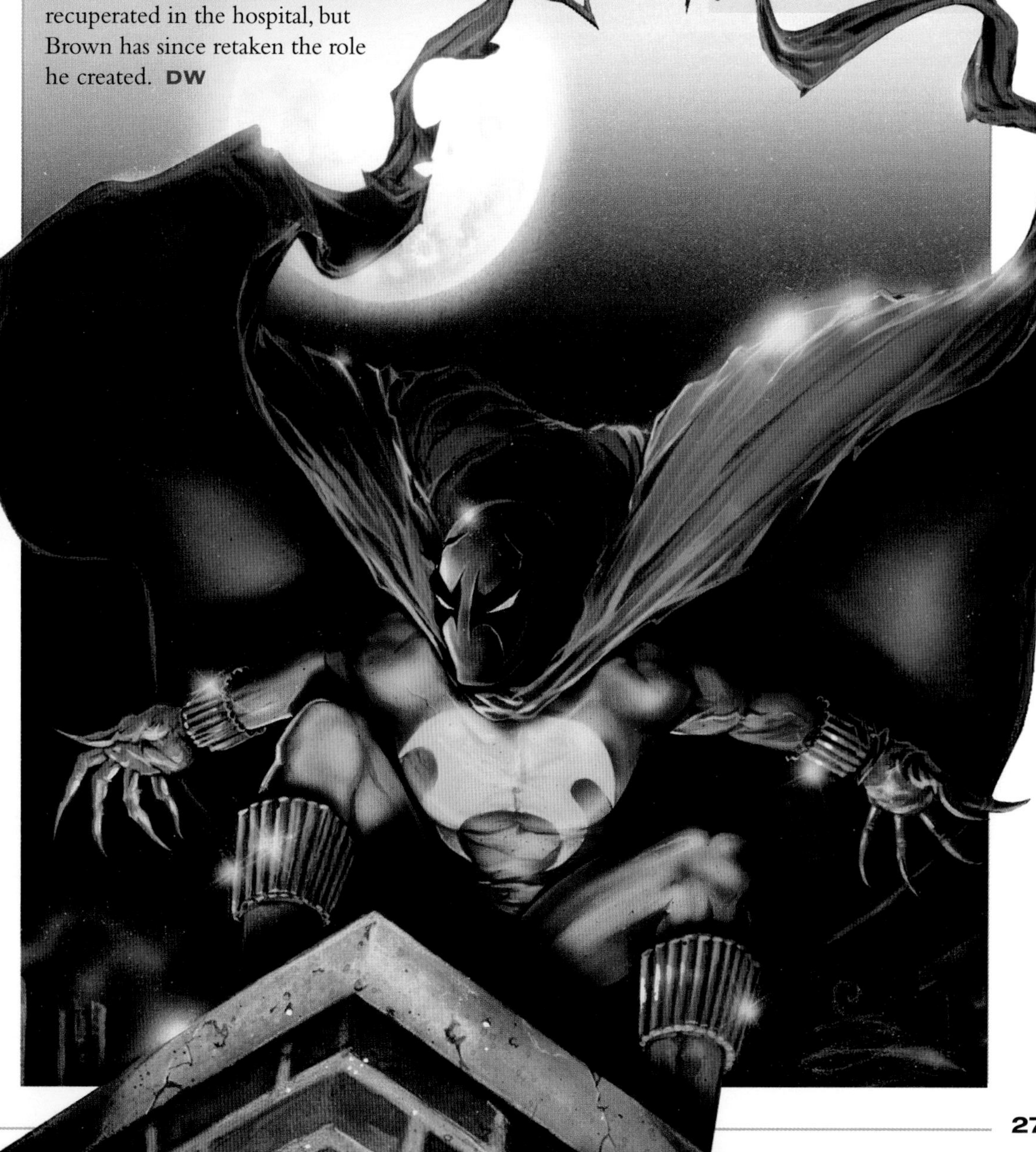

PROFESSOR X

Mastermind of the X-Men

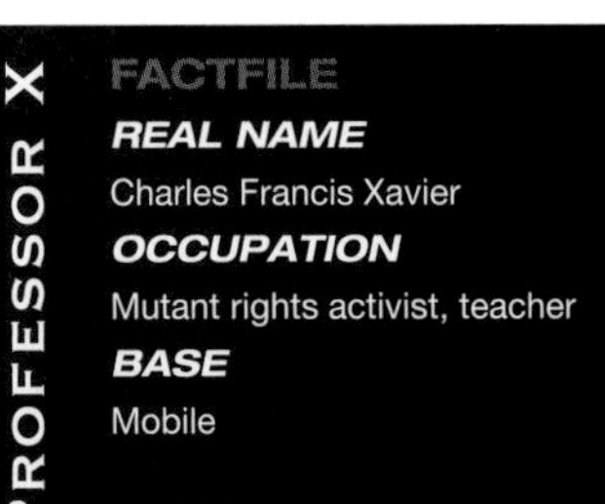

PROFESSOR X

FACTFILE

REAL NAME
Charles Francis Xavier

OCCUPATION
Mutant rights activist, teacher

BASE
Mobile

HEIGHT 6 ft
WEIGHT 190 lbs
EYES Blue
HAIR None

FIRST APPEARANCE
The X-Men #1 (September 1963)

POWERS

Vast psionic abilities including mind-reading, mind-erasing, astral projection, the projection of illusions, the ability to take mental control of others, and the ability to fire mental blasts.

ALLIES/FOES

ALLIES The X-Men, the Starjammers

FOES Magneto, Juggernaut, Cassandra Nova, the Sentinels, the Hellfire Club

ISSUE #1

In *X-Men* #1, Professor X's team unites to fight off the menace of Magneto, marking the first appearance of both the heroic X-Men and their arch-foe.

Growing up in a time before widespread superpowers, Charles Xavier hid his telepathic abilities to shield himself from unwanted attention.

Widely considered the most powerful mutant on Earth, Charles Xavier has dedicated his life to the ideal that humans and mutants can coexist peacefully. His father Brian died when Charles was a child. Kurt Marko, his father's research partner, married Charles's mother Sharon, but only valued her for her fortune. Charles became a rival of his stepbrother Cain (who one day gained the powers of the JUGGERNAUT), and saw both his mother and stepfather die in separate incidents.

FIRST LOVE

Xavier attended graduate school at Oxford University, England, where he fell in love with Moira MACTAGGERT; however their relationship ended when Charles joined the US Army.

Following his tour of duty, Xavier traveled the world. At a clinic for Holocaust survivors in Israel, he befriended the man who would become MAGNETO. Magneto and Xavier teamed up to fight BARON VON STRUCKER, but Magneto's ruthless methods made it clear that the two had incompatible philosophies concerning the use of violence. Xavier left Israel, leaving behind Gabrielle HALLER, not realizing that Haller was pregnant with his child (the boy, David, would grow up to become the mutant LEGION). A rockslide caused by the villainous alien LUCIFER, left Xavier a paraplegic.

IF THINGS HAD BEEN DIFFERENT, WE MIGHT HAVE BEEN FRIENDS...WE MIGHT HAVE TRULY BEEN BROTHERS! BUT YOU WOULD HAVE IT NO OTHER WAY! THIS FINAL CHAPTER WAS WRITTEN WHEN WE FIRST MET! THIS IS THE ONLY WAY IT COULD HAVE ENDED!

UHHHHHHHH....!

Professor X can disable opponents, such as the Juggernaut, with mental blasts.

THE X-MEN

As Professor X, Charles Xavier founded Xavier's School for Gifted Youngsters in Westchester County, New York to train mutant children in the use of their powers. Xavier identified potential students with the machine Cerebro, which amplified his telepathic powers and allowed him to pinpoint mutants from afar. His initial Super Hero team, the X-MEN, consisted of CYCLOPS, ANGEL, Marvel Girl (*see* Jean GREY), ICEMAN and BEAST, who sought to improve the image of mutants by selfless deeds.

The X-Men repeatedly faced off against Magneto, who had dedicated himself to subjugating humanity through his powers as the master of magnetism.

Professor X founded a second team of X-Men, whose members included NIGHTCRAWLER, COLOSSUS, STORM, BANSHEE, and WOLVERINE. The new X-Men helped Xavier battle SHI'AR emperor D'ken and the Imperial Guard. Xavier then fell in love with the new Shi'ar empress, LILANDRA. He entered into the Shi'ar equivalent of marriage with Lilandra, and adventured with the STARJAMMERS.

Although his love for Shi'ar empress Lilandra took him across the galaxy, Professor X eventually returned to the X-Men.

Back on Earth, Xavier organized a third grouping of students, the NEW MUTANTS, but fell under the influence of the alien BROOD. To prevent his transformation into a Brood Queen, Xavier shifted his consciousness into a clone body with fully-functional legs. After suffering injuries as a result of a hate crime, Xavier reunited with Lilandra to recuperate among the Shi'ar, leaving Magneto to run the academy in his absence. Xavier again lost the use of his legs battling the SHADOW KING, and brought together a fourth team of young mutants, GENERATION X.

The relationship between Magneto and Xavier took a turn for the worse, culminating in a terrible moment when Magneto ripped the adamantium from WOLVERINE's skeleton. Enraged by Magneto's brutality, Xavier mind-wiped his former friend, unwittingly creating a powerful psionic being known as ONSLAUGHT. All of Earth's heroes united to destroy Onslaught, leading to the apparent deaths of the AVENGERS and the FANTASTIC FOUR. In the aftermath, Xavier briefly lost his telepathic powers and became a prisoner of the US government. He later uncovered a SKRULL plot to infiltrate the X-Men, and trained a promising group of Skrull mutants calling themselves Cadre K.

BATTLING MAGNETO

The philosophies held by Professor X and Magneto are diametrically opposed, but share some similarities. Both men profess the goal of protecting mutantkind, but Magneto wants to subjugate or eliminate human opposition, while Professor X dreams of a world where humans and mutants can co-exist. After Professor X founded the X-Men, Magneto created the Brotherhood of Evil Mutants. Over the years, the two men have been friends and foes.

TRANSITIONS

Xavier's genetic twin, the sinister Cassandra Nova, had died in Sharon Xavier's womb yet somehow maintained her life-essence. Nova orchestrated the devastation of the mutant nation Genosha and took mental control of Xavier, outing him as a mutant to the world and inciting the Shi'ar Imperial Guard to attack the X-Mansion. Xavier's students helped free him from Nova's influence.

Xavier then founded the X-Corporation, stepping down as head of the academy. He tried to help Magneto's daughter, the Scarlet Witch, recover from a breakdown, but was unable to prevent her from removing the power from most mutants—including himself—on M-Day. The huge backlash of power reawakened Vulcan, and Xavier and a team of X-Men tracked him to the Shi'ar Empire. They failed to stop him, but when Vulcan threw Xavier into the M'Kraan Crystal, Xavier's powers were restored.

Professor X designed the Danger Room, not realizing it would develop a mind of its own.

As one of the ILLUMINATI, Xavier faced the Hulk's wrath during WORLD WAR HULK, until the Hulk realized that M-Day had cost the mutant enough. During the hunt for the first mutant baby born since M-Day, BISHOP accidentally shot Xavier in the head, putting him into a coma. He recovered but had lost much of his memory.

During the DARK REIGN, HAMMER captured Xavier, and MYSTIQUE impersonated him in an attempt to gain control over the X-Men. After being released, Xavier turned his attention to helping nurse his son David back to health.

When the Phoenix Force returned to Earth and possessed the Phoenix Five, Xavier stood against them and tried to convince Cyclops to give up the power. Cyclops lost control and killed his old mentor, then turned into the Dark Phoenix. **PS, MF**

ESSENTIAL STORYLINES

- ***Giant-Size X-Men #1*** Professor X recruits a new batch of X-Men to replace the originals, welcoming such future favorites as Nightcrawler and Storm.
- ***New X-Men #118–126*** The "Imperial" story arc sees Professor X's genetic twin, Cassandra Nova, impersonating Xavier to imperil the Shi'ar empire.
- ***Astonishing X-Men #7–12*** A failure from his past returns to haunt Professor X, as he confronts the self-aware consciousness of the X-Men's Danger Room.
- ***X-Men: Mutant Genesis, tpb*** The X-Men stand in the way of Magneto's world-conquering schemes.

Professor X's life tragically ended at the hands of Cyclops, his greatest student.

PRYDE, KATHERINE

Far from insubstantial

FACTFILE

REAL NAME
Katherine "Kitty" Pryde

OCCUPATION
Adventurer, student, former SHIELD employee

BASE
The Xavier Institute, Salem Center, New York State

HEIGHT 5 ft 6 in
WEIGHT 110 lbs
EYES Brown
HAIR Brown

FIRST APPEARANCE
The Uncanny X-Men #129 (October 1994)

POWERS
Mutant ability to pass ("phase") through solid matter by altering the vibratory rate of the atoms of her body, her clothing, and a limited amount of other matter. Highly adept with computers.

As a schoolgirl in Deerfield, Illinois, Kitty Pryde began suffering intense headaches. They were a sign that her mutant power to phase through solid matter and disrupt electronics was about to emerge. Emma Frost, the White Queen of the Hellfire Club visited Kitty's parents to recruit her as a student. Professor X and three of his X-Men soon followed, hoping to convince Kitty's parents to let her attend his School for Gifted Youngsters instead.

Kitty and Colossus often seem unable to make their relationship work, but their love still runs deep.

CHOOSING SIDES

After the White Queen kidnapped the visiting X-Men, Kitty helped Cyclops and Phoenix (Jean Grey) rescue them. Kitty entered Xavier's school and joined the X-Men. Kitty briefly adopted the codenames Sprite and Ariel. During an adventure in Japan, where Wolverine taught her martial arts, she chose the name Shadowcat, which she sometimes still uses today.

She and fellow student Colossus fell in love, although the relationship turned stormy and eventually ended. Kitty later became a founding member of the original Excalibur, a British-based team of adventurers. She also worked for the law enforcement agency SHIELD for a short time.

While on an adventure in space, Kitty met the small, dragonlike alien Lockheed, who took an instant liking to her. They became close friends for many years, until she discovered that he could speak—something he had never done before—and was spying on the X-Men for SWORD.

SAVIOR AND TEACHER

After Excalibur disbanded, Kitty rejoined the X-Men. She was lost while on a mission to Breakworld with them. She saved the Earth by phasing a gigantic bullet all the way through the planet, but the X-Men were unable to remove her from it after it sailed off into space. Much later, Magneto brought her back by returning the bullet and breaking it open. Having been forced to remain in her phase state for so long, she found she could not turn substantial again. The Breakworlder Haleena had to kill her and revive her to make her solid once more.

When the schism between the X-Men split them into two groups, Kitty helped Wolverine open the Jean Grey School for Higher Learning. She stayed out of the subsequent conflict between the Avengers and the X-Men, concentrating on the school instead. When the Beast brought the original X-Men from the past to visit the present, however, she took charge of taking care of them. **PS, MF**

Pryor, Madelyne

Madelyne Pryor was a clone of Jean Grey and created to meet Scott Summers.

Mr. Sinister was obsessed with obtaining the spawn of a union between Jean Grey and Scott Summers (*see* Cyclops), but it was only after Jean's death that he achieved his goal. Using stored genetic material, he successfully cloned Jean. He named his creation Madelyne Pryor, provided her with false memories, and manipulated Scott Summers into marrying her. Their relationship resulted in a son—Nathan Summers (*see* Cable)—but when the real Jean Grey was resurrected, Scott left Madelyne. Insanely jealous, Madelyne began to lose her grip on reality, and her journey towards madness accelerated when Sinister kidnapped Nathan. As Madelyne's mutant powers began to emerge, so did her thirst for vengeance, and she transformed herself into the Goblin Queen.

She was killed in a showdown with the X-Men. She later returned as a psychic ghost and then as the Red Queen. She recruited a Sisterhood of Mutants to help her acquire a new body. Cyclops tricked her into entering the wrong body, and she died again. **AD, MF**

As the Goblin Queen, Madelyne Pryor was a terrifying enemy for the X-Men.

Pryor, Madelyne

FACTFILE
REAL NAME
Madelyne Jennifer Pryor-Summers
OCCUPATION
Vengeance-seeker
BASE
Mobile

HEIGHT 5 ft 6 in
WEIGHT 110 lbs
EYES Green
HAIR Red

FIRST APPEARANCE
Uncanny X-Men #168 (April 1983)

POWERS
Most of Madelyne's abilities stem from her status as a clone of Jean Grey. She possesses vast psionic powers including telepathy and telekinesis, Madelyne is able to generate energy and manipulate it so that she can fly, project powerful force blasts, and create force fields that act as shields.

Psionex

FIRST APPEARANCE New Warriors #4 (October 1990)
BASE Mobile
MEMBERS AND POWERS **Asylum** Converts body to a mist that causes hallucinations, uses Darkforce. **Coronary** Controls the bodies of other, has crystal form. **Darkling** Controls Darkforce. **Impulse** Superhuman reflexes and speed. **Mathemanic** Can project math into others' heads. **Pretty Persuasions** Amplifies erotic urges and wields energy whip.

The Genentech corporation created a team of superpowered youths, led by Asylum, who battled the New Warriors. Mathemanic and Impulse were injured in an escape attempt and retired, but the rest of the team broke free. They later united under Darkling, who posed as Asylum. Some time later, Psionex became the Fifty-State Initiative team for Maryland. **MF**

Psycho-Man

FIRST APPEARANCE Fantastic Four Special #5 (November 1967)
REAL NAME Unrevealed
OCCUPATION Scientist; conqueror **BASE** Traan; his World-Ship
HEIGHT Indeterminate **WEIGHT** Indeterminate
EYES Unrevealed **HAIR** Unrevealed
SPECIAL POWERS/ABILITIES Superhuman intelligence; his main weapon projects a "psycho-ray" that stimulates fear, doubt, and hate.

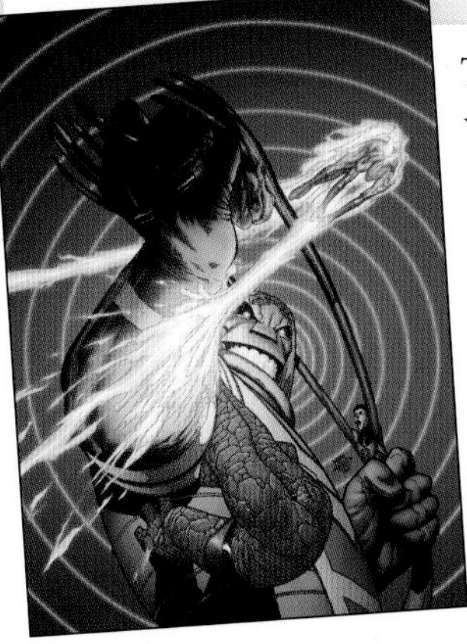

The Psycho-Man was chief scientist of Traan, a planet in a different dimension known as the Microverse. He traveled to Earth to conquer the planet by means of his "psycho-ray," but was thwarted by the Fantastic Four's Human Torch and Thing, the Black Panther, and the Inhumans' Royal Family. The Psycho-Man's true size and appearance are mysteries: on Earth he remained tiny while encased in a human-sized suit of body armor. He continues to clash with the Fantastic Four, both on Earth and within the Microverse. **PS**

Psyklop

FIRST APPEARANCE Avengers #88 (May 1971)
REAL NAME Psyklop
OCCUPATION Servant of the Dark Gods **BASE** Mobile
HEIGHT 8 ft **WEIGHT** 450 lbs **EYES** Red **HAIR** None
SPECIAL POWERS/ABILITIES Possessed of superhuman strength and durability, Psyklop can also fire beams of energy from his eye that can hypnotize an opponent, or make him experience illusions.

The devoted servant of the Dark Gods who ruled the Earth at the dawn of time, Psyklop hibernated for millennia until called upon to serve his masters once more. He tried to offer up the Hulk as a sacrifice to his sinister lords, but was prevented from doing so by the Avengers. The Hulk ended up miniaturized, and fell into the Microverse, alighting on the planet K'ai. Pursuing the Hulk, Psyklop engaged him in battle and was defeated. For his failure, the Dark Gods exiled Psyklop to K'ai, where he seemingly met his end, consumed by the spirits of all the people he had slain. **TB**

PSYLOCKE

FACTFILE

REAL NAME
Elisabeth "Betsy" Braddock

OCCUPATION
Adventurer

BASE
The Xavier Institute, Salem Center, New York State

HEIGHT 5 ft 11 in
WEIGHT 155 lbs
EYES (current body) blue
HAIR (current body) black, dyed purple

FIRST APPEARANCE
Captain Britain #8 (December 1976)

POWERS
Possesses telekinetic powers. Can focus her psionic powers into a "psychic knife" to stun or kill an adversary. Former telepath. Highly skilled in martial arts.

Psylocke

James Braddock Sr. was an inhabitant of Otherworld who came to Britain and fathered three children, James Jr., Brian, and Elizabeth. Brian became the hero Captain Britain, a role Betsy later briefly took over at the behest of the British government agency RCX. Blinded and nearly killed by the villain Slaymaster, Betsy was abducted by Mojo, who gave her new artificial eyes. She was rescued by the New Mutants and joined the X-Men as Psylocke. Spiral switched the minds of Psylocke and the Japanese assassin Kwannon into each other's bodies. Discovering that her new body was dying, Kwannon had the crimelord Matsu'o Tsurayaba kill her. Elizabeth survives in Kwannon's original body. Psylocke sacrificed her telepathy to defeat the X-Men's enemy, the Shadow King. Subsequently, she gained telekinetic abilities. While with the X-Treme X-Men, Psylocke was seemingly slain by their enemy Vargas. Psylocke returned, however, and after a spell with the X-Men, joined the Exiles. Betsy later returned to Earth-616 and has since worked mostly with X-Force.
PS, MF

Psylocke alongside her teammates in the Exiles, including alternate versions of Morph, Rogue, and Sabretooth.

Psylocke forfeited her telepathic powers in order to imprison the Shadow King, one of the X-Men's deadliest foes, in the Astral Plane.

PUCK

FACTFILE

REAL NAME
Eugene Milton Judd

OCCUPATION
Alpha Flight member

BASE
Tamarind Island

HEIGHT 3 ft 6 in
WEIGHT 225 lbs
EYES Brown
HAIR Black

FIRST APPEARANCE
Alpha Flight #1 (August 1983)

POWERS
Superb athlete and gymnast; formidable hand-to-hand combatant with unique fighting style; trained bullfighter; limited knowledge of sorcery.

Puck

Eugene Judd released the evil sorcerer Black Raazer and managed to trap him in his own body, which extended his life but reduced him to the height of a dwarf. Judd was later invited to join Beta Flight as Puck, and he worked his way up to the top-level Canadian team: Alpha Flight. He eventually rid himself of Black Raazer, which cost him his powers and caused him to gain both years and height. The Dreamqueen restored him to his former self so she could torture him longer, although he later escaped.

Later, Puck's daughter Zuzha Yu joined a new Alpha Flight, calling herself Puck, too. She inherited her father's powers and made good use of them. Both father and daughter died trying to stop the Collective (*see* Weapon Omega), a man imbued with all of the mutant energies lost on M-Day.

While Zuzha is still gone, the elder Puck helped Wolverine as he battled his way through Hell. This gave him a chance to escape so he could help his friends in Alpha Flight as they battled the Unity Party, which had taken over the Canadian government. He later joined X-Force.
AD, MF

Zuzha Yu only joined Alpha Flight after losing an arm-wrestling bout to Sasquatch.

PUMA

FIRST APPEARANCE The Amazing Spider-Man #256 (Sept. 1984)
REAL NAME Thomas Fireheart
OCCUPATION CEO of Fireheart Enterprises; mercenary
BASE Mobile **HEIGHT** 6 ft 2in **WEIGHT** 240 lbs
EYES Green **HAIR** Red; (as Fireheart) black
SPECIAL POWERS/ABILITIES As Puma, Fireheart has superhuman strength, agility, heightened senses, and claws.

Puma was the heir to a long tradition of mystical champions created by a Native American tribe. Raised to oppose the Beyonder, Thomas Fireheart donned the mantle of the Puma and kept his fighting skills sharp by becoming a mercenary, often fighting (or aiding) Spider-Man. Fireheart also served as the head of Fireheart Enterprises, which supplied him with high-tech weaponry and vehicles, but he constantly struggled to control his animalistic Puma persona. After the Civil War, he was accused of taking bribes and joined MODOK to make money to pay for his defense.
MF

PUNISHER, *see pages 282-283*

Puppet Master

PUPPET MASTER

FACTFILE

REAL NAME
Phillip Masters

OCCUPATION
Professional criminal

BASE
Sunshine City, Florida

HEIGHT 5 ft 6 in
WEIGHT 150 lbs
EYES Blue
HAIR None

FIRST APPEARANCE
Fantastic Four #8 (November 1962)

POWERS

A brilliant biologist and technician; able to control the actions and thoughts of others by making models of them out of special radioactive clay. He then turns the models into marionettes, attaching strings to their limbs.

A talented biologist, Phillip Masters became the research partner of Jacob Reiss. Resentful of Reiss's success, Masters killed his partner during a botched robbery of their lab, triggering an explosion that blinded Reiss's daughter, Alicia. Masters later married Reiss's widow and became Alicia's stepfather. Learning he could control others with his clay sculptures, Masters became the Puppet Master, one of the earliest enemies of the FANTASTIC FOUR. He also teamed up with the villains EGGHEAD, MAD THINKER, and DOCTOR DOOM. To his horror, his daughter Alicia fell in love with the THING, though in time the Puppet Master was reconciled to their relationship. The US government recruited the Puppet Master to run their Sunshine City project, where mind-controlled criminals safely served out their prison sentences. He returned to crime during the CIVIL WAR, using the YANCY STREET GANG. He seemed to blow himself up while facing Ms. Marvel but returned later to manipulate Misty KNIGHT. **DW, MF**

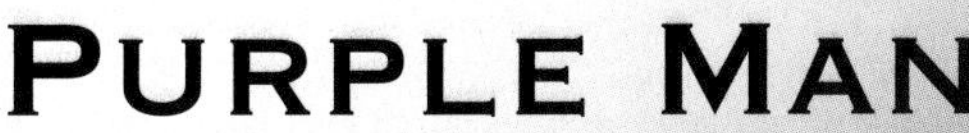

The Fantastic Four look on helplessly as the Puppet Master tinkers with a robot clutching a model of an atomic bomb. What can the villain be up to?

Pyro

FIRST APPEARANCE Uncanny X-Men #141 (January 1981)
REAL NAME St. John Allerdyce
OCCUPATION Professional criminal **BASE** Mobile
HEIGHT 5 ft 10 in **WEIGHT** 150 lbs **EYES** Blue **HAIR** Blond
SPECIAL POWERS/ABILITIES Could control and manipulate flames within his immediate vicinity, though he could not produce flames himself. His insulated costume had built-in flamethrowers.

Born in Sydney, Australia, St. John Allerdyce won fame as a novelist until MYSTIQUE convinced him to join her BROTHERHOOD OF EVIL MUTANTS. As the flame-shaping Pyro, Allerdyce battled the X-MEN and remained with his teammates when they transitioned into the US government-sanctioned FREEDOM FORCE. Pyro contracted the fatal Legacy virus and succumbed to its effects after saving Senator Robert KELLY from a new Brotherhood of Evil Mutants. The sorceress SELENE later briefly revived him. **DW, MF**

Purple Man

PURPLE MAN

FACTFILE

REAL NAME
Zebediah Killgrave

OCCUPATION
Former spy, professional criminal, conqueror

BASE
Mobile

HEIGHT 5 ft 11 in
WEIGHT 165 lbs
EYES Purple
HAIR Purple

FIRST APPEARANCE
Daredevil #4 (October 1964)

POWERS

Killgrave's body secretes psychoactive chemicals that deaden the will of people in his vicinity, rendering them susceptible to his commands. Individuals with unusually strong willpower can resist him.

Born in Yugoslavia, Zebediah Killgrave was a spy who was accidentally covered with an experimental nerve gas in liquid form. This permanently dyed his hair and skin purple and gave him the power to compel others to obey his commands. As the Purple Man, he was repeatedly defeated by DAREDEVIL, one of the few people able to resist his power. For a while, he made Jessica JONES his slave. She was so traumatized, she gave up being a Super Hero afterward.

He later tried to retire from crime, but the KINGPIN and DOCTOR DOOM exploited him still. He attempted to compel the mutant Nate Grey, alias X-MAN, to help him conquer the world, but Grey defeated him. He later controlled all of New York at the behest of BARON ZEMO, but the THUNDERBOLTS put a stop to that. For a time, he joined the HOOD's crime syndicate and ran a Las Vegas casino. He later set up his own organization known as Villains for Hire.

The Purple Man has a daughter, Kara Killgrave, with similar powers. She is known as PERSUASION. **PS, MF**

PUNISHER

War hero turned vengeful vigilante

PUNISHER

FACTFILE

REAL NAME
Frank Castle (born Castiglione)

OCCUPATION
Vigilante

BASE
Mobile

HEIGHT 6 ft 1 in
WEIGHT 200 lbs
EYES Blue
HAIR Black

FIRST APPEARANCE
The Amazing Spider-Man #129 (February 1974)

POWERS

The Punisher is seasoned combat veteran of exceptional skill. He has undergone SEAL (Sea, Air, Land), UDT (Underwater Demolition Team), and LRPA (Long Range Patrol) military training. He is an expert using all types of small arms and large caliber guns, he has extensive training using explosives and tactical weapons, and he is a superior martial artist and hand-to-hand combatant.

ALLIES/FOES

ALLIES Daredevil, Legion of Monsters, Microchip, Rachel Cole-Alves, the Red Hulk's Thunderbolts, Spider-Man

FOES Bullseye, Daken, The Exchange, the Hand, the Hood, the Kingpin, the Mafia, the Yakuza

ISSUE #1

The Jackal hires a vigilante named the Punisher to hunt down and kill Spider-Man. The Punisher eventually realizes that the wall-crawler is no criminal and vows vengeance on the Jackal.

Marine Captain Frank Castle was a decorated hero during the Vietnam War. Winner of the Bronze and Silver Star, and recipient of four Purple Hearts, Castle was an exceptionally skilled combat veteran. Then came the event that changed his life. While on leave in New York, Castle took his family for a picnic in Central Park. There they witnessed a mob murder. The mobsters then killed Castle's wife and two young children.

Frank Castle, family man, in happier days.

ONE-MAN ARMY

With his whole world destroyed, Castle deserted from the Marines and dropped out of sight for a few months. When he resurfaced, it was as a vigilante named the Punisher, who conducted a one-man, anti-crime campaign throughout New York City. Equipped with an arsenal of weapons, the Punisher took his vengeance on the mob gang who had killed his family, but he didn't stop there. He vowed to kill criminals of every kind.

The Punisher has devoted his life to destroying organized crime, drug dealers, street gangs, muggers, killers, or any other criminal element. His actions have brought him into conflict with several costumed heroes, such as SPIDER-MAN (with whom he has also cooperated), and DAREDEVIL, who strictly opposes Punisher's lethal methods.

The big white skull on Punisher's costume draws criminal fire to his heavily armored body rather than to his unprotected head.

ESSENTIAL STORYLINES

• Marvel Preview #2
Marine captain Frank Castle takes his wife and two children for a picnic in New York's Central Park. There, they witness a mob killing, after which the mobsters kill Castle's wife and children. Traumatized, Castle take vengeance against the killers and continues his one-man vigilante campaign against all criminals as the Punisher.

• The Punisher Vol. 1 Welcome Back, Frank (tpb)
After a long absence, the Punisher returns to the streets of Manhattan to take on Ma Gnucchi and her crime family.

The Punisher fiercely follows his own code of conduct. While he kills criminals on sight, during the Civil War, he refused to lift a finger to defend himself against Captain America.

When Spider-Man was on the run after switching sides during the Civil War, the Punisher stepped in to save him.

Weapons and Enemies

To carry out his war on crime, the Punisher uses firearms of all types, knives, grenade launchers, armor-piercing bullets, and explosives. His weapons are customized with tactical scopes, night-vision scopes, silencers, and tripods.

During the Civil War, the Punisher targeted Super Villains. In the aftermath of the Secret Invasion, he dedicated himself to killing one of the most powerful people in the world: Norman Osborn (Green Goblin). Under Osborn's orders, Daken cut the Punisher into pieces.

Death and Back

The Legion of Monsters recovered the Punisher's body, stitched the pieces together, and brought him back to life as Frankencastle. They asked him to help defend them against a group of monster-hunting samurai led by Robert Hellsgaard, an old friend of Ulysses Bloodstone, brought back from limbo. Frankencastle refused at first but eventually relented. He later used the Bloodstone itself to restore himself to life.

Soon after, the Punisher partnered with Marine Sergeant Rachel Cole-Alves, whose husband had been killed at their wedding reception, along with dozens of others. They worked together to bring down the Exchange, the organized crime ring that had ordered the killings. Rachel wound up on death row after exacting her vengeance, but the Punisher broke her out of jail just in time, letting himself be captured so she could escape. He later joined the Red Hulk's Thunderbolts team. **MT, MF**

Not even death can stop the Punisher.

Pym, Hank

Scientific genius behind Ant-Man, Giant-Man, and Goliath

PYM, HANK

FACTFILE

REAL NAME
Dr. Henry "Hank" Pym

OCCUPATION
Adventurer, biochemist, roboticist, manager of Avengers Compound

BASE
Cresskill, New York; Avengers Compound, LA, California

HEIGHT 6 ft
WEIGHT 185 lbs
EYES Blue
HAIR Blond

FIRST APPEARANCE
Tales To Astonish #27 (January 1962)

POWERS

By ingesting Pym Particles, either as a serum, gas, or capsule, Henry Pym can shrink to the size of an ant, or grow up to 100 ft tall. He can also change the size of objects. Using his cybernetic helmet, Pym can communicate with ants and control them.

ALLIES/FOES

ALLIES Ants, the Avengers, Captain America, Iron Man, Thor, Tigra, The Wasp

FOES Egghead, Kang the Conqueror, Morgan Le Fay, Ultron

Doctor Henry Pym shrinks himself down to the size of an ant—and leaves his growth serum out of reach.

As Ant-Man, Henry Pym could shrink himself so small that he could ride atop an ant.

Dr. Henry Pym, a brilliant scientist, discovered a rare group of subatomic particles which became known as "Pym Particles." When ingested through a serum (and later through a gas and a capsule) the particles could either shrink a person down to the size of an ant, or increase a person's size to 10, 25, even 100 feet in height.

Ant and Wasp

Undertaking a study of ants, Pym also developed a cybernetic helmet that allowed him to communicate with and control ants. Developing a costume to go along with his size-changing ability and helmet, Pym reduced himself to the size of an ant and fought evil as Ant-Man. Pym and his future wife Janet Van Dyne were founding members of the Avengers as Ant-Man and the Wasp.

Later, Pym decided to use his size-changing power to grow rather than shrink, and he began fighting crime as the costumed hero Giant-Man. Eventually, Pym realized that changing his size was putting too great a strain on his body and he stopped.

Janet did her best to cope with Hank's violent mood swings, but their marriage ended in divorce.

A Troubled Mind

When Janet was kidnapped by Attuma and the Collector, Pym helped the Avengers rescue her. He then became Goliath. While experimenting in his lab, an accident changed Pym's personality. He claimed that he had murdered Pym and became Yellowjacket. He married Janet, but they later divorced.

During the Secret Invasion, it was revealed that this Pym was a Skrull imposter. The real Pym returned to see the Wasp die due to modifications his Skrull impersonator had made to her powers. Pym renamed himself the Wasp in honor of Janet and formed a new Avengers team.

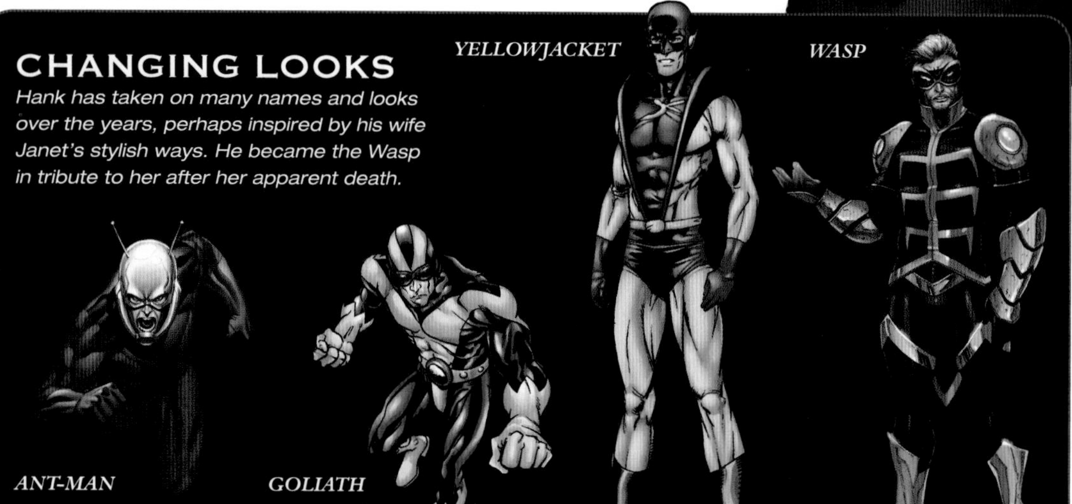

Changing Looks

Hank has taken on many names and looks over the years, perhaps inspired by his wife Janet's stylish ways. He became the Wasp in tribute to her after her apparent death.

Rededication

During the Dark Reign, Pym formed his own team of renegade Avengers to work against Norman Osborn (*see* Green Goblin). Following Osborn's downfall, Pym decided that he could do most good by doing something similar to what his Skrull impersonator had done: teaching the next generation of heroes how to handle their powers. To that end, he founded the Avengers Academy, which was similar to the Fifty-State Initiative training grounds at Camp Hammond.

Meanwhile, Pym studied the son of Tigra, who'd had a relationship with Pym's Skrull impersonator. Since the Skrull had duplicated Pym's genetic code, the boy turned out to be genetically Pym's, and Tigra asked Pym to take care of him should anything ever happen to her.

Meanwhile, Pym sought a way to bring Janet Van Dyne back from the dead. He finally decided that it was too risky, and returned to his Giant-Man identity, wearing his original costume.

After coming back from being replaced by a Skrull, Hank found a new purpose in his life: training the next generation of heroes at the Avengers Academy.

Bad Sons

Early in his career with the Avengers, Pym had invented a robot called Ultron, which grew to be one of the greatest villains of all time, dedicated to the eradication of organic life. Ultron had left the planet long ago, but he now returned and laid the world to waste. A few heroes survived, and they traveled to the Savage Land to find a time machine to stop Ultron (*see* Age of Ultron)

While most of the heroes went into the future, where Ultron had hidden himself, Wolverine and Invisible Woman traveled back in time. They found Pym working in his lab just before he created Ultron, and Wolverine killed him. However, this act eradicated all the good Pym had done as well as the bad, as Wolverine and Invisible Woman discovered when they returned to the present. They went back to stop *themselves*, and convinced Pym to send a secret message to his future self and then erase his memories of the entire event.

Pym eventually created a virus to defeat Ultron, but the virus evolved into Dimitrios, a sentient AI bent on revenge against humanity. Pym joined SHIELD to found a new Avengers AI team to combat the virus. In the meantime, he kept up his duties at Avengers Academy.

MT, MF

The younger Hank Pym didn't let Wolverine—who he'd not met before—take him down without a fight.

Avengers A.I.
1 Doombot ***2*** Protector
3 Vision ***4*** Victor Mancha
5 Hank Pym ***6*** Monica Chang

ESSENTIAL STORYLINES

- ***Tales to Astonish #49*** Hank Pym first uses his size-changing Pym Particles to grow in size, transforming himself from Ant-Man into Giant-Man.
- ***Avengers #54*** Hank Pym creates Ultron, an incredibly powerful robot, which he implants with his own brain patterns. However Ultron rebels against his inventor.
- ***Avengers Forever, tpb*** Pym (as Giant-Man) and the Avengers battle Kang with humanity's future at stake.

QUASAR

QUASAR

FACTFILE

REAL NAME
Wendell Vaughn

OCCUPATION
Protector of the Universe

BASE
Mobile

HEIGHT 5 ft 10 in
WEIGHT 168 lbs
EYES Blue
HAIR Blond

FIRST APPEARANCE
Captain America #217 (January 1978)

POWERS

Quantum Bands permit flight, teleportation, andnthe ability to form quantum energy constructs, including weapons and armor.

When Wendell Vaughn's graduation ceremony from the SHIELD academy was attacked by AIM terrorists, a desperate Vaughn donned Quantum-Band bracelets worn by a copy of 1950s MARVEL BOY. As the new Marvel Boy, Vaughn joined SHIELD's Super-Agent program, later calling himself Marvel Man before settling on Quasar. Vaughn had been chosen by the cosmic entity Eon to become the new Protector of the Universe, replacing the late CAPTAIN MAR-VELL. Quasar became a member of the AVENGERS, and worked with the FANTASTIC FOUR.

ANNIHILUS destroyed Vaughn during the ANNIHILATION event and the Quantum Bands were passed on to Phyla-Vell, the daughter of Mar-Vell. She became Quasar but after Vaughn's death, he was resurrected in solid light form. When Phyla-Vell was killed and became DEATH's new avatar, Vaughn gave the Quantum Bands to Richard Rider, who'd been stripped of his powers as NOVA. When Rider became Nova again, Vaughn resumed his duties as Quasar once more, joining the Annihilators to help protect the universe. **DW, MF**

Using his Quantum Bands, Quasar can project bubbles of energy that act as force shields. They can also transport things through space.

Quasar is Earth's foremost cosmic hero, regularly dealing with representatives from interstellar empires such as the Kree, the Skrulls, and the Shi'ar. He has even held his own against Galactus-level threats.

QNAX

FIRST APPEARANCE Tales to Astonish #74 (December 1965)
REAL NAME Qnax (also known as Amphibian)
OCCUPATION Gladiator **BASE** The planet Xantares
HEIGHT 7 ft 9 in **WEIGHT** 915 lbs **EYES** Green **HAIR** None
SPECIAL POWERS/ABILITIES A product of centuries of scientific breeding to create the ultimate fighting machine; can travel fast and breathe underwater.

Xantares' Council of Elders sent Qnax on a mission to obtain the Sphere of Ultimate Knowledge, telling him the Sphere was needed to save the planet. Arriving on the homeworld of the WATCHERS, Qnax encountered the HULK, who was also searching for the Sphere. They fought and Qnax was hurled into space. Exiled from Xantares for this failure, Qnax traveled the cosmos as a gladiator for hire. He eventually discovered that the Council of Elders wanted the Sphere in order to dominate Xantares. Dismayed by this, Qnax returned home, hoping to bring justice to his people. **AD**

QUASIMODO

FIRST APPEARANCE Fantastic Four Special #4 (November 1966)
REAL NAME Quasi-Motivational Destruct Organism
OCCUPATION Former computer **BASE** Mobile
HEIGHT 6 ft **WEIGHT** 1,350 lbs **EYES** White **HAIR** None
SPECIAL POWERS/ABILITIES Computer brain; superhuman strength (when in physical form); left eye projects force blasts; can exist as pure consciousness without a physical body.

Quasimodo originated as a sentient computer created by the MAD THINKER. Endowed with a grotesque face that appeared on a screen, Quasimodo longed for a more human form. However, despite promising to fulfill his wish, the Thinker abandoned him. The SILVER SURFER took pity on Quasimodo and transformed him into a mobile, humanoid creature, but the ungrateful Quasimodo fought the Surfer, who rendered him immobile. Eventually Quasimodo regained his mobility, and has since battled such champions as SPIDER-MAN, the BEAST, the VISION, and the original CAPTAIN MAR-VELL. During the DARK REIGN, he assembled files on heroes and villains for HAMMER. **PS, MF**

QUIRE, QUENTIN

FIRST APPEARANCE New X-Men #134 (January 2003)
REAL NAME Quintavius Quirinius Quire
OCCUPATION Adventurer, student **BASE** New York
HEIGHT 5 ft 8 in **WEIGHT** 129 lbs
EYES Brown **HAIR** Brown, dyed purple
SPECIAL POWERS/ABILITIES Quentin is an Omega-level telepath.

Quentin Quire became a star pupil at PROFESSOR X's Xavier Institute, but he also picked up an addiction to Kick, a designer drug that enhanced mutant powers. While using it, he formed the Omega Gang and started a student riot at the school. His abuse of Kick caused him to become a being of mental energy, only able to reformulate his body when the Phoenix Force arrived. When the X-MEN split up, WOLVERINE dragged him to the new Jean Grey School for Higher Learning, believing that CYCLOPS would only lock the boy up. **MF**

QUICKSILVER

The super-fast Super Hero

The son of MAGNETO, Pietro and his twin sister Wanda (SCARLET WITCH) grew up never knowing their father's identity. While pregnant with them, their mother, Magda, fled from Magneto and gave birth to them in the hills of Wundagore Mountain. The gypsy family of Django Maximoff raised the children, but when their mutant powers first showed, Pietro and Wanda were persecuted as demons.

VILLAINS AND HEROES

Magneto found them during his hunt for members of his BROTHERHOOD OF EVIL MUTANTS. As Quicksilver and Scarlet Witch, they engaged in a series of battles with the X-MEN, remaining with the Brotherhood only because of the debt they felt they owed Magneto. When the first incarnation of the Brotherhood dissolved, Pietro and his sister went into seclusion, vowing never

Quicksilver eventually turned against Magneto (in reality, his long-lost father), and became a valued member of the Avengers along with his sister.

again to use their powers for evil. Hearing that the AVENGERS needed new blood, Pietro and Wanda resumed their costumed identities and were accepted as members. Quicksilver did not approve of Wanda's marriage to the android VISION, and it caused a rift between them. Quicksilver was later injured during a mission and nursed back to health by CRYSTAL of the INHUMANS. The two were married and had a daughter, Luna.

When Wanda had a breakdown and destroyed the Avengers, Quicksilver persuaded her to use her powers to change the world into a place where mutants ruled, creating the House of M (Earth-58163). Once mainstream reality returned on M-Day, Quicksilver lost his powers. He used the Inhumans' Terrigen Mists to restore himself and others, but his plans went awry. Furious, Crystal announced that their marriage was over.

Hoping to redeem himself, Quicksilver joined Hank PYM's new Avengers during the DARK REIGN, and he later served on the staff of the Avengers Academy. He also sided with the Avengers during their battle with the X-Men over the Phoenix Force.

TB, MF

Since childhood, Quicksilver has been overly protective of his unstable sister, the Scarlet Witch.

QUICKSILVER

FACTFILE

REAL NAME
Pietro Maximoff

OCCUPATION
Adventurer

BASE
Various

HEIGHT 6 ft
WEIGHT 175 lbs
EYES Blue
HAIR Silver

FIRST APPEARANCE
X-Men #4 (March 1964)

POWERS

Quicksilver possesses the mutant ability to run at superhuman speeds over great distances. His top speed is alleged to be 175 mph. He can create a whirlwind by running in a circle; his temper can be a quick as his feet.

ESSENTIAL STORYLINES
- ***Avengers #16*** Quicksilver and his sister the Scarlet Witch join the Avengers.
- ***Avengers #127/Fantastic Four #150*** Quicksilver marries Crystal of the isolationist Inhumans.
- ***Avengers #185-187*** Quicksilver and the Scarlet Witch return to Wundagore Mountain in Eastern Europe to discover the strange secrets of their birth and their parentage.

While in the Brotherhood of Evil Mutants, Quicksilver experienced superhuman combat against the X-Men, including Cyclops.

Radioactive Man

FIRST APPEARANCE Journey Into Mystery #93 (June 1963)
REAL NAME Dr. Chen Lu
OCCUPATION Former scientist; criminal **BASE** Mobile
HEIGHT 6 ft 6 in **WEIGHT** 310 lbs **EYES** Brown **HAIR** None
SPECIAL POWERS/ABILITIES Manipulates radioactivity given off by body; emits radiation as heat or blinding light and can incinerate a city block; hypnotic abilities; superhuman strength.

Dr. Chen Lu was a nuclear physicist in the People's Republic of China, and was among those asked by the Chinese government to defeat Thor. Lu exposed himself to nuclear radiation, transforming him into Radioactive Man. He traveled to New York and battled Thor, but lost. Baron Zemo then enlisted him in his Masters of Evil. He later joined the Thunderbolts, and when he returned to China, he was made part of the People's Defense Force. A Russian mutant, Igor Stancheck, also used the Radioactive Man name. He was killed while attacking Wakanda. **MT, MF**

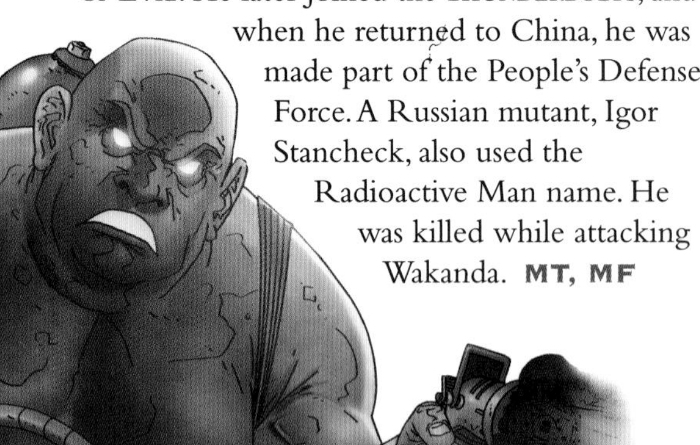

Ragnarok

FIRST APPEARANCE Civil War #3 (September 2006)
REAL NAME Ragnarok
OCCUPATION Warrior **BASE** Mobile
HEIGHT 6 ft 6 in **WEIGHT** 640 lbs **EYES** Blue **HAIR** Blond
SPECIAL POWERS/ABILITIES Ragnarok has superhuman durability, endurance, speed, and strength. He can project electric shocks from his hammer.

When the Civil War erupted, Henry Pym, Iron Man, and Mister Fantastic needed more power on their side. Thor would have been perfect, but he had died, so they made a cyborg clone of him, Ragnarok. In his first battle, Ragnarok murdered Goliath and had to be shut down. In the final Civil War battle, Hercules destroyed him. Revived, he hunted down the returned Thor, who slew him once more. He was rebuilt for HAMMER and destroyed again. He returned once more to join Luke Cage's Thunderbolts. **MF**

Rasputin, Mikhail

FIRST APPEARANCE Uncanny X-Men #284 (January 1992)
REAL NAME Mikhail Rasputin **OCCUPATION** Cosmonaut
BASE The Hill, in an unspecified dimension
HEIGHT 6 ft 5 in **WEIGHT** 255 lbs **EYES** Blue **HAIR** Black
SPECIAL POWERS/ABILITIES Manipulates matter on a sub-atomic level. He uses this power to fire destructive blasts, warp reality, and teleport through space and between dimensions.

During a spaceflight, Soviet cosmonaut Mikhail Rasputin entered another dimension. There he fell in love with and married a princess, but when he had to try to close the dimensional rift, the backlash killed hundreds of people, including his beloved wife. When he returned to Earth, he became leader of the Morlocks before massacring them and setting up the mutant terrorist group Gene Nation for Dark Beast. He later helped the X-Men defeat Apocalypse and his Horsemen. Eventually, he banished himself to another dimension to save his brother from Mister Sinister. **MT, MF**

Rage

FIRST APPEARANCE Avengers #326 (November 1990)
REAL NAME Elvin Daryl Haliday
OCCUPATION Student **BASE** Oatridge School for Boys
HEIGHT 6 ft 6 in **WEIGHT** 450 lbs **EYES** Brown **HAIR** None
SPECIAL POWERS/ABILITIES Exposure to alien radiation granted him the ability to fly and to understand the language of birds.

Twelve-year-old Elvin Haliday plunged into Newtown Creek to escape a gang of racist thugs. The chemicals in the water caused him to grow into an adult with superhuman strength. Although Elvin could have used his new powers for crime, his only relation, the devout Granny Staples, convinced him to become a hero. Elvin slipped from this road just once: when Granny Staples herself was murdered. Rage worked with both the Avengers and the New Warriors. He sided with Captain America during the Civil War, but later joined the Fifty-State Initiative at Camp Hammond. He is now part of the latest New Warriors team. **AD, MF**

Ravonna

NO ONE COMMANDS A *PRINCESS!*

In the 41st century of an alternate future, Kang had conquered all of Earth except the small kingdom of Princess Ravonna, who refused his offer of marriage. Kang's army ultimately overwhelmed Ravonna's kingdom but when Kang refused to execute Ravonna, his commander Baltag rebelled against him.

Kang joined forces with Ravonna and the Avengers to defeat Baltag and Ravonna fell in love with Kang. When the vengeful Baltag fired a blaster at Kang, Ravonna pushed him out of the way, and the blast struck her instead. To restore her to life, Kang played a game with the alien Grandmaster, who gave him temporary power over life and death when Kang won. However, Kang wasted this short-lived power in an unsuccessful attempt to kill the Avengers.

After this point various timelines diverge, in which Ravonna leads different lives. In one timeline Kang saves Ravonna from Baltag's attack, but she becomes the ally and consort of Kang's own future counterpart, Immortus. In another the Grandmaster revives Ravonna, who seeks vengeance on Kang. She assumes a number of identities, including Nebula, the Temptress, and the Terminatrix. A future counterpart will take the name Revelation. **PS**

FACTFILE

REAL NAME
Ravonna Lexus Renslayer

OCCUPATION
Princess

BASE
Originally an unnamed kingdom on 41st century Earth in an alternate future.

HEIGHT 5 ft 8 in
WEIGHT 142 lbs
EYES (as Ravonna) Brown; (as Nebula/Terminatrix) Blue
HAIR (as Ravonna) Red-brown; (as Nebula/Terminatrix) Blond

FIRST APPEARANCE
Avengers #23 (December 1965)

RAVONNA

POWERS
As Terminatrix or Revelation: has enhanced durability, speed, and agility, is a formidable hand-to-hand combatant, and uses highly advanced technology.

Rawhide Kid, The

FIRST APPEARANCE Rawhide Kid #1 (March 1955)
REAL NAME Johnny Bart
OCCUPATION Gunslinger **BASE** The American Old West
HEIGHT 5 ft 10 in **WEIGHT** 185 lbs
EYES Blue **HAIR** Red
SPECIAL POWERS/ABILITIES Skilled brawler and horseman; among the quickest draws in the Old West.

The Rawhide Kid learned to handle a six-shooter thanks to his adoptive father, a Texas Ranger, after his real parents were killed by Cheyenne warriors. When his adoptive father died in a rigged duel, the Rawhide Kid took revenge on the killers and then wandered the West astride his horse Nightwind, keeping one step ahead of the sheriff who suspected the Kid of murder. By means of time travel, the Rawhide Kid occasionally crossed paths with modern-era Super Heroes. **AD**

Reaper

FIRST APPEARANCE New Mutants #87 (March 1990)
REAL NAME Pantu Hurageb
OCCUPATION None **BASE** Unknown
HEIGHT/WEIGHT/EYES/HAIR Unrevealed
SPECIAL POWERS/ABILITIES Neurosynaptic energy generated by Reaper slows reflexes and movements of those nearby; scythes focus energy and can be used to paralyze others.

Not to be mistaken for the demon raised to battle Blade, nor for an adversary of the Phantom Rider, the Reaper known as Pantu Hurageb was a member of the Mutant Liberation Front. During his stint there, he lost a hand and a lower leg and replaced both with artificial limbs. Following Reaper's incarceration in Neverland, Nathan Summers (Cable) tried to pry the camp's location from his mind, causing him severe brain damage and turning him mute. He lost his powers on M-Day, but Quicksilver has since given them back. He was later trapped in the hellish Brimstone Dimension. **AD, MF**

Reavers

The cyborg mercenaries known as the Reavers originally operated from an underground complex in Cooteman's Creek, located in Australia's Northern Territory. They exploited the teleportation mutant Gateway in order to commit robberies around the world until the X-Men forced them from their base. Ex-Hellfire Club member Donald Pierce reorganized the team, bringing in Cole, Macon, and Reese, and Lady Deathstrike. The new Reavers nearly killed Wolverine, and launched a failed attack on Moira MacTaggert's Muir Island laboratory. A squad of Sentinels nearly destroyed the Reavers, though most members survived due to their half-machine physiologies.

The Reavers later won a contract from the psionic entity the Shadow King to kidnap Rogue of the X-Men, but failed to capture their quarry. Pierce chose to remake the Reavers into a grassroots anti-mutant movement, and swayed many citizens with his hateful propaganda. Lady Deathstrike formed her own Reavers by giving advanced cybernetics to members of the Purifiers, a fundamentalist Christian, anti-mutant terrorist movement. They were destroyed by X-Force. **DW MF**

FACTFILE
KEY MEMBERS
DONALD PIERCE (LEADER)
Adamantium-enhanced body, enhanced strength; morphing cyborg limbs emit energy blasts.
BONEBREAKER
Cyborg strength, tank treads, built-in weaponry.
PRETTY BOY
Extendible cyborg limbs and capture coils; reprograms the personalities of others.
SKULLBUSTER
Cyborg strength, robot legs; uses machine guns, grenade launchers.
SKULLBUSTER/CYLLA
Cyborg strength, reflexes; wrist claws, thermite launchers.
LADY DEATHSTRIKE
Augmented strength, reflexes; talons extend from fingertips.
COLE, MACON, AND REESE
Cyborg strength, reflexes; bionic scanners and tracking devices.
BASE Mobile
FIRST APPEARANCE
Uncanny X-Men #229 (May 1988)

THE REAVERS
(left to right) Skullbuster, Bonebreaker, Pretty Boy

Red Ghost

FIRST APPEARANCE Fantastic Four #13 (April 1963)
REAL NAME Ivan Kragoff **OCCUPATION** Villain
BASE Mobile **HEIGHT** 5 ft 11 in **WEIGHT** 215 lbs
EYES Brown **HAIR** White, balding
SPECIAL POWERS/ABILITIES Renders himself and nearby objects intangible and transparent; ingenious scientist and brilliant engineer.

Russian scientist Ivan Kragoff envied the achievements of the Fantastic Four. Determined to beat them to the Moon, he designed his spacecraft to maximize exposure to cosmic rays, hoping to duplicate the freakish accident that had created his rivals. Kragoff gained the ability to become intangible, and his three ape companions became smarter and obtained powers of strength, magnetism, and shapeshifting. As the Red Ghost, Kragoff and his Super-Ape companions clashed with the Fantastic Four, the Avengers, and Spider-Man. He became a member of the Intelligencia and was later killed by Doctor Octopus but revived by MODOK. **AD, MF**

RED GUARDIAN

FACTFILE

REAL NAME
Alexei Shostakov

OCCUPATION
Espionage agent for Soviet Union; later for People's Republic of China

BASE
Various secret KGB bases in USSR; later a military base in the People's Republic of China

HEIGHT 6 ft 2 in
WEIGHT 220 lbs
EYES Blue
HAIR Red

FIRST APPEARANCE
Avengers #43 (August 1967)

POWERS
Brilliant athlete and test pilot, trained in espionage techniques and hand-to-hand combat by the KGB. Disc on Red Guardian's belt could be detached and used as a throwing weapon; magnetic force returned the disc after throwing.

Red Guardian

A talented athlete and test pilot—and husband to Natasha Romanoff (Black Widow)—Alexei Shostakov faked his death and trained to become a top KGB operative codenamed Red Guardian, modeled after a Soviet hero from World War II. While Natasha became disillusioned with her KGB masters and defected to the USA, Alexei remained loyal and increasingly ruthless and vindictive. He was thought to have given his life to save her and Captain America, but he turned up alive again years later, trying to bring Natasha to justice for betraying her homeland.

Dr. Tara Belinsky became the next Red Guardian and even joined the Defenders for a while. When Presence gave her radioactive powers, she changed her name to Starlight. Five other Red Guardians followed after her, each athletic men. The latest became leader of the Winter Guard. **AD, MF**

After encountering the Avengers, the Red Guardian battles Hawkeye, Black Widow's lover.

The Red Guardian's identity is revealed.

RED HULK

FACTFILE

REAL NAME
General Thaddeus E. Ross

OCCUPATION
Adventurer, retired soldier

BASE
Mobile

HEIGHT 7 ft
WEIGHT 1200 lbs
EYES Yellow
HAIR Black

FIRST APPEARANCE
Hulk #1 (March 2008)

POWERS
Red Hulk has superhuman durability, endurance, and strength. As he gets angrier, he gets hotter. He can also absorb radiation to become more powerful.

Red Hulk

After World War Hulk, the Intelligencia took General Thunderbolt Ross—who'd faked his death—and transformed him into the Red Hulk, a smarter version of the Hulk. The Red Hulk grew hotter when angry rather than stronger. For a long time, the Red Hulk worked with them, never letting anyone outside the group know who he really was. He appeared in Russia and gunned down the Abomination with a pistol the size of a small cannon. He next arrived at the new SHIELD Helicarrier built by Iron Man and tore it from the sky. Soon after that, he attacked Rick Jones, who transformed into A-Bomb, a gamma-irradiated creature with armored, blue skin.

The Red Hulk attacked a SHIELD Helicarrier and singlehandedly brought it down, beating his way through She-Hulk, Iron Man, and countless SHIELD agents to do it.

When it came time for Red Hulk to help the Intelligencia take over America, he betrayed them and tried to take the country over for himself. The original Hulk stopped him, and Steve Rogers (Captain America), believing Ross could be redeemed, offered him a spot in the Avengers. During the events of Avengers vs X-Men, the Red Hulk battled Cyclops who sent him back to the Avengers with an X carved on his chest. He later formed and led a new Thunderbolts team. **MF**

The Red Hulk attacked Rick Jones but he got more than he bargained for when Jones transformed into A-Bomb, a new version of the Abomination.

Red Raven

FIRST APPEARANCE Red Raven Comics #1 (August 1940)
REAL NAME Unknown
OCCUPATION Adventurer **BASE** Mobile
HEIGHT 6 ft **WEIGHT** 180 lbs **EYES** Black **HAIR** Red
SPECIAL POWERS/ABILITIES Can fly using anti-gravity metallic wings, which can also deflect bullets and fire energy beams.

Raised by a lost tribe of Inhumans known as the Bird-People, on a hovering island in the Atlantic, Red Raven was a heroic member of the World War II-era Liberty Legion. After the war, he placed himself and his people into suspended animation to prevent aggression between them and humanity. Later, the Angel discovered Red Raven, who made it appear that his island had been destroyed to ensure the privacy of the Bird-People. His daughter Dania has also assumed the identity of Red Raven. Arcade kidnapped her for his latest Murderworld, and she died trying to escape it. **DW, MF**

Red Skull,
see pages 292-293

Red Wolf

FIRST APPEARANCE Avengers #80 (September 1970)
REAL NAME William Talltrees **OCCUPATION** Adventurer
BASE American Southwest **HEIGHT** 6 ft 4 in
WEIGHT 240 lbs **EYES** Brown **HAIR** Black
SPECIAL POWERS/ABILITIES Superhuman senses. Skilled hand-to-hand combatant. Expert tracker and archer. Employs a coup stick (a 6ft wooden staff used as a bo or javelin), tomahawk, and knife.

The first Red Wolf is believed to have tamed the first horse and conquered the American plains for the Cheyenne. Another was Johnny Wakeley, a Cheyenne orphan who forged peace between his people and the US Cavalry. The current Red Wolf is Will Talltrees, who grew up on a Cheyenne Reservation. After his family was murdered, the Wolf Spirit Owayodata granted his prayers for the power to avenge them. Talltrees later joined the Fifty-State Initiative's Texas team, the Rangers. His wolf friend, Lobo, turned out to be a Skrull and was killed during the Secret Invasion. **TD, MF**

Reptil

FIRST APPEARANCE Avengers: The Initiative Featuring Reptil #1 (May 2009) **REAL NAME** Humberto Lopez
OCCUPATION Hero-in-training **BASE** Avengers Academy
HEIGHT 5 ft 10 in **WEIGHT** 168 lbs
EYES Brown **HAIR** Brown
SPECIAL POWERS/ABILITIES Reptil can fully transform into any prehistoric animal, such as a dinosaur. At first he could only change parts of his body at a time.

Berto Lopez's paleontologist parents discovered a fossilized amulet and gave it to him. After they went missing, he discovered the amulet allowed him to change parts of his body into that of a dinosaur. He registered with the US government and was sent to be trained at Camp Hammond. After the Dark Reign ended, he joined the Avengers Academy instead. At one point, he swapped minds with his future self and learned he would have a child with fellow Avenger student Finesse. Later, Arcade kidnapped him and pitted him against other young heroes in a new Murderworld. **MF**

Redeemer

FIRST APPEARANCE Incredible Hulk #343 (May 1988)
REAL NAME Craig Saunders
OCCUPATION Former demolitions expert **BASE** New York
HEIGHT 6 ft 1 in **WEIGHT** 205 lbs **EYES** Brown **HAIR** White
SPECIAL POWERS/ABILITIES Bonded with combat suit armed with twin plasma canons on each hand, a rocket and grenade launcher, and rocket boots enabling 30 minutes of flight.

After joining the military as a demolitions expert, Craig Saunders' world came crashing down when he failed to defuse a bomb in an airport terminal, causing the death of two civilians. Desperate, he joined a new paramilitary team called the Hulkbusters, but their effort to defeat the Hulk also ended in disappointment. Taking advantage of Saunders' despair, the Leader persuaded him to become the Redeemer and integrated Saunders' body into a formidable yellow combat suit. Sadly, redemption was not to be his—Saunders died during his very first confrontation with old greenskin. **AD**

Revanche

FIRST APPEARANCE X-Men #17 (February 1992)
REAL NAME Kwannon **OCCUPATION** Assassin **BASE** Japan
HEIGHT (both bodies) 5 ft 11 in **WEIGHT** (both bodies) 155 lbs
EYES (original body) Blue, (Braddock's body) Violet
HAIR (original body) Black, (Braddock's body) Brown, dyed purple
SPECIAL POWERS/ABILITIES Martial arts; (as Revanche) telepath; manifested psychic energy in form of Samurai sword.

Kwannon was a Japanese assassin and the lover of crimelord Matsu'o Tsurayaba. When Kwannon was mortally injured, Tsurayaba made a deal with Spiral, who transferred Kwannon's mind into the body of Psylocke and swapped Psylocke's mind into Kwannon's body. Gaining Psylocke's memories and powers, Kwannon claimed to be her and called herself Revanche (French for "revenge"). Discovering that she was infected with the Legacy Virus, she begged Matsu'o to kill her with a ceremonial dagger. She was later revived to join the Sisterhood of Mutants, but Psylocke slew her soon after. **PS, MF**

Revengers, The

FIRST APPEARANCE New Avengers Annual #1 (November 2011)
BASE New York City
MEMBERS AND POWERS
Anti-Venom Wears a healing symbiote.
Atlas Grows to huge size. **Captain Ultra** Superhuman who can fly, become intangible, use X-ray vision and super breath.
Century Teleporting superhuman.
Demolition Man Superhuman durability, endurance, and strength. **Devil-Slayer** Teleporter with mystic, prehensile cloak that holds many things. **Ethan Edwards** A super-Skrull. **Goliath** Grows to huge size. **Wonder Man** Controls the ionic energy of which he's composed.

Angered at what he saw as the way the Avengers continued to endanger the world with their irresponsible adventures, Wonder Man assembled a team to stop them. They attacked Luke Cage's Avengers in the Avengers Mansion first and defeated them soundly, but the fully assembled Avengers captured them and put an end to the team. Wonder Man would later repent this action and go on to rejoin the Avengers, trying to lead through example. **MF**

Red Skull

The most dangerous of all Nazi agents

RED SKULL

FACTFILE

REAL NAME
Johann Schmidt

OCCUPATION
Terrorist; conqueror

BASE
Nazi Germany, later various secret bases around the world.

HEIGHT (original body) 6 ft 1 in; (cloned body) 6 ft 2 in
WEIGHT (original body) 195 lbs; (cloned body) 240 lbs
EYES (both bodies) Blue
HAIR (original body) Brown; (cloned body) Formerly blond, later none

FIRST APPEARANCE
Captain America Comics #5 (August 1941)

POWERS

Totally ruthless, brilliant subversive strategist; excellent hand-to-hand combatant and marksman. Uses lethal "dust of death," which causes a victim's head to resemble a ghoulish red skull.

ALLIES/FOES

ALLIES Adolf Hitler, Sin Crossbones, Doctor Faustus, Arnim Zola, the S-Men, Honest John

FOES Captain America, General Lukin, the Winter Soldier, the Avengers, Wolverine

ISSUE #1

In "The Ringmaster of Death" Cap and Bucky discover that a circus is a front of a gang of Nazi assassins. The Red Skull lurks behind the scenes.

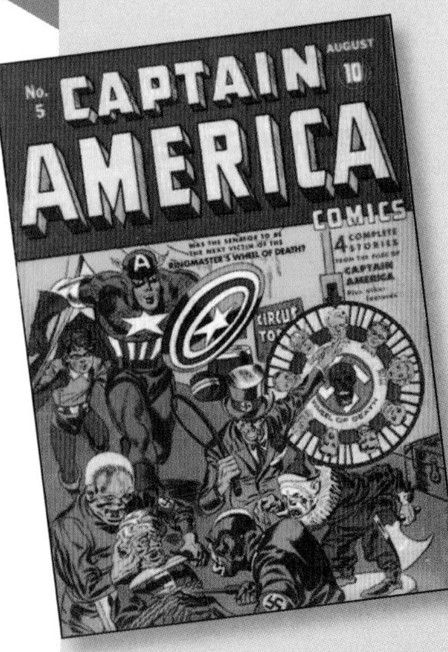

The Red Skull's Cosmic Cube, could alter reality.

Johann Schmidt was born in a German village. His mother died giving birth to him and, after failing to drown the newborn child, Johann's father committed suicide. The orphaned Schmidt became a beggar and thief, though he sometimes took menial jobs. Schmidt was working as a bellboy in a hotel when Adolf Hitler, the dictator of Nazi Germany, paid a visit there.

A Perfect Nazi

Recognizing in Schmidt's eyes a hatred of all humanity that mirrored his own, Hitler decided to turn him into "the perfect Nazi." Hitler oversaw Schmidt's training, presented him with a skull-like head mask, and named him "The Red Skull." Answerable only to Hitler himself, the Red Skull undertook a range of missions for the Third Reich, especially acts of terrorism.

In order to have an American counterpart to the Red Skull, the US government gave "super-soldier" Steve Rogers the identity of Captain America. Shortly before the US entered World War II, the Red Skull first battled Captain America, who would become his greatest foe. During the war, the Red Skull commanded numerous military missions. He rose to become the second most powerful man in the Third Reich, feared even by Hitler.

During the fall of Berlin, Captain America fought the Red Skull in Hitler's bunker. A bomb caused a cave-in that seemingly killed the Red Skull. However, an experimental gas kept the villain in suspended animation for decades.

During World War II the Red Skull repeatedly battled Captain America and his partner Bucky.

Back From the Dead

In the 1950s, communist agent Albert Malik impersonated the Red Skull, but eventually the original was found and revived. Since then, Captain America has repeatedly thwarted his bids for global domination. At one point, the Red Skull died, but Arnim Zola transferred the Skull's consciousness into a clone of Captain America. By accident, his own "dust of death" caused the Skull's new head to resemble a living red skull.

The Skull made many enemies, including General Lukin, who sent the Winter Soldier to kill him. Before dying, the Skull used a Cosmic Cube to transfer his mind into Lukin's body. With the help of his daughter, Sin, Crossbones, and Doctor Faustus, the Skull set up the assassination of Captain America at the end of the Civil War. This was, however, not just the end of his plans for Cap, but the beginning.

ESSENTIAL STORYLINES

- ***Tales of Suspense #66***
The first time that the fascinating origin of the Red Skull was revealed.
- ***Tales of Suspense #79–81***
The Red Skull is revived in modern times and steals the Cosmic Cube.
- ***Captain America #101–104***
The Red Skull unleashes the Fourth Sleeper robot and leads his Nazi army of Exiles.

The Enemy Returns

It seemed that Captain America had died from a bullet fired by the Skull's henchman Crossbones; however, the Red Skull had actually arranged for Doctor Faustus to brainwash Sharon Carter and she had shot Cap in the confusion caused by Crossbones' attack. She hadn't used a pistol, however, but a device designed to freeze Captain America in time. With the help of Arnim Zola, the Red Skull planned to pluck his foe back out of time and transfer his mind into Cap's body.

Carter foiled the Skull's plan by escaping from him and damaging Zola's machinery. This left Cap unstuck in time, but only temporarily. The Red Skull and Zola traveled to Latveria for help from Doctor Doom and completed the transfer. They then returned to Washington, DC, and fought the Avengers. The Red Skull planned to kill the new Captain America (Bucky Barnes), but as they battled, the original Captain America mentally broke through the Red Skull's controls and pushed him out of his brain.

The Red Skull returned to his robot body and battled the Avengers. Carter shot him with a weapon she thought would shrink him, but instead it grew him into a giant. While the Avengers kept the Red Skull occupied, Carter shot him with a barrage of missiles, destroying his body and putting an end to him.

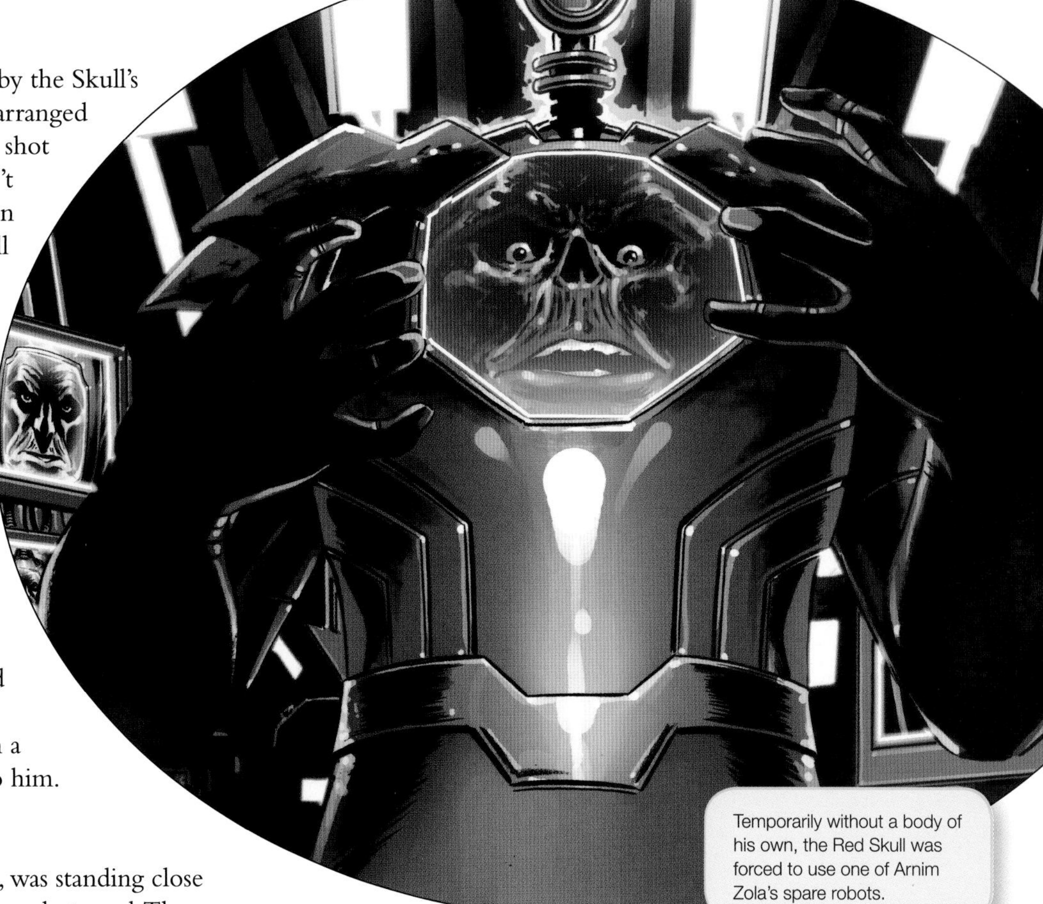

Temporarily without a body of his own, the Red Skull was forced to use one of Arnim Zola's spare robots.

With her face disfigured in the same way as her father's, Sin assumed his mantle of evil.

The Skull's Heir

The Red Skull's daughter, Sin, was standing close to him when his robot body was destroyed. The explosion blasted her, removing her hair and turning her burnt skin bright red. She took on his name and mantle, becoming the new Red Skull.

The new Skull returned to her father's secret bases to explore her inheritance. In one, she discovered his diary and learned of his attempt to invoke the Serpent of Norse myth to help the Nazis win World War II. This led her to an isolated fortress in which she found a mystical hammer. When she picked it up—something her father had been unable to do—it transformed her into Skadi, the herald of the Serpent. This launched Fear Itself.

Following the eventual defeat of the Serpent, Odin took Skadi's hammer, and the Red Skull changed back into herself, still disfigured. Despite her defeat, she managed to remain free. **MF**

Red Skull and the S-Men
1 Living Wind ***2*** Dancing Water
3 Mzee ***4*** Goat-Faced Girl
5 Red Skull ***6*** Dangerous Jinn
7 Insect ***8*** Tsar Sultan

THE NEW SKULL

The original Red Skull had died, but he wasn't done yet. After Sin's defeat, Arnim Zola revived a clone of the Skull he had kept in suspended animation since the end of World War II. Awakening in the middle of the conflict between the Avengers and the X-Men, the cloned Skull decided that mutants were the source of everything that was wrong with the world.

The Skull assembled a new force of S-Men—enhanced people loyal to him and bigoted against mutants—and stole Professor X's body. The Skull then took part of Xavier's brain and grafted it onto his own, giving him some semblance of Xavier's tremendous psychic powers. He then took to the streets of Manhattan, telepathically projecting his hatred of mutants to the people there.

The Skull tried to control a new team of Avengers led by Havok, mentally dominating Thor with the help of Honest John. He failed to do the same to Captain America, however, and he lost his hand to Wolverine, who sliced it off when he learned what the Skull had done to Xavier. Rogue managed to disrupt the Skull's powers, sending him and his S-Men fleeing to fight another day.

FACTFILE

REAL NAME
Aleksei Sytsevich

OCCUPATION
Criminal

BASE
Mobile

HEIGHT 6 ft 5 in
WEIGHT 710 lbs
EYES Brown
HAIR Brown

FIRST APPEARANCE
The Amazing Spider-Man #41 (October 1966)

POWERS
The Rhino possesses the strength and enhanced durability of his namesake due to his protective suit, which is bonded to his body.

The Hulk seemed to have killed the Rhino once, but Aleksei survived that too.

RHINO

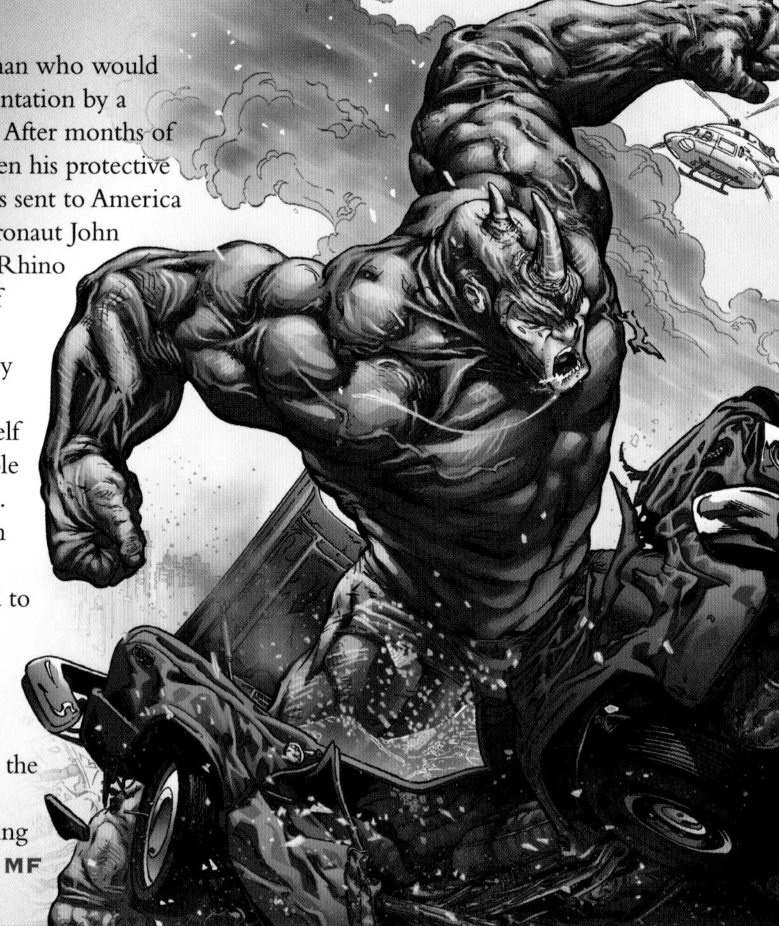

A career criminal in the Russian Mafia, the man who would become the Rhino was selected for experimentation by a group of spies because of his low intelligence. After months of chemical and radiation treatments, he was given his protective suit, which resembled rhinoceros hide. He was sent to America under the identity Alex O'Hirn to abduct astronaut John JAMESON, but was foiled by SPIDER-MAN. The Rhino subsequently used his strength in a number of criminal endeavors.

Believing himself to be trapped permanently within his costume, the Rhino was subject to bouts of insanity, but he eventually gave himself up to SHIELD, who were able to remove the suit from him. Released on parole, he fell in love with a waitress and got married. A new Rhino tried to destroy him but killed the Rhino's wife instead. Aleksei donned his old suit and killed the newcomer. Joining a new SINISTER SIX, the Rhino seemingly drowned SILVER SABLE, apparently dying himself in the process. **TB, MF**

FACTFILE

REAL NAME
Franklin Benjamin Richards

OCCUPATION
Occasional adventurer

BASE
New York City

HEIGHT 4 ft 8 in
WEIGHT 100 lbs
EYES Blue
HAIR Blond

FIRST APPEARANCE
Fantastic Four Annual #6 (1968)

POWERS
Formerly possessed vast powers of telepathy and telekinesis, as well as the ability to fire psionic blasts, reshape reality, appear in astral form, and perceive future events.

RICHARDS, FRANKLIN

Son of Reed and Sue Richards of the FANTASTIC FOUR, Franklin Richards was once one of the most powerful mutants on Earth. Before his birth, strange energies flowing through Sue's body nearly killed both mother and baby until ANNIHILUS' Cosmic Control Rod suppressed them. Agatha HARKNESS acted as Franklin's nanny in his earliest years. The boy soon began to exhibit immense psionic powers. Using his ability to see possible futures, he became a member of POWER PACK under the name Tattletale. Nathaniel RICHARDS, his grandfather, later raised him in a realm outside of time, where he became the adult adventurer Psi-Lord, and founded the Fantastic Force before Hyperstorm erased his adult form from existence. When the AVENGERS and the Fantastic Four seemingly perished fighting ONSLAUGHT, Franklin sent them to a "Counter-Earth" of his own creation. He used his powers to bring back GALACTUS and return his sister Valeria to his mother's womb and, in the process, seemed to lose his powers. As a member of his family's Future Foundation, however, he has quietly revealed that his powers have returned. **DW, MF**

RICHARDS, NATHANIEL

FIRST APPEARANCE Fantastic Four #272 (November 1984)
REAL NAME Nathaniel Richards
OCCUPATION Adventurer and scientist **BASE** Mobile
HEIGHT 6 ft 2 in **WEIGHT** 170 lbs
EYES Brown **HAIR** Gray
SPECIAL POWERS/ABILITIES Nathaniel is a super genius who can travel through time.

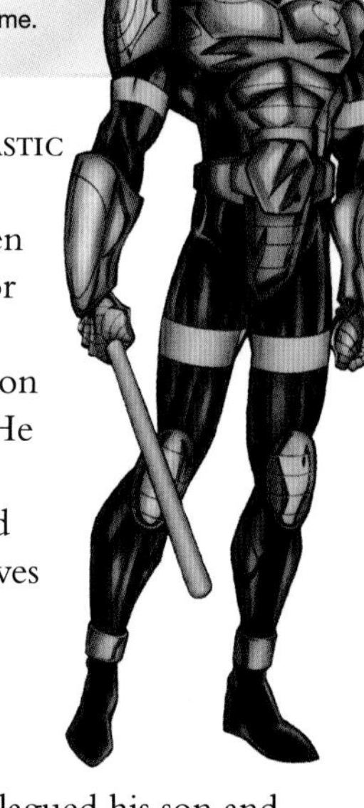

The father of MISTER FANTASTIC (Reed Richards), Nathaniel Richards left his family when Reed was young to work for the Brotherhood of the Shield, an ancient organisation created to safeguard Earth. He gained the power to travel through time and discovered that all of his multiversal selves had been gathered in one place by IMMORTUS, so that they would kill each other until only one remained. Hiding in time, Nathaniel plagued his son and his family for many years, kidnapping Franklin RICHARDS and even posing as DOCTOR DOOM. He later joined the Future Foundation to work with his family rather than against them. **MF**

Richards, Valeria

FACTFILE
REAL NAME
Valeria Meghan Richards
OCCUPATION
Student, adventurer
BASE
New York City

HEIGHT 3 ft 5 in
WEIGHT 50 lbs
EYES Blue
HAIR Blond

FIRST APPEARANCE
Fantastic Four #50 (February 2002)

POWERS
Valeria has superhuman intelligence and can generate force fields.

The second child of Mister Fantastic and the Invisible Woman, Valeria was conceived in the Negative Zone and thought to be stillborn. Instead, her brother Franklin took her to an alternate future where she was raised by the Invisible Woman and her husband, a heroic Doctor Doom. Valeria eventually returned to their time as a teenager calling herself Marvel Girl. When battling the universe-destroyer Abraxas with their family, Valeria and Franklin used their powers to revive Galactus to defeat him.

In the subsequent restructuring of reality, Valeria went back to being a fetus in her mother's womb. This time, Doctor Doom came to the Fantastic Four's aid and saved the girl. He asked only that he be able to name her, although he also cast a spell on her to bind her to him. The Fantastic Four eventually broke this. At one point, future versions of Valeria and her brother came back in time to help the Fantastic Four save the universe from the Mad Celestials. In time, Valeria joined the Future Foundation with the rest of her family. **MF**

Ricochet

FACTFILE
REAL NAME
Jonathon "Johnny" Gallo
OCCUPATION
College student
BASE
Los Angeles, California; formerly Brooklyn, New York

HEIGHT 5 ft 10 in
WEIGHT 155 lbs
EYES Blue
HAIR Blond

FIRST APPEARANCE
Slingers #0 (as Johnny Gallo, December 1998)

POWERS
Mutant with superhuman leaping, acrobatic, and gymnastic skills. Possesses a "danger sense," similar to Spider-Man's "spider-sense." Also uses throwing disks as weapons.

Ricochet can use his throwing disks to shatter opposing weaponry and stun his foes

When Spider-Man was falsely accused of murder, a $5 million reward was placed on his head and he was forced to adopt a new identity in order to find the real killer. Instead of temporarily assuming one new persona, he created four: Ricochet, Dusk, Hornet, and Prodigy. After clearing his name, Spider-Man discarded these identities and their costumes. The costumes came into the possession of a former Super Hero called the Black Marvel, who gave them to four teenagers and formed a new super-team called the Slingers. One of the members was Johnny Gallo, a troubled youth who had grown apart from his father after his mother was killed in a car accident. Johnny literally leaped at the chance to use his mutant powers in the Slingers, but like the other members of the team he was disillusioned when it emerged that the Black Marvel had obtained the costumes from Mephisto. Nevertheless, the Slingers battled to save the Black Marvel's soul from Mephisto and won, although the battle claimed the life of the Black Marvel. The Slingers then disbanded and Gallo moved to Los Angeles. He joined a group of former teenage heroes who were adjusting to civilian life and trying to dissuade other teenagers from becoming costumed heroes. **TD**

Rictor

FIRST APPEARANCE X-Factor #17 (June 1987)
REAL NAME Julio Esteban Richter
OCCUPATION Private Investigator **BASE** New York City
HEIGHT 5 ft 9 in **WEIGHT** 162 lbs **EYES** Brown **HAIR** Brown
SPECIAL POWERS/ABILITIES By touching objects can cause them to vibrate and crumble; applied to buildings his powers have earthquake-like effect.

As a boy, Julio Richter saw the mutant clone Stryfe murder his father. Julio later developed mutant powers and was captured by the Right to cause mayhem in San Francisco. Freed by X-Factor, he has since served with them as well as the New Mutants and X-Force. M-Day robbed him of his powers, but he still joined X-Factor Investigations. He later started a relationship with Shatterstar, and the Scarlet Witch restored his powers. **AD, MF**

Right, The

FIRST APPEARANCE X-Factor #17 (June 1987)
MEMBERS AND POWERS
Cameron Hodge (commander) Brilliant planner; made immortal through a mystical pact.
Ani-Mator Genius-level geneticist.
Other unnamed operatives and soldiers.
BASE Mobile

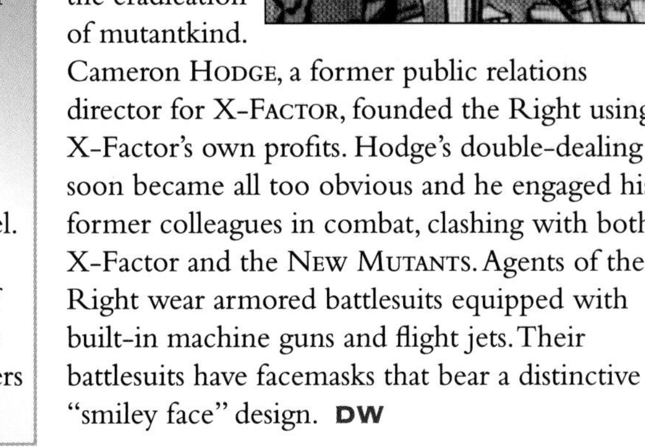

The Right is a secret organization dedicated to preserving human freedoms by the eradication of mutantkind. Cameron Hodge, a former public relations director for X-Factor, founded the Right using X-Factor's own profits. Hodge's double-dealing soon became all too obvious and he engaged his former colleagues in combat, clashing with both X-Factor and the New Mutants. Agents of the Right wear armored battlesuits equipped with built-in machine guns and flight jets. Their battlesuits have facemasks that bear a distinctive "smiley face" design. **DW**

RIORDAN, DALLAS

FIRST APPEARANCE Thunderbolts #1 (April 1997)
REAL NAME Dallas Riordan **OCCUPATION** Adventurer
BASE New York City **HEIGHT** 5 ft 1 in **WEIGHT** 150 lbs
EYES Blue **HAIR** Red
SPECIAL POWERS/ABILITIES Expert swordswoman and adept hand-to-hand combatant.

Dallas served as New York City's liaison to the THUNDERBOLTS until BARON ZEMO discredited the team and ruined Dallas' own reputation. Invited to become the new Citizen V, Dallas's career as a costumed crusader was cut short when she was crippled in battle. For a while, she could only walk when she merged her consciousness with that of her dead lover, Erik Josten (ATLAS). Erik has since returned—and the two have broken up—but they share a link that causes Dallas to become paralyzed when Erik draws on her powers. Dallas currently works for the COMMISSION ON SUPERHUMAN ACTIVITIES. **AD, MF**

RIOT SQUAD

The Riot Squad came into being when the villainous LEADER detonated a gamma bomb on the town of Middletown, Arizona. Amazingly, a few residents survived, mutated by gamma radiation in the same manner as the HULK. These five took the cover names Jailbait, Hotshot, Ogress, Omnibus, and Soul Man, and became the Leader's elite guards. Charged with protecting the Freehold base, where the Leader gave sanctuary to those suffering from radiation sickness, the team fought the Hulk on several occasions.

During an attack on the Freehold base by HYDRA, Soul Man was killed, and with the Leader also presumed dead, Omnibus took control of the Riot Squad. His teammates put him on trial after he orchestrated terrorist bombings in an effort to gain more power. Despite his protestations that he had been under the control of the Leader when he committed the crimes, they found him guilty and banished him to the Arctic. The Troyjans later decimated Freehold despite the efforts of Riot Squad. The team is likely to continue as a mercenary outfit. **DW**

CHARACTER KEY
1 Rock
2 Soul Man
3 Ogress
4 Hotshot
5 Jailbait
6 Redeemer

FACTFILE

CURRENT MEMBERS AND POWERS

JAILBAIT
Can project psionic force fields.

HOTSHOT
Can project psionic force fields.

OGRESS
Enhanced strength and damage resistance.

OMNIBUS
Super-genius intellect.

SOUL MAN (deceased)
Possessed ability to resurrect the dead.

FIRST APPEARANCE
(As normal humans) Incredible Hulk #345 (July 1988); (as Riot Squad) Incredible Hulk #366 (February 1990)

RIOT SQUAD

RISQUE

FIRST APPEARANCE X-Force #51 (August 1991)
REAL NAME Gloria Dolores Muñoz
OCCUPATION X-Corporation employee (deceased)
BASE Hong Kong **HEIGHT** 5 ft 9 in **WEIGHT** 120 lbs
EYES Brown **HAIR** Black
SPECIAL POWERS/ABILITIES Compresses matter, inorganic and organic; can destroy smaller objects, like a mobile phone, altogether.

Gloria Muñoz had a lonely childhood. Her parents divorced when she was 12 and she left home at 16. Forced to fend for herself, Gloria developed a cold, distant personality and her first encounters with the mutant group X-FORCE did not endear her to them. However, she became romantically involved with WARPATH, even falling in love with him, before betraying him to the DEVIANT known as Sledge. After making recompense for her misdeeds, Gloria was invited to join X-CORPORATION's Hong Kong office, but she wasn't there long. While investigating the trade in mutant body parts, Gloria was killed by the U-Men, a group of humans seeking mutant body parts to graft onto themselves. **AD**

ROBERTSON, JOE

Robertson defeated his nemesis Tombstone after years of trying.

Joseph "Robbie" Robertson, long-time editor-in-chief of the *Daily Bugle*, grew up in Harlem alongside the brutal Lonnie Thompson Lincoln (TOMBSTONE). While working as a reporter in Philadelphia, Robertson saw Tombstone kill a man, but he kept silent about the murder for nearly two decades. Years later, he finally gathered evidence of the murder and Tombstone's other crimes, only for Tombstone to break his back. Robertson recovered and testified against Tombstone in court, receiving a jail sentence of his own for withholding evidence. He resigned from the *Daily Bugle* when Norman Osborn (*see* GREEN GOBLIN) purchased the newspaper, but later returned to the job. His son Randy attended college with Peter Parker, and Robertson is believed to have guessed that Peter Parker was SPIDER-MAN. When Dexter Bennett bought the *Daily Bugle* following J. Jonah JAMESON's heart attack, Robertson left to go work for another newspaper, *Front Line*. After the *DB* was destroyed by ELECTRO, the Jamesons bought the paper back and gave Robertson the money to transform *Front Line* into the new *Daily Bugle*. **DW, MF**

FACTFILE

REAL NAME
Joseph Robertson

OCCUPATION
Editor-in-chief of the *Daily Bugle*

BASE
New York City

HEIGHT 6 ft 1 in
WEIGHT 210 lbs
EYES Brown
HAIR White

FIRST APPEARANCE
Amazing Spider-Man #51 (August 1967)

ROBERTSON, JOE

POWERS

Highly skilled writer and dogged investigative reporter.

Rock

FIRST APPEARANCE The Incredible Hulk #343 (May 1988)
REAL NAME Samuel J. Laroquette
OCCUPATION Warrior **BASE** Mobile
HEIGHT 6 ft **WEIGHT** Unrevealed
EYES Brown **HAIR** Black
SPECIAL POWERS/ABILITIES Able to shape his rock-like exoskeleton into any form he imagines.

A former explorer, Sam Laroquette became a member of the Hulkbusters at a time when the Hulk had been separated from Bruce Banner. Later recruited by would-be world conqueror the Leader, Laroquette received treatments that encased him in a rocklike substance responsive to his mental commands. As Rock, he went into action against the Hulk alongside his fellow operative Redeemer. The stone projections Rock created by reshaping his exoskeleton proved to be one of the few things capable of puncturing the Hulk's tough skin. The Rock has since worked alongside the U-Foes and the Riot Squad. **DW**

Rocket Raccoon

FIRST APPEARANCE Marvel Preview #7 (June 1976)
REAL NAME Rocket Raccoon
OCCUPATION Adventurer **BASE** Mobile
HEIGHT 4 ft **WEIGHT** 25 lbs
EYES Brown **HAIR** Black, brown, and white
SPECIAL POWERS/ABILITIES Rocket is an evolved raccoon who stands on his hind legs and speaks. He is an excellent combatant and tactician.

Rocket Raccoon was the chief guardian on Halfworld, a planet on which animals had been forcibly evolved to help provide care for an outpost of insane humanoids. The Hulk arrived and helped Rocket and his first mate Wal Rus rescue Rocket's girlfriend, the evolved otter Lylla, from the evolved mole Judson Jakes. He later helped Star-Lord stop the second Annihilation and then joined the Guardians of the Galaxy, helping to bring the team back together after it disbanded. **MF**

Rocket Racer

FIRST APPEARANCE Amazing Spider-Man #172 (September 1977)
REAL NAME Robert Farrell
OCCUPATION Student **BASE** New York City
HEIGHT 5 ft 10 in **WEIGHT** 160 lbs **EYES** Brown **HAIR** Black
SPECIAL POWERS/ABILITIES Rides jet-powered skateboard to which boots are magnetically attached; mini-rockets on gloves can tear holes in three-inch thick steel.

When Robert Farrell's mother died, he became responsible for his six younger siblings. Realizing he couldn't earn enough to support his family, he turned to a life of crime. He developed a superpowered skateboard and a weapon-equipped costume to become the Rocket Racer. After repeated defeats at the hands of Spider-Man—and several brushes with the law, including a short jail sentence—Robert decided to reform. Later, he joined the Fifty-State Initiative and trained at Camp Hammond. He was also with the Avengers Academy for a while. **AD, MF**

Rogue

Rogue has striking white streaks in her long hair.

Orphaned, Rogue ran away from her Mississippi home and was adopted by Mystique and Destiny. Her mutant power manifested itself when she kissed a boy and absorbed his memories. She joined Mystique's Brotherhood of Evil Mutants in her teens. While fighting Ms. Marvel, Rogue absorbed her superhuman strength, durability, and the power of flight. Unable to control her absorption power, Rogue turned to the X-Men for help. Professor X invited her to join them, and she fell in love with Gambit. After the villain Pandemic infected her with the 88 virus, Rogue's skin became lethal to anyone she touched. To save her, Mystique touched Rogue with the infant Hope Summers, which took away her lethal touch and all her absorbed powers and memories. Later, Professor X helped her remove the mental blocks that formed each time she used her powers, allowing her to control them. Afterward, she followed Wolverine to his new Jean Grey School for Higher Learning and joined the Avengers Unity Squad. **PS, MF**

Rogue stole and retained the powers of Ms. Marvel.

FACTFILE

ROGUE

REAL NAME
Unrevealed

OCCUPATION
Former terrorist, now adventurer

BASE
The Xavier Institute, Salem Center, New York State

HEIGHT 5 ft 8 in
WEIGHT 120 lbs
EYES Green
HAIR Brown

FIRST APPEARANCE
Avengers Annual #10 (1981)

POWERS

Mutant ability to absorb the memories, knowledge, talents, personality, and physical abilities of another person through physical contact with them.

Roma

FIRST APPEARANCE Captain Britain #1 (January 1985)
REAL NAME Roma **OCCUPATION** Sorceress
BASE Otherworld **HEIGHT** 5 ft 10 in
WEIGHT 135 lbs **EYES** Green **HAIR** Black
SPECIAL POWERS/ABILITIES Sorceress with mystical abilities; casts spells that restore life to the dead or block her own presence or others' presence from detection by organic or technological means.

Daughter of MERLYN, Roma appeared to Brian Braddock as the Goddess of the Northern Skies and gave him the Amulet of Right. The amulet's energy turned him into CAPTAIN BRITAIN, and Roma became one of his advisors. Thinking her father dead, she took over his duties as ruler of Avalon and guardian of the Omniverse, and she oversaw the formation of EXCALIBUR. When Merlyn returned, Roma helped Excalibur defeat him and gave her throne to Captain Britain. Roma died at her father's hand, but not before transferring her knowledge to the mutant SAGE. **MT, MF**

Ronan the Accuser

FIRST APPEARANCE Fantastic Four #65 (August 1967)
REAL NAME Ronan
OCCUPATION Supreme Public Accuser
BASE Citadel of Judgement, on planet Kree-Lar
HEIGHT 7 ft 5 in **WEIGHT** 480 lbs **EYES** Blue **HAIR** Unknown
SPECIAL POWERS/ABILITIES Wields Universal Weapon—fires concussive energy bolts, disintegrates matter, creates force fields.

Born to an aristocratic KREE family, Ronan was accepted into the Accuser Corps and rose to the position of Supreme Public Accuser. After failing to punish the FANTASTIC FOUR for defeating a Kree Sentry, his humiliation drove him to plot to take over the Empire himself during the Kree-SKRULL War, but Rick JONES stopped him. In the course of the ANNIHILATION, Ronan euthanized a lobotomized SUPREME INTELLIGENCE and finally took over as the Kree ruler. To strengthen the Kree, he agreed to cede his position to BLACK BOLT if CRYSTAL agreed to marry him. The pair grew to love each other, but separated at Black Bolt's request. He later joined the ANNIHILATORS. **AD, MF**

Ross, General T. E.

FIRST APPEARANCE Incredible Hulk #1 (May 1962)
REAL NAME Thaddeus E. Ross
NICKNAME Thunderbolt
OCCUPATION Lieutenant General, US Air Force **BASE** Mobile
HEIGHT 6 ft 1 in **WEIGHT** 245 lbs **EYES** Blue **HAIR** White
SPECIAL POWERS/ABILITIES Is a capable combatant and has an advanced military mind.

General Ross's troops nicknamed him Thunderbolt because he struck like a thunderbolt in combat. After Bruce Banner transformed into the HULK, General Ross became obsessed with him. Ross worked alongside Colonel Glenn TALBOT, who married his daughter Betty Ross. She later left Talbot and married Bruce. For a time, Ross possessed the electrical form of Zzzax. He later seemed to be killed, but the INTELLIGENCIA stole his body and transformed him into the RED HULK. **DW, MF**

Romulus

FIRST APPEARANCE Wolverine #50 (March 2007)
REAL NAME Romulus **OCCUPATION** Tyrant
BASE Unknown
HEIGHT 7 ft **WEIGHT** 300 lbs **EYES** Red **HAIR** Black
SPECIAL POWERS/ABILITIES Immortal Lupine.

Romulus was the leader of the Lupines, a group of feral mutants he claimed were descended from wolves instead of primates. Thousands of years old, he was once an emperor of Rome. In the 1940s, he murdered WOLVERINE's wife, Itsu, and cut the infant DAKEN from her womb, raising and training him, then pitting him against his father to see which one of them would triumph. Wolverine had CLOAK trap Romulus in the Darkforce Dimension, but SABRETOOTH broke him out. His twin sister Remus helped Wolverine capture him again. **MF**

Rose, The

FIRST APPEARANCE (JC) Daredevil #131 (March 1976); (RF) Amazing Spider-Man #83 (April 1970)
REAL NAME Jacob Conover; Richard Fisk **OCCUPATION** (JC) columnist; (RF) crime lord **BASE** (JC & RF) New York City
HEIGHT (JC) 6 ft; (RF) 6 ft 2 in **WEIGHT** (JC) 210lbs; (RF) 225lbs
EYES (JC) brown; (RF) brown
SPECIAL POWERS/ABILITIES (JC & RF) criminal masterminds, manipulators, and strategists.

The first leather-masked Rose was Richard Fisk, the son of criminal KINGPIN. Fisk believed that his father was an honest businessman. When he learned the truth, he tried to ruin his father's empire and became a member of HYDRA. Fisk eventually joined forces with his father and became the Rose but was killed by his mother. The second Rose was a police officer seeking revenge on the Kingpin. The third Rose was Jacob Conover, a *Daily Bugle* journalist given the identity as a reward for saving crime lord Don Fortunato. SPIDER-MAN put him in prison. The fourth Rose, Philip Hayes, worked with Jackpot in her secret identity and ordered her husband's murder. MORBIUS killed him. **TD, MF**

Ross, Betty

The Hulk's beloved

IT SEEMS ONLY YESTERDAY WHEN I FIRST MET BRUCE... BEFORE THE HORROR OF THE HULK CAME BETWEEN US!

Betty Banner met her one-day husband Bruce when she came to live on a New Mexico military base with her father, Thunderbolt Ross.

The only daughter of renowned military general Thaddeus "Thunderbolt" Ross, Betty spent her formative years firmly under her father's thumb. Thunderbolt Ross had wanted a son, and had no use for his unfortunate daughter; after her mother died during Betty's teenage years, she was sent away to boarding school. After graduating, she returned to her father's side, a repressed wallflower. Thunderbolt Ross was then in charge of a top-secret project to create a new type of weapon employing the limitless power of gamma radiation. The head scientist on the project was the quiet, bookish Bruce Banner, and an attraction between Betty and Banner soon developed.

FACTFILE

REAL NAME
Elizabeth Ross

OCCUPATION
Adventurer

BASE
Mobile

HEIGHT 5 ft 6 in
WEIGHT 110 lbs
EYES Blue
HAIR Brown

FIRST APPEARANCE
Incredible Hulk #1 (May 1962)

POWERS

No superhuman powers, but courageous and resourceful; steadfastly loyal to her husband Bruce Banner through many shared tribulations.

Tragic Love

Their relationship was forever changed when, during the gamma-bomb test, Banner was struck by the full force of the detonation, and its radiations transformed him into the HULK whenever he grew angry. Banner tried to keep his condition secret from Betty, which only served to alienate them. Betty was then ardently pursued by Major Glenn Talbot (*see* TALBOT, Col. Glenn), the new aide attached to her father's Hulkbuster task force. Eventually, the secret of Banner's dual identity became public knowledge, and his transformations and rampages created a rift between Betty and himself. With no one else to turn to, Betty married Major Talbot. Their union soon ended in divorce, however, and Talbot died attempting to destroy the Hulk.

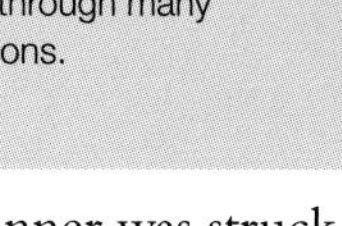

As the Red She-Hulk, Betty was far more aggressive than when she was her normal self

Hulks and Harpies

MODOK used gamma rays to turn Betty into a flying menace known as the Harpy, who attacked the Hulk, but Banner cured her. Despite her father's objections, she eventually married him. Later, the ABOMINATION used his gamma-irradiated blood to poison and kill Betty, hoping to pin the crime on Bruce. Her father kept her body in cryogenic storage. After he became the RED HULK, he urged the LEADER and MODOK to use the same process on Betty to revive her, turning her into the Red She-Hulk. No one outside of their group knew who she was until Hulk's son SKAAR stabbed her and she reverted to human form. She told Banner that their marriage was over because she'd been declared dead, but they have since struck up a new relationship.

TB, MF

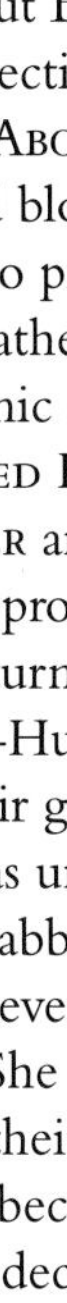

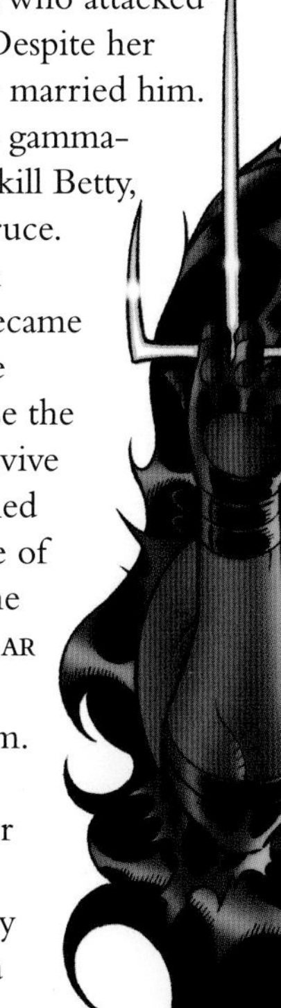

ESSENTIAL STORYLINES

- ***Hulk Vol. 2 #168–169***
MODOK transforms Betty into the Harpy.
- ***Hulk Vol. 2 #319***
After years of courtship and chaos, Bruce Banner finally marries Betty.
- ***Hulk Vol. 2 #465–469***
Betty is exposed to radiation poisoning; Bruce desperately tries to save her.

Roth, Arnold

FIRST APPEARANCE Captain America #270 (May 1982)
REAL NAME Arnold "Arnie" Roth
OCCUPATION Sailor, later publicist, later costume shop manager
BASE New York City
HEIGHT Unrevealed **WEIGHT** Unrevealed **EYES** Blue **HAIR** Grey
SPECIAL POWERS/ABILITIES Possessed the normal human strength of a man of his age who engaged in mild exercise.

Arnold Roth became friends with Steve Rogers when they were growing up in the 1930s. During World War II, Roth served in the US Navy and realized that Captain America was his friend Steve. While Captain America spent years in suspended animation, Roth aged normally. Learning of Roth's friendship with Captain America, Baron Helmut Zemo (see Baron Zemo) imperiled Roth and his life partner, Michael. Later, the Red Skull captured Roth. Captain America and Roth remained friends. Roth worked as the Avengers' publicist and managed Steve Rogers' costume shop before dying from bone cancer. **PS**

Ruiz, "Rigger"

FIRST APPEARANCE The Mighty Thor Vol. 1 #426 (Nov. 1990)
REAL NAME Margarita Allegra "Rigger" Ruiz
OCCUPATION Police officer **BASE** New York City
HEIGHT Unknown **WEIGHT** Unknown
EYES Unknown **HAIR** Black
SPECIAL POWERS/ABILITIES Adept with range of weaponry; she invented "port-a-pulley" for easy navigation of elevator shafts.

Margarita Allegra "Rigger" Ruiz is the armory specialist of Code: Blue, a SWAT team designated to deal with superpowered criminals. Bodybuilder Rigger has come face-to-face with these superhumans on a regular basis and her experiences have been many and varied. The strongest member of Code: Blue, Rigger has rescued hostages from the Wrecking Crew, been driven mad by the Super Villain Dementia, and posed as a slave during a mission to Asgard. During this last assignment, Rigger also flirted with Fandral the Dashing, an Asgardian noble—life is never dull in Code: Blue. **AD**

Russian, The

FIRST APPEARANCE Punisher Vol. 5 #8 (November 2000)
REAL NAME Unrevealed
OCCUPATION Mercenary **BASE** Mobile
HEIGHT 7 ft 2 in **WEIGHT** 573 lbs
EYES Blue **HAIR** Reddish-blond
SPECIAL POWERS/ABILITIES Post-reconstruction, the Russian possessed enhanced strength and damage resistance.

The mercenary nicknamed "The Russian" accepted a job from crime boss Ma Gnucci to kill the Punisher. After a brutal fight, the Punisher smothered the Russian, later taunting Ma Gnucci by showing her the Russian's severed head. A secret paramilitary agency then resurrected the Russian, giving him an enhanced body with boosted olfactory senses, three hearts, and a toughened skeleton. This new body required regular injections of female hormones. The Russian apparently died when he was caught in the explosion of a nuclear warhead on Grand Nixon Island. **DW**

Ryker, General J.

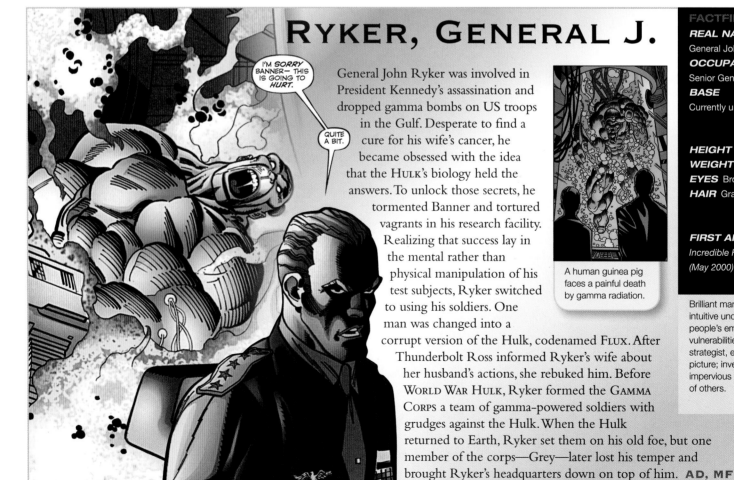

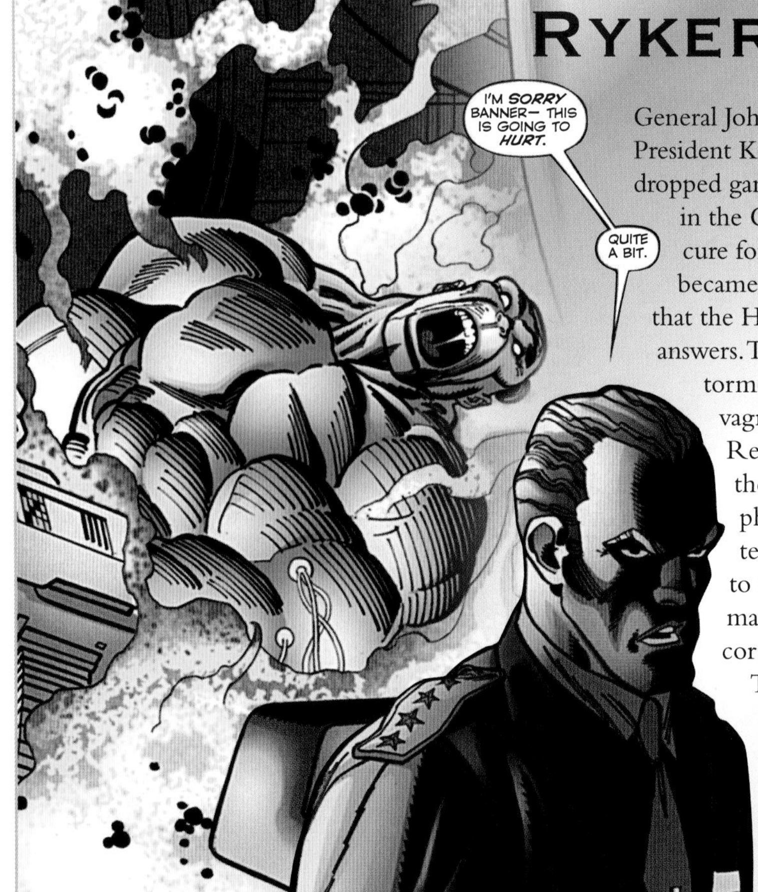

I'M SORRY BANNER— THIS IS GOING TO HURT.
QUITE A BIT.

General John Ryker was involved in President Kennedy's assassination and dropped gamma bombs on US troops in the Gulf. Desperate to find a cure for his wife's cancer, he became obsessed with the idea that the Hulk's biology held the answers. To unlock those secrets, he tormented Banner and tortured vagrants in his research facility. Realizing that success lay in the mental rather than physical manipulation of his test subjects, Ryker switched to using his soldiers. One man was changed into a corrupt version of the Hulk, codenamed Flux. After Thunderbolt Ross informed Ryker's wife about her husband's actions, she rebuked him. Before World War Hulk, Ryker formed the Gamma Corps a team of gamma-powered soldiers with grudges against the Hulk. When the Hulk returned to Earth, Ryker set them on his old foe, but one member of the corps—Grey—later lost his temper and brought Ryker's headquarters down on top of him. **AD, MF**

A human guinea pig faces a painful death by gamma radiation.

FACTFILE
REAL NAME
General John Ryker
OCCUPATION
Senior General in US Army
BASE
Currently unknown

HEIGHT 6 ft 2 in
WEIGHT 190 lbs
EYES Brown
HAIR Gray

FIRST APPEARANCE
Incredible Hulk Vol.3 #14 (May 2000)

RYKER, GENERAL JOHN

POWERS
Brilliant manipulator, possesses intuitive understanding of people's emotional vulnerabilities; exceptional strategist, excels at seeing big picture; inveterate liar; impervious to the suffering of others.

SABRETOOTH

Wolverine's nemesis

SABRETOOTH

FACTFILE
REAL NAME
Victor Creed
OCCUPATION
Assassin
BASE
Mobile

HEIGHT 6 ft 6 in
WEIGHT 275 lbs
EYES Amber
HAIR Blond

FIRST APPEARANCE
Iron Fist Vol. 1 #14 (August 1977)

POWERS
Sabretooth possesses an extended lifespan, thanks to the healing ability that also allows him to recover rapidly from almost any injury. He also possesses enhanced animalistic strength, speed and agility, and razor-sharp claws on each hand.

Sabretooth was chained up as a child due to his feral nature.

A vicious, psychotic killer, little is known about the early life of Victor Creed, the mutant called Sabretooth, save that he apparently came from an abusive background. His healing ability having kept him alive and youthful for decades, he first acquired the alias Sabretooth in the 1960s, when he did wetwork for the CIA.

ESSENTIAL STORYLINES
- ***Wolverine #10***
A flashback to an early Wolverine/Sabretooth face off.
- ***Sabretooth #1***
Sabretooth gets his own mini-series.

BITTER FEUD

Like WOLVERINE, Sabretooth's abilities were enhanced by the top-secret Weapon X project, and while the two men share much history in common, they are the bitterest of enemies. Sabretooth routinely returned to stalk and defeat Wolverine on the latter's birthday each year. And because of his enmity for Wolverine, Sabretooth has been pulled into the X-MEN's orbit time and again, sometimes in partnership with other villains such as MISTER SINISTER, sometimes on his own. But while there is still some humanity left within Wolverine's heart, Sabretooth's soul is as black as pitch. He is about as irredeemable an individual as has ever existed.

Sabretooth's claws are razor-sharp

A FALSE DEATH

Over the years, Sabretooth has been imprisoned by the X-MEN and even forced to work with X-FORCE several times, but his relationship with Wolverine never improved. Under the influence of ROMULUS, Sabretooth regressed to a beastlike state and murdered FERAL. In retribution, Wolverine killed him with the Muramasa Blade, a weapon no healing factor could counter.

This Sabretooth turned out to be a clone Romulus had created. The real Sabretooth re-emerged in the Far East and slaughtered the crimelords there, declaring himself the invisible king of Asia. He later joined Daken's new BROTHERHOOD OF EVIL MUTANTS and then another lineup under the leadership of MYSTIQUE. **TB, MF**

Sabretooth's powers made him a skilled tracker.

Sabretooth's "final" showdown with Wolverine, after years of conflict.

Sabra

FIRST APPEARANCE The Incredible Hulk #250 (August 1980)
REAL NAME Ruth Bat-Seraph
OCCUPATION Police officer; Israeli government agent
BASE Jerusalem, Israel **HEIGHT** 5 ft 11 in
WEIGHT 240 lbs **EYES** Brown **HAIR** Black
SPECIAL POWERS/ABILITIES Wrist bracelets equipped with neuronic-frequency stunners that shoot "energy quills." Cape has a device that neutralizes gravity, enabling flight; superhuman strength.

When Ruth Bat-Seraph's mutant powers emerged, the Israeli government sent her to live at a special kibbutz where she was trained to use them. As an adult, she became the first member of Mossad's super-agent program. After terrorists killed her son, she disobeyed orders and brought them down. She fought alongside the X-Men and worked for the X-Corporation in Paris. She registered with the US government during the Civil War. After that, she returned to Israel and fought the Skrulls during the Secret Invasion. **PS, MF**

Sage

FIRST APPEARANCE Uncanny X-Men #132 (April 1980)
REAL NAME Unrevealed, goes by "Tessa"
OCCUPATION Member of New Excalibur **BASE** England
HEIGHT 5 ft 7 in **WEIGHT** 135 lbs **EYES** Blue **HAIR** Black
SPECIAL POWERS/ABILITIES Able to remember everything she sees and hears; can "jump start" the mutant abilities of others; possesses limited telepathy.

Born in Eastern Europe, the mysterious Sage rescued an injured Professor X from Afghanistan and became one of his first mutant recruits. Rather than joining the original X-Men, Sage became a spy within the Hellfire Club, working as an advisor to Sebastian Shaw. When she tricked the mind-controlling Elias Bogan into losing a wager, he scarred her face. Rescued by Storm, Sage joined the X-Men and later New Excalibur. Later, she was recruited into the Exiles and went dimension hopping, but she's since returned to Earth. **DW, MF**

St. Lawrence, Col.

FIRST APPEARANCE Incredible Hulk #446 (October 1996)
REAL NAME Colonel Cary St. Lawrence
OCCUPATION US Army officer **BASE** Mobile
HEIGHT/WEIGHT Unrevealed **EYES** Brown **HAIR** Black
SPECIAL POWERS/ABILITIES Skilled military strategist, highly trained athlete, adept with variety of weaponry.

When she was a cadet at West Point academy, General "Thunderbolt" Ross was dismissive about Cary St. Lawrence's chances of a successful career in the military. Inspired to work even harder to prove him wrong, Cary graduated third in her class.

Assigned to capture the Hulk, Cary proved to be unusually effective in her dealings with the green fiend. At first she favored brute force during her encounters with the creature, but soon came to realize that there was no point in employing strong-arm tactics: after all, the Hulk only got more powerful the angrier he became. She thus began to use more subtle approaches to subdue the creature. Perhaps all the Hulk has ever needed is a woman's touch. **AD**

Sabreclaw

FACTFILE

REAL NAME
Hudson Howlett
OCCUPATION
Adventurer
BASE
New York City

HEIGHT 5 ft 10 in
WEIGHT 198 lbs
EYES Brown
HAIR Brown

FIRST APPEARANCE
J2 #8 (May 1999)

POWERS
Superhuman agility, reflexes, stamina, and strength, plus sharp teeth, adamantium-laced claws, and a healing factor.

The son of Wolverine in the alternate future of Earth-982, Sabreclaw felt jealous of his half-sister Rina (Wild Thing) because she had the chance to actually be raised by their father, who didn't know of Hudson's existence for many years. Sabreclaw started out as a villain, battling the A-Next (future Avengers) team alongside the Revengers and fighting Spider-Girl as part of the Savage Six. However, when Galactus returned to threaten the Earth, he joined the Avengers and their allied heroes to drive him away. Afterward, he asked to join Avengers, and despite some reservations was accepted. **MF**

Sabreclaw alongside his fellow Revengers.

Sabreclaw--!
He arrived without an appointment and demanded an immediate audience.
Ya miss me, Sweetie?

Sabreclaw faces off against American Dream.

SALEM'S SEVEN

The children of Nicolas SCRATCH lived in the isolated village of New Salem, where witches and warlocks held sway. When Scratch's mother, Agatha HARKNESS, left to become the governess of Franklin RICHARDS, Scratch put her on trial for treason, transforming his offspring into Salem's Seven to act as guards. They failed to stop the FANTASTIC FOUR from rescuing her, but later became rulers of New Salem and burned Harkness at the stake. Harkness's spirit led the VISION and the SCARLET WITCH to New Salem, and Salem's Seven died in the battle. When the Scarlet Witch returned them to life. Scratch tricked the Seven into releasing the demon Shuma-Gorath. DOCTOR STRANGE, the Fantastic Four, and DIABLO helped them to foil Scratch's plans. **DW, MF**

SALEM'S SEVEN
1 Brutacus
2 Hydron
3 Vakume
4 Vertigo
5 Thornn
6 Reptilla
7 Gazelle

Salem's Seven first appeared in the pages of the Fantastic Four as diabolical, sorcerous opponents for the science-based team led by Mr. Fantastic.

FACTFILE
FORMER MEMBERS
BRUTACUS
Enhanced strength.
GAZELLE
Superhuman agility and reflexes.
HYDRON
Able to blast water from left arm.
REPTILLA
Fanged arm-snakes could bite and constrict.
THORNN
Ability to fire explosive spines.
VAKUME
Could drain air or energy, and assume an intangible state.
VERTIGO
Power to induce dizziness in others.

BASE
New Salem, Colorado

FIRST APPEARANCE
Fantastic Four #186 (September 1977)

SANDMAN, *see page 304*

SASQUATCH

FACTFILE
REAL NAME
Walter Langkowski
OCCUPATION
Scientist, adventurer
BASE
Canada

HEIGHT 10 ft
WEIGHT 2000 lbs
EYES Red
HAIR Orange

FIRST APPEARANCE
Uncanny X-Men #120 (April 1979)

POWERS
Sasquatch possesses superhuman strength and greatly enhanced resistance to injury, and is able to leap enormous distances. He can shift between his normal human form and his Sasquatch body at will.

Inspired by Bruce Banner's metamorphosis into the HULK, Dr. Walter Langkowski was experimenting with gamma radiation when he breached the realm of the Great Beasts and was possessed by a spirit called Tanaraq, who gave him his powers. He became a member of ALPHA FLIGHT and was the only member of the team to survive WEAPON OMEGA's post-M-Day rampage. Afterward, he formed a new OMEGA FLIGHT but has since joined his resurrected friends to rebuild Alpha Flight. **TB, MF**

In Alpha Flight, Sasquatch often came to blows with members of the X-Men.

SATANA

FIRST APPEARANCE Vampire Tales #2 (October 1973)
REAL NAME Satana Hellstrom
OCCUPATION Hero **BASE** Mobile
HEIGHT 5 ft 7 in **WEIGHT** 120 lbs
EYES Black with red highlights **HAIR** Red
SPECIAL POWERS/ABILITIES Levitation and limited spellcasting; could feed on human souls and project bolts of "soulfire."

The half-human daughter of the demon Satan—and the half-sister of Daimon Hellstrom (HELLSTORM)—for a time Satana was forced to live as a succubus, draining the spirits of humans to survive. Rebelling at this, Satana became estranged from her father and started to appreciate human society. Learning that DOCTOR STRANGE was trapped in the form of a werewolf, Satana traveled to the astral realm where Strange's soul was held prisoner, and freed him. The price was her own life. Strange later resurrected her and she teamed up with Jennifer KALE and TOPAZ to form a coven of witches. **AD, MF**

SANDMAN

The villain who slips through Spidey's fingers

SANDMAN

FACTFILE

REAL NAME
William Baker

OCCUPATION
Former professional criminal

BASE
Brooklyn, New York

HEIGHT 6 ft 1 in
WEIGHT 450 lbs
EYES Brown
HAIR Brown

FIRST APPEARANCE
Amazing Spider-Man #4 (September 1963)

POWERS
Sandman is able to change all or part of his body into a sand-like substance which he can form into any shape. He can spread out the grains of sand in his body to avoid attack, project them outward at high speeds, or harden them into a super-powered weapon.

With the ability to change his body into grains of sand and reshape it at will, Sandman has proven to be a dangerous and slippery foe for Spider-Man, the Fantastic Four, and the Hulk. Born William Baker in one of the rougher areas of New York City, he had a bad start in life. His father abandoned him and his mother when William was three years old, and the boy grew up in poverty. He quickly learned to steal and cheat.

A LIFE OF CRIME

William was kicked out of high school for taking money to throw a big football game, but soon found work with a protection racket. He took the alias "Flint Marko," and became a success in New York's crime underworld. After an arrest and a jailbreak, Marko headed south. He was on a beach near a military testing site in Georgia when a nuclear reactor's steam system exploded, knocking him unconscious. Marko woke to find that his body now had the properties of sand. Reveling in his new ability, he called himself Sandman and set out on a major criminal career. Sandman battled Spider-Man (his main nemesis), and many other Super Heroes. He joined the Wizard, Trapster, and Medusa to form the Frightful Four and teamed up with five more of Spider-Man's foes to form the Sinister Six.

ESSENTIAL STORYLINES
- ***Amazing Spider-Man Annual #1*** Sandman, Vulture, Mysterio, Electro, Kraven the Hunter, and Doctor Octopus get together to form the Sinister Six.
- ***Amazing Spider-Man #217–218*** Sandman teams up with Hydro-Man, but a freak accident merges the two villains into a mud creature.

When he hardens the sand particles that make up his body into a solid block, Sandman packs an incredibly powerful punch.

Sandman can alter all of his body at once or just selective parts, as in this example of his right arm changing while the rest of his body remains in its human-looking form.

GOOD OR EVIL?

When Sandman teamed up with Hydro-Man, an accident caused the two to merge into a mud creature. After he was freed, Sandman gave up crime, becoming a probationary member of the Avengers. The Wizard brainwashed him into becoming a criminal again, thinking he'd been faking his turn toward good, and he rejoined the Sinister Six. Venom destroyed Sandman, but he reconstituted himself, and later discovered he could create duplicates of himself with distinct personalities. Some of these duplicates murdered the mother of his daughter Keemia without his knowledge. The Superior Spider-Man (Doctor Octopus) later stole him from where the Fantastic Four had imprisoned him and stored him in an underwater lab. **MT, MF**

When Sandman and Hydro-Man combined they became the Mud-Thing. The new creature proved to be a big attraction.

SAURON

FIRST APPEARANCE X-Men #59 (August 1969)
REAL NAME Dr. Karl Lykos
OCCUPATION Geneticist, hypnotherapist
BASE New York City, Savage Land
HEIGHT 7 ft **WEIGHT** 200 lbs **EYES** Red **HAIR** None
SPECIAL POWERS/ABILITIES Drains victims' life forces into his own body. Uses eye contact to hypnotize and induce hallucinations.

Young Karl Lykos was in Antarctica when he was bitten by a pteranodon from the Savage Lands. Thereafter, he had to feed off the life energy of others to survive. As an adult, he transformed into an evil half-human, half-pteranodon creature after attacking HAVOK. He took the name Sauron, became an enemy of the X-MEN, and returned to the Savage Land. During the SECRET INVASION, he fought beside KA-ZAR and SHANNA THE SHE-DEVIL against the SKRULLS. Later, he returned to the US and joined the Hellfire Academy. **MT, MF**

SCARLET CENTURION

In the year 3000 of Earth-6311, Earth is a utopia, founded centuries earlier by Nathaniel RICHARDS, father of Reed Richards (MR. FANTASTIC). However this paradise does not suit everyone. One distant descendant of Richards, a man known as the Scarlet Centurion, feels suffocated by his surroundings. Learning that one of his ancestors built a time machine, the Centurion recreates this device and wreaks chaos across multiple realities and times zones.

Arriving in ancient Egypt, the Centurion became the pharaoh Rama-Tut—until the FANTASTIC FOUR forced him back to the future. Since then, he has also become KANG the Conqueror and IMMORTUS at various times, as well as the YOUNG AVENGER known as Iron Lad. The one-time ruler of 30th-century Earth, he has tried to conquer the present-day world many times, only to be defeated by the Fantastic Four or the AVENGERS. One of his sons (the 23rd) also called himself the Scarlet Centurion and worked with him while he was Kang. After another failure to conquer the world, Kang stabbed him and put him in stasis. **AD, MF**

FACTFILE

REAL NAME
Nathaniel Richards
OCCUPATION
Conqueror
BASE
Mobile

HEIGHT 6 ft 3 in
WEIGHT 230 lbs
EYES Brown
HAIR Brown, later gray

FIRST APPEARANCE
Avengers Annual #2 (September 1968)

POWERS
Master of numerous far future technologies; wears battlesuit armed with electrical bolts and concussive force beams; adept time traveller.

For a short time, the second Scarlet Centurion ruled the Earth alongside his father.

SAWYER, GENERAL

FIRST APPEARANCE Sgt. Fury and his Howling Commandos #1 (May 1963)
REAL NAME Samuel "Happy Sam" Sawyer
OCCUPATION Adventurer **BASE** The Pentagon
HEIGHT 6 ft 2 in **WEIGHT** 230 lbs **EYES** Blue **HAIR** Gray
SPECIAL POWERS/ABILITIES Happy Sam Sawyer was a career military man and an expert at strategy.

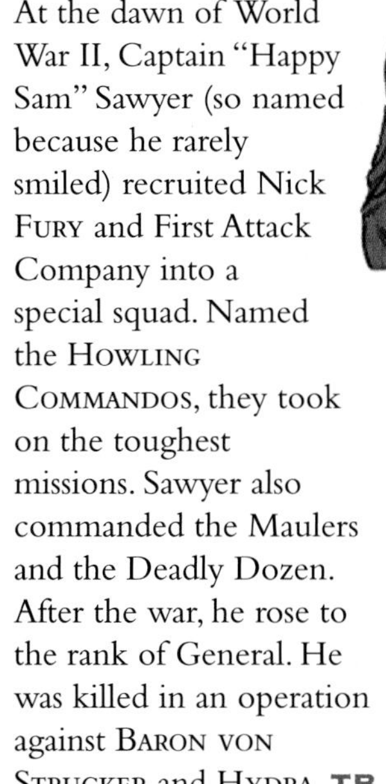

At the dawn of World War II, Captain "Happy Sam" Sawyer (so named because he rarely smiled) recruited Nick FURY and First Attack Company into a special squad. Named the HOWLING COMMANDOS, they took on the toughest missions. Sawyer also commanded the Maulers and the Deadly Dozen. After the war, he rose to the rank of General. He was killed in an operation against BARON VON STRUCKER and HYDRA. **TB**

SCARLET SPIDER

Professor Miles Warren, the criminal known as the JACKAL, created a clone of Peter Parker, alias SPIDER-MAN. He endowed the clone with Parker's memories and pitted him against Spider-Man. Seemingly killed, the clone revived and wandered America for years, calling himself Ben Reilly. In New York, he became a costumed hero, the Scarlet Spider. The original GREEN GOBLIN manipulated Parker and Reilly into believing that Reilly was the real Spider-Man, with Reilly even adopting Spider-Man's costumed identity. Ultimately, the Goblin killed Reilly, and Parker reclaimed his identity.

Reilly actually fought a second Scarlet Spider, one the second DOCTOR OCTOPUS (Carolyn Trainer) fashioned out of FBI agent Joe Wade and a virtual reality graft of holograph technology. Reilly and the NEW WARRIORS rescued him and turned him over to the FBI. Later, triplet clones of Michael VAN PATRICK donned suits of Spider-Man's Iron Spider armor, designed by IRON MAN. Two of them were killed in action. Later, another clone of Parker known as KAINE adopted the Scarlet Spider identity, after being killed by KRAVEN's family. He returned as a mutated TARANTULA but was healed by the Spider-Island cure. When Kaine moved to Texas, he wore a red version of Spider-Man's costume and was called the Scarlet Spider. **PS, MF**

FACTFILE

REAL NAME
Ben Reilly
OCCUPATION
Adventurer
BASE
New York City

HEIGHT 5 ft 10 in
WEIGHT 165 lbs
EYES Hazel
HAIR Brown

FIRST APPEARANCE
(as Scarlet Spider) Web of Spider-Man #118 (November 1994)

POWERS
Super-strength and agility, able to adhere to surfaces; spider-sense alerts him to danger. Wore web-shooters that projected artificial webbing.

SCARLET WITCH

Magical mistress of "Hex Power"

SCARLET WITCH

FACTFILE

REAL NAME
Wanda Maximoff, aka Wanda Frank, Wanda Magnus

OCCUPATION
Adventurer

BASE
Europe

HEIGHT 5 ft 7 in
WEIGHT 130 lbs
EYES Blue
HAIR Auburn

FIRST APPEARANCE
X-Men #4
(March 1964)

POWERS

Possessed ability to affect probability fields and cause unlikely events to occur. Could make objects spontaneously burst into flame, rust, or decay. Her "hex bolts" could also deflect flying objects and disrupt energy transmissions or fields. However, recent evidence seems to indicate that the Scarlet Witch has lost her mutant powers.

After Magneto rescued the Scarlet Witch from certain death, she and her brother Quicksilver became members of his Brotherhood of Evil Mutants. They didn't learn that Magneto was actually their father until many years later.

Studying witchcraft has helped the Scarlet Witch hone her control over her mutant abilities.

Wanda Maximoff is the daughter of the mutant criminal MAGNETO and the twin sister of Pietro Maximoff, the former Avenger QUICKSILVER. Wanda's mother ran away from Magneto while she was pregnant and, fearing her husband would exploit her unborn children, gave her twins up for adoption.

SOCIAL OUTCAST

The twins were raised in the eastern European country of Transia by a gypsy couple and Wanda soon learned that she could cause strange things to happen. After accidentally making a house burst into flames, she was about to be stoned as a witch when Magneto arrived and saved her. Not realizing that he was their real father, Wanda and Pietro took on costumed identities and joined his war against humanity. After many battles with the X-MEN, the twins abandoned Magneto and later joined the AVENGERS in return for full pardons for their past crimes. Over her brother's objections, Wanda became attracted to the synthozoid called the VISION and began a long romance with him. They were eventually married and set up house in New Jersey.

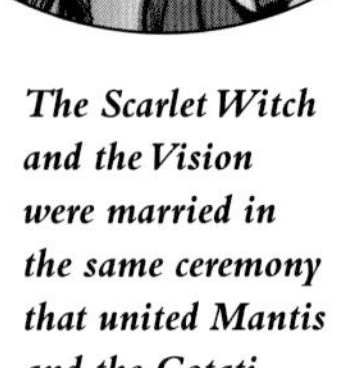

The Scarlet Witch and the Vision were married in the same ceremony that united Mantis and the Cotati.

Through gestures and mental concentration, the Scarlet Witch creates finite pockets of force that can disrupt reality. She can hurl these "hex-spheres" at her intended targets.

TROUBLED SOUL

Wanda also began to study real magic, combining it with her natural mutant abilities. She eventually grew powerful enough to defeat the dreaded DORMAMMU. However, her increased power came at a terrible cost. She conjured up imaginary children and experienced temporary bouts of insanity.

The Vision was disassembled by the US after trying to seize control of every computer on Earth. He was rebuilt, but he no longer possessed emotions. His relationship with Wanda ended in divorce.

Wanda later suffered another breakdown and destroyed the Avengers Mansion, killing a number of teammates. Unbalanced, she later used her powers to warp reality so that her father ruled the world (House of M), and when she was stopped she removed the mutant gene and powers from most of the world (M-Day). It turned out that DOCTOR DOOM had helped channel too much power in an effort to bring her children back, and driven her mad. He later stole her powers but was equally unable to handle them.

When the Avengers battled the X-Men over the Phoenix Force, Wanda returned to the Avengers, despite the Vision's objections. With Hope SUMMERS' help, she erased the Phoenix Force, repowering mutantkind again. **TD, MF**

Suffering from a breakdown, the Scarlet Witch drastically altered reality, disassembling the Avengers team and eliminating many of Earth's mutants.

ESSENTIAL STORYLINES

- ***Avengers: The Yesterday Quest (tpb)***
The Scarlet Witch learns her true origins.
- ***The Vision and Scarlet Witch #1–12***
The Vision and Scarlet Witch leave the Avengers and move to the suburbs.
- ***Avengers: Avengers Disassembled (tpb)***
The Scarlet Witch goes mad and attacks the Avengers, killing many of her former comrades.
- ***House Of M (tpb)***
The Scarlet Witch restructures reality and depowers most of Earth's mutants.

Schemer

FIRST APPEARANCE Amazing Spider-Man #83 (April 1970)
REAL NAME Richard Fisk
OCCUPATION Criminal mastermind **BASE** New York City
HEIGHT 6 ft 2 in **WEIGHT** 175 lbs **EYES** Blue
HAIR Reddish blond
SPECIAL POWERS/ABILITIES Had the normal strength of a man who engages in regular moderate exercise; was a cunning criminal strategist.

Richard Fisk was devoted to his father Wilson—until he learned that Wilson Fisk was the KINGPIN. Psychologically shattered, Richard secretly became a criminal leader himself, the Schemer, to take revenge on his father. As the Schemer, Richard disguised himself with a face mask that made him look much older. Subsequently Richard became head of a Las Vegas fragment of HYDRA. Still later, Richard took on two more masked identities, the original ROSE and the Blood Rose. Ultimately Richard was shot dead by his own mother, Vanessa. **PS**

Scorn

FIRST APPEARANCE Carnage #1 (December 2010)
REAL NAME Tanis Nieves
OCCUPATION Adventurer, psychiatrist **BASE** Mobile
HEIGHT 5 ft 5 in **WEIGHT** 115 lbs
EYES Brown **HAIR** Brown
SPECIAL POWERS/ABILITIES Scorn wears an alien symbiote that grants her superhuman durability, endurance, speed, and strength, as well as accelerated healing, a danger sense, webbing, and wall-crawling. The symbiote can also bond with technology.

Tanis Nieves was a psychiatrist working with SHRIEK until the CARNAGE symbiote bonded with her. Once it found its original host, it abandoned her, but it left an offspring that bonded to her prosthetic arm and later to her. As Scorn, she helped defeat Shriek and Carnage and later partnered with the MERCURY TEAM—a group of soldiers bonded with parts of a symbiote known as Hybrid—to take down Carnage again. Because the symbiote bonded with her arm first, it can change it at will. **MF**

Scratch, Nicholas

FIRST APPEARANCE Fantastic Four #185 (August 1977)
REAL NAME Nicholas Scratch **OCCUPATION** Warlock
BASE New Salem, Colorado **HEIGHT** 6 ft 3 in
WEIGHT 196 lbs **EYES** Blue **HAIR** Black with white streaks
SPECIAL POWERS/ABILITIES Nicholas Scratch possesses an encyclopedic knowledge of magical incantations and lore and a wide array of sorcerous abilities.

The son of Agatha HARKNESS, the witch who became governess to Franklin RICHARDS, Nicholas Scratch grew up to be leader of the witches of New Salem. Scratch convinced his followers that Agatha had betrayed their existence to the outside world and that she must be executed. When Agatha and Franklin were abducted, the FANTASTIC FOUR came to the rescue. Scratch and his most devoted followers, SALEM'S SEVEN, vainly sought revenge on the Fantastic Four and Agatha. For a while, he worked for the demon DORMAMMU, but after being banished to Hell, he struck a deal with MEPHISTO. **TB, MF**

Scorpion

Scorpion/Carmilla Black's parents worked for AIM, which genetically modified her in the womb to give her powers.

Scorpion controls his tail via a cybernetic link with his own spinal column. He can whip his tail at 90 mph.

Dr. Farley Stillwell had developed a method of giving animals the attributes of other creatures. When newspaper editor J. Jonah JAMESON found out, he asked Stillwell to test it out on a human guinea pig, a private investigator named Mac Gargan. Stillwell's amazing procedure gave Gargan the strength and agility of a scorpion. Stillwell also provided him with a specially designed mechanical tail.

Nothing comes without a price and the cost to Gargan—now calling himself the Scorpion—was the loss of his sanity. Contracted to put an end to SPIDER-MAN, it was only by his wits that the wallcrawler defeated the hugely powerful and vengeful Scorpion. Since then, Scorpion has become an assassin-for-hire, and his attempts to defeat Spider-Man being repeatedly foiled.

Gargan gave up his Scorpion suit to become the new VENOM. As part of the AVENGERS team assembled by Norman Osborn (GREEN GOBLIN), he impersonated Spider-Man. At the end of the DARK REIGN, however, he lost the symbiote. Alistair SMYTHE broke him out of jail and provided him with a new Scorpion suit, which he used to battle the Superior Spider-Man (DOCTOR OCTOPUS).

A woman named Carmilla Black also calls herself the Scorpion and wears a similar costume, although she has a stinger in her arm that can deliver deadly poison. She worked for SHIELD for a while but has since become a mercenary. A criminal named Elaine Coll wore an upgraded Scorpion suit, calling herself Scorpia. **AD, MF**

FACTFILE

REAL NAME
MacDonald "Mac" Gargan

OCCUPATION
Assassin-for-hire

BASE
New York City

HEIGHT 6 ft 2 in
WEIGHT 220 lbs
EYES Brown
HAIR Brown

FIRST APPEARANCE
The Amazing Spider-Man #20 (January 1965)

SCORPION

POWERS
Strength greater than Spider-Man's; mechanical tail can be used as a bludgeon or to propel Scorpion 30 ft into the air. Tail has also been equipped with a toxic "sting" and a mechanism to fire electric blasts.

SCOURGE

FACTFILE

ANGEL (Tom Halloway)
Financed Scourges of the Underworld.

SCOURGE I
Gunned down the Enforcer, started killing criminals around the US.

SCOURGE II
Killed Scourge I to keep him from talking.

SCOURGE III
Leaving the group, he became an agent of the Red Skull.

SCOURGE IV
Killed Scourge II, then went after Priscilla Lyons who left the group.

SCOURGE V (Priscilla Lyons)
Left Scourges, incurring their wrath.

CAPRICE (Scourge VI)
Master of disguise, espionage, brain washing, interrogation.

BLOODSTAIN (Scourge VII)
Master of armed and unarmed combat.

DOMINO (Dunsinane)
Encyclopedic knowledge of every costumed hero, villain, organization.

FIRST APPEARANCE
Iron Man #194 (May 1985)

SCOURGE

Scourge was the brother of the criminal known as the ENFORCER. Outraged by his brother's behavior, Scourge got a gun, disguised himself as an old woman, and gunned down the Enforcer. He then became obsessed with traveling the country ruthlessly exterminating criminal after criminal, all while disguised.

Known as Scourge of the Underworld, Scourges wanted to rid the world of crime.

Scourge was captured by CAPTAIN AMERICA and then shot by an unseen assailant. To date, there have been at least nine Scourges of the Underworld. Each Scourge has been assassinated by the following Scourge to keep the previous one from talking. Scourges relied on an investigator named Domino to feed them information about their targets and killed countless villains. BARON VON STRUCKER made Henry GYRICH force Jack Monroe (NOMAD) to become a Scourge. Gyrich later did the same thing to DEMOLITION MAN. **DW, MF**

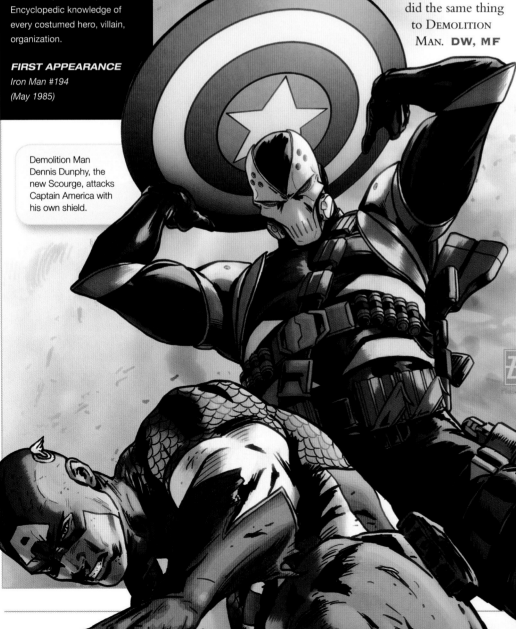

Demolition Man Dennis Dunphy, the new Scourge, attacks Captain America with his own shield.

SCREAM

FIRST APPEARANCE Venom: Lethal Protector #4 (May 1993)
REAL NAME Donna (full name unrevealed)
OCCUPATION Villain **BASE** Mobile
HEIGHT 5 ft 11 in **WEIGHT** 130 lbs **EYES** White **HAIR** Red
SPECIAL POWERS/ABILITIES Symbiote provides enhanced strength, speed, and stamina. Scream's prehensile hair can shape itself into deadly weapons.

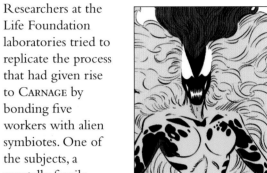

Researchers at the Life Foundation laboratories tried to replicate the process that had given rise to CARNAGE by bonding five workers with alien symbiotes. One of the subjects, a mentally fragile woman named Donna, found that the process drove her further into madness. The five test subjects sought out VENOM for help in controlling their symbiotes, but Donna killed her fellow hybrids. As Scream, Donna struggled to reform and help others with symbiotes. In the end, Venom (Eddie Brock) hunted her down and killed her. **DW, MF**

SCRIER

FIRST APPEARANCE The Amazing Spider-Man #394 (October 1994) **REAL NAME** Inapplicable (discovered to be an organization) **OCCUPATION** Criminal Cult **BASE** Unrevealed
HEIGHT/WEIGHT/EYES/HAIR Not applicable
SPECIAL POWERS/ABILITIES Each member of the Scrier is a formidable combatant. The Scrier also have access to an array of sophisticated weaponry.

By wearing identical garb, for centuries the Brotherhood of the Scrier maintained the deception that the Scrier was just one being. It was a clever ploy, disguising the true nature and scope of this worldwide criminal organization. United by their worship of a godlike being, itself called the Scrier, the Brotherhood became especially powerful under a new and mysterious leader who focused the organization's energies on SPIDER-MAN and his clone, Ben Reilly. It emerged that this new leader was in fact Norman Osborn (*see* GREEN GOBLIN). Following Osborn's defeat the fate of the Scriers remains uncertain. **AD**

SECRET INVASION
see pages 310-311

Secret Warriors

Nick Fury lost his job as director of SHIELD after a failed coup attempt in Latveria, but he didn't give up trying to save the world. During the Secret Invasion, he assembled a team called the Secret Warriors to help defeat the Skrulls. When Fury learned that Hydra had been controlling SHIELD since its founding—and was now taking over HAMMER from within—he moved to put an end to it, working with Dum Dum Dugan's Howling Commandos. The Secret Warriors also helped defend Asgard at the end of the Dark Reign.

Secret Warriors was composed of three teams. Fury ran the main team, Team White, and two covert teams. Deep-cover agent Alexander Pierce led Team Black, and Fury's son Mikel took charge of Team Gray. In the course of their work, Slingshot lost her arms, and Phobos was killed. Fury secretly killed Hellfire himself after the man betrayed the team to Hydra. **MF**

Fury lost many things, including his son Mikel and the rest of Team Gray.

Although no longer with SHIELD, Fury still worked with old friends like Steve Rogers (Captain America).

FACTFILE

DAISY JOHNSON, aka Quake. Can shake people and Earth.
DRUID Alchemist.
HELLFIRE Channels mystical fire through a chain.
MANIFOLD Teleporter.
NICK FURY Former director of SHIELD.
PHOBOS Young god of fear.
SLINGSHOT Superfast runner.
STONEWALL Property-absorbing strongman.

BASE
New York City

FIRST APPEARANCE
Mighty Avengers #13 (July 2008)

Selene

FIRST APPEARANCE New Mutants #9 (November 1983)
REAL NAME Selene Gallio
OCCUPATION Goddess, sorceress, conqueror **BASE** Mobile
HEIGHT 5 ft 10 in **WEIGHT** 130 lbs
EYES Brown **HAIR** Black
SPECIAL POWERS/ABILITIES Selene is immortal and can siphon the life force from others. She has superhuman durability, endurance, speed, strength, and telepathic powers, including pyrokinesis and the ability to control the minds of those from whom she's siphoned life. She can control darkforce (solid shadow) and has mastered magic.

Born over 17,000 years ago, Selene attempted to commit mass murders in order to ascend to godhood. After fleeing a failed plot in ancient Rome, she founded Nova Roma in Brazil and became the goddess of a cult. Intrigued after meeting the New Mutants, she went to New York and joined the Hellfire Club as its Black Queen. Later, she began animating dead mutants around the world, gathering them for a strike on Genosha. She revived them in a massive group and then sacrificed them all. The X-Men killed her, just as she achieved her dream. **MF**

Sentry

When meth addict Robert Reynolds broke into a secret lab and consumed a glowing Super-Soldier serum, he developed the power of a thousand exploding suns and went on to become the Sentry, the greatest hero the world had ever known. He later discovered that his archenemy the Void was actually part of his own repressed personality, and he had all memories of the Sentry erased from the world—and from his own mind.

When the memories began to return, Reynolds transformed into the Sentry once more, enlisting the help of other heroes against the Void. He wound up re-erasing himself. The only record of his existence survived in comic books.

Reynolds later turned up in the Raft super-prison when Electro started a jailbreak, and he joined the Avengers in trying to stop it. He continued to work with the Avengers while battling his mental health issues, sticking with the team even after Norman Osborn (Green Goblin) took it over. At the end of the Dark Reign, Sentry destroyed Asgard, and the Void burst out, trying to destroy the world. Thor eventually killed him and carried his body to burn in the sun. **MT, MF**

FACTFILE

REAL NAME
Robert Reynolds

OCCUPATION
Adventurer

BASE
Watchtower

HEIGHT 6 ft 2 in
WEIGHT 200 lbs
EYES Blue
HAIR Blond

FIRST APPEARANCE
Sentry #1 (September 2000)

POWERS
Serum provides super-strength, speed, and invulnerability. Can fly and control light.

Secret Invasion

Trust no one...

ISSUE #1

Once the Avengers finally realize that the Skrulls have infiltrated Earth, Queen Veranke launches the invasion. Sleeper agents around the world awaken, and the destruction begins.

At one time, the Skrull Empire ruled one of the most powerful interplanetary civilizations in the galaxy. However, a series of wars with the Kree, the destruction of the empire's capital planet by Galactus, and the loss of nearly all the empire's other planets to the Annihilation Wave drove the Skrulls to seek a new home. Because of the interference of humanity over the years—and owing to information the Skrulls gleaned after the Illuminati's botched mission to warn them off—the Skrulls resolved to fulfill an ancient prophecy and lay claim to Earth.

The Skrull who replaced Elektra reverted to her natural form when Echo killed her. The fact that none of the Avengers had realized she was a Skrull before told them an untold number of Skrulls had invaded Earth.

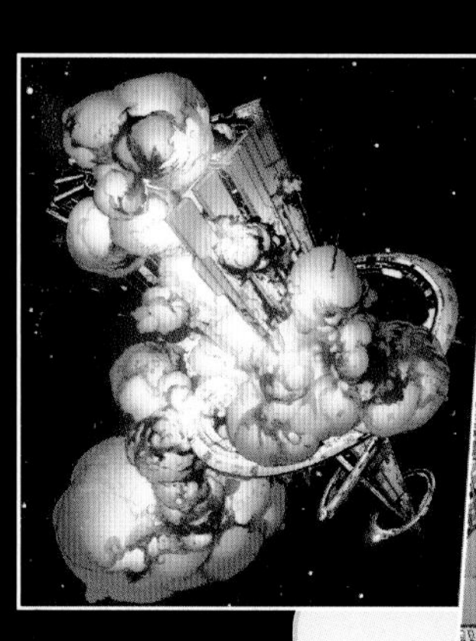

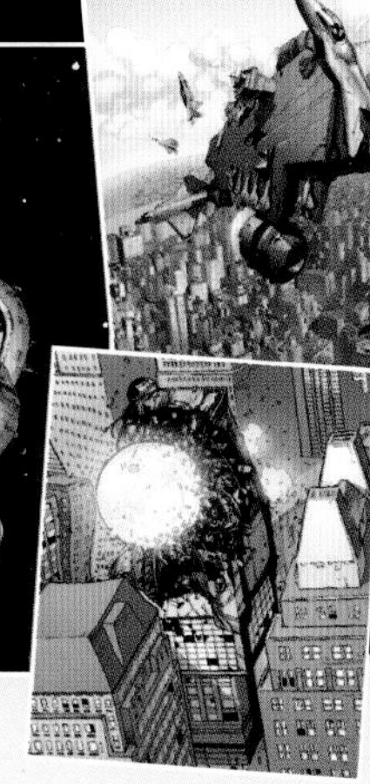

Disaster struck when the Skrulls launched their invasion. The Peak (the orbiting headquarters of SWORD), the SHIELD Helicarrier, the Fantastic Four's Baxter Building, and Thunderbolt Mountain were all destroyed.

THEY CAME TO CONQUER

The Skrull Queen Veranke began planning the invasion soon after ascending the throne. She began with an initiative to replace powerful and influential defenders of Earth with undetectable sleeper agents. When the Avengers discovered that Elektra had been replaced by a Skrull, Tony Stark (Iron Man) immediately suspected the potential Skrull threat. He called on the Illuminati to come up with a plan to counter an invasion. The other Avengers then learned that a Skrull had replaced Black Bolt long ago. Feeling that they could not even trust each other, the Super Hero team split to attack the problem on their own.

Realizing that the Avengers knew of the infiltration, Veranke—who had replaced Spider-Woman—gave the word to launch the invasion. Skrull agents simultaneously attacked several vital people and key points in Earth's defenses. Meanwhile, two teams of Avengers (one sanctioned by the US government and one not) raced to the Savage Land to investigate a crashed Skrull starship. There they faced off against each other and a third group of heroes who claimed to be the originals that the Skrulls had replaced over the years.

Manhattan became the central battleground in the invasion attempt. With the Avengers in the Savage Land, Nick Fury led a new crew of young heroes called the Secret Warriors to help the remaining heroes check the Skrull attacks. Even the Hood and his villains joined the heroes to fight the Skrulls. As the Hood remarked, "No more Earth is bad for business."

Once Reed Richards (Mr. Fantastic) came up with a way to identify the Skrulls, the Avengers raced back to New York and joined the battle there, along with Thor and every other hero in the area. In the course of the battle, Veranke fell, and one of her lieutenants, who had posed as Hank Pym, activated the growth serum he had given to the Wasp back when she thought he was her husband. This caused her to grow to giant size and give off a lethal biotoxin.

Thor stopped this, but only at the cost of the Wasp's life. Meanwhile, Veranke had recovered, but before she could escape, Norman Osborn (*see* Green Goblin) shot her dead. In the aftermath, Tony Stark took much of the blame for not stopping the invasion. The president disbanded SHIELD and replaced it with the Thunderbolts Initiative, placing Norman Osborn, now feted as a hero, in charge of overseeing the USA's registered superhumans. MF

The climactic conflict happened once Reed Richards had come up with a way to identify the Skrull infiltrators. The heroes of Earth and the invading Skrulls destroyed large chunks of New York City in a pitched battle that shook the streets.

When a Skrull infiltrator heard another Skrull say the words, "He loves you," his original personality resurfaced. Until then, the infiltrator was often unaware that he was a Skrull.

Norman Osborn formed a team of villains to help run the world after the Secret Invasion. Besides him, it included Doctor Doom, Loki, the Hood, the Sub-Mariner, and the White Queen.

THE SECRET IS OUT

The most terrifying part of the Secret Invasion was that the people of Earth had no way to tell whom they could trust. The embedded Skrulls were so well hidden that no one—not even they themselves—could tell who they were. Once the Skrulls revealed themselves to each other and united in the Secret Invasion, the heroes had to face off against a desperate army of foes who could not only shift shapes but also often had multiple sets of superpowers to draw upon. With no world left to call their own, the Skrulls fought hard for what they hoped would be their new home.

SENTINELS

Enormously powerful, mutant-hunting robots

SENTINELS

FACTFILE

MARK V MODEL

HEIGHT 20 ft

WEIGHT (including fuel) 7,400 lbs

MAX. CARGO 2,000 lbs

FLIGHT RADIUS 400 miles

MAX. LEVEL AIRSPEED (sea level) 600 mph

SERVICE CEILING 10,000 ft

MAX. RATE OF CLIMB 450 ft per second

FIRST APPEARANCE
X-Men #14
(November 1965)

POWERS

Most Sentinels possess superhuman strength and jet propulsion units in their feet which enable them to fly, and can fire lasers and electron beams from their eyes and hands. Mark II Sentinels could adapt to counter any opponent.

Dr. Bolivar Trask introduced the Sentinels to the world on live TV.

The Sentinels were created by Dr. Bolivar Trask to combat superhuman mutants. Trask had concluded that a superhuman mutant race was evolving that would conquer the rest of humanity. He organized the team of scientists and engineers who built the first Mark I models.

TAKING OVER

However, despite being programmed by Trask to protect humanity, the Sentinels decided to take control of the human race. They kidnapped Trask, and the lead Sentinel, the Master Mold, ordered him to create a Sentinel army. The X-MEN battled the Sentinels and Trask lost his life destroying the Master Mold and other Sentinels.

Trask's son, Larry, oversaw the creation of the Mark II Sentinels. However, once the Sentinels recognized that Trask was a mutant himself, they turned against him. The government then seized the Sentinel designs, and Dr. Steven Lang built the Mark III Sentinels; but both he and they were destroyed battling the X-Men.

After mutant terrorists tried to kill Senator Robert KELLY, the President initiated "Project: Wideawake." Shaw Industries constructed Sentinels to combat mutant threats to national security. Xavier's evil twin, Cassandra Nova, used Mega-Sentinels to devastate Genosha, a nation with a large mutant population. She also devised microscopic "nano-Sentinels," which attacked mutants' bloodstreams.

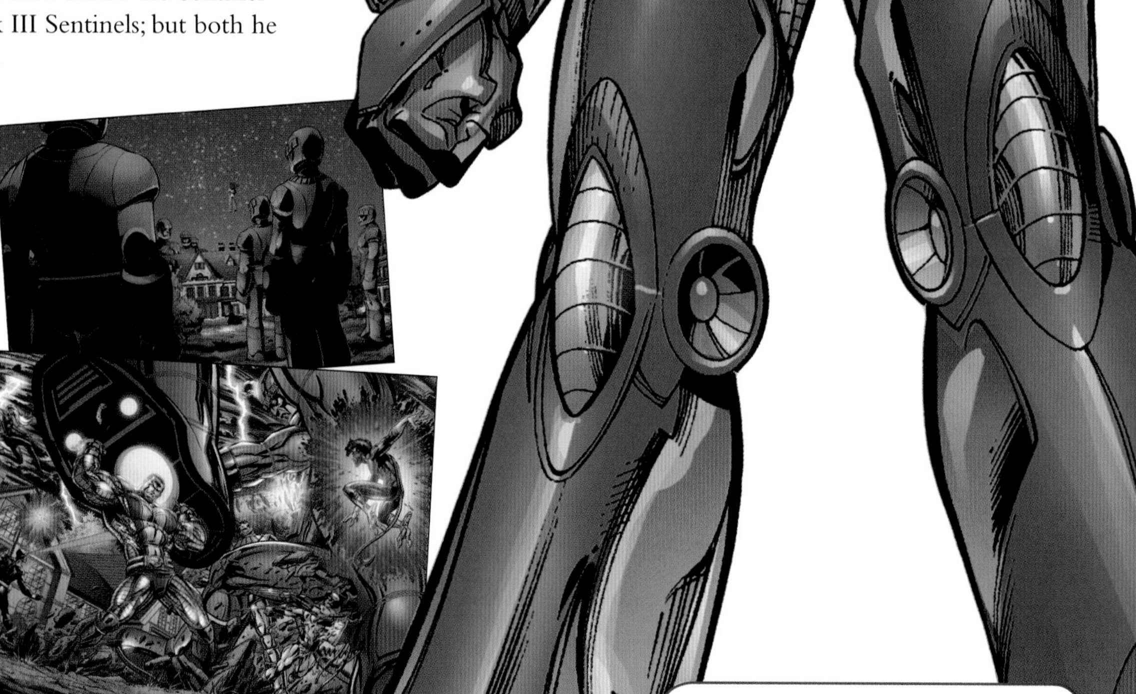

Following only their own logic, the Sentinels have repeatedly turned against their human masters as well as mutants.

SENTINEL TAKE OVER

Later, the US government created Sentinel Squad O★N★E, headed by Dr. Valerie COOPER and James Rhodes (WAR MACHINE) for defense against superhuman threats. These Sentinels were not robots but gigantic suits of armor with human pilots. However, Nano-Sentinels took over these pilots and their armor, forcing them to attack PROFESSOR X's mansion. Simon Trask (Bolivar's brother) later created a techno-organic virus that transformed people into Sentinels. **PS, MF**

The Sentinel Bastion created cyborgs known as Prime Sentinels that could pass as ordinary humans.

ESSENTIAL STORYLINES

- ***X-Men Vol. 1 #14–16***
Dr. Bolivar Trask creates the original Sentinel robots. He introduces them on live TV—and they promptly capture him.
- ***X-Men Vol. 1 #57–59***
Larry Trask's Mark II Sentinels capture and imprison mutants.
- ***Uncanny X-Men #141–142***
The Sentinels rule North America in the "Days of Future Past" storyline set in an alternate reality.

Sersi

A member of the Eternals, Sersi inspired the legend of Circe in Homer's *Odyssey* and encountered Merlin and King Arthur Pendragon. She proved her value during the Eternals' struggles against the Deviants. Sersi also joined the Avengers but Proctor manipulated her into battling her teammates. Seeking penance, she departed for an alternate reality with her lover the Black Knight. Upon her return, she joined Heroes for Hire, before returning to the Eternals' home, Olympia. Recently, fellow Eternal Sprite wiped the memories of all the Eternals, including Sersi. Once Sersi recovered, she decided to return to her fabricated but normal life. **DW, MF**

Sersi's playful personality can irritate some, and she is an incorrigible flirt around attractive men.

IT'S TOO LATE TO RUN, YOU ARMOR-HEADED HALFWITS! IT'S TIME YOU WERE IMPROVED!

Sersi has vast, advanced transmutational powers.

SERSI

FACTFILE

REAL NAME
Sersi

OCCUPATION
Adventurer

BASE
New York City

HEIGHT 5 ft 9 in
WEIGHT 140 lbs
EYES Blue
HAIR Black

FIRST APPEARANCE
Strange Tales #109 (June 1963)

POWERS
A powerful sorceress, Sersi can release cosmic energy, create illusions, and transmute matter. Capable of flight and virtually immortal.

Though it rarely mixes business with revenge, the Serpent Society has often made an exception in Captain America's case.

Serpent Society

The original Viper founded the first Serpent Squad with Eel and Cobra. The team changed its lineup several times, and it inspired one member, Sidewinder, to expand the squad into the Serpent Society and focus on treating their enterprise as a business. The leader assigned specific members to each job, supplying them with a detailed plan in return for a percentage of the take. Captain America put them out of commission several times.

Sin led a new Serpent Squad including Cobra, Eel, and Viper. During the Secret Invasion, the Serpent Society held a large group of people hostage, claiming to be protecting them from the Skrulls, but Nova and his teammates shut them down. Hope Summers stopped the latest crew from robbing a bank during the conflict between the Avengers and the X-Men. **TD, MF**

SERPENT SOCIETY
1 Death Adder ***2*** Rattler
3 Cottonmouth ***4*** Diamondback

SERPENT SOCIETY

FACTFILE

KEY MEMBERS
COBRA (Klaus Voorhees)
Super-flexible.
SIDEWINDER (Seth Voelker)
Interdimensional travel.
ANACONDA (Blanche Sitznski)
Elongates limbs; amphibious.
ASP (Cleo Nefertiti)
Energy field; fires venom-bolts.
BLACK MAMBA (Tanya Sealy)
Mesmerism; projects inky clouds of Darkforce.
BUSHMASTER (Quincy McIver)
Tail crushes his enemies.
COTTONMOUTH (Burchell Clemens) Bionic jaws.
RATTLER (Gustav Krueger)
Bionic tail generates sonic shockwaves.

FIRST APPEARANCE
Captain America #310 (October 1985)

Shadow Council

FIRST APPEARANCE Secret Avengers #1 (July 2010)
BASE Mobile
MEMBERS AND POWERS
Aloysius Thorndrake Immortal soldier.
Arnim Zola Mad genius in robot bodies.
Max Fury Superhuman android copy of Nick Fury.
John Steele Original Super Soldier.

The secretive Shadow Council has been operating since Confederate soldier Aloysius Thorndrake founded it around the time of the American Civil War, to pave the way for a mysterious alien called the ABYSS. Thorndrake recruited a brainwashed John STEELE and Max Fury (a Life Model Decoy of Nick Fury), along with a number of trained agents and a new MASTERS OF EVIL. The Secret AVENGERS—along with Nick Fury and TASKMASTER—foiled their plans and cured Steele of his brainwashing. **MF**

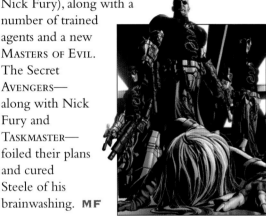

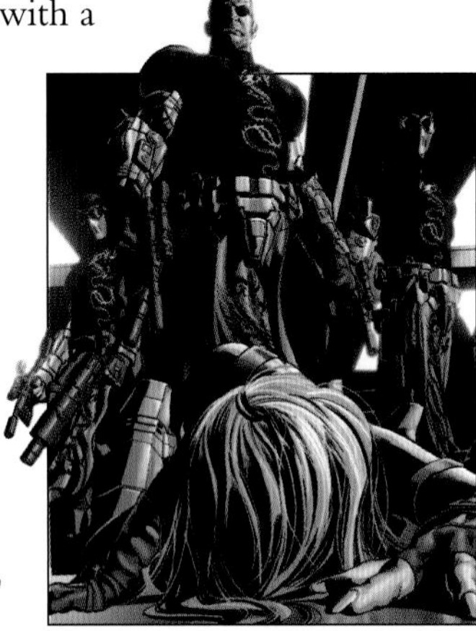

Shadowmasters

FIRST APPEARANCE Shadowmasters #1 (October 1989)
LINEUP Sojin Ezaki (deceased), Yuriko Ezaki, Phillip Richards
SPECIAL POWERS/ABILITIES Masters of ninjitsu

Demonstrating his martial arts skills, Phillip Richards wields a katana sword and *kyoketsu shoge* knife.

The original Shadowmasters were expert practitioners of the martial art of ninjitsu, who protected the Iga Province of Japan for centuries. Following the end of World War II, US Army Captain James Richards became friends with Shigeru Ezaki, one of the last Shadowmasters. Together they opposed renegade Japanese soldiers. Ezaki trained his children Sojin and Yuriko and Richards' son Phillip in martial arts. The renegades became the Sunrise Society, who killed James Richards and seemingly killed Shigeru Ezaki. Since then, Richards' son and Ezaki's children, as the new Shadowmasters, have opposed the Society, now renamed the Eternal Sun. **PS**

Shadow King

The Shadow King is an immortal demon that has lived on the astral plane. It possesses people in the real world, making them fat as it feeds upon the hatred it breeds. In the 1940s, it worked with BARON VON STRUCKER to try to replace King George VI of the UK with a Nazi puppet. Years later, the Shadow King reappeared as Amahl Farouk, an Egyptian crimelord and the first evil mutant PROFESSOR X ever met. Farouk's gang included a young thief who would one day become STORM. Professor X defeated Farouk in a psychic duel and believed him killed. However, he had only been banished back to the astral plane and remained an omnipresent threat to Xavier's dream of peaceful coexistence between mutants and normal humans. The Shadow King once controlled a group of X-MEN from a parallel world, dubbing them his Dark X-Men before EXCALIBUR defeated him. Bast, the Panther God of Wakanda, later devoured the Shadow King for daring to attack the BLACK PANTHER and his wife Storm. The remnants of him grew in power until he was able to take over a nuclear launch site and aim the bombs at the X-Men's island home of Utopia. He later joined DAKEN'S BROTHERHOOD OF MUTANTS, which X-FORCE stopped. **TB, MF**

Using his telepathic powers, Amahl Farouk came to rule Cairo's criminal underworld.

FACTFILE

REAL NAME
Amahl Farouk

OCCUPATION
Criminal

BASE
Various

HEIGHT Various
WEIGHT Various
EYES Various
HAIR Various

FIRST APPEARANCE
Uncanny X-Men #117 (January 1979)

POWERS
An entity composed solely of malevolent psionic power, the Shadow King can possess others, bending them to his will. He also possesses various telepathic and telekinetic abilities.

The Shadow King was the first mutant encountered by Professor X as he wandered the world, a tale told in *Uncanny X-Men #117.*

Shalla-Bal

FIRST APPEARANCE Silver Surfer #1 (August 1968)

REAL NAME Shalla-Bal

OCCUPATION Empress of the planet Zenn-La **BASE** Zenn-La

HEIGHT 5 ft 9 in **WEIGHT** 125 lbs **EYES** Blue **HAIR** Black

SPECIAL POWERS/ABILITIES Born with no special powers, Shalla-Bal was later invested with power to restore life to the soil of Zenn-La after it was devastated by Galactus.

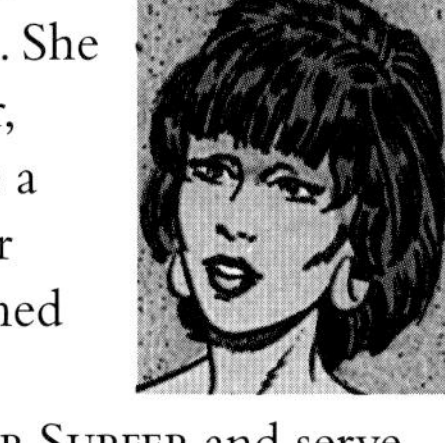

Shalla-Bal is a member of an alien race, the Zenn-Lavians. She was separated from her lover, Norrin Radd, after he made a bargain with the world-eater GALACTUS, who had threatened to destroy Zenn-La. Radd offered to become the SILVER SURFER and serve GALACTUS if he would spare Zenn-La, and Galactus agreed. For years the Silver Surfer traveled the universe, scouting out uninhabited planets for Galactus to consume. When the Surfer eventually decided to abandon Galactus and remain on Earth, Shalla-Bal became caught up in his struggle with MEPHISTO. Then Galactus returned to consume Zenn-La in revenge for the Surfer's betrayal. After the Surfer endowed Shalla-Bal with the power to restore life to Zenn-La, she was declared Empress, and so she remains to this day. **AD**

Shaman

FIRST APPEARANCE Uncanny X-Men #120 (April 1979)

REAL NAME Michael Twoyoungmen

OCCUPATION Medicine man, Super Hero **BASE** Mobile

HEIGHT 5 ft 10 in **WEIGHT** 175 lbs **EYES** Brown **HAIR** Black

SPECIAL POWERS/ABILITIES Vast magical powers. Able to fire energy bolts, change his appearance, control weather, levitate, and teleport. Powers are focused through the use of his medicine pouch.

Michael Twoyoungmen was a Canadian surgeon who embraced his heritage as a Native American medicine man after his wife's death. The spirit of his grandfather trained him in the use of magic, and he helped deliver Narya, the daughter of the Northern Goddess. Twoyoungmen and Narya took the codenames of Shaman and SNOWBIRD and joined ALPHA FLIGHT. Shaman's daughter Elizabeth was known as TALISMAN, an identity he had briefly used himself. He died at the hands of The Collective (*see* WEAPON OMEGA), but was resurrected during the CHAOS WAR. **DW, MF**

Shanna the She-Devil

FIRST APPEARANCE Shanna the She-Devil #1 (December 1972)

REAL NAME Shanna O'Hara Plunder

OCCUPATION Vet and adventurer **BASE** Savage Land

HEIGHT 5 ft 10 in **WEIGHT** 140 lbs **EYES** Hazel **HAIR** Red

SPECIAL POWERS/ABILITIES Trained veterinarian and extraordinary gymnast and athlete with superb hunting and foraging skills. Post-resurrection, she is tied to the Savage Land and knows its languages and history. She also has superhuman strength and speed.

Now living in the Savage Land with her husband KA-ZAR and their young son, Shanna O'Hara first worked in a New York zoo. Furious when a sniper casually killed most of the zoo's big cats, she chose to return the surviving animals to Africa and live with them in the wild. Shanna lost her friends and father to criminal organizations and was forced to team up with DAREDEVIL to defeat them. She was killed in the Savage Land and resurrected with the blood of a native MAN-THING, tying her to the land. **AD, MF**

The Savage Land in Antarctica is maintained at tropical temperatures. It has been stocked with species that are extinct elsewhere on Earth.

Shang-Chi

FACTFILE

REAL NAME
Shang-Chi

OCCUPATION
Former secret agent, fisherman

BASE
Formerly Fu Manchu's retreat in Honan, China, mobile for a while, then Yang Yin, China

HEIGHT 5 ft 10 ins
WEIGHT 175 lbs
EYES Brown
HAIR Black

FIRST APPEARANCE
Special Marvel Edition #15 (1973)

POWERS
Shang-Chi is the greatest living master of kung fu. He is also highly skilled in many other mental and physical disciplines. Although he has no superhuman powers, Shang-Chi has defeated superpowered enemies.

Shang-Chi was born in China, the son of the criminal mastermind Fu Manchu. Trained in the mental and martial arts at Fu Manchu's retreat, Shang-Chi was a brilliant pupil but grew up unaware of his father's crimes. When Shang-Chi was nineteen, his father sent him away on a mission of assassination. The boy assumed that his father's enemies must be evil and so went willingly, but he soon learned the truth. Feeling betrayed, Shang-Chi vowed to destroy his father. He also learned that his father had created a conscienceless clone of him, called Moving Shadow. Defeating them both, Shang-Chi retired, but during the CIVIL WAR he returned to action as a member of Heroes for Hire. He later worked with MI-13 and also joined the AVENGERS. **MT, MF**

Shang-Chi as he appears in the Ultimates series.

Passion fueled by vengeance against his father coupled with Shang-Chi's amazing martial arts skills make him an almost unstoppable adversary to those who oppose him.

This was the first issue to feature Shang-Chi's name in the title.

Shaper of Worlds

FIRST APPEARANCE The Incredible Hulk #155 (September 1972)
REAL NAME Unrevealed, perhaps inapplicable
OCCUPATION Reality manipulator **BASE** The known universe
HEIGHT 18 ft **WEIGHT** 5.6 tons **EYES** Blue **HAIR** None
SPECIAL POWERS/ABILITIES Restructures pockets of reality, and rearranges the molecular structure of objects and living beings. Can teleport himself, and perceive the dreams and imagination of others.

The Shaper of Worlds originated in the SKRULL empire as a Cosmic Cube, an object which can alter reality according to the thoughts of whoever holds it. In time the Cosmic Cube developed sentience, and took the form of a Skrull with a metallic trustrum and tractor treads as the lower body. The Shaper wants to use his powers to restructure reality, but has little creative imagination. So he seeks out those who can supply dreams and imaginative concepts with which he can work. **PS**

Shatterstar

FIRST APPEARANCE New Mutants #99 (March 1991)
REAL NAME Benjamin Russell **OCCUPATION** Adventurer
BASE The Xavier Institute, Salem Center, New York State
HEIGHT 6 ft 2 in **WEIGHT** 210 lbs **EYES** Black **HAIR** Gray
SPECIAL POWERS/ABILITIES Genetically engineered for enhanced strength, speed, stamina; converts sonic frequencies into a vibratory shockwave that he channels through weapons.

Born to DAZZLER and LONGSHOT a hundred years in the future on Mojoworld, Shatterstar's parents' memories of him were wiped. Trained as an arena warrior, he escaped and joined the Cadre Alliance, to overthrow MOJO. Shatterstar traveled back in time to Earth and joined CABLE to found X-FORCE. During a battle, Shatterstar was mortally wounded, and Longshot transferred his consciousness into the comatose body of Benjamin Russell. Later, Cortex (a rogue duplicate of the MULTIPLE MAN) possessed him and made him attack his friends in X-FACTOR. When cured, he and RICTOR started a new relationship. **TD, MF**

Shaw, Sebastian

FIRST APPEARANCE X-Men #130 (February 1980)
REAL NAME Sebastian Shaw **OCCUPATION** CEO of Shaw Industries, Inc. **BASE** Worldwide; Hellfire Club, New York City
HEIGHT 6 ft 2 in **WEIGHT** 210 lbs **EYES** Black **HAIR** Gray
SPECIAL POWERS/ABILITIES Mutant power to absorb kinetic energy, which enhances his strength, speed, and stamina. He can also absorb electrical energy.

Sebastian Shaw became a self-made millionaire by the age of 20. As head of Shaw Industries, he joined the elite HELLFIRE CLUB, and then became part of its secret Council of the Chosen, which schemed to achieve world domination. Seizing control of the club and becoming its Black King, he changed its name to the Inner Circle and teamed with Emma FROST, the White Queen, in secretly creating mutant-hunting SENTINELS. The X-MEN captured Shaw, and Frost wiped his mind so that he could only remember the faces of the Genoshans the Sentinels destroyed. Hope SUMMERS found him later and brought him to the X-Men, as he seemed to be a changed man. He later helped a group of mutants escape from the Avengers. **MT,**

She-Thing

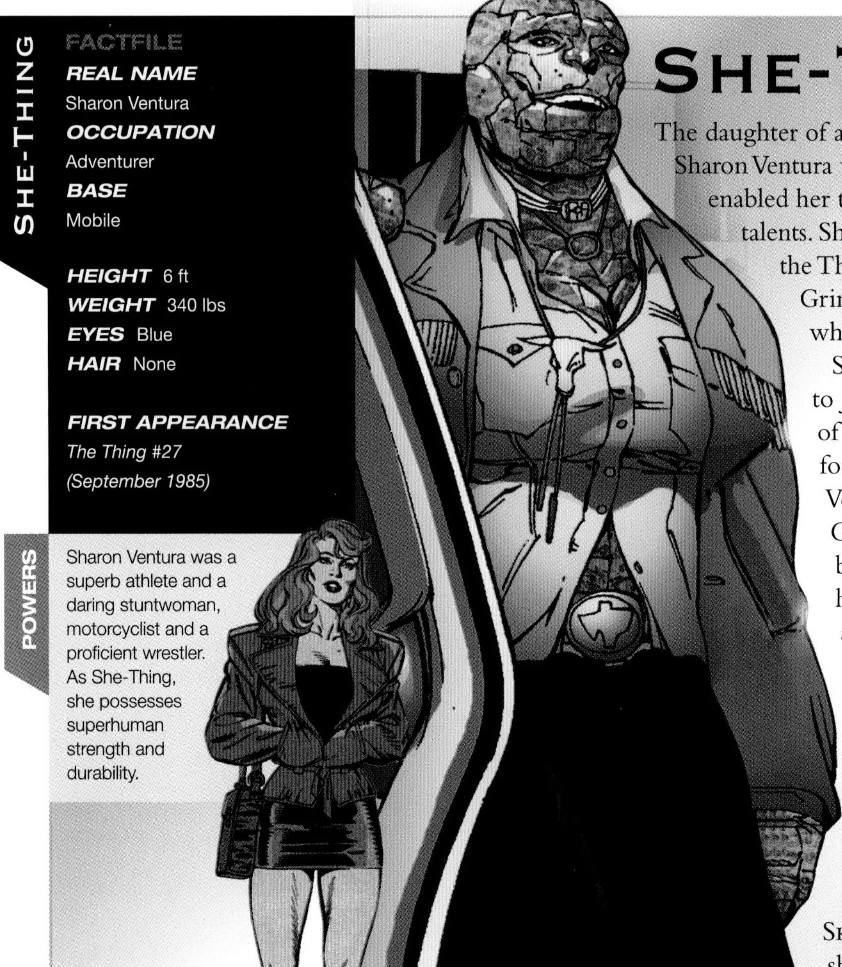

SHE-THING

FACTFILE
REAL NAME
Sharon Ventura
OCCUPATION
Adventurer
BASE
Mobile

HEIGHT 6 ft
WEIGHT 340 lbs
EYES Blue
HAIR None

FIRST APPEARANCE
The Thing #27 (September 1985)

POWERS
Sharon Ventura was a superb athlete and a daring stuntwoman, motorcyclist and a proficient wrestler. As She-Thing, she possesses superhuman strength and durability.

The daughter of a career officer in the US Army, Sharon Ventura worked in various professions that enabled her to make full use of her athletic talents. She was working as a stunt cyclist with the Thunderiders when she first met Ben Grimm, the THING of the FANTASTIC FOUR, who was immediately attracted to her.

Subsequently, Ventura accepted an offer to join the Grapplers, a professional team of superhuman female wrestlers. Working for the POWER BROKER, Dr. Karl MALUS augmented Ventura's strength to superhuman levels. As a Grappler, she adopted a costumed identity, becoming the second Ms. Marvel. The Thing helped her battle the Grapplers when they turned against her.

When Reed and Susan Richards temporarily left the Fantastic Four, Ben Grimm invited Sharon Ventura to join the team as Ms. Marvel. Shortly afterward she became the She-Thing.

Later, Ventura accepted the Thing's offer to join the Fantastic Four. During a mission in space, Ventura was exposed to cosmic rays, which mutated her into a female version of the Thing. She was later restored to her normal human appearance by DOCTOR DOOM.

Ventura later mutated into an even more grotesque version of the Thing. Worse, her intellect began to deteriorate. As the She-Thing, she even temporarily joined the WIZARD's FRIGHTFUL FOUR and battled her former friends the Fantastic Four. During the SECRET INVASION, the SKRULLS captured and replaced the She-Thing, but after the war was over she escaped. **PS, MF**

She-Hulk

Legal eagle and greenskinned crimefighter

Driven to madness by Scarlet Witch's hex power in *Avengers: Disassembled.*

The cousin of Bruce Banner, who would one day become the Hulk, Jennifer Walters pursued her dream of becoming a successful lawyer. Shot by criminals whose boss she was prosecuting, Jennifer received a life-saving blood transfusion from her cousin Bruce. But this infusion of gamma-irradiated blood had an effect on Jennifer's physiology similar to that experienced by Bruce himself: the repressed part of her personality began to manifest itself as a green-skinned powerhouse: the savage She-Hulk!

She-Hulk was one of the last characters created by Stan Lee.

She-Hulk

FACTFILE

REAL NAME
Jennifer Walters

OCCUPATION
Lawyer

BASE
The law offices of Goodman, Lieber, Kurtzburg & Holliway

HEIGHT 6 ft 7 in
WEIGHT 650 lbs
EYES Green
HAIR Green; brown as Jennifer Walters

FIRST APPEARANCE
The Savage She-Hulk #1 (February 1980}

POWERS
As the She-Hulk, Jennifer Walters possesses superhuman strength and durability; she can withstand extreme temperatures and her skin is highly resistant to injury

Rampaging Free

At first, Jennifer kept her dual role as the She-Hulk a secret. But over time, she found that she enjoyed being the She-Hulk, who, while definitely an extrovert, was far more controlled than her cousin's rampaging alter ego. She began to spend more time as the She-Hulk, using her gamma-spawned strength to battle villainy. Eventually, the She-Hulk was offered membership in the Avengers.

Thereafter, transported to the Battleworld created by the celestial Beyonder alongside her fellow Avengers, She-Hulk fought in the Secret Wars. Following that conflict, the Thing decided to remain on Battleworld, and asked the She-Hulk to take his place in the Fantastic Four, which she did for a while, becoming almost one of the family. During her time with the FF, Jennifer abandoned her identity as Jennifer Walters, remaining in her She-Hulk form full time.

Legal Troubleshooter

However, the She-Hulk's more boisterous personality created problems for her down the line, and she was asked to move out of Avengers Mansion. At this low point in her life, she was recruited by the law offices of Goodman, Lieber, Kurtzburg & Holliway, a firm specializing in superhuman law. But a condition of Jennifer's employment was that she had to pursue her duties in her normal human state, rather than as the She-Hulk.

After the Civil War, Jennifer helped train heroes in the Fifty-State Initiative. Disbarred for revealing privileged information about a client she thought guilty of murder, Jennifer later turned to bounty hunting with her Skrull friend Jazinda (daughter of the Super-Skrull). For a while, she was thought killed at the hands of the Red She-Hulk (Betty Ross) but Lyja found and freed her. Later, she served in a substitute Fantastic Four.

TB, MF

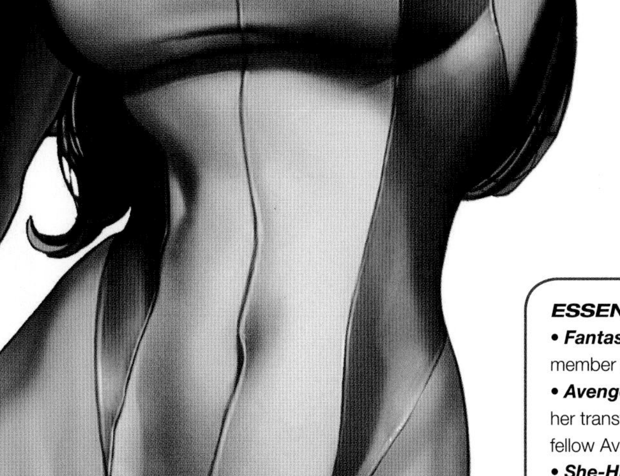

ESSENTIAL STORYLINES
- ***Fantastic Four #265*** Replaces the Thing as a member of the Fantastic Four.
- ***Avengers Vol. 3 #72-75*** Having lost control of her transformations, She-Hulk is pursued by her fellow Avengers and her cousin, the Hulk.
- ***She-Hulk #2*** Joins the superhuman law offices of Goodman, Lieber, Kurtzburg & Holliway.

As Jennifer Walters, She-Hulk practiced superhuman law for the legal firm of Goodman, Lieber, Kurtzburg & Holliway.

SHI'AR

Empire-building alien race

FACTFILE

NAME
THE SHI'AR
Enhanced strength and endurance

BASE
Chandilar (Aerie), Shi'ar Galaxy

FIRST APPEARANCE
Uncanny X-Men Vol. 1 #97 (February 1976)

SHI'AR

CURRENT MEMBERS AND POWERS
GLADIATOR (LEADER) Flight, enhanced strength, speed, near-invulnerability, heat vision.
ASTRA Ability to phase through solid objects.
ELECTRON Power over electricity and magnetism.
FANG (DECEASED) Enhanced strength, speed, and senses; razor-sharp claws.
HOBGOBLIN/SHAPESHIFTER (DECEASED) Could assume nearly any form.
IMPULSE/PULSAR Energy-based body can be released as concussive force.
MIDGET/SCINTILLA Can shrink to tiny size.
NIGHTSHADE/NIGHTSIDE Can draw others into the Darkforce dimension.
MAGIQUE Ability to cast illusions.
MENTOR Genius-level intelligence and boosted calculating speed.
ORACLE Telepathy, precognition, and ability to fire mental blasts.
QUASAR/NEUTRON Enhanced strength and damage resistance.
STARBOLT Flight, energy projection.
SMASHER Enhanced strength.
TEMPEST/FLASHFIRE Ability to release electrical bolts.
TITAN Can grow to giant size.

BASE
Chandilar (Aerie), Shi'ar Galaxy

FIRST APPEARANCE
Uncanny X-Men Vol. 1 #107 (October 1977)

IMPERIAL GUARD

Majestor D'ken failed to hold onto the Shi'ar throne.

The Shi'ar are an alien species descended from avians, who typically sport feathery hair and sometimes vestigial wings. Unlike the rival SKRULL and KREE empires, the Shi'ar Imperium consists of a patchwork of alien species, each absorbed into the empire through treaties or by force. A hereditary Majestor (male) or Majestrix (female) rules the Imperium, overseeing a High Council under the protection of the Elite Corps of the Shi'ar Imperial Guard.

ESSENTIAL STORYLINES
- ***Uncanny X-Men #107-109***
The X-Men battle the Shi'ar Imperial Guard in a fight involving D'ken, Lilandra, and the M'Krann crystal.
- ***New X-Men #118-126***
The "Imperial" story arc sees Cassandra Nova, the villainous genetic twin of Professor X, launching a scheme to ruin the Shi'ar empire.

CRUEL RULE

The Shi'ar are aggressive about absorbing other cultures into their empire, though the newcomers seldom receive the same rights as the Shi'ar themselves. Majestrix Lilandra has made strides to reverse this inequality, but under the leadership of Majestor D'ken, the cruel treatment of alien slaves triggered the formation of the pirates called the STARJAMMERS.

The M'Krann crystal is an artifact of immense power located on a lifeless world. It has the ability to destroy all of reality.

The first contact between the Shi'ar and Earth's heroes occurred when the X-MEN stopped Lilandra's brother D'ken from exploiting the powerful M'Krann crystal. Lilandra subsequently became the Majestrix of the Shi'ar Empire, briefly losing her throne to her sister DEATHBIRD until gaining it once more. Lilandra and PROFESSOR X of the X-Men enjoyed a romantic relationship for years.

When Skrull spies fanned the flames of war between the Shi'ar and the Kree, a team of AVENGERS tried to negotiate a cessation of hostilities with Majestrix Lilandra, but they could not prevent the detonation of the Nega-Bomb, a Shi'ar weapon that nearly destroyed the Kree. The Shi'ar annexed vast swaths of the Kree Empire, and Deathbird served as the viceroy of the conquered territories.

The X-Men have been staunch allies of Lilandra's, thanks to her romantic liaison with Professor Charles Xavier.

The mutant Vulcan later returned to the Shi'ar Empire to avenge his mother's death and become majestor by marrying DEATHBIRD and killing her brother D'Ken. He led the Shi'ar into a final war with the INHUMANS-led Kree, which they lost after Vulcan died in a battle with BLACK BOLT. The former GLADIATOR, Kallark, then became leader of the Shi'ar under the dominion of the Kree. **DW, MF**

THE IMPERIAL GUARD

The Elite Corps of the Shi'ar Imperial Guard, also known as the Superguardian Elite, are the protectors of the Majestor or Majestrix of the Shi'ar Empire. Most members of the Imperial Guard are not Shi'ar—they represent a cross-section of cultures from the multispecies mix that comprises the Shi'ar empire. Typically, each member has a distinct superpower that adds a needed component to the team's overall power mix.

Their leader, called the praetor, is currently the powerful Strontian called Gladiator. The Imperial Guard also has a larger, secondary division known as the Borderers, who are charged with enforcing local laws on member planets.

The Imperial Guard first came into conflict with the inhabitants of Earth when the X-Men followed a space warp and emerged on the desolate planet that housed the reality-altering M'Krann crystal. On the orders of Majestor D'ken, the Imperial Guard battled the X-Men and D'ken's sister Lilandra, though the Guard shifted its allegiance to Lilandra as soon as she assumed the throne. Later, the Imperial Guard fought the X-Men on Earth's moon, in an honor duel over the fate of the Dark Phoenix.

Throughout the changes in Shi'ar rule, the Imperial Guard has remained loyal to whomever holds the royal office. The Guard clashed with the Starjammers and Excalibur during Deathbird's time as Majestrix, and welcomed Lilandra back as leader after her return to power.

During the Kree-Shi'ar war, the Imperial Guard helped steal the nega-bands worn by Captain Mar-Vell from the late hero's tomb, which then went into the construction of the Shi'ar ultimate weapon, the nega-bomb. Following the apparent death of Earth's greatest heroes fighting Onslaught, Lilandra ordered Gladiator and several other Imperial Guard members to protect Earth, where the team uncovered a cell of undercover Kree agents.

The Imperial Guard served Vulcan during the War of Kings against the Kree. The newest ruler of the Shi'ar came from within their ranks: the former Gladiator, Kallark.

When they combine their powers, the Shi'ar Imperial Guard are nearly unstoppable. They are among the most feared combatants in the universe.

GLADIATOR

ASTRA

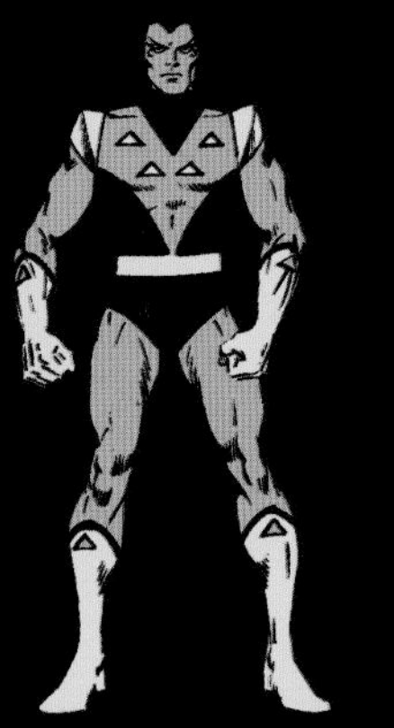

ELECTRON

FANG

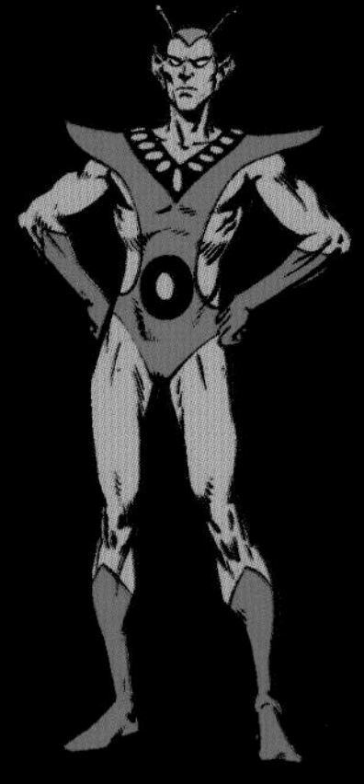

SHAPE-SHIFTER

IMPULSE

SCINTILLA

NIGHTSIDE

MAGIQUE

MENTOR

ORACLE

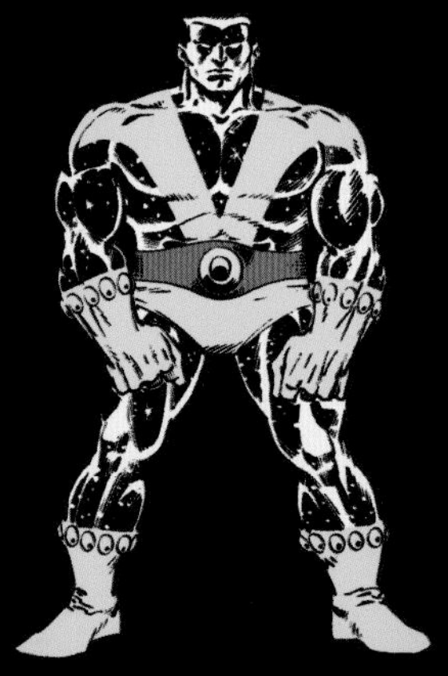

NEUTRON

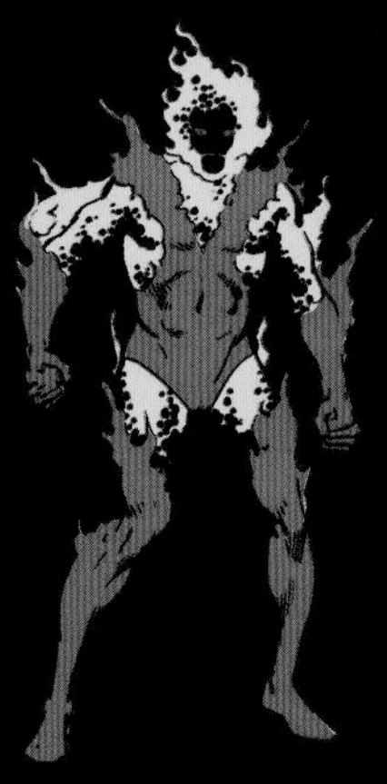

STARBOLT

SMASHER

FLASHFIRE

TITAN

SHIELD

Strategic Hazard Intervention, Espionage, and Logistics Directorate

SHIELD

FACTFILE

NOTABLE MEMBERS

NICK FURY Former director
CONTESSA VALENTINA ALLEGRA DI FONTAINE
YELENA BELOVA (Black Widow)
G. W. BRIDGE Former director
SHARON CARTER (Agent 13), former director, liaison officer to Captain America
JESSICA DREW (Spider-Woman)
THADDEUS "DUM-DUM" DUGAN former director
MARIA HILL Former director
Gabriel "Gabe" Jones
AL MACKENZIE CIA liaison officer
ALI MORALES
CLAY QUARTERMAIN
NATASHA ROMANOVA (Black Widow)
JASPER SITWELL
TONY STARK (Iron Man), former director
JIMMY WOO (Agents of Atlas)

BASE

The Helicarrier; mobile

FIRST APPEARANCE

Strange Tales #135 (August 1965)

The longest-serving director of SHIELD, not even Nick Fury knows the identity of the man he replaced.

SHIELD (Supreme Headquarters International Espionage Law-Enforcement Division; later changed to Strategic Hazard Intervention, Espionage and Logistics Directorate) is a counter-terrorism, intelligence, espionage, and peace-keeping organization. SHIELD runs covert as well as military operations, and works with governments and their military forces around the world.

SHIELD'S FORMATION

SHIELD was established to counter the threat posed by the technologically advanced neo-fascist subversive organization known as Hydra. The identity of SHIELD's founders remained classified, as did the identity of its first executive director, who was assassinated by Hydra operatives. SHIELD's second and longest-serving leader was Nick Fury, a colonel in the U.S. Army, who had also been a top CIA operative. Other top SHIELD members include Timothy "Dum-Dum" Dugan, Valentina Allegro De Fontaine, and Jasper Sitwell.

For many years, SHIELD's headquarters was the Helicarrier, a huge flying aircraft carrier that was kept airborne at all times. It carried a squadron of jet fighters and an ICBM. The Helicarrier was damaged and even destroyed several times over the years, but SHIELD rebuilt it every time and maintained many regional headquarters throughout the world.

As director of SHIELD, Maria Hill tried to cut the agency's dependency on Super Heroes and rely on human resources instead.

SHIELD also kept close ties to the Super Hero community and often called upon Captain America, the Avengers, and the Fantastic Four for help. In addition to battling earthly terrorist and military threats, SHIELD saved the world many times from extraterrestrial invasion and infiltration. As well as its human operatives, SHIELD also employed Life Model Decoys (LMDs), incredibly lifelike androids sent into extremely dangerous situations to help avoid human casualties. Nick Fury was known to deploy several LMDs of himself to confuse assassins and even the agents working beneath him.

Over the years, SHIELD's main adversaries included Hydra, AIM, Zodiac, the Corporation, the Yellow Claw, the Viper, the Red Skull, Centurius, and Doctor Demonicus. SHIELD provided intelligence and technical support to the Avengers and the Fantastic Four during the Kree-Skrull War, when a battle of the aliens took place very close to Earth.

Although chartered by the UN, SHIELD maintained close ties to the US. The UN also founded a number of sister organizations. ARMOR (Altered-Reality Monitoring and Operational Response) stopped invasions from other universes, and SWORD (Sentient World Observation and Response Department) defended the planet from alien invasions.

The terrorist organization Hydra, dedicated to world domination, is SHIELD's greatest and most persistent enemy.

ESSENTIAL STORYLINES

- ***Strange Tales #135*** Nick Fury, who will be the organization's top operative and eventual leader, is recruited by SHIELD.
- ***Strange Tales #158*** Hydra Island sinks, and Baron Wolfgang von Strucker, Hydra's leader is killed.

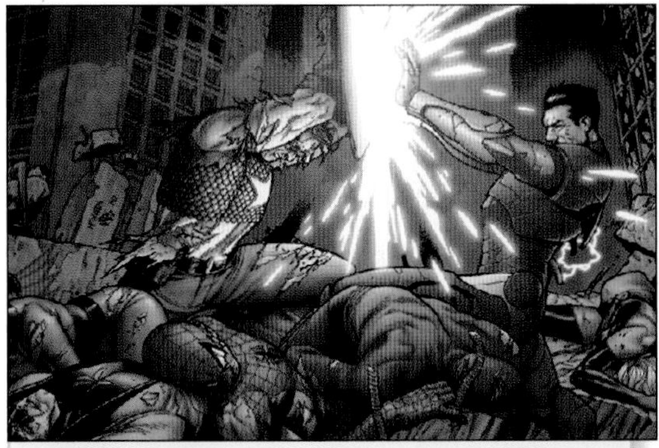
Iron Man was made director of SHIELD after defeating one of its staunchest allies, Captain America, during the Civil War.

Trouble at the Top

While acting as director of SHIELD, Nick Fury gathered a secret team of Super Heroes and launched a covert attempt to topple the government of Latveria, then run by Prime Minister Lucia von Bardas. Although helped by Captain America, Spider-Man, Luke Cage, Daredevil, Black Widow, Wolverine, and agent Daisy Johnson (Quake), the mission failed. Fury had all memories of the mission wiped from the heroes' minds.

A year later, Latveria launched an attack on New York City in revenge, and Fury's role in the disaster was exposed. He resigned soon afterward and then disappeared underground.

Eager to show a clean break with Fury, the UN appointed relative outsider Maria Hill as the next director of SHIELD. Hill was leading the organization when the Superhuman Registration Act was passed, placing her in charge of controlling all registered superhumans in the US—and of hunting down the rest. She served as director throughout the Civil War, but when the conflict finally resolved, she suggested that Tony Stark—who had led the pro-registration heroes as Iron Man—take over as director and that she serve as his deputy.

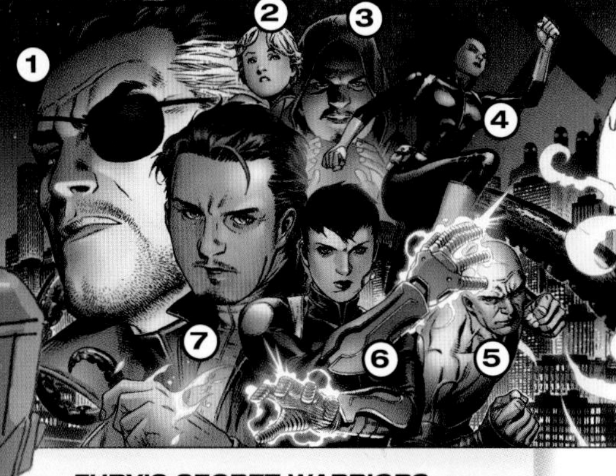

Fury's Secret Warriors
1 Nick Fury **2** Phobos **3** Druid **4** Slingshot **5** Stonewall **6** Quake **7** Hellfire

As SHIELD director, Stark launched the Fifty-State Initiative and ordered a new Helicarrier built using the latest Stark technology. He also used SHIELD money to fund the Avengers and their HQ in Stark Tower.

A Dark Reign

When SHIELD failed to prevent the Secret Invasion, Norman Osborn (Green Goblin) replaced Stark as director and SHIELD with a new organization called HAMMER. Osborn also formed a team of villains masquerading as Avengers, which he led as the Iron Patriot. Thus began the period known as the Dark Reign.

Nick Fury had resurfaced during the Secret Invasion with his Secret Warriors to help defeat the Skrulls. He discovered that Hydra had been controlling SHIELD from its founding, and he rededicated his team to bringing his old foes down, revealing to them in the end that they'd actually been working for him.

After the Dark Reign ended, Captain America ended HAMMER, rebuilt SHIELD, and put Daisy Johnson (Quake) in charge. She added new agents, including Nick Fury Jr. and Phil Coulson, and formed her own secret Avengers team. Maria Hill has since resumed the directorship. **MF**

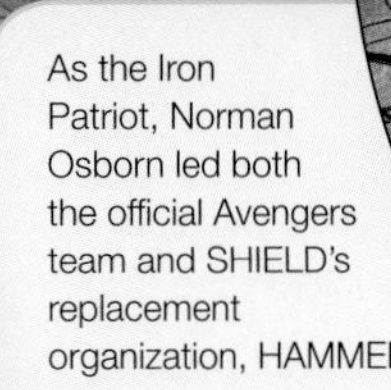
As the Iron Patriot, Norman Osborn led both the official Avengers team and SHIELD's replacement organization, HAMMER.

Shocker

FIRST APPEARANCE The Amazing Spider-Man #46 (March 1967)
REAL NAME Herman Schultz
OCCUPATION Burglar **BASE** New York City
HEIGHT 5 ft 9 in **WEIGHT** 175 lbs **EYES** Brown **HAIR** Brown
SPECIAL POWERS/ABILITIES Wears gauntlets containing "vibro-shock units" that project compressed air blasts creating highly destructive vibrations.

While imprisoned, safecracker Herman Schultz invented a new device for opening safes by projecting intense vibrations. He used it to shatter the prison walls and escape. Wearing an insulated costume to absorb the vibrations, Schultz became the Shocker. After SPIDER-MAN beat him several times, he joined a number of teams, including the SINISTER SIX, the SINISTER SYNDICATE, the Sinister Seven, the Sinister Twelve, and EGGHEAD'S MASTERS OF EVIL. Another criminal, Randall Darby, once called himself the Shocker, too, but later changed his name to Paralyzer. **PS, MF**

Shriek

FIRST APPEARANCE Spider-Man Unlimited #1 (May 1993)
REAL NAME Frances Louise Barrison **OCCUPATION** Patient
BASE Ravencroft Institute for the Criminally Insane
HEIGHT 6 ft **WEIGHT** 170 lbs **EYES** Blue **HAIR** Black
SPECIAL POWERS/ABILITIES Manipulates sound as a destructive force. Hypersonically generates emotions of fear, hate, or despair in others. Can employ sonic energy to fly.

After being mistreated by her mother for being overweight, Frances Louise Barrison turned to drugs, eventually becoming a dealer. She lost her fragile grip on reality when she was shot in the head by the police and spent a brief period in the dark dimension of the costumed adventurer known as CLOAK. Her powers may be the result of her time in that dimension, her injury, some latent mutant gene, or a combination of all three factors. She used her emerging powers to commit crimes and create chaos until she was committed to the Ravencroft Institute for the Criminally Insane. CARNAGE later freed her and they went on a murder spree until they were captured by a team of heroes led by SPIDER-MAN. Shriek has escaped Ravencroft on at least two other occasions, but is now responding to therapy. **TD**

Shroud

FIRST APPEARANCE Super-Villain Team-Up #5 (April 1976)
REAL NAME Unknown **OCCUPATION** Crime fighter masquerading as a criminal **BASE** Los Angeles
HEIGHT 6 ft 2 in **WEIGHT** 220 lbs **EYES** Blue **HAIR** Blond
SPECIAL POWERS/ABILITIES Though blind, has extrasensory perception that allows him to "see" his environment; can summon absolute darkness by opening a portal into another dimension.

After witnessing the murder of his parents as a boy, the Shroud dedicated his life to fighting crime. After college, he traveled to Nepal and joined a cult that trained him in mysticism and the martial arts. Seven years later, he was given the "Kiss of Kali" and branded with the imprint of the goddess on his eyes, cheeks, and forehead, trading his eyesight for a mystical perception. He often pretends to be a criminal and formed a gang called the Night Shift. He refused to register with the government during the CIVIL WAR and sided with CAPTAIN AMERICA. **TD, MF**

Shockwave

FIRST APPEARANCE Master of Kung Fu #42 (July 1976)
REAL NAME Lancaster Sneed
OCCUPATION Mercenary, professional criminal **BASE** Mobile
HEIGHT 5 ft 11 in **WEIGHT** 170 lbs **EYES** Green **HAIR** Black
SPECIAL POWERS/ABILITIES His protective armor can generate electric shocks upon contact. Agility, combat skills, and knowledge of explosives were gained during his years as an intelligence agent.

As a child, Lancaster Sneed loved to listen to his uncle's tales of his battles with crime lord Fu Manchu. As an adult, he became an explosives specialist for MI-6, but he was injured by a blast on his first mission. Rebuilt with metal plates, he traveled to Asia and studied martial arts. Going to the US, he donned a suit of armor that generated electricity, took the name Shockwave, and switched sides to join forces with Fu Manchu. The Heroes for Hire captured him during the CIVIL WAR, but during the SECRET INVASION, he broke out of prison and joined the HOOD'S forces to fight the SKRULLS. **MT, MF**

Sif

SIF

FACTFILE
REAL NAME
Sif
OCCUPATION
Warrior
BASE
Asgardia

HEIGHT 6 ft 2 in
WEIGHT 425 lbs
EYES Blue
HAIR Black

FIRST APPEARANCE
Journey Into Mystery #102 (March 1964)

POWERS
Sif is a god of Asgard, gifted with superhuman durability, endurance, speed, and strength. She's also an excellent combatant.

Sif was born with blonde hair, but LOKI cut it off as a prank. He hired trolls to replace it, but then stole it from them. When she wore her new hair, it turned jet black. Tired of her tears over the matter, her parents sent her to be trained to become a great warrior. As an adult, she dated THOR, and they pledged to marry (although they never have). Like the rest of the Norse gods (*see* GODS OF ASGARD), Sif died during Ragnarok. Thor returned and set about reviving the gods, finding them wearing the bodies of mortals on Midgard. He didn't find Sif, because Loki had taken her body, trapping her spirit in that of an elderly woman dying of cancer. Thor realized this and raced to restore Sif just moments before her host's body died. Sif returned to Asgard and helped defend it against HAMMER's attack at the end of the DARK REIGN. She also battled alongside Thor against the Serpent. Tired of seeing Asgard threatened, Sif found a witch who gave her new power—along with nearly uncontrollable bloodlust. She has since conquered it. **MF**

Silhouette

FACTFILE
REAL NAME
Silhouette Chord
OCCUPATION
Adventurer
BASE
Manhattan

HEIGHT 5 ft 6 in
WEIGHT 105 lbs
EYES Black with white pupils, formerly brown
HAIR Black

FIRST APPEARANCE
New Warriors #2 (August 1990)

POWERS
Able to pass through the Darkforce Dimension, allowing her to effectively teleport through the shadows. In her shadowy form, she can also phase through others, causing them injury. Her crutches variously house taser devices, anesthetic needles, pellet guns, and smoke capsules.

The daughter of Chord, the mentor of Night Thrasher, Silhouette's conception was part of a pact enacted by a squad of Vietnam soldiers and the protectors of a secret temple, intended as a mystic sacrifice that would convey great power. Unaware of her parentage, Silhouette and her brother Midnight's Fire grew up on the streets, a nemesis to the gangs that preyed there. In one foray against the underworld, Silhouette encountered the young Night Thrasher, and they began a torrid relationship. But then Silhouette was caught in the crossfire between the police and a street gang, losing the use of her legs. Midnight's Fire blamed Night Thrasher for this accident, and became his enemy. It was only to prevent her brother from slaying Night Thrasher that Silhouette came into contact with him again, and she thereafter joined his group the New Warriors. She eventually left both Night Thrasher and the New Warriors. During the Civil War, she sided with Captain America's resistance, but she registered with the government after his death. **TB, MF**

Silver Dagger

FIRST APPEARANCE Dr. Strange #1 (June 1974)
REAL NAME Isaiah Curwen
OCCUPATION Self-appointed mystic policeman **BASE** Mobile
HEIGHT 6 ft **WEIGHT** 220 lbs **EYES** Black **HAIR** Gray
SPECIAL POWERS/ABILITIES Spellcaster; can project mystic energy bolts, enlarge animals, and give himself superstrength; his silver dagger can cut through Doctor Strange's magical barriers.

The Pope's favored choice of successor, Isaiah Curwen harbored hopes of elevation to the Holy See. But the College of Cardinals failed to elect him, and Curwen decided to fight for the church in a different way. After studying the Vatican's library of black magic books, he set off to fight mystical masters across the world. A cruel psychopath, he has been a thorn in the side of Doctor Strange, even taking Strange's lover, Clea, and burning her soul in mystical fire. **AD**

Silver Sable

FACTFILE
REAL NAME
Silver Sable
OCCUPATION
CEO, Silver Sable International
BASE
Symkaria

HEIGHT 5 ft 5 ins
WEIGHT 125 lbs
EYES Blue
HAIR Silver

FIRST APPEARANCE
Amazing Spider-Man #265 (June 1985)

POWERS
Silver Sable is a master of martial arts and a highly skilled markswoman, swordswoman, gymnast, and strategist. She sometimes uses a samurai sword (katana), and the chai, a half-moon, weighted projectile of her own design.

Symkaria, a small country in the Balkans, had suffered under German occupation during World War II, and after the war ended, Sable's father had no trouble convincing the government to fund his hunt for Nazi war criminals. He formed a group called the Wild Pack that scoured the world to bring them to justice. Silver was only a child when her mother died in her arms, the victim of a terrorist attack. From that moment she devoted her entire life to preparing for the day she would take over the Wild Pack, training in all forms of martial arts and becoming an expert in the use of many different weapons. Silver began her leadership of the Wild Pack by continuing the fight to bring former Nazis to justice, but as the years passed she expanded the scope of the Wild Pack. She formed Silver Sable International, a company that provided security, apprehended wanted felons, and recovered stolen property for foreign governments, major corporations, and private individuals. Her company eventually became Symkaria's primary source of income and any citizen could be drafted into its service. She later drowned, sacrificing herself while fighting the Rhino with Spider-Man. Madame Web suggested that she may have survived the incident. **TD, MF**

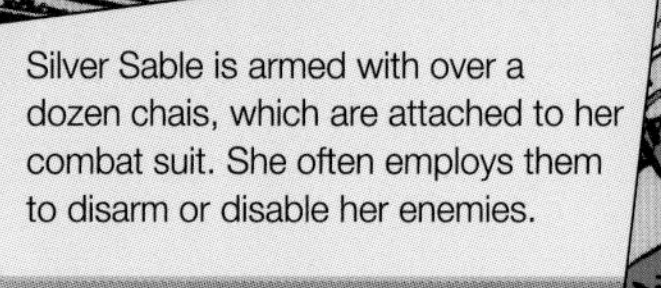

I'D BETTER USE A CHAI TO DISARM THE OTHERS BEFORE ANYONE GETS HURT!

Silver Sable is armed with over a dozen chais, which are attached to her combat suit. She often employs them to disarm or disable her enemies.

SILVER SAMURAI

Master with a deadly katana blade

FACTFILE

SILVER SAMURAI

REAL NAME
Keniuchio Harada

OCCUPATION *Mercenary*

BASE *Mobile*

HEIGHT *6 ft 6 in*

WEIGHT *250 lbs*

EYES *Brown*

HAIR *Black*

FIRST APPEARANCE
Daredevil #111 (July 1974)

POWERS
Body generates tachyon field that he focuses through his sword; skilled in ways of samurai—master of bushido and kenjutsu.

The illegitimate mutant son of a Japanese crimelord—and the half-brother of Mariko Yashida—Keniuchio (or Ken) mastered bushido before becoming a mercenary whose assignments included work for Hydra and pitted him against Daredevil, Spider-Man, and Black Widow. He often served as a bodyguard for Viper and once battled Spider-Man on the set of *Saturday Night Live*. After his father's death, Keniuchio struggled with Mariko for the leadership of Clan Yashida, but her lover Wolverine helped her prevail against him. When Mariko died, Keniuchio finally took on that mantle.

HERO OR CROOK

Keniuchio proved unsuited for the leadership of a large criminal organization. He reformed for a while and worked as a super hero in Japan. He was later brainwashed into believing that Professor X had telepathically compelled him to leave crime behind, so he returned to his old ways as a mercenary. However, he managed to lose his suspicion and become the head of security for the Prime Minister of Japan. Madame Hydra recruited him to become the leader of the Hand, but he refused that particular honor and helped the Avengers against them instead.

Keniuchio retained his powers after M-Day, but soon after that he lost a fight with Wolverine—along with his right hand. He survived, but was later attacked by black-suited samurai hired by the Red Right Hand—a group dedicated to destroying Wolverine and everything he held dear. He died defending his sister's grave.

The Silver Samurai met the new Avengers in their first adventure abroad.

SON OF THE SAMURAI

Keniuchio's son Shingen—Shin, for short, named after Keniuchio's father—took on the identity of the Silver Samurai after the original's death. He joined with Wolverine's adopted daughter Amiko Kobayashi (whom he was dating) to become thieves, but they ran afoul of the Hand and had to be rescued by Wolverine.

Some time afterward, Shin joined Mystique in her efforts to recruit mutants to her side, and he later attended the Hellfire Academy run by Kade Killgore. This put him in direct conflict with Wolverine's Jean Grey School for Higher Learning. **AD, MF**

As the son of the original Silver Samurai, Shin Yashida wore a new suit of armor and relied more on high-tech devices.

Silvermane

A leader of the Maggia crime syndicate, the elderly Silvermane ordered the theft of an ancient tablet bearing a formula for a youth serum. He forced Dr. Curt Connors to create the serum and drank it. As a horrified Spider-Man watched, Silvermane grew younger and younger until he seemingly disappeared completely. Fortunately the serum had a boomerang effect, and Silvermane rapidly aged back into his forties.

Silvermane briefly took over a New York-based splinter group of Hydra and then vainly attempted to unite New York City's organized crime under his leadership. He fell from a great height while fighting the third Green Goblin and Spider-Man. His injuries undid the effects of the youth serum, causing him to revert to old age. Nearly slain by the vigilante Dagger (*see* Cloak and Dagger), Silvermane had his brain, face, and vital organs transplanted into a robotic body. He was thought killed in a gang war with the Owl after his body was dropped into a garbage compactor. He seemed to reappear later, but it was only a trick by Mysterio. His head later turned up in a dump, however, still alive.

Silvermane counts Spider-Man, Daredevil, Cloak and Dagger, the Punisher, and the Kingpin among his foes. He is also the father of Joseph Manfredi, the criminal Blackwing. **PS, MF**

As a cyborg, the once frail Silvermane has amazing strength.

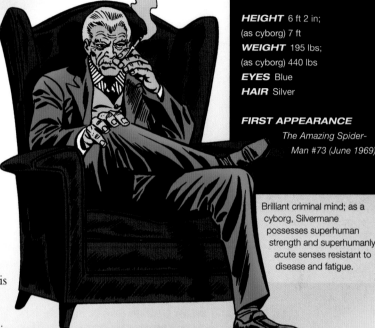

FACTFILE

REAL NAME
Silvio Manfredi

OCCUPATION
Criminal leader and mastermind

BASE
New York City

HEIGHT 6 ft 2 in;
(as cyborg) 7 ft
WEIGHT 195 lbs;
(as cyborg) 440 lbs
EYES Blue
HAIR Silver

FIRST APPEARANCE
The Amazing Spider-Man #73 (June 1969)

POWERS
Brilliant criminal mind; as a cyborg, Silvermane possesses superhuman strength and superhumanly acute senses resistant to disease and fatigue.

Sin

After her washerwoman mother died in childbirth, Synthia's father—the Red Skull—placed the infant girl into the care of Susan Scarbo, later known as Mother Night. When Synthia reached her teens, the Red Skull returned to claim her. He then used a strange machine to accelerate her aging and grant her superpowers, transforming her into Mother Superior. Encouraged by his success, he repeated the process on four orphaned girls and used them to form a team of Super Villains named the Sisters of Sin.

When Captain America later used the same machine to reverse the Skull's attempts to age him to death, Synthia and the other Sisters of Sin reverted to girlhood again. This cost Synthia her powers, but she still returned to a reformed Sisters of Sin—under Mother Night's leadership—as Sister Sin.

SHIELD tried to reform her by erasing her memories, but her lover Crossbones kidnapped her and tortured her until she recovered them. She was later injured in the blast that killed her father, scarring her face and transforming her into a new Red Skull, determined to carry on her father's legacy. **MF**

Since the Red Skull ordered Crossbones to retrain Sin, she has been deadlier than ever and central to the Skull's plans.

FACTFILE

REAL NAME
Synthia Schmidt

OCCUPATION
Terrorist

BASE
Mobile

HEIGHT 5 ft 8 in
WEIGHT 120 lbs
EYES Green
HAIR Red

FIRST APPEARANCE
Captain America #290 (February 1984) as Mother Superior; Captain America #355 (July 1989) as Sin

POWERS
As Mother Superior: intangibility, telepathy, telekinesis, and teleportation. These powers have been lost.
As Sin: experienced with a range of weapons.

Due to years of training, Sin is one of the world's deadliest killers.

SILVER SURFER

Sentinel of the Spaceways

SILVER SURFER

FACTFILE

REAL NAME
Norrin Radd

OCCUPATION
Spacefaring adventurer

BASE
Mobile

HEIGHT 6 ft 4 in
WEIGHT 225 lbs (variable)
EYES Silver (blue as Radd)
HAIR None (black eyebrows as Radd)

FIRST APPEARANCE
Fantastic Four #48 (March 1966)

POWERS

Navigates the galaxy at faster-than-light speeds, riding virtually indestructible board; can channel cosmic energy to augment strength, heal others, and restructure matter.

ALLIES/FOES

ALLIES Fantastic Four, Shalla-Bal, Alicia Masters, Al B Harper, the Defenders, Mantis, Nova

Foes Galactus, Mephisto, Loki, Terrax, Yarro Gort, the Abomination, Doomsday Man

ISSUE #1

Pre-warned by Uatu the Watcher, the Fantastic Four stand ready for their first encounter with the herald of Galactus—the Silver Surfer.

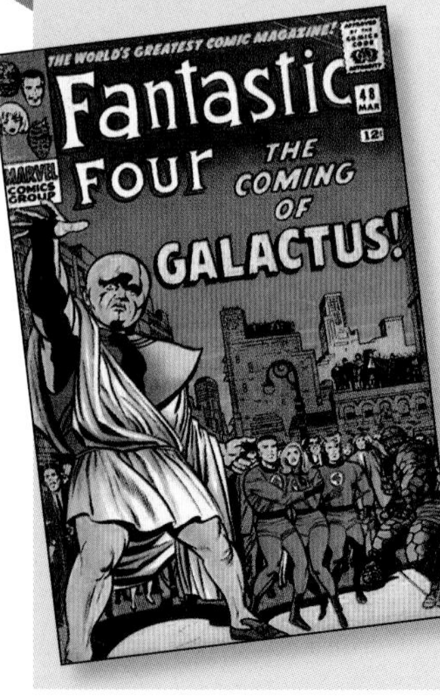

Bored and frustrated by life on Zenn-La, Norrin Radd sought a more challenging existence.

Over the years the Earth has played host to a variety of extraordinary beings: super-powered heroes and villains, mutants and Norse Gods, but few creatures have been as powerful yet restless as that enigmatic alien entity, the Silver Surfer. A galactic wanderer frustrated by the hedonism and complacency of his own world, the Silver Surfer developed a similarly ambivalent relationship with the Earth, where the good intentions of so many were sullied by the wanton malice of a few.

THE ZENN-LAVIANS

Born Norrin Radd on the faraway world of Zenn-La, even as a child Norrin was something of an outcast. Wanting for nothing, the Zenn-Lavians were an easy-going people, whereas Norrin hungered for a more meaningful, vibrant life. Even Norrin's lifelong companion, Shalla-Bal, could not calm his restless spirit. It was only when the Zenn-Lavians detected the approach of an alien entity—GALACTUS, Devourer of Worlds—that Norrin came into his own.

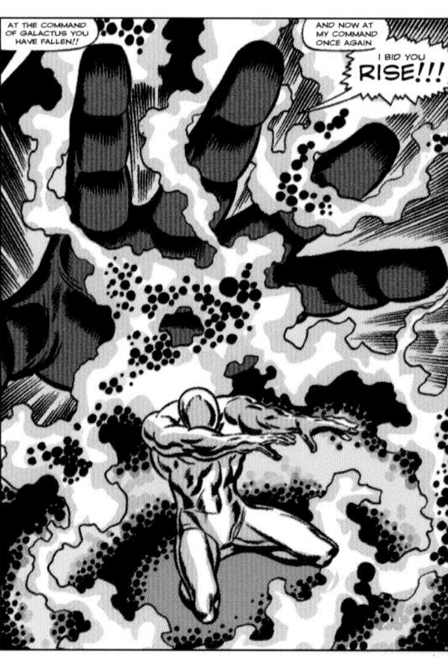

Galactus imbues Norrin Radd with the Power Cosmic, transforming him into the Silver Surfer.

In exchange for Galactus sparing Zenn-La, Norrin offered to become the entity's herald—to scour the galaxy for planets devoid of life but suitable for Galactus' needs. To empower Norrin for this role, Galactus plucked an old adolescent fantasy from the young Zenn-Lavian's mind and transformed him into a silver-skinned creature who could travel the galaxy on a silver board. Norrin became the Silver Surfer.

ESSENTIAL STORYLINES

- ***Fantastic Four #48–50*** The Silver Surfer and Galactus' first encounter with Earth.
- ***Silver Surfer Vol. 1 #1*** Stan Lee tells the story of the Silver Surfer's origins in the character's first stand-alone series.
- ***Silver Surfer Vol. 2 #1*** Returning to Zenn-La the Surfer discovers it has been devastated by the world-devouring Galactus.

Herald of Galactus

Over time it became increasingly difficult for the Surfer to find suitable worlds for his master, and so Galactus began to make subtle changes to the Silver Surfer's mind. He was made to care less about avoiding sentient life, and countless worlds and peoples were sacrificed. Until, that is, the Silver Surfer arrived on planet Earth.

There the Surfer encountered the Fantastic Four and Alicia Masters. Their compassion and heroism reawakened the Silver Surfer's suppressed emotions and he aligned himself with them. Threatened with the Ultimate Nullifier, a weapon used by Reed Richards (Mister Fantastic), Galactus was driven off, but not before punishing the Silver Surfer for his treachery: Galactus wrapped a field around the Earth to prevent the Silver Surfer from ever leaving. Galactus returned to Earth several times, wishing to reclaim the Silver Surfer as his herald. Each time the Fantastic Four helped drive Galactus away.

His conscience awoken by Alicia Masters, the Silver Surfer stood ready to oppose Galactus for the very first time.

Innocence Lost

The Silver Surfer arrived on Earth as something of an innocent. The malevolent Doctor Doom played on this naivety, befriending him and stealing his powers. When Doom attempted to leave the Earth he ran into Galactus' cosmic barrier, losing control of these powers and enabling the Silver Surfer to regain them.

As the Silver Surfer traveled the world, he became appalled by people's bigotry and cruelty. Hoping that humanity would improve if threatened by a common enemy, he transformed himself into humanity's nemesis. Only a "Sonic Shark" missile, created by Reed Richards, ended the threat that he posed.

Love Life

Although his heart remains with his first love, Shalla-Bal, during his interstellar voyages, the Silver Surfer has romanced several other women. The most significant of these was Alicia Masters who, during their first encounter, had revived him from his Galactus-induced mental stupor. For a time, Alicia journeyed across the stars with the Surfer, but she eventually decided to return to Earth. Years earlier, the Surfer had been linked to the Celestial Madonna, an Earth-born cosmic heroine, but she died during their battle against the Elders of the Universe. Tragedy also ended his relationship with Nova. A former Herald of Galactus, Nova died battling her successor as herald, the evil Morg.

The Celestial Madonna was also known as Mantis.

Freedom Regained

Essentially exiled to the Earth, the Silver Surfer never stopped yearning to travel among the stars once more. With Reed Richards' help he found a way of doing this, but his wanderings were not without upset. Returning to his home world Zenn-La, the Surfer discovered that, although his people still survived, Galactus had returned and ravaged the planet.

The Surfer's visit to Zenn-La was curtailed when he learned that his former lover, Shalla-Bal, had been kidnapped by the demon Mephisto—a creature bent on corrupting the Silver Surfer's soul. Arriving back on Earth, the Silver Surfer freed Shalla-Bal and provided her with some of his own cosmic power—sufficient to heal their home planet.

His exile on Earth over, the Silver Surfer set out to explore the cosmos.

Not the best of friends, the Silver Surfer and Galactus regularly face each other in battle.

Annihilator

When the Annihilation Wave threatened the galaxy, the Silver Surfer fought Galactus, Tenebrous (Lord of All Sorrows) and Aegis (Lord of the Darkness Between). In the aftermath, he joined a team of some of the greatest powers in the cosmos, the Annihilators.

The Silver Surfer often returns to Earth, either with Galactus or on his own, and sometimes works with the Defenders. He has even become close with Earth women from time to time, including Alicia Masters and Frankie Raye, who became another herald of Galactus under the name Nova.

The Silver Surfer fought alongside Galactus during the Chaos War, and he nursed him back to health afterward. In gratitude, Galactus released him from his service once more.

AD, MF

As Nova, Frankie Raye was one of Galactus' more recent heralds.

Sinister Six

Super Villain team out to get Spider-Man

Sinister Six

FACTFILE

ORIGINAL MEMBERS

DOCTOR OCTOPUS
Mastermind, mechanical arms.
VULTURE Mechanical wings.
ELECTRO Human dynamo.
KRAVEN THE HUNTER
Super-strong combatant.
LIZARD Bloodthirsty human/ reptile hybrid.
MYSTERIO Master of illusion.

BASE
Secret

FIRST APPEARANCE
The Amazing Spider-Man Annual #1 (January 1964)

Determined to beat Spider-Man, Doctor Octopus contacted five of the webslinger's greatest enemies and formed a team of Super Villains dedicated to destroying their common foe. He decided that each member of the Six would take on Spider-Man in turn, wearing him down until they could kill him. As the mastermind, Doctor Octopus, of course, would be the final foe. Despite starting out against the original Sinister Six without his powers, Spider-Man regained his abilities along with his self-confidence and prevailed against them.

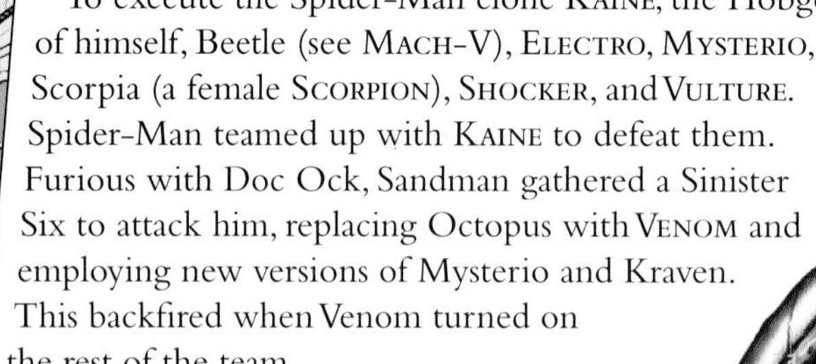

The original Sinister Six appeared in the first-ever Spider-Man annual.

Several Sinisters

The membership, size, and leadership of the team has varied, depending on the villains available. The second time Octopus gathered the six together, he replaced Kraven (who had died) with the Hobgoblin, but the Sandman, who was trying to reform, betrayed them all.

The third Sinister Six replaced the Sandman with a lizard-like alien named Gog. Armed with alien weapons, this group beat Spider-Man at first, and it eventually took the combined efforts of Spider-Man, the Fantastic Four, the Hulk, Nova, and Solo to end their spree.

To execute the Spider-Man clone Kaine, the Hobgoblin formed a Sinister Seven consisting of himself, Beetle (see Mach-V), Electro, Mysterio, Scorpia (a female Scorpion), Shocker, and Vulture. Spider-Man teamed up with Kaine to defeat them. Furious with Doc Ock, Sandman gathered a Sinister Six to attack him, replacing Octopus with Venom and employing new versions of Mysterio and Kraven. This backfired when Venom turned on the rest of the team.

SINISTER SIX
1 Sandman ***2*** Vulture
3 Doctor Octopus
4 Electro ***5*** Kraven
6 Mysterio

Deadly Dozen

The Green Goblin formed the Sinister Twelve. Mac Gargan (the new Venom) led the team to break Osborn out of jail. Boomerang, Chameleon, Electro, Hammerhead, Hydro-Man, Lizard, Tombstone, Sandman, Shocker, and Vulture rounded out the deadly dozen. Captain America, Daredevil, the Fantastic Four, Iron Man, and Yellowjacket rallied to help Spider-Man and stop the Goblin's plans.

During the Civil War, Doctor Octopus rallied a new team with help from Grim Reaper, Lizard, Shocker, Trapster, and Vulture. The rebel Avengers led by Captain America made short work of them.

The Avengers helped Spider-Man once more against the version of the Sinister Six formed just before Doctor Octopus' death. With Chameleon, Electro, Mysterio, Rhino, and Sandman by his side, Doc Ock held the entire world hostage.

After Doctor Octopus took over Spider-Man's body, Boomerang started a new group with Beetle, Living Brain, Overdrive, Shocker, and Speed Demon. Spider-Man stopped them and then started to capture Sinister Six members for some mysterious new plan.

TD, MF

THE SUPERIOR FOES OF SPIDER-MAN
1 Overdrive ***2*** Beetle ***3*** Speed Demon
4 Shocker ***5*** Boomerang

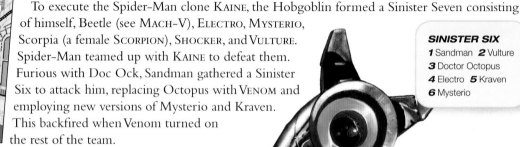

Sinister Syndicate

FIRST APPEARANCE Amazing Spider-Man #280 (Sept. 1986)

BASE New York City **MEMBERS AND POWERS**

Rhino Nearly invulnerable, with superhuman strength [1].

Beetle Armored, multi-weaponed battlesuit [2].

Speed Demon Able to run at superhuman speeds [3].

Boomerang An expert with his specially equipped boomerangs [4].

Hydro-Man Can convert all or part of body into water [5].

Shocker Gauntlets generate highly destructive vibrations [6].

After defeats by the Human Torch and Spider-Man, the Beetle decided to stop being a solo act and organize a super-team. Inspired by the Sinister Six, the Beetle called his group the Sinister Syndicate. The Beetle was soon contacted by international mercenary Jack O'Lantern who hired the Syndicate to assassinate Silver Sable. Spider-Man and the Sandman interfered and foiled this scheme. The Syndicate was then hired by Doctor Octopus to kidnap the royal family of Belgriun, a small European country. Once again, Spider-Man and Silver Sable defeated the Syndicate and eventually forced the team to disband. **TD**

Siryn

FIRST APPEARANCE Spider-Woman #37 (April 1981)

REAL NAME Theresa Rourke (Cassidy)

OCCUPATION Private investigator

BASE New York City **HEIGHT** 5 ft 7 in **WEIGHT** 130 lbs

EYES Blue **HAIR** Blond

SPECIAL POWERS/ABILITIES Combination of psionic ability and sonic waves produced by her voice can shatter steel, enable flight, and generate force blasts.

Theresa Rourke was born when her father, Sean Cassidy—Banshee—was on a secret mission. When her mother died, Theresa's uncle Black Tom Cassidy took her in and tried and failed to lead her into a life of crime. When Black Tom was arrested, he told her who her father was and Theresa and Sean were joyfully united. Teresa joined X-Force and served as its deputy leader. After that, she worked with X-Factor Investigations. She gave birth to a baby fathered by Jamie Madrox, the Multiple Man, but when he held the baby, it merged into his body. She later took the name Banshee after her father and, after becoming the latest incarnation of an Irish goddess called the Morrigan, disappeared. **AD, MF**

Sisters of Sin

FIRST APPEARANCE Captain America #294 (June 1984)

BASE Mobile **MEMBERS AND POWERS**

Raunch (formerly Sister Pleasure): Master hypnotist [1].

Hoodwink (formerly Sister Dream): Master hypnotist [2].

Slash (formerly Sister Agony): Has lacerating metal claw [3].

Torso (formerly Sister Death): Enhanced strength [4].

Sin (formerly Mother Superior): Ability to fire psionic bolts [5].

Mother Night (formerly Suprema): Ability to cloud minds.

The Sisters of Sin are the brainchildren of the Red Skull, created to spread his ideology of hate. Synthia Schmidt (*see* Sin), the Red Skull's daughter, took the name Mother Superior after receiving an artificial boost into adulthood. Four orphan girls received similar rapid-aging treatments. As the Sisters of Sin they battled Captain America and Nomad. After the Sisters had become teenagers again, the villain Suprema took control as Mother Night. The Sisters took new names, and founded Camp Rage to incite runaways to violent rebellion. **DW**

Six Pack

FIRST APPEARANCE Cable #1 (Oct. 1992) **BASE** Mobile

MEMBERS AND POWERS

Domino Can influence the laws of probability.

G. W. Bridge Skilled combatant and weapons expert.

Anaconda Can stretch limbs and use them to crush enemies.

Solo Able to teleport himself and weapons.

Hammer Weapons designer and technician.

Constrictor Has electrically powered cables mounted on wrists.

Originally known as the Wild Pack, Cable's mercenary team included him, Deadpool, Domino, Grizzly, Hammer, and Garrison Kane. Six Pack often clashed with the mutant villain Stryfe. On one mission, Stryfe threatened to kill Kane if he didn't receive a data disc, and Cable shot Hammer in the back to stop the trade. Outraged, the rest of Six Pack cut ties with Cable. A later incarnation of Six Pack, assembled by SHIELD, added Solo, Constrictor, and Anaconda under agent G. W. Bridge, but they broke up after Cable defeated them. **DW, MF**

Skaar

The son of the Hulk (who'd conquered the planet Sakaar) and Caiera—a warrior of the native Shadow People—Skaar was born after his father had left for Earth to exact revenge on the Illuminati for his mother's death (*see* World War Hulk). He emerged from a cocoon, already grown to the size of a 10-year-old boy. He failed to save Sakaar from Galactus and headed to Earth to kill the Hulk. Bruce Banner, his father, who had been robbed of the ability to become the Hulk by the Red Hulk, trained him how to kill the Hulk should he return, as an excuse to get to know the boy. In the end, surprised by the Hulk's compassion for the innocent, Skaar couldn't kill him. Skaar later joined the Green Goblin's Avengers while secretly working for Captain America. **MF**

FACTFILE

REAL NAME
Skaar

OCCUPATION
Warrior

BASE
Planet Sakaar

HEIGHT 6 ft 1 in
WEIGHT 500 lbs
EYES Brown
HAIR Black

FIRST APPEARANCE
World War Hulk #5 (November 2007)

SKAAR

POWERS

Skaar is a master warrior with superhuman strength and limited invulnerability. Like the Hulk, when calm he turns to a more human form.

Nothing on Sakaar could stand before Skaar's wrath.

Skrulls, The

Shape-changing alien race

SKRULLS, THE

FACTFILE

BASE
Tarnax IV, Andromeda Galaxy

FIRST APPEARANCE
Fantastic Four #2 (January 1962)

Skrull warships are designed to protect the paranoid species.

POWERS

Shapeshifting permits radical changes in size, shape, and color; lifespans reach 200 years on average.

The Skrulls are an ancient humanoid species from the Andromeda galaxy, with reptilian physiologies. The cosmic beings known as the CELESTIALS visited the species' birthworld of Skrullos long ago and created Skrullian equivalents to Earth's ETERNALS and DEVIANTS. The Deviant Skrulls exhibited the ability to shapeshift and soon wiped out all competing racial branches.

THE KREE WAR

After forging an interstellar empire, the Skrulls encountered the primitive KREE, who murdered the Skrull contact team and stole their starship technology. A Kree armada soon attacked the Skrulls, triggering the eons-long Kree-Skrull War. Skrull scientists later developed the first Cosmic Cube, which gained sentience and decimated the Skrull Empire, eventually evolving into the exceptionally powerful SHAPER OF WORLDS. The Skrulls bounced back from this tragedy, establishing an Imperial throneworld on Tarnax IV.

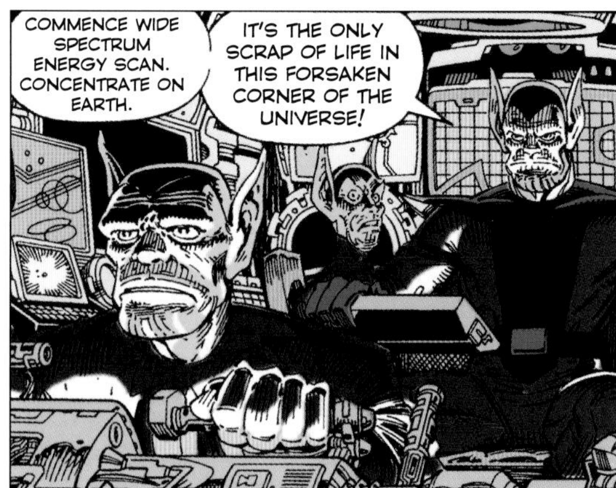

COMMENCE WIDE SPECTRUM ENERGY SCAN. CONCENTRATE ON EARTH.
IT'S THE ONLY SCRAP OF LIFE IN THIS FORSAKEN CORNER OF THE UNIVERSE!

The Skrulls have taken a secret role in Earthly affairs, using their shapeshifting powers to impersonate world leaders.

SECRET AGENTS

The Skrulls placed agents on Earth, but these were defeated by the FANTASTIC FOUR. In response, the Skrull emperor Dorrek VII created the SUPER-SKRULL, who possessed the combined powers of the Fantastic Four. The Skrulls also engineered an elite class of Warskrulls, agents that could duplicate the powers of other beings when they assumed those beings' shapes. After GALACTUS devoured Tarnax IV, the Skrull Empire fell into civil war. The mad Skrull Zabyk detonated a hyper-wave bomb that removed the shapeshifting ability from all Skrulls. The Super-Skrull escaped the bomb's effects and eventually managed to restore the species' shapeshifting powers.

Skrulls can alter their appearance to duplicate anyone, but can be shocked into dropping their disguise if they are hurt or knocked out.

WHICH IS WHY THE UNSUSPECTING EARTHMEN WILL NEVER KNOW THAT WE SKRULLS HAVE IMPERSONATED THEIR FAMOUS FANTASTIC FOUR.

During the ANNIHILATION, the Skrulls lost nearly all of their planets. They turned to VERANKE and made her their queen. Relying on Skrull prophecies, she led the SECRET INVASION to make Earth the new Skrull homeworld. The people of Earth banded together to root out the Skrulls and repel their attack, leaving the few remaining Skrulls homeless once more. AMATSU-MIKABOSHI then slew their gods. Small groups of them were later found on Earth, fleeing the advance of the BUILDERS during INFINITY. **DW, MF**

ESSENTIAL STORYLINES
- ***Avengers #89-97*** The devastating Kree-Skrull War reaches Earth, and the Avengers assemble to prevent innocents from being caught in the crossfire.
- ***Avengers Annual #14*** The insane Skrull warrior Zabyk detonates a hyper-wave bomb, removing the shapeshifting abilities of all Skrulls.
- ***Secret Invasion #1-8*** The Skrulls invade Earth.

Skids

FIRST APPEARANCE X-Factor #7 (August 1986)
REAL NAME Sally Blevins
OCCUPATION Adventurer **BASE** Mobile
HEIGHT 5 ft 5 in **WEIGHT** 115 lbs **EYES** Blue **HAIR** Blond
SPECIAL POWERS/ABILITIES Skids possesses a protective, frictionless force field which shields her from harm, and which she can extend to envelop others.

Born a mutant, Skids lived among the sewer-dwelling MORLOCKS until the Mutant Massacre by the MARAUDERS caused her to flee. Rescued by X-FACTOR, for a time she became a trainee with that team, and she fought alongside their junior members, the X-Terminators. Brainwashed into serving with the MUTANT LIBERATION FRONT, Skids eventually regained her freedom after her boyfriend Rusty COLLINS was killed battling HOLOCAUST, and she herself was injured. She kept her powers after M-Day and became an undercover agent of SHIELD. **TB, MF**

Slapstick

FIRST APPEARANCE Slapstick #1 (November 1992)
REAL NAME Steve Harmon
OCCUPATION Adventurer **BASE** Mobile
HEIGHT 5 ft 7 in **WEIGHT** 145 lbs **EYES** Blue **HAIR** Blond
SPECIAL POWERS/ABILITIES Indestructible, stretchable, and gains strength from electricity, plus superhuman strength, speed, endurance, and agility.

While facing the Overlord and his evil Clowns of Dimension X, Steve Harmon's molecules were transformed into unstable molecules. He also gained a pair of high-tech gloves: the left allowed him to change from human to Slapstick and back, while the right featured an extra-dimensional storage pocket. Steve managed to defeat the Overlord and rescue all of his captives. Later, he joined the NEW WARRIORS for a time, working with his friend SPEEDBALL. After the CIVIL WAR, Slapstick became one of the first of the FIFTY-STATE INITIATIVE recruits at Camp Hammond. Disillusioned with the program, he left and joined the rebuilt New Warriors. **MF**

Sloan, Fred

FIRST APPEARANCE Incredible Hulk #231 (January 1979)
REAL NAME Frederick Sloan
OCCUPATION Author **BASE** Unrevealed
HEIGHT/WEIGHT Unrevealed **EYES** Blue **HAIR** Blond
SPECIAL POWERS/ABILITIES Fred Sloan possesses no superhuman powers save a peculiarly positive outlook on life; possesses the strength and endurance of an average man.

Fred Sloan first encountered the incredible HULK while he was being thrown bodily out of a bar. The childlike Hulk interceded on the drifter's behalf, and the two became fast friends. Sloan helped the Hulk to elude the authorities, and the two traveled together for a time. Eventually they encountered WOODGOD and his band of similar human-animal hybrids known as the Changelings, and Sloan decided to remain with them. In time, he wrote a book, entitled *Hulk Encounter: A Survivor's Story,* which painted the green behemoth in an unusually positive light. **TB**

Skyhawk

FIRST APPEARANCE Thor #395 (September 1988)
REAL NAME Winston Manchester **OCCUPATION** Entrepreneur
BASE New York City **HEIGHT** (as Skyhawk) 6 ft 3 in
WEIGHT (as Skyhawk) 210 lbs **EYES** Blue **HAIR** Brown
SPECIAL POWERS/ABILITIES As Skyhawk, possesses superhuman strength and the ability to fly; formerly a high-achiever working 20 hours a day, he now leaves the office at 5 o'clock.

Businessman Manchester collapsed in the office and was taken to the same hospital where the god Hogun (*see* GODS OF ASGARD) was staying. Manchester opened his eyes to find that he was with two other patients. They had all attracted the attention of Seth, god of death, (*see* GODS OF HELIOPOLIS). Claiming that Hogun was a threat to the Earth, Seth branded their left palms with the sign of Aton, the glowing disc of the sun, and gave them all superhuman powers. Manchester and his teammates learned that Seth was the real menace and they helped THOR defeat him. **TD**

Slater, Jink

FIRST APPEARANCE The Incredible Hulk #36 (March 2002)
REAL NAME Jink Slater
OCCUPATION Professional assassin **BASE** Mobile
HEIGHT/WEIGHT Unrevealed **EYES** Brown **HAIR** Black
SPECIAL POWERS/ABILITIES Excellent marksman; expert with guns and knives; a formidable hand-to-hand combatant; above average in strength and endurance; ruthless in pursuit of his quarry.

Jink Slater was hired by unidentified parties to capture the HULK. Despite his objections, his employers ordered Slater to work with a partner, Sandra VERDUGO, on the assignment. Eventually, Slater and Verdugo found the Hulk in his human identity of Bruce Banner in a diner. Their attempt to capture him was thwarted by the arrival of DOC SAMSON. Not trusting his partner, Slater shot Verdugo in the head and escaped. Subsequently, Slater found Banner and Verdugo together in a cabin. Slater shot Verdugo in the shoulder. Verdugo retaliated by setting off explosives that killed Slater. **PS**

Smasher

FIRST APPEARANCE Avengers #1 (February 2013)
REAL NAME Isabel Kane
OCCUPATION Astronomer, Imperial Guard **BASE** Mobile
HEIGHT 5 ft 8 in **WEIGHT** 135 lbs **EYES** Blue **HAIR** Black
SPECIAL POWERS/ABILITIES Izzy wears Exospex, which grant her a life-support system and access to one power at a time: vision powers, energy blasts, hyperspace travel, superhuman durability, strength, and speed. Her suit also allows her to fly.

Smasher is a role in the SHI'AR Imperial Guard, in which a Superguardian of each type commands a number of Subguardians. The first known Smasher Superguardian was Vril Rokk, who served many years, until VULCAN killed him. The next, Salac Turr, attacked the wedding of RONAN THE ACCUSER and CRYSTAL and was slain by KARNAK. Izzy Kane—an astronomer who found a Smasher's Exospex on her family's farm—was the first human member of the Guard, and she quickly rose to Superguardian. She also served with the AVENGERS. **MF**

Smythe, Alistair

FIRST APPEARANCE The Amazing Spider-Man Annual #19 (1985) **REAL NAME** Alistair Smythe
OCCUPATION Criminal inventor **BASE** New York City
HEIGHT 6 ft **WEIGHT** 220 lbs **EYES** Brown **HAIR** Brown
SPECIAL POWERS/ABILITIES Ultimate Spider-Slayer armature provides enhanced strength, and features built-in cutting blades and web shooters.

Alistair Smythe grew up hating Spider-Man. His father, Professor Spencer Smythe, built the first robotic Spider-Slayer units, and Alistair continued that legacy. Following a stint in the employ of the Kingpin, Alistair constructed ever more deadly Spider-Slayers until an accident left him in a wheelchair. He fashioned a cyborg armature for himself and emerged as the Ultimate Spider-Slayer. He later rebuilt the Scorpion's costume for him and murdered J. Jonah Jameson's wife. The Superior Spider-Man (Doctor Octopus) killed him in a final battle. **DW, MF**

Smythe, Professor

FIRST APPEARANCE The Amazing Spider-Man #25 (June 1965)
REAL NAME Spencer Smythe
OCCUPATION Professor, criminal inventor
BASE New York City **HEIGHT** 5 ft 10 in **WEIGHT** 175 lbs
EYES Gray **HAIR** Gray
SPECIAL POWERS/ABILITIES Genius-level expertise in engineering and robotics.

Professor Spencer Smythe's life was marked by an irrational hatred for Spider-Man. He used his engineering expertise to construct the Spider-Slayer, a Spider-Man hunting robot, and persuaded *Daily Bugle* publisher J. Jonah Jameson to pay for it. He followed up with several improved generations of Spider-Slayers, but the radiation used in their construction gradually poisoned him. He died during a revenge plot hatched against both Spider-Man and Jameson, leaving his son Alistair (*see* Smythe, Alistair) to carry on his work. **DW**

Snarks

The Snarks are perennial enemies of the super-powered children of the Power Pack.

A malevolent, warlike, reptilian race, the Zn'rx or "Snarks" are based on a planet in the Milky Way galaxy known on Earth as Snarkworld. The Snarks first came to notice when their ages-long conflict with the horselike Kymellians spilled over to Earth.

The Queen Mother, Maraud, sent raiding parties to Earth in order to learn the secrets of a new scientific breakthrough discovered by Dr. James Power, and use it as a weapon against their ancient foes. Sent by his people to prevent this from happening, Kymellian champion Aelfyre Whitemane was slain by the Snarks, but not before he passed on his abilities to Dr. Powers' four children. These children, now known as the Power Pack, defeated the Snark menace. Thereafter, the Snarks became obsessed with taking Whitemane's powers for themselves, and repeatedly staged attacks on the Power children, to no avail.

Although convinced of their own importance, the Snarks remain only minor players on the galactic stage. **TB**

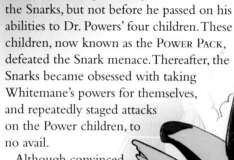

FACTFILE

REAL NAME
Zn'rx (pronounced "Snarks")

BASE
The planet Snarkworld

HEIGHT 8 ft (average)
WEIGHT 400 lbs (average)
EYES Red
HAIR None (green scales)

FIRST APPEARANCE
Power Pack #1 (August 1984)

SNARKS

POWERS

Snarks are larger, stronger, and live longer than human beings. As well as various high-tech weapons (their technology is generally more advanced than Earth's), they have a vicious array of teeth and sharp claws. Like Earth's reptiles they are cold-blooded and so are vulnerable to extremes of cold.

The Snarks were given their name by Aelfyre Whitemane after the monster in the famous poem "The Hunting of the Snark" by Lewis Carroll.

Snowbird

Nelvanna, goddess of the Northern Lights, mated with a human to produce a child that could defend humanity from the mystical Great Beasts. The infant, named Narya, was raised by Native American sorcerer Michael Twoyoungmen (Shaman). She grew to adulthood within a few years, and James MacDonald Hudson invited her and Shaman to join Alpha Flight. Narya took the name Snowbird, and the cover identity of Anne McKenzie, an officer in the Canadian Mounties. When Alpha Flight teammate Walter Langkowski (Sasquatch) fell under the mental control of Tanaraq, one of the Great Beasts, Snowbird slew his physical body.

Anne McKenzie married a fellow officer in the RCMP and they had a son. A menace called Pestilence subsequently took mental possession of Snowbird. Hudson's wife Heather defeated Pestilence by killing Narya's physical form. Langkowski's spirit took over Narya's resurrected body, becoming the new Sasquatch. Snowbird's spirit later gained a new body and returned to Alpha Flight. She was not with the team when the Collective (*see* Weapon Omega) destroyed it. During the Secret Invasion, she helped destroy the Skrull god Kly'bn. **PS, MF**

FACTFILE

REAL NAME
Narya

OCCUPATION
Goddess; adventurer

BASE
Canada

HEIGHT 5 ft 10 in
WEIGHT 108 lbs
EYES (Snowbird) White; (Anne McKenzie) blue
HAIR Pale blonde; (in animal form) White

FIRST APPEARANCE
(as Anne McKenzie) Uncanny X-Men #120 (April 1979)

SNOWBIRD

POWERS

Snowbird can assume the form of a human woman or of any animal native to the Canadian Arctic. She has superhuman strength and the ability to fly.

FACTFILE

KEY MEMBERS

GENERAL CHEN
The first Supreme Serpent; a grossly overambitious individual.

DAN DUNN
Co-leader; talk-show host, white right-winger.

MONTAGUE HALE
Co-leader and black, left-winger.

J.C. PENNYSWORTH
Head of Richmond Enterprises; sponsor of Sons of the Satan.

HATE-MONGER
Foments hatred and anger.

RUSSELL DABOIA
Mystic powers.

SKINHEAD
Superhuman neo-Nazi.

BASE California

FIRST APPEARANCE
Avengers #32 (September 1966)

Sons of the Serpent

"As the first serpent drove Adam and Eve from Eden, so shall we drive all foreigners from this land." This is the mantra of the Sons of the Serpent—an organization fueled by hatred and sponsored by a few wealthy businessmen. Targeting non-whites, immigrants, and the infirm, the Sons of the Serpent is dedicated to making the US a citadel of white racial supremacy.

During their first bid for power, they took Captain America hostage to try to force the Avengers into publicly supporting their evil cause. When this failed, the Sons developed further plots aimed at dividing America and black against white, one of which actually culminated in a mind-controlled Captain America fighting against his black partner, the Falcon. After repeated knock backs, their plans have become increasingly desperate. They have even resorted to crude mysticism, perhaps a sign of their waning influence. **AD**

Serpent Signs can be used to record and leave messages.

Southern, Candy

FIRST APPEARANCE X-Men #31 (April 1967)
REAL NAME Candace Southern **OCCUPATION** CEO Southern Industries **BASE** New York City, Colorado Rocky Mountains
HEIGHT/WEIGHT Unknown **EYES** Blue **HAIR** Black
SPECIAL POWERS/ABILITIES Normal human strength of woman who engaged in regular exercise. Had great leadership abilities.

Archangel Warren Worthington was unable to prevent Candy's murder.

Candace "Candy" Southern began dating Warren Worthington III when they were teenagers. Southern discovered that Worthington was the Angel, a member of X-Men, when his uncle, the original Dazzler abducted her. Southern and Worthington later shared a home in the Rocky Mountains which became the Defenders' headquarters. Southern was the team's business manager and government liaison. She was killed by Worthington's enemy, Cameron Hodge. Southern's mind was assimilated into the group consciousness of the techno-organic Phalanx. She sacrificed herself to destroy Hodge. **PS**

Soviet Super Soldiers

Created to be the Soviet Union's answer to the Avengers, the Soviet Super-Soldiers functioned as that nation's defenders through much of the latter part of the Cold War. Eventually, questioning some of the orders given to them by the State, they rebelled, and began to operate independently. The Russian government sent their replacement team, the Supreme Soviets, to reclaim the members of the Soviet Super Soldiers and bring them back into line—an attempt that met with failure.

Thereafter, with the fall of communism and the dissolution of the Soviet Union, the surviving members of both the Soviet Super Soldiers and the Supreme Soviet joined forces with other new heroes to become first the People's Protectorate, then the Winter Guard, still dedicated to using their great powers to defend their homeland, no matter who ruled it. **TB**

SOVIET SUPER SOLDIERS
1 Red Guardian ***2*** Unicorn ***3*** Ursa Major ***4*** Vanguard ***5*** Crimson Dynamo ***6*** Darkstar ***7*** Synthesizer ***8*** Perun ***9*** Titanium Man (The Gremlin) ***10*** Vostok ***11*** Fantasma ***12*** Blind Faith ***13*** Firefox ***14*** Sibercat ***15*** Stencil

FACTFILE

NOTABLE MEMBERS

CRIMSON DYNAMO (5)
In armor, has superhuman strength, durability, and can fly.

URSA MAJOR (3)
Transforms into a large bear; retains his intelligence while in bear form.

VANGUARD (8)
Forcefield repels virtually all electromagnetic and kinetic energy. By crossing his hammer and sickle in front of his body, he can redirect energy repelled by his natural force field

DARKSTAR (6)
Manipulates extradimensional energy called the Darkforce.

TITANIUM MAN (GREMLIN) (9)
Armor provided superhuman strength, durability flight; fired force blasts from hands.

BASE
The former Soviet Union, now Russia

FIRST APPEARANCE
Incredible Hulk #258 (April 1981)

Space Phantom

FIRST APPEARANCE Avengers #2 (November 1963)
REAL NAME Unknown **OCCUPATION** Agent of Immortus
BASE Limbo **HEIGHT** 6 ft 6 in **WEIGHT** 215 lbs **EYES** Blue
HAIR Red **SPECIAL POWERS/ABILITIES** Space Phantom can change his appearance to look like any living being. If they have superpowers, then he assumes those powers as well. The being whose form is taken is instantly sent to the dimension of Limbo.

The Space Phantom is an alien from the planet Phantus, which shifted into the timeless dimension of Limbo when the space-time continuum ruptured. Or so it was thought. There are actually several Space Phantoms, and anyone trapped in Limbo for too long forgets their past life and becomes one. IMMORTUS took advantage of this to mold them into his servants and send them out to kidnap others for his examination. Since they can impersonate anyone, including each other, it's difficult to determine which Space Phantoms are responsible for what. **MF**

Spaceknights

FIRST APPEARANCE Rom #1 (December 1979)
BASE The planet Galador
NOTABLE MEMBERS
Breaker Red, with radiation powers. **Firefall** Red, with magical fire. **Rom** Silver, with neutralizer gun. **Scanner** Blue, with incredible senses. **Seeker** Red, with missiles.
Starshine Golden, with magical light. **Terminator** Black, with optic blasts. **Unseen** White, with invisiblity. **Ikon** Silver, wields an energized polearm
SPECIAL POWERS/ABILITIES The powers of the Spaceknights vary, but they usually include superhuman durability, endurance, speed, and strength, and each can expose the shape-changing Dire Wraiths and achieve spaceflight.

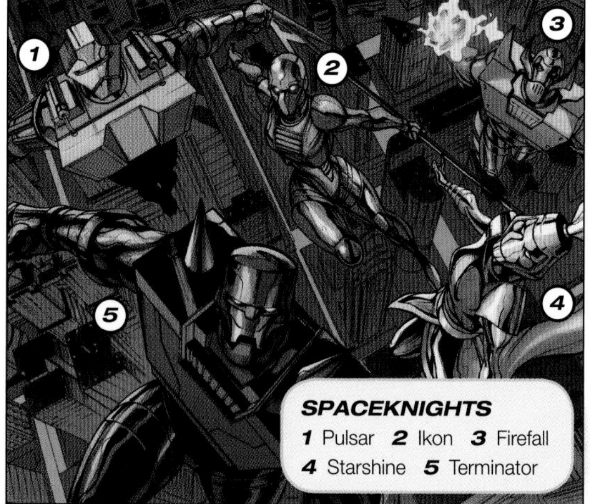

SPACEKNIGHTS
1 Pulsar ***2*** Ikon ***3*** Firefall
4 Starshine ***5*** Terminator

When the planet Galador came under threat of invasion by DIRE WRAITHS, a number of Galadorians volunteered to be transformed into cyborg warriors known as Spaceknights, each with their own style, weapon, and powers. The first of these was Rom, who became a legend among the Spaceknights. After rescuing Galador, the Spaceknights hunted down the Dire Wraiths scattered on planets throughout the galaxy, including Earth. There have been four generations of Spaceknights, improving them each time. The ancient BUILDERS later evaluated Galador and, judging it unworthy, destroyed it, including every Spaceknight on it. **MF**

With the help of the Annihilators, the Spaceknights made peace with the Dire Wraiths.

Spectrum

SPECTRUM

FACTFILE
REAL NAME
Monica Rambeau
OCCUPATION
Adventurer
BASE
New Orleans; New York City

HEIGHT 5 ft 8 in
WEIGHT 145 lbs
EYES Black
HAIR Black

FIRST APPEARANCE
The Amazing Spider-Man Annual #16 (1982)

POWERS
Photon can turn into any type of energy, including light, electricity, microwaves, radio waves, ultra-violet waves, gamma rays, or lasers. She can travel at the speed of light and fire blasts of whatever type of energy she becomes.

Monica Rambeau was working as a lieutenant in the New Orleans Harbor Patrol when she was struck by extradimensional energy from an "energy disruptor" weapon being developed by a South American terrorist. This exposure gave Rambeau her superpowers. Dubbed "Captain Marvel" by the media, she tried to put her new abilities to good use. Early in her career she met SPIDER-MAN who introduced her to the AVENGERS. They agreed to help train her to use her powers more skillfully. In time she became a valuable member of the AVENGERS, and was even their leader for several stints.

When Genis-Vell, the son of CAPTAIN MAR-VELL, wanted to use his father's name, Rambeau gladly gave up the name and became PHOTON. Later, Genis-Vell changed *his* name to Photon, forcing Rambeau to change her Super Hero name yet again, this time to PULSAR.

Monica led the team NEXTWAVE against the terrorist organization SILENT and the Beyond Corporation. She sided with CAPTAIN AMERICA during the CIVIL WAR but later registered with the FIFTY-STATE INITIATIVE. She has since changed her codename to Spectrum and joined Luke CAGE's Avengers team. To this day, she fears using her powers underwater after having nearly died while leading the Avengers against MARRINA, who'd become a sea monster. **MT, MF**

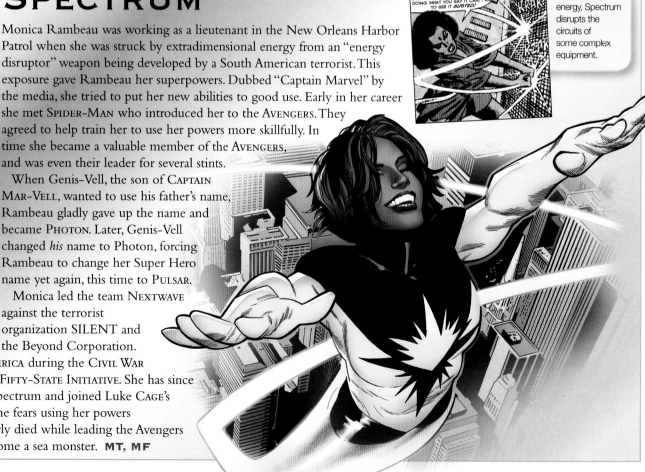

Firing electrical energy, Spectrum disrupts the circuits of some complex equipment.

Speed

FIRST APPEARANCE Young Avengers #10 (February 2006)
REAL NAME Thomas Shepherd
OCCUPATION Adventurer **BASE** New York City
HEIGHT 5 ft 10 in **WEIGHT** 182 lbs **EYES** Blue **HAIR** White
SPECIAL POWERS/ABILITIES Superhuman speed, plus atomic destabilization, which can cause touched objects to explode.

Tommy Shepherd thought he'd been born and raised in New Jersey to Frank and Mary Shepherd. In fact, he and Billy Kaplan (*see* WICCAN) of the YOUNG AVENGERS were products of the SCARLET WITCH's powers. Desperate for children, the Scarlet Witch had created twin boys for herself out of lost souls, but MEPHISTO eventually came to reclaim them. When the Scarlet Witch remade the world on M-Day, she remade the boys too, placing them in different homes. Soon after the VISION and SUPER-SKRULL had figured this out, Tommy took the codename Speed and joined his twin brother Billy in the Young Avengers. **MF**

Tommy bears a striking resemblance to his uncle Quicksilver.

Speedfreek

FIRST APPEARANCE Incredible Hulk #388 (December 1991) **REAL NAME** Leon Shappe
OCCUPATION Assassin **BASE** Mobile
HEIGHT/WEIGHT Unrevealed **EYES** Brown **HAIR** Brown
SPECIAL POWERS/ABILITIES Combat suit of titanium steel alloy that is virtually indestructible; rocket-powered boots enable flight and travel at 150 mph; uses two long adamantium blades.

Drug addict Leon Shappe stole a sophisticated combat suit from an inventor and became the assassin Speedfreek. He clashed with the HULK a few times. When a protestor erroneously gunned down Shappe's daughter outside an abortion clinic, the Hulk stopped him from murdering the killer. While dodging Speedfreek's blades, the Hulk threw a car battery at him. Speedfreek sliced right through it with his blades, accidentally showering himself with battery acid. He was part of the band of villains the NEW WARRIORS were battling in Stamford, Connecticut, when NITRO destroyed the place. Speedfreek died in the blast. **AD, MF**

Speedball

FIRST APPEARANCE The Amazing Spider-Man Annual #22 (1988)
REAL NAME Robert Baldwin **OCCUPATION** High-school student **BASE** New York City, formerly Springdale, Connecticut
HEIGHT 5 ft 6 in **WEIGHT** 133 lbs **EYES** Blue **HAIR** Blond
SPECIAL POWERS/ABILITIES Personal force field allows him to absorb all kinetic energy directed at him and reflect it back at a greater velocity, which he often does by bouncing off objects.

Bombarded with energy bubbles from another dimension, Robert Baldwin gained strange powers. Once he learned to control them, he created a costume and took the name Speedball, becoming a crimefighter in his hometown. He co-founded the NEW WARRIORS and was with them when NITRO exploded, destroying a city and launching the CIVIL WAR. Surviving Nitro's blast, Baldwin joined the THUNDERBOLTS, calling himself PENANCE and donning a suit of armor with 612 internal spikes, one for every person who had died in the explosion. He later returned to being Speedball and worked at the AVENGERS Academy, then reformed the New Warriors. **TD, MF**

Speed Demon

FIRST APPEARANCE The Amazing Spider-Man #222 (Nov. 1981)
REAL NAME James Sanders
OCCUPATION Professional criminal **BASE** New York City
HEIGHT 5 ft 11 in **WEIGHT** 175 lbs **EYES** Black **HAIR** Gray
SPECIAL POWERS/ABILITIES A super speedster, able to run at up to 160 mph; also possesses superhuman strength.

The GRANDMASTER gave James Sanders his powers when he recruited the chemist for his Squadron Sinister. Sanders called himself the WHIZZER at first, but then changed it to Speed Demon. He regularly fought SPIDER-MAN and later joined the SINISTER SYNDICATE. After that, he took up with BARON VON STRUCKER's THUNDERBOLTS, but he returned to the Squadron Sinister when the Grandmaster called him again. Speed Demon tried to help them find the Wellspring of Power, but the Thunderbolts stopped him. **DW, MF**

Sphinx

FIRST APPEARANCE Nova #6 (October 1999)
REAL NAME Anath-Na Mut
OCCUPATION Wizard **BASE** Mobile flying pyramid
HEIGHT 7 ft 2 in **WEIGHT** 450 lbs **EYES** Red **HAIR** None
SPECIAL POWERS/ABILITIES Enhanced strength; Ka stone permitted immortality, flight, telepathy, energy transference, and the ability to fire concussive beams.

Anath-Na Mut, an ancient Egyptian mutant given further powers by the Caretaker of Arcturus, served in the court of Ramses II until his failure to defeat Moses branded him an exile. He became the immortal Sphinx through the energies of the Ka stone, wandering for five thousand years until absorbing the extraterrestrial Xandar living computer with unwitting help from the hero NOVA. Now nearly omnipotent, the Sphinx met defeat at GALACTUS' hands. Later, Anath-Na Mut returned to life. When he merged with his reincarnated Egyptian lover, Meryet Karim (Sphinx II), the two formed the "Omni-Sphinx." **DW**

SPIDER-GIRL, *see page 342*

SPIDER-MAN

Your friendly neighborhood webslinger

SPIDER-MAN

FACTFILE

REAL NAME
Peter Benjamin Parker

OCCUPATION
Freelance photographer, science teacher

BASE
New York City

HEIGHT 5 ft 10 in
WEIGHT 170 lbs
EYES Hazel
HAIR Brown

FIRST APPEARANCE
Amazing Fantasy #15 (August 1962)

POWERS

Possesses the proportionate strength, speed, agility, and reflexes of a spider. Can cling to any surface and generate organic webbing. Also possesses a "spider-sense" that warns him of danger and can psychically align him with his environment. Invented spider-tracers that he can track across the city with his spider-sense.

ALLIES/FOES

ALLIES Ben and May Parker, Mary Jane Parker, Captain America, the Avengers, the Fantastic Four, the X-Men, Eugene "Flash" Thompson, Betty Brant Leeds.

FOES Chameleon, Vulture, Doctor Octopus, Sandman, Kingpin, Green Goblin, Lizard, Electro, Kraven the Hunter, Black Cat, Venom, Mysterio, Carnage, Scrier, Judas Traveller.

ISSUE #1

While attending a scientific demonstration, Peter Parker was bitten by a spider that had been exposed to radioactivity. Feeling nauseous, the teenager immediately headed home and began to exhibit the most amazing powers—like the ability to stick to walls and crawl up sheer surfaces!

Before gaining his spider-powers, Peter Parker was weaker than most of the kids his age.

Peter Parker's parents died in a plane crash while he was still a child. When they said goodbye at the airport, his parents told him to be a good boy for his Aunt May and Uncle Ben PARKER, who later raised him as their own son. Peter always thought of his Uncle Ben as his best friend. Not only did Ben Parker spend quality time with the boy, he had a great sense of humor and spent many hours telling jokes and pulling gags on Peter, who developed a real appreciation for quips and pranks. Peter studied hard in school and became an honor student. Although his teachers praised him, the other students had little use for a know-it-all like puny Parker. The girls thought him too quiet, and the boys considered him a wimp.

ORIGIN OF SPIDER-MAN

On the day his life changed forever, Peter went to a science exhibition by himself where he was bitten by a common house spider that had been exposed to a massive dose of radiation. Within a few hours, Peter discovered that he could stick to walls and had gained other amazing arachnid abilities.

Anxious to cash in on his new powers he designed a distinctive costume that concealed his identity, built a pair of web-shooters and went into showbusiness using the Amazing Spider-Man as his stage name.

One night, after a performance, he was walking toward an elevator when a security guard asked him to stop a fleeing man. However, Peter Parker did nothing and the burglar escaped.

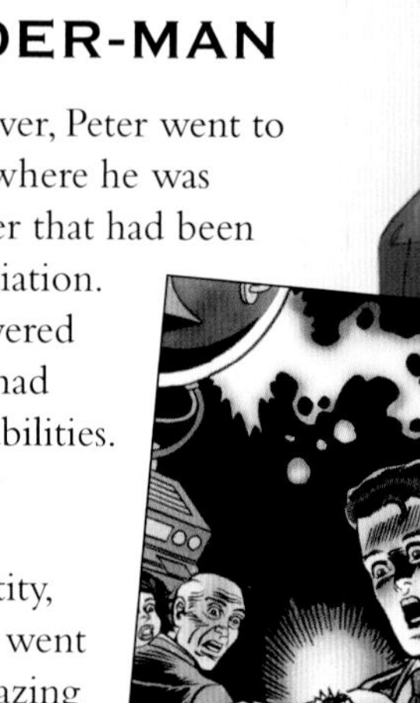

Peter began to suspect that his powers might be the result of paranormal forces.

MY FAULT -- ALL MY FAULT! IF ONLY I HAD STOPPED HIM WHEN I COULD HAVE! BUT I DIDN'T -- AND NOW -- UNCLE BEN -- IS DEAD...

A few days later the same thief murdered Peter's Uncle Ben! Filled with remorse, Peter vowed that he would never allow another innocent person to suffer because Spider-Man had failed to act. He had learned, in the hardest possible way, to use his great powers in a responsible manner.

High-School Hero

Spider-Man soon found himself battling criminals such as the Chameleon, the Vulture, Doctor Octopus, the Sandman, Doctor Doom, the Lizard, Electro, Mysterio, the Green Goblin, the Scorpion. and many more. He attempted to join the Fantastic Four and began a feud with the Human Torch.

J. Jonah Jameson, publisher of the *Daily Bugle,* hated masked vigilantes and claimed Spider-Man was a menace to the public. Peter saw an opportunity to exploit Jameson's campaign and began taking pictures of himself as Spider-Man. He was soon supporting himself by selling these pictures to the *Daily Bugle* on a freelance basis.

Peter eventually graduated from Midtown High with the highest scholastic average in the school's history. However, he almost missed the graduation ceremony. While the other seniors were donning caps and gowns, he was busy battling the Molten Man. He won his fight and arrived at the ceremony just in time to learn that he had won a full scholarship to Empire State University.

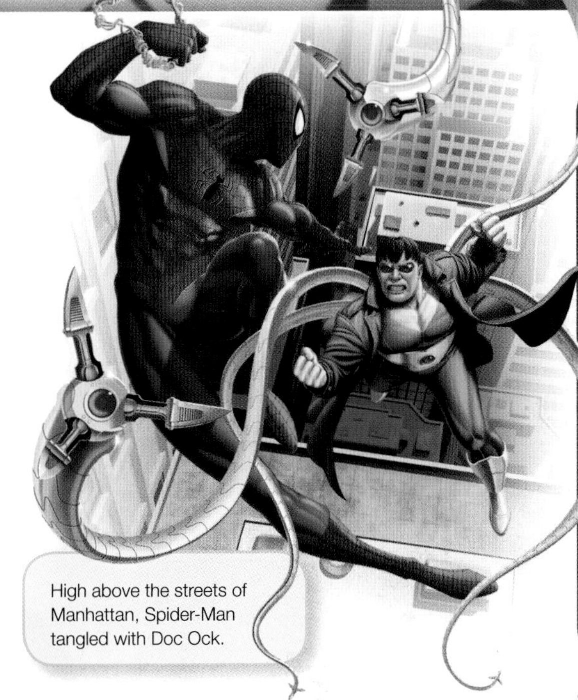

High above the streets of Manhattan, Spider-Man tangled with Doc Ock.

ESSENTIAL STORYLINES

- ***Amazing Spider-Man #31–33*** Spider-Man battles the Master Planner in order to obtain a rare serum that can save Aunt May's life.
- ***Amazing Spider-Man: Fearful Symmetry or Kraven's Last Hunt (tpb)*** Kraven the Hunter kidnaps Spider-Man and takes his place in a battle against the deadly Vermin.
- ***Amazing Spider-Man: The Saga of the Alien Costume (tpb)*** Spider-Man learns that his new black costume is actually an alien symbiote.
- ***Amazing Spider-Man vs. Venom (tpb)*** Spider-Man meets his match when Venom enters his life.
- ***Amazing Spider-Man: Identity Crisis (tpb)*** When a $5 million bounty is placed on his head for a murder he didn't commit, Spider-Man must adopt four new costumed identities to find the real murderer.
- ***Amazing Spider-Man: Coming Home (tpb)*** Spider-Man meets the man called Ezekiel and learns that there may be a lot more to his origin than he ever realized.

The Green Goblin murdered Gwen Stacy, Peter's first true love.

College Years And Beyond

While in college, Peter met Mary Jane Watson (his future wife), but began to date Gwen Stacy. (Gwen would later die tragically at the hands of the Green Goblin.) Peter became best friends with Harry Osborn and later learned that the Green Goblin was secretly Harry's father Norman. Spider-Man also encountered such villains as Kingpin, the Rhino, the Shocker, Silvermane and the Prowler.

After graduating from college, Peter encountered the acrobatic cat burglar Black Cat (his girlfriend for a while), and the criminals Hydro-Man, Speed Demon and the Hobgoblin. He also battled the unstoppable Juggernaut and cosmically-powered Firelord. He temporarily donned a new black costume that possessed some additional new powers, but later proved to be an alien symbiote. Meanwhile, his relationship with the beautiful model Mary Jane Watson had grown serious and they were married.

Further Developments

After leading a European crime cult for many years, Norman Osborn reentered Peter's life. Peter also met a man called Ezekiel who claimed that Spider-Man's powers were the result of magic and not a radioactive spider. Peter later confronted the Queen, who had the power to control insects and she mutated him into a giant spider. After returning to his human form, Peter learned that his powers and strength had been increased and that he had gained the ability to produce organic webbing. Peter also joined a new Avengers team.

After a battle with the mysterious, super-strong, vampiric villain Morlun, in which Peter appeared to have been killed, Peter temporarily accepted a new armored costume and a job working for Tony Stark (*see* Iron Man). However he has since returned to his traditional look. **TD**

The Alien Suit

Along with other heroes, Spider-Man was transported to a planet created by a near-omnipotent being called the Beyonder and forced to fight in a series of "Secret Wars". When his original red and blue costume was torn in battle, the web-spinner tried to repair it, but mistakenly activated a device that released a little black ball. The ball spread across him, duplicating the costume worn by the Julia Carpenter Spider-Woman.

Spider-Man's new suit could instantly mimic any kind of clothing, could carry his camera and spare change, was equipped with its own web-shooters and possessed a seemingly endless supply of webbing. He eventually discovered that the alien suit was a symbiote with a mind of its own. Spider-Man had to enlist the scientific help of Mr. Fantastic to remove it, using soundwaves at a certain frequency.

Rejected by Spidey, the symbiote grafted itself to Eddie Brock to become Venom (top).

SPIDER-MAN

Peter sided with Iron Man (Tony Stark) during the Civil War, even going so far as to register with the government and expose his true identity during a televised press conference. He quickly came to regret this decision when he saw the tactics the pro-registration forces used to win, and he switched sides to join Captain America's resistance. For a short time, he returned to his black costume while he, Mary Jane, and Aunt May went into hiding, but he soon returned to his red and blue suit.

Peter heeded his spider-sense and dodged the bullet. It hit Aunt May instead.

Aunt May Shot

Besides the government hounding him, Peter now had to deal with the fact that all his old foes knew who he was. From inside prison, the Kingpin hired an assassin, who waited outside the hotel room in which Peter, Mary Jane, and Aunt May were staying. When Peter's guard was down, he fired. Peter's spider-sense enabled him to dodge the bullet, but it struck Aunt May. Peter and Mary Jane rushed her to the hospital, where the doctor informed them that she was too frail to survive.

I TRUSTED YOU! I LET YOU GET CLOSE TO ME... YOU WERE LIKE A FATHER TO ME!
I TRUSTED YOU WHEN YOU SAID I HAD TO EXPLORE MY IDENTITY! THAT IT WAS THE ONLY EAY! I KEPT IT SECRET TO PROTECT MAY, AND MJ, BUT YOU SAID THEY'D BE SAFE! YOU SAID--

Peter Parker tangled up Iron Man in his webs, forcing Tony Stark to listen to his pleas for financial help to save Aunt May's life.

Needing money to pay for Aunt May's treatment, Peter turned to the wealthiest man he knew: Tony Stark. Tony immediately changed into Iron Man and tried to arrest Peter, but Peter managed to entangle Iron Man with his new webs, which now sprang directly from his wrists rather than from a webshooter. While Iron Man was trapped, Peter accused Tony of misleading him into making the worst mistake of his life. Then he demanded that Tony help Aunt May.

Tony refused, saying that he couldn't be seen aiding and abetting a known criminal like Peter. Breaking free from the webs, he flew off without trying to arrest Peter again, but he made it clear that he could not help. Later, Tony's butler, Edwin Jarvis—who had been dating Aunt May—arrived at the hospital with a check for two million dollars to help pay for her care. Despite the money, however, the doctor believed that Aunt May would not live long.

Mephisto's Deal

Torn apart with guilt over Aunt May's shooting, Peter scoured the city for a cure. He visited Doctor Strange, who transported Spider-Man's astral form around the globe to ask for help, but no one could do anything to save her. Peter even tried to travel back in time to stop the shooting, but failed.

Then Mephisto approached Peter and Mary Jane with an offer. He would save Aunt May and alter reality so that no one would remember that Peter was Spider-Man. All he wanted in exchange was their greatest source of happiness: their marriage.

Searching their souls, Peter and Mary Jane agreed to Mephisto's offer. The next morning, Peter awoke alone—but with Aunt May alive and well and cooking him a stack of wheatcakes—and with no one aware that anything had ever been different.

All Change

While Mephisto had supposedly only made a couple of changes, their effect was to alter Peter's life drastically. He was alone once again, living at his Aunt May's and looking for an apartment in Manhattan. His old friend Harry Osborn had returned after being presumed dead. And without Mary Jane in his life, Peter was unlucky in love.

An anguished Peter and Mary Jane waited by Aunt May's hospital bed, realizing that only a miracle could save her. It would come from a most unexpected source.

Tired of bargaining for souls, Mephisto demanded something far more rare from Peter and Mary Jane: the pure happiness found in their true love for each other.

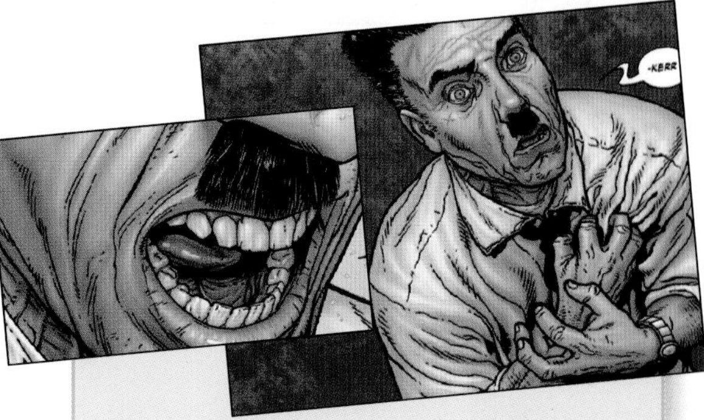

Peter saved Jameson's life by giving him CPR after he collapsed during an argument. Later, as Spider-Man, he had to do so again when he inadvertently told Jameson that his wife had sold the *Daily Bugle* while he was ill.

Some things, however, stayed the same. With the *Daily Bugle* having cash troubles, J. Jonah Jameson hadn't paid Peter for several photos he'd bought. When Peter confronted Jameson about the money he was owed, they fell into a shouting match, and Jameson collapsed from a heart attack. Jameson survived, but the paper had to be sold, and Peter wound up working as a paparazzo. He soon gave that up to become a photographer for Ben Urich's new paper, *Front Line.*

Altered States

Many of Spider-Man's foes cropped up soon after Peter's life changed. With his secret identity once more intact, however, he could fight them on his own terms.

Aunt May now did volunteer work at a homeless shelter, working under the philanthropist Martin Li, who was secretly Chinatown crimelord Mr. Negative. Eddie Brock returned, no longer as Venom but as the new Anti-Venom. Norman Osborn (*see* Green Goblin) showed up as the leader of the Thunderbolts and even, eventually, the Avengers—a separate team from the secret Avengers with which Spider-Man still worked. He also battled a new villain called Menace, who used many of the Green Goblin's old tricks.

A new hero—Jackpot—entered Peter's life too. As she was a tall, beautiful redhead, Peter suspected her of actually being Mary Jane, with whom he still had a romantic—but apparently sour—history. Instead, she turned out to be Alana Jobson, a woman who'd bought the identity from Sara Ehret. Alana died soon after Peter learned her secret, destroyed by the drugs she'd been taking to gain her powers.

While Peter enjoyed the fact that no one but he knew his secret identity, he recently told a few of his friends on his Avengers team his true name. **MF**

Menace turned out to be none other than Lily Hollister, the woman who Peter's unwitting friend Harry Osborn (the second Green Goblin) hoped to marry. As Menace, she publicly attacked her father to drum up sympathy support for his mayoral campaign.

Essential Storylines

- ***Civil War #1–7*** During the Civil War, Spider-Man registers with the government and reveals his identity to the world—and then comes to regret it.

- ***One More Day, tpb*** With Aunt May at death's door after taking a sniper's bullet meant for Peter, he and Mary Jane cut a deal with Mephisto to trade their marriage to save her life.

Amazing Spider-Man #546 His marriage erased—along with any knowledge anyone has about his secret identity—Spider-Man starts again fresh, but alone.

Both Peter Parker and Spider-Man started all over again with a Brand New Day—but Mary Jane was no longer by Peter's side.

SPIDER-MAN *continued*

A flashback story revealed that in the timeline Mephisto had modified, Peter and Mary Jane had never married because he'd missed their wedding day.

Dark Days

During the Dark Reign, Peter had to deal with the fact that his worst enemy—Norman Osborn (Green Goblin)—had taken charge of security in the US. To make matters even worse, Osborn recruited villains to pose as well-known heroes and form a new Avengers team loyal to him, with Venom (Mac Gargan) posing as a black-suited Spider-Man. Because of this, Peter felt compelled to reveal his identity to the Avengers, and later to the Fantastic Four. He discovered that his deal with Mephisto (which he didn't remember making) had given the world a psychic blind spot when it came to Spider-Man's identity. Once he revealed his identity to someone, the blind spot was removed, and any memories a person had about Spider-Man's identity came flooding back.

When Peter Parker met Miles Morales—the new Spider-Man from Earth-1610 (the Ultimate universe)—he was shocked to discover that the Peter Parker of that world had been killed. Miles had received his powers from the bite of a genetically enhanced spider, but he hadn't felt the responsibility to use them until the Spider-Man of his world died.

Desperate for the return of their patriarch, Kraven the Hunter, the Kravinoff family turned to the ritual sacrifice of his greatest foe: Spider-Man. But they weren't all thrilled with the results.

The Kravinoffs

The surviving family of Kraven the Hunter—his children Ana and Aloysha, helped by the Chameleon (Kraven's half-brother) and led by his wife Sasha Kravinoff—decided to take their revenge on Spider-Man. They started by kidnapping Madame Web and Mattie Franklin, the third Spider-Woman. Using Madame Web's powers, they forced Spider-Man to battle a gallery of his old foes, weakening him until they were ready to launch their ultimate plan.

The Kravinoffs sacrificed Mattie to revive the dead Vladimir Kravinoff—Kraven's son, known as the Grim Hunter. However, he came back to life as a half-lion creature rather than himself. Using what they learned from this attempt, they sacrificed Spider-Man to bring Kraven himself back from the dead. It turned out that they'd killed Spidey's clone Kaine instead, who'd swapped himself with Peter.

When he worked for the Future Foundation, Spider-Man wore an all-new, white-and-black costume.

Working-Class Hero

Peter always had a hard time holding on to a job, but he had been working as a science teacher at his old school, Midtown High in Queens. After his Aunt May married John Johan Jameson Sr. (the father of J. Jonah Jameson), however, May and John asked Jonah—who had become the mayor of New York City—if they could find Peter a better job. Jonah's wife Marla Madison recommended Peter to Horizon Labs, where he became one of the think-tank's top scientists.

Meanwhile, after the apparent death of his pal the Human Torch, Spider-Man joined the Fantastic Four, as the Torch had requested in his will. He served with their Future Foundation until the Torch returned. He also served with the Avengers after Norman Osborn was removed from power at the end of the Dark Reign.

Spider-Island

The Jackal, who had been behind all of Peter's problems with clones, returned with a new plot. Working for the Spider Queen and with Kaine revived as a new, Jackal-controlled Tarantula, the Jackal infected most of the citizens of Manhattan with a virus that gave them superpowers. Fortunately, Mister Fantastic created a cure for the virus, using the symbiote of Anti-Venom.

During this time, Peter displayed the use of his spider-powers on live TV. This weakened the psychic blind spot the world had about his identity as Spider-Man. His girlfriend at the time—forensic police officer Carlie Cooper—suspected who Peter was, and she broke up with him. **MF**

Superior Spider-Man

The enfeebled and dying Doctor Octopus returned as Spider-Man's greatest foe. Using a specialized Octobot, he managed to swap his mind with that of Spider-Man, trapping Peter in his body. Despite his best efforts, Peter could not reverse this before Doc Ock's body died. A repentant Doc Ock took up Peter's life as his own, determined to do a better job than Peter had managed.

Still, some part of Peter's mind survived in his body, and he eventually managed to communicate with Doc Ock inside their shared head. They wound up in a psychic battle in which Doc Ock triumphed. Soon after, he deleted all of Peter's memories from his mind. Wishing to make himself the superior Spider-Man, Doc Ock went back to school to finish the doctorate Peter had never managed to achieve. He also dated a new woman, worked closely with Mayor Jameson to fight crime, and used hirelings and a slew of Spider-Bots to help him patrol the city.

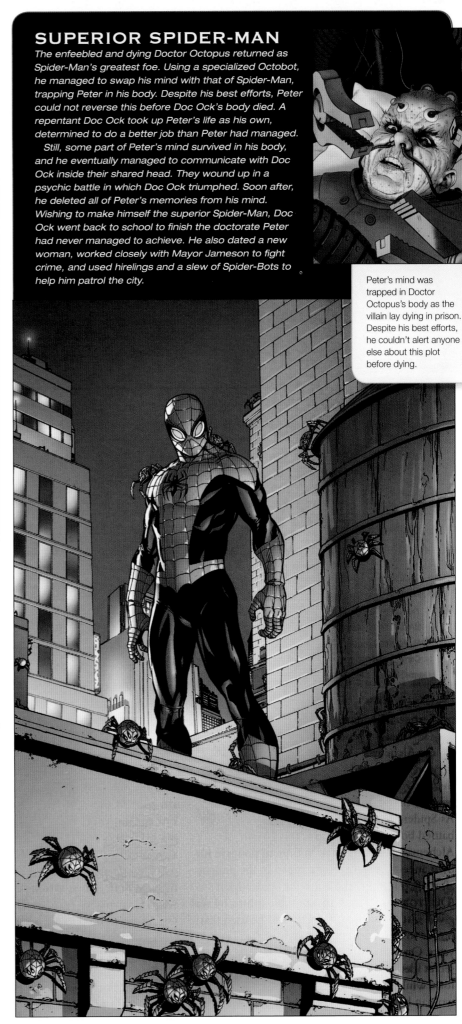

Peter's mind was trapped in Doctor Octopus's body as the villain lay dying in prison. Despite his best efforts, he couldn't alert anyone else about this plot before dying.

SPIDER-GIRL

FACTFILE

REAL NAME
May "Mayday" Parker

OCCUPATION
Student, adventurer

BASE
New York City

HEIGHT 5 ft 7 in
WEIGHT 119 lbs
EYES Blue
HAIR Brown

FIRST APPEARANCE
What If? #105 (February 1998)

POWERS
Similar powers of agility, strength, and climbing ability as Spider-Man; uses web-shooters, developed by her father, to travel across the city or trap enemies.

Spider-Girl

In a possible future, Mayday Parker (left) inherited her father Peter's spider-powers—and his fashion-sense. In the present day, Anya Corazón (below) was no relation to Peter, and she soon established her own look.

On Earth-982, Spider-Man and his wife Mary Jane Watson had a daughter named May. Sometime after that, the Green Goblin maimed Spidey in battle, and he retired to become Peter Parker, NYPD forensic scientist.

As a teenager, May inherited Peter's powers and became Spider-Girl. She battled new villains—such as Funny Face and Killerwatt—plus the descendants of her dad's foes—like Raptor, and Normie Osborn (Norman Osborn's grandson). Recently, she and her father battled the Green Goblin's ghost, along with a symbiote-hybrid clone of May, named April. They defeated the Goblin, and May welcomed April into her family. April later sacrificed herself to save May's life.

In the main timeline, Brooklyn high-school student Anya Corazón nearly died in a battle between the Spider Society and the Sisterhood of the Wasps. Miguel, the sorcerer of the Spider Society, endowed her with a spider-shaped tattoo which gave her spider-like powers and an exoskeleton. She called herself Araña (Spanish for spider). During the Civil War, Anya registered with the government and lost her exoskeleton in a fight. Anya later became Spider-Girl when she received Julia Carpenter's old Spider-Woman outfit. She later joined a group of super teens called the Young Allies. TD, MT, MF

Spider-Man 2099

FIRST APPEARANCE Spider-Man 2099 #1 (November 1992)
REAL NAME Miguel O'Hara
OCCUPATION Genetic engineer, adventurer
BASE New York City **HEIGHT** 5 ft 10 in **WEIGHT** 170 lbs
EYES Brown **HAIR** Brown
SPECIAL POWERS/ABILITIES Superhuman strength, speed, and agility. Can adhere to surfaces and project webbing from spinnerets in forearms. Retractable talons and fangs that secrete poison.

In the year 2099 on Earth-928, Miguel O'Hara, head of genetics for the Alchemax corporation, gained Spider-Man's powers in a episode of industrial intrigue. As Spider-Man 2099, he battled both criminals and Alchemax. Traveling back in time to preserve his own ancestry, Miguel was trapped in the present after encountering the Superior Spider-Man (Doctor Octopus). In a possible future, he was given Thor's hammer Mjolnir, and he used that power to rule Earth peacefully for a thousand years. On Earth-6375, after Spider-Man 2099's secret identity was exposed, he joined the Exiles for a while. He later returned to be with the woman he loved Dana D'Angelo. PS, MF

Spider-Man 2211

FIRST APPEARANCE Spider-Man 2099 Meets Spider-Man (November 1995) **REAL NAME** Dr. Jamoff "Max" Borne
OCCUPATION Adventurer **BASE** New York City
HEIGHT 6 ft **WEIGHT** 187 lbs **EYES** Brown **HAIR** Bald
SPECIAL POWERS/ABILITIES Armor grants superhuman strength, flight, and four additional telescopic arms.

Max Borne is a TimeSpinner, charged with maintaining the continuity of the timeline of Earth-9500. He first encountered the original Spider-Man (of Earth-616) when Max's daughter, the Hobgoblin of 2211, chased back through time, killing various Spider-Men as she went. He managed to stop her, but before he could return to his own time, he was shot and killed by the Chameleon of 2211, disguised as Ben Parker. Max's costume shared the colors of the original, but it also featured an open-mouthed helmet and a set of mechanical arms, much like those of Doctor Octopus. MF

Spider-Queen

FIRST APPEARANCE The Spectacular Spider-Man #15 (August 2004) **REAL NAME** Adriana (Ana) Soria
OCCUPATION Conqueror **BASE** New York City
HEIGHT 5 ft 10 in **WEIGHT** 125 lbs
EYES Brown **HAIR** Black
SPECIAL POWERS/ABILITIES Ana has superhuman strength and can emit a sonic blast. She is also telepathic with insects and humans who have insect DNA, and can control their minds.

Ana Soria was the first female marine to enter combat as part of the US military's Super-Soldier program. Exposed to radiation during the Bikini Atoll atomic bomb tests, she developed spider powers. She arrived in modern times and controlled Spider-Man's mind, but Captain America stopped her. She arose years later with a plan to infect everyone in Manhattan with spider powers so she could control them. She transformed into a spider-monster nearly thirty stories tall, and many heroes attacked and killed her. MF

SPIDER-WOMAN

Investigator with irresistible powers

The daughter of scientist Jonathan DREW, Jessica gained her powers before birth, when a laser laced with spider DNA hit her mother's womb. Born and raised on Wundagore Mountain, her powers manifested when she was six years old. She was in stasis for a long time and when she woke found herself in the care of HYDRA.

It was originally believed that Jessica's powers stemmed from an experiment conducted by her father.

REAL NAME
Jessica Drew

OCCUPATION
Adventurer

BASE
Mobile

HEIGHT 5 ft 10 in
WEIGHT 130 lbs
EYES Green
HAIR Brown (dyed black)

FIRST APPEARANCE
Marvel Spotlight #32 (February 1977)

Enhanced strength, speed, and hearing; flight; superhuman healing factor; emits mood-altering pheromones that attract both sexes; ability to adhere to walls and fire electric "venom blasts."

Wings let Spider-Woman glide, and she can now fly unassisted.

SUPER SPY

Trained by the TASKMASTER—and with her mind warped by MENTALLO—Jessica became an agent of Hydra. Captured by SHIELD on her first mission and then released, she went underground. She resurfaced to become an agent of SHIELD for a short time, after which she struck out on her own. Calling herself Spider-Woman, Jessica became a private investigator, a bounty hunter, and a sometime Super Hero. At one point, she saved the life of Giant-Man (Bill Foster) through a blood transfusion, and lost some of her powers in the process.

Others took on the name of Spider-Woman but when Hydra offered to restore Jessica's powers if she would become their agent, she accepted the deal, then contacted Nick FURY and became a double agent for SHIELD. Shortly thereafter, she was kidnapped by the SKRULLS and replaced by Queen VERANKE.

While posing as Jessica, Veranke led the SECRET INVASION. Norman Osborn (*see* GREEN GOBLIN) shot and killed Veranke in the final battle of the Skrull invasion. Jessica, along with several other replaced heroes, was found in a Skrull prison ship and brought back to Earth. She has since joined the Avengers team led by CAPTAIN AMERICA (Bucky Barnes).

Julia Carpenter as Spider-Woman.

KEY STORYLINES

- ***The Spider-Woman #1*** The first issue of her original, self-titled series sees Jessica Drew striking out on her own as a hero.
- ***Spider-Woman: Origin #1–6*** This limited series retells Spider-Woman's beginnings, from a HYDRA pawn to a member of the New Avengers.
- ***New Avengers #1*** Jessica Drew returns as Spider-Woman in the New Avengers... or does she?

THE OTHERS

Julia Carpenter (now MADAME WEB) was made Spider-Woman by the COMMISSION ON SUPERHUMAN ACTIVITIES. Later, Mattie Franklin became the third Spider-Woman after taking her father's place during a ceremony called the Gathering of the Five. DOCTOR OCTOPUS gave Charlotte Witter the ability to absorb spider-powers only to have Mattie reclaim them, along with the name. Mattie worked with the Loners for a while, but she was on her own when the KRAVEN family hunted her down and killed her. **DW, MF**

Charlotte Witter was the only villainous Spider-Woman. Doctor Octopus bestowed her with powers sufficient to kill Spider-Man. Witter also possessed the ability to drain the powers of the other Spider-Women, but lost them when defeated by the third Spider-Woman—Mattie Franklin.

Spirit of '76

FIRST APPEARANCE The Invaders #14 (March 1977)
REAL NAME William Nasland
OCCUPATION Costumed adventurer **BASE** Mobile
HEIGHT 6 ft 2 in **WEIGHT** 215 lbs **EYES** Blue **HAIR** Black
SPECIAL POWERS/ABILITIES Top level athlete and formidable hand-to-hand combatant; wore a bullet-proof cape; as Captain America he had a steel shield, which was not indestructible.

Inspired by Captain America's World War II exploits, William Nasland became the costumed adventurer, Spirit of '76. After battling Nazi spies in Philadelphia, Nasland moved to Great Britain and joined the Crusaders team of heroes, until its leader was revealed to be a German agent. Nasland continued to contribute to the war effort, partnering Captain America on a mission to Berlin. Following the Cap's apparent demise, Nasland agreed to become a second Captain America but his career as this emblematic figurehead was cut short when he died preventing the assassination of would-be congressman John F. Kennedy. **AD**

Spitfire

FIRST APPEARANCE The Invaders #7 (July 1976)
REAL NAME Jacqueline Falsworth Crichton
OCCUPATION Adventurer **BASE** Falsworth Manor, England
HEIGHT 5 ft 4 in **WEIGHT** 110 lbs **EYES** Blue **HAIR** Blond
SPECIAL POWERS/ABILITIES Spitfire can move at speeds up to 50 mph for up to four hours. She has a vampire's fangs, superhuman strength, and a healing factor, but feels no bloodlust.

During World War II, Jacqueline Falsworth served in England's Home Guard and was attacked by the Nazi vampire Baron Blood. She was rescued by the original Human Torch, an android who gave her a transfusion of his artificial blood. The combination of the vampire bite and the android blood gave Falsworth superhuman speed. She adopted the name Spitfire and teamed up with the Invaders, a group of Allied heroes who battled the Axis powers. Over time her powers faded, but another transfusion from the Human Torch restored them. In modern times, she served with the New Invaders and with MI-13. After her romance with Blade, she was seen helping Captain Britain at Braddock Academy. **MT, MF**

Spiral

FIRST APPEARANCE Longshot #1 (September 1985)
REAL NAME "Ricochet" Rita **OCCUPATION** Warrior sorceress
BASE Mobile
HEIGHT 5 ft 10 in **WEIGHT** 150 lbs
EYES Blue **HAIR** Silver
SPECIAL POWERS/ABILITIES Enhanced strength; spellcasting abilities allow teleportation between dimensions; excellent swordswoman who can wield six weapons at once.

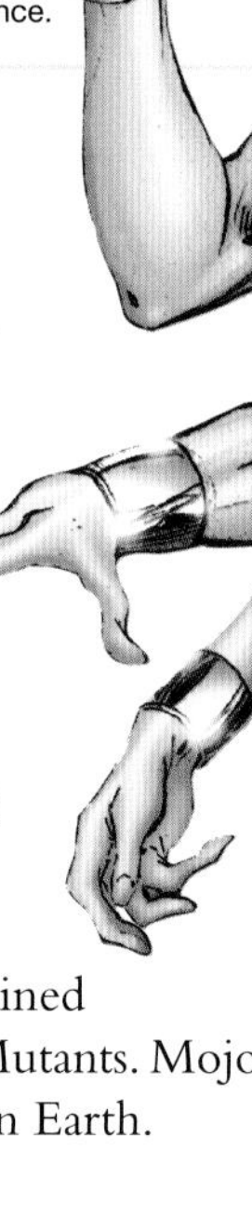

Spiral is a six-armed sorceress who worked as an aide to Mojo. An actress in her former life, Spiral received genetic alterations in the Mojoverse, which gave her the ability to manipulate magic. On Earth, she briefly served in Freedom Force and opened a cybernetics store, the Body Shoppe, whose customers included Lady Deathstrike. She later conquered Earth-2055 until Shatterstar defeated her, then joined Madelyne Pryor's Sisterhood of Mutants. Mojo fired her afterward, stranding her on Earth. **DW, MF**

Spot

FIRST APPEARANCE Peter Parker, The Spectacular Spider-Man #98 (January 1985) **REAL NAME** Dr. Jonathan Ohnn
OCCUPATION Criminal, research scientist
BASE New York City **HEIGHT** 5 ft 10 in
WEIGHT 170 lbs **EYES** Blue **HAIR** Brown
SPECIAL POWERS/ABILITIES Ohnn's body is covered with black spots that can teleport items from one of them to another. The spots are movable and can even be removed and placed off his body.

While researching teleportation for the Kingpin, Dr. John Ohnn was transported into the Spotted Dimension, and when he returned, he found his body covered with portable wormholes. He clashed with Spider-Man and the Black Cat soon after. When he opened up a spot into the Negative Zone, he ran afoul of the Fantastic Four. While in prison, he helped Tombstone escape, for which the crook broke his neck. He survived only to be killed by Elektra and resurrected by the Hand. Another villain called the Coyote captured him to use his powers against Daredevil. **MF**

Spymaster, *see page 346*

Squadron Supreme

Another world's mightiest heroes

In a 12-issue series, the Squadron Supreme explores absolute power.

The Squadron Supreme is a force of superhuman champions inhabiting the Earth of an alternate reality. They have crossed paths with the AVENGERS many times, including an early team-up to eradicate the evil influence of the serpent-god Set's Serpent Crown.

A new Hyperion recently arrived from a doomed dimension that had been part of an incursion on the main reality. He was the only survivor.

THE SINISTER ONES

The Avengers first encountered the Squadron Sinister, a team of villains the GRANDMASTER created in the main universe after he'd discovered the Squadron Supreme in his travels through the multiverse. They included DOCTOR SPECTRUM, HYPERION, NIGHTHAWK, and WHIZZER (later known as SPEED DEMON). The Avengers defeated them, but they later clashed with the DEFENDERS as well. Appalled at the team's plans, Nighthawk betrayed them, after which he joined the Defenders.

When the Avengers later found themselves in the Squadron Supreme's world (Earth-712), they initially thought they were facing the Squadron Sinister again. They soon sorted out their mistake, and together they defeated a mad scientist who called himself Brain-Child, saving the Squadron Supreme's world.

FACTFILE

NOTABLE MEMBERS

HYPERION (leader)
Flight, enhanced strength, super-speed, near-invulnerability, atomic vision.

AMPHIBIAN
Enhanced strength, able to live underwater at ocean depths.

DOCTOR SPECTRUM
Power prism permits flight and the projection of hard-energy objects.

GOLDEN ARCHER
Unsurpassed skill with a bow and arrow.

NIGHTHAWK
Brilliant strategist, top-level combatant.

POWER PRINCESS
Enhanced strength, skilled warrior.

THE WHIZZER
Super-speedster.

BASE Squadron City

FIRST APPEARANCE
Avengers #85 (March 1971)

Power Corrupts

The Squadron Supreme faced their greatest challenge when the OVERMIND and Null the Living Darkness conquered their planet. Hyperion escaped to mainstream Earth and recruited the Defenders, who successfully defeated the Overmind. The damage to their world from the Overmind war was so great that the Squadron Supreme implemented the Utopia Program, seizing control of the government and forcibly implementing new methods of policing and social engineering.

Nighthawk left the Squadron in protest and organized the Redeemers to act as a rebel insurgency. The Redeemers forced the Squadron's surrender, but at the price of Nighthawk's life, and the two groups dismantled the Utopia Program. The Squadron Supreme later became marooned on Earth, where they adventured alongside QUASAR.

The Squadron eventually returned to their own world, where they found that a Global Directorate had taken the reins of power they'd abandoned, fulfilling their nightmares. Working with a new underground movement called the Nighthawks—and led by Neal Richmond, the son of Nighthawk—they successfully liberated their world from the grip of various monolithic corporations who were seeking to gain control of the planet.

DW, MF

SQUADRON SUPREME
1 Tom Thumb ***2*** Whizzer ***3*** Nuke ***4*** Redstone ***5*** Shape
6 Power Princess ***7*** Hyperion ***8*** Lamprey ***9*** Doctor Spectrum
10 Firefox ***11*** Arcanna ***12*** Blue Eagle ***13*** Black Archer ***14*** Ape X

SPYMASTER

FIRST APPEARANCE Iron Man #33 (January 1971)
REAL NAME Unrevealed
OCCUPATION Industrial spy **BASE** Mobile
HEIGHT 6 ft **WEIGHT** 195 lbs **EYES** Blue **HAIR** Blond
SPECIAL POWERS/ABILITIES Master of disguise; expert saboteur; exceptional hand-to-hand combatant; expert with high-tech weaponry; bulletproof costume; used hoverjet for transport.

From his first days as IRON MAN, Tony Stark was dogged by the Spymaster. Initially working with his Espionage Elite team, Spymaster tried many times to steal Stark's technology. ZODIAC, SHIELD, and MADAME MASQUE all employed him, but Justin HAMMER benefited most. The first Spymaster died at the hands of a rival named the Ghost. A second Spymaster discovered Iron Man's identity and beat Stark badly only to be stopped by the BLACK WIDOW. A third Spymaster killed the second and then plagued Stark before nearly dying in the fall that killed Happy HOGAN. He was later killed by the police. **AD, MF**

SQUIRREL GIRL

FIRST APPEARANCE Marvel Super-Heroes #8 (December 1991)
REAL NAME Doreen Green
OCCUPATION Adventurer, babysitter, student
BASE New York City **HEIGHT** 5 ft 3 in **WEIGHT** 100 lbs
EYES Brown **HAIR** Brown
SPECIAL POWERS/ABILITIES Doreen has enhanced agility, speed, and strength, plus small claws and large, sharp incisors, as well as a knuckle spike and a tail; she can also communicate with squirrels.

As a teenager, Doreen discovered her mutant powers, which included an uncanny rapport with squirrels. She tried to convince IRON MAN to let her be his sidekick, but he declined her offer, even after she rescued him from DOCTOR DOOM. She later became a founding member of the Great Lakes AVENGERS, later known as the Great Lakes X-Men, the Great Lakes Champions, and the Great Lakes Initiative. She retained her powers through M-Day, and after the DARK REIGN, she became the nanny of Luke CAGE and Jessica JONES's baby Danielle. **MF**

STACY, CAPTAIN GEORGE

FIRST APPEARANCE Amazing Spider-Man #56 (January 1968)
REAL NAME George Stacy
OCCUPATION NYPD captain **BASE** New York City
HEIGHT 6 ft 1 in **WEIGHT** 190 lbs
EYES Blue **HAIR** Gray
SPECIAL POWERS/ABILITIES
Captain Stacy was a sharp policeman.

George Stacy—father of Gwen STACY—was a decorated member of the NYPD, along with his brother Arthur. He injured his leg in a battle with the Proto-Goblin (a predecessor of the GREEN GOBLIN), but continued to work to semi-retirement. He became a fan of SPIDER-MAN and took an instant liking to his daughter's new boyfriend Peter Parker. During a battle between Spider-Man and DOCTOR OCTOPUS, George saved a boy from falling rubble, paying for his heroism with his life. With his dying breath, he revealed he knew who Spider-Man was, and he exhorted Peter to take care of Gwen. **MF**

STACY, GWEN

FACTFILE
REAL NAME
Gwendolyn Stacy
OCCUPATION
Student
BASE
Empire State University, New York City

HEIGHT 5 ft 7 in
WEIGHT 130 lbs
EYES Blue
HAIR Blond

FIRST APPEARANCE
Amazing Spider-Man #31 (December 1965)

POWERS
Gwen Stacy possessed an aptitude for science, but no special powers of any kind.

The daughter of NYPD Captain George Stacy, Gwen first met Peter Parker (SPIDER-MAN) at Empire State University. Although attracted to him, his frequent moodiness and his apparent cowardliness put her off. Eventually, she and Peter became a couple, despite competition from Mary Jane WATSON, but the Parker-Stacy relationship was an uneasy one. After her father was slain during a battle between Spider-Man and DOCTOR OCTOPUS, Gwen came to hate Spider-Man, a fact that weighed heavily on Peter's mind. Not long after, Gwen was captured by the GREEN GOBLIN and hurled from the top of a bridge. When Spider-Man attempted to save her with his webbing, the sudden shock of deceleration snapped Gwen's neck, causing her death. It was later revealed that Gwen had had an affair with Norman Osborn (GREEN GOBLIN) and bore twins by him, Gabriel and Sarah STACY, who have now grown to adulthood by accelerated aging. **TB, MF**

Hurled off of a bridge by the Green Goblin, Gwen Stacy perished without ever learning that her boyfriend Peter Parker was secretly Spider-Man.

Stacy, Gabriel & Sarah

FIRST APPEARANCE Amazing Spider-Man #509 (August 2004)
REAL NAMES Gabriel and Sarah Stacy
OCCUPATION Criminal/research scientist **BASE** New York City
HEIGHT 6 ft/5 ft 7 in **WEIGHT** 180 lbs/115 lbs
EYES Blue/Blue **HAIR** Reddish-brown/Blond
SPECIAL POWERS/ABILITIES Both were born with enhanced durability, speed, and healing. Gabriel has been injected with Goblin Formula, granting superhuman strength and toughened skin.

Gwen Stacy had an affair with Norman Osborn (Green Goblin) and gave birth to twins Gabriel and Sarah, who aged faster due to their father's powers. Norman raised them and told them Peter Parker (Spider-Man) was their father and had killed their mother. When Peter told them the truth, Sarah believed it, but Gabriel injected himself with Goblin Formula and became the Gray Goblin. He was defeated by Sarah and Spider-Man. During the Dark Reign, Gabriel returned and battled his half-brother Harry Osborn for the American Son armor Norman made. MF

Stane, Obadiah

Orphaned when his father killed himself in a game of Russian roulette, Obadiah Stane regarded life as a game that he was determined to win.

His preferred tactic was to wage psychological warfare against his opponent. Stane became the head of a multinational corporation that produced munitions. Knowing that Anthony Stark, head of Stark International, was a reformed alcoholic, Stane manipulated events to drive Stark back to drinking. Buying up the debts of Stark International, Stane took control of the company, renaming it Stane International, and froze Stark's personal fortune. Stark duly became a drunken derelict.

Eventually Stark stopped drinking and resumed his secret identity as Iron Man. Stane had his scientists create his own armored battlesuit, called the Iron Monger. In the Iron Monger armor, Stane personally battled Iron Man, who defeated him. Removing his helmet, Stane committed suicide by firing a repulsor ray blast at his head. PS

Stane's Iron Monger armor was larger than Iron Man's, but he could not defeat him.

FACTFILE
REAL NAME
Obadiah Stane
OCCUPATION
President and chairman of the board of Stane International
BASE
Stane International headquarters, Long Island, New York

HEIGHT 6 ft 5 in
WEIGHT 230 lbs
EYES Blue
HAIR Bald

FIRST APPEARANCE
Iron Man #163 (October 1982)

POWERS
"Iron Monger" battlesuit amplified his strength to superhuman levels; boot jets enabled flight; projected repulsor rays (force beams) and laser blasts.

Stane, Obadiah

Stane, Ezekiel

FIRST APPEARANCE The Order #10 (April 2008)
REAL NAME Ezekiel (Zeke) Stane
OCCUPATION High-tech inventor and futurist **BASE** Mobile
HEIGHT 5 ft 11 in **WEIGHT** 223 lbs
EYES Brown **HAIR** Bald
SPECIAL POWERS/ABILITIES Superhuman intelligence andbio-upgrades granting various superpowers.

The son of Obadiah Stane, Ezekiel inherited his father's fortune and promptly turned it and his incredible intellect toward making Tony Stark (Iron Man) obsolete. He started by coordinating attacks against the Order, the California team for the Fifty-State Initiative. When his efforts failed, he went after Stark directly. Zeke reverse-engineered Stark technology that was available on the black market. Instead of building a better Iron Man suit, however, he upgraded his body directly. He sometimes wears a suit as a heat sink for his powers. The Mandarin later enslaved Zeke to help capture Stark. Zeke and Tony worked together to turn the tables on the Mandarin. MF

Star Brand

The Star Brand is a mark of great power that has appeared in many universes, and the bearer is often known as Star Brand. The first such person was Ken Connell from Earth-148611, who gained the brand during the White Event from the Old Man, who'd grown bored with it. It was later granted to Quasar in the main universe, and it fell into the hands of the Stranger, who then moved Earth-148611 into the same universe, where the Star Brand was quarantined for being too dangerous.

A White Event (a cosmic upheaval) happened in the main universe when Ex Nihilo tried to give the Earth sentience, and the Star Brand wound up with college student Kevin Connor, who destroyed his entire campus by accident. He worked with Nightmask to understand what had happened, and in the course of their investigations, he accidentally killed the Earth's new sentience. The Avengers captured and imprisoned him after this, placing him in the Dyson sphere that Iron Man was building in outer space. Kevin now works with them to save the universe. MF

FACTFILE
REAL NAME
Kevin Connor
OCCUPATION
Adventurer, student
BASE
Mobile

HEIGHT 5 ft. 9 in.
WEIGHT 155 lbs.
EYES Blue
HAIR Blond

FIRST APPEARANCE
Star Brand #1 (October, 1986)

POWERS
The Star Brand gives its bearer nearly infinite power limited only by their imagination.

The Star Brand first appeared as part of Marvel's New Universe line of titles, debuting in 1986.

Star Brand

Starfox

FIRST APPEARANCE Iron Man #55 (February 1973)
REAL NAME Eros
OCCUPATION Adventurer **BASE** Mobile
HEIGHT 6 ft 1 in **WEIGHT** 190 lbs **EYES** Blue **HAIR** Red
SPECIAL POWERS/ABILITIES Flight; enhanced strength; telekinesis; ability to generate personal force fields; the power to stimulate the brain's pleasure centers.

Eros is an ETERNAL, raised on the Saturn moon of Titan by his father, Mentor. His buoyant outlook is the opposite of that of his older brother THANOS. For years Eros wandered in search of sensual pleasure, but he returned to Titan when Thanos and the SUPER-SKRULL attacked it. After the death of CAPTAIN MAR-VELL, Eros looked after Mar-Vell's son, Genis-Vell, and he eventually joined the AVENGERS as Starfox. He helped to foil Thanos's efforts to assemble the Infinity Gauntlet. When the SHE-HULK discovered that he'd used his powers to influence her to marry John JAMESON, she beat him badly. **DW, MF**

Starhawk

FIRST APPEARANCE Defenders #27 (September 1975)
REAL NAME Stakar Vaughn Ogord
OCCUPATION Adventurer **BASE** Arcturus IV
HEIGHT/WEIGHT/EYES/HAIR Unknown
SPECIAL POWERS/ABILITIES Starhawk can fly at light speed and can manipulate cosmic energy. He also has the power of precognition, knowing events that will occur before they happen.

On Earth-691, Stakar Vaughn Ogord is the child of the superpowered beings QUASAR and Kismet, making him half human and half artificial. Born on the planet Vesper, Stakar was kidnapped as an infant and taken to the planet Arcturus IV, where he was adopted by Ogord, a REAVER. Stakar eventually married Ogord's daughter Aleta. When an accident merged Stakar and Aleta, they became a single being known as Starhawk. Starhawk fled Arcturus IV and joined the GUARDIANS OF THE GALAXY. Being precognitive, Starhawk relives his life over and over, making changes and adjustments each time. Another version of Starhawk recently battled the modern-day Guardians. **MT**

Starjammers

The Starjammers' leader, Corsair, is quick-witted and skilled with a blade.

CORSAIR—real name Christopher Summers, father of CYCLOPS, HAVOK, and VULCAN—was abducted and enslaved by the alien SHI'AR. After his wife died for Emperor D'ken's pleasure, Corsair staged a jailbreak with fellow prisoners Ch'od, Raza, and Hepzibah. The group became the Starjammers, space pirates who fought against the cruel excesses of Shi'ar rule. The team helped the X-MEN defeat D'ken in his bid to possess the M'Krann crystal, and later teamed with the X-Men to rescue D'ken's sister Lilandra. The Starjammers accepted Carol Danvers (*see* MS. MARVEL) as a member when she was known as Binary, while both Lilandra and PROFESSOR X worked with the team during the fight against DEATHBIRD.

Later, Vulcan returned to Shi'ar space, killed Corsair, and took over the Shi'ar Empire. Havok then led the Starjammers in their attempt to stop his brother. They were imprisoned, but broke free and headed for the KREE Empire, and then to Earth. **DW, MF**

FACTFILE

MEMBERS AND POWERS
CORSAIR (3) (Christopher Summers) Excellent pilot, swordsman, and combatant.
CH'OD (1) Natural strength, tough skin, slashing claws.
HEPZIBAH (2) Feline reflexes, night vision, retractable claws.
RAZA (4) Cyborg strength, vision and reflexes, skilled with bladed weapons.
SIKORSKY Advanced medical knowledge.
KEEYAH Skilled pilot.
CR'REEE Ch'od's semi-intelligent, white-furred pet.
BASE Mobile
FIRST APPEARANCE
Uncanny X-Men #104 (April 1977)

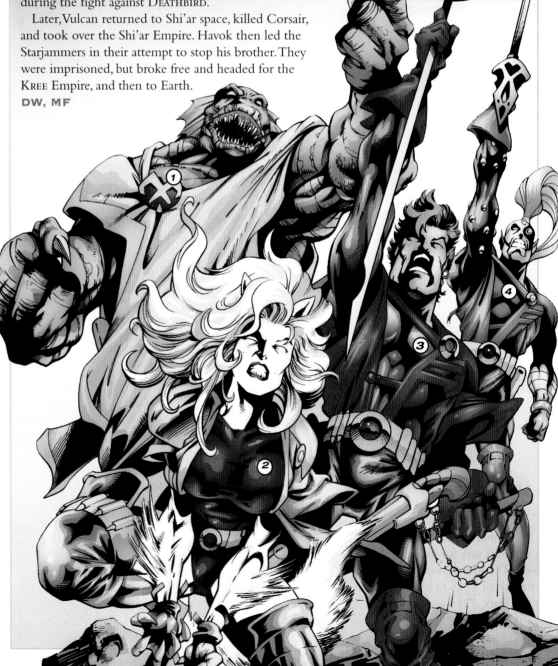

Stark, Howard

FIRST APPEARANCE Iron Man #28 (August, 1970)
REAL NAME Howard Stark
OCCUPATION Inventor, industrialist **BASE** New York City
HEIGHT 6 ft **WEIGHT** 170 lbs
EYES Blue **HAIR** Gray, white at the temples
SPECIAL POWERS/ABILITIES Howard was a genius inventor, a ruthless businessman, and a scrapper in a fight.

As a young man, Howard Stark founded Stark Industries with his father. During World War II, he worked on the Manhattan Project and afterward joined the Brotherhood of the Shield, where he helped Nathaniel Richards try to save the world. He married Maria Carbonell, who bore their son Tony (Iron Man). Maria had pregnancy troubles, so Howard sought the help of a Rigellian Recorder to save his son, and the Recorder genetically improved the baby with Kree technology. Howard's greatest battle was with his own alcoholism. He and Maria died in a suspicious car crash. MF

Starlord

When Peter Quill's father—J'Son of Spartax, future ruler of the Spartoi Empire—crash-landed on Earth, Meredith Quill took him in and cared for him. When J'Son headed for the stars, he left two things behind: his high-tech gun and a pregnant Meredith. When Peter was ten, Badoon warriors came to kill him and his mother. Meredith died, but Peter secretly escaped. As an adult, he joined NASA to get into space and wound up in a galactic prison after a fight with the Fallen One, a former herald of Galactus. During the Annihilation, Nova broke Peter out of prison, and they helped defeat both Annihilus and the Phalanx. Believing the universe needed protecting, Peter formed the Guardians of the Galaxy. When the others discovered he'd asked Mantis to mentally push them into joining his group, the Guardians banished him. Peter later joined a new Guardians team formed by Rocket Raccoon and traveled through time to try to save the future. Afterward, he and Nova sacrificed themselves to save the galaxy from Thanos and the Cancerverse, a place in which death had been conquered, filling it with a horrible unlife. He returned to Earth with a third team of the Guardians of the Galaxy. MF

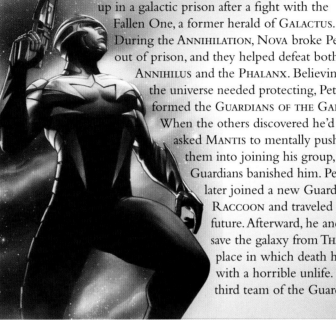

FACTFILE
REAL NAME
Peter Quill
OCCUPATION
Adventurer
BASE
Mobile

HEIGHT 6 ft 2 in
WEIGHT 175 lbs
EYES Blue
HAIR Blond

FIRST APPEARANCE
Marvel Preview #4 (January 1976)

POWERS
Peter's half-Spartoi heritage grants him top human durability, endurance, intelligence, speed, and strength. He also has triple the normal life expectancy.

Stark, Morgan

FIRST APPEARANCE Tales of Suspense #68 (August 1965)
REAL NAME Morgan Stark **OCCUPATION** Businessman
BASE New York City **HEIGHT** 5 ft 11 in **WEIGHT** 175 lbs
EYES Hazel **HAIR** Brown
SPECIAL POWERS/ABILITIES None.

The cousin of Tony Stark (Iron Man), Morgan was jealous of his famous cousin, believing that Tony's father had stolen Stark Industries from his own father. He worked with Count Nefaria to try to discredit Tony but failed. He returned years later during the Dark Reign to pose as Tony and take control of Stark Solutions. While there, he drank a vial of Ultimo Virus—a weaponized version of Ultimo—which converted him into a giant robot. War Machine used the robot's programming against it, and it self-destructed, presumably killing Morgan. MF

Star Stalker

FIRST APPEARANCE (Star Stalker I) Avengers #123 (May 1974), (Star Stalker II) Power Pack #56 (May 1990)
REAL NAME Unrevealed **OCCUPATION** Predator
BASE Planet Vormir in the Kree Galaxy (Greater Magellanic Cloud)
HEIGHT 16 ft 6 in **WEIGHT** Unrevealed **EYES** Black **HAIR** None
SPECIAL POWERS/ABILITIES Superhuman strength; could drain planetary energy and travel through outer space without protection.

The original, red Star Stalker was part of the reptilian alien Vorns. He used his tail as a weapon and his mutant powers to form an ionic cocoon to drain energy from other planets. His enemies were the Priests of Pama, a cult of Kree who knew his vulnerability to intense heat. Following the massacre of the Priests of Pama living on Earth, he journeyed there to absorb its energies. The Vision slew him with heat beams, but he returned later as part of the Grim Reaper's Legion of the Unliving. The Star Stalker's son, who inherited his father's powers, but had green skin, later menaced Earth. He was apparently destroyed by Nova (Frankie Raye). PS, MF

Stature

FIRST APPEARANCE Marvel Premiere #45 (April 1979)
REAL NAME Cassandra Eleanore "Cassie" Lang
OCCUPATION Adventurer **BASE** New York City
HEIGHT Varies **WEIGHT** Varies **EYES** Blue **HAIR** Blond
SPECIAL POWERS/ABILITIES Can grow and shrink to extremes.

When Cassie Lang was a young girl, her father Scott became the second Ant-Man so he could save her life. Because of Scott's life as a Super Hero, Cassie's mother (Scott's ex-wife) sued for and won full custody of Cassie. After her father's death, Cassie joined the Young Avengers to continue his legacy. She sided with Captain America during the Civil War, but after his death she joined the Fifty-State Initiative and trained at Camp Hammond. Cassie started dating the Vision and joined the new Avengers team led by Henry Pym. She died battling Doctor Doom, and Iron Lad took her body into the future to try to revive her. The Young Avengers stopped him, believing they should let the dead rest. MF

Steele, John

FIRST APPEARANCE Daring Mystery Comics #1 (January 1940)
REAL NAME John Steele
OCCUPATION Adventurer **BASE** Mobile
HEIGHT 6 ft 1 in **WEIGHT** 187 lbs
EYES Brown **HAIR** Black
SPECIAL POWERS/ABILITIES Superhuman durability, endurance, speed, and strength; heals faster and ages slower; an expert combatant.

John Steele—America's first Super-Soldier—has been part of the country's conflicts since the American Civil War. He fought in World War I, and was later captured by the German army and placed into stasis for study. Freed in 1940, he set to fighting Nazis. He disappeared after the Allies invaded Normandy, and was captured by the Shadow Council and brainwashed into working for them. Steve Rogers (Captain America) helped cure him, and John fought the Shadow Council's Masters of Evil until the android named Max Fury killed him. **MF**

Stein, Chase

FIRST APPEARANCE Runaways #1 (July 2003)
REAL NAME Chase Stein
OCCUPATION Adventurer **BASE** Mobile
HEIGHT 5 ft 11 in **WEIGHT** 188 lbs **EYES** Blue **HAIR** Blond
SPECIAL POWERS/ABILITIES An excellent pilot and athlete; uses gear stolen from his parents. Fistigon gloves allow him to manipulate fire; X-Ray Specs give X-ray vision. When his girlfriend Gert died, he inherited an empathic link to her dinosaur, Old Lace.

The son of evil geniuses who are part of an organization called the Pride, Chase joined with the Pride's other children to flee their parents, including Chase's abusive father, after witnessing them ritually sacrifice a girl. He fell in love with fellow runaway Gertrude Yorkes, who was killed. Later, Chase was one of the sixteen youths Arcade pitted against each other in his latest Murderworld, and he became the latest Darkhawk after recovering Chris Powell's Darkhawk amulet. **MF**

Stepford Cuckoos

FIRST APPEARANCE New X-Men #118 (November 2001)
MEMBERS AND POWERS Celeste, Esme, Mindee, Phoebe, and Sophie, Identical telepaths. **BASE** New Xavier's School for the Gifted, Canada

As part of the Weapon Plus program, John Sublime harvested eggs from Emma Frost and used them to create thousands of age-accelerated clones of her, a project called Weapon XIV. Five of the telepathic clones were activated and sent to the Xavier Institute. Sophie died while using the power-enhancing drug Kick to defeat Quentin Quire. Esme was later killed by the mutant Xorn, with whom she'd been using Kick. The remaining three gained Phoenix powers for a short time and destroyed the unactivated clones. They remained loyal to Cyclops through his troubles and joined his mutant revolution. **MF**

Stick

FACTFILE
REAL NAME
Unrevealed
OCCUPATION
Sensei
BASE Mobile

HEIGHT 5 ft 9 in
WEIGHT 135 lbs
EYES Blue
HAIR White

FIRST APPEARANCE
Daredevil #176 (November 1981)

POWERS
Martial arts expert; "proximity sense" allows him to detect others despite his blindness; some telepathic abilities; an inspirational teacher.

Despite being blind, Stick, who took his name from his combat staff, was the sensei of an elite warrior school called the Chaste. When young Matt Murdock (*see* Daredevil) lost his vision in a toxic waste accident, Stick helped him develop his remaining senses to compensate. Stick also trained the assassin Elektra, although he expelled her when she could not control her rage in combat. When the evil ninjas of the Hand attacked Stick and his allies, Stick absorbed the life essences of his attackers, killing himself. His spirit later reincarnated, and Daredevil and the Chaste defended the baby against the Hand. **DW, MF**

As the leader of the mystical Ninja clan known as the Chaste, Stick was one of the world's best martial artists and used his knowledge to train Matt Murdock.

Stilt-Man

FIRST APPEARANCE Daredevil #8 (June 1965)
REAL NAME Wilbur Day **OCCUPATION** Criminal
BASE New York City **HEIGHT** 5 ft 10 in (variable)
WEIGHT 185 lbs **EYES** Brown **HAIR** Black
SPECIAL POWERS/ABILITIES Legs of armored costume can extend up to 60 feet in length; costume also contains a formidable array of built-in weaponry.

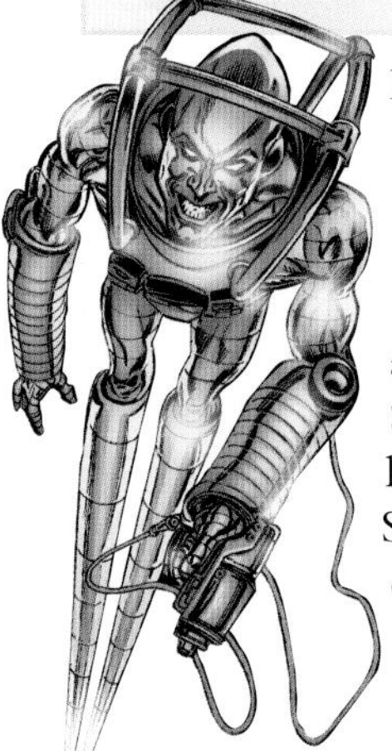

Lab assistant Wilbur Day made off with his boss's revolutionary hydraulic ram technology and—after adapting the device to an armored costume—became the Stilt-Man and embarked on a life of crime. Daredevil and Spider-Man regularly foiled his efforts. After becoming a laughing stock, Day tried to give up his costumed identity, but he found himself pulled back into the underworld. He later married Princess Python and registered with the government, but the Punisher killed him on one of his missions. A couple of others have worn Stilt-Man suits, including a woman who called herself Lady Stilt-Man. **TB, MF**

Stingray

FIRST APPEARANCE Tales to Astonish #95 (Sept. 1967) **REAL NAME** Walter Newell **OCCUPATION** Adventurer, oceanographer
BASE Mobile within Atlantic Ocean
HEIGHT 6 ft 3 in **WEIGHT** 200 lbs **EYES** Hazel **HAIR** Brown
SPECIAL POWERS/ABILITIES Costume incorporates built-in rebreathing apparatus and provides enhanced strength, the ability to travel underwater at great speed, and to fire electrical bolts.

The US government gave a seemingly impossible task to oceanographer Walter Newell: bring in Namor the Sub-Mariner for questioning. Newell designed a revolutionary submersible suit and actually succeeded in his task, in the process becoming the adventurer Stingray. Subsequent adventures saw him fighting the Atlantean warlord Attuma, and becoming a reserve member of the Avengers. He helped the resistance during the Civil War but later joined the Point Men, Hawaii's Fifty-State Initiative team. **DW, MF**

Stone, Lt. Marcus

FIRST APPEARANCE Thor #404 (June 1989)
REAL NAME Marcus Stone
OCCUPATION Police officer **BASE** New York City
HEIGHT 6 ft 2 in **WEIGHT** 225 lbs **EYES** Brown **HAIR** Bald
SPECIAL POWERS/ABILITIES A dedicated and tenacious police officer who never gives up on a case; an expert marksman and highly trained hand-to-hand combatant.

After serving as one of New York's Finest for 25 years, Marcus Stone was ready to retire. His marriage to his childhood sweetheart was in trouble because he kept bringing his police work home with him. Stone knew the time had come to choose between his job and his wife. On what should have been his last day, he stumbled upon a battle between the mighty Thor and Ulik, the unconquerable rock troll. After Thor fell, Stone pursued Ulik and managed to arrest him. Having proved that normal cops can handle super-menaces, Stone was later assigned to head up Code: Blue, a special New York City strike-force that takes on Super Villains. **TD**

STONE TIBERIUS, *see page 352*

Stinger

FIRST APPEARANCE Spider-Girl #1 (October 1998)
REAL NAME Cassandra Lang **OCCUPATION** Adventurer
BASE New York City (Earth-982) **HEIGHT** 5 ft 5 in
WEIGHT 105 lbs **EYES** Blue **HAIR** Reddish-blond
SPECIAL POWERS/ABILITIES Synthetic wing implants enable flight; armored costume protects from harm; possesses ability to shrink to the size of a wasp.

On Earth-982, Stinger is the superpowered pseudonym of Cassandra Lang, the daughter of the second Ant Man. Cassandra combined the powers and costume of her father with those of the Wasp, and she demonstrated a natural aptitude for organization and leadership. With a new generation of heroes emerging, Cassandra helped reform the Avengers and was in charge of the resurrected superteam when Loki attempted to rid the world of heroes. A scientist in her mid-20s, Cassandra is the oldest and best-educated member of the team. **AD, MF**

Stranger, The

The Stranger is an immeasurably powerful cosmic being, created from the life-energies of a vanished species from the planet Gigantus in the Andromeda Galaxy. The Gigantians built the Stranger to stand against the Overmind, a villainous composite entity fashioned by the Gigantians' traditional enemies, the Eternians. The Stranger wandered for eons until he encountered Earth. Convinced that Earth's superhuman mutants posed a threat to the greater galaxy, the Stranger attempted to destroy the Earth on multiple occasions. The heroism of champions such as the Hulk won him over, and the Stranger agreed to spare Earth for the immediate future. For a while he used the Abomination as a servant.

The Stranger eventually faced and defeated the Overmind, then selected an Earth from the New Universe (Earth-148611) as an object of study for his Labworld. The Stranger subsequently posed as the Beyonder and gathered a number of superpowered people to battle for him as an experiment. It was revealed that he created Ego the Living Planet and Alter-Ego as part of an experiment. **DW, MF**

FACTFILE
REAL NAME
Unrevealed
OCCUPATION
Surveyor of Worlds
BASE
The Stranger's own Labworld

HEIGHT Variable
WEIGHT Variable
EYES Black
HAIR White

FIRST APPEARANCE
Uncanny X-Men #11 (May 1965)

POWERS
Vast strength; wields cosmic power to emit energy blasts, reshape matter, generate force fields, levitate, and change his own size.

STONE, TIBERIUS

FIRST APPEARANCE Iron Man #37 (February 2001)
REAL NAME Tiberius "Ty" Stone **OCCUPATION** Owner of Viastone, a multinational corporation **BASE** Mobile
HEIGHT 6 ft **WEIGHT** 210 lbs **EYES** Blue **HAIR** Blond
SPECIAL POWERS/ABILITIES Brilliant business strategist; a totally ruthless sociopath, driven by jealousy and revenge.

Ty Stone and Tony Stark (IRON MAN) were childhood friends, although their parents were business rivals. Stark's father eventually drove Stone's to the verge of bankruptcy. Pretending to still be Stark's friend, Stone vowed to get revenge. He planted news stories that tarnished Stark's reputation, stole Stark's girlfriend, Rumiko Fujikawa, and attempted to take over Stark Industries. He later worked for the KINGPIN and infiltrated Horizon Labs to sabotage the work of Peter Parker (SPIDER-MAN). He also turned out to be an ancestor of SPIDER-MAN 2099. **TB, MF**

STRONG GUY

FIRST APPEARANCE New Mutants #29 (July 1985)
REAL NAME Guido Carosella **OCCUPATION** Special Enforcer for X-Factor Investigations **BASE** New York City
HEIGHT 7 ft **WEIGHT** 750 lbs **EYES** Blue **HAIR** White
SPECIAL POWERS/ABILITIES Absorbs kinetic energy—failure to release it quickly causes physical distortions and damages heart; kinetic energy enhances strength.

Guido Carosella worked as the bodyguard for Lila CHENEY until he wound up on Muir Island under the SHADOW KING's control. After X-FACTOR freed him, he joined their team and became friends with MULTIPLE MAN. He joined X-Factor Investigations, then served as the sheriff of New York's Mutant Town. He kept his powers after M-Day but was later killed while saving J. Jonah JAMESON from an assassination attempt. Layla MILLER resurrected him, but without his soul—for now. **AD, MF**

SUGAR MAN

FIRST APPEARANCE Generation Next #2 (April 1995)
REAL NAME Unknown
OCCUPATION Adventurer, former assassin **BASE** Mobile
HEIGHT 6 ft 9 in **WEIGHT** 400 lbs **EYES** White **HAIR** Black
SPECIAL POWERS/ABILITIES Enhanced strength and reflexes; razor-sharp extendible tongue; four arms; advanced regenerative abilities; can control his size and mass.

Sugar Man comes from the future of Earth-295—the Age of Apocalypse—where he operated the Seattle Core slave camp. When COLOSSUS came to rescue his sister Illyana Rasputin (MAGIK), Sugar Man shrank down and hid in Colossus's boot, emerging in Earth-616, 20 years in the past. From there, he built up the island nation of Genosha by supplying genetic technology to create a population of mutant slaves. Sugar Man survived the Genosha holocaust, but he took a brutal beating at the hands of CALLISTO. He later returned to his home timeline to help the new APOCALYPSE, but was captured by the Human Resistance. **DW, MF**

STRAW MAN

FIRST APPEARANCE Dead of Night #11 (August 1975)
REAL NAME Skirra Corvus
OCCUPATION Mystic guardian **BASE** An unnamed magical realm
HEIGHT 5 ft 10 in **WEIGHT** 60 lbs **EYES** Red **HAIR** Yellow
SPECIAL POWERS/ABILITIES Incarnates himself in bodies composed of straw, projects fear, can command crows and local plant life, and has assorted other mystic attributes.

A being indigenous to an extra-dimensional realm bordering that of Earth, the Straw Man can access our universe through a mystic painting that depicts him. The painting's origins are shrouded in mystery; it is coveted by the Cult of Kalumai, who can summon their demonic master and his underlings through it. However the Straw Man considers himself a guardian of the Earth, and has successfully kept Kalumai in check. Recruited by the Dweller-In-Darkness as one of his Fear Lords, the Straw Man refused to go along with the demonic entity's plan to subjugate Earth, and he incarnated himself as Skirra Corvus, a television personality, in whose form he was able to warn DOCTOR STRANGE of the Dweller's plan. **TB**

STRYFE

Infected with a techno-organic virus, the infant Nathan Summers was taken nearly two millennia into the future of Earth-4935 to save his life. In case he should die, Mother Askani of the Askani Sisterhood had him cloned. The tyrant APOCALYPSE kidnapped and raised the clone, who he called Stryfe. The original Nathan grew up to become the hero CABLE, leader of the freedom fighters that battled armies commanded by Stryfe. Both men traveled back to the present day, where they continued to bitterly oppose each other. Although his original form was destroyed, Stryfe's consciousness managed to take over other bodies. He later sacrificed himself to save the Earth. Stryfe returned in his original form to help BISHOP hunt for Hope SUMMERS, but he was captured by Apocalypse. **PS, MF**

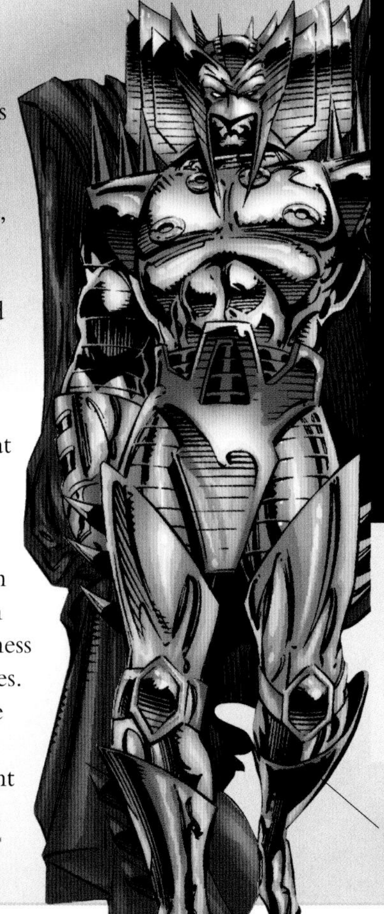

Ironically, since Stryfe is free from the techno-organic virus, he must wear metal armor for protection.

FACTFILE

REAL NAME
Stryfe

OCCUPATION
Terrorist leader

BASE
Mobile

HEIGHT 6 ft 8 in
WEIGHT 350 lbs
EYES Blue
HAIR White

FIRST APPEARANCE
The New Mutants #87 (March 1990)

STRYFE

POWERS
A mutant possessing superhuman strength and other physical abilities, Stryfe also has vast telepathic and telekinetic powers. Unlike his clone Cable, he does not have to waste any of these powers keeping a techno-organic virus in check.

STORM

The Mutant Queen of Wakanda

Goddess, mutant, and queen, Storm is a woman of many facets.

Ororo Munroe is descended from a long line of African witch-priestesses. Her mother married an American photographer, and Ororo was born in New York City. When the child was six months old, the family moved to Egypt. Five years later, Ororo's parents were killed during an Arab-Israeli conflict. Young Ororo was buried under the rubble of her home beside her dead mother's body, an experience that gave her intense claustrophobia.

THE YOUNG GODDESS

Ororo wandered the streets of Cairo and eventually became an accomplished thief and pickpocket. She even robbed PROFESSOR X, who was in Cairo to battle the SHADOW KING. By the age of 12, her amazing mutant power to control the weather began to emerge. She traveled throughout Africa, where she used her abilities to help several tribes, the members of which came to worship her as a goddess of rain.

Professor X later returned to Africa and convinced Ororo to use her powers to help all of humanity. She joined the X-MEN under the codename Storm and quickly became one of Professor X's most trusted students. At times, she even served as the team's leader.

POWERLESS

At one point, Henry Peter GYRICH shot Ororo with a weapon that removed her powers. Shortly after this, she met and fell in love with FORGE, the man who designed that weapon. She continued to work with the X-Men, eventually regaining her powers. She gave her life to defeat the ADVERSARY, but ROMA (the daughter of MERLYN) restored her.

Ororo evolved from a thief on the streets of Cairo to the leader of the X-Men.

ESSENTIAL STORYLINES

- ***Ororo: Before the Storm #1-4***
  The story of Ororo's early days, before she became an X-Man.
- ***Uncanny X-Men #253–272***
  Storm is regressed to the age of a young girl by Nanny and the Orphan Maker.
- ***Black Panther Vol. 3 #14–18***
  Ororo's courtship with and marriage to the Black Panther.

FACTFILE

REAL NAME
Ororo Munroe

OCCUPATION
Adventurer

BASE
Wakanda

HEIGHT 5 ft 11 in
WEIGHT 127 lbs
EYES Blue
HAIR White

FIRST APPEARANCE
Giant-Size X-Men #1 (1975)

POWERS
Mutant ability to manipulate the weather. Storm can control the creation of rain, snow, sleet, fog, hail, and lightning. She can create hurricane-force winds or lower the temperature around her to freezing point and below.

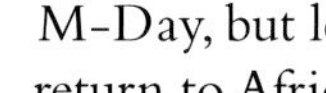

THE MUTANT QUEEN

Ororo retained her powers after M-Day, but left the X-Men to return to Africa. While there, she married the BLACK PANTHER (T'Challa), becoming the queen of Wakanda. She returned to the X-Men to help them search for Hope SUMMERS. She later helped defeat the Shadow King, who had possessed her husband's form. She was forced to take over as the sole ruler of Wakanda after DOCTOR DOOM critically injured T'Challa. She initially sided with the X-Men in their conflict against the AVENGERS, putting her on the opposite side to her husband. Afterward, he had their marriage annulled, and she returned to the X-Men full time. **MT, MF**

Storm is one of the most powerful members of the X-Men and the Queen of Wakanda.

Although now the queen of Wakanda, Ororo refuses to abandon her mutant friends in their times of need.

FACTFILE
REAL NAME
Hope Summers
OCCUPATION
Savior
BASE
New York

HEIGHT 5 ft 6 in
WEIGHT 105 lbs
EYES Green
HAIR Red

FIRST APPEARANCE
X-Men #205 (January 2008)

POWERS
Can copy the powers of any nearby mutant; telepathic and telekinetic powers.

SUMMERS, HOPE

As the first mutant born after the SCARLET WITCH erased most mutant powers on M-Day, Hope became a point of massive conflict, with mutants from both the future and the present trying to control, kidnap, or even kill her. CABLE escaped with her into the future and raised the orphaned girl as his own daughter, while BISHOP continued to chase them throughout time. As a teen, Hope returned to the present and immediately became a target of BASTION, but she defeated him and his helpers with her newly manifesting mutant powers.

Joining the X-MEN, Hope helped in their efforts to track down other new mutants. She stayed with CYCLOPS on Utopia when WOLVERINE left. She became the focal point of a conflict between the AVENGERS and the X-Men when the Phoenix Force returned to Earth. She became the Phoenix Force's host but, with the help of the Scarlet Witch, she wished it away. Afterward, she joined the Jean Grey School for Higher Learning and tried to live a more normal life. **MF**

Although not related to Jean Grey, Hope adopted a uniform much like the one Jean wore as Phoenix.

FACTFILE
REAL NAME
Shiro Yoshida
OCCUPATION
Adventurer
BASE
Department H, Canada, (formerly) Tokyo, Japan.

HEIGHT 5 ft 10 in
WEIGHT 175 lbs
EYES Brown
HAIR Black

FIRST APPEARANCE
X-Men #64 (January 1970)

POWERS
Can project "solar fire" and create super-heated air currents to fly; has a psionic protective force field; trained in karate, Japanese Samurai swordsmanship, and kendo.

SUNFIRE

Sunfire's mother was exposed to radiation when the US dropped an atomic bomb on Hiroshima. When his mutant power surfaced, Sunfire vowed vengeance on the US, destroying a monument at the United Nations and clashing with the X-MEN. PROFESSOR XAVIER invited Sunfire to join a new group of X-Men and he did, temporarily. Preferring to go on special missions for Japan, Sunfire was hypnotised by DR. DEMONICUS to fight the West Coast AVENGERS. He subsequently served with ALPHA FLIGHT and BIG HERO 6. He lost his legs in a battle with LADY DEATHSTRIKE and then lost his powers on M-Day. He later became APOCALYPSE's latest version of Famine and, after Apocalypse's defeat, joined the MARAUDERS in their hunt for Hope SUMMERS. Repowered, he later joined the Avengers Unity Squad. **TD, MF**

On Earth-2109, Shiro's cousin (and Wolverine's love) Mariko Yashida became Sunfire and later served with the Exiles until her death.

Sunfire's temper runs as hot as the temperatures his powers can conjure and has cost him much over the years.

Summers, Rachel

Mutant child from another time

In an alternate future Ahab brainwashed Rachel into serving as his telepathic mutant "hound."

Rachel Summers is the daughter of Scott Summers (Cyclops) and Jean Grey (alias Phoenix) in an alternate timeline known as the "Days of Future Past" or Earth-811. In this reality, the US government activated mutant-hunting robot Sentinels after Senator Robert Kelly was assassinated by mutant terrorists. Federal troops attacked Professor X's mansion, and captured Rachel.

Phoenix

Rachel was brainwashed into becoming a mutant "hound," using her telepathic powers to track down other mutants. Her face was branded with tattoos (which nowadays she uses her powers to conceal). Eventually Rachel rebelled and attacked her master, Ahab. As punishment, she was confined to a mutant concentration camp. By now the Sentinels had taken control of North America. In an effort to change history, Rachel used her powers to send the astral self of her friend Kate Pryde (a middle-aged version of Kitty) back in time. Kate's spirit journeyed to the "mainstream" reality of the X-Men, where she thwarted Kelly's assassination. After returning to their alternate future, Kate sent Rachel back through time to the "mainstream" reality, where she joined the X-Men. Rachel bonded with the Phoenix Force, enabling her to tap its energies, and adopted the name "Phoenix." Subsequently she became a founding member of Excalibur.

Mother Askani

Rachel was cast two thousand years into the alternate future of Earth-4935, a world ruled by Apocalypse. There she founded a group of rebels, the Askani. Decades later, as the elderly Mother Askani, she sent one of her followers back in time to retrieve the infant Nathan Summers. Mother Askani also transported the astral selves of Scott Summers and Jean Grey into new bodies in this alternate future, where they raised Nathan for ten years. Then Mother Askani sent Scott and Jean's astral selves back to their proper time and bodies, before she herself perished. Nathan grew up to become Cable. After an alteration in the timestream, Rachel was a living teenager once more, though she lost her connection to the Phoenix Force. She was held captive in an alternate future by a being named Gaunt. Cable returned her to the X-Men's time, and she rejoined the team. To honor her mother, Rachel started to call herself "Rachel Grey" in private and "Marvel Girl" at work.

After the Shi'ar murdered most of the Grey family, Rachel joined Professor X in his pursuit of her uncle Vulcan. When her grandfather Corsair was killed, she joined his Starjammers in their effort to overthrow Vulcan. She later returned to Earth and joined the staff of the Jean Grey School of Higher Learning. She helped the X-Men in their battle with the Avengers. **PS, MF**

In honor of Jean Grey, Summers has assumed her mother's identities of Phoenix and Marvel Girl.

SUMMERS, RACHEL

FACTFILE

REAL NAME
Rachel Anne Summers, now Rachel Grey

OCCUPATION
Adventurer

BASE
Mobile

HEIGHT 5 ft 7 in
WEIGHT 125 lbs
EYES Green
HAIR Red

FIRST APPEARANCE
The Uncanny X-Men #141 (January 1981)

POWERS

Rachel Summers has considerable telepathic and telekinetic abilities. She formerly served as the host of the Phoenix Force, which greatly amplified her psionic powers.

As Phoenix, Rachel could use the cosmic Phoenix Force, though not to the same extent as Jean Grey.

...FOR THE PERFECT VESSEL.
ONE DEAR TO ALL OUR HEARTS--
-- NATHAN CHRISTOPHER SUMMERS
WHICH IS WHY I ARRANGED TO GRAB THE CHILD FIRST.
BUT HE WAS DESPERATELY ILL. I DID WHAT I COULD TO SAVE HIM FROM THE RAVAGES OF THE TECHNO-ORGANIC VIRUS.
BUT TIME WAS RUNNING OUT AS A FAIL-SAFE, WE CREATED A HEATHLY CLONE.

As Mother Askani, Rachel created a clone of the infant Cable, called Stryfe.

ESSENTIAL STORYLINES

• New Mutants Vol. 1 #18, Excalibur Vol. 1 #52
In her timeline, Rachel witnesses the federal attack on Xavier's mansion and becomes Ahab's "hound."

• Uncanny X-Men #184-199
Rachel journeys to the "mainstream" timeline, joins the X-Men and becomes the New Phoenix.

• Adventures of Cyclops and Phoenix #1-4
As the elderly Mother Askani, Rachel brings Scott Summers and Jean Grey to a distant future to raise the young Cable.

Sunspot

FIRST APPEARANCE Marvel Graphic Novel #4 (1982)
REAL NAME Roberto da Costa
OCCUPATION Leader of Hellfire Club **BASE** New York City
HEIGHT 5 ft **WEIGHT** 130 lbs **EYES** Brown **HAIR** Black
SPECIAL POWERS/ABILITIES Solar powers provide super-strength, thermal updrafts for flight, projection of heat and light, and concussive blasts of solar energy.

Sunspot grew up as a wealthy heir in Rio de Janeiro, Brazil. In his powered-up form, his mutant powers transform him into a being of black, crackling force. He has worked with several teams, including the New Mutants, the Fallen Angels, and X-Force. More recently, he accepted a position as a Lord Imperial of the Hellfire Club. Later, he joined the rebooted New Mutants and, when that team dissolved, the Avengers. After leaving the Hellfire Club, he joined the X-Men in San Francisco and agreed to help Danielle Moonstar train the Young X-Men. Sunspot's genetic copy—Reignfire—was a terrorist with the Mutant Liberation Front, but he has been killed. **DW, MF**

The Young X-Men were tricked into thinking Sunspot was the new leader of the Brotherhood of Evil Mutants.

Super-Adaptoid

FIRST APPEARANCE Tales Of Suspense #82 (October 1966)
REAL NAME None **OCCUPATION** Super-assassin
BASE Mobile **HEIGHT/WEIGHT/EYES/HAIR** Variable
SPECIAL POWERS/ABILITIES Android that can duplicate the appearance and powers, clothing and weaponry of anyone who passes within 10 ft of the scanning instruments in its eyes. It can mimic a maximum of eight beings at a single time.

The criminal organization AIM built the Super-Adaptoid and powered it with a sliver from the Cosmic Cube. Sent to destroy Captain America, it copied the powers and appearances of several heroes, but the Avengers defeated it time after time. Other versions of the Adaptoid have plagued the Earth, including one merged with Yelena Belova (Black Widow). The Ultra-Adaptoid infiltrated the criminal group MODOK's 11 for AIM. At the end of the Dark Reign, HAMMER outfitted Norman Osborn (*see* Green Goblin) with the powers of the Super-Adaptoid. **TD, MF**

Super-Apes

Over time, the savage Super-Apes gained human level intelligence.

Reed Richards wanted to test a new rocket fuel in a ship designed to take the Fantastic Four to the moon. They hoped to get to the moon before the Soviets. But unknown to Reed, a Soviet scientist named Ivan Kragoff had built his own ship, which he hoped would get him to the moon first. Kragoff had trained three apes, a gorilla, a baboon, and a orangutan to help him operate the ship. Aware of the cosmic rays that gave the Fantastic Four their powers, Kragoff intentionally exposed himself and the apes to cosmic rays during their journey to the moon. Kragoff, now calling himself the Red Ghost, and the three apes all gained different super-powered abilities.

Once on the moon, the Super-Apes battled the Fantastic Four but quickly turned against Kragoff, who starved them to keep them controlled. As their powers developed, each of the Super Apes gained human-level intelligence, and they allied with the Red Ghost again. Miklho died at the hands of the Red Hulk, and was replaced by Grigori, a young ape with the same powers. **MT**

Super-Apes
1 Igor the baboon
2 Miklho the gorilla
3 Peotor the orangutan
4 Red Ghost

FACTFILE
MEMBERS
IGOR
A baboon
MIKLHO
A gorilla
PEOTOR
An orangutan

BASE Mobile

FIRST APPEARANCE
Fantastic Four #13 (April 1963)

SUPER-APES

POWERS
Igor: possesses the ability to shapeshift.
Miklho: possesses super-strength.
Peotor: possesses the ability to control magnetism.

SUPER-SKRULL

Super-Skrull projects a beam that briefly paralyzes his foes and makes them do his will.

After the FANTASTIC FOUR prevented the SKRULLS from conquering Earth, the Skrull Emperor vowed to develop a super-weapon that could destroy them. His scientists created the Super-Skrull, a warrior bionically re-engineered to possess all the powers of the Fantastic Four. The Super-Skrull's first battle ended in failure and he was imprisoned by the Fantastic Four.

The Super-Skrull battled the AVENGERS and CAPTAIN MARVEL during the KREE-Skrull War, and over the years he has clashed with SPIDER-MAN, MS. MARVEL, SASQUATCH, IRON FIST, Luke CAGE, and the YOUNG AVENGERS. He was killed defending his people during the ANNIHILATION, but later returned and helped the Kree fight the PHALANX invasion. During the SECRET INVASION, he saved the life of NOVA and then came to Earth to kill his daughter Jazinda, but ended up saving her instead. Dozens of other Super-Skrulls with different sets of powers followed in Kl'rt's wake. **TD, MF**

FACTFILE

REAL NAME
Kl'rt

OCCUPATION
Warrior

BASE
Mobile, usually within the Skrull Empire

HEIGHT 6 ft
WEIGHT 625 lbs
EYES Green
HAIR None

FIRST APPEARANCE
Fantastic Four #18 (September 1963)

SUPER-SKRULL

POWERS

The Super-Skrull is an extraterrestrial possessing the combined abilities of the Fantastic Four, and the physical malleability common to all Skrulls. He can project hypnotic energy from his eyes.

SUPREME INTELLIGENCE

SUPREME INTELLIGENCE

FACTFILE

REAL NAME
Supremor

OCCUPATION
Planetary leader

BASE
Kree-Lar

HEIGHT n/a
WEIGHT n/a
EYES Black with yellow pupils
HAIR Green stalks

FIRST APPEARANCE
Fantastic Four #65 (August 1967)

POWERS

The Supreme Intelligence possesses the combined intellect of the greatest minds in Kree history. In the past, the Supreme Intelligence has projected its consciousness into a powerful artificial body in order to actively engage in battle.

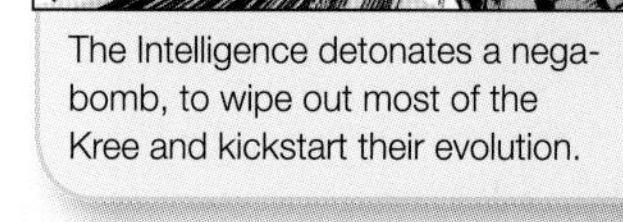

The Intelligence detonates a nega-bomb, to wipe out most of the Kree and kickstart their evolution.

Decades ago, the KREE race learned that their ancient intergalactic enemies, the SKRULLS, had created a cosmic cube. To maintain parity, they created the Supreme Intelligence, an entity made up of the finest minds ever to exist within the Kree empire. Upon their deaths, those brains deemed worthy of being added to the great repository were absorbed into the Supreme Intelligence, adding their knowledge and experience to its own. The Supreme Intelligence seized control of the Kree empire, becoming at once its dictator and an object of religious worship.

After CAPTAIN MARVEL (Genis-Vell) destroyed and rebuilt the universe, House Fiyero led the Kree instead, keeping the Supreme Intelligence in a state of undeath. RONAN THE ACCUSER tried to euthanize it, but it survived. Ronan later resurrected the Supreme Intelligence to lead the Kree again, by merging two alternate-universe MISTER FANTASTICS with a Supremor Seed. **TB**

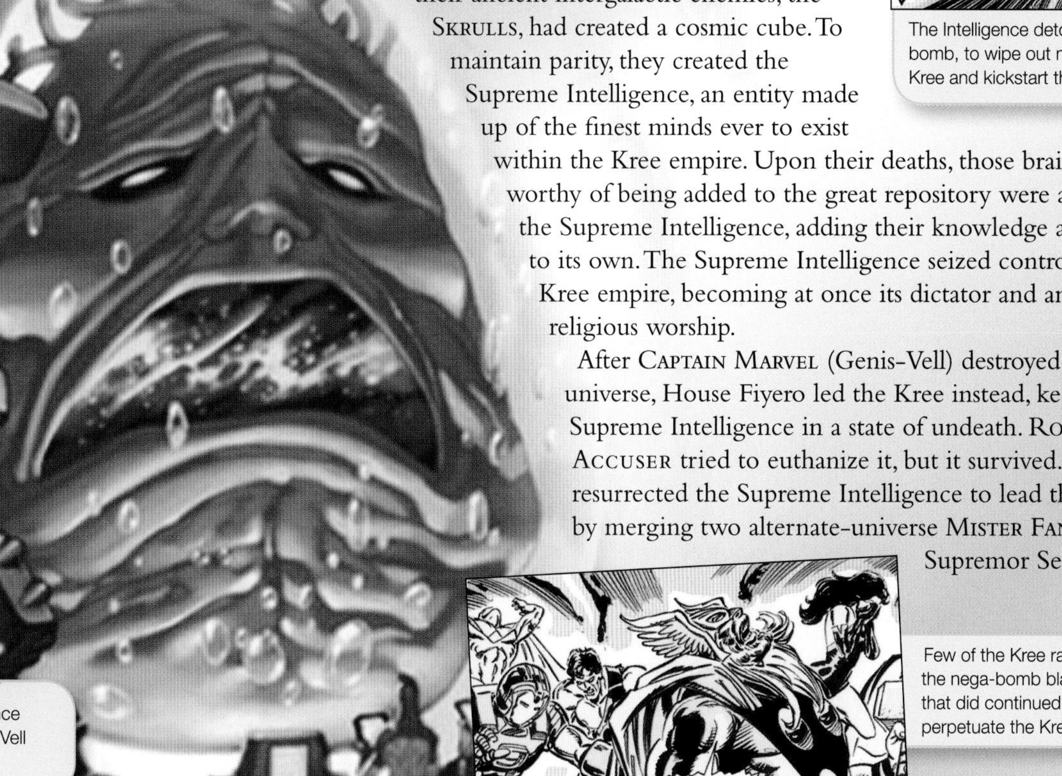

At one point, the Supreme Intelligence wished to add Rick Jones and Mar-Vell to its brain bank.

Few of the Kree race escaped the nega-bomb blast, but those that did continued to evolve and perpetuate the Kree empire.

Surge

FIRST APPEARANCE New Mutants #8 (January 2004)
REAL NAME Noriko "Nori" Ashida
OCCUPATION Student
BASE Xavier Institute **HEIGHT** 5 ft 7 in **WEIGHT** 137 lbs
EYES Brown **HAIR** Black (dyed blue)
SPECIAL POWERS/ABILITIES Absorbs electricity and transforms it into electric bolts or bursts of speed.

Raised in Japan, Nori came to the US after her parents kicked her out of their home after she displayed mutant powers. She joined the Xavier Institute, and Beast made her a pair of gauntlets with which she could control her powers, something she had only been able to do with drugs before. Taking the codename Surge, Nori became part of the New Mutants and struck up a relationship with Prodigy. She remained with the X-Men on Utopia after her team disbanded, and after Cyclops was put into prison, she joined the Jean Grey School for Higher Learning. **MF**

Swarm

FIRST APPEARANCE The Champions #14 (July 1977)
REAL NAME Fritz Von Meyer
OCCUPATION Scientist, conqueror **BASE** Mobile
HEIGHT 6 ft 5 in **WEIGHT** Unrevealed **EYES** None **HAIR** None
SPECIAL POWERS/ABILITIES Von Meyer's consciousness can mentally control a mutant queen bee, and through her, vast numbers of mutant bees.

Nazi scientist Fritz Von Meyer was attacked by a colony of bees whose exposure to radiation had given them unusually high intelligence. His body was consumed, but his consciousness survived and took control of the bees, which swarmed in the configuration of a human body around his skeleton. Thus was created Swarm. Seeking world conquest, Swarm has battled the Champions of Los Angeles, Spider-Man, and the Runaways. When he faced the Thunderbolts, Venom devoured his skeleton. He later cropped up with a new hive in Buenos Aires. **PS, MF**

Switzler, Beverly

FIRST APPEARANCE Howard the Duck #1 (January 1976)
REAL NAME Beverly Switzler
OCCUPATION Former art model and actress
BASE Cleveland, Ohio
HEIGHT/WEIGHT Unrevealed **EYES** Blue **HAIR** Red
SPECIAL POWERS/ABILITIES As an art model, she can stand perfectly still.

A former art model, Beverly Switzler's life was transformed by an encounter with that extradimensional waterfowl, Howard the Duck. After Howard rescued her from financial wizard, Pro-Rata, the pair began a life together in Cleveland, Ohio. Things weren't easy—they had difficulty paying the rent and, despite Howard's desire for the quiet life, they were constantly getting embroiled in the shenanigans of nefarious characters. Doctor Bong proved to be the most intransigent of these. Lusting after Beverly, he eventually forced her to marry him, but when he failed to consummate their relationship she returned to Howard and had the marriage annulled. **AD**

SWORD

FACTFILE

NOTABLE MEMBERS

ABIGAIL BRAND
Director.

BEAST
Mutant genius.

DEATH'S HEAD
Cyborg bounty hunter.

HENRY GYRICH
Co-director.

LOCKHEED
Mini-dragon spy.

SPIDER-WOMAN
Spider-powered hero.

SYDREN
Alien hacker/telepath.

BASE
The Peak space station, orbiting Earth

FIRST APPEARANCE
Astonishing X-Men #6 (December 2004)

(Sentient World Order and Response Department) was the semi-autonomous division of SHIELD charged with protecting Earth from alien threats. Abigail Brand has been in charge of the organization since its founding, sharing the directorship responsibilities with Henry Gyrich only during the Dark Reign. The organization concentrates on diplomacy as much as espionage or military action and specializes in communication with new alien races from its space station headquarters, known as the Peak. **MF**

Orbiting the Earth, SWORD's base The Peak is ideal for surveillance of the world's trouble spots.

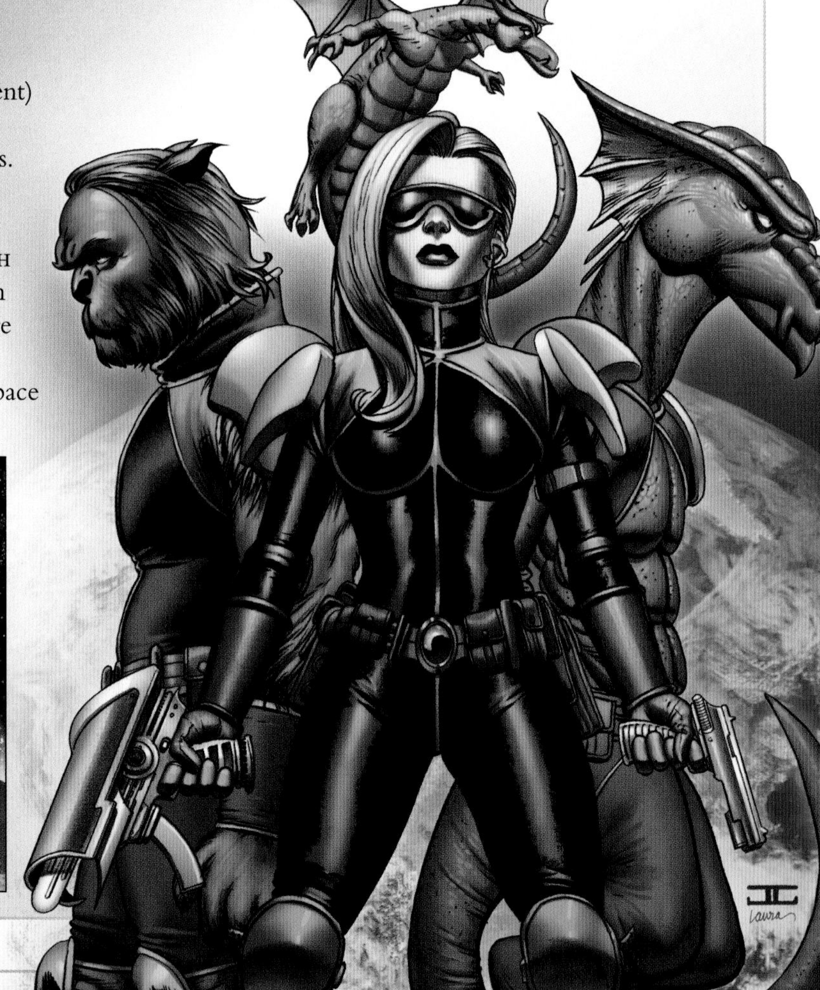

SWORDSMAN

FACTFILE

REAL NAME
Philip Javert

OCCUPATION
Adventurer

BASE
Mobile

HEIGHT 6 ft 4 in
WEIGHT 250 lbs
EYES Blue
HAIR Black

FIRST APPEARANCE
Avengers #343 (January 1992)

POWERS

The Swordsman was a skilled swordfighter and combatant; expert with all bladed weapons; usually carried a set of throwing knives as well as his sword; a superb athlete; excelled in unarmed combat.

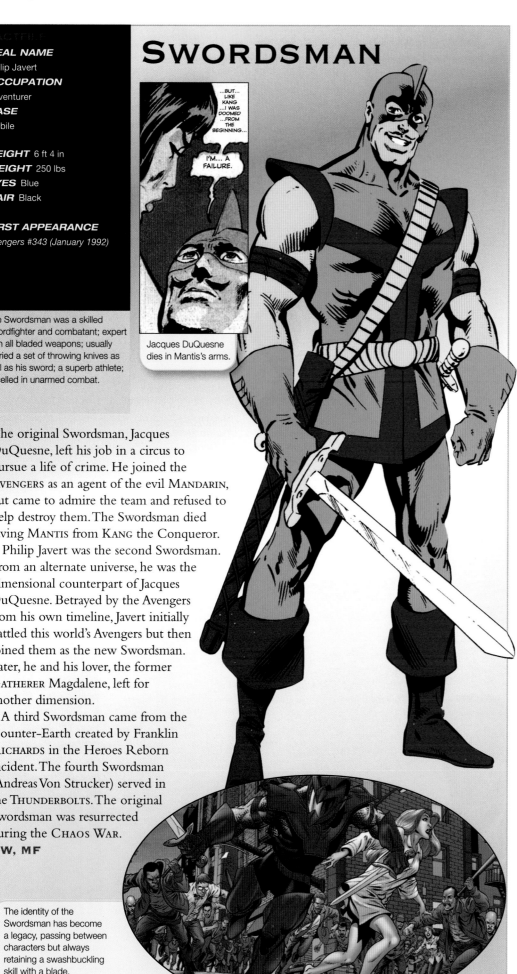

SWORDSMAN

Jacques DuQuesne dies in Mantis's arms.

The original Swordsman, Jacques DuQuesne, left his job in a circus to pursue a life of crime. He joined the Avengers as an agent of the evil Mandarin, but came to admire the team and refused to help destroy them. The Swordsman died saving Mantis from Kang the Conqueror.

Philip Javert was the second Swordsman. From an alternate universe, he was the dimensional counterpart of Jacques DuQuesne. Betrayed by the Avengers from his own timeline, Javert initially battled this world's Avengers but then joined them as the new Swordsman. Later, he and his lover, the former Gatherer Magdalene, left for another dimension.

A third Swordsman came from the Counter-Earth created by Franklin Richards in the Heroes Reborn incident. The fourth Swordsman (Andreas Von Strucker) served in the Thunderbolts. The original Swordsman was resurrected during the Chaos War.
DW, MF

The identity of the Swordsman has become a legacy, passing between characters but always retaining a swashbuckling skill with a blade.

SYNCH

FIRST APPEARANCE X-Men #36 (September 1994)
REAL NAME Everett Thomas
OCCUPATION Student **BASE** Massachusetts Academy
HEIGHT 5 ft 11 in **WEIGHT** 165 lbs **EYES** Brown
HAIR Black (shaved bald)
SPECIAL POWERS/ABILITIES Able to take on the superhuman powers of others while they remain in his immediate vicinity.

When teenager Everett Thomas' mutant power emerged, the entity Harvest tried to experiment on him. Rescued by Emma Frost, Jubilee, and Sabretooth, Thomas joined with them to free Husk, M, Skin, and Blink from Harvest. Everett enrolled at the Massachusetts Academy, joining Generation X as Synch. While battling the villain Emplate, who fed off the bone marrow of mutants, Synch became a creature like Emplate himself. He was rescued from Emplate's influence by his teammates. Synch sacrificed his life to save the Generation X students by trying to disarm a bomb planted by Adrienne Frost, elder sister of Emma Frost, at the time Generation X's headmistress. Selene later resurrected Synch for her attack on the X-Men and then killed him.
MT

Taine, Sydney

FIRST APPEARANCE Nightside #1 (December 2001)
REAL NAME Sydney Taine
OCCUPATION Police detective **BASE** New York City
HEIGHT/WEIGHT/EYES Unrevealed **HAIR** Black and gray
SPECIAL POWERS/ABILITIES Skilled in a variety of martial arts, including capoeira; adept in various forms of weapons combat; no known superpowers.

Sydney Taine is the only detective in the NYPD trusted by the Others, individuals that appear human but who are driven by sinister thirsts and passions. While investigating the death of three crime bosses, Sydney, partnered by Ape Largo, uncovered a plot by the Others to obtain the Three Lost Treasures of Tao. Defeating them with cunning and fighting prowess, Sydney returned the stolen treasures to Suzuki Shosan, her former teacher. Sydney may be a member of the Players, a powerful alien race. **AD**

Talbot, Major Matt

FIRST APPEARANCE Incredible Hulk #436 (December 1995)
REAL NAME William M. "Matt" Talbot
OCCUPATION US Air Force Major
BASE Mobile
HEIGHT 6 ft **WEIGHT** 210 lbs
EYES Blue **HAIR** Brown
SPECIAL POWERS/ABILITIES None.

Major William M. "Matt" Talbot is the nephew of Colonel Glenn Talbot. Matt Talbot is furious at his uncle's wife Betty (*see* Ross, Betty) for dumping his uncle in favor of the Hulk.

Matt went to Betty's house and appeared to rescue her from a berserk soldier, but then he slapped her and called her names for hurting his uncle. Out of control, Talbot shot Betty in each leg. When the Hulk came to rescue Betty, he was hit by Talbot's plasma blasts, but it turned out that the gun Talbot used contained stun pellets that soon wore off. Talbot escaped having exacted some measure of revenge for his uncle's broken heart. **MT**

Talisman

FIRST APPEARANCE Alpha Flight #5 (December 1983)
REAL NAME Elizabeth Twoyoungmen
OCCUPATION Student **BASE** Canada
HEIGHT 5 ft 10 in **WEIGHT** 175 lbs **EYES** Blue **HAIR** Black
SPECIAL POWERS/ABILITIES Has natural mystical abilities and can control magical energy; when wearing the "circlet," she can command spirits and manipulate mystical energies.

The latest in a long line of North American shamans, Elizabeth Twoyoungmen transformed into the long-prophesied Talisman when she place a circlet of enchantment on her forehead. She later went on to join Alpha Flight. The circlet gradually corrupted Elizabeth and caused her to grow farther apart from her father Michael Twoyoungmen. Michael took the circlet to defeat the mystical creature Pestilence, but he later returned it to his daughter. After her father's death, she joined Sasquatch's Canadian team, Omega Flight, subsequently retiring from active duty in order to return to her tribe. **TB, MF**

Talbot, Colonel Glenn

TALBOT, COLONEL GLENN

FACTFILE
REAL NAME
Glenn Talbot
OCCUPATION
Major, later Colonel in US Air Force; head of security, Desert Base; later adjutant to General T. E. "Thunderbolt" Ross; later commanding officer, Gamma Base
BASE
Desert Base, New Mexico; later Gamma Base, New Mexico

HEIGHT 6 ft 1 in
WEIGHT 215 lbs
EYES Blue
HAIR Brown

FIRST APPEARANCE
Tales to Astonish #61 (November 1964)

POWERS
Normal human strength

General Thaddeus E. "Thunderbolt" Ross installed Major Glenn Talbot as security head of Desert Base, New Mexico, to investigate Dr. Bruce Banner. Talbot became Banner's rival for Ross's daughter, Betty (*see* Ross, Betty).

He eventually learned that Banner was the Hulk. For years Talbot aided General Ross in attempts to capture or kill the Hulk. Betty married Talbot, but she later divorced him, realizing she still loved Banner. Promoted to colonel, Talbot was killed by an electrical overload while attacking the Hulk. **PS**

Glenn Talbot married Betty Ross, but she never stopped loving his rival Bruce Banner, alias the Hulk.

Tanaka, Kenjiro

FIRST APPEARANCE Quasar #5 (December 1989)
REAL NAME Kenjiro Tanaka
OCCUPATION Former SHIELD agent **BASE** New York City
HEIGHT 5 ft 10 in **WEIGHT** 160 lbs **EYES** Black **HAIR** Black
SPECIAL POWERS/ABILITIES None; received combat training from SHIELD.

Kenjiro "Ken" Tanaka attended SHIELD academy alongside Wendell Vaughn, who later became the cosmic hero Quasar. After graduation, Tanaka took an undercover position within International Data Integration and Control (IDIC) and became its director of design. He eventually left IDIC to join his former classmate at Vaughn Security Systems. Tanaka discovered the link between Wendell Vaughn and Quasar but agreed to keep the secret safe. He now heads up Vaughn Security Systems while Quasar is away saving the galaxy. **DW**

TARANTULA

Hero for Hire with a sting

A criminal used the name Tarantula during the days of the Old West, but the first modern Tarantula, Anton Miguel Rodriguez, was a brutal revolutionary from the small, South American country of Delvadia. Government officials gave him his powers with a variant of the super-soldier formula, intending to make him a national symbol, like CAPTAIN AMERICA.

KILLER FOR HIRE

Instead, he became a professional criminal and assassin. In New York, where he hijacked a boat on the Hudson River, SPIDER-MAN and the PUNISHER thwarted his plans. He later mutated into a humanoid spider due to treatments from Roxxon Oil, and he killed himself in a police standoff. His daughter donned the Tarantula costume and teamed up with the daughter of BATROC THE LEAPER before dying at the hands of the TASKMASTER.

Captain Luis Alvarez of Delvadia became the second official Tarantula. On a mission to the US to execute Delvadian refugees, he battled SPIDER-MAN and lost. Exiled from his country, Alvarez died when the armed vigilante team the Jury executed him.

MARIA VASQUEZ

During the Civil War, a new Tarantula joined Misty Knight's Heroes for Hire. Maria Vasquez had abilities and weapons similar to those of her predecessors, but no other connection. She hoped to avenge her sister, who died when Nitro blew up Stamford, Connecticut. After World War Hulk, she nearly died when her teammate Humbug offered her to No-Name, the Brood member of the Warbound, but Shang-Chi saved her.

Enhanced reflexes and military training allowed the Tarantula to make deadly stabs with his venomous boot-spikes.

Carlos LaMuerto was a criminal known as the Black Tarantula. He fought Spider-Man and later became Daredevil's lieutenant and helped him lead the Hand.

TARANTULA

FACTFILE

REAL NAME
Maria Vasquez

OCCUPATION
Hero for hire

BASE
New York

HEIGHT Unrevealed
WEIGHT Unrevealed
EYES Green
HAIR Black with red streak

FIRST APPEARANCE
Heroes For Hire #1 (August 2006)

POWERS
Martial arts and knife fighting expert. Spiked blades in the wrists and toes of her costume.

ESSENTIAL STORYLINES
- ***Amazing Spider-Man #134***
First appearance of the original Tarantula.
- ***Heroes for Hire #1***
Maria Vasquez appears for the first time.
- ***Heroes for Hire #15***
Maria Vasquez is left in a coma as the team go their separate ways.

THE OTHERS

Spider-Man's clone KAINE became a new Tarantula for a while. Slain by KRAVEN's family to resurrect their patriarch, Kaine returned from the dead in a half-spider form. The JACKAL and the SPIDER QUEEN controlled him until he was given the cure for the Spider-Island outbreak, returning him to a more stable state than he'd ever known. **DW, MF**

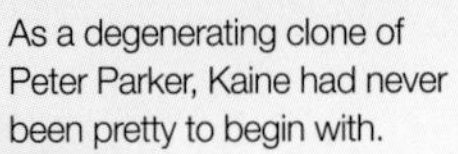

As a degenerating clone of Peter Parker, Kaine had never been pretty to begin with.

TASKMASTER

FACTFILE

REAL NAME
Tony Masters

OCCUPATION
Mercenary, teacher

BASE Mobile

HEIGHT 6 ft 2 in
WEIGHT 220 lbs
EYES Brown
HAIR Brown

FIRST APPEARANCE
Avengers #195 (May 1980)

POWERS
Can copy other people's movements, regardless of complexity, after watching them once.

TASKMASTER

The Taskmaster has the unique ability to duplicate physical movements he's seen, something he calls photographic reflexes, but at the cost of his own memories. He combined these new skills with a set of weapons similar to those used by Super Heroes to transform himself into a highly dangerous villain, a match even for the AVENGERS. Eventually he decided that training criminals made more sense than committing crimes, so he set up a series of academies to train henchmen. Later, while in prison, he even trained John Walker (USAGENT) for his position as the new CAPTAIN AMERICA.

Taskmaster became an instructor at Camp Hammond, teaching the youths of the FIFTY-STATE INITIATIVE. Afterward, he returned to working as a mercenary and started filling the gaps in his memories. He discovered that he'd been an agent of SHIELD who'd accidentally ingested a Nazi serum that granted him his strange abilities, and that he'd been married to Mercedes Merced. Forced to copy the combat moves of a man called Redshirt, he managed to kill the man but forgot who his wife was again. He later joined SHIELD's secret Avengers team. **DW, MF**

TAURUS

FIRST APPEARANCE The Avengers #72 (January 1970)
REAL NAME Cornelius Van Lunt
OCCUPATION Criminal mastermind **BASE** New York City
HEIGHT 6 ft 2 in **WEIGHT** 260 lbs **EYES** Brown **HAIR** Black
SPECIAL POWERS/ABILITIES Utilized Star-Blazer handgun, which fired blasts of stellar energy.

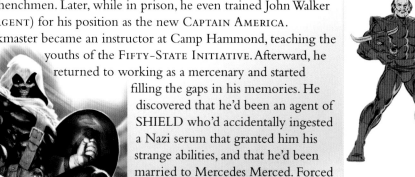

Fascinated by astrology, multimillionaire Cornelius Van Lunt secretly founded the criminal organization ZODIAC to achieve political and economic domination of the world. Each of Zodiac's 12 leaders was named after his or her astrological sign and was based in a different American city: Van Lunt became Taurus, based in New York. Both in his true identity and as Taurus, Van Lunt clashed with the AVENGERS. Van Lunt ended up battling MOON KNIGHT aboard a plane and died when it crashed. There have since been various other versions of the Zodiac organization, each with its own Taurus. **PS**

TATTERDEMALION

FIRST APPEARANCE Werewolf By Night #9 (September 1973)
REAL NAME Arnold Pattonroth (alias Michael Wyatt)
OCCUPATION Tap-dancer, actor **BASE** Los Angeles
HEIGHT 5 ft 9 in **WEIGHT** 165 lbs **EYES** Blue **HAIR** Brown
SPECIAL POWERS/ABILITIES Enhanced strength, speed; gloves treated with a solvent that dissolves paper and fabric; Kevlar body armor; cloak contains chloroform capsules; indestructible scarf.

Pattonroth was swindled of his life's savings by Las Vegas mobsters. He joined an army of derelicts on the streets of LA and declared war on the rich. Defeated by the WEREWOLF and SPIDER-MAN, he moved back to Las Vegas and attacked the criminals who had stolen from him. He later returned to LA and was recruited into the criminal organization Night Shift, run by the SHROUD. During the CIVIL WAR, he was forced to fight for the THUNDERBOLTS. Later, in Los Angeles, COUNT NEFARIA killed him and the rest of Night Shift. **TD, MF**

TEEN BRIGADE

FACTFILE

MEMBERS
RICK JONES (founder), **CANDY**, **RIDER**, **SPECS**, **WHEELS**, plus other unnamed volunteers.

BASE
Mobile

FIRST APPEARANCE
Incredible Hulk #6 (March 1963)

The original Teen Brigade was a group of teenaged shortwave radio enthusiasts, founded by Rick JONES to keep tabs on the HULK. A Teen Brigade call for help assembled the AVENGERS for the very first time, and another helped CAPTAIN AMERICA track down a suspect who had turned the Avengers to stone. The group was a precursor to Captain America's Stars and Stripes computer hotline network.

Many years later, a new Teen Brigade composed of Super Heroes formed. It included Angel Salvadore, Barnell Bohusk (BLACKWING), the IN-BETWEENER, the new MISS AMERICA, and the Ultimate Nullifier. Jack Truman, a former agent of SHIELD, guided them as they fought demons called the Braak'nhüd and faced off against the YOUNG MASTERS, traveling to Latveria to stop them from assassinating Kristoff VERNARD. **DW**

The Teen Brigade used short-wave radios and Internet-enabled computers to keep in touch with each other.

Temugin

FIRST APPEARANCE Iron Man #53 (June 2002)
REAL NAME Temugin
OCCUPATION Criminal leader **BASE** China
HEIGHT/WEIGHT Unrevealed **EYES** Brown **HAIR** None
SPECIAL POWERS/ABILITIES Supreme martial artist; harnesses the power of his Chi to perform feats of incredible strength, speed, and agility; possesses the Mandarin's rings of power.

The illegitimate son of the Mandarin, Temugin was raised in a monastery and trained in the mystic martial arts. As an adult, he received a package containing the Mandarin's ten rings of power (each of which endowed the wearer with a different ability), and felt honor-bound to seek revenge on Iron Man for his father's death. Taking over the Mandarin's criminal empire, Temugin clashed with Iron Man but failed to discharge this honor-debt. He later lost a hand, along with five rings, to Puma. He subsequently joined the Agents of Atlas. Sasha Hammer was his half-sister. **TB, MF**

Terminus

FIRST APPEARANCE Fantastic Four #269 (August 1984)
REAL NAME Terminus **OCCUPATION** Destroyer of worlds
BASE Mobile **HEIGHT** 150 ft **WEIGHT** unrevealed
EYES Inapplicable **HAIR** None
SPECIAL POWERS/ABILITIES Immeasurable strength, nearly indestructible; can regenerate body parts; carries a lance that fires atomic energy.

Terminus is an intelligent creation made from living metal, grown by the alien Terminex in a failed attempt to protect them from the Celestials. A continuum of Termini exist, from Stage 1 metallic microbes to the Stage 4 behemoths represented by Terminus. Taking revenge on planets that the Celestials had spared, Terminus claimed Earth for his own but met defeat at the hands of the Fantastic Four. The Deviant called Jorro wore the Terminus armor and destroyed the Savage Land. Terminus defeated a duplicate and emerged as the Stage 5 "Ulterminus," only to be vanquished by Thor. **DW**

Terrax

FIRST APPEARANCE Fantastic Four #211 (October 1979)
REAL NAME Tyros
OCCUPATION Interstellar traveller **BASE** Mobile
HEIGHT 6 ft 6 in **WEIGHT** 2,750 lbs **EYES** Gray **HAIR** None
SPECIAL POWERS/ABILITIES Body covered with supple, rocky shell; animates rock and commands it to do his bidding; lifted Manhattan into orbit around Earth.

Galactus was looking for a new herald and chose Tyros, a despot from the planet Birj. Tyros, rechristened Terrax, remained a restless, rebellious soul, and before long he betrayed his overbearing master. Terrax traveled to Earth and battled the Fantastic Four, who handed him over to Galactus. After being killed and reborn a number of times, he returned to space. He was swept up in the Annihilation, but survived. He returned to conquer Birj and died defending it against the Phoenix Force. The Illuminati later captured a version of Terrax from another universe, its only survivor. **AD, MF**

Terror

FIRST APPEARANCE St. George #2 (1988)
REAL NAME Unknown (possibly Shreck) **OCCUPATION** Criminal
BASE San Francisco **HEIGHT** 6 ft 2 in **WEIGHT** 170 lbs
EYES Variable **HAIR** None
SPECIAL POWERS/ABILITIES Able to replace parts of his body with those of humans or animals, gaining the powers of those body parts, as well as their "memories." If Terror takes a body part from a superhuman being he gains that being's power; removes limbs or other parts by generating a special acid that allows him both to tear off a body part and to bond it to his own; expert with firearms.

At some point in the distant past, the virtually indestructible being now known as Terror battled a green, bear-shaped demon. The only way to defeat the demon was to sacrifice his own form, but in doing so he took on the form of the dead demon. He also gained the demon's power to bond the limbs of others to his body. His body is now made up of a collection of dead or decaying body parts. His associate Boneyard helped him collect body parts. He was also befriended by a half-human, half-demon being named Hellfire. Terror formed Terror Inc., an assassination bureau. **MT**

The spikes on Terror's face came from a demon. He can remove them and use them as weapons, then regrow them.

FACTFILE
REAL NAME
Thanos
OCCUPATION
Conqueror
BASE
Sanctuary III

HEIGHT 6 ft 7 in
WEIGHT 985 lbs
EYES Red
HAIR None

FIRST APPEARANCE
Iron Man #55 (February 1973)

POWERS
Synthesizes ambient cosmic energy for use in a variety of ways, from increasing strength to firing energy blasts; also possesses a personal force field and other devices.

THANOS

Born one of the ETERNALS on Saturn's moon Titan, young Thanos was ostracized because of his hideous mutant nature. Morose and withdrawn, he became obsessed with DEATH. Gathering an army of mercenaries, he set out to conquer and destroy. He slaughtered thousands on his homeworld with nuclear bombs, including his mother, and then went on a quest for a Cosmic Cube for the power to rule the universe and romance Death. Working with the AVENGERS, CAPTAIN MAR-VELL stopped him, and Death deserted him.

Infamous as the Mad Titan, Thanos committed many more atrocities in the name of wooing Death, including eradicating half of the lifeforms in the universe with the Infinity Gauntlet. He joined forces with ANNIHILUS during the cosmic ANNIHILATION, but DRAX THE DESTROYER killed him. Death resurrected him, making him unkillable, and he journeyed to the Cancerverse, a perverted place where Death had been destroyed. He killed that universe's ruler, Lord Mar-Vell, but Death spurned him again, driving him into an insane rage. NOVA and STAR-LORD sacrificed themselves to trap him there. Accompanied by the Black Order, a new coalition of aliens bent on conquest, he returned to Earth, determined to kill his son, Thane, who'd been raised by a secret group of INHUMANS. **TB, MF**

Thanos believed the power the Infinity Gauntlet gave him was the key to winning back Death's affections.

THENA

FIRST APPEARANCE The Eternals #5 (November 1976)
REAL NAME Azura, changed by royal decree to Thena
OCCUPATION Warrior, scholar **BASE** Olympia, Greece
HEIGHT 5 ft 10 in **WEIGHT** 160 lbs **EYES** Blue **HAIR** Blond
SPECIAL POWERS/ABILITIES Superhuman strength; mental control over body gives virtual immortality; psionic abilities include flight through levitation; projects cosmic energy from eyes or hands.

Thena is the daughter of Zuras, ruler of the ETERNALS, and his wife Cybele. In a pact between the Eternals and the GODS OF OLYMPUS, Zuras renamed Azura "Thena" after the goddess Athena. Thousands of years ago, Thena met Kro, a member of the DEVIANTS. They became lovers, and they had twin children. Upon the demise of Zuras, Thena succeeded him as Prime Eternal, but she subsequently lost this position to another Eternal, IKARIS. Her mind wiped, Thena resurfaced recently with a human husband and son. She has since regained her memories of her former life. **PS, MF**

THING, *see pages 366-367*

THOMPSON, EUGENE "FLASH"

Eugene Thompson's athletic prowess made him a football hero at Midtown High School, helping him overcome the insecurities of having a father—Harry, an alcoholic cop—who regularly beat him. He dated Liz ALLAN, the most popular girl in the school, and bullied bookish Peter Parker (SPIDER-MAN). Ironically, Flash was Spider-Man's biggest fan. Flash went on to attend Empire State University with Parker and, in time, the two became friends. Flash later joined the military and served in South-East Asia.

After returning, he had an affair with Betty BRANT, wife of *Daily Bugle* reporter Ned Leeds, who framed Flash as the HOBGOBLIN. For a while, Flash worked at Midtown High as a gym teacher, but he re-upped with the Army to fight in Iraq, where he lost both legs trying to save his commanding officer.

When the US government removed the VENOM symbiote from Mac Gargan (SCORPION), they gave it to Flash, turning him into Agent Venom. Flash fled rather than return the symbiote, but his heroism convinced CAPTAIN AMERICA to invite him to join his secret AVENGERS. Flash later gave part of the symbiote to save a student who joined him as a new hero, Mania. **DW, MF**

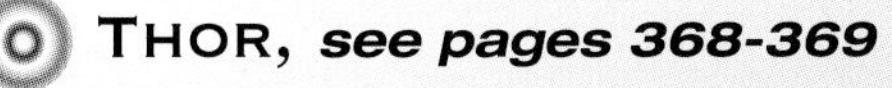

THOR, ***see pages 368-369***

As Venom, Flash became the hero he'd always hoped to be.

FACTFILE

REAL NAME
Eugene Thompson

OCCUPATION
Unemployed

BASE
New York City

HEIGHT 6 ft 2 in
WEIGHT 185 lbs
EYES Blue
HAIR Reddish-blond

FIRST APPEARANCE
Amazing Fantasy #15 (August 1962)

POWERS

Formerly a gifted athlete, nicknamed "Flash" because of his speed. He was a star of Midtown High's football and baseball teams.

THOR GIRL

FIRST APPEARANCE Thor #22 (August 2000)
REAL NAME Tarene **OCCUPATION** Adventurer
BASE New York City **HEIGHT** 5 ft 9 in
WEIGHT 317 lbs **EYES** Blue **HAIR** Blond
SPECIAL POWERS/ABILITIES Immortal, superhuman strength, invulnerability, plus a mystic hammer that grants flight, weather control, and energy blast that can transform her to human and back.

Tarene is the Designate prophesied by X'Hoss to elevate all life to greatness. Before she could manage this, THANOS destroyed her homeworld and stripped her of much of her power. THOR and Orikal, a powerful being from an extra-dimensional realm, helped her defeat Thanos. She came to Earth and took the codename Thor Girl to emulate her hero. She joined the FIFTY-STATE INITIATIVE, assigned to Georgia's team, the Cavalry. During SECRET INVASION, she was impersonated by a SKRULL but later returned. After fending off people attacking her during FEAR ITSELF, she went back to being the Designate. **MF**

3-D MAN

FIRST APPEARANCE Marvel Premiere #35 (April 1977)
REAL NAME Charles "Chuck " Chandler
OCCUPATION Test pilot, adventurer **BASE** None
HEIGHT 6 ft 2 in **WEIGHT** 200 lbs **EYES** Blue **HAIR** Blond
SPECIAL POWERS/ABILITIES Strength, stamina, agility, and speed three times that of a normal human; a brilliant pilot with the ability to sense the presence of alien Skrulls.

In 1958, SKRULLS captured NASA test pilot Chuck Chandler in midflight. He escaped, causing their ship to explode. He crash-landed his plane, and Skrull radiation imprinted his essence onto the glasses worn by his brother Hal. By concentrating on the glasses, Hal could resurrect his brother as 3-D Man. However, side effects caused Hal to put his glasses aside. Years later, Hal brought his brother back permanently. Chuck had not aged a single day and began his life anew. Later, the hero TRIATHLON gained the 3-D Man's powers, too. Soon after, he joined the AGENTS OF ATLAS. **AD, MF**

THUNDERBIRD

FIRST APPEARANCE Giant-Size X-Men #1 (1975)
REAL NAME John Proudstar **OCCUPATION** X-Man (deceased)
BASE New York City; mobile; New York State
HEIGHT 6 ft 1 in **WEIGHT** 225 lbs **EYES** Brown **HAIR** Black
SPECIAL POWERS/ABILITIES Super strength and stamina; can run at 35mph for long periods; leathery skin protects him from harm.

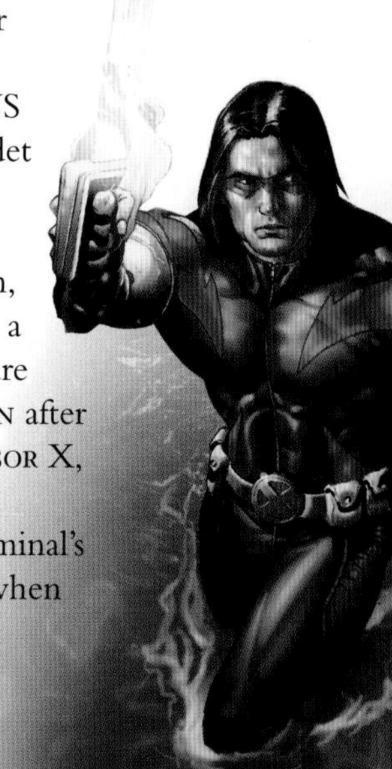

Eager to emulate his warrior ancestors, Native American John Proudstar joined the US Marines as an under-age cadet and served with distinction. John's mutant powers emerged relatively late when, at the age of 20, he wrestled a rampaging bison with his bare hands. He joined the X-MEN after being sought out by PROFESSOR X, but died on only his second mission: jumping onto a criminal's escape plane, he was killed when the aircraft blew up. John's brother, James, eventually followed in his footsteps as Warpath. **AD, MF**

THING, THE

Big-hearted tough guy of the Fantastic Four

THING, THE

FACTFILE

REAL NAME
Benjamin Jacob Grimm

OCCUPATION
Adventurer, former test pilot, wrestler

BASE
New York City

HEIGHT 6 ft
WEIGHT 500 lbs
EYES Blue
HAIR (human form) Brown; (Thing) none

FIRST APPEARANCE
Fantastic Four #1
(November 1961)

POWERS
Superhuman strength, endurance, and durability. He can lift 85 tons, absorb the blast of an armor-piercing bazooka shell, withstand temperature extremes, and needs no suit to survive in space or in the ocean depths.

ALLIES/FOES
ALLIES Reed Richards, Sue Richards, Franklin Richards, Valeria Richards, Johnny Storm, Alicia Masters, Sharon Ventura, Captain America, Edwin Jarvis, Iron Man, Jack of Hearts, Thundra, Tigra.

FOES Hulk, Beetle, Trapster, Namor, Mad Thinker, Puppet Master, Sandman, Doctor Doom, the Beyonder, Annihilus.

ISSUE #1
The story of the Fantastic Four's creation. Pilot Ben Grimm becomes the orange, scaly-skinned, super-strong Thing.

Ben Grimm, alias the Thing, is a hot-headed member of the FANTASTIC FOUR, using his abilities to fight evil, almost as often as he does battle with himself. Ben grew up in New York City in poverty. Like his older brother, Daniel, he got involved with a street gang (*see* YANCY STREET GANG). After his parents died, Ben was taken in by his uncle Jake, a doctor, who helped set the boy on the right track. Ben ended up going to Empire State University on a football scholarship. His first-year roommate was brilliant science student Reed Richards, who became Ben's best friend.

A GRIMM TALE

When Reed told Ben of his plan to one day build a starship, Ben jokingly said that he would pilot the ship.

After college, Ben joined the US Air Force and became an excellent pilot and astronaut. Reed's starship reached the test stage but the government threatened to cut off funding. Reed decided to stage a test flight. Ben agreed to pilot the ship, though he worried that the radiation shields weren't strong enough.

Reed and Ben blasted into space along with Reed's fiancée, Susan Storm, and Sue's brother Johnny. In space, the foursome was bombarded with high levels of cosmic radiation.

LET THE CLOBBERIN' BEGIN!

The crew were altered on a genetic level and gained unusual powers. Ben's skin turned orange and rocky, and his strength grew tremendously, earning him the nickname the Thing. Reed convinced the others that they should use their powers to help humanity as the Fantastic Four. Ben would sometimes revert back to his human form unexpectedly, but neither he nor Reed could control this change. In the early years after he became the Thing, Ben dated the blind sculptor, Alicia MASTERS. Because she had fallen in love with him while he was in his rocky form, he worried that she might not feel the same way about him if he managed to become human again.

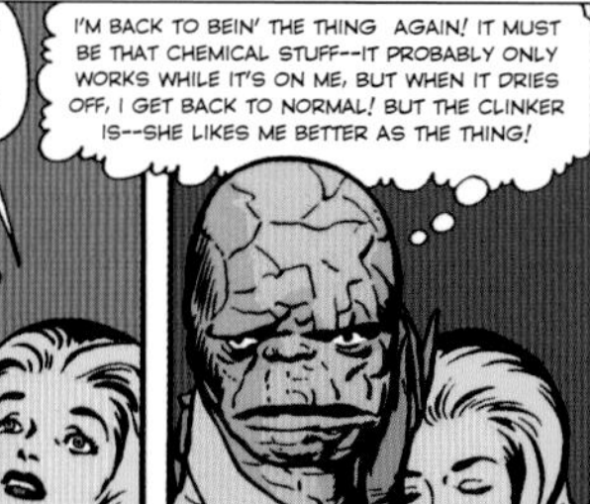

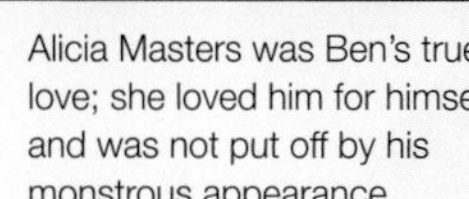
Alicia Masters was Ben's true love; she loved him for himself and was not put off by his monstrous appearance.

Ben and Debbie Green hit it off fast. He asked her to marry him after they'd only been dating for six weeks.

The Lonely Monster

After fighting in the first of the secret wars involving the Beyonder, Ben stayed on Battleworld for months, able to change back and forth from his human form to the Thing. While there, he fell for Tarianna of Leenn, whom he eventually learned the Beyonder had created as a simulacrum of Ben's ideal woman.

When Ben returned, stuck as a monster once more, he discovered that, in his absence, the Human Torch and Alicia had not only struck up a relationship, they were soon to be married. The fact that this Alicia turned out to be a Skrull named Lyja masquerading as Alicia did little to help, as by that time Ben had gotten over his heartbreak. He and Alicia remained friends but nothing more.

Ben has also dated other women over the years, including Sharon Ventura, who was Ms. Marvel at the time but later transformed into the She-Thing. He became engaged to a teacher named Debbie Green, but left her before the wedding, fearful of exposing her to the extreme dangers that were an everyday part of his life.

For his uniform as the Thing, Ben usually preferred to wear just blue shorts, but he went with more coverage for his white Future Foundation outfit.

The People's Hero

While Ben has strong opinions, he doesn't care to argue for the sake of it. When the Civil War erupted, he initially sided with the government, following the lead of Iron Man and Reed Richards. When an innocent man died in a battle on Yancy Street, however, Ben left the conflict disgusted at both sides' apparent lack of regard for folks caught in the crossfire. To avoid getting dragged back into the war, he left for France.

Always fiercely loyal to the Fantastic Four, Ben sometimes split his time with other teams, such as the Avengers.

With the Civil War at its height, Ben returned to protect New York City's civilian population. He was happy when Captain America called an end to the fight to stop any more people getting hurt. After Captain America died, Ben was honored to serve as one of the pallbearers at Cap's funeral.

A depowered Ben was prepared to sacrifice himself to save the Future Foundation (*see* Fantastic Four) and the world from Annihilus when the portal to the Negative Zone was forced open. To Ben's dismay, the Human Torch tossed him to safety and took his place. While trying to get back into the Negative Zone to stand beside his pal, Ben morphed into the Thing again. He was delighted when the Human Torch returned safely from his battles in the Negative Zone. **MT, MF**

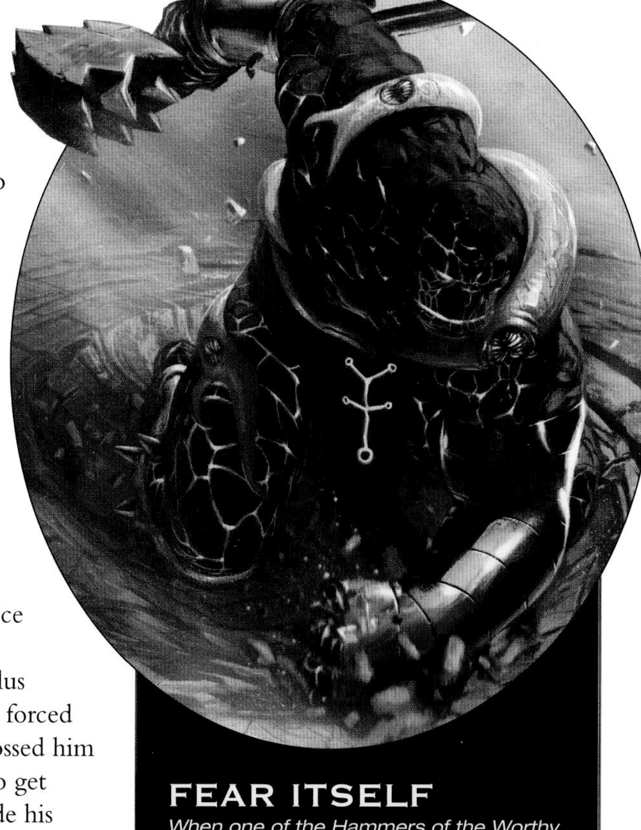

FEAR ITSELF

When one of the Hammers of the Worthy fell on Yancy Street, the Thing picked it up and found himself possessed and transformed into Angrir, Breaker of Souls.

ESSENTIAL STORYLINES

- ***Fantastic Four #1*** An accident in space changes pilot Ben Grimm into the orange-colored-rock-encrusted the Thing.
- ***Fantastic Four #8*** The Thing meets Alicia Masters and a long love affair begins.
- ***Fantastic Four #310*** Having quit the Fantastic Four, the Thing decides to join the West Coast Avengers, when he mutates into an even more grotesque creature, and sets off for Monster Island to find Mole Man.

THOR

The Asgardian God of Thunder

THOR

FACTFILE

REAL NAME
Thor Odinson (alias Donald Blake, Eric Masterson, Jake Olson)

OCCUPATION
God of Thunder

BASE
Asgard

HEIGHT 6 ft 6 in
WEIGHT 640 lbs
EYES Blue
HAIR Blond

FIRST APPEARANCE
Journey Into Mystery Vol. 1 #83 (August 1962)

POWERS

Enhanced strength, near-invulnerability, longevity, and vast magical abilities provided by the Odinforce. Wields the unbreakable hammer of Mjolnir which can open interdimensional portals, permit flight, channel storms, and fire energy blasts.

ALLIES/FOES

ALLIES The Avengers, Beta Ray Bill, Sif, Warriors Three

FOES Loki, Surtur, the Enchantress, the Absorbing Man

ISSUE #1

In *Journey into Mystery,* Thor leads a double life as the Thunder God and the mortal man Donald Blake. Later, Thor dropped the Blake identity.

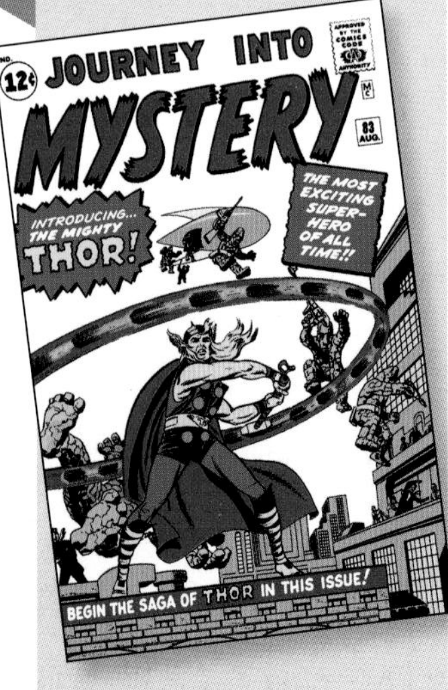
12¢
JOURNEY INTO
MYSTERY
83
AUG.
INTRODUCING... THE MIGHTY THOR!
THE MOST EXCITING SUPER-HERO OF ALL TIME!!
BEGIN THE SAGA OF THOR IN THIS ISSUE!

Thor could transport himself to Midgard via Asgard's rainbow bridge, or by using the powers of his hammer Mjolnir.

Thor was the God of Thunder, the beloved champion of Asgard (*see* GODS OF ASGARD) and a figure of worship among the ancient Norse. He loved his people so much that he triggered their destruction in the end battle of Ragnarok, finally breaking a repeating cycle of futility. Thor was born to ODIN, the ruler (sky-father) of Asgard, and Gaea, the mother goddess of Earth (a place known to the Asgardians as Midgard).

EARLY LIFE

Groomed to assume his father's throne, Thor grew up with his best friend Balder and his first love, Sif. But Thor's half-brother Loki hated him, and schemed to become ruler of Asgard himself.

When Thor proved himself worthy of carrying the uru hammer Mjolnir, he took up the identity as the Thunder God. Thor mingled with his Earthly worshippers throughout the 9th century, leading the Vikings into battle. He later abandoned his followers after several of them butchered a Christian monastery. Over the succeeding centuries he spent most of his time in Asgard, venturing to Earth to battle Loki in the Old West and mistakenly becoming a pawn of the Nazis during World War II.

THE TEEN BRIGADE! THEY'RE LOCATED IN THE SOUTH WEST! IF THIS CONCERNS THE HULK, IT MUST BE SERIOUS! AND SO, THE TIME HAS COME...

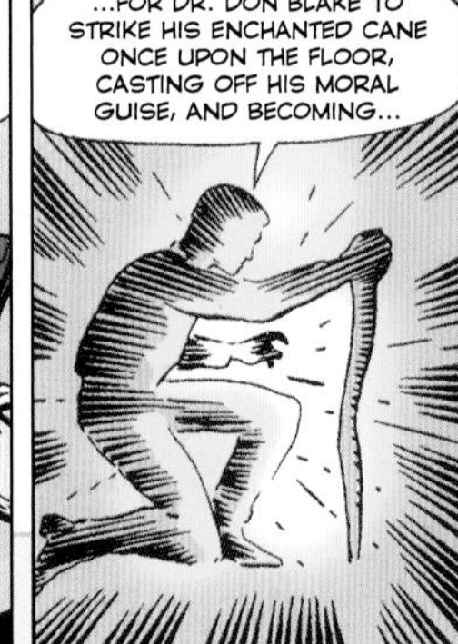
...FOR DR. DON BLAKE TO STRIKE HIS ENCHANTED CANE ONCE UPON THE FLOOR, CASTING OFF HIS MORAL GUISE, AND BECOMING...

...THE MIGHTY THOR, GOD OF THUNDER!

Originally, Thor transformed from Donald Blake to the Thunder God by striking a simple wooden staff on the ground.

Deciding that his son needed to learn humility before assuming the title of sky-father, Odin exiled Thor to Earth. There, the Thunder God believed himself to be the mortal doctor Donald Blake, and walked with the aid of a

As one of the core members of the Avengers, Thor defeated the robot Ultron and crushed countless other threats to humanity.

STORMY TIMES

A second incarnation of the Thunder God appeared when Thor merged his spirit with Earth architect Eric Masterson. Thor entered temporary exile for apparently killing Loki, and Masterson carried on, posing as Thor while wielding the hammer of Mjolnir. Masterson later received the identity of Thunderstrike, before perishing in battle against the Egyptian god Seth and overcoming a curse laid upon Masterson by the weapon of Bloodaxe. Thor subsequently assumed the civilian identity of dead EMS worker Jake Olson, though he soon gave this up and let a resurrected Olson continue his life. Eric Masterson's son, Kevin, later took up the role of Thunderstrike in a possible future timeline also inhabited by Spider-Girl.

Thor and Thunderstrike unite their mystical hammers to unleash even greater power. Thor, who considered Eric Masterson one of the most noble mortals he had ever encountered, greatly mourned his death.

wooden cane. When he struck the cane on the ground it transformed into Mjolnir, and Thor regained his powers and all memories of his life on Asgard. For years, he lived a dual identity as Thor and Blake, battling threats such as the Radioactive Man and the Absorbing Man. Loki sought to entrap Thor by drawing him into conflict with the Hulk, but only succeeded in uniting a group of heroes that would become the Avengers. Thor became a founding member of the team, and fought alongside such heroes as Captain America, Iron Man, and Hercules.

Few beings ever bested Thor in combat, but the alien Beta Ray Bill defeated the Thunder God and proved worthy of wielding the hammer of Mjolnir. Impressed, Odin forged a new hammer, Stormbreaker, for Bill to wield. Thor gave up his Blake alter ego at this time, briefly trying out a new identity as construction worker Sigurd Jarlson. New trials continued to vex Thor—his father Odin seemingly perished in combat against the fire demon Surtur, but Thor refused the throne, the honor passing to Balder. Thor then suffered terrible torment when a curse rendered him incapable of death. Wounds nearly disintegrated his body until the spell was reversed.

RAGNAROK

The events that led to the end of Asgard began with the true death of Odin, killed battling Surtur. Thor took up the mantle of rulership and became empowered with the mystical Odinforce. Wishing to take a more direct role over earthly affairs, Thor moved Asgard to Earth and transformed the planet into a dictatorship that endured for two hundred years. At last, realizing the error of his actions, he unwound the previous two centuries through time travel.

Loki enlisted Surtur to forge new weapons comparable in power to Mjolnir. He rallied his followers and conquered Asgard. Thor, realizing that Loki's actions presaged the final conflagration of Ragnarok, followed the Odinforce on a spiritual journey. The Thunder God uncovered the truth of the Ragnarok cycle—its endless loop of creation and rebirth had been orchestrated by the godlike Those Who Sit Above in Shadow for their amusement. Unwilling to endure his people's dishonor through yet another cycle, Thor severed the tapestry that wove the reality of Asgard's dimension, wiping himself and Asgard from existence.

Desperate for Thor's power during the Civil War, Mister Fantastic and Hank Pym created a biomechanical Thor clone. It proved hard to control and killed Giant-Man (Bill Foster). It later attacked the Fifty-State Initiative's headquarters at Camp Hammond.

Later, in the void of the afterlife, Thor reunited with his old alter ego Donald Blake and returned to Earth, rebuilding Asgard on an island floating in the sky over Oklahoma. He then set out to find the other gods, who now lived unknowingly as mortals, and restore them to their rightful places. **DW, MF**

Ragnarok, the twilight of the gods, spelled an end to all of the five races of the dimension of Asgard.

Beta Ray Bill proved he could fight alongside the Asgardians, and briefly became Beta Ray Thor.

ESSENTIAL STORYLINES

- ***The Mighty Thor #337***
Beta Ray Bill explodes into action as a rival, and later an ally, of the Thunder God.
- ***Thor: Son of Asgard #1–12***
This limited series explores the early adventures of a young Balder the Brave, Sif, and Thor.
- ***The Mighty Thor #582–588***
It's Ragnarok, the Asgardian apocalypse, and the long-running series comes to an end with the total destruction of Asgard and all who live there.

THOR *continued*

FAMILY FIGHTS

Loki brought Odin's father Bor back from the dead and tricked him into attacking everything in sight. Thor was forced to kill Bor, unaware that Bor was his grandfather. Since Bor had technically become the ruler of Asgard upon his return, Balder—who had previously assumed rule of Asgard with Thor's blessing—had to banish Thor from the home of the Norse gods. With Thor gone, Loki persuaded Balder to evacuate the Asgardians to Latveria, the home of his ally DOCTOR DOOM, another member of the CABAL.

Thor's hammer Mjolnir had been damaged during his battle with Bor, and he asked DOCTOR STRANGE to help repair it. They managed this by transferring some of Thor's power to Mjolnir, strengthening the bond between them. With Mjolinir fixed, Thor finally managed to find the lost goddess Sif and return her to the body that Loki had stolen from her. Angry with Loki, Balder ordered his people back to Asgard.

Thor killed his crazed grandfather Bor with a blow that broke his hammer Mjolnir.

Banished from Asgard, Thor walked the Earth alone—until he came back to save the Asgardians from the Sentry.

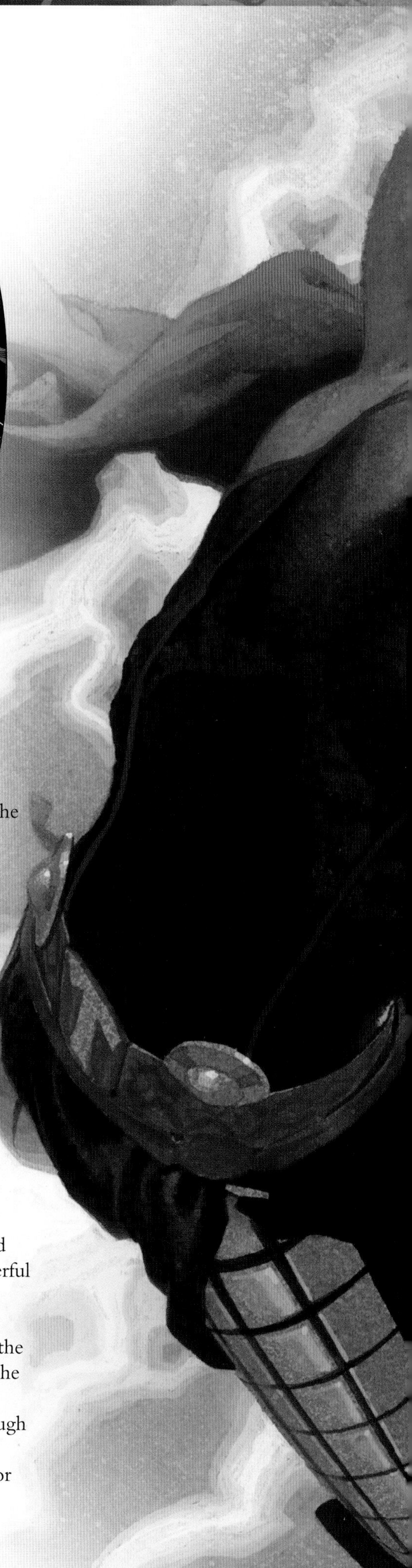

THE SIEGE OF ASGARD

Loki persuaded the leader of the Cabal—Norman Osborn (*see* GREEN GOBLIN)—that the return of the Norse gods to the skies above Oklahoma presented a threat to his power as head of national security. Loki convinced Osborn by staging a fight between the U-FOES and Volstagg (of the WARRIORS THREE) that killed tens of thousands of innocents during a football game at Chicago's Soldier Field. Osborn decided to launch a preemptive assault on Asgard.

Despite his banishment, Thor joined the fight to defend Asgard against HAMMER (Osborn's version of SHIELD) and Osborn's villainous team of AVENGERS, buttressed by DAKEN (posing as WOLVERINE) and SENTRY. During the battle, Sentry razed Asgard, reducing it to rubble, and his dark side—embodied as the evil and powerful Void—threatened to destroy the world. Even Loki decided that this was too much, and he tried to help the Avengers with the magic of the Norn Stones. Once the Void figured this out, he slew Loki.

Enraged, Thor kept the Void busy long enough for IRON MAN to crash the HAMMER Helicarrier into him. After Sentry's death, Thor wrapped him in his cape and hurled his old friend into the sun. In return for his service, Balder lifted Thor's banishment.

Family Reunion

Thor learned that Loki's spirit was not in Hel, and he set out to find him. He located him in a boy's body in Paris, reborn without any memories of his past, including his many misdeeds. Thor brought this Kid Loki back to Asgard and sought to protect him from the hostility the other gods still harbored for him.

Thor later brought Odin back to life, too. The All-Father was furious with Loki for what he had done and with Thor for bringing them both back when he could have lived in peace. When the event known as FEAR ITSELF began with the return of Odin's brother Cul, also known as the Serpent, Odin retreated from Earth and created a new Asgard in a realm apart so that he and his people could prepare for war with the Serpent and his generals, known as the Worthy.

Thor remained on Earth, against his father's wishes, and led the fight against Cul and his forces. In the end, he slew the Serpent, but at the cost of his own life, as Odin had prophesied long ago. In his grief, Odin sealed himself up alone in Asgard and gave rule of his people to Freyja, Gaea, and Idunn, a trinity of All-Mothers. They helped recreate their home (with the help of Iron Man's technology) as the all-new Asgardia, floating over Oklahoma once more. **MF**

Thor missed his brother Loki, no matter how horrible he had been, and he was thrilled to have him back.

Thor first fought Gorr a thousand years ago, but the God Butcher's menace grew with every passing year.

The Thunder Returns

From the fires of Thor's funeral pyre emerged Tanarus, a new God of Thunder whom everyone but Loki remembered as the god Thor had been. This turned out to be a trick of the sorceress KARNILLA, who had substituted the rock troll Ulik in Thor's place. With the help of the SILVER SURFER, Loki hunted down Thor's old alter ego, Donald Blake, and brought his brother back to life. Together, they revealed Karnilla's treachery and stopped a troll attack on Asgardia.

Soon after, Thor tangled with GORR THE GOD BUTCHER, an alien god who amassed power through the destruction of other gods. Gorr planned to detonate a Godbomb that would destroy every god in all space and time. He enslaved scores of gods to build it for him—including Thor and his younger and older selves. With all those gods praying to Thor, he managed to foil Gorr's plot.

THUNDERBOLTS

Reformed Super Villains with the "best intentions"

THUNDERBOLTS

FACTFILE

NOTABLE MEMBERS

CITIZEN V (Baron Zemo)
Team leader.

TECHNO (The Fixer)
Varies her molecular density.

MACH-1 (Beetle)
Wears a suit that enables him to fly, fire weapons, and resist attack.

SONGBIRD (Screaming Mimi)
Can transform the sound of her voice into physical forms.

ATLAS (Goliath) Can increase his size and mass.

METEORITE (Moonstone)
Superhuman strength and invulnerability.

JOLT Exceptional strength, speed, agility.

CHARCOAL Can change his body into charcoal, creating flames or diamonds.

HAWKEYE Expert archer.

BASE Mobile

FIRST APPEARANCE
The Incredible Hulk #449 (January 1997)

The Thunderbolts came into conflict with Captain America.

When the FANTASTIC FOUR and the AVENGERS disappeared after their first battle with ONSLAUGHT, BARON ZEMO transformed his MASTERS OF EVIL into the Thunderbolts, giving members new identities to escape their criminal pasts. He himself became the patriotic Citizen V, leader of the new team. When the lost heroes returned, Zemo realized that his team had come to enjoy the lives of heroes, so he exposed their secret to the world, hoping to force them to stay with him, but they turned on him instead.

NEW THUNDER

With Zemo gone, HAWKEYE took over the team, and they faced off against Henry GYRICH and a new SCOURGE. Mach-I turned himself in for a murder he'd committed as the Beetle, hoping to earn the rest of the team a pardon, but this never came. They then defeated the CRIMSON COWL's Masters of Evil and took their headquarters in Colorado, renaming it Thunderbolt Mountain. Hawkeye finally won the team its pardon by blackmailing Gyrich and turning himself in.

Valerie COOPER's Redeemers replaced the Thunderbolts for a while, but after GRAVITON destroyed them, the Thunderbolts reformed. After they disbanded, Mach-III (now Mach-IV) reformed the team once more, and they became heroes on the Counter-Earth on which the Fantastic Four and the Avengers had been stranded. Meanwhile, Hawkeye broke out of jail and formed a new team from members of the Masters of Evil, whom the Crimson Cowl was trying to enslave. The two teams later united to stop her plan. Zemo continued to work against them, both in the open and in secret.

With the Thunderbolts, it was often hard to tell who were the heroes and who were the villains.

DARK HEROES

During the CIVIL WAR, the Thunderbolts registered with the US government and forced many villains to join the Thunderbolts Army. Zemo's plans were ruined when Songbird shattered his Moonstones, which sent him into a cosmic vortex.

Soon after, Norman Osborn (GREEN GOBLIN) formed a brand-new Thunderbolts team. When Osborn became the head of US national security after the SECRET INVASION, he took command of the Avengers as well and made the Thunderbolts his secret hit squad.

When Osborn's DARK REIGN ended, Luke CAGE headed up a new Thunderbolts operating out of the Raft super-prison. One part of the team wound up jumping through time before finally reuniting in the present and becoming a new Dark Avengers team.

The RED HULK subsequently started up his own team of Thunderbolts, with no government supervision. **MT, MF**

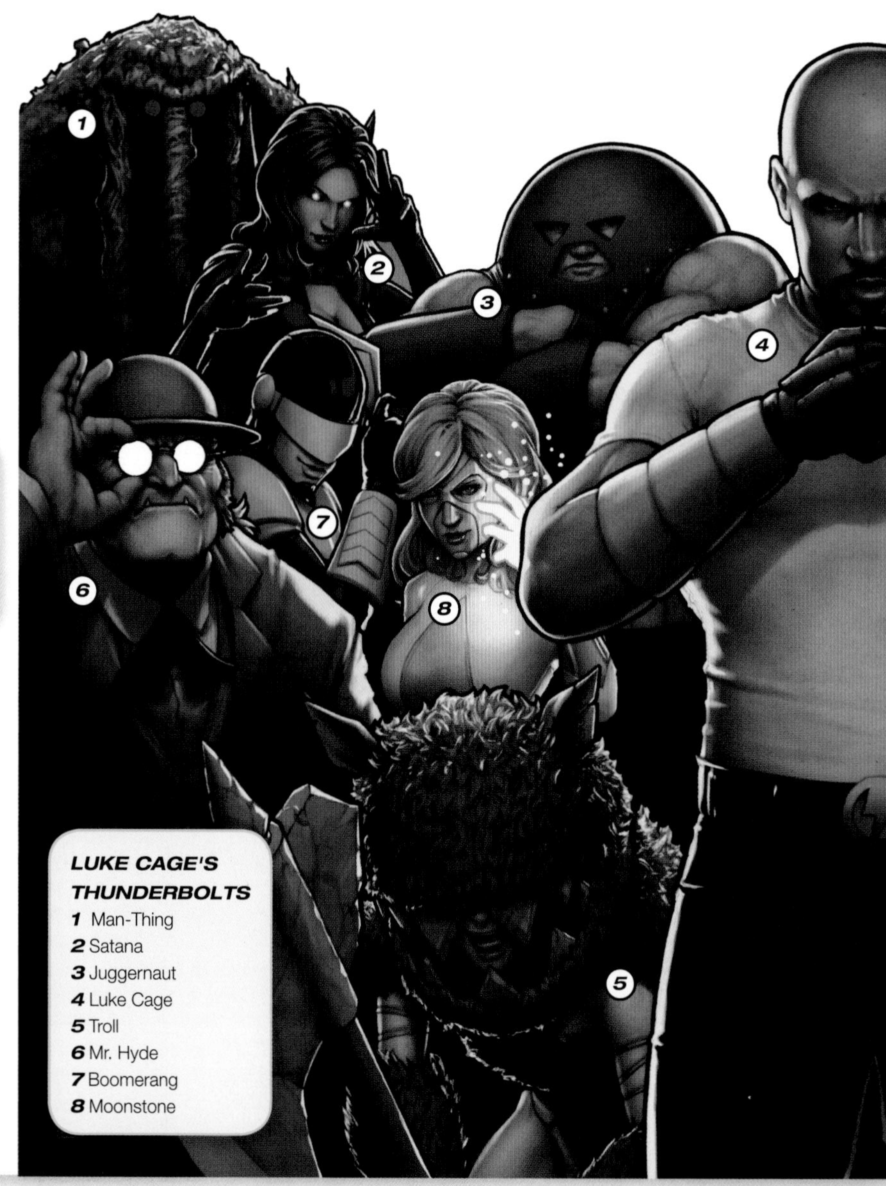

LUKE CAGE'S THUNDERBOLTS
1 Man-Thing
2 Satana
3 Juggernaut
4 Luke Cage
5 Troll
6 Mr. Hyde
7 Boomerang
8 Moonstone

THUNDERSTRIKE

Divorced and with sole custody of his young son, Eric Masterson was an architect who was working at a building site where Thor, under a secret identity, was also employed. Thor was attacked by the assassin Mongoose and, during the battle, Eric was injured by falling girders. He was left with a permanent limp. After becoming friends with Thor, Eric was wounded again, this time mortally, and Odin merged him with the Thunder God to save his life. Thereafter, Masterson would assume the form of Thor whenever the hero was needed on Earth.

The original Thunderstrike is one of many Avengers who died in the line of duty.

When Thor seemingly slew his brother Loki and was banished from this plane of reality, Eric took his place as Thor II. Eventually the real Thor returned, and Eric was given his own enchanted mace and became Thunderstrike. He later died battling the god Seth.

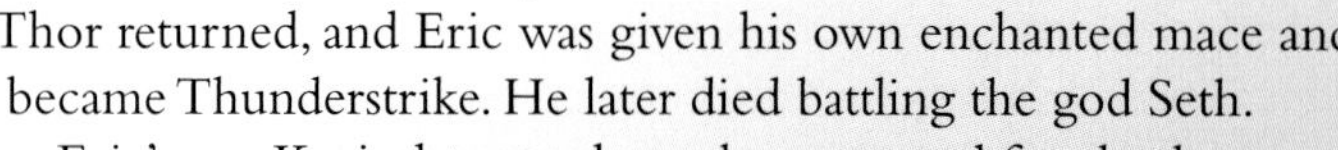

Eric's son Kevin later took up the mace and fought the super villain Man-Power. In the future of Earth-982, Kevin forms A-Next. He lost powers after Galactus devoured Asgard, but Thor's daughter Thena helped him regain them. **TD, MF**

Like his father, Kevin Masterson can physically transform into Thunderstrike through intense concentration.

FACTFILE

REAL NAME
Eric Masterson (father)
Kevin Masterson (son)

OCCUPATION
Architect (father); college student (son)

BASE
New York City

HEIGHT 6 ft 6 in (father); 6 ft (son)
WEIGHT 640 lbs (father); 585 lbs (son)
EYES Blue
HAIR Blond

FIRST APPEARANCES
Thor #391 (father); Thor #392 (son); Thor #432 (father as Thunderstrike); What If #105 (son as Thunderstrike)

THUNDERSTRIKE

POWERS
(Father) Super-strong, owns enchanted uru mace that projects concussive blasts of mystical energy. Flies by throwing mace and gripping its strap. (Son) Super-strong; projects concussive blasts of mystical energy, which can be used to propel him through the air.

THUNDRA

FIRST APPEARANCE Fantastic Four #129 (December 1972)
REAL NAME Thundra
OCCUPATION Warrior
BASE United Sisterhood Republic of North America
HEIGHT 7 ft 2 in **WEIGHT** 350 lbs **EYES** Green **HAIR** Red
SPECIAL POWERS/ABILITIES Enhanced strength, endurance, reflexes, and damage resistance; skilled at wielding a chain.

In the 23rd century of Earth-715, women ruled the world and raised men as servants and breeding stock. Thundra, born into the United Sisterhood Republic of North America, became one of its finest warriors. She was sent back in time to defeat the Thing but eventually took a liking to him and brought him to her time to help liberate her world. At the time of the Secret Invasion, Thundra had started an all-female settlement on Earth-616. Her people captured a Skrull and turned him over to the Inhumans. She later infiltrated the Intelligencia for the Red Hulk and she has worked with the Fearless Defenders. **MF**

TIGER SHARK

FIRST APPEARANCE Sub-Mariner #5 (September 1968)
REAL NAME Todd Arliss
OCCUPATION Amphibious criminal **BASE** The deep blue sea
HEIGHT 6 ft 1 in **WEIGHT** 450 lbs **EYES** Gray **HAIR** Brown
SPECIAL POWERS/ABILITIES Amphibious—able to withstand great water pressure and swim at up to 60mph; also possesses superhuman strength.

His genes spliced with those of Namor the Sub-Mariner and a tiger shark, Todd Arliss, former Olympic-level swimmer, became a superpowered amphibian. Namor and Tiger Shark became vengeful foes, and when Tiger Shark's powers began to fade, he kidnapped Namor's father, Leonard MacKenzie, and blackmailed Namor into donating more powers. Chaos ensued during the transfer process and Tiger Shark ended up killing MacKenzie with a lead pipe. He later joined the Thunderbolts, and he helped conquer Atlantis during Fear Itself.

TIGRA

FIRST APPEARANCE The Cat #1 (November 1972)
REAL NAME Greer Grant Nelson
OCCUPATION Adventurer **BASE** New York City
HEIGHT 5 ft 10 in **WEIGHT** 180 lbs **EYES** Green
HAIR (human form) black; (cat form) orange fur with black stripes
SPECIAL POWERS/ABILITIES Enhanced strength, slashing claws, and heightened senses of smell, hearing, and vision.

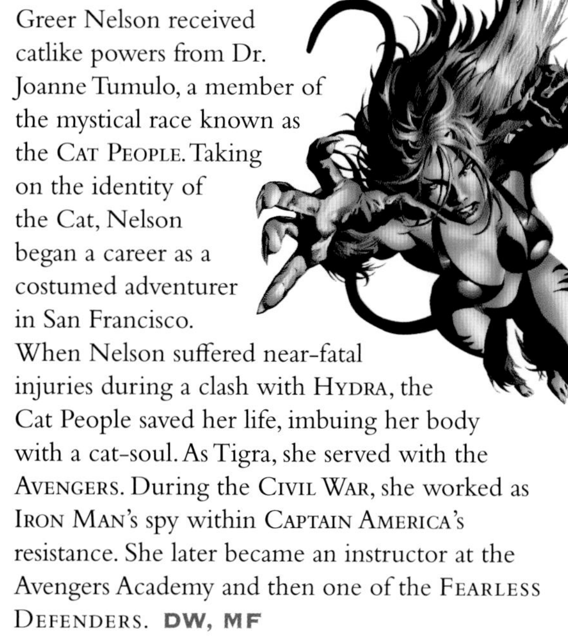

Greer Nelson received catlike powers from Dr. Joanne Tumulo, a member of the mystical race known as the Cat People. Taking on the identity of the Cat, Nelson began a career as a costumed adventurer in San Francisco. When Nelson suffered near-fatal injuries during a clash with Hydra, the Cat People saved her life, imbuing her body with a cat-soul. As Tigra, she served with the Avengers. During the Civil War, she worked as Iron Man's spy within Captain America's resistance. She later became an instructor at the Avengers Academy and then one of the Fearless Defenders. **DW, MF**

Timebreakers, The

FIRST APPEARANCE Exiles #62 (June 2005)
BASE Panoptichron
SPECIAL POWERS/ABILITIES None, but they have access to the Panoptichron.

The Timebreakers are an alien insectoid race that found the Panoptichron, a crystal palace that sits at the nexus of all realities, outside of time and space. Not knowing what they were doing when they arrived, they made mistakes that damaged many different realities. Hoping to repair the problems they'd caused, they created a human-looking illusion called the Timebroker to gather heroes known as EXILES and send them out on missions. Timebreakers come in different castes, including cockroach-like workers and mantis-like sovereigns. **MF**

Tinkerer, The

FIRST APPEARANCE The Amazing Spider-Man #2 (May 1963)
REAL NAME Phineas Mason
OCCUPATION Criminal inventor **BASE** New York City
HEIGHT 5 ft 8 in **WEIGHT** 175 lbs **EYES** Gray **HAIR** White
SPECIAL POWERS/ABILITIES Genius-level ability to create sophisticated gadgets and deadly weapons from everyday pieces of machinery or scrap metal.

Phineas Mason, the "Terrible Tinkerer," is unparalleled in his ability to create and repair machinery, and long ago became the premiere gadget-maker for the criminal underworld. Among his works are DIAMONDBACK's throwing diamonds and the SCORPION's tail. His son, Rick Mason, worked for SHIELD as the Agent until he was killed on a mission. Later, the PUNISHER stabbed the Tinkerer, putting him in a wheelchair. Incarcerated in the Negative Zone, he helped the THING and HUMAN TORCH escape during the SECRET INVASION, winning his freedom. **DW, MF**

Titanium Man

FIRST APPEARANCE Tales of Suspense #69 (Sept. 1965)
REAL NAME Boris Bullski **OCCUPATION** Former Russian champion **BASE** Moibile **HEIGHT** (without armor) 7 ft 1 in **WEIGHT** (without armor) 475 lbs **EYES** Blue **HAIR** Black
SPECIAL POWERS/ABILITIES Unusual strength proportionate to his giant size; armor provided flight, enhanced strength, near-invulnerability, and the ability to fire energy blasts from hands.

Russian inventor Boris Bullski devised the Titanium Man armor in order to crush IRON MAN and win favor with his superiors. As Titanium Man, Bullski lost to IRON MAN in a televised slugfest of East vs. West. A second Titanium Man, the mutant known as the GREMLIN, died when his armor exploded. Boris Bullski later returned as an agent of AIM, but died in battle with Iron Man. A new Titanium Man appeared later, working as a mercenary with villains like DOCTOR OCTOPUS and SPYMASTER. **DW, MF**

Time Keepers, The

FIRST APPEARANCE Thor #282 (April 1979)
BASE Citadel at the End of Time
MEMBERS AND POWERS
Ast, Vort, Zanth: All Time Keepers possess nearly unlimited powers of time-manipulation, including time travel and the ability to rapidly age or devolve people and things.

The Time Keepers are guardians of the timestream, created by He Who Remains (the final chairman of the Time Variance Authority) at the end of time to replace his flawed agents, the Time Twisters. The Time Keepers sought to preserve their existence at all costs, which led them to enlist IMMORTUS to destroy the meddling AVENGERS and powerful "nexus beings" such as the SCARLET WITCH. KANG, with help from Rick JONES, seemingly wiped out the Time Keepers after they attempted to eliminate a host of alternate realities. **DW**

Titania

Davida DeVito, the first Titania, was the leader of the original Grapplers, a team of female professional wrestlers. Titania and her teammates were hired by the Roxxon Oil company to sabotage the government's Project: PEGASUS. They were defeated and sent to prison. After her release, Titania's strength was enhanced to superhuman levels by the POWER BROKER. She continued to lead an expanded Grapplers team. However, Titania was assassinated by a new Grappler called GOLDDIGGER, who appeared to have been working with the vigilante SCOURGE.

Mary "Skeeter" MacPherran lived in a Denver suburb that was transported by the BEYONDER to his "Battleworld." There DOCTOR DOOM gave her super-strength to serve in his army of criminals during the first "Secret War." This new Titania and her teammate, "Crusher" Creel, the ABSORBING MAN, were attracted to one another. After returning to Earth, Titania had a feud with SHE-HULK. She also served as a member of the MASTERS OF EVIL and the FRIGHTFUL FOUR. She attacked the She-Hulk but was shrunk down and imprisoned by Hank PYM. She escaped and, still tiny, attacked the She-Hulk again but was eaten by a shark. During FEAR ITSELF, she wielded the hammer of Skirn, Breaker of Men. **PS, MF**

FACTFILE
REAL NAME
Mary "Skeeter" MacPherran
OCCUPATION
Criminal
BASE
Formerly a suburb of Denver, Colorado, later New York City

HEIGHT 6 ft 6 in
WEIGHT 545 lbs
EYES Blue
HAIR Red-blond

FIRST APPEARANCE
Marvel Super Heroes Secret Wars #3 (July 1984)

POWERS
Possessed superhuman strength—able to lift about 90 tons; superhuman stamina and durability. Resistant to heat, cold, injury, and disease.

Tombstone

FIRST APPEARANCE Web of Spider-Man #36 (March 1988)
REAL NAME Lonnie Thompson Lincoln
OCCUPATION Professional hitman **BASE** Mobile
HEIGHT 6 ft 7 in **WEIGHT** Unknown **EYES** Pink **HAIR** White
SPECIAL POWERS/ABILITIES Enhanced strength, speed, stamina, and reflexes; skilled hand-to-hand fighter and assassin.

Lonnie Lincoln was born an African-American albino. He grew up in Harlem, New York City, with Joe "Robbie" Robertson, whom he coerced into keeping quiet regarding a murder that Lincoln had committed. Lincoln became an assassin for mob figures such as the Kingpin, and gained superhuman powers after exposure to an experimental gas. Following a stint with the Sinister Twelve—a team of Spider-Man enemies formed by Norman Osborn (Green Goblin)—Tombstone worked with the Hood and with Doctor Octopus between stints in jail. **DW, MF**

Torpedo

FIRST APPEARANCE Daredevil #126 (October 1975)
REAL NAME Brock Jones
OCCUPATION Crimefighter **BASE** Clairton, West Virginia
HEIGHT 6 ft **WEIGHT** 200 lbs **EYES** Blue **HAIR** Blond
SPECIAL POWERS/ABILITIES Battlesuit provides damage resistance; turbojets at wrists and ankles add power to punches; suit also generates shockwaves, and permits supersonic flight.

Inventor Michael Stivak became the first Torpedo when his uncle, Senator Eugene Stivak, convinced him to build a battlesuit. In truth, Senator Stivak had been prodded to do so by the extraterrestrial Dire Wraiths, who wanted to possess a weapon capable of defeating their enemy Rom the Spaceknight. After the younger Stivak's death, Brock Jones fought crime while wearing the costume and fended off Senator Stivak's efforts to retrieve it. He died in his adopted hometown of Clairton, West Virginia while battling the Dire Wraiths. **DW**

Trapster

FIRST APPEARANCE Strange Tales #104 (January 1963)
REAL NAME Peter Petruski
OCCUPATION Criminal **BASE** New York City
HEIGHT 5 ft 10 in **WEIGHT** 160 lbs **EYES** Brown **HAIR** Brown
SPECIAL POWERS/ABILITIES Carries assorted weapons at all times, most of them applications of his paste-formula.

Chemist Peter Petruski happened upon a formula for a super-strong, quick-hardening adhesive. He constructed a special handgun that could project it without clogging, and set out to make his name among the criminal fraternity as Paste-Pot Pete. However, not even a name-change to the Trapster and an alliance with the Wizard, the Sandman, and Medusa as the Frightful Four brought him the respect he craved. After the Tinkerer upgraded his weapons, the Trapster became far more dangerous and he won a number of battles. He worked with Hammerhead's criminals during the Civil War. **TB, MF**

Topaz

FIRST APPEARANCE Werewolf By Night #13 (January 1974)
REAL NAME Unrevealed; possibly Topaz
OCCUPATION Sorceress **BASE** New York City
HEIGHT 5 ft 3 in **WEIGHT** 100 lbs **EYES** Brown **HAIR** Black
SPECIAL POWERS/ABILITIES A trained sorceress with a multitude of mystic spells at her command, primarily empathy-based in nature.

Branded a witch after she made a flower bloom in the desert as a child, Topaz was incarcerated in a prison camp, where she was adopted and trained in the mystic arts by Taboo. Topaz served as the familiar for Taboo's sorcery until, in pursuit of Jack Russell, the Werewolf By Night, Topaz turned against her mentor rather than allow Russell and his friends to come to harm. Topaz later joined forces with Jennifer Kale and Satana as the Witches to recover the stolen Tome of Zhered-Na. A prophecy states that, one day, Topaz will be capable of wiping away the evils of the world. **TB**

Trainer, Dr. Seward

FIRST APPEARANCE Peter Parker: Spider-Man #54 (January 1995)
REAL NAME Seward Trainer
OCCUPATION Geneticist **BASE** New York City
HEIGHT 5 ft 10 in **WEIGHT** 200 lbs **EYES** Brown **HAIR** Brown
SPECIAL POWERS/ABILITIES A genius in the fields of biology and genetic engineering.

So brilliant that he was once employed by the High Evolutionary, geneticist Seward Trainer gave in to Green Goblin Norman Osborn's blackmailing and participated in a plot to crush Spider-Man Peter Parker's morale. By tampering with the Jackal's research, Trainer made it appear that Parker was a clone. Dr. Trainer became a father figure to the real clone, Ben Reilly (Scarlet Spider), but died at the hands of Norman Osborn (Green Goblin) before he could confess his role in the scheme. His daughter Carolyn Trainer briefly took the identity of Doctor Octopus. **DW, MF**

Trauma

FIRST APPEARANCE Avengers: The Initiative #1 (March 2007)
REAL NAME Terrance Ward
OCCUPATION Adventurer **BASE** Camp Hammond
HEIGHT 5 ft 10 in **WEIGHT** 175 lbs
EYES Brown **HAIR** Black
SPECIAL POWERS/ABILITIES Can shape-shift into whatever a foe fears most.

Terrance joined the Fifty-State Initiative and became one of the first cadets to be trained at Camp Hammond. His power allows him to read someone's mind, discover their worst fear, and then morph into a physical manifestation of that fear. In early combat training, this ability resulted in tragedy, when Armory panicked upon seeing her worst fear and accidentally killed Michael Van Patrick. MVP's evil clone later killed Terrance, but Terrance revived in his coffin. The source of his powers is the fact that his real father is secretly Nightmare. Terrance served as a counselor at Camp Hammond but left after Nightmare possessed him while he slept. **MF**

TRAVELLER, JUDAS

FIRST APPEARANCE Web of Spider-Man #117 (October 1994)
REAL NAME Dr. Judas Traveller
OCCUPATION Adventurer **BASE** Currently unknown
HEIGHT 6 ft 7 in **WEIGHT** 245 lbs **EYES** Blue (pupils turn red when he uses his powers) **HAIR** White
SPECIAL POWERS/ABILITIES Possesses limited psionic powers and the mutant ability to alter people's perceptions of reality.

Famous criminal psychologist Dr. Judas Traveller was lecturing in Europe when he became aware of the Brotherhood of SCRIERS, a secret criminal organization. The Scriers sent an assassin to inject Traveller with a fatal drug. Instead of killing him, the drug triggered Traveller's mutant abilities and he suffered a nervous breakdown. The Scriers supervised his recovery and assigned four agents—Mr. Nacth, Medea, Boone, Chakra and a Scrier—to watch over him 24 hours a day. After SPIDER-MAN freed him from the Scriers' control, Traveller went into hiding. **TD**

TRIATHLON

FIRST APPEARANCE Avengers #8 (September 1998)
REAL NAME Delroy Garrett Jr.
OCCUPATION Adventurer **BASE** New York City
HEIGHT 6 ft 3 in **WEIGHT** 200 lbs **EYES** Brown **HAIR** Brown
SPECIAL POWERS/ABILITIES Garrett has superhuman strength, speed, and agility three times greater than the human peak, is fast enough to dodge bullets, and can identify hidden Skrulls.

Former Olympic sprinter Delroy Garrett Jr. joined the Triune Understanding movement, and its leader, Jonathan Tremont, merged the energy shard of 3-D MAN into him, giving him his powers. As Triathlon, Garrett joined the AVENGERS and fought Tremont, who had betrayed his cause. During the CIVIL WAR, Garrett sided with CAPTAIN AMERICA but later joined the FIFTY-STATE INITIATIVE as 3-D Man and was assigned to the Hawaii team, the Point Men. During the SECRET INVASION, he found he could detect SKRULLS and joined the Skrull Kill Krew. He later joined the AGENTS OF ATLAS. **DW, MF**

TRICK SHOT

Buck Chisholm met Clint Barton (HAWKEYE) when they were working for a carnival. Clint's mentor, the SWORDSMAN, asked Buck to train Clint with the bow. When Clint balked at robbing the carnival, Buck kept the Swordsman from killing him. Later, Buck decided to rob a crook named Marko and brought Clint with him. Buck apparently killed Clint's brother Barney, who was Marko's bodyguard. When Clint objected, Buck pinned him to a tree with an arrow.

Years later, Buck—now the mercenary Trick Shot—contracted cancer and challenged Clint—now the hero Hawkeye—to a final duel. Clint beat Buck but couldn't bring himself to kill him. BARON ZEMO made a bargain with Buck to cure his cancer if he'd train the revived Barney as an archer. Zemo then double-crossed Buck and sent him, dying, to the Avengers as a cruel gift for Hawkeye.

Calling himself the new Trick Shot, Barney fought Clint, who defeated him. Despite his hatred for his brother, Barney provided bone marrow for a transplant to save Clint's eyesight. Broken out of prison, Barney joined the second team of AVENGERS assembled by Norman Osborn (GREEN GOBLIN), posing as his Hawkeye. He later reconciled with Clint. **MF.**

TRICKSHOT

FACTFILE
REAL NAME
Buck Chisholm
OCCUPATION
Assassin, mercenary
BASE
Mobile

HEIGHT 6 ft 2 in
WEIGHT 287 lbs
EYES Brown
HAIR Grayish brown

FIRST APPEARANCE
Solo Avengers #1 (December 1987)

POWERS

Buck was one of the greatest archers ever as well as a trained combatant.

TRITON

FIRST APPEARANCE Fantastic Four #45 (December 1965)
REAL NAME Unrevealed
OCCUPATION Scout **BASE** Washington, D.C.
HEIGHT 6 ft 1 in **WEIGHT** 210 lbs **EYES** Green **HAIR** None
SPECIAL POWERS/ABILITIES Can breathe underwater but cannot survive on land without special equipment; superhuman strength and other physical adaptations for undersea living.

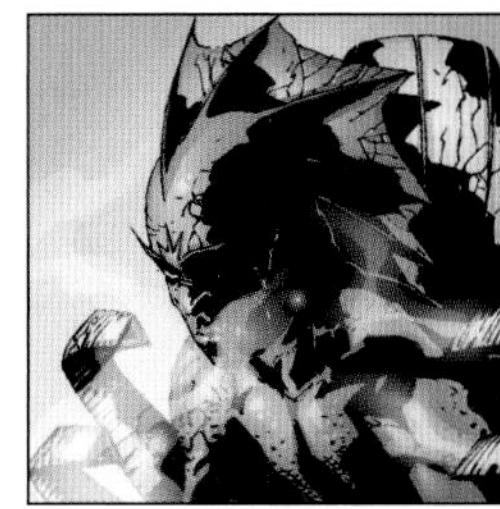

Triton is a member of the royal family of the INHUMANS, a genetic offshoot of the human race. The son of the Inhuman priest and philosopher Mander and his biologist mother Azur, Triton was exposed to mutagenic Terrigen Mist when a year old. The resulting mutations adapted him to live and breathe underwater. Along with other members of the royal family, Triton was banished when MAXIMUS first usurped the throne. While in exile, Triton first encountered and fought the FANTASTIC FOUR. Since then, however, Triton has become the ally of the Fantastic Four and Prince NAMOR. **PS**

TWELVE, THE

In the final days of World War II, during the Battle of Berlin, Nazis captured a dozen American heroes and placed them in suspended animation in a secret bunker. The bunker remained undiscovered until some sixty years later when construction crews stumbled upon it. The US government brought the heroes back home and revived them on a set constructed to resemble 1945. The heroes soon figured out that something was wrong and had to endure the shock of entering a world in which most of the people they knew and loved were dead.

Soon after, the Phantom Reporter discovered the Blue Blade dead and vowed to find the killer. It turns out he was murdered by the robot Electro, who was under the control of the bigoted Dynamic Man, who—unknown to the others—was an android. Cornered, Dynamic Man killed Fiery Mask, who passed his powers on to the Phantom Reporter. Captain Wonder held Dynamic Man down, suffering terrible burns as the Reporter destroyed him. The survivors all built new lives for themselves in this brave new world. **MF**

FACTFILE
MEMBERS
BLUE BLADE
Swashbuckling swordsman.
BLACK WIDOW
Mystical mistress of vengeance.
CAPTAIN WONDER
Superstrong flyer.
DYNAMIC MAN
Superhuman flying android shapeshifter.
ELECTRO
Super strong and fast robot.
FIERY MASK
Superhuman pyrokinetic.
LAUGHING MASK
Expert gunman and combatant.
MASTERMIND EXCELLO
Precognitive telepath.
MISTER E
Athlete.
PHANTOM REPORTER
Investigator.
ROCKMAN
Superhuman bruiser.
WITNESS
Precognitive superhuman.
BASE
New York
FIRST APPEARANCE
Twelve #0 (December 2007)

FACTFILE
REAL NAME
Michiko "Mickey" Musashi
OCCUPATION
Adventurer, journalist
BASE
Mobile

HEIGHT 5 ft 7 in
WEIGHT 125 lbs
EYES Brown
HAIR Black

FIRST APPEARANCE
New Warriors #28 (October 1992)

POWERS
Turbo's suit is fitted with jet turbines. It allows Turbo to fly faster than a commercial jet, and the powerful turbines on her wrists allow her to deliver turbine-powered hyper-punches. The suit can also fire energy bursts, and its visor has telescopic sights.

TURBO

Mickey Musashi never wanted to be a hero. In fact the journalism student thought that being a Super Hero was a ridiculous notion...until she came across the Turbo suit. This remarkable piece of equipment was created by a human scientist, Michael Stivak, under the orders of the DIRE WRAITHS. When the suit's inventor learned that the suit was to be used for evil purposes, he gave it to a man named Brock Jones, who donned it to fight crime as the hero TORPEDO.

Eventually, the Wraiths found and killed Brock Jones, and the suit passed to Brock's cousin Mike Jeffries, who shared it with Musashi. As it turned out, the suit worked better for her than for Jeffries and she reluctantly became the hero known as Turbo.

While teamed with the NEW WARRIORS, Turbo battled the Dire Wraiths, as well as the criminal team known as Heavy Mettle.

Musashi quit life as a hero and pursued her journalism career, also setting up a support group called Excelsior to dissuade super-powered teenagers from risking their lives as heroes. The group disbanded, but several members, including Musashi, enrolled at the AVENGERS Academy. **MT, MF**

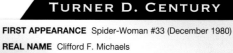

TURNER D. CENTURY

FIRST APPEARANCE Spider-Woman #33 (December 1980)
REAL NAME Clifford F. Michaels
OCCUPATION Former vigilante and reformer
BASE New York City; mobile; New York State
HEIGHT 6 ft 1 in **WEIGHT** 185 lbs **EYES** Blue **HAIR** Black
SPECIAL POWERS/ABILITIES Extensive engineering expertise; carries umbrella that doubles as flame-thrower; rides flying bike.

Wealthy Morgan MacNeil Hardy adopted Clifford Michaels and sealed him away from the world for decades. When he emerged, he hated what he saw as the terrible moral state of the Earth. Calling himself Turner D. Century, he went on a crime spree to protest this decline. During a clash with SPIDER-WOMAN, Hardy died in a fire. Michaels hoped to avenge him, but the SCOURGE killed him first. Arnim ZOLA made a clone of Michaels, but it was killed, too. The HOOD later revived Michaels, but only for thirty days. **TB, MF**

TYPHOID MARY

FACTFILE
REAL NAME
Mary (last name possibly Mezinis or Walker)
OCCUPATION
Criminal
BASE
New York City

HEIGHT 5 ft 10 in
WEIGHT 140 lbs
EYES Brown
HAIR Brown

FIRST APPEARANCE
Daredevil #254 (May 1988)

POWERS
Telekinesis, pyrokinesis, and also limited hypnotic ability; a skilled hand-to-hand combatant and expert with various bladed weapons.

TYPHOID MARY

Childhood abuse caused Mary to develop a disassociative identity disorder, giving her three distinct personalities: timid Mary, lustful Typhoid, and vicious Bloody Mary. Through therapy, a fourth personality emerged as a stable combination of all three. Typhoid Mary worked as an assassin for the KINGPIN and played a cruel game with DAREDEVIL by charming him as Mary and tormenting him as Typhoid. To join the FIFTY-STATE INITIATIVE, she disguised herself as Mutant Zero, and later she worked with Daredevil when he ruled the HAND. **DW, MF**

TYRANT

FIRST APPEARANCE Silver Surfer #81 (June 1993)
REAL NAME Unrevealed
OCCUPATION Conqueror of Worlds
BASE Star-Traveling Fortress
HEIGHT 29 ft **WEIGHT** 20 tons **EYES** Red **HAIR** None
SPECIAL POWERS/ABILITIES Virtually unlimited cosmic power on a par with Galactus.

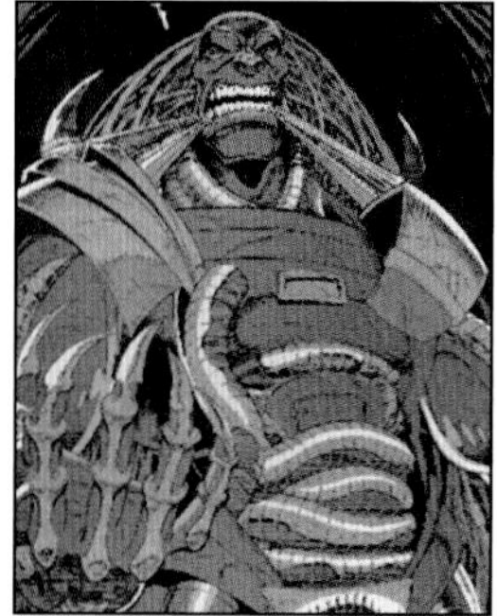

Created by GALACTUS billions of years ago, Tyrant draws his power from living worlds, and thus loses energy each time a planet is consumed by Galactus. Driven by a lust for power, Tyrant enslaved entire civilizations and protected himself with a robot army. Among the few who successfully opposed him were the women warriors of the Spinsterhood. In the modern era, Tyrant nearly succeeded in killing Galactus until Galactus' herald Morg unleashed the unstoppable energies of the Ultimate Nullifier. Tyrant and Galactus both vanished, though Galactus has since returned. **DW**

TYRANNUS

FACTFILE
REAL NAME
Romulus Augustulus
OCCUPATION
Would-be conqueror
BASE
Subterranea

HEIGHT 6 ft 2 in
WEIGHT 225 lbs
EYES Light brown
HAIR Blond

FIRST APPEARANCE
Incredible Hulk #5
(January 1963)

POWERS
Psychic powers including mind-control, telepathy, and the ability to drain life energy. The Fountain of Youth provides Tyrannus with immortality, giving him plenty of time for devising ways to conquer the surface world.

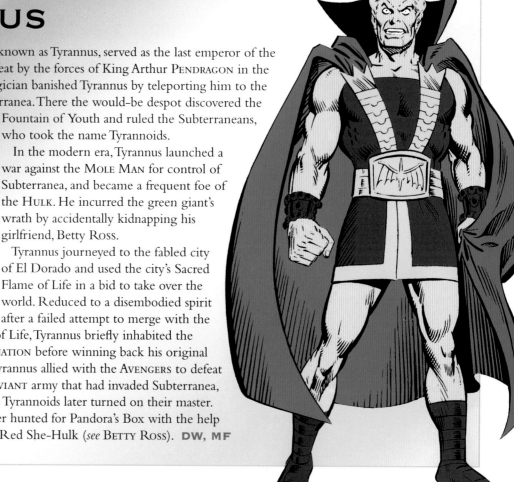

Tyrannus' planned invasion of the surface world was smashed by Hulk.

TYRANNUS

Romulus Augustulus, better known as Tyrannus, served as the last emperor of the Roman Empire, until his defeat by the forces of King Arthur PENDRAGON in the 6th century. MERLIN the Magician banished Tyrannus by teleporting him to the underground world of Subterranea. There the would-be despot discovered the Fountain of Youth and ruled the Subterraneans, who took the name Tyrannoids.

THOUGH I WAS BANISHED TO THE CENTER OF EARTH CENTURIES AGO BY THE ACCURSED MERLIN THE MAGICIAN, THIS MAGIC ELIXIR HAS KEPT ME ALIVE AND YOUNG ALL THESE YEARS-- WHILE I PLANNED MY REVENGE UPON MANKIND!
TYRANNUS DRINKS THE POTION! GREAT IS TYRANNUS! BOW DOWN TO THE ALL POWERFUL TYRANNUS!

Tyrannus gulps a goblet of the Fountain of Youth.

In the modern era, Tyrannus launched a war against the MOLE MAN for control of Subterranea, and became a frequent foe of the HULK. He incurred the green giant's wrath by accidentally kidnapping his girlfriend, Betty Ross.

Tyrannus journeyed to the fabled city of El Dorado and used the city's Sacred Flame of Life in a bid to take over the world. Reduced to a disembodied spirit after a failed attempt to merge with the Flame of Life, Tyrannus briefly inhabited the ABOMINATION before winning back his original body. Tyrannus allied with the AVENGERS to defeat the DEVIANT army that had invaded Subterranea, but the Tyrannoids later turned on their master. He later hunted for Pandora's Box with the help of the Red She-Hulk (*see* BETTY ROSS). **DW, MF**

Uatu, The Watcher

FIRST APPEARANCE Fantastic Four #13 (April 1963)
REAL NAME Uatu **OCCUPATION** Observer
BASE Mobile; New York State **HEIGHT** Variable
WEIGHT Variable **EYES** No visible irises **HAIR** None
SPECIAL POWERS/ABILITIES Virtually immortal; has superhuman intelligence, is telepathic and can teleport from the Earth to the Moon.

Self-appointed observers of the universe, the WATCHERS vowed never to interfere in the affairs of others. As the Watcher responsible for Earth and its solar system, Uatu has broken this rule several times since encountering the FANTASTIC FOUR. His most significant intervention in human affairs came just before Earth's first visit from GALACTUS and the SILVER SURFER, when he warned the Fantastic Four of the impending alien threat. Cautioned for his repeated interference, Uatu was stripped of his role as Watcher but he has since been reinstated. **AD**

U-Go Girl

FIRST APPEARANCE X-Force #116 (July 2001)
REAL NAME Edith ("Edie") Constance Sawyer
OCCUPATION Adventurer **BASE** Los Angeles
HEIGHT 5 ft 7 in **WEIGHT** 135 lbs
EYES Green **HAIR** Red
SPECIAL POWERS/ABILITIES Teleportation, which makes her narcoleptic.

Born in the Midwest, Edie became pregnant at 15 and gave the baby up to her parents to adopt. When she saw her daughter's face, she reflexively teleported away to LA, only to return soon after. Years later, the blue-skinned young woman returned to LA and joined X-FORCE. After saving her teammate Orphan from his suicidal tendencies, she became romantically involved with him. The team's relationship with its owners eventually broke down, and they hired the Bush Rangers to kill them all. Edie died at their hands. When Orphan died much later, they finally reunited in the afterlife. **MF**

Ultimo

FIRST APPEARANCE Tales of Suspense #76 (April 1966)
REAL NAME Ultimo
OCCUPATION Destroyer **BASE** Mobile
HEIGHT Varies **WEIGHT** Varies
EYES Yellow **HAIR** None
SPECIAL POWERS/ABILITIES Monstrous strength, endurance, and invulnerability.

Ultimo was an ancient alien robot that slaughtered the people of the planet Rajak and then crashed on Earth while pursuing the last Rajaki. The MANDARIN claimed it and used it to battle IRON MAN and an Iron Legion of Tony Stark's friends in armor, led by WAR MACHINE. Stark figured out how to shut it down by accessing its programming. It was later turned into an Ultimo virus that Morgan STARK consumed, turning him into a giant robot made from morphable liquid metal. **MF**

U-Foes

Hoping to duplicate the process by which the FANTASTIC FOUR had gained their powers, millionaire Simon Utrecht enlisted rocket pilot Mike Steel, engineer Jimmy Darnell, and technical specialist Ann Darnell to accompany him into space. The experiment worked, and the cosmic radiation they were exposed to gave each a unique power: Steel became a metal-coated being, Jimmy gained control over radiation, his sister Ann converted into a gaseous state, and Utrecht himself discovered that he could repel objects.

As Ironclad, Vapor, X-Ray, and Vector, they formed the U-Foes and unleashed their powers on Bruce Banner (HULK), whom they blamed for grounding their test flight prematurely. Over time, they found work as professional mercenaries. During the CIVIL WAR, they worked for the THUNDERBOLTS Army and then the HOOD's gang. During the DARK REIGN, they became the FIFTY-STATE INITIATIVE's North Carolina team. They helped launch the siege of Asgard by battling Volstagg (*see* WARRIORS THREE) and framing him for killing thousands during a football game at Soldier Field. **DW, MF**

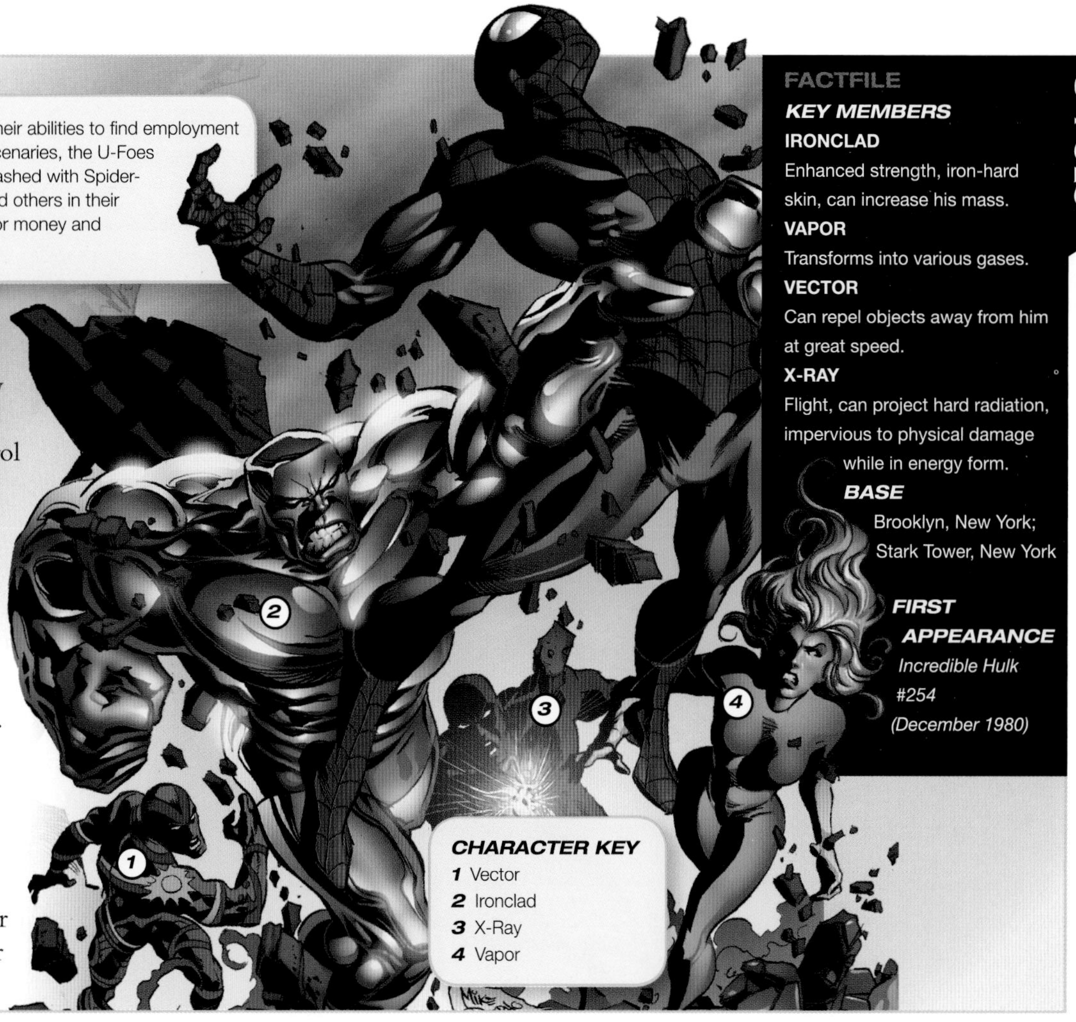

Using their abilities to find employment as mercenaries, the U-Foes have clashed with Spider-Man and others in their quest for money and power.

CHARACTER KEY
1 Vector
2 Ironclad
3 X-Ray
4 Vapor

FACTFILE

KEY MEMBERS

IRONCLAD
Enhanced strength, iron-hard skin, can increase his mass.

VAPOR
Transforms into various gases.

VECTOR
Can repel objects away from him at great speed.

X-RAY
Flight, can project hard radiation, impervious to physical damage while in energy form.

BASE
Brooklyn, New York; Stark Tower, New York

FIRST APPEARANCE
Incredible Hulk #254 (December 1980)

FACTFILE

ULTRAFORCE

KEY MEMBERS

BLACK KNIGHT Wields the Ebony Blade; rides winged horse.

CONTRARY Master manipulator.

GHOUL Undead man who can speak with the dead.

HARDCASE Nanotech man with superhuman senses and strength.

PIXX Technological genius who can project illusions.

PROTOTYPE Energy blasts and flight; armor grants superstrength.

SIREN Superstrength; control over liquids.

TOPAZ Superstrong; fires energy blasts from staff.

BASE

Headless Cross, Arkansas

FIRST APPEARANCE

Ultraforce #0 (June 1994)

ULTRAFORCE

On Earth-93060, superpowered people were known as Ultras. The members of Ultraforce banded together to protect their Earth from evil Ultras and other threats. Hardcase and Contrary brought together the initial members of the team—which included them and Ghoul, Pixx, Prime, Prototype, and Topaz—and received sanctioning from the US government. Contrary outfitted them with technology from the subterranean Fire People so that they could try to keep them from invading the surface world.

Later, the BLACK KNIGHT arrived from Earth-616 (the main Marvel universe) and joined the team. They also teamed up with the AVENGERS and fought against SERSI of the ETERNALS. During the Black September event, they served as LOKI's champions in a contest with the GRANDMASTER. **MF**

CHARACTER KEY

1 Prime ***2*** Hardcase ***3*** Topaz ***4*** Contrary ***5*** Prototype ***6*** Ghoul ***7*** Pixx

ULTRA GIRL

FIRST APPEARANCE Ultra Girl #1 (November 1996)
REAL NAME Tsu-Zana (Suzy Sherman)
OCCUPATION Adventurer **BASE** Camp Hammond
HEIGHT 5 ft 6 in **WEIGHT** 233 lbs **EYES** Blue **HAIR** Blond
SPECIAL POWERS/ABILITIES Flight, superhuman strength, speed, and durability, healing factor, and ability to see energy auras.

Suzy discovered her powers while on a modeling shoot, when a SENTINEL attacked her. Soon afterward, she joined the NEW WARRIORS, at which point her best friend revealed that she was actually a KREE destined to revive her people's empire. Suzy joined CAPTAIN AMERICA's side during the CIVIL WAR. After his death, she registered with the US government and joined the FIFTY-STATE INITIATIVE. For a short while, she wore CAPTAIN MARVEL's (Carol Danvers) original costume, but she surrendered it to HAMMER, which grabbed the rights to the name and outfit. She later left the Initiative to join the New Warriors. **MF**

UMAR

FIRST APPEARANCE Strange Tales #150 (November 1966)
REAL NAME Umar
OCCUPATION Sorceress **BASE** Dark Dimension
HEIGHT/WEIGHT Unknown **EYES** Black **HAIR** Black
SPECIAL POWERS/ABILITIES Umar possesses extensive mystic knowledge, which allows her to cast powerful spells for a variety of purposes

The sister of the dreaded DORMAMMU and a member of the mystical Faltine race, Umar was exiled along with her brother from their home dimension and sought sanctuary within the Dark Dimension. But Dormammu, who had altered himself to become a being of pure energy, conquered the Dark Dimension, and banished Umar, the only threat to his power base. With Dormammu's defeat at the hands of DOCTOR STRANGE, Umar was freed, and she battled Strange to avenge her brother and expand her power base, despite the fact that her daughter, CLEA, became involved with Strange. Dormammu returned to join Umar against Strange, but the two betrayed each other at every turn. Umar was thought killed, but a wishing well resurrected her and she captured the HULK, making him her consort. She was forced to let him and the Red She-Hulk (*see* BETTY ROSS) go rather than see her world destroyed. **TB, MF**

UNICORN

FIRST APPEARANCE Tales of Suspense #56 (August 1964)
REAL NAME Milos Masaryk
OCCUPATION Intelligence agent, later criminal **BASE** Mobile
HEIGHT 6 ft 2 in **WEIGHT** 220 lbs **EYES** Blue **HAIR** Red
SPECIAL POWERS/ABILITIES Possesses superhuman strength and durability; wears helmet with "power horn" that can project concussive energy blasts, lasers, and microwaves; wears rocket belt permitting flight.

A Russian intelligence agent, Milos Masaryk guarded Professor Anton Vanko's lab. Vanko invented the harness, helmet, and "power horn" that Masaryk wore as the Unicorn. While spying on Stark Industries, the Unicorn first battled his longtime enemy IRON MAN. The Unicorn underwent treatment that endowed him with superhuman strength but caused rapid cellular deterioration. The BEYONDER revived him after his death, however, and the Unicorn fought for the THUNDERBOLTS during the CIVIL WAR. **PS, MF**

ULTRON

Robot with an evil mind of its own

AVENGERS
THE NEW MASTERS OF EVIL!
Ultron assembled a team of Masters of Evil to combat the Avengers.

Henry Pym built Ultron as a robot servant programmed with his own brain patterns. Ultron rebelled against his maker, escaping to plot the extermination of all humanity. Engineering a succession of upgraded bodies for himself, he emerged as Ultron-5 to fight Pym's Avengers teammates.

... A CRUDE, YET WORKABLE ROBOT... A FALTERING STEP ON THE PATH TO SYNTHETIC LIFE!
SKRAWWK! DA-DA...WANT DA-DA--- SKRAWWK!
WH..? IT'S SPEAK-ING...MOVING!
BUT, I HAVEN'T EVEN TURNED IT ON YET...!

FACTFILE

REAL NAME
Ultron

OCCUPATION
Would-be world conqueror

BASE
Mobile

HEIGHT 6 ft
WEIGHT 535 lbs
EYES Glowing red
HAIR None

FIRST APPEARANCE
Avengers #54 (July 1968)

ULTRON

POWERS
Enhanced strength, near-invulnerability, energy projection; and flight; uses encephalo-ray to hypnotize others or put them into a coma.

BODYHOPPING

By posing as the villainous Crimson Cowl, Ultron assembled a second grouping of the Masters of Evil. He then created the android Vision, using a duplicate body from the original Human Torch and brainwave patterns from Wonder Man. Ironically, just like Ultron himself, the Vision rebelled against his creator and defected to the Avengers, setting the pattern for most of Ultron's subsequent creations.

Ultron incorporated indestructible adamantium into his frame beginning with the Ultron-6 body. Ultron-7 was a gargantuan construct, while Ultron-8 created a robotic "wife," Jocasta.

Ultron-9 perished in a vat of molten adamantium, and Machine Man deactivated Ultron-10. Ultron-11 participated in the Beyonder's Secret Wars. Ultron-12, initially a member of the Lethal Legion, repented and tried to atone for his criminal past until destroyed by Ultron-11. Doctor Doom programmed Ultron-13 with all previous personalities running simultaneously, making it easy for Daredevil to beat the addled robot. Ultron-14 created a new mate called Alkhema, though the two robots could not agree on their differing approaches to genocide.

MULTIPLYING MACHINES

Ultron-15 built hundreds of duplicates and conquered Slorenia, meeting defeat when exposed to metal-disintegrating vibranium. Later, Ultron infected Iron Man's Extremis armor and took over his body, but Hank Pym foiled him with a counter-virus. Soon after, Ultron led the Phalanx in an attempt to conquer the universe (*see* Annihilation). When he failed, he stored his mind in the body of a Galadorian Spaceknight sent back to Earth, where he created an Age of Ultron. He was stopped by the time-traveling Wolverine and Invisible Woman. **DW, MF**

Ultron returned as leader of the Phalanx, threatening the entire universe.

ESSENTIAL STORYLINES

- ***Avengers Vol. 3 #19-22***
In "Ultron Unlimited," the robot tyrant annihilates a tiny European nation with an army of duplicates.
- ***Runaways Vol. 2 #1-6***
Ultron is revealed as the creator of a teenage cyborg, leading to a battle with the Runaways in the story arc "True Believers."

The Vision and Ultron had a shared history, but still found themselves to be bitter enemies.

UNION JACK

FACTFILE
REAL NAME
Joseph Chapman
OCCUPATION
Adventurer
BASE
Great Britain

HEIGHT 6 ft
WEIGHT 195 lbs
EYES Brown
HAIR Light brown

FIRST APPEARANCE
Captain America #253 (January 1980)

POWERS
Enhanced strength and speed; wears a bulletproof costume, carries a variety of guns, and a silver dagger.

UNION JACK

The original Union Jack, Lord James Falsworth, fought for the British during World War I as a member of the heroic team Freedom's Five. After an injury, he was succeeded as Union Jack by his son, Brian (formerly known as the Destroyer), while his daughter Jacqueline went on to become SPITFIRE. Both heroes joined the World War II-era Invaders, where they fought alongside CAPTAIN AMERICA and NAMOR the Sub-Mariner; Brian also founded the heroic post-war V-Battalion.

The third Union Jack is Joey Chapman, who took up the mantle when Spitfire's son, Kenneth Crichton, refused to follow in his uncle's footsteps. Chapman joined the Knights of Pendragon and received superhuman abilities through possession of the Pendragon spirit. As Union Jack, Chapman has served with the most recent Invaders team. **DW**

Union Jack is a member of the New Invaders. The team's proactive role in ending world threats puts them at odds with traditional heroes, including Captain America's Avengers.

URICH, BEN

FIRST APPEARANCE Daredevil #153 (July 1978)
REAL NAME Benjamin Urich
OCCUPATION Reporter for the *Daily Bugle*
BASE New York City
HEIGHT 5 ft 9 in **WEIGHT** 140 lbs **EYES** Brown **HAIR** Gray
SPECIAL POWERS/ABILITIES None; a skilled and responsible investigative journalist.

Ben Urich started his journalism career as a copy boy at the *Daily Bugle*. He worked his way up to become a reporter. Urich began gathering information about DAREDEVIL, and soon learned the hero's true identity and personal history. He left the *Daily Bugle* to join the new *Front Line*, which later became the new *Daily Bugle*. His wife died during the SECRET INVASION, leaving him blocked until he started writing about the DARK REIGN. **MT, MF**

U.S.AGENT

FIRST APPEARANCE Captain America #323 (November 1986)
REAL NAME John F. Walker **OCCUPATION** Adventurer; government agent **BASE** Washington, D.C.
HEIGHT 6 ft 4 in **WEIGHT** 270 lbs **EYES** Blue **HAIR** Blond
SPECIAL POWERS/ABILITIES Superhuman strength and stamina; carries a shield made of Vibranium, which can absorb the vibrations from concussive forces directed against it.

Ex-soldier John Walker struck a deal with the POWER BROKER to become the Super-Patriot. Later, Walker replaced Steve Rogers as CAPTAIN AMERICA. When Rogers reclaimed his shield, Walker assumed Rogers' costume as the Captain and became the US Agent. During the CIVIL WAR, he joined the new OMEGA FLIGHT. Fighting alongside the AVENGERS at the end of the DARK REIGN, he lost his left arm and leg and later became the warden of the Raft super-prison. Trapped in an alternate reality with the Dark Avengers, he bonded with a lobotomized VENOM symbiote to restore his limbs. **TD, MF**

UNUS

FIRST APPEARANCE X-Men #8 (November 1964)
REAL NAME Angelo Unuscione
OCCUPATION Professional criminal **BASE** Mobile
HEIGHT 6 ft 1 in **WEIGHT** 220 lbs
EYES Blue **HAIR** Black
SPECIAL POWERS/ABILITIES Generates an impenetrable force field around body; redoubtable hand-to-hand combatant.

Unus was invited to join the BROTHERHOOD OF EVIL MUTANTS if he could defeat an X-Man. Fighting BEAST, Unus was beaten when his opponent employed a device to magnify Unus' force field out of his control. He disappeared for years and was thought dead until he turned up in Genosha. He lost his powers on M-Day, but QUICKSILVER returned them to him. They became unstable, though, and he suffocated to death in his own force field. **AD, MF**

UPSTARTS

FIRST APPEARANCE Uncanny X-Men #281 (October 1991)
FORMER MEMBERS AND POWERS
Gamesmaster Telepath who reads billions of minds simultaneously [1].
Siena Blaze Controlled the Earth's electromagnetic field [2].
Shinobi Shaw Can change his body from rock-solid to intangible [3].
Fabian Cortez Could overload the abilities of other mutants [4].
Trevor Fitzroy Drained victims' life energy to control time [5].
Andrea and Andreas von Strucker (Fenris Twins) Could project energy blasts when in contact with one another [6] and [7].
Graydon Creed Wore strength-boosting battle armor [8].

Looking for a new challenge, the GAMESMASTER gathered a group of young humans and mutants to compete in a murderous game. The contestants, who called themselves the Upstarts, earned points if they killed powerful targets such as members of the X-MEN, the NEW MUTANTS, or the HELLFIRE CLUB. The Upstarts launched a number of high-profile hits during their short career, and often fought each other. Eventually many members died, and the survivors, bored with the sport, disbanded. **DW**

Valkyrie

Odin made Brunnhilde the leader of the Valkyrior, giving her the task of bringing worthy warriors from among the slain to Valhalla. The Enchantress trapped her spirit within a crystal and kept it there for centuries, using it to invest herself and others with Valkyrie powers. In modern times, she gave the powers of Valkyrie to the socialite Samantha Parrington and later to Barbara Norriss, intending to use them as pawns. However, Brunnhilde restored her consciousness into Norriss' body and won back her original body. As Valkyrie, Brunnhilde joined the Defenders and seemingly sacrificed her life to defeat the evil entity the Dragon of the Moon. She returned by inhabiting new host bodies, but perished in the events surrounding Ragnarok. She returned to fight in Fear Itself and then to track down the hammers of the Worthy. Under the instructions of the All-Mother, she formed a new team of Valkyries called the Fearless Defenders. When archaeologist Annabelle Riggs sacrificed herself to save Valkyrie, she resurrected Riggs by bonding with her.

The Samantha Parrington version of Valkyrie regained her powers and continued her adventuring career. **DW, MF**

Wielding a mystical sword, Valkyrie deflects an energy attack.

The Defenders were Valkyrie's extended family. As a core member, she helped the team fight off countless threats to the planet.

FACTFILE

REAL NAME
Brunnhilde

OCCUPATION
Adventurer, former Chooser of the Slain

BASE
Asgard

HEIGHT 6 ft 3 ins
WEIGHT 475 lbs
EYES Blue
HAIR Blond

FIRST APPEARANCE
Avengers #87 (April 1971)

POWERS
Valkyrie has enhanced strength, longevity, and stamina; can perceive the onset of death, can teleport to the realm of the dead.

Vamp

FIRST APPEARANCE Captain America #217 (January 1978)
REAL NAME Denise Baranger
OCCUPATION Secret agent **BASE** Mobile
HEIGHT 5 ft 2 in **WEIGHT** 125 lbs **EYES** Blue **HAIR** Black
SPECIAL POWERS/ABILITIES A trained secret agent, the Vamp wore an absorbo-belt that allowed her to duplicate the strength and physical skills of anyone around her.

Due to her excellent fighting skills, the woman known as the Vamp was selected to become one of the first Super-Agents of SHIELD. Unfortunately, the Vamp was a double-agent, secretly working for the criminal Corporation, and assigned to infiltrate SHIELD. She had also been subjected to a genetic modification, which allowed her to transform into a psionically-powered creature called Animus. Eventually, the Vamp's true loyalties were exposed and she was incarcerated. She subsequently became yet another victim of the notorious serial killer of Super Villains the Scourge of the Underworld. **TD**

Vanguard

FIRST APPEARANCE Iron Man #109 (April 1978)
REAL NAME Nicolai Krylenko
OCCUPATION Adventurer **BASE** Belarus
HEIGHT 6 ft 3 in **WEIGHT** 230 lbs **EYES** Blue **HAIR** Red
SPECIAL POWERS/ABILITIES Generates force field that repels most energy directed at him; also uses hammer and sickle to redirect the repelled energy.

Born in Soviet Russia with mutant powers, Nicolai Krylenko and his twin sister Laynia were adopted by the state after their mother died in childbirth and their father (the Presence) was told they were stillborn. Raised to be a counterweight to the increasingly prolific US mutants, Nicolai and Laynia became members of the Soviet Super-Soldiers, he as Vanguard and she as Darkstar. He later became the latest Red Guardian, a member of the Winter Guard. **AD**

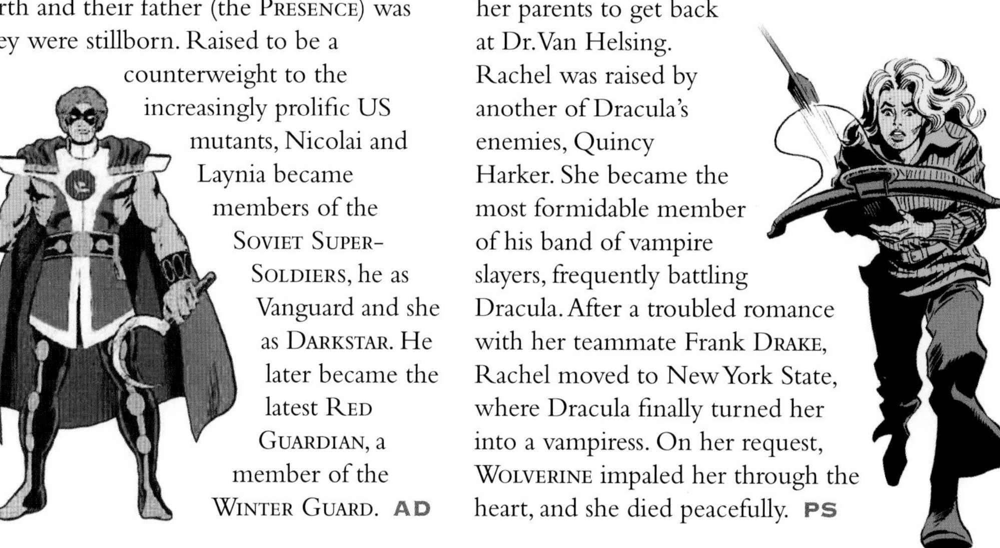

Van Helsing, Rachel

FIRST APPEARANCE Tomb of Dracula #3 (July 1972)
REAL NAME Rachel Van Helsing
OCCUPATION Vampire slayer **BASE** London, England
HEIGHT 5 ft 8 in **WEIGHT** 135 lbs **EYES** Blue **HAIR** Blond
SPECIAL POWERS/ABILITIES Expert vampire slayer whose preferred weapon was the crossbow; was also a parapsychologist and anthropologist.

Rachel Van Helsing was the descendant of Dr. Abraham Van Helsing, the 19th century nemesis of Dracula. As a child she saw Dracula murder her parents to get back at Dr. Van Helsing. Rachel was raised by another of Dracula's enemies, Quincy Harker. She became the most formidable member of his band of vampire slayers, frequently battling Dracula. After a troubled romance with her teammate Frank Drake, Rachel moved to New York State, where Dracula finally turned her into a vampiress. On her request, Wolverine impaled her through the heart, and she died peacefully. **PS**

VAN PATRICK, MICHAEL

Heroes die, but their clones live on

VAN PATRICK, MICHAEL

FACTFILE

REAL NAME
Michael Ian Van Patrick

OCCUPATION
Adventurer

BASE
Camp Hammond, Connecticut

HEIGHT 6 ft
WEIGHT 200 lbs
EYES Blue
HAIR Brown

FIRST APPEARANCE
Avengers: The Initiative #1 (April 2007)

POWERS
MVP is a gifted athlete in top physical condition, with perfect DNA but without any superhuman powers.

Michael Van Patrick was the most gifted athlete in his hometown of Liberty, Kentucky. However, when word got out that his great-grandfather had been Dr. Abraham Erskine, the creator of the Super-Soldier Serum, he was suspected of having superpowers, and all his records were taken away. In truth, Michael's father Brian had simply used Erskine's studies to train his son to perfection from birth.

MVP's short career ended while saving his friend Cloud 9.

THE INITIATIVE

After the CIVIL WAR, Vance Astrovik (*see* MARVEL BOY) recruited Van Patrick to join the FIFTY-STATE INITIATIVE. As MVP, Van Patrick reported for training at Camp Hammond in Connecticut, under the command of GAUNTLET. Sadly, MVP was killed during his first combat exercise. After TRAUMA terrified ARMORY by morphing into a giant spider, she fired her Tactigon in panic. MVP rescued CLOUD 9 from a stray blast, but the next shot killed him.

KIA was born bent on revenge for MVP's death.

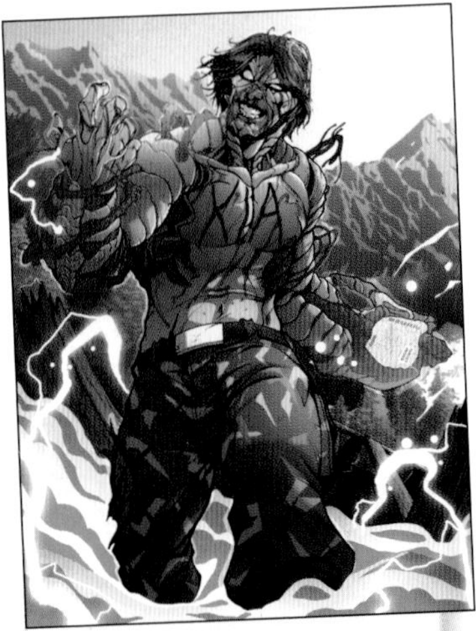

KIA wears the Tactigon, the alien weapon that killed MVP.

COVER-UPS AND CLONES

Henry Peter GYRICH ordered MVP's killing covered up and the Tactigon removed from Armory. Soon after, Baron VON BLITZSCHLAG set to work making his first clone of MVP, an exact duplicate sent back to Kentucky to take the place of the original. Von Blitzschlag quickly created three more clones, giving them copies of the "Iron Spider" armor that IRON MAN made for SPIDER-MAN. As the SCARLET SPIDERS, the three separated out MVP's name, calling themselves Michael, Van, and Patrick.

A CLONE TOO FAR

Delighted with the success of the Scarlet Spiders, Von Blitzschlag created another clone he called Ian, after the original MVP's middle name. In addition to MVP's memories, he gave the clone Armory's memories of the Tactigon and then attached the device to Ian. The feedback drove Ian insane. Realizing he was not the original MVP, he called himself KIA and then set out to kill everyone involved in MVP's death and cover-up. During this, he injured many Initiative heroes and murdered the clone Van and several SHIELD agents.

To defeat him, the Initiative trainees found the original MVP clone, hoping to transfer his mind into a helmet and then copy it into MVP, but at the cost of wiping the first clone's mind. The first clone used the helmet to wipe KIA's mind instead.

Afterward, Michael and Patrick joined the NEW WARRIORS. Michael died while battling RAGNAROK, an insane clone of THOR. Distraught, Patrick revealed his identity to the media, exposing the cover-up over MVP's death. MF

ESSENTIAL STORYLINES
- ***Avengers: The Initiative #1*** MVP is introduced and killed, all in a single issue.
- ***Avengers: The Initiative #7*** The Scarlet Spiders make their public debut and display their independence by helping Spider-Man.
- ***Avengers: The Initiative #8–11*** KIA is created and nearly destroys the Initiative.

Vanisher

FIRST APPEARANCE Uncanny X-Men #2 (November 1963
REAL NAME Telford Porter
OCCUPATION Professional criminal **BASE** New York City
HEIGHT 5 ft 5 in **WEIGHT** 175 lbs
EYES Green **HAIR** None
SPECIAL POWERS/ABILITIES Mutant ability to teleport himself and others by accessing the Darkforce dimension.

The Vanisher stole US defense plans until the original X-Men foiled him. After that, he mentored a gang called the Fallen Angels. The being called Darkling set him against the New Warriors. The Vanisher then joined a new team of Enforcers. Later, he moved to South America and sold Mutant Growth Hormone. He survived M-Day with his powers, and X-Force forced him to work with them. At one point, he was shot and killed trying to escape from Bastion, but he appeared later with the Marauders. **DW, MF**

Varnae

FIRST APPEARANCE Bizarre Adventures #33 (December 1982)
REAL NAME Varnae
OCCUPATION Lord of Earth's Vampires **BASE** Mobile
HEIGHT 10 ft **WEIGHT** 475 lbs **EYES** Red **HAIR** Green
SPECIAL POWERS/ABILITIES Near-immortality, enhanced strength, ability to grow in size and become a wolf, a bat, or a cloud of mist; can telepathically influence and vampirize others.

Varnae became the first vampire in the days of ancient Atlantis, when the Darkholders who worshipped the Elder God Chthon subjected him to anti-death experiments. Over the millennia, Varnae battled the Catholic Church's Montesi lineage, to prevent them from discovering the Montesi Formula that would destroy all vampires. In the year 1459, Varnae died and passed his title as Lord of the Vampires to Dracula. Through sorcerous incantations, Varnae returned in the modern era, and battled enemies including Doctor Strange and Blade. Varnae is also responsible for reversing the effects of the Montesi Formula, which had temporarily eradicated Earth's vampires. **DW**

Veil

FIRST APPEARANCE Avengers Academy #1 (August 2010)
REAL NAME Madeline Berry
OCCUPATION Student **BASE** Mobile
HEIGHT 5 ft 7 in **WEIGHT** 130 lbs
EYES Green **HAIR** Red
SPECIAL POWERS/ABILITIES Able to fly and change her body into any naturally occurring gas.

Maddy registered for the Fifty-State Initiative during the Dark Reign, and was later admitted to the inaugural class of the Avengers Academy under Hank Pym. After being attacked during Fear Itself, she decided to leave the Academy and take a job with Briggs Chemical. As it became harder for her to maintain herself as a solid, she accepted Jeremy Briggs offer to remove her powers. When she discovered that he planned to depower most heroes, leaving only those he judged worthy with their powers, she warned her friends away from him. Powerless, she retired. **MF**

Vapor

FIRST APPEARANCE The Incredible Hulk #254 (December 1980)
REAL NAME Ann Darnell **OCCUPATION** Life support technologist turned criminal **BASE** Mobile
HEIGHT 5 ft 6 in **WEIGHT** (in human form) 122 lbs
EYES (in human form) Green; (as Vapor) White **HAIR** Auburn
SPECIAL POWERS/ABILITIES Can transform herself into any kind of gas; can resume her original human form for brief periods only.

Millionaire industrialist Simon Utrecht built his own unshielded spaceship and sent it through the cosmic rays, like the Fantastic Four. His crew consisted of Ann Darnell, her brother Jimmy, and pilot Mike Steel. The radiation converted Ann Darnell's body into a gaseous state, and the four became known as the U-Foes, longstanding enemies of the Hulk. During the Civil War, they worked for the Thunderbolts Army, and afterward they joined the Hood's mob. During the Dark Reign, they served as the North Carolina team for the Fifty-State Initiative and helped frame Volstagg (*see* Warriors Three) for destroying Soldier Field. **PS, MF**

Varua

FIRST APPEARANCE (unnamed) Thor #300 (October 1980)
REAL NAME Mira **OCCUPATION** Pupil of the Celestials
BASE Celestial Mothership, previously Ruk Island
HEIGHT/WEIGHT/EYES Unrevealed **HAIR** Brown
SPECIAL POWERS/ABILITIES Posesses telepathy, teleportation, flight, and ability to generate the Blue Flame, which changes her and others into the Uni-Mind, a psionic entity.

Born in 1405 on Ruk Island, Mira began life as a priestess. In 1419, she was recruited into the Young Gods by the goddesses of Earth's pantheons. Mira was taken to train in combat under Katos on the Celestial Mothership where she became Varua. After the Sea Witch had a prophetic dream, the Celestials granted the Young Gods three days on Earth to investigate evil threats. Varua was held captive by the Deviants who used a brain mine to make her help them reawaken Ghaur. Varua was forced by Ghaur to create a Uni-Mind with other prisoners to give its power to him. This was cut open by the Black Knight, which set everyone free. Varua left with Delta Force. **MF**

Vengeance

FIRST APPEARANCE Ghost Rider #21 (December 1976)
REAL NAME Michael Badilino **OCCUPATION** Detective
BASE New York City **HEIGHT** (Badilino) 5 ft 10 ins, (Vengeance) 6 ft 6 ins **WEIGHT** (Badilino) 195 lbs, (Vengeance) 235 lbs
EYES Green **HAIR** Black
SPECIAL POWERS/ABILITIES Can project cold fire that causes others physical pain; his penance stare causes mental anguish.

Mephisto tricked the Ghost Rider into blasting detective Michael Badilino's father with hellfire. Unaware of Mephisto's involvement, Badilino bargained with him to gain the power to destroy the Ghost Rider. Known as Vengeance, he learned the truth, made peace with the Ghost Rider, and joined the Midnight Sons to battle demons like Mephisto. Vengeance appeared to destroy himself in a huge explosion but returned to help Ghost Rider battle the demon Blackheart. Deputy Kowalski became the new Vengeance after Badilino was freed, and he later joined the Shadow Council's Masters of Evil. **TB**

VENOM

The costume makes the villain

FACTFILE

REAL NAME
MacDonald "Mac" Gargan

OCCUPATION
Assassin-for-hire

BASE
New York City

HEIGHT 6 ft 2 in
WEIGHT 220 lbs
EYES Brown
HAIR Brown

FIRST APPEARANCE
The Amazing Spider-Man #298 (March 1988)

POWERS
Venom possesses superhuman strength, speed, and agility. Like Spider-Man, his hands and feet can adhere to most surfaces. Can project web-like substance from his "costume."

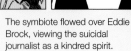

The symbiote flowed over Eddie Brock, viewing the suicidal journalist as a kindred spirit.

While SPIDER-MAN was on the BEYONDER's "Battleworld," he acquired a black costume, which turned out to be an alien being that bonded itself to him. Spider-Man rejected this alien symbiote, which then latched onto ex-*Daily Globe* columnist Eddie Brock, transforming him into Venom.

THE ORIGINAL VENOM

A disgraced ex-reporter, Brock blamed Spider-Man for ruining his career by revealing Brock's error in identifying the wrong man as the Sin-Eater. Stricken with cancer, he was about to kill himself when the symbiote bonded with him and put his disease into remission. Angry at Spider-Man for spurning it, the symbiote urged Brock to take his revenge on Spider-Man, and the bonded pair set out to do just that. Armed with the knowledge of Spider-Man's secret identity—and being hidden from Spider-Man's spider-sense—Brock became one of his most dangerous foes. At times, however, the two declared a truce, and during such periods Brock sometimes worked as an antihero, killing those who would threaten innocents.

ESSENTIAL STORYLINES
- ***The Amazing Spider-Man #299–300*** The first appearance of Eddie Brock as Venom.
- ***Marvel Knights: Spider-Man #7–8*** Brock auctions off the Venom symbiote to Angelo Fortunato for $100 million.
- ***Marvel Knights: Spider-Man #9-12*** Mac Gargan becomes the new Venom.

MULTIPLYING MACHINES

The Venom symbiote has reproduced a number of times, its children finding hosts of their own. This included SCREAM, CARNAGE and his spawn Toxin, plus Riot, Phage, Lasher, and Agony, who later combined to form Hybrid. When Brock's cancer returned, the symbiote wanted to leave him. Brock auctioned the creature for $100 million to gang lord Don Fortunato, who gave the suit to his son Angelo. Disgusted by Angelo's cowardice, the suit abandoned him in mid-air to die.

When Gargan attacked Brock, Brock turned into Anti-Venom.

Venom saw himself as a protector of the innocent. However, he had few qualms about killing criminals

NEW HOSTS

The symbiote offered itself to Mac Gargan (the SCORPION), who eagerly accepted the creature's incredible powers. The new Venom was more monstrous than ever, devouring some of his victims.

Gargan fought Spider-Man and then joined the THUNDERBOLTS during the CIVIL WAR. Subsequently the symbiote tried to reclaim his old host, Brock. Instead, Brock turned into Anti-Venom and nearly killed Gargan. Gargan recovered and fought the SKRULLS during the SECRET INVASION. Afterward, he joined Norman Osborn's (GREEN GOBLIN) new AVENGERS, posing as Spider-Man. When the DARK REIGN ended, the US government removed the symbiote from Gargan and gave it to Spider-Man's biggest fan, Flash THOMPSON, for him to work as a secret operative. Flash was only allowed to wear the suit for a maximum of 48 hours at a time to prevent permanent bonding. **MF**

Venus

FIRST APPEARANCE Venus #1 (August 1948)
REAL NAME Victoria Nutley Starr
OCCUPATION Adventurer **BASE** Washington, D.C.
HEIGHT 5 ft 6 in **WEIGHT** 280 lbs
EYES Blue **HAIR** Blond
SPECIAL POWERS/ABILITIES Mesmerizing voice. Also, superhuman durability and immortality.

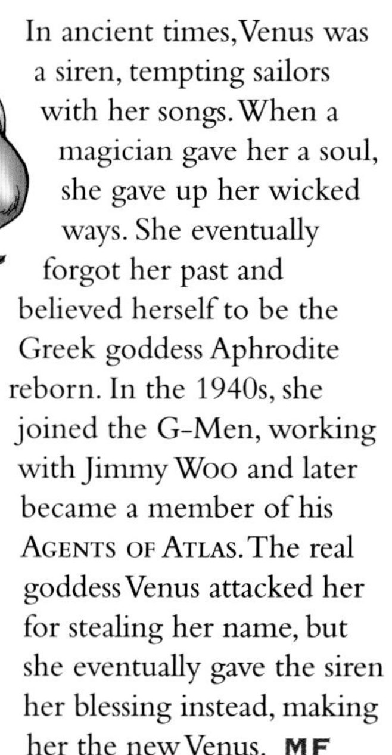

In ancient times, Venus was a siren, tempting sailors with her songs. When a magician gave her a soul, she gave up her wicked ways. She eventually forgot her past and believed herself to be the Greek goddess Aphrodite reborn. In the 1940s, she joined the G-Men, working with Jimmy Woo and later became a member of his Agents of Atlas. The real goddess Venus attacked her for stealing her name, but she eventually gave the siren her blessing instead, making her the new Venus. **MF**

Verdugo, Sandra

FIRST APPEARANCE Incredible Hulk #36 (March 2002)
REAL NAME Sandra Verdugo
OCCUPATION Mercenary, Home Base operative **BASE** Mobile
HEIGHT 5 ft 8 in **WEIGHT** 122 lbs **EYES** Black **HAIR** Black
SPECIAL POWERS/ABILITIES Recipient of H-Section Programming: is able to recover from most injuries and revive from death; brilliant markswoman, athlete, and hand-to-hand combatant.

A one-time member of the US Special Forces, Sandra Verdugo worked as a mercenary before becoming pregnant by Doc Samson. When Sandra's eight-year-old son was kidnapped, the clandestine organization Home Base offered her a deal. Home Base would retrieve her son if Sandra would agree to become one of their operatives. Her mission would be to capture the Hulk. Sandra agreed but it wasn't long before she turned on her new employers. With the help of Doc Samson and the Hulk, Sandra was reunited with her son just before Home Base's headquarters were destroyed. Mother and child are thought to have perished in the conflagration. **AD**

Vernard, Kristoff

FIRST APPEARANCE Fantastic Four #247 (October 1982)
REAL NAME Kristoff Vernard
OCCUPATION Ruler of Latveria **BASE** Latveria
HEIGHT 4 ft 11 in, (in suit) 6 ft 7 in **WEIGHT** 103 lbs, (in suit) 293 lbs
EYES Brown **HAIR** Brown
SPECIAL POWERS/ABILITIES Enhanced strength; damage resistance; ability to generate force fields or fire concussion beams.

Some believe Kristoff Vernard to be the biological son of Nathaniel Richards, making him the half-brother of Mister Fantastic. After the death of Kristoff's mother in Latveria, Doctor Doom adopted the boy and groomed him as his heir. When Doom appeared to have died, his Doombots brainwashed Kristoff into believing that he was Doom. He donned an armored suit and attacked the Fantastic Four, though he eventually recovered his true identity. Nathaniel Richards later helped him regain the Latverian throne when Doom had disappeared. Doom and Kristoff have since reconciled. **DW, MF**

Veranke, Queen

FIRST APPEARANCE New Avengers #1 (January 2005) as Spider-Woman; New Avengers #40 (June 2008) as Veranke.
REAL NAME Veranke **OCCUPATION** Ruler
BASE Skrull empire **HEIGHT/WEIGHT/EYES/HAIR** Variable
SPECIAL POWERS/ABILITIES Shapeshifting, plus Spider-Woman's powers. Ruler of the Skrull empire.

A Skrull princess from Tyeranx 7 province, planet Satriani, Veranke challenged King Dorrek for ignoring Skrull prophecies. She was banished for her trouble. After Galactus devoured the Skrull homeworld and the Annihilation Wave destroyed most of the empire, Veranke was seen as a visionary and elevated to queen. She declared that Earth was to be the new Skrull homeworld and so launched the Secret Invasion. As part of this, she replaced Spider-Woman just before the reformation of the Avengers. At the climax of the Secret Invasion, she was killed by Norman Osborn (*see* Green Goblin). **MF**

Vermin

FIRST APPEARANCE Captain America #272 (August 1982)
REAL NAME Edward Whelan
OCCUPATION Unknown **BASE** Mobile
HEIGHT 6 ft **WEIGHT** 220 lbs **EYES** Red **HAIR** Brown
SPECIAL POWERS/ABILITIES Superhuman strength and speed. Teeth and nails can cut through soft metals; greatly enhanced sense of smell; can command rats to attack an enemy.

Villains Baron Zemo and Arnim Zola found Whelan living on the streets of Manhattan and genetically modified him into a rat-man. They sent him to kill Captain America, but he failed. He was unstable, and often turned on his masters. During the Civil War, he helped out both the Thunderbolts and the Hood. Later, Vermin battled the new Kraven the Hunter and also tangled with his old foe Spider-Man, who was wearing a Daredevil costume at the time. **MF**

Vibraxas

FIRST APPEARANCE Fantastic Four #390 (July 1994)
REAL NAME N'Kano
OCCUPATION Adventurer **BASE** Mobile
HEIGHT 5 ft 10 in **WEIGHT** 165 lbs
EYES Brown **HAIR** Brown
SPECIAL POWERS/ABILITIES Can generate intense vibratory force.

The young Wakandan N'Kano gained his powers when an experimental Vibrasurge project backfired, seemingly killing his mother. Taken in by the Black Panther, he traveled to America and became a member of the Fantastic Force under the name Vibraxas. When he accidentally murdered a gang member, Vibraxas went back to Wakanda to stand trial, but he was exonerated. After the Fantastic Force disbanded, Vibraxas found love with Queen Divine Justice, a member of the "Dora Milaje" who serve the Wakandan king as bodyguards and wives-in-training. **DW**

Vindicator

FIRST APPEARANCE Uncanny X-Men #139 (November 1980)
REAL NAME Heather McNeil Hudson
OCCUPATION Member of Alpha Flight
BASE Tamarind Island, British Columbia, Canada
HEIGHT 5 ft 5 in **WEIGHT** 120 lbs **EYES** Green **HAIR** Red
SPECIAL POWERS/ABILITIES Thermal-energy battlesuit provides ability to fly, generate force fields and fire concussive blasts.

Heather Hudson and her husband James helped found the Canadian team ALPHA FLIGHT. James led the team as GUARDIAN and, after his apparent death, Heather took over as Vindicator, wearing a modified version of her husband's battlesuit. She and James later had a baby girl and left on a mission to deep space. After M-Day, the Collective—a man burning with the power of most of the world's mutants—slaughtered Heather and the rest of Alpha Flight, but they were resurrected during the CHAOS WAR. Controlled by the MASTER OF THE WORLD, she betrayed the team and later escaped with her daughter. **DW, MF**

Virgo

FIRST APPEARANCE Avengers #72 (January 1970)
REAL NAME Elaine McLaughlin
OCCUPATION Professional criminal
BASE Denver, Colorado
HEIGHT 5 ft 6 in **WEIGHT** 125 lbs **EYES** Green **HAIR** Red
SPECIAL POWERS/ABILITIES Sharp criminal mind; good organizer; a skilled hand-to-hand combatant.

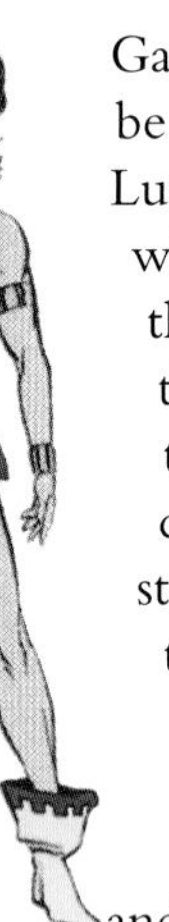

Gang boss Virgo was recruited to be a member of Cornelius Van Lunt's ZODIAC crime cartel, in which each member would adopt the guise of a different sign of the zodiac, and control a territory in a different American city. Zodiac was equipped with state-of-the-art weaponry and their ultimate goal was global domination. However, their bid for power was foiled by the combined forces of SHIELD and the AVENGERS. Later, a rogue ZODIAC faction led by former Cartel member SCORPIO and using androids to represent the twelve zodiological symbols targeted the original Zodiac leaders. In the end, Virgo was slain by her robot counterpart. **TB**

Von Blitzschlag, Baron

FIRST APPEARANCE Avengers: The Initiative #1 (April 2007)
REAL NAME Werner von Blitzschlag
OCCUPATION Scientist **BASE** Camp Hammond
HEIGHT 5 ft 10 in **WEIGHT** 165 lbs **EYES** Gray **HAIR** Gray
SPECIAL POWERS/ABILITIES Genius who can produce and control electricity.

During World War II, von Blitzschlag worked as a scientist for the Nazis. After the war, he disappeared until he became the head of research for the FIFTY-STATE INITIATIVE, working at Camp Hammond. After the death of Michael VAN PATRICK, von Blitzschlag cloned the young man many times, producing the SCARLET SPIDERS and KIA. KIA's attack left the old man bound to a wheelchair and stuck on life support. When THOR's clone later tried to kill him with lightning, the attack strengthened von Blitzschlag instead. Von Blitzschlag worked at Camp Hammond until the end of the DARK REIGN and was arrested for his crimes. **MF**

Viper

VIPER

FACTFILE

REAL NAME
Ophelia Sarkissian

OCCUPATION
Terrorist

BASE
Mobile

HEIGHT 5 ft 9 ins
WEIGHT Unknown
EYES Green
HAIR Black with green highlights

FIRST APPEARANCE
Captain America #110 (February 1969)

POWERS

Viper is a superb strategist and a trained terrorist with extensive knowledge of weaponry, tactics, and fighting styles. She is skilled in a number of martial arts and an expert in the use of various weapons, including whips.

Her face scarred at some point in her nebulous past, the woman who would one day be known as Viper began her career as a member of the international terrorist organization called HYDRA. After the leadership of Hydra was captured by Nick FURY and SHIELD, she assumed command of the remnants of the organization and, as MADAME HYDRA, excelled at creating panic and terror until CAPTAIN AMERICA brought her down. Madame Hydra later resurfaced in Virginia, where she murdered Jordan Stryke, a costumed criminal known as Viper, as he was being escorted by US marshals to Washington D.C. to testify about his criminal connections. She stole his costume and, assuming his name, took command of the Serpent Squad he had assembled. Under the new Viper's leadership, the Serpent Squad became a terrorist unit. Since then, both alone or in concert with allies such as the SILVER SAMURAI, BARON STRUCKER, and the RED SKULL, Viper has continued to hatch plans resulting in chaos and anarchy. She and the SILVER SAMURAI were lovers, although she once forced WOLVERINE to marry her (it didn't last). For a while, Viper ran the nation of Madripoor as its dictator, but SHIELD and IRON MAN overthrew her. A third Viper, Leon Murtagh, surfaced as part of SIN's new Serpent Squad, but he was killed after entering the witness protection program. **TB, MF**

Von Doom, Cynthia

FIRST APPEARANCE Astonishing Tales #8 (October 1971)
REAL NAME Cynthia von Doom
OCCUPATION Sorceress **BASE** Astral plane
HEIGHT 5 ft 8 in **WEIGHT** 150 lbs **EYES** Brown **HAIR** Brown
SPECIAL POWERS/ABILITIES Knowledge of magic allowed her to contact demons; however she often unleashed forces that were beyond her ability to control.

Cynthia von Doom was a sorceress who belonged to a group of Latverian gypsies called the Zefiro. She married Werner von Doom, a healer. Their son Victor grew up to become DOCTOR DOOM. Cynthia summoned the demon MEPHISTO, who offered her great power so she could overthrow Latveria's ruthless king and give her people a homeland. She unleashed terrible magic but could not control it. One of the king's guards killed her, and her soul joined Mephisto in Hell. Doom devoted himself to saving her from Mephisto's realm. With the help of DOCTOR STRANGE, she has moved on to a higher plane. **AD, MF**

VISION

Synthozoid with a human heart

The synthozoid who would become the Vision was programmed with the brain patterns of WONDER MAN, who was believed to be deceased at the time. The synthozoid was created by ULTRON, the AVENGERS' robotic archenemy, with the help of Professor Phineas T. Horton, the scientist responsible for the original HUMAN TORCH.

WH-WHY DO YOU WANT A NEW FACE FOR HIM, ULTRON?
BECAUSE HE MUST HAVE A COMPLETELY NEW LIFE, DIVORCED ENTIRELY FROM HIS PREVIOUS DAYS AS A HERO, WE SHALL ALSO PROVIDE HIM WITH NEW, FANTASTIC POWERS!
STILL, I DO DESIRE THAT HIS NEW FACE BE SCARLET--

Ultron forced Horton to help him build the Vision. Horton then programmed the Vision for independent thoughts.

FACTFILE
REAL NAME
Inapplicable
OCCUPATION
Adventurer
BASE
New York City

HEIGHT 6 ft 3 in
WEIGHT 300 lbs; however weight may vary from nothing to 90 tons.
EYES Gold
HAIR None

FIRST APPEARANCE
Avengers #57
(October 1968)

POWERS
Superhuman strength, endurance; jewel on brow discharges blasts of solar energy; can make all or part of body hard as diamond; can decrease his mass to become a wraith; can partially materialize within another person, causing extreme pain.

EMOTIONAL SIGNALS

Ultron sent the Vision to lure the Avengers into a trap, the Vision grew to admire the Avengers and couldn't betray them. He broke free of Ultron's control and helped the Avengers defeat him. The grateful heroes rewarded the Vision by inviting him to join the team. He was so shaken by the gesture that he actually shed a tear. The Vision's human emotions began to surface over time and he slowly realized that he was falling in love with Wanda Maximoff, the SCARLET WITCH. When she returned his feelings, they were married and took a leave of absence from the Avengers, settling in Leonia, New Jersey.

A MATTER OF TRUST

The Vision later returned to action to aid the Avengers against ANNIHILUS, and was severely injured. STARFOX attempted to cure him by linking him with ISACC, a massive computer complex that controlled the moon of Saturn called Titan. ISACC tapped into a control crystal left in the Vision by Ultron and used it to alter the android's way of thinking. When the Vision was elected chairman of the Avengers, he decided to bring a new golden age to humanity by taking control of every computer on Earth. However, the other Avengers convinced him to abandon his ambitious plan. Believing he could no longer be trusted, the government kidnapped and disassembled the Vision.

Infected by a virus, the Vision's body was completely liquefied.

The Vision was rescued by the AVENGERS WEST COAST and rebuilt, but he had lost his emotions and could no longer return the Scarlet Witch's love. Their marriage eventually ended in divorce. The Vision's android body was later destroyed when the Scarlet Witch went mad and disassembled the Avengers. IRON MAN rebuilt him after FEAR ITSELF, and he joined Hank Pym's Avengers AI team after being forced to serve his creator in the AGE OF ULTRON.

ESSENTIAL STORYLINES
- ***Giant-Size Avengers #4*** The Vision and Scarlet Witch are married.
- ***The Vision and Scarlet Witch #1–12*** The Vision and Scarlet Witch leave the Avengers and move to the suburbs.
- ***Avengers #251-254*** The Vision attempts to take over every computer on Earth.
- ***West Coast Avengers #42–45*** The government kidnaps and disassembles the Vision.

JONAS

A second version of the Vision was created when his programming was integrated into the armor of the YOUNG AVENGER known as Iron Lad. When Iron Lad removed the armor, it turned into a new, sentient Vision, who called himself Jonas. He fell in love with teammate STATURE and they joined Pym's Avengers team during the DARK REIGN.

After DOCTOR DOOM killed Stature, Jonas protested Iron Lad's plan to bring her into the future and revive her, fearing this would bring Iron Lad closer to becoming his future self, KANG. In response, Iron Lad destroyed him. **TD, MF**

Vulcan

FIRST APPEARANCE X-Men: Deadly Genesis #1 (January 2006)
REAL NAME Gabriel Summers
OCCUPATION Former adventurer **BASE** Shi'ar Empire
HEIGHT 6 ft **WEIGHT** 178 lbs **EYES** Black **HAIR** Black
SPECIAL POWERS/ABILITIES Gabriel can psionically control, manipulate, and absorb energy of any kind.

Vulcan is the brother Cyclops and Havok didn't know they had.

Christopher (later Corsair of the Starjammers) and Katherine Summers were flying in a small plane with their sons Scott (Cyclops) and Alex (Havok) when they spotted a Shi'ar starship. Scott and Alex got away, but the Shi'ar captured their parents. The Shi'ar killed Katherine and placed her unborn child in a machine that turned him into an adolescent, then made him a slave on Earth. The boy escaped and was taken in by Moira MacTaggert, who named him Gabriel. When the original X-Men were captured, Professor X trained Moira's wards, including Gabriel, to rescue them. Instead, they were killed, and Professor X erased Cyclops' memory of his newfound brother. After M-Day, the burst of energy taken from the Earth's mutants revived Gabriel. Calling himself Vulcan, he killed Banshee, exposed Professor X's betrayal, then left to take his revenge on the Shi'ar. In the process, he killed his father and later declared himself the Shi'ar emperor. He tried to conquer the Kree and was killed in an explosion while battling their ruler, Black Bolt. **MF**

Vulture

Adrian Toomes gained self-esteem from criminality. A founder of B&T Electronics with his friend Gregory Bestman, Toomes had just completed his electromagnetic harness—which enabled him to fly—when he discovered his partner had been defrauding the company. Desperate for revenge Toomes destroyed the company's factory and found a substantial cache of money. He then embarked upon a life of crime, throughout which he has been continually dogged by Spider-Man.

Several others used the Vulture name over the years, including Blackie Drago (Toomes' cellmate), Professor Clifton Shallot (who mutated into a vulture-man), a trio of crooks calling themselves the Vulturions, and mob cleaner Jimmy Natale (who mutated into an acid-spitting flyer). Toomes' latest gang included children in Vulture outfits, a crime for which the Superior Spider-Man (Doctor Octopus) beat him nearly to death. **AD, MF**

For a short time, two Vultures soared the skies of Manhattan.

FACTFILE

REAL NAME
Adrian Toomes

OCCUPATION
Inventor; criminal

BASE
Staten Island

HEIGHT 5 ft 11 in
WEIGHT 175 lbs
EYES Hazel
HAIR None

FIRST APPEARANCE
Amazing Spider-Man #2 (May 1963)

POWERS

Electromagnetic harness worn beneath costume enables the Vulture to fly at speeds of up to 95 mph. It also augments his strength, agility, and endurance to superhuman levels.

War

FIRST APPEARANCE X-Factor #11 (December 1986)
REAL NAME Abraham Lincoln Kieros **OCCUPATION** Former Horseman of Apocalypse **BASE** Unknown
HEIGHT 6 ft 6 in **WEIGHT** 270 lbs **EYES** Blue **HAIR** Brown
SPECIAL POWERS/ABILITIES As the Horseman of the Apocalypse War, Abraham could shatter objects just by concentrating on them and clapping his hands.

Vietnam war veteran Abraham Kieros was forced to live out his days in an iron lung. When Apocalypse offered to heal Abraham if he became one of his Four Horsemen, Abraham seized the opportunity. As the Horseman War, Abraham helped the group to win their first victory over X-Factor, but after that they suffered repeated defeats. Eventually, Apocalypse disbanded the group and Abraham returned to his paralyzed state. He would have remained in this condition if Angel, another former Horseman, had not healed him. Abraham is now determined to make the most of this new life. The Hulk, Deathbird, the mutant Gazer and Decimus Furius of ancient Rome have all been War at one time. **AD, MF**

Warp

FIRST APPEARANCE Avengers Next #1 (January 2007)
REAL NAME Unrevealed
OCCUPATION Adventurer, former thief **BASE** New York City
HEIGHT 5 ft 11 in **WEIGHT** 175 lbs **EYES** Brown **HAIR** Bald
SPECIAL POWERS/ABILITIES Can open teleportation portals.

In a possible future Marvel Universe known as Earth-982, Warp used his powers to teleport to any location to become an uncatchable thief. He sided with the troll Ulik and Sylene, the daughter of Loki, in what he thought was a plot to kidnap Kevin Masterson (*see* Thunderstrike) for ransom from the A-Next. When he learned that they planned to kill everyone on Earth and recreate Asgard—which Galactus had devoured, he helped A-Next save the day, after which he joined the team. **MF**

War Machine *see page 393*

Warbound

During training on the planet Sakaar, the Hulk bonded with his fellow gladiators—Hiroim, Miek, No-Name and Korg—and the group became "warbound," warriors dedicated to helping each other. Later, Caeira helped lead their revolt against the Red King and then married the Hulk. When the Hulk's starship exploded, killing millions—including the pregnant Caiera—the Warbound traveled to Earth to exact the Hulk's revenge during World War Hulk.

At the end of that battle, the Hulk and the traitorous Miek (who had let the starship explode) were captured. The others escaped SHIELD only to be caught in a plot by the Leader to irradiate Earth with gamma rays. SHIELD agent Kate Waynesboro helped them put a stop to this, and Hiroim bequeathed his Oldstrong power to her when he was killed. They later relocated to the Savage Land. **MF**

WARBOUND
1 Elloe Kaifi ***2*** Korg
3 Kate Waynesboro
4 No Name ***5*** Lavin Skee

FACTFILE

MEMBERS AND POWERS
CAIERA Shadow Sakaarian warrior with Oldstrong power: superhuman strength and near invulnerability.
ELLOE KAIFI Red Sakaarian warrior.
HIROIM Shadow Sakaarian warrior priest; Oldstrong power.
HULK Gamma-powered superhuman strength, agility, invulnerability, and healing factor.
KORG Kronan warrior with superhuman strength and durability.
LAVIN SKEE Red Sakaarian warrior.
MIEK Insectoid Sakaarian warrior with armor plating, flight, and four arms.
NO-NAME Sakaarian Brood queen with six limbs, flight, armor plating, vicious teeth, tail stingers.
KATE WAYNESBORO SHIELD agent now has Oldstrong power.
BASE Planet Sakaar. Later, Earth.

FIRST APPEARANCE
Incredible Hulk #94 (June 2006)

Warlock

Warlock is an alien of the Technarchy, a race of techno-organic creatures from the planet Kvch that survive by infecting living matter with a transmode virus that transforms them into similar material, which can then be absorbed. The ruler of the Technarchy is Magus, the father of Warlock. As a mutant of his race, Warlock didn't want to battle his father to the death, as was the way with his people. Instead, he fled to Earth, where he became a member of the New Mutants. Later, Cameron Hodge killed Warlock in an attempt to steal his powers, and his ashes were scattered over his friend Cypher's grave.

A group of mutant-haters who wished to become living Sentinels injected themselves with transmode virus taken from Warlock's ashes. They called themselves the Phalanx, and one of their number was Douglock, a revived Warlock given Cypher's memories. Warlock eventually regained his own memories and resumed his original form. On a trip back to Kvch, he helped defeat Ultron and the Phalanx in the second wave of the Annihilation. Upon returning to Earth, he found Cypher resurrected by a transmode virus employed by Selene. Freeing him from her influence, they both rejoined the New Mutants. **MF**

FACTFILE

REAL NAME
Warlock
OCCUPATION
Adventurer
BASE
Mobile

HEIGHT Varies
WEIGHT Varies
EYES Black
HAIR None

FIRST APPEARANCE
New Mutants #18 (August 1984)

POWERS

Warlock was a techno-organic alien who could shapeshift, changing not only his appearance but creating weapons and defenses on the fly.

WARLOCK, ADAM

Genetically created life form

WARLOCK

FACTFILE
REAL NAME
Adam Warlock
OCCUPATION
Avenger, Savior of Worlds
BASE
Counter-Earth

HEIGHT 6 ft 2 in
WEIGHT 240 lbs
EYES White
HAIR Blond

FIRST APPEARANCE
Fantastic Four #66 (September 1967)

POWERS
Body can trap cosmic energy which enhances his strength, endurance, and healing powers; also uses this energy to reduce gravity enabling him to fly; projects energy blasts from his hands.

Adam Warlock was the genetic creation of a group of scientists known as the ENCLAVE. He was the prototype for what they hoped would be an invincible army, with which they planned to conquer the world. While forming in his cocoon, Warlock overheard his creators' plans. When he hatched, he rebelled against them, destroyed their base, and used his cosmic power to take off into space.

When he emerged from his developmental cocoon, Warlock refused to go along with the plans his creators had for him, rebelling against them.

At first Adam Warlock was known simply as "Him."

HIGH EVOLUTIONARY

Warlock met the HIGH EVOLUTIONARY, a human who had learned how to control evolution, who was creating an artificial world called "Counter-Earth." He was hoping to create a planet free from evil, but MAN-BEAST brought evil to this pure world. The High Evolutionary gave Warlock the Soul Gem, which could draw souls into another dimension, and Warlock battled Man-Beast. In the end, however, Warlock was unable to defeat evil on Counter-Earth, and left to fight the good fight elsewhere.

Adam Warlock has golden-colored skin

THE MAGUS

Warlock subsequently battled THANOS, who mortally wounded him. Warlock's soul retreated into the Soul Gem, where it lived peacefully for many years until he emerged to battle Thanos once more to keep him from the Infinity Gauntlet. After this second victory, Warlock formed a group called the Infinity Watch to keep the Infinity Gems safe.

The backlash from the number of people killed in the Annihilation Wave sent Warlock into a coma, but QUASAR (Phyla-Vell) and MOONDRAGON revived himto help fight the PHALANX. He later joined the new GUARDIANS OF THE GALAXY, but in an effort to repair damage done to the timeline, he became the MAGUS and was killed. **MT, MF**

Awakened by Quasar and Moondragon, Warlock bursts from his healing cocoon to fulfil his destiny as "Saviour of the Kree," in the Annihilation story arc.

ESSENTIAL STORYLINES
- ***The Infinity Abyss Miniseries*** While living in one of his self-generated cocoons, Warlock is revived to battle six clones of Thanos.
- ***Warlock Miniseries*** The Enclave create another Warlock to rule the Earth, but he turns out to be an illusion in the mind of Janie, placed there by the real Adam Warlock to teach her compassion.

War Machine

Super Hero willing to stand in for Iron Man

As a pilot, Jim was prepared for flight-equipped armor.

While serving with the US Marines in Southeast Asia, helicopter pilot James "Rhodey" Rhodes met Tony Stark (Iron Man), who had just escaped from a warlord by creating his first suit of powered armor. Rhodes became Stark's pilot, and he even became Iron Man during one of Stark's battles with alcoholism. He reprised this role several more times over the years, even though he suffered mentally and physically for it.

FACTFILE

REAL NAME
James Rupert Rhodes

OCCUPATION
Adventurer

BASE
Mobile

HEIGHT 6 ft 1 in
WEIGHT 210 lbs
EYES Brown
HAIR Brown

FIRST APPEARANCE
Iron Man #118 (January 1979)

WAR MACHINE

POWERS
Armor provides flight, enhanced strength, damage resistance, and the ability to project destructive energy.

Nobody's Substitute

When Stark seemed to have been killed, Rhodey inherited Stark Enterprises, along with a new suit of armor built specially for him and geared up for full-out war. When Stark returned, Rhodes kept the armor at his request and eventually took the codename War Machine.

Working with the human-rights organization Worldwatch in the African nation of Imaya, Rhodey accepted the offer to serve as the company's executive director. This put him into conflict with Stark, who demanded the armor back. After they were captured and then defeated the Mandarin together, though, Stark ceded the armor to Rhodey again, along with its blueprints.

Rhodey lost the armor during a time-traveling adventure, but he wound up wearing an alien construct called the Eidolon Warwear to fight Stark, who was controlled by Immortus. With Stark thought dead and his company purchased by Fukijawa Industries, Rhodey strove to keep all information about Iron Man technology out of Fukijawa's hands. This also destroyed his own armor, and he retired.

While working as a military consultant in Dubai, Rhodey was torn to pieces in combat. Stark had Bethany Cabe rebuild him as the ultimate cyborg. During the Civil War, Rhodey worked with the Fifty-State Initiative, and he played an important role in defeating the Skrulls during the Secret Invasion. During the Dark Reign, Rhodey faced off against Eaglestar International, a corrupt private military contractor using Ultimo technology. While rooting out this technology, Rhodey foiled Norman Osborn (Green Goblin) in his plan to take it for himself. In retribution, Osborn put Rhodey on trial for war crimes in the Hague, but Rhodey prevailed and soon found himself restored into a clone body.

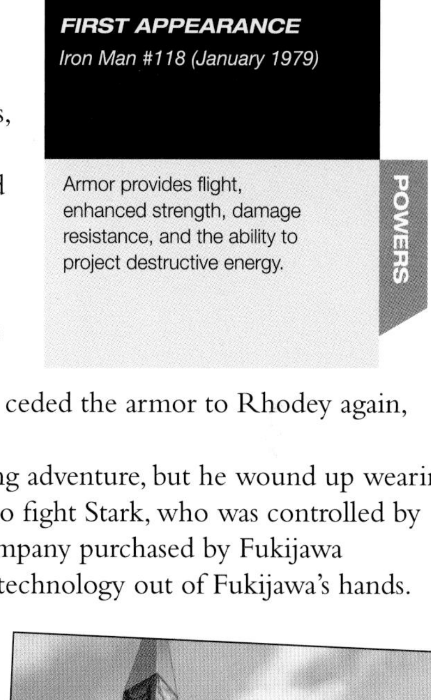

War Machine has always emphasized the benefits of superior firepower.

True Patriot

Outfitted in new armor, Rhodey rejoined the army as a lieutenant colonel. He later faked his death so he could take over for Stark as Iron Man until they managed to defeat the Mandarin.

Rhodey later helped SHIELD stop a squadron of Iron Patriot drones, and they gave him his own set of Iron Patriot armor in which to lead them. **DW, MF**

WARPATH

FACTFILE
REAL NAME
James Johnathan Proudstar
OCCUPATION
Adventurer
BASE
San Francisco

FIRST APPEARANCE
New Mutants #16 (June 1984

POWERS
Superhuman strength, speed, endurance, agility, and reflexes, and the ability to fly. Trained in unarmed combat techniques.

WARPATH

Native American brothers John and James Proudstar were born mutants. When John (the original THUNDERBIRD) died on a mission, James blamed PROFESSOR X, and calling himself Thunderbird, joined the HELLIONS. He reconciled with the professor and joined the NEW MUTANTS, later taking the name Warpath. He kept his powers after M-Day and joined the X-MEN officially for the first time. He later became part of X-FORCE. He killed his brother after SELENE reaniminated him with a techno-organic virus, and he later slew her, too. **AD, MF**

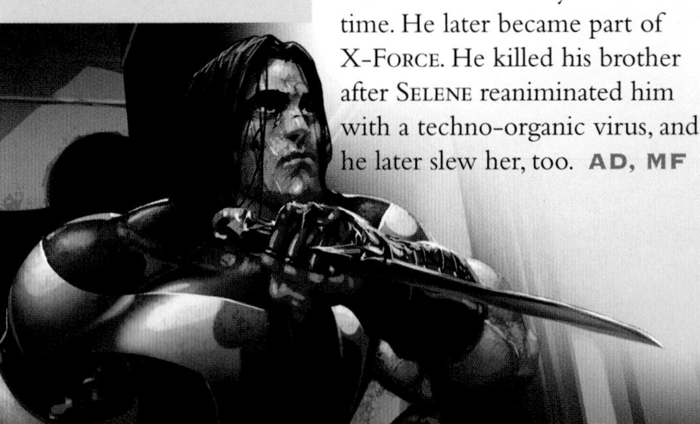

WARRIORS THREE

The Warriors Three were champions of Asgard, although their reckless exploits also brought them notoriety. Fandral was dashing, as quick with a blade as he was with his wit. Taciturn Hogun, nicknamed the Grim, came from a faraway land in Asgard's dimension and wielded a mace in battle. Volstagg was the heart of the band, though his boisterous nature often got the others into trouble.

The Three often fought at the side of THOR. They were killed during Ragnarok (see GODS OF ASGARD), but were restored to their former selves. Later, LOKI set up Volstagg to fight the U-FOES in an incident that slaughtered everyone at a football game in Chicago and gave Norman Osborn (GREEN GOBLIN) an excuse to invade Asgard. Volstagg helped make things right by knocking out Osborn as the madman tried to escape after the fall of Asgard. **DW, MF**

WARRIORS THREE
1 Hogan
2 Volstagg
3 Fandral

FACTFILE
MEMBERS AND POWERS
FANDRAL
Enhanced strength, master swordsman.
HOGUN
Enhanced strength, superb hand-to-hand combatant.
VOLSTAGG
Enhanced strength and endurance, ability to consume vast quantities of drink.
BASE Asgard

FIRST APPEARANCE
Journey into Mystery #119 (August 1965)

WARRIORS THREE

WATCHERS, THE

FACTFILE
NOTABLE MEMBERS
THE ONE
(the leader of the Watchers),
IKOR, EMNU, UATU, ECCE, ARON (the renegade watcher)
BASE
The Watchers' homeworld is unknown, but believed to be in a galaxy other than the Milky Way.

FIRST APPEARANCE
Tales of Suspense #53 (May 1964)

POWERS
All Watchers possess vast mental and physical powers, and the ability to manipulate energy. They are telepathic, can alter their appearance using their mental powers, and teleport through space at hyper-light speeds.

WATCHERS, THE

The Watchers are an ancient race of extraterrestrials who, eons ago, took upon themselves the task of observing the planets, peoples, and phenomena of the universe, without taking an active part in the affairs of the peoples under observation.

The Watchers adopted their policy of passive observation after a disastrous experiment. A group of Watchers, including UATU THE WATCHER who eventually came to observe Earth, once gave the knowledge of atomic power to the inhabitants of the planet Prosilicus, believing this would advance the race technologically.

However the Prosilicans used the knowledge to create nuclear weapons and waged war on their own planet, and against others. After this, the Watchers vowed to only passively observe, never to interfere. Uatu, however, met Reed Richards (MR. FANTASTIC) and came to look kindly on the FANTASTIC FOUR. He has helped the team numerous times, especially during their conflicts with the world-eater GALACTUS. **MT**

The Watchers have all sworn a sacred oath not to interfere in a planet's affairs.

WATSON, ANNA MAY

FIRST APPEARANCE Amazing Spider-Man #15 (August 1964)
REAL NAME Anna May Watson
OCCUPATION Retired **BASE** Florida
HEIGHT 5 ft 8 in **WEIGHT** 180 lbs
EYES Blue **HAIR** White
SPECIAL POWERS/ABILITIES A kind and loving heart.

The aunt of Mary Jane WATSON, in her youth Anna Watson shared many of the same hopes and dreams as her young niece. As a young woman harboring hopes of an acting career, she moved to California and married. Sadly, her acting dream came to nought and her marriage collapsed following an affair. Returning to New York, Anna looked after Mary Jane following her parents' separation and the two became close. The nextdoor neighbor and best friend of May PARKER, Anna helped pair off Peter Parker (*see* SPIDER-MAN) and Mary Jane, but has now moved to Florida to enjoy her twilight years. **AD**

WASP

Buzziest hero of the Avengers team

Janet Van Dyne was with her scientist father Vernon when he visited Dr. Henry PYM to ask him to collaborate on a project to use an energy beam to detect signals from extraterrestrial civilizations. Pym declined, but was attracted to Janet, who reminded him of his late wife Maria. Van Dyne proceeded with his experiment. However, a criminal from the Kosmosian race tracked Van Dyne's beam to Earth and murdered him.

Pym implanted cells in Janet that would enable her to grow antennae to communicate with insects. The antennae cells died early in her career.

The Wasp's bioelectric "stings" can inflict pain on even superhumanly strong foes.

PYM PARTICLES

Janet told Pym she was determined to bring her father's killer to justice. Pym revealed his dual identity as ANT-MAN and offered to endow her with superhuman abilities and make her his crimefighting partner. Janet agreed and became the Wasp. Pym taught her to use gas containing subatomic "Pym particles" to shrink herself and regain normal size. He also implanted cells beneath her shoulder blades that enabled her to grow wings at insect size. Ant-Man and the Wasp duly defeated the "creature from Kosmos." Pym and Janet also fell in love. It was Pym who suggested that he, the Wasp, the HULK, IRON MAN, and THOR band together, and Janet who suggested the name "THE AVENGERS."

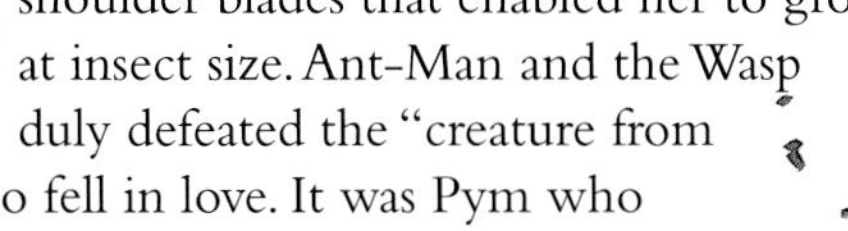

AREN'T YOU EVER GONNA GROW UP, WASP? HAVEN'T YOU ANYTHING ELSE ON YOUR MIND??

WELL, HAPPY DAY! DO I FINALLY SEE A GLINT OF GREEN IN THOSE BIG BLUE EYES OF YOURS??

NOW, PUT ME DOWN, YOU BIG SHOWOFF! THIS IS VERY UNDIGNIFIED!!

The fun-loving Wasp enjoyed teasing her partner Henry Pym, here in Giant-Man mode.

A STORMY MARRIAGE

Pym adopted other costumed identities, Giant-Man and GOLIATH, and then an alternate, aggressive personality named YELLOWJACKET. Realizing that he was still Pym, Janet married him anyway, and he soon regained his true personality. Pym later had a nervous breakdown, and he and Janet they divorced; however time healed the rift and they became friends, and eventually lovers again.

After the CIVIL WAR, the Wasp joined Iron Man's team of pro-registration Avengers. She fought the SKRULLS during the SECRET INVASION and was stunned to learn that a Skrull had been posing as Pym for months. After Queen VERANKE was killed, the Skrull Pym turned the Wasp into a fast-growing bio-bomb, and THOR had to kill her to keep her from detonating. THE AVENGERS later discovered she was alive in the Microverse and rescued her. She joined and helped fund the Avengers Unity Squad (Uncanny Avengers).

PS, MF

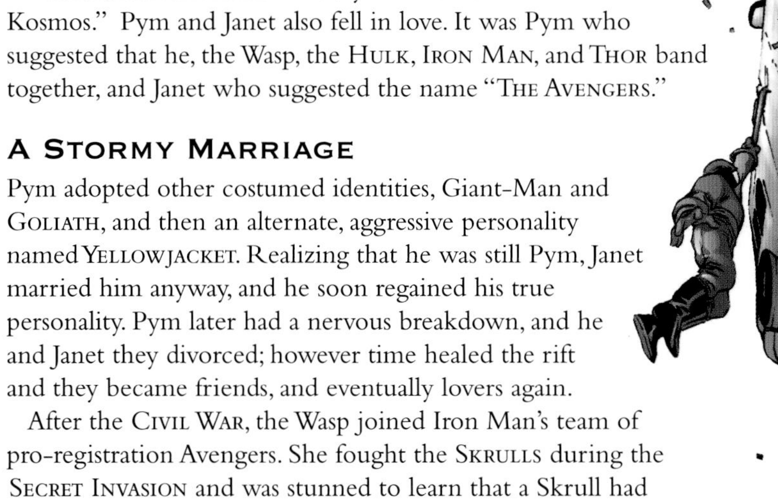

Janet Van Dyne briefly used her size-changing powers to grow to gigantic size, but soon went back to fighting evil as the Wasp.

FACTFILE — WASP

REAL NAME
Janet Van Dyne

OCCUPATION
Adventurer, fashion designer

BASE
Avengers Mansion, New York City; Cresskill, New Jersey; later Oxford, England

HEIGHT 5 ft 4 in
WEIGHT 110 lbs
EYES Blue
HAIR Auburn

FIRST APPEARANCE
Tales to Astonish #44 (June 1963)

POWERS
Ability to shrink in size down to a half inch in height. When the Wasp is 4 ft 2 in or less in height, wings appear from her body, enabling her to fly. Can discharge bioelectric force bolts from her hands.

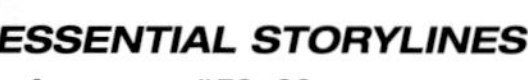

ESSENTIAL STORYLINES
- ***Avengers #59–60*** Janet Van Dyne marries Henry Pym in his new Yellowjacket identity.
- ***Avengers #214–219*** Janet Van Dyne divorces Henry Pym and becomes Avengers chairman.
- ***Avengers #270–277*** In her final mission as chairman, Wasp leads Avengers in thwarting Masters of Evil's takeover of Avengers Mansion.

WATSON, MARY JANE

The Webslinger's wife and one true love

WATSON, MARY JANE

FACTFILE

REAL NAME
Mary Jane Watson

OCCUPATION
Fashion model, "B" movie actress, former star of daytime TV drama.

BASE
New York City

HEIGHT 5 ft 8 in
WEIGHT 120 lbs
EYES Green
HAIR Red

FIRST APPEARANCE
Amazing Spider-Man #25, (June 1965)

POWERS
Mary Jane has no special powers, but she is a talented dancer, model, and actress; retains her fun-loving and optimistic outlook despite the numerous dangers and trials of being friends with Spider-Man.

Mary Jane was the daughter of Philip and Madeline Watson. Her mother was a drama student who dreamed of being an actress, while her father was an aspiring novelist. They met and fell in love at college, and married as soon as they graduated, with Philip taking a teaching job to support his family while he worked on his first novel. The couple had two daughters, Gayle and Mary Jane, and Madeline put her acting career on hold to stay at home and care for the girls.

After always missing each other, Peter finally met Mary Jane.

UNSETTLED YOUTH

Frustrated with his inability to complete his novel, Philip began switching jobs, hoping each new location would spark his creativity. As a result, Mary Jane was constantly changing schools and having to make new friends. To cope with this, she developed an extrovert personality and became a bit of a class clown. The marriage of Mary Jane's parents was never happy, and they eventually broke up. But Madeline and the girls had a good relationship with Philip's elderly sister, Anna Watson, who lived next door to the Parker family, and kept in touch with her after the split.

FIRST MEETING

Gazing out of her Aunt Anna's window, Mary Jane first saw Peter Parker when she was 13 years old. She later discovered that he was SPIDER-MAN when she spotted him sneaking out of his Aunt May's house (*see* PARKER, Aunt May). Aunt Anna kept trying to get them together, but the outgoing Mary Jane didn't want anything to do with the bookish, sensitive boy who hid behind a mask. When they eventually met, however, she discovered that she was attracted to Peter. Feigning indifference, she flirted with his rival Flash THOMPSON and dated Harry Osborn (*see* GREEN GOBLIN), his best friend and roommate.

After repeatedly refusing to marry Peter, Mary Jane finally accepted his proposal. They were married at City Hall.

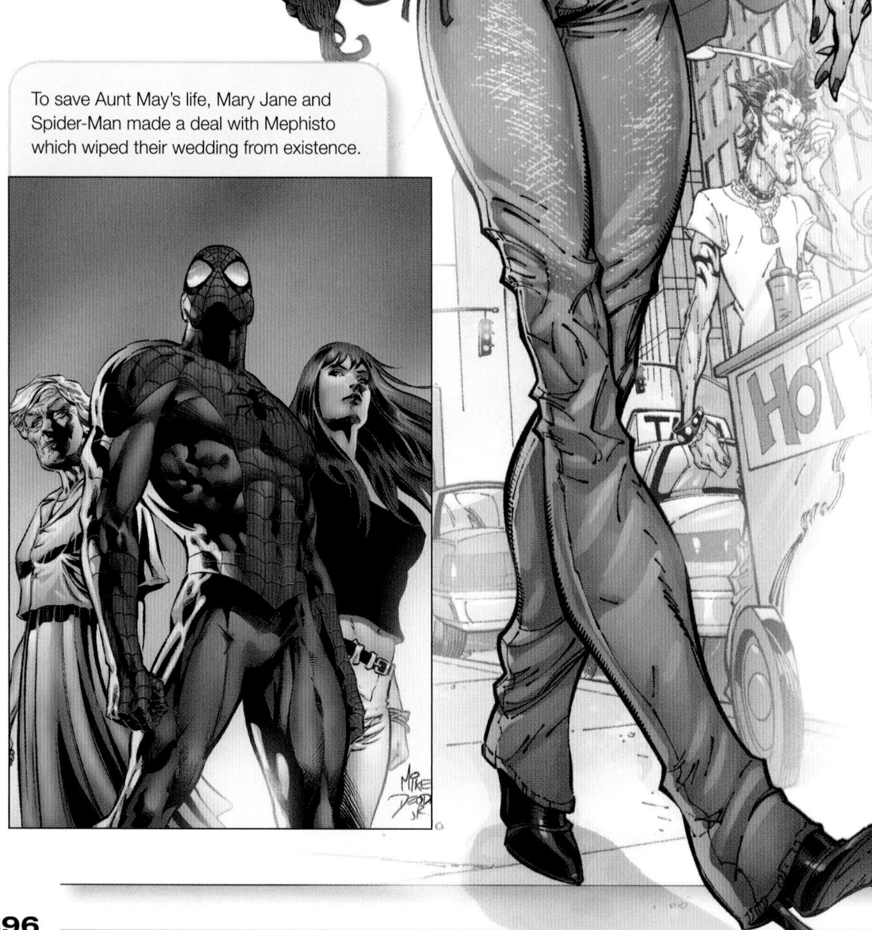

To save Aunt May's life, Mary Jane and Spider-Man made a deal with Mephisto which wiped their wedding from existence.

STARTING OVER

Mary Jane and Peter dated for years and eventually married. However, when Aunt May was shot by a sniper targeting Peter, Mary Jane and Peter were forced to make a deal with the demon Mephisto in order to save her life, and they agreed to erase their happy marriage from reality. This caused them to retroactively break up after Peter missed their wedding while fighting crime. Peter later had Doctor Strange remove everyone's memory of his identity—unless he informed them of it again, which he did with Mary Jane.

On her own, Mary Jane left New York and established herself as a successful model and actress. She later returned to Manhattan and started a hot new nightclub called MJ's. She seemed ready to start dating Peter once again, right up until Doctor Octopus took over Peter's body, becoming the Superior Spider-Man, and broke off their relationship. **TD, MF**

ESSENTIAL STORYLINES
- ***Amazing Spider-Man #42*** After months of missing each other, Peter Parker finally meets Mary Jane Watson for the first time.
- ***Amazing Spider-Man: Parallel Lives, tpb*** The early lives of Mary Jane and Peter are shown to have a lot in common.
- ***Amazing Spider-Man Annual #21*** Mary Jane finally marries Peter Parker!

Weapon Omega

FIRST APPEARANCE New Avengers #16 (April 2006)
REAL NAME Michael Pointer **OCCUPATION** Adventurer
BASE Canada **HEIGHT** 5 ft 11 in
WEIGHT 190 lbs **EYES** Blue **HAIR** Blond
SPECIAL POWERS/ABILITIES Mutant power to drain and redirect the energy of other mutants. Suit allows him to convert that energy into energy blasts, flight, and superhuman durability.

When the Scarlet Witch removed the powers of most mutants on M-Day, innocent postal worker Michael Pointer absorbed the energy, becoming the Collective. Xorn's absorbed personality drove him to slaughter Alpha Flight and attack Magneto. Captured, Michael was given a suit to help him control his power and a spot on Omega Flight as the new Guardian for a shot at redemption. He later changed his codename to Weapon Omega (and then Omega) as well as his costume. Overwhelmed by his powers, he was put into a coma at the Jean Grey School for Higher Learning. **MF**

Wendigo

An ancient curse dooms anyone who consumes human flesh in the Canadian wilderness to become a Wendigo, a savage and near-mindless being covered with shaggy white fur. The hunter Paul Cartier became one of the earliest Wendigos, after resorting to cannibalism to survive in a snowed-in cave. Cartier tried to transfer the curse to the Hulk, but his hunting companion Georges Baptiste voluntarily became the new Wendigo.

Many more Wendigos have since appeared, including fur trapper François Lartigue and cryptozoologist Michael Fleet. The Canadian government, apparently hoping to exploit the creature's superhuman attributes, employed a Wendigo operative codenamed Yeti as part of its Weapon PRIME program. During its time with Weapon PRIME, Yeti attacked Cable's X-Force as well as the hero Northstar. Several others have appeared since, including a pack in the Bering Straights and ones working for Biggs Chemical, Omega Flight, and the Hellfire Academy. **DW, MF**

Wendigo uses his mystically powered strength to go toe-to-toe with superpowered opponents.

FACTFILE
REAL NAME
Various
OCCUPATION
Forest creature
BASE
Mobile in Canadian wilderness

HEIGHT 9 ft 7 in
WEIGHT 1,800 lbs
EYES Red
HAIR White

FIRST APPEARANCE
Incredible Hulk #162 (April 1973)

POWERS
Mystically enhanced strength, stamina, and reflexes; nearly indestructible, slashing claws on hands and feet.

WENDIGO

Weapon X

In 1945, a liberated concentration camp unearthed the genetics research of Mister Sinister, giving birth to the US government's Weapon Plus program. The government's previous Super-Soldier project (which produced Captain America) retrospectively became Weapon I. Weapons II and III used animal subjects, Weapons IV, V, and VI experimented on ethnic minorities, and Weapons VII, VIII, and IX relied on mutants. In the 1960s, Weapon X (conducted in conjunction with the Canadian government's Department K) produced memory-wiped operatives including Wolverine and Sabretooth, and used Shiva robots to eliminate rogue agents. Wolverine escaped and became a member of the X-Men.

Weapon X eventually disbanded, but Weapon Plus continued under the leadership of John Sublime, who took the program up to Weapon XV. Sublime reopened Weapon X, recruiting mutants as field operatives and executing surplus mutants in the Neverland concentration camp. Wolverine teamed with Agent Zero and Fantomex to investigate the program, but found that it had gone underground. A new Weapon X program later produced X-23, and Cyclops set up his mutant revolution's headquarters in one of the old Weapon X facilities. **DW, MF**

WEAPON X
1 Sauron
2 Brent Jackson, Director
3 Wild Child
4 Aurora

FACTFILE
NOTABLE MEMBERS
WOLVERINE Mutant healing factor, enhanced senses, adamantium-bonded skeleton, retractable claws.
SABRETOOTH Similar powers to Wolverine.
MAVERICK/AGENT ZERO Absorbs and discharges energy; age suppressant.
SILVER FOX Artificial healing factor and age suppressant.
DEADPOOL Artificial healing factor, enhanced reflexes, teleportation device.
MARROW Bone growth; agility; recuperative powers.
MESMERO Hypnosis.
SAURON Drains life force from others; transforms into pterosaur.
CHAMBER Blasts of psionic energy from chest furnace.
BASE Weapon X facility, Alberta, Canada

FIRST APPEARANCE
Marvel Comics Presents #72 (March 1991)

WEAPON X

Werewolf By Night

WEREWOLF

FACTFILE

REAL NAME
Jacob Russoff, later changed to Jack Russell

OCCUPATION
Adventurer

BASE
Los Angeles, California

HEIGHT 5 ft 10 in
WEIGHT 200 lbs
EYES Blue; (as Werewolf) Red
HAIR Red; (as Werewolf) Brown

FIRST APPEARANCE
Marvel Spotlight #2 (February 1972)

POWERS
Superhuman strength, agility, reflexes, stamina, and senses.

Jack Russell's ancestor, Grigori Russoff, had the misfortune to be bitten by a female werewolf in 1795 in his home country of Transylvania. The curse eventually afflicted Jack. When he turned 18, Jack was transformed into a mindless, savage werewolf during the three nights of the full moon.

The mystical beings known as "The Three Who Are All" gave Jack the power to change into a werewolf at will, while retaining his human mind. He used this ability as a crimefighter. However, on the nights of the full moon, he still changes into a werewolf involuntarily and his mind becomes that of the beast. On those nights, he protects others by locking himself away in an escape-proof room.

Jack worked with many heroes over the years, including joining the Midnight Sons in defeating a zombie invasion from Earth-2149. He was part of the Legion of Monsters that turned the Punisher into Frankencastle, and he became the guardian of Wolfsbane's child after she rejected the cub. **MT, MF**

Werewolf's senses of sight, hearing, and smell are as sharp as a wolf's. He can leap 18 ft into the air, run at speeds up to 35 mph, and is immune to normal injury.

Whirlwind

FIRST APPEARANCE Tales to Astonish #50 (December 1963)
REAL NAME David Cannon
OCCUPATION Criminal **BASE** New York State
HEIGHT 6 ft 1 in **WEIGHT** 220 lbs **EYES** Blue **HAIR** Brown
SPECIAL POWERS/ABILITIES Able to revolve at amazingly high speed, rendering himself untouchable; throws wrist blades while spinning, to deadly effect; never becomes dizzy.

David Cannon began his criminal career as the Human Top before becoming Whirlwind and joining the MASTERS OF EVIL. For a while he worked as the WASP's chauffeur. After returning to his costumed identity, he joined the Thunderbolts. The Mandarin later upgraded his powers and planted a bomb inside him, but David joined Iron Man's rebellion against him. He has since returned to crime. **AD, MF**

Whiplash

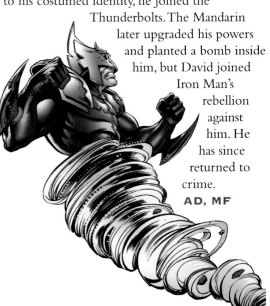

WHIPLASH

FACTFILE

REAL NAME
Mark Scarlotti

OCCUPATION
Assassin-for-hire

BASE
Mobile

HEIGHT 6 ft 1 in
WEIGHT 196 lbs
EYES Blue
HAIR Blond

FIRST APPEARANCE
Tales of Suspense #97 (January 1968)

POWERS
Expert with whip and nunchakus. Possesses two cybernetically-controlled whips, anti-gravity bolas, and a necro-lash releasing electrical energy generated by gauntlets.

As a MAGGIA engineer, Mark Scarlotti developed his own super-weapons and, calling himself Whiplash, battled IRON MAN to a draw. As Mark Scott, he worked undercover for Stark International. Later, Justin HAMMER hired Scarlotti, and he upgraded his arsenal and changed his name to Blacklash. For a time, he gave up crime, but he later returned as Whiplash and was killed by Iron Man's armor.

Leeann Foreman, a mutant with adamantium wires snapping from her gloves, became the second Whiplash. She worked with the Band of Baddies, the Femme Fatales, and the Femizons. During the CIVIL WAR, an unrelated pair of villains called Whiplash and Blacklash joined the THUNDERBOLTS.

Later, Russian scientist Anton Vanko's village was attacked by a killer in a stolen suit of IRON MAN armor. Vanko captured the suit's chest plate and used it to reverse engineer his own suit of armor, complete with energy whips. He then hunted down Tony Stark to exact his revenge. Upon discovering Stark had been framed, Vanko turned his rage against Russian Prime Minister Vladimir Putin instead. He later joined the SHADOW COUNCIL's MASTERS OF EVIL. **TD, MF**

Whitemane, Aelfyre

FIRST APPEARANCE Power Pack #1 (August 1984)
REAL NAME Aelfyre Whitemane
OCCUPATION Scientist **BASE** His sentient starship, Friday
HEIGHT 6 ft **WEIGHT** 320 lbs **EYES** Pink **HAIR** White
SPECIAL POWERS/ABILITIES Like all Kymellians, Whitemane was born with the potential to project energy, teleport, and fly. These powers required much practice and training to master.

Aelfyre Whitemane, nicknamed "Whitey" was a scientist of the Kymellian race. He discovered that Dr. James POWER was working on a matter/antimatter converter. Whitey knew the dangers of this device, which had destroyed his homeworld. His message back home was intercepted by the Z'nrx (*see* SNARKS), who wanted to use Dr. Power's invention as a weapon. They shot down Whitey's starship. Near death, the Kymellian transferred his powers to Dr. Power's children, who became the POWER PACK. **MT**

Whiteout

FIRST APPEARANCE Uncanny X-Men #249 (October 1989))
REAL NAME Unknown
OCCUPATION Unknown **BASE** The Savage Land
HEIGHT 5 ft 11 in **WEIGHT** 144 lbs
EYES White **HAIR** Unknown
SPECIAL POWERS/ABILITIES Creates flash of brilliant light which has the potential to blind anyone she chooses.

A native of the Savage Land, situated somewhere in Antarctica, little is known about the creature known as Whiteout. She was briefly a member of ZALADANE's Savage Land mutants, and it is thought that her first and only mission with this group involved an attack on the X-MEN in Chile, where that mutant team was searching for their lost team-mate, POLARIS. Subsequently, Whiteout was a member of Superia's Femizons and their effort to put women in charge of the world. Her appearances since have been both sporadic and fleeting. **AD**

White Wolf

FIRST APPEARANCE Black Panther #4 (February 1999)
REAL NAME Hunter **OCCUPATION** Leader of the Hatut Zeraze
BASE Wakanda, later mobile
HEIGHT 6 ft 2 in **WEIGHT** 210 lbs **EYES** Blue **HAIR** Black
SPECIAL POWERS/ABILITIES A formidable hand-to-hand combatant and master spy. His costume is made of vibranium microweave fabric, protecting him from physical impact.

When his parents died in a plane crash in Wakanda in Africa, Hunter, a Caucasian, was adopted by Wakanda's king, T'Chaka. Later T'Chaka fathered an heir, T'Challa, and Hunter lost his status as the king's favored son, developing a jealous hatred of T'Challa. Hunter was made the leader of the Hatut Zeraze ("Dogs of War"), who served as the Wakandan secret police. But when T'Challa became king, he disbanded the Hatut Zeraze, objecting to their brutality. Hunter and his men left Wakanda and became mercenaries. T'Challa and Hunter became enemies as the BLACK PANTHER and the White Wolf. **PS**

Whitman, Debra

FIRST APPEARANCE Amazing Spider-Man #196 (September 1979) **REAL NAME** Debra Whitman
OCCUPATION Former secretary at Empire State University
BASE The Midwest
HEIGHT 5 ft 6 in **WEIGHT** 120 lbs **EYES** Green **HAIR** Blonde
SPECIAL POWERS/ABILITIES None; only the strength of a woman of her age and weight who indulges in moderate exercise.

Debra Whitman dated Peter Parker (SPIDER-MAN) while they were both at university. Suffering from mental illness, she became convinced Peter was Spider-Man. At her psychologist's urging, Peter wore a Spider-Man costume to shock her into seeing she was wrong, and she left town to get help. During the CIVIL WAR, Peter revealed to the world that he really was Spider-Man, and Debra wrote a tell-all memoir about their relationship. During the Brand New Day event, this revelation was erased and so, presumably, was Debra's book. **DW, MF**

White Tiger

After her uncle Hector Ayala, the White Tiger, was slain, FBI agent Angela Del Toro inherited the tiger amulets that granted him his powers. She fought against the Yakuza and brought down the international criminal organization called the Chaeyi. Later, Lady BULLSEYE killed her and then brought her back to life as an unwilling assassin for the HAND. She is unrelated to the White Tiger created by the HIGH EVOLUTIONARY, or to the NYC vigilante associated with the BLACK PANTHER.

Hector's sister Ava became the latest White Tiger and joined the AVENGERS Academy. **TB, MF**

FACTFILE

REAL NAME
Angela Del Toro

OCCUPATION
Former FBI agent, now assassin

BASE
New York City

HEIGHT 5 ft 8 in
WEIGHT 125 lbs
EYES Brown
HAIR Brown

FIRST APPEARANCE
Daredevil #58 (May 2008)

WHITE TIGER

POWERS

Amulets that grant enhanced strength and agility and training in the martial arts.

WHIZZER

FACTFILE

REAL NAME
Robert Frank

OCCUPATION
Adventurer

BASE
New York City

HEIGHT 5 ft 10 in
WEIGHT 180 lbs
EYES Brown
HAIR Brown, later gray

FIRST APPEARANCE
Giant-Size Avengers #1 (August 1974)

POWERS

The Whizzer possessed superhuman speed, which allowed him to run at several hundred miles per hour.

WHIZZER

Bitten by a poisonous snake as a child, Bob Frank's scientist father gave him a transfusion of mongoose blood in an attempt to save his life. This transfusion sparked Bob's latent mutant abilities, and granted him superspeed. Reaching manhood, Bob became the Whizzer, and set out to battle crime and the Axis powers. During World War II, the Whizzer was a member of the Liberty Legion, where he met MISS AMERICA, his future wife, and then the INVADERS. After the war, both the Whizzer and Miss America served in the ALL-WINNERS SQUAD; they then retired from the heroic life to raise children.

Tragically, Miss America died in childbirth, and the Whizzer's son was a horrifically mutated radioactive mutant known as Nuklo.

Years later, while trying to cure his son's condition, the Whizzer was attacked and suffered a fatal heart attack. The Whizzer should not be confused with the member of the Squadron Sinister, who now operates as SPEED DEMON, nor with the member of the other-Earth SQUADRON SUPREME. **TB**

WILD THING

FIRST APPEARANCE J2 #5 (February 1999)
REAL NAME Rina Logun **OCCUPATION** High-school student
BASE Saddle River, New Jersey
HEIGHT 5 ft 2 in **WEIGHT** 98 lbs **EYES** Brown **HAIR** Black
SPECIAL POWERS/ABILITIES Superhuman strength, speed, agility, and a healing factor giving immunity from poisons, gases, or drugs; psychic claws can cut through virtually any substance.

In a possible future, the former assassin ELEKTRA marries WOLVERINE of the X-MEN and has a daughter. Named Rina, she inherits many of her father's physical powers and also possesses the mutant ability to generate psychic claws. Over her parents' objections, Rina hones her powers and becomes Wild Thing. When J2, son of the original JUGGERNAUT, reveals himself to the public, she hunts him down and challenges him to a fight, which Wolverine breaks up. Rina later joins with SPIDER-GIRL and the AVENGERS to prevent the god LOKI from ending the age of heroes. **TD**

WICCAN

FIRST APPEARANCE Young Avengers #1 (April 2005)
REAL NAME William "Billy" Kaplan
OCCUPATION Adventurer
BASE New York City
HEIGHT 5 ft 4 in **WEIGHT** 135 lbs **EYES** Blue **HAIR** Black
SPECIAL POWERS/ABILITIES Able to cast spells, generate light, and fly.

Billy Kaplan thought he was the eldest son of Jeff and Rebecca Kaplan. In fact, he and SPEED of the YOUNG AVENGERS were products of the SCARLET WITCH's powers. Desperate for children, the Scarlet Witch had created twin boys for herself out of lost souls, but MEPHISTO eventually came to reclaim them. When the Scarlet Witch remade the world on M-Day, she remade the boys too, placing them in different homes. Billy originally patterned himself on the mighty THOR and called himself Asgardian, but he later switched to the codename Wiccan. He recently outed himself as gay and is in a relationship with HULKLING. **MF**

WILD CHILD

FIRST APPEARANCE Alpha Flight #1 (August 1983)
REAL NAME Kyle Gibney
OCCUPATION None **BASE** Mobile
HEIGHT 5 ft 8 in **WEIGHT** 152 lbs
EYES Green-blue **HAIR** Blond
SPECIAL POWERS/ABILITIES Superb hand-to-hand combatant; superhuman senses and claw-like fingernails; can see in the dark.

Thrown out by his parents when his feral mutation manifested, Kyle Gibney took to the streets until agents of the Secret Empire captured him. Their experiments made him wilder than ever. Freed, he joined Canada's Department H, which assigned him to Gamma Flight. He has since worked with OMEGA FLIGHT, ALPHA FLIGHT, and WEAPON X, slipping back and forth between his more bestial and human forms and outlawed and sanctioned teams. He lost his powers on M-Day but later regained them. OMEGA RED killed him by throwing him into molten steel. **AD, MF**

WILL O'THE WISP

FIRST APPEARANCE Amazing Spider-Man #235 (December 1982)
REAL NAME Jackson Arvad
OCCUPATION Scientist; Adventurer **BASE** Mobile
HEIGHT 6 ft 1 in **WEIGHT** 195 lbs
EYES White **HAIR** Blond
SPECIAL POWERS/ABILITIES Controls sub-atomic particles in his body to become intangible, fly, and increase strength; uses limited telepathic ability to compel others to do his will.

While working for the Brand Corporation, Jackson Arvad fell asleep during an experiment, and his body became trapped in an electromagnetic field. His boss, James Melvin, left him to die. Reconstituting himself as Will o'The Wisp, Arvad found he could manipulate every molecule in his body. SPIDER-MAN and TARANTULA stopped him from killing Melvin, but he eventually forced him to confess his crime. When Spider-Man unmasked during the CIVIL WAR, Arvad joined the CHAMELEON's plot to exact revenge on the webslinger. **AD, MF**

Wilson, Jim

FIRST APPEARANCE Incredible Hulk #131 (September 1970)
REAL NAME Jim Wilson
OCCUPATION Former thief **BASE** Mobile
HEIGHT 6 ft **WEIGHT** 200 lbs
EYES Brown **HAIR** Black
SPECIAL POWERS/ABILITIES No superhuman powers, but a loyal friend despite—or because of—his tough upbringing.

Growing up as tough street kid no one ever gave Jim Wilson a break. So it was perhaps no surprise that he was destined to become friends with that well known outsider the Hulk. Jim was homeless and starving when he snatched a woman's purse. However, he became overcome with guilt and left the purse where the woman could find it. Jim was hiding out in an abandoned tenement when he encountered the Hulk and offered him his last candy bar. Wilson agreed to help the Hulk find Banner and avoid the army, and the Hulk's sense of loyalty to Wilson grew. Sadly, a few years later, Jim Wilson would die from AIDS. **MT**

Wind Warrior

FIRST APPEARANCE Thor #395 (September 1988)
REAL NAME Pamela Shaw **OCCUPATION** Adventurer
BASE New York City **HEIGHT** (Shaw) 5 ft 2 in; (Wind Warrior) 5 ft 11 in **WEIGHT** (Shaw) 135 lbs; (Wind Warrior) 143 lbs
EYES Blue **HAIR** (Shaw) Auburn; (Wind Warrior) Unknown
SPECIAL POWERS/ABILITIES Enhanced strength; flies by controlling wind updrafts; transforms herself into a living whirlwind.

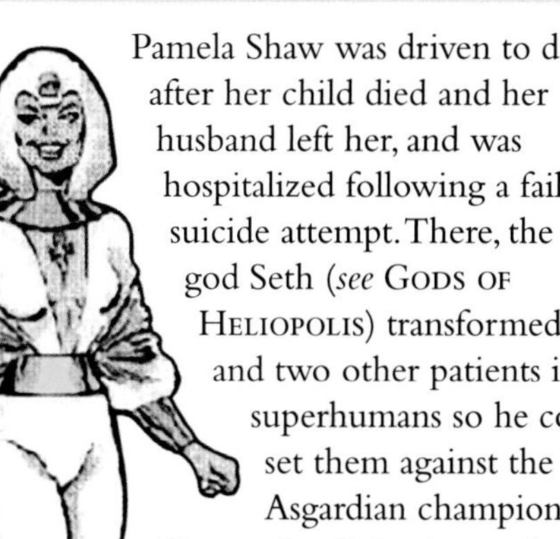

Pamela Shaw was driven to despair after her child died and her husband left her, and was hospitalized following a failed suicide attempt. There, the death god Seth (*see* Gods of Heliopolis) transformed her and two other patients into superhumans so he could set them against the Asgardian champion Hogun the Grim (a member of the Warriors Three). As Wind Warrior, Shaw joined Earth Lord and Skyhawk to form a team they called Earth Force. Later, learning of Seth's malevolent intentions, Earth Force turned on its creator and the members became independent agents. **DW**

Wingfoot, Wyatt

FIRST APPEARANCE Fantastic Four #50 (May 1966)
REAL NAME Wyatt Wingfoot **OCCUPATION** Adventurer
BASE Fantastic Four HQ, Keewazi Reservation, Oklahoma
HEIGHT 6 ft 5 in **WEIGHT** 269 lbs **EYES** Brown **HAIR** Black
SPECIAL POWERS/ABILITIES No superhuman powers, but extremely skilled in hand-to-hand combat; also a brilliant horseman, tracker, motorcyclist, and trainer of animals.

Wyatt Wingfoot is a member of the Keewazi tribe of Native Americans. Born on a reservation in Oklahoma, Wingfoot went to Metro College near New York City, where Johnny Storm, the Human Torch, was his roommate. The two became close friends, and soon Wingfoot was accompanying the Fantastic Four on their adventures proving to be a valuable ally. Wingfoot eventually went to live with the Fantastic Four and began a romance with Jennifer Walters, the She-Hulk. However, when oil was discovered on the Keewazi reservation, he returned home to help his people manage their newfound resource and ensure they were not exploited by multinational oil companies. **MT**

Windshear

FIRST APPEARANCE Alpha Flight #95 (April 1991)
REAL NAME Colin Ashworth Hume
OCCUPATION Adventurer **BASE** Mobile
HEIGHT 6 ft **WEIGHT** 183 lbs **EYES** Brown **HAIR** Brown
SPECIAL POWERS/ABILITIES Flight; can create solid molecules of air and project them as force waves; can transform liquid into gas.

A former operative of Roxxon Oil, Windshear used his air-shaping abilities to further Roxxon's corrupt schemes. Ashamed of his role with Roxxon, Windshear joined the Canadian superteam Alpha Flight to fight on the side of heroism. When the Canadian government temporarily disbanded Alpha Flight, Windshear used the opportunity to retire from adventuring, returning to his native England to open a curio shop selling hard-air constructs. **DW**

Wing, Colleen

FIRST APPEARANCE Marvel Premiere #19 (November 1974)
REAL NAME Colleen Wing
OCCUPATION Private detective **BASE** New York City
HEIGHT 5 ft 9 in **WEIGHT** 135 lbs **EYES** Blue **HAIR** Brown
SPECIAL POWERS/ABILITIES Excellent swordswoman and martial arts expert; also a very fine detective.

Half Japanese, Colleen was raised in Japan and trained as a samurai. Soon after moving to New York, she became friends with Misty Knight, and they formed Nightwing Restorations, a private detective agency. During the Civil War, she registered with the US government and formed a new Heroes for Hire with Misty. After World War Hulk, Colleen became disgusted with a deal Misty struck for help to save her, and she broke off their friendship. At Daredevil's request, she took over the Nail, an all-women division of the Hand, but she later betrayed them. **AD, MF**

Winter Guard

FIRST APPEARANCE Iron Man #9 (October 1998)
MEMBERS **Crimson Dynamo** Powered armor. **Darkstar** Manipulates Darkforce. **Ursa Major** Bear-man.
BASE Moscow

The Winter Guard was the Russian super team formed after the fall of the Soviet Union disbanded groups like the Soviet Super Soldiers. They have had many members over the years, but they have a core of three positions—Crimson Dynamo, Darkstar, and Ursa Major—that many individuals have filled, with new heroes coming in as others retire or are killed. Other members included Fantasia, Powersurge, Red Guardian, Sibercat, Steel Guardian, and Vostok. **MF**

Winter Soldier

The American hero destroyed and rebuilt

WINTER SOLDIER

FACTFILE

REAL NAME
James Buchanan Barnes

OCCUPATION
Assassin, spy

BASE
Russia

HEIGHT 5 ft 9 in
WEIGHT 260 lbs
EYES Brown
HAIR Brown

FIRST APPEARANCE
Captain America #1 (January 2005)

POWERS

The Winter Soldier is a trained assassin and spy. His bionic left arm grants him superhuman strength.

In World War II, young Bucky BARNES served as CAPTAIN AMERICA's sidekick. Toward the end of the war, the pair clashed with BARON ZEMO and hopped on a drone plane filled with explosives. Captain America watched the plane explode seconds after he fell from it. He awakened decades later—having been frozen in a block of ice—believing that he had watched his friend die.

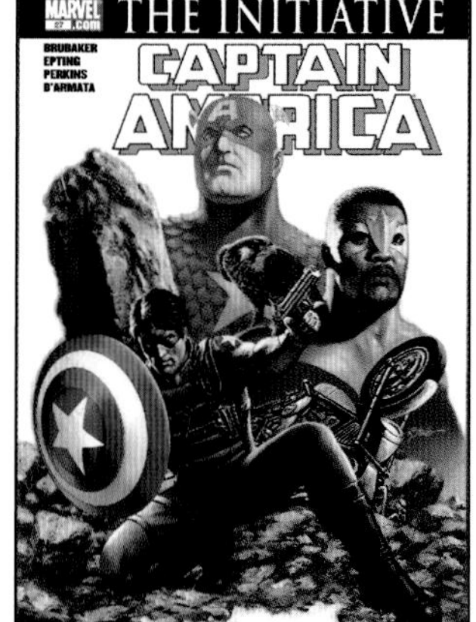

After Captain America's death, Barnes stole his shield from SHIELD.

A COLD-WAR SOLDIER

Bucky lost his left arm in the explosion, but the cold waters into which he fell preserved him until a Soviet submarine found and rescued him. Taken to Moscow, he awoke with amnesia and with a crude bionic arm in place of his missing limb.

General Vasily Karpov, who had fought alongside Captain America and Bucky in the war, took advantage of this opportunity to brainwash Bucky into becoming the Winter Soldier, a coldly efficient assassin and spy. Because of his strong will, however, Bucky's mind kept trying to break through his programming, so Karpov kept him in suspended animation between missions. Each time the Soviets revived him, they reinforced his brainwashing and upgraded his bionics.

Barnes's bionic arm can be detached when necessary.

Unlike Captain America's sidekick Bucky, the Winter Soldier regularly used guns.

COSMIC CUBE

This went on for decades until Karpov died and his protégé General Aleksander LUKIN took over the Winter Soldier program. Lukin used Bucky to kill the RED SKULL with a sniper's bullet and steal the Skull's newly made Cosmic Cube. Under Lukin's orders, Bucky also killed NOMAD and launched an attack on Philadelphia designed to charge the Cube. Captain America eventually got his hands on the Cube and used it to restore Bucky's memories. Afterward, Bucky disappeared and began hunting for Lukin.

With his training and cybernetics, Barnes could take on Super Heroes and win.

BACK IN THE USA

Together with Captain America, Bucky saved London from a giant Nazi robot Lukin unleashed. During the CIVIL WAR, Nick FURY—no longer with SHIELD—recruited Bucky to work as an undercover operative. After Captain America's death, Bucky accepted IRON MAN's offer to become the new Captain America. He accepted on two conditions: that SHIELD would clean his mind of all brainwashing and that he would answer only to himself.

Bucky served as the new Cap even after Steve Rogers returned, but when he was thought killed during FEAR ITSELF, he gave up that identity and went back to being the Winter Soldier, but this time as his own man. He set out to make amends for the things he had done while brainwashed, and found himself facing off against the RED GHOST and Lucia von Bardas, the former prime minister of Latveria. MF

ESSENTIAL STORYLINES
- ***Captain America #1*** The Winter Soldier kills the Red Skull.
- ***Captain America #8–9, 11–14*** Captain America confronts the Winter Soldier and brings him to his senses.
- ***Captain America #31-33*** The Winter Soldier comes in from the cold after the death of Captain America.

Wisdom, Peter

FIRST APPEARANCE Excalibur #86 (February 1995)
REAL NAME Peter Wisdom
OCCUPATION Adventurer **BASE** United Kingdom
HEIGHT 5 ft 9 in **WEIGHT** 140 lbs **EYES** Hazel **HAIR** Black
SPECIAL POWERS/ABILITIES Possesses the mutant power to create intense heat in the form of "hot knives," which he then projects from his hands.

Peter Wisdom worked as an agent for Black Air, a division of the British government that investigated paranormal phenomena. When he discovered his superiors were in league with the HELLFIRE CLUB, he turned against them and joined EXCALIBUR instead. For a while, he led the young mutant team X-FORCE, but he faked his death to leave them. He kept his powers after M-Day and went back to work for MI-13 and joined the new Excalibur. During the SECRET INVASION, he led the defense of Britain, striking a deal with demons for the nation's protection. He later led the defense of the UK against an invasion of vampires led by DRACULA. **PS, MF**

Wiz Kid

FIRST APPEARANCE X-Terminators #1 (October 1988)
REAL NAME Takashi "Taki" Matsuya
OCCUPATION Student **BASE** New York City
HEIGHT 4 ft 7 in **WEIGHT** 87 lbs **EYES** Brown **HAIR** Black
SPECIAL POWERS/ABILITIES Mutant ability to technoform machinery: able to mold objects into any configuration that his imagination can conceive.

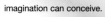

The accident that killed his parents left Takashi Matsuya (Taki to his friends) wheelchairbound. Taki focused his attentions on building sophisticated devices. When his ability to technoform objects manifested, his engineering abilities became even more prodigious. Captured by N'ASTIRH, Taki agreed to create a bridge between the Limbo dimension and Earth. However, when he realized the devastation being caused, Taki helped to foil N'astirh's plan. He lost his powers on M-Day but later regained them and joined the AVENGERS Academy. **AD, MF**

Wizard

Once an inventor and escapologist who performed as the Wizard, Bentley Whitman became jealous of the attention heroes gained and turned to villainy to reclaim the spotlight. He first tried to destroy the HUMAN TORCH but failed. After several defeats, he organized the FRIGHTFUL FOUR—a sinister counterpart to the FANTASTIC FOUR—varying its lineup many times, seeking a combination that would work. During the CIVIL WAR, he joined the HOOD's criminal crew, and he fought alongside those criminals against the SKRULLS during the SECRET INVASION. His young clone Bentley 23 was rescued from him and joined the Future Foundation. **TB, MF**

FACTFILE
REAL NAME
Bentley Whitman
OCCUPATION
Criminal
BASE
New York City

HEIGHT 5 ft 8 ins
WEIGHT 150 lbs
EYES Hazel
HAIR Brown

FIRST APPEARANCE
Strange Tales #102 (November 1962)

POWERS
Costume features an anti-gravity disk that enables him to fly, and "wonder gloves," which give him heightened strength and a protective force field.

Wolfsbane

Born in Scotland, the orphaned Rahne Sinclair was raised by a fanatical minister, Reverend Craig. At puberty, her mutant power to transform into a wolf emerged. Believing she was possessed by the devil, Reverend Craig led a mob in pursuit of Rahne, who fled in wolf form. Shot by one of the mob, Rahne transformed back to human form. Geneticist Dr. Moira MACTAGGERT rescued Rahne, and made Rahne her ward.

Rahne joined the NEW MUTANTS, organized by MacTaggert's colleague PROFESSOR X, remaining with the team after CABLE reorganized it into X-FORCE. Sinclair eventually joined the second version of X-FACTOR. After X-Force collapsed, Sinclair lived with MacTaggert at her Muir Island base. Rahne fell in love with Hrimhari, the wolf prince of Asgard, and became pregnant by him. AGAMEMNON captured her just before the birth, but when the baby, Tier, was born, it tore the man to pieces. Traumatized, Rahne fled from her son, but WEREWOLF BY NIGHT took him in to raise him. Tier grew to adolescence quickly but was killed by STRONG GUY as he battled demons in Hell. Afterward, Rahne decided to study to become a deacon in the Episcopal church. **PS, MF**

FACTFILE
REAL NAME
Rahne Sinclair
OCCUPATION
Adventurer
BASE
Mutant Town, New York City

HEIGHT (lupine form) Up to 12 ft standing on hind legs
WEIGHT (lupine form) Up to 1,050 lbs
EYES Blue-green
HAIR Reddish-brown

FIRST APPEARANCE
Marvel Graphic Novel #4: The New Mutants (1982)

POWERS
Mutant ability to transform herself into a wolf while retaining most of her human intellect, or into a transitional form which combines human and lupine aspects. Has more acute senses in lupine form.

WOLVERINE

The best there is at what he does—but what he does isn't pretty!

WOLVERINE

FACTFILE

REAL NAME
James Howlett; often goes by Logan

OCCUPATION
Adventurer

BASE
The Xavier Academy, Salem Center, Westchester, New York

HEIGHT 5 ft 3 in
WEIGHT 195 lbs
EYES Brown
HAIR Black

FIRST APPEARANCE
Incredible Hulk #180 (October 1974)

POWERS

Wolverine possesses a "healing factor" that allows him to recover from almost any injury in seconds. His skeleton has been laced with the unbreakable metal adamantium, which makes his bones unshatterable. Wolverine also possesses three foot-long adamantium claws that retract from either hand, capable of slicing through almost any substance known to man.

ALLIES/FOES

ALLIES X-Men, New Avengers, Nick Fury.

FOES Sabretooth, Omega Red, Silver Samura.

ISSUE #1

After a successful limited series in 1982, Wolverine was awarded his own ongoing title in November, 1988, a series devoted to his solo adventures apart from his fellow X-Men. The title has been published ever since.

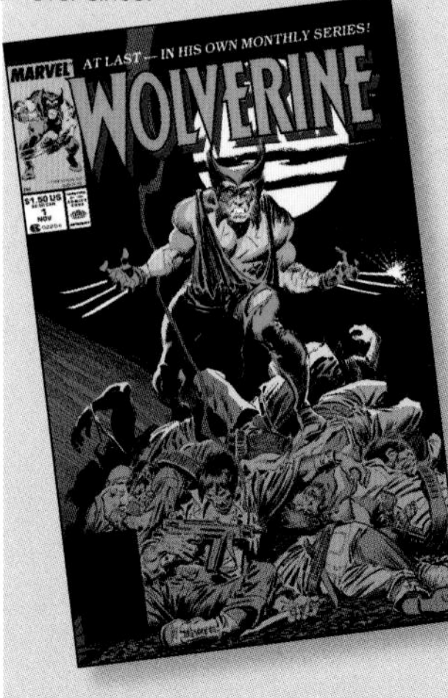

Childhood traumas were repressed by a mutant healing factor.

Born at the turn of the century, James Howlett, the man who would one day become known and feared as Wolverine, was a sickly child. But he was also born a mutant, gifted with the remarkable ability to heal virtually instantaneously from almost any wound. He also had razor-sharp claws made of bone, a fact he first became aware of when, during a domestic dispute, he accidentally unsheathed his claws for the first time, killing his assailant.

ESSENTIAL STORYLINES

- ***Origin #1–6***
The secret beginnings of Wolverine are revealed for the first time.
- ***Wolverine Limited Series #1–4***
Wolverine must wage a war of honor in Japan to protect the woman he loves, and to prove that he is more man than beast.
- ***Wolverine Vol. 2 #21–34***
Brainwashed by Hydra, Wolverine is sent to kill the greatest Super Heroes in the Marvel Universe.

THE WANDERER

Forced by his nature to leave behind the pampered world in which he grew up, Howlett began a life of wandering, moving from place to place. His own healing factor acted upon his mind to suppress the traumatic memories of his childhood, leaving him a man without a past. Over the years, he took a succession of menial jobs, building up his strength and stamina, and losing himself in the repetitiveness of simple work. He had also adopted the name Logan, after the groundskeeper at the Howlett estate, who might have been his real father. But both the man and the estate were long lost among the indistinct memories buried deep within his mind.

A haunted figure, Logan spent much of his youth wandering the world.

Logan lived the life of a drifter, moving from one adventure to another, learning all there was to know about fighting along the way. He fought in both world wars, spent time in Japan, and made his home-away-from-home in the tiny city of Madripoor, a haven for smugglers and pirates. His miraculous healing factor prolonged his natural lifespan, making him appear far younger than he truly was. For a time, he operated as a secret agent for the Canadian government, a vocation and association that would come to have dire ramifications.

A secret project of the Canadian government was attempting to create a super-soldier along the lines of the famous Captain America.

Wolverine's claws have been reinforced with adamantium.

With an unbreakable adamantium skeleton, retractable razor-sharp claws, and a healing factor that also prolongs his lifespan, Wolverine is an almost unbeatable opponent.

Selected as a subject for enhancement due to his incredible healing factor, the mysterious forces behind the Canadian Weapon X project laced Logan's skeleton and claws with the unbreakable metal, adamantium.

Kidnapped and used as a guinea pig, Logan, now referred to as Weapon X, was subjected to unimaginable tortures as his captors attempted to mold him to their liking. Realizing that Logan's healing factor would allow him to survive procedures which would kill any ordinary man, the scientists of the Weapon X project laced his skeleton with a nearly-unbreakable metal alloy known as adamantium. They also attempted to control his mind by brainwashing, which only served to scramble Logan's memories even further.

But eventually they could contain Logan no longer. Reduced to a bestial state, Logan broke free, annihilated the Weapon X project and all of its personnel, and fled into the Canadian wilderness. He lived there many years, hunting game to survive. A chance meeting with James MacDonald Hudson and his wife Heather put Logan on the road back to humanity. They took the beast-man into their home, and nursed him back to health. Hudson was a scientist working for the Canadian government, where he had developed a battlesuit that he hoped would make him a hero on a par with the newly-revealed American group, the Fantastic Four.

A New Name

Attempting to put together an equivalent team of Canadian Super Heroes, Hudson brought Logan into Alpha Flight, where he was given the codename Wolverine. Hudson had intended Wolverine to be the leader of this new strike force, but all that changed when a man in a wheelchair entered the scene: Professor Charles Xavier (Professor X), the mutant telepath who had founded the clandestine team of mutant heroes the X-Men.

Recognizing Wolverine's mutant nature, Professor X offered him a place among others of his kind. Wolverine accepted Xavier's offer and went to live in his School for Gifted Youngsters, which doubled as the X-Men's headquarters.

Wolverine leaped at the chance to join Professor Charles Xavier's mutant team of X-Men.

While his savage nature initially alienated his fellow mutants, Wolverine found friendship among them, and came to be one of the strongest believers in Professor X's dream of co-existence between mutants and normal humans—though this belief was tinged with a healthy cynicism.

In addition to his duties as an X-Man, Wolverine joined the new Avengers. He continued to work with the underground Avengers who formed the core of Captain America's resistance during the Civil War (*see* pp 85–5). He helped restore reality after the Scarlet Witch had a breakdown and altered everything, and when most things turned back to normal on M-Day, he not only retained his powers but regained all of his lost memories, too.

Since then, Wolverine discovered that Romulus, leader of the Lupines, had engineered the death of his wife Itsu and torn her unborn son from her womb. He erased many of Wolverine's memories and trained the child, named Daken, to be a ruthless killer.

TB, MF

As a result of the reality-altering powers of the Scarlet Witch, Wolverine gained possession of all of his lost memories. This knowledge remained with Logan even after the world returned to its normal state.

WOLVERINE *continued*

FAMILY TROUBLES

Knowing that Daken was trained to kill him, Wolverine had the WINTER SOLDIER hire Deadpool to assassinate him. The Winter Soldier put a carbonadium bullet in Daken's head instead, which kept his healing factor from kicking in.

Wolverine then took his son away to see if he could free him from the evil influence of Romulus, but Sebastian SHAW kidnapped Daken.

In the resulting conflict, Daken's memories were repaired, and he agreed to join his father in the fight against Romulus. Before they could manage this, however, a wedge was driven between them. Daken joined the Dark Avengers that Norman Osborn (GREEN GOBLIN) assembled, wearing his father's costume and taking his codename.

Wolverine and Daken clashed several other times; eventually Daken formed his own BROTHERHOOD OF EVIL MUTANTS to capture and kill Wolverine and destroy his reputation. Eventually, Wolverine turned the tables on him and drowned him.

Daken's cruelty and the way he embraced his nature as a killer hurt Wolverine more than his claws.

Even Wolverine's most powerful friends couldn't stand against the Hellverine.

No longer as much a loner as he once was, Wolverine made so many friends that he sometimes had to choose between them.

To Hell and Back

A mysterious group of Wolverine's enemies called the Red Right Hand helped a demon possess his body and sent his spirit to Hell. While he struggled to find a way back, his possessed form—Hellverine, which had all of his powers but none of his humanity—went on a killing spree. In an effort to regain control, Wolverine hunted the Devil himself with the help of Puck and a man he later realized was the first person he had ever killed: his father. With the help of Ghost Rider, Hellstorm, Mystique and his ex-girlfriend, reporter Melita Garner, Wolverine returned from Hell and expelled the demon.

Wolverine then hunted down the Red Right Hand, determined to kill every one of its members. He first had to fight his way through their muscle, a group of mercenaries known as the Mongrels. After he slaughtered them, he discovered that the members of the Red Right Hand preferred to commit suicide rather than die at his hand. To make matters worse, Wolverine discovered that the Mongrels group he had killed had all been his own illegitimate children.

Leading the Way

At Cyclops' request, Wolverine headed up a new X-Force, a black-ops team willing to do the kind of wetwork most of the X-Men would balk at. Warpath, Wolfsbane, and Wolverine's young female clone X-23 made up his original team, with Domino coming on board later. Eventually word about the team leaked out, and Cyclops lost the nerve to keep it together. Wolverine, however, reformed the team on his own, asking Archangel (*see* Angel), Deadpool, Fantomex, and Psylocke to join him.

The split between Wolverine and Cyclops deepened. Wolverine believed mutant children should grow up normally, while Cyclops wanted to train them for battle as X-Men. Wolverine led a group of mutants back to the grounds of the old Xavier estate and founded the Jean Grey School of Higher Learning. **AD, MF**

When the vampire lord Xarus attacked the X-Men, Wolverine allowed Cyclops to shut down his healing factor so he could infiltrate the vampiric forces.

VS. The X-Men

When the Phoenix Force returned, the Avengers decided they should take custody of Hope Summers in case it took her as its host. Wolverine sided with them against Cyclops and his part of the X-Men, but he couldn't stop the fight from escalating. Nor could he keep Cyclops from killing Professor X and becoming the Dark Phoenix.

After that conflict ended and the Phoenix Force was destroyed, Wolverine rejoined the Avengers. He became part of the main team once again, as well as a new Avengers Unity Team, led by Havok and featuring a number of powerful mutants.

WONDER MAN

FACTFILE
REAL NAME
Simon Williams
OCCUPATION
Adventurer
BASE
New York City

HEIGHT 6 ft 2 in
WEIGHT 380 lbs
EYES Red
HAIR Gray

FIRST APPEARANCE
Avengers #9 (October 1964)

POWERS
Body composed of ionic energy, which provides enhanced strength, stamina, flight, longevity, virtual invulnerability, and freedom from the need to eat or even breathe. Wonder Man is virtually immortal because his ionic body reforms whatever injuries he receives.

WONDER MAN

Born the wealthy inheritor of a family business, Simon Williams ran the company into near-bankruptcy and embezzled funds to invest with the criminal MAGGIA. Nursing a grudge toward the competing Stark Industries and its champion, IRON MAN, Williams underwent ionic energy treatments from BARON ZEMO and the original MASTERS OF EVIL. As Wonder Man, he infiltrated the AVENGERS, but refused to follow through on Zemo's scheme to destroy the team, and perished after aiding his AVENGERS teammates. The homicidal robot ULTRON later copied Wonder Man's brain patterns to help program the android VISION.

Wonder Man has adventured throughout known space and encountered thousands of alien cultures.

BACK TO LIFE

Believed dead, Wonder Man hibernated in an ionic coma until restored, in a zombie-like state, by his unstable brother Eric, the GRIM REAPER. The resurrected Wonder Man returned to the Avengers, befriending the BEAST and forging a close bond with the Vision, whom he viewed as a brother due to their shared brain patterns. Wonder Man became a part-time actor and stuntman, and also helped to establish the Avengers West Coast. At this time, he realized he loved the SCARLET WITCH, who had since married the Vision.

After the Vision's dismemberment and reassembly, Wonder Man refused to allow his brain patterns to be copied a second time, driving a wedge between him and the Scarlet Witch. Nevertheless, as time went by, the two began a romance, and Wonder Man pursued a successful acting career in Hollywood movies.

SECOND CHANCES

After the Avengers West Coast disbanded, Wonder Man joined FORCE WORKS and was killed. However, he lived on as disembodied ionic energy, occasionally materializing via the Scarlet Witch. Eventually, he reconstituted himself.

During the CIVIL WAR, Simon became an agent of SHIELD. He left when HAMMER took over from SHIELD, disillusioned with heroes of all stripes. He later gathered a group of REVENGERS to attack the Avengers and show how their methods were flawed. Afterward, he redeemed himself by helping rescue the WASP. He then joined the Avengers Unity Squad, declaring himself a pacifist. **DW**

WONDRA

FIRST APPEARANCE Uncanny X-Men #244 (May 1989)
REAL NAME Jubilation Lee
OCCUPATION Adventurer **BASE** New York City
HEIGHT 5 ft 5 in **WEIGHT** 105 lbs **EYES** Blue **HAIR** Black
SPECIAL POWERS/ABILITIES Technology that grants superhuman strength, limited invulnerability, and flight (as Wondra); generates and controls plasmoids (as Jubilee).

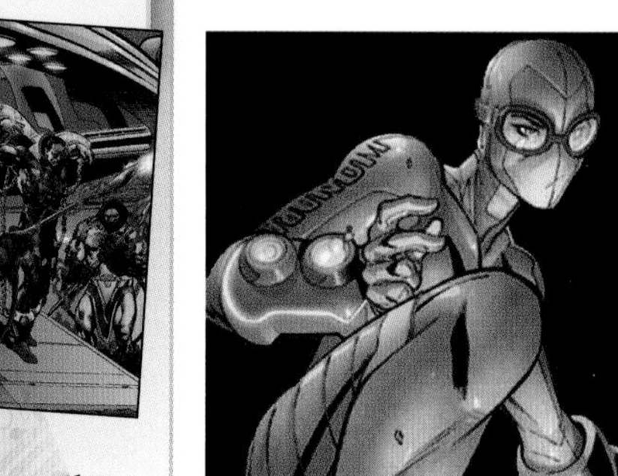

As the young mutant JUBILEE, Jubilation Lee joined the X-MEN for a while, and then became part of GENERATION X. After it dissolved, she joined BANSHEE'S X-CORPS instead. When that fell apart, she came back to the X-Men. On M-Day, Jubilation lost her powers. With the help of NIGHT THRASHER, she obtained technology that gave her superpowers and, under the new codename Wondra, she joined the latest incarnation of the NEW WARRIORS. The group disbanded, and she gave up being a hero. She was later turned into a vampire and adopted a child. **MF**

WONG

FIRST APPEARANCE Strange Tales #110 (July 1963)
REAL NAME Wong **OCCUPATION** Manservant
BASE Doctor Strange's Sanctum Sanctorum, New York City
HEIGHT 5 ft 8 in **WEIGHT** 140 lbs
EYES Brown **HAIR** Shaved
SPECIAL POWERS/ABILITIES Expert martial artist, although he has not actively practiced his skills in several years. A highly efficient manservant, utterly loyal to Doctor Strange.

The youngest surviving member of a bloodline whose members served the mystical ANCIENT ONE, Wong was offered into the service of the master mage at the time of his birth. He was tutored in the martial arts of Kamar-Taj. When he became an adult, the Ancient One dispatched him to the US, so that he could become the manservant of DOCTOR STRANGE. The two have since become peers instead, with a mutual respect for each other. Wong has also worked for the AVENGERS in the Avengers Mansion. **TB, MF**

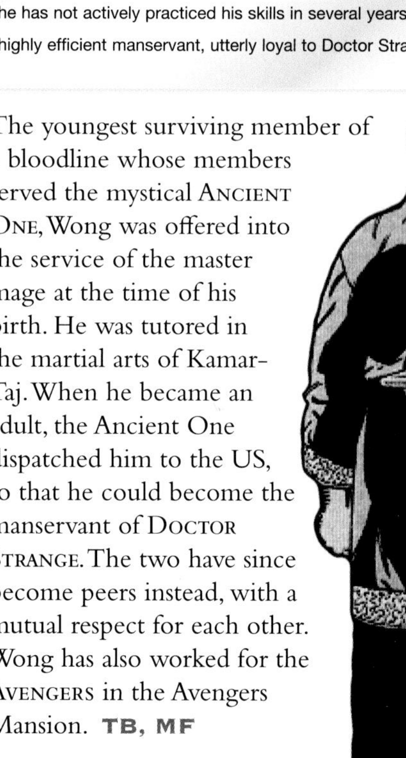

Woo, Jimmy

FIRST APPEARANCE Yellow Claw #1 (October 1956)
REAL NAME James "Jimmy" Woo **OCCUPATION** Adventurer
BASE San Francisco **HEIGHT** 5 ft 8 in **WEIGHT** 170 lbs
EYES Brown **HAIR** Black
SPECIAL POWERS/ABILITIES Investigative agent specializing in infiltration and information.

In the 1950s, Jimmy worked for the FBI against the forces of the YELLOW CLAW. In 1958, he led an early super group called the G-Men, but it disbanded and he joined SHIELD. He was nearly killed in action against the Atlas Foundation, but MARVEL BOY healed him, restoring his youth but at the cost of his memories. Reuniting the G-Men, Jimmy discovered that the Yellow Claw had been grooming him to be an heir for his empire, based on his lineage from Genghis Khan. Jimmy accepted the offer, hoping to turn the AGENTS OF ATLAS into a force for good. **MF**

Woodman, Senator

FIRST APPEARANCE Avengers: The Initiative #7 (December 2007)
REAL NAME Arthur Woodman
OCCUPATION Congressman, HYDRA leader
BASE Washington, D.C.
HEIGHT 6 ft **WEIGHT** 220 lbs **EYES** Brown **HAIR** Brown
SPECIAL POWERS/ABILITIES Powerful and cunning politician and leader.

Arthur Woodman led a double life for a long while, playing both the prominent politician and rising through the ranks of HYDRA at the same time. When VIPER, the Hydra leader, was discovered to be a SKRULL, Woodman stepped into the vacuum she left behind and declared himself Hydra's supreme leader. Woodman blackmailed HARDBALL into becoming a Hydra agent. When the Initiative caught Woodman and Hardball trying to steal KOMODO's lizard serum for Hydra, Woodman injected himself with the serum and became a giant lizard-man. Hardball killed him and then took over his position as the leader of Hydra. **MF**

Wraith

FIRST APPEARANCE Marvel Team-Up #48 (August 1976)
REAL NAME Brian DeWolff **OCCUPATION** Vigilante crimefighter
BASE New York City **HEIGHT** 5 ft 11 in **WEIGHT** 190 lbs
EYES Blue **HAIR** Reddish-blond
SPECIAL POWERS/ABILITIES Able to affect the minds of others, controlling them, casting illusions, or rendering himself invisible; also able to evade Spider-Man's "spider-sense."

Four people have used the name Wraith. Brian DeWolff was crippled in the line of duty before his controlling father gave him psionic powers. The second, Hector Rendoza, was a mutant who could turn his flesh translucent. He lost his powers on M-Day. The third, the KREE warrior Zak-Del, became infected with Exolon, a soul-eating parasite. He helped defeat the PHALANX. The fourth, Captain Yuri Watanabe of the NYPD, pretended to be the ghost of Brian's sister, Captain Jean DeWolff, using equipment stolen from an evidence room. **AD, MF**

Woodgod

FIRST APPEARANCE Marvel Premiere #31 (August 1976)
REAL NAME Woodgod
OCCUPATION Lawgiver of the Changelings
BASE The Rocky Mountains, Colorado
HEIGHT 6 ft 3 in **WEIGHT** 265 lbs
EYES Red **HAIR** Reddish-brown
SPECIAL POWERS/ABILITIES Woodgod possesses superhuman strength and an immunity to nerve gas.

Woodgod is a genetically engineered being, created by scientists David and Ellen Pace. Combining human and animal genetic material, the Paces created Woodgod, who resembles the half-human, half-goat Satyr of Greek myth. The townsfolk of Liberty, near the Pace's farm in New Mexico, convinced themselves that Woodgod was a dangerous monster. They tried to kill the creature using a canister of a deadly nerve gas invented by David Pace. Woodgod proved to be immune to the gas, but the Paces were both killed. The grief-stricken Woodgod discovered the Paces' notes and created a race of half-human, half-animal beings, which he called Changelings. The Changelings found a secret home away from humanity in the Colorado Rockies. Woodgod dreams that one day the Changelings will be able to come out of hiding and live in harmony with the human race. **MT**

WW HULK *see pages 410-411*

Wrecker

FIRST APPEARANCE Thor #148 (January 1968)
REAL NAME Dirk Garthwaite
OCCUPATION Criminal **BASE** Mobile
HEIGHT 6 ft 3 in **WEIGHT** 320 lbs **EYES** Blue **HAIR** Brown
SPECIAL POWERS/ABILITIES Superhuman strength and invulnerability; mental link to his enchanted crowbar allows him to transfer his powers into the crowbar, and then back to himself.

Wrecker was a violent criminal who used a crowbar to demolish the scenes of his crimes, thereby hindering investigation. When he was accidentally given magic powers by KARNILLA, the Norn Queen, Wrecker went on a rampage that attracted the attention of THOR. Placed in prison by the Asgardian automaton named Destroyer, Wrecker escaped with three other inmates who took on the costumed identities of THUNDERBALL, Bulldozer, and Piledriver, collectively known as the Wrecking Crew. He worked with the HOOD and helped him battle the SKRULLS during the SECRET INVASION. **MT, MF**

WORLD WAR HULK

A Story of Revenge

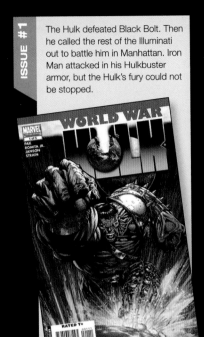

ISSUE #1 The Hulk defeated Black Bolt. Then he called the rest of the Illuminati out to battle him in Manhattan. Iron Man attacked in his Hulkbuster armor, but the Hulk's fury could not be stopped.

The ILLUMINATI decided that the HULK had become too dangerous to be permitted to remain on Earth. Discovering that a Life Model Decoy robot of Nick FURY had sent the Hulk into space on a mission, they turned his rescue vehicle away from Earth and sent it toward an uninhabited planet. On its way, the ship entered a wormhole and wound up on the planet Sakaar. There, the Hulk became a gladiatorial slave of the Red King—until he and his WARBOUND friends led a rebellion that installed him as the planet's king instead.

Black Bolt was the only Super Hero who had ever defeated the Hulk. Because of this, the Hulk made sure to take him out first when he returned to Earth.

MADDER THAN EVER

As king, the Hulk married the Red King's lieutenant CAIERA, making her his queen. His happiness was shattered, however, when the ship in which he'd traveled to Sakaar exploded, killing millions of people, including the pregnant Caiera. Believing the Illuminati was responsible, the Hulk gathered his Warbound allies and returned to Earth.

On his way to Earth, the Hulk stopped at the Moon to pick up BLACK BOLT. He and his Warbound then appeared in their starship over Manhattan and gave the people 24 hours to evacuate. IRON MAN, wearing his latest Hulkbuster armor, attacked, but the Hulk defeated him and brought his Warbound to help beat the AVENGERS. He then took on the FANTASTIC FOUR and captured MR. FANTASTIC.

While General Ross led the US Army against the Hulk, DR. STRANGE tried to help his old friend. The Hulk broke his hands, making it difficult for him to cast spells. Then he set up Madison Square Garden as a gladiatorial arena.

Desperate, Dr. Strange unleashed and merged with the demon Zom, becoming as angry and powerful as the Hulk. When he nearly killed a group of bystanders, however, doubts overcame him, and the Hulk brought him down.

Back in Madison Square Garden, the Hulk permitted those with grievances against BLACK BOLT, DR. STRANGE, IRON MAN, and MR. FANTASTIC to demand justice. He then unleashed a monster from Sakaar on the heroes. When they survived that, he used slave disks implanted in each of them to set the four against each other.

At the last moment, the Hulk spared the Illuminati, stating that he had come for justice, not murder. Having exposed them for what they were, he and the Warbound would raze Manhattan and then leave. Before he could do so, the SENTRY finally showed up and attacked. He and the Hulk battled each other until they both reverted to their human forms.

Unwilling to let the conflict end, Miek—the first of the Warbound that the Hulk had ever met—stabbed the Hulk's oldest friend, Rick JONES to enrage Bruce Banner and make him turn back into the Hulk. Miek also revealed that he had seen a band of Red King loyalists set the explosion on Sakaar but had said nothing so that the Hulk would go to war.

Too angry to control himself, the Hulk begged Iron Man to stop him. Iron Man fired a coordinated blast from several orbital satellites, causing the Hulk to become Bruce Banner once more. Unconscious, he was captured and imprisoned three miles beneath the earth. MF

Doctor Strange was desperate enough—after the Hulk broke his hands—to merge himself with the spirit of the vicious demon Zom. But even this action wasn't sufficient to stop the Hulk.

The Gamma Corps charged into action against the Hulk for the first time, each hungry for revenge. When he showed them who was really to blame for their troubles, they changed their target to the Illuminati instead.

Although most people fled Manhattan before the battle began, many New York landmarks fell in the battle with the Hulk, including Stark Tower and Madison Square Garden

HULK VS. EVERYONE

When the Hulk returned to Earth for his revenge, he was ready to fight anyone who came between him and the Illuminati. Black Bolt, Mr. Fantastic, Iron Man, and Dr. Strange had a lot of friends willing to stand by them, no matter what they might or might not have done; nevertheless, the Hulk and his Warbound beat them all. The Illuminati were bound with slave disks and brought to Madison Square Garden. There they were forced to fight each other. Despite his rage, the Hulk remained true to his claim that he had returned not for murder but justice. None of the heroes—nor anyone else—died at his hand.

X-23

FACTFILE
REAL NAME
Laura Kinney
OCCUPATION
Adventurer
BASE
San Francisco

HEIGHT 5 ft 6 in
WEIGHT 147 lbs
EYES Green
HAIR Black

FIRST APPEARANCE
NYX #3 (February 2004)

POWERS
X-23 possesses superhuman agility, reflexes, speed, and senses. She can also extend adamantium-coated, retractable bone claws from her hands and feet.

X-23

Cloned from a damaged sample of WOLVERINE's DNA, which was missing the Y chromosome, X-23 was raised in the WEAPON X program as the daughter of geneticist Dr. Sarah Kinney. As soon as she was old enough, she was sent on covert killing missions, sometimes influenced by a trigger scent that sent her into a berserker rage. When Dr. Kinney discovered Weapon X had dozens of clones of X-23, she ordered her daughter to destroy them all. X-23 smelled her trigger scent during this operation and killed her mother, too.

The X-MEN found her in the Mutant Town neighborhood of New York City, and Wolverine took her under his wing. She kept her powers after M-Day, and she became an X-Men trainee. After the X-Men moved to California, CYCLOPS made her part of the black-ops X-FORCE team. She later joined the AVENGERS Academy, and was one of the teens abducted to ARCADE's latest Murderworld. **MF**

When X-23 goes berserk, nothing can stop her.

X-CORPS

FIRST APPEARANCE Uncanny X-Men #401 (January 2002)
BASE Paris, France
MEMBERS AND POWERS
Blob Superhuman size and strength; can create a gravity field that makes him immovable [1]. **Avalanche** Generates destructive vibrations from his hands [2]. **Banshee** Projects sonic screech [3]. **Husk** Biomorph: sheds skin to reveal transformed body beneath [4]. **Jubilee II** Projects "fireworks" from her fingers [5].

Following the death of his lover, Moira MACTAGGERT, and the collapse of the Massachusetts Academy where he was headmaster, Sean Cassidy lost his way. Establishing X-Corps, a paramilitary operation, Sean sought to enforce good behavior between mutants. After releasing a number of criminal mutants from jail, he imprisoned the telepathic mutant, Mastermind and used her to control these mutants' activities. It wasn't long before the organization began to collapse, a process accelerated by the shapechanger MYSTIQUE who brought X-Corps to its knees by freeing Mastermind and stabbing Sean in the throat. **AD**

X-CUTIONER

FIRST APPEARANCE X-Men Annual #1 (1970)
REAL NAME Carl Denti
OCCUPATION Vigilante; former FBI agent
BASE Washington, D.C.
HEIGHT 6 ft 1 in **WEIGHT** 210 lbs **EYES** Brown **HAIR** Brown
SPECIAL POWERS/ABILITIES Possesses neuro-stun gauntlet, psi-lance, laser sword, teleporter, cloaking field, phasing unit, grappling claws, propulsion boots, and a genetic scanner. Shi'ar battle-armor enhances strength to almost superhuman levels.

Special Agent Denti had been partnered with Fred Duncan, who had secretly aided PROFESSOR X on occasion. Duncan stored equipment and weaponry that the X-MEN had confiscated from alien races and other threats. After Duncan was murdered, Denti vowed revenge. He discovered Duncan's connections to the X-Men and used the impounded weaponry to hunt down mutants who had not been convicted for their crimes. He clashed with the X-Men, and also assisted the PUNISHER. After Denti gave up his hunt, he was briefly replaced by a second X-Cutioner, an alternate-reality version of GAMBIT, who died in action. **PS, MF**

X-CELL

FIRST APPEARANCE X-Factor #18 (June 2007)
BASE Mobile
MEMBERS AND POWERS
ELIJAH CROSS Increases his mass without slowing him down.
ABYSS Shapeshifter, dimensional transport.
CALLISTO Superhuman senses, strength, speed, agility, and reflexes, plus healing factor.
FATALE Teleportation and light manipulation, including invisibility [1].
MARROW Bone growth, healing factor, superhuman strength, agility, and durability [2].
REAPER Cybernetic hands and leg, plus a scythe that paralyzes.
BLOB Superhuman strength and durability, immovable [3].

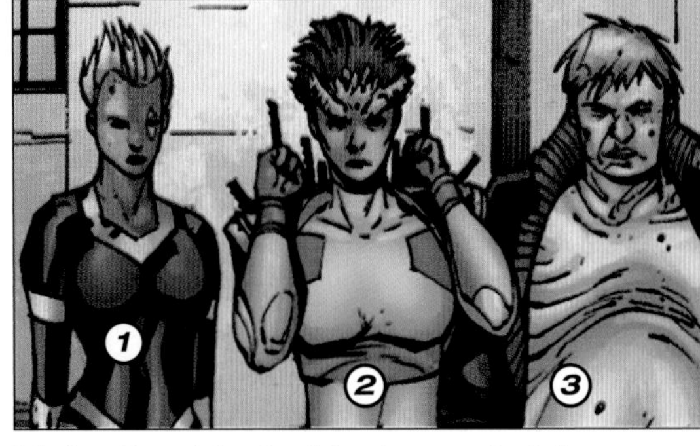

After most of the world's mutants were depowered on M-Day, Elijah Cross banded together a group of ex-mutant terrorists who believed the US government was behind a conspiracy that caused them to lose their powers. Under Cross's leadership, they tracked down QUICKSILVER to see if he could repower them with the Terrigen Crystals he can produce from his body. He did so for ABYSS, Cross, Fatale, REAPER, and RICTOR. After Cross literally exploded from becoming overpowered, Abyss grabbed Fatale and Reaper and disappeared. The others managed to escape on their own. Their current whereabouts and status is unknown. **MF**

X-FACTOR

Mutant investigators

A number of teams have used the name X-Factor. The first was comprised of the original X-MEN, who had left PROFESSOR X's team over the fact that he had installed their old foe MAGNETO as the team's new leader. Posing as mutant hunters, ANGEL, BEAST, CYCLOPS, Jean GREY, and ICEMAN set up shop in Manhattan. They pretended to bring mutants in to face justice, but instead trained them in the use of their powers and in how to blend into regular society. Their recruits included Artie, Boom Boom, Rusty COLLINS, LEECH, RICTOR, and SKIDS.

Madrox is the heart of the latest X-Factor.

UNDERCOVER HUNTERS

When in costume, X-Factor pretended to be the outlaw X-Terminators. Eventually, however, they gave up on this ruse, believing it to cause more harm than good. The original members opted to rejoin the X-Men. Rather than let X-Factor fade away, the US government formed a new team using the name. This started out with HAVOK, Jamie Madrox, POLARIS, QUICKSILVER, STRONG GUY, and WOLFSBANE, with Valerie COOPER as their governmental liaison. A later version of the team, led by FORGE, included the criminals MYSTIQUE, SABRETOOTH, Shard, and WILD CHILD.

X-FACTOR I
1 Archangel
2 Iceman
3 Cyclops
4 Jean Grey
5 Beast

X-FACTOR III
1 Strong Guy ***2*** Rictor ***3*** Wolfsbane
4 Madrox ***5*** Siryn ***6*** M

FACTFILE

NOTABLE MEMBERS

MADROX
Creates duplicates of himself.

STRONG GUY
Transforms kinetic energy directed against himself into strength.

SIRYN
Vocal chords can create sonic blasts.

M
Super-strength, durability, and flight.

RICTOR
Currently powerless; formerly could creates seismic shifts in the Earth.

BUTTERFLY
Instinctively understands causality, and creates a desired effect through a small action.

WOLFSBANE
Can transform into a wolflike creature.

BASE
Mutant Town, New York City

FIRST APPEARANCE
X-Factor #1 (June 2002)

A third version of this team reunited many members of the various government teams. However, it broke up after an exploding time machine sent Havok to Earth-1298, in which many of the roles of the mainstream heroes and villains of Earth were swapped. Later, a governmental Mutant Civil Rights Task Force used the X-Factor name for a short while.

After M-Day, Jamie Madrox opened up a private investigations firm called X-Factor Investigations with many of his old friends. This included M, Layla MILLER (Butterfly), SIRYN, Strong Guy, Wolfsbane, and a powerless Rictor. The team set out to determine what happened on M-Day and became embroiled in the hunt for Hope SUMMERS.

During this, Madrox and Miller traveled to the future of Earth-1191, in which the birth of Hope led to mutants being rounded up into concentration camps. Madrox managed to escape to the present and returned later to find an older Miller and help foment a rebellion. LONGSHOT and Darwin also joined the team. MF

Despite its low profile, X-Factor Investigations still deals with larger threats—like Sentinels.

ESSENTIAL STORYLINES

- ***X-Factor #6***
The first regular appearance of Apocalypse.
- ***X-Factor #149***
X-Factor disbands, and Havok is sent to Earth-1298.
- ***X-Factor Vol. 2 #1***
In the wake of M-Day, Jamie Madrox forms X-Factor Investigations.

X-FORCE

FACTFILE

NOTABLE MEMBERS

BEDLAM
(Jesse Aaronson)
Can disrupt electronic devices.

DOMINO
Can alter luck in her favor, formidable combatant.

CANNONBALL
Can propel himself through the air by releasing energy.

DANIELLE MOONSTAR
Could create images from the minds of others.

WARPATH (PROUDSTAR)
Superhuman strength, speed, and durability.

MELTDOWN (BOOM BOOM)
Creates explosive energy balls.

SUNSPOT
Absorbs solar energy for superhuman strength.

SIRYN
Sonic scream.

BASE
Various

FIRST APPEARANCE
X-Force #1
(August 1991)

X-FORCE

Cable, founder and mentor of X-Force.

PROFESSOR X founded a young mutant team, the NEW MUTANTS, for training. After he had journeyed into outer space and a new headmaster, MAGNETO, had come and gone, CABLE became the team's mentor. He trained his charges to become soldiers against mutant threats and renamed the team X-Force. The roster included Boom Boom (later MELTDOWN) and CANNONBALL, FERAL, SHATTERSTAR, WARPATH, and the shapeshifter COPYCAT, who posed as Cable's ally DOMINO. The real Domino later joined X-Force, as did Bedlam, Caliban, MOONSTAR, RICTOR, SIRYN, and SUNSPOT.

After Cable left, former British intelligence agent Peter WISDOM briefly took over as leader. There have been several other X-Force teams. The first, which predated Cable's team, featured artificially mutated US soldiers. The second turned into X-STATIX. The third was a black-ops team formed by CYCLOPS. After he disbanded that team, WOLVERINE secretly gathered another. Cable later returned to reform a team, while PSYLOCKE simultaneously built another. **PS, MF**

X-FORCE
1 X-23 ***2*** Wolverine ***3*** Domino
4 Warpath ***5*** Archangel

X-MAN

FACTFILE

REAL NAME
Nathan "Nate" Grey

OCCUPATION
Shaman

BASE
Mobile

HEIGHT 5 ft 9 in
WEIGHT 171 lbs
EYES Blue
HAIR Brown

FIRST APPEARANCE
X-Man #1
(March 1995)

POWERS

A telepath of vast power; able to read and control minds, project his astral form across the world, and create complex psionic illusions, and "psionic spikes." Also possessed considerable telekinetic powers, allowing him to move heavy objects at will.

X-MAN

When moved to anger, X-Man's psionic fury was almost unstoppable.

Even on the alternate Earth known as the Age of Apocalypse, MISTER SINISTER is as obsessed with the progeny of Jean GREY and Scott Summers (*see* CYCLOPS) as the Mister Sinister of Earth-616. After obtaining genetic material from these two individuals, he created their child artificially, naming him Nathan Grey. By greatly accelerating the child's growth and development Sinister intended to use Nathan's mutant powers to fight APOCALYPSE.

Ultimately, the Age of Apocalypse timeline was doomed. After killing MISTER SINISTER, Nate managed to escape to the mainstream Earth and made it his goal to prevent this Earth from suffering the same fate. He eventually joined the X-MEN before becoming a shaman. He died saving Earth from the alien Harvester. He returned during the DARK REIGN and fought Norman Osborn, releasing Norman's GREEN GOBLIN personality, but he lost and had his powers drained, leaving him only with limited telekinesis. He later joined the NEW MUTANTS. **AD**

X-MEN ***see pages 416-421***

The X-Men 2099 were initially based in the mountains of New Mexico.

X-Men 2099

In an alternate future, the Earth is ruled by malevolent, self-serving corporations and mutants have been outlawed—forced underground.

In the year 2099, one mutant dedicated himself to overthrowing this oppressive world order. Gathering some of the surviving mutants together to form a new band of X-Men, the almost messianic Xi'an Chi Xan (also known as the Desert Ghost) began challenging this status quo.

Initially based at a mountain fortress in New Mexico that had once belonged to an enemy named Master Zhao, these X-Men were to become the protectors of Halo City in California, which had been declared a safe haven for mutants. However, when an approaching Phalanx planetoid caused severe flooding, mutants and humans were forced to flee to the Savage Land in the Antarctic. Following the Phalanx's defeat, humanity is now in a position to rebuild. On Earth-96099, an alternate set of X-Men 2099 led by by a bald, one-armed Wolverine fought to help repair their damaged timeline. **AD**

X-MEN 2099
1 Bloodhawk ***2*** Krystalin
3 Desert Ghost ***4*** Skullfire ***5*** Metalhead
6 Cerebra ***7*** Meanstreak

FACTFILE

MEMBERS AND POWERS

XI'AN CHI XAN
With his left hand he disintegrates matter, with his right hand he heals injuries.

CEREBRA
Detects mutants with her mind.

KRYSTALIN
Creates crystals from thin air.

MEANSTREAK
Travels at superhuman speeds.

METALHEAD
Touches any metal and assumes its properties.

SKULLFIRE
Absorbed energy makes his skeleton glow.

BLOODHAWK
Transmutes body to develop red skin and bat-like wings.

BASE
The Savage Land, Antarctica

FIRST APPEARANCE
X-Men 2099 #1 (October 1993)

X-MEN 2099

SHE'S DOWN!
HERE'S OUR CHANCE TO STAGE AN ALL-OUT ASSAULT!
DUHHH! LISTEN TO SIMIAN THE MASTER STRATEGIST!
ENOUGH, SPANNER--!
STOP BICKERING... AND SPREAD OUT!

CHARACTER KEY
1 Angry Eagle
2 Simian
3 Spanner
4 Torque
5 Jubilee

X-People

The X-People inhabit an alternate future in which the Earth's superhuman population is dominated by a new generation of champions. In this reality, the X-Men have been recast as the X-People. Under the leadership of an adult Jubilee, the team upholds the principles of Professor X, who envisioned the peaceful coexistence of humans and mutants.

The new faces making up the roster of the X-People include the winged Angry Eagle, the gymnastic Simian, shapeshifting Spanner, and superfast Torque. Former members included the speedster Bluestreak, and an aging Cyclops, who still maintains connections to the team. The X-People battled J2 (son of Juggernaut) when the villainess Enthralla used her hypnotic abilities to coerce them into violence. Later, the X-People trained Wild Thing (daughter of Wolverine), but she declined the team's offer of membership. **DW**

FACTFILE

CURRENT MEMBERS AND POWERS

JUBILEE (leader)
Generates explosive energy bursts.

ANGRY EAGLE
Flight, enhanced eyesight.

SIMIAN
Enhanced agility, talented acrobat.

SPANNER
Can elongate limbs and change shape.

TORQUE
A super-speedster.

BASE
Mobile

FIRST APPEARANCE
J2 #1 (October 1998)

X-PEOPLE

X-MEN

Earth's mightiest team

X-MEN

FACTFILE

MEMBERS AND POWERS

PROFESSOR X (Charles Xavier)
Telepathy.

CYCLOPS (Scott Summers)
Optic power beams.

PHOENIX (Marvel Girl I, Jean Grey) Telepathy, telekinesis.

ARCHANGEL (Angel, Warren Worthington III) Flight.

BEAST (Henry McCoy)
Superhuman strength and agility.

ICEMAN (Bobby Drake)
Generates intense cold.

COLOSSUS (Peter Rasputin)
Turns to "organic steel."

NIGHTCRAWLER (Kurt Wagner)
Teleportation.

ROGUE (Real name unrevealed)
Absorbs memories and abilities.

SHADOWCAT (Kitty Pryde)
"Phases" through solid objects.

STORM (Ororo Munroe)
Controls weather.

WOLVERINE (Logan)
Adamantium skeleton and claws.

BASE The Xavier Institute, Salem Center, New York State

FIRST APPEARANCE
X-Men #1 (September 1963)

ALLIES/FOES

ALLIES The New Mutants, Excalibur, X-Factor, Generation X, the Fantastic Four, the Avengers, Spider-Man, Doctor Strange

FOES Magneto, the Juggernaut, the Sentinels, Apocalypse, Mister Sinister, Mystique, Brotherhood of Evil Mutants, the Hellfire Club, the Brood

ISSUE #1

Professor X trains his X-Men and the team are confronted with arch-enemy Magneto.

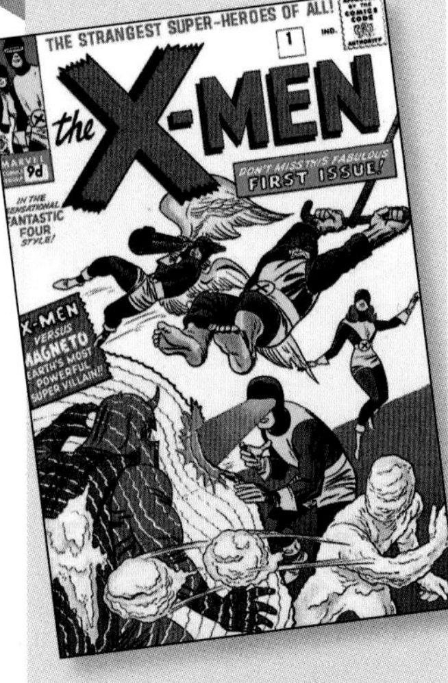

The X-Men is a team of superhuman mutants that was founded by Professor Charles Xavier (PROFESSOR X), who is not only a mutant himself, but is also one of the world's leading authorities on mutation. In founding the X-Men, Xavier had two principal purposes. First, he sought to find young mutants and to train them in utilizing their superhuman powers. Second, Xavier intended the X-Men to serve as a combat team to defend "ordinary" humans against attack by other mutants. Further, Xavier recognizes that "normal" humans tend to fear and distrust the mutants, who are appearing in their midst, and that therefore mutants often suffer persecution.

XAVIER'S DREAM

By founding the X-Men, Xavier created a community of mutants living together on his estate. Xavier is a visionary who hopes to help bring about peaceful coexistence between mutants and the rest of the human race. The X-Men are dedicated to this goal, which they call "Xavier's dream." Xavier has explained that he named the team "X-Men" after the "extra" powers that his mutant students possess. (Of course, "X" is also the first letter of Xavier's last name.) As a young man, Xavier battled another mutant telepath, Amahl Farouk, alias the SHADOW KING, in Egypt. This encounter made him aware of the need to protect humanity from malevolent mutants.

ROAD TO RECOVERY

Xavier subsequently lost the use of his legs in a clash with an alien who called himself LUCIFER. Deeply depressed, Xavier led a reclusive existence at his family mansion. However, he began treating a ten-year-old girl named Jean Grey whose mutant powers had prematurely emerged.

Years later, the FBI initiated an investigation of mutants, headed by agent Fred Duncan. Xavier met

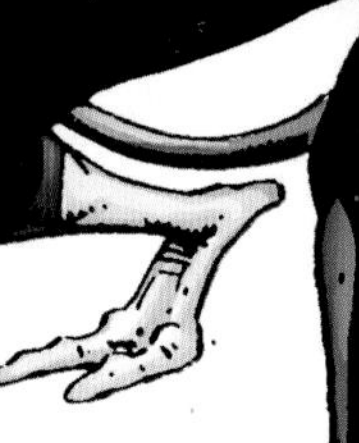

ESSENTIAL STORYLINES

- ***Giant-Size X-Men #1***
Charles Xavier forms a new international team of X-Men.
- ***The Uncanny X-Men #129–137***
"The Dark Phoenix Saga": the X-Men try to stop the mad Phoenix (Jean Grey) from wreaking havoc through the cosmos and save her from insanity.
- ***The Uncanny X-Men #141–142***
"Days of Future Past": present day X-Men try to prevent a future America ruled by Sentinels.

THE X-MEN
1 Storm ***2*** Banshee ***3*** Angel
4 Sunfire ***5*** Iceman ***6*** Havok
7 Polaris ***8*** Marvel Girl (Jean Grey)
9 Colossus ***10*** Nightcrawler
11 Wolverine ***12*** Cyclops
13 Thunderbird

The X-Men are based in Charles Xavier's Westchester County mansion.

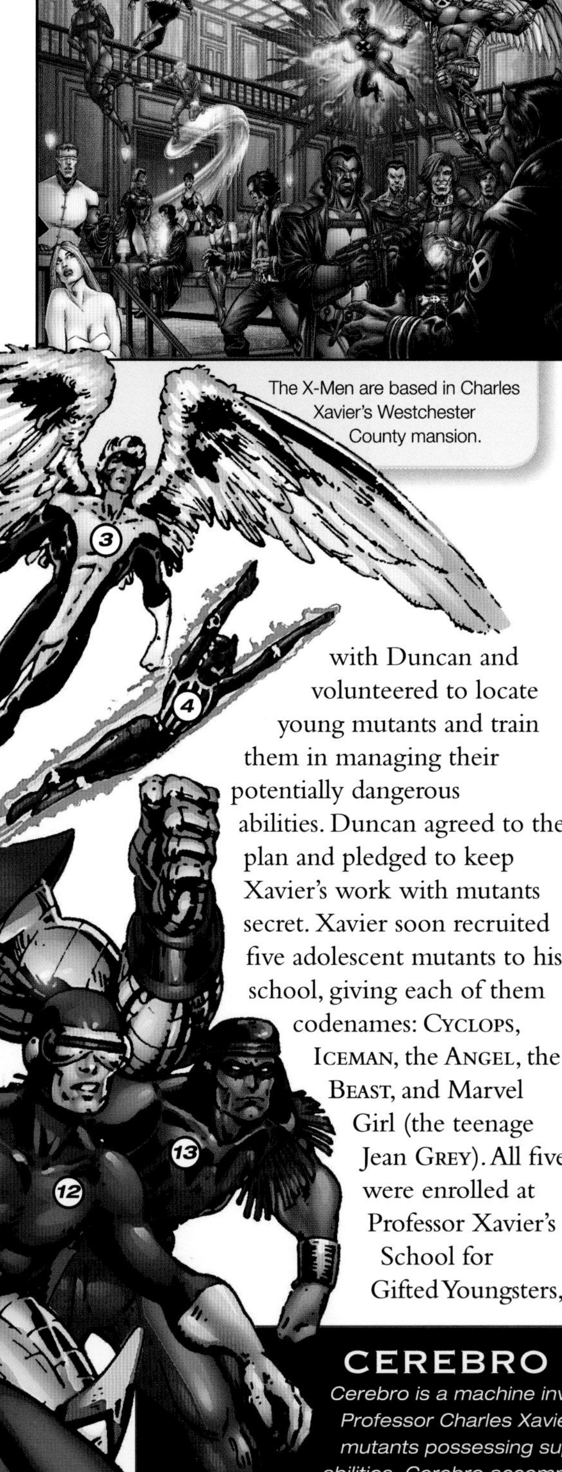

with Duncan and volunteered to locate young mutants and train them in managing their potentially dangerous abilities. Duncan agreed to the plan and pledged to keep Xavier's work with mutants secret. Xavier soon recruited five adolescent mutants to his school, giving each of them codenames: CYCLOPS, ICEMAN, the ANGEL, the BEAST, and Marvel Girl (the teenage Jean GREY). All five were enrolled at Professor Xavier's School for Gifted Youngsters, a private school based in Xavier's mansion, in the town of Salem Center in New York City's Westchester County.

There Xavier educated them in conventional academic subjects, while secretly teaching them how to utilize their mutant abilities.

The next member of the X-Men, who served only briefly, was the MIMIC, who was not a mutant but had the ability to imitate mutant powers. During a period when Xavier was in seclusion, he was impersonated by the CHANGELING, a shapeshifting mutant who died heroically. The mutants HAVOK and Lorna Dane, later known as POLARIS, subsequently joined the team.

New Recruits

Most of the X-Men became trapped on the island of Krakoa, which proved to be a gigantic mutant organism. Xavier then recruited a new team of X-Men from various countries. The new members included the BANSHEE, from Ireland; COLOSSUS, from Russia; NIGHTCRAWLER, from Germany; STORM, from equatorial Africa; SUNFIRE, from Japan; THUNDERBIRD, a Native American; and WOLVERINE, from Canada.

Led by Cyclops, the new recruits rescued the X-Men from Krakoa. After their return, the senior X-Men left the team, except for Cyclops, who remained as deputy leader. Sunfire quit, and Thunderbird was killed during the new X-Men's second mission.

Over subsequent years, many other members have joined the X-Men, including Kitty PRYDE, alias Shadowcat; ROGUE; Rachel SUMMERS, known both as the second Phoenix and the current Marvel Girl; PSYLOCKE; the DAZZLER; and LONGSHOT. During a temporary reformation, even the X-Men's archfoe MAGNETO joined the team.

Xavier formed a new international team of X-Men after the immense mutant Krakoa the Living Island captured the original team.

After forming their own group, X-FACTOR, the five founding X-Men returned to their original team. Xavier's school was renamed the Xavier Institute. Further new members included FORGE, JUBILEE, GAMBIT, BISHOP, REVANCHE, CANNONBALL, JOSEPH (a clone of Magneto), Dr. Cecilia Reyes, MARROW and MAGGOTT. Storm organized a short-lived spinoff team called the X-Treme X-Men, which included, SAGE, the third THUNDERBIRD, LIFEGUARD and Slipstream. Most of these members joined the main X-Men team.

Open Secret

Many other heroes have joined the X-Men over the years, including CABLE, CHAMBER, HUSK, NORTHSTAR, Stacy X, and the traitor XORN. Even former foes like Emma FROST, JUGGERNAUT, and MYSTIQUE have been part of the team. Ever since Professor X's evil twin sister Cassandra Nova exposed him as a mutant, the world has known that the Xavier Institute was the headquarters of the X-Men. This made it possible for the Institute to openly advocate for mutant rights. In the aftermath of M-Day, the government made the X Mansion a sort of reservation for mutants, keeping the few remaining ones there, purportedly for their safety.

PS, MF

CEREBRO

Cerebro is a machine invented by Professor Charles Xavier to locate mutants possessing superhuman abilities. Cerebro accomplishes this by detecting psionic energy emitted by the minds of superhuman mutants. Cerebro operates best when it is linked to the mind of a telepath, such as Xavier or Jean Grey, through a headset. Xavier utilized an early version of Cerebro, called Cyberno, to locate Scott Summers, who became Cyclops. On combining with the Sentinel Bastion's nanotechnology, Cerebro became sentient. It posed a menace until Xavier destroyed it. Since then Xavier has created an advanced version, called Cerebra.

Among the X-Men's adversaries are Sabretooth (left, fighting Wolverine), the insect-like alien Brood (battling Cyclops), and their leading nemesis Magneto (top right, attacking Bishop).

X-MEN *continued*

Disgusted with Magneto, the Scarlet Witch removed 90 per cent of the world's mutants on November 2.

M-Day

One of the world's most powerful mutants, the SCARLET WITCH, had a breakdown, during which she tore apart the team with which she worked: the Avengers. Later, as the X-Men discussed the Scarlet Witch's fate, her brother, QUICKSILVER, encouraged her to use her powers to remake the world. At her bidding thousands more people became mutants, and her father, MAGNETO, ruled the planet as the leader of the House of M. To keep others from looking too closely at their new reality, she gave them whatever they wanted: respectability, money, love, power.

Once the Scarlet Witch had been made to realize what she'd done, she changed everything back to normal—with a few twists. Among these were the fact that 90 per cent of the world's mutants lost their powers, including Magneto, Professor X, and herself.

The Aftermath

With the mutant population decimated, the US government estimated that 198 mutants were left with their powers intact. The Office of National Emergency (ONE) under Valerie COOPER moved to gather these mutants at the Xavier Mansion and keep them there, guarded by SENTINELS.

This lasted until the CIVIL WAR, during which the X-Men officially remained neutral. As the war progressed, the restrictions on the mutants living at the X Mansion were lifted, with the SENTINELS left in place to guard the residents from outside attacks.

The power of the mutants had been stripped from them, but it could not be destroyed. Many of the powers banded into a being known as the Collective, which possessed mutant Michael Pointer (GUARDIAN) and used him to cut a swathe of destruction across North America. The Collective then traveled to Genosha to converse with Magneto before racing off into space. As it left the planet, it brushed past Krakoa—the island-sized mutant that nearly killed the original X-Men—and awakened the missing Summers brother, Gabriel (VULCAN). Gabriel returned to Earth and, after killing BANSHEE, revealed that he had been part of a team of young mutants sent to save the original X-Men from Krakoa. After they had all been apparently killed, Professor X had erased the memory of their existence. Learning this, Cyclops informed the professor that he would no longer be welcome with his X-Men.

As the Collective, Michael Pointer and Xorn slaughtered Alpha Flight, repowered Magneto, and awakened Vulcan.

Interplanetary Problems

Trying to make up for his mistakes, Professor X led a team of X-Men—including Darwin, Havok, Nightcrawler, Polaris, Rachel Summers, and Warpath—into space to stop Vulcan. They failed to keep Vulcan from killing his father, Corsair, but they and the rest of the Starjammers rescued Lilandra. After Xavier regained his powers, he and half the team returned to Earth, leaving the others to form a new Starjammers to stand against Vulcan, who had become the new ruler of the Shi'ar Empire.

The other X-Men, under Cyclops, traveled to the planet Breakworld, where its leader was preparing to fire a gigantic missile at the Earth, large enough to destroy the planet. Kitty Pryde phased into the missile to try to defuse it but discovered it was actually a solid bullet. Using all her might, she managed to phase the bullet through Earth, but she remained trapped inside of it and was presumed dead.

Professor X's X-Men consisted of Vulcan, Sway, Petra, and Darwin. They were lost fighting Krakoa.

When the Hulk returned to Earth to have his revenge on the Illuminati, he went to the X-Mansion to confront Xavier. After a pitched battle, the Hulk learned about all of the horrible things that had happened to the mutants in his absence and concluded that they had suffered plenty as a people.

Messiah Complex

It looked like there would be no more mutants to join the 198 or so left on the planet. While using his Cerebra mutant-finding machine, though, Professor X spotted one amazingly powerful new mutant in Cooperstown, Alaska, and Cyclops led a team of X-Men to investigate. The anti-mutant militants known as the Purifiers, and Mr. Sinister's new team of Marauders, beat the X-Men there.

The Purifiers, realizing that they were looking for a young mutant, killed every child in town, even the infants still in the hospital. This tipped the X-Men—along with X-Factor and the Young X-Men—off to the fact that the first mutant since M-Day had been born—and manifested its powers at birth. They later learned that Cable had gotten there first and taken the baby to safety.

Meanwhile, Predator X, a monster the Purifiers had created to destroy the "Mutant Anti-Christ," found the baby's scent and began killing mutants to sate its hunger as it tracked the infant down. While many X-Men were out hunting for the baby, the Nano-Sentinels infected the human pilots of the Sentinels assigned to guard the mansion. They attacked, nearly destroying the place. In response to this, Cyclops formed an all-new X-Force as a black-ops team. MF

Gambit joined Mr. Sinister's new Marauders—not to help with their plans but to advance his own.

The US government agency ONE positioned Sentinels around the X-Mansion to keep hostile humans out—and the mutants in.

X-MEN *continued*

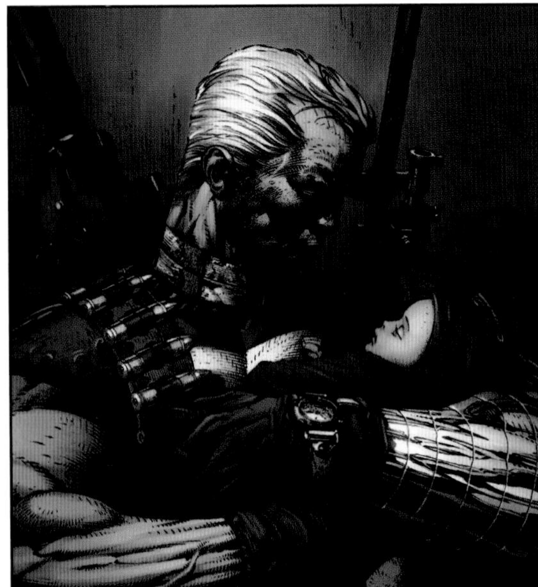

Sent into the future as a baby himself, Cable hoped to save the baby he would raise as Hope Summers the same way.

The Future of Mutantkind

When Cable went to Forge for a time machine so he could escape with the baby, he discovered Bishop had already shot Forge. In the future from which Bishop came, the first mutant baby became the Mutant Messiah and later killed a million humans. Bishop meant to stop that by murdering the infant. The Marauders prevented that and stole the child. Before Sinister could get his hands on the infant, Mystique killed him and used the baby to bring Rogue out of a coma caused by her absorbing too many minds at once.

X-Force managed to kill Predator X while the Young X-Men defeated the remaining Marauders. Professor X took the baby from Gambit, who'd rescued her from Mystique, and gave her back to Cable, just before Cyclops and the X-Men caught up with them. While the baby held the potential to cause Bishop's horrible future, Cyclops saw that it also could bring Cable's better future to pass. Revealing a long-buried optimistic side, Cyclops let Cable escape into the future with the baby.

As Cable and the baby disappeared, Bishop caught up with them and shot at them. A bullet hit Professor X, nearly killing him. Cyclops took Bishop down, but he soon escaped to chase Cable through time, still pursuing the baby, who Cable named Hope Summers.

A New Home

With the mansion destroyed and Professor X now missing, Cyclops decided to end the X-Men—or so he told Iron Man when he came to ask the X-Men to register with the Fifty-State Initiative.

He moved the team to the Marin Headlands near San Francisco, where the mayor rejected the help of the Fifty-State Initiative and made the X-Men the city's official protectors. They set up shop in an abandoned military complex they renamed Graymalkin Industries (after the road where they had had their original headquarters), placing a mutant embassy on top of a facility that extended three miles below the Earth's surface. Then, through Emma Frost, Cyclops telepathically declared the city of San Francisco a mutant sanctuary.

Professor X resurfaced with his powers intact to lead another group of X-Men aiming to find and rescue Rogue from Danger, the personification of the Danger Room. At the same time, Cyclops and his X-Men and X-Force teams were gearing up for the Messiah War, the next round in the battle over Hope Summers.

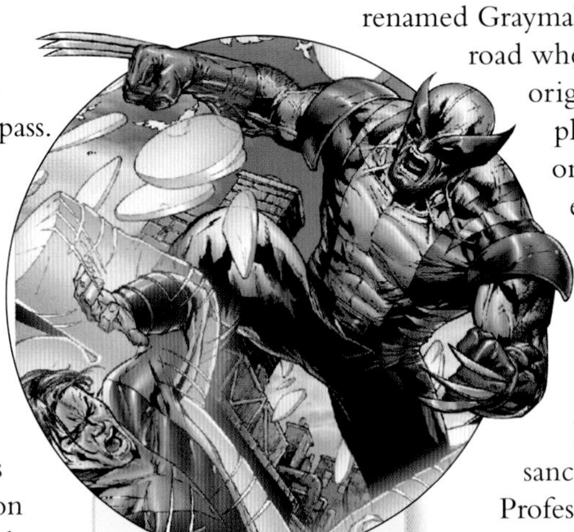

Cyclops picked Wolverine to lead the new black-ops X-Force team.

Predator X was designed to hunt down and devour mutants of any kind, but it hungered for the mutant baby most of all.

Pixie and the rest of the X-Men have settled into their new headquarters in San Francisco with a renewed sense of both determination and hope.

HOUSE OF M

Quicksilver believed that the X-Men and their friends might put his sister the Scarlet Witch to death for disassembling the Avengers. He encouraged her to use her powers to reshape reality. After a flash of light, the world became one in which mutants were plentiful and Magneto and his House of M ruled. No one remembered things ever being any other way. With the help of Layla Miller—a mutant who could restore to others the memories they had lost—Wolverine led a movement and an assault to put things right.

Darkness and Hope

During the Dark Reign, Norman Osborn (Green Goblin) set up a fake team of X-Men, led by Emma Frost, to help control the rest of the X-Men by turning public opinion against them. When Emma and Namor betrayed Osborn, Cyclops moved the real X-Men to a floating island constructed from the remains of Asteroid M, Magneto's former headquarters, which had crashed into the ocean. As the island, Utopia, was in international waters, Cyclops declared it to be outside of the USA and Osborn's jurisdiction. At Magneto's suggestion, Namor later had the Atlanteans build a column beneath Utopia to support it and to house New Atlantis.

Cable brought Hope Summers—now a teenager—back to the present day, where they found their foes, led by Bastion, waiting for them. Working with the X-Men and traveling back and forth in time, they destroyed Bastion, but at the cost of the life of Nightcrawler, who sacrificed himself to save Hope.

The mutant detector Cerebra announced that it had started to find new mutants arising around the globe, the first since the events of M-Day. The X-Men went to find and help the first of these, five mutants known as the Lights.

As the leader of the X-Men, Cyclops became more militant and determined to protect the mutants still left. Wolverine accused Cyclops of abandoning Professor X's dream of peaceful cooperation between mutants and humans. Taking half the mutants on Utopia with him, Wolverine left to found the Jean Grey School for Higher Learning on the site of the X-Men's old school. Hoping to show Cyclops how far he'd fallen from his ideals, Beast brought the original X-Men back from the past to visit. **MF**

When Beast brought the original X-Men to the future, they didn't all want to leave, no matter how dangerous that might turn out to be.

VS. THE AVENGERS

The schism between Cyclops and Wolverine came to a head when the Phoenix Force returned to Earth and the Avengers decided that they needed to take Hope into custody to protect her (and the planet) from it. Wolverine sided with them in their battle against the X-Men, even after Iron Man broke the Phoenix Force into five parts, each of which chose a host: Colossus, Cyclops, Emma Frost, Magik, and Namor.
While the Phoenix Five started out helping the planet, their power corrupted them, and they fell one by one. Eventually Cyclops took the last of the power from Emma to defend himself against the Avengers. The surge in power caused him to kill Professor X and become the Dark Phoenix. Hope and the Scarlet Witch stopped him and destroyed the Phoenix Force.

The Phoenix Five
1 Magik ***2*** Emma Frost
3 Colossus ***4*** Cyclops
5 Namor

X-STATIX

FACTFILE

MEMBERS AND POWERS

HENRIETTA HUNTER Empathic powers, could resurrect herself.

VIVISECTOR Could shapeshift into wolflike form.

EL GUAPO Could levitate while riding a skateboard.

DEAD GIRL Can return to life, can become intangible and communicate with the dead.

VENUS DEE MILO Body composed of pure energy, could self-teleport and project energy blasts.

DOOP Self-levitation

ANARCHIST Acidic sweat generated energy bolts.

MISTER SENSITIVE (ORPHAN) Self-levitation, superhuman speed, heightened senses.

PHAT Could increase the size of any part of his body

BASE Mobile

FIRST APPEARANCE
(as X-Force) X-Force #116 (May 2001); (as X-Statix) X-Statix #1 (September 2002)

Mr. Sensitive and Venus were lovers until both died on their final mission.

X-STATIX

Rather than hide their mutant abilities from a bigoted humanity, the members of X-Statix took a completely opposite approach. They used their mutant powers to become rich and famous. The team was known as X-FORCE, having stolen the name from another mutant band.

The members of this new X-Force battled criminals to protect the public. But their adventures were telecast as a reality show, and members became celebrities. They paid for their success with their lives. During one show, most of the team, including the leader Zeitgeist, were massacred. Only the Anarchist, the teleporter U-GO GIRL, and Doop survived.

Guy Smith, alias the Orphan and MISTER SENSITIVE, became the leader. Other recruits included Bloke, Dead Girl, El Guapo, Phat, Saint Anna, the Spike, Venus Dee Milo, and the Vivisector. Smith was succeeded as leader by the Anarchist and mutant pop star Henrietta Hunter. To avoid potential legal action, the group changed its name to X-Statix. The team continued to suffer fatalities, and the roster was completely wiped out on X-Statix's final mission. Their adventures continued, however, in the afterlife. **PS, MF**

X-STATIX
1 Henrietta Hunter **2** Vivisector **3** El Guapo
4 Dead Girl **5** Venus Dee Milo **6** Doop
7 Anarchist **8** Mister Sensitive **9** Phat

XARUS

FACTFILE

REAL NAME
Xarus

OCCUPATION
Vampire lord

BASE
Mobile

HEIGHT 6 ft 2 in
WEIGHT 200 lbs
EYES Red
HAIR Blond

FIRST APPEARANCE
Death of Dracula #1 (August 2010)

POWERS

Xarus is a vampire. He has a pendant that allows him to withstand daylight.

Not even Blade could kill Xarus. It took Dracula's might instead.

XARUS

The son of DRACULA, Xarus was the brother of Janus and the half-brother of Lilith and Vlad Tepulus. Frustrated with his father's leadership, Xarus stepped up at the once-a-century meeting of the vampire clans and slew Dracula with the help of his allies. He then led the vampires to attack San Francisco, hoping to transform it into a new vampire homeland, but the X-MEN stood in his way. He had JUBILEE transformed into a vampire, using her as bait for the other mutants. He turned WOLVERINE and then set his sights on the mutant island of Utopia.

He landed on Utopia, confident of victory. When he tried to order Wolverine to attack the X-Men, however, CYCLOPS revealed that Xarus had only been able to take control of Wolverine because his healing factor had been turned off by nanites. Cyclops turned off the nanites, and Wolverine became human again. Meanwhile, the X-Men and their ATLANTEAN allies had revived Dracula. With Xarus' forces routed, Dracula removed Xarus' head. **MF**

XANDU

FIRST APPEARANCE Amazing Spider-Man Annual #2 (1965)
REAL NAME Unknown
OCCUPATION Sorceror **BASE** New York City
HEIGHT/WEIGHT Unrevealed **EYES** Blue **HAIR** White
SPECIAL POWERS/ABILITIES Xandu possesses numerous abilities derived from his sorcery, most notably a hypnotic gaze that makes other people do his bidding.

A would-be master sorcerer into whose possession half of the mystic Wand of Watomb fell, Xandu desired the power that would be his if he could unite both halves of this magical talisman. Recruiting several toughs at the waterfront and casting a spell that turned them into robots, Xandu sent them to recover the other half of the wand from DOCTOR STRANGE. But Strange gained an unexpected ally when SPIDER-MAN stumbled on the robbery, and together they defeated Xandu's agents. Strange caused Xandu to forget all of his magical knowledge, but this didn't prevent the renegade sorcerer from returning again and again to challenge the two heroes. **TB**

XEMNU

FIRST APPEARANCE Journey into Mystery #62 (November 1960)
REAL NAME Xemnu **OCCUPATION** Former ruler
BASE Mobile **HEIGHT** 11 ft **WEIGHT** 1,100 lbs
EYES Red **HAIR** Reddish-brown; more recently white
SPECIAL POWERS/ABILITIES Consciousness able to survive without body for indefinite periods; psionically manipulate individuals through vast hypnotic abilities.

Although he cuts a lonely, tragic figure, Xemnu the Titan remains a very real threat to mankind. The one-time ruler of his native world, Xemnu left there to travel the galaxy. Upon returning home, he discovered it had been ravaged by plague, and his people were dead. Having felt most at home on Earth, Xemnu returned there and made several attempts to transform its citizens into members of his own race. He was repeatedly rebuffed, the HULK, DOCTOR STRANGE and the THING taking turns to defeat him. Xemnu looks set to be the last of his kind. **AD**

XORN

FIRST APPEARANCE New X-Men Annual 2001 (September 2001)
REAL NAME Kuan-Yin Xorn
OCCUPATION Teacher, adventurer, terrorist **BASE** Mobile
HEIGHT 6 ft 2 in **WEIGHT** 210 lbs **EYES** N/A **HAIR** N/A
SPECIAL POWERS/ABILITIES Xorn had a miniature star in his head which emitted magnetism and a blinding, incinerating light, and could be converted to a black hole. He didn't need food, water, or air and he could heal others.

Kuan-Yin Xorn and his twin brother Shen were born in China and imprisoned, forced to wear special iron helmets to keep those around them safe. Their warden sold Kuan-Yin to John Sublime, but the X-MEN managed to free him first.
He worked as a teacher at the Xavier Institute until, claiming to be MAGNETO, he slaughtered many people in Manhattan. WOLVERINE beheaded Xorn, and Magneto showed up alive after the funeral. Shen later confirmed this, but he disappeared soon after. Kuan-Yin's consciousness later controlled the Collective (*see* WEAPON OMEGA) on M-Day. **TB**

XAVIERS'S SECURITY ENFORCERS

In an alternate future in which Earth's population rose up against their oppressors, the SENTINELS, a mutant police force, was formed to ensure peace between mutants and humans. This group called itself Xavier's Security Enforcers in tribute to the idealism of the X-MEN's PROFESSOR X. The XSE eventually arrived in our world's current reality while pursuing renegade member Trevor Fitzroy.

A traitorous splinter group, Xavier's Underground Enforcers, included Greystone, Archer, and Fixx. **DW**

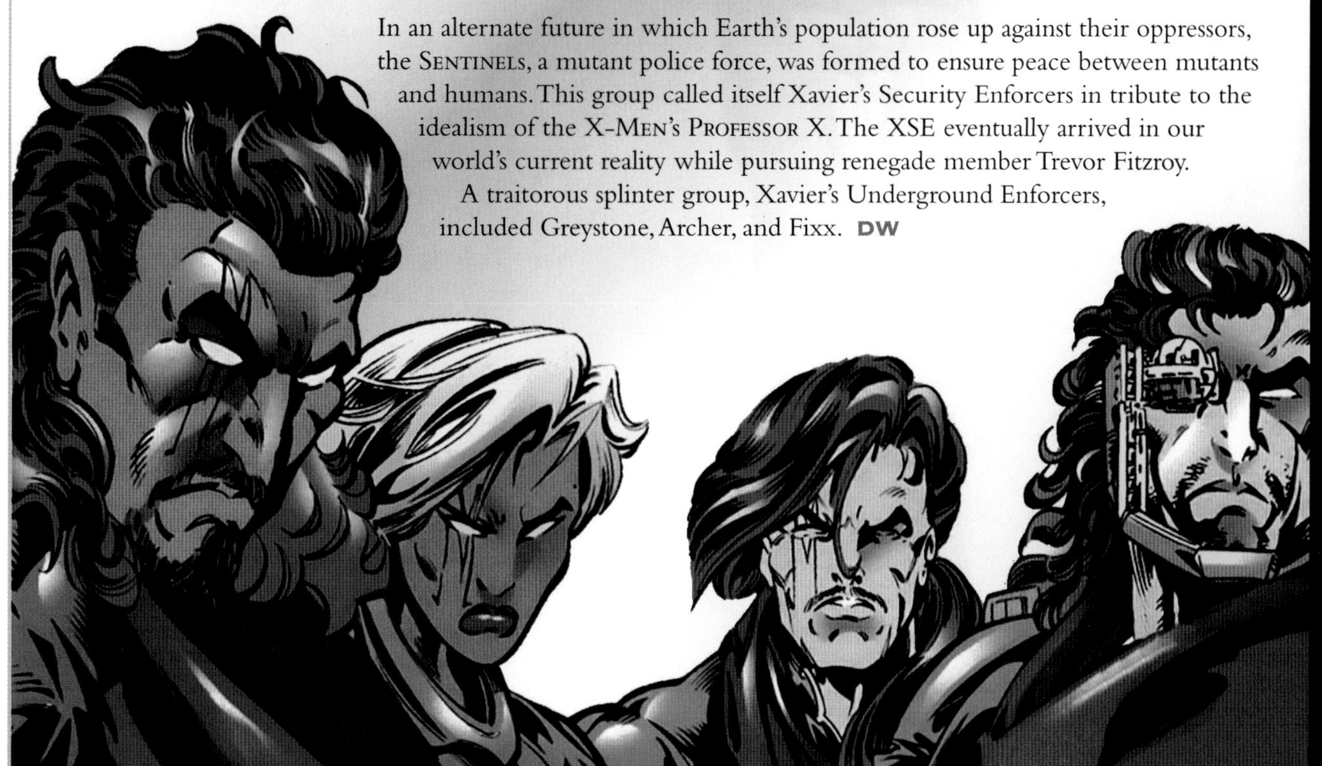

FACTFILE

MEMBERS AND POWERS
BISHOP Absorbs and releases any form of energy.
RANDALL (deceased) Immune to radiation, skilled combatant.
MALCOLM (deceased) Could distinguish between humans and mutants.
SHARD (deceased) Could absorb light and emit it as shockwaves.
HECATE Projects a null-light field that causes others to see their fears.

BASE Mobile

FIRST APPEARANCE
Uncanny X-Men #282 (November 1991)

Yama, Jimmy

FIRST APPEARANCE Spider-Girl #1 (October 1998)
REAL NAME Jimmy Yama
OCCUPATION High-school student **BASE** New York City
HEIGHT 5 ft 5 in **WEIGHT** 145 lbs **EYES** Brown **HAIR** Black
SPECIAL POWERS/ABILITIES Jimmy is an ordinary teenager with no special powers.

In a future timeline populated by a second generation of Earth's heroes, Jimmy Yama is a Midtown High School student and friend to May Parker (Spider-Girl). Yama's nemesis is Midtown bully Moose Mansfield. When Yama lashed out at Moose and inadvertently injured him, he stood trial for punitive damages until Moose's parents dropped the case. Yama has tried several times to establish a romantic relationship with May, but his efforts have been hindered by his shyness. **DW**

Yancy Street Gang

FIRST APPEARANCE Fantastic Four #6 (September 1962
BASE Yancy Street, on the Lower East Side of Manhattan

Based around the tough neighborhood of Manhattan's Lower East Side, the Yancy Street Gang was at one time led by Daniel Grimm, the wayward older brother of Ben Grimm, fated to transform into the Thing. Daniel was killed during a rumble between the Yancy gang and a rival street gang, and Ben eventually replaced his brother as the leader. But when Ben moved out west after the death of his mother, the Yancy Gang took it as a betrayal. After Ben was transformed into the Thing and became one of the Fantastic Four, the Yancy Street Gang made it their mission to heckle and bedevil their former member. During the Civil War, the gang sided with the outlaw heroes. The Puppet Master and Mad Thinker used them to incite a riot in which the gang's leader was killed. **TB, MF**

Yashida, Mariko

FIRST APPEARANCE X-Men #118 (February 1979)
REAL NAME Mariko Yashida
OCCUPATION Head of Clan Yashida **BASE** Japan
HEIGHT 5 ft **WEIGHT** 100 lbs **EYES** Brown **HAIR** Black
SPECIAL POWERS/ABILITIES An exceptional businesswoman; had the normal fitness of a woman of her age and weight, but no special powers.

For many years, Mariko Yashida was the love of Wolverine's life. Meeting her during a mission to Japan, their relationship blossomed in New York, and they remained in contact even after her forced marriage to a brutal criminal associate of her father. The deaths of Mariko's husband and her father presented them with the opportunity for marriage, but Mariko wanted to wait—she had inherited the family business and wished to sever its criminal links first. In the end, the pair never wed—when she was poisoned by an assassin, Wolverine was forced to kill Mariko in order to end her terrible suffering. **AD**

Yellow Claw

FIRST APPEARANCE Yellow Claw #1 (October 1956)
REAL NAME Plan Tzu **OCCUPATION** Conqueror
BASE Various hidden bases around the world
HEIGHT 6 ft 2 in **WEIGHT** 210 lbs **EYES** Brown **HAIR** Bald
SPECIAL POWERS/ABILITIES Knowledge of biochemistry, genetics, robotics, and sorcery (can reanimate the dead); can mentally create illusions in the minds of others.

Born in China in the 1800s, Plan Tzu (aka Master Plan) became the latest in a line of conquerors stretching back to Genghis Khan. He chose a young Jimmy Woo as his successor, but Woo's parents moved to the US to avoid that fate. When Woo joined the FBI in the 1950s, Tzu became Woo's nemesis, the Yellow Claw. He then clashed with SHIELD after Woo joined that agency. In modern times, he finally revealed his plot to Woo and his Agents of Atlas. When Woo accepted his heritage, Tzu allowed the dragon Mr. Lao to devour him. **PS, MF**

Yellowjacket

FIRST APPEARANCE Avengers #264 (February 1986)
REAL NAME Rita DeMara
OCCUPATION Adventurer; former criminal **BASE** Mobile
HEIGHT 5 ft 5 in **WEIGHT** 115 lbs **EYES** Blue **HAIR** Blond
SPECIAL POWERS/ABILITIES Battlesuit provided flight, the ability to shrink via Pym particles, and gloves that fired "disruptor sting" blasts of electricity.

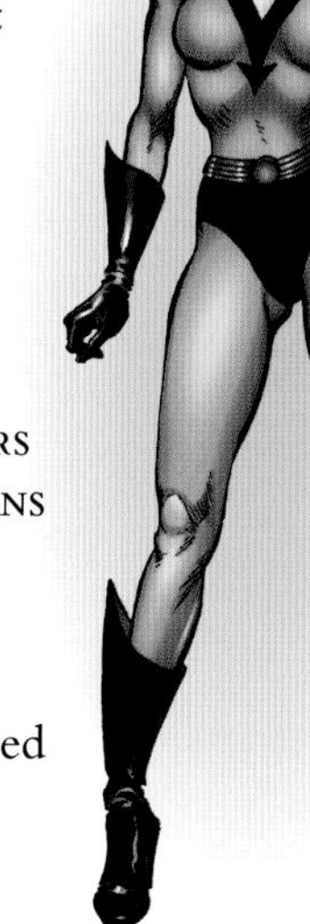

Rita DeMara adopted the identity of Yellowjacket after stealing Hank Pym's original battlesuit from Avengers Mansion. She embarked on a life of crime, joining the Masters of Evil before turning against that group. Her efforts to go straight earned her reserve member status in the Avengers and a place with the Guardians of the Galaxy. Iron Man killed her while under the mental control of Immortus. She was temporarily resurrected years later, during the Chaos War. **DW, MF**

Young Allies, *see page 426*

Young Avengers

The next generation of justice

In a possible alternate year 3016, a young robotics student named Nathaniel Richards was saved from death by his future self. Nathaniel learned that he was destined to grow up to become Kang the Conqueror. Horrified, the 16-year-old fled to modern-day Earth, hoping to circumvent his fate by securing help from the Avengers, Kang's greatest enemies.

A New Plan

Unfortunately, Nathaniel arrived soon after the Scarlet Witch went mad and disassembled the current team. Desperate, he broke into Stark Industries (*see* Iron Man) and examined the central processing unit of the recently destroyed android the Vision, finding a failsafe program that pinpointed the next generation of super-powered youths. Calling himself Iron Lad, Nathaniel quickly recruited them and trained them for a battle with Kang.

When Captain America and Iron Man learned of this new team, they tried to convince the teenagers to disband before they could be hurt, but Kang arrived and demanded the return of Iron Lad so that destiny could fulfill its preordained course. Otherwise Kang would not exist! In the resulting battle, Kang was killed, and Iron Lad decided he must accept his destiny in order to prevent the destruction of the current timeline.

Iron Lad used data from the Vision's central processing unit to locate the next wave of heroes. He found and enlisted Patriot, Hulkling, and Wiccan for the battle against Kang.

FACTFILE

MEMBERS AND POWERS

IRON LAD (Nathaniel Richards)
Scientific genius with a suit of psychokinetic armor that responds to his thoughts.

WICCAN formerly Asgardian (Billy Kaplan) Projects mystical energy.

KATE BISHOP
Olympic-level athlete and weapons-master.

STATURE (Cassie Lang)
Size-changing abilities.

HULKLING (Teddy Altman)
Shapeshifter with healing factor.

PATRIOT (Eli Bradley)
Enhanced speed and agility.

BASE

Formerly Avengers Mansion, New York City

FIRST APPEARANCE

Young Avengers #1 (February 2005)

THE NEXT GENERATION OF JUSTICE

1 Wiccan
2 Kid Loki
3 Miss America
4 Hawkeye (Kate Bishop)
5 Hulking
6 Marvel Boy

New Beginnings

The team later added the superfast Speed to the squad after breaking him out of prison. When Nathaniel took off his armor at one point, it transformed into a new version of the Vision called Jonas. Captain America gave Hawkeye's bow and quiver to Kate Bishop, along with the hero's codename.

During the Civil War, the Young Avengers sided with Cap's resistance. Stature switched sides after the death of Goliath at the hands of Ragnarok. When the conflict ended, the rest registered with the government, except for Hawkeye, Patriot, and Speed. During the Dark Reign, the team joined with a new team of Young Avengers to fight the Dark Avengers under the control of Norman Osborn (Green Goblin). Later, Wiccan and Speed hunted for the Scarlet Witch, believing they were the reincarnations of her children. The quest took them to Latveria, and in an ensuing battle Doctor Doom killed Stature. Determined to save her, Iron Lad decided to take her into the future, even though this would eventually result in him becoming Kang. When Jonas objected, Iron Lad destroyed him.

Months later, Kid Loki gathered Hawkeye, Hulkling, and Wiccan together with Marvel Boy and Miss America to form a new team and take on new challenges. **TD, MF**

After leading the team against Mr. Hyde (left), Patriot admitted he had taken a mutant growth hormone to increase his physical powers.

Young Allies

FACTFILE

NOTABLE MEMBERS

BUCKY Captain America's sidekick.

TORO Original Human Torch's sidekick.

FIRESTAR Flaming mutant.

NOMAD Former Bucky from Counter-Earth.

EL TORO Super-soldier resembling a bull.

SPIDER-GIRL Spider-powers.

GRAVITY Controls gravitons.

BASE Mobile

FIRST APPEARANCE
Young Allies #1 (Summer 1941)

The first team of Young Allies were a group of regular boys who joined up with Bucky Barnes and Toro, the sidekick of the original Human Torch in the days before and during World War II. They were Henry "Tubby" Tinkle, Jefferson Worthing "Jeff" Sandervilt, Percival Aloysius "Knuckles" O'Toole, and Washington Carver "Whitewash" Jones. They fought foes like the Red Skull and Lotus. They stayed in touch over the years, but Bucky is the only one left.

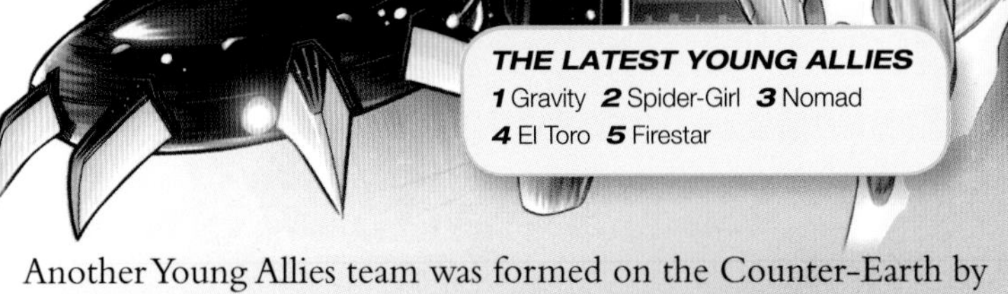

THE LATEST YOUNG ALLIES
1 Gravity *2* Spider-Girl *3* Nomad *4* El Toro *5* Firestar

The Young Allies learned that Superior created the rest of the Bastards of Evil by giving teens powers and brainwashing them to join him.

Another Young Allies team was formed on the Counter-Earth by Franklin Richards. This consisted of that world's Bucky (Rikki Barnes/Nomad), IQ (a brilliant, quadriplegic telepath), Jolt (a girl with shocking punches), Kid Colt (a human-Kymelian hybrid), and Toro (a half-bull boy). They stayed on Counter-Earth when the other heroes left.

A new team formed on Earth in the present day to fight the Bastards of Evil. This included El Toro, Firestar, Gravity, Nomad (Rikki Barnes), and Spider-Girl (Anya Corazon). They later banded together against Onslaught and worked alongside the Avengers Academy. **MF**

Young Masters

FACTFILE

MEMBERS AND POWERS

BIG ZERO Size control.

BLACK KNIGHT Armored fighter.

COAT OF ARMS Coat gives her four working arms.

EGGHEAD Android.

ENCHANTRESS Sorceress.

EXECUTIONER Skilled fighter.

MAKO Atlantean clone.

MELTER Melts matter.

RADIOACTIVE KID Emits radiation.

BASE New York

FIRST APPEARANCE
Dark Reign: Young Avengers #1 (July 2009)

A young artist who took the name Coat of Arms brought the Young Masters—a junior version of the Masters of Evil—together as an art project. Many of the members were named for older heroes and villains they had little to do with, like the Egghead, Enchantress, and Executioner. Melter wanted to be a hero, but some of the others had mixed emotions about such commitments.

The original team started out calling itself the Young Avengers, but the real Young Avengers took issue with that and asked them to audition to join their team. When most of them failed, Melter called Norman Osborn (Green Goblin), who sent in his team of Avengers to deal with the Young Avengers.

The team called itself the Young Masters after that, but many of them moved on, leaving only Egghead and Executioner from the original crew. A mysterious villain calling himself Zodiac helped them recruit Mako, Black Knight (who again had nothing to do with the original), and Radioactive Kid, and they set up in an old Hydra base. They tried to commit a few major crimes, including killing Doctor Octopus and Kristoff Vernard, but they failed. **MF**

YOUNG MASTERS
1 Enchantress
2 Egghead
3 Executioner
4 Melter
5 Big Zero
6 Coat of Arms

Yukio

FIRST APPEARANCE Wolverine #1 (September 1982)
REAL NAME Yukio (full name unrevealed)
OCCUPATION Adventurer, former assassin **BASE** Mobile
HEIGHT 5 ft 9 in **WEIGHT** 130 lbs **EYES** Brown **HAIR** Black
SPECIAL POWERS/ABILITIES Highly skilled athlete, martial artist, and knife-thrower.

Yukio started out as a thief, running with Gambit, before becoming an assassin in the service of Japanese crimelord Lord Shingen of Clan Yashida. Her employer sent her after Wolverine, but she eventually befriended him and his X-Men teammates, particularly Storm. Wolverine grew to trust Yukio so much that he left his foster daughter Amiko Kobayashi in her care. They were attacked by Omega Red and Lady Deathstrike, and later by a possessed Wolverine, who put Yukio in a wheelchair. **DW, MF**

YOUNG X-MEN

Young and foolish

In the aftermath of M-Day, Cyclops—the leader of the X-Men—assembled a new team of mutants called the Young X-Men to bring down a new Brotherhood of Evil Mutants. Ironically, this new Brotherhood was composed of former New Mutants Cannonball, Magma, Dani Moonstar, and Sunspot, who'd become the new leader of the Hellfire Club.

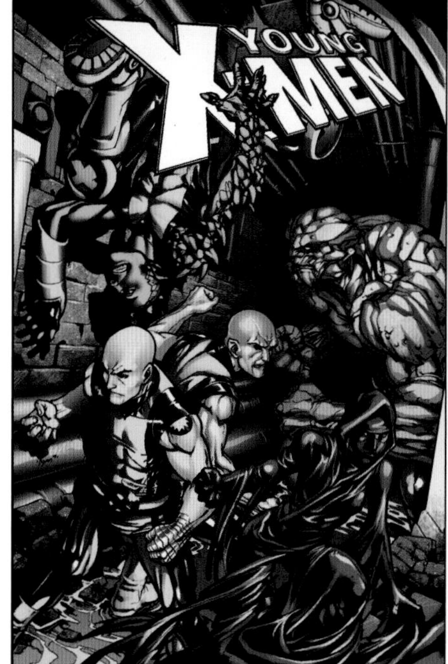

Discovering they'd been brought together by an imposter didn't drive the Young X-Men apart but made them a closer unit.

FACTFILE

MEMBERS AND POWERS

ANOLE Superhuman speed, reflexes, and coordination, plus regeneration, wallcrawling, and camouflage.

BLINDFOLD Telepath able to see past, future, and present.

CIPHER Undetectability and phasing.

DUST Living sandstorm.

GRAYMALKIN Superhuman strength, invulnerability, and night vision, which all increase in darkness.

INK Tattoos that grant various abilities.

MIRAGE (Dani Moonstar) None.

ROCKSLIDE Psionic creature who can telekinetically form a superstrong body from rock.

SUNSPOT Solar power control, superhuman strength, and flight.

WOLF CUB Wolfman form and enhanced senses.

BASE San Francisco

FIRST APPEARANCE
Young X-Men #1 (May 2008)

MEMBERSHIP CHANGES

Initially, the Young X-Men members included Blindfold, Dust, Ink, Rockslide, and Wolf Cub—and secretly Cipher—but when they discovered that their Cyclops was actually X-Men foe Donald Pierce, they united with their targets in the Brotherhood to defeat him. Before he was captured, however, Pierce managed to kill Wolf Cub.

Afterward, the real Cyclops made the team official and asked Sunspot and Moonstar to train the Young X-Men. Blindfold left the team, but Anole joined to replace her. Ink also left the team after it was revealed he wasn't a mutant but had gained his powers through Leon Nunez, a mutant who could give people powers via tattoos. While investigating, the Young X-Men found a group of criminals called the Y-Men, who had forced Leon to give them powers too. Ink persuaded Leon to give him a Phoenix Force tattoo so he could help his friends. While the strain put Leon into a coma, it provided the edge the team needed against the Y-Men, and afterward Ink was allowed to stay with the team, if only so Cyclops could keep an eye on him.

Faced with death and betrayal, the Young X-Men hung together right until the very end.

DOOMED

Soon after, Dust realized that she was slowly dying after having survived Magma temporarily fusing her body of sand into glass. Donald Pierce, who'd been held prisoner on the X-Men's island of Utopia, persuaded her that he could save her, but she died while helping him escape. Ink used his Phoenix Force tattoo to resurrect her, but the effort put him into a coma as well.

Soon after, the team broke up. Many of its members joined the reformed New Mutants. **MF**

YOUNG X-MEN
1 Rockslide ***2*** Anole
3 Graymalkin
4 Dani Moonstar
5 Dust ***6*** Sunspot
7 Ink

ESSENTIAL STORYLINES
- ***Young X-Men #1–5*** The Young X-Men form and realize they've been tricked.
- ***Young X-Men #6–10*** The Young X-Men face off against the Y-Men and learn the truth behind Ink's powers.
- ***Young X-Men #11–12*** Dust dies, but Ink revives her, although at a high cost.

ZABU

FIRST APPEARANCE X-Men #10 (March 1965)
REAL NAME Zabu **OCCUPATION** Companion to Ka-Zar
BASE The Savage Land, Antarctica **HEIGHT/WEIGHT** Unrevealed
EYES Green **HAIR** Orange
SPECIAL POWERS/ABILITIES Two long, saber-like teeth; great strength and agility; unusually intelligent for a saber-tooth tiger; lifespan extended by gases in the Savage Land's "Place of Mists."

Zabu is the last known saber-tooth tiger on Earth. Saber-tooths survived in the Savage Land until recent times but even there are now all but extinct. When Maa-Gor and his Swamp Men slew Zabu's mate, the infuriated tiger hunted them down. Zabu attacked Maa-Gor just as he was about to kill Kevin Plunder, the orphaned son of an explorer. In the ensuing struggle, Kevin shot Maa-Gor, saving Zabu's life. Ever since, Zabu and Kevin have been loyal companions, and Kevin is known today as the jungle lord Ka-Zar, which means "Son of the Tiger." Zabu also joined the Pet Avengers under the leadership of Lockjaw. **PS, MF**

ZARAN

FIRST APPEARANCE Master of Kung Fu #77 (June 1979)
REAL NAME Maximillian Zaran
OCCUPATION Mercenary **BASE** Mobile
HEIGHT 6 ft 1 in **WEIGHT** 235 lbs **EYES** Blue **HAIR** Red
SPECIAL POWERS/ABILITIES Skilled with a wide range of ancient weapons, including nunchakus, shurikens, maces, bows and arrows, staffs, and knives; he can also fire a gun.

A former British MI6 agent and now a mercenary, Maximillian Zaran's career has been chequered to say the least. After defecting from the British secret service, Zaran worked for Fah Lo Suee, Fu Manchu's daughter, but she cut his contract short. For a time, his apprentice took over his identity, but once that was resolved Zaran joined Batroc's Brigade. During the Civil War, he was forced to work for the Thunderbolts. He later registered with the US government and joined the Fifty-State Initiative. **AD, MF**

Z'NOX

FIRST APPEARANCE X-Men #65 (February 1970)
BASE Z'nox, Huz'deyr solar system, Andromeda galaxy
SPECIAL POWERS/ABILITIES Villainous race boasts highly sophisticated technology and are able to move their homeworld through space.

OUR VICTIMS LAUNCH YET ANOTHER PROJECTILE AT US!

Although unable to subvert the Skrull dominance of their home galaxy Andromeda, the warlike Z'nox were a highly sophisticated and deadly race of world conquerors. When Professor X learned that a Z'nox invasion force was heading towards Earth, he went into complete seclusion, leaving the mutant shapeshifter the Changeling to stand in for him. As the fleet approached, Xavier combined his mind with those of the X-Men and the Earth's entire population to psionically repel the attack. **AD**

ZALADANE

FIRST APPEARANCE Astonishing Tales Vol. 1 #1 (December 1970)
REAL NAME Zala Dane (allegedly)
OCCUPATION High priestess **BASE** The Savage Land
HEIGHT 5 ft 9 in **WEIGHT** 125 lbs **EYES** Blue **HAIR** Black
SPECIAL POWERS/ABILITIES Zaladane is a sorceress who possesses assorted spell-based abilities.

The High Priestess of Garokk, Zaladane led believers against the other tribes of the Savage Land in a bid for power. Zaladane's sorcery transformed Kirk Marston into the avatar of Garrok on Earth, and she supported him as his second in command. After her bid to conquer the Savage Land had been foiled, Zaladane's mutates abducted Lorna Dane, the X-Man known as Polaris. Posing as Lorna's long-lost sister, Zaladane succeeded in transferring Polaris' magnetic abilities to herself, albeit temporarily. Thereafter, in a failed bid to control all of the magnetic forces on Earth, Zaladane ran afoul of Magneto, who overwhelmed her with his own superior magnetic might, and left her for dead. **TB**

ZARATHOS

FIRST APPEARANCE Marvel Spotlight Vol. 1 #5 (August 1972)
REAL NAME Zarathos **OCCUPATION** The Spirit of Vengeance
BASE The netherworld dimension of Mephisto
HEIGHT 20 ft **WEIGHT** 225 lbs **EYES/HAIR** Not applicable
SPECIAL POWERS/ABILITIES Uses magic to enhance strength, height, weight. Employs levitation and projects blasts of concussive force. Projects cold fire that sears his enemies' souls.

Zarathos is a demon who journeyed to Earth before the Dawn of Man. A sorcerer offered to trade souls for his aid. Mephisto, lord of the underworld, grew jealous of a cult that grew around Zarathos and enslaved him, sending him to possess humans in the causes of sin, corruption, and vengeance. Zarathos became bound to stunt motorcyclist Johnny Blaze and later to bike messenger Danny Ketch and (still later) to Alejandra Blaze, transforming each into Ghost Rider. **TD, MF**

ZOLA, ARNIM

FIRST APPEARANCE Captain America Vol. 1 #208 (April 1977)
REAL NAME Arnim Zola **OCCUPATION** Criminal biochemist
BASE Weisshorn Mountain, Switzerland
HEIGHT 5 ft 10 in **WEIGHT** 200 lbs
EYES Brown **HAIR** None
SPECIAL POWERS/ABILITIES Brilliant geneticist; can mentally project his intelligence into any of his creations.

During the late 1930s, Swiss geneticist Arnim Zola discovered a tome of Deviant science and learned how to create artificial life. He built himself a new body with a brain inside its chest, a holographically projected face, and an ESP box for a head. Zola became a valued member of Hitler's Third Reich, preserving Hitler's consciousness in the form of the Hate-Monger. A frequent foe of Captain America, Zola often worked with the Red Skull. Zola escaped to and ruled Dimension Z, where Cap found him and led a rebellion against him. **DW, MF**

FACTFILE

MEMBERS AND POWERS

ARIES
Shoots fire from his horns.

AQUARIUS
Carries a gun that fires blasts of electricity.

CANCER
Superhuman strength, ability to create and control torrents of water.

CAPRICORN
Superhuman leaping and climbing abilities.

GEMINI
Can split into two bodies, can grow to huge size and strength, can project energy.

LEO
Superhuman strength and leaping ability.

LIBRA
Can fly, can become intangible.

PISCES
Can easily maneuver underwater.

SAGITTARIUS
Advanced archery skills.

SCORPIO
Wields the powerful Zodiac Key.

TAURUS
Superhuman strength.

VIRGO
Highly skilled in creating and using machines.

BASE Mobile

FIRST APPEARANCE
(in shadow) Defenders #49 (July 1977); (fully seen) Defenders #50 (August 1977)

ZODIAC

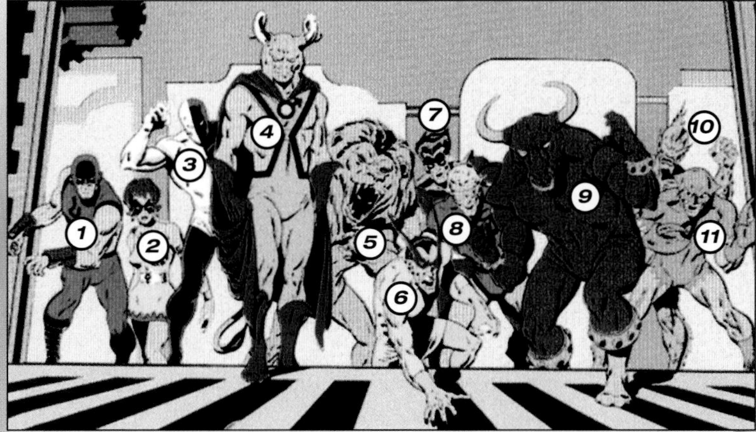

ZODIAC
1 Aquarius ***2*** Virgo ***3*** Gemini ***4*** Aries ***5*** Leo ***6*** Capricorn ***7*** Sagittarius ***8*** Libra ***9*** Taurus ***10*** Pisces ***11*** Cancer

The first public Zodiac was a criminal team in which each of its 12 members had powers based on a zodiac sign. Cornelius Van Lunt (Taurus) and Jake Fury (Scorpio) formed it, intending to rule humanity. One of this group—Aquarius—later appeared as the One-Man Zodiac.

The second Zodiac was formed when an android Scorpio slaughtered the original Zodiac and replaced them all with androids. The third Zodiac group was composed of humans hired by Canada's Department H to test Alpha Flight, but they turned rogue and a Weapon X team murdered them.

ZODIAC ATTACK

A fourth group faced off against the New Warriors, and that team's Cancer killed the overconfident hero Longstrike. When Thanos returned from the dead, he formed a Zodiac of his own. A solo villain calling himself Zodiac appeared during the Dark Reign to harass Norman Osborn (Green Goblin). He murdered over 100 HAMMER agents and lent support to the Young Masters.

MT, MF

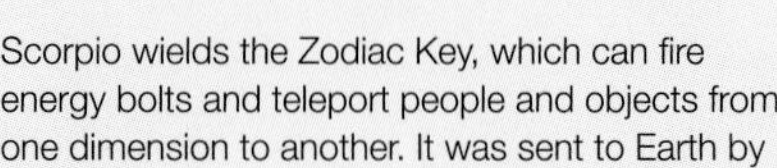

Scorpio wields the Zodiac Key, which can fire energy bolts and teleport people and objects from one dimension to another. It was sent to Earth by the Brotherhood, a cult from another dimension that believes that the Key's existence depends on constant conflict between good and evil.

ZOMBIE

FIRST APPEARANCE Tales of the Zombie #1 (August 1973)
REAL NAME Simon William Garth
OCCUPATION Former businessman **BASE** New Orleans
HEIGHT 6 ft 2 in **WEIGHT** 220 lbs
EYES White **HAIR** Black
SPECIAL POWERS/ABILITIES Superhuman strength and regenerative ability.

Ruthless businessman Simon Garth so upset his gardener Gyps that he killed Garth and resurrected him as a zombie. For two years, the zombiefied Garth wandered the Earth, initially controlled by Gyps with an amulet, and later by one despicable individual after another. The love of a good woman restored Garth to life for a short spell, enabling him to put his affairs in order before going to his rest. He returned later to hunt for the missing amulet and then to fight against a zombie invasion from an alternate dimension.

AD, MF

ZZZAX

FIRST APPEARANCE Incredible Hulk #166 (August 1973)
REAL NAME Inapplicable **OCCUPATION** Purveyor of destruction
BASE Mobile **HEIGHT** Variable (max. 40 ft)
WEIGHT Negligible **EYES /HAIR** Inapplicable
SPECIAL POWERS/ABILITIES Unlimited electricity-manipulating powers including flight, super strength, and the ability to fire electrical bolts of concussive force.

Zzzax is a living electromagnetic field formed by a bizarre accident at a nuclear power plant. By absorbing the electromagnetic brainwave energies of its victims, Zzzax gained a limited sentience and fashioned itself into a crude humanoid form. Zzzax can grow in size by draining energy from its surroundings, a tactic it used against its most frequent foe, the Hulk. For a while, General Ross' consciousness controlled the creature, but he soon abandoned that. Zzzax later escaped from the Raft super prison, but She-Hulk recaptured him. It later worked with MODOK and fought against the Red Hulk.

DW, MF

The Multiverse

Countless Universes of Heroes

The mainstream Marvel Universe is only one of countless possible universes in the multiverse. Most full universes are known by the name "Earth" attached to an identifying number. The regular Marvel Universe is Earth-616, although almost no one in that universe knows of it as anything other than "home." Many of the universes have their own versions of familiar characters, although they may be drastically different from each other. Most people live their lives in a single universe, never knowing anything of places beyond their own. A rare few, however, travel between the universes frequently. We live on Earth-1218.

1602

In an alternate world (Earth-460), the Purple Man uses his powers of persuasion to become US President and exiles Captain America into the past of Earth-311. This disrupts that universe's timeline so badly that modern heroes begin to appear at the turn of the 17th century; for instance, Sir Nicholas Fury works for Queen Elizabeth of England. Later, after the timeline has been fixed by the removal of Captain America, many of the heroes move to the New World, which is populated by dinosaurs along with the native peoples.

EARTH X

The future of Earth-9997 is a dark time. Black Bolt has released the Terrigen Mists into the atmosphere, causing many humans to become mutants. Controlling the US food supply, Norman Osborn (Green Goblin) makes himself US President and has Iron Man build robotic versions of the Avengers for him. The new Galactus (Franklin Richards) eventually saves the world. Later, Captain Mar-Vell persuades Thanos to use the Ultimate Nullifier on Death, then helps to make Mr. Fantastic—who has built a Paradise for the dead in the Negative Zone—into the new Eternity.

The transparent Machine Man served as the eyes for Earth X's Watcher.

Alternate versions of regular heroes and villains band together to save the multiverse as the Exiles.

EXILES

The Exiles are a Super Hero team assembled by the mysterious Timebroker to solve problems in the multiverse. The Timebroker is actually part of an insectoid alien race that is trying to repair the damage it did to the multiverse. The creatures live in the Panoptichron, a transdimensional space from which they can monitor several other realities at once. The leader of the Exiles uses a device called a Tallus to communicate with the Timebroker, helping to keep the team on track. Due to the dangerous nature of their jobs, the Exiles have a high turnover rate, but there are always replacements ready to take the place of the fallen.

ULTIMATES

On Earth-1610, the heroes who have been around the mainstream universe for decades have just developed, and sometimes have done so in unique ways. Spider-Man, for instance, is just a teenager in high school, Nick Fury is African-American—although he still wears an eye patch—and the Avengers are known as the Ultimates. There are far fewer superpowered people in this world, and the number was recently reduced when Magneto went on a murderous rampage to avenge the deaths of Quicksilver and the Scarlet Witch and flooded New York City with a tidal wave.

Until recently, the Ultimate universe seemed like a younger version of Earth-616, but it has now diverged in important and substantial ways.

SQUADRON SUPREME

One of the most enduring crossovers between universes happened when the Avengers traveled to Earth-712 and met the top hero team there, the Squadron Supreme. Years later, the Squadron's members decided to try taking over and running the world, but when this went bad they exiled themselves to Earth-616. They returned to find their homeworld overrun by ruthless corporations. They've also had encounters with people from the Ultimate universe (Earth-1610) and a darker version of their own team from Earth-31916.

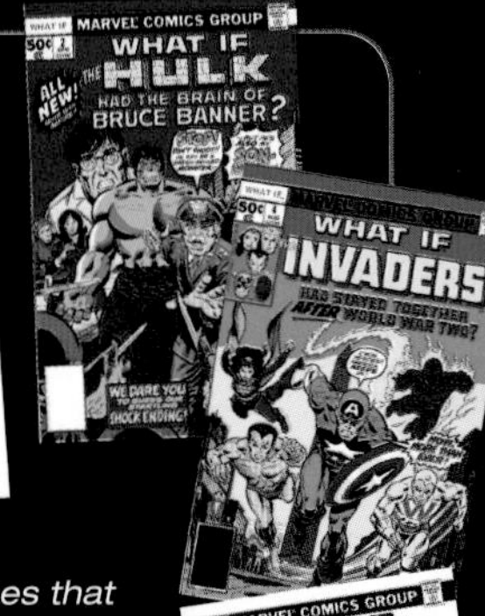

WHAT IF....

The WATCHER often travels to different universes that are extremely close to Earth-616 but diverge at one critical point or another, such as "What if Uncle Ben had lived?" Sometimes he visits universes in which a regular hero appears in a different time, like Captain America as a fighter in the Revolutionary War. Other times, the issues the Watcher examines are more complex and posit a series of different paths taken during massive events like the Civil War (see pp. 84–5) or the Secret Invasion (see pp. 326–7).

ZOMBIES

A zombie version of the Sentry entered Earth-2149 and, with the help of Magneto, began infecting superpowered people with a virus that turned them into the living dead. Magneto mistakenly thought the infection would only harm humans, leaving mutants alive. The zombies retain most of their powers, but their hunger for human flesh regularly overpowers them. After they run out of food, the superpowered zombies try traveling to new universes filled with fresh meat. They have managed to reach Earth-1610 and Earth-616 universes.

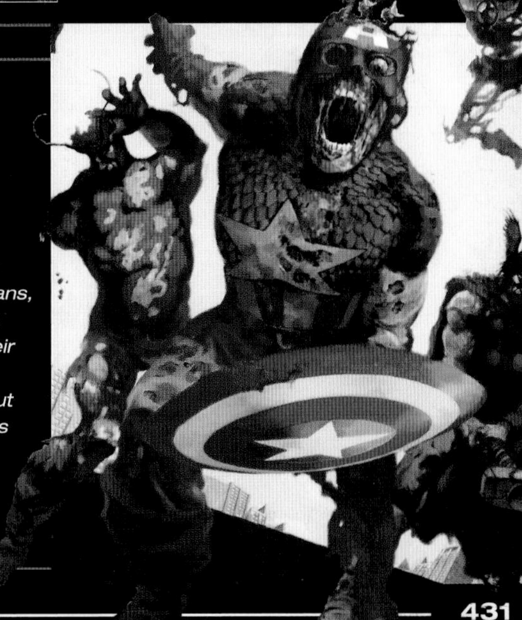

INDEX

Entries in bold signify that a character has his, her or its own entry.

A

B

C

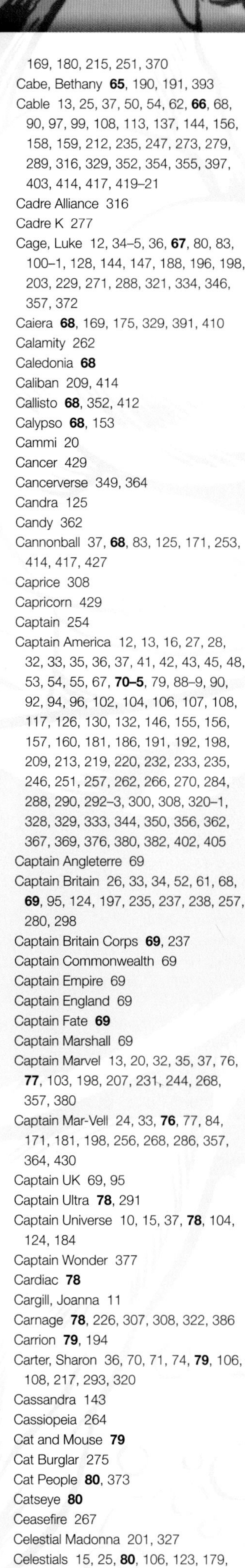

E

F

G

H

I

J

K

L

M

N

ACKNOWLEDGMENTS

TOM DEFALCO would like to thank Mark Gruenwald who believed that people would enjoying reading books like this and was the driving force behind the original Official Handbooks of the Marvel Universe. HOO-HA, my friend!

TOM BREVOORT would like to thank Stan, Jack, Steve and all the rest, for doing the hard part and coming up with all of these characters and concepts in the first place.

MICHAEL TEITELBAUM would like to thank Danny Fingeroth for the invaluable loan of the books and for his generosity in sharing his knowledge of the Marvel Universe, and Peter Sanderson for his help in identifying some of the characters; Alastair Dougall for bringing me on board and for his endless help and patience; Mike Hobson and John Romita, Sr. for the magazine (nod to Tom D. there as well!); Stan Lee, Steve Ditko, and Jack Kirby for starting all this; and my mom and dad, who—back when you could buy two comic books and a piece of gum for 25 cents—always gave me that quarter.

ANDREW DARLING would like to thank Keith Martin for those hyper-detailed responses to tricky questions, and the guys at Travelling Man in Manchester, who rescued me more than once. Big cheers go to Simon Beecroft for putting me forward for this gig, Alastair Dougall, who kept coming back for more, and Laura Gilbert, who couldn't quite get away. Finally, special thanks go to Ruth, who now knows a lot more about the Marvel Universe than she did, and Elijah—always a welcome distraction.

DANIEL WALLACE would like to dedicate my work on this book to the memory of my friend Dan Zoch, who introduced me to Marvel comics.

PETER SANDERSON would like to thank Jeff Christiansen, Tom Brevoort, Mike Fichera and Sean McQuaid for helping me resolve some continuity conundrums.

DORLING KINDERSLEY would like to thank Chelsea Alon, C.B. Cebulski, David Gabriel, Thomas Murphy, Brian Overton, Jeff Poulin, and Jeff Youngquist at Marvel; Mark Perry at Avalon Comics and Will at 30th Century Comics; Lindsay Kent, Amy Junor, Elizabeth Noble, Laura Gilbert, Alan Cowsill, Laura Baxter, Lynne Moulding, Cynthia O'Neill, and Zoe Hedges for editorial assistance; Guy Harvey for design assistance; Ann Barrett for the index.